THE OXFORD HANDBOOK OF

BUSINESS ETHICS

THE OXFORD HANDBOOK OF

BUSINESS ETHICS

Edited by

GEORGE G. BRENKERT
TOM L. BEAUCHAMP

OXFORD

UNIVERSITY PRESS

OXFORD

UNIVERSITY PRESS

Oxford University Press, Inc., publishes works that further
Oxford University's objective of excellence
in research, scholarship, and education.

Oxford   New York
Auckland   Cape Town   Dar es Salaam   Hong Kong   Karachi
Kuala Lumpur   Madrid   Melbourne   Mexico City   Nairobi
New Delhi   Shanghai   Taipei   Toronto

With offices in
Argentina   Austria   Brazil   Chile   Czech Republic   France   Greece
Guatemala   Hungary   Italy   Japan   Poland   Portugal   Singapore
South Korea   Switzerland   Thailand   Turkey   Ukraine   Vietnam

Copyright © 2010 by Oxford University Press, Inc.

Published by Oxford University Press, Inc.
198 Madison Avenue, New York, New York 10016
www.oup.com

First issued as an Oxford University Press paperback, 2012.

Oxford is a registered trademark of Oxford University Press.

Library of Congress Cataloging-in-Publication Data

The Oxford handbook of business ethics /
edited by George G. Brenkert,
Tom L. Beauchamp.
p.   cm.
Includes index.
ISBN 978-0-19-530795-5 (hardcover); 978-0-19-991622-1 (paperback)
1. Business ethics—Handbooks, manuals, etc.   2. Professional
ethics—Handbooks, manuals, etc.   I. Brenkert, George G.   II. Beauchamp,
Tom L.
HF5387.O95 2009
174'.4—dc22   2008049464

1 3 5 7 9 8 6 4 2

Printed in the United States of America
on acid-free paper

PREFACE

When Oxford University Press asked us to prepare a volume on business ethics, we eagerly agreed. We believe that business ethics is deserving of much greater attention by philosophers and ethicists than it has received. To this end, we have solicited chapters from leading philosophers who have made important contributions to our understanding of central issues in business ethics. This volume is unabashedly aimed at those who seek a philosophical approach to these issues. This focus does not exclude the practical implications and importance of these essays, but it does mean that the conceptual, theoretical, and normative nature of the issues discussed is given precedence in this volume.

The chapters in this Handbook are all original essays that develop prominent areas of business ethics. The reader will note that the authors come from the full spectrum of views on business ethics—from those who place special emphasis on individual liberty to those who give more emphasis to the social context of business. Though business ethics has come a great distance from its founding a half century ago, it still has much further to go. We hope that these essays will be useful to the readers of this volume and help spur additional work in business ethics that will continue the development of this intellectually rich and important field.

The preparation of this volume has taken several years. We greatly appreciate the willingness of several of our authors who have encountered personal difficulties to persist through them and complete their work. We are likewise grateful for the readiness of all our authors to go through numerous drafts of their chapters as this book was being brought to completion.

Washington, D.C.   GGB
July, 2009   TLB

Contents

Contributors, xi

Introduction, 3

Part I Basic Philosophical Issues

1. The Methods of Business Ethics, 21
   Ronald M. Green and Aine Donovan

2. The Place of Ethical Theory in Business Ethics, 46
   Robert Audi

Part II Competitive Markets and Corporate Responsibility

3. The Idea and Ideal of Capitalism, 73
   Gerald Gaus

4. The Public Authority of the Managers of Private Corporations, 100
   Christopher McMahon

5. Corporate Responsibility and Its Constituents, 126
   Kenneth E. Goodpaster

Part III Economic Justice and Consumer Rights

6. Executive Compensation: Unjust or Just Right?, 161
   John R. Boatright

7. Just Access to Health Care and Pharmaceuticals, 202
   Paul T. Menzel

PART IV UNIVERSAL NORMS AND THE RELATIVITY
OF MORAL JUDGMENTS

8. Relativism, Multiculturalism, and Universal Norms: Their Role
in Business Ethics, 235
Tom L. Beauchamp

9. Business and Human Rights: A Principle and Value-Based
Analysis, 267
Wesley Cragg

10. Moral Issues in Globalization, 305
Carol C. Gould

PART V THE USE AND PROTECTION OF INFORMATION

11. Deception and Information Disclosure in Business
and Professional Ethics, 335
Thomas L. Carson

12. Informational Privacy, 366
Richard A. Spinello

13. The Moral Problem in Insider Trading, 388
Alan Strudler

14. Intellectual Property Rights, 408
Richard T. De George

PART VI INCENTIVES AND INFLUENCE

15. Conflicts of Interest, 441
Wayne Norman and Chris MacDonald

16. Corruption and Bribery, 471
Manuel Velasquez

17. Business in Politics: Lobbying and Corporate Campaign
Contributions, 501
Andrew Stark

PART VII EMPLOYEE RIGHTS AND CORPORATE RESPONSIBILITIES

18. Discrimination, Affirmative Action, and Diversity in Business, 535
    Bernard Boxill

19. Whistle-Blowing, Moral Integrity, and Organizational Ethics, 563
    George G. Brenkert

20. Employment at Will and Employee Rights, 602
    John J. McCall and Patricia H. Werhane

21. Working Conditions: Safety and Sweatshops, 628
    Denis G. Arnold

PART VIII SAFETY, RISK, AND HARM

22. Environmental Ethics and Business, 657
    Lisa H. Newton

23. The Mirage of Product Safety, 677
    John Hasnas

PART IX CREATING MORAL ORGANIZATIONS

24. Organizational Integrity and Moral Climates, 701
    Norman E. Bowie

Index, 725

Contributors

DENIS G. ARNOLD, Department of Philosophy, Department of Management, Belk College of Business, University of North Carolina, Charlotte

ROBERT AUDI, Department of Philosophy, Department of Management, Mendoza College of Business, University of Notre Dame

TOM L. BEAUCHAMP, Department of Philosophy, Kennedy Institute of Ethics, Georgetown University

JOHN R. BOATRIGHT, Department of Management, Graduate School of Business, Loyola University of Chicago

NORMAN E. BOWIE, Department of Strategic Management and Organization, Carlson School of Management, University of Minnesota

BERNARD BOXILL, Department of Philosophy, University of North Carolina, Chapel Hill

GEORGE G. BRENKERT, McDonough School of Business, Georgetown University

THOMAS L. CARSON, Department of Philosophy, Loyola University of Chicago

WESLEY CRAGG, Department of Philosophy, Department of Business Ethics, Schulich School of Business, York University

RICHARD T. DE GEORGE, Department of Philosophy, University of Kansas

AINE DONOVAN, Ethics Institute, Medical School, Dartmouth College

GERALD GAUS, Department of Philosophy, University of Arizona

KENNETH E. GOODPASTER, Department of Ethics and Business Law, Opus College of Business, University of St. Thomas

CAROL C. GOULD, Department of Philosophy, Department of Political Science, Temple University

RONALD M. GREEN, Department of Religion, Dartmouth College

JOHN HASNAS, McDonough School of Business, Georgetown University

CHRIS MacDONALD, Department of Philosophy, St. Mary's University

JOHN J. McCALL, Department of Philosophy, Department of Management, Erivan K. Haub School of Business, Saint Joseph's University

CHRISTOPHER McMAHON, Department of Philosophy, University of California, Santa Barbara

PAUL T. MENZEL, Department of Philosophy, Pacific Lutheran University

LISA H. NEWTON, Department of Philosophy, Business Law and Ethics Department, Charles F. Dolan School of Business, Fairfield University

WAYNE NORMAN, Department of Philosophy, Duke University

RICHARD A. SPINELLO, Department of Operations & Strategic Management, Carroll School of Management, Boston College

ANDREW STARK, Department of Political Science, Department of Strategic Management, Rotman School of Management, University of Toronto

ALAN STRUDLER, Department of Legal Studies and Business Ethics, Wharton School, University of Pennsylvania

MANUEL VELASQUEZ, Department of Management, Leavey School of Business, Santa Clara University

PATRICIA H. WERHANE, Department of Philosophy and College of Commerce, DePaul University, Darden Graduate School of Business, University of Virginia

THE OXFORD HANDBOOK OF

BUSINESS ETHICS

INTRODUCTION

BUSINESS ethics has long existed in the form of reflection on the ethical dimensions of business exchanges and institutions. As such, business ethics is traceable to ancient times. However, only in the last half century has business ethics developed as an identifiable field of study. About the same time that biomedical ethics was taking shape in the 1970s, conferences were being held and articles and books on business ethics were being published. This book reflects the work that has been done in these last four decades.

TWO UNDERSTANDINGS OF BUSINESS ETHICS

"Business ethics" is understood in two distinctive ways by those who have a major interest in its development. One group approaches it from a background in philosophy, and the other group approaches it primarily from the business community. Since this volume has been prepared for those who view business ethics from a philosophical approach, we start with an explanation of this very important distinction.

Business Ethics from a Philosophical Orientation

The philosophical ethics orientation consists of the analysis of moral problems and case studies using categories such as justice, utility, rights, obligations, and personal virtues. Problems of business ethics involving these concepts include issues internal to businesses such as problems of discrimination in hiring and promotion as well as issues external to them such as consumer, governmental, and environmental problems. In this approach, a consideration of moral theory is basic for a proper understanding of how to treat moral problems and engage in the analysis of perplexing cases in business ethics.

A reason for using the theoretical orientation to business ethics preferred by philosophers is to avoid situations in which discussion of moral problems in business is little more than an exposure to the prejudices of persons who do not generalize beyond their own viewpoint. Discussion and reflection on issues of sexual harassment, executive salaries, whistle-blowing, and the like may lack critical distance due to cultural blindness, rash analogy, or mere popular opinion. For example, if one limits one's study of some issue to the facts of cases and to problems of management, the outcome might only be that one becomes immersed in the current system of doing business without achieving any distance from the prejudices or blindness of the current system. The philosophical goal is to reach moral understanding through a general and impartial framework or theory. This approach does not assert that philosophical reflection is a fully adequate basis for business ethics, but it does assert that reflection through theory and principle allows us to examine and, where appropriate, depart from certain dominant or tradition-bound assumptions.

Business Ethics from a Business Orientation

By contrast, the business orientation tends to view its endeavor in terms of various relationships that obtain largely within business. In this conception business ethics pertains to relations between employer and employee, between manager and workers, and between supervisors and supervisees. This understanding of business ethics has developed in the United States in step with practical developments such as the U.S. Federal Sentencing Guidelines, the Defense Industry Initiative, and the Ethics and Compliance Officer Association. Each of these has been concerned with developing programs to foster employee compliance with legal and regulatory strictures as well as background values, motivation formats, rules, and norms that would help foster employee legal and ethical behavior. As a result, many major U.S. businesses have ethics officers who oversee these programs. Their focus is practical rather than theoretical by design and by the nature of the institutions in which they function.

The business approach is often focused on moral problems and apparent dilemmas that could have been avoided or minimized through more skillful management. Particularly difficult and important case studies are often used to stimulate reflection on whether, by whom, and when certain actions should be taken. Often cases and problems are examined in terms of alternative strategies and actions. Usually such a rich array of alternatives is available that it is not feasible to reach agreement on a single best solution; however, complete agreement or a single solution may not be the purpose of the investigation. Learning how to spot and manage problems is of high importance. The focus is meant to be practical.

The business orientation sometimes stays close to empirical work on subjects under study. Problems of environmental pollution, for example, are studied by detailing empirical facts about pollution and disease and by examining social processes that have diminished the scope of decision making in business and have created new responsibilities through government requirements. The economic aspects of pollution control are an influential example. The responses of corporations to changing legal and regulatory situations may be emphasized, as may considerations of what has been and may become public policy. Tax policies and the economic consequences of proposed public policies may be studied in detail and are likely to be viewed as central to the investigation.

The two different orientations to business ethics mentioned in this section are not mutually exclusive, though the philosophical orientation is probably the broader of the two. The most constructive approach is to acknowledge that moral problems and the analysis of cases invite multiple forms of productive analysis. The editors of this volume strongly encourage this way of thinking about the field. However, this book is committed almost entirely to philosophical approaches. This is not because the editors see this approach as superior or of greater significance. The commitment of this volume is to see how far and in what ways philosophy can help us develop an impartial and probing business ethics.

REGRETTABLE WAYS IN WHICH BUSINESS ETHICS HAS BEEN VIEWED

In both of the ways just outlined, business ethics is a matter of serious study and investigation. Almost everyone engaged in business ethics views the field in this way. However, business ethics is not always regarded by others as having an important status as an area of investigation. It has, especially in its philosophical forms, received less recognition and acceptance than some areas of practical ethics—many believe that it is derivative from other areas of philosophy and possibly even conflicted as a result of the connection to business. It is sometimes suggested that the idea of ethics is not taken seriously as a constraint on business conduct, and some even hold that there is no ethics in business. It has also been said that business is not a profession and therefore cannot have a professional ethics of the sort expected in medical ethics and legal ethics.

These perspectives need to be heard, but they also need to be restrained and carefully stated. They have often been stated inaccurately, and they also are likely to retard development of good moral practices in business. Business is, perhaps, the premier institution that influences the lives of everyone in society, from hourly workers to physicians and philosophers. It is regrettable when an institution of such significance is treated in the discipline of philosophy as if it has only a subordinate status and is not an important subject of ethical analysis and evaluation. Business raises some of the most important and difficult ethical issues ethicists and philosophers need to consider—conflicts between self-interest and the interests of others, manipulation and cooperation, trust and distrust, honesty and deception, responsibility for future generations, and so on. Business ethics also does not use different methods or forms of reasoning than those found in other areas of applied ethics, nor does it have less connection to some of the most important public policy issues of our times. As this book goes to press, the United States and much of the world face a financial crisis that was fed by unethical conduct and lax oversight. Some of the conduct underlying this crisis is now considered scandalous, yet little moral reflection had been invested in the practices involved. Both activities in business and failures of government oversight of business are involved. These kinds of issues deserve the closest kind of ethical and philosophical attention.

THE ORGANIZATION AND CONTENTS
OF THIS VOLUME

This book is divided into nine parts ranging from basic philosophical issues to the moral culture of business organizations. Each part provides the relevant background history in business ethics, presents the major current issues, and offers solutions to leading problems.

Part I: Basic Philosophical Issues

We all grow up with an understanding of how to meet society's moral expectations, but philosophical assessment of this morality and of how its scope can be extended involve a different kind of understanding and practice than that provided in our moral upbringing. The terms "ethical theory" and "moral philosophy" refer to reflection on the nature and justification of right actions as well as the nature and role of moral character. Philosophers seek to introduce clarity, substance, and precision of argument into the discussion of moral rightness and wrongness, the virtues, social justice, and intrinsic value. Their goal is usually to justify a system of standards or some moral point of view on the basis of carefully analyzed and defended norms of distributive justice, human rights, trustworthiness, contractual relationships, and the like. The writers in this book take such a philosophical approach to the topics in business ethics they address.

A number of different methods have been employed in business ethics, and not all of them are either distinctly philosophical or attempts to justify a position. Some approaches are descriptive and do not involve taking moral positions. Other approaches are normative and make explicit appeals to ethical theory in order to develop arguments to support their positions. Still other approaches are almost purely conceptual. They pay close attention to one or more central concepts in business ethics, such as capitalism, whistle-blowing, conflict of interest, and liability.

Both the nature of ethical theory and the methods used in the work of business ethics are studied in part I. In "The Methods of Business Ethics," Ronald M. Green and Aine Donovan examine how the mission of business ethics has fostered several methodological approaches—chiefly drawn from philosophical analysis and descriptive methodologies. They treat the work of several leading business ethics scholars and include in the scope of their discussion a number of ways in which these methods have affected methods of teaching business ethics. In "The Place of Ethical Theory in Business Ethics," Robert Audi explains the nature of ethical theory, provides an account of the leading theories, and explores the ways in which these theories form a critical resource for the treatment of practical moral problems. He discusses how theory connects to practice and provides several concrete illustrations of how ethical theory helps address practical problems in business ethics. In particular, he shows how theory can be helpful in the analysis of problems of affirmative action, whistle-blowing, and advertising,

Part II: Competitive Markets and Corporate Responsibility

A famous maxim is that "the business of business is business," meaning that the responsibilities of a business should be confined to the business world of contracts, stockholders, profits, record keeping, taxes, and the like. This position resists the encroachment of government into competitive markets and rejects the proposition that corporations have moral and social responsibilities other than responsibilities that the corporation voluntarily assumes. However, corporations are chartered by society. This charter permits a corporation to conduct business only within contractually imposed limits, and there are, in addition, moral and social norms that further limit and prescribe the activities of business. Precisely what this free market system is and how much freedom it gives to corporations are topics taken up in this part.

"Capitalism" is generally understood in these discussions as a market-based, economic system governed by capital—that is, the wealth of an individual or an establishment accumulated by or employed in its business activities. Entrepreneurs and the institutions they create generate the capital with which businesses provide goods, services, and payments to workers. Defenders of capitalism argue that this system maximally distributes social freedoms and desirable resources, resulting in the best economic outcomes for everyone in society. On this view, business's only social responsibilities are to maximize legally generated profits. However, over the past several decades there has been a significant reaction against this view. It is argued that businesses have responsibilities far beyond following the law and profit making. When society accepts capitalism, this view holds, it need not also accept the view that economic freedom always has priority over competing conceptions of the collection and distribution of social goods, or of other responsibilities owed to employees, customers, society, and the environment.

In "The Idea and Ideal of Capitalism," Gerald Gaus considers what a relatively pure form of capitalism would look like if we were to have one. He then asks what would be required for its justification and asks whether traditional justifications work. Gaus analyzes what he calls the rather vague idea of "capitalism" into distinct elements and asks how each element might be justified. The main aim is not to defend capitalism but to analyze it in order to better understand the context in which business, and therefore business ethics, occurs. His chapter, Gaus says, is not so much an essay *in* business ethics as it is an essay on the foundations of the very practices of business and business ethics—the idea of a capitalist economic order.

Christopher McMahon notes in "The Public Authority of the Managers of Private Organizations" that it is a commonplace of political philosophy that authority must be legitimate. Less discussed is what establishes the legitimacy of managerial authority. One view is that a consent model is at work: Employees voluntarily join the corporations where they work and accept managerial authority. McMahon argues that matters are not so simple. He proposes that we view managers of private corporations as exercising the same kind of authority as governmental officials. McMahon argues for what he calls "a political theory of the corporation." Through this lens he sees business ethics as grounded in values and norms that apply to a whole society, including its collective life.

In "Corporate Responsibility and its Constituents," Kenneth E. Goodpaster addresses an issue of corporate responsibility that has, in recent years, attracted a great deal of attention. Often this issue is referred to as "corporate social responsibility," but increasingly business ethicists maintain that the inclusion of "social" misrepresents the responsibilities that business has. Goodpaster develops his position by first examining stockholder and stakeholder views of corporate responsibility. He finds both views inadequate and in need of supplementation by a "comprehensive moral thinking" that makes for a better model of corporate responsibility.

Part III: Economic Justice and Consumer Rights

Economic disparities among individuals and nations generate many controversies over systems for distributing goods and services and for taxing income and wealth. Central issues are the justification of structures of taxation, international debt relief, uses of corporate profits, corporate gifts, executive salaries and bonuses, plant closings, and exploitative conditions in factories. What a person deserves or is entitled to is often decided by specific rules and laws, such as those governing health care coverage, salary scales, and procedures for hiring and firing. These rules need to be evaluated, criticized, and revised by reference to moral principles and theories.

The word *justice* is often used in the discussion of these principles and specific rules. A basic question is whether the market itself is a fair arrangement. If so, what makes it fair? If not, what makes it unfair? If health care and other critical goods and services are distributed nationally or internationally with vast inequality, on what basis do we say the system is unfair? If a multinational company has a monopoly on an essential foodstuff, is there no such thing as a price that is unjust? What would constitute an executive compensation package that is unjust? These questions of fairness fall under the topic of distributive justice.

If people have a right to a minimal level of material means to items such as health care (a right many do not acknowledge), it seems to many writers that their rights are violated whenever economic distributions leave persons with less than the minimal level. A commitment to individual economic rights, then, may go hand in hand with a theory of justice that requires an activist role for government. This may be true even if one starts with free market assumptions. Almost everyone agrees with the premise that economic freedom is a value deserving of respect and protection, but they disagree over the claim that the principles and procedures of unmitigated capitalist markets adequately protect the basic values of individual and public welfare. Many theories adopt some form of a principle specifying human need as basic to economic justice.

In "Executive Compensation: Unjust or Just Right?" John R. Boatright tackles the controversial issue of executive compensation that has provoked a great deal of moral outrage in many quarters. In order to narrow the discussion of this large topic, Boatright assumes that some form of capitalism is morally justified and that consequently "both the principles of compensation in a free market and the patterns of distribution of income and wealth produced by the market are just." Given these assumptions, Boatright argues that the normative and empirical issues that surround executive compensation lead to the conclusion that high levels of executive compensation can be justified. However, he also argues that there have been significant abuses and excesses in the compensation packages of some executives.

In "Just Access to Health Care and Pharmaceuticals," Paul T. Menzel discusses why access to health care is a subject of interest to business and its employees, particularly in the United States, where businesses commonly supply health care insurance as a benefit for employees. Eventually, access to health care, including pharmaceuticals, came to be discussed in terms of employee rights and employer obligations. But are there such rights or obligations? Menzel also treats concerns about consumers, especially the alleged obligations of health insurance companies and pharmaceutical companies to their consumers. In his final section, he explores just access to health care and pharmaceuticals from a society-wide perspective. Menzel is optimistic that there is a possibility at present of finding common moral ground on today's contentious issues about health care access.

Part IV: Universal Norms and the Relativity of Moral Judgments

Multinational corporations often find themselves perplexed by the laws, rules, and customs of a host country in which they conduct business or have subsidiaries. They wonder whether they should do as the locals do or conform to the different and even conflicting cultural guidelines of their home states. For example, should a Canadian firm follow the rules of financial disclosure required in Canada or the rules in certain Arab countries in which it has subsidiaries? Should a U.S. firm that does business in Japan sanction payments for services that are encouraged in Japan but legally prohibited in the United States? Should a company liquidate its stock of artificially sweetened fruit by selling to customers in Germany, Spain, or Third World countries when the product has been declared hazardous and outlawed in the home country? Would it make any difference if a culture has rules that are inconsistent with human rights?

No international body has answered these questions authoritatively, and there is currently no uniform agreement about the measure of control that governments and corporations should introduce for circumstances in which standards or expectations vary. The multinational setting presents numerous ethical complexities of universality and particularity—for example in the treatment of employees and consultants, in practices involving consumers and clients, and in different government expectations and types of government-industry relationships. An employer engaged in manufacturing or marketing in a foreign culture cannot simply assume that workers should be governed by the same salary standards, grounds for dismissal, workplace standards, requirements of company loyalty, and promotional standards as those prevalent back home. Some writers hold that morality has no place in a country that demands that a business participate in immoral actions to survive, but others take the position that some moral values transcend any policy imposed by another country and that these values may not be ignored.

In "Relativism, Multiculturalism, and Universal Norms: Their Role in Business Ethics," Tom L. Beauchamp considers the question whether moral standards are merely personal opinions and cultural conventions or whether some moral standpoints transcend the personal and cultural. He discusses moral relativism, how universal morality can be distinguished from particular moralities, moral conflict and disagreement, human rights as universal standards, multiculturalism, cultural moral imperialism, and global social justice. Beauchamp argues that some moral standards are universal, whereas others are particular forms of institutional or social custom. He also argues that a true multiculturalist point of view requires universal morality, not merely cultural standards. He concludes that certain norms constrain corporate activities in all cultures, whereas other norms constrain corporate conduct only in specific contexts.

In "Business and Human Rights: A Principle and Value-Based Analysis," Wesley Cragg examines the responsibilities businesses have to conform their practices to human rights standards. With the creation of the United Nations Global Compact for Business and appeals to the U.S. Alien Tort Claims Act, this topic has become increasingly important for business. Cragg examines three models for understanding the human rights obligations of business organizations each of which, he argues, is seriously flawed. In their place, he defends a "hybrid model" that allocates human rights responsibilities to business organizations based upon the contexts in which a business is active.

In "Moral Issues in Globalization," Carol C. Gould focuses on the forms of globalization that are "often thought to be the defining social, political, and economic development of our times." Her chapter examines several key issues in business ethics raised by globalization, including global poverty, labor standards, and outsourcing. Underlying these issues are fundamental moral notions of global justice, transparency, and sustainability. After providing the reader with an analysis of these issues and ethical concepts, Gould traces the implications for business ethics. In her final major section, she devotes attention to corporate social responsibility, human rights, and social inequality.

Part V: The Use and Protection of Information

Information about products, employees, strategies, and resources forms the core of business. Its value is of unquestioned importance. Some of this information is rightfully private to business, for example, information about pricing strategies and intended mergers and acquisitions. Business has a responsibility to make other information public, such as that regarding the actual price it will charge customers for its products, its environmental impacts, and the results of pharmaceutical drug trials. Some information regarding employees, customers, and competitors business ought not to collect at all. Business goes beyond the rightful bounds of information collection when it pries into certain areas of the private lives of its employees or customers or when it uses illegal means to obtain information on competitors. Some information regarding its products—such as how they are produced, what goes into their production, or simply information that constitutes the product itself—ought to be protected for a business's own benefits and perhaps for those of society. For example, consumers do not have a right to know the exact ingredients and their proportions that go into the creation of Coca-Cola. How to sort out these difficult issues is the common thread that unites the articles in this part.

In "Deception and Information Disclosure in Business and Professional Ethics," Thomas L. Carson focuses on moral questions about deception and the many circumstances in which there are obligations to disclose information. He defends a definition of deception and connects it to related concepts of lying and withholding information. He also proposes a version of what he calls the Golden Rule and argues that it affords a strong moral presumption against deception even in cases in which deceptive practices may be common in business. He provides a general account of the duties of salespeople and analyzes several cases of deception and the withholding of information in sales. He also argues that advertising and bluffing in negotiations, though generally wrong, can sometimes be justified on grounds of "self-defense." His treatment includes a discussion of the fiduciary obligations of professionals to act for the benefit of their clients by giving truthful answers to questions.

Richard A. Spinello discusses the subject of "Informational Privacy" in his chapter. He starts with the body of problems of privacy that have been introduced in recent years through the arrival of cybertechnology, which allows large amounts of information to be rapidly collected and manipulated at minimal cost, affording businesses greater access to information about prospective customers, employees, and other key stakeholders. Cybertechnology creates many business opportunities that threaten personal privacy. Spinello proposes a definition of informational privacy and then distinguishes the concept of privacy from the value of privacy and the right to privacy. He notes that his stance on informational privacy is very different than traditional concerns about "physical privacy," that is, protection from an unwarranted intrusion into homes and similarly private spaces. He argues that the appearance of the computer and its capacity to gather massive amounts of information have changed our sense of privacy and about what will be required to maintain it.

Information that may affect the price of a corporation's stock raises other issues. If a person is able to gain inside information regarding new mineral finds that a company has discovered, or about the impending resignation of an effective CEO, then the price of that company's stock may be significantly affected. In his essay, "The Moral Problem in Insider Trading," Alan Strudler identifies the moral wrongness involved in insider trading. His discussion assumes a standard legal view of insider trading in which "a corporate insider engages in a securities transaction on the basis of material, nonpublic information." Given this understanding, Strudler examines both consequential and deontological accounts of the moral wrong of insider trading. He argues that standard consequentialist and deontological accounts are unpersuasive. Arguments morally condemning insider trading based upon harm, deception, theft, unfairness, or breaches so fiduciary duties are either normatively or empirically inadequate. Strudler argues it is the unconscionability of insider trading that is the most persuasive moral basis for wrongfulness of insider trading.

Finally, the chapter by Richard T. De George delves into the complex issues of "Intellectual Property Rights." He begins with a discussion of the complex notion of intellectual property that leads the reader through some of the crucial features of trademarks, patents, copyrights, and trade secrets. The upshot is that our understanding of intellectual property is closely tied to the various laws that protect its different forms. De George then examines three different justifications of intellectual property rights: a natural rights and justice argument; a utilitarian argument; and an argument based upon property being an extension of one's personality. Each has its strengths and weaknesses, but De George argues that the first two best stand up to critical scrutiny. These justifications apply only to the most general forms of intellectual property. Finally, De George considers more particular relations of legal and ethical considerations regarding intellectual property, with special emphasis on cases of copyright with respect to software and the digital information that constitutes music and film.

Part VI: Incentives and Influence

Business organizations involve wealth, valuable information, and the power to affect people and societies in which they operate. Of course, they may also be affected by the similar qualities of other businesses as well as the legal, regulatory, and political power of the societies in which they operate. How and on what bases businesses make decisions within this complex situation are crucial questions of business ethics.

Entering into this decision process are some danger zones. For example, if ethical decisions are to be made on the basis of objective considerations, unbiased by personal advantage, then how should business persons make decisions when their own personal interests, or those of others close to them, are involved? When do their interests conflict with the responsibilities they have as a result of the positions they occupy in the business? Unless business people can sort out these questions they may be accused of being involved in a conflict of interest.

In other situations, people in business may attempt to use their power, wealth, or valuable knowledge to influence or provide incentives to others to act in ways that may unjustly advantage them. Some of these situations involve various forms of corruption and bribery, as when businesses provide valuable incentives to government officials to persuade them to make official decisions that they would not otherwise make. Sometimes government officials use their position to try to force businesses to provide items of value to them. This may occur on a grand scale, or simply on a petty level such as passing expeditiously through customs. In either case, a question of bribery arises as well as the corruption of the system with which one does business.

Businesses have any number of interests that they may rightfully seek to pursue. Businesses may legitimately seek to make their views and interests known to the public and to members of the government. The question is how they may do so in a manner that is ethically justified. One extreme view holds that they may not present their views in any manner to an elected official. A more widely accepted view is that they may do so as long as they do not offer the official something of value that will sway his or her vote on issues of importance to the business. Which view is correct and where the lines of undue influence, manipulation, or even bribery run raise questions any ethical business must seek to answer.

In "Conflicts of Interest," Wayne Norman and Chris MacDonald remind us of the importance of the concept of conflict of interest to our ethical thinking about business. Though they do not defend a particular definition of "conflict of interest," they aim to give the reader a sense of the progress made, over recent decades, on settling various disputes regarding this concept. They sketch an agenda of empirical and normative questions that deserve attention and draw our attention to mid-level questions rather than micro- or macrolevel questions regarding conflicts of interest. They argue that the next stage in the development of our understanding of conflicts of interest should merge micro- and macrolevel studies with a middle realm. In the end, they aim to give the reader insight into "why our contemporary concept of conflict of interest was only dimly appreciated before the second half of the twentieth century even though we cannot now think our way through the challenges of organizational and professional ethics without it."

In "Corruption and Bribery," Manuel Velasquez focuses on the ethical issues that arise when business engages in bribery and corrupt activities. Though it is widely assumed that it is ethically wrong for business to engage in such activities, Velasquez notes that this assumption is often not closely examined. He contends that the main arguments that have been offered why corruption and bribery are wrong each have significant limitations. Still each of these arguments shows that corruption and bribery are generally unethical within modern Western cultural contexts. However, Velasquez argues, these arguments do not show that "corruption is unethical where the norms governing institutional roles are not widely known or accepted and where government is not understood as having the kind of public purpose that it is assumed to serve by members of Western societies." Given this provocative view, Velasquez concludes by considering how business should address the issues of corruption and bribery.

Andrew Stark argues in "Business in Politics: Lobbying and Corporate Campaign Contributions" that corporate political activity in the form of lobbying must be carried out between the principle of freedom of expression and the principle of a government free from corruption. By examining the interplay of these two democratic principles, Stark proposes "eight guidelines that should govern eight of the most common types of corporate political activity." Four involve corporate lobbying and four pertain to corporate finance. Though all eight involve risks of corruption, Stark argues that in four of these cases the form of expression is more democratically valuable than in the remaining four and may be permitted, though subject to various safeguards. In other cases, where the risk of corruption is greater and the form of expression less democratically valuable, Stark argues that corporations ought not to engage in these forms of political activity.

Part VII: Employee Rights and Corporate Responsibilities

However one looks at business, employees are central to the design, innovation, production, and distribution of its products. How business should treat its employees has been a major topic in business ethics since its beginning. Though some businesses still treat their employees simply as commodities to be used and then discarded, this view is in decline these days, at least in many leading businesses. However, what criteria should a business use in deciding whether or not to hire a person? May race or gender issues be counted either for or against a potential employee? Though blatant forms of discrimination are less and less frequent in many countries, they are prevalent in some countries and many important ethical questions remain regarding the justification of forms of preference, diversity, and affirmative action.

Once a person has been hired, the ethical issues do not end. May an employee be fired for no reason or bad reasons? The view that they may be dismissed without any kind of due process is one form of the "employment at will" doctrine that continues to hold considerable support in the United States. If a person remains employed, what conditions of health and safety must a business fulfill in order to treat an employee ethically? The highly hazardous conditions we sometimes find in sweatshops are unacceptable. But where is the ethical line in business's responsibilities regarding these conditions?

Finally, suppose that an employee has been properly hired and enjoys appropriate safety and health conditions, but suppose that the employee learns about something unethical or illegal that some other employee in the business has committed or is planning on committing. Are there responsibilities to report this action? If such reporting is discouraged, does he or she have a responsibility to blow the whistle on those involved in such acts? These are the kinds of questions and issues that frame this important topic in business ethics.

Bernard Boxill takes up the topic of "Discrimination, Affirmative Action, and Diversity in Business." Many writers on this subject have treated various U.S. policies and laws that encourage or require corporations and other institutions to advertise jobs fairly and to promote the hiring and promotion of members of groups formerly and currently discriminated against, most notably women and minority ethnic groups. Boxill takes a notably philosophical approach to these issues, by contrast to one that merely examines the letter and the spirit of federal laws and requirements. He examines whether several major philosophical theories can lead us to the correct conclusions. In particular, he argues that utilitarianism supports many forward-looking arguments for affirmative action based on good consequences and that natural rights theory can be used to support both forward-looking and backward-looking arguments for affirmative action. He also defends a version of the currently popular view that diversity in the workplace is an important grounding for affirmative action.

In "Whistle-Blowing, Moral Integrity, and Organizational Ethics," George G. Brenkert tackles the difficult topic of whistle-blowing, of how employees should respond when something illegal, immoral, or contrary to company policies becomes known to them. In his chapter, Brenkert surveys three prominent theories of when an employee would be justified in blowing the whistle. He identifies both strengths and weaknesses in each of these theories and defends an integrity account of whistle-blowing in their stead. At the end, he places whistle-blowing in its broader context of an organization that has permitted wrongdoing to take place and briefly surveys some organization design issues businesses should undertake to avoid the ethical issue of whistle-blowing arising in the first place.

John J. McCall and Patricia H. Werhane examine our understanding of the employment relation in their chapter, "Employment at Will and Employee Rights." In the United States, as opposed to Western Europe (and most of the rest of the world), a common law doctrine of Employment at Will is the predominate model by which this relationship is understood. Central to this view are norms emphasizing individualism, liberty, and property. These norms promote a bargaining relation between employer and employee. In contrast, European views of this relationship emphasize a partnership between employer and employee. McCall and Werhane ask whether there are good moral reasons to prefer one view or the other. They do so in light of purported employee rights against abusive treatment and arbitrary termination, due process and grievance procedures, and political free expression in the workplace. They conclude that there are good moral reasons for "holding that employees are entitled to employment-related rights that extend beyond those currently recognized in U.S. law." In their final section they discuss the outlook for their view given trends in globalization.

Another issue that has attracted considerable worldwide attention has been the working conditions that businesses put in place in their operations, not only in their home countries but particularly in developing countries. Denis G. Arnold discusses these issues in his chapter, "Working Conditions: Safety and Sweatshops." The issue is not whether employers have obligations to protect workers from workplace hazards but the extent of these obligations and whether they may be mitigated by other obligations or interests. Two general duties concerning safety play a key role in Arnold's analysis: the obligation to inform workers in advance regarding workplace hazards and the obligation to ensure minimum health and safety conditions. In response to the former, Arnold defends a reasonable-person standard that calls for managers to ask themselves, "What information about occupational health and safety conditions the manager would want prior to deciding whether or not to accept a job?" With regard to sweatshops, Arnold rejects various defenses of sweatshops. Instead, he contends that corporations must adhere to local labor laws, disclose workplace hazards to employees in accord with his reasonable-person standard, and fulfill an obligation, whose conditions he specifies, to improve workplace safety beyond legally mandated minimal standards. Finally, Arnold defends the view that a respectful treatment of workers requires that they be paid a weekly wage consistent with human dignity.

Part VIII: Safety, Risk, and Harm

Corporate activities present several types of risk of harm, including risks of psychological harm, physical harm, legal harm, and economic harm. For example, there are risks to consumers (and their families) from prepared foods (increased fat and sugar), drugs (side effects such as gastrointestinal bleeding), cigarettes (lung cancer), and so forth. Risks are also presented to workers (and their families) and to the public and the environment from carbon and other fuel emissions, toxic chemicals, and the like. The essays in part VIII concentrate on judgments of acceptable risk for consumers, workers, and the environment. The focus is primarily on the responsibilities of corporations to reduce risks to acceptable levels.

It is difficult for corporations and government agencies to adequately grasp the extent of the risks inherent in thousands of toxic chemicals, foods, drugs, energy sources, machines, and environmental emissions. Some conditions have serious, irreversible consequences; others do not. The *probability* of exposure to a risk may be known with some precision, whereas virtually nothing may be known about the harm's *magnitude*, or the magnitude may be precisely expressible, whereas the probability remains too indefinite to be calculated accurately. "Wild guess" sometimes best describes the accuracy with which chemical risks, for example, may be determined for products, for workers, or for the environment.

Over the last several decades the subjects of corporate environmental responsibility and product safety have become staples of work in business ethics. The public as well as writers in business ethics have become increasingly concerned about the environmental impact of chemical dumping, airborne emissions, nuclear power, oil pipelines and shipping, endangered species, and the like. Product safety too has had a long history of discussion in business ethics. Household and office accidents caused by many products are common. While major responsibility for the occurrence of a variety of harms rests primarily on the consumer, many risks can be described as inherent in the product and may or may not be reducible. Still other problems of risk derive from use of cheap materials, careless design, poor construction, or new discoveries about risk in an already marketed product.

In "Environmental Ethics and Business," Lisa H. Newton analyzes patterns of interaction between the for-profit corporation and the natural environment. She presents the history of concern about the environment, including the rapid growth of environmental awareness since the 1960s. Newton also traces corporate responses to environmental regulation and other environmental initiatives. She addresses new duties that she thinks now must be acknowledged, the new ethical frameworks in which the natural environment must be included and the emerging environmental agenda to be addressed in the twenty-first century. She argues that the issues should today be framed in business ethics so that there is no barrier between the interests of business and the protection of the environment.

In "The Mirage of Product Safety," John Hasnas takes up questions of product safety and product liability. He asks how we are to understand the idea that businesses have an ethical obligation to produce safe products. Hasnas argues that the answer is far from clear. He doubts whether the question can even be made meaningful and finds the business ethics literature thin and unconvincing. He argues that the concept of safety is inherently a matter of subjective evaluation, that the concept of an obligation to produce safe products is not well-formed, and that businesses do not have an ethical obligation to produce safe products. He concludes by arguing that businesses do have an ethical obligation not to produce deceptively dangerous products, but that this obligation derives from the general duty of honest dealing, not from a distinct duty of product safety.

Part IX: Creating Moral Organizations

The preceding parts of this book discuss ethical issues business faces on a variety of levels—from that of individual employees who must decide which information to provide customers or whether to blow the whistle, to managers who confront insider trading, corruption, and privacy, to organizational and societal levels concerned with lobbying and topics of justice that competitive markets raise. A remaining issue is how individual business organizations might be designed so that they foster moral action both within as well as outside their organizational walls. This has been a topic of considerable concern for businesses for decades. Most large North American businesses now have ethics and compliance officers who are charged with monitoring both the legal compliance and ethical behavior of employees. Corporate social responsibility officers have similar charges with respect to at least some of the external relations and activities of business. In recent years, the U.S. Federal Sentencing Guidelines has directed U.S. businesses to develop systems to ensure legal compliance as well as an ethical culture. Thus, what an "ethical culture" amounts to and how a business should go about creating one has become a matter of considerable importance for businesses.

In the concluding chapter, Norman E. Bowie writes on the subject of "Organizational Integrity and Moral Climates." He starts with the assumption that business organizations have personalities that can be called a culture or a moral climate. He considers what distinguishes an organization with integrity and which factors hinder organizational integrity. Detailing the characteristics of a moral climate is the general goal of this essay. Bowie argues that achieving organizational integrity may require that managers de-emphasize or even, in certain situations, ignore issues of personal responsibility and that an organization with integrity must put in place certain kinds of organizational structures and incentives. He points to the great importance of a commitment to stakeholder management and a commitment to seeing the purpose of the organization as a cooperative enterprise. Finally, he considers the role of incentives as they support or inhibit organizational integrity and raises questions about whether for-profit organizations can instill organizational integrity and remain profitable.

A reader who has read through the preceding parts and their chapters will come away with a current, philosophically oriented understanding of some of the major ethical issues and dilemmas that business faces. Upon this basis he or she should be well prepared to engage in further discussion and reflection on some of the most important ethical issues facing individuals, business, and society in the coming decades.

PART I

BASIC PHILOSOPHICAL ISSUES

CHAPTER 1

THE METHODS OF BUSINESS ETHICS

RONALD M. GREEN
AINE DONOVAN

Bob Collingwood was President and Chief Executive Officer of the U.S. subsidiary of Woodland International, a large multinational company headquartered in Europe. Bob was responsible for all of Woodland's activities in the U.S. His functional responsibilities included manufacturing as well as public affairs. As he checked his appointment calendar for the upcoming two weeks, he could see that the schedule listed appointments with one external group after another, with agendas ranging from traditional labor management issues to concerns with Woodland's social responsibility.

On Monday a state legislature in the Northeast where Woodland had major manufacturing facilities would open two days of hearings on a bill requiring companies to notify the state government before moving a plant out of state.... On Saturday, the leaders of a coalition of consumer organizations would arrive to hear his talk about the merits and safety of several of Woodland's products. And, on Sunday an environmental group was going to hold a demonstration to protest air pollution caused by a Woodland plant.... The following week Collingwood was scheduled to go to Washington for a meeting concerning his compliance with the newest set of regulatory guidelines....

> Collingwood had risen rapidly at Woodland
> International, and was headed for "stardom" in company
> headquarters in Europe if he so desired. However, Bob did
> not feel prepared for the diverse mix of situations which he
> now faced....Bob knew that he needed a framework and a
> strategy for managing diversity and turbulence, to get out of
> the crisis-reaction-crisis cycle. This book is about Bob and
> the thousands of managers around the world like him who
> meet all the criteria for "good managers," yet who do not
> seem able to manage well in today's fast changing business
> environment.

Thus begins R. Edward Freeman's *Strategic Management: A Stakeholder Approach* (1984),[1] a pioneering book in the field of business ethics. In this work, Freeman outlines a vision of managerial responsibility that goes beyond the firm's owners or shareholders to embrace all of its stakeholders, whom he defines as "any group or individual who can affect or is affected by the achievement of the firm's objectives."[2] In the years following publication of *Strategic Management*, hundreds of influential articles and several books on the stakeholder approach have emerged.[3] More than twenty years later, Freeman and coauthors published *Managing for Stakeholders*.[4] Like its predecessor, the later work opens by focusing on the decisional challenges facing Bob Collingwood, still a senior manager of Woodland International, which is now portrayed as an even larger firm facing business and ethical challenges around the world.

Freeman's stakeholder account is just one approach to business ethics found in the vast literature on this topic that has appeared over the past few decades. Nevertheless, it provides an important introduction to the methods of business ethics because it exhibits some of the key objectives of those who work in the field. The methods that are employed in any field of human endeavor flow from an understanding of its goals and objectives, what might be called its *mission*. The mission of medicine, for example, is to prevent or cure illness. In pursuing its mission, medicine has privileged scientific research into the causes of disease and, even when lacking such understanding, it has favored practices such as the use of drugs or surgery that provide patient benefit.

Business ethics, too, is a field with a mission that has greatly influenced its choice of methods. Freeman's opening narrative about Bob Collingwood provides insight into this mission. We can summarize it by saying that business ethics, especially as it has been developed by scholars in the United States, aims at improving the quality of business managers' ethical thinking and performance. The goal is not just to understand the ethics of business people and business organizations but to *improve* them. This goal extends to all aspects of business activity, from the design, sales, and marketing of products to the quality of relationships with the firm's key constituencies, whether they are its stockholders, customers, or employees.

This mission of improving managers' ethical performance has at least three implications for the methods of inquiry, teaching, and practice of business ethics. First, it tells us that, at its core, business ethics is a morally intentioned activity. It starts from the assumption that business firms *should* act ethically and that the people who direct them should likewise express and develop a commitment to ethical conduct. In terms of its academic basis, business ethics has been rooted in law, philosophy, theology, and the liberal arts. A focus on ethics and a commitment to humanistic values are among its defining features. Although moral reasoning aimed at supporting managers' ethical obligations has not always represented the bulk of work in business ethics, it remains central because it both stimulates and guides work in the field.

A second implication of the practical and ethical mission of business ethics points in a seemingly opposite direction. The centrality of ethical concerns and methods has not ruled out significant employment in much business ethics scholarship of descriptive and social scientific methodologies. Almost all ethical theories, even those that appeal to abstract principles, recognize the need to understand the context and consequences of moral decision. This is especially true of fields such as business ethics, where choices affect so many people and where the implications of those choices must be well understood. It is also true, however, that the copresence of both normative and descriptive methodologies creates an inherent tension in the field. We will see that this tension often expresses itself in business ethics scholarship and in the institutions in which business ethics is studied and taught. In business ethics education today, this tension has even led to a shift away from the philosophical toward pragmatic and economic approaches.

Third, the ethical mission of the field has led to its being focused primarily on the *individual* business manager, whether as a member of the board of directors, the CEO of the firm, a middle-level executive, or a newly graduated MBA seeking a first job. This focus, in turn, has shaped the field's choice of methodologies by highlighting issues or areas that are within the orbit of managerial discretion and that pertain to managers' responsibilities. Graduate education for business leaders reflects this orientation toward the manager, with cases that focus on executive misconduct and expressions of greed that create mistrust among stakeholders.[5] However, this focus has also tended to draw attention away from the structural features of the business environment, such as legal, social, cultural, political, or economic systems that concern managers as citizens but are not generally seen as pertaining to the domain of managerial decision making. Managers are presumed to work within these systems, but their business responsibilities have not usually been perceived as extending to shaping them. It is true that one subfield of business ethics—the interest in corporate social responsibility (CSR)—has encouraged discussion of the role of the corporation in alleviating social problems.[6] CSR encourages companies to maintain their financial performance while addressing social ills, even when those ills are not a result of the company's business practices. But CSR, like business ethics generally, retains its focus on the decisions of the individual manager or corporate officer. It does not usually extend to attempting to change the legal, social, or cultural environments that shape corporate decision making. We will see that this relative lack of attention to the larger context of managerial conduct places limits on how well business ethics can accomplish its mission of improving the performance of business managers and their firms.

In what follows we examine how the mission of business ethics has shaped its choice of methodological approaches, explaining the central importance of philosophical and ethical analysis, the copresence of descriptive methodologies, and the focus on individual managerial decision making. Referring to the work of leading business ethics scholars, we will show that these features describe a field that is both limited and also intellectually ambitious. We conclude with an examination of the ways in which these features have influenced the method adopted in the teaching of business ethics.

The Centrality of Philosophical
and Ethical Methodologies

Business ethics today emerges from a series of ethical discussions that began during the early 1970s in the United States about the social responsibilities of business. Against a background of turmoil generated by the war in Vietnam, the Watergate scandal, foreign investment in South Africa's Apartheid regime, and racial conflict in the United States, many people were calling for business to take more of an activist role in addressing social problems. Amid this debate, the economist Milton Friedman, writing in the *New York Times Magazine* in 1970, challenged the concept of the corporate social responsibility of business by arguing that the primary duty of managers is to serve the interests of shareholders. The manager, in his view, is "an employee of the owners of the business," and is required to "conduct the business in accordance with their desires, which generally will be to make as much money as possible."[7]

Friedman's point was a moral one, based on a conception of the property rights of stockholders and business owners. Nevertheless, his argument was also taken as supportive of the concept of the "amoral manager," the individual who puts most moral values aside in the name of maximizing profit. This view was buttressed by others who defended the essential independence of business from most moral constraints. Albert Z. Carr likened business to the game of poker in an influential essay that appeared in the *Harvard Business Review* in 1968 titled "Is Business Bluffing Ethical?" Both are activities untouched by one's personal moral values. They evidence a "special ethics" in which deception is routine and winning and losing are the supreme value considerations.[8] Friedman and Carr appeared to agree that businessmen and women must obey the law, but when no laws are broken or none exist (as is often the case in the international context), managers are not obligated to consider the welfare of nonshareholders who might be negatively affected by their actions.

Stakeholder theory was largely a reaction against these positions. It was driven by the strong intuitive sense that managers have responsibilities to other people affected by a firm, not just to its shareholders. From its start, stakeholder theory has had important descriptive, instrumental, and normative dimensions.[9] That is, it has sought to describe stakeholder relationships, to offer the stakeholder perspective as one that is conducive to successful management, and to provide an underlying moral justification of managers' responsibilities to stakeholders. In Freeman's earliest expressions of stakeholder theory, the underlying moral idea was only suggested. His primary emphasis—stimulated by a series of major corporate scandals that marked the preceding decade—was instrumental and focused on the connection between attention to stakeholders and organizational survival and success. But the normative moral foundations became clearer in his later writings. Collaborating with Daniel R. Gilbert, William M. Evan, and others, Freeman sought to base managers' obligations to stakeholders on both Kantian and Rawlsian grounds,[10] a line of thinking that was further developed by Robert Phillips.[11] These approaches appealed to notions of fairness and respect for persons as the basis for stakeholder obligations. In their 1988 volume, *Corporate Strategy and the Search for Ethics*, Freeman and Gilbert describe the stakeholder approach as seeking to "infuse corporate strategy with an understanding of values and ethics."[12] Eventually Freeman and others working on stakeholder theory attempted to establish these obligations on a variety of theoretical grounds, ranging from a utilitarian position of greatest social benefit,[13] to American pragmatism,[14] and a feminist ethics of care.[15] In his book *Business Ethics: A Kantian Perspective*, Norman Bowie applied Kant's three formulations of the categorical imperative to argue that managers' obligations extend beyond the shareholders of the firm. Bowie used a Kantian perspective to criticize the narrow "economic paradigm" governing most management theories. He insisted that managers should focus "less on profit" and "more on doing the right thing," which means "treating the humanity of all corporate stakeholders as an end and managing in accord with the principles of the moral firm."[16]

Although stakeholder theories have been a main avenue of response to the challenge posed by those denying the moral responsibilities of business managers, they are not the only way that business ethicists have responded to the narrowly economic or "amoral" shareholder view. Business ethicists have also appealed directly to various types of moral theories to ground the responsibilities of managers to others than shareholders. The aim has been to show that sound moral reasoning leads to the conclusion that managers are responsible not only to the owners of firms who employ them but also to a wide range of constituents, including communities, employees, consumers, and others. Almost every major philosophical approach has been enlisted for this purpose, ranging from Kant's strict, duty-oriented position[17] to utilitarianism, and a host of positions seeking to combine both consequentialist and duty-oriented principles.[18] Virtue theories,[19] religious-ethical positions,[20] and varieties of contractualism drawing on the work of the philosopher John Rawls[21] have all been invoked. Theorists have also offered strategic visions for the firm resting on moral premises[22] or have developed business leadership positions emphasizing ethical integrity.[23]

These efforts to bring approaches from the field of moral philosophy into business ethics have posed some difficult challenges for the field. Different moral theories frequently offer radically different guidance in cases of practical decision. What is one to do when theories are unhelpful or point in opposite directions? For example, a manager relying on utilitarianism and heeding that theory's overarching requirement to seek "the greatest good overall" might well be led to misrepresent the dangers of a defective product if the net costs of a recall appeared to outweigh the product's dangers. In contrast, a Kantian in this situation might feel duty bound to tell the truth regardless of consequences.

Conflicts of this sort raise the question of the place of moral theory in business ethics. Is theory meant to guide decision making? If so, what are business ethics scholars and teachers, and also managers to do in the face of this conflicting advice? Are real instances of business decision making meant to inform theorizing and perhaps lead to greater refinement and choice on the theoretical side? Within moral philosophy, there is a long-standing view, perhaps best represented by John Rawls's concept of "reflective equilibrium," that theory and our intuitive judgments in instances of decision should ultimately correspond and reinforce one another.[24] Theories that consistently run counter to our intuitive judgments are unacceptable, although this does not rule out a viable theory's leading us to revise one or more of our intuitive judgments if we become convinced that it is wrong. Is business ethics, then, a search for reflective equilibrium in this sense? Are theories meant to be "in conversation" with real managerial choices, the aim being the development of theories that in philosophical and practical terms are both compelling and useful?

Unfortunately, despite the widespread resort to philosophical theories and methods in much work in business ethics, these questions have not often been well addressed. In a survey of leading business ethics texts in the early 1990s, Green and Derry showed that philosophical theories are often used in a rather wooden manner in many such texts.[25] Theories are often introduced without adequate attention to their potentially opposing implications. When these implications are noted and efforts are made to overcome the problem, the efforts are often less than satisfactory. In some instances, students using the texts are advised to apply all the available theories to cases for decision. In other instances, students are encouraged to combine different aspects of the theories to help resolve cases, taking elements from utilitarianism, for example, and aspects of principled reasoning from duty-oriented theories. Some theorists argued for the employment of mid-level theories that share elements of several competing views.[26] Finally, some of the texts, after introducing theory at the outset, simply point the students/readers to the cases and ask them to do as best they can on their own. By leaving students with the impression that theory is either employed ad hoc or irrelevant, however, these approaches often support a trend to relativism or amoralism among business students.

Integrating philosophical theory into business ethics remains one of its most persistent challenges of the field. As suggested here, that integration has not always been successful. The problem crops up again in business ethics teaching. As we will see, it has often been very difficult to integrate either moral philosophy or the moral philosopher into the management curriculum or programs of business ethics. Despite this serious problem, however, the methods of philosophy remain seminal to the field of business ethics. The justification of managers' moral responsibilities, an essentially moral and philosophical enterprise, has marked the field from its start.

Although the justification of managers' and firms' ethical responsibilities has been one major focus of normative business ethics, philosophically inclined business ethicists have also paid attention to a host of other matters. Much work in business ethics has involved the formulation of moral judgments about a wide array of issues, from ethical conduct in sales, marketing, or purchasing to the challenges posed by doing business in the international setting.[27] There are many opinions on precisely how the principles of morality should be applied to business ethics, but it has generally been understood in the field that normative ethical theory provides the tools necessary for analysis and informed discussion of ethical issues in business. This gives normative ethics a primacy of place in business ethics.

Finally, we should observe that attention has also sometimes been focused on metaethical issues regarding the meaning and application of moral concepts in the business setting. Such issues involve the very meaning of basic moral terms and concepts. Perhaps foremost among these questions in business ethics are those relating to the moral status of the corporation. Can we regard the corporation as a moral entity to which we can apply the concepts of praise and blame as we commonly do to individuals? Anglo-American law regards the corporation as a legal person. During the 1980s, philosophers attracted to business ethics began asking what this means for our understanding of the corporation's moral responsibilities?[28] Their inquiries were spurred, in part, by catastrophes such as the release of toxic gas at Union Carbide's plant in Bhopal, India, or Firestone's manufacture and marketing of its defective 500-series tires. In these and similar cases, blame seemed less appropriate for individual managers caught up in massive organizational misconduct than for the corporation that fostered the misbehavior. By stressing the role of corporate intention and corporate structures in the process of decision making, philosophers have argued that corporations have the essential features we ordinarily associate with responsibility and accountability in individual decision making.[29]

The use of moral theory in business ethics has been far from perfect. We will see that these shortcomings have sometimes encouraged a flight from philosophical ethics in business ethics education and, more recently, have had the effect of frequently sidelining philosophers and ethicists in the teaching of business ethics. These problems, in turn, have been accentuated by the heavy reliance in business ethics education on the case method. This pedagogical method is not unique to business education. It was initially developed for legal education but has been brilliantly adapted to business by leading educators.[30] Cases are rich narratives that bring readers to the center of real business dilemmas and force decision. The case method personalizes abstract theory and encourages both active learning, and depending upon its use, teamwork. The full development of the case method, as evidenced in the Harvard Business School's publication program and numerous case textbooks, is one of the achievements of the field of business ethics.

Nevertheless, the ethical resolution of complex cases, as opposed to their mere discussion, requires resort to adequate philosophical argumentation. This again points to the centrality of philosophical analysis, and to the fact that it often receives only cursory attention.

THE COPRESENCE OF EMPIRICAL METHODS

Even though the analysis of moral arguments and justification of moral positions associated with moral philosophy has had pride of place since the inception of the field, this has not eclipsed an enormous amount of work in the field by scholars utilizing empirical methodologies. Various empirical methods deriving from such social-scientific fields as economics, political science, psychology and social psychology, ethnography, anthropology, and sociology have been employed. Survey research received an impressive start in an article titled "How Ethical Are Businessmen?" by Ray C. Baumhart that appeared in the *Harvard Business Review* in 1961,[31] and that was followed in 1968 by his book *An Honest Profit: What Businessmen Say about Ethics in Business*.[32] Since that beginning, survey-based studies have had an important place in the field.[33] These studies have employed multiple regression and ANOVA (analysis of variance) experimental designs. Much less frequently, some theorists have used computer-based experiments[34] or other "experiments" (often using students) to test theories regarding factors affecting behavior in organizations, such as the link between pay cuts and employee theft.[35] The field of Organizational Behavior (OB), which has often, though not exclusively,[36] been the home of business ethics in many business schools, utilizes all these disciplines and methods in a "systems approach" that stresses the interaction of many causal processes within the complex social system of the business organization.[37]

These empirical studies have a common interest in understanding the causal factors associated with ethical misconduct (or, less commonly, good ethical performance) within organizations. Social science approaches are used to explain and/or predict such behaviors as lying, cheating, stealing, or whistle-blowing or the factors that lead to serious forms of corporate misconduct such as environmental abuse and bribery or corruption. Researchers have identified factors influencing managers' reasoning and choices[38] and the roles played by peers and supervisors in unethical behavior.[39] At the organizational level, investigators have studied the impact on ethical behaviors of the firm's ethical climate,[40] cultures,[41] organizational size,[42] financial performance or its relationship to competitors,[43] and corporate codes of conduct.[44] Emerging fields such as behavioral economics, which applies scientific research on human emotional biases to better understand economic decisions, have also been used to better understand organizational ethical dynamics. Game theory and behavioral studies motivated Frans de Waal, professor of primate behavior and psychology at Emory University, to refute the assumption that human beings are profit maximizers driven by selfishness. He concludes that humans, like the primates studied, have a natural interest in cooperation that benefits the entire community.[45] All of these new fields of inquiry and methods indicate the complexity of business decision making. Their findings are essential for responsible ethical choice in the organizational context.

This plethora of empirical methodologies illustrates how both normative and empirical approaches have played an important role in business ethics. Nevertheless, the centrality of practical and normative concerns is evidenced by the fact that much empirical research in the field has been stimulated by the effort to defend normative positions or answer normative questions. The central questions persist. Are there alternatives to an ethics of strict profit maximization? Which factors in an organization's leadership, culture, or incentive systems enhance ethical performance? Which invite ethical misconduct?

In some cases, ethical theorists have sought to incorporate empirical/descriptive components into their normative positions in order to render them more applicable to managerial decision making. A leading example of this is the "integrated social contract theory" (ISCT) of Thomas Donaldson and Thomas Dunfee.[46] ISCT seeks to address what its authors see as a major problem in normative business ethics: the abstraction and generality of many ethical theories and their seeming irrelevance to the concrete norms, values, and practices with which business managers must work. In the words of Donaldson and Dunfee:

> The theory promises...to reach beyond the generality of, say, Kantian deontology or "virtue" ethics to allow a more detailed normative assessment of particular ethical problems in business. ISCT is heavily contextual and thereby establishes an agenda for empirical research as a means for establishing authentic ethical norms in industries, corporations, alliances, and regional economic systems.[47]

We will see that what makes norms "authentic" is one of the more controversial issues raised by Donaldson and Dunfee's theory. Nevertheless, the authors point to the theory's value in the arena of global business where high-level moral norms elaborated by philosophers are often challenged by different local cultural values and practices. The hallmark of ISCT is its refusal to dismiss these diverse normative patterns, even while it resists ethical relativism, the view that holds that whether an action is right or wrong depends on the moral norms of the society in which it is practiced. ISCT is built on the importance of "contracts" in managerial decision making at two different levels. First, there is a high-level "macrosocial contract" that is hypothetical in nature and similar to Rawls's "original position." In Rawls's theory, the basic norms of justice are derived by agreements within this position by rational decision makers who are rendered radically impartial by being thought of as deprived of all knowledge of their strengths and weakness and their place in society. For Donaldson and Dunfee, a contract of this type eventuates in "hypernorms" that apply everywhere and take precedence over all other norms identified by the theory. Although the hypernorms are generally derived by rational and conceptual analysis from the circumstances of this hypothetical contract, so-called "substantive hypernorms" are empirically discoverable and have their source in the "convergence of human experience and intellectual thought."[48] These substantive hypernorms open ISCT to high-level, empirically discernible normative input, including global ethical conventions such as the 1948 United Nations Universal Declaration of Human Rights or the 1994 Caux Round Table, intergovernmental compacts (e.g., the OECD Guidelines), and evolving patterns of religious, cultural, and philosophical belief.[49]

The second kind of contract is "microsocial" and is exemplified by the many agreements found in individual communities. These can include such matters as the very different norms governing business entertainment and gift giving that prevail from firm to firm, industry to industry, region to region, or country to country. Similarly, individual corporations and national cultures can allowably differ on such issues as the role of family and interpersonal loyalty in business versus efficiency and profit. In keeping with ISCT, each economic community or business firm is allowed to develop its own practices in these and related areas. The norms implicit in these practices must be respected, so long as they do not involve the violation of hypernorms and are "authentic" in the sense that they are freely adopted and are "supported by the attitudes of a clear majority of the community."[50] A community is understood to be "a self-defined self-circumscribed group of people who interact in the context of shared tasks, values, or goals and who are capable of establishing norms of ethical behavior for themselves."[51] Authentic communities can include individual business organizations, industrial associations, and regional or national economic groups. By making provision for such microsocial contracts, ISCT seeks to maximize the "moral free space" available to business managers, allowing them to discern and respect local norms and even create new norms for new situations. Donaldson and Dunfee believe that ISCT bridges the normative/descriptive divide by encouraging attention to existing practices and norms in the communities in which managers work (both within and outside of the firm).

As an effort within normative theory to integrate the normative and descriptive sides of business ethics, ISCT is not free of problems. Noting the importance of hypernorms in the theory as a whole, critics have pointed to the relative lack of development of this idea,[52] especially the tension between the conceptual/normative and empirical/descriptive sides of the theory.[53] For example, Donaldson and Dunfee assert that a commitment to gender equality in the workplace is a hypernorm, although they do not offer any conceptually normative argument for this assertion and sometimes appear to suggest that it is somehow empirically discoverable. At the same time, they acknowledge that many communities appear to have "authentic" microsocial norms—norms "supported by the attitudes of a clear majority of the community"—that do not support gender equality in the workplace and elsewhere. In asserting the priority of gender justice without fully developing its normative basis in hypernorms or the reasons that these norms trump opposing microsocial contracts, ISCT shows that it is not entirely successful in developing or integrating either the normative or empirical elements in its theory. The same is true of its attempt to overcome the tension between high-level, allegedly universal moral norms in such areas as bribery or the neglect of intellectual property rights and the reality of microsocial contracts that tolerate these practices.

The tension between normative and empirical approaches evidenced in ISCT also characterizes the field of business ethics as whole. In a survey of methods in business ethics, Linda Trevino and Gary Weaver point to this tension in describing major differences in the assumptions and underlying scholarly commitments of normative and empirical researchers in the field.[54] They point out that normatively inclined business ethicists, reflecting their academic specialty in philosophy, theology, or the liberal arts, tend to use a language that involves critical rational analysis of arguments. They also presume the autonomy and moral agency of those working in business environments. In contrast, empirical researchers use a language of description and empirical methods to measure, explain, and predict behavior in organizations. Their scientific orientation leads them to hold a more deterministic view of human nature, the view that human conduct is less freely chosen than people believe and the result of more identifiable causal factors inside or outside the individual. Trevino and Weaver believe these different methodologies and perspectives can complement one another. They have argued for the need to move beyond symbiosis of these methods to full theoretical integration or "hybridization,"[55] but they also acknowledge the tension between philosophical analysis and empirical studies. "It is not clear," they observe, "why or how one should stop short of thinking in terms of a single field of inquiry, rather than two related fields."[56]

We will see that these tensions also characterize the teaching of business ethics. When MBA students are taught ethics in a course that is distinctly humanities oriented, they often lose the connection to the more pragmatic and empirically grounded course offerings needed in business: finance, marketing, strategy, and the like. However, what some perceive to be a problem for the field can also be regarded as one of its strengths. Unlike many scholarly pursuits, business ethics from its start has been unashamedly normative. It has cherished the goal of guiding the way that business organizations approach their ethical responsibilities. It has also recognized that values and ideals make no sense and will not be accepted by business managers unless they are conjoined with an understanding of the realities of the business world. The tensions resulting from this mix of methodologies are the unavoidable consequence of the attempt to have a real impact on the ethical practices of managers like Bob Collingwood.

The Focus on Individual Managerial Decision Making

Despite the tension between empirical and philosophical approaches, most work in business ethics retains a focus on informing and educating the individual manager. This focus, however, creates methodological problems by narrowing the scope of some work in the field. We saw that the modern field of business ethics emerged as a response to the narrowly economic or "amoral" view of management. As such, it tends to maintain the individualistic focus, while replacing the single line of responsibility to the shareholder with a network of stakeholder ties. Managers are typically viewed as the central agents of business ethics and the subjects to whom its guidance is directed. The philosopher Robert Solomon expresses this notion when he says,

> Corporate life and consequently corporate success will be determined by the character and personality of the individuals who are its constituents, and though the nature of the corporation will have much to do with the formation of that character, it will also be the product of the totality of personalities that guide and run it.[57]

Solomon is a virtue theorist who believes that individual moral exemplars provide our norms of moral conduct and that the creation of such exemplars is a goal of our moral efforts. But this focus in business ethics on informing the conduct of individual managers is by no means confined to virtue theorists. Whether they are utilitarians, Kantians, or proponents of a feminist or other type of theory, business ethicists have always assumed that educating the individual manager—and through that manager others in the firm—is the primary activity of the field. With the manager's instruction as its pivot, business ethics reaches backward to the selection of normative approaches likely to be persuasive to individuals, and it reaches forward, often drawing on empirical studies, to the development of these approaches so that managers can use them effectively.

In addition to the need to respond to the challenge posed by the concept of the "amoral manager," there are several reasons why this individualized and managerial focus has predominated in the field. One is the placement of business ethics courses within the context of business education. Although, these courses, at least in their earliest stages, were frequently introduced and taught by faculty trained in philosophy, the courses themselves tend to flourish in business or pre-business undergraduate programs or in graduate business (MBA) programs. This has tended to shift the curriculum of the field from broad scholarly inquiry about the relations between business and society to a pre-professional approach aimed at shaping the thinking of students who will someday assume managerial responsibilities. The presence of business ethics in executive education programs has had a similar effect. Directed at improving organizational performance by changing managers' assumptions and processes of thinking, these programs appeal by design to the professional needs and interests of managers.

The focus on guiding individual managers has had two further effects on the content of business ethics scholarship and teaching. First, it has striven to show the link between ethics and corporate flourishing. If individual managers are to commit to business integrity, they must be persuaded that this commitment will not undermine personal and organizational success, and that it should even contribute to success. But the preponderance of short-term and bottom-line thinking in business continues to pose a challenge to those who argue for the link between profitability and ethics.

From its inception, stakeholder theory tried to redress the disconnection between theorists and practitioners. We have already noted that this theory has an "instrumental" dimension in addition to its descriptive and normative commitments. Freeman has always insisted that it be regarded as belonging to the sphere of strategic management. As such, it is integrally related to the task of organizational survival, profitability, stability, and growth. In *Managing for Stakeholders,* Freeman and his coauthors distinguish stakeholder theory from the concept of Corporate Social Responsibility (CSR). They believe that the latter stresses the social responsibilities of businesses and in doing so places ethical responsibility in a region separate from good business management. In contrast, the goal of stakeholder theory "is to promote a different way of doing business that integrates considerations of business, ethics, and society."[58] Freeman and his colleagues believe that a business's productivity derives from its effort to create value for all its stakeholders. As a result, "The more we can begin to think in terms of how to better serve stakeholders, the more likely we will be to survive and prosper over time."[59] The work of Freeman and colleagues thus epitomizes what might be called "a business case for business ethics." One may question whether this confidence in the union of ethical integrity and long-term business success is fully justified. Nevertheless, it remains a fundamental premise of the field. It is also a premise that justifies and motivates much of the normative and descriptive work in business ethics.[60]

A second effect of the focus on guiding individual managers is an emphasis on providing tools for making appropriate decisions in this context and for understanding organizational factors that lead to or detract from ethical conduct. With some important exceptions, this has drawn attention away from understanding some of the larger forces or structures that shape and are shaped by the ethics of individuals and firms. Although often present elsewhere in the business curriculum, attention to the political and legal environments in which business works or the social and cultural realities that interact with corporations tends to be less prevalent in the business ethics context. So, too, are questions about the inherent justice of the economic and political system(s) in which businesses operate.

This point was made as early as 1991 in an article by Richard L. Lippke that criticized the approach to business ethics found in many standard texts of the field.[61] Lippke noted that a concern to provide guidance to business practitioners forms the dominant approach to the field. This "concern to get moral considerations of a relatively basic and uncontroversial sort in the corporate door" leads, however, to a relative neglect of larger issues of social justice as they bear on the conduct of business firms. While some foundational texts in the field, such as Richard De George's *Business Ethics*, try to address competing theories of social justice as they bear on the justification of free market capitalism and its institutions, these excursions into complex matters of political philosophy do not fit well within the "practitioner model" and are usually left unresolved. In Lippke's view, this neglect of theory as it relates to the broader context of business life has serious consequences for the adequacy of the field. For example, it makes it difficult, if not impossible, to assess accurately such key business ethics issues as employees' right to participate in decision making in the workplace.[62] Today, it would make difficult a critique of the enormous gap in compensation between the average worker and many corporate CEOs.

A similar criticism was voiced by John Boatright in a provocative 1998 presidential address to the Society of Business Ethics titled "Does Business Ethics Rest on a Mistake?"[63] Boatright observed that business ethicists have tended "to focus in our teaching and research on the high-level corporate manager, typically a CEO, who shapes the environment of an organization and makes the key strategic decisions."[64] He calls this "the Moral Manager Model," but adds that if it describes the aim of business ethics, "we are fighting a losing battle." The uninterrupted series of corporate ethics scandals shows that the field has so far had little impact on managerial behavior. "Reports from the front do not describe trends that favor the Moral Manager Model," says Boatright. "The most admired corporate executives fit the conventional view of the hard-headed, business-savvy decision maker."[65]

What has gone wrong? Boatright's answer is that the Moral Manager Model rests on the assumption that the business organization is the fundamental unit of analysis for business ethics, when the reality is that other structures may be more important. One structure is the market itself. Although economic theory often presumes perfect markets, "many ethical problems in business arise from market and regulatory failures." As such, a leading question for business ethics is "how best to overcome these failures."[66] The answers to this question, however, take us beyond individual managerial decision making and raise political and legal questions for all members of society. In place of the Moral Manager Model, Boatright proposes what he calls the Moral Market Model, which emphasizes that ensuring moral markets would place responsibility on all of us to improve the business system by creating more efficient markets and more effective regulation.[67] The goal might be to develop a form of corporate governance and economic oversight that reduces individual managerial discretion and favors rules or structures that better shape the conduct of individual actors. The German model of codetermination (*Mitbestimmung*), according to which workers and employees have appointed places on corporate boards, illustrates a dramatically different approach to the social understanding of corporate governance against a background of larger social and legal frameworks.[68]

Not too differently, George Brenkert has called into question what he calls the "Moralist Model" of the firm as a way of understanding its responsibilities to the environment.[69] This model treats the firm as an agent that, through its individual managers, is able to act, exercise moral judgment, and make moral decisions.

In doing so, the Moralist Model approach treats problems "on the level of the particular institution, not the system of business institutions." That system, however, can exhibit significant constraints such as limited information, powerful organizational incentives, and intense competition with other firms that prevent a business or its managers from acting on moral grounds. Progress in fostering corporate environmental responsibility may not be made unless the business system itself is restructured. Brenkert points to the need for changes in such matters as the firm's systems of authority and accountability, its willingness to cooperate with other corporations, the government, and the public; the openness of its conduct to others' scrutiny; and the extent of democratization of its decision making.[70]

Lippke's, Boatright's, and Brenkert's critiques apply well beyond the economic or business system. Once ethical attention is shifted from informing and guiding the individual manager or firm, it might focus instead on the laws and regulations that shape all aspects of society, including political and legal systems.[71] For example, restructuring laws that govern corporate contributions to election campaigns might have much more of an effect on ethical business conduct than all the admonitions to managerial civic responsibility found in stakeholder analysis. The passage of the Foreign Corrupt Practices Act (FCPA) in 1977 provides one example of a legal initiative that had an external, transformative effect on much managerial practice. Among other things, this legal initiative stimulated the development of new, voluntary ethics codes in various parts of the world.[72] Some business ethicists such as Richard De George have recognized the importance of such inter-firm structural approaches in addressing the challenges of international business.[73]

Two other examples illustrate the point. In 1991, strict federal sentencing guidelines providing legal guidance to judges on how to sentence those involved in white-collar crime were modified to permit more lenient penalties if companies could demonstrate that they had in place measures to prevent unethical behavior. These adjusted guidelines both reflected and gave momentum to corporate efforts to institutionalize ethical oversight through compliance offices and written codes of conduct. This illustrates how social and legal factors beyond the sphere of managerial initiative could have a positive impact on organizational behavior.

The other example of legal-structural reform is offered by the Sarbanes-Oxley Act, a 2002 legislative response to unprecedented levels of corporate corruption and fraud. The aim of Sarbanes-Oxley legislation was to restore investor confidence by improving corporate financial reporting. In the circumstances that led to that legislation, Enron overstated its net income by $586 million and became the symbol of corporate greed and corruption for the 1990s, while Arthur Andersen, Enron's auditing firm, destroyed potentially incriminating financial records and was eventually indicted for criminal misconduct. Similarly, WorldCom overstated its cash flow by $3.8 billion, and Tyco committed a variety of financial misdeeds. The rush to remedy the situation led to numerous policies and programs, all of which were eventually folded into the Sarbanes-Oxley Act. The challenge for business ethicists is in restoring the shared responsibility of stewardship among employee, shareholder, and board member.

A 2006 *Fortune Magazine* article by Andrew Serwer cited Mallory Factor, chairman of the Free Enterprise Fund, as claiming that Sarbanes-Oxley coincided with the loss of $1.4 trillion of shareholder wealth.[74] Factor's assertion was largely anecdotal. He failed to provide evidence for those staggering costs. How much these programs are costing U.S. business has not yet been calculated, but it is known that confidence is being restored in public companies. According to Serwer, the Wilshire 5000 index—a proxy for all public companies in the United States—has increased by 54 percent since the passage of Sarbanes-Oxley. Conducting business in ethically better ways, which may involve externally imposed constraints on managers' conduct, can have a positive effect on corporate profits.

These considerations suggest that the curriculum and methods of business ethics must be enriched with subject matter well beyond much of their current content. On this model, business law, political science, political philosophy, and other fields germane to the ethical shaping of societies become as relevant to the fields of business ethics as moral philosophy. To some extent, a larger series of perspectives is already evident among European scholars of business ethics who tend to stress collective, rather than an individual, responsibility for ethics, with government, trade unions, and corporate associations as key actors (rather than corporations and individual managers).[75]

There is an irony in this. With its focus on guiding individual managers, the field of business ethics has placed a premium on managers' freedom to act. It also promises to enhance that freedom. By respecting stakeholders' interests, Freeman says, "directors and managers can achieve the goals of reformers voluntarily while keeping a substantial amount of control over their own future."[76] He adds, "We need to have a philosophy of voluntarism to actively engage stakeholders and manage the relationships ourselves, rather than leaving it to government."[77] Similar thinking applies to labor relations, where enhanced attention to stakeholders is seen as an alternative to adversarial union-management encounters.[78]

However, if some of the factors that hinder ethics in business are social and structural in nature, then it may be that society must *reduce* managers' freedom in order to enhance business' ethical performance. If it appears odd to say that an ethical stance requires limiting the sphere of individual choice, that is because the full array of ethical obligations extends not just to areas of personal discretion but to the social, economic, and cultural systems in which we act. They are obligations incumbent on us all as citizens, not just on business managers. The grounding for this insight was provided in the late 1960s by the ecologist Garrett Hardin in a landmark article titled "The Tragedy of the Commons."[79] In that article, Hardin used the example of the overgrazing of shared lands to argue that the unfettered pursuit of personal advantage can sometimes damage all participants in a cooperative scheme. To prevent this, he maintained, participants must sometimes utilize "mutual coercion mutually agreed upon." In the business world, such mutual coercion can take the forms of legislative restraints and administrative regulations that equally constrain all economic players and create a level playing field for efficient cooperation. But this dimension of business ethics can easily be missed if the larger social and legal context of business conduct is replaced by a narrow focus on managerial decision making alone. In methodological terms, this requires the expansion of business ethics from ethics per se to law, political philosophy, sociology, and cultural studies.

THE TENSION BETWEEN METHODS WITHIN BUSINESS ETHICS EDUCATION

The tensions between traditional philosophical analysis of moral arguments and empirical studies of business behaviors, between efforts to inform the individual manager and the need to effect social, structural change all evidence themselves in the content and methods of business education. The last three decades witnessed a dramatic increase in the level of corporate misconduct. From CEOs and CFOs to mid-level managers, the 1980s mantra of "greed is good" seemed to have been an accepted rule of thumb. Two or three years of federal prison and the mandatory fine of several million dollars often left convicted business leaders still wealthy beyond the average person's wildest dreams. The risk, it seemed, was worth the reward, but with the increasingly negative image that business was gaining came the call for introduction of ethics training in the workplace and in the curriculum of business schools. The business school community itself was not immune to the trends toward unethical behavior found in the business world. Research by Don McCabe at Rutgers University indicates that of all academic disciplines, business students cheated more than any other group.[80] This problem, which often begins in school and is carried over to the corporate environment, underlies the repeated calls for enhanced business ethics education. But how is this to be accomplished? What pedagogical and curricular approaches are relevant to improving the ethical sensitivities and performance of business people?

To assess the state of business ethics instruction we gathered information from eighteen[81] of the leading MBA programs in the United States and analyzed what was taught, why it was taught, and—perhaps most significantly—who was teaching it. This survey was not intended to serve as a comprehensive overview of the field, but instead to offer a snapshot of the trends in methods of teaching business ethics. Of the eighteen schools surveyed in 2006, nine required a stand-alone ethics course as a core component of the curriculum, two offered an interdisciplinary course, and seven offered ethics electives. Most had an ethics component included in the orientation that all students are required to attend. However, as Marjorie Kelly, the editor of *Business Ethics Magazine*, noted in 2003, "it would be too simplistic to say that business ethics is missing from business schools, but its emphasis is uneven and at too many schools it is diminishing."[82]

Since 2003, business schools have recognized the need for a normative dimension in the educational experience that demonstrates the correlation between good business and ethical behavior. To that end, a variety of approaches have arisen, most with a distinct emphasis on integration of ethics into the curriculum, rather than a stand-alone course. MIT, for example, redesigned its entire curriculum as part of its fiftieth anniversary and made the decision to integrate ethics throughout its curriculum rather than introduce a new course that would be taught by philosophers. Harvard also offers an integrated approach to infusing ethics into the MBA program by having core faculty from economics, psychology, and organizational behavior team-teach a course that emphasizes the leadership challenges facing those who will work in a global economy. While all these efforts properly reflect the practical nature of business ethics, it can be asked whether they successfully pay attention to the core normative and moral concerns, and whether they adequately address the key moral justifications that are so essential to the field.

Our survey found surprising disparity in what is considered "ethics" and how it is placed in the curriculum. The subtitle of many of the required ethics courses placed an emphasis on leadership, compliance, business law, or professionalism. The ethics electives include CSR, business through literature, leadership in theater, sexual harassment, work-life balance, and courses on codes of conduct and compliance. The textbooks used in these courses range from a small number that use a standard business ethics text, to collections of short stories, to Thomas L. Friedman's *The World is Flat*, a largely optimistic assessment of globalization with relatively little attention to its ethical challenges. The lack of uniformity in teaching business ethics is not necessarily a negative. However, the fact that so few of the courses are taught by professors who are trained as ethicists is at odds with the normative emphasis that has always been so central to the field.[83]

The survey of these eighteen schools found only three philosophers teaching the business ethics class—the rest were taught by economists, lawyers, marketing and/or strategy professors, or interdisciplinary professors. The correlation between a professor's academic specialty (e.g., economics) and the method for teaching the business ethics course is evidenced in the selection of texts. The diffuse method for producing better business managers is notable. The American Academy of Collegiate Schools for Business (AACSB) has urged ethics instruction, but has fallen short of calling for mandatory ethics education. They do, however, acknowledge a crisis in business today, stating "at issue is no less than the future of the free market system, which depends on honest and open enterprise to survive and flourish."[84] Do current approaches to business ethics education, with their reduced attention to the ethical theory and moral analysis really respond to this call for reform?

In a 1979 report, Harvard's president Derek Bok wrote about the need for business to serve as an instrument of social change. He called for four specific changes in the curriculum of business education:

> (1) a reconsideration of objectives, especially those not linked with profit,
> (2) a study of ethical conflicts that people are likely to encounter in business,
> (3) a study of the proper roles of government and business with respect to each other, especially with regard to matters of regulation, and (4) a deeper consideration of consumer involvement in corporate affairs.[85]

Bok's recommendations contributed to the increasing emphasis on ethics in business education at Harvard and elsewhere. His four goals suggested the outlines of a fairly comprehensive approach to business ethics teaching and research, one that unites moral theory, practice, and the formation of the individual manager with attention to the larger social context of business. By its nature, business ethics requires precisely this plurality of methodological approaches. It is clear that while much has been accomplished, much remains to be done.

NOTES

1. R. Edward Freeman, *Strategic Management: A Stakeholder Approach* (Boston: Pitman, 1984), 3–4.

2. Ibid., 25, 46.

3. M. B. E. Clarkson, "Introduction," in *The Corporation and Its Stakeholders: Classic and Contemporary Readings*, ed. M. B. E. Clarkson (Toronto: University of Toronto Press, 1998), 1–9.

4. R. Edward Freeman, Jeffrey S. Harrison, and Andrew C. Wicks, *Managing for Stakeholders: Survival, Reputation, and Success* (New Haven, Conn.: Yale University Press, 2007).

5. Barbara Alpern and David Odett, "Enhancing the MBA: Ethics Linked to an Organizational Communication Specialization," in *Proceedings of the 2003 Association for Business Communication Annual Convention*, http://www.businesscommunication.org/convsentions/Proceedings/2003/PDF/10ABC03.pdf.

6. Richard N. Farmer and W. Dickerson Hogue, *Corporate Social Responsibility* (Chicago: Science Research Associates, 1973); Archie B. Carroll, "A Three-Dimensional Conceptual Model of Corporate Social Performance," *Academy of Management Review* 4 (1979): 497–505; Howard F. Sohn, "Prevailing Rationales in the Corporate Social Responsibility Debate," *Journal of Business Ethics* 1 (1982): 139–144; Douglas J. Den Uyl, *The New Crusaders: The Corporate Social Responsibility Debate* (Bowling Green, Ohio: The Social Philosophy and Policy Center, 1984); Bill Shaw and Frederick R. Post, "A Moral Basis for Corporate Philanthropy," *Journal of Business Ethics* 12 (1993): 745–751; Archie B. Carroll, "Ethical Challenges for Business in The New Millennium: Corporate Social Responsibility and Models of Management Morality," *Business Ethics Quarterly* 10 (1) (2000): 33–42; Jacob M. Rose, "Corporate Directors and Social Responsibility: Ethics versus Shareholder Value," *Journal of Business Ethics* 73 (2007): 319–331; Steven K. May George Cheney and Juliet Roper, eds., *The Debate over Corporate Social Responsibility* (New York: Oxford University Press, 2007).

7. Milton Friedman, "The Social Responsibility of Business is to Increase its Profits," *New York Times Magazine*, September 13, 1970.

8. Albert Z. Carr, "Is Business Bluffing Ethical," *Harvard Business Review* 46 (1) (1968): 143–153.

9. We draw these distinctions from Thomas Donaldson and Lee E. Preston, "The Stakeholder Theory of the Corporation: Concepts, Evidence, and Implications," *Academy of Management Review* 20 (1) (1995): 65–91.

10. R. Edward Freeman and W. M. Evan, "Corporate Governance: A Stakeholder Interpretation," *Journal of Behavioral Economics* 19 (1990): 337–359; W. M. Evan and

R. Edward Freeman, "A Stakeholder Theory of the Modern Corporation: Kantian Capitalism," in *Ethical Theory and Business*, 2nd ed., ed. T. Beauchamp and N. Bowie (Englewood Cliffs, N.J.: Prentice Hall, 1988).

11. R. A. Phillips, "Stakeholder Theory and a Principle of Fairness," *Business Ethics Quarterly* 7 (1997): 51–66, and R. A. Phillips, *Stakeholder Theory and Organizational Ethics* (San Francisco: Berrett-Koehler, 2003).

12. Edward Freeman and Daniel Gilbert, *Corporate Strategy and the Search for Ethics* (Englewood Cliffs, N.J.: Prentice-Hall, 1988), 10.

13. Freeman et al. *Managing for Stakeholders*, 75.

14. Rogene A. Buchholz and Sandra B. Rosenthal, "Toward a Contemporary Conceptual Framework for Stakeholder Theory," *Journal of Business Ethics* 58 (2005): 137–148.

15. A. C. Wicks, D. R. Gilbert Jr., and R. E. Freeman, "A Feminist Reinterpretation of the Stakeholder Concept," *Business Ethics Quarterly* 4 (1994): 475–498. For a subsequent and independent development of this position, see Brian K. Burton and Craig P. Dunn, "Feminist Ethics as Moral Grounding for Stakeholder Theory," *Business Ethics Quarterly*, 6 (1996): 133–137.

16. Norman E. Bowie, *Business Ethics: A Kantian Perspective* (Oxford: Blackwell, 1999), 132.

17. Ronald M. Green, *The Moral Manager* (New York: Macmillan, 1994).

18. Richard T. De George, *Business Ethics* (New York: Macmillan, 1990); Laura L. Nash, "Ethics without the Sermon," *Harvard Business Review* 59 (6) (1981): 78–90; Manuel Valasquez, *Business Ethics: Concepts and Cases*, 3rd ed. (Englewood Cliffs, N.J.: Prentice Hall, 1992). For approaches that combine various normative methods, see Lester F. Goodchild, "Toward a Foundational Normative Method in Business Ethics," *Journal of Business Ethics* 5 (1986): 485–499, and Surendra Arjoon, "Ethical Decision-Making: A Case for the Triple Font Theory," *Journal of Business Ethics* 71 (2007): 395–410.

19. See Robert C. Solomon, *Ethics and Excellence: Cooperation and Integrity in Business* (New York: Oxford University Press, 1992). Also Daryl Koehn, "A Role for Virtue Ethics in the Analysis of Business Practice," *Business Ethics Quarterly* 5 (3) (1995): 533–539; John Dobson and Judith White, "Toward the Feminine Firm: An Extension to Thomas White," *Business Ethics Quarterly* 5 (3) (1995): 463–478; Geoff Moore, "Humanizing Business: A Modern Virtue Ethics Approach," *Business Ethics Quarterly* 15 (2) (2005): 237–255, and Geoff Moore, "Corporate Character: Modern Virtue Ethics and the Virtuous Corporation," *Business Ethics Quarterly* 15 (4) (2005): 659–685.

20. The December 1986 (5/6) issue of the *Journal of Business Ethics* is devoted to the relation between religion and business ethics. See especially the challenge to a religious methods posed by Richard De George, "Theological Ethics and Business Ethics," 421–433, and the replies by Thomas F. McMahon, "Creed, Cult, Code and Business Ethics," 453–464; John T. Leahy, "Embodied Ethics: Some Common Concerns of Religion and Business," 465–473; Oliver F. Williams, "Can Business Ethics Be Theological? What Athens Can Learn from Jerusalem," 473–484; David A. Krueger, "The Religious Nature of Practical Reason: A Way into the Debate"; and Richard T. De George, "Replies and Reflections on Theology and Business Ethics," 521–525. See also William J. Byron, "Twin Towers: A Philosophy and Theology of Business," *Journal of Business Ethics* 7 (1988): 525–530, and Gerard Magill, "Theology in Religious Ethics: Appealing to the Religious Imagination," *Journal of Business Ethics* 11 (1992): 129–135. Similarly, volume 7, issue 2 (1997) of *Business Ethics Quarterly* is devoted to religious approaches to business ethics. See the "Introduction" and "Enlarging the Conversation" by Stewart W. Herman, 1–3, 5–20. See also, Manuel Velasquez and F. Neil

Brady, "Natural Law and Business Ethics," *Business Ethics Quarterly* 7 (2) (1997): 83–107; and Moses L. Pava, "Religious Business Ethics and Political Liberalism: An Integrative Approach," *Journal of Business Ethics* 17 (1998): 1633–1652.

21. Thomas Donaldson, *Corporations and Morality* (Englewood Cliffs, N.J.: Prentice Hall; 1982); Thomas Donaldson and Thomas W. Dunfee, *Ties That Bind: A Social Contracts Approach to Business Ethics* (Boston: Harvard Business School Press, 1999); Ben Wempe, "In Defense of a Self-Disciplined, Domain-Specific Contract Theory of Business," *Business Ethics Quarterly* 15 (1) (2005): 113–135.

22. Lynn Sharp Paine, "Managing for Organizational Integrity," *Harvard Business Review* 72 (2) (March-April 1994): 106–117, and Lynn Sharp Paine, *Value Shift: Why Companies Must Merge Social and Financial Imperatives to Achieve Superior Performance* (New York: McGraw-Hill, 2003).

23. Al Gini, "Moral Leadership and Business Ethics" in *Ethics, The Heart of Leadership*, ed. Joanne B. Ciulla (Westport, Conn.: Praeger, 1998), 27–45.

24. John Rawls, *A Theory of Justice* (Cambridge, Mass.: Harvard University Press, 1971).

25. Ronald M. Green and Robbin Derry, "Ethical Theory in Business Ethics—A Critical Assessment," *Journal of Business Ethics* 8 (1989): 521–533.

26. For a discussion of such approaches, see Richard L. Lippke, "A Critique of Business Ethics," *Business Ethics Quarterly* 1 (4) (1991): 367–384.

27. Thomas Donaldson, *The Ethics of International Business* (New York: Oxford University Press, 1991); Richard T. De George, *Competing with Integrity in International Business* (Oxford: Oxford University Press, 1993); Georges Enderle, ed., *International Business Ethics: Challenges and Approaches* (Notre Dame, Ind.: University of Notre Dame Press, 1999); John M. Kline, *Ethics for International Business: Decision-Making in a Global Political Economy* (Oxford: Routledge, 1995); Gerald F. Cavanagh, "Global Business Ethics: Regulation, Code, or Self-Restraint," *Business Ethics Quarterly* 14 (4) (2004): 625–642.

28. John Ladd, "Morality and the Ideal of Rationality in Formal Organizations," *The Monist* 54 (1970): 488–516; Peter A. French, "The Corporation as a Moral Person," *American Philosophical Quarterly* 16 (1979): 208–210; Kenneth Goodpaster, "The Concept of Corporate Responsibility," in *Just Business*, ed. T. Regan (New York: Random House, 1984), 292–323; Virginia Held, "Corporations, Persons, and Responsibility," in *Shame, Responsibility, and the Corporation*, ed. Hugh Curtler (New York: Haven, 1986), 161–181; Patricia H. Werhane, *Persons, Rights, and Corporations* (Englewood Cliffs, NJ: Prentice Hall, 1985), chap. 1–2; Michael J. Phillips, "Corporate Moral Personhood and Three Conceptions of the Corporation," *Business Ethics Quarterly* 2 (4) (1992), 435–459; William G. Weaver, "Corporations as Intentional Systems," *Journal of Business Ethics* 17 (1998), 87–97.

29. Peter French, "The Corporation as a Moral Person," in *The Spectrum of Responsibility*, ed. Peter French (New York: St. Martin's Press, 1991), 290–304; Thomas Donaldson, *Corporations and Morality* (Englewood Cliffs, N.J.: Prentice-Hall, 1982), 109–128.

30. For a classic discussion, see Louis B. Barnes, C. Roland Christensen, and Abby J. Hansen, *Teaching and the Case Method: Texts, Cases, and Readings* (Boston: Harvard Business School Press, 1995).

31 "How Ethical Are Businessmen?" *Harvard Business Review* 39 (4) (1961): 6–8.

32. Raymond Baumhart, *An Honest Profit: What Businessmen Say About Ethics in Business* (New York: Holt, Rinehart and Winston, 1968).

33. This was the conclusion of a 1990 examination of ninety-four empirical studies that had appeared in leading journals up to that time. See D. M. Randall and A. M. Gibson,

"Methodology in Business Ethics: A Review and Critical Assessment," *Journal of Business Ethics* 9 (1990), 457–471.

34. W. H. Hegarty and H. P. Sims, Jr., "Some Determinants of Unethical Decision Behavior," *Journal of Applied Psychology* 63 (4) (1978): 451–457; Holmes Miller and Kurt J. Engemann, "A Simulation Model of Intergroup Conflict," *Journal of Business Ethics* 50 (2004): 355–367.

35. J. Greenberg, "Employee Theft as a Reaction to Underpayment Inequity: The Hidden Cost of Pay Cuts," *Journal of Applied Psychology*, 75 (5) (1990): 561–568; Ann E. Tenbrunsel, "Misrepresentation and Expectations of Misrepresentation in an Ethical Dilemma: The Role of Incentives and Temptation," *Academy of Management Journal* 41 (3) (1998): 330–339; Maurice E. Schweitzer, Lisa Ordóñez, and Bambi Douma, "Goal Setting as a Motivator of Unethical Behavior," *Academy of Management Journal* 47 (3) (2004): 422–432; and Bryan Church, James C. Gaa, S. M. Khalid Nainar, and Mohamed M. Shehata, "Experimental Evidence Relating to the Person-Situation Interactionist Model of Ethical Decision Making," *Business Ethics Quarterly* 15 (3) (2005): 363–383.

36. Business ethics also frequently is housed in business school departments of finance, strategy, and law.

37. Stephen P. Robbins and Timothy A. Judge, *Organizational Behavior*, 12th ed. (Upper Saddle River, N.J.: Pearson/Prentice Hall, 2007).

38. L. K. Trevino and S. A. Youngblood, "Bad Apples in Bad Barrels: A Causal Analysis of Ethical Decision-Making Behavior," *Journal of Applied Psychology* 75 (4) (1990): 378–385; J. Weber, "Managers' Moral Reasoning: Assessing Their Responses to Three Moral Dilemmas," *Human Relations* 43 (7) (1990): 687–702.

39. O. C. Ferrell and L. G. Gresham, "A Contingency Framework for Understanding Ethical Decision Making in Marketing," *Journal of Marketing* 49 (1985): 87–96. M. Zey-Ferrell and O. C. Ferrell, "Role Set Configuration and Opportunity as Predictors of Unethical Behavior in Organizations," *Human Relations* 35 (1982): 587–604.

40. B. Victor and B. J. Cullen, "The Organizational Bases of Ethical Work Climates," *Administrative Science Quarterly* 33 (1988): 101–125; Deborah Vidaver Cohen, "Moral Climate in Business Firms: A Framework for Empirical Research," *Academy of Management Journal*, Best Papers Proceedings 1995, 386–390; David J. Fritzsche, "Ethical Climates and the Ethical Dimension of Decision Making," *Journal of Business Ethics* 24 (2000): 125–140; Craig V. van Sandt, Jon M. Shepard, and Stephen M. Zappe, "An Examination of the Relationship Between Ethical Work Climate and Moral Awareness," *Journal of Business Ethics* 68 (2006): 409–432; James W. Westerman, Rafik I. Beekun, Yvonne Stedham, and Jeanne Yamamura, "Peers versus National Culture: An Analysis of Antecedents to Ethical Decision-Making," *Journal of Business Ethics* 75 (2007): 239–252.

41. K. E. Kram, P. C. Yeager, and G. E. Reed, "Decisions and Dilemmas: The Ethical Dimension in the Corporate Context," in *Research in Corporate Social Performance and Policy*, vol. 11, ed. J. E. Post (Greenwich, Conn.: JAI, 1989), 21–54; M. Pastin, *The Hard Problems of Management: Gaining the Ethics Edge* (San Francisco: Jossey-Bass, 1986); Robert Jackall, *Moral Mazes: The World of Corporate Managers* (New York: Oxford University Press, 1989); Patricia Casey Douglas, Ronald A. Davidson, and Bill N. Schwartz, "The Effect of Organizational Culture and Ethical Orientation on Accountants," *Journal of Business Ethics* 34 (2001): 101–121; Chia-Mei Shih and Chin-Yuan Chen, "The Effect of Organizational Ethical Culture on Marketing Managers' Role Stress," *Journal of American Academy of Business* 8 (1) (2006): 89–95; David F. Caldwell and Dennis Moberg, "An Exploratory Investigation of the Effect of Ethical Culture in Activating Moral Imagination," *Journal of Business Ethics* 73 (2007): 193–204.

42. P. L. Cochran and D. Nigh, "Illegal Corporate Behavior and the Question of Moral Agency," in *Research in Corporate Social Performance and Policy*, vol. 9, ed. W. Frederick (Greenwich, Conn.: JAI, 1987), 73–81; B. M. Staw and E. Szwajkowski, "The Scarcity-Munificence Component of Organizational Environments and the Commission of Illegal Acts," *Administrative Science Quarterly* 20 (1975): 345–354.

43. J. B. McGuire, A. A. Sundgren, and T. Schneeweis, "Corporate Social Responsibility and Firm Financial Performance," *Academy of Management Journal* 31 (1988): 854–872; Bert van de Ven and Ronald Jeurissen, "Competing Responsibly," *Business Ethics Quarterly* 15 (2) (2005): 299–317.

44. M. C. Mathews, "Codes of Ethics: Organizational Behavior and Misbehavior," in W. Frederick, *Research in Corporate Social Performance and Policy* 9 (1987): 107–130; Betsy Stevens, "An Analysis of Corporate Ethical Code Studies: Where Do We Go from Here?" *Journal of Business Ethics* 13 (1994): 63–90; D. L. McCabe, L. K. Trevino, and K. D. Butterfield, "The Influence of Collegiate and Corporate Codes of Conduct on Ethics-Related Behavior in the Workplace," *Business Ethics Quarterly* 6 (4) (1996): 461–466; Thomas J. von der Embse, Mayur S. Desai, and Seema Desai, "How Well are Corporate Ethics Codes and Policies Applied in the Trenches?" *Information Management & Computer Security* 12 (2–3) (2004): 146–153.

45. Frans B. M. de Waal, *Our Inner Ape* (New York: Riverhead, 2005); also *Primates and Philosophers: How Morality Evolved* (Princeton, N.J.: Princeton University Press, 2006).

46. Thomas Donaldson and Thomas W. Dunfee, *Ties That Bind a Social Contracts Approach to Business Ethics* (Boston: Harvard Business School Press, 1999).

47. Ibid., 47.

48. Ibid., 53.

49. Ibid., 59, 64.

50. Ibid., 38.

51. Ibid., 39.

52. John R. Rowan, "How Binding the Ties: Business Ethics as Integrative Social Contracts: Review of *Ties That Bind: A Social Contracts Approach to Business Ethics*," *Business Ethics Quarterly* 11 (2) (1999): 379–390.

53. D. Mayer and A. Cava, "Social Contract Theory and Gender Discrimination," *Business Ethics Quarterly* 5 (2) (1995): 257–270; Edward J. Conry, "A Critique of Social Contracts for Business," *Business Ethics Quarterly* 5 (2) (1995): 187–212.

54. Linda Klebe Trevino and Gary R. Weaver, "Business ETHICS/BUSINESS ethics: ONE FIELD OR TWO?" *Business Ethics Quarterly*, 4 (2) (1994): 113–128.

55. Gary R. Weaver and Linda Klebe Trevino, "Normative and Empirical Business Ethics: Separation, Marriage of Convenience, or Marriage of Necessity?" *Business Ethics Quarterly* 4 (2) (1994): 129–143.

56. Ibid., 135.

57. Solomon, *Ethics and Excellence*, 188.

58. Freeman et al., *Managing for Stakeholders*, 99.

59. Ibid., 80.

60. See R. Edward Freeman and Jeffrey S. Harrison, "Stakeholders, Social Responsibility, and Performance: Empirical Evidence and Theoretical Perspectives," *Academy of Management Journal* 42 (5) (1999): 479–485; Shawn L. Berman, Andrew C. Wicks, Suresh Kotha; Thomas M. Jones, "Does Stakeholder Orientation Matter? The Relationship between Stakeholder Management Models and Firm Financial Performance," *Academy of Management Journal* 42 (5) (1999): 488–506; and LaRue Tone Hosmer and

Christian Kiewitz, "Organizational Justice: A Behavioral Science Concept with Critical Implications for Business Ethics and Stakeholder Theory," *Business Ethics Quarterly* 15 (1) (2005): 67–91.

61. Richard L. Lippke, "A Critique of Business Ethics," *Business Ethics Quarterly* 1 (4) (1991): 367–384.

62. Ibid., 371, 377–378.

63. J. R. Boatright, "Does Business Ethics Rest on a Mistake?" *Business Ethics Quarterly* 9 (4) (1999): 583–591.

64. Ibid., 584.

65. Ibid., 585.

66. Ibid.

67. Ibid.

68. Hans Pohl, ed., *Mittbestimmung und Betriebsverfassung in Deutschland, Frankreich und Grossbritannien seit dem 19. Jahrhundert. Tagungsband zum 16. wissenschaftlichen Symposium auf Schloss Quint bei Trier 1993* (Stuttgart: Steiner, 1996).

69. George G. Brenkert, "The Environment, the Moralist, the Corporation and Its Culture," *Business Ethics Quarterly* 5 (4) (1995): 675–697.

70. Ibid., 687–690.

71. See, for example, Jeffrey Nesteruk, "The Ethical Significance of Corporate Law," *Journal of Business Ethics* 10 (1991): 723–27.

72. Susan Ariel Aaronson, "'Minding Our Business': What the United States Government Has Done and Can Do to Ensure that U.S. Multinationals Act Responsibly in Foreign Markets," *Journal of Business Ethics* 59 (2005): 59, 175–198; James Weber and Kathleen Getz, "Buy Bribes or Bye-Bye Bribes: The Future Status of Bribery in International Commerce," *Business Ethics Quarterly* 14 (4) (2004): 695–711.

73. De George, *Competing with Integrity in International Business*, 97.

74. "Stop Whining about SarbOx! Critics Want to Repeal the Law, but It's Been a Boon to the Market, says Fortune's Andy Serwer," *Fortune*, August 1, 2006, http://money.cnn.com/magazines/fortune/fortune_archive/2006/08/07/8382589/index.htm.

75. Laura J. Spence, "Review Article: European Business Ethics: Still Playing Defense," *Business Ethics Quarterly* 15 (4) (2005): 123–132.

76. Freeman et al., *Managing for Stakeholders*, 212.

77. Ibid., 55.

78. Ibid., 240.

79. Garrett Hardin, "The Tragedy of the Commons," *Science*, 162 (1968): 1243–1248.

80. Donald McCabe, "Cheating Among College and University Students: A North American Perspective," *International Journal for Educational Integrity* 1 (1) (2005), http://www.ojs.unisa.edu.au/index.php/IJEI/issue/view/3.

81. The eighteen schools were chosen by reputation and not intended to be fully representative of what is currently being taught in the hundreds of business programs throughout the United States. They are merely representative of "best practices" in the field. The schools surveyed were the University of Chicago, Columbia, University of Virginia, Duke, University of California at Berkeley, Harvard, Cornell, Northwestern, University of Michigan, Massachusetts Institute of Technology, Stanford, New York University, Dartmouth College, University of Pennsylvania, Yale, Carnegie Mellon, University of North Carolina, and University of California at Los Angeles.

82. Marjorie Kelly, "It's a Heckuva Time to be Dropping Business Ethics Courses,"*Business Ethics Magazine*, Fall 2003, http://www.business-ethics.com/BizSchlsDropEthics.htm.

83. E. R. Klein, "The One Necessary Condition for a Successful Business Ethics Course: The Teacher Must Be a Philosopher," *Business Ethics Quarterly* 8 (3) (1998): 561–574.

84. AACSB Report of the Ethics Education Task Force, *Ethics Education in Business Schools,* June 2004.

85. Carter Daniel, *MBA: The First Century* (Lewisburg, Pa.: Bucknell University Press, 1988), 238.

SUGGESTED READING

Beauchamp, Tom L., Norman Bowie, and Denis Arnold, eds., *Ethical Theory and Business,* 8th ed. Englewood Cliffs, N.J.: Prentice Hall, 2008.

Bowie, Norman. *Business Ethics: A Kantian Perspective.* Oxford: Blackwell, 1999.

Brenkert, George. "The Environment, the Moralist, the Corporation and its Culture."*Business Ethics Quarterly* 5 (4) (1995): 367–384.

Carr, Albert. "Is Business Bluffing Ethical?" *Harvard Business Review*46 (1) (1968): 143–153.

Clarkson, M. B. E. "Introduction." In *The Corporation and Its Stakeholders: Classic and Contemporary Readings.* Edited by M. B. E. Clarkson, 1–9. Toronto: University of Toronto Press, 1998.

De George, Richard. *Business Ethics.* New York: Macmillan, 1990.

Donaldson, Thomas. *Corporations and Morality.* Englewood Cliffs, N.J.: Prentice Hall, 1982.

Donaldson, Thomas, and Lee F. Thomas. "The Stakeholder Theory of the Corporation: Concepts, Evidence, and Implications." *Academy of Management Review* 20 (1) (1995): 85–91.

French, Peter. "The Corporation as a Moral Person," *American Philosophical Quarterly* 16 (1979): 208–210.

Friedman, Milton. "The Social Responsibility of Business is to Increase its Profits," *New York Times Magazine,* September 13, 1970.

Green, Ronald M. *The Moral Manager.* New York: Macmillan, 1994.

Green, Ronald M. and Robin Derry. "Ethical Theory in Business Ethics—A Critical Assessment," *Journal of Business Ethics* 8 (1989): 521–533.

Jackall, Robert. *Moral Mazes: The World of Corporate Mangers.* New York: Oxford University Press, 1989.

Ladd, John. "Morality and the Ideal of Rationality in Formal Organizations." *The Monist* 54 (1970): 488–516.

McCabe, Donald. "Cheating Among College and University Students: A North American Perspective." *International Journal for Educational Integrity* 1 (1) (2005): 3–14.

Paine, Lynn Sharp. "Managing for Organizational Integrity." *Harvard Business Review* 72 (2) (March–April 1994): 106–117.

Solomon, Robert. *Ethics and Excellence: Cooperation and Integrity in Business.* New York: Oxford University Press, 1992.

Werhane, Patricia. *Persons, Rights and Corporations.* Englewood Cliffs, N.J.: Prentice Hall, 1985.

CHAPTER 2

THE PLACE OF ETHICAL THEORY IN BUSINESS ETHICS

ROBERT AUDI

ETHICAL theory is a major critical resource for serious discussion of ethical problems, including those in business ethics. Why this is so will become clear once we frame an adequate conception of ethical theory and describe the scope of business ethics. I begin with a section that considers what kind of enterprise ethical theory is and what sorts of problems in business it can help address. I then proceed to explore some dimensions of ethical theory, some leading theories important for business ethics, and some concrete illustrations of the connections between ethical theory and specific problems in business ethics.

ETHICAL THEORY, APPLIED ETHICS, AND BUSINESS ETHICS

Ethical theory is the branch of inquiry concerned with understanding morality, in the wide sense in which morality is constituted by standards of right and wrong, and of the good and the bad, in human conduct.[1] There are at least two senses of "morality." In the objective sense, it designates sound standards of right and wrong, and we can thus speak of what morality objectively requires in employment policy and of what it objectively prohibits in advertising. In the personal sense, morality designates an individual's or group's particular standards of right and wrong, which may or may not be sound. Ethical theory is concerned mainly with morality in the objective sense, but one of its questions is what it means for objective moral standards to be *realized* in an individual's thought and conduct. For instance, how closely does a person's behavior have to conform to sound moral standards in order for the person to qualify as genuinely moral?

We may also speak of an ethical (or moral) theory, such as utilitarianism. In common terminology, an ethical theory is a statement of standards of right and wrong and includes an account of at least their content and application to decision problems. An ethical theory need not contain answers to theoretical questions *about* morality, such as whether it embodies universally valid standards of conduct. Although the major proponents of an ethical theory of this sort also address such questions, there are ethical theories—including those called *metaethical*—that contain no endorsement of any moral standard. The latter theories will not be of primary concern here.

Ethical theory is commonly contrasted with applied ethics. The latter is moral inquiry concerned with answering specific questions of right and wrong, such as whether it is wrong for employers to require blood tests to determine drug use even for employees not in certain risky occupations such as operating dangerous machines. Applied ethics seeks generality in its answers, but it does not address theoretical questions about, for instance, the meanings of highly general moral terms, the nature of moral properties, or the kinds of evidence possible for moral judgments. These questions are often grouped under the term *metaethics*. An ethical theory such as Kantianism or utilitarianism, however, will often have implications for specific moral questions and will imply that certain answers are sound. These theories are normative, whereas metaethics is generally conceived as nonnormative.

Applied ethics was originally conceived as the application of one or more ethical theories or of at least of some general moral standard to specific problems of right and wrong. Now, however, the term also encompasses any kind of practical ethics, including an approach that might examine, in an intuitive and nontheoretical way, a particular question of right and wrong, such as one concerning drug testing, with no appeal to anything beyond what might be called intuitive moral sensitivity, a kind usually taken to reflect a commonsense understanding of human conduct. Practical ethics is not, however, always an application of a general moral standard. A manager's decision whether to blame an employee for losing a potentially profitable contract may be reached by reflection on the details of the case, with background ethical intuition playing the role that some people would accord to moral rules. This is not to say that the manager cannot, after the decision, formulate a rule that subsumes the case. We will here leave open the question whether every decision is an implicit application of an already presupposed rule or, by contrast, at least some rules emerge only in the light of reflection on a particular case.

Business ethics may be conceived as a branch of applied ethics, parallel to legal and medical ethics. Where a legal or medical practice constitutes a business, business ethics encompasses moral questions about its business conduct, and there business ethics may overlap with legal or medical ethics. Business ethics is neither narrow nor isolated from other branches of ethics. It overlaps legal ethics, for instance, in addressing the question of the kind and extent of business leaders' obligation to follow the law of the country in which they operate. It overlaps medical ethics in addressing the question of whether an incorporated medical group, pharmaceutical company, or hospital is a business and the related question of whether it has the same kinds of ethical obligations as other businesses.

Among the kinds of questions pursued in business ethics are both internal and external questions. Internal questions concern, among other things, the conduct of management toward employees under its authority: How, for instance, should one determine fair compensation, preserve privacy, and maintain a proper health insurance program? Internal questions also concern the rights of employees, most aspects of corporate governance—including ethics training for employees—and how to conduct research, particularly when it poses risks to persons. External questions concern, among other things, the relation of businesses to people and institutions outside them: What is the place of business in society and how does this bear on its responsibilities toward customers and environmental preservation? What are the standards of fair competition with other businesses? What criteria of remuneration and safety must businesses abide by, particularly when operating in countries with less stringent standards than their own, such as countries that permit the operation of sweatshops? Some external questions concern not only what roles, ethically speaking, businesses should voluntarily play in society but also what legal restrictions should be placed on their operations. There are also a multitude of questions, such as what constitutes truth in marketing, that might be conceived as mainly internal or mainly external, depending on whether their focus is on intra-company activity or on the relation between the company and other elements in society, as is the case with advertising in public media.

Some of these questions will be considered below. First, however, it is important to develop a more detailed picture of ethical theory and its major concerns.

Major Dimensions of Ethical Theory

How ethical theory in the disciplinary sense bears on business ethics can be clarified by describing some subfields of ethical theory and articulating some of the major questions they explore. This section will not presuppose any particular ethical theory, though some theories are cited for illustration.

Moral Judgment

There is no brief way to distinguish sharply between, on the one hand, moral judgments or the *oughts* they commonly express and, on the other hand, aesthetic and, especially, pragmatic judgments and *oughts*. In the moral case, more than in the aesthetic and pragmatic case, taking the moral point of view implies receptivity to a kind of criticism. We are not taking the moral point of view in making a judgment on an action unless we meet at least three conditions. First, we must consider the effects of the action on the well-being of persons. Second, we must be open to being held to a standard of consistency in treating like cases alike. Third, we are aware that something serious is at stake—sufficiently serious to make the emotions of guilt and shame appropriate if, with no mitigating circumstance, we err. Some of these conditions may apply to a lesser degree in aesthetic and pragmatic matters. What is it, then, that sets the moral point of view apart and indicates the broad subject matter of ethical theory?

Certain notions are, in their normal uses, intrinsically moral. Consider a judgment about justice. Judgments and decisions applying this notion represent the moral point of view. Similarly, we can plausibly say that acts such as cheating, defrauding, and exploiting people are paradigms of what is morally wrong; hence, to judge such an act to be wrong is to make a moral judgment. The judgment that an act is one of cheating implies wrongdoing by providing a criterial ground for it, the kind of ground whose relevance must be acknowledged by anyone who adequately understands the judgment.[2]

One approach to understanding the moral point of view depends on finding moral *terms*. A wider approach proceeds, as in the examples just given, with reference to *grounds* of moral judgment. Moral judgments and decisions commonly employ the concepts of what is right or wrong or of what we ought or ought not to do, or of what is fair or unfair, just or unjust. There are, as already noted, nonmoral senses of "right" and "wrong," for instance, senses applicable from the point of view of self-interest. This point of view in particular needs comment in connection with understanding business ethics. Not only is self-interest different from the moral point of view; the latter is to be understood as a point of view capable of conflicting with that of self-interest and even the wider point of view of prudence. In many business decisions there is no conflict, but there may be, as in the greedy pursuit of profits.[3]

I have presupposed that the point that we ought not to do injustices can serve as a model for understanding the notion of the moral ought. To determine precisely what counts as an injustice one must make a moral determination. One can do this from the point of view of a particular ethical theory, but there is a core notion of injustice recognizable without presupposing any particular theory. Consider a judge who fines one company $50,000 for pollution of a river and a second company $100,000 for it, where the *only* differences are in what part of town they dumped their effluent—and in the judge's friendship with the management of one but not the other. This is not a controversial case; it is the kind of uncontroversial example that anchors the concept of justice that competing theories seek to analyze. The same holds for other moral notions, such as being an act of reparation or of making amends for injuring someone, and—to shift to descriptions of character—for being virtuous or vicious. We can identify moral judgments and decisions in part in terms of nonmoral grounds for them—"facts" in one commonsense meaning of the term. The idea is roughly that *descriptive* factual judgments, such as that one person lied to another, broke a promise to a customer, or allowed a lethal gas to escape and burn people, often tell us that a judgment of moral wrongdoing is being made. These descriptive judgments are not normative—they are not, for instance, moral in content or evaluative, though they are a *basis* for moral judgments and in that sense not morally neutral. This distinction is a very important matter when it comes to explaining and justifying moral judgments— for example, that a business ought to compensate someone for an injury or ought not to have lied about who released gas into the air. Their grounding in descriptive facts is perhaps the major reason for their objectivity and universal applicability. Let us consider some of the crucial domains of descriptive factual grounds.

One pertinent domain of (nonmoral) facts is that of bodily harms and injuries. Typical examples would be killing, raping, burning, and beating. Calling the facts in question nonmoral needs comment. The point is the narrow one that, like the fact that the judge gave different fines for the same offense, they are not moral *in content*: determining them does not require using moral or other normative concepts. But they *are* moral *in upshot*: they are by their very nature the kinds of facts that are criterial evidence for moral judgment. It is a very important fact about ethics (a fact recognized by virtually all ethical theories) that moral judgments can be justified and even known on the basis of facts to which we have access by observation and scientific investigation. Indeed, sound moral judgments may be considered anchored in descriptive facts in a way that yields objectivity of a kind that makes them acceptable across different cultures.

There are domains besides harming and injury in which factual affirmations enable us to identify moral judgments and moral decisions and to determine that they represent the moral point of view. One is veracity. A judgment that an act is *wrong* because it is a lie is a moral judgment. It has moral content in calling the act *wrong*. Similarly for fidelity to one's word: a judgment that an act is *obligatory* because it is the keeping of a promise is also moral. The same holds for a judgment that a deed ought to be done because otherwise a person who can be saved will die.

Moral judgments, then, are normative judgments with roughly the content that an action or kind of action ought, or ought not, to be performed. Sound moral judgments are justifiable on the basis of correct identifications of morally relevant facts, such as that someone lied to stockholders or poisoned a stream. Ethical theory is concerned with the nature of these judgments and their interconnections. Particular *normative* ethical theories demand action identified in relation to the facts they take to be morally relevant. For instance, utilitarianism is concerned with the consequences of actions for pleasure and pain. Sound moral judgments are anchored in facts accessible to observation or scientific inquiry, and this anchoring is the main basis of *objectivity* in moral judgment.

Metaphysical Dimensions of Ethical Theory

The metaphysics of ethics is concerned with whether there is any moral reality: whether there are *in fact* properties such as being *obligatory* or being *wrong* or being *good*. Moral realists hold that there are in fact such properties; antirealists deny that there are. The previous discussion has not presupposed realism but is written in a way that suggests that it is highly plausible. Some readers may wonder why antirealism is plausible enough to need mention. The reason, as many in business fields who are social scientists know, is that empirical testability is a standard requirement for scientific acceptability—or, on a view still influential—of making sense at all in assertions intended to be true. An underlying motivation for the testability requirement has been memorably expressed by Wilfrid Sellars: "Science is the measure of all things, of what is that it is and of what is not that it is not."[4] If this is so, then any moral properties there are must be empirical—that is, ascertainable by scientific means.

Common sense and ordinary language appear to favor realism, at least in the form in which it says simply that there are such properties as being obligatory and being wrong that acts may have in virtue of having the descriptive properties of being promised and being lies. This simple realism leaves open whether ascriptions of moral properties are empirically verifiable. Clearly they are empirically *evidence-able*, since the descriptive properties that justify them are accessible to observation and scientific inquiry.

A point that apparently gives support to moral realism is that in many languages one can say that a person did not *know* that an action was wrong, that someone did not *see* that an action was obligatory, and that it is *true* that someone did wrong. I am aware of no natural language in which some equivalent of these statements is not considered to have a clear meaning, and those who reject realism must explain why such terms as "true" have a different meaning than in ascriptions of descriptive properties. It has been argued that to speak of truth here is only to *express* something, not to *ascribe* a property. Moral language is here said to be expressive rather than factual, prescriptive rather than descriptive, or emotive rather than truth-valued.[5] The widest term for these positions is "noncognitivism," so called because it denies that moral statements express anything cognizable in the way objects of cognition—truths and falsehoods—do.

This is not the place to establish the cognitive status of the ethical, and even the best developed antirealist positions make room for some kind of objectivity. Even if one thinks that calling the cheating of employees wrong is expressive, rather than descriptive, one is likely to grant that people have *reasons* for taking this attitude and that they should hold the same negative attitude in any precisely parallel case. It can turn out that the relevant reasons, such as that children will starve if the company does not provide emergency flood assistance, are the same kinds of reasons realists would adduce for the same judgment. Thus, for those whose criteria for realism in a body of discourse are so strict as to require a belief in antirealism, business ethics can be pursued without further addressing this question. Realism is simply not a requirement for well-ordered discussion of moral questions in business ethics. This point is especially important for those who think that objectivity in moral judgments can be achieved only if they are reducible to descriptive empirical judgments. Objectivity reaches beyond the empirical.

Epistemology

Epistemology is concerned with the nature of knowledge and justification. Scarcely anyone doubts that we have knowledge in logic and mathematics (which are not empirical disciplines), but ethics is another matter. *Ethical skeptics* hold that we do not have moral knowledge or, if they are *strongly* skeptical, that we also lack justification for moral claims. The commonsense view is that we sometimes achieve both, as in our judgments that the dictators who perpetrated the atrocities of the twentieth century did wrong. A great deal must be said to defend common sense here, and this is not the place to say it. I shall simply presuppose that at least some moral judgments are justified.

Empiricism implies that only testable claims or those that are true in virtue of certain relations of ideas can be known or justifiably believed. The main contrasting view in epistemology is *rationalism*, understood as the position that reason—our rational capacity—reveals substantive truths. Versions of rationalism have been held by Plato, Aquinas, Clarke, and, in twentieth-century ethics, W. D. Ross, Thomas Nagel, and others.[6]

The epistemological aspects of ethical theory bear more directly on business ethics than the metaphysical aspects. For moral empiricists, there will be a sense that ethical claims may be established by empirical information such as facts about the impact of an action on the material well-being of persons. This information will be central for utilitarians. For moral rationalists, empirical information will also be essential, but it will not play the same role. Adequate reflection of a qualitative and often intuitive kind will be central for justification of moral decisions. Specifically, rational reflection will supply the general principles underlying moral judgments and decisions, but their application will require appraising facts pertinent to the circumstances. Consider veracity. For moral empiricists the obligation not to lie is based on empirical facts, such as facts about the negative consequences of lying. For moral rationalists this obligation is knowable by reflection—*a priori*, in one terminology—though whether it is *overriding* in a given case will depend on facts such as whether an innocent person will die if a lie is not told. Although rationalists in moral epistemology maintain that moral principles can be known through pure reason or some form of rational reflection, they commonly grant that the obligations these principles express may conflict. Hence they do not hold that the application of the principles in specific cases yields a decision independent of facts about those particular cases.

Methodologically, there is something neutral among empiricism, rationalism, and indeed antirealism, and also applicable to questions of business ethics. It is *theoretical method*. This is a general method of building and rebuilding theories while raising questions, hypothesizing, comparing, and evaluating hypotheses in relation to data, revising theories in the light of the comparisons and evaluations, and adopting theories through assessing competing accounts of the same or similar problems. An element in this method is the attempt to achieve *reflective equilibrium*: a kind of integration between one's general beliefs and one's judgments concerning the kinds of cases they apply to.[7] A plausible principle for determining raises in salary may, for instance, be compared with intuitions about what certain specific employees deserve. These intuitions may force one to revise the principle. One might then compare the revised principle with a new case and revise it yet again. Hypothetical cases may also play a role in refining a principle. There also may be competing principles—say, those concerning how much should be given to shareholders. Theoretical method, with the search for reflective equilibrium as a part of the method, may help one to improve principles already in place or to discover new ones needed for new challenges. The aim is to achieve a combination of plausible ethical judgments in specific cases and a coherent framework of principles that justifies them.

Moral Psychology

Ethical theory often considers questions about the psychology of human agents, particularly as it bears on our capacity to act on moral judgments and on the kind and degree of responsibility we have for our actions. Let us consider these two areas in turn.

Since antiquity, moral philosophers have debated the question whether holding moral judgments entails being motivated to act accordingly. The view that it does is often called *motivational internalism*. It is so called because its central idea is that some degree of motivation is internal to the holding of a moral judgment, as with judgments that one (morally) must do something. Sometimes this view is associated with moral rationalism, on the ground that, in ascribing motivational power to reason—which is assumed to be represented by the moral judgments in question—it expresses the wider scope attributed to reason by rationalists by contrast with empiricists. But nonrationalists can hold motivational internalism (as David Hume did), and it seems best to consider internalism to be neutral on epistemological matters.

Motivational internalism has some important implications for business ethics. It reinforces the view that actions speak louder than words. It implies that those who claim to hold moral principles and moral judgments, but do not act accordingly, must either be seen as motivated but hindered or be liable to suspicion of insincerity or of self-deception—itself a sometimes blameworthy condition. They are at the very least properly subject to being challenged to explain why they failed to act accordingly. This is one way motivational internalism bears on moral assessment.

Motivational internalism also bears on moral instruction, including the kind possible in the ethics programs of business schools and companies: if it is true, then in educating the intellect we to some extent direct the will. Even if the moral judgments people hold do not entail *enough* motivation to produce action in accordance with them, they must, on a defensible motivational internalism, produce some motivation and will thereby assist whatever other motivation people have to be moral, such as a desire to be prudent. Everyday experience, however, shows sufficient disparity between people's apparent moral beliefs and their actions to suggest that moral instruction alone—even when it produces morally sound beliefs—cannot be the only ethical incentive in business or any other domain. This is one reason for the importance of ethical climate in a company—a notion that is best understood in terms of moral and social psychology.

Moral psychology also concerns the conditions for moral responsibility. One widely accepted result of analysis is that weakness of will—conceived as action against one's better judgment—does not entail mental compulsion. This implies that such weakness is not excusatory or even (necessarily) mitigatory. A fund manager may judge that an insider trade is wrong but, out of greed, do it. The "irresistible" deed here is not at all like action under a coercive threat of death. Another implication of a sound moral psychology is that self-deception, rationalization, and other possible sources of unconscious motivation are not necessarily excusatory. Unconscious hatred can and must be resisted. In these matters, among others, moral psychology can both help to refine moral judgment and expand the scope of our understanding of moral responsibility. Doing that can help in articulating a company's ethics code, devising an ethics training program for all who work in it, and in deciding who to judge those who act wrongly.

Conceptual Analysis of Important Notions

There is a central activity that ethical theorists engage in regardless of their views in epistemology or metaphysics. They make explicit and clarify the concepts and judgments to be examined. This is crucial for both ethics and empirical inquiry. Some examples of morally important results of conceptual analysis will illustrate its value in business contexts.

1. Veracity. What is the difference between lying and deceiving? The question in the abstract is theoretical, but how we answer it may determine what kind of business we may and may not do. An advertisement, for instance, may deceive without lying (since it says nothing false) and people may lie without deceiving (since a lie need not be believed). Is some deception, then, permissible? And does the answer depend on still other notions needing analysis, such as those of "normal" or "reasonable" consumers? A related notion is *being deceptive*. This notion applies to both persons and their statements and independently of whether they *succeed* in producing false belief. This also differs from lying, although lying normally implies an *attempt* to be deceptive. Clarification of these concepts is central to ethical accounts of advertising and marketing.

2. Improper influence. Must gifts in business become bribes when their value rises to a certain level? The question for ethical theory here is what distinguishes an attempted bribe from an actual bribe given by one person to another with an understanding concerning a payoff. No gift *necessarily* produces an actual bribe, but some kinds of gift giving are reasonably taken as attempted bribes. It does not follow, however, that as a gift becomes more valuable, it automatically becomes an attempted bribe.

These points should make it clear that a great deal of conceptual sorting is needed to determine ethical standards for gift giving in business. For example, there are many forms of undue influence, which is a central issue in the area of corporate campaign contributions and lobbying.

3. Equal treatment. Equal treatment of persons is commonly considered a requirement of justice. The question for ethical theory is what equal treatment means if vast differences exist in, for example, compensation.

One answer is *proportionate equality*. What variables, however, are crucial for determining the proportions? A major one is productivity. But is that, in business, just a monetary variable? And are there not other variables, such as the degree of importance of an employee for the survival of a company? The determination of these variables and their proper weighting are challenges to ethical analysis in business, and different normative ethical theories in business ethics give different answers. Discussion of compensation of CEOs is but one of many examples.

Are these issues purely linguistic? Language is important, and its proper use is a major source of evidence, but concepts need not be taken to be peculiar to any given language. A linguistic issue—in the sense of one concerning the correct analysis of terms in a natural language—is not about mere words. Often the issue concerns the meaning of underlying concepts. Anyone lacking in linguistic competence and basic concepts will need help in being understood when addressing ethical questions and will be in a poor position to contribute to the articulation and promotion of high ethical standards in the company. Consider criticism vs. harassment, warnings vs. threats, incentives vs. temptations, and ambition vs. opportunism—all are significant concepts in business ethics. Ethical conduct in business requires distinguishing these, and managers who want to create an ethical climate should be articulate about the differences.

Ethics and Religion

One other dimension of ethical theory needs mention: the issue of autonomy of ethics in relation to religion. Many ethical works are written from a religious point of view, and many concrete moral judgments are influenced by religion. A question in ethical theory is whether ethics has some kind of evidential dependence on religion.

Consider the question whether moral knowledge—say, that lying is (with certain exceptions) wrong—requires knowing any religious truth. This does not seem so. To say this is not to claim (as some would) that we can know moral truths even if there *are* no theological or religious truths. The point is theologically neutral on this matter. It is that *knowledge* of moral truths does not depend on *knowledge* of God or of religious truths. This view that moral knowledge is possible independently of religion is not antireligious, and indeed it has often been held by religiously committed philosophers and by theologians.

A person's ethics, in business or any other realm, may be enriched by reflection on religious texts and traditions, and secular ethical reflection can enhance one's understanding of religious texts and traditions. Many religious traditions, for instance, give a special place to the Golden Rule. Each tradition interprets the rule in the light of its own scriptures and practices.[8] The related question for ethical theory is whether treating others as we would have them treat us implies, for example, an endorsement of *good* treatment, or of some kind of *equal* treatment, or of what one would *rationally* want for oneself. It is possible for religiously committed people in business ethics to benefit on either side, the perspective of ethical theory or that of religion, from reflection on the other. This does not entail that there is always complementarity between any plausible ethical position and any given religious viewpoint, but such complementarity is often possible and commonly achieved.

Major Ethical Theories as Resources in Business Ethics

So far our focus has been on ethical theory in the disciplinary sense, as used mainly by philosophers. Ethical theory of this kind has often been presented in the form of specific comprehensive positions in ethics spanning both normative ethics and metaethics. Four kinds of historically important, comprehensive ethical theories have received widespread attention in business ethics. These four are described below, with reference to the kinds of resources they provide for business ethics.

Virtue Ethics

The central demand of virtue theories is that one concentrate on being a person of good character—a virtuous person. Honesty, fairness, fidelity, and beneficence are important moral virtues, and they empower their possessor to make and adhere to sound ethical decisions. For a virtue ethics, agents and their traits, as opposed to rules of action, are morally basic: we are, for instance, to understand what it is to behave justly through studying the nature and tendencies of the just person, not the other way around. We do not construct a notion of just deeds as those that treat people equally, and then, on that basis, define a just person as one who characteristically does deeds of this sort. For virtue ethics, as commonly understood, moral traits of character are ethically more basic than moral *acts*.[9] Here, in ordinary life as in business, role models are crucial for moral learning. Everyone can be a role model for others, but virtue ethics particularly calls on management and other business leaders to model good character and conduct. For Aristotle, as for many later virtue theorists, the person of practical wisdom is the chief role model in ethics—such people exemplify many of the moral virtues and also tend to be good advisers in ethical decisions. They are prudent and insightful, as well as morally upright.

If, however, we take *traits* as ethically more basic than *acts*, we must ask: How does a virtue theory tell us what to *do*? Ethics largely concerns *conduct*. How do we determine what counts as, for instance, being just or beneficent? Virtue ethics has resources for answering this question. For instance, Aristotle calls virtue "a state that decides, consisting of a mean, the mean relative to us, which is defined by reason.... It is a mean between two vices, one of excess and one of deficiency."[10] Consider beneficence. If, relative to my resources, I am selfish and ignore others' needs, this is a deficiency; if I give so much at once that I am prevented from providing much better things for others later, I am excessive. Good ethical decisions, on this view, are seen in the light of such comparisons.[11]

The term "mean" suggests a kind of kind of weighting that virtue ethicists, and indeed virtually all ethical theorists, take to be unavailable in ethics. One case might be the kind in which there is already a quantitative baseline. If you already have an employee whose monetary compensation is *n* and you are hiring one who is in every way comparable, then the relevant mean calls for equality of compensation. Suppose, however, that you are determining bonuses. Now you may have no such beacon. Still, some figures will be clearly too high, others clearly too low. Moreover, virtue ethics would have us not only avoid extremes but also formulate the general standards of virtue by which we are to judge. The manager should want to be, for example, just, generous, and prudent; in employees, virtuous managers look for virtues such as productivity, cooperativeness, and beneficence toward coworkers and customers. These refinements in the perspective of judgment, together with progressive elimination of what is too much or too little, can lead to good judgments. The judgments may, as in this case, be financial, but virtue bears on nonmoral decisions as well as moral ones. Plainly, such financial decisions as determinations of bonuses also have a moral aspect.

Kantian Ethics

A contrasting ethical theory centers on rules, and this kind of theory is even more prominent than virtue ethics in contemporary discussions of business ethics. Many business ethicists are substantially guided by the master principle of Immanuel Kant, a principle called the Categorical Imperative. In one formulation, it says that we are always to act in such a way that we can rationally will the principle we are acting on to be a universal law: *So act as if the maxim of your action* [that is, the principle of conduct underlying the action] *were to become through your will a universal law of nature.*[12] Thus, I should not mislead potential buyers in an advertisement I can legally publish if I could not rationally will the universality of the practice—say, when *I* am the victim. We would not want to universalize, and thus live by, the callous principle that "one should mislead others when this is legal and will be profitable."

Kant also gave a less abstract formulation of the Categorical Imperative: *Act so that you use humanity, as much in your own person as in the person of every other, always at the same time as an end and never merely as a means.*[13] The requirement is that we always treat persons never merely as means, but also as ends in themselves. In part, the imperative seems to say: never *use* people, as in manipulating them by deceptive advertising. Instead, respect them. Treating people as ends clearly requires (nonselfishly) caring about their good. They matter as persons, and one must to some extent act *for their sake* whether or not one benefits from it. This formulation applies to oneself as well as others. It requires a kind of respect for persons, and this includes self-respect. If we take Kant's two formulations together (and he considered them equivalent), then apparently we must not only treat persons as ends but *equally* so. Everyone matters and matters equally.[14]

The Kantian approach has at least a twofold emphasis. The universalizability principle calls on us both to act on principle and to be willing to apply our principle in any relevantly similar situation, including one in which we are on the receiving end of the decision in question. This has obvious application to determining compensation in employment, but the variables that go into such a decision are often numerous, and it should not be thought that formulating the rules that account for one's actual decision is easy. Just as one can follow rules of linguistic usage without being readily able to formulate them, one can follow a moral principle yet find difficulty formulating it with precision. The effort to do so, however, is often both morally desirable and economically rewarding.

Managerial judgments, whether in rewarding merit or in punishing violations, are *precedential*, and both clarity in the ethical climate of a business and incentives toward ethical conduct are often well served by articulating the rules guiding managerial decision. The second Kantian formulation of the Categorical Imperative is, in emphasis at least, very different: it says that no one is to be treated merely as a means to someone else's ends and, positively, that people are to be treated with respect for their value as persons (as ends in themselves). Exploitive treatment, as in sending employees on dangerous missions without adequate warning and their proper consent is thus ruled out. Creating a climate of respect is essential for ethical business, and the good of all stakeholders must be given due weight.

Utilitarianism

It is sometimes said that whereas Aristotle's ethics is a virtue ethics, Kant's is a rule ethics. (Kant's is also sometimes called an ethics of duty.) There is a point in this contrast, but it must not be taken to imply that practitioners of one must always differ with practitioners of the other in concrete ethical judgments on cases. The same holds for a quite different kind of rule ethics, one suggested by the question: what *good* are rules unless they contribute to our well-being—that is, unless (above all) following them enhances human happiness and reduces human suffering? This kind of concern leads to *utilitarianism*, the position of Jeremy Bentham and John Stuart Mill. For Mill, the central requirement of ethics is roughly this: choose that act from among your options which is best from the twin points of view of increasing human happiness and reducing human suffering (an ethically permissible act may be such by increasing happiness or decreasing suffering *or both*). In Mill's words: "The creed which accepts as the foundation of morals 'utility'…holds that actions are right in proportion as they tend to promote happiness, wrong as they tend to produce the reverse of happiness. By happiness is intended pleasure, and the absence of pain."[15] If one act produces more happiness than another, it is preferable, other things being equal. If the first also produces suffering, other things are not equal. Ideally, our actions would be doubly good, as in providing good jobs for unemployed poor people. We would be producing pleasure *and* reducing suffering.

The ethical aim for action is to find options second to none in total value, understood in terms of happiness. For instance, lying causes suffering, at least in the long run, and truthfulness contributes, over time, to our well-being—roughly, how well off we are from the point of view of happiness as the positive element and suffering as the negative one. Mill argued similarly in support of other morally required conduct, such as fairness in dealing with others and noninterference with other people's conduct.[16]

From the point of view of ethical theory, utilitarianism has advantages of a kind that are appealing to many businesspeople. It is empirical, in the sense that the question whether an act is right is answerable in terms of its predictable consequences for happiness and unhappiness. This makes it correspondingly objective and as quantitative as one can be about measurements of pleasure and pain and the probabilities of producing them. Many ethical theories have noted, however, that pleasure and pain are difficult to measure and that the task of predicting their consequences is complex, especially if one tries to take account of an indefinitely long future. One response to this problem is to take the maximization of happiness standard to apply not to individual acts but to rules of action. For this "rule utilitarianism," such everyday rules as those requiring promise keeping and veracity are often endorsed as normally giving good moral guidance. Their *internalization* by actors is what rule utilitarianism calls for.

In business ethics, then, utilitarians can claim to have a method that enables them to bring empirical techniques to bear on ethical decisions much as they bear on cost-benefit analysis in purely economic decisions aimed at maximizing profit. However, consider the difficulty of deciding when a working mine is sufficiently safe to permit sending miners into it. How should one weight the unhappiness value of an accidental death? One would need to take account of the expected value of the otherwise remaining life, as well as the suffering caused by loss and grief. Less dramatically, is one to pay one employee more than another because, although they are equal in productivity and other professional variables, one is healthy and single, the other is the sole support of three children, and we can find no further basis of a differentiation in happiness value? Here one might have a rule of justice calling for equal treatment, but cases like these raise the question whether such rules are actually supported by the overall maximization aim. The literature on utilitarianism is enormous, and here we can only note some of the advantages and disadvantages of giving it a major role in business decisions.[17]

Commonsense Intuitionism

A rule theory need not have a master principle. Many writers in ethics hold a pluralistic, multiple-rule view that categorizes our basic obligations. W. D. Ross did so by considering the kinds of grounds on which moral obligations rest; for instance, making a promise to help you review an inventory statement is a ground of an obligation to do it, and damaging someone's computer in delivery is a ground of an obligation to make reparations. For Ross, the basic prima facie obligations—roughly, obligations that constitute our overall obligation when there is no at least equally strong conflicting obligation—include obligations to (1) keep promises, (2) act justly, (3) express gratitude for services rendered, and (4) do good deeds toward others. Ross also stressed (in the same chapter) the obligations to (5) avoid injuring others, (6) make reparations for wrongdoing, (7) avoid lying, and (more positively) (8) improve oneself. He considered it intuitively clear and even self-evident that we have these eight obligations: you can see that we do by simply engaging in sufficiently clear and deep reflection—a kind of intuitive thinking—on the moral concepts in question in relation to representative applications of them to actual or hypothetical acts.[18] Hence the name "intuitionism" for the position that morality is to be conceived in terms of the principles expressing these commonly recognized obligations.[19]

Ross thought that in at least the majority of cases in which two or more prima facie obligations conflict, we need practical wisdom (wisdom in human affairs) to determine which is *final*, that is, which obligation is, all things considered, the one we ought to fulfill, as opposed to our prima facie obligation, our obligation relative to the moral grounds in the situation. Our final obligation is what we ought to do "in the end," and it will be the same as our prima facie obligation *if* no other such obligation of equal weight should conflict. Consider two cases in which most businesspeople would agree on the resolution, regardless of their orienting theories among those considered. If I promise to deliver a new computer to you and this turns out to be so expensive, owing to bad weather and shipping costs, that I would make no profit, this promissory obligation overrides my obligation to protect my profit. Similarly, if a computer is damaged in shipment, I may face a choice between replacement and equally costly repairs, but it would be wrong to hold the buyer responsible. These ethical preferences would often be intuitive and readily apparent to a person of practical wisdom, but they might also be justifiable by one or more ethical theories.

There is, then, both an Aristotelian element in Ross's common sense ethics and an openness to theoretical justifications of intuitive moral judgments. Practical wisdom is what Aristotle took to be essential in determining what kinds of acts express virtue; and Ross thought, as Aristotle may have, that sometimes it is intuitive, or even obvious, which of two conflicting obligations takes precedence. Saving a dying person may be quite obviously a stronger obligation than keeping a promise to help harvest corn. That the morally right choice is obvious does not prevent its being explained by, for instance, a Kantian categorical imperative. By contrast, the choice of one good candidate over another good one to fill an important position may rarely be obviously right. Here *morality* counsels humility—and the constant retrospective self-scrutiny that helps us both to rectify past mistakes and to avoid future errors. But even in difficult cases like this one may still be able to find—and to defend to higher management—good resolution with the help of an ethical theory.

Given a conscientious use of practical wisdom and appeals to a morality that we all commonly share, do we really need an ethical theory at all? And if we do, must it be "high-level" as are virtue ethics, Kantianism, and utilitarianism, or may it be more nearly "ground-level," as with the kinds of everyday moral generalizations Ross thought morally sufficient? Arguably, people are guided by one or another kind of high-level theory even if they are unaware of it. Be that as it may, there is wide agreement on this point: an act that is right—including the mental act of deciding to do something—is not just brutely right, it is right in virtue of being, say, an equal division of profits, a keeping of a promise, a relieving of suffering, or an expression of respectfulness. The reference here is to *grounds*—grounds that represent verifiable descriptive *facts*. These grounds represent the things ethical theorists have stressed: equal treatment in Kantian ethics, promise making in commonsense intuitionism, reduction of suffering in utilitarianism, and, in virtue ethics, acting from virtue. Ethical decisions by any conscientious and morally committed person tend to be guided by taking account of grounds of these sorts.

This brings us to the role of ethical theory in making such decisions. Ethical decisions are *precedential*: if we (morally) ought to do a certain deed in circumstances C, then we ought to do the same type of thing in exactly similar circumstances or—to take the more common case—in relevantly similar ones. A conscientious ethical decision, then, implies a rule that calls for the same act in circumstances that are at least relevantly similar. Kant's universalizability idea partly rests on, and calls attention to, this important point. Utilitarianism is in part an attempt to summarize the kinds of grounds that matter under the broad "welfarist" headings of pleasure and pain. Commonsense pluralism of the sort embraced by Ross provides a wider account of such grounds. Virtue ethics indicates connections between such grounds and right action as those connections are seen in the light of such virtues of character as justice, fidelity, and sincerity.

All conscientious people are *ground guided* in making moral decisions. Often, they are influenced by one or another kind of theory in deciding what the relevant grounds are and what action they call for. Ethical theories help one to find and articulate grounds, to justify decisions by appeal to them, and to generalize from good decisions to rules that can guide future conduct and facilitate good decisions in the future. A special merit of commonsense pluralism is that it provides a practical and readily applicable meeting ground for people whose theoretical orientations may be quite different. The principles Ross formulated are common in the moral education of many cultures: (1) they describe much of the ethical conduct of the virtuous; (2) they are "theorems" rationalized by Kant's central principles; (3) they are widely and plausibly thought to promote human well-being; and (4) they operate on the basis of familiar empirically accessible grounds for action.

SOME ILLUSTRATIVE PROBLEMS
IN BUSINESS ETHICS

Some illustrations of the practical uses of ethical theory in business ethics will help clarify the more theoretical matters discussed so far. The importance of virtue ethics, utilitarianism, Kantian ethics, and commonsense intuitionism will be presupposed, but it should be clear that other views might have similar applications to the problems in question.

Affirmative Action

Affirmative action is, roughly speaking, giving preferential treatment to members of a group identified by a characteristic not normally a qualification for doing the job in question. Gender and ethnicity are the main cases discussed in business ethics. Affirmative action comes in degrees. Among the importantly different degrees revealed by ethical analysis are (1) extra effort to bring the preferred group into the applicant pool, say to maximize female applications; (2) giving hiring preference when other things are *equal* in terms of qualifications; and (3) giving preference when a member of a nonpreferred class is perceptibly (but not substantially) better qualified.

The two most important rationales for affirmative action are that (1) it is needed, for some period of time, to compensate for past discrimination against the designated group (a rationale defensible by appeal to some of the commonsense intuitive principles or on Kantian lines) and (2) that it is beneficial for society as a whole (a rationale most readily defensible on utilitarian lines or by some nonutilitarian principle of beneficence). Consider African Americans whose ancestors were slaves and who may themselves have been victims of discrimination. It may be argued that there is an obligation of reparation owed to them, at least by government on behalf of society. The obligation of reparation, in general, is one Ross stressed. Fulfilling it here may also be considered a requirement of treating the persons in question as *ends*, in the sense required by Kant's categorical imperative. As to the social benefit argument, this may be supported by utilitarian considerations or even by appeal to the obligation of beneficence applied at the level of society as a whole. From the point of view of virtue ethics, both the character traits of benevolence and justice may be appealed to in support of an affirmative action policy: goodness toward others requires helping those at socioeconomically low levels, and justice toward those disadvantaged by wrongdoing calls for compensatory action. Both the reparation and the social benefit argument are controversial, and there is a huge literature on affirmative action. The aim here is to show some of the ways in which the major theories might be brought to bear on the issue.

The major ethical theories may, however, also be appealed to in challenging policies of affirmative action. Both the Kantian emphasis on universalizability and the commonsense principle of justice, for instance, call attention to the other side of the issue: *equal opportunity*. People commonly claim rights to it and argue that it requires assessing persons solely on their merits for the position in question. Rights of equal opportunity, many say, outweigh affirmative action considerations. These writers usually hold that there is no *right* to affirmative action and that even a right of reparation for wrongdoing could be satisfied by measures other than employment preference, say by enriched early childhood education programs, with some preference for the group owed the reparations. At the same time, since rights are not absolute—an important point of ethical theory that must here be assumed without argument—a case for some *degree* of affirmative action could still be made, at least in societies like that of the United States today. But what degree of affirmative action and for how long?

This problem is of the kind that Ross thought called for practical wisdom. Practical wisdom, however, may be significantly assisted by theory. Consider the requirements of justice and their bearing on affirmative action. Presumably, hiring preference is given only when other things are *equal* in terms of qualifications. Under this policy, no one should suffer the prima facie injustice of having someone less qualified preferred. It is true that there would not be perfect equality of opportunity, but do we have a right to have a prospective employer choose arbitrarily between us and someone equally qualified, so that our chance is equally good? An employer might claim a right in such cases to choose on other criteria within a morally acceptable range, including beneficence toward a member of a historically disadvantaged group. Both utilitarian and virtue ethical criteria may be helpful here. When the relevant details are clear, it may also help to frame a principle for deciding such cases and to consider, as Kantians would, whether whatever policy is considered is rationally universalizable.

Suppose that a good case can be made for affirmative action that calls for preference for a minority candidate whose qualifications for performing the job are not *quite* equal to those of the best majority candidate, though they are very close. Utilitarian considerations (among others) suggest an appeal to the economic value of diversity: the claim is that at least many businesses tend to succeed better when their workforce matches, in gender and ethnic proportionality, the population in which it operates. In a sense, this makes minority status a kind of economic merit. If the diversity argument is economically sound, does giving it some weight create a policy that would do an injustice to certain applicants or at least fail to treat them as ends? Is the argument truly a *justification* of some level of affirmative action, or is it a rationalization for violations of the equal opportunity standard? The answer is perhaps not obvious, but the question is an important one that ethical theory can at least help us clarify and think through.

Whistle-Blowing

In mining, construction, engineering, security firms, and industrial manufacture there are sometimes failures to maintain adequate safety conditions. Employees may face the question whether to "blow the whistle," that is, go to authorities higher in the business, or outside the business, or to the press or some other (usually outside) person(s) in order to rectify the wrong in question. The question can be difficult because blowing the whistle can harm other employees and even destroy the company, yet not doing so can lead to accidents or, on the economic side, loss of jobs for employees and suppliers and, for stockholders, loss of vast sums of money. Employees who discover serious wrongs will likely face conflicts of obligations— conflicts between obligations of fidelity to coworkers, who will likely be hurt by damage to the company, and to people, such as customers or stockholders, who will be harmed if nothing is done.

Suppose that tunnels in a mine are not sufficiently secured against collapse, with the result that there is a significant chance of a cave-in—one that neither good judgment nor the law would tolerate if it should come to light. Given the obligation of fidelity to coworkers and to one's company, one might favor a *priority of internal resolution* principle: it says that a reasonable attempt to solve the problem should be made through internal channels if there is a significant chance of success. But suppose nothing is done in response. It will take courage to go above one's supervisor. But what if it turns out that no one within the company is at all likely to solve the problem? It may be hard to determine this, but there have been cases in which it is clear that the top management is corrupt or at least unwilling to correct a wrong. This appears to have been the case with Enron and with WorldCom, though the circumstances at both were complicated. In the mining case, the miner (or other employee) may, and perhaps ethically must, blow the whistle.

This case illustrates the relevance of probability calculations in ethics. There is always some chance of disasters in mining. One question is what constitutes an "acceptable risk." It also may matter which ethical theory, if any, guides us. A utilitarian calculation is one route to an answer, but for cases like whistle-blowing a Kantian universalizability principle may be more pertinent: all concerned, from the mine operator to the person considering blowing the whistle, should ask whether the risk is one we could knowingly and rationally take or let our friends take. If the answer is negative, that person morally should take some action. Suppose that, as has often happened, there is an inadequate attempt at remedy within the company. From the point of view of a pluralism of moral norms, several obligations are relevant: the obligations of fidelity to coworkers, of justice, of beneficence, and of noninjury must be considered. It is clearly reasonable to minimize harm to the company, but the need to protect innocent people also looms large, and prevention of injury and injustice may together require blowing the whistle.

Another ethical question about whistle-blowing is how to state the appropriate degree of protection to provide for those who do it. One approach is a utilitarian calculation in which we compare, say, the good of strong protections against firings or prosecutions against the bad effect of the likelihood of false charges that would come with this system. Another approach is to appeal to the principle of noninjury (nonmaleficence), which calls for abstaining from injuring or harming others. This would imply that a truthful, judicious whistle-blower should have protection, but penalties should be assessed against those who make false charges, especially if they are negligently or quite detectably false. The results of these two approaches might or might not coincide, but they differ in their central focus.

Other approaches to whistle-blowing might also be used (as chapter 19 in this volume makes clear). Any approach should be tested by framing the principles it leads to and testing them against actual and hypothetical cases on which a clear intuitive judgment can be made. This procedure is usable in any field, and the attempt to achieve what was above called reflective equilibrium is an important goal in arriving at operating standards to govern whistle-blowing.

Advertising and the Ethics of Creating Desire

Advertising succeeds only if adequate desire exists on the part of consumers. The ethical appraisal of advertising requires conceptual analysis, and it benefits from moral psychology. To begin with motivation, three important kinds of desire should be considered. The main division is between need-based desire and non-need-based desire. But what is need? We here require a further distinction. Needs are relative to some state or outcome for which the needed thing is essential. Food and shelter are needed for survival; an all-terrain vehicle is needed for certain kinds of recreation or for war. The respect of others is needed for a good life.

A good life is not definable in biological terms and can be the object of ethical needs and of desires an ethical person would have. For example, that people need the respect of others is an ethical statement. A plausible ethical theory can help us to determine what human beings need. In the virtue-ethical tradition since Aristotle, the notion of human flourishing has been used to describe a pattern of human existence in which what is sometimes called "the human good" is realized. A broad guideline is that, from the moral point of view, people need to flourish. They need to develop and use their talents, to enjoy social interaction, and to express themselves intellectually and spiritually. Ethical theorists who give *rights* a central place tend to agree that there is a basic human right to an *opportunity* to flourish.[20] What level of support this right requires businesses to give to their employees and other "stakeholders"—and what it requires governments to provide for citizens—are difficult questions. No ethical theory of the basic kinds we have considered gives a precise answer, but no answer that is not defensible in relation to some general moral grounds is likely to succeed.

Need-based desires of either biological or ethical kinds are natural for human beings and are ethically proper targets of advertising and marketing. Whether need-based or not, desires met by marketing divide into two kinds: those existing *antecedently* to marketing—especially advertising—and those *created* by it. A desire for a good night's sleep is need based and antecedent to advertising; a desire for a particular kind of sleeping pill may well not be antecedent to advertising. A desire for a powerful all-terrain vehicle for recreational use is (generally) not need based. It may or may not be created by advertising. Is it ethical for a business to create it and sell such products? Is doing so unjustifiably manipulative—a way of treating people merely as means or at least not as ends?

It would be a mistake to claim that creating and meeting desires that are not need based is always unethical. Many things that make life enjoyable are not needed either biologically or for ethical reasons. However, one could market cigarettes to minors or otherwise create desires for something harmful that is not needed. Here one would violate the obligation of noninjury. One could also create desires that have *disproportionate strength*. They are disproportionate in that, though not themselves need based, they come to outweigh need-based desires. This would apply to desires for hard drugs that are not medically needed but create a chemical dependency.

People who want to enter the business world have choices, and businesses themselves have latitude regarding what they will create or market. Here it is important to ask what kind of person one wants to be, as virtue ethics demands of us, and to have a good understanding of what is called for in business conduct by one or another answer. Given a manufacturing or marketing plan, we should be able to explore how it bears on the promotion of human good, which in turn requires distinguishing between need-based desires and other desires, and between evoking desire for what advances well-being and manipulatively evoking desires that simply lead to consumption and, like excessive energy consumption, to harms. Connected with this is the difference between persuading potential customers with arguments based on their needs and manipulating them with images and information that produce consumption by evoking non-need-based desires.

CONCLUSIONS

Ethical theory is often developed purely metaethically in a way that is neutral on substantive moral questions. It is also frequently represented by a variety of well-developed positions that include both metaethical and normative ethical components. These positions include virtue, Kantian, utilitarian, and commonsense theories. These theories either contain or can be readily integrated with positions in epistemology and metaphysics, moral psychology, and philosophical theology. These theories center on certain kinds of descriptive factual grounds for ethical decision, such as promises made, harms done to persons, or consequences for human happiness. All require conceptual analysis for their interpretation and application. In some cases of ethical decision, these theories lead one in different directions; in others, they converge in support of a decision or resolution, even if for quite different reasons. None makes ethical decisions in complicated cases easy. But the theories agree in recognizing a wide range of human conduct in which ethics provides helpful answers. In the majority of business decisions, it is clear that, negatively, harms, lies, and broken promises are to be avoided and that, positively, the welfare of human beings is to be promoted. Where hard cases require decisions that are controversial, ethical theory enables us to explain their basis, frame tentative principles that support the decisions, and critically compare the cases with other cases that fall under the principles and may confirm them or, in some instances, lead us to revise them. This use of ethical theory reduces the chance of error, facilitates nonviolent resolution of disagreement, sets a precedent for dealing with problems that will likely arise, and provides a basis for better procedures and decisions in the future.[21]

NOTES

1. The domain of the right and the wrong is called *deontic*, that of the good and the bad *axiological*, but I will not use these terms and will instead speak of what is right, wrong, obligatory (wrong *not* to do), and permissible (not wrong *to* do, though not necessarily obligatory), and of what is good as an end (good in itself) as opposed to good as a means (instrumentally).

2. The difference between a judgment that is moral in content and one that is moral in force is essential for showing that moral judgments have criteria of application not *themselves* dependent on *prior* moral judgment. If you give $20 for an item selling for $12 and are (intentionally) shortchanged by receiving $7 in change, it is a simple verifiable fact that you are cheated. There are moral uses of "cheat," but the point here is that we can specify the moral point of view in part by finding terms with nonmoral content whose application entails the applicability of a moral judgment. Some would call *cheating* a "thick" moral concept, presumably on the ground that it has definite content self-evidently entailing a prima facie wrong.

3. Kenneth Goodpaster analyzes various excessive pursuits of profit and other goals under the heading of "teleopathy," *Conscience and Corporate Culture* (Oxford: Blackwell, 2007), 28.

4. This is from Sellars's paper "Empiricism and the Philosophy of Mind," in his *Science, Perception and Reality* (London: Routledge and Kegan Paul, 1963), 173 (originally published in *Minnesota Studies in the Philosophy of Science* 1, 1956).

5. For a major recent statement of noncognitivism with references to earlier writers in this tradition see Allan Gibbard, *Wise Choices, Apt Feelings* (Cambridge, Mass.: Harvard University Press, 1990).

6. Ross is a prominent defender of the view that certain basic principles are self-evident. He suggests that people who have a certain mental maturity and reflect sufficiently can know them in the way we know rules of inference in logic. See W. D. Ross, *The Right and the Good* (Oxford: Oxford University Press, 1930), 29. Supporting theory is given by Thomas Nagel, *The View from Nowhere* (Oxford: Oxford University Press, 1986).

7. John Rawls, *A Theory of Justice* (Cambridge, Mass.: Harvard University Press, 1971) is largely responsible for giving reflective equilibrium prominence in ethical theorizing; see, especially, 48–51. There is now a large literature on it, and the method has been claimed by both people who think justification for beliefs and judgments comes chiefly from coherence among them and those who think it comes chiefly from their grounding in experience or reason taken to provide evidence for beliefs and judgments. Rawls is also a major proponent of a contractualist approach to understanding social justice. For a short statement of how such an approach bears on business ethics see Thomas W. Dunfee and Thomas Donaldson, "Social Contract Approaches to Business Ethics: Bridging the

'Is-Ought' Gap," in *A Companion to Business Ethics*, ed. Robert E. Frederick (Oxford: Blackwell, 2002), 38–55.

8. For an indication of how the Golden Rule is formulated in many different religious traditions—African as well as Western and Eastern—see Patrick E. Murphy et al., *Ethical Marketing* (Upper Saddle River, N.J.: Pearson/Prentice-Hall, 2005), 36.

9. Aristotle described just acts as the kind that a just person would perform; a just person is not to be defined as one who performs just acts. He took moral traits of character to be ethically more basic than moral acts. He said, regarding types of acts that are right, "Actions are called just or temperate when they are the sort that a just or temperate person would do" (*Nicomachean Ethics*, 1105b5ff). It is virtues such as justice and temperance rather than acts that are ethically basic for Aristotle: "Virtue makes us aim at the right target, and practical wisdom makes us use the right means" (1144a).

10. Aristotle, *Nicomachean Ethics*, ed. Roger Crisp (Cambridge: Cambridge University Press, 2002), 1107a1–4.

11. For discussion of virtue ethics in the business domain, with applications to many problems treated in this volume, see Robert C. Solomon, *Ethics and Excellence: Cooperation and Integrity in Business* (Oxford: Oxford University Press, 1992). Also instructive for business ethics is Edwin Hartman, "Can't We Teach Character? An Aristotelian Answer," *Academy of Management Learning and Education* 5 (2006): 68–81.

12. Immanuel Kant, *Groundwork of the Metaphysics of Morals*, trans. Allen Wood (New Haven, Conn.: Yale University Press, 2002), 38, sec. 422. Kant apparently has *rational universalizability* in mind in this and the other universalizability formulations of the Categorical Imperative. There is a large literature on how he should be interpreted, but nothing highly controversial about his view will be presupposed here.

13. Ibid., 46–47, sec. 429.

14. A account of Kantian ethics in business is provided by Norman E. Bowie, *Business Ethics: A Kantian Perspective* (Oxford: Blackwell, 1999). A shorter statement of his view is his "A Kantian Approach to Business Ethics," in *A Companion to Business Ethics*, ed. Robert E. Frederick (Oxford: Blackwell Publishers, 2002), 3–16.

15. John Stuart Mill, *Utilitarianism*, ed. George Sher (Indianapolis: Hackett, 1979).

16. Utilitarianism is popularly formulated as the position that for an act to be morally right is for it to produce "the greatest good for the greatest number." This misrepresents the view. Utilitarians are concerned above all to maximize the good. Some ways to produce good for all concerned, such as providing education for all children, are quantitatively better than others because of how many people they help; but the idea that doing good for more people rather than less is not a *basic* concern of utilitarianism and is not appropriate to defining the position. For instance, if providing public parks only in poor communities would produce more good than providing them equally to a whole population (where this entails their being of lower quality), the former, narrower distribution would be preferred.

17. For critical explication and an analytical treatment of utilitarianism, see my "Can Utilitarianism Be Distributive?" *Business Ethics Quarterly* 17 (4) (2007): 593–611.

18. See W. D. Ross, *The Right and the Good*, 21–34.

19. For clarification, modification, and extension of Ross's position, see Robert Audi, *The Good in the Right: A Theory of Intuition and Intrinsic Value* (Princeton, N.J.: Princeton University Press, 2004), 40–79, which proposes a *Kantian intuitionism*, an integration between the Rossian, commonsense pluralist approach and a version of the categorical imperative. Clearly, an ethical theory may draw on elements in more than one of the four major kinds of positions introduced in section 2, and my statement argues for an integrated view with advantages over Kant's and Ross's positions.

20. It is difficult to say what constitutes a moral right. On the most plausible understandings of the notion, *rights* do not exhaust *oughts*, and hence are not the entire basis of moral standards.

21. Acknowledgments: For many helpful comments on earlier versions of this essay or parts of it, I thank my colleagues Georges Enderle and Patrick E. Murphy and, especially, the editors of this volume.

SUGGESTED READING

Aquinas, Thomas. *Disputed Questions on the Virtues.* Edited by E. M. Atkins and Thomas Williams. Cambridge: Cambridge University Press, 2005.

Aristotle. *Nicomachean Ethics.* Edited by Roger Crisp. Cambridge: Cambridge University Press, 2002.

Audi, Robert. *The Good in the Right: A Theory of Intuition and Intrinsic Value.* Princeton, N.J.: Princeton University Press, 2004.

Bowie, Norman E. *Business Ethics: A Kantian Perspective.* Oxford: Blackwell, 1999.

Dunfee, Thomas W., and Thomas Donaldson. "Social Contract Approaches to Business Ethics: Bridging the 'Is-Ought' Gap." In *A Companion to Business Ethics.* Edited by Robert E. Frederick, 38–55. Oxford: Blackwell, 2002.

Gert, Bernard. *Common Morality.* Oxford: Oxford University Press, 2004.

Gibbard, Allan. *Wise Choices, Apt Feelings.* Cambridge, Mass.: Harvard University Press, 1990.

Harman, Gilbert, and Judith Jarvis Thomson. *Moral Relativism and Moral Objectivity.* Oxford: Basil Blackwell, 1996.

Hooker, Brad. *Ideal Code, Real World.* Oxford: Oxford University Press, 2000.

Hume, David. *A Treatise of Human Nature.* Edited by David Fate Norton and Mary J. Norton. Oxford: Clarendon Press, 2007.

Kant, Immanuel. *Groundwork of the Metaphysics of Morals.* Translated by Allen Wood. New Haven, Conn.: Yale University Press, 2002.

Mill, John Stuart. *Utilitarianism.* Edited by George Sher. Indianapolis, Ind.: Hackett, 1979.

Nagel, Thomas. *The View from Nowhere.* Oxford: Oxford University Press, 1986.

Nozick, Robert. *Anarchy, State and Utopia.* New York: Basic Books, 1974.

Parfit, Derek. *Reasons and Persons.* Oxford: Oxford University Press, 1984.

Rawls, John. *A Theory of Justice.* Cambridge, Mass.: Harvard University Press, 1971.

Ross, W. D. *The Right and the Good.* Oxford: Oxford University Press, 1930.

Scanlon, T. M. *What We Owe to Each Other.* Cambridge, Mass.: Harvard University Press, 1998.

Swanton, Christine. *Virtue Ethics: A Pluralistic View.* Oxford: Oxford University Press, 2003.

PART II

COMPETITIVE
MARKETS AND
CORPORATE
RESPONSIBILITY

CHAPTER 3

THE IDEA AND IDEAL
OF CAPITALISM

GERALD GAUS

CONSIDER a stylized contrast between medical and business ethics. Both fields of applied ethics focus on a profession whose activities are basic to human welfare. Both inquire into obligations of professionals and the relations between goals intrinsic to the profession and ethical duties to others and to the society. I am struck, however, by a fundamental difference: whereas medical ethics takes place against a background of almost universal consensus that the practice of medicine is admirable and morally praiseworthy, the business profession is embedded within the framework of firms in a capitalist market economy, and for the last century and a half there has been sustained debate about the moral and economic justifiability of such an economy. To be sure, even under socialism there might be an "ethics of socialist managers," and there would be some overlap between such an ethic and contemporary business ethics. Nevertheless, many of the characteristic problems of business ethics—for example, what are the obligations of a corporation to its shareholders?—arise only in the context of a private property-based market economy.

This raises a deep question for business ethics: can one develop an account of ethical practices for an activity (i.e., business) while ignoring that the context in which this activity occurs (i.e., capitalism) is morally controversial? It is as if work in medical ethics proceeded in the midst of widespread disagreement about whether medicine was a good thing.[1] Another way of thinking about the problem is, if you teach business ethics, does this commit you to accepting that business can be ethical? And does this commit you to accepting that capitalism is justifiable? I suspect that this is a serious problem for many teachers of business ethics. Many were trained in academic philosophy, and within academic philosophy there are many who think—or at least suspect—that capitalism is basically unjust, or perhaps that only a greatly modified capitalism would be acceptable. The great economist John Maynard Keynes articulated a view that is probably shared by many teachers of business ethics:

> For my part I think that capitalism, wisely managed, can probably be made more efficient for attaining economic ends than any alternative system yet in sight, but that in itself it is in many ways extremely objectionable. Our problem is to work out a social organisation which shall be as efficient as possible without offending our notions of a satisfactory way of life.[2]

Indeed, many teachers and students of business ethics may not even incline as far as Keynes in thinking that capitalism can be made acceptable: in the end, Keynes was more a liberal reformer than a radical critic of capitalism.

If the practice of business ethics is embedded in a capitalist economic system, students and teachers of business ethics should have an appreciation of what a relatively pure form of capitalism would look like. We can then begin to think about what would be required for its justification. Knowing that, we will then be in a position to reflect on whether we think there can be truly ethical business practices. If, after seeing what a pure form of capitalism would be, and what would be required for its justification, a student or teacher of business ethics concludes that such justification is not to be had, then her task is basically Keynes's: to determine what, if any, alteration of this system retains the important benefits of capitalist business while conforming to her notion of "a satisfactory way of life." Perhaps reflecting on contemporary versions of capitalism, she will decide that the current versions depart from the pure form, and because of that they are consistent with her notion of a satisfactory way of life; then again, it is possible that contemporary capitalism is objectionable just because it departs too much from the pure form.

My task in this chapter is to sketch what I see as the elements of a pure form of capitalism and to indicate some of the ways that proponents of capitalism have sought to justify these elements. The rather vague idea of "capitalism" is better grasped if we analyze it into distinct elements. And each element might be justified in different ways. I believe that once we reflect on the elements of capitalism we will see that Keynes and many others have woefully underestimated its power as an ideal way to organize economic—and indeed many social—relations. However, my main aim is not to defend capitalism as an ideal, but to analyze capitalism into its constitutive elements. This will not only allow us to better understand the context in which business occurs but it will also help the reader to better identify just what aspect of capitalism, if any, offends her notion "of a satisfactory way of life." This chapter, then, is not so much an essay *in* business ethics as it is an essay on the foundations of the very practices of business and business ethics—the idea of a capitalist economic order.

PRIVATE PROPERTY

Classical debates about the justifiability of capitalism, and especially the contrast between capitalism and communism, focused on the right to private property. John Stuart Mill (a defender of a modified version of capitalism) and Karl Marx (the most famous critic of all) supposed that capitalism is essentially defined by a system that relies on private property rights, and so they thought that the rejection of capitalism just *is* the rejection of private property. "Communism is the positive abolition of private property," wrote Marx.[3]

Maximally Extensive Feasible Property Rights: Capitalist Ownership

The *complete* abolition of private property has rarely been advocated. In Plato's ideal republic, it is true, the ruling class was to live under complete communism— including communism of wives—but that is an extreme view indeed.[4] Even Soviet Communism recognized personal private property in the form of consumer goods such as clothes, household items, and books. Perhaps, then, capitalism requires private property in nonpersonal goods—we might think that capitalism is defined in terms of the private ownership of capital goods (i.e., goods required for the production of other goods). Although there is something to this, throughout almost all of human history capital goods such as tools and farm equipment have been privately owned, yet we would not want to say that capitalism has been the dominant mode of production throughout all human history.[5] Just what is the relation between capitalism and private property?

The ideal of capitalism—that is, a pure version of capitalism—is characterized by *maximally extensive feasible property rights* along two different dimensions. The *first* dimension concerns the extent of an individual's ownership right or, as philosophers often put it, the extent of the bundle of rights that make up a person's property. Most scholars today conceive of property in terms of a set of rights that might vary. For some person (call him Alf) to have *full private property rights* over P, Alf must have:[6]

- The right to use P as he wishes so long as this is not harmful to others or their property;
- The right to exclude others from using P.
- The right to manage: Alf may give permission to any others he wishes to use P, and determine how it may be used by them.
- The right to compensation: If someone damages or uses P without Alf's consent, Alf has a right to compensation for the loss of P's value from that person.

- The rights to destroy, waste, or modify: Alf may destroy *P*, waste it, or change it.
- The right to income: Alf has a right to the financial benefits of forgoing his own use of *P* and letting someone else use it.
- Immunity from expropriation: *P* (or any part of *P*) may not be made the property of another or the government without Alf's consent, with the exception of a few items such as taxation.
- Liability to execution: *P* may be taken away from Alf by authorized persons for repayment of a debt.
- Absence of term: Alf's rights over *P* are of indefinite duration.
- Rights to rent and sale (transfer rights): Alf may temporarily or permanently transfer all or some of his rights over *P* to anyone he chooses.

To say that someone who holds these rights over *P* has maximally extensive feasible property rights over *P* is to say that his control over *P* is as complete as possible (the maximal claim) given the like control of others over their property (the feasibility claim). If we drop the feasibility requirement we can give Alf an even more extensive control over *P*: he might have the right to use his property in ways that harm others, or has no liability to execution. But this increase in his control would limit others' control over their property. If Alf has the right to use his property in ways harmful to others, their use of their property will be impaired. If Alf is free from liability to execution, he can avoid paying compensation when he damages the property of others. So we can think of the above as approaching the maximally extensive control of Alf over *P* consistent with the like control of others over their property.

The concept of maximally extensive feasible property rights is part of an ideal, pure, conception of capitalism. Real world economic systems, even those that we would all agree are appropriately deemed "capitalist," may limit Alf's control over *P* by limiting, or even removing, some of these rights. Zoning laws limit the uses to which Alf may put his property; historical district regulations limit his rights to destroy, waste, or modify his residence; business licensing laws limit his ability to transfer his property; laws setting a maximum interest rate limit his right to an income. Sometimes, however, real-world systems actually expand these rights. A long-established public policy has been to limit the extent to which consumers can claim rights to compensation against harm from certain public utilities; thus the utilities have less liability than other property owners.[7] All these are rightly seen as ways of qualifying full capitalist ownership of some people. It is clear, though, that as these qualifications accumulate, we are apt to wonder whether the remaining property rights are sufficiently extensive to provide the basis for capitalism. And certainly some of these rights are more fundamental to capitalism than others. The rights to use, to exclude, to income, to modify, to manage, to transfer, to compensation, and to immunity from expropriation are basic to a capitalist order. An economic system that is based on some qualifications on them may still be recognizably capitalist: one that drastically curtails any of them over a wide range of property begins to loose its capitalist character. A system that does not generally recognize the rights to income or to transfer, for example, may be said to have a sort of private property, but not capitalist property.

The right against expropriation raises deep questions about the justifiability of taxation. Nonconsensual takings of property limit or abridge this right; if such takings are extensive, the resulting system will be far from the capitalist ideal.[8] As John Locke insisted, if government may legitimately take away people's property without their consent, "this would be in effect to leave them no *Property* at all."[9] Given this, the most extreme capitalist position is "anarcho-capitalism," which maintains that, because all taxation is nonconsensual, government is inherently illegitimate.[10] Locke took a more moderate view. Though he held that government may not raise taxes without the people's consent, insofar as a legitimate legislature rests on the consent of the governed, taxation approved by a representative legislature does not constitute an expropriation, and so is not a violation of property rights.[11] Thus the famous rallying cry of the American Revolution—"No taxation without representation!"—expresses a strong commitment to capitalist property rights. Only if government is organized in a certain way can its taxes, which take a citizen's property, be legitimate.[12]

Maximally Extensive Feasible Property Rights: What Can Be Owned?

One dimension along which the ideal of capitalism endorses maximally extensive feasible property rights is, then, the extent of the bundle of rights one has over P. The other dimension concerns the range of objects[13] over which one can have property rights. The capitalist ideal is to extend as far as possible the range of things that are privately owned. Of course under the capitalist ideal, consumer and productive goods are privately owned. So too are natural resources. Recently, advocates of capitalism have argued that many of our environmental problems stem from the *absence* of private property rights over such resources. Many environmental problems concern what are called "common pool resources," which are characterized by (1) relatively open ("public") access and (2) private consumption. Clean air and fresh water are common pool resources: they are accessible to everyone but consumed privately. The "tragedy of the commons" arises in situations in which individuals (or groups) make individually rational decisions about how much of the relevant resource (e.g., water, air) to consume that, collectively, leads to the overharvesting of that resource and depleting its sustainable capacity.[14] Pollution is a prime example of a common pool problem: overuse of the air's ability to dissipate waste gasses leads to the depletion of that ability. When goods remain in the common pool, if some restrain their current consumption (e.g., fish less) while others do not, those who restrain themselves will not only end up with less today but very likely will have no more in the future: those who do not restrain themselves may well overharvest the resource, depleting future stocks. If so, no one has an incentive to restrain themselves today and all will overharvest. Most of our worst resource depletion problems—the ability of the atmosphere to absorb carbon dioxide, fresh air, fresh water, fisheries, coral reefs, wild animals—stem from *lack* of private property rights. When a resource is privately owned, the owner will be confident that she will benefit from her restraint on present use: she will reap less today but she will gain the benefit—future sustainable yields. As David Schmidtz has convincingly argued, only if resources are taken out of the common pool will depletions be minimized. As he tellingly puts it, "leaving goods in the common practically ensures their destruction."[15] When dealing with resources that cannot be renewed such as petroleum, capitalist ownership induces efficient pricing (see section 3 below), which in turn encourages searches for additional supplies and alternative technologies.

Advocates of the capitalist ideal thus have sought to extend as far as feasible the range of objects subject to private property rights. This includes maximal rights over one's body and labor, so that one is free to sell any services to others that do not harm third parties (again, one's use of one's property does not uncontroversially extend to harmful uses). Although Marx sometimes saw private property as characteristic of capitalism, at other times he stressed that capitalism's truly distinctive feature was the "commodification of labor": that labor itself is a commodity to be bought and sold like any other good.[16] This "commodification" of labor and services is embraced by capitalism: defenders of capitalism not only endorse the sale of labor in the usual contexts but may also support—even strongly support— more controversial applications such as the right to sell sexual services in the form of prostitution, sell pornography, create clubs with strippers, and so on. The terms "sex industry" and "workers in the sex industry" expresses this "commodification" of sexual services. Indeed, many friends of capitalism push the "commodification" even further, arguing for property rights in body parts, and thus for the right to sell parts of one's body such as a kidney[17]—or, more radically, any body part. The upshot of this conception of capitalism is a "permissive society": in "competitive capitalism…the businessman will make money by catering to for whatever it is people wish to do—by providing pop records, or nude shows, or candyfloss."[18] At the extreme, this leads some advocates of capitalism to allow that an individual may transfer the property over himself to another, becoming a slave or a source of many body parts for research and transplantation.[19]

Justifying Capitalist Property Rights

I have been describing a regime of maximally extensive feasible property rights; as figure 3.1 shows, there are numerous regimes of property that lie between such a regime (point A) and communism (point D).

The Space of Capitalist Property

One might speculate that, say, current U.S. capitalism is closer to point C than to A, the capitalist ideal: the range of things that can be owned is quite extensive (though

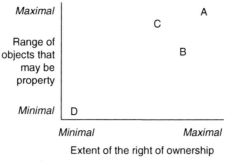

Figure 3.1

certainly not maximal—think of the absence of property over heroin, certain sexual services, and kidneys), but ownership rights are qualified in numerous ways (licensing regulations, environmental regulations, health and safety rules, and so on). However, John Stuart Mill seemed to support a system closer to B: fuller property rights over what can be owned but significant limitations on what should be owned. For Mill, the justification of private property—that people deserve the fruits of their labor—does not apply to land: "No man made the land. It is the original inheritance of the whole species."[20]

To justify an impure regime of capitalist property rights, then, is to justify a system of property rights somewhere *in the neighbourhood* of point A. To justify the capitalist ideal is to justify the sort of maximally extensive feasible property rights *at* A. Although we cannot even begin to fully survey the arguments that have been advanced to justify such extensive property rights, it will help to get some idea of why advocates of capitalism have thought property rights approaching point A can be justified. I consider briefly two important lines of justification advanced by political philosophers (I turn to economists in section 3).

Self-Ownership

Perhaps the most influential justification holds that (1) to be a free person is to have maximally extensive feasible property rights over oneself and (2) there is some mechanism that allows these extensive self-ownership rights to yield extensive rights over objects in the world. For Locke, one's property is not just one's "estates" but one's "life," "liberty," and "person."[21] In this sense we are self-owners, and our ownership over parts of the world is an extension of our self-ownership. For Locke, when a person mixes his labor (which is his property) with unowned parts of the world, he can extend his property in his person to include those parts of the world. This type of view was by no means unique to Locke. As Stephen Buckle shows in his study of the natural law theories of property, Hugo Grotius, Samuel Pufendorf, and Locke all insisted on an intimate connection between a person's rights and what "belongs" to her. This idea of what belongs to a person or her "*suum*" concerns a set of "essential possessions": life, limbs, and liberty. Thus understood, says Buckle, the *suum* is "what naturally belongs to a person because none of these things can be taken away without injustice."[22] Now, crucially, natural law theorists held that one's *suum* could be—indeed, if we are to survive, must be—extended into the world. As Buckle says, concerning Locke, "the property in one's own person thus has a dynamic quality, in that it needs to grow to survive—it requires the acquisition of certain things. The *suum* must be extended—'mixed' with things—in order to be maintained."[23] Thus by extending one's *suum* into the external world—in Locke's theory, by mixing one's labor with parts of the world—external private property in goods is generated. External ownership involves property rights over things that are as extensive as property rights over oneself: they are an extension of the attributes of personhood itself.

If the self-ownership argument is to justify the sort of extensive capitalist property rights we have been analyzing, (1) it must be shown that the extension process applies to a suitably wide range of objects and (2) that these new property rights are characterized by the full bundle of capitalist rights. Both of these tasks look daunting. As Buckle notes, at the heart of self-ownership theories such as Locke's was the idea that our right of self-ownership is inalienable: we have property in our own person, but no right to destroy or waste it.[24] But if one's property rights over one's self constitute less than full capitalist property, it is hard to see how one's extension of this right of self-ownership creates full capitalist property rights: the extended property rights would be more complete than the property right on which they are based. Moreover, if the point of the extension of one's *suum* is to provide for our maintenance, then it seems that this process could not justify property rights that would ultimately be harmful to us, such as property rights over heroin or alcohol. To be sure, some advocates of the self-ownership view have insisted that a pure self-ownership doctrine would accord us full capitalist property rights over our body and labor.[25] An implication of this position would be that others would have a right of execution over your body for purpose of compensation and nonpayment of debts—a radical view.

Agency Justifications

A more adequate justification of maximally extensive property seeks to derive them from the very idea of agency. Loren Lomasky, for example, argues that persons, understood as pursuers of projects, have a natural and important interest in possessing things:

> Persons…have a natural interest in having things. The relation of *having* is
> conceptually more basic and not to be confused with a *property right*. It amounts
> to the actual ability to employ some object in the furtherance of one's designs and
> does not presuppose the existence of any structure of rights. Having *I* and enjoying
> property rights in *I* are conceptually and empirically distinguishable…. However,
> these are not two unrelated concepts. It is because of a person's interests in having
> objects that there is an interest in being accorded property rights.[26]

Thus, as Lomasky understands them, property rights protect one's possession of things: "Property rights demarcate a moral space within which what one has is marked as immune from predation."[27] Such morally secure possession is required for successful project pursuit.

The crucial task for the agency justification is to move from a general argument that *some* property is necessary for agency to a defense of *maximally extensive* property rights. The agency argument has an easier time than self-ownership accounts in showing that our rights of ownership should approximate full property rights (our first dimension of capitalist property rights): agency requires that one be able to control parts of the world as part of one's projects, and full capitalist property maximizes control. But can it also be shown that the agency justification leads to the desirability of maximal property rights over the other dimension—the things over which one can have property? This looks more dubious. The key, it would seem, is to show that (1) agency is a great, perhaps the supreme value and (2) to limit what parts of the world a person may own, or what services she may sell, always to some extent limits her agency and so (3) it takes an extremely strong case, in terms of competing values, to justifiably set a limit on what can be owned, or what services can be sold. Thus, for example, an advocate of the agency justification may object to John Rawls's suggestion that one's interest in agency is adequately advanced by a system that grants private property over personal items but prohibits it over productive goods.[28] Such a socialist system prohibits "capitalist acts between consenting adults"[29]—and that looks like a significant limitation on the types of projects that one is free to pursue.

Capitalism and Markets

To fully understand why capitalism endorses maximally extensive property rights we need to turn from philosophic justifications to the analysis of the market and efficiency.

Markets and Efficient Property: Full Capitalist Property Rights

In his classical paper on "The Problem of Social Cost," R. M. Coase showed that, regardless of the initial distribution of property rights, if there are no transaction costs, free exchange in the market yields an efficient outcome.[30] Consider an example. As we all know, there is a great demand for solar panels in the West; environmentalists, those concerned about global warming, and those interested in national energy independence all are urging increased use of solar power. Now the production of solar panels requires polysilicon, but manufacturing polysilicon produces toxic waste. In Western countries this waste is recycled; in China, however, recycling technologies are not well developed, and recycling is not required by law.[31] Waste is either stored or, after minimal reprocessing, released into the environment. It is estimated that to recycle the waste would increase the cost of Chinese polysilicon by somewhere between 50 to 400 percent. It is disputed how great the resulting pollution is, but it is safe to say that enough waste leaks on to adjoining land to severely curtail agriculture on surrounding farms. Suppose, as does Coase, that we ignore transaction and bargaining costs and simply focus on the Polysilicon Factory and say, the group of Affected Farmers. The Polysilicon Factory clearly produces what economists call a *negative externality* on the Affected Farmers: its productive activity negatively impacts their livelihood. Now if the Polysilicon Factory does not take this negative impact into account it has an incentive to produce polysilicon up to the point where its marginal costs equal its marginal benefits: that is, up to the point where its costs for producing another ton of polysilicon equals the profits of doing so. (That this is so is a standard axiom of economics.) If the Polysilicon Factory is at a level of production such that the benefits of producing another ton of polysilicon exceed the total costs of producing that unit, it clearly has an incentive to produce that additional ton; if it is at the point where the total costs of producing another ton of polysilicon exceed the benefits of producing that unit, it clearly has an incentive *not* to produce that ton. But the problem for society is that at the point at which the Polysilicon Factory's marginal costs equal *its* marginal benefits, the *total social costs* will have exceeded the total social benefits. This is because the Polysilicon Factory does not take into account the costs imposed on the Affected Framers; if it considers these costs in its calculations, it would have ceased production at a lower level of output (at an extreme, zero).

To see this better, let us assume some figures. Suppose that a Polysilicon Factory would incur a one-time cost of $500,000 to build an improved storage facility that would not leak on to neighboring properties: suppose such a facility would last twenty years, so the yearly cost is roughly $25,000. Now assume that the pollution causes a collective loss of $40,000 a year to the Affected Farmers. Even if there is no law against the pollution, an efficient result can still be achieved: the Farmers can pay the Factory $25,000 a year to build the improved facility. They will be $15,000 a year better off, and the factory will be no worse off (if the farmers pay $26,000, both will be better off than in the current situation). It is important that this "theorem" applies regardless of how the property rights are divided between the two parties. An efficient outcome can be reached whether the Factory has a right to pollute or the Farmers have a right that it not pollute. Suppose that there is indeed a law against pollution, but to totally stop pollution would require a much larger expenditure, say $10,000,000; suppose the Factory could not afford to pay this and would close down. Assume that the Farmers still suffer a total loss of $40,000 a year and that the Farmers have the right to bring suit against the Factory. Now it is efficient for the Factory to pay the Farmers something more than $40,000 a year not to bring suit. This would be better for both the Farmers and the Factory than shutting down the Factory.

According to Coase, then, in the absence of transaction and bargaining costs, parties to activities with negative externalities will agree to some efficient allocation of resources regardless of the initial distribution of property rights. Coase's theorem challenges one of the main principled justifications for government activity. In the absence of a perfect scheme of property rights that fully internalizes costs and benefits (i.e., an economic actor reaps the full benefits, but also pays the full costs, of her activity), it has been widely argued that government action is necessary to regulate the "market failure" that results from externalities (when an actor imposes costs on another that are not considered in her calculations). But Coase argues that, at least ideally, market transactions can solve the problem of externalities and get us to efficient outcomes (though the actual costs involved in negotiation, etc. may preclude this, and then government action may be required as a second-best strategy). But— and this is the important point—if markets are to approach efficient outcomes in which people are compensated for externalities, people must have extensive rights to make agreements. Restrictions on to what they can agree to—what trades they can make, what aspects of their rights they can transfer to others, how they can use their property, and so on—will undermine efficiency and the possibility of mutual benefit. Suppose that the Factory is doing $1,000,000 damage to the Farmers, but that strict enforcement of the pollution code would raise the price of Factory's polysilicon by 200 percent, which would drive it out of business. It would obviously be mutually beneficial for the Factory and the Farmers to agree to, say, a payment to the Farmers of $1,500,000 a year: both would be better off than if the factory closed. If such agreements are precluded—if the parties cannot trade their rights in these ways—then the efficient outcome may not be possible. Thus we see how full capitalist ownership rights are conducive to efficiency—and "efficiency" is simply a term for mutual benefit. Unless each is free to trade her rights as she sees fit, opportunities for mutually beneficial exchanges will be blocked.

Markets, Mutual Benefit, and Mutual Respect

The account I have been presenting conceives of markets as arenas of mutual benefit. The idea that exchange is generally mutually beneficial is at the heart of what we might call that capitalist view of social life (and most of modern economics). In contrast, in the eyes of many opponents of capitalist markets, market exchanges are what game theorists call "zero-sum" transactions: for every gain by one party, there is a corresponding loss by another. The market is seen as a realm of dog-eat-dog competition: some win by devouring others, but the devoured lose. For every one who eats there is someone who is eaten. In the words of a former French prime minister, "What is the market? It is the law of the jungle, the law of nature."[32] Capitalism rejects this conflict-ridden view of social life and the market. If I possess two bottles of beer, and you possess two slices of pizza, an exchange of a slice of pizza for a bottle of beer will make us both better off.[33] As Adam Smith saw it, our propensity to "truck, barter and exchange one thing for another"[34] is at the root of mutual benefit, and the growth of wealth:

> Give me that which I want and you shall have this which you want, is the meaning of every such offer; and it is in this manner that we obtain from one another the

> far greater part of those good offices which we stand in need of. It is not from the benevolence of the butcher, the brewer, or the baker, that we expect our dinner, but from their regard to their own interest.... Nobody but a beggar chooses to depend chiefly on the benevolence of his fellow-citizens.[35]

In commenting on this passage Stephen Darwall stresses that, though certainly it is about mutual advantage, it presumes far more than mere self-interested agency. Smith stresses that exchange relations presuppose agents who conceive of each other of having distinct points of view, which demand respect:

> Smith evidently thinks of exchange as an interaction in which both parties are committed to various normative presuppositions, for example, that the exchange is made by free mutual consent, that neither party will simply take what the other has.... Both parties must presume that the other is dealing fairly.[36]

Market transactions are built on a foundation of trust and a type of mutual respect: without that, we are apt to invade for gain (a true zero-sum interaction) rather than trade for mutual gain.

As Smith famously shows, markets both rely on and provide the main impetus to the division of labor. If someone is a butcher, another a brewer, and another a baker, an immensely greater amount of food and drink is available than if each is her own butcher, brewer, and baker. According to David Hume, this is the very essence of society: "By the partition of employments, our ability encreases."[37] Indeed, for Hume market relations are even more basic than property or justice: the rules of property and justice evolve out of market relations based on the division of labor. As cooperation proceeds, conventions arise about the terms of our cooperative interactions—hence the genesis of our principles of justice.

Are Market Exchanges Always Beneficial?

A fundamental claim of capitalism, then, is that markets respect full private property rights and allow for mutual benefit among independent agents. We have been assuming that each of the parties to the exchange has full information about what they are exchanging. Economists generally assume that both parties to an exchange are equally informed; only recently has there been a sustained interest in how asymmetric information can affect market transactions.[38] To the extent that one party does not know what he is buying, we can no longer suppose that market exchanges are truly mutually beneficial. Of course classical exponents of the market economy insisted that mutual gain through markets presupposed the absence of fraud and force (recall the idea that markets are based on trust and a sort of mutual respect), but the problems of asymmetric information run deeper.

A related problem is asymmetric bargaining power. One of the main justifications for labor laws regulating hours and factory conditions in the early part of twentieth century was that employers and workers had asymmetric bargaining power, so that workers were forced to accept disadvantageous bargains. This line of analysis is more complex and controversial than it first appears. Hardly any bargains are made from equality of bargaining power, yet the fact that some need the bargain more than others does not show that the exchange is not mutually beneficial. However, in extreme cases, unequal bargaining power can undermine the moral legitimacy of market outcomes. As Robert Nozick, a staunch defender of capitalism, has argued, "a person may not appropriate the only water hole in a desert and charge what he will. Nor may he charge what he will if he possesses one, and unfortunately it happens that all the water holes in the desert dry up but his."[39] Under these conditions an offer of a glass of water for all your property would be a *coercive offer*: an offer that exploits one's bargaining power and simply cannot be refused.[40] Instead of mutual advantage we have a sort of exploitation of those in great need.

Thus far we have been considering the conditions under which an individual market transaction is genuinely mutually beneficial. But it might be objected that a *series* of market transactions, each of which is unobjectionable, may have an outcome in which some (i.e., the workers) have no real choices, and so their freedom and self-ownership is undermined. Nozick appears to deny this:

> Consider the following example. Suppose that there are twenty-six women and twenty-six men each wanting to get married. For each sex, all of that sex agree on the same ranking of the twenty-six members of the opposite sex in terms of desirability of marriage partners: call them A to Z, and A´ to Z´ respectively in decreasing preferential order. A and A´ voluntarily choose to get married, each preferring the other to any other partner. B would most prefer to marry A´, and B´ would most prefer to marry A, but by their choices A and A´ have removed these options. When B and B´ marry, their choices are not made nonvoluntary merely by the fact that there is something else they would rather do. This other most preferred option requires the cooperation of others who have chosen, as is their right, not to cooperate.... This contraction of the range of options continues down to Z and Z´, who face a choice between marrying the other or remaining unmarried.[41]

Nozick argues that Z and Z´ are still free to choose whether or not to get married, despite their extremely restricted range of options. After all, the others have simply chosen other partners, a decision that was fully within their rights. Z and Z´ are not unfree simply because no one has chosen them. Nozick goes on to insist that this same reasoning applies to workers who may face extremely restricted employment options: their freedom and self-ownership have not been undermined by the legitimate choices of others. Suppose a business ethics teacher at a small college complains that she is not free to move to some other position because no one wishes to give her a job—Nozick insists she is perfectly free, the problem is that her services simply are not desired by any other institution. G. A. Cohen disagrees: he believes that a series of legitimate choices can lead to an outcome that undermines the freedom of some and so some are forced to accept offers.[42] Suppose that each person in a community acts within their rights to erect a fence on their property, preventing others from crossing it. Now also suppose that Alf is surrounded by such fences, and can no longer leave his property. Betty makes an offer: half his wealth for free passage through her property. Do we really want to say that, as a result of a series of legitimate choices, Alf's self-ownership and freedom have not been compromised? It seems that they have been.

A defender of markets must, I think, show that the overall effect of markets, far from radically decreasing options, is to increase them, providing a greater range of choice.[43] To be sure, just what we mean by a greater range of choice is open to various interpretations: it might mean simply how many options a person has, how many options a person values, the breadth of options (not simply a lot of options to do basically similar things), and so on. These are difficult issues in the philosophy of freedom. However, on almost any interpretation, modern capitalist-like market economies have astronomically increased people's range of options. Consider Eric Beinhocker's comparison of two tribes: the Yanomamö, a tribe living along the Orinoco River between Brazil and Venezuela, and the New Yorkers, a tribe living on Hudson River along the border of New York and New Jersey. The Yanomamö have an average income of $90 a year, the New Yorker $36,000:

> But it is not just the absolute level of income that makes the New Yorkers so wealthy: it is also the incredible variety of things their wealth can buy. Imagine you had the income of a New Yorker, but you could only spend it on things in the Yanomamö economy. If you spent your $36,000 fixing up your mud hut, buying the best clay pots in the village, and eating the finest Yanomamö cuisine, you would be extraordinarily wealthy by Yanomamö standards, but you would still feel far poorer than a typical New Yorker with his or her Nike sneakers, televisions and vacations in Florida. The number of economic choices the average New Yorker has is staggering. The Wal-Mart near the JFK Airport has over 100,000 different items in stock, there are over 200 television channels offered on cable TV, Barnes and Noble lists over 8 million titles, the local supermarket has 275 varieties of breakfast cereal, the typical department store offers 150 types of lipstick, and there are over 50,000 restaurants in New York City alone.[44]

Beinhocker points out that the 400-fold difference in income does not even begin to estimate the difference in options; the New Yorker, he estimates, has an order of 10^{10} more choices—an astronomical number.[45] And with these consumer choices come occupational, educational, and religious ones as well. When we compare capitalist modern market economies with simple nonmarket economies (and Soviet-type planned economies), what is striking is not simply the difference in the absolute level of wealth, but in the range of options—the jobs one can perform, the goods one can consume, the lives one can have.

Markets and Efficiency: The Extent of Property

As we have already seen in the case of common pool resources, extending the range of things that can be privately owned is of fundamental importance if our aim is to ensure efficient sustainable use. Efficiency is also nearly always enhanced when services are privately rather than publicly provided. There is evidence of the greater efficiency of private over public ownership in, among other things, airlines, banks, municipal bus services, cleaning services, debt collection, fire protection, hospitals, housing insurance claims processing, military aircraft repair, ocean tanker maintenance, preschool education, garbage collection, removal of abandoned vehicles, slaughterhouses, and weather forecasting.[46]

F. A. Hayek provides one of the most compelling arguments for extending as far as possible the range of things subject to private ownership. As Hayek understands a modern society, each individual has her own projects and plans (think again of the agency justification in section 2); whether she is successful depends on whether she can mesh her plans with those of others.[47] If plans come into constant conflict, people will find their aims and projects frustrated. Two things are needed for this meshing. First, there must be settled rules of conduct that allow each to anticipate the actions of others: repeated interventions by government to change regulations and the rules of the market undermine our ability to anticipate others. Second, however, we require knowledge: we need to know what others are doing. If we are to efficiently pursue our own goals we must have an idea of whether the resources necessary for our plans are being demanded by others, whether others will be interested in the outputs of our plans and projects, and so on. But how can we know that? Modern society is literally composed of hundreds of millions of people; the knowledge required for meshing the plans of these great societies is of an incredible magnitude:

> The economic problem of society is thus not merely a problem of how to allocate "given" resources—if "given" is taken to mean given to a single mind which deliberately solves the problem set by these "data." It is rather a problem of how to secure the best use of resources known to any of the members of society, for ends whose relative importance only these individuals know. Or, to put it briefly, it is a problem of the utilization of knowledge which is not given to anyone in its totality.[48]

The problem is this: each of us has both personal and local knowledge not generally available to others, and yet the success of our plans often depends on knowing the personal and local knowledge of others. Personal knowledge consists of one's knowledge of one's own plans and goals. Local knowledge is "the knowledge of the particular circumstances of time and place. It is with respect to this that practically every individual has some advantage over all others because he possesses unique information of which beneficial use might be made, but of which use can be made only if the decisions depending on it are left to him or are made with his active cooperation."[49] I wish to employ my local knowledge to exploit those possibilities of which I know. But for me to successfully do this requires that I know about events in far off places that might affect my plans: what do others want, what alternative uses do they have for resources, what local new possibilities do they see that I do not? How can I possibly know all this? Now—and here is Hayek's great contribution—this knowledge of remoter events is conveyed by the price system. The relative prices for goods do not tell us why goods are wanted, or why they are in short supply: it is a summary measure conveying just the crucial information—that others want the good, or that they are having a hard time getting hold of enough: "The marvel [of the market] is that in a case like that of a scarcity of one raw material, without an order being issued, without more than perhaps a handful of people knowing the cause, tens of thousands of people whose identity could not be ascertained by months of investigation, are made to use the material or its products more sparingly; i.e., they move in the right direction."[50] The market, then, sums up the local and personal knowledge of actors across the world and converts it into the crucial information that each of us must have so that we can use our own local and personal knowledge to efficiently satisfy our aims. If, though, the market is to convey as much information as possible about plans, resources, and opportunities, as many resources as possible must be subject to the price mechanism. To take something out of the market limits the spread of information about it, impairing the effectiveness of plans throughout the market.

Consider the use of central city streets. In most large metropolitan areas, streets in the central business district are jammed: it is very difficult for anyone to make reasonable progress in their journeys. It is the perfect case where plans fail to mesh: in fact, they often gridlock. The system does not tend to promote efficient outcomes: the increased demand for city streets does not sufficiently raise the price, which would induce people to use alternative methods of transport, or simply avoid the central city. To be sure, as congestion becomes horrible, there is some movement to other modes of transport or avoiding the city center, but it is very difficult to gauge what are the relative costs or benefits. The problem is that use of city streets is not a tradable good, and so no price emerges. This could be remedied by a system in which those who placed a higher value on using central city streets could pay others not to use them. Transactions costs, though, would be extraordinarily high in this case. A more realistic proposal that would tend toward efficiency would be to auction a limited number of permits to use central city streets. Those who place more value on using the streets would pay more and, if these permits could be traded, those who lost out on the auction could buy permits from others: we would then have a useful social signal about how much value people place on using nonjammed streets. Moving yet further away from a market solution, cities might follow London in placing a fee on using city center streets. This limits congestion, but the price does not provide much information about how much people value using the streets, since it is set by a central authority and not by market interactions.

The Commodification Objection to a Market with Extensive Property Rights

"The market," Cass Sunstein tells us, "is typically the sphere for use."[51] The things bought and sold on the market are typically commodities. But humans also have a wide range of nonuse values such as friendship, life, health, enlightenment. They are not only different goods, they are valued in different ways: friends—true ones, at any rate—do not value each other because of their use to each other. Or, according to Elizabeth Anderson's somewhat different analysis, sometimes "higher" and "lower" valued goods cannot really be compared, and if they cannot be compared, they cannot be traded, for the market "commensurates" goods: it scores all goods on a common, monetary, scale of value:

> Two goods are incomparable in intrinsic worth if they are not candidates for the same mode of valuation. One good is of incomparably higher worth than another if it is worthy of a higher mode of valuation than the other—worthy of love, awe, respect or honor beyond what is owed to persons in general, worthy of respect beyond the consideration owed to animals, worthy of consideration beyond mere use.... [O]ne way to express this difference in demands is to prohibit tradeoffs between states of affairs concerning the goods that express a lower kind of valuation for the higher good than it merits.[52]

Thus, argue critics, because markets turn all goods into mere tradable commodities, they violate our sense of value.

When thinking about these matters, it is important to be careful how we relate the idea of "price" (or "economic value") to our wider notions of what is valuable. Consider two "commodities" that in some ways appear of widely different types: Norman Rockwell's 1943 *Rosie the Riveter* and an endowed chair in philosophy. Rockwell's painting has sold for almost $5 million; a fully endowed chair in philosophy costs between $3 million and $4 million. If price is meant to sum up the total values of *Rosie the Riveter* and a chair in philosophy, and if to accept the market is to accept that *Rosie the Riveter* is, overall, more valuable than a philosophy professorship, then the market certainly would do violence to *my* values. There is more to values than that. But it is not—or at least it should not be—a claim of friends of market that price fully captures what we mean by the "value" of two "commodities." Ideally, the market price of X indicates the amount of resources the marginal buyer is willing to allocate to secure X. I can, and do, hold that the philosophy professorship is more valuable than *Rosie the Riveter*, and in so saying I do not claim that there has been a market failure. We do not all place the same value on each commodity: that is precisely why trades take place. It is our differences, not agreements, in valuations that underlie market exchange. If we all valued everything to the same extent, no one would trade her goods for anyone else's. As Hayek stressed, it makes no sense to say that the market price is *the* value of anything; market prices are the result of our differences in how we value goods.[53] The mistaken idea that goods in the market that have equal prices must have equal value inherent in them, and so the market exchange somehow expresses—or purports to express—the true value of goods, is at the heart of the Marxist criticism of markets (see below).[54]

THE HIERARCHICAL, PROFIT-MAXIMIZING FIRM

It might seem that once we have described a market based on maximally extensive property rights we have completed our task of characterizing the capitalist ideal. Not so.

The Master-Servant Relation

In his *Principles of Political Economy*—the most influential economic text of the nineteenth century—John Stuart Mill sketches an *alternative* to capitalism that embraces both private property and markets. Mill endorsed the private ownership of firms, but not firms in which some were hired and were required to obey the instructions of the owners—the "master":

> Hitherto there has been no alternative for those who lived by their labour, but that of labouring either each for himself alone, or for a master. But the civilizing and improving influences of association, and the efficiency and economy of production on a large scale, may be obtained without dividing the producers into two parties with hostile interests and feelings, the many who do the work being mere servants under the command of the one who supplies the funds, and having no interest of their own in the enterprise except to earn their wages with as little labour as possible.... [T]here can be little doubt that the status of hired labourers will gradually tend to confine itself to the description of workpeople whose low moral qualities render them unfit for anything more independent: and that the relation of masters and workpeople will be gradually superseded by partnership, in one of two forms: in some cases, association of the labourers with the capitalist; in others, and perhaps finally in all, association of labourers among themselves.[55]

As workers become better educated and more public spirited, Mill argued, the master-servant relation characteristic of the capitalist firm will be replaced by a regime of worker cooperatives: worker-owned firms that compete in the market. The idea was that workers would be collective owners of the firms and democratically decide important strategic matters, though-day-to-day operations would still be directed by a manager instructing workers what to do—but a manager who could be dismissed by the workers. Thus the worker cooperatives were privately held firms in a competitive market economy without the master-servant relation (in which the owners are masters and the workers simply hired servants). Unfortunately for this view, the worker cooperative movement barely outlived Mill; worker cooperatives appear to have succumbed to the greater efficiency of capitalist firms based on the master-servant relation.[56]

Hierarchy and Efficiency

Why did Mill's hope for the future—firms owned by the workers and, ultimately, managed by them—succumb to traditional capitalist firms in which, either, the owner managed the firm and hired workers as his "servants," or (see below) the owners hired managers, who in turn instructed the workers about what to do, when to do it, and so on? As we have seen, Coase had a fundamental impact on our thinking about markets, property, and efficiency. Another of his papers fundamentally changed our thinking about "The Nature of the Firm."[57] Coase agrees with Mill: the "master and servant" relation is fundamental to the capitalist firm (it is widely thought that this relation is at least partly constitutive of capitalism).[58] This, of course, is a hierarchical, authority relation: those who own (or at the behest of the owners, who manage) make the decisions about what is to be produced, how, by whom, and so on. The job of the workers is to do as they are instructed by their "boss." Coase and his followers show that organization via such an authority relation reduces transaction costs. Transactions organized through the market and its price mechanism entail, for instance, negotiating costs and information costs: we must find out who is selling a product, whether we wish to pay his price, and so on. Typically these costs are not so great as to make market exchange inefficient; however, in some cases the negotiations would be quite costly. Suppose that one is building a new computer. One might buy all the components in the market, but perhaps one's aim is to design a new computer. This would involve a new motherboard unit, a video display that works well with it, effective power sources, and so on. Now these new units must work well together, and this may require constant cooperation by the individual design teams (focusing on the motherboard, display, etc.) as they are building the unit. If so, it may greatly reduce transaction costs to have a central coordinator who directs each specialist team and their activities, giving them design parameters so that the designs work well together. So one may organize a hierarchical firm. The firm, then, is a way to decrease some transaction costs. In this sense the hierarchical firm is an engine of efficiency.[59]

The Socialist Character of the Capitalist Firm

The division of labor in the market is based on individual producers and consumers, each contracting with each other; one's reward is directly based on one's production of what others want. The division of labor in the firm is very different. It is based on a central coordinator—the boss—who decides the relevant targets, and then designs systems that divide up tasks in order to achieve the goals. Of course the boss may seek input and feedback from her subordinates, but this is up to her. Those with authority make plans and instruct the "servants" how to go about implementing them. The values *within* the firm are in many ways the opposite of the values *between* participants in the market: whereas the latter stress independence, contract, and reward based on satisfaction of demand, the former stresses the values of leadership, teamwork (directed by leaders), tasks based on instruction from above, and reward based on the boss' evaluation of the subordinates' usefulness to the firm.

It is interesting that the values within the firm were attractive to many communists. N. I. Bukharin and Evgenii Preobrazhensky sought to organize all of society as one large factory. They wrote in their *ABC of Communism*:

> We must know in advance how much labour to assign to the various branches of industry; what products are required and how much of each it is necessary to produce; how and where machines must be provided. These and similar details must be thought out beforehand, with approximate accuracy at least; and the work must be guided in accordance with calculations.... Without a general plan,

without a general directive system, and without careful calculation and
book-keeping, there can be no organization. But in the communist social
organization, there is such a plan.[60]

Just as a factory manager seeks to organize and plan production, so too, it was
thought, must communist planners organize and plan production for the entire
economy. Thus many early communists had great regard for capitalist techniques
of production *within* enterprises; it was the "anarchy" of the market that provoked
their deepest ire.[61]

Because most people in capitalist societies spend their lives within large corporations, in nonprofit organizations such as universities, or in government service,
we arrive at the surprising conclusion that most people in capitalist societies spend
their lives in organizations whose values are in many ways more "socialist" than
"capitalist." This is an important theme in Hayek's work. In large organizations subordinates expect to be rewarded according to their merit: they were given tasks to
perform and if, on some set of criteria, they performed well, they merit a higher pay.
As Hayek points out, this is very different than reward in the market: "Reward for
merit is reward for obeying the wishes of others in what we do, not compensation
for the benefits we have conferred upon them by doing what we thought best."[62] In
the market one's reward *does* depend on how much others benefit from your action;
and a good deal of luck may be involved in this. An entrepreneur may gain because
she was in the right place at the right time, and so able to perceive a way to satisfy
others' wants. In the market two entrepreneurs may have tried equally hard, done
everything in their power, and one entirely fail and the other be a great success.
It is not the case that such luck is simply about the way a "deliberate gamble" works
out: the luck may be that the entrepreneur's local situation was such that she had
possibilities of gain that were simply unknowable by others.[63]

Because most of us spend most of our time in organizations not informed
by market values, when we come to politics—where market outcomes are often
the subject of debate—we tend to apply our "socialist" (i.e., nonmarket) values to
market outcomes. For example, in contemporary political philosophy one of the
most influential doctrines of distributive justice is that property should track the
distinction between "choice and chance": although one should be held responsible
for one's choices, one should not be held responsible for what results from mere
brute chance.[64] Distributive justice, it is said, should compensate people for bad
brute luck.[65] This claim resonates with all of us who have spent our life within large
organizations: if things go wrong for us and it was through no fault of our own,
then we insist that this does not detract from our merit, or the rewards we are due
from our bosses. "It was simply bad luck" is a relevant reply in one's end-of-the-
year review. But, as Hayek points out, this makes no sense in the market, which in
many ways runs by brute luck. Entrepreneurs are confronted by options many of
which are not of their own devising; efficiency is promoted by them taking advantage of this "brute luck" (a sort of local knowledge) to satisfy additional wants and
aims.[66] To "compensate" entrepreneurs for their bad luck (not having the same local
knowledge as others) would undermine the very core of the market as a device for

generating information. For the market to function, differential local knowledge must crucially enter into an entrepreneur's profits. In Hayek's eyes the upshot of this is a certain moral instability of capitalism: most people in capitalist economic systems have moral views about justice and distribution that they apply to the market and are destructive of the very economic prosperity on which all depend.

What Is the Aim of the Capitalist Firm?

Ever since Marx it has been said that a constitutive characteristic of capitalism is the profit-maximizing firm.[67] Given that the capitalist ideal is based on full property rights, this cannot be literally true: a full owner can do anything he wishes with his property. Think of the familiar story of the *Christmas Carol*.[68] The firm of Scrooge and Marley was profit maximizing with a vengeance: the *only* thing that Scrooge and Marley ever cared about was maximizing their profit. But the firm at which Scrooge apprenticed as a lad, run by Mr. Fezziwig, moderated profit maximization with special kindness to its employees. Now it does not seem that Fezziwig's firm departs from any of the core commitments of capitalism: Fezziwig owned his firm and competed in the market. Still there is something right about identifying Scrooge and Marley as the "more" capitalist firm. After all, Fezziwig cannot go too far in ignoring profitability: if he runs his firm simply as a way to be kind to employees, it will fail. If Fezziwig's costs are too high he will be out-competed—consumers will not buy his product; if his returns are too low, he will not be able to loan funds from banks. (Indeed, he does go out of business in the 1951 movie version.) So we might think of Fezziwig as compromising the firm's profitability with his concern for his employees.[69] Scrooge and Marley can run their firm simply and purely as a way to maximize profit, and that will not cause it to fail. Market competition does reward firms that excel at earning profits.

In contrast to Dickens's Victorian-era capitalism, in which firms are often managed by those who privately own them, modern-era large capitalist firms are largely owned by shareholders, and their shares are very often publicly traded. And they are managed by nonowners, or at most by partial owners. This raises a host of difficult issues about what the aim of such firms should be.[70] Instead of owner-managers, we are confronted by a world composed of principals and agents: the managers of the firm are agents of the principals, the shareholders. This leads to a host of possible complications and problems: agents may pursue aims not approved by principals, and which are not in the principals' interests—a possibility that simply did not arise in owner-managed firms.[71] We cannot explore these difficult issues here, but one thing seems clear: in anything approaching the capitalist ideal, the shareholders own the firm, and it is their wishes and interests that should guide the agents. Capitalism, we have seen, is based on full ownership: if the firm is not managed according to the wishes or interests of the shareholders, their ownership rights are abridged. Apart from contractual obligations and basic market norms of fair dealing, the interests of employees *as such*—simply as "stakeholders" in the firm—are not ultimate aims of managers in an ideal capitalist order. Of course the shareholders may desire that such stakeholders be accorded consideration: like modern Fezziwigs, they may compromise some profit in order to improve the lot of their nonowning stakeholders. But when firms are publicly traded, conveying this information to prospective investors may be costly and difficult. In capitalist economies there is a presumption that managers are the agents of the shareholders: firms that have included nonowners among their principals run the risk of misleading potential investors about their ownership rights.

Profit

But what is profit? In his important essay on the concept of profit, James Child remarks that there is no accepted understanding of the concept.[72] One remarkable feature of debates about profit is that to friends of capitalism "profit" has strongly positive connotations, while to critics it is a strongly pejorative term. Hayek argues that intellectuals, from Aristotle to Bertrand Russell and Albert Einstein, all misunderstand the idea, a misunderstanding summed up by the slogan "Production for use, not for profit."[73] This familiar hostility to "production for profit" derives from seeing economics as an engineering problem: knowing what people want and what resources are available, the problem is to maximize the production of goods to maximize the satisfaction of wants. But, as we saw previously, Hayek stressed that economics is precisely the study of how wants are satisfied when no one knows everyone's wants, no single person knows all the available resources, or the possible ways to satisfy these (largely unknown) wants. The "search for profit" by the entrepreneur is the probing of the entrepreneur "beyond known uses and ends" in order to best satisfy the "*multiplicity* of human ends."[74]

In contrast, for Marx "profit and wages remain in inverse proportion": profits come out of the possible wages of laborers.[75] For Marx the key to profit under capitalism is that in the market the exchange value of a commodity is determined by its cost of production, in particular by the amount of labor it takes to produce a good.[76] Because capitalist markets treat the ability to labor as itself a commodity, it too has an exchange value—the amount of labor it takes to produce a unit (e.g., a day) of the ability to work (or, we might say, "labor power"). The key to understanding capitalism, Marx insists, is that labor power is "a source not only of value, but of more value than it has itself."[77] The price of a unit of (say, a day's) labor power is the amount of labor it takes to produce it; suppose it takes four hours of labor to produce a day's worth of labor power. This would include all the labor that goes into the worker's food for the day, his clothes for the day, supporting his family for the day, and so on. But the worker labors ten hours a day and so creates ten hours of value; the price of his labor power was only four hours of labor. The six hours of surplus value—that which the worker creates above and beyond the cost of producing his ability to work for the day—is the source of profit. Hence profit directly comes out of what the worker produced and, in other systems of production, might have constituted his reward for his work. For Marx, capitalist profit is a sort of theft.

Child proposes that these different attitudes toward profit derive from the two opposed attitudes toward exchange that we have observed: exchange as a zero-sum versus positive-sum, cooperative, interaction. If exchange is viewed as zero-sum, then one party's profits must come out of the other party. If we focus on the firm and the sale of labor power, the capitalist's profits must be someone's loss—the workers'. Where else could profits come from? In contrast, on the positive-sum view, "*One makes profits by benefiting those one transacts with, while benefiting oneself.*"[78] Capitalism insists that the pursuit of profit is not only socially useful but also benefits all parties to the exchange.

CONCLUSION

In this chapter, I have sketched the elements of the capitalist ideal: maximally extensive property rights, efficient markets employing such rights, and hierarchical firms run in the interest of the owners. I have focused here on an ideal or pure version of capitalism: real-world systems often described as "capitalist" modify one or more of these elements. To know one's attitude to capitalism is to know one's evaluation of these elements: someone who strongly supports them all is a fervent defender of capitalism. Others may advance criticisms of one or more elements, and so approve of a modified form of capitalism. As one rejects more elements, either on moral or economic grounds, one begins to move to a noncapitalist economic system. The question for teachers and students of business ethics is whether their evaluation of the elements still endorses a recognizably capitalist business firm. If not, they are confronted with problem with which we began: studying the ethics of an organization embedded in a system that we ought not to have.

NOTES

1. Or perhaps business ethics is some sort of theory of the morally second best: it instructs one how to act ethically in a morally unjustifiable context. Is that what business ethics does?

2. John Maynard Keynes, "The End of Laissez-Faire," in his *Essays in Persuasion* (London: Macmillan, 1972), 294.

3. Karl Marx, *Economic and Philosophic Manuscripts of 1844*, in *Marx/Engels Collected Works*, vol. 4 (London: Lawrence & Wishart, 1975–2002), 293. Compare John Stuart Mill, *Principles of Political Economy with Some of Their Applications to Social Philosophy*, in *The Collected Works of John Stuart Mill*, ed. J. M. Robson (Toronto: University of Toronto Press, 1977), vol. 2, bk. 2, chap. 1.

4. Plato, *The Republic*, in *The Dialogues of Plato*, translated into English with Analyses and Introductions by B. Jowett, 3rd ed. revised and corrected (Oxford: Oxford University Press, 1892), 106ff.

5. On this point, see Jürg Niehans, *A History of Economic Theory: Classic Contributions, 1720–1980* (Baltimore: Johns Hopkins University Press, 1990), 143.

6. This list draws on A. M. Honoré "Ownership," in *Oxford Essays in Jurisprudence*, ed. A. G. Guest (Oxford: Clarendon Press, 1961), 107–147; and Frank Snare, "The Concept of Property," *American Philosophical Quarterly* 9 (April 1972): 200–206. For an excellent and accessible discussion, see Lawrence C. Becker, *Property Rights: Philosophical Foundations* (London: Routledge & Kegan Paul, 1977), chap. 2.

7. See Paul Finn, "Public Function—Private Action: A Common Law Dilemma," in *Public and Private in Social Life*, eds. S. I. Benn and G. F. Gaus (New York: St. Martin's, 1983), 93–111.

8. The now-classic work on this matter is Richard A. Epstein, *Takings: Private Property and the Power of Eminent Domain* (Cambridge, Mass.: Harvard University Press, 1985).

9. John Locke, *Second Treatise of Government*, ed. Peter Laslett (Cambridge: Cambridge University Press, 1960), sec. 139, emphasis in original.

10. See David Friedman, *The Machinery of Freedom* (New York: Harper and Row, 1973); Murray Rothbard "Society without a State," in *NOMOS XIX: Anarchism*, eds. J. Roland Pennock and John W. Chapman (New York: New York University Press, 1978), 191–207.

11. Locke, *Second Treatise*, sec. 142. On the range of antitaxation anarcho-capitalist views, see Eric Mack and Gerald F. Gaus, "Classical Liberalism and Libertarianism: The Liberty Tradition," in *The Handbook of Political Theory*, ed. Gerald F. Gaus and Chandran Kukathas (London: Sage, 2004), 115–142.

12. For a contemporary criticism of this view, see Liam Murphy and Thomas Nagel, *The Myth of Ownership: Taxes and Justice* (New York: Oxford University Press, 2002).

13. I use "objects" broadly here to include financial instruments, such as mortgages.

14. See Garret Hardin, "The Tragedy of the Commons," in *Managing the Commons*, ed. Garrett Hardin and John Baden (New York: W. H. Freeman, 1977).

15. David Schmidtz, *The Limits of Government: An Essay on the Public Goods Argument* (Boulder, Colo.: Westview Press, 1991), 21. 16. Karl Marx, *Capital*, vol. 1, in *Marx/Engels Collected Works*, vol. 35, chap. 6.

17. See James Stacey Taylor, *Stakes and Kidneys: Why Markets in Human Body Parts Are Morally Imperative* (Aldershot, U.K.: Ashgate, 2005). Compare Stephen R. Munzer, "An Uneasy Case Against Property Rights in Body Parts," *Social Philosophy & Policy* 11 (Summer 1994): 259–286. I do not mean to suggest that only friends of the capitalist ideal support such markets.

18. Samuel Brittan, *A Restatement of Economic Liberalism* (Atlantic Highlands, N.J.: Humanities Press, 1988), 1.

19. See Robert Nozick, *Anarchy, State, and Utopia* (New York: Basic Books, 1974), 331.

20. Mill, *Principles of Political Economy*, bk. 2, chap. 2, sec. 6.

21. Locke, *Second Treatise*, secs. 27, 123.

22. Stephen Buckle, *Natural Law and the Theory of Property* (Oxford: Clarendon Press, 1991), 29.

23. Ibid., 171. Buckle argues for the applicability of the concept of *suum* to Locke's theory, 168–174. See also A. John Simmons, *The Lockean Theory of Rights* (Princeton, N.J.: Princeton University Press, 1992), 226–227.

24. Buckle, *Natural Law and the Theory of Property*, 191ff.

25. Nozick, *Anarchy, State, and Utopia*, 58.

26. Loren E. Lomasky, *Persons, Rights and the Moral Community* (New York: Oxford University Press, 1987), 120–121, emphasis in original.

27. Ibid., 121.

28. John Rawls, *Justice as Fairness: A Restatement*, ed. Erin Kelly (Cambridge, Mass.: Harvard University Press, 2001), 136ff. I have in mind here Rawls's support of "liberal (democratic) socialism."

29. Nozick, *Anarchy, State, and Utopia*, 163.

30. See Ronald Coase, "The Problem of Social Cost," *Journal of Law and Economics* 3 (1960): 1–44. My explication follows Dennis Mueller, *Public Choice III* (Cambridge: Cambridge University Press, 2003), 27–30.

31. See Ariana Eunjung Cha, "Solar Energy Firms Leave Waste Behind in China," *Washington Post*, March 9, 2008, A1.

32. Edouard Balladur, quoted in Martin Wolf, *Why Globalization Works* (New Haven, Conn.: Yale University Press, 2004), 4.

33. For an explanation of this notion of allocative efficiency, see my *On Philosophy, Politics, and Economics* (Belmont, Calif.: Wadsworth-Thomson-Cengage, 2007), chap. 3.

34. Adam Smith, *An Inquiry Into the Nature and Causes of the Wealth of Nations*, ed. W. B. Todd (Indianapolis: Liberty Fund, 1981), bk. 1, chap. 2, para. 1.

35. Smith, *Wealth of Nations*, bk. 1, chap. 2, para. 2.

36. Stephen Darwall, *The Second-person Standpoint: Morality, Respect, and Accountability* (Cambridge, Mass.: Harvard University Press, 2006), 47.

37. David Hume, *A Treatise of Human Nature*, 2nd ed., eds. L. A. Selby-Bigge and P. H. Nidditch (Oxford: Oxford University Press, 1978), bk. 3, pt. 2, sec. 2, para. 3.

38. See Todd Sandler, *Economic Concepts for the Social Sciences* (Cambridge: Cambridge University Press, 2001), chap. 7.

39. Nozick, *Anarchy, State and Utopia*, 180.

40. Joel Feinberg, *The Moral Limits of the Criminal Law*, vol. 3, *Harm to Self* (New York: Oxford University Press, 1986), 250.

41. Nozick, *Anarchy, State, and Utopia*, 263.

42. See G. A. Cohen, *Self-Ownership, Freedom and Equality* (Cambridge: Cambridge University Press, 1995), 35–37.

43. See Eric Mack, "Self-ownership, Marxism, and Egalitarianism, Part II: Challenges to the Self-ownership Thesis," *Politics, Philosophy and Economics* 1 (June 2002): 237–276.

44. Eric D. Beinhocker, *The Origin of Wealth* (Cambridge, Mass.: Harvard Business School Press, 2006), 9.

45. Ibid., 9.

46. Charles Wolff Jr., *Markets or Governments: Choosing between Imperfect Alternatives* (Cambridge, Mass.: MIT Press, 1993), appendix B.

47. See Hayek, *Law, Legislation and Liberty*, vol. 1, *Rules and Order* (Chicago: University of Chicago Press, 1973), 99.

48. F. A. Hayek, "The Use of Knowledge in Society," *American Economic Review* 35 (September 1945): 519–520.

49. Ibid., 522.

50. Ibid., 527.

51. Cass R. Sunstein, *Free Markets and Social Justice* (Oxford: Oxford University Press, 1997), 94.

52. Elizabeth Anderson, *Values in Ethics and Economics* (Cambridge, Mass.: Harvard University Press, 1993), 70.

53. Hayek, *The Mirage of Social Justice*, 76.

54. Marx, *Capital*, vol. 1, pt. 1, chap. 1, sec. 1.

55. Mill, *Principles*, bk. 4, chap. 7, sec. 4. Shares could not be sold.

56. For an excellent analysis of cooperative production, see P. J. D Wiles, *Economic Institutions Compared* (New York: Wiley, 1977), chap. 6. See also Oliver E. Williamson's analysis of the "Peer Group" system in *The Economic Institutions of Capitalism* (New York: Free Press, 1985), 217ff.

57. Coase, *The Firm, The Market and the Law*, chap. 2.

58. See, for example, Talcott Parsons's "Introduction" to Max Weber, *The Theory of Social and Economic Organization*, trans. A. M. Henderson and Talcott Parsons (New York: Free Press, 1947), 51; Niehaus, *A History of Economic Theory*, 144; Karl Marx, *Capital*, chap. 14, sec. 5.

59. See Williamson, *The Economic Institutions of Capitalism*.

60. Nikolai Bukharin and Evgenii Preobrazhensky, *The ABC of Communism*, quoted in Michael Ellman *Socialist Planning* (Cambridge: Cambridge University Press, 1979), 9, emphasis added.

61. See Bukharin and Preobrazhensky's views on the "anarchy of production" in Ellman, *Socialist Planning*, 8. See also Marx, *Capital*, chap. 14, sec. 4.

62. F. A. Hayek, *The Constitution of Liberty* (London: Routledge and Kegan Paul, 1960), 100.

63. On the distinction between "option" luck and "brute" luck, see Ronald Dworkin, *Sovereign Virtue: The Theory and Practice of Equality* (Cambridge, Mass: Harvard University Press, 2000), 73ff.

64. Ibid., 287ff.

65. Whether *good* brute luck should be compensated for is a matter of disagreement. See Peter Vallentyne, "Self-Ownership and Equality: Brute Luck, Gifts, Universal Dominance and Leximin," in *Real Libertarianism Assessed*, eds. Andrew Reeve and Andrew Williams (New York: Palgrave Macmillan, 2003), 29–52.

66. Indeed, believing that one's property is deserved, Hayek says, encourages "an air of self-righteousness." Hayek *Law, Legislation and Liberty*, vol. 2, *The Mirage of Social Justice* (Chicago: University of Chicago Press, 1976), 74.

67. See, for example, Niehans, *A History of Economic Theory*, 144.

68. Charles Dickens, *A Christmas Carol*, in *Five Christmas Novels* (New York: Heritage, 1939).

69. See Wiles, *Economic Institutions Compared*, 67.

70. For complexities, see Wiles, *Economic Institutions Compared*, 69–70.

71. On economic analyses of principal-agent relations, see Sandler, *Economic Concepts for the Social Sciences*, 120ff.

72. James W. Child, "Profit: The Concept and its Moral Features," *Social Philosophy & Policy* 15 (Summer 1998): 243ff.

73. F. A. Hayek, *The Fatal Conceit*, ed. W. W. Bartley III (Chicago: University of Chicago Press, 1988), 104.

74. Ibid., 104–105.

75. Karl Marx, "Wage Labour and Capital" ("The general law that determines the rise and fall of wages and profit"), in *Marx/Engels Collected Works*, vol. 9.

76. Marx, *Capital*, pt. 1, chap. 1, sec. 1–3; pt. 2, chap. 6.

77. Ibid., pt. 3, chap. 8, sec. 2, emphasis in original.

78. Child, "Profit," 282, emphasis in original.

SUGGESTED READING

Anderson, Elizabeth. *Values in Ethics and Economics*. Cambridge, Mass.: Harvard University Press, 1993.

Brittan, Samuel. *A Restatement of Economic Liberalism*. Atlantic Highlands, N.J.: Humanities Press, 1988.

Buchanan, Allen. *Ethics, Efficiency and the Market*. Oxford: Clarendon Press, 1986.

Buckle, Stephen. *Natural Law and the Theory of Property*. Oxford: Clarendon Press, 1991.

Child, James W. "Profit: The Concept and its Moral Features," *Social Philosophy & Policy* 15 (Summer 1998): 243–282.

Coase, R. H. *The Firm, the Market and the Law*. Chicago: University of Chicago Press, 1998.

Cohen, G. A. *Self-Ownership, Freedom and Equality*. Cambridge: Cambridge University Press, 1995.

Gaus, Gerald F. *On Philosophy, Politics and Economics*. Belmont, Calif.: Thomson Wadsworth, 2007.

Hayek, F. A. *Law, Legislation and Liberty*. 3 vols. Chicago: University of Chicago Press, 1973–1979.

Heath, Joseph. "Business Ethics without Stakeholders," *Business Ethics Quarterly* 16 (2006): 533–557.

Mack, Eric, and Gerald F. Gaus. "Classical Liberalism and Libertarianism: the Liberty Tradition." In *The Handbook of Political Theory*. Edited by Gerald F. Gaus and Chandran Kukathas, 115–142. London: Sage, 2004.

Marx, Karl. *Capital*. Edited by Friedrich Engels, translated by Samuel Moore and Edward Avling. London: W. Glaisher, 1909.

Mill, John Stuart. *Principles of Political Economy with Some of Their Applications to Social Philosophy*. In *The Collected Works of John Stuart Mill*, Vols. 2 and 3. Edited by J. M. Robson. Toronto: University of Toronto Press, 1977.

Nozick, Robert. *Anarchy, State, and Utopia*. New York: Basic Books, 1974.

Schmidtz, David. *The Elements of Justice*. Cambridge: Cambridge University Press, 2006.

Smith, Adam. *An Inquiry into the Nature and Causes of the Wealth of Nations*, 2 vols. Edited by R. H. Campbell and A. S. Skinner. Indianapolis, Ind.: Liberty Press, 1981.

Waldron, Jeremy. *The Right to Private Property*. Oxford: Clarendon Press, 1988.

Wiles, P. J. D. *Economic Institutions Compared*. New York: Wiley, 1977.

Williamson, Oliver E. *The Economic Institutions of Capitalism*. New York: Free Press, 1985.

Wolff, Charles, Jr. *Markets of Governments: the Choice between Imperfect Alternatives*, 2nd ed. Cambridge, Mass.: MIT Press, 1994.

CHAPTER 4

THE PUBLIC AUTHORITY OF THE MANAGERS OF PRIVATE CORPORATIONS

CHRISTOPHER MCMAHON

THE managers of private corporations occupy positions of authority in societies where their corporations operate. It is a commonplace of political philosophy that authority must be legitimate. What, then, establishes the legitimacy of managerial authority? To answer this question we need to know who is subject to managerial authority. Managerial decisions can have effects throughout society, and indeed the world. As we shall see, this fact is relevant to the question of what makes managerial authority legitimate. But in general, an authority relation obtains when the members of a group are prepared to defer to the directives emanating from some source, such as a government, where deferring to a directive means doing what one is directed to do. This gives us the result that, in the first instance, managerial authority is exercised over employees. So we can begin by asking what makes this authority legitimate.

It might seem that this question hardly deserves discussion. In modern societies, it is commonly said that the authority exercised by the government is grounded in the consent of the governed. Consent, in turn, is understood as involving something like a promise to obey. That is, deferring to the directives emanating from the government, obeying the laws and regulations of the state, is justified because the recipients of these directives have promised to obey. This idea has, however, been subjected to criticism and is almost certainly untenable. Only a few members, at most, of a typical modern polity can be regarded as having consented to the authority of the government in a way that constitutes a promise to obey.[1] One important reason for this is that most people are born into a given polity and realistically have no choice about whether to remain members of it. The legitimacy of political authority must then be established in some other way. The corporate case, by contrast, seems to fit the consent model: Employees voluntarily join the corporations where they work. Taking a job means putting oneself in a position where one will be told what to do by one's employer. There is thus a straightforward sense in which employees have consented to being told what to do. Moreover, there appears to be no problem about regarding this consent as having promissory force, as creating a promissory obligation on the part of the employee to do what he or she is told. The employee can be understood as having promised to obey in return for pay.[2]

In what follows, I present some reasons for thinking that matters are not so simple. The managers of private corporations are best understood as exercising the same kind of authority as governmental officials. The reason for this is that consent that has promissory force is not actually capable of doing what is required to establish the legitimacy of managerial authority. Nothing has yet been said about how the authority of governmental officials, such as legislators, is to be understood. But we do know that the mechanism of authorization is not consent that has promissory force.

Authority is a political concept. Consequently, providing an account of the authority exercised by the managers of private corporations requires the construction of a political theory of the corporation. It is customary to distinguish between the public sector and the private sector. The distinction suggests that, politically, private corporations are fundamentally different from states. I do not believe, however, that this idea accords with social reality. In a modern society, government and management form two parts of a single, integrated structure of social authority. Thus we need a similarly integrated theory of the legitimacy of this authority. In particular, we need a theory that establishes the legitimacy of the integration. If management and government form two parts of a single, integrated structure of social authority, the authority that managers exercise is a kind of public authority. Managers function as public officials of a certain sort, whose ultimate task is to serve the public good generally.

It might be suggested that while the project I have described—formulating a political theory of the corporation—has a natural place in political philosophy, it does not belong in business ethics. Business ethics is usually regarded as a branch of professional ethics that identifies and elaborates moral principles governing the actions of men and women functioning in a certain professional capacity. But business ethics can also be understood as grounded in values and norms that apply to a whole society, guiding its thinking about how a central aspect of its collective life, business, is to be structured. Viewed in this way, business ethics is actually a branch of political philosophy.

POWER AND AUTHORITY

My argument has three main parts. First, I present reasons for thinking that the authority of corporate managers cannot be grounded in the consent of employees. Second, I propose a way of thinking about the authority of governments and suggest that it, suitably interpreted, has application to the corporate case. This gives us the integrated structure of legitimate authority that I just mentioned. Third, I consider in more detail how the integrated structure is to be understood. But before turning to these issues, it is necessary to say more about the concept of authority. This will also enable us to reject another suggestion that might be made about what grounds the authority of corporate managers, the suggestion that the ownership of productive property brings with it legitimate authority over the people the owners employ.

It is customary in political philosophy to make a distinction between power and authority. When we talk about power, we are talking about an actual ability to make things happen. Authority, however, or to be more precise, legitimate authority, is a normative concept. It is concerned with what people ought to do. For the purpose of establishing a contrast between power and authority, we can narrow our focus to what I shall call *directive power*. This is the ability to get people to do certain things by telling them to do these things. Often directive power is created by the fact that some agent is able to offer incentives for doing what he, she, or it tells people to do. In the governmental case, the most important incentives are negative, such as the threat of punishment for failure to comply with directives. Thus one reason that governments have directive power is that they can threaten imprisonment or fines if one fails to obey the law.

The ability to offer rewards for compliance with directives can also create directive power, but this case shades into the case where negative incentives are employed. Once a relationship in which rewards are being offered is established, the threat of termination of the relationship can function as a reason for complying with directives, especially if the recipient of the rewards has come to depend on them. Of course, these points have the consequence that the managers of corporations have directive power with respect to the employees. They have the ability to promise payment for compliance with their directives, and to threaten the termination of employment for noncompliance.

Now let us turn to authority. Earlier I said that an authority relation obtains where the members of a group are prepared to defer to the directives emanating from some source. When a source of directives has authority in a group, compliance does not depend on the ability to offer incentives. The recipients of the directives comply because they think that complying is the right thing to do. They may have a variety of reasons for thinking this. They might, for example, comply because they were taught by their parents to "respect authority," where respecting authority means deferring to the directives issued by people who occupy various institutional roles. A teacher in a classroom can have authority of this sort.

This kind of authority is called *de facto* authority. It consists simply in the social fact that the members of a group are prepared to comply with the directives emanating from some source even in the absence of external incentives for complying. It is actually a form of directive power, an ability to get people to do things by telling them to do these things. De facto authority is an extremely important social phenomenon. Governments, for example, cannot rely solely on the threat of punishment or fines to secure compliance with the law. The effectiveness of these threats depends on the fact that most people comply with the law simply because it is the law. That makes it possible for the police to focus on the few who do not.

For a source of directives to possess *legitimate* authority, however, it is not enough that the recipients of directives can be relied upon to comply with them. The recipients must have reasons sufficient to justify complying, where this means reasons sufficient to establish that it would really be wrong, wrong in an objective sense, not to comply. A source of directives possesses legitimate authority within a group if it possesses legitimate authority with respect to almost all the members of that group. It is not possible to be precise, but to make the point concrete, let us say that it must be legitimate with respect to 99 percent of the members of the group. It is unrealistic to insist, as a condition of legitimacy within a large group, on legitimacy with respect to everyone in the group. There will always be a few members for whom the conditions of legitimacy are not met. But if a substantial subset of the people to whom directives are being issued cannot regard the source of those directives as exercising legitimate authority over them, the source cannot claim legitimate authority within the group as a whole. This point will play an important role in the argument that follows.

Of course, these general observations apply to the corporate case. As has been mentioned, the managers of corporations have directive power deriving from the fact that they are able to reward compliance with their directives and punish noncompliance. The reward is payment of a wage or salary, and the punishment is termination of employment. Further, as a matter of social fact, many employees may comply with managerial directives because they have been taught to respect authority. So managers also typically have de facto authority within the groups they manage, and top managers have de facto authority within the whole corporation. But the fact that managers possess directive power of these two kinds does not establish that they exercise legitimate authority. It does not establish that an employee would be acting wrongly in some objective sense if she failed to comply with managerial directives. The question of what establishes the legitimacy of managerial authority is the focus of the present essay.

Is Legitimacy Necessary?

Legitimate authority is not an alternative to directive power. A source of directives cannot claim to be exercising legitimate authority unless it also has the de facto ability get people to do things by telling them to do these things.[3] One reason for this is that in many cases, whether an individual is justified in complying with the directives emanating from some source will depend on whether the other people to whom directives are issued will in fact comply. Establishing that a source of directives possesses legitimate authority then involves showing both that it possesses directive power and that it satisfies some further condition. We can take it for granted that managers possess directive power with respect to employees. Our task is thus to determine what the further condition is in the managerial case.

We should be clear about the method to be followed in answering this question. To establish that a source of directives is exercising legitimate authority, we must identify a reason for compliance with the directives that operates independently of any incentives the source is able to offer. Otherwise, we merely have directive power. In the political case, this requirement can be given a simple formulation. Citizens must have a reason for complying with the official directives of the state, its laws and regulations, that would justify doing this even if the state were not able to punish violation of the law.

The situation in the managerial case is in some respects similar. Employees must have a reason for complying with managerial directives that would justify compliance even if managers lacked the ability to monitor performance to ensure that employees were doing their jobs. However, we cannot put this point by saying that employees must have a reason for complying with managerial directives that would operate even in the absence of incentives. Only rarely will an employee have a reason for complying with managerial directives when the employer lacks the ability to pay him. Still, something must be added to the ability to offer incentives if we are to speak of legitimate authority. Otherwise managers are simply exercising directive power.

Confronted with this observation, some might be tempted to say, "So much the worse for legitimate authority."[4] It is important, we all now think, for political authority to be legitimate. We all acknowledge the distinction between mere political power and legitimate political authority. But when it comes to corporate governance, it might be suggested, we can do without the concept of legitimate authority. In this case, we should simply accept that all we have is directive power. Further, this power will not be completely unregulated. If a polity determines that the power possessed by managers is being abused, it can enact laws requiring that the power be exercised, or not be exercised, in particular ways.

To make the latter point, however, is to concede that there is a difference between the appropriate and the inappropriate exercise of the directive power that managers possess. And once this is admitted, it is not clear on what ground the question of legitimacy can be set aside. Or at least this is so after a culture has evolved to the point, as Western culture has, of acknowledging a general distinction between power and authority in institutional settings. For such a culture, a claim that directive power is being appropriately exercised must ultimately be expressed in the language of legitimacy. The abuse of power in an institutional setting is avoided when and only when those issuing directives possess legitimate authority. The abuse of power is avoided when and only when those to whom the directives are addressed would be acting wrongly, in some objective sense, if they failed to comply with the directives.

AUTHORITY AND PROPERTY

Property rights provide the basis for the classification of corporations as private entities. Corporate property is privately owned. As I noted in the introduction, if the authority exercised by the managers of corporations is ultimately to be understood as occupying, along with the authority exercised by governmental officials, a position within an integrated structure of legitimate social authority, there will be an important sense in which managers are public officials. This means that there will be an important sense in which corporations are not, after all, private entities. But it will remain the case that corporate property is privately owned.

The ability that managers have to offer external incentives, both positive and negative, derives from the fact that they exercise property rights. This can be seen in the case of the negative incentive provided by the threat of termination for noncompliance with managerial directives. The ultimate source of the ability of managers to terminate employment is a system of legal property rights. The termination of employment involves, in the first instance, the exclusion of the terminated individual from the premises of the employer. The right to exclude is one of the components of ownership.[5]

To establish the legitimacy of managerial authority, we need to show that employees have a reason, over and above the incentives managers are able to provide, for complying with managerial directives. But it might be thought that property rights themselves could provide such a reason. That is, it might be thought that property rights not only ground the directive power that managers possess but also give employees an independent reason to comply with managerial directives. Respect for the property rights of the employer requires compliance with managerial directives. But this idea is mistaken. Property rights cannot establish the legitimacy of managerial authority.

A simple example shows this. The property rights of the owner of a car give him the power to order out of the car a driver who is unwilling to comply with his directives. For a driver who does not want to be ordered out, the threat of the application of this power will provide a reason to comply with the owner's directives. But the owner's property rights do not give the driver the sort of reason for compliance that is required to establish the legitimacy of authority. Legitimacy requires the existence of a reason over and above that provided by negative sanctions for noncompliance. Property rights cannot provide such a reason. An owner of a car does not, by virtue of his ownership, have the right to direct a passer-by to drive him someplace. One has a reason to comply with the directives of someone exercising property rights only if one has an independent desire not to be excluded from the property. This desire makes the prospect of exclusion threatening and gives the owner directive power.

It is important to be clear about the force of this example. The managers of corporations can be regarded as agents of the owners. They can be regarded as managing the corporation on behalf of the owners. They are thus authorized to exercise the property rights of the owners. Put another way, they have been given the authority to exercise these rights. But authority to exercise property rights is not the same thing as authority over employees. The owners cannot give managers authority over the employees, cannot delegate such authority to managers, unless the owners have it in the first place. And as we have just seen, ownership by itself does not create legitimate authority. By authorizing the managers to exercise their property rights, the owners give the managers directive power. They give managers the ability to offer employees incentives for complying with managerial directives. But directive power is not legitimate authority.

The Insufficiency of Consent

If property rights cannot ground managerial authority, what can? As we have seen, a natural suggestion is that the legitimacy of managerial authority is established by the consent of the employees. That is, what justifies employees in complying with managerial directives is that they have consented to being told what to do by managers, where this involves a promise to do what they are told to do. To be more precise, the employee has promised to comply with managerial directives in return for pay. The prospect of pay provides an incentive to comply, but what establishes that we are dealing with legitimate authority rather than mere directive power is the fact that the employee has made a promise to comply if she is paid. The promise will rarely be explicit. The words, "I promise," will rarely be used. There is, however, such a thing as tacit promising, and we can suppose that it is operative in this case. In accepting employment, the employee tacitly promises to comply with managerial directives.

Does this suffice to establish the legitimacy of managerial authority? Of special interest is the case where the directed actions are judged by an employee to be morally objectionable. When the source of directives is a government, the question of legitimacy, in a case of this sort, is the question of whether there can be good reason to obey laws that one regards as morally mistaken. In managerial contexts, the question of legitimacy has a somewhat different character. Corporate activities are subject to the law, so the question whether to obey laws that one regards as morally mistaken can arise in connection with doing one's job. But an employee may think there are moral objections to doing what he is told to do even when the activities of his corporation are perfectly legal. If consent that has promissory force is to ground the legitimacy of managerial authority, it must be able to justify compliance with managerial directives in situations of this sort.

It might be replied that even if there are moral objections to corporate activities, it does not follow that employees will be doing anything morally wrong simply by doing their jobs. But there is a sense in which all employees of a corporation, even those assembling products in a factory, could regard themselves as acting in a morally inappropriate way. Compliance with routine managerial directives sustains the corporation as a collective agent. So an employee who regards as morally objectionable various elements of the policies that have been put in place by her employer, or elements of the business strategy pursued by the employer, will be associating herself with an outcome that she views as morally unacceptable when she complies with routine managerial directives.

I say more about why this is so shortly. But before turning to that, it will be useful to explore more fully the idea that employees may find what their employers are doing morally objectionable. The requirements of morality include norms governing how individuals may treat other individuals. Thus murder and assault are morally prohibited. But when we are considering issues in political philosophy, it is necessary to acknowledge the existence of moral considerations of a different sort. These are not moral norms but rather values that establish certain social states of affairs as morally desirable. I call them *morally important social values*. They include social justice, the defense of national territory, the maintenance of the rule of law (or, more generally, social peace), the promotion of social prosperity (that is, the prosperity of the population as a whole), the protection of the environment, the fostering of community, the preservation of the health of the population, the advancement of knowledge (understood broadly as including the creation of an informed populace), and the development of culture. An employee who regards corporate policy as, on the whole, hindering the social promotion of these values will have a reason to view herself as acting inappropriately when she complies with routine managerial directives.

Can the fact that an employee has consented, in a way that has promissory force, to being told what to do by his or her employer, or by managers acting as agents of the employer, justify compliance with managerial directives in a situation like this? There are reasons for thinking that it cannot. A promissory obligation constitutes a single, substantive moral reason for action. For employees who regard the policies of their employers as morally objectionable, this obligation will be in conflict with other substantive reasons, such as those provided by the morally important social values, that count against compliance. For example, when an employee regards the activities of his employer as damaging the health of the elements of the general population, which might include the employees themselves, the promissory obligation he has to comply with managerial directives will be in conflict with a contrary reason provided by a morally important social value. I mention some other examples in the next section.

Moreover, it can be expected that a significant number of employees will find themselves in a situation of this general kind. In modern pluralistic societies, there is much disagreement about the moral permissibility of the policies of particular corporations, and the employees of any large corporation will be a cross-section of the society as a whole. So it is likely that a significant number of the employees of a corporation—usually not a majority, but a significant number nonetheless—will find the policies of that corporation morally objectionable. Some of these may conclude that the promissory obligation to comply with managerial directives has sufficient moral force to outweigh the objections. But if we suppose that there are strong moral reasons on both sides, it is plausible that a similar number will come to the opposite conclusion. They will judge that the moral objections to corporate policy have greater weight than the promissory obligation. And as was noted in the section on power and authority, when a substantial subset of the people receiving directives from some source lacks sufficient reason, independent of any incentives, to comply with those directives, the source cannot claim to exercise legitimate authority in the group of recipients as a whole.

It may be useful to put these points another way. The reason that consent possessing promissory force cannot establish the legitimacy of managerial authority is that a promise is just one moral consideration among many, and thus may be outweighed, in the minds of some of those who have made the promise, by other considerations that count against complying with managerial directives. Because they need to make a living, it is likely that employees who hold such views will nevertheless comply. They will do what they are told to do. But compliance for this reason is irrelevant to legitimacy of managerial authority.

The Reason Not to Comply

Before considering a way of establishing the legitimacy of managerial authority that avoids the problem just described, it may be useful to explore further a few issues raised by the argument just given. The first concerns the idea that by complying with managerial directives, an employee who finds corporate policies morally objectionable will be associating herself with those policies. This might be understood in explicitly causal terms. If it is, the argument could elicit the reply that the causal contribution made by almost all employees, as individuals, to any given corporate action will be slight. Thus the moral objection to a particular employee's making her designated contribution will be slight as well. Elsewhere, I have attempted to meet this objection by proposing that if employees who object to corporate actions act together with like-minded others, they can block these actions. Thus employees who decline to take such opportunities for joint action can be regarded as causally responsible for corporate actions that they judge objectionable.[6]

This argument can be questioned, but causal contribution is not the only issue.[7] The preservation of what Bernard Williams calls moral integrity provides a reason to dissociate oneself from something one regards as morally objectionable even when dissociation will have no causal consequences.[8] For example, this reason can justify one in declining to purchase clothing made in a sweatshop even though this will have no causal impact on what happens there. Similarly, it can justify an employee in declining to contribute to an overall corporate effort that he finds morally problematic, even if declining will have no effect on this effort. In this sort of case, an employee will have a reason for declining to comply with managerial directives that conflicts with the reason to comply provided by consent that has promissory force.

Parallel points have application in the political sphere. The perceived moral impermissibility of a particular governmental policy can provide a reason to withhold some or all taxes. Thus during the Vietnam War, some people regarded the moral impermissibility of the war as a reason to withhold taxes. But the causal impact of such an action, when undertaken by a single individual, will be negligible. The reason for withholding taxes must have a different basis, and considerations of moral integrity are capable of providing this. By paying taxes, one associates oneself with the actions of one's country, even if one makes no significant causal contribution to these actions. Conversely, by not paying, one dissociates oneself from them. The same can be said about complying with routine managerial directives. By complying, one associates oneself with corporate actions that one finds objectionable, and, by not complying, one dissociates oneself from such actions.

A second issue that warrants further exploration concerns the role of systemic considerations in the argument I have made. It would be natural to reply to the foregoing argument that an employee who finds corporate policy morally objectionable, and who regards reasons of integrity as outweighing her promissory obligation to comply, should quit. Surely this would be the most effective way for her to dissociate herself from something she regards as morally objectionable.[9] But while employees often have the opportunity of working for a different employer, the other employment opportunities available to an employee who has moral reservations about what her present employer is doing may place her in the same position. She may find the policies of all the corporations where she could find employment morally objectionable in some way or other. If so, "exit" will not solve her problem.[10]

A final point should also be mentioned. Employees who find corporate policies morally objectionable may have a variety of reasons for this judgment, some reflecting political convictions on the Right and some reflecting political convictions on the Left. Some possible objections on the Left are that the corporation is promoting distributive injustice by opposing efforts to unionize the workforce, that it is preventing the alleviation of poverty in poor countries by lobbying for tariff protection for its products, that it is contributing unacceptably to global warming, or that it (an insurance company, for example) is obstructing the preservation of the health of the population by lobbying against national health insurance. A natural reply to such objections is that abandoning these policies would cost jobs. What is the significance of this consideration for the question of legitimacy?

The fact that a corporation's pursuing a different policy would cost jobs creates, for an employee who regards current policy as morally objectionable, a conflict between morality and self-interest. The corporation's doing the right thing, as he understands this, could be bad for him. Morality, however, is often regarded as permitting one to decline to pursue certain morally desirable courses of action if pursuing them would be extremely costly personally. For example, one need not contribute to charity up to the point where one is no better off than those one is helping, even though this would arguably do more good than making a more modest contribution. This means that an employee in the situation we are now considering might, after all, be justified in complying with managerial directives when he finds corporate policy morally objectionable.

But this sort of justification for complying does not establish the legitimacy of managerial authority. To establish the legitimacy of authority, in situations where a recipient of a directive judges that there are genuine moral objections to compliance, it is not enough to show that there are limits on the sacrifices the recipient can be expected to make. Otherwise a source of directives could guarantee its status as a legitimate authority simply by arranging things so that alternatives to its policies were personally costly for the recipients of the directives. Indeed, it could secure its legitimacy by the simple expedient of threatening punishment for non-compliance with its directives. This last point has application to the corporate case. An employee who regards corporate policy as morally objectionable might be justified, nevertheless, in complying with managerial directives simply because failure to comply would result in the termination of employment, and this would be very costly personally. But again, the justification is not of the right sort to establish the legitimacy of authority.

To summarize: it is plausible to suppose that employees have a promissory obligation to comply with managerial directives. But some employees of large corporations will have moral reservations about corporate policy serious enough to outweigh, in their minds, this obligation. The argument I have been making is not that they should refuse to comply. This might involve sacrifices that morality cannot demand. The argument is that the compliance they can usually be expected to exhibit requires some other kind of justification.[11]

AUTHORITY AND COOPERATION

If the foregoing argument is correct, consent that has promissory force is not capable of justifying routine compliance with managerial directives by almost all the employees of a large corporation. This means that it is not capable of establishing that the managers of those corporations exercise legitimate authority within the group of employees as a whole. How might we do better?

The problem that we have been addressing, the problem of justifying compliance with a directive that one finds morally objectionable, also arises in the political case. Just as in the managerial case, many members of a political community will judge particular policies pursued by the community to be morally objectionable. Further, by obeying the official directives of the state, its laws and regulations, the members of those communities will be contributing to, or otherwise associating themselves with, these policies. They will thus have a moral reason not to obey the official directives of the state. As was mentioned earlier, it is not plausible to suppose that those subject to political authority have consented to the exercise of that authority in a way that has promissory force. What, then, can establish the legitimacy of political authority?

Often, whether the policies pursued in a political community are morally objectionable admits of reasonable disagreement.[12] When this is the case, no complete profile of policies will be found fully acceptable by everyone. It follows that no member of a political community can reasonably insist on moral perfection, as he or she understands this. No one can reasonably insist that political cooperation take precisely the form that he or she thinks morally correct. Rather, reasonableness requires that each member live with a certain amount of what that individual regards as moral error. Reasonableness requires each member to live with at least some policies that seem to have been adopted in moral error.

These observations imply that political association is, in a particular way, cooperative. People with different political views cooperate with each other to produce a condition of life that each can regard as at least morally tolerable. The fact that each must be able to regard the resulting condition of life as morally tolerable, together with the fact of reasonable disagreement, means that no one can expect to find the resulting condition of life exactly as she thinks it ought to be. Thus, part of being cooperatively disposed, in the political case, is being prepared to accept arrangements that one judges morally suboptimal.

This gives us a way of understanding legitimate political authority. The official directives of the state can be regarded as facilitating the cooperation just described. So the members of a political community, as cooperatively disposed individuals, will have sufficient reason to comply with the official directives of the state. They will be acting wrongly, in some objective sense, if they do not comply. In particular, they will be acting contrary to a requirement of practical reason.[13] Or at least this will be so if they can regard the policies of the state as morally tolerable overall. If they cannot, if they regard the negative features of political cooperation as outweighing the positive, they will have no reason to comply with the official directives of the state. But if the state is well governed, only a minuscule percentage of the population will hold this view, which means that the authority exercised by the government will be legitimate.

THE INTEGRATED STRUCTURE
OF SOCIAL AUTHORITY

Can we extend this way of understanding legitimate authority to the managerial case? The basic idea is that the legitimacy of authority is grounded in the fact that general compliance with the directives that are being issued brings about a form of mutually beneficial cooperation among people who reasonably disagree about what morality requires. As we have seen, corporate policies, and corporate actions generally, have moral implications. In particular, they have consequences for the promotion of morally important social values such as social justice, the protection of the environment, or the preservation of the health of the population. And it is to be expected that there will be disagreement among the employees of large corporations about whether the policies and activities of the corporation are morally objectionable. In this respect, the corporate situation resembles the political situation.

There is, however, an obstacle to applying the political model to the corporate case. The model requires that almost all the people over whom authority is exercised regard what they are contributing to as morally tolerable overall. But in arguing against the idea that the legitimacy of managerial authority can be grounded in the consent of employees, I claimed that there is reason to suppose that this condition will not be met in the corporate case. The employees of a large corporation will represent a cross-section of the society as a whole, and there is much disagreement within most modern societies about the moral acceptability of the actions and policies of the corporations the society contains. So it is to be expected that a significant number of the employees of a large corporation will find its policies morally objectionable overall. We might call these people corporate dissidents, although they will often keep their dissent to themselves. They comply with managerial directives only because they need to make a living. Most employees of large corporations will not be corporate dissidents in this sense, but there is reason to suppose that a sizable fraction will be. Some dissidents may regard the promissory obligation they incurred in taking their jobs as sufficient to outweigh the moral reasons they have not to comply with managerial directives. But since there are important moral considerations on both sides, it is likely that a similar number will come to the opposite conclusion. And a source of directives can claim legitimate authority in a large group only if almost all the members of the group—I earlier suggested at least 99 percent—regard compliance as justified.

This obstacle is not insurmountable, however. It has the consequence that we cannot apply the political model to the corporate case on a piecemeal basis. We cannot establish the legitimacy of managerial authority by showing that each corporation, considered separately, can be regarded as comparable from the standpoint of legitimacy to a sovereign state. But this is not the only possibility. We can instead regard each corporation as a subordinate center of cooperation facilitating authority in a larger, society-wide cooperative endeavor controlled by political authority—by government. That is, we can regard the whole society as engaged in a single cooperative endeavor that has component parts, some of which are constituted by the cooperation that takes place in corporations.

We have been focusing so far on the fact that corporate activities can have negative effects on the morally important social values. But corporate activities can also have positive effects. Corporations play an important role in the promotion of the morally important social values. This is especially true in the case of the value of social prosperity. I characterized this earlier as the prosperity of the population as a whole. By producing goods and services for sale, and providing the employment that enables members of the population to purchase these goods and services, corporations contribute to the promotion of social prosperity.

For corporate dissidents, these positive effects on prosperity, and any other morally important social values that their corporation can be regarded as promoting, are outweighed by various negative effects. But when corporations are regarded as subordinate centers of cooperation within a larger, integrated system of social cooperation, the situation may look different. This system can be regarded as promoting the public good, understood as a condition of life displaying an appropriate balance among all the different morally important social values. Because the relevant moral issues admit of reasonable disagreement, so does the question of what would promote the public good. But many of the employees who regard their corporation's policies as morally objectionable overall may have a different view of the total cooperative endeavor that is in place in their society. While regarding it as morally suboptimal in various respects, they may judge that on the whole, the good that is being done outweighs the bad. Thus, if corporate cooperation is understood as a component part of this larger cooperative endeavor, these dissident employees will be able to reconcile themselves to complying with managerial directives.

Let us consider this idea in more detail. A dissident employee of the sort we are considering will regard the good that is being done by her corporation as outweighed by the bad. Thus she will not be able to regard participation in corporate cooperation, considered in isolation from what is happening in the rest of the society, as having the kind of justification that is necessary to establish the legitimacy of authority. She will comply with managerial directives, but only because she needs to make a living. For her, the managers of the corporation will possess only directive power.

But when what the corporation is doing is considered as part of a larger cooperative enterprise coordinated by political authority, our dissident employee may be able to come to a different conclusion. In this case, she will add the bad things she regards the corporation as doing to the bad things happening in society as a whole, insofar as these are produced by the total system of cooperation that is in place. She will also add any good that she regards the corporation as doing to the other good things happening in the society, insofar as these produced by the total system of social cooperation that is in place. And when the moral horizon is expanded in this way, the good may be judged to outweigh the bad. This means that our dissident employee will be able to regard herself as having sufficient reason to participate in the integrated system as a whole, and thus to comply with the directives that maintain this system. But if corporations are understood as subordinate centers of cooperation with within the integrated system, the sufficient reason the employee has to comply with the directives that maintain the system as a whole will translate into sufficient reason to comply with managerial directives. So by viewing the corporations as such subordinate centers of cooperation, we may be able to establish the legitimacy of managerial authority.

It must be emphasized that this result follows only if corporate cooperation is understood as playing a subordinate role in a single, overarching system of cooperation that is in place in the society as a whole. This overarching cooperative endeavor is politically coordinated. Thus the result follows only if corporate cooperation is understood as ultimately guided by the existing political authorities. This is what enables a dissident employee to regard herself, in complying with the directives she receives immediately from her managers, as making a contribution to an integrated system of social cooperation.

There is no guarantee that a particular corporate dissident will take this view of the matter. He may also be a dissident in the larger political community. He may judge the total cooperative effort coordinated by the ultimate political authority in his society to be morally unacceptable on balance. In that case, he will regard neither managerial authority nor political authority as legitimate. But expanding the moral horizon in the way I have described means that corporate activities that are judged to be morally objectionable will be supplemented by other forms of social cooperation that may be regarded as morally desirable. So there is reason to suppose that expanding the moral horizon will enable many corporate dissidents to regard themselves as justified, after all, in complying with managerial directives. And if the number of corporate dissidents who find themselves in this position is large enough, as it typically will be if the relevant governments can be regarded as exercising legitimate political authority, corporate managers will possess legitimate authority within their corporations.

Corporate Democracy

The basic idea behind cooperation facilitating authority is that those exercising authority serve those over whom it is exercised by facilitating cooperation within the latter group. It is a natural extension of this idea to suppose that cooperation facilitating authority should take a democratic form. In this way, those served by authority control its exercise. More generally, democracy can be understood as the fairest way to distribute the burden of living with perceived moral error, a burden that is unavoidable when there is reasonable disagreement about the form that coop-eration should take. There is thus a moral presumption, grounded in the value of fairness, that cooperation facilitating authority should be democratically exercised.

This last point is relevant to the argument of the previous section. I suggested that corporate dissidents may be able to judge the overall system of social coopera-tion to be morally tolerable. But they would judge the overall system to be better still if the policies of their corporations were different. If the integrated system of social cooperation is ultimately under democratic control, however, they will have a reason to reconcile themselves to the fact that the system as a whole is not struc-tured exactly as they would like. The question of how the integrated system is to be structured will admit of reasonable disagreement, and some people may hold a different view about what the corporations that form part of the system should be doing. Democracy constitutes a fair way of resolving these disputes.

Still, it does not follow that corporations themselves should be democratically managed. When cooperation facilitating authority is hierarchically organized, with some centers of cooperation facilitating authority subordinate to others, the presumption in favor of democracy applies only to the top-most level of authority, that is, the authority exercised by the national government. It can decide that the presumption in favor of the democratic exercise of authority at lower levels is outweighed by other considerations. So if we view corporate management as playing a subordinate role in an integrated structure of social authority, the top-most political authority can decide that the public good would be best served by allowing nondemocratic forms of corporate organization.

One reason for taking this step is that expertise of various kinds is relevant to the decisions that corporations make, and it is often appropriate for nonexperts to defer to experts (who are exercising their expertise). Another reason is provided by the role of investment in a market system. Investment in such a system is for the most part provided by nonemployees, and those providing it are unlikely to be happy with an arrangement in which they simply surrender control of their investments to managers implementing the democratic will of the employees, even if it is understood that the investors have a right to the profits. But ensuring an adequate level of investment is important for the promotion of social prosperity. It makes possible the production of more goods and services and the employment of more people.

These considerations are not by themselves decisive. The reason to allow control by experts or investors is that particular morally important social values, especially the value of social prosperity, will be more effectively promoted in this way. But in deciding what forms of corporate governance to allow, the higher level political authorities cannot simply disregard the moral presumption, grounded in the value of fairness, in favor of the democratic exercise of cooperation facilitating authority. Stipulating arrangements that give employees some sort of role in corporate decision making may thus be appropriate all things considered. There are a number of possibilities. Mandating employee representation on boards of directors is one possibility; active encouragement, by appropriate legislation, of the unionization of corporate workforces is another.

Two Kinds of Subordinate Authority

I have suggested that by regarding corporations as subordinate centers of cooperation facilitating authority in an integrated structure of authority that is under political control, we can vindicate the legitimacy of the authority exercised by the managers of corporations. Or at least this can be done if most dissident employees are not also dissident citizens who reject the integrated structure itself. More, however, must be said about how the subordinate authority exercised by managers is to be understood.

If we look to the larger system of political authority generally, we find two forms that subordinate authority can take. One is the subordinate authority exercised by lower level governments, such as state governments and municipal governments, in a federal system. Thus in the United States, the national government facilitates cooperation within the national territory to promote the public good. But some space is left for more local forms of cooperation that possess the same character. The governments of the several states are subordinate to the national government in the sense that their efforts to promote the public good locally are constrained by various directives emanating from the national government. Similar points apply to municipal governments. For our purposes, the key feature of a federal system is that at each level, the exercise of authority involves making decisions about how to reconcile the claims of a number of different morally important social values. Let us call authority that does this *legislative* authority. The national government, state governments, and municipal governments all exercise legislative authority.

The subordinate authority exercised by managers in the integrated system I have described can be understood, in some respects, as possessing a legislative character. This will be the picture we get if we suppose that managerial decision making involves balancing the claims of different morally important social values within a framework of constraints established by higher level political authorities. To the extent managers make such decisions, corporations will take a place alongside state and municipal governments as subordinate centers of legislative activity. Though many corporations operate in a number of different political jurisdictions, the most dramatic example is provided by multinational corporations. If the argument I have given is correct, managerial authority counts as legitimate by virtue of playing a subordinate role in an integrated system of social authority that is ultimately under political control. Thus the preservation of legitimacy requires that the corporate activities that take place within the territory of each political unit constitute component parts of a coordinated effort under ultimate political control to promote the public good in that unit.[14]

The other possibility is to model managerial authority, understood as a subordinate form of authority in an integrated structure of social authority, on the authority exercised by the public officials in charge of governmental departments and agencies. That is, we could model managerial authority on what might be called *bureaucratic* authority. Bureaucratic authority facilitates cooperation within a group of employees. But as Henry Richardson has argued, the basic social role of bureaucratic authority is to give specific form to more general goals set by legislation.[15] That is, the basic task performed by these centers of cooperation is the resolution of such general goals into more specific goals, or the identification and implementation of specific means by which general goals set by legislation can be achieved. Richardson gives the example of the Biaggi Amendment to the Urban Mass Transit Act of 1970. This mandated that steps be taken to make mass transit systems accessible to the elderly and the disabled. But it was left to the Department of Transportation to sort through different definitions of access and craft a specific policy.[16]

In most corporations some managerial decisions will have a bureaucratic character and some a legislative character. Let us consider these possibilities in more detail.

THE BUREAUCRATIC AUTHORITY
OF MANAGEMENT

The plausibility of viewing managerial decision making as possessing a bureaucratic aspect is most easily seen by considering the role it plays in a planned economy. In the planned economy characteristic of the former Soviet Union, consumption and employment were not directed by central authorities. Citizens made their own decisions concerning what, of the items available, to buy, and where to seek employment, but production was centrally planned. Thus the managers of productive units functioned as bureaucrats within what was, in effect, a single governmental department focused on the promotion of social prosperity. We might speak here of a department of production. The job of managers was to translate goals set for them by the plan into specific policies guiding the activities of the productive units they managed. They were responsible for finding specific ways to achieve more general goals set by higher authority. This responsibility is the mark of bureaucratic decision making.

On the surface, a market system seems different. Producers compete with other producers. They decide what to produce by considering what will maximize profit, or some other index of success, such as market share, in a competitive environment. The task of coordinating overall social production is performed by the market. Precisely for this reason, it becomes possible to view the entire system of firms competing in the market, or the various markets that make up an economy, as comprising the society's department of production. This interpretation is especially plausible if the managers of corporations are understood as exercising subordinate authority in an integrated structure of authority. This fact, together with the coordinating role of the market, gives the market order as a whole the character of a subordinate form of cooperation within an integrated system of social cooperation.

The idea that corporate managers exercise bureaucratic authority receives further support from another consideration. In modern economies, market interactions take place within a legal framework that reflects legislative and regulatory decisions intended to ensure the promotion of social goals that normal market operations will not achieve. This is accomplished partly through legal prohibitions, and partly through the creation of incentives beyond those the market can provide, which are typically subsidies or tax breaks. The more market activity can be understood as unfolding within a framework of this sort, a framework of legislatively mandated constraints and incentives, the more the characteristic feature of bureaucratic decision making—the translation of goals set by higher authority into specific policies—will be displayed by the decisions that managers make.[17]

I said in the introduction that managerial authority is exercised in the first instance over employees. The heads of governmental departments and agencies possess authority of this sort. Governmental departments and agencies have many employees, but bureaucratic authority in the political case is also exercised over the population at large. Governmental departments and agencies are authorized by legislatures to craft directives that constrain in various ways what the larger population can do.

Recent work in political philosophy has stressed the importance of creating procedures that allow affected parties to participate in bureaucratic decision making.[18] Bureaucracies give specific form to legislative mandates, and the people affected by bureaucratic decisions have a chance to participate—by voting for legislators—in crafting the mandates. But leading theorists now suppose that those affected also need to be given a role in the process of specification. In particular, these people need to be given an opportunity to voice their concerns and to present bureaucratic decision makers with arguments supporting one or another of the options among which a decision is to be made. Thus a governmental agency is expected to hold public hearings on its regulatory proposals.

The managers of corporations are not authorized by legislatures to issue directives to the population at large, but the decisions they make concerning how to promote social prosperity and any legislatively mandated goals typically have consequences for the population at large. So the parallel with the governmental case suggests that procedures must be established that give those affected in this way by managerial decisions an opportunity to voice their concerns and present arguments supporting one or another of the available options. The resulting picture bears some resemblance to that associated with stakeholder theory in business ethics, insofar as stakeholders are understood as having a right to be heard but not to vote.

We should be clear, however, about the rationale for participation by the various groups that have a stake in managerial decisions. The people who have a right under democratic principles to participate in decisions concerning what a collective agent will do are not those who will be affected by its actions. The people who have a right to participate are the members of that collective agent, the people who will cooperate to implement the decisions that are made.[19] In this respect, decision making by collective agents is like decision making by individual agents. Those potentially affected by an action of mine have a right to my consideration of their concerns. But they do not have a right to vote on what I will do. The decision about how to reconcile their concerns with other morally relevant considerations falls to me. The role that investors often have in managerial decision making can be reconciled with this observation if we suppose that one is partly responsible for what is done with one's property when one has made it available for the performance of certain actions.[20] The rationale for establishing procedures by which stakeholders who are neither employees nor investors can voice their concerns is not, then, that they have a right, under democratic principles, to participate in these decisions. The rationale is that establishing procedures by which they can make their concerns and arguments known to corporate decision makers is a fair and efficient way to ensure that these concerns and arguments receive consideration in any internal decision-making procedure.

THE LEGISLATIVE AUTHORITY
OF MANAGEMENT

Bureaucratic authority decides the specific form that will be given to the social effort to promote goals established by higher authority. The legislative decisions that set these goals balance the claims of various morally important social values. The balancing of such claims is the mark of reasoning about the public good, so legislative decision making establishes a conception of the public good. Legislative decision making can take place in subordinate centers of cooperation within the integrated structure. This will be the case when the decision makers setting policy for a subordinate unit have been given discretion by higher authority to decide how to resolve conflicts among the morally important social values affected by the activities taking place in that unit. To the extent that subordinate decision makers possess this discretion, their decisions will determine, in part, the conception of the public good that the integrated structure as a whole puts into effect. This is true of decisions made by state and municipal governments, and it can also be true of decisions made by corporate managers.

The subordinate legislative authority found within a federal structure of political authority is typically exercised democratically, but this is not essential. The essential feature of subordinate legislative authority is that the decisions made by those exercising authority balance the claims of different morally important social values. Thus the fact that corporate democracy is almost always severely abridged poses no obstacle to regarding managerial authority as legislative. To the extent that some form of participation by nonmanagers in corporate legislative decision making is deemed appropriate, the points made in the previous section apply. The rationale for participation by the people whose cooperative efforts are organized by managerial directives is different from the rationale for participation by those who are merely affected by the corporate actions that result.

Before exploring the legislative dimension of managerial decision making, we need to say more about the moral considerations that managers making legislative decisions must take into account. I have suggested that a system of firms competing in a market can be understood as oriented in the first instance toward the promotion of one morally important social value, the value of social prosperity—the prosperity of the population as a whole. But how is prosperity itself to be understood? If prosperity is what efficient markets produce, it would seem that people are prosperous to the extent that the wants they have for goods and services are satisfied. Social prosperity is a moral value, but the goods and services the enjoyment of which constitutes social prosperity need not be understood as possessing any moral value. They may simply be things that people happen to want.

The market system promotes social prosperity, but prosperity can also be promoted in other ways. In particular, it can be promoted by the regulation of market activity. A standard example concerns the good of clean air. Much production creates air pollution, and when the costs imposed by pollution are taken into account, the overall cost to society of producing particular items may exceed the benefit. The purchasers benefit from the items, but the price they pay does not reflect the full social cost of production. Market failure of this sort is familiar from economic theory. There are external diseconomies of production associated with productive processes that create pollution. The usual remedy is the legislative mandating, and the bureaucratic specification, of measures that have the effect of internalizing costs, so that consumers pay the full social cost of producing the things they want. Thus a government might mandate the installation of pollution control equipment in power plants, with the cost being passed on to the users of the electricity.

The fact that people want clean air suggests that taking steps to clean up the air will promote social prosperity, but these actions are also required by another morally important social value: the value of protecting the environment. So in this case, the promotion of social prosperity brings with it the promotion of a further morally important social value. Similar points can be made about the other morally important social values. People often want what accompanies the promotion of these values, so the promotion of social prosperity, by market activity or governmental action, can involve the promotion of these other values. But in regarding these other values as possessing moral importance in their own right, we are supposing that the claim they have on us does not depend on what people happen to want. If preserving the environment has moral importance in its own right, a society should take steps to preserve the environment even if this means that its members go without some things they merely happen to want.

In the first instance, the decisions concerning what steps to take are made by governments. Legislators must decide how to balance the claims of applicable morally important social values and then craft laws giving practical effect to these judgments. Governmental departments and agencies also have a role to play, since legislative mandates must be converted into specific policies. These legislative and bureaucratic activities can involve imposing constraints on producers or consumers, or creating incentives for producers or consumers to act in certain ways. The goal of all these measures will be to ensure that social values other than prosperity are adequately promoted.

But to the extent that governments refrain from micromanaging corporations, they will be delegating some of these decisions about how to reconcile different morally important social values to managers. When this happens, managerial decision making takes on a legislative character. The decisions that managers make determine in part the conception of the public good that the integrated structure as a whole will put into effect. The legislative character of managerial decision making is especially pronounced in corporations that can be regarded as having the social job of promoting particular morally important social values other than social prosperity. These corporations play a role that, in a different system, might be played by a governmental agency. For example, media companies promote, in addition to social prosperity, the morally important social values of the advancement of knowledge, understood as above, and the development of culture. They thus do a job that, in Britain, is done by the BBC.[21] And companies operating in the health care industry, including insurance companies, promote, in addition to social prosperity, the preservation of the population's health. They thus do a job that, in Britain, is done by the National Health Service.

That such companies promote social prosperity means that they act to satisfy wants that people happen to have by producing goods and services for purchase in a market. It is not plausible, however, to suppose that the courses of action that will maximize profit in companies of this sort, and thus contribute to the promotion of social prosperity by the market system generally, will always be optimal from the standpoint of the additional social values. Thus media companies, for instance, may be driven by the imperative to maximize profit to provide more entertainment and less news, or to report the news in a bland way that will be found acceptable by all the people they want to attract as customers. And the profit motive may lead pharmaceutical companies to under- or overproduce medicines, thus compromising the health of the population as a whole. Similar points can be made about medical insurance companies. Considerations of profit maximization may lead them to price insurance in such a way that the people most in need of it cannot afford it, again compromising the health of the population as a whole.

The managers of corporations in this position will face the legislative task of balancing the value of social prosperity, understood as promoted by normal, profit-seeking activity, against the claims of other morally important social values. The discretion they have been given to make these decisions constitutes, in effect, a license to determine an aspect of the conception of the public good that the integrated structure as a whole will put into effect. Thus the managers of media companies are licensed to determine, in part, how the integrated structure as a whole balances the claims of general want-satisfaction against those of the advancement of knowledge and the development of culture.

Particular corporations will not, however, pursue policies that put them at a competitive disadvantage. So if the claims of morally important social values other than prosperity are to be honored in a market system, some measures must be put in place that allow firms to promote these values without losing out to competitors. The upshot is that a society that acknowledges the moral importance of social values other than prosperity, but also wants to take advantage of the decentralized decision making associated with a market system, will face a delicate task. It must create a legal framework that enables the managers of corporations of the sort we are now considering to exercise their legislative authority responsibly while preserving the viability of their corporations as profit-making entities.

Ultimately, the achievement of this goal requires the recognition by the general population of the distinction between social prosperity and the other morally important social values. It requires a recognition that satisfying wants that people merely happen to have is not all that matters. Only when this condition is met can a democracy craft a legal framework of the requisite sort. Moreover, if the citizenry does recognize that mere want-satisfaction is not all that matters, corporations will operate in a climate of opinion that by itself, independently of legal regulation, constrains and rewards the requisite corporate actions.

Conclusion

The fact that people need to make a living, and thus must do what they are told by employers, does not establish that the managers of private corporations exercise legitimate authority. It merely establishes that they possess directive power. I have argued that consent that has promissory force is not enough to convert this directive power into legitimate authority. The managers of private corporations can be regarded as exercising legitimate authority only if their authority is understood as a subordinate form of cooperation facilitating authority, a form of such authority located within a larger, integrated structure that is ultimately under political control—control by the relevant governments. This means that when managers exercise legitimate authority, they are functioning as public officials of a certain sort.

NOTES

1. See A. John Simmons, *Moral Principles and Political Obligations* (Princeton, N.J.: Princeton University Press, 1979), chap. 3 and 4. (I have received helpful comments on earlier versions of this paper from Jeffery Smith and, especially, from the editors.)

2. It may be that the moral work here is actually being done by an obligation not to disappoint reliance intentionally induced, but for present purposes, we can set this possibility aside.

3. The observation that legitimate authority presupposes de facto authority is made by Joseph Raz in "Authority and Justification," *Philosophy and Public Affairs* 14 (1985): 3–29.

4. This possibility is broached by Jeffrey Moriarty in "McMahon on Workplace Democracy," *Journal of Business Ethics* 71 (April 2007): 339–345. This paper is his contribution to a symposium on my book *Authority and Democracy: A General Theory of Government and Management* (Princeton, N.J.: Princeton University Press, 1994), the proceedings of which have been published in the mentioned issue of the *Journal of Business Ethics*. The symposium was organized by Jeffery Smith. The other participants were Nien-hê Hsieh and J. (Hans) van Oosterhout.

5. Ownership of an item involves a number of different rights. See A. M. Honoré, "Ownership," in *Oxford Essays in Jurisprudence*, ed. A. Guest (Oxford: Clarendon Press, 1961), 107–148. What Honoré calls the right to possess is a right to exclude others from an item.

6. I make this argument in *Authority and Democracy*.

7. My claim in *Authority and Democracy* that a promise to obey is not capable of grounding managerial authority is questioned by Nien-hê Hsieh in his contribution to the symposium on that book, "Managers, Workers, and Authority," *Journal of Business Ethics* 71 (April 2007): 347–357. In my reply (371–77), I suggest that even if substantive moral reasons like that provided by consent that has promissory force can in fact ground the routine exercise of managerial authority, there is still a sound basis for regarding managerial authority as cooperation facilitating. This gives us the result that the legitimacy of managerial authority is overdetermined. As I indicate in the main text, however, I am now inclined to reaffirm my original view the promissory obligation is inadequate to establish the legitimacy of managerial authority.

8. See Bernard Williams, "A Critique of Utilitarianism," in *Utilitiarianism For and Against*, eds. J. J. C. Smart and Bernard Williams (Cambridge: Cambridge University Press, 1973), 108–118, and "Utilitarianism and Moral Self-indulgence," in *Moral Luck*, ed. B. Williams (Cambridge: Cambridge University Press, 1981), 40–53. Williams uses the notion of moral integrity to justify an agent's declining to perform a morally repugnant action that would prevent something worse. But the idea that one can have a strong moral reason to decline to associate oneself with something that one regards as morally objectionable seems to have broader application, as the example of purchasing a garment made in a sweatshop shows.

9. As an editor has observed, whistle-blowing is another possibility. But normally, this will be available only when what the employee objects to is illegal. Many corporate activities that are the subject of moral controversy are perfectly legal.

10. In "Toward an Ethics of Organizations," *Business Ethics Quarterly* 9 (October 1999): 619–638, Robert A. Phillips and Joshua D. Margolis suggest that the possibility of exit constitutes one important difference between corporations and political societies. They cite this fact in arguing that it is not appropriate to ground organizational ethics in political philosophy. But later in their paper, they seem to qualify their claim about exit. They write: "those with less power within an organization lack complete volition over their commitment to join and have limited freedom to exit. They have less volition and freedom to join or exit both the organization as a whole as well as single activities within the organization" (632).

11. It might be suggested that there is a further reason that consent that has promissory force cannot establish the legitimacy of managerial authority. The promise is a promise to comply with managerial directives in return for pay. An employee thus has a moral reason to comply if she accepts pay, and to deny herself pay if she does not comply. But this simply means that she has a moral reason to collaborate in the exercise of the directive power that managers possess. An employee who acts on this reason exercises the directive power of her employer on the employer's behalf, and directive power is not legitimate authority. Compare the discussion of authority and property in the third section.

12. I explore the phenomenon of reasonable disagreement in *Reasonable Disagreement: A Theory of Political Morality*, forthcoming from Cambridge University Press.

13. I defend the idea that displaying a cooperative disposition is a requirement of practical reason in chapter 1 of *Collective Rationality and Collective Reason* (New York: Cambridge University Press, 2001), 50–54. The directives emanating from some source can

facilitate cooperation among cooperatively disposed individuals only if each recipient has good reason to believe that the others will do their parts. Common knowledge, in the relevant group, of the source's possession of directive power can provide this assurance. I discuss the connection between authority and assurance in *Collective Rationality and Collective Reasoning*.

14. Employment of the concept of the public good may be restricted to political units, and thus not make sense on a global scale, at least at this point in human history. For a related discussion, see Thomas Nagel, "The Problem of Global Justice," *Philosophy and Public Affairs* 33 (2005): 113–147.

15. Henry S. Richardson, *Democratic Autonomy* (Oxford: Oxford University Press, 2002).

16. See *Democratic Autonomy*, chap. 7. Richardson notes that the decision the Department of Transportation ultimately made was later legislatively mandated in the Americans with Disabilities Act of 1990.

17. The role of incentives and tax breaks deserves emphasis. Corporations that benefit from this sort of legislative activity probably do not think of it as the regulation of business by government, but it is.

18. See, for example, Richardson, *Democratic Autonomy*, chap. 16, and Philip Pettit, *A Theory of Freedom* (Oxford: Oxford University Press, 2001), chap. 7, especially 169–171.

19. For an opposing view, see Robert Goodin, "Enfranchising All Affected Interests, and Its Alternatives," *Philosophy and Public Affairs* 35 (2007): 40–68. Goodin's argument, taken at face value, seems to have the consequence that autonomous moral decision making—an agent's autonomously deciding how to treat the other agents with which he, she, or it interacts—should play no role in human affairs. If there is a place for the idea that agents should decide for themselves what morality requires, it is found only in connection with voting on the policies to be pursued by a single collective agent of which everyone in the world is a member.

20. The question whether managerial authority encompasses investors is discussed by J. (Hans) van Oosterhout in his contribution to the symposium on *Authority and Democracy*, "Authority and Democracy in Corporate Governance?" *Journal of Business Ethics* 71 (April 2007): 359–370.

21. The United States has the Public Broadcasting Service, but given the role of private media companies in American life, they must take on part of the job of promoting the advancement of knowledge and the development of culture.

SUGGESTED READING

Goodin, Robert. "Enfranchising All Affected Interests, and Its Alternatives." *Philosophy and Public Affairs* 35 (2007): 40–68.

Honoré, A. M. "Ownership." In *Oxford Essays in Jurisprudence*. Edited by A. Guest, 107–148. Oxford: Clarendon Press, 1961.

Hsieh, Nien-hê. "Managers, Workers, and Authority." *Journal of Business Ethics* 71 (April 2007): 347–357.

McMahon, Christopher. *Authority and Democracy: A General Theory of Government and Management*. Princeton: Princeton University Press, 1994.

———. *Collective Rationality and Collective Reasoning*. New York: Cambridge University Press, 2001.

———. "Comments on Hsieh, Moriarty and Oosterhout." *Journal of Business Ethics* 71 (April 2007): 371–79.

Moriarty, Jeffrey. "McMahon on Workplace Democracy." *Journal of Business Ethics* 71 (April 2007): 339–345.

Nagel, Thomas. "The Problem of Global Justice." *Philosophy and Public Affairs* 33 (2005): 113–147.

Oosterhout, J. (Hans) van. "Authority and Democracy in Corporate Governance?" *The Journal of Business Ethics* 71 (April 2007): 359–370.

Pettit, Philip. *A Theory of Freedom*. Oxford: Oxford University Press, 2001.

Phillips, Robert A., and Margolis, Joshua D. "Toward an Ethics of Organizations." *Business Ethics Quarterly* 9 (October 1999): 619–638.

Raz, Joseph. "Authority and Justification." *Philosophy and Public Affairs* 14 (1985): 3–29.

Richardson, Henry, S. *Democratic Autonomy*. Oxford: Oxford University Press, 2002.

Simmons, A. John. *Moral Principles and Political Obligations*. Princeton, N.J.: Princeton University Press, 1979.

Smith, Jeffery D. "Managerial Authority as Political Authority: A Retrospective Examination of Christopher McMahon's Authority and Democracy." *Journal of Business Ethics* 71 (April 2007): 335–38.

Williams, Bernard. "A Critique of Utilitarianism." In *Utilitarianism For and Against*. Edited by J. J. C. Smart and Bernard Williams, 108–118. Cambridge: Cambridge University Press, 1973.

———. "Utilitarianism and Moral Self-Indulgence." In *Moral Luck*. Edited by B. Williams, 40–53. Cambridge: Cambridge University Press, 1981.

CHAPTER 5

CORPORATE RESPONSIBILITY AND ITS CONSTITUENTS

KENNETH E. GOODPASTER

IT has been standard practice over the past quarter century to think of the field of business ethics as involving three levels of analysis: (1) the individual responsibility of the businessperson, (2) corporate responsibility, and (3) the responsibility of the societal system as a whole.

At the level of individual responsibility, the focus is on the values by which self-interest is balanced by a concern for fairness and the good of others, both within and outside the company. At the level of corporate responsibility, the focus is on the acknowledged or unacknowledged obligations that every company has as it pursues its economic objectives. This is the level at which scholars and practitioners debate the ethical aspects of corporate policy. Finally, at the level of the societal system itself, business ethics examines the pattern of cultural, political, and economic forces that drive individuals and firms, values that define democratic capitalism in a global environment. From a moral point of view, is a market economy to be preferred to a socialistic or managed economy?[1]

At each level, the language of ethical responsibility enters the picture (see figure 5.1) and at each level there are both descriptive and normative questions, including questions about the adequacy of market-based and law-based reasoning in decision making. The challenge before us in this essay relates primarily to the *second* of these three levels of analysis, the corporation, though it must be acknowledged that the three levels interact with one another in important ways.

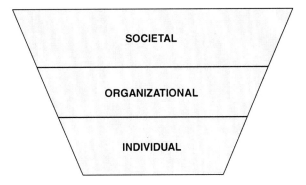

Figure 5.1. Levels of Ethical Responsibility

Another aspect of "locating" the subject of corporate responsibility in the field of business ethics is that our focus will be on the responsibilities *of* corporations—in contrast to reciprocal responsibilities *toward* corporations. Accounts of the idea of responsibility, to be complete, would typically consider mutuality, that is, the fact that an individual or an organization to which we attribute responsibility often deserves to be the *recipient* of respect by external parties who have responsibilities to those individuals or organizations. While the latter theme will not be explored in this essay, it is an important dimension of our subject and one that seldom gets sufficient attention in either descriptive or normative discussions.[2]

A Tripartite Model

The conventional interpretation of corporate responsibility in the literature of business ethics uses some version of "stakeholder thinking" as shorthand, almost as a synonym for "ethical thinking in business." Commentators often point out that publicly held business organizations need to move beyond a preoccupation with *stockholders* and guide their behavior with attention to all *stakeholders*, parties whose interests or rights are affected by corporate decision making.[3] Essentially the model is dualistic, involving a presentation or comparison of two paradigms (figure 5.2).

The upper-left array in figure 5.2 depicts the corporation and its stakeholders with the shaded circle (representing the shareholders) as the principal focus of attention. The other stakeholders may enter into the decision-making consciousness of the corporation on this model, but they do so either instrumentally or in some other subordinate way. Instrumental concern by the corporation for these stakeholders implies considering the satisfaction of their interests or the recognition of their rights as useful means to the end of adding shareholder value. Subordinate consideration by the corporation for these stakeholders may not see them as *means* to shareholder value, but may see their interests and rights as overridden or

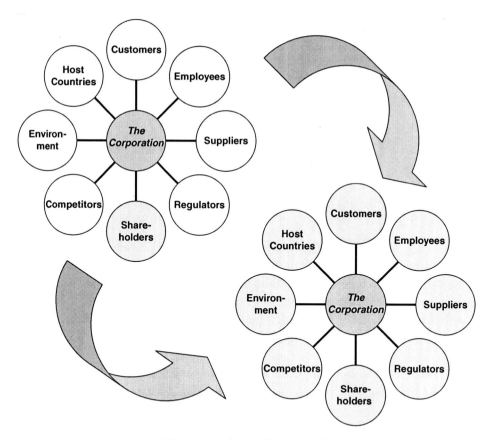

Figure 5.2. The Dualistic Model

"outranked" by those of the shareholders. The lower-right array depicts the same set of stakeholders, except that in this view, all of the stakeholder circles are shaded, indicating ethical *parity* with shareholders. The ethical attention of the corporation must, on this view, include all stakeholders and must not give special (much less exclusive) attention to shareholders.[4]

Some argue for the displacement of the upper paradigm by the lower, while others argue for the retention of both perspectives in a somewhat paradoxical relationship (see "Paradox?" section below). In either case, the model is dualistic in the sense that it assumes essentially two frameworks for corporate decision making.

In this essay, I will explore both the *necessity* and the *sufficiency* of understanding corporate responsibility in stakeholder categories. In other words, the idea of moving *beyond* stockholder thinking to stakeholders seems to be a salutary step in the direction of forming an ethical corporation, but it may not be quite so simple or *enough*. There may be more to institutionalizing ethical values in the marketplace than meets the eye. And we might overlook this fact if our account of corporate responsibility were to stop at stakeholder thinking. The missing factor I will call *comprehensive moral thinking,* and I will suggest that it is essential to a credible account of corporate responsibility—because it is essential to responsible corporate

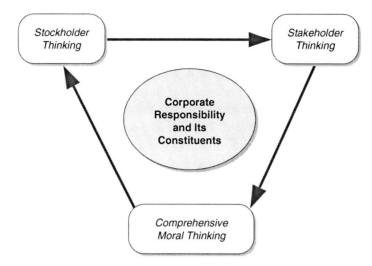

Figure 5.3. The Tripartite Model

decision making in a global economy. Thus I will be arguing for a *tripartite* model of corporate responsibility, rather than a *dualistic* one (see figure 5.3).

By "tripartite," I mean that the thinking being recommended to corporate leaders (mirrored by the elements of a *theory* of corporate responsibility) involves three reflective lenses in contrast to the two lenses of the dualistic model. In other words, while it might be tempting to interpret the phrase "corporate responsibility and its constituents" to mean something like "corporations and the stakeholders to whom they are responsible," this will *not* be the approach taken in this essay. Thus when I refer to "constituents," I will not mean "stakeholders," even though this is one possible meaning of the term (as when it is urged that leaders "pay attention to their constituents"). The word "constituent" in this essay signals a component part of a larger whole—and the larger whole is an understanding of corporate responsibility that includes attention to stockholders and stakeholders, but it also calls for another, more holistic perspective—comprehensive moral thinking.

A responsible corporation, on the model depicted in figure 5.3, is one that approaches decisions first in the conventional fiduciary manner, with special attention to profitability and return to stockholders. But second, such a corporation expands its consideration to include other stakeholders toward whom it has obligations. And finally, I will argue, such a corporation also considers the implications of its decision making using principles aimed at cooperation among sectors to achieve a common good and social justice. Thus a full account of the responsible corporation calls for a three-stage reflective process (suggested by the arrows in figure 5.3).

I have organized this essay around three basic ideas, each of which corresponds to one of the three "constituents" of the tripartite model. Each of these ideas will be discussed in the pages that follow.

1. Progress. Stakeholder thinking is *a moral advance* on stockholder thinking as a constituent of corporate responsibility, although it does not *eliminate* the special fiduciary obligations of corporate management.

2. Insufficiency. Stakeholder thinking is *not sufficient* as an account of corporate responsibility for several reasons, even though it is an essential constituent. Those reasons include "open questions" about stakeholder desires and social arrangements, questions of the form "Yes, this corporate decision satisfies key stakeholders, but does it really demonstrate social responsibility?"

3. Comprehensiveness. As one seeks a more satisfactory account of corporate responsibility, one discovers that it must be more comprehensive. Such comprehensiveness must eventually be anchored in (1) principles of human dignity and a just community and (2) a distinction between *categorical* responsibility and *qualified* (or *conditional*) corporate responsibility.

PROGRESS

Like a *mantra*, the exhortation to go beyond stockholder thinking in the context of the modern publicly held corporation has been repeated with intensity during the last three decades. But Peter Drucker has argued persuasively that "going beyond" is not simply a matter of eliminating organizational single-mindedness. It is a matter of balancing "two apparently contradictory requirements":

> Organizations must competently perform the one social function for the sake of which they exist—the school to teach, the hospital to cure the sick, and the business to produce goods, services, or the capital to provide for the risks of the future. They can do so only if they single-mindedly concentrate on their specialized mission. But there is also society's need for these organizations to take social responsibility—to work on the problems and challenges of the community.[5]

Should the responsible corporation be single-minded or not? Eventually, I will suggest that Drucker's exhortation really involves balancing not just two requirements but three.

The emergence of stakeholder language signals genuine moral progress for democratic capitalism. It has opened up the consciousness of business leaders to go beyond the single-mindedness to which Drucker referred, and it has for many decades offered a humanizing or socializing framework for decision making. In the wake of the collapse of the Soviet Union at the end of the 1980s, this language offered hope that the globalization of market economies could stand up to moral scrutiny.

Nevertheless, while the emergence of stakeholder thinking represented genuine moral progress, it should not blind us to the fact that the special fiduciary obligation owed by managers to shareholders is an *essential* ingredient in any account of corporate responsibility.

The idea that stakeholder thinking is an advance in our thinking about corporate responsibility, even though a focus on stockholders is legitimate, can be illuminated by reflecting on the moral development of human individuals. For in many ways, *corporate responsibility is the institutional analogue of personal conscience*. Let us explore this analogy.

From the Individual to the Corporation: Moral Projection

Philip Selznick in his classic *Leadership in Administration* describes institutional character by drawing upon an analogy between individual personality and organizational development:

> The study of institutions is in some ways comparable to the clinical study of personality. It requires a genetic and developmental approach, an emphasis on historical origins and growth stages. There is a need to see the enterprise as a whole and to see how it is transformed as new ways of dealing with a changing environment evolve.[6]

This idea—that organizations are in many ways macroversions (projections) of us as individuals—is as old as Plato. Because of this, we can sometimes see more clearly in organizations certain features that we want to understand better in ourselves. And the reverse is true as well. Managers of organizations can profit from what we understand about personal decisions—especially in the case of personal moral decisions. This is an example of my earlier observation that the three levels of analysis "interact with one another in important ways."

The dynamics of goal-directed motivation and ethical values are present in both arenas (individuals and organizations) and offer useful comparisons. This analogical approach has been called the "moral projection" principle.[7]

The field of business administration frequently relies upon projections—attributions to organizations of traits that originate in our understanding of individuals. This may occur in "strategy," for example, but also in business learning, intelligence, memory, perception, competitiveness, discipline, and even "control consciousness." Organizations are groups of human individuals with decision-making structures. It should come as no surprise that we can profit from the understanding that we have of individuals by applying this to the organizational context (and vice versa). There is no reason to think that individual ethics-related traits are any less illuminating in their application to the responsibility of corporations.

Corporate Analogues: Stockholders and Stakeholders

Josiah Royce, writing at the end of the nineteenth century, insisted that all of ethics was grounded in something he called the *moral insight* (a gateway to what philosophers today call the "moral point of view"). Royce described the moral insight as "the realization of one's neighbor," a liberation from the illusion that one's neighbor is unreal, the "illusion of selfishness."[8]

The natural organizational analogue to Royce's discussion of a self-centered "illusion" is a publicly traded company that is preoccupied with the interests of "shareholders" (recall figure 5.2, upper left).[9] And the natural organizational analogue to Royce's "realization of one's neighbor" is "stakeholder thinking" on the part of management (recall figure 5.2, lower right). John Boatright summarizes these two perspectives on corporate responsibility in the following passage:

> The prevailing system of corporate *governance* may be expressed in three related propositions: (1) that shareholders ought to have control; (2) that managers have a fiduciary duty to serve shareholder interests alone; and (3) that the objective of the firm ought to be the maximization of shareholder wealth. The main theses of stakeholder management can then be stated by modifying each of these propositions as follows: (1) all stakeholders have a right to participate in corporate decisions that affect them; (2) managers have a fiduciary duty to serve the interests of all stakeholder groups; and (3) the objective of the firm ought to be the promotion of all interests and not those of shareholders alone.[10]

To the extent that one can generalize about "findings" in the field of business ethics, the shift from a "stockholder" or "shareholder" paradigm to a "stakeholder" paradigm for corporate responsibility is probably the most widely accepted change in thinking during the last half century, among academics and among practitioners.[11]

The most persuasive arguments behind this shift in thinking center on the nature of private property itself. Even the classic defenses of private property, such as we find in the writings of John Locke, contain "provisos" about the claims that can be made in the name of property rights when other parties are left wanting. The idea that the shareholders of a corporation are its owners, and that therefore management and the board of directors owes an *exclusive* allegiance to them—and only *conditional* allegiance to other stakeholders—depends upon a questionable moral assumption that during the last century has become increasingly problematic.

The assumption is that the fiduciary relationship between management and shareholders (governed by the law of agency) carries a kind of moral immunity when it comes to the claims of other parties to the corporate enterprise. But this assumption is not plausible because we know that nobody has moral immunity. No one should expect of an *agent* behavior that is ethically less responsible than what he would expect of himself. Shareholders cannot (ethically) *hire* something done on their behalf that they may not (ethically) *do* themselves.[12] Thus the legitimacy of stakeholder thinking becomes clearer once we recognize that the responsibilities of management toward stakeholders are largely extensions of the obligations that *stockholders themselves* would be expected to honor independently of the corporate form. The analogy between individual responsibility and corporate responsibility is not serendipitous—it is a product of the ethical norms surrounding promises and fiduciary relationships themselves.

All this being said, there is not a consensus on the *way* in which the concerns of "stakeholders" should enter into managerial decision making. For many today still argue that *all stakeholders* are better served when boards of directors represent stockholders and when managers are primarily focused on quarter-to-quarter activity aimed at improving stockholder value. Boatright seems to espouse this view:

> From the premise that corporate activity should benefit all stakeholder groups, it does not follow that ensuring this outcome is a task for management.... To conclude that it is management's task to ensure that all stakeholders benefit would be to commit a rather elementary mistake in reasoning that might be called the stakeholder fallacy. Just because every stakeholder group ought to benefit from participation in a firm, it does not follow that the task of ensuring this outcome belongs to management—or, indeed, to any persons.[13]

Boatright's identification of a "stakeholder fallacy" brings to mind an oft-quoted essay by Milton Friedman, "The Social Responsibility of Business Is to Increase Its Profits."[14] Commentators seldom notice that Friedman's position is quite consistent with a stakeholder perspective—at least in terms of the ultimate beneficiaries of corporate decision making. The reason for this consistency is that Friedman could, and probably did, hold that the greatest good for all is best achieved by a rule or norm for some individuals or organizations to make decisions with other objectives in mind. Friedman believed that the *proximate* beneficiaries should be the stockholders, because he held that the system of democratic capitalism is designed to create wealth and thereby be socially successful.

There are, in other words, politically conservative ways of supporting the idea that corporate responsibility is about taking stakeholders (not just stockholders) seriously.[15] According to some, the benefit to nonstockholders (such as employees, customers, suppliers, etc.) has to come in large measure from contracts, statutes, regulations, and the working of the competitive system itself, rather than from the day-to-day managerial decisions of corporate executives.[16]

Corporate executives frequently imply that maintaining competitiveness is the best path to doing what is right, even though this may not *seem* right on the face of it. Here is an example of one such executive reflecting on her situation:

> I operate in a hypercompetitive global marketplace. My primary responsibility is to be profitable in order to serve my shareholders. I have to obey the local laws, for sure. I must also follow the laws imposed by the country in which I am headquartered if they apply overseas. But if I go beyond that—if I pay wages or uphold environmental standards that are higher than legally required in a foreign country, and if that causes my company to be less competitive than my rivals and hence to be less profitable, am I doing the right thing?[17]

On the more politically progressive side of the argument, however, the idea of stakeholder management has often given rise to radical suggestions about stakeholder governance and control—proposals to include stakeholder representatives on corporate boards of directors, implying that management duties to employees, customers, suppliers, and others are modeled on *fiduciary* duties owed to stock-holders. In this context, stakeholder thinking amounts to both a governance struc-ture and an executive decision-making process that aims at maximizing positive outcomes for as many different groups of affected parties as possible.[18] On this view, the idea appears to be that unless all stakeholder groups are represented in the deci-sion-making process in the same way as stockholders are represented, they will not be taken seriously enough.

It is important to note in this context that both the politically conservative and the politically liberal approaches to stakeholder thinking share a conviction about the place of legal and regulatory compliance in achieving corporate responsibility. Both approaches ask the corporation to think about stakeholders as part of their operating consciousness, not simply as external pressure groups backed by social authority.

Accordingly, the unfolding of responsibility or moral concern in the life of a private sector enterprise is similar in important ways to its unfolding in the life of an individual person. In the terms used by Josiah Royce earlier in this section, we see a shift to the "realization" of stakeholders in addition to stockholders, and then a shift to understanding that laws and regulations (social authorities) are not enough to do justice to our understanding of corporate responsibility. As in the lives of indi-viduals, corporations can come to acknowledge the decision-making relevance of parties other than their providers of capital. Employees, customers, suppliers, and local communities represent the business analogues to an individual's "neighbors."

Paradox?

Advocates of the conservative view usually concede that the purpose of their emphasis on stockholders is a matter of *means*, not of *ends*. In other words, they believe strongly that the purpose of the firm (or of the economic system in which the firm functions) is to benefit all, not just some stakeholders. Thus even in prac-tice, Boatright acknowledges, the default to stockholder interests calls for awareness and (if needed) correction—*guidance* rather than *governance* with all stakeholders in mind. Managers must acknowledge that "shareholder primacy benefits *all* stake-holders" and must not "use it as a reason for *disregarding* other stakeholders."[19]

The difference of opinion about executive obligations in this arena has been called the "stakeholder paradox."[20] A paradox is "a statement or proposition that seems self-contradictory or absurd but in reality expresses a possible truth."[21] In the case of an ethical proposition, the seeming contradiction presents itself as two conflicting obligations. Those who advocate *impartiality* in relation to stakeholder groups contradict those who believe that *partiality* toward stockholders is the only legitimate posture for business to adopt, given its economic mission and the law of agency. Milton Friedman, who defends the latter view, also questions the *compe-tence* of business leaders to manage impartially.

The paradox, then, is that *it seems essential, yet illegitimate, to guide corporate deci-sions by ethical values that go beyond stockholder considerations to impartial stakeholder considerations.* Ethics seems both to forbid and to demand a partial (vs. impartial) mindset. The issue arises from managers' fiduciary duty to investors, essentially the duty to be good stewards, to keep a profit-focused promise. Shareholders, after all, are in many ways *residual* stakeholders, that is, their returns are available only if there is a surplus after other stakeholder obligations are met.[22] This fact appears to be at the root of the special fiduciary obligation owed to providers of capital.

To embrace impartiality through a stakeholder approach, in the eyes of some, cuts managers loose from accountability to investors for their property and leads to a *betrayal of trust*. Such an approach *dilutes*, critics claim, the fiduciary obligation to stockholders (by extending it to customers, employees, suppliers, etc.) and thereby threatens the "privacy" of the private sector organization. If corporate responsibility is modeled on public sector institutions with impartiality toward all constituencies, the providers of capital lose status.

The stakeholder paradox seems to call for an account of corporate responsibility that (1) recognizes moral obligations on the part of management toward stakeholders (2) *without* interpreting these as *fiduciary* duties (thus protecting the uniqueness of the principal-agent relationship between management and stockholders).

The solution to the paradox may lie in appreciating a *difference in kind* between the *fiduciary* relationships managers have to their shareholders while still acknowledging significant nonfiduciary obligations to other stakeholders. Such *nonfiduciary* obligations are not merely contingent, but they may be discharged (for example) by candor in labor negotiations or special attention to product safety rather than by putting employees and consumers into the *governance* structures of the corporation. A board of directors that rejects a hostile tender offer for its company's stock may not be acting in the financial interest of the shareholders (at least in the short term), but the board may invoke nonfiduciary obligations to the local community, the employees, and/or the customers that outweigh shareholder obligations in the situation at hand.

The former CEO of Medtronic, Inc., Art Collins, and Steve Mahle, head of Medtronic's Cardiac Rhythm Management division, had to face a product quality issue that called for courage and humility. The issue and their decisive response are summarized in the following company press release:

> MINNEAPOLIS, February 11, 2005—Medtronic, Inc., today said it is voluntarily advising physicians about a potential battery shorting mechanism that may occur in a subset of implantable cardioverter-defibrillator (ICD) and cardiac resynchronization therapy defibrillator (CRT-D) models. In a letter to physicians, Medtronic reported that nine batteries (0.01 percent, or approximately 1 in 10,000) have experienced rapid battery depletion due to this shorting action. If shorting occurs, battery depletion can take place within a few hours to a few days, after which there is loss of device function. There are no reported patient injuries or deaths....
>
> ICDs shock or pace the heart into normal rhythm after patients suffer rapid, life-threatening heart rhythm disturbances originating in the lower chambers of the heart that can lead to sudden cardiac arrest (SCA). CRT-Ds can also provide electrical pulses to the heart's two lower chambers to improve heart failure symptoms. An ICD or CRT-D device is surgically implanted in the chest in a procedure typically lasting one to two hours.

"We were able to identify this possible risk through our stringent product testing," said Steve Mahle, president of Medtronic Cardiac Rhythm Management. "Even though the potential for rapid battery depletion is extremely low, we see it as our obligation to alert all implanting physicians to the potential issue and provide ways to help them and their affected patients successfully manage the situation."[23]

This incident, and others like it in other companies, illustrates the kind of decision making that takes seriously (nonfiduciary) obligations to customers or other stakeholders without departing from a shareholder-based governance structure. The seeming contradiction between a special obligation to shareholders and a legitimate concern for the safety of employees or customers is avoided by clarity of purpose and a view of corporate responsibility that instinctively honors both.

It is useful to note in this connection that the laws in most jurisdictions seldom decide these matters preemptively in favor of the shareholders. Most U.S. states have "constituency statutes" in place that protect corporate decision makers from narrow constructions of their fiduciary duties. And rarely are threats of shareholder lawsuits more intimidating to senior management than lawsuits from customers or employees when moral responsibilities to stakeholders are at issue.

The argument in this section has been that stakeholder thinking is *a moral advance* on stockholder thinking as a constituent of corporate responsibility, even though it does not *eliminate* the special fiduciary obligations of corporate management. There can be little doubt that the ideas of "stakeholder awareness" and even "corrective stakeholder management" have gained wide acceptance during the closing decades of the twentieth century. This fact represents, in the eyes of most observers, genuine progress.

There has been an expansion, but not a complete shift in our cultural "paradigm," our way of thinking about the ultimate beneficiaries of business organizations. Charles Handy offers the following explanation for this change:

> We cannot escape the fundamental question, Whom and what is a business for? The answer once seemed clear, but no longer. The terms of business have changed. Ownership has been replaced by investment, and a company's assets are increasingly found in its people, not in its buildings and machinery. In light of this transformation, we need to rethink our assumptions about the purpose of business.[24]

Handy continues:

> The purpose of a business, in other words, is not to make a profit, full stop. It is to make a profit so that the business can do something more or better. That "something" becomes the real justification for the business. Owners know this. Investors needn't care.[25]

With this last point, Handy suggests that the shareholder relationship to management has become more technical over time—"owners" having become simply "investors." We have seen above, however, that this fact does not give shareholders moral immunity in the demands they make on managers.

Handy's central assertion is that corporate responsibility must be anchored not *simply* in the achievement of profits for stockholders but in a true contribution to the lives of other stakeholders.[26] Profits may be a reward for that contribution. But failure to recognize the "real justification" of business leads to "suspicions about capitalism [that] are rooted in a feeling that its instruments, the corporations, are immoral in that they have no purpose other than themselves." In the case of Medtronic example above, the "something" that provided the justification for its business was articulated in the first element of its mission statement: "To contribute to human welfare by the application of biomedical engineering [to] alleviate pain, restore health, and extend life."

Our expectations of corporations, like our expectations of human individuals, change over time as they exhibit the capacity for conscience. Handy's observations in "What's a business for?" provide a natural segue to the theme of the second main section of this essay: Stakeholder thinking is *not sufficient* as an account of corporate responsibility, even though it is an essential constituent.

INSUFFICIENCY

We have seen in our discussion above that despite disagreements over the best way to structure corporate *governance*, many observers agree that the shift in paradigm—and in imagination—signaled by the use of the phrase "stakeholder management" represents genuine moral progress. Now we must look more closely at the *significance* of this progress. We can take cues in discussing the sufficiency of stakeholder thinking in relation to *corporate responsibility* as we did before—from our understanding of *individual conscience*.

Two Kinds of Moral Awareness: Thomas Nagel

Three decades ago, Thomas Nagel wrote about an aspect of moral maturity that challenges us once we achieve the moral insight discussed earlier:

> The real issue is the relative priority, in regard to action, of two ways of looking at the world. On the one hand there is the position that one's decisions should be tested ultimately from an external point of view, to which one appears as just one person among others.... This point of view claims priority by virtue of greater comprehensiveness.... On the other hand there is the position that since an agent lives his life from where he is, even if he manages to achieve an impersonal view of his situation, whatever insights result from this detachment need to be made part of a personal view before they can influence decision and action.[27]

Nagel reminds us of our capacity for different perspectives in the moral life—an *agent-centered perspective* that contextualizes our decision making in the "here and now" and a more detached or *agent-neutral perspective* that steps out of the situation to assess our responsibilities impartially and comprehensively.

These are not just *different* perspectives, however; they sometimes appear to be *opposing* perspectives. It is not just that we can look at our actions from two distinct points of view; it is that each of these points of view claims a certain priority in our decision making and may direct us to different actions. For example, our relationships to significant others (family, friends, workplace colleagues, clients) from an agent-centered perspective make moral claims on us that might conflict with a more detached, impartial perspective, emphasizing loyalties to persons and communities that may be remote and unrelated. Arguments about the risks associated with a U.S. signing of the Kyoto Protocol exhibit Nagel's distinction. From an agent-centered point of view, the consequences to the U.S. economy might well be damaging, but from an impartial agent-neutral point of view, the assessment might be positive.

It is essential to note that when Nagel refers to an "agent-centered perspective," he is *not* referring to egocentrism or self-interest. He means a perspective that acknowledges responsibilities to others as well as to oneself—but responsibilities that can influence action because they belong to an *embedded* agent (or corporation) in a concrete decision-making situation. The agent-centered perspective by its very nature calls for an operating framework that is "partial" to the set of relationships and circumstances surrounding the person or corporation making the decision.

The literature of ethics is replete with talk about "moral frameworks" just as the literature of management refers consistently to "decision-making frameworks." And as we reflect upon the concept of an operating "framework," we can discern the idea of a surrounding border that limits inputs and outputs in a more or less orderly manner. In fact, the very word "decision" comes from a Latin root that means "to cut off," suggesting a discontinuity, a limit on the potentially indefinite consideration of informational inputs. Operating frameworks allow us to organize, and ultimately to manage, the decision-making process.[28] The central point is that the "stakeholder thinking" we have been discussing in relation to corporations corresponds to the agent-centered framework described by Nagel in relation to individuals.

While Nagel does not use the language of conscience, he can be interpreted as suggesting that conscience has a kind of subjective authority that comes from an agent's situational role in decision making, but it *also* seeks authority from a more objective and impartial source. Conscience must be an *action guide*, and yet it must also be validated in a way that *transcends* our subjectivity, joining our humanity to others.[29] "We are faced with a choice," Nagel insists,

> For the purposes of ethics, should we identify with the detached, impersonal will that chooses total outcomes, and act on reasons that are determined accordingly? Or is this a denial of what we are really doing and an avoidance of the full range of reasons that apply to creatures like us? *This is a true philosophical dilemma; it arises out of our nature, which includes different points of view on the world.*[30]

It is difficult to be both engaged and detached at the same time—and yet this appears to be Nagel's view of the moral life. We must be *engaged* to take action in our network of circumstances; yet we must be *detached* to guard against the biases that our engagement carries with it. On the one hand, action in the real world calls for a limited perspective that is anchored in a person's motivational framework, character, and relationships. On the other hand, a person must be vigilant about the contingency that accompanies such a limited perspective. We seem to be creatures that are called to be both "special" (partial) *and* "no different" (impartial) in our moral lives.[31]

Nagel is drawing our attention to a *tension* at the core of moral judgment between subjective and objective. He is contrasting the perspective of the decision maker who must act in a context using an operating framework with a perspective that is anchored in a more holistic awareness of moral truth. And he is *not* suggesting that the tension be *eliminated*. On the contrary, he sees the tension as part of the inner dynamism of conscience itself. We must *follow* our convictions, but we must also *examine* and *discipline* our convictions, seeking their justification in a larger vision of human good. In the spirit of an observation once made by F. Scott Fitzgerald, conscience asks us to "hold two opposed ideas at the same time, and still retain the ability to function."[32]

The two perspectives to which Nagel draws our attention create a dilemma, of course, only if they are ultimately incapable of being united in the same moral life. Yet we are frequently able to join the motivational intimacy of the agent-centered point of view with the impartial point of view. We do this in the spirit of Socrates' chariot allegory in the *Phaedrus*: "The charioteer directs the entire chariot/soul, trying to stop the horses from going different ways, and to proceed towards enlightenment."[33] Indeed, the "Golden Rule" is something of a managerial exhortation to take *both* perspectives seriously.

Most of us believe that Nagel's two dimensions of moral judgment are, or can be rendered, ultimately consistent with one another.[34] Let us now consider the importance of this understanding of conscience for an account of corporate responsibility.

The Embeddedness of Stakeholder Thinking

The framing of an organizational decision in stakeholder terms—if it is to be practical—needs to concretize variables to make alternatives or options ethically *comparable*. To be sure, stakeholder *theory* as a general account of right and wrong in business decision making is not the same as stakeholder thinking in practice.[35] But to the extent that stakeholder thinking is intended to be a theory *in use* by corporate decision makers, it has to be used in a specific time and place, taking into account specific parties (employees, customers, vendors, local communities, etc.). In these respects, stakeholder thinking is the corporate analogue of agent-centered (or subjective) thinking in the moral life of the individual.

For any given corporate decision, the set of stakeholders will vary according to (1) time and place, (2) *which* parties are affected, (3) the *magnitude* and the *significance* of the effects upon those in each stakeholder group,[36] (4) the *boundaries* of each stakeholder group,[37] or even (5) the degree to which individuals in each stakeholder group have interests or obligations that limit the obligations owed to them.[38]

A more *comprehensive* perspective would involve stepping outside of the limitations of this time, this place, and these specific stakeholder relationships. It would search for impartiality with attention to the ways in which markets, laws, and social norms might lead well-intended actors to outcomes that undermine their good intentions. If a convenience food company focuses attention on satisfying its various specific consumers, employees, and vendors, it might not take a more comprehensive view of nutrition patterns on a national or global scale. A number of alcoholic beverage producers have, in taking note of the more comprehensive view, included phrases like "Enjoy in Moderation" on product labels.[39]

The *benefits* (ethically) of stakeholder thinking are (1) that it expands moral consideration from a single group (stockholders) to several groups, and (2) that it makes ethical decisions more systematic and operational. Indeed, talk about "balanced scorecards" and "triple bottom line" reporting reinforces this perception. Executives who would use stakeholder thinking do so against a backdrop of operating assumptions that are institutionally given: a specific network of customers, employees, suppliers, shareholders, competitors, and regulators.

The *risks* (ethically) of stakeholder thinking in practice are (1) that it might accept uncritically the idea of stakeholder *satisfaction* as a surrogate for stakeholder *value*, and (2) that it might substitute *aggregation* of stakeholder satisfactions for normative principles that are less amenable to such a reductive methodology (e.g., "social justice" and "the common good"). In the words of Jeffery Garten, "besides considering all the stakeholders of a company—employees, customers, suppliers, communities—business leaders must also consider the concerns of society, such as a cleaner environment and a higher level of integrity in business dealings."[40]

Moral ideals like human dignity and a just community may or may not underlie the "satisfactions" of any given corporation's embedded stakeholder portfolio. Its consumers may not care much about how minorities are treated; its shareholders may not care much about nonfinancial "returns"; and its employees may be more worried about wage increases than about cutting back on the company's environmental pollution.

Just as *stockholders* must recognize a moral proviso in the context of the fiduciary demands they may place on corporate management, so too other *stakeholders* must recognize moral provisos. As we shall see presently, this proposition is central to the need for a Tripartite Model of corporate responsibility.

Stakeholder thinking is the thinking of a corporate actor that is embedded in a network of transactions with parties whose conceptions of their own goods, their own interests, and their own rights may or may not survive scrutiny from a more objective point of view. Moreover, the framing of *this* set of stakeholders at *this* time with *this* set of civic constraints may not permit us to advance the public good or social justice in the community. Let us consider three examples to help clarify these observations.

Illustrations

The proposition I am defending here is that corporate responsibility calls for a stakeholder perspective, but that it *also* calls for a shift to a more comprehensive perspective. Corporate responsibility asks of business leaders *more* than simply maximal stakeholder satisfaction. Consider the following examples.

First, certain cigarette companies pay regular attention to their stakeholders. British American Tobacco (BAT), for example, emphasizes this in its "Core Beliefs":

> We believe in creating long term shareholder value.
> We believe in engaging constructively with our stakeholders.
> We believe in creating inspiring working environments for our people.
> We believe in adding value to the communities in which we operate.
> We believe that suppliers and other business partners should have the
> opportunity to benefit from their relationship with us.[41]

The company implements its beliefs and verifies its stakeholder effectiveness using focus group feedback. It also is generous in the philanthropic domain. Yet a more comprehensive (less "embedded") consideration of public health and the common good would probably call for *diversification away from tobacco products entirely.* Such a diversification would adhere to the legitimate concerns of stockholders while respecting the moral proviso associated with their investments. And it is worth noting that such a corporate reorientation might be achieved by responsible choice rather than legal force (making tobacco products illegal). Wholesale "prohibition" of controlled substances in its many forms is often ineffective anyway, as Americans know from Prohibition. If BAT wishes to use phrases like "long term shareholder *value*" and "adding *value* to communities" in their most robust sense, want-satisfaction as measured by focus groups and surveys may need to survive more demanding scrutiny from a comprehensive moral perspective.

A decision to transform a corporation's product line to avoid contributing to life-threatening disease (lung cancer) is *different* from a decision to comply with statutes and regulations and court orders, even if some of the consequences may overlap. And while it may seem to be a decision that goes *against the will of the company's cigarette consumers* (as stakeholders), in the final analysis it is likely to be a decision for the good of all.

Judge Gladys Kessler in a U.S. federal court ruled against a tobacco company in early August 2006. She found that for forty years U.S. cigarette companies had "marketed and sold their lethal product with zeal, with deception, with a single-minded focus on their financial success and without regard for the human tragedy or social costs that success exacted."[42] But is it possible that during those forty years, such a company might *not* have been single-minded? That is, could such a company have actually done "embedded" stakeholder thinking along the lines of British American Tobacco above—considering the conventional list of loyal customers, employees, suppliers, government regulators, state and federal tax authorities, local communities, and (of course) shareholders—measured in conventional ways?[43] If so, then what might be missing from the corporate responsibility equation? Perhaps the tripartite model offers the clearest explanation.

Second, certain producers of interactive video games appear to market them uncritically to adolescents even though there is some evidence that such games are addictive and that explicit sex and violence in these games actually does influence behavior.

More to the point, might "stakeholder thinking" fail to lead companies in this industry to an appropriate level of social awareness? A 2006 statute in Minnesota aimed at protecting game players younger than seventeen was recently struck down by a U.S. federal judge as unconstitutional: "Backers [of the statute] pointed to games such as 'God of War,' in which players gouge out eyes, sever limbs and make human sacrifices, and 'Manhunt,' in which a serial killer uses a nail gun and chain saw to slay victims."[44] The video game industry argued that the law "violated constitutional rights of game makers and customers." After it was struck down, the legislator who sponsored the law commented:

> The judge's conclusion that the current body of research didn't show violent video games harm children and teens defies logic. "You score points for how many women you rape, how many cops you kill," Pappas said. "How could that not affect them psychologically?"[45]

As in the example of cigarette companies, it is possible that video game producers have actually done "embedded" stakeholder thinking—considering talented employees, suppliers, market competition, legal compliance, rights of free speech, and consumer desires. The question is whether another kind of thinking may be called for.

One must grant, in this context, that evidence of causal linkage between video game products and negative psychological or behavioral effects is contested, and that significant research must be done to answer the central question. It is enough for our present purpose to note that embedded stakeholder thinking might not provide a sufficient impetus for a corporation to support or to participate in such research.

Third, the growth of the pharmaceutical industry has surely been a societal good, developing cures for many diseases throughout the world. But the social side effects of marketing pharmaceuticals with great intensity can result in drugs, effective against rare diseases, not being developed by pharmaceutical companies because they do not provide a sufficient economic payback to the company.[46] Pharmaceutical advertising may also foster a culture of overmedication when we might be better served by habits of healthier living (e.g., proper nutrition and regular exercise). What I have been calling the more comprehensive perspective on corporate responsibility is more apt than the embedded stakeholder perspective to explore these issues and to do research needed to respond to them reliably out of a concern for the common good.[47]

These examples have in common an appeal for a *comprehensive* social awareness on the part of corporate leadership that steps outside of embedded stakeholder frameworks, laws, and market forces to discern whether (or not) the identified decision-making patterns are damaging to the *community* even when the community cannot reasonably be construed as a stakeholder. If they are, then stakeholder thinking needs to be balanced by the larger perspective—as a check on the embeddedness of the status quo.

Reflections about the larger social implications of corporate decision making are typically *not* framed in stakeholder terms. I have in mind here reflections regarding the family, the moral and spiritual development of children, public health, civic virtue, and the natural environment. This is mostly because they involve stepping "outside of the box" and turning a critical eye toward the influence of business behavior on *the system as a whole*.[48]

Philosophers will appreciate that these reflections are reminiscent of the "Open Question Argument" used a century ago by G. E. Moore in his classic treatise, *Principia Ethica* (1903). Moore could say today: Yes, this business practice is warranted by the market, but is it good? Or yes, this corporate policy is permitted by the law, but is it right? And in the present context: "*This proposed strategy satisfies key stakeholders, but is this all there is to corporate responsibility?*"

As with individuals, the responsibility of corporations involves a kind of partiality or subjectivity, *even* when they appreciate the importance of stakeholders (beyond profitability for stockholders and beyond legal compliance). And like individual responsibility, corporate responsibility must seek more objective validation lest it become unduly committed to stakeholder demands that are not, in fact, sustainable from a more comprehensive perspective.

Adjustments to the social system itself may need to be made to avoid tragic trends emerging from stakeholder thinking by corporations operating autonomously. Such adjustments may come in the form of interventions by the public sector, but they may not. Other influences on corporate decision making over many decades have also proved to be effective, such as appeals by NGOs, education, boycotts, industry associations, social investment screens, community-sponsored ethics awards, and the like.[49] The most challenging question, however, is, Can we expect adjustments to come in the form of *company* initiatives—*and in the name of corporate responsibility*? This question leads us to the third part of the argument.

Toward Comprehensiveness

In 1991, John Paul II, reflecting on the fall of Soviet Communism and addressing not only Catholics but all persons of good will, wrote: "Of itself, an economic system does not possess criteria for correctly distinguishing new and higher forms of satisfying human needs from artificial new needs which hinder the formation of a mature personality."[50] He insisted that even a regulated and stakeholder-driven economic system depends profoundly on a "comprehensive picture of man" and of the human community that guides its business leaders and corporate practitioners.

One must look at the system *as a whole* to fully appreciate its effects on human persons. And just as democracy—as a political system—can be dysfunctional if the voters are poorly educated or poorly informed, so too the economic system can become dysfunctional despite the best intentions of its decision makers and their stakeholders. The practical imperative, according to John Paul II, was a fresh understanding of "responsibility" in a capitalistic economy—on the part of consumers, corporations, the media, and the public sector:

> Thus a great deal of educational and cultural work is urgently needed, including the education of consumers in the responsible use of their power of choice, the formation of a strong sense of responsibility among producers and among people in the mass media in particular, as well as the necessary intervention by public authorities.[51]

I have been arguing that stakeholder thinking is necessary but not *sufficient* because it must be attentive to a more "comprehensive picture" (see figure 5.3, "The Tripartite Model"). As I introduced the notion of comprehensive moral thinking, I said that it needed to be anchored in the moral point of view and added that a distinction was needed between *categorical* responsibility and *qualified* (or *conditional*) corporate responsibility for securing certain core values like human dignity and a just community. Let us clarify these ideas both conceptually and managerially.

Responsibility beyond Stakeholders: Human Dignity and a Just Community

If Royce reminded us that a self-centered perspective is insufficient—indeed, illusory—and that we must also respect ("realize") our neighbors (stakeholders), Nagel reminded us that an (embedded) stakeholder perspective is also insufficient, and that responsibility in its fullest sense calls for a more embracing point of view.

One way to interpret Nagel's idea of an "impartial perspective" (or what he sometimes called an "agent-neutral" perspective) is to think of it as aiming dispassionately at satisfying the interests of all affected parties (or as many as possible). But this is not the only interpretation of an "agent-neutral" perspective. Agent-neutrality *could* be a perspective that is not solely trained on interest groups. It could be a perspective anchored in overarching values that emerge directly from the moral point of view. Two of these values would be human dignity and the ideal of a just community. Of course, such values would need to be carefully developed to perform their function as critical guides in relation to embedded stakeholder thinking. The purpose of this essay is not to develop and articulate these values but *to identify the need for them* in a robust model of corporate responsibility.

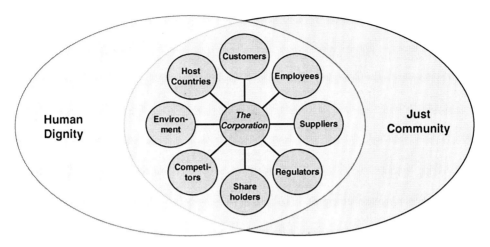

Figure 5.4. Comprehensive Moral Thinking

As to *why* there should be a *second* (agent-neutral) perspective rather than just a single (agent-centered) one—a fact that causes consternation for Nagel—I believe that each represents a normative implication of Royce's moral insight: (1) the *dignity* of the human person or subject, and (2) the importance of a *just community* (the common good combined with social justice).[52] The dignity of the person creates an agent-centered zone of respect around each of us that we sometimes call autonomy or freedom of conscience. But the principle of a just community reminds us that the zone of respect must be extended—and ultimately made consistent with *both* freedom of conscience *and* the good of all.[53]

My experience with business leaders suggests that human dignity and just community are central to their moral intuitions. For fifteen years, I have worked actively with an executive group called the Caux Round Table (CRT).[54] The CRT *Principles for Business* (available in over a dozen languages) have influenced corporate leaders around the world. And because the members of this group come from Asia, Europe, and North America, their agreement on these principles supports an initial characterization of them as transcultural.

Even though the Caux executives had never heard of Nagel's claim about the duality of perspective at the heart of ethics, it was clearly in evidence in the discussions that ended up framing the CRT *Principles*. Those discussions identified two fundamental ethical values: (1) the dignity of the human person, and (2) the Japanese concept of *kyosei*. The first insists on valuing each human being as an end, implying that an individual's worth can never be reduced to his or her utility as a means to someone else's purpose. The value of *kyosei* was defined by Ryuzaburo Kaku, the late chairman of Canon, Inc., as "living and working together for the good of all." *Kyosei* tempers individual, organizational, and even national self-interest by emphasizing the common good and justice.[55] Figure 5.4 depicts the way in which these two values can be seen as providing a normative backdrop for corporate responsibility, reminding us that embedded stakeholder thinking is not sufficient—that it calls for a more comprehensive perspective.

While systematic research would be required to support the suggestion of a transcultural consensus among business practitioners, there is reason to suppose that the two values of human dignity and a just community are widely recognized as fundamental. And to call them fundamental is to say that they provide a context within which stakeholder-based decision making can be both conducted and critiqued.

Comprehensive Moral Thinking in Action: Cases in Point

It will be helpful to have before us some concrete examples of business organizations whose stakeholder thinking seemed to call for something more comprehensive.

During 1983 and 1984, Velsicol Chemical Corporation, a Chicago-based producer of agricultural chemicals, attempted to initiate industry reform in the export of hazardous chemicals by proposing a "One World Communication System" for pesticide labeling. The idea was to create an industry-wide system of pictograms to convey information on the safe use of pesticides—especially for agricultural workers in developing countries who were often illiterate or could not understand the precautionary information on conventional labels. Sales of Velsicol's products (to farmers, of course, not to their field workers) were strong, employees were enthusiastic, and suppliers and local communities were quite satisfied with the company's success. Stock values, as a result, were up. Conventional stakeholder thinking suggested responsibility—but a comprehensive view seemed to call for more. The transfer of these chemicals to developing countries was blind to hidden casualties—and solutions to this problem would require both industry (private sector) and government (public sector) cooperation. Each had some responsibility for the problem.

The social values of Velsicol, however, were not congruent with those of the dominant players in its industry. Enthusiasm at the National Agricultural Chemical Association (NACA) for Velsicol's pictogram initiative was not sufficient to move the idea forward, with the result that the CEO decided on economic grounds that Velsicol could not—unilaterally—continue the project.[56] The moral aspiration of fewer lives lost to the misuse of dangerous pesticides—surely a reflection of concern for human dignity and a just global community—was not realized because the coordination of corporate efforts was not achieved. Several executives at Velsicol, disheartened at this outcome, left the company.

Corporate *lobbying*, in relation to industry associations or governmental entities (state or federal), is another way of trying to find value congruence between organizations and their social environments. To be sure, lobbying has a mixed reputation because it is often thought to be simply a self-serving activity on the part of an industry or even a single corporation. But viewed more dispassionately, lobbying can be a form of mutual accommodation between organizations and their societies, sometimes leading to good for *both*. Perhaps we do not pay sufficient attention to the idea of "lobbying in the public interest" as a corporation's way to eliminate competitive dilemmas that undermine human dignity and a just community, for example, in the context of mileage or emissions regulations for automobiles and safety regulations for consumer goods.

The Velsicol case, of course, is an example of a company's *lack of success* in influencing its industry association. It illustrates the distinction between a company's *categorical* responsibility and its *qualified* (or *conditional*) responsibility for securing comprehensive solutions. Comprehensive moral thinking—thinking outside the conventional stakeholder "box"—often calls in its implementation for collaborative efforts on the part of responsible corporations. But because there can be competitive dilemmas involved in breaking ranks within an industry, there may be a need for business-government or business-NGO cooperation to address problems effectively. Child labor practices by U.S. and European manufacturers who outsource from developing countries illustrate how competitive dilemmas can prevent progress. In such circumstances, NGOs and governments can be effective catalysts.

The key point to be emphasized is that even if a company does not have a *categorical* responsibility, a responsibility to resolve the moral challenge *on its own*, it can still have a *qualified* responsibility to make an effort—or to *participate* in the efforts of others in seeking a collaborative resolution. If, as in the Velsicol case, such a qualified responsibility was exercised unsuccessfully, then perhaps no further responsibility remains. "Ought categorically" implies "can"—but "ought conditionally" simply implies "can try."

Criteria for discharging qualified responsibilities can be complex. How would Velsicol—or any company—know whether it had *continuing* responsibilities after an unsuccessful effort to modify an economic playing field based on comprehensive moral thinking? Certainly cost considerations will play a significant *limiting* role, but factors like employee morale, consumer loyalty, new legislation, and even socially responsible investor (SRI) initiatives might *extend* qualified responsibilities. The significance of a given threat to human dignity or justice in the community might raise our reasonable expectations of a corporation's responsibility, even if we acknowledge that, in the end, we are dealing with a *qualified* responsibility.

There are many cases of *effective* industry collaboration in the public interest. One recent example is the voluntary *Code of Ethics on Interactions with Health Care Professionals* adopted by the Advanced Medical Technology Association ("AdvaMed") in January 2004. Sometimes industry associations can be vehicles for the private sector to reduce competitive behavior that is corrosive in relation to society's needs or expectations. In this case, those needs and expectations had to do with the proper delivery of health care.

Medical device manufacturers had for decades experienced competitive pressure in connection with business practices aimed at attracting and retaining physician loyalty to their branded products. The incremental escalation (one-upsmanship) in this arena led to questionable behavior (e.g., travel inducements and perks for physicians and their spouses) that was neither good for patients nor in the interests of industry competitors generally. Nevertheless, stakeholder reasoning for decades had failed to change corporate decision making. Patients were not the immediate customers—physicians and hospitals were. Employees and stockholders had few complaints.

The situation called for *comprehensive moral thinking*, and Medtronic, Inc., under the leadership of CEO Art Collins, guided the development and adoption of the AdvaMed Code of Ethics, the *Preamble* of which reads as follows:

> [AdvaMed] is dedicated to the advancement of medical science, the improvement of patient care, and in particular to the contribution that high quality, cost-effective health care technology can make toward achieving those goals. In pursuing this mission, AdvaMed members ("Members") recognize that adherence to ethical standards and compliance with applicable laws are critical to the medical device industry's ability to continue its collaboration with health care professionals. Members encourage ethical business practices and socially responsible industry conduct related to their interactions with health care professionals. Members also respect the obligation of health care professionals to make independent decisions regarding Member products. Consequently, AdvaMed adopts this voluntary Code of Ethics, effective January 1, 2004, to facilitate Members' ethical interactions with those individuals or entities that purchase, lease, recommend, use, arrange for the purchase or lease of, or prescribe Members' medical technology products in the United States ("Health Care Professionals").[57]

The AdvaMed Code that follows this preamble sets strict guidelines for member behavior, prohibiting practices that led to excesses in spending on "hospitality," meals, travel, and lodging for physicians' educational seminars. Also, it includes rules about consulting agreements, gifts, and reimbursements. The AdvaMed Code, by most accounts effective in its implementation, is only one example of industry self-regulation aimed at fulfilling society's ethical expectations of corporate behavior *when marketplace pressures were taking companies in dysfunctional directions.* Recalling the words of John Paul II, such problems often require "the formation of a strong sense of responsibility among producers" or the consequence will be a "necessary intervention by public authorities."

There are clear analogues in the pharmaceutical industry of problematic behaviors (from promotional practices aimed at physicians to direct-to-consumer advertising) that would lend themselves to the kind of comprehensive moral thinking that we see in the AdvaMed narrative. The effectiveness of such initiatives will vary, to be sure, depending on the authenticity of the efforts and the consequences of noncompliance. Nevertheless, these examples illustrate the value of the Tripartite Model of corporate responsibility and they clarify the practical meaning of *comprehensive moral thinking.*

Between 2000 and 2007, a number of large retail banks, including Bank of America, Wells Fargo, and US Bancorp began to compete with money-transfer organizations like Western Union and MoneyGram for the business of Hispanic immigrants who wished to send money "back home" in the form of remittances.[58] A question was raised, in the wake of the 9/11 tragedy, as to whether these financial institutions should require documentation from account applicants that would establish their legal residence in the United States. The U.S. Treasury Department permitted banks to accept the *matricula consular* card issued by immigrants' home countries, but this form of identification did not attest to a person's legal presence in the United States.[59] Most banks decided to accept the *matricula* card, insisting that it was not their responsibility to do the job of Immigration and Customs Enforcement (ICE), despite protests from those who saw this practice as "aiding and abetting" illegal immigration. Stakeholders included customers, stockholders, employees, local communities, and families in home countries (the recipients of remittances). But stakeholder thinking alone seems insufficient to address the question of the private sector's responsibility for social goods like the rule of law.

It is possible that the value of human dignity and the value of a just community are in tension on this issue, but it seems wholly unsatisfactory for the financial services industry to ignore the possible social implications of their policies and practices because they are not ICE. Individual banks (indeed, the financial services industry as a whole) may not be subject to *categorical* responsibilities for immigration enforcement in this arena, but it is certainly a reasonable proposition for debate whether they are subject to *qualified* or *conditional* responsibilities.

Preventing illegal immigration may not be the *categorical* task of banks, insurance companies, automobile license bureaus, providers of housing, or even employers. But do we really wish to leave questions about human dignity and immigration fairness exclusively in the hands of law enforcement? Charles Handy's counterpoint is salutary: "Business needs to take the lead in areas such as environmental and social sustainability instead of forever letting itself be pushed onto the defensive."[60]

If a "just community" is not seen as a responsibility by most or any of its individual and institutional members, then whose responsibility is it? Recall Peter Drucker's question earlier in this essay: "In the society of organizations, each…is concerned only with its own purpose and mission. It does not claim power over anything else. *But it also does not assume responsibility for anything else.* Who, then, is concerned with the common good?"[61] The answer, surely, is that in at least a *qualified* sense, each of us is responsible—individuals and corporations alike.

Philip Selznick (quoted earlier) reminds us of the stakes when corporations embrace responsibility in the robust way described here:

> From the standpoint of social systems rather than persons, organizations become infused with value as they come to symbolize the community's aspirations, its sense of identity. Some organizations perform this function more readily and fully than others. An organization that does take on this symbolic meaning has some claim on the community to avoid liquidation or transformation on purely technical or economic grounds.[62]

In 1987, Dayton Hudson Corporation (DHC), headquartered in Minneapolis, Minnesota, was a hostile takeover target by a company whose record of social and community involvement was considerably less impressive than that of the legendary DHC (today, Target Corporation).[63] The Minnesota legislature responded with a public statute that had the effect of slowing the takeover process by raising the hurdle for purely financially motivated takeover attempts. Eventually, Dayton Hudson succeeded in defeating the takeover attempt. One interpretation of this result was that the company had, in Selznick's words "some claim on the community to avoid liquidation or transformation on purely technical or economic grounds."

The fate of Arthur Andersen & Co may illustrate the other side of the coin. In this case we saw a company pursue stockholder and embedded stakeholder thinking as it sought to satisfy the interests of key affected parties. Sadly, the company failed to look comprehensively at the incentive structure driving its relationships with Enron and other large clients, an incentive structure in which consulting revenue dwarfed auditing revenue, creating a powerful motive to maintain large consulting clients even at the cost of unethical behavior. Andersen's conviction on the charge of obstruction of justice in June of 2002 led to the company's dissolution.[64] The prosecution portrayed the partnership as a repeat offender that destroyed records to shield itself from potential regulatory punishment. The contrast between the Dayton Hudson and Arthur Andersen cases is, in Selznick's terms, that unlike Dayton Hudson, Andersen renounced its "claim on the community to avoid liquidation."

In many ways, an entire industry was convicted for not performing its social function as a "gatekeeper" to protect investors.[65] The passage of the Sarbanes-Oxley Act in the United States represented a form of "comprehensive moral thinking" *after* the corporate scandals of 2001–2002. Perhaps the institutions surrounding business will do this kind of thinking on their own if corporate responsibility defaults.

SUMMARY AND CONCLUSION

It seems clear that *comprehensive moral thinking* by corporations, in addition to stockholder thinking (fiduciary responsibility) and broader (but embedded) stakeholder thinking, is essential. But some companies *embrace* this responsibility while others do not.

I have puzzled in this paper over the necessity and the sufficiency of stakeholder thinking as an account of corporate responsibility. In exploring these questions with the help of some reflections on personal conscience, I have argued that the tripartite model of corporate responsibility offers a more promising approach than the conventional dualistic model. The grammar of stakeholders can be liberating, to be sure; however, it can also *blind* corporations by preforming their ethical awareness, actually *inhibiting* moral imagination.

Corporate responsibility can be seen in terms of relationships to various specific stakeholders, and the morality of those relationships is certainly an important part of business ethics. But there is another dimension to corporate responsibility. There is a whole greater than the sum of the parts (stakeholders) that does not show up in conventional stakeholder analysis. Without attention to the whole, corporate leaders are in danger of missing their moral responsibilities for *collective* action—action as a part of a just human community, when they see the direction of the system itself tilting in a tragic way. In the words of Marvin Brown,

> The conversations between corporations and government agencies can develop new possibilities for the enhancement of human flourishing in civic life. Corporations cannot facilitate the flourishing *by themselves*. They need public corporations and government agencies, just as public corporations and government agencies need them. For these conversations to have integrity, each participant needs to cooperate with the other, guided by the mission of the city and the dynamics of civic life.[66]

Stakeholder thinking is an important advance upon the narrow construction of corporate responsibility that limits it to providers of capital (stockholders or owners). Providers of capital must acknowledge that their claims are conditioned by a moral proviso. But while attending to their relationships with multiple interested parties, corporations can overlook the challenges of *participation* in a wider community. Stakeholders too must acknowledge moral provisos relating to their claims on management.

The "tripartite model" discussed in this essay sees the constituents of corporate responsibility as three imperatives for guiding decision making. First, there is the imperative of fiduciary awareness—to manage the organization with special accountability to the providers of capital. Second, there is the imperative of stakeholder awareness—to manage the organization with accountability toward all of its key stakeholders. Third, there is the imperative of comprehensive moral awareness—to manage the organization with attention to its qualified or conditional responsibilities to advance human dignity and a just community. The third constituent of the model means joining with others to build a city (or a state or a nation or a global community) that none can build separately—a city that is good.

NOTES

1. See Kenneth Goodpaster, "Business Ethics," in the *Encyclopedia of Ethics*, ed. Lawrence C. Becker and Charlotte B. Becker (New York: Garland, 1997), 170–175. The article adds:

> If the focus is the organization, for example, a background assumption is that the values of the organization are not a simple or straightforward function of either the values of the surrounding system or the values of the individuals in the organization. If the values of the organization were completely determined by either the individuals in it or the social system surrounding it (or both), then one would have to apply one's ethical prescriptions to them, and not to the organization. Positing multiple levels of analysis to the field of business ethics, therefore, carries a presumption (one that can, of course, be debated) that the levels are

prima facie distinct and do not collapse into one another, even if there are significant causal relationships among them.

2. For a discussion of obligations toward corporations, see Jerry D. Goodstein and Andrew C. Wicks, "Corporate and Stakeholder Responsibility: Making Business Ethics a Two-Way Conversation," *Business Ethics Quarterly*, 17 (3) (2007): 375–398.

3. Typically these parties include—in addition to owner/investors—employees, customers, suppliers, competitors, local communities, and "the environment." See the new anthology *Stakeholder Theory*, ed. Abe J. Zakhem, Daniel E. Palmer, and Mary Lyn Stoll (New York: Prometheus, 2007) for a representative sampling of the literature. The work of Edward Freeman is particularly important in this connection. See for example R. Freeman, K. Martin, and B. Parmar, "Stakeholder Capitalism," *Journal of Business Ethics*, 74 (4) (2007): 303–314. Also see the work of Thomas Donaldson, Thomas Dunfee, and Lynn Paine, each of whom has clarified and elaborated stakeholder-based accounts of corporate responsibility (see "Suggested Reading" below).

4. Throughout this essay, I will use the terms "stockholder" and "shareholder" interchange-ably—which is also the case in the quoted literature on the subject of corporate responsibility.

5. Peter Drucker, "The Age of Social Transformation," *The Atlantic Monthly*, November 1994, 53–80.

6. Philip Selznick, *Leadership in Administration: A Sociological Interpretation* (New York: Harper & Row, 1957), 141.

7. Formally, it can be stated as follows: "It is appropriate not only to *describe* organizations and their characteristics by analogy with individuals, it is also appropriate *normatively* to look for and to *foster* moral attributes in organizations by analogy with those we look for and foster in individuals." See "moral projection, principle of" in *Blackwell's Encyclopedic Dictionary of Business Ethics*, ed. Werhane and Freeman, (Oxford: Blackwell, 1997), 432. Also see Kenneth Goodpaster, *Conscience and Corporate Culture* (Oxford: Blackwell, 2007), chap. 1 and 2.

8. Josiah Royce, *The Religious Aspect of Philosophy*, (1865) reprinted (Gloucester, Mass.: Peter Smith, 1965), 155–156.

9. In the case of private or closely held firms, the analogue might be preoccupation by management with the interests of the controlling group or family.

10. John R. Boatright, "What's Wrong—and What's Right—with Stakeholder Management?" *Journal of Private Enterprise* (Spring 2006): 106–130.

11. See Lynn Paine, *Value Shift* (New York: McGraw-Hill, 2003).

12. See Kenneth Goodpaster, "Business Ethics and Stakeholder Analysis," *Business Ethics Quarterly* 1 (January 1991): 52–71. Also see Goodpaster, *Conscience and Corporate Culture*, chap. 4.

13. Boatright, "What's Wrong," 119–120.

14. Milton Friedman, "The Social Responsibility of Business Is to Increase Its Profits," *New York Times Magazine*, 1970.

15. Royce might call this "the realization of one's stakeholders."

16. Philosophers will recognize in this arena echoes of the familiar distinction between "act-based" and "rule-based" theories of obligation. If one has a moral criterion (such as utility), does it get applied to the system as a whole or does each decision maker apply the criterion to the action alternatives that present themselves whatever other decision makers might do?

17. Jeffrey Garten, *The Politics of Fortune* (Boston: Harvard Business School Press, 2002), 139. Conservatives would applaud the language of *The Economist* (January 20, 2005): "The proper business of business is business. No apology required."

18. Note that stakeholder thinking might be orchestrated in different ways, but whatever the orchestration, it involves an analysis of impacts on specific groups within the context of an assumed economic and political system. In other words, stakeholder thinking functions alongside the decision making that corporations already do in other (nonethical) arenas. This point is revisited later in this essay.

19. Boatright, "What's Wrong," 127 (emphasis mine). Says Boatright earlier in his article, "Just as we all have a responsibility to make sure that markets work as they should to produce a benefit for all, so too do we all, including managers, have a responsibility for ensuring the proper functioning of firms" (124–25). Other examples of the stockholder primacy view include Ian Maitland, "Distributive Justice in Firms: Do the Rules of Corporate Governance Matter?" *Business Ethics Quarterly* 11(1) (2001):129–143, and Alexei Marcoux, "A Fiduciary Argument against Stakeholder Theory," *Business Ethics Quarterly* 9 (2) (1999): 207–223.

20. Kenneth Goodpaster, "Stakeholder Analysis," in *The Encyclopedia of Ethics*, rev. and exp. ed., vol. 3, ed. Lawrence C. Becker and Charlotte B. Becker (New York: Garland, 2001), 1645–1649.

21. *Random House Webster's Unabridged Dictionary*, first definition.

22. "Equity capital is money provided to a firm in return for a claim on profits— or, more precisely, for a claim on residual revenues, which are the revenues that remain after all debts and other legal obligations are paid. Just as customers buy a company's products, equity capital providers "buy" the future profits of a firm; or alternatively, in order to raise capital, a company "sells" its future profits to investors. In addition, since future profits are risky, investors not only provide capital but also assume much of the risk of a firm" (Boatright, "What's Wrong," 10).

23. http://www.girardgibbs.com/medtronic-press-release.asp (accessed December 2007).

24. Charles Handy, "What's a Business For?" *Harvard Business Review*, December 2002: 49–55. Also see Lynn Paine's book *Value Shift* for a discussion of this paradigm change.

25. Handy adds: "We need to eat to live; food is a necessary condition of life. But if we lived mainly to eat, making food a sufficient or sole purpose of life, we would become gross." Later in the same article, he adds: "This is a moral issue…. To mistake the means for the end is to be turned in on oneself, which Saint Augustine called one of the greatest sins."

26. Boatright puts it this way: "Everyone can benefit from the productive activity of a firm only if there is a vision for creating a valuable product or service as well as a strategy for achieving this vision" (126).

27. Thomas Nagel, "Subjective and Objective," in his *Mortal Questions* (Cambridge University Press, 1979), 205.

28. In other contexts, the word "ideology" is used with a similar connotation: "a body of doctrine or belief that guides an individual, social movement, institution, class, or large group…along with the devices for putting it into operation." (*Random House Webster's Unabridged Dictionary*). And in some ways, what we call the "culture" of a social group has a similar function.

29. Originally, according to the *Oxford English Dictionary*, "conscience" was understood as a common quality in which individuals *shared*: "a man or a people had more or less conscience," as persons or groups had more or less science, knowledge, intelligence, prudence, and the like. Eventually, the word came to be used as an individual faculty or attribute, so that "*my conscience*" and "*your conscience*" were understood no longer as "our respective shares or amounts of the common quality *conscience*," but as "two distinct individual consciences,

mine and yours." Perhaps this etymology lies behind the conceptual tension that Nagel finds so challenging: conscience as a *social* asset and conscience as a *private* faculty.

30. Thomas Nagel, *The View from Nowhere* (New York: Oxford University Press, 1986), 185, emphasis added. Nagel goes on: "When we ask ourselves how to live, the complexity of what we are makes a unified answer difficult. I believe the human duality of perspectives is too deep for us reasonably to hope to overcome it. A fully agent-neutral morality is not a plausible human goal."

31. A friend of mine once "reminded" me (when, frankly, I needed it) that: "You're *special*, but you're *no damn different!*" Painful as it was for me to hear such a message, it expressed the very essence of Nagel's account of the moral point of view. See Goodpaster, *Conscience and Corporate Culture*, chap. 3.

32. "The test of a first-rate intelligence is the ability to hold two opposed ideas in the mind at the same time, and still retain the ability to function." Quoted in Mark Sagoff, "Can Environmentalists Keep Two Ideas in Mind and Still Function?" *Philosophy & Public Policy Quarterly* (Winter/Spring 2007): 2–7.

33. See the entry under "chariot allegory" in *Wikipedia*, http://en.wikipedia.org/wiki/Chariot_Allegory.

34. Some argue, for example that a Creator has "written in our hearts" a natural law that, if accessed by reflection, unites the external with the internal, the impartial with the partial, the detached with the embedded. See my paper "Stakeholders and the Common Good" in *Business, Globalization and the Common Good*, ed. H-C DeBettignies and François Lépineux (London: Peter Lang, 2009).

35. Robert Phillips, R. E. Freeman, and Andrew C. Wicks, "What Stakeholder Theory Is Not," *Business Ethics Quarterly* 13 (4) (2003): 479–502.

36. For example, are these stakeholders affected strictly in economic terms, or are the effects psychological or spiritual—involving rights or levels of well-being more significant than, say, material disappointment?

37. For example, in corporate healthcare decisions about stem cell research, are human embryos counted as stakeholders?

38. For example, it may be that members of a stakeholder group (employees) would be obliged to take a pay cut for the good of the corporation as a whole, or to avoid layoffs as a more drastic cost-saving measure.

39. See "Alco Beverage Company and Moderation Advertising," *Harvard Business School Case Services*, 9-387-070 (1987). Reprinted in *Policies and Persons: A Casebook in Business Ethics*, 3rd ed., ed. Goodpaster and Nash (New York: McGraw-Hill, 1998).

40. Garten, *The Politics of Fortune*, 11.

41. See the British and American Tobacco company Web site, http://www.bat.com/oneweb/framework.nsf/F/MB1?opendocument.

42. As quoted in *Ethics Newsline* by Rush Kidder, August 28, 2006. Kidder goes on to describe those who are cynical about the judge's decision and about critics who would urge investors not to buy tobacco stocks: "Investors, they argue, have a perfect legal right to invest in tobacco. That's true. But the beauty of this case is that it so clearly exemplifies the difference between what's legal and what's ethical. Can we as a nation tolerate a disconnect between ethics and law so deep that 'adjudicated racketeers' not only are free to continue racketeering, but are encouraged to do so by investors excitedly bidding up their shares?" One wonders whether a similar point might be made about other stakeholders besides investors. If so, the insufficiency of stakeholder thinking begins to reveal itself.

43. And even if one lists various NGOs and health advocacy groups among the (secondary, if not primary) stakeholders of a tobacco company, it seems possible, indeed

likely, that these stakeholder interests, when aggregated with the interests of shareholders, customers, employees, suppliers, and others would not carry the day.

44. Shannon Prather, "US Judge Throws Out Minnesota Video Game Law," *Pioneer Press* (August 1, 2006), A1. "Attorney General Mike Hatch said he will consider appealing the ruling. 'There are psychologists who believe the reward mechanism of more points, more games and higher levels of play in video games condition children to be rewarded by reenacting violence in the real world,' Hatch said."

45. Shannon Prather, "US Judge Throws Out Minnesota Video Game Law," *Pioneer Press* (August 1, 2006), A1.

46. The *Orphan Drug Act of 1983* in the United States and similar legislation in the European Union are examples of the kind of cross-sector collaboration between business and government that can provide a social remedy to the problem. See the entry under "orphan drug" in *Wikipedia*, http://en.wikipedia.org/wiki/Orphan_drug.

47. I refer here *not* to what might be called "micro" side effects—since those will presumably be noticed as part of stakeholder thinking in connection with the FDA and consumer product safety. The "macro" side effects on society as a whole seem to call for a different logic than the conventional stakeholder approach.

48. Kant invoked ideas like a "kingdom or community of ends" and "universalizability" in relation to objective ("categorical") moral imperatives, and Rousseau invoked "the General Will." Today the concept of "sustainability" is used by those who seek to remind us of a "macro" point of view. These ideas recall the comprehensive perspective to which Nagel refers, no longer compartmentalizing affected parties or politically segmenting the moral community. This also appears to be Marvin Brown's advice when he insists that corporations "need to care about the integrity of civil society." See his book *Corporate Integrity* (Cambridge: Cambridge University Press, 2005), 155. Brown's "principle of civic cooperation" is straightforward and applicable whether the community in question be a city, a nation, or humankind itself: "Business corporations have an obligation not to prevent and sometimes to promote the mission of the city."

49. On this point, we might return to the video game topic and the article by Shannon Prather, "US Judge Throws Out Minnesota Video Game Law": "David Walsh, president of the Minneapolis-based National Institute on Media and the Family...said education and public pressure is ultimately how parents will force change. 'While we might be tempted to wish for a legislative solution, the real solution has to be education, which is what we've been advocating for years,' Walsh said. 'Parents need to be media wise and watch what our kids watch. We can't always look to law to solve this problem.'"

50. *Centesimus Annus*, 36 (1991). John Paul II continues: "In singling out new needs and new means to meet them, one must be guided by *a comprehensive picture of man* which respects all the dimensions of his being and which subordinates his material and instinctive dimensions to his interior and spiritual ones."

51. Ibid.

52. William Frankena, in his famous primer on ethics, argued persuasively that normative ethics needed to rest upon two principles (beneficence and justice). See William K. Frankena, *Ethics*, 2nd ed. (Englewood Cliffs, N.J.: Prentice-Hall, 1988). In articulating these basic principles, Frankena echoes earlier moral philosophers like W. D. Ross and has been acknowledged by numerous philosophers and practitioners since.

53. Philosopher Richard M. Hare, in the title of his classic *Freedom and Reason* (New York: Oxford University Press, 1960), emphasized the centrality of autonomy or freedom in normative ethics. At the same time, however, his title suggested a second central aspect of moral thinking (*reason*).

54. The Caux Round Table (CRT) *Principles for Business* originated in July 1994. The CRT, which had been founded in 1986 by a small group of Japanese, European, and U.S. executives, embraced the mission of promoting *principled business leadership*. Each year, this group gathered in the peaceful village of Caux-sur-Montreux, overlooking Lake Geneva. The *Principles for Business* were fashioned in part from a document that one of the U.S. members shared with the group—a document known as the *Minnesota Principles*, which came out of the *Minnesota Center for Corporate Responsibility* (MCCR) in 1992. Today the MCCR is known as the *Center for Ethical Business Cultures* (CEBC) and is formally affiliated with the University of St. Thomas. See http://www.cauxround-table.org.

55. See R. Kaku, "The Path of Kyosei," *Harvard Business Review* 75 (4) (1997): 55–63. In its July 2003 Global Dialogue in Switzerland, the CRT heard from three prominent representatives of Christianity, Judaism, and Islam about the strong fit between the CRT's foundational ideals and these faith traditions. In the words of one representative: "Both the individual and the collective must stand before the Lord, and *servant leadership* must minister to both. You—the Caux Round Table—are acting out of the two principles that undergird our Abrahamic faith traditions."

56. See Goodpaster, "Velsicol Chemical Corporation (A)," *HBS Case Services*, 9–385–021.

57. For the full text of the AdvaMed code, see http://www.advamed.org.

58. See Kenneth Goodpaster, "U.S. Citizen Bank: The Remittance Business (A) and (B)," University of St. Thomas (2006), available through McGraw-Hill *Primis* online database at http://www.primisonline.com/cgi-bin/POL_primisearch.cgi?srchtype=all&srch phr=goodpaster.

59. The U.S. Homeland Security Department and the FBI both *discouraged* the acceptance of the *matricula consular* as a valid form of identification for financial services.

60. Charles Handy, "What's a Business For?" 49–55.

61. Peter Drucker, "The Age of Social Transformation," *The Atlantic Monthly*, November 1994, 78 (emphasis mine).

62. Philip Selznick, *Leadership in Administration: A Sociological Interpretation* (New York: Harper & Row, 1957).

63. See "Dayton Hudson Corporation: Conscience and Control (A) (B) and (C)," in *Business Ethics: Policies and Persons*, 4th ed., ed. Kenneth Goodpaster, Laura Nash, and Henri-Claude de Bettignies, (New York: McGraw-Hill, 2006).

64. See the note "The Corporate Scandals of 2002 (B): Arthur Andersen" and "An Introduction to the Sarbanes-Oxley Act of 2002," written by T. Dean Maines under my supervision, Spring 2003, published in *Business Ethics: Policies and Persons*.

65. John C. Coffee, in his book *Gatekeepers: The Role of the Professions in Corporate Governance* (New York: Oxford University Press, 2006), looks at the institutional pressures that caused "gatekeepers" (like Arthur Andersen) to neglect their responsibilities, and he suggests changes that can restore gatekeepers as the loyal agents of investors.

66. Marvin Brown, *Corporate Integrity* (Cambridge: Cambridge University Press, 2005), 159 (emphasis mine). Peter Drucker expressed a similar sentiment when he wrote, "The emergence of a strong, independent, capable social sector—neither public sector nor private sector—is thus a central need of the society of organizations. But by itself it is not enough—*the organizations of both the public and the private sector must share in the work*." See "The Age of Social Transformation," *Atlantic Monthly*, November 1994, 53–80 (emphasis mine).

SUGGESTED READING

Boatright, John R. "What's Wrong—and What's Right—with Stakeholder Management?" *Journal of Private Enterprise* (Spring 2006): 106–129.

Bowie, Norman. *Business Ethics: A Kantian Perspective*. Hoboken, N.J.: John Wiley & Sons, 1998.

Coffee, John C. *Gatekeepers: The Role of the Professions in Corporate Governance*. New York: Oxford University Press, 2006.

Donaldson, Thomas, and Dunfee, Thomas. *Ties That Bind: A Social Contracts Approach to Business Ethics*. Cambridge, Mass.: Harvard Business School Press, 1999.

Drucker, Peter. "The Age of Social Transformation." *The Atlantic Monthly*, November 1994, 53–71.

Frankena, William K. *Ethics*, 2nd ed. Englewood Cliffs, N.J.: Prentice-Hall, 1988.

Freeman, R. Edward. *Strategic Management: A Stakeholder Approach*. London: Pitman, 1984.

Garten, Jeffrey. *The Politics of Fortune*. Boston: Harvard Business School Press, 2002.

Goodpaster, Kenneth. *Conscience and Corporate Culture*. Oxford: Blackwell, 2007.

Goodpaster, K. Nash, L. and de Bettignies, H-C., eds. *Business Ethics: Policies and Persons*. New York: McGraw-Hill, 2006.

Handy, Charles. "What's a Business For?" *Harvard Business Review* (December 2002): 49–55.

Marcoux, Alexei. "A Fiduciary Argument Against Stakeholder Theory." *Business Ethics Quarterly* 9 (2) (1999), 207–223.

Nagel, Thomas. *The View from Nowhere*. New York: Oxford University Press, 1986.

Paine, Lynn S. *Value Shift*. New York: McGraw-Hill, 2003.

Royce, Josiah. *The Religious Aspect of Philosophy*, (1865), reprint. Gloucester, Mass.: Peter Smith, 1965.

Selznick, Philip. *Leadership in Administration: A Sociological Interpretation*. New York: Harper & Row, 1957.

Zakhem, A. D. Palmer, and M. Stoll, eds. *Stakeholder Theory: Essential Readings in Ethical Leadership and Management*. New York: Prometheus, 2007.

PART III

ECONOMIC JUSTICE AND CONSUMER RIGHTS

CHAPTER 6

EXECUTIVE COMPENSATION: UNJUST OR JUST RIGHT?

JOHN R. BOATRIGHT

EXECUTIVE compensation has provoked considerable moral outrage. A great many people are convinced that *something* is wrong with it, even if they cannot say exactly *what* is wrong. Although critics of executive pay fervently believe that current levels of compensation for chief executive officers (CEOs) are unfair or unjust in some way, they seldom articulate the grounds for their convictions or the standards for just pay. This chapter examines executive compensation with the ultimate aim of determining whether high CEO pay is morally justified.[1]

The task of justifying executive compensation is difficult because it involves complex normative and empirical considerations. The central normative question concerns the principles for determining CEO pay or, indeed, the pay of anyone in a business organization. Any principles for justifying compensation cannot be identified in isolation from an economic system, and their justification depends on the justification of the economic system of which they are a part. In addition, the principles for justifying compensation cannot be established without addressing broader issues about the just distribution of income and wealth in society. Consequently, a complete justification of executive compensation would involve the justification of the economic system within which the compensation is received and the distribution of income and wealth in society.

Both of these topics—the justification of an economic system and the just distribution of income and wealth—extend far beyond the narrow topic of executive compensation. In order to focus solely on the justification of CEO pay, some simplifying assumptions must be made. This chapter assumes that capitalism, in its main outlines, is a justified economic system[2] and that, as a result, both the principles of compensation in a free market and the patterns of distribution of income and wealth produced by the market are just. These assumptions are necessary because otherwise this chapter would be an examination not of executive compensation *per se* but of capitalism and the distribution of income and wealth in society. These are large assumptions to make, although the latter one is less serious than the former because any distribution that occurs in a market can be altered by taxing away compensation to achieve any desired pattern of distribution. Compensation is not the only factor affecting distribution; taxation is another; so any moral problems with distribution can be addressed by either one.

One conclusion of this chapter is that the principles of compensation in a free market capitalist system are easily identified and widely accepted. There is general agreement that CEOs ought to be paid their worth in a market for managerial talent and that the just level of pay is whatever amount results from arm's-length bargaining between a CEO and the shareholders. The chief sources of controversy are the crucial empirical questions of whether the CEO labor market works efficiently and whether bargaining occurs at arm's length. These factual matters are the subjects of extensive, inconclusive debates. Resolving them is beyond the scope of this chapter, but the normative implications of the various positions are identified and examined.

The main conclusion reached in this chapter is that high levels of executive compensation can be justified in a free market capitalist system if certain conditions are met. The conditions are that the bargaining between a CEO and shareholders not involve fraud or a breach of fiduciary duty. If these conditions are met, then the agreements made by arm's-length bargaining are not morally objectionable. However, even in the absence of fraud or breach of fiduciary duty, the market for CEOs may be imperfect in ways that are not morally objectionable but are possibly socially undesirable. Thus, there are prudential grounds, but not moral reasons, for objecting to high levels of CEO pay that result from imperfect markets.

This market-based justification of high levels of executive compensation must also make a plausible case that CEOs are usually worth what they are paid and that their pay really is in the shareholders' interest. Another conclusion of this chapter is that the appropriate level of pay depends on what CEOs are being paid to do. The case is made that in recent decades, chief executives are paid to act not like bureaucrats but like entrepreneurs. This has been achieved by tying pay to performance, chiefly by means of stock options. If CEOs are able to bring greater shareholder returns by exploiting new opportunities, then shareholders may choose to pay more for an entrepreneurial CEO, and this higher pay may be justified for being chosen by the shareholders.

However, the right of shareholders to determine executive compensation solely with regard to their own interests raises questions about what constraints, if any, should be placed on shareholder power. A final conclusion of this chapter is that a main driver of high executive compensation is the power that shareholders have in corporate governance. This power is less constrained in the United States than in Europe and Japan, and this difference in corporate governance accounts for different levels of CEO compensation between these parts of the world. Ultimately, the debate over executive compensation becomes a question of the justification of a shareholder-centered system of corporate governance.

Overall, this chapter presents a rather unscandalized view of executive compensation, although this is not to deny that there have been some egregious abuses and excesses. The current high level of executive pay is due to significant changes in the world economy in the past few decades. Once these changes are understood, then high levels of CEO pay can be shown to be justified by widely accepted normative principles. The conclusion reached is rather tentative, however, because of unresolved controversies over many empirical issues in CEO pay. Normative analysis alone is unable to yield more definitive conclusions in the absence of greater empirical certainty.

THE BACKGROUND OF EXECUTIVE COMPENSATION

In order to examine the justification of executive compensation, it is necessary, first, to understand the pay-setting process for top executives and the various components of their pay packages, as well as the evolution of the process that resulted in the high compensation in recent decades.

The Structure of CEO Pay

The compensation of the CEO and other top executives of a publicly held company is set by a compensation committee of the board of directors. This committee consists normally of three or four independent directors.[3] Typically, the compensation committee does not conduct studies of executive pay or engage consultants but instead relies on recommendations that are prepared by the human resources department of the company, usually with the aid of compensation consultants. The typical pay package for a CEO and other top executives consists of four parts: the base salary, an annual bonus tied to certain performance measures, stock grants and stock options, and long-term incentive plans. Compensation often includes fringe benefits in addition to those received by other employees, most notably a supplemental executive retirement plan (SERP).[4] CEOs may also negotiate compensation to be paid after leaving the position. Examples of such "golden handshakes" include consulting contracts and continued perks of housing, medical care, and transportation. Contracts may also include "golden parachutes" that open in the event of a departure due to termination or change of control.

The base salary is typically determined by comparison with CEO pay in companies of similar size in the industry. As a result, firm size is generally accepted as the best predictor of the level of pay.[5] As a practical matter, base salaries seldom exceed $1 million. This is due to a change in the tax code made by Congress in 1993 to deny a tax deduction for any salary over this amount unless it was based on board-approved performance goals that were disclosed to shareholders.[6] Although this provision was enacted by Congress to rein in executive compensation, it had, ironically, the opposite effect of accelerating the use of stock options, which vastly increased total compensation.[7]

Annual bonus plans award compensation above the base salary in proportion to meeting some performance measure, such as annual revenue or accounting profits. Long-term incentive plans (LTIPs) are structured like bonus plans but are usually based on longer periods, typically three- to five-year rolling averages. LTIPs are less common than annual bonuses and constitute a small portion of total pay.[8] Generally, a bonus is not paid until some minimal performance threshold is met, and then the bonus increases in proportion to an increase in the performance measure until a cap is reached. The sensitivity of the bonus to performance is determined by the increase in the bonus for any given increase in the performance measure. For example, a bonus plan that awards $2 million for meeting a certain performance measure is more sensitive to performance than a plan that awards only $1 million for the same performance. The success of bonus plans depends on the performance measures chosen, although most plans use the same simple measures.[9]

The most substantial component of present-day CEO pay packages is stock options, which have been responsible for the recent rapid increase in total compensation. This form of compensation was virtually nonexistent in 1970, but in 2000, the average value of stock options in the compensation of S&P 500 CEOs was $7 million, dropping in 2002 to $4.2 million.[10] Between 1980 and 1994, the amount of increase in total executive compensation due to stock options was thirty times greater than the increase due to salary and bonuses.[11]

An employee stock option is a contract that allows the holder to buy stock at some time in the future at a fixed price (called the exercise or strike price). Employee stock options cannot be exercised before the end of a certain holding period (the vesting period) nor after a certain date (the expiration date). Typically, the exercise or strike price of an option is the value of a share on the date of issue (so-called at-the-money options), but the exercise price can be lower than the price on the date of issue (in-the-money options) or above the current price (out-of-the money).[12] A stock option produces a gain for the holder only if the price of the stock rises above the exercise or strike price. If that occurs, then the holder can exercise the option and either retain the stock or sell it for an immediate profit. Thus, if a holder has an option to buy 1,000 shares of stock at a strike price of $20 and the stock has risen to $30, then the holder may buy the stock for $20,000, immediately sell it for $30,000, and pocket the $10,000 difference. An employee who retains the stock has been able to buy stock worth $30,000 for only $20,000.

Employee stock options provide a strong incentive to increase the price of a company's stock.[13] Their incentive effect is greater than that of bonuses because bonuses are typically capped whereas stock options, as well as stock grants, have unlimited upside potential. The incentive effects of stock options also differ from those of stock grants in several important ways. Options encourage riskier behavior since they have no value unless the stock price rises, and their incentive effect is lost completely if the stock price falls (unless they are repriced, which is often done to regain the incentive effect). Options, unlike stock grants, discourage CEOs from paying dividends since retained earnings, but not dividends, contribute directly to stock price appreciation.[14]

The Evolution of CEO Pay

Popular concern over executive compensation is a relatively recent phenomenon. Before the mid-1980s, few chief executives received more than a few million dollars. As late as 1993, the total compensation of the average S&P 500 CEO was less than $4 million, and CEOs of smaller companies made considerably less. The explosion took place between 1995 and 2000, when the average increased from $4.8 million to $17.4 million, a rise of more than 360 percent.[15] This rapid increase coincided with the bull market of the late 1990s, and the bursting of the bubble in 2000 was followed by a sharp decline, with the average of $9.1 million in 2003 equal to the average pay in 1997.

However, the bull market alone does not account for the huge increase between 1995 and 2000, nor was this increase the sole target of criticism. Indeed, widespread criticism of executive compensation began around 1990 and was prompted not so much by high compensation as by the rapid restructuring of U.S. companies, often involving downsizing. Moreover, the bull market would not have increased executive compensation but for the increased use of stock options to tie compensation more closely to performance. This change in how executives were compensated was the result, in turn, of a transformation in U.S. corporations in response to the challenges of technological innovation, the expansion of capitalism around the world, and the globalization of trade.

High executive compensation in the late 1990s was due directly to the attempt to tie pay to performance by means of stock options. This much is obvious. What is not as well known is how the pressure for performance-based compensation arose. The story, in brief, is that the pay practices in the post–World War II years up through the 1960s were effective at inducing U.S. CEOs to create value by increasing firm size and expanding production. This growth, which benefited not only investors but workers, consumers, and society in general, was made possible by high returns on capital, low costs for capital and raw materials, and expanding consumer demand. Under these favorable economic conditions, executives thought that their job was to expand their enterprises, and this is what they were rewarded for doing.

The business environment changed sharply in the 1970s. This transformation, which Michael Jensen has called "the modern industrial revolution,"[16] created the need for companies to downsize and to exit some lines of business and to enter others. Jensen argues that rapid technological development, the worldwide expansion of capitalism, and the globalization of trade in the 1970s and early 1980s led to massive excess capacity, which required companies to contract instead of continuing to grow. At the same time, growth became difficult because the returns on capital declined precipitously, reaching a postwar low in the recession of 1982,[17] while the costs of capital and of many resources, most notably oil, were increasing. Under these conditions, continued growth could not be undertaken profitably and, if attempted, would destroy value rather than create it. However, the same factors created new opportunities for start-up companies and established firms that were agile enough to exploit them.

The changed economic conditions, which Jensen dates from the oil shock of 1973, required that companies downsize by closing plants, laying off workers, selling assets, buying back stock, and returning money to shareholders. However, the pay practices of the time, which were designed to increase growth, discouraged CEOs from undertaking these steps.[18] As a result, investors put great pressure on corporate boards to change the compensation of CEOs away from growth to value creation, thus leading to pay tied directly to stock price instead of firm size and accounting profits. Those companies that failed to change their compensation practices were subject to hostile takeovers by raiders who recognized that they could unlock value by forcing the companies they took over to undergo the downsizing that its previous managers had resisted. In Europe and Japan, where takeovers were not feasible and where CEO compensation was still tied to growth, the economies endured a long period of stagnation.[19]

Tying pay more closely to performance by means of stock options, along with the hostile takeovers of companies that resisted downsizing, had the intended effect of rapidly increasing stock prices in the 1980s and 1990s. However, this success was achieved by imposing great hardships on workers, who experienced stagnant wages, greater insecurity, and actual job loss. In this difficult period for ordinary workers, executive compensation, which had yet to reach the lofty heights of the late nineties, was thought to be gained at the workers' expense. Thus, this transformation can be viewed as the triumph of investors over workers, which explains the understandable protest against high executive compensation by workers who suffered hardships during this period. However, the same factors that produced excess capacity and the need for downsizing also opened up new opportunities for growth that created new and better jobs elsewhere in the economy. The hardships imposed on workers were thus offset to some degree by the eventual creation of new jobs and also by the avoidance of the even greater job loss that would have occurred had the downsizing not occurred.

The shift to stock-based compensation in the 1980s and 1990s, which tied compensation more closely to performance, was accompanied by an important change in the role of the chief executive. Prior to this time, corporate managers adhered to a professional creed in which they were bureaucrats whose control over the immense productive resources of a firm was legitimated by their sound business judgment and their commitment to the public weal.[20] Corporate leaders were quasi-public servants who could be trusted to create wealth for shareholders, while, at the same time, satisfying employees, customers, and other stakeholder groups. This bureaucratic creed developed in the 1920s and 1930s in the wake of the rise of large corporations and the separation of ownership and control noted by Adolf Berle and Gardiner Means[21] and was firmly adopted by the public and executives themselves in the 1945 to 1973 period. When corporations responded to the modern industrial revolution described by Jensen after 1973 with pay tied to performance by means of stock options, CEOs were gradually transformed from bureaucrats to a special kind of shareholder who acted like an entrepreneur.[22]

This shift from bureaucrat to entrepreneur was not readily adopted by executives, who still saw their legitimacy and their wealth tied to their bureaucratic role. Also, they did not initially welcome stock options since the variable pay was much riskier than a fixed salary and bonuses. However, they were not slow to observe the immense wealth that was being captured by self-employed entrepreneurs and the financiers who were conducting hostile takeovers.[23] The tide turned when CEOs discovered that stock options could not only make them wealthy but confer on them a new legitimacy as shareholder advocates.[24] In adopting a new entrepreneurial creed, CEOs were supported by investors, who viewed bureaucratic management as an impediment to increasing shareholder value. The same investors who welcomed hostile takeovers for their potential to unlock value also favored stock-based compensation as a means of enlisting executives in their struggle against the bureaucratic creed.[25] The legitimacy of this new role was based on the restoration of shareholder control of corporations. By turning the CEO into a new type of shareholder—an entrepreneur instead of a bureaucrat—stock-based pay overcame problems with the separation of ownership and control and reclaimed control of corporations for shareholders.

This brief account of the evolution of executive compensation in the United States since the 1970s is important because a central question in the justification of CEO pay is what chief executives are being paid to do. Should they be asked to act like bureaucrats who merely manage a large enterprise and get paid accordingly? Or will shareholders benefit more if CEOs assume the role of entrepreneur and are given incentives to create the greatest amount of value for the firm? If shareholders choose the latter, then it will be in their interest to tie pay to performance and allow high compensation for superior performance. This account of the structure and evolution of executive compensation provides an essential background for understanding the objections that have been raised by critics of executive compensation, as well as the justification of CEO pay.

Objections to High Executive Compensation

The business press in the United States and abroad is filled with stories of exceptionally rich CEO pay packages and examples of alleged abusive practices. Newspapers and magazines also feature annual surveys of CEO pay at major companies and frequent editorials calling for reforms. These sources are a useful starting point for identifying people's concerns with executive compensation.

First, the size of executives' annual total compensation, which sometimes runs in the tens or hundreds of millions of dollars, is enough to draw criticism. Executive pay became big news in 1994 when it was announced that Michael Eisner received $203 million in the previous year, although the next year his pay was a mere $10.6 million.[26] The highest paid executive in 2005 was the media magnate Barry Diller, with a pay package worth $469 million.[27] For most CEOs, the pay is far lower. According to one study, the average total executive compensation for CEOs of S&P 500 companies peaked in 2000 at $17.4 million and declined in 2003 to $9.1 million.[28] In 2003, the average compensation for the CEO of mid-cap 400 companies was $4 million, and for small-cap 600 companies $2 million. It is estimated that between 1999 and 2003, the aggregate total compensation of the top five executives of the S&P 1500 companies was about $122 billion, slightly more than 8 percent of corporate earnings.[29]

Second, the press and vocal critics focus on cases in which high compensation is unrelated to performance.[30] A CEO who receives a handsome payoff while the company slumps is a poster child for pay without performance. However, it is not possible to determine the relation of pay and performance merely by correlating how much a CEO earns and how well the company does.[31] It is necessary to determine the performance "sensitivity" of the pay package, which is the percentage and amount of compensation that are contingent on performance. Performance is important for critics of executive pay because most people understand and accept high pay that rewards an executive for a job well done. One kind of compensation that appears to be especially unrelated to performance is the package that many CEOs receive upon departure from a company. This "golden handshake" typically consists of deferred pay, vested stock options, pension, a consulting contract, and an early termination payment if a departure occurs before the end of a contract. When companies are acquired or merged, the executives who are forced out often receive payments as part of a "golden parachute." That a CEO should receive so much at a time when his or her value to the company has ended strikes many observers as unrelated to performance.[32]

Third, many critics decry a lack of appropriate proportion between CEO compensation and the pay of lower-level employees and also the fact that CEO pay has increased far more rapidly than most workers' wages. The ratio of CEO pay to the average or lowest-paid worker is cited by some as a significant measure. Aristotle reported Socrates' view that no member of a community should possess more than five times the common landholding.[33] Both financier J. P. Morgan and management guru Peter Drucker favored 20 to 1 as the maximum ratio of CEO pay to the average employee.[34] When Ben & Jerry's Homemade was founded, the unconventional company, which marketed premium ice cream with a socially aware message, adopted a ratio of 7 to 1 between the CEO and the lowest paid worker.[35] The ratio of the average S&P 500 CEO's salary plus bonus to the average production work was 30 to 1 in 1970, and by 1996, CEO pay was ninety times that of the average worker.[36] However, including stock options, which has constituted the preponderance of executive compensation since 1970, the ratio has increased during the period 1970–1996 from 30 to 1 to 210 times the average worker's pay. For more recent years, figures of 400 to 1 and 500 to 1 have been cited based on different comparison groups.[37]

Fourth, a related concern is the rapid increase in executive compensation when compared with most employees of U.S. corporations. From 1983 to 2003, the average total compensation of the CEO of an S&P 500 corporation increased six-fold, from less than $2 million to roughly $11 million.[38] The increase from 1993 to 2000, the peak year for CEO compensation in S&P 500 companies, was approximately 470 percent, while the average total compensation of CEOs of mid-cap 400 and small-cap 600 firms was 232 percent and 192 percent respectively.[39] During this time, average worker pay increased a mere 42 percent, six percentage points above the rate of inflation.[40] Between 2000 and 2006, the productivity of the average nonfarm worker increased 18 percent, but the inflation-adjusted wages of these workers rose by just 1 percent.[41] Such disparities create a concern that the gains in workers' productivity are not being fairly shared and that rich pay for executives is at the expense of ordinary employees.

Fifth, critics charge that executive compensation does not have the right incentive effect. Although bonuses, stock grants, and stock options create powerful incentives, some critics argue that the same effort could be achieved at much lower cost. As Derek Bok, a former president of Harvard University observes, "But there is no reason to suppose that American executives would work less hard if they were paid several hundred thousand dollars a year instead of several million. It is at least as plausible to assume that executives who were paid less would value a raise much more and hence might be motivated to work even harder."[42] In a similar vein, other critics argue that anyone who requires tens or even hundreds of millions to exert maximum effort must be very lazy. Commenting on Barry Diller's $469 million pay package for 2005, *New York Times* columnist Nicholas Kristof complained if it takes $150,000 an hour to get him motivated, he may be "the laziest man in America."[43] Another criticism is that pay is not a very effective motivator. Beyond a certain amount, CEO-caliber executives are more concerned about power, prestige, and other nonmonetary benefits. Indeed, too much reliance on extrinsic rewards can be counterproductive by "crowding out" the intrinsic rewards of a job and other effective sources of motivation.[44]

Sixth, some critics charge that the problem with incentive pay is not that it is ineffective but that it is *too* effective: It leads people to focus solely on what they are being paid to do, regardless of the consequences. The problem with the powerful effects of large monetary rewards is that they may generate unintended counterproductive results.[45] Because the measures that can be devised by shareholders for rewarding executives are not precise indicators of value creation, executives may operate in ways that are value destroying. Thus, a CEO may succeed in raising the stock price in time to exercise his or her stock options but do so in a way that reduces the price in the future, say by cutting back on research.[46] Strong monetary incentives may also lead to questionable accounting or financial practices and even massive fraud that result in legal complications, financial distress, and eventual bankruptcy.[47]

Seventh, many critics charge that the process by which executive compensation is determined is deeply flawed because of the improper power that CEOs exert in the pay-setting process. In theory, executive pay is determined by the compensation committee of the board of directors in arm's-length bargaining with the executive. However, critics point out that CEOs control the selection of the board of directors, so that its members, who want to be reappointed, are dependent on the approval of the person whose pay they set. Board members frequently have strong personal and social relations with a company's CEO that make it difficult for them to resist pay demands. Also, board members who are themselves CEOs of other companies are accustomed to high executive compensation, which they have an interest in maintaining. In addition, board members have neither the time nor the expertise, even if they had the incentive, to bargain effectively with a CEO. Furthermore, boards are advised by compensation consultants hired by the human resources department, who have no incentive to offend the CEO if they also provide other lucrative consulting services to the company. When consultants use comparisons of CEO pay in peer companies, the result is a "ratchet" effect on pay because boards are reluctant to pay a CEO less than the peer group average. Since a CEO's compensation takes many forms, it is possible to camouflage the total amount, so that it can be hidden from shareholders and sometimes the board itself.

Eighth, as stock options have become a larger portion of executive pay packages and the main cause of the large increases in total pay, they have drawn heavy criticism. One charge against stock options is that they result in "windfall" gains for executives when a company's stock price increases for reasons unrelated to the performance of the company's executives.[48] In particular, the bull market of the late 1990s increased the value of most stock options regardless of firm performance, while stock price increases in some industries, such as petroleum, were due to rapidly increasing commodity prices. When such windfall gains are unrelated to what executives have done, they appear to be undeserved. In addition, critics charge that stock options create perverse incentives for executives.[49] Because the value of stock options increases in proportion to the rise in a company's stock, executives may take great risks to boost the stock price. The result may be to make executives less risk averse and willing to engage in risky strategies in the hope of a high payout. Finally, some object that during the 1990s, boards simply awarded too many stock options, perhaps in the mistaken belief that they were nearly free to grant.[50]

A final, ninth, criticism of executive compensation is the greed factor. Many newspaper and magazine stories portray CEOs as extraordinarily greedy people who ought to be ashamed but are not.[51] This "moral fault" thesis is articulated by *Washington Post* economic columnist Robert J. Samuelson in the following way:

> But they [CEOs] have contrived a moral code that exempts them from self-control—a moral code that justified grabbing as much as they can. They unduly enrich themselves at shareholders' expense and set a bad leadership example. Because almost everyone else sees their code as self-serving and selfish, CEOs have undermined their moral standing and their ability to be taken seriously on other issues. They are slowly becoming a threat to the very system they claim to represent.[52]

It is not clear that highly paid CEOs are any greedier than most people; it may be that they are merely more successful at being greedy. However, Samuelson's charge has force if even only a few pay packages are not justified because the moral taint extends to all CEOs.

These objections to high executive compensation must be taken seriously. Rather than meeting these objections directly by supporting or refuting them, however, it is more instructive to determine how compensation ought to be set by identifying the relevant ethical principles in the pay-setting process.

JUSTIFYING EXECUTIVE COMPENSATION

In searching for a justification of executive compensation, this chapter assumes the justness of a free market capitalist system and seeks to identify within capitalism the common-sense or intuitive principles that most people would accept about pay-setting practices. Such a reliance on our considered moral beliefs is used by John Rawls, for example, in his methods of "reflective equilibrium"[53] and "overlapping consensus."[54] A strength of this approach is that the principles employed should gain the assent of most people and not depend on the acceptance of specific ethical theories. However, a possible weakness is that it may merely enshrine our preconceived political views and involve what R. M. Hare describes as "politics masquerading as philosophy."[55]

The Relevant Ethical Principles

In a capitalist economy, the compensation of a CEO occurs within a firm operating in a market, and every group that participates in production receives some portion of the total revenues of a firm. Some revenues are distributed to workers as wages, to suppliers as payments, to lenders as loan payments, and, of course, to shareholders as profits. The revenues of a firm come from customers, who receive in return a product or service. CEO pay is another cost to a firm that must be paid out of the total revenues. The justified level of pay can be understood, then, in the same way that other participants in a firm receive a return from productive activity.

Each participant in a firm has some resource or input that is contributed to production through a process of market exchange. In theory, the return on what a participant has contributed to production is the amount that results from mutual agreement or voluntary contracting. This amount can be considered just precisely because it results from a free market exchange. The relevant ethical principle here is the right to transact with others so as to exchange our property rights to a thing in return for something that we value more. Thus, a worker, who has a property right in his or her labor (which is the sum of a person's knowledge, skills, and talents), has a right to exchange this labor for wages, and subsequently has a right to whatever wage an employer is willing to offer and the worker is willing to accept. The same principle applies to the suppliers of raw materials and, with certain complications, to capital.[56] CEOs, too, contract with a firm, offering his or her services in return for some compensation.

This principle is the same as the principle of just transfer in Robert Nozick's entitlement theory: "A person who acquires a holding in accordance with the principle of justice in transfer, from someone else entitled to the holding, is entitled to the holding."[57] One means of just transfer is a voluntary exchange, and so one has a right to whatever one can gain in a free market transaction. Although Nozick's principle of just transfer provides one justification for voluntary exchange, such economic transactions can be justified by any theory that justifies capitalism since voluntary exchange and property rights—of which voluntary is an exercise—are central to this system.[58] Questions can be raised in Nozick's account about whether holdings were originally acquired justly or whether a given transfer is just. There is also debate about whether natural talents and abilities are the property of the person who has them or are common property.[59] However, the objections to executive compensation are not commonly based on such considerations. Most people accept that executives have a right to "sell" their services like any other owner of property.

Thus, the first principle of distributive justice for income in a business firm can be expressed as follows: *P1—Each person has a right to whatever he or she gains by exchanging his or her property through voluntary transactions.* This principle has limits, of course. Some voluntary transactions are not permitted by the state, such as drug dealing, prostitution, and working below a minimum wage; others raise questions about what may be considered property, such as body organs. However, none of these limits are relevant to executive compensation.[60]

The gain or return that any person may rightly receive from a business firm through market exchange is determined by that person's contribution to productivity. Since all payments by a firm are limited to its revenues—that is, a firm can pay out only what it takes in—each input provided by a person must contribute to production. Thus, a worker's labor must be combined with other inputs, such as raw materials and machines, to yield products that customers will buy, thereby creating revenue for the firm. In addition to whatever amount is reached by mutual agreement, it can also be said that a worker's just share of the resulting revenues is the amount that he or she contributes to production. In economic terms, the return for labor or any other input is its *marginal product*, which is the output of a given unit of input. The principle that a person has a right to his or her marginal product is expressed in Milton Friedman's prescription for the distribution of income in a free market: "To each according to what he and the instruments he owns produces."[61]

The second principle of distributive justice for income in a business firm can thus be expressed as follows: *P2—Each person has a right to the full value of whatever he or she produces.*[62] The possibility exists for conflict between P1 and P2 if the amount that a person can obtain in voluntary exchange is less than the full value of the marginal product. In theory, at least, a worker, for example, can hold out for wages that equal his or her marginal product, and an employer will continue to hire workers until the wage equals the marginal product. Consequently, in a market in equilibrium, each input should receive its marginal product.[63]

Although principles P1 and P2 are sufficient to justify wages in a market economy, including the compensation of CEOs, they are unlikely alone to justify high executive compensation since they cannot easily provide support for the massive income and wealth that capitalism creates, some of which goes to CEO pay. Although some wealth can be gained purely by means of market exchanges and thus be justified by P1, most inputs contributed by market exchanges have limited outputs, so that there is not much created wealth to be justified by P2. Thus, a person may acquire moderate wealth by a series of advantageous trades or by mere luck, but the creation of great wealth requires some additional element not yet identified, which is crucial to the justification of executive compensation. This element is "pure profit," which is considered next as the return to the entrepreneur.

The Entrepreneur's Return

Normal profit is the return on capital as an input of production. In addition to labor, raw materials, machines, and managerial direction (which is really another kind of labor), production requires capital with which to purchase productive assets. Because capital is an input, its cost will generally be equal to its contribution to the output, in which case the return to the owners of capital can be justified by P1 and P2.[64] However, in addition to this kind of profit, there is the profit that is gained by an entrepreneur who conceives a new way of combining inputs so that the value of the resulting output greatly exceeds the cost of the inputs. An entrepreneur is an innovator who develops a new product or a method of production and thereby exploits an opportunity to earn an above-market rate for his services. Frank Knight termed such returns "pure profit."[65]

Although the pure profit gained by an entrepreneur might be analyzed merely as a gain resulting from market exchanges and thus the element that an entrepreneur provides to production, a number of economists have recognized that this element is not just another input. Knight himself attributed the gain to luck, so that the gain is a windfall profit to someone who was willing to assume risk in a world of uncertainty. In his famous analysis of entrepreneurship, Joseph Schumpeter saw this kind of activity as part of the "perennial gale of creative destruction" of capitalism whereby the entrepreneur creates "new combinations" of products or methods of production that no one else has seen or has been able to realize.[66] Building on Schumpeter and Ludwig von Mises, who saw pure profit as an arbitrage opportunity,[67] Israel Kirzner has developed a theory of entrepreneurship as a matter of *discovery*.[68]

What an entrepreneur brings to the productive process is alertness. Kirzner notes that in the standard economic view, profit is understood "either as the deliberately achieved goals of human effort, or as windfall attributable to sheer luck."[69] However, Kirzner argues,

> We wish to insist that a third possible source for economic gain, a source entailing ethical implications of an entirely different character, must be recognized. This source is deliberate human discovery, not to be attributed to unaided luck, but (at least in part) to the alert attitude on the part of the discoverer. It is the alertness of human beings that enables them to notice and profit by what they find.[70]

If income from pure profits is neither a contribution to production from an input nor a windfall due to luck or external circumstances, how can it be justified? Kizner's answer is the finders-keepers rule, which asserts that "an unowned object becomes the justly-owned private property of the first person who, discovering its availability and its potential value, takes possession of it."[71] Kirzner claims that this rule, which has obvious similarities to Locke's justification for the initial acquisition of property[72] and Nozick's principle of justice in acquisition,[73] is in accord with our common moral intuitions about the ownership of created objects. He writes:

> When an entity owes its existence, in every morally relevant sense, to the creative act of an individual, we feel very strongly that no one else has any right to deprive that individual of the enjoyment of that which he has created.[74]

The entrepreneur's claim to have created something truly original lies in the fact that he or she has taken materials in which no one else saw potential value and fashioned them into an object of value. Quite literally, the entrepreneur has brought the object of value into existence from nothing—it has been created *ex nihilo*.[75]

Kirzner's finders-keepers rule is not the only way to justify the pure profit that results from entrepreneurial activity.[76] However, if pure profits are justified in the way Kirzner suggests, then a third principle for distributing income and wealth can be formulated as: *P3—Each person has a right to the pure profit resulting from entrepreneurial activity*.[77]

In a free market, pure profits are typically temporary. They arise because of a market disequilibrium in which an opportunity exists to exploit the mispricing of inputs, and this opportunity disappears once competitors recognize the same opportunity and prices adjust to reach a market equilibrium. Henry Ford was able to build a fortune because the price of labor at the time was low due to workers' low productivity. When this low-priced labor was set to work on an assembly line, this innovation enabled Ford to produce automobiles at lower cost than the competition, which handcrafted their products. In a similar manner, Sam Walton conceived a business model for selling goods that cut sourcing costs and enabled Walmart to offer lower prices than competitors. Bill Gates saw that computer code could expand the possible uses of desktop computers and became wealthy developing new software products. However, as soon as competitors are able to duplicate the innovations of entrepreneurs, the market returns to equilibrium and pure profits disappear. Nevertheless, many entrepreneurs are able, before competitors intervene, to make fortunes that we consider to be justly earned.

To summarize this part of the discussion, in a capitalist, market economy, individuals create income for themselves by making advantageous economic exchanges with the assets they possess. This is true not only when people trade material possessions, which are tangible property, but also when they employ their talents, skills, and knowledge in productive activity. Income thus results from the workings of a labor market. The income that people obtain in a labor market is justified by the same principles that apply to all market transactions, which are expressed in principles P1 and P2. Although these principles are not necessarily linked to any particular theory of distributive justice, they are nevertheless central to a free market economy, which may be justified by many different theories. Anyone who rejects these two principles is rejecting essential elements of a capitalist economic system.

Principle P3 is more controversial and less essential to capitalism. However, entrepreneurial activity is an increasingly important feature of modern capitalism that produces "pure" or supernormal profits, which stand in need of justification. Kirzner's finders-keepers principle is one means for justifying such profits and is expressed in principle P3. P3 is important to the present discussion because it justifies high executive compensation if CEOs are viewed as entrepreneurs rather than mere bureaucrats, which is argued below. The next step in the argument, though, is to describe and defend the pay of chief executives in a market for CEO labor.

THE ECONOMIC FRAMEWORK

The three principles for justifying executive compensation cannot be applied without understanding how executive compensation is determined in a market. If a CEO contracts with the shareholders of a corporation for compensation of a certain amount, then that amount is just, according to P1, because it is the result of mutual voluntary agreement. A crucial question, though, is what amount the shareholders—or, more precisely, the compensation committee of the board of directors, acting for the shareholders—ought to offer. What is a just amount? The brief answer is that the directors, who have a fiduciary duty to act in the shareholders' interest, ought to offer whatever amount provides the greatest benefit to shareholders. But how do directors determine *this*? The answer to this question depends, in turn, on the factors that determine CEO pay in a market. In economic theory, two factors are relevant, namely the market forces of supply and demand, which create a market for CEOs, and agency problems, to which CEO pay offers a solution.

The CEO Labor Market Argument

In a market economy, all compensation is set by the labor market, which exists not only for ordinary workers but also for CEOs. Such a market operates according to the laws of supply and demand. On the demand side, the board of directors should offer compensation equal to the market worth of the executive. This is an amount that does not exceed the value that the person adds to the net revenues or profits of the firm, which is equivalent to saying that an executive should be paid his or her marginal product. The supply side is determined by the availability of potential CEOs and their reserve price for accepting an offer of employment.[78] As long as a firm offers a position with compensation that does not exceed a potential CEO's marginal product and exceeds this person's reserve price, then a deal can be made, and anyone who accepts the three principles should readily admit that the amount agreed upon is just.

However, CEOs and other top executives are not merely hired labor, and the market for CEO services has certain inefficiencies or imperfections. Most workers are hired merely to work as directed or to accomplish specific tasks, but CEOs are charged with achieving the overall objective of a firm, namely the maximization of shareholder value. Consequently, they cannot be motivated merely to work diligently as directed because they have to work largely without direction. Nor can they be motivated to accomplish only specific tasks. They must be motivated instead to pursue the objective of the firm to the best of their abilities. Unlike most workers, whose work can be directly monitored, CEOs effort cannot be adequately gauged except by results. Consequently, pay packages must be designed to motivate CEOs to pursue the objective of the firm in ways that can be measured.

Determining the appropriate level of compensation is difficult, then, because the market for CEOs is characterized by asymmetric and incomplete information. First, in designing pay packages, the board is not able to know fully the level of effort or commitment of the CEO. Thus, the CEO has information that the board lacks (asymmetric information). Second, the ability of the CEO to achieve the expected results is unknowable, both to the board and to the CEO (incomplete information). Furthermore, it is difficult to know whether performance, good or bad, is due to the CEO or to outside forces over which management has little control. It may be difficult, therefore, to know the extent to which any level of performance should be rewarded.

The market for CEOs may be inefficient for several other reasons. The supply of CEOs may be constricted by the inability of firms to identify suitable candidates or even the relevant talent pool. Although hiring boards may be aided by executive search firms, the best candidates may not be obvious, and the resulting shortage of supply may drive up prices.[79] The tendency of firms to hire from inside and the influence of compensation consultants, who tend to recommend pay based on comparative pay data, further inhibit the efficient functioning of the CEO labor market. In practice, CEO pay is compressed within a range that would not occur in an efficient market where CEOs are paid for their marginal product. Sydney

Finkelstein and Donald Hambrick observe, "CEO pay, while often substantial, still falls short of the marginal product of the most effective CEOs and greatly exceeds the contributions of others."[80]

Fortunately, contractual means exist to overcome, at least partially, the problems of asymmetric and incomplete information. In particular, bonuses tied to performance targets enable boards to pay a CEO in accord with an expected level of performance with an "insurance policy" that guards against the possibility that the targets are not reached. An executive who fails to perform as expected simply does not receive the bonus. If a CEO is worth $2 million for meeting targets that add more than this amount to the earnings of a company, and if the ability of the CEO to deliver this level of performance is unknown, then offering this compensation as a bonus and not, say, as a fixed salary, compensates for the lack of knowledge. However, since variable pay is less valuable to an executive because of the uncertainty, more will have to be offered to compensate for the risk. Thus, the total pay to a successful CEO, including the variable portion, will be higher than fixed compensation without any variable component. In other words, the "insurance policy" that variable pay provides to overcome the problem of asymmetric and incomplete information comes at a cost to the shareholders, but, lacking any better alternatives, it may still be a price worth paying.

To summarize, one way of justifying CEO compensation is to understand the pay as the result of a market for CEO services. Insofar as this is the case, the compensation, whatever its level, is justified by P1 and P2. The reserve price of CEO candidates will be determined by their prospects for other employment of their services, which may be quite promising. Such candidates may be considering not only work as a CEO in a public firm but also the opportunities as an entrepreneur, a private investor, or the leader of private company. Furthermore, the marginal product of CEO candidates, which is the value they can bring to the firm, although uncertain, may be quite high. For example, Warren Buffett has been quoted as saying, "You'll never pay a really top-notch executive...as much as they are worth. A million, $3 million, or $10 million, it's still peanuts."[81] However, the pay of CEOs is determined not solely by ordinary market forces of supply and demand. Another factor in executive compensation is the need to solve an agency problem, which is addressed by the principal-agent approach.

The Principal-Agent Approach

The principal-agent approach shares with the CEO labor market argument the assumption that the contract between a CEO and the shareholders represents a mutually beneficial exchange but differs in its understanding of what CEOs are paid for. Instead of being paid solely for their marginal product, this approach holds that the pay is intended, at least in part, to overcome an agency problem that occurs in the modern corporation with a separation of ownership and control. Put simply, on this approach the shareholders are "buying" not merely a CEO's services but also the person's loyalty.

Standard economic analysis views the firm as a nexus of contracts among the various corporate constituencies including the contract between the shareholders and a CEO.[82] When the owners of a firm exercise day-to-day responsibility, these owners presumably operate the firm in their own interests. However, as the task of management comes to require specialized skills, the shareholder-owners may hire professional management to operate the firm. This development, which was noted by Berle and Means in 1932, has been termed the separation of ownership and control.[83] In the language of agency theory, the shareholders are *principals*, who seek to make mangers their *agents*, who act in place of the principals and serve their interests.[84]

Because professional managers, in their role as agents, cannot be assumed to pursue shareholder wealth maximization with the same diligence as the shareholder-principals, it is necessary that the contracts contain sufficient incentives for managers to pursue the objective of the firm as the shareholders would themselves. One purpose of executive pay, then, is to induce them to become loyal agents and to act solely in the shareholders' interest. The amount that principals pay to secure the loyalty of their agents is termed an *agency cost*. No matter how much they are paid, though, managers will not always be perfect agents: they will act in some ways to benefit themselves at the expense of shareholders. Any amount that principals lose from failing to induce their agents to act solely in their interests is termed an *agency loss*. The agency-principal approach assumes that shareholders and CEOs write optimal contracts that reduce agency costs and agency loss in ways that represent the best bargain between shareholders and CEOs. Thus, the principal-agent approach is also called the optimal contracting and the efficient contracting approaches.[85]

In theory, then, CEO compensation can exceed the marginal product of an executive's services to a firm because, in addition to a person's managerial abilities, the firm is paying for agency costs resulting from the separation of ownership and control. Alternatively, it may be said that the benefit to the firm of overcoming agency problems is part of a CEO's marginal product. However the point is expressed, it explains the willingness of shareholders to pay a CEO enough to motivate the person to pursue the objective of shareholder wealth maximization. The additional amount of CEO compensation that can be attributed to the solution of agency problems thus represents some portion of the extra value achieved by professional management.

Insofar as executive compensation is intended to solve an agency problem, it is justified in the same way as pay in a market for CEO labor, namely, it results from voluntary contracting between shareholders and CEOs. It is justified, in other words, by P1 and P2. The same justification applies to the determination of all wages in a free market and indeed to all income derived from economic exchange. The enormous earnings of athletes and performers are also due to the demand for their services and the limited supply of great talent. If fans voluntarily pay high prices for tickets to the concerts of a rock star, for example, then the resulting income is just, at least within the normative principles of a free market economy.[86]

The principles justifying compensation in a free market economy entail that if a compensation package represents an optimal contract between shareholders and a CEO, then the amount, whatever it is, is justified. The main source of dispute over CEO pay is a factual or objective element, namely, whether most of the contracts in question are optimal. Is executive compensation really the result of efficient labor markets, or is the market for CEOs "rigged"?[87] The labor market may be inefficient or rigged if CEOs have the power to unduly influence the pay-setting process. That they have this power is asserted by the managerial power thesis.

THE MANAGERIAL POWER THESIS

The managerial power thesis, which is presented most prominently in the book *Pay without Performance* by Lucien Bebchuk and Jesse Fried,[88] accepts the normative core of the optimal contracting approach that executive compensation *ought* to be set with a view to maximizing shareholder wealth. More precisely, boards of directors should negotiate optimal contracts with CEOs that best serve the shareholders' interests, and this contract is whatever agreement would result from true arm's-length bargaining. Indeed, they do not object to the high level of pay *per se* but to the lack of arm's-length bargaining and transparency in the pay-setting process and to a lack of linkage between pay and performance.[89] Their complaint is that boards are unable or unwilling to negotiate such contracts due to the power that executives have over the process. As a result, the contracts between CEOs and the shareholders are not, in fact, optimal or efficient, *as they should be*, and CEOs are able to use their power to extract above market returns or "rents."

Evidence for the Managerial Power Thesis

The managerial power thesis and the evidence marshaled for it can only be outlined here. It is not necessary for purposes of this chapter to determine whether the thesis is true as an explanation of high executive compensation. The relevant normative question is whether executive compensation, if this explanation is correct, is thereby unjustified.

In support of their factual or empirical claim that CEO pay does not result from arm's-length bargaining, Bebchuk and Fried argue, first, that incumbent CEOs have extensive control over the nomination and remuneration of board members. Since nomination to the board virtually guarantees election, the composition of the nominating committee is critical. Unlike the audit committee of the board, which usually has a majority of outside directors, this generally is not true of nominating committees.[90] To the extent that board members owe their appointment to the CEO, they may be reluctant to oppose him or her, especially over matters of pay, which have less bearing on shareholder interests than many other decisions made by the board. Board members also have an incentive to appease the person who controls the pay and other benefits that accrue to them, which can take such forms as doing business with board members' own companies and making philanthropic contributions to their favored charities.

Second, board members are often tied to the CEO by social and business networks, as well as, in many cases, friendship. As a result, they may feel pressure to show respect to the CEO and maintain collegial relations with other board members, both of which are incompatible with open dissent. Third, board members are often CEOs themselves, and so they have a common interest in maintaining high levels of compensation and may share convictions about the appropriateness of such pay. Fourth, even directors who were determined to engage in hard bargaining with a CEO would be hampered by a lack of skill, time, and information. Board members typically lack the skills to bargain effectively, and they also do not have adequate time to consider all the relevant information, assuming that it is available. Boards seldom engage their own consultants but generally rely on the company's human resources department or on compensation consultants engaged by this department, who have even less incentive than board members to engage in hard bargaining.[91]

Fifth, some of the possible checks on compliant boards are weak. Shareholders have little power to influence boards on matters of pay. Although they may complain, they have little recourse by means of either shareholder voting or court suits. The market has little disciplining force except in extreme cases where excessive compensation might invite a takeover bid. Finally, regulatory bodies, such as the Securities and Exchange Commission and the New York Stock Exchange have issued rules requiring disclosure of compensation packages (SEC) and independent directors on nominating and compensation committees (NYSE), but these measures, too, have limited effect. The most powerful force to reduce executive compensation, according to Bebchuk and Fried, is the "outrage" constraint, which imposes reputation costs on directors and the firm. However, outrage can be avoided by the use of "camouflage" to hide compensation from the public eye,[92] and a rising market, such as bull market of the 1990s, further weakens the outrage constraint.[93]

The argument offered by Bebchuk and Fried for the managerial power thesis consists mostly of the ways in which executive compensation is insensitive to performance. The argument is that the managerial power thesis serves better than the optimal contracting approach or the CEO labor market model to explain many features of current pay practices in which pay is not closely tied to performance. These features include bonuses with easily attainable targets, payments upon a CEO's departure, retirement benefits, and executive loans (now prohibited by the 2002 Sarbanes-Oxley Act).[94] The common trait of these forms of compensation is that they have limited incentive force. Even the motivating force of stock options, which are justified as aligning CEO interests with those of shareholders, is reduced when holders can "unwind" their options by exercising them quickly or hedge the options against loss by personal portfolio trading, or when options can be repriced[95] or reloaded.[96] All of these features reduce the incentive effect of stock options. Finally, the authors cite the failure of stock option plans to cancel out the effect of windfall gains from a rising stock market, in which CEOs' awards are related not to their performance but to improvements in the whole economy. In this case, the windfall gains do little to increase the incentive force of the stock options.[97]

Assessing the Managerial Power Thesis

As a factual or empirical account of how executive compensation is determined, the book *Pay without Performance* has drawn strong critical responses.[98] Although the debate is still open, critics raise many solid objections. First, because CEOs have had considerable power for some time, the managerial power thesis is, at best, incomplete; something else must have occurred around 1990 that allowed this power to result in increased compensation.[99] Second, the use of equity-based pay and the accompanying rise in total compensation have occurred not only in publicly held companies but also in family companies and private equity companies, including leveraged buyouts, where shareholders have greater control and more incentive to reduce CEO compensation.[100] Third, there is no evidence that total compensation is less in companies with more independent boards of directors, which is a useful proxy for a lack of managerial power.[101] Indeed, there appears to be no correlation between board independence and firm performance generally.[102] Fourth, the managerial power thesis predicts high executive compensation only for incumbent CEOs or inside hires, but the evidence shows that outside hires, who presumably have little power coming in, receive compensation that is as high if not higher than that of incumbent CEOs.[103]

Another line of criticism notes that even if managers have extensive power, it does not follow that the resulting contracts are suboptimal. First, it may be argued that such contracts, formed when a CEO is first hired and thus lacks power, already anticipate future managerial power and compensate for this future power *ex ante*.[104] Second, what appear to be suboptimal contracts may, in fact, be optimal (or at least relatively efficient) once the costs of contracting and the objective of contracting are taken into account.[105] If the ultimate objective of contracting by the board is to maximize shareholder wealth, then the contract with a CEO must be evaluated in terms of its contribution to total firm value. A board that is determined to hire the best CEO candidate at the lowest amount that person will accept—that is, at his or her reservation price—may not develop a working relationship with a CEO that will maximize shareholder wealth. Thus, it may not be desirable to negotiate at arm's length because such an adversarial relationship may not be conducive to effective interaction between a board and a CEO.[106]

In addition, boards must be selected and operate with a view to all the decisions they will make. A board that is well composed to negotiate optimal compensation packages may not be well suited for making decisions on other, more important matters. If total shareholder return is the test of whether contracts with CEOs are optimal, then the superior performance of U.S. companies in recent years suggests that they are, especially when compared with those of other countries. Bengt Holmstrom and Steven Kaplan observe:

The fact that the shareholders of U.S. companies earned higher returns *even after* payments to management does not support the claim that the U.S. executive pay system is designed inefficiently; if anything, shareholders appear better off with the U.S. system of executive pay than with the systems that prevail in other countries.[107]

To summarize the discussion of the managerial power thesis so far, the empirical debate over whether CEO contracts are the optimal—which is to say that they would result from arm's-length bargaining—is inconclusive. There is good reason to believe that they are optimal once the uncertainties and imperfection of contracting are taken into account, but evidence for the presence of managerial power is strong. At best, the Bebchuk and Fried argument is suggestive but not conclusive. However, it is not necessary for purposes of this chapter to determine the correctness of the managerial power thesis. The relevant question is, what are the ethical or normative implications if the thesis is true?

Ethical Implications of Managerial Power

Suppose that Bebchuk and Fried are right about the influence of managerial power on the bargaining process. What follows about the justification of executive compensation? In economic terms, managers' power enables them to extract rents.[108] An economic rent is payment for a good in excess of what would be required for it to be supplied in a market. With regard to wages, any worker who is paid more than the amount that would induce that worker to do a job receives an economic rent. Probably most employees enjoy the benefit of some rents.[109] Bebchuk and Fried, who hold that managerial power enables executives to extract rents, explain their use of term this way:

> We will use the term [rents] to refer to the additional value that managers obtain beyond what they would get in arm's-length bargaining with a board that had both the inclination to maximize shareholder value and the necessary time and information to properly perform that task.[110]

The question about the ethical or normative implications of the managerial power thesis can be rephrased by asking whether a person is justified in obtaining economic rents. Is there anything morally objectionable about rent-seeking activity?

Although some writers hold all rents to be unjustified,[111] the principles of distribution in a free market economy would justify rents unless some other moral wrong is present. That is, voluntary exchange creates a presumption of justness that may be rebutted by other factors that renders the outcome unjust. Fraud is one obvious factor, but two other factors that may be present are breaches of fiduciary duty and market failures.

As an example of fraud, Richard Grasso's $140 million pension has been challenged on the grounds that not all members of the board of the New York Stock Exchange were kept informed about the impact of his high compensation on the calculation of his retirement benefits.[112] If Mr. Grasso and his allies on the board withheld material information from other board members, then his total compensation cannot be justified merely by citing the board's approval. Any compensation package with stock options is also subject to fraud if the executive uses improper accounting to boost stock price in order to increase their value. For example, Joseph P. Nacchio, CEO of Qwest, was convicted in April 2007 of nineteen counts of insider trading for selling more than $100 million in stock from options while lying to investors about the financial condition of the company, which was under investigation for accounting fraud.[113] Fraud may also be involved in the backdating of options. Option backdating occurs when the date of issue is changed to a day on which the stock had a low price, thus increasing the eventual payoff.[114] Backdating is not illegal if it is properly approved by the board, reported to shareholders, and correctly treated for accounting and tax purposes, but such conditions are often not met.[115]

In cases where managerial power is a factor, there may also be a breach of fiduciary duty. In the theory of executive compensation, the members of a board of directors—or more precisely, of the compensation committee of the board—have a fiduciary duty to the corporation and its shareholders to bargain at arm's length with the CEO and to offer compensation that best serves the shareholders' interest. Insofar as the directors are induced by the CEO or any other force to fail in this duty, the outcome cannot be justified. If board members allow themselves to show favoritism to the CEO, then they have violated their fiduciary duty, and if a CEO improperly seeks to gain the board's favor, then he or she has acted wrongly by inducing a breach of fiduciary duty.

Although a breach of fiduciary duty is a clear moral wrong, it must be distinguished from two other problems that are less clear in their moral import. First, boards may make mistakes in judgment that lead to less-than-optimal contracts. For example, boards may significantly misjudge the ability of a CEO to implement a plan or the soundness of the plan itself. They may also make mistakes about the actual effect of different components of executive pay, especially stock options. Some observers suggest that stock options have been used extensively because boards thought them cheap and failed to appreciate their full cost.[116] It is generally agreed that boards failed to anticipate the bull market of the 1990s and the effect this broad rise in stock prices would have on the value of stock options. Because boards must also decide upfront on compensation in the event of termination, even a CEO who fails is guaranteed a certain payout. Although, in retrospect, a board may overpay an executive, the amount may have seemed reasonable at the time it was offered. In all matters, boards cannot be expected to make perfect decisions but only to act reasonably under the circumstances.

Second, CEOs, aided by their own compensation consultants, may be very effective bargainers because of their own capabilities and resources. In the role of CEO, an individual has a fiduciary duty to act in the shareholders' interest in all matters, but this duty does not extend to negotiating compensation as a CEO. Similarly, the fiduciary duty that a lawyer has to act in a client's interest does not preclude being self-interested in negotiating the fees for the lawyer's service. There seems to be nothing unjust when people gain some advantage in negotiation due to their own abilities. Indeed, Bebchuk and Fried hold that any advantage gained by a CEO from his or her bargaining skill is "not inconsistent with arm's-length bargaining."[117]

These factors, namely, mistakes in judgments and ineffective bargaining by boards, are both instances of imperfect markets. As previously noted, the CEO labor market has certain imperfections, due mainly to asymmetric and incomplete information. In particular, boards do not have perfect information about the available CEO candidates or about the capabilities and potential of any given one. In addition, boards are not dealing with homogenous products, and there are not large numbers of buyers and sellers, with freedom of entry and exit from the market. All of these are features of imperfect markets. The outcomes of imperfect markets are not necessarily unjust. However, since these outcomes affect people's well-being, regulation is often introduced to increase the welfare of society. For example, without labeling laws for products, consumers would be at a disadvantage, which producers could exploit. The outcome would be that in otherwise voluntary market exchanges, producers would gain at consumers' expense. In passing laws requiring certain information on labels, legislatures are expressing the judgment that the welfare of society will be increased when consumers have certain information that corrects a market imperfection.

The main justification for correcting the outcomes of imperfect markets is consequentialist or utilitarian: it leads to increased social welfare. Rent-seeking in imperfect markets not only affects the distribution of income but can produce distorting effects in an economy that reduce total wealth.[118] However, the mere act of rent-seeking in an imperfect market is not itself morally wrong. Indeed, investing with superior information and entrepreneurial activity are both possible only in imperfect markets. Exploiting imperfect markets in these ways is not only morally permissible but moral praiseworthy because of its generally beneficial effects. So with respect to executive compensation, it does not follow that high CEO pay that results from imperfect markets is morally wrong, barring fraud or breach of fiduciary duty.

This said, utilitarianism would justify any legal restrictions on rent-seeking in imperfect markets that would increase societal welfare. The main justification for labeling laws, for example, is that the market will be more efficient if buyers have certain information and that the seller can provide this information at less cost than buyers would incur in obtaining it. Overall, the welfare of society is increased by enacting such laws. Similarly, it may be argued that the market for CEOs can be made more efficient by providing shareholders with more information about compensation packages and also by giving them more power in the nomination of board members.[119] The former argument—that the market for CEOs can be made more efficient by providing shareholders with certain information—lies behind the regulation issued by the Securities and Exchange Commission that requires the disclosure of executive and director compensation in annual reports and other documents.[120] Most of this disclosure must be provided in "plain English." In issuing the SEC's regulation, Chairman Christopher Cox explained:

The better information that both shareholders and boards of directors will get as a result of these new rules will help them make better decisions about the appropriate amount to pay the men and women entrusted with running their companies. Shareholders need intelligible disclosure that can be understood by a lay person without benefit of specialized expertise or the need for an advanced degree. It's our job to see that they get it.[121]

The SEC has also considered controversial proposals to allow shareholders to nominate directors and permit contested elections, although no regulations have been issued.[122]

Any laws or regulations that reduce rent-seeking in imperfect markets may be justified on utilitarian grounds for increasing market efficiency and, with it, social well-being. Whether any restrictions are morally justified, however, depends on whether they, in fact, have the effect of increasing social welfare. Although greater disclosure to shareholders is unlikely to do any harm, there is little evidence so far that shareholders and directors will make better decisions as a result. The more controversial proposals to allow shareholder nomination of directors and contested elections are opposed by many critics on the grounds that they would have significant adverse effects on corporations.[123] The more important point is that disclosure requirements are fully compatible with the principle that executive compensation should be determined by arm's-length bargaining between shareholders and the CEO. Indeed, this principle provides the rationale for requiring greater disclosure. If such requirements reduce CEO pay, then this shows that higher levels of compensation are not justified. However, the reverse is also true: that whatever level of compensation is approved by (better informed) shareholders is just.

The conclusion to be drawn about the normative implications of the managerial power thesis is that seeking compensation above what would result from arm's-length bargaining, which is a form of economic rent, is morally wrong when it is done by morally impermissible means, such as fraud or breach of fiduciary duty. However, rent-seeking in imperfect markets is not morally wrong *per se* but may be morally undesirable because of its impact on social welfare. Thus, rent-seeking may be rightly limited on consequentialist grounds in much the same way as labeling requirements are justified. The justification for both kinds of measures is that correcting for the underlying market imperfections increases social well-being. However, correcting for such market imperfections is wholly compatible with the optimal contracting view and, indeed, strengthens it by ensuring more efficient markets.

The managerial power thesis rejects the optimal contracting view on the grounds that CEO pay contracts do not always result from arm's-length bargaining. Another objection to the optimal contracting view is that it assumes that the amount of compensation paid in recent years would, in fact, be approved by the shareholders. As a justification of CEO pay, the optimal contracting thesis holds that these high compensation packages reflect the marginal product of CEOs and hence are a good deal for shareholders.[124] It is incumbent on the optimal contracting approach, however, to explain why CEOs really are worth what they are paid.

Aside from the explanations already offered, another is that CEOs should be paid not like bureaucrats but as entrepreneurs.

COMPENSATING EXECUTIVES
AS ENTREPRENEURS

Chief executives today are expected not merely to manage organizations like bureaucrats but to create as much wealth as possible. This can be done only if CEOs act like entrepreneurs in exploiting new opportunities for wealth creation. In the 1990s, conditions were right for companies to be very entrepreneurial, and executives seized on this development to change the rationale for their compensation. Jack Welch of General Electric characterized himself and his fellow chief executives as entrepreneurs who stand above the corporate hierarchy.[125] In the words of Ernie Englander and Allen Kaufman, "The CEO was in effect the intrafirm entrepreneur, who had battled managerial bureaucrats to uncover new wealth-creating opportunities."[126] Louis V. Gerstner, who transformed IBM, titled his book about this experience *Who Says Elephants Can't Dance?*, reflecting his view that he had turned a lumbering bureaucratic organization into a nimble entrepreneurial one.[127]

The practical effect of expecting CEOs to be entrepreneurs and paying them as such is that compensation is closely tied to performance. By using stock options for compensation, not only are boards of directors inducing executives to pursue the most promising business opportunities but they are also permitting successful CEOs and other top officers to benefit directly from increases in stock price. When executives' compensation consists largely of a portion of the wealth they create, their role changes from that of a bureaucrat, who merely manages the corporation on behalf of the shareholders, to an important shareholder, who acts like an entrepreneur. There are two main questions to be asked about this development: Are CEOs really being paid for performance, and should they be paid in this way? The answers are yes and yes, but compensating executives as entrepreneurs raises certain ethical issues about this new role of the CEO and about shareholder control of corporations that need examination.

Tying Pay to Performance

Historically, executive compensation has been correlated with firm size or span of control, and when firms increase in size or complexity, as many have done in recent years, the amount of compensation can be expected to rise as well. From a moral point of view, it seems just to pay executives more for leading larger, more complex organizations, although how much more is open to question. As previously noted, this rationale for CEO pay changed around 1973, when it became necessary for shareholders to modify compensation in order to induce chief executives to downsize companies. Under such conditions, compensation was no longer tied to firm size—because the CEO might be leading a smaller, but more productive, company—but was tied instead to increases in stock price, which reflect greater wealth creation. Although the use of stock options became more common in the 1970s, this was not a significant source of compensation because of relatively stagnant stock prices through the decade. However, the value of stock options as a component of CEO pay packages increased dramatically in the 1980s with the beginning of a long bull market.

Although this bull market was accompanied by some overvaluation of firms—which Alan Greenspan termed "irrational exuberance"[128]—much of the rise in stock prices reflected genuine increases in productivity that resulted from corporations' successful response to the challenges and opportunities of the period. According to a study by Xavier Gabaix and Augustin Landier, the capitalization of S&P 500 corporations increased six-fold between 1983 and 2003, which neatly corresponds to a six-fold increase in CEO compensation.[129] The six-fold increase in the capitalization of the S&P 500 corporations did not necessarily result from an increase in the size of firms in terms of the number of employees, plants or divisions; it reflected, rather, a rise in the price of the companies' stock from increased productivity.[130] Thus, in the aggregate, the level of CEO pay between 1983 and 2003 was closely linked to performance, with the increase in compensation proportional to the wealth that was created.

Not only has executive compensation increased proportionately with the profitability of firms, it has also remained a relatively constant percentage of the value created. Michael Jensen and Kevin Murphy found that in the period 1974 to 1983, the dollar amount of CEO received for each increment in net revenues or profit for the firm was .0325 percent or $3.25 for each $1,000 increase in shareholder wealth.[131] For the period 1980 to 1994, Brian J. Hall and Jeffrey B. Liebman find a slightly higher percentage but confirm the finding of Jensen and Murphy that CEO pay is closely correlated with performance.[132]

Critics might admit that firms increased in value during this period and that CEO pay rose proportionately but deny that this increase was due to the CEO's performance—or even if the CEO is responsible for the increase that he or she deserves to receive a proportionate share of the increased value. Although the contribution of CEOs to the increased value of firms may be questioned,[133] this matter is irrelevant as long as shareholders believe that the performance of CEOs is important and are willing to pay for performance. In a market, the terms of CEO compensation are determined by negotiations, in which the amount of incentive needed to achieve certain results is a major factor. This increase in value belongs to shareholders, and if they willingly share it with the CEO in the belief that that person is responsible for the increase and that the increase would not have occurred otherwise, then the pay is morally unobjectionable, even if the belief turns out to be mistaken.[134]

Critics may also question the link between pay and performance by citing the number of cases in which fired CEOs leave with a very substantial "golden handshake." The directors of Home Depot came under strong criticism, for example, when CEO Robert L. Nardelli received an exit package of more than $200 million after presiding over six years of disappointing performance, during which time the company's stock dropped more than 17 percent.[135] One reason for such cases is that some portion of a pay package must be set in advance based on anticipated performance, which may turn out to be incorrect.[136] CEO compensation almost always includes a guaranteed amount plus some performance-based pay.[137] This situation is little different from that of baseball pitchers who are paid large sums in anticipation of a winning season but who fail to perform as expected. Only a pure pay-for-performance system can avoid the mistakes that arise from imperfect knowledge of the future. However, in such a system, the pay for performance would be very high to compensate for the added risk. For example, a pitcher who is offered $1 million guaranteed pay with a bonus of another $1 million for a winning season might demand $3 million in a package that offers nothing in the event of a losing season.

In summary, the main factor responsible for high executive compensation is the linking of pay to performance, mainly through the use of stock options. The data show that since the early 1980s, shareholders have been willing to reward CEOs with a share of the value they add to firms and that the percentage of the added value awarded has been relatively constant. In linking pay with performance, shareholders are inducing CEOs to strive for maximum wealth creation by acting like entrepreneurs rather than mere bureaucrats. This account describes what has, in fact, happened with executive compensation, but it does not answer the normative question of whether this development is justified. Morally, should executives be paid for performance?

Justifying Pay for Performance

This chapter has assumed that the shareholders, through the board of directors, rightly control executive compensation, so that whatever amount of pay that would be approved by the shareholders is justified. Shareholder control of corporations includes not only the right to determine how much CEOs should be paid but also what they should be paid to do. If shareholders want CEOs to act like entrepreneurs and are willing to allow CEOs to share in the profits as an incentive for maximal performance, then it follows from the assumption of shareholder control that they have a right to do this.

The evidence suggests that paying for performance through the use of stock options is, in general, in the shareholders' interest. That CEOs in recent decades have received on average $3.25 or slightly more for every $1,000 of added value probably represents a good bargain for shareholders. Percentages in range of .0325 do not seem to be unreasonable if CEOs create value that would not be achieved otherwise. Investors in mutual funds willingly pay annual fees of 1 or 2 percent for the management of their assets, and hedge fund managers typically charge 2 percent of assets under management and 20 percent of all profits. If a hedge fund manager could achieve a higher return after all fees are paid than could be obtained from any alternative investments, then it would be irrational for investors not to pay the fees. Increased value comes at a price, and investors find it reasonable to pay some percentage of an increase in order to obtain it.

Moreover, how much would rational shareholders pay to achieve the desired results? There is no easy answer to this question except to accept the amount that would result from arm's-length bargaining in a free market. Although the CEO labor market is not wholly efficient or perfect, there is little reason to believe that the amount that executives receive through stock options is very far from the outcome of a better functioning market. However, it may be questioned whether shareholders ought to have the power to determine the level of executive compensation solely with a view to their own interests. Such power, which results from a shareholder-centered system corporate governance, raises two significant ethical issues.

First, the high-risk strategies that benefit diversified shareholders, who hold financial capital, may not be optimal for a firm's employees and managers, whose human capital is tied to one company and, hence, is undiversified. Even when some companies fail because of excessive risk-taking, the shareholders may gain overall as long as other stocks in their portfolios outperform the average when the high-risk strategies of other companies succeed. The main ethical issues here are what is the appropriate level of risk for a firm and who should determine this level. In general, shareholders prefer more risk than other stakeholders, and when they control the level of risk, they can gain at the expense of other groups. Although the level of risk taken by firms is a contributing factor to high CEO pay, these questions are a matter of corporate governance, and their answers lie beyond the focus of this chapter on executive compensation.

A second and more general ethical issue concerns the constraints on shareholders in selecting executives who will act like entrepreneurs in exploiting opportunities. High executive compensation is mainly a U.S. phenomenon; European and Japanese CEO pay did not experience the same dramatic rise in the 1990s. However, during the 1970s and 1980s, corporations outside the United States also did not experience the same restructuring that U.S. firms underwent, nor did they achieve the same productivity growth in the 1990s. This was due to many factors including labor laws that prevent layoffs, the lack of a market for corporate control to facilitate hostile takeovers, and legal obstacles to entrepreneurial start-up ventures.[138] The use of stock options to tie compensation more closely to performance was hindered by tax, securities, and accounting laws. Ownership patterns also play a role. Shareholders in Europe and Japan, which are typically large institutions with multiple relationships, consider objectives other than mere shareholder wealth, whereas the dispersed shareholders typical in the United States seek only a financial return. In addition, labor unions, which are concerned about pay equity, have board representation in some European countries but not in the United States.

All of these factors, which account for the differences in the level of compensation between the United States and much of the rest of the world, raise ethical issues about the legal structure of business. The laws in question reflect many values and moral judgments about business practice, as well as deep cultural forces. For example, if people in a country believe that job security is a right and that it is wrong to lay off workers, then shareholders will be constrained in undertaking restructurings that require massive layoffs. Corporate governance affects the balance of power between shareholders and other constituencies or stakeholders. For example, systems such as those of Germany and Japan, which are less shareholder-centered than U.S. corporate governance, have been adopted for many reasons, including considerations of fairness and social stability. A major factor, perhaps the decisive factor, in the current high levels of CEO pay in the United States is the considerable power of shareholders. How much power shareholders should have to insist that corporation pursue entrepreneurial opportunities, without regard for their impact on other groups, is a crucial ethical question in the justification of executive compensation.

CONCLUSION

The ethical justification of executive compensation is at once very simple and exceedingly complex. Considering the matter within the framework of the U.S. capitalist economic system and setting aside broader concerns about inequalities of income and wealth in society, there is general agreement on one proposition: The amount paid to CEOs is justified if it results from arm's-length bargaining between executives and the shareholders. The ultimate aim of this contracting is maximum wealth creation for shareholders. Many thoughtful people question this shareholder model of corporate governance as well as capitalism as an economic system, but it is assumed here in order focus solely on CEO pay.[139]

In a market for CEO talent, the prices for chief executives are determined in the same way as the prices of automobiles or houses, which is what well-informed buyers and sellers voluntarily agree to. Economic theory teaches that CEOs are paid not only for their marginal product but also to overcome an agency problem inherent in the separation of ownership and control. The principles P1 and P2 express the basic moral intuitions behind such free market exchanges: That each person has a right to whatever he or she gains by exchanging property rights through voluntary transactions, and that each person has a right to the full value of whatever he or she produces. In addition to such gains from voluntary contracting and production is the wealth created by entrepreneurial activity, the right to which is justified by Kirzner's finders-keepers rule, which is expressed in principle P3.

This is the simple part. Beyond this area of broad, but not universal, agreement, matters become much more difficult. The managerial power thesis denies that arm's-length contracting commonly occurs. Although the book by Bebchuk and Fried, *Pay without Performance*, has virtually defined the current debate on executive compensation, critics have succeeded in casting doubt on many of its main points. At best, the thesis is only a partial explanation of the high level of CEO pay. Even if the thesis is correct, though, it does not show that high compensation is unjustified but only that contracting over CEO pay involves rent-seeking in imperfect markets. Such rent-seeking is not morally wrong, except when accompanied by fraud or breach of fiduciary duty. Like other instances of imperfect markets that affect social welfare, it may be undesirable on consequentialist or utilitarian grounds. However, any laws or regulations that seek to correct imperfections in the market for CEOs—such as greater disclosure of pay packages to shareholders or changes in the nomination and election procedures—are wholly compatible with the principle that executive compensation should be set by arm's-length bargaining.

Another difficult part of the controversy over executive compensation is explaining how chief executives are really worth the amounts that are being paid. Justifying CEO pay depends crucially on what they are being paid to do. Before the 1980s, U.S. executives were paid essentially to act like bureaucrats in managing large, stable enterprises. This bureaucratic role has been the norm in Europe and Japan to the present day. If CEOs are expected to be bureaucrats, then it is difficult to understand how exceptionally high compensation can be justified. However, beginning in the 1980s and especially in the period 1995–2000, when CEO pay was at its peak, compensation was strongly tied to performance in order to induce executives to be highly entrepreneurial. The evidence is that CEOs have received a relatively constant percentage of the extra value they create for firms, so that pay is being tied to performance. Although it is generally agreed that the levels of compensation reached in 2000, when the average S&P 500 CEO garnered $17.4 million, resulted from the same excessive optimism that spawned a stock market bubble, the average of $9.1 million in 2003 probably represents good value for shareholders.

Whether CEOs have excessive power to influence their compensation and whether their pay would be agreed to by shareholders in arm's-length bargaining are factual or empirical questions, about which there is ongoing debate. The more critical normative question is whether executives ought to be paid as entrepreneurs by tying pay to performance in order to achieve the maximum return for shareholders. On the assumption that shareholders have a right to determine the level of CEO pay that best serves their own interest, paying CEOs to be entrepreneurs who seek a maximum return is justified. This result may be questioned, however, if unconstrained shareholder power itself is not just. If shareholder power is constrained, as it is in Europe and Japan, in order to advance other values, then CEO pay cannot be justified merely by considerations of shareholder interests, and its justification depends on the choices about corporate governance systems. To pursue this objection, though, would lead to a debate about comparative corporate governance.

The ultimate conclusion is that the high levels of executive compensation today are *probably* justified. This tentative outcome is unavoidable because the subject of executive compensation involves unresolved empirical considerations. Executive compensation is thus an example of a business ethics problem that demonstrates the limitations of normative analysis in the absence of greater empirical knowledge.

The argument for this conclusion also makes a number of assumptions about the justification of free market capitalism, including the distribution of income and wealth in such a system and a shareholder-centered system of corporate governance. These assumptions can be questioned, and any complete justification of executive compensation would have to provide a complete justification for them. Such a complete justification would eventually lead to questions about what we want from business corporations. Do we, as employees, consumers, investors, and citizens want to live in a society devoted to wealth creation with all its consequences or do we prefer to temper wealth creation with other values? Executive compensation, like all moral matters, comes down to the age-old question of how we should live.

NOTES

1. In this chapter, the terms "executive" and "CEO" are used interchangeably to refer to the chief executive officer of a publicly held corporation. In most U.S. corporations, the chief executive officer (CEO) is also the chairman of the board of directors, although the two positions are sometimes held by different persons. The "top executives" of a company generally comprise the officers (chief financial officer, chief operating officer, and so on) and anyone with the title of president. Generally, these persons are hired by the board, which also sets their compensation. The compensation of all other employees is set at the level of the CEO or lower.

2. Capitalism is not a single system but takes diverse forms, some more justified than others. For an account of different kinds of capitalism, see Charles Hampden-Turner and Fons Trompenaars, *The Seven Cultures of Capitalism: Values Systems for Creating Wealth in the United States, Japan, Germany, Britain, France, and the Netherlands* (New York: Doubleday, 1993). An assessment of each form is provided in William J. Baumol, Robert E. Litan, and Carl J. Schramm, *Good Capitalism, Bad Capitalism, and the Economics of Growth and Prosperity* (New Haven, Conn.: Yale University Press, 2007). For a comparison of U.S.-style market capitalism and the welfare capitalism of Japan and Germany, see Ronald P. Dore, *Stock Market Capitalism, Welfare Capitalism: Japan and Germany versus the Anglo-Saxons* (New York: Oxford University Press, 2000). Capitalism also changes over time in the same country. In Robert B. Reich, *Supercapitalism: The Transformation of Business, Democracy, and Everyday Life* (New York: Knopf, 2007), the author finds a difference in U.S. capitalism before and after the 1970s. The former he calls democratic capitalism, and the latter supercapitalism.

3. Independent directors are not current or former employees of the company and do not have any relation to the company beyond being a director. Being independent is thought to make such directors more objective in their judgment.

4. SERPs are "nonqualified" pension plans, which means that the company may not take a tax deduction for them. The value of SERPs is generally excluded from studies of executive compensation because they are difficult to value and are not commonly disclosed. However, the available evidence suggests that their value is often very high, and, given the lack of disclosure, some have called this the ultimate form of "stealth compensation." Kevin J. Murphy, "Executive Compensation," in *Handbook of Labor Economics*, ed. O. Ashenfelter and D. Card (New York: Elsevier Science B.V., 1999). See also Lucien Bebchuk and Robert Jackson, "Putting Executive Pensions on the Radar Screen,"

Discussion Paper No. 507, John M. Olin Center for Law, Economics and Business, Harvard Law School.

5. Peter F. Kostiuk, "Firm Size and Executive Compensation," *Journal of Human Resources* 25 (1) (1990): 90–105.

6. The Omnibus Budget Reconciliation Act of 1993 added Section 162(m) to the Internal Revenue Code, which removed the tax deductibility of salary compensation over $1 million. For its effect see Nancy L. Rose and Catherine Wolfram, "Has the 'Million Dollar Cap' Affected CEO Pay?" *American Economic Review* 90(2) (2000): 197–202; and Brian J. Hall and Jeffrey B. Liebman, "The Taxation of Executive Compensation," in *Tax Policy and the Economy*, vol. 14, ed. James Poterba (Cambridge: NBER & MIT Press, 2000).

7. Christopher Cox, the chairman of the Securities and Exchange Commission, in testimony to the Senate Banking Committee commented, "This tax law change deserved pride of place in the Museum of Unintended Consequences." Eric Dash, "Congress Is Urged to Hold Off Acting on Options and Pay," *New York Times*, September 7, 2006, C3.

8. Murphy reports that in 1996, approximately 27 percent of S&P 500 CEOs received income from LTIPs and that the amount for those CEOs was 20 percent of total compensation. Murphy, "Executive Compensation," 2516.

9. See Murphy, "Executive Compensation," 2500–2503, for an analysis of performance measures.

10. Michael C. Jensen, Kevin J. Murphy, and Eric G. Wruck, *Remuneration: Where We've Been, How We Got Here, What Are the Problems, and How to Fix Them*, Harvard Business School NOM Research Paper No. 04–28 (2004), 25.

11. Brian J. Hall and Jeffrey B. Liebman, "Are CEOs Really Paid Like Bureaucrats?" *Quarterly Journal of Economics* 113 (3) (1998): 653–691.

12. In-the-money options are obviously worth more than ones out of the money, but they are seldom issued because they must be immediately recorded as an expense to the company and as a tax liability for the employee since they have cash value on the day of issue.

13. Companies issue stock options not only to top executives but to employees at all levels. The purpose of stock options issued to lower level employees is generally not to provide an incentive, as is the case of top executives, but to provide more compensation than the company is able to pay current revenues. Stock options to lower level employees have been used most extensively in high-tech start-up firms that lack sufficient revenues to pay employees their market worth.

14. Murphy, "Executive Compensation," 2510.

15. Lucian Bebchuk and Yaniv Grinstein, "The Growth of Executive Pay," *Oxford Review of Economic Policy* 21 (2) (2005): 283–303.

16. Michael C. Jensen, "The Modern Industrial Revolution, Exit, and the Failure of Internal Control Systems," *Journal of Finance* 48 (3) (1993): 831–880.

17. Margaret M. Blair, "CEO Pay: Why Such a Controversy?" *Brookings Review* 94 (1) (1994): 23–31.

18. Kevin J. Murphy, "Politics, Economics, and Executive Compensation," *University of Cincinnati Law Review* 63 (1995): 713–746.

19. Dore, *Stock Market Capitalism, Welfare Capitalism*. Dore defends the Japanese and European systems despite the slow economic growth of these regions compared to the United States.

20. The points in this and the next paragraph are due to Ernie Englander and Allen Kaufman, "The End of Managerial Ideology: From Corporate Social Responsibility to Corporate Social Indifference," *Enterprise and Society* 5 (3) (2004): 404–450.

21. Adolf A. Berle Jr., and Gardiner C. Means, *The Modern Corporation and Private Property* (New York: Macmillan, 1932).

22. Although stock options were issued to executives in the 1945–1973 period, they were intended primarily to respond to high marginal tax rates by providing nonsalary compensation that was taxed at a lower rate than ordinary income. The use of stock options declined between 1955 and 1973 due to the stagnation of stock prices. See Wilbur G. Lewellen, *Executive Compensation in Large Industrial Corporations* (New York: Columbia University Press, 1958), 211–226.

23. Englander and Kaufman, *The End of Managerial Ideology*, 425.

24. "Managers saw in shareholder advocacy the opportunities that had eluded them as impartial, public-spirited technocrats" (Englander and Kaufman, *The End of Managerial Ideology*, 428).

25. Englander and Kaufman, *The End of Managerial Ideology*, 428. Englander and Kaufman note that CEOs were also supported in this shift by economic conservatives, who had long rejected the bureaucratic thesis and looked to competitive markets and property rights as the basis of corporate governance (440).

26. John A. Byrne, "CEO Pay: Ready for Takeoff," *Business Week*, April 24, 1995, 88–119.

27. Nicholas D. Kristof, "America's Laziest Man?" *New York Times*, November 7, 2006, A21.

28. Bebchuk and Grinstein, "The Growth of Executive Pay." These figures, which are based on the ExecuComp database of the S&P 1500 companies, excludes the value of pension plans, which Bebchuk and Grinstein say is a "significant source" of compensation.

29. Bebchuk and Grinstein, "The Growth of Executive Pay," 296.

30. Lucian Bebchuk and Jesse Fried, *Pay without Performance: The Unfulfilled Promise of Executive Compensation* (Cambridge, Mass.: Harvard University Press, 2004). Graef S. Crystal, *In Search of Excess: The Overcompensation of American Executives* (New York: W. W. Norton, 1991).

31. John M. Abowd and David S. Kaplan, "Executive Compensation: Six Questions that Need Answering," *Journal of Economic Perspectives* 13 (4) (1999): 145–168.

32. See Philip L. Cochran and Steven L. Wartick, "'Golden Parachutes': A Closer Look," *California Management Review* 26 (4) (1984): 111–125.

33. Aristotle, *Politics*, 1265b21, 1266b6.

34. Graef S. Crystal, "The CEO Factor," *Columbia Journalism Review* 32 (4) 1993: 49–50.

35. This policy was abandoned in 1994 when CEO Ben Cohen retired and no replacement could be found for less than twice his modest salary of $133,212. Barbara Carton, "A Ben & Jerry's Principle Hits a Melting Point," *Boston Globe*, June 4, 1994, Metro 1. The salary is exclusive of retirement, stock options, and the return on the substantial stock he held as a cofounder of the company. When the company was sold in 2000 to Unilever, Cohen personally received $46 million.

36. Murphy, "Executive Compensation," 2553.

37. Scott Klinger, Chris Hartman, Sarah Anderson, John Cavanagh, and Holly Sklar, "Executive Excess 2002: CEOs Cook the Books, Skewer the Rest of Us," Ninth Annual CEO Compensation Survey, Institute for Policy Studies and United for a Fair Economy, 2002, cites the figure 411 to 1. Bebchuk and Fried, *Pay without Performance*, 1, accepts the figure of 500 to 1.

38. Xavier Gabaix and Augustin Landier, "Why Has CEO Pay Increased So Much?" Unpublished Manuscript, July 21, 2006.

39. Bebchuk and Grinstein, "The Growth of Executive Pay," 285.

40. Klinger et al., "Executive Excess 2002," 14.

41. Bob Herbert, "Working Harder for the Man," *New York Times*, January 8, 2007, A19.

42. Derek Bok, *The Cost of Talent: How Executives and Professionals Are Paid and How It Affects America* (New York: Free Press, 1993), 102.

43. Kristof, "America's Laziest Man?"

44. Bruno S. Frey, *Not Just for the Money: An Economic Theory of Personal Motivation* (Cheltenham, U.K.: Edward Elgar, 1997); Edward Deci, *Intrinsic Motivation* (New York: Plenum Press, 1975).

45. George P. Baker, Michael C. Jensen, and Kevin J. Murphy, "Compensation and Incentives: Practice vs. Theory," *Journal of Finance* 43 (3) (1988): 597.

46. Brian J. Hall and Kevin J. Murphy, "The Trouble with Stock Options," *Journal of Economic Perspectives* 17 (3) (2003): 49–70.

47. Shane A. Johnson, Harley E. Ryan, and Yisong S. Tian, "Executive Compensation and Corporate Fraud," Unpublished Manuscript, April 21, 2005. Merle Ericson, Michelle Hanlon, and Edward Maydew, "Is There a Link between Executive Compensation and Accounting Fraud?" Unpublished Manuscript, February 24, 2004. Jared Harris and Philip Bromiley, "Incentives to Cheat: The Influence of Executive Compensation and Firm Performance on Financial Misrepresentation," *Organization Science*, 18 (3) (2007): 350–367.

48. Murphy, *Executive Compensation*, 2486; Bebchuk and Fried, *Pay without Performance*, 137–146.

49. Murphy, *Executive Compensation*, 2510.

50. Hall and Murphy, "The Trouble with Stock Options," 65–67.

51. For example, see Jerry Useem, "Have They NO Shame?" *Fortune*, April 28, 2003, 58.

52. Robert J. Samuelson, "Delinquency of the CEOs," *Washington Post*, July 13, 2006, A23.

53. John Rawls, *A Theory of Justice* (Cambridge, Mass.: Harvard University Press, 1971), 20, 48–51.

54. John Rawls, *Political Liberalism* (New York: Columbia University Press, 1993), 15.

55. R. M. Hare, "Liberty and Equality: How Politics Masquerades as Philosophy," in *Liberty and Equality*, ed. Ellen F. Paul, Fred D. Miller Jr., and Jeffrey Paul (Oxford: Basil Blackwell, 1985), 5.

56. The capital provided by shareholders raises problems because its return, namely profit, is not easily secured by contracts of the kind that protect employees, suppliers, and other participants in a firm. The main purpose of corporate governance is to protect the vulnerable contribution of shareholders to the productive process.

57. Robert Nozick, *Anarchy, State, and Utopia* (New York: Basic Books, 1974), 151.

58. The question of the justification of free market exchange is not considered further here. Allan Gibbard distinguishes two kinds of justifications. One kind of justification holds the right to liberty or property to be of ultimate value; the other kind justifies free market exchanges for the value of their outcome, such an enhancing welfare. Allan Gibbard, "What's Morally Special about Free Market Exchange?" in *Ethics and Economics*, eds. Ellen Frankel Paul, Fred D. Miller Jr., and Jeffrey Paul (Oxford: Basil Blackwell, 1985).

59. Rawls, *A Theory of Justice*, 72.

60. As previously noted, in adding Section 162(m) to the Internal Revenue Code, Congress limited to $1 million the amount of executive salary that is tax deductible for the corporation. Although this was an attempt to reduce executive compensation, it is not an outright prohibition, which might be considered an unjustified interference in the right of contract between a corporation and an executive, but it is within the taxation powers of government. The fact that this amount may be exceeded by a board-approved plan based on performance that is disclosed to shareholders further recognizes the right of the corporation and an executive to transact freely.

61. Milton Friedman, *Capitalism and Freedom* (Chicago: University of Chicago Press, 1962), 161–162.

62. Typically, workers receive less than the value of what they produce. This difference is called by Marxists "surplus value" and is the basis of the charge that capitalism exploits workers. However, the productivity of a worker requires other inputs, including raw materials, machinery, and capital. The cost of these inputs must be paid out of the revenues generated by what workers produce. Wages represent the value of workers' contribution net of other costs of production. And profit, which is what remains after all costs are paid, is the return on capital. The error in the Marxist doctrine of surplus value is the failure to recognize the legitimacy of profit as the return on capital.

63. Although such a result follows from economic theory, it is well known that it is not true in practice, and various explanations have been offered for this deviation from theoretical predictions, including the difficulty of measuring each person's marginal product, workers' risk aversion, and a concern about status. See Armen A. Alchian and Howard Demsetz, "Production, Information Costs, and Economic Organization," *American Economic Review* 62 (December 1972): 777–795; Joseph E. Stiglitz, "Incentives, Risk, and Information," *Bell Journal of Economics* 6 (1975): 552–579; and Robert H. Frank, "Are Workers Paid Their Marginal Product?" *American Economic Review* 74 (4) (1984): 549–571. Baker, Jensen, and Murphy note that many explanations by behaviorists are "distinctly uneconomic" and focus on such considerations as fairness, morale, and trust. George P. Baker, Michael C. Jensen, and Kevin J. Murphy, "Compensation and Incentives: Practice vs. Theory," *Journal of Finance* 43 (3) (1988): 593–616.

64. A fuller account would involve separate treatments of debt capital and equity capital, only the latter of which receives profit as a return. However, both kind of capital involve a contract between capital providers and the firm such that its receipts (debt payments and profits, respectively) are justified by P1 and P2.

65. Frank H. Knight, *Risk, Uncertainty and Profit* (Chicago: University of Chicago Press, 1971). Such profits are also called "supernormal" and "abnormal."

66. Joseph Schumpeter, *The Theory of Economic Development* (Cambridge, Mass.: Harvard University Press, 1950).

67. "An entrepreneur can make a profit only if he anticipates future conditions more correctly than other entrepreneurs. Then he buys the complementary factors of production at prices the sum of which…is smaller than the price at which he sells his product." Ludwig von Mises, *Human Action* (New Haven, Conn.: Yale University Press, 1949), 291. See also Israel M. Kirzner, *Competition and Entrepreneurship* (Chicago: University of Chicago Press, 1973).

68. Israel M. Kirzner, *Discovery, Capitalism, and Distributive Justice* (Oxford: Basil Blackwell, 1989), 49.

69. Israel M. Kirzner, "The Nature of Profits: Some Economic Insights and Their Ethical Implications," in *Profits and Morality*, ed. Robin Cowan and Mario J. Rizzo (Chicago: University of Chicago Press, 1995), 39.

70. Ibid.

71. Kirzner, *Discovery, Capitalism, and Distributive Justice*, 98.

72. John Locke, *An Essay Concerning the True Original Extent and End of Civil Government*, sec. 27.

73. Nozick, *Anarchy, State, and Utopia*, 151.

74. Kirzner, *Discovery, Capitalism, and Distributive Justice*, 153.

75. Ibid., 150.

76. N. Scott Arnold justifies pure profit on the grounds that it "best promotes the essential goal of the market" by combining control over productive resources with personal

responsibility for results. N. Scott Arnold, "Why Profits Are Deserved," *Ethics* 97 (January 1987): 387–402.

77. What the entrepreneur has discovered and has a right to under the finders-keepers rules is an economic opportunity, which may be a new product, a method of production or a business model, not the income from it. However, if the economic opportunity belongs to the discoverer as a kind of property, then he or she also has a right, by principles P1 and P2 to derive income through economic exchange. Thus, P1 and P2 are essential for justifying the entrepreneur's income from his or her discovery by means of the finders-keepers rule.

78. A reserve price is the minimum amount that a person is willing to accept in trade for some good, the good in this case being an executive's services.

79. Sydney Finkelstein and Donald C. Hambrick, "Chief Executive Compensation: A Synthesis and Reconciliation," *Strategic Management Journal* 9 (1988): 543–558, 546.

80. Finkelstein and Hambrick, "Chief Executive Compensation," 547–548.

81. D. Wechsler, "Would Adam Smith Pay Them So Much?" *Forbes*, May 28, 1990, 210.

82. The contractual theory has been developed by economists using an agency or transaction-cost perspective. See Alchian and Demsetz, "Production, Information Costs, and Economic Organization"; Benjamin Klein, Robert A. Crawford, and Armen A. Alchian, "Vertical Integration, Appropriable Rents, and the Competitive Contracting Process," *Journal of Law and Economics*, 21 (1978): 297–326; Michael C. Jensen and William H. Meckling, "Theory of the Firm: Managerial Behavior, Agency Costs, and Ownership Structure," *Journal of Financial Economics* 3 (1983): 305–360; Eugene F. Fama and Michael C. Jensen, "Separation of Ownership and Control," *Journal of Law and Economics* 26 (1983): 301–325; Steven N. S. Cheung, "The Contractual Theory of the Firm," *Journal of Law and Economics* 26 (1983): 1–22; and Oliver E. Williamson, *The Economic Institutions of Capitalism* (New York: Free Press, 1985). An authoritative development of the theory of the firm in corporate law is Frank H. Easterbrook and Daniel R. Fischel, *The Economic Structure of Corporate Law* (Cambridge, Mass.: Harvard University Press, 1991). See also William A. Klein, "The Modern Business Organization: Bargaining under Constraints," *Yale Law Journal* 91 (1982): 1521–1564; Oliver Hart, "An Economist's Perspective on the Theory of the Firm," *Columbia Law Review*, 89 (1989): 1757–1773; and Henry N. Butler, "The Contractual Theory of the Firm," *George Mason Law Review* 11 (1989): 99–123.

83. Berle and Means, *The Modern Corporation and Private Property*.

84. For a survey of the agency structure of a firm, see John W. Pratt and Richard J. Zeckhauser, eds., *Principals and Agents: The Structure of Business* (Cambridge, Mass.: Harvard University Press, 1985).

85. Bebchuk and Fried, *Pay without Performance*, 3.

86. See Sherwin Rosen, "The Economics of Superstars," *American Economic Review*, 71 (5) (1981): 845–858. This point is also expressed in Robert Nozick's example involving Wilt Chamberlain. Nozick, *Anarchy, State, and Utopia*, 161–163.

87. See, for example, Joe Nocera, "What If CEO Pay Is Fair?" *New York Times*, October 13, 2007, C1: "But what offends me most is…that the market for executive compensation is so clearly rigged."

88. The thesis of the book is also developed in Lucian Arye Bebchuk, Jesse M. Fried, and David L. Walker, "Managerial Power and Rent Extraction in the Design of Executive Compensation," *Chicago Law Review* 69 (2002): 751–846.

89. Bebchuk and Fried, *Pay without Performance*, 9.

90. Ibid., 26.

91. See Gretchen Morgenson, "Gilded Paychecks: Troubling Conflicts; Outside Advice on Boss's Pay May Not Be So Independent," *New York Times*, April 10, 2006, A1.

92. Bebchuk and Fried, *Pay without Performance*, 67.

93. Ibid., 74.

94. Public Company Accounting Reform and Investor Protection (Sarbanes-Oxley) Act, Pub. L. No. 107–204, 116 Stat. 745, section 402.

95. Repricing occurs when the strike price of an option is lowered. Typically, this is done when the price of a stock declines and the options become worthless, and the reason for repricing is to restore their incentive effect.

96. Reloadable option plans allow executives to exercise options and receive new options for the same number of shares with the same expiration date as the old options. Reloadable options enable a holder to lock in some gains while still having the opportunity to benefit from future gains and to benefit from temporary price rises even if the long-term stock price is flat. Reloadable options reduce the risk of holding the options and provide an incentive to increase volatility instead of long-term appreciation. Bebchuk and Fried, *Pay without Performance*, 169–170.

97. Bebchuk and Fried, *Pay without Performance*, 137–146.

98. Most notably, William Bratton, "The Academic Tournament over Executive Compensation," *California Law Review* 93 (2005): 1557–1584; John E. Core, Wayne R. Guay, and Randall S. Thomas, "Is U.S. CEO Compensation Inefficient Pay without Performance?" *Michigan Law Review* 103 (2004–2005): 1142–1185; and Stephen M. Bainbridge, "Executive Compensation: Who Decides?" *Texas Law Review* 83 (2004–2005): 1615–1662.

99. Bengt Holmstrom, "*Pay without Performance* and the Managerial Power Hypothesis: A Comment," *Journal of Corporation Law* (Summer 2005): 703–715, 704.

100. Bengt Holmstrom and Steven N. Kaplan, "The State of U.S. Corporate Governance," European Corporate Governance Institute, Working Paper No. 23/2003, 11.

101. Iman Anabtawi, "Explaining Pay Without Performance: The Tournament Alternative," *Emory Law Journal* 54 (2005): 1557–1602. One study shows a positive correlation between low executive compensation and another proxy for managerial power, namely a large shareholder. Marianne Bertrand and Sendhi Mullainathan, "Are CEOs Rewarded for Luck: The Ones without Principals Are," *Quarterly Journal of Economics* 116(3) (2001): 901–932. However, Anabtawi rejects a large outside shareholder as a useful proxy for a lack of managerial power.

102. Sanjai Bhagat and Bernard Black, "The Non-Correlation between Board Independence and Long-Term Firm Performance," *Journal of Corporation Law* 27 (2001–2002): 231–273.

103. Kevin J. Murphy, "Explaining Executive Compensation: Managerial Power versus the Perceived Cost of Stock Options," *University of Chicago Law Review* 69 (2002): 847–869.

104. Core et al., "Is U.S. CEO Compensation Inefficient Pay without Performance?" 1164.

105. Ibid., 1165–1166.

106. Bevis Longstreth, "A Real World Critique of *Pay without Performance*," *Journal of Corporation Law* 30(4) (2005): 767–771. Longstreth observes that a person may want to bargain at arm's-length with a car salesman but not a brain surgeon: "You and the surgeon have an ongoing relationship to carry forth. So, too, does the board with the CEO" (768).

107. Holmstrom and Kaplan, "The State of U.S. Corporate Governance," 4.

108. Bebchuk and Fried, *Pay without Performance*, 62.

109. The test would be whether a worker could quit a current job and obtain another job with the same or greater pay. If any other job would entail a pay loss, then the worker enjoys a rent, which is the difference between the pay of the current job and the next best alternative.

110. Bebchuk and Fried, *Pay without Performance*, 62.

111. David Gauthier, *Morals by Agreement* (Oxford: Clarendon Press, 1986). Gauthier focuses on the income that star athletes whose services are in high demand are able to

command. His argument is that the actions of everyone contribute to the conditions that make rents possible, and so everyone should share in these rents. For criticism, see Eric Mack, "Gauthier on Rights and Economic Rent," *Social Philosophy and Policy* 9 (1) (1992): 171–200.

112. Landon Thomas Jr., "The Winding Road to the Huge Payday," *New York Times*, June 25, 2006, C1.

113. Dan Frosch, "Ex-Chief at Qwest Found Guilty," *New York Times*, April 20, 2007, C1.

114. Charles Forelle and James Bandler, "The Perfect Payday: Some CEOs Reap Millions by Landing Stock Options When They Are the Most Valuable; Luck—or Something Else?" *Wall Street Journal*, March 18, 2006, A1. See also Randall Heron, Erik Lie, and Tod Perry, "On the Use (and Abuse) of Stock Option Grants," *Financial Analysts Journal* 63 (3) (2007): 17–27.

115. Backdated options are "in-the-money options" because the strike price is below the value of the stock on the day of issue. Because the option would have cash value if it were immediately exercised, it must be recorded as an expense to the corporation and as taxable income for the recipient.

116. Jensen et al., "Remuneration," 37.

117. Bebchuk and Fried, *Pay without Performance*, 62.

118. Anne O. Krueger, "The Political Economy of the Rent-Seeking Society," *American Economic Review* 64 (3) (1974): 291–303. Krueger demonstrates that when regulation creates rents, firms may compete for the benefit of regulation instead of competing in the products market. With regard to executive compensation, CEOs may seek to structure pay in ways that benefit themselves but destroy value for the firm. Bebchuk and Fried, *Pay without Performance*, 63.

119. Although shareholders elect members of the board of directors, the slate of nominees for election is prepared by the nominating committee of the board. The power of shareholders is typically limited to deciding whether or not to vote for the board-prepared slate of nominees.

120. "Executive Compensation and Related Person Disclosure," Securities and Exchange Commission, *Federal Register*, vol. 71, No. 174, September 8, 2006.

121. "SEC Votes to Adopt Changes to Disclosure Requirements Concerning Executive Compensation and Related Matters," U.S. Securities and Exchange Commission, press release, 2006–123.

122. Stephen Labaton, "A Public Airing for Proposals on Shareholders," *New York Times*, July 26, 2007, C3.

123. For one critical view, see Lynn Stout, "Corporations Shouldn't Be Democracies," *Wall Street Journal*, September 27, 2007, A17.

124. Or more precisely the *expected* marginal product since some compensation must be committed in advance and cannot be tied wholly to performance. In anticipating the value of a CEO's contribution, shareholders can, of course, make mistakes.

125. Jack Welch and John Byrne, *Jack: Straight from the Gut* (New York: Warner Books, 2001).

126. Englander and Kaufman, "The End of Managerial Ideology," 438.

127. Louis V. Gerstner, *Who Says Elephants Can't Dance? Leading a Great Enterprise through Dramatic Change* (New York: Collins, 2003).

128. Remarks by Chairman Alan Greenspan at the Annual Dinner and Francis Boyer Lecture of The American Enterprise Institute for Public Policy Research, Washington, D.C., December 5, 1996.

129. Gabaix and Landier, "Why Has CEO Pay Increased So Much?"

130. The capitalization of a corporation is its stock price multiplied by the number of outstanding shares. This amount represents the market price of the company and its value to shareholders.

131. Michael C. Jensen and Kevin J. Murphy, "Performance Pay and Top Management Incentives," *Journal of Political Economy* 98 (2) (1990): 225–265.

132. Hall and Liebman, "Are CEOs Really Paid Like Bureaucrats?" Hall and Liebman do not provide an average percentage but seek rather to correlate the amount of CEO pay with quality of performance.

133. See, for example, Rakesh Khurana, *Searching for a Corporate Savior: The Irrational Quest for Charismatic CEOs* (Princeton, N.J.: Princeton University Press, 2002).

134. Generally, the mistakes of market participants are held to be their own fault, absent any fraud. For example, the purchase of a house at too high a price is not unjust because the buyer had the opportunity to gain more information that might have led him or her to pay less. If shareholders overpay a CEO, then they have only themselves to blame, and they pay the cost of the mistake. Moreover, the right price for a house or a CEO cannot be determined in advance except through a market. Even though people may make mistakes in a market, the only remedy is to make the market work better.

135. Eric Dash, "An Ousted Chief's Going-Away Pay Is Seen by Many as Typically Excessive," *New York Times*, January 4, 2007.

136. Other reasons include the fact that exit packages typically include deferred compensation, which could have been taken earlier, as well as vested stock options. Moreover, most terms of a CEO's contract are negotiated before employment with a view by both the executive and the company of its expected value. Although Robert Nardelli's departure package exceeded his combined compensation during his six-year tenure, which was $64 million, his total compensation amounted to $45.8 million a year. In order to judge whether his golden handshake was excessive, one would have to ask whether expected annual compensation of $45.8 million would have been viewed as fair at the time of his hiring. That Nardelli, a former GE executive, was subsequently hired to be CEO of Chrysler Corporation suggests that he has high potential. Because the new owner of Chrysler is a private equity firm (Cerberus), it is likely that his compensation is heavily based on performance. See Micheline Maynard, "Once Tainted, Nardelli Now Has Chrysler's Keys," *New York Times*, August 7, 2007, A1.

137. A few CEOs—Steven Jobs at Apple is one—receive a salary of $1 per year, with the rest of the compensation in performance-based bonuses and stock options. Very few CEOs are willing to base their pay entirely on performance.

138. Brian R. Cheffins, "Will Executive Pay Globalize Along American Lines?" *Corporate Governance: An International Review* 11 (1) (2003): 8–24.

139. For an argument in support of the shareholder model of corporate governance, see John R. Boatright, "Ethics and Corporate Governance: Justifying the Role of Shareholder," in *The Blackwell Guide to Business Ethics*, ed. Norman E. Bowie (Malden, Mass.: Blackwell, 2002).

SUGGESTED READING

Abowd, John M. and David S. Kaplan. "Executive Compensation: Six Questions that Need Answering." *Journal of Economic Perspectives* 13 (1999): 145–168.

Bebchuk, Lucian and Jesse Fried. *Pay Without Performance: The Unfulfilled Promise of Executive Compensation*. Cambridge, Mass.: Harvard University Press, 2004.

Bebchuk, Lucian and Yaniv Grinstein. "The Growth of Executive Pay." *Oxford Review of Economic Policy* 21 (2005): 283–303.

Blair, Margaret M. "CEO Pay: Why Such a Controversy?" *Brookings Review* 94 (1994): 23–31.

Crystal, Graef S. *In Search of Excess: The Overcompensation of American Executives* (New York: W. W. Norton, 1991).

Englander, Ernie and Allen Kaufman. "The End of Managerial Ideology: From Corporate Social Responsibility to Corporate Social Indifference." *Enterprise and Society* 5 (2004): 404–450.

Finkelstein, Sidney and Donald C. Hambrick. "Chief Executive Compensation: A Synthesis and Reconciliation." *Strategic Management Journal* 9 (1988): 543–558.

Gabaix, Xavier and Augustin Landier. "Why Has CEO Pay Increased So Much?" Unpublished Manuscript, 2006.

Hall, Brian J. and Jeffrey B. Liebman. "Are CEOs Really Paid Like Bureaucrats?" *Quarterly Journal of Economics* 113 (1998): 653–691.

Kirzner, Israel M. *Discovery, Capitalism, and Distributive Justice.* Oxford: Basil Blackwell, 1989.

Kolb, Robert W. ed. *The Ethics of Executive Compensation.* Malden, Mass.: Blackwell Publishers, 2006.

Jensen, Michael C. "The Modern Industrial Revolution, Exit, and the Failure of Internal Control Systems." *Journal of Finance* 48 (1993): 831–880.

Jensen, Michael C., and Kevin J. Murphy. "CEO Incentives: It's Not How Much You Pay, but How." *Harvard Business Review* May–June 1990: 138–149.

Jensen, Michael C., Kevin J. Murphy, and Eric G. Wruck. *Remuneration: Where We've Been, How We Got Here, What Are the Problems, and How to Fix Them.* Harvard Business School NOM Research Paper No. 04–28, 2004.

McCall, John J. "Assessing American Executive Compensation: A Cautionary Tale for Europeans." *Business Ethics: A European Review* 13 (2004): 243–254.

Moriarty, Jeffrey. "Do CEOs Get Paid Too Much?" *Business Ethics Quarterly* 15 (2005): 257–281.

Murphy, Kevin J. "Politics, Economics, and Executive Compensation," *University of Cincinnati Law Review* 63 (1995): 713–746.

———— "Executive Compensation." In *Handbook of Labor Economics.* Edited by Orley Ashenfelter and David Card. New York: Elsevier Science B.V., 1999.

Piketty, Thomas and Emmanuel Saez. "The Evolution of Top Incomes: A Historical and International Perspective." National Bureau of Economic Research, Working Paper 11955 (2006).

CHAPTER 7

JUST ACCESS TO HEALTH CARE AND PHARMACEUTICALS

PAUL T. MENZEL

ACCESS to health care has been a subject of long-standing interest to business and its employees, particularly in the United States, which does not have a comprehensive system of universal coverage provided or mandated by the government. Once health care came to be seen as significantly related to health by the mid-twentieth century, health insurance not only became a benefit employees wanted but it also became a benefit that business owners, too, were interested in providing if they could competitively afford it. A healthy workforce not exposed to the financial ravages of uninsured illness is likely to be more productive. Eventually, access to health care, including pharmaceuticals, came to be discussed in terms of employee rights and employer obligations. Such alleged rights and obligations can be approached as moral matters, including a concern for justice and fairness, not merely employee and employer self-interest.

A very different dimension of moral discussion about just access to health care occurs in certain businesses' relationship to their consumers. Pharmaceutical and health insurance companies confront questions about just consumer access to their products. Many health insurance companies justly segment the market and "experience rate" premiums, charging likely ill subscribers more for equivalent coverage—often much, much more—than they charge less likely ill subscribers. What are the limits to a just price that drug companies may charge for "orphan drugs"—drugs for rare conditions that cost companies more to develop per prospective customer than typical research and development (R&D) expense? May pharmaceutical companies justifiably insist, as a matter of the fair distribution of the costs of R&D, that U.S. consumers not be allowed to buy "reimported" drugs at discount prices from Canadian distributors, or is it U.S. consumers who can legitimately complain that drug companies are denying them affordable access to drugs that have become too expensive for their health plans to cover if reimportation is banned? Many such questions abound in the literature on this subject.

First, I treat the concerns that are directly about consumers in two sections: one on consumer rights as related to alleged obligations of health insurance companies, and another on drug consumers' rights and the correlative obligations of pharmaceutical companies. In the subsequent third section, I will treat the concerns about employees and employers as related to just access to care. In a fourth section, I explore just access to health care and pharmaceuticals within a broader, society-wide perspective, not just as matters of concern for employees and employers or consumers and companies.

My intent is more to reveal and clarify issues than, in all cases, to lay out the strongest arguments for my own conclusions, but I will not hesitate to note where I believe persuasive arguments lead. Some important themes, claims, and arguments are found throughout my analysis, chiefly these three: (1) The ideological polarization of views about just access to health care and pharmaceuticals that tends to pit egalitarians, individual rights libertarians, and collective-good utilitarians against each other will often break down when the issues and arguments are closely examined;[1] (2) most of the rights and obligations of particular parties in relation to just access to health care in the United States are contingent on larger principles and ideas widely shared in U.S. society; and (3) both of the previous two themes point to the real possibility of finding common moral ground on contentious issues between consumers and companies, and employees and employers.

I will also attend to "free-riding" issues more frequently than in the usual treatment of just access to health care. Free-riding occurs when an individual or organization obtains a benefit without paying its alleged fair share of the cost. Not all conceptions of justice in access to vital goods centrally feature principles about free-riding. However, some do. In any case, conceptions of fairness that involve anti-free-riding principles are particularly prominent in the business world. The notion of fair competition in a marketplace inherently involves claims about when businesses would be cheating on other competitors by trying to get the advantages of well-ordered market competition without paying their fair share of adhering to the rules of that competition. Even if the dominant philosophical milieu for business is one in which ambitious notions of distributive justice (along the lines of "*redistributive, social* justice") are suspicious, business persons are more likely to view a discussion of fair and just access as naturally fitting into their perspective if it significantly focuses on claims about free-riding.

CONSUMERS AND HEALTH INSURANCE COMPANIES

In a society like the United States that neither provides universal insurance to basic health care nor mandates that everyone be insured, what justice-based obligations ought to temper the competitive behavior of for-profit insurance companies? Many of the same moral rights and obligations that apply to other businesses, of course, will apply here—truth in advertising, faithful execution of contracts, and the like. However, health insurance is different than most other business sectors in the centrality and depth of its tensions between the needs of consumers and the competitive incentives of insurers, tensions that easily generate moral controversies.

One source of these tensions is an understandable element of insurance behavior, the avoidance of "adverse selection." The term refers to choices ("selection") of different levels of insurance—robust compared to lean, for example, or even whether to insure at all—that *subscribers* make on the basis of what they believe is their likelihood of needing the care the insurance will cover. Such choices by subscribers, made for their own perceived advantage, will often be "adverse" for insurers. Subscribers get the advantage of adjusting coverage, or insuring at all, according to what they believe is their propensity to incur costs of care, a propensity the insurer is usually not able as accurately to discern—one tends to know, or at least sense, one's propensity to illness and accident better than prospective insurers can detect it from information accessible to them. Insurers' very livelihood is jeopardized by such informational imbalance. Understandably, they develop strategies in response—they must to survive. As defensible as these strategies are for insurers, however, collectively the strategies are not benign. One type of response, market segmentation, is commonplace in private insurance unless it is prohibited, and a particularly offensive form of it, genetic discrimination, lurks in the background as our knowledge about genetic propensity for illness expands.

Market Segmentation

For both individual and group policy insurance markets, a common response of insurers to the prospect of adverse selection is to use "experience" as opposed to "community" rating: set premiums for a particular individual or group by the actual experience of paying for their care, not by the average expense in a much larger pool of persons in the community. At the point of initial insurance purchase, particularly with individual policies, insurers may have little information to go on, so they protect themselves by measures such as preexisting condition exclusions and implicit surcharges simply because the policy is individual. Once a person or group has been insured for a while, actual expense experience can become the guide, and adverse selection greatly reduced, if not eliminated. The result is that for both individual and group policies, the market of subscribers divides into many different high and low cost segments.

While the initial logic of these divide-and-charge-accordingly strategies is defensive—and guards against adverse selection, in a heavily pressured, for-profit competitive framework—the logic quickly becomes more ambitious. The quickest way for companies to profit is to minimize coverage for higher-risk persons, a highly ironic development since these are precisely the people most in need of coverage. A competitive voluntary insurance market is thus likely to reflect what might be called the Inverse Coverage Law: The more that people need coverage, the less likely they are to get it—either because they are denied coverage altogether or charged much more, which also makes it less likely that they will insure.[2] Selective marketing becomes not just temporary preexisting condition exclusion clauses and waiting periods but coverage caps, claims harassment, and rapid policy switching ("churning"), among other techniques.[3] Moreover, the competitive for-profit context must always be kept in mind: If even a few insurers use these techniques, others fall under pressure to follow on pain of losing market share of the persons most profitable to insure. People with disabilities and disease then suffer the double burden of uncovered medical bills and higher premiums, in addition to limited ability to work. Those persons, even with good income, are often forced to use up their savings and impoverish themselves.[4] The relatively well, on the other hand, often like such arrangements, though they may not realize the harmful effects on others.

In health insurance, all market segmentation techniques raise moral questions of just access. At the extreme, market segmentation blocks access by making insurance unaffordable to those who need it most. Even where it does not have that great an effect, it still places a high burden of expenditure on the ill. To the extent that illness is not the result of choices for which the individual is clearly responsible, a basic, broader principle of justice is violated: People should not be significantly worse off than others through no fault or voluntary choice of their own.[5] Sometimes we express principles of justice through the language of consumer rights. If we did that here, we could speak of consumer rights to a just premium for health insurance (a premium that is fair between the likely ill and the likely well). Premiums that are fair between well and ill will generally not be experience-rated premiums, but will, to an at least considerable extent, be community rated. Rights claims may not always take the form of claims of fairness and justice, of course, but they can, and they often do.

However, it is important not simply to blame insurance companies and say that *they* are violating the consumer's right to a fair premium if they use market segmentation strategies. Insurers need to defend themselves against the adverse selection that can doom them financially, and even when their segmentation techniques are more aggressive than that, emulation of other equally aggressive insurers may be necessary for financial survival in a competitive economy. As we shall see later, the solutions, both for consumers and for insurers, involve *collective* steps such as making insurance mandatory. To the extent that private insurers oppose such collective action—perhaps fearing that it will lead to the displacement of most private insurance—they can indeed be plausibly accused of violating their obligations to work for just access.

Another effect of market segmentation in health insurance that may seem less related to principles of justice should also be mentioned. It is not only that the likely ill will pay a great deal more for insurance than will the likely well. Segmentation's effect is arguably a great deal of waste as well. A study of the mature market in the Seattle area in the late 1990s, for example, found that a sample of 2,277 people were covered by 755 different policies linked to 189 different health care plans.[6] The expense of designing, marketing, and servicing so many policies and of establishing and operating so many plans, all of which claim to be "better" than the others, amounts to much greater overhead than a public system like Medicare: Seven times more, by one prominent estimate ($420 billion, or 31 percent of total plan expense).[7] In their analysis of why U.S. health care costs so much, Anderson and Reinhardt point to the fragmented purchasing power that results in higher prices, larger transaction costs, and steeper increases than are found in countries with universal health care insurance.[8]

This waste in the system created by aggressive market segmentation exposes insurance companies to particular moral temptation. Much of the wasteful expense of designing, marketing, and servicing a complex array of policies and plans is money in the pockets of those in the private insurance industry who would not be there in a system simplified by regulation. (The ultimate simplification is a state-administered, single payer system.) Thus, private insurers, though they could survive well in a "voucher" system for universal coverage,[9] may fiercely oppose many efforts toward universal coverage. At the least, they lobby strongly to have roles and revenues for themselves built into new policies and regulations. The mandatory but partial coverage in Medicare for pharmaceutical costs that was adopted by the U.S. Congress in 2005 exemplifies their power, resulting in a complex and more expensive structure costing taxpayers more than in any country with universal insurance where coverage and administration are simpler. Ultimately such decisions make it more difficult to realize other expansions of access. Failure by insurance companies to understand the larger picture and work toward a fairer, more bridled market is morally short-sighted, a genuine failure to assist in expanding fair access to those who need insurance, not merely make an acceptable profit.

Genetic Discrimination

One particular way for insurers to segment their market is to use genetic information to charge higher premiums to subscribers genetically disposed to incur higher expenses, and insurers will charge less for those who are discernibly genetically lucky. Good luck seldom raises complaints of unfairness, but bad luck—suffering a discernible disadvantage due to factors clearly beyond one's control—does, at least when it becomes the basis for further human action that adds to the disadvantage. Since one's own genetic characteristics are among the clearest cases of elements over which one has no control and stay with one for life, genetic discrimination in insurance is commonly thought to be among the most unfair forms of differential pricing.[10] The clarity of people's convictions about the unfairness of genetic discrimination in insurance is reflected in the fact that all but one of the fifty U.S. states prohibit it, and the federal government bars insurers from using genetic information to set rates for group health plans.[11] Such prohibition arguably prevents the genetically unlucky from being priced out of the affordable market for insurance merely by the bad luck of their genetic indicators.

Here again, as in other cases of market segmentation, one needs to account for adverse selection to see the complexity of the matter. A key argument against prohibiting genetic discrimination in insurance is driven by adverse selection and claims that prohibition actually *decreases* access to insurance.[12] Persons who, because of their genetic characteristics, know that they will likely need more care than most people, will tend to sign up for insurance more readily than those who know they are genetically less likely to need care. To the former, insuring when premiums rates are flattened as a result of banning genetic discrimination will be a financial bargain; to the latter, insuring at those rates will appear statistically a financial loser. Accordingly, the pool of those who insure will shrink to accommodate a higher proportion of expensive-to-insure subscribers, premiums will climb, and still more people (the healthier ones) will decide that insurance is not a financially wise investment. Then premiums will climb more yet for those who remain. The cycle continues mercilessly. The end result is ironic and alarming: Barring insurance companies from using genetic information will eventually have the effect of *decreasing* access. As unfair as differential pricing based on genetic discrimination is, prohibiting it while leaving in place other elements of a voluntary, private insurance market will not improve access.

This argument also holds more broadly against banning experience rating and mandating community rating when the other primary elements of a voluntary market are left in place. The market segmentation reflected in experience-rated premiums may well violate our sense of justice between likely ill and likely well subscribers. Simply prohibiting it, however, will only discourage the likely well from buying insurance because, to them, insurance will then seem more than ever to be excessively expensive for the protection against the actual risk that it affords. Like the mere prohibition of genetic discrimination, simply banning experience rating is likely to increase the number of individuals and employers who decide not to purchase insurance. Moreover, as a matter of moral fairness, insurance companies can justifiably object if they are merely prohibited from genetically discriminating or experience rating. This has an important moral consequence for consumers: They cannot claim to have any simple right, by itself, not to be subject to experience rating or genetic discrimination.

Adverse Selection and Mandatory Insurance

These difficulties in avoiding the unfairness of differential pricing while simultaneously improving access to health care can only be resolved by recognizing the more complex web of steps needed to advance just access. *Mere prohibition by the society of differential pricing will not do. An essential complementary step is to require that everyone be insured.* Only by mandating insurance will prohibiting genetic discrimination, for example, not lead to the adverse selection that is unfair and financially threatening to insurers. If everyone must be insured at some basic level of coverage we refer to as "basic care," people will not be able to avoid insurance simply because they think they are unlikely to need it, only conveniently hopping in to subscribe and pay when they sense that they are headed toward treatment.

How does one effectively advocate mandatory, compulsory insurance as a solution to the problems of adverse selection and unfair discrimination in a moral culture that highly values liberty, including the liberty of the consumer of insurance? Arguments for universal access to basic health care are usually made on the basis of equality,[13] but equality is not the only basic value driving moral judgments about a preferred structure for health care. The key to the case for mandating insurance is to see that allowing people to go uninsured is dubious not only in respect to equality between well and ill but also in respect to liberty. To see this one needs to understand how the prevention of free-riding is fundamentally important to liberty and individual responsibility and how much free-riding occurs when people are allowed to go uninsured.[14]

The paradigm of free-riding is a person who gets benefits from a collective enterprise without paying her fair share. This is what usually happens when people lack health insurance. Uninsured persons in the United States, for example, do not just go without care, imposing no costs on others. Even without insurance they nonetheless need and receive a great deal of care, much of which is paid for, explicitly or implicitly, by others. In the United States in 2001, the uninsured used $98.9 billion in health care, $34.5 billion of which was "uncompensated"—paid for neither out of pocket by the uninsured nor by any discrete source of private or public insurance.[15] In a major 2005 report, Families USA calculated that for that year $43 billion of care for the uninsured was "uncompensated," and in turn, $29 billion of that was cost-shifted to those who paid higher premiums for private health insurance. As a result, private insurance premiums were 8.5 percent higher than they would otherwise have been, adding $922 to the annual cost of family health insurance provided by private employers.[16] The thousands of employers who do not offer health insurance or offer only thin coverage, as well as the millions of individuals who choose not to buy coverage, cause this cost-shifting. In other words, whether they think they will need care or not, collectively they will use a considerable amount of it anyway, and much of it will be paid for by others without any explicit decision about the fairness of that way of distributing its cost.

To make matters worse, from this cost-shifting there unfolds a vicious cycle similar to what we have already seen to afflict simple prohibitions of experience rating and genetic discrimination. When some people go without insurance, premiums rise for others, including those who are most likely to need care. Most of these—statistically the less healthy—are still likely to stay insured, even if they have to pay the rising cost-shifted expenses of patients who are un- and underinsured. In turn, the rising premiums that result lead even more people to drop out of insurance, causing premiums to rise still further for those who remain. Then still more drop insurance, causing an even higher portion of insurance premiums to be needed to cover cost-shifted, uncompensated care. When combined with other factors causing increases in health care costs, these rising premiums render health insurance unaffordable to more and more people.[17]

One might suggest that those who eventually pay much of the cost of the rising volume of care for the uninsured simply stop paying it. This is much easier said than done, however, in a moral culture where a rescue ethic trumps other values when health care providers encounter uninsured patients with serious medical needs. In a traffic accident involving serious injuries to 100 persons in need of ambulances to transport them to care facilities, uninsured patients are not going to be weeded out from insured ones. Not providing care to the uninsured who land on providers' doorsteps may be a theoretically conceivable response, but it is not an option that even conservative opponents of mandatory insurance support. Most of them have also supported the "antidumping" legislation that requires hospitals to treat the uninsured in emergency situations.[18] Many liberty-emphasizing and otherwise "conservative" physicians are proud to be among those who provide considerable care to patients who cannot realistically be expected to pay their bills. The end result is that most uninsured patients still get treated in good facilities for many conditions (though often, of course, in nonideal situations such as emergency rooms). The cost of this care must be shifted largely to individuals and employers who pay insurance premiums.

If they are thus going to be rescued anyway, those going without insurance (or employers not providing it) are gaining a critical benefit without paying their share—that is, they are free-riding. The principle against free-riding that makes such cost-shifting objectionable is based on larger values about individual responsibility that are fundamentally conservative.[19] Observations similar to those made about the free-riding inherent in a voluntary health insurance system have led to making automobile liability insurance mandatory. This mandate is apparently widely accepted by conservatives as well as liberals to correct an analogous instance of free-riding, drivers who go without liability insurance and shift costs for their negligence onto other drivers, who then feel compelled to defend themselves by purchasing "uninsured motorist" insurance at their own expense. The free-riding created by leaving health insurance in the United States a voluntary market should similarly lead to mandating health insurance for basic care.

Amid this argument for mandatory insurance driven by the moral need to prevent unfair free-riding, we should hold blameless those who truly cannot afford to be insured. The onus of the "free-riding" label should not be laid on that portion of the uninsured. Nonetheless, the entire picture of a voluntary insurance market that shifts many of the costs of the uninsured onto those who can hardly be seen as the appropriate parties on whom that cost would justly fall, is still marked by significant free-riding. The way out is to abandon voluntary insurance for basic care, governmentally mandate it, and then directly provide or governmentally subsidize this insurance for those deemed unable to afford what they are required to have.

I conclude that it is misleading to speak *simply* of a consumer right not to be exposed to the differential prices for insurance that emerge from experience rating or genetic discrimination. Mere prohibition of these pricing practices creates another morally objectionable situation, the adverse selection that puts insurers at an unfair disadvantage vis-à-vis strategically behaving subscribers. In the larger picture, however, just access to health care is still incompatible with genetic discrimination and most experience rating of premiums. Those practices ought to be disavowed, but in combination with requiring everyone to be insured for basic care. Within such a framework that includes mandated insurance, consumers can justifiably claim a moral right not to be exposed to the varying prices that are inevitable if insurers are allowed to segment the market for basic care into insurance for some who are likely to run up high expenses and others who are not.

CONSUMERS, PHARMACEUTICAL COMPANIES, AND SHAREHOLDERS

Large pharmaceutical companies have come under intense ethical fire for a wide range of practices. Media reports, books, articles, and government documents all serve up searing criticisms of the power and influence of the pharmaceutical industry. The issues involve alleged injustices and corruptions such as aggressive and deceptive marketing schemes, exploitative uses of research subjects, a corrupting influence on universities, suppression of vital data, bias and amateurism in the presentation of data, conflicts of interest that bias research investigators, corruption of the clinical judgment of medical students and practicing physicians, and a shameful use of lobbying. These accusations, one by one, may or may not be correct, and even when they are, they may be largely the fault of others (e.g., the FDA).

One of the dimensions of just access to pharmaceuticals, amid all these controversies, is their price. Because medicinal drugs can hold dramatically big stakes for consumers whose life or basic quality of life is threatened, and because the consumer demand for them is thus often "inelastic," as economists say (not decreasing much as price rises), drug companies are in a powerful position over consumers, and this makes drug pricing of moral interest. The standard defense of drug prices, as high as they are, almost always involves appeal to the costs of their research and development (R&D). A common social strategy for ensuring that these companies can recoup their high costs of R&D is to grant monopolistic control over pricing through temporary patents. At the same time, drug companies run considerable risk in many particular investments of R&D, because the prospectively useful and lucrative drug may not emerge.

The combination of these characteristics—big stakes for consumers, monopolistic control of producers over prices, and large risks for the companies and their investors—is guaranteed to generate moral tension. One particular clash occurs in the "reimportation" of price-discounted drugs back into the United States from other countries. Another occurs in setting prices for "orphan drugs," disease-specific drugs for patients with rare diseases. While these are by no means the only or the most important issues of business ethics in the pricing of pharmaceuticals, they are examples in which moral analysis can be revealing.

Reimportation and the Costs of R&D

Are U.S. consumers failing to pay their fair share of research and development (R&D) expenses if they procure their drugs through a country such as Canada where distributors have legally negotiated large discounts from manufacturers? Are U.S. consumers who do this free-riding on the rest of us who buy within the United States and pay more? We need to understand the facts about R&D expenditure and examine elements of our moral convictions about free-riding and paying one's "fair share" before we can provide insightful answers to these questions.

Here are some basic facts we need before us:

—Expenditures to purchase pharmaceuticals in the United States totaled $250 billion in 2004, or 3 percent of GDP—roughly one-fifth of the more than 15 percent of GDP spent on health care. One-tenth of that 3 percent—$25 billion, or 0.3 percent of GDP—was spent on pharmaceutical R&D.[20] Annual R&D spending worldwide by the corporate members of Pharmaceutical Research & Manufacturers of America (PhRMA) exceeded $30 billion in 2004. The spending of these same companies for marketing and administration exceeded $60 billion.[21]

—Patent protection may increase the cost of drugs worldwide by as much as $400 billion annually, though a safer, conservative figure is probably $100 billion.[22]

—A high proportion of the new drugs developed with the roughly $30 billion in annual R&D spending by PhRMA are noninnovative drugs (colloquially referred to as "me-too" drugs). Of the 415 new drugs approved by the FDA from 1998 through 2002, only 32 percent were "new molecular entities" (NMEs—containing new active elements). In 2002, 17 of 78 were NMEs, and only 7 of those (9 percent of the total) were regarded by the FDA as improvements over older drugs. Arguably, only about 10–15 percent of newly approved drugs provide important benefits over existing drugs.[23]

—In developed countries the percentage of GDP spent for pharmaceutical R&D varies from roughly 0.1 percent in Canada, France, Germany, and Italy to over 0.3 percent for Sweden and the United Kingdom and upwards of 0.5 percent for Switzerland. The United States is in the middle, with 0.24 percent. On average, pharmaceutical companies commit a *larger* percentage of *sales revenue* to R&D in Europe than they do in the United States, but since European drug prices are approximately 65 percent lower than U.S. prices, the average level of R&D spending there turns out to be roughly equal to that in the United States (see table 7.1).[24]

Table 7.1 Europe, Canada, and the United States, Year 2000

	Canada	France	Germany	Italy	Sweden	Switz.	U.K.	U.S.
% of GDP	0.08	0.14	0.11	0.06	0.35	0.55	0.32	0.24
% of US Price	63.6	55.2	65.3	52.9	63.6	69.2	68.6	100

From Light and Lexchin, "Foreign Free Riders."

While Sweden, Switzerland, and the United Kingdom devote a higher percentage of their GDP to pharmaceutical R&D than does the United States, the United States appears to spend slightly more than twice the percentage of its GDP on R&D as Canada, France, Germany, and Italy do. Whether that constitutes free-riding by Canada, France, Germany, and Italy on U.S. R&D depends on several other factors. For example, if two-thirds of U.S. pharmaceutical R&D is spent on noninnovative drugs and only one-third on innovative ones, and if the proportions of this division in these four other countries are typically the reverse (of their R&D spending, two-thirds is for innovative drugs), then they and the United States are still making roughly equal contributions to *innovative* drug development as a percentage of GDP. This one-third/two-thirds proportion and its reverse turn out to be close to what actually obtains in the United States (on the one hand) and in France and Germany (on the other hand).[25]

Pharmaceutical R&D can reasonably be viewed as a "public good": (1) Its benefits eventually accrue even to those who do not pay the initially higher, patent-protected price that funds it (those who later buy generic versions, as well as those who benefit from other drugs whose later development is enabled by the knowledge accrued in earlier drugs' development); (2) It is not possible to block people who pay little of the R&D from gaining benefits. A different instance of a public good, outside the world of medicine and pharmaceutical drugs, is a city park that provides light and beauty to passersby, better air and morale for those living in the surrounding area, an outlet for youth who might make even more trouble otherwise, and so on.

To determine whether the reimportation of drugs constitutes free-riding by consumers who gain the discount, we need to pursue the question of how we ought to deal with the free-riding that can easily surround the sort of benefit referred to as a "public good." Any comprehensive understanding of when and why we see free-riding as wrong will speak to these situations where a good takes effort and expense to produce but people can readily gain its benefit without paying much if any of that expense. A plausible statement of our sense of when steps may be taken to prevent someone from free-riding on the public goods is this: A person should be required to pay her share of a collective enterprise, even one that she did not choose to form or join, if it produces benefits from which she cannot be excluded, *as long as she would not actually prefer to lose the benefits of the enterprise to avoid paying what is deemed to be her fair share of its costs.*[26]

To illustrate this principle, take the previous park example in a more specific form. A number of individuals dedicated to preserving open green space own a significant plot of land in a community and have already shaped and protected it to function as an accessible, rudimentary park. A variety of circumstances, both for the owners and for the small park district for this local area, have spurred a proposal that the district buy this land and make it officially a park. It would do that with funds procured by a marginal property tax increase. If the land is not thus purchased to be a park, it will likely be sold for typical development. Suppose that I were a resident near the park before any of this prospective purchase arose, and I did not move into the neighborhood because of the park-like property. Can I justifiably object to paying taxes to fund the purchase? If I do not have to contribute through taxation, I will not, but I also then will not try to enter the park to use it. I contend that the park's use should be limited to those willing to buy a park membership and voluntarily fund the purchase that way. The park, however, provides some benefits that naturally accrue to me regardless of my choice to forgo entering it. My claim that I should not have to pay an assigned fee to help purchase the park would be plausible if, *were* I to have a choice between no park at all and paying some allegedly fair share to live near the park, I would, honestly, select no park at all. If, however, my choice in such a constrained circumstance would be to pay my share rather than forgo the naturally accruing benefits of the park, I ought not object to being forced to pay to prevent me from free-riding on a public good.

This same principle about controlling free-riding when a public good is present can be applied to pharmaceutical R&D. First, as previously explained, the development of new medicines is to some considerable extent a public good. It is thus plausible to use the collective power of the state, either through taxes or legal arrangements such as patents that allow producers to exclude competition and protect prices, to extract fair share payments for pharmaceutical R&D. But second, the moral justification for using this state power will depend on the accuracy of the claim that the persons from whom fair share contributions to R&D are extracted *really would prefer to pay that share rather than go without developing the new medicines involved.* It would seem that drug companies are already appealing to such a framework to justify their pricing power deriving from state-enforced patent protection. On one very plausible interpretation, their advertisements are effective because they ask rhetorically: "Would you actually want to live with a lower prospect of some wonderful drug being developed for the condition that might someday afflict you? You should be proud to pay the drug prices that generate ample amounts of funds for aggressive R&D!"

Within this framework, however, things get problematic for using strong patent rights to enforce prohibitions on reimportation of drugs at reasonable levels of discount. Note the second point in the previous paragraph, which leads us to ask: What actually are we paying for with patent-protected prices? If a large share of R&D is devoted to development of *noninnovative* drugs for purposes of profitable capture of market share, not the creation of improved medicine, those who are asked to pay for the R&D do not reap a degree of health benefit remotely proportionate to the size of that investment. Nexium is an example of such a noninnovative, "me-too" drug. Introduced by AstraZeneca—just as its earlier drug for heartburn, Prilosec, was going off patent—Nexium contained only the active, not also an inactive, form of omeprozole. To meet FDA and patent-granting criteria, all AstraZeneca had to show was that Nexium was effective in treating heartburn, not that it was *more* effective than other soon-to-be-generic drugs like Prilosec, nor that it was effective *for different conditions.*[27]

The case against reimportation at discount gets even more problematic when another factor is considered. If pharmaceutical companies use a major part of the enhanced net revenues they gain from patent protection to finance large marketing and promotion efforts, this would be another element of dubious benefit to consumers. Consumers could claim that if they had a choice of paying to fund R&D at only the level provided by the revenues from Canadian level prices, or paying to fund both the R&D and promotion and advertising budgets at levels made feasible by U.S. prices, they would clearly choose the former.

On both of these counts, the facts provide operative fuel for a defense of reimported drugs. Arguably, much of the R&D funding procured by pharmaceutical companies through patent protected prices *is* devoted to developing noninnovative drugs that often turn great profits for their companies but provide little benefit to consumers.[28] And the increased revenues from patent-protected prices *are* partially devoted to much greater investment by U.S. firms in promotion and advertising (the need for which may well be generated by the intense competition to sell noninnovative drugs!). Why should costs of such dubious value to the consuming public be extracted from them? The public good, fair-share defense of patent protection depends straightforwardly on constructing a cogent argument that what is done with the *greater* R&D funding and other greater revenues created by patent protection is indeed *worth consumers' investment.* Heavy investment by competing pharmaceutical companies in "me-too" drugs and high advertising and promotion efforts make any such cost-worthiness highly questionable.

Arguably, consumers would, upon rational examination of the matter, prefer to lose the marginal benefits of the portion of the higher revenue from patent protection that goes toward developing many noninnovative drugs and aggressive advertising and promotion. But then consumers cannot fairly be asked to pay non-discounted prices. To force consumers to pay the higher domestic price over the discounted reimported price is not forcing them to pay a fair share *of what is for their benefit*, but forcing them to pay what is essentially *for other parties' benefit*—pharmaceutical companies and their stockholders. A noninnovative drug like Nexium is a case in point.

One can also look at paying fair shares for pharmaceutical R&D as a matter of national shares, not individual consumer shares. In relation to whether other *nations* are free-riding on U.S. drug companies' R&D (not the immediate reimportation issue per se), Light and Lexchin claim that the figures in table 7.1 imply that other nations are not generally free-riding. Such a conclusion is strengthened—or more strictly, *enabled*, depending on one's interpretation of the data—by consideration of the fact that other countries generally devote a higher percentage of their R&D to basic research and a lower percentage to noninnovative drugs. The two perspectives, however, can then be joined. *If Canadian consumers are not free-riders at fault for failing to support a U.S. level of R&D that includes heavy investment in noninnovative drugs and aggressive promotion and advertising, U.S. consumers who gain access to discounted Canadian prices are not free-riders either.*[29]

"Orphan" Drugs and the Costs of R&D

Suppose one disease is rare, another common. Assume that the former afflicts 10,000, while the latter afflicts 1,000,000. Assume that everyone afflicted with either of these diseases will use a drug developed specifically for their disease. For the common disease, $800 million spent on R&D will amount to a per-patient share of $800, compared to a $80,000 per patient share for the rare disease.[30] Companies developing the drug for the rare disease—a so-called "orphan drug"—will need to see those who may pay for it as willing to pay, on average, $80,000 on top of the cost of manufacture, distribution, profit, and so on. Moreover, suppose that less than half of those with the rare disease are either sufficiently insured or wealthy enough to be able to purchase the medication. The individual purchaser's share of R&D will jump to perhaps $200,000, which still fewer can afford.

Many examples roughly fit this hypothetical profile for an orphan drug. One that fits it well is Soliris, developed by Alexion Pharmaceuticals to treat PNH (paroxysmal nocturnal hemoglobinuria). PNH afflicts only 10,000 persons worldwide in any given year. Its expected price before release was expected to be $100,000–$300,000 for a year's supply, but upon release in March 2007 was announced to be $389,000,[31] which per patient *per year* seems much more than is necessary to recoup development costs if there are 10,000 customers. Perhaps, though, far fewer than 10,000 will buy the drug, and Alexion's revenue from developing this drug will have to cover the company's risk in the many other drug development efforts that fail.

How should a private, for-profit drug company behave in this situation? How much effort should it invest in developing drugs for rare diseases? If it does invest and succeeds, how should it price the products? These questions are about moral obligations, not merely about financial obligations to a company and its investors. Psychologically, demand will be high if development succeeds and the drug is the only good treatment option for a given disease, either for living comfortably and functionally with it, or for living at all. Looking down the line, however, nonaffordability for consumers is a chilling prospect to any drug company. Moreover, there may be many other, likely more profitable fish to fry in its development kitchen— a relatively noninnovative drug, for example, that could capture one-tenth of the large market for a hundred times more common disease.

To counter such disincentives to develop drugs for persons with rare conditions who individually need medical assistance just as much as people with more widespread ones, the United States passed the Orphan Drug Act of 1983. To come under the act's protection, the drug must have been developed for a disease with fewer than 200,000 sufferers (at any one point in time). For any qualifying drug, a company gains a seven-year marketing protection without going through the lengthy process of getting a patent. Moreover, once the FDA grants a company orphan drug status for a drug, it is barred from approving any other drug with the same active ingredient "unless it is proven clinically superior for that disease"—that is, no "me-too" drugs can get FDA approval for orphan diseases.[32] This act has been hugely successful in stimulating the production of new orphan drugs. Before 1983, only ten had been developed in the previous ten years. By 2006, 260 were on the market, and 1,400 were in development.[33]

From a typically nonviable investment before 1983, these drugs now often become financial profit centers. Genzyme, for example, set the price for Cerezyme, to treat Gaucher's disease, at $200,000 per year for a minimal dosage and up to $1 million for the maximum dosage that some patients need. Those prices earned the company over $1 billion in revenue in 2006 alone, while its R&D cost was just $29.4 million.[34] With inelastic demand from desperate patients, profits far beyond those necessary to defray the R&D cost of the drug in question can be achieved, even after statistically accounting for the fact that many drug research efforts fail. Is this unfair exploitation? The industry sees these apparently windfall profits as useful in providing the capital for other R&D efforts in turn.

Pharmaceutical companies often argue that prices such as $100,000 per year seldom affect patients adversely. An executive for Calgene Corporation, maker of the $74,000 per year cancer drug Revlimid, has bluntly claimed that "either people are wealthy enough to pay or health insurance pays or our company gives the medicine available for free."[35] To be sure, for the uninsured, including those who are otherwise insured but by companies that refuse to cover the drug in question, pharmaceutical companies often create assistance programs that selectively discount a medicine or even dispense it for free. At profit margins remotely as high as they are in cases like Cerezyme, drug companies have the room to do that. In turn, insurers may be tempted to exclude such highly priced drugs, especially if they have some reason to be confident that most of their subscribers will then qualify for the drug company's assistance program. The assistance programs are wary of such strategic behavior, and as dispensers of "compassionate use," they remain essentially in the driver's seat in regard to any strategic games that may unfold. Patients can get caught in the middle. Even when an expensive orphan drug is covered by insurance, they are exposed to the lifetime caps of many insurance policies ($1 million). Such limits are quickly reached in situations where the annual cost of a drug is, say, $300,000.[36]

Advocacy groups for particular diseases fight battles on various fronts—both to get insurers to cover the medication regardless of its price and to get particular drug companies to keep their orphan drug prices moderate, $20,000 per year, say, compared to $200,000, when $20,000 may well be sufficient to recoup R&D. The CEO of Lev Pharmaceuticals, one of several companies vying in 2005 to bring to market the first treatment for hereditary angiodema, which affects 6,000 people at any given moment in the United States, acknowledged facing such pressures. However, he also noted, another pressure pulling in the opposite direction: Lev's investors were looking for it to price the drug closer to other blood product treatments for other diseases that are priced at over $100,000 per year.[37] If insurers will pay such prices for these other treatments, why should Lev accept any less for its drug for hereditary angiodema?

To investors this question may seem rhetorical—in their favor. It harbors, however, various moral questions: Does Lev need to charge as much as insurers are paying for some other treatments in order to recoup its R&D expenses in the case of this drug and the surrounding efforts that fail? If a lower price would be ample, but it also would be for other companies with their analogous drugs, why should we assume that just because one company is allowed to make far more than is necessary to recoup its R&D costs, the similarly situated company is doing nothing wrong if it does, too? While economic competition may allow it to do so, that is only a descriptive fact and hardly constitutes a *moral* argument. Insurers, caught in their own pressures from advocacy groups, may often pay $100,000 per year for a treatment, but why does that morally justify a drug manufacturer charging prices distinctly higher than are necessary to recoup its orphan drug R&D costs? From the perspective of investors, the absolutely maximum price that the market will bear may appear best, but any moral force behind such prices would have to derive from a more general principle that pharmaceutical company management is morally obligated first and foremost to maximize investor profits, not serve the interests of its other stakeholders as well (particularly the patients who are its actual or prospective customers). To abide by such a principle, however, would simply be taking the side of shareholders in the classic debate between "stakeholder" and "shareholder" theories of the obligations of corporate management.[38] There is a strong case here for saying that pharmaceutical company executives' obligations are not merely to investors but also to patients and insurers—insurers whose premiums, forced up as much as they are by high orphan drug prices, will likely diminish access to other care for other patients.

Moral Questions for Investors, Not Only Companies

This discussion also pushes to another crucial, additional level. Even if we should say that management is morally obligated more to the wishes of its shareholders than the interests of its other stakeholders, the discussion of moral obligation does not end there. If investors are the proper focus, we still need to ask, *what are the moral obligations of investors?*, not merely, *what is in their financial self-interest?*[39] Should they be willing to hang with a company long enough for it to reap good profits from its products and reputation, without demanding maximal return in the immediate year or quarter? Especially when access to medicines that are crucial to consumers' welfare, even to their very lives, is involved, it hardly seems justifiable for investors to say, "No," they will not settle for a good return over five years but will insist on a greater one right now. Yes, there may be other better opportunities for short-term investment, but *should one be a merely short-term investor in a business like pharmaceuticals?*

If pharmaceutical companies' obligations are not merely to investors but also to patients, then why is it not their obligation to look frankly for investors who are willing to take the pressure off of quarterly returns enough to enable management to price new drugs for a more ordinary, longer-term payoff of R&D? If we believe that corporate leaders need to articulate company mission and moral ideals to their employees and their customers, why not expect them also to be articulate on moral matters to their investors? Articulate corporate leadership arguably includes the ability to portray forcefully to investors the dependence of many rare disease patients on investors' moral decency.

Analogous questions arise in the case of insurance company behavior. The investors behind for-profit insurers also need to be asked hard questions about the pressure for quick returns that they may be putting on management, pressure that finds its outlet in market segmentation of extreme sorts, including genetic discrimination. Behind many interesting and morally demanding questions of management ethics lie equally important questions of investor ethics. There is a tendency to bring discussion of "business ethics" forcefully to bear on management and consumers, but not also on investors. In the ethics of health insurance and pharmaceuticals, we would be particularly remiss to be so limited in our scope. The "ethical investor" movement has injected its influence at various important points—human rights and environmental responsibility are cases in point. Yet when we launch into a discussion of the moral aspects of pharmaceutical company behavior, we usually fail to note that investor behavior, not just management behavior, should be put under the ethical microscope.

Access to Health Care: Employees and Employers

Nations vary considerably in the role that employers play in providing health insurance. It is sometimes thought that countries that guarantee universal access to basic health care do not do it through the workplace, but sometimes they do—witness the truly universal access insurance systems of Germany and France that still involve a significant role for employers.[40] Especially in the United States, however, where universal access is not provided, employers face major questions about their moral obligations. When they have a large amount of discretion about what sort of insurance, if any, to provide or arrange *morally*, what coverage, if any, are they morally obligated to provide? The importance of this question is heightened when, as is often the case in the United States, employees will have no insurance at all except that provided by the employer.

An important background question is whether as a matter of public policy a significantly employer-based health insurance system can be just.[41] That larger systemic question about the role of government, however, will not be the focus of this section (at least not initially). I will instead assume the context of an employer-based system that does not provide universal access, and where the issue of whether to replace the system is not the question at hand. In such a circumstance, how much, if any, insurance are employers obligated to provide their employees?

Particular facts about the United States are relevant to the question. One is that the federal government is not at all neutral about employer-provided insurance. After World War II, in order to encourage employment-based insurance, employer-paid health insurance premiums became excluded from taxable income.[42] The policy continues to this day. The resulting $126 billion annual subsidy has been a huge boost to employer provided insurance, which now covers close to 160 million of the 300 million U.S. population.[43] It needs to be noted, however, that this taxable income exclusion is an economically regressive subsidy, benefiting less those in the lower tax brackets with lower incomes.[44] Moreover, even with the encouragement of this subsidy, employment-based insurance is still not close to universal, and it has recently diminished. In 2000, 69 percent of employers offered coverage, but by late 2005, only 60 percent did,[45] and between 2001 and 2007 the percentage of small business providing insurance dropped from 68 to 59 percent.[46] The explanation is not hard to find: The average cost of insurance premiums is rising several times faster than either the Consumer Price Index or typical earnings. On the one hand, competition among employers for the best employees inclines them to offer a relatively robust coverage. Prospective employees often do not have other reasonably priced ways of getting their insurance, certainly not on the individual policy market, so paying higher wages in lieu of good insurance coverage is not likely to be appealing. On the other hand, many employers face the opposite pressure: In an employer's particular sector of the economy, competitors may be keeping their labor costs (and prices) down by providing little or no insurance. If employer-based insurance is going to close much of the current large gap of the uninsured and underinsured, more sizable and much less regressive subsidies for low-income workers will be needed, or basic insurance will have to be legally mandated.[47]

Such altered subsidies and a mandate that all be insured may gain business support. Noncontributing firms are competitively advantaged free-riders in the system of funding health care, and for this reason firms that supply health insurance for their employees increasingly favor mandatory contributions in an enforceable system of health care insurance. This so-called *mandating* is a way of leveling the playing field fairly by not allowing free-riders to avoid paying their fair share while shifting costs to others. This argument need not move to the conclusion that firms should be required to supply private health insurance. Economic realities such as wage levels, corporate finance, and various costs might make this approach to mandating inefficient and unfair compared to more publicly sponsored insurance. The appropriate conclusion is that a more efficient and equitable system is needed, but not necessarily a system featuring either exclusively public or exclusively private insurance, and not necessarily an egalitarian system.

When Competitors Do Generally Provide Insurance

Suppose that there is no legal mandate to be insured. In that context, the claim that a particular employer is *morally* obligated to offer health coverage is more clearly justified if most of its competitors offer coverage. Not providing insurance contributes to the number of uninsured and thus increases the volume of costs shifted onto other premium payers, including many employers. When most competitors are providing insurance, and especially if the considerable financial encouragement of the taxable income exclusion is also present, we are inclined to see employers who do not provide reasonably comprehensive, basic insurance as free-riding on other employers and their workers, who end up indirectly paying part of others' health care tab. (See the cost-shifting discussion in the first section above.) When most competitors are providing insurance, an otherwise plausible competitive financial "survival" defense is not available to the employer who does not provide insurance. The reference point for competition already includes insurance. Moreover, a basic moral concern for any employer is whether, among one's employees, there is some modicum of justice in the relationship between those who are well and those who end up ill. When much heavier financial burdens that befall a person are little if any of that person's fault and could have been reasonably prevented by insurance, and when the "survival" defense of pressure from an employer's competitors who are getting by without providing insurance is *not* available, an employer who allows the situation to continue would seem to be responsible for injustice.

At this point the argument might turn on the same basic conflict between shareholder and stakeholder theories of the moral obligations of management that inserted itself into the previous discussion of pharmaceutical company obligations about orphan-drug pricing: Even if the "survival" defense that one's competitors do not provide insurance is not available, why not increase shareholder profits by avoiding insurance premiums, anyhow? In answering this question, as we did in the pharmaceutical discussion, we should focus part of our moral attention on investors. With either focus—on the moral obligations of management or of investors—the situation in which one's competitors do not provide the "survival" defense noted above argues strongly for an employer's obligation to provide basic insurance. If companies in these circumstances typically have a moral obligation to provide insurance to their employees, investors have an obligation not to undercut them in fulfilling that obligation by being excessively demanding of higher profit margins.

When Competitors Do Not Typically Provide Insurance

The moral situation may change considerably when competitors are not providing basic coverage, or at most slim coverage. Small-business owners frequently find themselves in this circumstance,[48] and certain large retail sectors such as fast food or cut-rate general stores such as Walmart and Target may, too. Even if a society has decided that employment-based insurance is a primary mode through which insurance will be disbursed throughout the society, if one's direct competitors are providing their employees little or no insurance, why should we say that *a particular company* is obligated to do that which may endanger its survival? The issue is whether the playing field between business competitors is level. If the service the product provides is sufficiently valuable that consumers are readily willing to pay for it even at higher, insurance-inclusive prices, to be sure, all producers should provide employees insurance—they *can*, without endangering their businesses. Even then, why should individual business be the producer who takes the fall in stepping out courageously and doing the right thing by providing insurance? What would be fair about that, especially when the employees will probably end up worse off if their business fails than they would be if it survived without providing insurance? This is precisely the kind of moral defense that is often marshaled by struggling small businesses that do not provide insurance. One can imagine convenience marts, for example, being in this circumstance.

Acknowledging this reasonable moral defense for failing to provide insurance in the applicable situations, however, we ought to note that in some contexts its reasoning is arguably shortsighted. Is it really true that one is less likely to survive if one provides basic insurance when competitors are not? Employers have a great deal of self-interest in hiring very able employees, and perhaps, especially with a taxable income exclusion for employment-based premiums in place, one is better off, in sheer business investment terms, in providing insurance even if it means one must pay lower wages.

This discussion calls attention to larger systemic problems. Before we emphasize obligations of individual businesses, we should emphasize the obligation of either the whole society, or of many private parties in a whole sector of the economy acting collaboratively, to organize the larger insurance pools that can protect a business from such exposure. Social structure is everything in these matters. Individual businesses ought to fight for the kinds of structures that embody the collaboration needed to produce more just outcomes, including the prevention of free-riding by overly aggressive competitors. *If employers are participating constructively in those efforts, even if in the meantime they are not providing insurance, they may be meeting their moral obligations.* The first essential steps of collaborative action should be acts of individual businesses; it is they who can get the ball rolling.

Specific Exclusions from Coverage

Such conditional conclusions about the obligations of businesses to provide insurance for their employees still leave open another range of questions about the *extent* of the coverage employers should provide. Some of these questions concern various strategies for restraining costs: Cost-sharing (copayments and deductibles), limited panels of providers, exclusion of "experimental" and low benefit care, and so on.

Some such strategies may have their most adverse impact on lower income employ-ees. Cost-sharing, for example, almost certainly does unless it is graduated with income—a $50 copayment or $1,000 deductible, for example, hurts more, the lower one's income.[49] It quickly raises objections of distributive justice.[50]

Another quite different discussion about the extent of coverage employers should provide involves exclusions of specific categories of medical services rather than broad categories like "experimental." A much discussed example is abortion services. Another is various techniques of assisted reproduction such as in vitro fer-tilization (IVF) and surrogacy (contracted motherhood). Is it unjust, for example, for an employer to offer insurance that excludes the more aggressive techniques of assisted reproduction such as IVF and surrogacy?

The infertility that creates the demand for assisted reproduction is as arguably an impairment of physiological health as virtually any other condition for which medical care is used. Infertility, though, is not an ultimate barrier to having children, but only to having children that are genetically one's own. Adoption is a readily available alternative, especially once prospective adoptive parents include children of other nations and colors, children for whom adoptive parents are relatively scarce and whose lives, unless they are adopted, are likely to be especially difficult. No one suggests *prohibiting* parents from having genetically their own children, but a legiti-mate question remains: Should prospective parents be *positively assisted, at typically great expense*, in their efforts to accomplish that? This question in turn becomes: Should the other employees be willing to sacrifice take-home pay by incurring the higher health insurance premiums that would result from including assisted repro-duction in coverage, to allow some of their fellow employees afflicted by infertility to have genetically their own children and not need to adopt? It is not at all clear that they ought to, especially not in a community where adoption is an influential, admired, and not rare phenomenon. The coverage issue is not like most obligations of the well to help share the costs of illness for the ill; in this case the "ill" have a viable option to expensive therapy.

Arguably, employers are fully within their moral rights if the insurance options they provide exclude assisted reproduction. They are not failing to meet their obligations of justice and fairness, and they are not violating the moral rights of aggrieved employees. How far other specific exclusions of care can go and still be fair is an open and delicate question. I make no attempt here to articulate a general principle of fair exclusion, though it does seem clear that some exclusions are reasonable and justifiable.

WIDELY SHARED PRINCIPLES RELATED TO JUST AND FAIR ACCESS

In the previous sections we have seen that a business's moral obligations to consum-ers and employees concerning health care cannot be divorced from larger questions about the overall societal structures necessary for just and fair access to health care. Denial that a particular business is obligated to do this or that for its customers or employers may often—or at least sometimes—be justified when the core of the moral problem lies in some wider social structure. Because of the intensely competitive nature of business activity, it would be unfair to expect a particular business to act in what is to it a costly way without requiring its competitors to act similarly. We might call this the "why me?" defense. At the same time, however, it is likely that the businesses that can avail themselves of such a defense are obligated to work to build the societal structures that will further just access—for example, making insurance mandatory in order to reduce unfair adverse selection and prevent free-riding, or revising the federal Orphan Drug Act to moderate any excessive pricing power that ends up reducing access through prices that are higher than necessary to provide incentive and recoup R&D.

It may be helpful to review some of the principles and considerations that reach across most of the previous discussion.

Free-Riding

People often impose costs on others without others' consent of any sort, or they benefit from the activities in which others invest, without the others who supply the effort and resources for those activities being able to extract payment from them through any market exchange. In both cases, something unfair has happened that we call "free-riding": A person has failed to pay her fair share, either her fair share of the costs she has imposed on others, or her fair share of the costs that others have incurred in creating a benefit that she, too, enjoys. We can state a principle which captures these convictions that we might call the Anti-Free-Riding Principle: *To avoid free-riding, a person should help to pay for costs she imposes on others through voluntary action that she initiates without their consent. A person should also be required to pay her share of a collective enterprise that produces benefits from which she cannot be excluded, unless she would actually prefer to lose the benefits of that enterprise rather than pay her fair share of its costs.*[51]

Businesses can invoke this principle (qualified as stated) to object to paying for the partly collective benefit of health insurance when their competitors do not make a similar contribution: The more some pay and help to create the collective enterprise, the more others are free-riding. Those who are inclined to pay are logical in wanting a level playing field, and arguably correct in insisting on it. The Anti-Free-Riding Principle, also, however, creates obligations for the same businesses that invoke it to ward off the alleged obligation to step out ahead of the pack and provide insurance when competitors do not. All businesses are obligated to work politically, or in other ways that can be effective, to help achieve the societal structures (laws, if necessary) that will create a level playing field for improving access to health care and prevent free-riding amidst profit-motivated competition.

The Anti-Free-Rider Principle also creates a defense for insurance companies against adverse selection by subscribers who are more than typically likely to be ill.

The principle can be used to defeat, however, the common defense that U.S. pharmaceutical companies make against reimporting discounted drugs from Canada. People skirting U.S.-level prices may well prefer to go without the benefits of the marginally greater pharmaceutical R&D that goes largely toward "me-too" drugs and much more vigorous advertising.

Just Sharing between Well and Ill

One cannot discern the moral obligations of businesses in relation to just access to health care and pharmaceuticals without some principle about the fairness of people carrying various burdens of illness. One of the important aspects such a principle would speak to is the distribution of financial burdens. We can express this aspect as the Principle of Just Sharing. A plausible version would be: *Except when individuals can reasonably be expected to control the misfortunes of illness by their own choices, the financial burdens of those misfortunes ought to be shared equally by well and ill alike.* This principle is reflected in employers' and employees' desire for access to basic health insurance, so that widely different financial burdens of illness do not aggravate what are usually already considerable differences in income among employees. The principle also drives particular arguments about market segmentation and the need for some sort of "community rating" as well as the arguments for preventing genetic discrimination in insurance.

The principle may seem disputably egalitarian within the presumably individualist moral culture of the United States that highly prizes the often competing values of liberty and efficiency. The version stated here, however, can be derived from a more general principle, Equal Opportunity for Welfare, that is relatively conservative and liberty-friendly: *People should not be worse off than others through no fault or voluntary choice of their own.*[52] Such a principle tolerates situations in which people are worse off than others, by contrast, because of their own sufficiently blameworthy actions or choices.

This principle obviously has a wider reach than the previous Principle of Just Sharing focused more narrowly on the financial burdens of illness. It has the capacity to explain, among other things, the moral need for some sort of special incentive structure to encourage pharmaceutical companies to develop drugs for "orphan" diseases.

Efficiency and Long-Term Benefit

Businesses are usually keen on selecting health care plans that restrain their costs and can provide employers and employees coverage with relatively modest premiums. Few plans admit, much less proudly proclaim, that they attempt to keep patients from receiving care that is of such low added benefit ("marginal benefit," economists say) so as to not be worth its cost. Some of these omissions of care— "prioritizing" or "rationing," if you will—are accomplished by so-called "managed" care. Others are accomplished by explicit coverage limitations. A constant tension plays itself out between providing patients with everything that they want, or that they see as somehow benefiting themselves, and prioritizing out the care that is not "cost-worthy." An inherent problem in any medical insurance economy is that once patients are insured, both they and providers have strong incentive to use care even when its statistical benefits approach zero and its costs are enormous. Knowledgeable subscribers selecting what level of insurance to purchase, all the way from a very inclusive "no questions asked" approach to highly managed care intent on weeding out care of dubious value, are arguably in a less biased position than ill patients to discern care that is not worth its cost.[53]

Businesses are among the parties in the society most keenly aware of the need to keep health care within cost-worthy bounds. Efficiency, properly interpreted in human benefit terms, is not a mere monetary or economic shibboleth, but a core moral value. In occupying a skeptical perspective about the high costs of health insurance, businesses should be seen as commendably adding cost-restraining discipline to the medical marketplace. This is especially appropriate morally if they are able to incorporate employee input into the decisions about what their health plans will not provide. Cost-restraining discipline is laudable not only because of its inherent connection with human-benefit efficiency but also because of its strategic connection with justice and fairness. Arguably one of the essential elements in achieving universal access to basic health care is achieving some control over the much higher per-person total cost that health care runs up in the United States.[54] Only then are people likely to perceive it as politically feasible to mandate basic coverage for everyone.

Even in its own right, of course, efficiency matters. Perhaps one of the clearest instances of inefficiency in the current U.S. medical economy is the prevalence of noninnovative "me-too" drugs among the medicines that pharmaceutical companies choose to develop and market. Market incentives aplenty explain such decisions, though the policies of the FDA and particular interpretations of federal drug patent law undoubtedly also play a considerable role. Awareness of such drugs' dubious efficiency—their low marginal benefit of human health as well as the high costs they run up—can lead us to different views of the obligations of pharmaceutical companies and rights of consumers than we otherwise would have. Reimportation, for example, may be legitimate because companies should not be rewarded with patent protected prices for drugs that add little to any health benefit that could not have been achieved without them.

Discerning the obligations of businesses and the rights of consumers concerning just access to health care requires us to be aware both of the wider structure of a health care economy outside a particular business and of moral principles about free-riding, just sharing, and controlling costs for efficiency in achieving human benefit. Coverage for basic care should be universally mandated. Premiums for likely ill and likely well subscribers, respectively, should not be allowed to vary greatly. Drug pricing should not provide R&D fuel for inefficient but often highly profitable noninnovative drugs, and it should not allow pharmaceutical companies to parlay orphan drugs into windfall profits.

NOTES

1. For development of this line of thought, see Paul Menzel, "Justice and the Basic Structure of Health-Care Systems," in *Medicine and Social Justice: Essays on the Distribution of Health Care*, ed. R. Rhodes, M. Battin, and A. Silvers (New York: Oxford University Press, 2002), 24–37. Related observations are contained in Paul Menzel and Donald W. Light, "A Conservative Case for Universal Access to Health Care," *Hastings Center Report* 36 (4) (July–August 2006): 36–45.

2. Donald W. Light, "The Practice and Ethics of Risk-Rated Health Insurance," *Journal of the American Medical Association* 267 (1992): 2503–2508.

3. Donald W. Light, "Life, Death, and the Insurance Companies," *New England Journal of Medicine* 330 (1994): 498–500, and Stephen D. Boren, "I Had a Tough Day Today, Hillary," *New England Journal of Medicine* 330 (1994): 500–502.

4. This is not just logical conjecture. Medical bankruptcy, which is virtually unknown in the rest of the developed world, is common in the United States: 40 percent of U.S. personal bankruptcies are attributed to medical bills people are unable to pay, and out-of-pocket costs that total 10 percent or more of household income are not uncommon, especially among the working class. See Scott Gottlieb, "Medical Bills Account for Forty Percent of Bankruptcies," *British Medical Journal* 320 (2000): 1295, and George Shearer, *Hidden from View: The Growing Burden of Health Care Costs* (Washington, D.C.: Consumers Union, 2000).

5. For the general principle of Equal Opportunity for Welfare and the more specific principle of Just Sharing that is derived from it concerning the financial burdens of medical misfortune, see Paul Menzel, "Justice and the Basic Structure of Health Care Systems," in *Medicine and Social Justice*, ed. Rosamond Rhodes, Margaret Battin, and Anita Silvers (New York: Oxford University Press, 2002), 24–37.

6. David E. Grenbowski, Paula Diehr, Louise C. Novak, Amy Elizabeth Roussel, Diane P. Martin, Donald L. Patrick, Barbara Williams, and Cornelia M. Ulrich, "Measuring the 'Managedness' and Covered Benefits of Health Plans," *Health Services Research* 35 (2000): 707–734.

7. Steffie Woolhandler, Terry Campbell, and David U. Himmelstein, "Costs of Health Care Administration in the United States and Canada," *New England Journal of Medicine* 349 (2003): 768–775. See also Steffie Woolhandler and David U. Himmelstein, "The Deteriorating Administrative Efficiency of the U.S. Health Care System," *New England Journal of Medicine* 324 (1991): 1253–1258, correspondence at 331 (1994): 336, and Steffie Woolhandler and David U. Himmelstein, "Costs of Care and Administration at For-profit and Other Hospitals in the United States," *New England Journal of Medicine* 336 (1997): 769–774, correspondence at 337 (1997): 1779–1780.

8. Gerard F. Anderson, Uwe E. Reinhardt, Peter S. Hussey, and Varduhi Petrosyan, "It's the Prices, Stupid: Why the United States Is So Different from Other Countries," *Health Affairs* 22 (2003): 89–105.

9. The classic articulation of a full voucher system for universal coverage is still Mark Pauly, Patricia Danzon, Paul Feldstein, and John Hoff, *Responsible National Health Insurance* (Washington, D.C.: American Enterprise Institute, 1992).

10. See, for example, Francis S. Collins and James D. Watson, "Genetic Discrimination: Time to Act," *Science* 302 (October 31, 2003): 745. Some may wonder why differential pricing based on genes is so widely and quickly thought to be morally objectionable "genetic discrimination," but the practice of insurance companies taking the youthfulness

of a driver into account in pricing auto insurance is not "age discrimination" (or any other kind of it). The two are quite different, though: all older persons, gaining the advantages now of lower premiums, have gone through the disadvantaging younger age brackets. In most persons' lifetimes, then, the various stages balance out. In health insurance, by contrast, some, through no fault of their own, will have to pay higher premiums all of their lives. Bad genes do not leave.

11. Health Insurance Portability and Accountability Act of 1996 (HIPAA). In addition, HIPAA's privacy rules generally limit the collection and disclosure of genetic information without a person's consent. Thus, to a large extent, genetic discrimination is effectively banned in individual as well as group insurance policies. See America's Health Insurance Plans [AHIP] (2007), "Use of Genetic Information," http://www.ahip.org/content/default. aspx?bc=39|341|326, and "Genetic Testing and the Use of Genetic Information," http://www. ahip.org/content/default.aspx?bc=31|44|16888|16892 (both accessed June 17, 2007).

12. Ben Eggleston, "Genetic Discrimination in Health Insurance: An Ethical and Economic Analysis," paper delivered at the Pacific Division meetings of the American Philosophical Association, April 5, 2007 (unpublished, Department of Philosophy, University of Kansas).

13. The most well-known philosophical articulation is probably Norman Daniels, *Just Health Care* (Cambridge: Cambridge University Press, 1985).

14. Much of the rest of this section is adapted from Menzel and Light, "A Conservative Case."

15. Jack Hadley and John Holahan, "How Much Medical Care Do the Uninsured Use, and Who Pays For It?" *Health Affairs* 22 (February 12, 2003), Web exclusive, http://www. healthaffairs.org/WebExclusives/Hadley_Web_Excl_021203.htm (accessed July 15, 2007). See also Committee on the Consequences of Uninsurance, Board of Health Care Services, Institute of Medicine, *Hidden Costs, Value Lost: Uninsurance in America* (Washington, D.C.: National Academies Press, 2003), 38–61.

16. Families USA (Kathleen Stoll, author, with data analysis by Kenneth Thorpe), *Paying a Premium: The Added Cost of Care for the Uninsured* (New York: Families USA, 2005), http://www.familiesusa.org/site/PageServer?pagename=Paying_a_Premium (accessed June 22, 2005).

17. Uwe E. Reinhardt, "Forum: The Future of Health Insurance. Is There Hope for the Uninsured?" *Health Affairs* 22 (August 27, 2003), Web exclusive, http://www.healthaffairs. org/WebExclusives/Reinhardt_Web_Excl_082703.htm (accessed July 15, 2007).

18. EMTALA, "The Emergency Medical Treatment and Active Labor Act" (1998). Public Law 99–272, 100 Stat. 164 (codified as amended at 42 U.S.C. § 1395dd).

19. This is not to say that the values involved are only conservative. The sense of fairness and responsibility expressed in the anti-free-riding principle transcends most liberal and conservative lines.

20. James Love, "CPTech Comments on U.S. Department of Commerce Study of International Drug Pricing," Consumer Project on Technology, July 1, 2004, http://www. cptech/ip/health/rndtf/drugpricestudy.html (accessed June 14, 2006), and Marcia Angell, *The Truth about the Drug Companies: How They Deceive Us and What To Do about It* (New York: Random House, 2004), 3. One sees conflicting figures on this. PhRMA reports that its companies invest on average 18–19 percent of domestic sales into research. The U.S. National Science Foundation's data show only 12.4 percent of gross domestic sales spent on R&D—10.5 percent in house and 1.9 percent contracted out. See Donald W. Light and Joel Lexchin, "Foreign Free Riders and the High Price of U.S. Medicines," *British Medical Journal* 331 (October 22, 2005): 958–960.

21. Angell, *The Truth about the Drug Companies*, 48. Expenditures for 2001 reported by members of the Pharmaceutical Research and Manufacturers of America (PhRMA), including R&D performed outside the United States by U.S. companies or U.S. divisions of foreign companies and R&D that occurs after a drug has gone on the market, were marginally higher, at $35 billion; see the Congressional Budget Office study, "Research and Development in the Pharmaceutical Industry," October 2006, http://www.cbo.gov/ftpdocs/76xx/doc7615/10-02-DrugR-D.pdf (accessed January 22, 2008). By one frequently cited estimate, the so-called Tufts University study, each new drug costs $802 million to develop: Joseph A. Dimasi, Ronald W. Hansen, and Henry G. Grabowski, "The Price of Innovation: New Estimates of Drug Development Costs," *Journal of Health Economics* 22 (2003): 151–185, and Merrill Goozner, *The $800 Million Pill: The Truth behind the Cost of New Drugs* (Berkeley: University of California Press, 2004), 3, 237. Other reputable estimation methods that attend carefully to *after-tax* costs, to the fact that the Tufts study's estimate was for R&D costs for *new molecular entity* drugs, and to other elements involved in the $800 billion figure, however, put the average new drug's R&D cost as low as $100 million. See Angell, *The Truth about the Drug Companies*, 40–46, 271n5, and Goozner, *The $800 Million Pill*, 246, and the excellent comprehensive discussion that accounts for the Tufts study by the Congressional Budget Office cited just above.

22. Love, "CPTech Comments." The claim here is a fairly crude one, and a large set of puzzles can be seen to surround it. First and foremost, if there were no (or less) patent protection, such drugs may well not have been developed and they would not exist. Then how would we know what the marginally higher costs for those drugs is that is attributable to patents, as distinct from these drugs without patent protected prices? Perhaps the claim can be made more precise only with assumptions about which drugs would have been developed even with weaker patent protection. I owe these trenchant observations about the claim to George Brenkert (correspondence).

23. Angell, *The Truth about the Drug Companies*, 16, 75. Light and Lexchin, "Foreign Free Riders," citing NIHCM [National Institute for Health Care Management Research and Education Foundation], *Changing Patterns of Pharmaceutical Innovation* (Washington, D.C.: NIHCM, 2002). Recent examples are provided by Benedict Carey, "Study Finds Little Advance in New Schizophrenia Drugs," *New York Times*, September 20, 2005, D1, D16.

24. One may question how meaningful these comparisons are, given that the companies are usually highly globalized. Also, regulatory agencies' requirements may vary between Europe and the United States. I owe these qualifying points to Tom Beauchamp (correspondence).

25. Ibid.

26. Menzel, "Justice and the Basic Structure," 25–26, and Paul T. Menzel, *Strong Medicine: The Ethical Rationing of Health Care* (New York: Oxford University Press, 1990), 29–31.

27. Angell, *The Truth about the Drug Companies*, 76–79, and more generally, all of chapter 5, 74–93.

28. Admittedly, many ambiguities attend the term "noninnovative." Nonetheless, what we do know, for example, is that of the 415 new drugs approved by the FDA from 1998 through 2002, only 32 percent were "new molecular entities" (NMEs—containing new active elements); in 2002 specifically, only 17 of 78 new drugs approved were NMEs, and only seven of those (9 percent of the total) were regarded by the FDA as improvements over older drugs. See Angell, *The Truth about the Drug Companies*, 16 and 75. It is important to distinguish "NME" from "innovative drug": some NME's are not innovative, though only in rare cases is an innovative new drug not a NME. Light and Lexchin,

"Foreign Free-Riders," cite the NIHCM (National Institute for Health Care Management Research and Education Foundation) report, *Changing Patterns of Pharmaceutical Innovation* (Washington, D.C.: NIHCM, 2002), to claim that generally, 10–15 percent of newly approved drugs provide important benefits over existing drugs.

29. Much of this argument, and many other points in this section, are developed in Paul T. Menzel, "Are Patents an Efficient and Internationally Fair Means of Funding Research and Development for New Medicines?" in *Ethics and the Business of Biomedicine,* ed. Denis G. Arnold (Cambridge: Cambridge University Press, 2009). For an alternate defense of reimportation, see James Love and Sean Flynn, "Legal and Policy Issues Concerning Parallel Trade (aka Re-Importation) of Pharmaceutical Drugs in the United States," March 31, 2004, http://www.cptech.org/ip/fsd/love03312004.pdf (accessed July 15, 2007).

30. I use $800 million as the figure here because it is arguably the most famous estimate of the average cost to develop and bring a new drug to market. See Goozner, *The $800 Million Pill,* and discussion in footnote 22.

31. Janice Podsada, "Who'll Pay for Orphan Drugs?" *Hartford Courant,* April 22, 2007.

32. Geeta Anand, "How Drugs for Rare Diseases Became Lifeline for Companies," *Wall Street Journal,* November 15, 2005, http://online.wsj.com/article/SB113202332063297223.html.

33. Janice Podsada, "Who'll Pay…?"; and Anand, "How Drugs for Rare Diseases."

34. Anand, "How Drugs for Rare Diseases," and Podsada, "Who'll Pay…?" Perhaps $29.4 million is calculated too narrowly, without adequately factoring in the statistically predictable failures in attempting to develop other orphan drugs. Suppose the more realistic figure that includes coverage for failed attempts is $400 million. Even that is small, however, compared to the $1 billion *annual* profit in the case of Cerezyme.

35. Anand, "How Drugs for Rare Diseases."

36. Podsada, "Who'll Pay…?" A very important general moral issue about insurance decisions to cover high-priced orphan drugs is whether the rarity of one's disease should give one any ground at all to claim that insurers—and ultimately other premium payers—should be willing to pay a higher cost per health benefit gained than they ought to be willing to pay for treatments for more common diseases. See Christopher McCabe, Karl Claxton, and Aki Tsuchiya, "Orphan Drugs and the NHS: Should We Value Rarity?" *British Medical Journal* 331 (October 29, 2005): 1016–1019.

37. Anand, "How Drugs for Rare Diseases."

38. Two classic statements of the shareholder and stakeholder theories of the purpose of the corporation, respectively, are Milton Friedman, "The Social Responsibility of Business Is To Increase Its Profits," *New York Times Magazine,* September 13, 1970, and R. Edward Freeman, "A Stakeholder of the Modern Corporation," in *Ethical Theory and Business,* 7th ed., ed. Tom L. Beauchamp and Norman E. Bowie (Upper Saddle River, N.J.: Pearson/Prentice Hall, 2004), 55–64. The Friedman article is reprinted in the same *Ethical Theory and Business* anthology, 50–55.

39. An insightful short article on investor responsibilities is Michael Lewis, "The Irresponsible Investor," *New York Times Magazine,* June 6, 2004, 68–71.

40. Daniel Callahan and Angela A. Wasunna, *Medicine and the Market: Equity vs. Choice* (Baltimore: Johns Hopkins University Press, 2006), and Laurence A. Graig, *Health of Nations: An International Perspective on U.S. Health Care Reform,* 3rd ed. (Washington, D.C.: Congressional Quarterly, 1999).

41. Nancy S. Jecker, "Can an Employer-based Health Insurance System be Just?" *Journal of Health Politics, Policy, and Law* 18 (1993): 657–674. Alternative version available in

Gary S. Belkin and James A. Morone, eds., *The Politics of Health Care Reform: Lessons from the Past, Prospects for the Future* (Durham, N.C.: Duke University Press, 1994), 259–275.

42. William P. Brandon, "Health-Related Tax Subsidies," *New England Journal of Medicine* 307 (1982): 947–950.

43. Daniel Akst, "Why Should the Boss Pay for Your Health Care?" *New York Times,* November 13, 2005, B4. The $126 billion figure is for 2006. The 160 million number includes children and family members covered through an employed parent or spouse.

44. Menzel, *Strong Medicine,* 137–38, and Jack Meyer, William R. Johnson, and Sean Sullivan, *Passing the Health Care Buck: Who Pays the Hidden Cost?* (Washington, D.C.: American Enterprise Institute, 1983), 10–24. For a recent interesting related discussion, see Len Burman, Jason Furman, Greg Leiserson, Roberton Williams, Jason Furman, Greg Leiserson, and Roberton Williams, *The President's Proposed Standard Deduction for Health Insurance: An Evaluation,* a report of the Tax Policy Center (Washington, D.C.: The Urban Institute and Brookings Institution, 2007).

45. Reed Abelson, "Employer-Backed Health Care is Here to Stay, for Lack of a Better Choice," *New York Times,* December 5, 2005, C11. These percentages are of employers. The percentage of employees nationwide would be considerably higher, since virtually all large employers offer coverage.

46. Fran Hawthorne, "To Keep Health Plans, Many Firms Shift Costs," *New York Times,* September 26, 2007, C7.

47. See, for example, John Holahan, *Increasing Health Insurance Coverage in Missouri Through Subsidies,* Report 9 of the Cover Missouri Project (St. Louis: The Missouri Foundation for Health, and Washington, D.C.: The Urban Institute, 2006).

48. Eve Tahmincioglu, "Health Care at a Premium: Business Start-Ups Struggle with High Cost of Insurance," *New York Times,* November 30, 2006, C8.

49. Deductibles of $1,000, at a minimum, are common strategies to keep premiums affordable. Improvements in Walmart's benefits in late 2007, for example, still involved $2,000 deductibles for the lowest premium plans. Michael Barbaro, "A Wal-Mart Health Plan Cuts Costs," *New York Times,* September 19, 2007, C1, 8.

50. Paul T. Menzel, *Medical Costs, Moral Choices: A Philosophy of Health Care Economics in America* (New Haven, Conn.: Yale University Press, 1983), 119–125, and Norman Daniels, Donald W. Light, and Ronald L. Caplan, *Benchmarks of Fairness for Health Care Reform* (New York: Oxford University Press, 1996), 44–50, 88–92.

51. Menzel, "Justice and the Basic Structure," 24–27. There are, admittedly, a huge number of complications that need to be pursued if we are going to be reasonably certain that we have discerned a plausibly correct statement of the principle. It is also helpful to understand that some sort of anti-free-riding principle may be extremely basic in any larger structure of moral principles, because it may, more than any other principle, provide us with an understanding of *why we should be moral* (as distinct from what it is to be moral): once people have some set of moral rules and principles with which to guide their behavior, the noncompliant person is free-riding on others who are compliant, gaining the benefits of living in a reasonably morally well-ordered society without paying the most fundamental, fair cost of that enterprise, compliance. Some anti-free-riding principle may be necessary to explain why we should be moral at all; it may not be merely one principle alongside others, or a principle generated from any other principle. (I owe this observation to Calvin Normore.)

52. Richard Arneson, "Equality and Equal Opportunity for Welfare," *Philosophical Studies* 56 (1989): 77–93. Both for this principle and the previously stated Principle of Just Sharing, see Menzel, "Justice and the Basic Structure," 32–34, which includes an explanation

of the extent to which the Equal Opportunity of Welfare principle is a relatively conservative, liberty-protecting principle of distributive justice.

53. For a defense of rationing out care that is not cost-worthy, and for explanations of cost-worthiness as care which subscribers beforehand ("prepatients") would not view as worth their financial investment at the margins of insurance coverage, see Menzel, *Strong Medicine*, 3–29, and Menzel, "Justice and the Basic Structure," 29–31.

54. Menzel and Light, "A Conservative Case for Universal Access to Health Care," 3, 6, and Norman Daniels and James E. Sabin, *Setting Limits Fairly: Can We Learn to Share Medical Resources?* (New York: Oxford University Press, 2002), 13–24.

SUGGESTED READING

Anand, Geeta. "How Drugs for Rare Diseases Became Lifeline for Companies." *Wall Street Journal*, November 15, 2005. Http://online.wsj.com/article/SB113202332063297223.html.

Anderson, Gerard F., Uwe E. Reinhardt, Peter S. Hussey, and Varduhi Petrosyan. "It's the Prices, Stupid: Why the United States Is So Different from Other Countries." *Health Affairs* 22 (2003): 89–105.

Angell, Marcia. *The Truth About the Drug Companies: How They Deceive Us and What to Do about It*. New York: Random House, 2004.

Arnold, Denis G., ed. *Ethics and the Business of Biomedicine*. Cambridge: Cambridge University Press, 2009.

Callahan, Daniel, and, Angela A. Wasunna. *Medicine and the Market: Equity vs. Choice*. Baltimore: Johns Hopkins University Press, 2006.

Committee on the Consequences of Uninsurance, Board of Health Care Services, Institute of Medicine. *Hidden Costs, Value Lost: Uninsurance in America*. Washington, D.C.: National Academies Press, 2003.

Daniels, Norman. *Just Health Care*. Cambridge: Cambridge University Press, 1985.

———. *Just Health: Meeting Health Needs Fairly*. New York: Cambridge University Press, 2008.

Daniels, Norman, and James E. Sabin. *Setting Limits Fairly: Can We Learn to Share Medical Resources?* New York: Oxford University Press, 2002.

Daniels, Norman, Donald W. Light, and Ronald L. Caplan. *Benchmarks of Fairness for Health Care Reform*. New York: Oxford University Press, 1996.

Light, Donald W., and Joel Lexchin. "Foreign Free Riders and the High Price of U.S. Medicines." *British Medical Journal* 331 (October 22, 2005): 958–960.

Jecker, Nancy S. "Can an Employer-based Health Insurance System be Just?" *Journal of Health Politics, Policy, and Law* 18 (1993): 657–674. Alternative version in *The Politics of Health Care Reform: Lessons from the Past, Prospects for the Future*. Edited by Gary S. Belkin and James A. Morone, 259–275. Durham, N.C.: Duke University Press, 1994.

McCabe, Christopher, Karl Claxton, and Aki Tsuchiya. "Orphan Drugs and the NHS: Should We Value Rarity?" *British Medical Journal* 331 (October 29, 2005): 1016–19.

Menzel, Paul T. "Justice and the Basic Structure of Health Care Systems." In *Medicine and Social Justice: Essays on the Distribution of Health Care*. Edited by Rosamond Rhodes, Margaret P. Battin, and Anita Silvers, 24–37. New York: Oxford University Press, 2002.

Menzel, Paul T. *Strong Medicine: The Ethical Rationing of Health Care*. New York: Oxford University Press, 1990.

Menzel, Paul, and Donald W. Light. "A Conservative Case for Universal Access to Health Care." *Hastings Center Report* 36 (4) (July–August 2006): 36–45.

Nussbaum, Martha C. *Frontiers of Justice: Disability, Nationality, Species Membership*. Cambridge, Mass.: Harvard University Press, 2006.

Pauly, Mark, Patricia Danzon, Paul Feldstein, and John Hoff. *Responsible National Health Insurance*. Washington, D.C.: American Enterprise Institute, 1992.

Pogge, Thomas, ed. *Freedom from Poverty as a Human Right: Who Owes What to the Very Poor?* Oxford: Oxford University Press, 2007.

Powers, Madison, and Ruth Faden. *Social Justice: The Moral Foundations of Public Health and Health Policy*. New York: Oxford University Press, 2006.

Rhodes, Rosamond, Margaret Battin, and Anita Silvers, eds. *Medicine and Social Justice: Essays on the Distribution of Health Care*. New York: Oxford University Press, 2002.

Sen, Amartya. *Inequality Reexamined*. Cambridge, Mass.: Harvard University Press, 1992.

Woolhandler, Steffie, Terry Campbell, and David U. Himmelstein. "Costs of Health Care Administration in the United States and Canada." *New England Journal of Medicine* 349 (2003): 768–775.

PART IV

UNIVERSAL NORMS AND THE RELATIVITY OF MORAL JUDGMENTS

RELATIVISM, MULTICULTURALISM, AND UNIVERSAL NORMS: THEIR ROLE IN BUSINESS ETHICS

TOM L. BEAUCHAMP

ARE moral beliefs merely personal opinions and cultural conventions, or is there a moral standpoint that transcends the personal and cultural? In one type of theory, moral views are based on how a person feels, what a corporation decides, or how a culture accommodates the desires and aspirations of its people. The idea of objective principles or properties plays no role in this theory. In another type of theory, valid moral standards such as human rights govern all conduct and are not relative to cultures, nations, organizations, or individuals. Could it be that both perspectives are correct, or do we have two competing moral philosophies that cannot be rendered coherent? This issue is the thread connecting the several sections of this chapter.

The primary topics to be addressed are moral relativism, universal morality and particular moralities, moral conflict and disagreement, human rights, multiculturalism, cultural moral imperialism, and global social justice. Questions of whether there are universal moral norms and, if so, whether some norms are relative to groups or individuals are discussed in all sections. I argue that although a relativism of all moral standards is an untenable position, a lower-level relativism of moral judgment and multiculturalism are morally warranted. I conclude that there is a universal common morality, but that it allows for moral disagreement and legitimate differences of opinion about how to render universal norms specific for business contexts. Accordingly, certain norms constrain corporate activities in all cultures, but other norms constrain corporate conduct only in specific contexts.

Moral Relativism

Moral relativism is an ancient problem about cultural differences and one still vibrant today. Two types of relativism are examined in this section: cultural (or descriptive) relativism and normative (or ethical) relativism. I begin with the first.

Cultural Relativism

Defenders of relativism have claimed that the discoveries of anthropologists constitute evidence of a vast diversity of moral practices. These discoveries suggest that notions of moral rightness and wrongness derive from cultural histories that should be understood in terms of their cultural contexts.[1] These anthropological discoveries indicate that cultural practices and belief structures vary, but they do not demonstrate that morally committed people in diverse cultures disagree about the *basic* moral standards that underlie their particular moral codes. For example, moral principles of honesty, fair dealing, freedom of association, and respect for human dignity are remarkably similar in cultures in all regions of the world, which is not to say that there are no dissimilarities.

Cultures may agree on the basic principles of morality, such as keeping promises and making truthful disclosures, yet disagree profoundly about how to live by these principles in particular circumstances. For example, consider issues of insider trading—that is, trading in the stock of a corporation based upon material nonpublic information obtained by virtue of a close relationship with the corporation. Culture *A* may hold that rules against insider trading are essential to preserve the fairness and integrity of the securities markets and that investors who have nonpublic inside information are unfairly advantaged. It may also be believed that inside traders violate fiduciary duties to not disclose confidential information. In culture *B*, by contrast, it may be held that insider trading is not unfair and that permitting insider trades would make the securities markets more efficient while also reducing government interference with markets. The idea is that the activity of the traders would quickly be spotted and the market would respond almost immediately to information. From this perspective, a person who locates undervalued shares in a company through inside information provides a valuable service to the market.

Despite the differences between cultures *A* and *B*, their underlying moral principles may not be relative. Persons in *A* and *B* both appeal to the right to pursue accurate information in a free market, principles of market efficiency, the vital role of appropriately incentivized markets, and the like in the attempt to justify their policies on insider trading. While the customs and beliefs are different in A and B, the basic moral principles need not differ, even if the people of the two cultures utilize and specify these general principles in competing ways. It is primarily an empirical question whether cultures do in fact differ in their fundamental principles, but true cultural relativists subscribe to the thesis that no objective moral principles are shared across cultures. If even a single fundamental principle of morality such as the proscription of lying transcends cultural beliefs and practices, cultural relativism cannot be correct in asserting that all norms are culturally relative.

A *fundamental* conflict between cultural moral values would occur only if *basic* moral principles are relative to the cultures. A principle is basic if it cannot be reduced to or justified in terms of some other principle or moral notion. For example, the principle that one ought not to cause harm to others by one's actions is a basic principle. A moral conflict is fundamental if the conflict cannot be removed even if there were perfect agreement about the facts of a case, about the concepts involved, and about background beliefs. Accordingly, the problem of cultural relativism ultimately turns on whether there are basic, universal principles that cross cultural lines. This idea is considered below in the two sections titled "Universal Morality" and "Particular Moralities." It is also considered in the sections on "Human Rights" and "Multiculturalism."

Whatever the merits of the reports of anthropologists about cultural differences, their descriptive reports do not support any normative position about what *is* right and wrong or about what one *ought* to believe. This issue of normativity takes us to the second type of relativism.

Normative Relativism

In this type of relativism, the statement "What is right at one place or time may be wrong at another" is interpreted to mean that *it is right* in one context to act in a way that *it is wrong* to act in another. "When in Rome, do as the Romans do" is a famous saying about what is right that dates from St. Ambrose's explanation of how he handled the different traditions and practices that he encountered when he visited different churches. His saying might by reformulated as the prescription, "Romans and visitors to Rome should act according to the rules of Rome." This statement determines standards of right and wrong behavior. One form of normative relativism asserts that one ought to do what one's society determines to be right (a *group* form of normative relativism), while a second form holds that one ought to do what one personally believes is right (an *individual* form of normative relativism). St. Ambrose's original formulation appears to have been about what is right for *him* to do, but he also may have been giving advice to St. Augustine about what is right for *groups* of church visitors to do when in another church.[2]

According to group normative relativism, one ought to do what the group (a culture, perhaps) determines to be the norm. In Japan and in Japanese institutions one should act as the Japanese act, and in the United States or in American institutions one should act as Americans act. However, cultures such as those in Japan and North America often are cemented together in social institutions that embrace norms from both cultures. Here the advice of normative relativism can become muddy. Some managers in a firm may come largely from a cultural history in Japan and others from a cultural history in the United States. Cultural normative relativism is based on *cultural beliefs* and institutions, not merely on beliefs that appear only within the borders of nation states. Accordingly, normative relativism does not merely say that when one is in Japan one should act as the Japanese do or when in the United States as the Americans do. It is a cultural, not a geographical theory.

Consider a case involving allegations of sexual harassment at a Mitsubishi Motors plant in the United States. Problems at the plant were said by a number of witnesses to be due to "cultural factors." It was reported that traditions of loyalty of Japanese employees to their employer and of employer control were different from U.S. traditions. Employees at the Mitsubishi plant reported efforts by major figures in management to foster Japanese attitudes in order to counter various U.S. traditions of confrontation between management and union employees. It was also reported that there were different cultural understandings of the nature of sexual harassment and of the appropriate role and treatment of women. Press reports in Japan generally deviated from U.S. press reports. A strong opinion in the Japanese press was that the affair had been blown out of proportion and that the cultural criticisms that arose from the U.S. plant represented an instance of "Japan bashing" in the United States. However, many Japanese citizens, primarily younger workers and women, expressed disdain for the behavior of Mitsubishi male executives and workers and criticized the protective responses of the Japanese press. The issues, they judged, were more generational and gender-based than cultural.[3]

Normative relativists commonly assert that there is no criterion independent of one's culture or group for determining whether a practice is right or wrong. However, normative relativism could be relativized to parties other than cultures, including religions, individuals, and conceptual frameworks.[4] Normative relativism can be portrayed, in general, as the view that anything is right or wrong whenever some group, culture, religion, or individual judges that it is right or wrong. However, more guarded formulations can be provided. For example, when expressed in terms of individual belief, the account can be stated as the view that to be right some norm must be conscientiously and not merely customarily believed; and the group theory likewise can be formulated as the view that whatever is believed to be right is right if it is part of a traditional moral code of rules or set of practices, such as a business code of ethics or a set of practices customary in a trade.

Whether stated in the individual or the group form, normative relativism is difficult to defend because it is inconsistent with basic and cherished moral norms in effectively all moral traditions and all moral theories. Normative relativism offers no justification for its view that a norm is acceptable merely because a group believes it in a certain way or because an individual believes it in a certain way. This commitment is at the heart of the theory and cannot be jettisoned without abandoning the theory. But the idea that the slave trade, sexual harassment under a severe threat by a boss, firing good workers for no cause, and blocking women from holding executive positions ought to be practiced because an individual or group believes they should has no justification or credibility.

If right and wrong are entirely relative to a society's standards, no person could ever maintain that his or her society's standards are wrong. Internal criticism of social standards would be impossible no matter what the standards are.[5] Similarly, if there are no moral norms in a business or a society about exposing employees to toxic chemicals, coercion and exploitation of employees, unacceptable occupational risk, unethical accounting practices, and the like, then normative relativism implausibly maintains that the absence of such standards is morally normative for that business and society. While societies generally have a body of rules that can be used to criticize such an absence of norms, that fact misses the main point, which is that *if* there is a complete void of available standards, then there is no basis on which to criticize conduct.

Consider the so-called Enron scandal, when Enron executives learned that the U.S. Securities and Exchange Commission (SEC) was beginning an investigation of Enron's accounting irregularities. Enron and its accounting firm, Arthur Andersen, shredded all company documents. According to normative relativism (here relativized to the corporate culture), since the culture at Enron was to shred documents when litigation loomed, it was right to have shredded the documents.[6] This example focuses only on the corporate culture at Enron. If that culture is accepted as the relevant cultural unit, then it was right and not wrong to shred the documents. It is one thing to suggest that such beliefs and practices might be *excused*, which has plausibility in many contexts; it is quite another to suggest that the beliefs or practices are *right*.

Normative relativism, then, is a vague and implausible moral theory. However, we will later consider a distantly related and far more plausible theory now widely referred to as "multiculturalism" (see the section below on "Multiculturalism"). This theory has sometimes mistakenly been thought to be a form of normative relativism, but, as we will see, the theory is deeply in conflict with all forms of normative relativism.

Relativism of Judgment and Relativism of Basic Norms

Despite the problems with the types of relativism thus far assessed, a distinction needs to be made between *relativism of judgments* and *relativism of basic norms*. Relativism of moral judgment is so pervasive in social life that it would be foolish to deny it. For example, when people differ about whether one policy for keeping client or customer information confidential is more acceptable than another policy or about whether it should be legal to sell pornography through Internet sites and shopping mall outlets, they differ in their *judgments*. It does not follow, as noted earlier, that they differ in the basic moral norms used to justify the judgments.

I turn to the question of whether there is a reliable nonrelativism of basic norms.

Universal Morality

Relativity of moral judgment is a social fact, but it is no less a social fact that every morally sensitive person accepts certain cross-cultural norms. The set of norms shared by all persons committed to morality constitutes what will here be called "the common morality." This morality is not merely *a* morality in contrast to *other* moralities.[7] The common morality is normative for everyone, and all persons are rightly judged by its standards. The common morality is composed of *rules, virtues,* and *ideals.* I start with examples of each of these three categories.

Shared Moral Rules

The following are a few examples (but not a complete list) of rules of obligation in the common morality: (1) Do not kill; (2) Do not cause pain or suffering to others; (3) Prevent evil or harm from occurring; (4) Rescue persons in danger; (5) Tell the truth; (6) Nurture the young and dependent; (7) Keep your promises; (8) Do not steal; (9) Do not punish the innocent; and (10) Obey the law. These norms should be classified as basic or fundamental in the sense previously mentioned. This classification does not mean that the norms have no justification by appeal to more general norms, a point that will become clearer later. These norms are also implemented in different ways in different cultural or corporate settings, and some measure of relativism of judgment will arise in interpreting and implementing them, but the norms themselves are cross-cultural, not relative to cultures. In their influential work in business ethics, Thomas Donaldson and Thomas Dunfee have referred to norms of this sort as "hypernorms," meaning principles that are "so fundamental to human existence that they serve as a guide in evaluating lower level moral norms" found in particular communities.[8] Their hypernorms are fundamentally identical to what I am designating the moral rules in the common morality.

Shared Moral Virtues

The common morality also contains moral character traits, or standards of virtue, that should be distinguished from norms of obligation. Here are ten examples (but not a complete list) of moral character traits, or virtues, recognized in the common morality, and these too should be considered basic or fundamental norms: (1) Nonmalevolence; (2) Honesty; (3) Integrity; (4) Conscientiousness; (5) Trustworthiness; (6) Fidelity; (7) Gratitude; (8) Truthfulness; (9) Lovingness; and (10) Kindness. These virtues are universally admired,[9] and a person is deficient in moral character if he or she lacks such traits. Negative traits amounting to the opposite of these virtues are *vices* (malevolence, dishonesty, lack of integrity, cruelness, etc.). They are substantial moral defects and are universally so recognized. In an influential body of work in business ethics, Robert Solomon attempted to give a prominent place to a framework of virtues in order to understand acceptable and unacceptable corporate roles and actions.[10]

Shared Moral Ideals

All morally committed persons share views about moral ideals such as charitable goals, community service, dedication to one's job that exceeds expected levels, and service to the poor. These aspirations exceed obligations. The moral ideals are not *required* of persons, but they are universally *admired* when found in persons who accept and act on them.[11] However, only some, not all, moral ideals are shared, and some ideals are inherently contestable and not shared. A particularly contentious moral ideal that is not shared is whistle-blowing by company employees who disclose information regarding behavior in the organization that the whistle-blower believes to be wrongdoing.[12]

All persons committed to a moral way of life accept the universal moral rules, moral virtues, and moral ideals just mentioned. This does not mean that such persons always act in accordance with the rules, and certainly they do not always conform their behavior to the moral ideals. Nonetheless, they accept the relevance and importance of these norms. Likewise, the literature of ethics does not debate the merit or acceptability of these norms, which are basic to morality itself.[13] It would, however, be absurd to assert that all persons do in fact accept and act on the norms of the common morality. Many amoral, immoral, or selectively moral persons do not care about or identify with moral demands. Nonetheless, all persons in all cultures who are committed to a moral way of life accept the norms of the common morality. In recent years, the favored language in public discourse to express the basic norms in the common morality has been "human rights," to which an entire section below is devoted.

The common morality need not be understood as a body of timeless principles disconnected from human history. A body of rules can be a product of human experience and history and still be a universally shared product. The origin of the norms of the common morality is no different in principle from the cultural origins of the norms of what will now be discussed as particular moralities.

PARTICULAR MORALITIES

The universal common morality, from the perspective of the practical concerns of business ethics, is not sufficiently specific to give adequate guidance on many context-sensitive problems. These specific matters are often governed by distinct moralities in the form of moral rules and beliefs that spring from cultural, group, national, and religious sources. For example, one reason why moral norms about proper human treatment of animals on factory farms vary from society to society, and even from person to person, is that norms about the permissible treatment of animals are not a part of the common morality. No part of it has a specific focus on the treatment of animals and certainly not on something as specific as what agribusinesses and laboratories that own animals may and may not do with those animals. The universal common morality only supplies the core moral concepts and principles on the basis of which we can and should reflect on problems in many areas of the moral life, including business ethics. To be a practical, action-guiding morality, the common morality needs to be molded to capture the complexities and realities of business situations.

Particular Moralities as Nonuniversal

Whereas the common morality contains moral norms that are abstract, universal, and content-thin, particular moralities present concrete, content-rich norms. These particular moralities share the common morality with all other particular moralities, but particular moralities also include the responsibilities, aspirations, ideals, sympathies, attitudes, and sensitivities found in diverse cultural traditions, religious traditions, professional practice standards, and institutional rules and expectations. A moral relativism of judgment commonly arises in these contexts, but this relativism does not undercut the universal standards of the common morality. All specific moralities are appropriately judged harshly by the common morality when they violate universal norms.

Business organizations and associations understandably vary in their specific moral norms. Some include provisions that others do not. For example, some businesses have open-door grievance policies stating that management, and management only, hears complaints by employees. By contrast, some corporations use peer review panels to resolve employees' complaints and grievances. In a peer-review structure, a majority of peer employees and a minority of managers hear each grievance case. It is understandable that one approach to grievances works best in one corporation and a different approach works best in another corporate setting. Neither violates universal moral norms, and a reasonable moral case can be made for both. (One may be able to make a better moral case for one procedure than for another. I am here assuming only that the arguments on both sides are sufficient to justify each procedure.)

To turn to another example, some corporations allow the reporting of perceived corporate wrongdoing through *anonymous* channels of whistle-blowing. Other corporations do not permit anonymous whistle-blowing. Similarly, rules about conflict of interest vary. For example, an executive's hiring of his own family members might constitute an unjustified conflict of interest in one business and be routine and justified in another. Again, rules about permissible gift giving notoriously vary from one culture to another. Although rules governing whistle-blowing, conflict of interest, and gift giving can legitimately vary, they all have moral limits in the sense that some formulations of specific norms will violate the norms of the common morality. For example, conflict of interest rules could become a way of gaining access to legitimately private employee financial information, and rules about gift giving might be formulated as a way of allowing bribery of public officials.

Persons who accept a particular morality often suppose that they speak with an authoritative moral voice for all persons. They have a false belief that they have the authority of the common morality behind them and therefore can insist on the rightness of their positions and the wrongness of others' positions. Such particular moral viewpoints may even be morally praiseworthy without binding other persons or communities. For example, persons who believe that it is immoral to manufacture gasoline-inefficient automobiles or to sell low-fiber, high-calorie cereals in grocery stores may have very good reasons for their views, but they cannot claim direct support in the common morality for those views. At best they can claim indirect support by using premises drawn from the common morality.

Professional Moralities as Particular Moralities

Professional moralities are particular moralities found in codes, organizational rules, and standards of practice in business. Just as there is a general common morality with shared norms, so many professions contain, implicitly or by tradition, a professional morality with shared standards of behavior. Particular codes written for professional groups such as industrial hygienists, engineers, marketers, advertising agencies, chemical companies, architects, and the like usually spring from attempts to discover and develop an already inchoate morality in the profession. A diverse literature has emerged in business ethics that addresses the extent to which there are universal norms that can be made practically meaningful for multinational corporations.[14]

"Codes of ethics" are usually attempts to clarify, specify, explain, and expand the inchoate morality. Professional codes foster and reinforce member identification with the prevailing values of the profession. These codes should be encouraged when they incorporate defensible moral norms, but professional codes often oversimplify moral requirements, make them indefensibly rigid, or make excessive and unwarranted claims about their completeness and authoritativeness. Professionals sometimes mistakenly suppose that they are satisfying all relevant moral requirements by strictly following the rules of the code, just as many people believe that they fully discharge their moral obligations when they meet all legal requirements. However, a code may be poorly prepared, biased, incoherent, or deficient in implementing requirements of the common morality.

MORAL CONFLICT

Despite the common morality and related forms of convergent agreement in particular moralities, moral disagreements often run so deep that we despair of reaching agreement. Even the norms of the common morality can come into conflict with no clear resolution.

Conflicting Moral Norms

Whether in universal morality or in particular moralities, moral norms are not categorical or absolute standards. They can be justifiably overridden by the significance of other moral norms with which they conflict. For example, we might justifiably not tell the truth to prevent a terrorist from hijacking an airplane. We also might justifiably exclude pregnant women from certain jobs in the chemical industry to protect their fetuses from potentially harmful exposures. Even human rights are not absolute. A right generates obligations on others only if the obligation is not counteracted by conflicting and compelling moral considerations. For example, when conflict occurs between a person's right and public health emergencies or the rights of others, the person's right may legitimately be overridden or balanced with the other interests. In some cases the rights of business conflict with the rights of individuals. There is no a priori reason to think that one right holder is to be preferred over another. Some rights may be so carefully delineated that they can never be overridden or suspended, but such rights are comparatively rare.

W. D. Ross introduced a famous distinction between *prima facie* and *actual* obligations. A prima facie obligation must be fulfilled unless it conflicts, on a particular occasion, with an equal or stronger obligation. A prima facie obligation is always binding unless a competing moral obligation outweighs it. In a circumstance of contingent conflict, agents must determine what they ought to do by finding an actual or overriding obligation. They must locate what Ross called "the greatest balance" of right over wrong. What agents ultimately ought to do is determined by what they ought to do, *all things considered.*[15]

For example, imagine that a corporate executive has obtained confidential medical information about an employee. The employee is seeking advancement in a stress-filled position, and the executive has good reason to believe that this advancement would be devastating to both the employee and other employees. The executive has several obligations, including those of confidentiality, preventing harm, and fairness in promotions. Should the executive break confidence to meet the other obligations? Addressing such questions through a process of moral deliberation and justification is required to establish an agent's actual obligation in the face of conflicting prima facie obligations.

No moral theory or professional code of ethics has successfully presented a system of rules free of conflicts and exceptions, but this fact is no cause for skepticism about moral judgment. Almost daily we confront situations that force us to choose among conflicting values in our personal and work lives. Some choices are moral, whereas many are nonmoral or at least not entirely moral. For example, a company's low profit in a given year might compel executives to choose between (1) allocating an annual bonus that is usually provided and (2) raising rather than freezing salary levels. This choice is not easy when employees have become used to both, but in such situations we are usually able to think through the alternatives, deliberate, and reach a conclusion. The moral life presents similar problems of choice, and they rarely stymie us even if they cause agony and regret.

Residual Obligation and Moral Regret

When we must choose which act is best under circumstances of a conflict of moral norms, we will rarely be able to discharge all of the original moral obligations through the act selected. Even a correct decision about the morally best action usually leaves residual, continuing obligations.[16] We have residual obligations when the obligations we were unable to discharge create new ones. As Ross puts it, in the case of breaking a promise, we feel deep regret and a sting of conscience, and we realize that "it is our duty to make up somehow to the promisee for the breaking of the promise."[17] Although we cannot keep an obligation once we failed to act on it, we often can make up for it. For example, we may be able to notify persons in advance that we will not be able to keep a promise, to apologize in a manner that heals a relationship, to create a change of circumstance so that the conflict does not occur again, or to provide compensation. An agent who walks away with no sense of a continuing obligation deserves moral criticism, although it is sometimes difficult to determine with precision what the ongoing obligation is.

The use of corporate policies of mandatory testing of employees for drugs is an example of a situation in which it is confusing and uncertain whether there is a residual and continuing obligation and, if so, what the obligation is. In some industries, including those presenting hazards such as possible hand injuries or chemical explosions, significant percentages of employees have been found to use drugs on the job, and drug testing programs have been found highly effective in some of those industries. They raise productivity, cut costs, reduce accidents and injuries, and reduce waste.[18] Nonetheless, employers often feel misgivings about initiating these programs because the testing is invasive, often requires urination in the presence of a monitor, and in general is embarrassing and humiliating to many employees. Employees regard their personal integrity as challenged. Confidentiality of records cannot be guaranteed: In medical testing there is a standard expectation of privacy of information when testing bodily fluids, but drug testing by corporations realistically cannot carry this guarantee. It is no surprise that, with respect to employees who pass the tests, employers sometimes feel an obligation to apologize for the necessity of the testing, to try to heal damage to management-employee relationships, or to provide additional compensation.

Specifying Moral Norms

Many problems about conflicting norms can and should be handled by making the norms more specific in content and more restricted in scope. Rules must be made context specific to become practical. For example, we have previously referred to rules of disclosure, confidentiality, and workplace safety, all of which can be made more specific for particular settings. An example of a rule that sharpens the requirements of a more general norm is "Supervisors must avoid conflicts of interest by recusing themselves whenever friends under their supervision are under consideration for a promotion." This rule specifies the more general rule, "Avoid conflicts of interest in personnel decisions." The initial norm of avoiding conflicts endures while made more specific.

Consider the need for specification in the brokerage industry. Although a broker has a fiduciary responsibility to make recommendations on the basis of the financial best interest of the client, the broker is also a salesperson who earns a living by selling securities and is obligated to attempt to maximize profits for the brokerage house. The broker needs a significant number of trades, and commissions are a constant temptation even though brokers are obligated to present alternatives objectively and discerningly. The client wants a minimal number of trades consistent with a good return and would like a disclosure of the reason for every trade. Accordingly, a brokerage house should have rules that specify the kinds of disclosures that ought to be made, rules regarding when trades should not be made because of a conflict, and the like.

Specification is a process of reducing the indeterminate character of abstract norms and generating more specific action-guiding content.[19] Specifying the norms with which one starts, whether those in the common morality or norms from a source such as a professional code, is accomplished by *narrowing the scope* of the norms, not by explaining what the general norms *mean*. As Henry Richardson puts it, specification occurs by "spelling out where, when, why, how, by what means, to whom, or by whom the action is to be done or avoided."[20] To act in an informed manner in a business situation, one will need a solid understanding of the relevant business relationships, the social consequences of a change of policy, prevailing economic arrangements, and the like.

All norms are subject to specification, and many already specified rules will need further specification to handle new circumstances of conflict.[21] Progressive specification often must occur to handle the variety of new problems that arise, gradually reducing or eliminating the conflicts. Progressive specification can continue indefinitely. Consider again the earlier specification, "Supervisors must avoid conflicts of interest by recusing themselves whenever friends under their supervision are under consideration for a promotion." This norm could confront situations in which it is impractical and risky not to secure the advice and recommendation of a person with immediate supervisory capacity, and therefore it would be inadvisable to require recusal of the supervisor. The specified rule would need to be further specified, perhaps as follows:

> Supervisors must avoid conflicts of interest whenever friends under their supervision are under consideration for a promotion by recusing themselves from all deliberation on the promotion *unless* information from a supervisor is essential for meaningful deliberation, in which case the supervisor should not recuse but still must not vote on the promotion.

MORAL DISAGREEMENT

Moral conflicts are not always eliminable or reducible either by determining which norm is overriding or by a process of specification. Intractable disagreements can persist even after concerted efforts to resolve them. Different persons and groups will sometimes offer differing and competing specifications. These specifications may be offered by reasonable and fair-minded parties who are committed to the norms in the common morality. Nothing in the model of specification suggests that we can avoid moral disagreement or a relativism of judgments, and we have every reason empirically to believe that we sometimes cannot avoid them.

Throughout this volume we encounter moral disagreements while treating issues such as those about unjust levels of executive compensation, whistle-blowing, preferential hiring policies that use criteria of race and gender, conflict of interest in giving financial advice, high-interest loans to the poor, corporate contributions to political campaigns, bans on certain forms of advertising, environmental protection measures, and so on. These disagreements are sometimes about the best moral view to take, and these may be called *pure* moral disagreements. These disagreements include: (1) disagreement about the relative weights or rankings of the relevant norms, (2) disagreements about appropriate forms of specification or balancing, (3) disagreements springing from a genuine moral dilemma, and (4) scope disagreements regarding precisely who should be protected by a moral norm.

However, moral disagreements often derive from one or more *nonmoral* elements. These may be called *impure* moral disagreements. For example, controversy can emerge because of (1) factual disagreements, (2) disagreements resulting from insufficient or biased information, insufficient evidence, or false belief, (3) disagreements about which norms are applicable or relevant in the circumstances, and (4) conceptual disagreements about a crucial moral notion such as "stakeholder" (e.g., about who counts as a stakeholder) or "cause" (e.g., in the assertion that a chemical "causes" cancer).

To illustrate the point, consider two categories on the second list of impure moral disagreements. As an example of (1) on the second list, people often disagree because they differ over facts such as whether an act will have an intended effect, whether one outcome is more likely than another, and whether available data are adequate. They may not, however, disagree over any basic moral standards in environmental ethics or business ethics, even though the disagreement is seemingly about a moral issue. Disagreement may be caused by different assessments of facts such as whether certain discharges of chemicals and airborne particles will or will not affect an environment or workplace. Similarly, debates over the allocation of resources to prevent accidents or disease in the workplace often become mired in factual issues of whether measures such as the use of protective masks or lower levels of exposure to toxic elements function best to prevent death and disease.

As an example of (4) on the second list, controversies are often needlessly complicated because different meanings of central terms are employed. Disputing parties may have invested heavily in their particular definitions or conceptual understandings. Controversies in business ethics have often turned on the meaning of terms such as "acceptable risk," "bribery," "sexual harassment," and "affirmative action." The last term, for example, refers to policies that require positive steps to rank, admit, hire, or promote persons who are members of groups previously or presently discriminated against. It has been used to refer to everything from open advertisement of positions to quotas in employment and promotion. "Affirmative action" originally meant safeguarding equal opportunity, advertising positions openly, ensuring fair recruitment, and creating scholarship programs for specific groups.[22] However, "affirmative action" has acquired broader meanings, some advanced by proponents and others by opponents. Stern critics of affirmative action hold that the term "affirmative action" today means little more than naked preference by race.[23] Proponents of affirmative action reject this suggestion. They see affirmative action as confined to policies that favor qualified women and minority candidates over similarly qualified men or nonminority candidates if and only if there is an immediate objective of remedying persistent discrimination, achieving diversity, and achieving a sex-blind and color-blind society.[24]

If there is no common point of agreement about the meaning of crucial terms, conceptual assumptions will lead persons to address different issues and so to shadow box with an opponent. Often these parties will not have bona fide *moral* disagreement, only a *conceptual* one (even if they take it to be a moral disagreement). Although reaching conceptual agreement provides no guarantee that a disagreement will be dissolved, it often facilitates discussion of issues or a refocusing of them.

Finally, when conscientious and reasonable moral agents disagree over even a clearly *moral* matter involving a contingent conflict of moral norms, it should not be assumed that the disagreement is indicative of moral ignorance, moral defect, or mere stubbornness of will. We simply lack a reliable way to resolve all disagreements. If evidence is incomplete or different sets of evidence are available to different parties, an individual or group may be justified in reaching a conclusion that another individual or group is justified in rejecting. We cannot hold persons to a higher standard than to make judgments conscientiously in light of the relevant norms and the relevant evidence.

THE MORAL POINT OF VIEW

Some writers seek to steer a course around problems of the relativity of judgment and moral disagreement by focusing on choosing and acting from the right moral perspective. They advocate taking "the moral point of view." Principally, the moral point of view is an impartial, by contrast to partial, perspective. Moral judgments are judged acceptable in this theory when they derive from this viewpoint rather than a viewpoint that is self-interested or partial to self, family, community, culture, or nation.

A celebrated representative of one version of this theory, often called the "impartial spectator theory," is economist and moral theorist Adam Smith.[25] Smith held that in commercial transactions in market societies "it is in vain" for a businessperson to expect other businesspersons to act impartially or from "benevolence only" in commercial transactions. Businesspersons can be expected to act to "their own advantage." In a famous passage, he says that sales, contracts, and bargains depend on self-interest in acquisition and exchange:

> It is not from the benevolence of the butcher, the brewer, or the baker, that we expect our dinner, but from their regard to their own interest. We address ourselves, not to their humanity but to their self-love, and never talk to them of our own necessities but of their advantages.[26]

Smith does not mean that morals have no place in business. He means that it is unreasonable to think of business transactions as involving the taking of an impartial perspective. However, when moral judgments are called for in business relationships, as in other relationships, they must be taken from a perspective that transcends personal interest (self-love). Here Smith calls on his model of the impartial spectator. He argues that we have a moral capacity to judge our own acts and motives by placing ourselves in the position of another person. We then consider what the other would think of us were we to perform or not perform a certain action. We become spectators of our own behavior, like a second self looking at our judgments. Smith suggests that we are morally obligated to place ourselves in this light.[27] This general point of view constitutes the moral perspective, and only from this view do truly moral sentiments and judgments arise.[28]

Some recent moral philosophers have characterized the moral point of view in a somewhat different light. Kurt Baier, for example, maintains that the moral point of view should be understood in terms of *reversibility* of viewpoint: One takes the moral point of view if and only if one would recommend that an action be performed in the same way if the role of any party involved in the action is reversible.[29] For example, a salesperson takes the moral point of view in making disclosures to a customer about a product (e.g., a tire for an automobile) if and only if the salesperson would, under relevantly similar circumstances, accept being treated identically by another salesperson. Whatever one wills for oneself when treating others as customers, one must be willing to abide by when in the reverse position of customer. This position is closely related to the golden rule, which has been appealed to by a number of writers in business ethics.[30] It is invoked, for example, in the chapter in this volume by Thomas Carson in a discussion of "Deception and Information Disclosure in Business and Professional Ethics."

A third influential statement of the moral point of view is found in John Rawls's theory of the "veil of ignorance." Here a moral judgment should be formed from a viewpoint that does not allow consideration of the fortuitous advantages or disadvantages of persons affected by the judgment, because these properties bias judgment. The objective is an unbiased evaluation without regard, for example, to a person's race, sex, nationality, institutional affiliation, or economic circumstance. One is acting from the moral point of view if one makes judgments without knowledge of any properties and interests that would bias judgments. In this conception, a salesperson takes the moral point of view in making disclosures about a product if and only if the salesperson acts without any predisposing bias such as racial preference or personal economic gain.[31] Rawls himself does not attempt to use his theory of the veil of ignorance to reach particular judgments such as those involved in my salesperson example, but his theory has stimulated others to see such practical commitments latent in his theory.

Although theories of the moral point of view differ, they all attempt to provide a statement of *universal* morality in at least three respects. First, they assert that the moral point of view should be maintained by all persons. Second, they assert that judgments reached from this point of view are morally justified. Third, they assert that any judgment reached from this perspective applies universally to all persons in relevantly similar circumstances.

While these theories foster understanding of the idea of a universal moral viewpoint, they are notoriously content-thin and difficult to apply to practical situations in which hard choices must be made. These theories seem to offer more in the way of procedural advice than directive and practical moral advice when we confront difficult choices in business settings. Nonetheless, these theories afford a critical insight into the proper standpoint for moral deliberation. Moreover, almost all moral theories have abstract beginnings and need to be made more concrete. If the moral point of view can generate general moral principles of the sort endorsed in the common morality (as its advocates have claimed), then the theory seems, much like common-morality theory, in need of an account of specification rather than theoretical adjustment. If this is correct, theories of the common morality may have no significant advantage over theories of the moral point of view.

Human Rights

Though the language of rights has been only in the background of the theories considered thus far, from an international perspective human rights are today the most frequently mentioned dimension of universal morality. Rights protect life, liberty, freedom of expression, and property. They protect against oppression, unequal treatment, intolerance, and arbitrary invasion of privacy. Rights language is widely used in the business ethics literature, in which appeals have been made to rights to fair employment conditions, the rights of women to equal pay, the right to a workplace free of sexual harassment, the right to a smoke-free and drug-free workplace, the right to know about workplace hazards, and many other rights. Many corporations have come to see the importance of protecting human rights in their operations and have taken an aggressively pro-rights position.

Human rights are understood as universally valid claims and are not advanced as contingent on whether a culture confers the rights. The whole point of human rights language is to transcend unduly limited cultural moral systems. Human rights are possessed by being a human person, whether or not the rights are recognized in any particular society. Although these rights are often interpreted as legal rights, they should be understood as universally valid claims that are independent of structures of law. For example, rules legitimating the slave trade are unacceptable independent of any particular cultural framing of ethics. Slavery is inconsistent with morality itself, and rights against such treatment are cross-cultural moral norms that no culture can legitimately oppose. It is no surprise that attempts to outlaw and shut down trafficking in slaves were among the earliest attempts to enforce internationally the idea of human rights.[32]

The Concept of Rights and Their Connection to Obligations

Rights are *justified claims* that individuals and groups can make upon other individuals or upon a social group or nation. To have a right is to be in a position to determine by one's choices what others should or should not do.[33] What makes rights discourse distinctive is being able to make claims on others. Claiming is a norm-governed activity, and the relevant norms may be legal, moral, institutional, or rules of the sort found in games. *Legal* rights are justified by normative structures in law and *moral* rights are justified by normative structures in morality. Both universal morality and particular moralities provide norms that support rights claims, but claims about human rights (as discussed below) should be justified by appeal to universal morality. However, there is a priority issue: It is not clear that a right is always best understood as derived from or justified by a rule. Perhaps rules are at least sometimes derived from or grounded in rights. For example, perhaps the right to free speech is the basis of various rules of freedom of expression, rather than the converse. I leave the precise basis of rights and rules of obligation an open question.[34]

I will, however, assume what has been called "the correlativity of rights and rules of obligation." Here the claim is that for any right, if X has the right then some party Y has an obligation either not to interfere if X does Z or to provide X with Z. Likewise, if any party has an obligation to X, then X has a right to the discharge of that obligation. In some cases in which we know that a person, group, or business has a right, we may not know exactly who the holder of the correlative obligation is. Also, a change of circumstances—for example, an oil tanker spill—may lead to new holders of obligations (in this case likely an oil company or tanker company) based on an old right, such as the right to an unpolluted environment.[35]

The Recent Turn to Scrutiny of Corporations

Although the history of rights discourse has been principally about the protection of individuals from governmental abuses, multinational businesses have recently come under similar human rights inspection. This scrutiny is called for because corporations today can have as much effect on human welfare and often as much power or impact as governments.

Scrutiny of corporations has often come from widely respected organizations such as Human Rights Watch and Amnesty International. Their objective is not to critique capitalism or to denigrate the goals of international businesses. These organizations seek to correct corporate behavior that undermines or violates human rights. For example, in 1999, Human Rights Watch criticized Shell, Mobil, and other oil companies operating in Nigeria for collusion with the government to suppress political dissent.[36] Likewise, Texaco has been sharply criticized for taking advantage of the weak human rights record of the government of Ecuador, which long ignored the rights of indigenous native peoples and other marginalized groups. Texaco stands accused of turning a blind eye to these human rights issues while violating the human rights of Ecuadorean citizens to a clean and healthy environment. The charges were based on Texaco's drill site practices, construction of new roads, clear-cutting of forests, improper waste disposal, bulldozing of native people's land, spraying oil on dirt roads, and the like.[37]

As multinationals have expanded their activities in the developing world, sometimes with exploitative intent, human rights criticism has increased. Particularly close scrutiny has been given to failures to provide adequate safety standards for employees, activities that contribute to environmental pollution, and actions in support of governments that violate human rights. An example of the practical problems that confront the implementation of human rights is found in allegedly exploitative labor conditions in the manufacture of products for clothing and shoe manufacturers, an issue now to be addressed.

The Example of Sweatshops

The term "sweatshop" has been adopted to designate hazardous working conditions under which workers have few, if any, rights or even ways to discuss their situation. Both extreme temperatures and extreme abuse from employers have sometimes been observed, as have long working hours for what in developed countries are considered unjustly low wages. (The chapter in this volume by Denis Arnold considers these environments and the issues that arise from them.)

Concern has focused primarily on workers in third-world countries. Nike, Kathie Lee Gifford, Walmart, Liz Claiborne, L. L. Bean, and other companies have been involved in the controversies. Gap, Nike, New Balance, and adidas have changed their policies, and many companies, including Old Navy, Donna Karan, and Victoria's Secret, have made public pledges that conditions in all shops from which they buy are monitored for proper working conditions and to ensure that no children are hired.

Hundreds of thousands of workers are potentially affected by these policies. Activists have appealed to corporations not to do business in countries that have a poor human rights record on sweatshop conditions. However, the social, economic, and political contexts in these countries are often complicated by the conflicting pressures and interests at work. Sometimes there are questions about precisely which rights should prevail and problems in the implementation and enforcement of rights. Workers often want the jobs that are offered because they are the best jobs available, and governments want the jobs to remain in order to build infrastructure and bring in revenue. Each circumstance therefore needs a careful assessment of whether rights are being violated, and, if so, which rights.[38]

Although companies and business associations may have no legal obligation to comply with human rights standards, there is a general appreciation in many nations that businesses will suffer substantial losses of reputation in today's environment if they do not carefully monitor for human rights abuses. Shoe and apparel companies have confronted a battery of accusations of abusive practices because of their suppliers' toleration of low wages and dangerous working conditions. These corporations have learned not to respond by appealing to the cultural relativity of norms or tolerance of cultural diversity. The goal of preserving their reputation has motivated them to agree with their critics that they should insist that their suppliers and partners not violate human rights. Many corporations today assert that a local culture's beliefs and traditional practices in business do not provide an adequate standard. It is an unresolved question, however, whether multinationals should sever all connections with suppliers in those countries in which *governments* engage in violations of human rights.

MULTICULTURALISM

No one disputes that there are diverse cultures and many forms of cultural conflict. However, there are puzzles about how cultural conflicts should be framed and about whether theories of multiculturalism create doubts about universal norms. In this section I argue that multiculturalism requires rather than rejects universal norms.

The term "multiculturalism" is a general label for a group of theories holding that persons from diverse cultures are owed respect and that they should not be forced to accept cultural values that are foreign to their ways of life. These theories demand that cultural traditions, institutions, perspectives, and practices be respected. They seek especially to protect the values of cultures that have been marginalized or oppressed by some dominant culture(s). Multiculturalists argue that respect is owed to cultural traditions because morality itself demands it: It would be unjust and disrespectful to marginalize, oppress, or dominate persons from other cultures or subcultures.[39]

Multiculturalism asserts that it would be morally wrong not to accept particular moralities rooted in cultural histories. (I shall here assume that these particular moralities are composed of justified specifications of universal morality.) The key demand in multiculturalism is that people of one culture tolerate and recognize the legitimacy of the views of others. This norm is independent of any particular culture's values and is universally valid.[40] Multiculturalists therefore deny that all moral values are relative to cultures. Without universal norms of toleration, respect, restraint, and the like, a multiculturalist could not justify multiculturalism. The motivation and goal of the theory is to show that dogmatic cultural demands that are forced on subcultures or other cultures—for example by controlling elites—are moral wrongs of marginalization and devaluation. The moral obligation to respect other cultures is not confined to cultures that *recognize* the obligation—this limitation would be self-defeating from the perspective of the multiculturalist. Moral obligations of respect and tolerance apply to all cultures whether or not they recognize these norms, and even if they reject these norms.[41] As Harvey Siegal puts it, "multiculturalism is itself a culturally transcendent or universal moral, educational, and social ideal in the sense that it is applicable to all cultures…and rests upon other equally transcendent, moral imperatives and values."[42]

CULTURAL IMPERIALISM

What, then, is the difference between insistence on transcendent, universal moral standards and a mere cultural imperialism?

Persons outside of a given culture who press for recognition within that culture of the human rights of women, workers, children, the disabled, the oppressed, the marginalized, the unemployed, low-wage workers, and other vulnerable groups are often criticized as "cultural imperialists" who insist on "Western values" that are simply assumed to be universally valid values. Corporate values, when assumed by corporate officers as the normatively correct values, have likewise been criticized as forced on non-Western societies in which the corporations do business. Such imperialism is seen as heavy-handed, insensitive, and in need of replacement by culturally sensitive standards.

Cultural Imperialism as Western Domination

Charges of cultural imperialism have their roots in hundreds of years of Western political and economic domination. In the early modern period, European companies became significant actors in the economic exploitation of colonial territories. In concert with trading companies such as the British East India Company and the Dutch East India Company various colonial powers forcibly imposed their cultures, languages, and political systems on other peoples, often showing little respect for local culture and tradition. Companies exploited African farmlands, mineral wealth in many countries, and later vast petroleum resources. These business activities were described as investments, but local communities received little in the way of economic benefits from the ventures and often had no recourse or avenue of complaint.

Eventually, many host nation states successfully gained a measure of control over the power of multinationals, but decolonization has been a slow process, and arguably its remnants survive today. Globalized corporations still are, in many geographical regions, as powerful in the economic marketplace as the governments of nation states. In terms of economic development, markets often have more impact than many governments.[43]

Critics of so-called Western nations sometimes say that current talk of universal human rights is a guise for the continuation of Western dominance. They see many human rights initiatives as strategies designed to take advantage of and fundamentally alter local cultures and force them to adopt Western political, business, and economic policies that will enrich the West at their expense. To return to the example of sweatshop controversies, critics of the critics of sweatshops have argued that Western nations impose their standards of good working conditions and fair wages on factories in developing nations even when those factory conditions are welcomed by governments and workers, who receive a higher wage in the factories than in other jobs in their country.[44] Johan Norberg, a Swede, refers to these views (including his own original approach to the problems) as "naively Eurocentric."[45] From this perspective, insistence on human rights in sweatshops is simply an unwarranted imposition of Western values. Some critics maintain that powerful Western nations support human rights when it suits their own economic or political interests, but then ignore human rights issues when dealing with rights-impoverished, pro-Western governments such as Saudi Arabia.

Despite the perplexing history of dominance by colonial powers, the notion of "cultural imperialism" conceptually has nothing to do with a particular history of imperialism or with any particular region of the world. Some cultural traditions, past and present in all parts of the world, have held that their cultural values are universal values to which everyone should conform. This claim might be correct in the sense that one culture might have captured one or more universal norms not captured in another culture. A genuinely universal norm is applicable in all cultures, whether those cultures accept it or not. However, the imposition of a nonuniversal norm on another culture in the pretence that it is a universal norm is simply an example of cultural imperialism.

The Dangers of Local Control Unconstrained by Universal Norms

Despite numerous unresolved issues, there is today a convergence of opinion in many Western and non-Western nations that cultural arrogance must be restrained and that cultural and class differences ought not be allowed to obscure the injustice of the many forms of oppression that flourish under cultural disguises.[46] Among the human rights most vigorously defended in recent years are rights against oppression. Vulnerable groups such as ethnic minorities, women, and children have been the subject of treatises that defend a range of rights against oppression. Many nations that are signatories to the Universal Declaration of Human Rights of the United Nations do not vigorously protect the basic human rights of their women and children, or at least have a narrow vision of what those rights are. When complaints arise, governments often claim that they are treating women and children in accordance with *their* cultural and religious traditions.

The premise that every culture contains protected values, beliefs, and rituals that are of overriding importance to the culture is a dangerous view if expressed to dampen or thwart moral criticism of cultural practices that violate human rights. If cultures prevent women from educational opportunities, tolerate oppressive child labor, or discriminate against minorities or disenfranchised populations, these practices can legitimately be criticized.

Susan Okin has been concerned about this problem when group rights are defended on grounds that they preserve a group's culture. Cultural subordinations of women to men are her principal focus.[47] She rightly sees that conflict between traditional cultural practices and women subordinated to those practices cannot be resolved by a misguided multiculturalism. She argues that conflict ought always to be resolved in terms of the rights of the oppressed, not by appeal to cultural traditions. She calls not for a mere balancing of competing interests, but for the enforcement of human rights that override even longstanding values in cultural traditions: "There can be no justification for assuming that these groups' self-proclaimed leaders—invariably composed mainly of [older men]—represent the interests of all of the groups' members." She notes that appeals to "groups" and "cultures" often mean that, at most, the preferences of only 50 percent of the members of the larger social group will be taken into consideration.[48]

Widely shared norms are often overstated to suggest that the *entire culture* embraces them. There is also often a time lag in the gathering of evidence about the depth of certain beliefs in cultures. In some self-proclaimed "cultures" the societies are more *multi*cultural than *mono*cultural. Often societies have remarkably diverse moral and political commitments even if those societies cannot be said to be multicultural. It also should not be assumed that there are distinctly Eastern values, Asian values, African values, and the like. Even U.S., European, and Russian moral values are highly suspect categories.

Amartya Sen, who is from India, has argued that the idea of "Asia as a unit" with a set of Asian values makes little sense. About 60 percent of the world lives in Asia, with virtually nothing to solidify it as a uniform culture: "There are no quintessential values that apply to this immensely large and heterogeneous population, that differentiate Asians as a group from people in the rest of the world." He notes that violations of basic rights of freedom occur routinely in many parts of Asia and that those in control of governments use the excuse that "Asian nations" do not accord the same value to freedom as do Western countries and are not supportive of the rights to freedom found in the West. These authoritarian regimes attempt to justify their methods of control on grounds that it is necessary for proper economic development. Sen points out that data do not support the claim that rapid economic growth in countries such as China and South Korea was achieved by a suppression of civil rights. The idea of "Asian values" and "the Orient" were originally the products of a Eurocentric perspective that viewed the whole of the Asian region as united by a body of non-Western standards. The values often cited by European observers were drawn largely from East Asia, principally east of Thailand, but even this region has vast diversity of value and virtually nothing in the way of identifiably Asian values. Sen briskly criticizes Western governments, including the United States and European nations, for indirectly backing the idea of Eastern values and allowing it to serve as an excuse for not giving primacy to human rights.[49]

Yael Tamir has likewise challenged the hypothesis that *group rights* are essential to a group's identity. She argues that many cultural practices are not necessary for the survival of the group's identity, and therefore numerous human rights changes could be introduced in a group's traditional practices without affecting cultural identity. Tamir maintains that within any large population numerous subgroups embrace the larger group but take different views of what it means to be part of that group. She proposes that every member of every group and subgroup ought to be given equal human rights so that "the less powerful and less conservative members of each group [may] live their lives and preserve their identity the way they see fit."[50]

While reasonable persons affirm that we should be "culturally sensitive" in exporting moral values to other cultures, some groups may simply have values that constitute a failure to treat one human being as he or she ought to be treated. This is not to say either that moral imperialism is not a bona fide moral threat or that corporations are obligated always to follow the standards that they believe are morally best or ideal. As some authors in business ethics have argued, there is some "moral free space" in which local rules and practices do not violate universal norms of the common morality but still may vary from the norms a corporation typically accepts. Within this free space corporations may legitimately endorse local customs up to the point that they do not violate one or more universal norms. Defenders of this position recognize that local communities are entitled to some deference even when their norms are distinctive and comparatively uncommon. For example, in some countries advertising that presents one product as superior to another competitor product is considered unethical, whereas it is considered acceptable in other countries. Under this conception of free space, corporations as well as professional associations and codes may legitimately conform their policies to the standards operative in the many regions in which they do business. Local norms, in this conception, have moral legitimacy contingent upon their not violating the universal norms of the common morality.[51]

Global Social Justice

Globalization has brought a realization that the solution to many moral problems will require a restructuring of the global order. Here questions of human rights have been treated under the heading of "social justice." These issues have also been classified as questions of "global justice" and "cosmopolitanism."

Cosmopolitan theories take as their starting point major problems resulting from catastrophic or severely detrimental social conditions—in particular, famine, poverty, and epidemic disease. Problems of sweatshops, very low wages, and poorly distributed resources are possible examples in business ethics. A key issue is what globalized institutions—including globalized corporations and international organizations such as the World Trade Organization, the World Health Organization, globalized pharmaceutical companies, and globalized communications companies—owe to workers and to all who are impoverished and oppressed.

An early and abiding influence on cosmopolitan thinking came from Peter Singer's work on global obligations. Singer turned philosophers' attention in a global direction through his trenchant way of pointing to the gap between fundamental principles of morality and the practice of those principles at the international level. Singer convinced many philosophers that morality demands more of us than most of us have thought, especially in addressing global poverty, ill health, and economic deprivation. Singer has attempted to explain the almost universal lack of serious concern for global poverty relief as a failure to draw the correct implications from the moral principle(s) of beneficence that he believes all moral persons accept.

Singer has called his most important principle "the obligation to assist," which is the principle that "if it is in our power to prevent something bad from happening, without thereby sacrificing anything of comparable moral importance, we ought, morally, to do it." Thus, if we can prevent something bad (harmful) from happening by simply *not acting*—for example, by not polluting the environment—we ought to do so. Likewise, if we can prevent something bad (harmful) from happening *by acting*—for example, by donating money to prevent disease from spreading after an earthquake—we ought to do that as well.[52]

While Singer's theory is grounded in utilitarian beneficence, much recent thinking is grounded in an egalitarian theory of justice that evaluates social institutions and their responsibilities, legitimacy, and weaknesses. The focus is not on the morality of the individual choices of persons, but on the morality of the basic structure of society from within which moral choices are made, including the basic evaluative commitments embedded in social institutions. The basic structure of society is composed of the rules and institutions that affect almost everyone, including institutions of commerce and public policy. Today's most influential cosmopolitan theories attempt to extend John Rawls's theory of justice to achieve global institutional reform.

Thomas Pogge, a prominent defender of cosmopolitan theory, argues that Rawls's famous thesis that principles of justice are limited to the formation of rules in specific nation states unduly limits the scope of a theory of justice. A consistent theory, Pogge argues, will apply principles of justice universally. If the worst-off—extremely low-wage, temporary workers—are the focal point of concern, as they are in Rawls's theory, we should address their situation of poverty wherever they may be. National citizenship, from the point of view of justice, is as morally arbitrary as race, class, or gender.[53]

In this account, social justice is not relative to cultural views about justice. The goal of social justice everywhere is to reduce inequality in the face of human misery. Concerns about social justice begin with the world as we encounter it—a world characterized by profound inequalities in well-being and resources, especially in scarcity of food and level of disease. Internationally, there are radical inequalities in almost every respect, most notably in life expectancies.[54] Around twenty million people in the developing world die each year, including several million young children, from malnutrition and diseases that can be inexpensively prevented or treated by cheap and available means. If the reach of social justice is global, this inequality, born of disadvantaging conditions, should be at the top of the conditions to be remedied. Pogge argues that it would be immoral to stymie efforts to alleviate this human misery merely because of local customs and traditions[55] and that it would be misleading to suppose that failures to address global poverty stem only from a lack of beneficent giving by individuals, corporations, and governments. This makes it sound as if we are bystanders who see conditions of deprivation from afar and as having no connection to this deprivation ourselves. Pogge sees three morally significant connections between economically advantaged persons and the global poor: First, their disadvantaged condition and our relatively advantaged condition have historically emerged from a global historical process that pervasively involved wrongdoing through the infliction of harm. Historical processes such as colonialism and the slave trade have played a central role in causing poverty in many locations, while leading to affluence in others. Second, people all over the world depend on natural resource bases from which local benefits are derived, and often millions of people in those locations have resources removed without their consent and without compensation to them. Instead, the benefits accrue to economic players in developed nations and to elites in developing nations. The majority of humankind is thereby excluded from such benefits. Third, we all coexist in a single global economic order that tends to perpetuate global economic inequality.[56]

Assuming this global connectedness, failures of poverty reduction should not be approached merely as the result of a lack of charitable beneficence, but as the way the world has worked to impoverish, starve, and kill millions of innocent people. Pogge views the activities of many corporations as contributing to this process: Corporate activities have historically caused, and continue to cause, poverty, loss of natural resources without adequate compensation, and increasing gaps in levels of economic inequality. This is not to say that these harms are intended or even that they were foreseen when today's global economic order was initiated. It is only to say—now that we understand the consequences of the global economic system and the role of corporations in producing those consequences—that our perpetuation of it is a serious moral failure.[57]

These problems about global social justice will not be further pursued in this chapter, but their importance should be marked. In all of moral theory and business ethics, there are today no issues more important than those mentioned in the last few pages of this chapter. Pursuit of human rights and global justice have the potential to radically alter the way we have previously understood the moral obligations of governments, corporations, and international organizations. These topics also deserve a larger presence in the literature of business ethics than they now have.

CONCLUSION

This chapter started with the question: "Are moral beliefs merely personal opinions or cultural conventions, or is there a moral standpoint that transcends the personal and cultural?" Arguments throughout the chapter moved to the conclusion that there is a universal set of moral norms, comprising what I have called the common morality. These norms are very general and therefore thin in their action-guiding force. They afford a starting point for business ethics, but they rarely have sufficient content to handle complex moral problems about business that corporations and governments face. It is therefore essential that we engage in specification: the process of reducing the indeterminate character of abstract norms and generating more specific action-guiding content. All general norms must be specified for particular contexts, often creating what I have called particular moralities. These moralities may vary from group to group or individual to individual, and in this sense are relative. They are, however, justified only if they have a transparent connection to and are supported by the norms in the common morality. I have argued that although a relativism of all moral standards is an unacceptable position, a lower-level relativism of moral judgment that allows for legitimate differences in moral judgment and specification is morally acceptable and to be expected.

The literature of business ethics draws on both universal morality and particular moralities in the attempt to reach practical conclusions about the conduct of business and public policy. However, it would be incorrect to characterize the field of business ethics as a particular morality. It is often a more innovative and critical enterprise, but, as with particular moralities, innovation must be confined to judgments that can be justified by appeal to the common morality. This is true of the many issues in business ethics that have been considered in this chapter, including the grounding of human rights claims, the nature of a justified multiculturalism, the lack of justification in cultural moral imperialism, and the need for a more discerning account of global justice.

NOTES

1. For a history and analysis, see Elvin Hatch, *Culture and Morality: The Relativity of Values in Anthropology* (New York: Columbia University Press, 1983).

2. See David Wallechinsky and Irving Wallace, in "The People's Almanac" series of books, posted online in Trivia-Library Home, http://www.trivia-library.com/b/origins-of-sayings-when-in-rome-do-as-the-romans-do.htm (accessed April 13, 2008).

3. I am grateful to Jonathan Larkin, Jennifer Esposito, and George R. Lucas Jr. for calling the following sources to my attention and for assembling this literature as a case study: EEOC, Chicago District Office, U.S. Equal Employment Opportunity Commission Press Release: "Monitors Say Mitsubishi in Compliance with EEOC Consent Decree; Sexual

Harassment 'Firmly Under Control' at U.S. Plant," September 6, 2000, and see EEOC, U.S. Equal Employment Opportunity Commission Press Release, "EEOC Responds to Final Report of Mitsubishi Consent Decree Monitors," May 23, 2001; "Why Men Stay Silent: Fear of Retaliation Fostered Abusive Atmosphere, Mitsubishi Workers Say," *Washington Post*, May 26, 1996, H7; "Fighting Back: A Mitsubishi U.S. Unit Is Taking a Hard Line in Harassment Battle," *Wall Street Journal*, April 22, 1996, A1; Reed Abelson, "Can Respect Be Mandated? Maybe Not Here," *New York Times*, September 10, 2000, sec. 3, 1.

4. For many such categories and classification schemes, see William Max Knorpp Jr., "What Relativism Isn't," *Philosophy* 73 (1998): 277–300.

5. See the discussion of this problem in George Sher, "Moral Relativism Defended?" *Mind* 89 (1980): 589–594, especially 592–593.

6. The Powers Report, as discussed in CNNMoney, "Enron Scathed in Report," http://money.cnn.com/2002/02/02/companies/enron_report (accessed May 4, 2008). Enron had a "Vision and Values" statement in which it spoke about basic principles, respect, and the like. Someone might therefore argue that some of Enron's members violated their own principles. The stated principles, however, were not embedded in practice or taken seriously. The operative norms in the culture were very different from the "norms" put forward to foster a good public image.

7. Although there is only one universal common morality, there is more than one *theory* of the common morality. For a variety of theories, see Alan Donagan, *The Theory of Morality* (Chicago: University of Chicago Press, 1977); Bernard Gert, *Common Morality: Deciding What to Do* (New York: Oxford University Press, 2007); Tom L. Beauchamp and James F. Childress, *Principles of Biomedical Ethics*, 6th ed. (New York: Oxford University Press, 2009), chap. 1, 10; and W. D. Ross, *The Foundations of Ethics* (Oxford: Oxford University Press, 1939).

8. Thomas Donaldson and Thomas Dunfee, "Toward a Unified Conception of Business Ethics: Integrative Social Contracts Theory," *The Academy of Management Review* 19 (1994): 252–284, quote from 265. See further Donaldson and Dunfee, *Ties that Bind: A Social Contracts Approach to Business Ethics* (Cambridge, Mass.: Harvard Business School Press, 1999), 43–59. For a compelling criticism of the Donaldson-Dunfee theory and an account that links their theory to mine, see Edward Soule, "Managerial Moral Strategies," *Academy of Management Review* 27 (2002): 114–124, especially 117–123. I do not mean that the list of rules I have given is identical to those discussed by Donaldson and Dunfee. They identify three basic categories of hypernorms: substantive, procedural, and structural. My categorization is quite different, though I do not disagree with them that there are various types of basic norms.

9. See Martha Nussbaum's assessment that, in Aristotelian philosophy, certain "nonrelative virtues" are objective and universal: "Non-relative Virtues: An Aristotelian Approach," in *Ethical Theory, Character, and Virtue*, ed. Peter French et al. (Notre Dame, Ind.: University of Notre Dame Press, 1988), 32–53, especially 33–34, 46–50.

10. Robert C. Solomon, "Corporate Roles, Personal Virtues: An Aristotelian Approach to Business Ethics," *Business Ethics Quarterly* 2 (1992): 317–339; *Ethics and Excellence: Cooperation and Integrity in Business* (New York: Oxford University Press, 1993); and *A Better Way to Think about Business: How Personal Integrity Leads to Corporate Success* (New York: Oxford University Press, 1999).

11. See Bernard Gert, *Common Morality: Deciding What to Do*, 20–26, 76–77; Richard B. Brandt, "Morality and Its Critics," in his *Morality, Utilitarianism, and Rights* (Cambridge: Cambridge University Press, 1992), chap. 5.

12. See the chapter by George Brenkert in this volume, and also Sissela Bok, "Whistleblowing and Professional Responsibility," in *Honest Work: A Business Ethics Reader*,

eds. Joanne B. Ciulla, Clancy Martin, and Robert C. Solomon (New York: Oxford University Press, 2006).

13. The conclusion I reach has often been said by anthropologists and philosophers to be incorrect, but they offer no reasons for this conclusion. For a particularly blunt statement that views of the sort I am defending are incorrect, see Elvin Hatch, "The Good Side of Relativism," *Journal of Anthropological Research* 53 (1997): 371–381. Hatch paradoxically acknowledges the validity of some universal principles, but it is not clear exactly which ones or why they reach this status.

14. See Thomas Donaldson, *The Ethics of International Business* (New York: Oxford University Press, 1989); Richard T. De George, *Competing with Integrity in International Business* (New York: Oxford University Press, 1993); Thomas Donaldson and Thomas W. Dunfee, *Ties that Bind: A Social Contracts Approach to Business Ethics*; Laura P. Hartman, Denis G. Arnold, and Richard Wokutch, eds., *Rising Above Sweatshops: Innovative Management Approaches to Global Labor Practices* (Westport, Conn.: Praeger, 2003); Elaine Sternberg, "The Universal Principles of Business Ethics," in *Business Ethics in the Global Market*, ed. Tibor R. Machan (Stanford, Calif.: Hoover Institution Press, 1999).

15. W. D. Ross, *The Right and the Good* (Oxford: Clarendon Press, 1930), especially 19–36, 88; and *The Foundations of Ethics* (Oxford: Clarendon Press, 1939).

16. See Thomas E. Hill Jr, "Moral Dilemmas, Gaps, and Residues: A Kantian Perspective"; Walter Sinnott-Armstrong, "Moral Dilemmas and Rights"; and Terrance C. McConnell, "Moral Residue and Dilemmas"—all in *Moral Dilemmas and Moral Theory*, ed. H. E. Mason (New York: Oxford University Press, 1996). See also Robert Nozick, "Moral Complications and Moral Structures," *Natural Law Forum* 13 (1968): 1–50; and James J. Brummer, "Ross and the Ambiguity of Prima Facie Duty," *History of Philosophy Quarterly* 19 (2002): 401–422.

17. Ross, *The Right and the Good*, 28.

18. For general information on the problem, see http://www.dol.gov/asp/programs/drugs/workingpartners/dot.htm (accessed May 4, 2008).

19. Henry S. Richardson, "Specifying Norms as a Way to Resolve Concrete Ethical Problems," *Philosophy and Public Affairs* 19 (Fall 1990): 279–310; and "Specifying, Balancing, and Interpreting Bioethical Principles," in *Belmont Revisited: Ethical Principles for Research with Human Subjects*, ed. James F. Childress, Eric M. Meslin, and Harold T. Shapiro (Washington, D.C.: Georgetown University Press, 2005), 205–227.

20. Richardson, "Specifying, Balancing, and Interpreting Bioethical Principles," 289.

21. Ibid., 294.

22. See President of the United States, Executive Order 11246, 3 C.F.R. § 339 (1964–1965). This order required all federal contractors to develop affirmative action policies along the lines here mentioned. The U.S. Department of Labor still today explains government policy in terms of the practical implications of this order: "Facts on Executive Order 11246—Affirmative Action," as revised January 4, 2002: www.dol.gov/esa/regs/compliance/ofccp/aa.htm (as posted 2007). For various historical and definitional issues, see Carl Cohen and James P. Sterba, *Affirmative Action and Racial Preference* (New York: Oxford University Press, 2003), 14, 18–20, 25, 40, 101, 200–201, 253, 279, 296.

23. See the arguments by Carl Cohen in Cohen and Sterba, *Affirmative Action and Racial Preference*.

24. See Elizabeth S. Anderson, "Integration, Affirmative Action, and Strict Scrutiny," *New York University Law Review* 77 (November 2002): 1195–1271; Barbara R. Bergmann, *In Defense of Affirmative Action* (New York: Basic Books, 1996); Steven M. Cahn, ed., *The Affirmative Action Debate* (New York: Routledge, 2002); Robert Fullinwider, "Affirmative

Action," in *The Stanford Encyclopedia of Philosophy*, Spring 2008 ed., ed. Edward N. Zalta, http://plato.stanford.edu/archives/spr2005/entries/affirmative-action/.

25. See Patricia Werhane, *Adam Smith and His Legacy for Modern Capitalism* (New York: Oxford University Press, 1991); and J. Ralph Lindgren, "Adam Smith," in *Encyclopedia of Ethics*, eds. L. C. Becker and C. B. Becker (New York: Garland, 1992).

26. Adam Smith, *An Inquiry into the Nature and Causes of the Wealth of Nations*, ed. R. H. Campbell, A. S. Skinner, and W. B. Todd (Oxford: Clarendon Press, 1976), 26ff.

27. Adam Smith, *The Theory of Moral Sentiments*, eds. A. L. Macfie and D. D. Raphael (Oxford: Clarendon Press, 1976), 110–13, 158ff.

28. Ibid., pt. 3.

29. Kurt Baier, *The Moral Point of View* (Ithaca, N.Y.: Cornell University Press, 1958).

30. See the articles on "The Golden Rule" by Corey A. Ciochetti, and "Principle of Universalizability" by Melissa Mosko in the *Encyclopedia of Business Ethics*, vol. 2, 5, ed. Robert W. Kolb (Los Angeles: Sage, 2008), 1026–27, 2145–48.

31. John Rawls, *A Theory of Justice* (Cambridge, Mass.: Harvard University Press, 1971), especially 20ff, 46–50, 579–580 (revised 1999 ed.: 17ff, 40–45, 508–9); *Political Liberalism* (New York: Columbia University Press, 1996), especially 8, 381, 384, 399; "The Independence of Moral Theory," *Proceedings and Addresses of the American Philosophical Association* 48 (1974–75): 8.

32. Although the slave trade is today regarded as a relatively minor international problem, it flourishes in many countries in which it has a history of providing cheap labor, especially for farming and manufacturing. See Suzanne Miers, *Slavery in the Twentieth Century: The Evolution of a Global Problem* (Walnut Creek, Calif.: AltaMira, 2003); and United Nations Commissioner for Human Rights, Fact Sheet No.14, "Contemporary Forms of Slavery," www.unhchr.ch/html/menu6/2/fs14.htm (accessed June 5, 2008). On the history of human rights, as originally expressed through ideas of natural rights, see Anthony Pagden, "Human Rights, Natural Rights, and Europe's Imperial Legacy," *Political Theory* 31 (2003): 171–199, and Thomas Cottier, "Trade and Human Rights: A Relationship to Discover," *Journal of International Economic Law* 5 (2002): 111–132.

33. Compare H. L. A. Hart, "Bentham on Legal Rights," in *Oxford Essays in Jurisprudence*, 2nd series, ed. A. W. B. Simpson (Oxford: Oxford University Press, 1973), 171–198.

34. Cf. Joel Feinberg, *Social Philosophy* (Englewood Cliffs, N.J.: Prentice-Hall, 1973), 67.

35. See Joseph Raz, *The Morality of Freedom* (Oxford: Clarendon Press, 1986), 171.

36. Human Rights Watch, "The Price of Oil: Corporate Responsibility and Human Rights Violations in Nigeria's Oil Producing Communities" (1999), www.hrw.org/reports/1999/nigeria, as cited by Ratner, "Corporations and Human Rights."

37. Denis G. Arnold, "Libertarian Theories of the Corporation and Global Capitalism," *Journal of Business Ethics* 48 (2003): 155–173, especially 160–64.

38. See Denis G. Arnold and Norman E. Bowie, "Respect for Workers in Global Supply Chains: Advancing the Debate Over Sweatshops," *Business Ethics Quarterly* 17 (January 2007): 135–145; Ellen Israel Rosen, *Making Sweatshops: The Globalization of the U.S. Apparel Industry* (Berkeley: University of California Press, 2002).

39. See the essays in Robert K. Fullinwider, ed., *Public Education in a Multicultural Society* (Cambridge: Cambridge University Press, 1996).

40. See the philosophical essays by Charles Taylor, Amy Gutmann, Steven C. Rockefeller, Michael Walzer, and Susan Wolf, in *Multiculturalism and "The Politics of Recognition,"* ed. Amy Gutmann (Princeton: Princeton University Press, 1992). For crit-

ical analysis of the anthropological literature, see Hatch, "The Good Side of Relativism," 376ff.

41. This possibility seems denied by Jack Donnelly, "Cultural Relativism and Universal Human Rights," *Human Rights Quarterly* 6 (1984): 400–419.

42. This paragraph draws on the argument in Siegel, "Multiculturalism and the Possibility of Transcultural Educational and Philosophical Ideals," *Philosophy* 74 (1999): 387–409; he is himself drawing on the work of Robert K. Fullinwider, Amy Gutmann, and Charles Taylor, in Fullinwider, *Public Education in a Multicultural Society.*

43. See Stephen R. Ratner, "Corporations and Human Rights," *Yale Law Journal* 111 (2001): 443–545, especially 452ff; "Development and International Economic Co-operation: Transnational Corporations," UN Escor, Second Session, UN Doc. E/1990/94 (1990); Susan Strange, *The Retreat of the State: The Diffusion of Power in the World Economy Series,* Cambridge Studies in International Relations, No. 49 (Cambridge: Cambridge University Press, 1997).

44. See Paul Krugman, "In Praise of Cheap Labor: Bad Jobs at Bad Wages are Better than No Jobs at All," *Slate—Dismissal Science* (March 20, 1997), http://web.mit.edu/krugman/www/smokey.html (accessed April 20, 2008); Paul Krugman and Maurice Obstfeld, *International Economics: Theory and Policy,* 7th ed. (New York: Pearson Addison Wesley, 2006), 289–290; Nicholas D. Kristof, "Brutal Drive," in *Thunder From the East: Portrait of a Rising Asia,* ed. Nicholas D. Kristof and Sheryl WuDunn (New York: Alfred A. Knopf, 2000); and Kristof and WuDunn, "Two Cheers for Sweatshops," *New York Times Magazine,* September 24, 2000, 70.

45. Johan Norberg, *In Defense of Global Capitalism* (Washington, D.C.: Cato Institute, 2003); and Johan Norberg, "The Noble Feat of Nike," *Spectator* (June 7, 2003), http://findarticles.com/p/articles/mi_qa3724/is_200306/ai_n9251504 (accessed April 20, 2008).

46. See Martha Nussbaum and Jonathan Glover, eds., *Women, Culture, and Development* (Oxford: Oxford University Press, 1995); and Marcia Angell, "The Ethics of Clinical Research in the Third World," *New England Journal of Medicine* 337 (1997): 847–49.

47. Susan Moller Okin, "Is Multiculturalism Bad for Women?" in her *Is Multiculturalism Bad for Women?*, published as an anthology, eds. Joshua Cohen, Matthew Howard, and Martha C. Nussbaum (Princeton: Princeton University Press, 1999), 20–22.

48. Okin, "Is Multiculturalism Bad for Women?" 23–24.

49. Amartya Sen, *Human Rights and Asian Values* (New York: Carnegie Council, 1997). The quote is on page 13. See also Sen's *Resources, Values and Development* (Cambridge, Mass.: Harvard University Press, 1997).

50. Yael Tamir, "Siding with the Underdogs," in *Is Multiculturalism Bad for Women?*, 52; also Tamir's *Liberal Nationalism* (Princeton, N.J.: Princeton University Press, 1995), 95–116; and Okin, "Is Multiculturalism Bad for Women?" 22.

51. Donaldson and Dunfee, "Toward a Unified Conception of Business Ethics," 262; Dunfee et al., "Social Contracts and Marketing Ethics," especially 18–19.

52. The classic source of Singer's views is "Famine, Affluence, and Morality," *Philosophy and Public Affairs* 1 (1972): 229–243. Singer defended and updated his lines of argument in his 2007 Uehiro Lectures, "Global Poverty," Lectures 1–3, Oxford Uehiro Centre for Practical Ethics, Uehiro Lectures 2007 (in book form, 2009), http://www.practicalethics.ox.ac.uk/Events/Uehiro%20Lectures/nuehirolectures.htm (accessed 5/20/08). See also Singer, *Practical Ethics,* 2nd ed. (Cambridge: Cambridge University Press, 1993), 246.

53. Thomas Pogge, ed., *Freedom from Poverty as a Human Right: Who Owes What to the Very Poor?* (Oxford: Oxford University Press 2007); Pogge, "Human Rights and Global Health: A Research Program," *Metaphilosophy* 36 (2005): 182–209.

54. Madison Powers and Ruth Faden, *Social Justice: The Moral Foundations of Public Health and Health Policy* (New York: Oxford University Press, 2006), especially 64–79.

55. For an expansive list focused on capabilities, see Martha Nussbaum's writings, including *Frontiers of Justice: Disability, Nationality, Species Membership* (Cambridge, Mass.: Harvard University Press, 2006); *Sex and Social Justice* (New York: Oxford University Press, 1999); and *Women and Human Development* (Cambridge: Cambridge University Press, 2000). In part, Nussbaum is extending Amartya Sen's work—see, for example, his *Development as Freedom* (New York: Oxford University Press, 1999).

56. Thomas Pogge, "Priorities of Global Justice," in *Ethical Theory and Business*, 8th ed., eds. Tom L. Beauchamp, Norman E. Bowie, and Denis G. Arnold (Upper Saddle River, N.J.: Pearson Prentice Hall, 2008); and Pogge, "Responsibilities for Poverty-Related Ill Health," in *Contemporary Issues in Bioethics*, 7th ed., eds. Tom L. Beauchamp et al. (Belmont, Calif.: Thomson-Wadsworth-Cengage, 2008), 575–581.

57. In the sources listed in the previous footnote, Pogge argues that this conclusion is suggested by sec. 28 of the Universal Declaration of Human Rights of the United Nations: "Everyone is entitled to a social and international order in which the rights and freedoms set forth in this Declaration can be fully realized."

SUGGESTED READING

Bok, Sissela. *Common Values*. Columbia: University of Missouri Press, 1995.

De George, Richard T. *Competing with Integrity in International Business*. New York: Oxford University Press, 1993.

Donaldson, Thomas. *The Ethics of International Business*. New York: Oxford University Press, 1989.

Donaldson, Thomas, and Dunfee, Thomas W. *Ties that Bind: A Social Contracts Approach to Business Ethics*. Cambridge, Mass.: Harvard Business School Press, 1999.

———. "Toward a Unified Conception of Business Ethics: Integrative Social Contracts Theory," *Academy of Management Review* 19 (1994): 252–284.

Dunfee, Thomas W., N. Craig Smith, and William T. Ross. "Social Contracts and Marketing Ethics." *Journal of Marketing* 63 (1999): 14–32.

Frederick, William C. "The Moral Authority of Transnational Corporate Codes." *Journal of Business Ethics* 10 (1991): 165–177.

Gert, Bernard. *Common Morality: Deciding What to Do*. New York: Oxford University Press, 2007.

Harman, Gilbert. *Explaining Value and Other Essays in Moral Philosophy*. Oxford: Clarendon Press, 2000.

Harman, Gilbert, and Judith Thomson. *Moral Relativism and Moral Objectivity*. Cambridge, Mass.: Blackwell, 1996.

Hartman, Laura P., Denis G. Arnold, and Richard Wokutch, eds. *Rising Above Sweatshops: Innovative Management Approaches to Global Labor Practices* (Westport, Conn.: Praeger, 2003).

Hasnas, John. "The Normative Theories of Business Ethics: A Guide for the Perplexed." *Business Ethics Quarterly* 8 (1998): 19–42.

Human Rights Watch (an organization dedicated to global protection of rights). http://www.hrw.org/

Mackie, John. *Ethics: Inventing Right and Wrong.* London: Penguin, 1977.

Moser, Paul K., and Thomas L. Thomas, eds. *Moral Relativism.* New York: Oxford University Press, 2001.

Nussbaum, Martha. *Frontiers of Justice: Disability, Nationality, Species Membership.* Cambridge, Mass.: Harvard University Press, 2006.

Pogge, Thomas W., ed. *Freedom from Poverty as a Human Right: Who Owes What to the Very Poor?* Oxford: Oxford University Press, 2007.

Powers, Madison, and Ruth Faden. *Social Justice: The Moral Foundations of Public Health and Health Policy.* New York: Oxford University Press, 2006.

Ratner, Stephen R. "Corporations and Human Rights." *Yale Law Journal* 111 (2001): 443–545.

Sen, Amartya. *Human Rights and Asian Values.* New York: Carnegie Council on Ethics and International Affairs, 1997.

Siegal, Harvey. "Multiculturalism and the Possibility of Transcultural Educational and Philosophical Ideas," *Philosophy* 74 (July 1999): 387–409.

Singer, Peter. *One World: The Ethics of Globalization.* New Haven, Conn.: Yale University Press, 2002.

Soule, Edward. "Managerial Moral Strategies: In Search of a Few Good Principles." *Academy of Management Review* 27 (2002): 114–124.

Velasquez, Manuel. "International Business, Morality, and the Common Good." *Business Ethics Quarterly* 2 (1992): 27–40.

Walzer, Michael. *Thick and Thin: Moral Argument at Home and Abroad.* Notre Dame, Ind.: University of Notre Dame Press, 1994.

CHAPTER 9

BUSINESS AND HUMAN RIGHTS: A PRINCIPLE AND VALUE-BASED ANALYSIS

WESLEY CRAGG

Introduction

The thesis that business firms have human rights responsibilities is one of the least and, at the same time, one of the most contested theses in the field of business ethics. Explaining why this is the case and how it has come to be the case is the central task of this chapter.

Until very recently, for reasons explored in Section One, the protection and promotion of human rights has been thought to rest more or less exclusively with the state. As a result, it has been taken for granted that the human rights obligations of corporations were indirect and legal in nature. That is to say, it has been widely assumed that the human rights obligations of corporations were those assigned to them by the laws of the countries in which they had operations. Since virtually all countries do assign human rights obligations to corporations, and virtually all corporations accept that they have a moral obligation to obey the law, it follows uncontroversially that corporations have human rights obligations. It is in this sense that the proposition that business firms have human rights obligations is uncontested.

Under conditions of globalization, however, assumptions about the nature of the human rights obligations of business firms, but more particularly multinational corporations, are undergoing significant reevaluation. A reevaluation of the relation of business and human rights in a global economy is being fostered by the importance of the modern shareholder-owned multi- or transnational corporation in shaping economic development worldwide, allegations of human rights abuses on the part of multinational corporations, and limitations in the capacity of nation states to control the international operations of corporations.

Evidence of these shifts can be seen in the emergence of voluntary codes of corporate conduct. Some of these codes are articulated by corporations themselves; some are set out by international government institutions like the United Nations, the Global Compact, for example; some are formulated by international NGOs (nongovernmental organizations) like Amnesty International; and yet others are developed by international private-sector organizations and associations like the International Council for Mining and Metals (ICMM).[1]

The UN "Draft Norms on the Responsibilities of Transnational Corporations and other Business Enterprises with Regard to Human Rights" is the most recent and dramatic example of this process of reevaluation. The "Draft Norms" document has caused wide debates and controversy. If adopted, its effect would be to create an international legal framework allocating direct legal human rights obligations to multinational corporations in their international operations.[2]

The idea that corporations have direct human rights duties or obligations is changing what Peter Muchlinski argues is "the very foundation of human rights thinking."[3] It is this extension of direct human rights obligations to corporations that has made, and is making, the topic of business and human rights one of the most contested areas of business ethics.

The purpose of this chapter is to track and evaluate evolving views about the human rights obligations of corporations.[4] Specifically, my goal in what follows is to determine whether corporations have direct, morally grounded human rights obligations, and if so, the character and scope of those obligations.

My analysis has three sections. Section 1 addresses two questions: (1) What are human rights? and (2) Why historically has the responsibility for protecting and promoting human rights been thought to rest more or less exclusively with the state?

Section 2 will look at three models that dominate contemporary debates regarding our understanding of the human rights obligations of corporations. The first model, the one most deeply entrenched in current management and legal thinking, takes the position that corporations have no human rights obligations beyond those legal obligations imposed by nation states through legislation. Evaluating this model will lead us to explore why, given the historically grounded view that human rights protection and promotion are a state responsibility, corporations are now caught up in human rights debates. The second model is a voluntary self-regulation model. This model accepts the idea that corporations have direct human rights obligations. It assumes, however, that determining what those obligations are should be undertaken voluntarily by corporations themselves. The third model takes the view that corporations have direct human rights obligations similar in nature to those of nation states. It proposes that corporations should be held directly responsible for protecting and promoting human rights by national and international courts and legal tribunals.

Each of these models will be shown to be seriously flawed. As a consequence, in Section 3, I evaluate and endorse a fourth "hybrid" model that argues that corporations have direct, morally grounded human rights obligations and that the scope and character of those obligations are a function of two things: (1) The social, cultural, political, legal, environmental, and economic settings in which a given corporation is active, and (2) the nature and scope of the actual or potential human rights impacts of a given corporation in the settings in which it is doing—or is proposing to do—business.

Section One: Human Rights as a Philosophical Concept and a Historical Phenomenon

What Human Rights Are

Human rights are typically encountered today as values, principles or standards that find expression in laws or statutes enacted by legislative authorities, in the constitutions of national states, for example, the Canadian Charter of Rights and Freedoms, or in proclamations by international political bodies or institutions like the United Nations.

The Universal Declaration of Human Rights, passed by the General Assembly of the United Nations in 1948, is a paradigmatic example. This Declaration consists of a preamble and thirty articles that set out the human rights and fundamental freedoms to which all men and women are equally entitled, regardless of differentiating characteristics such as the color of their skin, their religious beliefs, their nationality, or ethnic origin. As I explain in more detail below, human rights define behavior that human beings have a right to expect of each other, and assign obligations that human beings share as human beings.

The Moral Foundations of Human Rights

The idea that human beings have rights by virtue of their status as human beings emerges clearly for the first time in the twelfth and thirteenth centuries. Seen from a historical perspective, human rights are grounded on the view that the defining characteristic of human beings is their status as moral agents. In this respect, they are born both free and equal. Moral agency requires both the capacity and the freedom to make choices based on moral considerations and to act on them. Human beings are equal because, as moral agents, they share equally the capacity and the freedom that capacity confers to make moral choices.

As James Griffin points out, early justifications of human freedom and equality derived from the view that:

> we are all made in God's image, that we are free to act for reasons, especially for reasons of good and evil. We are rational agents; we are more particularly moral agents.[5]

Human freedom and equality then led to the idea of human dignity, which was also theologically grounded in its earliest expression by early Renaissance philosophers like Pico della Mirandola, who argued that

> God fixed the nature of all other things but left man alone to determine his own nature. It is given to man "to have that which he chooses and be that which he wills." This freedom constitutes... "the dignity of man."[6]

The idea that human freedom itself confers dignity is subsequently taken up by both Rousseau and Kant. Emerging from their philosophical accounts is the realization that if it is a moral agent's capacity to make moral judgments that constitutes human freedom, and if it is human freedom that confers dignity, then theological supports for human freedom, equality and dignity are no longer necessary.[7]

Human rights enter the picture as values, principles or standards designed to protect and enhance the capacity of human beings to make and act on choices guided by moral considerations. That is to say, human rights give expression to human freedom, human equality, and human dignity as core moral values. They define what counts as being treated with dignity and respect.

The role of human rights, then, is to ensure that every human being has the freedom needed as a moral agent to pursue goals and objectives of his or her own choosing. Their justification is grounded on the need to ensure what all human beings share, namely, the freedom required to make the choices that the exercise of moral agency and moral autonomy requires.

The existence and importance given to human rights today reflects the perceived need to create rules, principles, and laws that, if respected, will ensure that everyone has the freedom required to exercise their moral autonomy. To provide people with the freedom required for the exercise of moral autonomy is to treat them with dignity and respect. To provide or allow that freedom for some but not others is to engage in discrimination.

It follows, as Alan Gewirth points out, that the need all human beings share equally for the moral space or freedom required for the exercise of moral autonomy generates a common interest in ensuring that the freedom to exercise moral autonomy is acknowledged and respected. Human rights serve to protect this interest that all human beings share with each other as human beings. There can be no justification, therefore, for restricting the freedom of some, but not others, to make and act on choices guided by moral reflection. If some human beings are human rights bearers, all human beings are rights bearers. If human dignity requires respect for human rights, human rights ought to be respected by all human beings since all human beings are worthy of being treated with dignity.[8]

Where and when they are respected, human rights have both intrinsic and instrumental value. They are intrinsically valuable because they affirm that the bearers of human rights are human beings equal in moral status to all other human beings and worthy, therefore, of equality of treatment on all matters impacting their capacity as moral agents to lead lives of their own choosing. They are also of significant instrumental value in as much as their respect ensures that the bearers of human rights will not be prevented by arbitrary barriers from living self-directed lives. Consequently, all human beings have an equal interest in ensuring that their human rights are protected and promoted.

This account of human rights is important for present purposes for several reasons. It explains why human rights are properly regarded as fundamental moral principles or values inasmuch as they map the conditions for the respect of human beings as persons, that is to say as moral agents. It grounds human rights on human freedom, dignity, and equality and gives those three values foundational moral significance. It provides a basis for understanding the historical emergence of human rights as significant practical, moral, and legal tools for protecting human dignity and advancing the principles of human freedom and human equality. It offers a framework for understanding the nature and character of the obligations and duties that the acknowledgement of the existence of human rights generates. And it links respect for human rights directly to human well-being.

Human Rights and Their Characteristics

Human rights as just described have a number of distinctive, interrelated characteristics:

1. They are intrinsically moral in nature. Human rights are moral rights. They set the fundamental conditions for the moral treatment of human beings as human beings because they connect directly to human well-being.[9]

2. They are universal. All human beings are the bearers of human rights by virtue of their common status as human beings.[10] This means, as Campbell points out, that "they apply to everyone, whatever the existing societal and legal rights may be within particular states." They are "those rights that ought to be respected globally."[11]

3. They generate parallel, correlative moral obligations or duties quite independently of the actions, decisions, status or role of human rights obligation bearers. From a moral point of view, this characteristic sets the obligations generated by human rights apart from other kinds of moral obligations.

Typically, moral duties and obligations are triggered by a specific act, decision, or differentiating human characteristic. Further, normally, an obligation is to someone in particular. The obligation when triggered is specific and direct. For example, the obligation to keep one's promises might well be described as universal in its application. Anyone making a promise has a (prima facie) obligation to keep that promise. The obligation to keep a promise, however, can only be triggered by making a promise.

Obligations also flow from roles. Parents have obligations as parents. Professionals have obligations as professionals. Members of legislatures have obligations as elected legislators. However, only those assuming those roles have those specific obligations. The obligations that come with the assumption of a specific role are specific to the people assuming the role: one's own children, clients or patients, members of one's constituency, and so on.

The obligations generated by human rights are quite different in character. Like human rights themselves, the obligations they impose are universal. They are not triggered by specific actions, decisions, or roles on the part of those bearing the obligations. Rather they attach to anyone and everyone in a position to impact a rights bearer's capacity to exercise his or her rights.[12]

Two very important conclusions follow from the fact that the obligations imposed by human rights are universal obligations. If I have a right to be treated with respect by virtue of my status as a human being, then everyone I encounter has an obligation to treat me with respect regardless of any act or decision on their part.[13] This means that just as all human beings are the bearers of human rights, all human beings are the bearers of human rights obligations. However, while the human rights of human beings are uniform and universal, the obligations generated by those rights, while universal, are not identical. They vary with the situations in which people find themselves. Understanding the conditions under which it is morally appropriate to assign human rights obligations (to governments, corporations, or individuals) is therefore fundamental to understanding what human rights are.[14]

4. Human rights are important because they are closely linked to human autonomy and well-being. Respect for human rights creates conditions that allow human beings to exercise their uniquely human capabilities and, as human beings, to live, and assist others to live, in ways of their own choosing.

5. Human rights are overriding. That is to say, they trump or take precedence over all other moral and nonmoral values and principles and the obligations they generate. They are overriding because of their importance. That is to say, the function of rights is to ensure that rights bearers are not arbitrarily prevented by other individuals, groups, or their society from realizing their potential as human beings, as they understand it, and in so far as they so choose to do so.[15] When embedded in legal systems, this feature of human rights is most graphically illustrated by the power of judges to strike down or nullify laws that clash with the exercise of human rights as laid down in constitutions in the form of charters or bills of rights.[16]

Human rights are overriding, also, because they are of fundamental moral importance for building societies where exercising the full range of human capacities is a genuine possibility and available to everyone.[17]

6. Human rights must be institutionalizable.[18] Campbell describes this as a "practicality requirement," which he interprets to mean "that it is possible or practicable to embody the right in actual societal or legal rules that promote the interests to which the right in question is directed."[19]

This sixth feature of human rights is crucially important for our discussion. It follows from the Kantian principle that "ought implies can." Rights generate obligations. It cannot be the case, therefore, that someone has a right where the obligation generated by the right is not realizable. Neither can it be the case that someone has a right where the obligations implied by what is claimed to be a right are so abstract or vague that it is unclear what obligations are entailed.

Most particularly, it cannot be the case that someone has a human right that is universally worthy of respect unless that right is capable in principle and practice of being embodied in a matrix of rules capable of guiding human behavior.[20] For this to be the case, the rules, principles, or practices that generate human rights obligations must be capable in principle and practice of being monitored and enforced.

Three important conclusions emerge from this discussion. First, the function of human rights is to instantiate conditions in which human dignity, freedom, and equality are respected. The obligations flowing from the existence of human rights, therefore, cannot be understood to be voluntary or matters of choice. To the contrary, respect for human rights must be societal or society-wide in nature. Second, human rights must be capable in principle and in practice of being institutionalized or embedded within a system of universal, binding, and overriding rules or principles capable in principle and practice of guiding behavior. Further, the implementation of those rules and principles must be capable in principle and practice of being monitored and enforced.

Third, to say that someone or some organization, institution, or state has human rights responsibilities is to say one of two things: There are rules or practices in place that the obligation bearer has an obligation to respect and observe; alternatively, the obligation bearer has a moral obligation to institutionalize rules designed to ensure that the human rights of individuals are protected and respected.

As we shall see, until very recently, responsibility for institutionalizing rules designed to protect and ensure respect for human rights was assumed to be the exclusive prerogative of the nation state. It is this assumption the claim that corporations have human rights obligations challenges.

Human Rights and the Law

In today's world, responsibility for embodying human rights in an actual, functioning social system is virtually universally accepted to be a responsibility of the state using its power to create and enforce law. It does not follow from the practicality requirement, however, that the institutionalization of human rights must take place exclusively within legal systems in the form of constitutional provisions or laws. This may be a practical requirement for a society like our own. However, it would certainly seem an open possibility, and perhaps historically a reality, that a society could exist in which the freedom, dignity, and equality of human beings were generally respected though not embedded in the form of human rights laws subject to legal enforcement.[21]

From their first appearance in modern Western societies, however, protecting and promoting human rights have been seen as more or less the exclusive responsibility of the state. This does not alter the fact that human rights are essentially moral constructs grounded on moral principles and moral conceptions of what it is to be a person or a human being. Neither does it suggest that in the absence of legal enforcement, people cannot be said to have human rights. What it does mean, however, is that the moral obligation for ensuring respect for human rights has been thought, until very recently, to fall on the shoulders of governments responsible for directing the affairs of state. This fact may help to explain why the legal dimensions of human rights have come to dominate human rights discourse today both nationally and internationally.

This fact about the allocation of human rights obligations in modern societies raises two significant questions:

(1) Why, historically, has responsibility for ensuring respect for human rights fallen so exclusively to governments?

(2) What rules and principles are thought today to embody respect for human rights?

Human Rights as Legal Constructs

Assigning responsibility to the state for ensuring that human rights are respected has obvious merits for two reasons in particular. First, the state, by virtue of its legislative, judicial, and executive powers, has a unique capacity to institutionalize rules required to promote and protect the interests to which human rights are directed. Second, historically, the abuse of the power of the state by governments has been the most obvious and significant obstacle to securing respect for human dignity, freedom, and equality of treatment.

It is not surprising, therefore, that both abstract philosophical examination of natural and human rights and the practical assignment of the responsibility for ensuring their respect have focused historically on discerning the limits to the morally acceptable uses of state power. Neither is it surprising that it is the abuse of state power that has provided the occasion and the motivation for addressing human rights issues.

Philosophical debates occasioned by the abuse of government power have focused on grounding discussions of human dignity, liberty, and equality on secure moral foundations. Political debates have focused on the more practical challenge of translating these fundamental moral values into laws and legal systems capable of constraining government exercise of political, police, and military power.

Accordingly, the significant advances in the institutionalization of human rights rules have come in response to the abuse of government power. The Magna

Carta has often been cited as one of the earliest practical human rights victories because it stands as a landmark example of the institutionalization of rules, constraining the exercise of the power of the British Crown. The American Declaration of Independence is a second frequently cited example with its proclamation:

> We hold these truths to be self-evident, that all men are created equal and that they are endowed by their creator with certain unalienable Rights."

The French Declaration of the Rights of Man and Citizen, with its proclamation that "men are born and remain free and equal in rights," echoes the American Declaration in affirming the values thought to be essential to the recognition of the inherent dignity of all human beings.

It is no coincidence that these historically significant attempts to embed moral conceptions of rights in legal frameworks, as well as the philosophical debates on which they were based, were made in revolutionary environments generated by the arbitrary and discriminatory exercise of state power. Hence they illustrate the reality that defining human rights has typically occurred in environments where the capacity of people individually or collectively to pursue goals and objectives seen as morally legitimate and/or morally required was arbitrarily constrained by the exercise of state power.[22]

Neither is it a coincidence that the remedies for these abuses have taken the form of laws embedded as bills of rights in national constitutions and national statutes. States and their governments have a unique legal capacity to create rules that apply uniformly to all their citizens, thus giving human rights society-wide application. There are no other societal institutions that have had until very recently that power and reach. The only drawback from a human rights perspective is that the reach of state law is territorial in nature and therefore geographically restricted. Human rights, by contrast, are universal rights that create obligations for all human beings. The fact that the protection and promotion of human rights has come to be seen as primarily a responsibility of nation states has, therefore, a somewhat paradoxical character that has led some to question whether the concept of human rights is in fact a meaningful one.[23]

It was abuses perpetrated by Fascist governments, on the countries, people, and peoples over which they gained control before and during World War II that refocused world attention on the central importance and the universal character of human rights. Those abuses included genocide, arbitrary police search and seizure, imprisonment, torture, execution without public trial, slavery, as well as economic exploitation and impoverishment.

The explicit response was the drafting of the Universal Declaration of Human Rights and its subsequent endorsement by the General Assembly of the United Nations.[24] In adopting the Universal Declaration, the General Assembly set the Declaration as "a common standard of achievement for all peoples and all nations." The response was therefore a global response, and the responsibility for protecting and advancing protection of human rights identified as a global responsibility.

The Universal Declaration of Human Rights holds the key, therefore, to answering our second question, namely: What rules and principles are thought today to embody respect for human rights?

The Internationalization of Human Rights

The Universal Declaration of Human Rights and the two covenants,[25] endorsed by the members of the United Nations a decade or so later, are today a widely endorsed international human rights benchmark. The UN Declaration sets out the moral principles on which human rights rest. It then sets out the specific rights whose respect, the Declaration's authors concluded, were essential to the realization of the moral values on which the Declaration grounded human rights.

Both in the preamble and the body of the document, the values of freedom (liberty), dignity, and equality are identified as the three moral values or principles on which human rights are grounded. Thus, the preamble identifies the "inherent dignity and the equal and inalienable rights of all members of the human family" as the "foundation of freedom, justice and peace in the world" and goes on to assign to member states responsibility for the promotion of human rights and fundamental freedoms.[26]

The Universal Declaration then sets out the full range of rules and principles its drafters and signatories concluded required protection and promotion if the three fundamental values of freedom, equality, and dignity were to be respected. Thus, article 3 sets out a basic cornerstone right, namely the right to life, liberty, and security of person, a right essential to the enjoyment of all other rights. Articles 4 to 21 elaborate on the political and civil rights[27] that drafters and signatories understood to be essential for securing the freedom required if human beings were to be able to exercise their uniquely human faculties and abilities.

Article 22 asserts the universal "right to social security," the economic, social, and cultural rights indispensable for human dignity, and "the free development of the human personality." Articles 23 to 27 detail the specific rights entailed by the right to social security and related economic, social, and cultural rights, rights perceived as essential for the achievement of social equality.[28] Articles 28 and 29 point in the direction of solidarity rights that entitle the individual "to a social and international order in which the rights and freedoms set forth in the Declaration can be fully realized," while assigning moral duties to the community "in which alone the free and full development of (one's) personality is possible."[29]

The preamble of the UN Declaration calls on every individual and every organ of society to keep this Declaration constantly in mind and to promote by teaching and education "respect for these rights and freedoms and by progressive measures, national and international, to secure their universal and effective recognition and observance." The obligation for ensuring respect for human rights, however, is clearly and unambiguously assigned to states that are instructed to ensure that all human rights are "protected by the rule of law."[30]

John Ruggie, in his report to the Human Rights Council of the United Nations (2007) titled "Business and Human Rights: Mapping International Standards of

Responsibility and Accountability for Corporate Acts," emphasizes the significance of the way in which human rights responsibilities are assigned in the UN Declaration. He points out that the obligation to protect and ensure the enjoyment of human rights as set out in all modern treaties, declarations, and covenants rests exclusively with governments with an emphasis on legislation and judicial remedies.[31] He points out further that:

> The traditional view of international human rights instruments is that they impose only 'indirect' responsibilities on corporations—responsibilities provided under domestic law in accordance with states' international obligations.[32]

Finally, he points out that where the Declaration provisions have entered "customary international law... it is generally agreed that they currently apply only to states (and sometimes individuals)."[33]

Thus, the prevailing conventional and therefore standard view of human rights is the view that the moral responsibility for ensuring respect for and the enjoyment of human rights lies with states or governments. Further, the normal and most efficacious way for states to effect their responsibilities is through the use of legislative powers and judicial institutions. It is to this view I now turn.

SECTION TWO: CORPORATIONS AND HUMAN RIGHTS

Model One: The Legal Model

The standard view assigns exclusive responsibility for the protection and promotion of human rights to the state. It does not follow that corporations have no human rights obligations. The standard interpretation holds that all human rights obligations of corporations are indirect. That is to say, they flow through the law.

On this model, the human rights obligations of a corporation are assumed to be limited to meeting the human rights laws and regulations set out by the states in whose jurisdictions it is active. That is to say, the moral obligation to respect and promote human rights is indirect and circumscribed by a corporation's legal and moral obligation to obey the law. It is therefore to the state that rights holders must turn for support and for remedies where their rights are not respected.

This historically grounded account of the human rights obligations of corporations has clear strengths. It is supported by both the conventional legal view of human rights, as we have seen, and what remains to a large extent the dominant conventional management view and theory that the primary moral and legal obligation of private sector managers is to maximize profits for shareholders.

The conventional management view is captured most graphically by Milton Friedman, who argues in various forums[34] that the sole responsibility of managers is "to make as much money as possible while conforming to the basic rules of the society, both those embodied in law and those embodied in ethical custom."[35] It is a view that, like its legal counterpart, is deeply embedded in corporate law, institutional investment, and management practice, particularly in North America. It is a view, furthermore, that is supported by a number of influential theories of the firm.[36]

Rejection of the thesis that corporations have direct, morally grounded human rights responsibilities rests on two kinds of considerations. The first consists of four distinct but related considerations.

1. Corporations do not have the requisite powers required to institutionalize human rights standards. They are not capable of ensuring that human rights are universally or even widely respected in the countries in which they are active.

2. To assign to corporations the obligation to ensure respect for human rights is inconsistent with a commitment to democratic principles which requires that the responsibility for serving public interests should be carried out by publicly elected officials. Corporate boards and their managers do not have democratically determined mandates. They are accountable in any formal sense only to their shareholders and not to the general public. The interests they serve are private, not public interests.

3. Managers do not have human rights training or competence. Managers of corporations are trained to make intelligent decisions as agents of their stockholders in market environments in anticipation of and response to market demands. They are not competent to set human rights standards (the role of legislators), to determine the proper application of those standards (the role of civil servants), or to respond to breaches of those standards (the role of police and the courts.) There are no grounds for confidence, therefore, that they are likely to exercise human rights responsibilities well. Milton Friedman puts the point bluntly when he says of business people: "They are capable of being extremely far-sighted and clear-headed in matters that are internal to their business. They are incredibly short-sighted and muddle-headed in matters that are outside their business."[37] On this view, it is important that business leaders and the corporations they lead stick to their business or commercial role and leave human rights standard setting and enforcement to those who have the mandate and the competence, namely, governments and public servants.[38]

4. A final, and perhaps the most fundamental, objection to the view that corporations have and should exercise human rights responsibilities is that the human rights and market economy values are fundamentally incompatible. On this view, to impose direct (and in the view of some even indirect) human rights obligations on corporations is to undermine the functioning of competitive markets.[39]

In contrast to these weaknesses, the second set of considerations points to significant virtues.

5. The Legal Model is clear that responsibility for ensuring respect for human rights fall squarely and unequivocally on the state. Further, the state's responsibilities cannot be delegated or shared.

6. It locates the moral responsibility for the enforcement of human rights with an authority that has the range of powers required to institutionalize their protection.

7. From a business perspective, it creates a level playing field for corporations and provides the kind of certainty about "the rules of the game" that allows business to focus on economic objectives.

8. It makes lines of accountability clear. Corporations are accountable to the state for obeying the law. The state is accountable to its citizens and the international community for ensuring that its laws provide adequate protection for human rights.

Finally, for all these reasons, allocating the moral obligation to ensure respect for human rights to the state is efficient from the point of view of government, business, society, and people generally by making the responsibilities of each clear. Government is morally responsible for protecting human rights. Business is morally responsible for obeying the law. Society and people generally are morally responsible for ensuring that government lives up to its moral responsibilities.[40]

In spite of these clear strengths, however, the Legal Model has come under sustained critical scrutiny. The fact that it is commonplace for corporations to acknowledge a direct moral responsibility for human rights observance in their corporate codes of ethics is one such indication. The gradual extension of national (domestic) law to encompass corporate liability for international crimes, and the gradual extension of responsibility for international crimes to corporations under international law are all harbingers of evolving understandings of the moral responsibility of corporations with respect to human rights.[41]

What would appear to underlie these changes is globalization. Understanding the impact of globalization on shifting conceptions of the human rights obligations of corporations is therefore our next task.

Globalization and the Shifting Responsibilities of Business and Government

Three significant changes integral to globalization are central to understanding the growing dissatisfaction with the traditional allocation of direct human rights responsibilities exclusively to governments. First, under conditions of globalization, corporations have acquired what would appear to be government-like powers. Second, globalization has been accompanied by both a diminished capacity and a diminished will on the part of governments to meet their human rights obligations. Third, the shifting powers of governments and corporations under conditions of globalization have opened the door to significant and very harmful human rights abuses on the part of corporations.

Each of these factors has been set out and analyzed at length elsewhere.[42] It is possible here to point simply to some of the key factors undermining what constitutes the dominant conventional legal and economic understanding of the human rights responsibilities of corporations.

1. Under conditions of globalization, the private sector, dominated by the growth of large multinational corporations, has come to play an increasingly significant role in the economies of developed, developing, and underdeveloped countries worldwide. Throughout the world, the investment decisions of corporations have displaced governments as the key determinants of economic development. The implications of decisions taken by transnational corporations for the welfare of the people and communities of the countries in which they do business are, therefore, on these grounds alone, substantial.

The access of large multinational corporations to huge pools of capital allows them to generate the technology required to put "nature altering science" to work.[43] As a result, corporations have acquired the power to change in very significant ways natural, social, and economic environments, not only locally, but also globally. New technologies, products, and systems are now global in their reach and impact. Applications of nuclear technology have global implications, as Chernobyl demonstrated. The use of fossil fuels in North America, Asia, and Western Europe is impacting the global climate as evidenced by global warming. Hedge funds can destabilize national and international financial institutions.[44] In short, science and technology under conditions of globalization are putting in the hands of the modern multinational corporation a kind of power that was the subject of science fiction just a few short decades ago.

The increasing power of corporations to impact the lives of those affected by their decisions and activities is not restricted simply to the supply of goods and services. Corporations have acquired also the capacity to shape in significant ways the legal environments in which they operate. Thus, under conditions of globalization, corporations have become a great deal freer to choose where the goods and services they provide will be produced and by implication the legal and regulatory standards that will govern their production. The products that appear on the retail shelves of a department store, the produce in the local grocery store, or the voice from a call center may originate anywhere in the world. This factor has greatly expanded the power of corporations to determine the regulatory environments in which they do business.

The power to choose the regulatory environments in which they operate has also increased their power to shape the regulatory environments in which they operate through bargaining, negotiation, and lobbying. Governments under conditions of globalization must compete with each other for private-sector investment. Reducing regulatory constraints is one way of winning the competition. The resulting impact on health, safety, wages, and the natural environment, to take just a few examples, has inevitable implications for the protection and the promotion of human rights.

The powers and opportunities resulting from globalization have also resulted in an enhanced capacity on the part of corporations to become directly involved in setting standards of operation in the various countries in which they operate. There are three dimensions to this power. First, as John Ruggie points out, "what once was external trade between national economies increasingly has become *internalized* within firms as global supply chain management functioning in real time and directly shaping the daily lives of people around the world."[45] This gives corporations extensive and direct power to set standards under which goods and services are produced by suppliers in their supply chain.

Corporations have played and continue to play an influential role in shaping trade agreements, for example, bilateral investment treaties, which grant them significant legal rights. In some economic sectors, as Ruggie points out, corporations have acquired the right to participate directly in setting the standards governing their own operations. Further, a significant range of disputes related to foreign investments "is settled by private arbitration and not by national courts. Accordingly, corporate law firms and accounting firms add yet additional (corporately controlled) layers to routine transnational rule-setting."[46]

Finally, corporations are active participants in international standard-setting organizations like the International Labour Organization (ILO), the World Health Organization (WHO), and various other UN bodies. Thus, multinational corporations are playing a direct role in setting international standards governing their own operations. This involvement in the regulatory activities of international institutions, traditionally the preserve of state governments, is a relatively recent phenomenon that illustrates the growing power of corporations internationally.[47]

2. By contrast, globalization has diminished the power of national governments to set regulatory standards in important ways. The doors to globalization and the creation of international markets have been opened by international regulatory systems whose function is to regulate governments. The WTO and regional free trade agreements like NAFTA have significantly constrained the freedom of national governments to regulate their own economies. To take just one example, national governments that are members of the WTO are significantly restricted in the ways in which they can regulate the conditions under which goods and services are produced. Thus, a member government of the WTO cannot prevent the import of clothing because it is produced under sweatshop conditions.[48]

In many developing countries, multinational corporations are essentially unregulated, except insofar as they impose environmental, social, and economic standards of performance on themselves. Individuals, communities, and indeed entire countries may thus become subject to the ethical standards that these corporations implicitly or explicitly espouse.

The capacity of even the most sophisticated governments to evaluate the risks posed by new technologies and the products they generate is limited. Access to the financial resources that will allow governments to compete for the intellectual expertise required to evaluate new products and economic development initiatives has been limited often in response to corporate pressure to reduce taxes. New technologies are spawning new products, chemicals for example, so quickly that government regulation has difficulty keeping up. Governments increasingly rely on the companies producing new products to self-evaluate the risks they may pose to users and the public more generally. As a result, serious questions about both the capacity and willingness of governments to set appropriate social, economic, and environmental parameters for economic activity in global and local markets have emerged.

3. Finally, globalization has opened the door to significant potential and actual abuses of human rights on the part of multinational corporations in the pursuit of profits. Abuses range across virtually every section of The International Bill of Rights, the international human rights benchmark against which corporate conduct is commonly evaluated. Abuses have occurred with regard to the use of public and private security forces by mining companies and governments; land tenure, water, and labor violations on the part of food, beverage, apparel, and footwear industries; and privacy and freedom of expression infringements on the part of corporations in communications and information technology.[49]

The widespread use of bribery as a corporate strategy for accomplishing strategic objectives is another door leading to human rights abuses that globalization has opened.[50] Corruption, as Transparency International has pointed out, is near pandemic proportions in many parts of the world. Bribery by itself is an important moral issue. It always involves an abuse of a position of responsibility by an individual. Its ethical, or perhaps better put, its unethical character, attaches directly to that abuse of authority. Where public officials are involved, it is easy to think of the problem as one simply of unjust enrichment related to the winning or retaining of contracts. In fact, however, bribery typically impacts law enforcement. Its point is to relieve those paying the bribe of the need to meet legal and regulatory standards. The result is often human rights abuses. When laws and regulations governing drinking water, safe working conditions, building codes, abduction, the protection of property, the administration of justice, and the management of prisons are subverted through bribery, human rights inevitably suffer.[51]

Cataloguing the abuses of the modern corporation, particularly the modern transnational corporation, has become over the past two decades a major preoccupation of a cadre of critics and NGOs. The revolution in communications technology that has provided the essential framework for globalization has also opened the door to the global sharing of information about the impacts of corporate business activities in every part of the world and the critical evaluation of those impacts.[52]

To summarize, globalization has opened the door to significant and harmful human rights abuses by multinational corporations, abuses of a kind that have led in the past to the assignment of the obligation to both respect and ensure respect for human rights to the state by their citizens and more recently by the United Nations. Globalization has also conferred on corporations government-like powers to control the conditions under which the goods and services they provide are produced and distributed. Further, while the power of corporations has been enhanced by globalization, the power of governments to set and monitor human rights standards has been diminished, leaving a human rights vacuum. It follows, therefore, that having acquired government-like powers, corporations must assume at least some of the moral burden for protecting and promoting respect for human rights.

This argument is powerful. It seriously undermines the Legal Model. Finally, it has led many to conclude that like governments, corporations have an obligation to respect but also ensure respect for human rights.

The argument, however, leaves three questions of fundamental importance unanswered:

1. If we accept that corporations have direct, morally grounded human rights obligations, as this argument suggests, what are those obligations?

2. Is the proposal that corporations have human rights obligations compatible with the requirement that human rights obligations must be institutionalizable?

3. Is the assignment of government-like human rights obligations to corporations compatible with the effective and efficient operation of a market economy?

Two models have emerged in response to these questions. Evaluating those models is the task for what follows.

Model Two: A Self-Regulatory Model

The Self-regulatory Model is a response to the deficiencies of the Legal Model and is built largely around voluntary codes of ethics. The codes on which the model is built may be created by individual corporations, industry-wide associations like the International Council on Mining and Metals (ICMM) and the International Chamber of Commerce (ICC), intergovernmental institutions like the Organization for Economic Cooperation and Development (OECD), and international governmental institutions like the World Bank and the International Financial Organization (IFO), to give just a few examples.[53]

The strengths of this model are twofold. First, it endorses the view that corporations have direct human rights obligations. As such, it captures the perceived need to articulate the human rights responsibilities of corporations more specifically with a view to strengthening corporate awareness of their human rights obligations locally and internationally.

A second clear strength is that virtually all voluntary codes acknowledge the universal character of human rights by acknowledging the global application of the human rights identified in their codes. This constitutes a kind of practical universalization of human rights that national legal systems cannot provide.

Like the first model, however, this model is severely flawed.[54] First, and most significantly, it understands human rights obligations to be voluntary and self-assigned. This feature of the model collides with the concept of human rights in two ways. To begin with, it carries with it the implication that the assumption of human rights responsibilities is a voluntary corporate act. However, if corporations have human rights obligations, they are not voluntary. They are entailed by the human rights that generate them.

In addition, voluntary codes both in theory and in practice imply that determining the nature and scope of a corporation's human rights obligations is a matter of self-formulation. The practical implications of this implied view are best reflected in the wide variation in the human rights contents of voluntary corporate codes of ethics. Some are quite general, for example, the OECD Guidelines; others are more detailed, for example, the UN Global Compact; and some are quite detailed, for example, the Apparel Industry Partnership Workplace Code.[55] This conflicts with the fact that the bearers of human rights obligations are not free to pick and choose among the human rights they are prepared to acknowledge and respect, as earlier discussion indicates.

Second, and equally significant, most voluntary codes and the corporations that endorse them are silent on issues of accountability. Consequently they are silent on questions of verification and enforcement. And once again, where codes and the corporations endorsing them set out concrete provisions for verification and enforcement, they imply in so doing that any assumption of responsibility in these regards is again voluntarily assumed.

In summary, the weakness of the Self-regulatory Model is the fact that voluntary codes are voluntary. The model implies that corporations have a right to pick and choose the standards that apply to their own conduct. Further, it assumes that how voluntary codes are applied and interpreted is a matter, when all is said and done, of corporate discretion.[56] As we have seen in Section One, this approach is incompatible with fundamental features of human rights.

Model Three: The Draft Norms Model

The third model is a response to the weaknesses of the Legal and the Self-regulatory Models. Although it is in many respects the mirror opposite of the first, nonetheless it shares with the first the view that laws are the only effective tool for institutionalizing the human rights responsibilities of corporations and ensuring that those responsibilities are carried out.

The Legal Model proposes that corporations have no morally grounded human rights responsibilities beyond those set out by law. The Draft Norms Model takes the opposite position. It proposes that the acquisition of government-like powers entails the assumption of human rights obligations parallel and similar in nature and scope to those of governments.

The UN "Draft Norms on the Responsibilities of Transnational Corporations and Other Business Enterprises with Regard to Human Rights" is a product of more than five years of deliberation and negotiation on the part of the UN Commission on Human Rights Sub-Commission on the Promotion and Protection of Human Rights. Clause 1 of the UN Draft Norms asserts that corporations have a (moral) obligation to "promote, secure the fulfillment of, respect, ensure respect of and protect human rights," an assignment of obligations that is identical in wording to what in the preamble, paragraph 3, the authors of the Draft Norms understand to be the obligations of states. The obligations assigned to corporations by the Draft Norms cover the entire panoply of treaties and international instruments to which states are subject and include: the right to equal opportunity and nondiscriminatory treatment; personal security rights; the rights of workers; respect for national sovereignty and human rights; obligations with respect to consumer protection; and obligations with respect to environmental protection. Finally, as is the case for states, the rights in question, and by implication the obligations they generate, are described in the preamble, paragraph 13, as universal, indivisible, interdependent, and interrelated.

The very comprehensive character of the Draft Norms is perhaps reflected most dramatically in clause 12, which says:

> Transnational corporations and other business enterprises shall respect economic, social and cultural rights as well as civil and political rights and contribute to their realization, in particular the rights to development, adequate food and drinking water, the highest attainable standard of physical and mental health, adequate housing, privacy, education, freedom of thought, conscience, and religion and freedom of opinion and expression, and shall refrain from actions which obstruct or impede the realization of those rights.

What is distinctive about this model, then, is that it understands that the scope and nature of the human rights obligations assigned to corporations parallel the scope and nature of the human rights obligations of states.

To ensure that the moral obligations of corporations are respected, the Draft Norms propose that corporations be formally monitored and that the human rights obligations of corporations be embedded in international law and national legal systems. Clause 18 asserts that

> transnational corporations and other business enterprises shall provide prompt, effective and adequate reparation to those persons, entities and communities that have been adversely affected by failures to comply with these Norms through *inter alia* reparations, restitution, compensation and rehabilitation for any damages done or property taken.

The same clause assigns responsibility "for determining damages, in regard to criminal sanctions, and in all other respects" to "national courts and/or international tribunals pursuant to national and international law."

In summary, the Draft Norms Model proposes to move from a system of institutionalization in which the human rights obligations of corporations are indirect, to a system in which corporations are directly responsible to rights bearers for protecting and promoting the full range of human rights "recognized in international and national law" previously understood to be the sole responsibility of governments.

Strengths and Weaknesses of Model Three

This third model has clear strengths:

1. By assigning broad human rights responsibilities to corporations, it gives human rights a global character and reach that locating human rights obligations exclusively with the nation state cannot achieve.

2. It connects the human rights obligations of corporations to widely endorsed international standards.

3. It calls for both monitoring and enforcement; and

4. It proposes to embed the human rights obligations of corporations within current national and international legal structures.

It is not surprising, therefore that the model has attracted the wide support of lawyers and international NGOs.

Despite its initial appeal, however, the model is seriously flawed. What the model fails to take into account is the different roles of governments and private sector corporations in the pursuit of public and private interests. Equally, the model fails to take into account the role of human rights in protecting the right of individuals to pursue private interests.

The central obligation of governments is to serve the public interest, or the public or common good.[57] In modern societies protecting and promoting human rights is essential to the achievement of that goal. By protecting and promoting human rights, a government commits itself to ensuring equality of access to the benefits that human rights extend to rights bearers. By protecting and promoting human rights, governments commit to removing arbitrary barriers to the resources and opportunities needed to pursue individual and therefore private interests.

Human rights are core moral values, as we have seen, because their respect is a necessary condition for the exercise of human autonomy or freedom. Further, inasmuch as human rights are universal and overriding they are public or common goods.[58] Protecting or generating public goods is perfectly consistent with the exercise of power by governments because protecting and promoting the public good is their explicit obligation. These two characteristics combined generate an obvious tension, however, when they intersect with values fundamental to commercial activities in market environments. Markets are environments in which individuals and groups pursue private interests. One of the fundamental interests of individuals is the right to social, economic, and cultural environments in which they are free to pursue their private interests. Absent this right, the capacity to make autonomous moral decisions disappears.

Corporations are the contemporary tool of choice in market economies for the pursuit of private economic interests. To impose on corporations an overriding obligation to protect and promote human rights, and thereby to ensure the protection and promotion of the full range of interests that human rights are designed to protect, is, in effect, to remove from corporations the right to serve private interests as their primary obligation.

For example, clause 12 of the Draft Norms requires transnational corporations and other business enterprises to respect political and civil but also social, economic, and cultural rights. Among other things, the Draft Norms would require them to contribute to the realization of the rights to development, adequate food and drinking water, the highest attainable standard of physical and mental health, adequate housing, privacy, education, and so on. If these rights are taken as overriding, a fundamental characteristic of human rights, the capacity of individuals or corporations to choose the purposes for which to enter into contractual relationships is either removed or very seriously attenuated.

This conflict between commercial values and human rights becomes inescapable if the principle that human rights obligations are overriding obligations is combined with the indivisibility principle,[59] a principle that proposes that human rights obligations are all of one piece and must all be accepted as an integral package.[60] That is to say, the conflict is inescapable if the indivisibility principle is understood to mean that human rights obligations, by their nature, come in a comprehensive bundle imposing obligations uniformly and universally across the whole range of human rights on corporate obligation bearers. It is inescapable because it entails that corporations must give overriding priority to the full range of human rights in all aspects of their operations.

The effect of the model, therefore, is to collapse the distinction between private and public interests, and to require that corporations and business enterprises assume a role similar to that of governments by giving priority to the public interest in all aspects of their operations. To put the matter concretely, a corporation wishing to contract with a supplier in a developing country like Bangladesh would have to decide first whether this was the appropriate place to invest given a global or universal "right to development." Having resolved that issue, it would then have to give overriding priority among other things to the right to economic development, healthcare, and education in that country.

Once the implications of this model for the prioritization of public versus private goods and interests are clear, the exposure of this model to a Legal Model type critique of the assignment of human rights obligations to corporations also becomes clear. Managers are not equipped to determine what the public interest requires with respect to the economic development of a country, or the provision of education or healthcare. They do not have a public mandate to undertake these tasks. Prioritizing these kinds of objectives is not consistent with their fiduciary obligations to their shareholders. Finally, undertaking public responsibilities required by this understanding of their human rights responsibilities would eliminate the use of corporations for the pursuit of private goals and objectives.

It is not surprising, therefore, that while the Draft Norms Model won the approval of the international NGO community, it was widely opposed by corporations and governments. Indeed, it would appear that the Draft Norms Model has resurrected fundamental issues and disagreements about the social responsibilities of corporations that the Self-regulatory Model-type voluntary commitments by corporations and other bodies had given the appearance of resolving. Not surprisingly, in rejecting the Draft Norms Model, the business community appealed, among other things, to the dangers of collapsing the role of private sector actors, whose principal focus is the private interests of shareholders and other stakeholders, for example, employees, customers, clients, and suppliers, into the role of governments, whose principal focus is the public interest.[61]

Summary

Let me summarize the conclusions to be drawn from our discussion of the three models of the human rights obligations of corporations.

First, I have rejected the view that corporations have no direct morally grounded human rights obligations beyond those imposed by law. With the power of corporations to impact the enjoyment of human rights on the part of those affected by their operations comes the responsibility to protect and respect human rights in the exercise of that power.

Second, voluntary self-regulation and the voluntary assumption or determination of human rights obligations by corporations is not a valid foundation on which to build an understanding of the human rights obligations of corporations. Human rights obligations are not voluntary. They are obligatory, universal, and overriding.

Third, the assumption that the human rights obligations of corporations are similar in nature or parallel to those of the state is mistaken. The human rights obligations of corporations are those obligations that flow from the role and powers of corporations, particularly corporations in international markets. The primary role of corporations is to serve private not public interests. Furthermore, though the powers of corporations are substantial, they are nonetheless different in significant ways from those of governments.

Finally, it follows from these conclusions taken together, that it cannot be the case that the indivisibility principle endorsed by the United Nations and built into the Draft Norms holds true of corporations, however valid its application might be to the state. The effect of the indivisibility principle applied to the human rights obligations of corporations is to convert private-sector entities into public-sector organizations whose primary purpose is the advancement of public not private interests.

Section Three: Identifying the Human Rights Obligations of Corporations

What our discussion shows is that corporations have human rights responsibilities. What we have been unable to determine thus far is the specific nature of those responsibilities. As we shall see, however, discussion in Sections 1 and 2 has provided us with the building blocks required to find what will turn out to be rather surprising answers to the three questions at the center of this inquiry.

The Nature and Scope of Corporate Human Rights Obligations

What then are the specific human rights responsibilities of corporations? We know from previous discussion that they do not cover the full spectrum of human rights as set out, for example, in such instruments as the International Bill of Rights in a manner that is identical or similar to the state. We know also from previous discussion that, in spite of the fact that they differ in significant respects to those of states, they are not voluntary. That is to say, corporations are not free to pick and choose what their human rights obligations are. What our findings also imply, though only obliquely, is that the human rights obligations of corporations are difficult to specify in concrete terms because they are in fact variable. That is to say, if the human rights obligations are limited but not voluntarily assumed, then, as we shall see, they must vary with the settings in which corporations operate.

What is it about human rights that suggest that the human rights obligations of corporations are variable? First is the fact that a corporation, operating in a country in which human rights are embedded in a functioning legal system, does not, for the most part, have to address questions about its human rights obligations simply because they are more or less comprehensively set out in law. In that kind of setting, a corporation's human rights obligations will be met simply by obeying the letter and the spirit of the law. In contrast, the human rights obligations of a company operating in a country where respect for human rights is not embedded in the law, or if embedded not enforced, will be different. Similarly, a company operating in a country whose government and people simply do not have the economic or social capacity to defend human rights in the face of their abuse by powerful economic actors, will face different human rights obligations.

In a country like Canada with its universal healthcare system, a corporation can leave any basic human rights related responsibilities for assuring adequate medical treatment for its employees to the state. In a country like the United States, what a company's healthcare obligations are becomes a matter to be determined through deliberation and negotiation. This is true across the full range of possible corporate social responsibilities. Where environmental protection regulation is robust, the primary obligation of a corporation will be to live up to its legal and regulatory responsibilities. If a corporation does not do so, there is a robust enforcement system in place to require compliance. Where environment protection on the part of the state is weak or absent, a corporation is faced with the need to define its environmental responsibilities for itself.[62]

Where human rights are concerned, where the law establishes adequate minimum wages, provides adequately for the formation of and participation in a union, ensures reasonable protection against arbitrary arrest or confiscation of property, and so on across the full range of human rights, a corporation will not need to address the human rights issues and standards involved beyond understanding its obligations as set out by law. In so far as human rights issues arise, any obligations will most likely involve participating in public policy dialogue around those issues openly and in good faith.[63]

A second reason for variability flows from the first. The role of human rights is to create an environment where the dignity, equality, and freedom of people are respected. The morally mandated task of a corporation seeking to understand its human rights obligations, where they are not defined adequately by the legal and regulatory system in place, is to mitigate the negative human rights impacts of its activities and enhance positive impacts. Inevitably, these impacts will vary from company to company and from setting to setting.

A commitment on the part of a corporation to respect the human rights of those whose human rights are impacted by its actions or activities will require that the corporation in question determine how those affected view those impacts on their freedom, equality, and dignity and what for them would constitute the mitigation of negative and the enhancement of positive impacts. This is true in part because those impacted are likely to be the best judges of the implication of those impacts for their own lives. It is also true because a failure to take into account the interpretations and conclusions of those affected is to ignore their interest in participating in the creation of a social, cultural, political, natural, and economic environment in which freedom, equality, and dignity are protected and promoted, since it is these interests that human rights are put in place to protect.

Corporations faced with the need to determine their human rights obligations where they are not adequately defined by law, can therefore meet their moral obligations only by engaging in a process of dialogue or moral deliberation. For reasons just set out, this process of moral deliberation must include "the free and informed and equal participation of all those who are affected by a particular decision."[64] The virtue of this process, as Tom Campbell points out, is that

> It captures a social situation which pressures participants to take an impartial and inclusive view. It encourages the provision of all available evidence or information which is relevant to the matter in hand. It is tolerant with respect to the criteria of relevance that are involved. It holds the promise of limiting the extent of any coercion that might result from the decision in question.[65]

Even more important, however, is the fact that if human rights are at stake, fundamental interests of those rights bearers likely to be impacted are at stake. Any decisions in which the interests of rights bearers are not directly represented or engaged will be a breach of their human rights. It is exactly the capacity to engage issues of this nature that human rights are put in place to protect.

An example will illustrate these conclusions. One of the obligations of corporations in global markets around which there is wide consensus is the obligation not to be complicit in the abuse of human rights on the part of the state. The challenge in carrying out this obligation on the part of a corporation is to determine what counts as complicity. Given that human rights are those rights required for the protection and enhancement of human freedom, dignity, and equality, complicity will involve any action or activity that endorses, encourages, or supports, explicitly or implicitly, behavior on the part of a state that undermines the freedom, equality, or the dignity of those impacted.

Determining complicity thus requires the assessment of the impact a corporate action or activity is having or is likely to have on the lives of those impacted. Equally, respect for the human rights of those impacted requires that those impacted or likely to be impacted participate in the assessment of those impacts.[66]

What, for example, would a corporation have to do to avoid complicity in human rights abuse in a country under a brutal military dictatorship? For some, the answer is clear: avoid doing business in such countries. But is this obvious?

Could a sound decision be arrived at without significant consideration of the impacts of not investing or divesting if already invested? And could the impact of not investing or of divesting be reliably determined without input on the part of those impacted as to the nature of the impacts that divestment, for example, would have? Clearly, the use of forced labor would count as morally unacceptable complicity because of its obvious negative implications for the autonomy of those forced to work against their will. But what would the prohibition against complicity imply for a corporation that is able to resist the use of forced labor and willing to pay a living wage? Equally, what would the prohibition against complicity require of a corporation with regard to the payment of royalties to an oppressive regime?[67]

Examples abound. What is to count as complicity in a country like South Africa under conditions of Apartheid, or the employment of women in a Muslim country like Saudi Arabia, or freedom of expression or association in a country like China under communism or Tanzania under Mugabi?

What is at stake here is not simply a matter of interpreting what respect for freedom of association or expression means in a country like China under communism. Rather, it is a matter of determining which human rights should take priority in these various circumstances and why. Accordingly, the problem is to determine not simply the proper implementation of a specific right like freedom of association, but rather the specific human rights obligations of a corporation in the specific social, cultural, legal, environmental, and economic circumstances in which it finds itself. It is the variability of the circumstances and the options available given the capacity of a company to respond that blocks the determination of a general, overarching set of concrete corporate human rights obligations.[68]

Three things follow from this discussion. First, the human rights obligations of corporations will vary with the environment in which they are active or thinking of becoming active. Second, determining those human rights obligations requires human rights impact assessments. This being the case, one of the central human rights obligations of corporations as well as other organizations and institutions with human rights responsibilities and interests is to develop effective and authoritative human rights impact assessment tools and methodologies.[69]

Third, protecting the interests of those whose human rights are impacted or are likely to be impacted will require the involvement of those whose human rights interests are at stake in determining what would count as protection and what would count as enhancement of their rights.

It does not follow from the fact that the human rights obligations of corporations are context relative that they are also culturally relative. Human rights are universal. However, the obligations they entail will vary with obligation bearers and the settings in which obligation bearers find themselves. This is true not just of human rights. It follows from the nature of moral obligations. Parents, teachers, doctors, and engineers all have obligations by virtue of their roles that others do not have. People who can swim have obligations to save someone who is drowning that those without those skills do not have. And so it is with human rights.

Neither is it the case that because the obligations of corporations vary that the obligations they do have are voluntarily assumed. Though the human rights obligations of corporations are a function of the social, political, cultural, environmental, and economic setting in which they are active, they are not discretionary.

Corporations and the Institutionalization of Human Rights

As noted earlier, one of the requirements for the existence of a human right is that its protection should be institutionalized or capable of being institutionalized. Does this account of the human rights obligations of corporations meet that requirement?

To institutionalize human rights is to embed them in "stable, valued and recurring patterns of behavior"[70] that are rule governed and "define actions in terms of relations between roles and situations."[71] Institutionalization enables "predictable and patterned interactions which are stable, constrain individual behavior and are associated with shared values and meaning."[72]

Institutionalization of corporate human rights obligations thus requires several things. It must be possible in theory and practice to embed the rules, in this case the human rights to be protected and promoted, in the management systems of those corporations to which they apply. It must be possible to monitor the implementation of the rules to determine compliance and to communicate findings in publicly available reports. The reports must be subject to verification. Unless these conditions are satisfied, it will not be possible to determine whether the rights in question have been institutionalized and whether a corporation's human rights obligations are being met.

As it turns out, these conditions are all realizable. Management systems are being developed and refined that allow training, monitoring, reporting, and auditing. These systems and training programs are designed to ensure that the ethical values and principles to which a corporation commits itself are effectively institutionalized. These systems are now commonplace. The Global Reporting Initiative has taken great strides in developing transparent monitoring and reporting systems. AccountAbility, Social Accountability International, the Caux Roundtable, Transparency International, and a variety of other public-, private-, and voluntary-sector organizations are engaged in developing sophisticated management systems for embedding ethical standards in organizations, and monitoring, reporting, and auditing the effective implementation of those standards throughout an organization's operations.[73]

The institutionalization of rule systems designed to guide corporate protection and promotion of human rights requires two additional elements. The human rights standards to be institutionalized must be credible. To be credible, they must emerge from public dialogue that incorporates the perspectives of those whose interests the standards are put in place to secure. Second, organizations engaged in supporting, facilitating, and promoting international trade must recognize that they too have a key role in ensuring that corporations they are engaged with live up to their human rights obligations. Such organizations include financial institutions like banks and export development agencies; international financial institutions like the World Bank, the International Finance Organization and regional banks like the Asian Development Bank; industry associations like the International Council for Mining and Metals (ICMM); NGOs setting reporting and auditing standards like the Global Reporting Initiative and AccountAbility, and so on. It requires that all these organizations engage in open and transparent discussion of the standards they endorse. And it requires that the process of public discussion and negotiation include a significant role for those whose freedom, equality, and dignity the standards being negotiated and implemented are meant to protect and enhance.

Further, the institutionalization of human rights requires that organizations and agencies playing a supporting, facilitating, or promotional role also require that the corporations whose activities they support embed their responsibilities in their management systems throughout their operations. Financial institutions, for example banks and export development agencies, can require human rights impact assessments and set relevant, setting-specific requirements for loans and other forms of financial support.[74] This would mean that a corporation could not get a loan unless it could persuade the financial agency to which it was turning for assistance that it had taken the steps necessary to identify its human rights obligations and ensure that it had the management systems in place to ensure that its human rights obligations were met. Industry organizations can set standards for membership, for example, impact assessment, reporting, and auditing requirements. International financial institutions can create transparent procedures for setting and enforcing their human rights standards as a condition of financial support.

Model Four: The Hybrid Model and Issues of Practicality and Effectiveness

As our discussion shows, the assertion that human beings are rights bearers is of little practical value or ethical import unless the assertion finds concrete expression in rules and practices that protect and promote human equality, freedom, and dignity. Are there practical examples of specific rule systems that are and have been effective?

A detailed answer to this question is not possible here. However, a brief summary account points persuasively in a positive direction. There is, to begin with, little evidence that general and sweeping endorsement of human rights obligations by corporations, or international government or nongovernment organizations, taken by themselves, are of much practical import. By way of contrast, there are examples of codes that are setting-specific, that, arguably, have made a difference.

The Sullivan Principles for South Africa are perhaps the best example. Other examples include the McBride Principles for Northern Ireland and the Miller Principles for China.[75]

More recent examples of setting-specific rule systems are even more persuasive. Three examples illustrate the emergence of industry-specific rules that articulate setting-specific corporate human rights obligations. The Voluntary Principles on Security and Human Rights are a first example. These principles promote human rights risk assessments and the provision of security provider training in the resource extraction sector. The Kimberly Process Certification Scheme is focused specifically on blocking the sale of blood or conflict diamonds. The Extractive Industries Transparency Initiative is a third example of an industry-specific initiative that is designed for country-specific application, in this case with a view to inhibiting public-sector bribery and corruption in resource rich countries in the developing world.

Each of these examples illustrates rule systems designed to protect the human rights interests of people impacted by corporate activity. Each is setting-specific. Each has emerged from broadly inclusive and transparent stakeholder dialogues. Each would appear to be having significant, practical impacts on those whose interests they are designed to protect.[76]

Equally significant, these and similar initiatives are intersecting with rules systems whose contents corporations do not control. Increasingly these other rules systems are forming an interconnected "web of rules" that are mutually reinforcing. Although corporations can ignore these interlocking sets of rules in principle, in practice this freedom is increasingly truncated. Obtaining loans for international projects is an example. Without access to loans, many projects are out of reach. Increasingly, national and international financial institutions, for example, the World Bank, the International Finance Organization, the international regional banks, national export development and credit agencies, and private sector banks, are setting performance standards for loan applicants. The Equator Principles are an example. These standards are in a sense voluntary. It is also true that these rule systems set uneven standards and do not always emerge from transparent and inclusive, consensus-oriented dialogue as the history of the development of the Equator Principles shows. However, individually and collectively they have impacts that are increasingly difficult for multinational corporations to avoid.

In summary, multinational corporations as well as public, private, and NGO institutions, organizations, and agencies are increasingly involved in the creation and administration of practical, setting-specific rule systems that have significant human rights content and are based on processes of collective moral deliberation that aspire to transparency and inclusiveness.

One of the important elements of the Legal Model is that model's implicit critique of the alternatives:

1. Corporations do not have the requisite powers required to institutionalize human rights standards.

2. Corporate attempts to acquire or exercise human rights responsibilities are clearly inconsistent with a commitment to democratic principles.

3. Managers do not have human rights training or competence.

4. Human rights and market economy values are fundamentally incompatible.

Is the Hybrid Model vulnerable to these objections?

The first three objections are countered relatively easily. The human rights obligations of corporations are neither identical nor broadly similar to those of the state because their power to impact the enjoyment of human rights while similar in some respects, nonetheless differs in significant ways from that of the state. For this reason, the human rights obligations of corporations are both limited and vary with the social, political, cultural, legal, environmental, and economic settings in which they are active. However, once their human rights obligations are clearly identified, corporations do have the management tools required to structure their operations so as to ensure that their human rights obligations, like all their other obligations, for example their contractual obligations, are met. The same is true of institutions, organizations, and agencies that support, facilitate or promote corporate activity in international markets.

The view that the exercise of human rights responsibilities by corporate managers is inconsistent with democratic political principles is equally mistaken. The human rights obligations of corporations can only be determined on the Hybrid Model through transparent and inclusive dialogue, debate, and negotiation. Further, once identified, the obligations involved are not voluntary or discretionary. The execution of human rights obligations will be undemocratic only if it involves the exercise of corporate power to exclude stakeholders with a legitimate interest in the outcome from participation, or, alternatively, if it involves the use of corporate power to dictate the outcome.

The third objection is also mistaken. The Hybrid Model does not require that managers determine unilaterally what their human rights obligations are or whether their firm's human rights obligations have been satisfied. It does require credible human rights impact assessments. It also requires participation in a process of moral deliberation that is transparent and inclusive. Finally it requires credible monitoring, reporting, and verification of corporate success in meeting its obligations. All of these are skills and competencies that managers require in other areas of their work.

The fourth objection is in many respects the most fundamental. It is also the most ideological. It is certainly true that respect for human rights constrains what corporations can and cannot do in the pursuit of their commercial interests. However, the Legal Model, which assigns responsibility for setting and enforcing human rights standards more or less exclusively to the state, does not leave corporations free to ignore human rights in their market activities. It simply relieves them of the need to determine for themselves what those standards should be. Thus, with respect to this fourth objection, there is no relevant difference between the Legal and the Hybrid Models. Both models accept that corporations have human rights obligations. Both models require that corporations respect rules not of their own making. The only real difference between the two models is how the rules are determined, implemented, and enforced, and by whom.

It follows that if there is a fundamental conflict, tension, or incompatibility between human rights and free market values or principles, then that tension or incompatibility holds equally for both the Legal and the Hybrid Models.[77] This wider and ideologically oriented issue, then, takes as its focus the values that should frame market economies and the role of the state in regulating market economies. While this is without question a significant problem, addressing it is beyond the scope of this discussion.

CONCLUSIONS

Understanding the role of human rights in the management of the contemporary private-sector corporation is one of the most challenging tasks of business ethics. There are several reasons for this. Human rights have a character that sets them apart from other moral values that frame human behavior. They are universal and thus not as such variable across social, cultural, political, environmental, or economic settings in which human activity takes place. However, the moral obligations they generate are variable, unlike the rights that trigger them.[78] For the state, they come in a package, a state of affairs frequently captured by the suggestion that human rights are interrelated and indivisible. For corporations, however, as we have shown, human rights, while interrelated, are not indivisible.

For many, the suggestion that the human rights obligations of corporations vary with the social, cultural, political, environmental, and economic settings in which they are or might become active implies what might be described as human rights relativism. This conclusion, however, is unwarranted. The fundamental moral importance of human freedom, equality, and dignity is not variable or relative. Neither do the rights, whose protection and respect are required if human freedom, equality, and dignity are to be realized, vary from setting to setting. What do vary from setting to setting are first, the human rights impacts corporate activities are likely to have and second, the means available to corporations to mitigate negative and promote positive impacts. In countries with well-developed human rights laws and democratic political structures (each probably a necessary condition of the other) the obligations of corporations will be defined by those laws. Where there are deficiencies and ambiguities with regard to the human rights practices of a corporation, correcting those deficiencies or resolving the ambiguities will require a process of dialogue and negotiation in which those impacted or their surrogates are active participants.

In countries lacking fully developed human rights laws and democratic governments, the obligations of corporations will be quite different. They will also be variable from company to company and from industry to industry. Assessing the human rights obligations of corporations in this kind of setting will require moral deliberation that must be transparent and inclusive if the values of freedom, equality, and dignity, on which human rights rules are grounded, are to be respected. If those foundational values do not guide the deliberative process leading to a determination of a corporation's human rights obligations, then the outcome of the deliberative process will be morally flawed.

What will not vary from company to company is the obligation to put in place management systems that ensure that a company-wide commitment and the capacity to fulfill that commitment are embedded in the company's management systems. This will include an obligation to monitor, report, and verify success in meeting those commitments. These obligations also extend to public- and private-sector organizations and agencies engaged in supporting, facilitating, or promoting corporate activity in environments in which human rights standards are not adequately defined, monitored, and enforced by the state.

Because human rights obligations, understood as variable, are capable of being institutionalized and are in fact (even if inadequately) being institutionalized, this approach to understanding the human rights responsibilities of corporations meets the test of practicality to which human rights are subject.

On this account, the human rights obligations of corporations are context dependent but not morally relative. The obligations of corporations will vary with the nature of the human rights impacts of their activities and their capacity to respond in morally appropriate ways to those impacts. However, corporations that are alike in the impacts that are likely to result from their activities and in their ability to mitigate negative impacts and promote positive one, will have the same obligations. It does not follow that companies lacking the capacity to mitigate negative impacts or promote positive ones will have less onerous obligations. It follows only that they will be different. Thus, for example, a company unable to avoid the use of forced labor in a country like Myanmar will have moral obligations that differ in this respect from a company that is able to carry out its economic activities without the use of forced labor. Accordingly, this approach or model meets the basic moral requirement that like cases be treated alike and different cases treated differently.

In short, globalization has undermined the Legal Model, in which the moral responsibility for preventing human rights abuses and promoting respect for human rights rests largely or exclusively with the state. Globalization has resulted in significant shifts in the power of the state to prevent human rights abuses and enforce and promote respect for human rights laws. Equally, globalization has resulted in shifts in the capacity of corporations, particularly multinational corporations, to avoid the human rights constraints it has been traditionally the obligation of the state to impose on their activities. Corporations today have powers that they did not previously have. With their shifting power comes shifting moral obligations. The task in this chapter has been to understand the implications of these changes for the human rights obligations of corporations.

NOTES

1. For a comprehensive collection of international codes, see *Voluntary Codes: Principles, Standards and Resources*, http://www.businessethicscanada.ca/capacity/tools/index.html or http://www.yorku.ca/csr.

2. The Draft Norms were tabled at the 55th Session of the Commission on Human Rights Sub-Commission on the Promotion and Protection of Human Rights, document reference E/CN.4/Sub.2/2003/12/Rev.2.

3. Peter Muchlinski, "Human Rights and Multinationals: Is There a Problem?" *International Affairs* 77 (2001): 32.

4. Note that because corporations are dominant expressions of private-sector economic activity in contemporary economies, our focus throughout this chapter will be privately and publicly held private sector corporations.

5. James Griffin, "Human Rights: Whose Duties," in *Human Rights and The Moral Responsibilities of Corporate and Public Sector Organizations*, ed. Tom Campbell and Seumas Miller (Dordrecht: Kluwer, 2004), 32.

6. Ibid.

7. Ibid.

8. Alan Gewirth explores and develops these ideas at length in chapters 1–3 of *Reasons and Morality* (Chicago: University of Chicago Press, 1978), and much more briefly in *The Community of Rights* (Chicago: University of Chicago Press, 1996), 16ff.

9. They contribute to human well-being both because their respect enhances human freedom, dignity, and equality and because of their instrumental value. Tom Campbell explores these ideas in *Rights: A Critical Introduction* (London: Routledge, 2006), 34.

10. Gewirth, *Community of Rights*, 9.

11. See Campbell, *Rights*, 103.

12. This observation is crucial to the discussion to follow. The central question for this chapter is determining the human rights obligations of corporations. The answer I give to this question is that the human rights obligations of corporations are a function of their human rights impacts. (See the chapter's conclusions for a summary.) Corporations, I argue, have an obligation to mitigate negative human rights impacts and enhance potentially positive impacts. It follows, I argue, that while the human rights obligations of governments are uniform across countries and societies, the human rights obligations of corporations vary with the social, cultural, legal, environmental, and economic contexts in which they operate.

13. Gewirth makes this point in *Community of Rights*, 9.

14. This is a crucially important point. It provides the foundation for the argument in section 3 of this chapter.

15. Griffin, "Human Rights," 33, and Campbell, *Rights*, 34.

16. If, when embedded in legal systems, "human rights" did not have this overriding character, they would not be human rights.

17. Human rights are typically described in Western societies as individual rights, which of course they are. Western societies have as a consequence focused heavily on civil and political rights, or what are sometimes referred to as first generation human rights. However, from the first formulations of the human rights declarations following World War II, the role of human rights in building social conditions in which human beings can flourish has been emphasized. The preamble to the UN Universal Declaration provides a good example of this vision. The insistence that economic, social, and cultural rights be

given the same moral status as civil and political rights illustrates the perceived importance of human rights for the creation of societies in which human beings can flourish. More recently, attention has shifted to the role of human rights in fostering conditions favorable to economic developments. Amartya Sen, *Development as Freedom* (New York: Anchor, 1999), illustrates this shift in focus. It is this shift that has motivated much of the emphasis on the human rights obligations of corporations, since in today's world, it is widely agreed that corporate investment is the key to economic development, as I discuss at more length in Section 2 of this chapter.

18. I return to a discussion of what counts as the institutionalization of human rights in section 3 below.

19. Campbell, *Rights*, 35. The importance of this "practicality" requirement is echoed by James Griffith, "Human Rights," 33.

20. To take education as an example, we might say that it is a human right that ought to be respected universally. However, it would not be the case that it could be claimed as a human right in a situation where it was the case that fulfilling that right was beyond the practical capability of the community or the government or governments within whose jurisdiction the community fell. Creating the conditions in which such a right could be said to exist in particular cases might then be said to be a moral obligation, though for whom it was an obligation would have to then be analysed and determined.

21. It is worth pointing out that if rights can be either or both societal and legal in nature, as Campbell argues in *Rights*, 35, then it would seem to follow relatively uncontroversially that they need not be formalized into law to be respected.

22. For a more detailed account of the emergence of rights discourse, see Campbell, *Rights*, chap. 1.

23. See for example Yanaki Stoilov, "Are Human Rights Universal?" in *Human Rights in Philosophy and Practice*, ed. Burton M. Leiser and Tom D. Campbell (Aldershot, U.K.: Ashgate, 2001), 87–105.

24. Clause 2 of the preamble is explicit on this point. It begins: "Whereas disregard and contempt for human rights have resulted in barbarous acts which have outraged the conscience of mankind..."

25. When the General Assembly of the United Nations adopted the Universal Declaration, they requested the drafting of a covenant on human rights to include measures of implementation. It was explicitly decided in 1950 that this covenant should include economic, social, and cultural rights as well as civil and political rights. After debate, however, it was decided to draft two covenants, one to set out civil and political rights and the other to focus on economic, social, and cultural rights. The International Covenant on Economic, Social and Cultural Rights and the International Covenant on Civil and Political Rights were adopted by the General Assembly in 1966.

26. See also article 1 that states: "All human beings are born free and equal in dignity and rights," and article 3 that states: "Everyone has the right to life, liberty and security of person."

27. These rights are sometimes referred to as first-generation rights. They derive primarily from the seventeenth and eighteenth centuries. They played a particularly formative role in the writing of the American Declaration of Independence and the French Declaration of the Rights of Man and Citizen.

28. These rights are sometimes referred to as second-generation rights.

29. These solidarity rights are sometimes referred to as third-generation rights.

30. For an example, see the third clause of the preamble.

31. Report of the Special Representative of the Secretary-General (SRSG) on the issue of human rights and transnational corporations and other business enterprises, by John

Ruggie titled "Business and Human Rights: Mapping International Standards of Responsibility and Accountability for Corporate Acts," A/HRC/4/035, February 9, 2007. See page 5, No. 12, for example.

32. See Ruggie, "Business and Human Rights," 11, No. 35.

33. Ibid., 12, No. 38.

34. Milton Friedman, *Capitalism and Freedom* (Chicago: University of Chicago Press, 1962) is perhaps his most significant contribution to this debate.

35. Milton Friedman, "A Friedman Doctrine—The Social Responsibility of Business Is to Increase Its Profits," *New York Times Magazine*, September 13, 1970, 33, 122–24.

36. The view of the firm on which these theories are grounded is based in the first instance on the work of a number of influential economists, which include Friedman and Hayek. More recent defenses have been mounted by business ethicists. One such defense is argued by Kenneth Goodpaster, "Business Ethics and Stakeholder Analysis," *Business Ethics Quarterly* 1 (1) (1991): 53–73. A second detailed analysis and defense is offered by John Boatright in *Ethics in Finance* (Oxford: Blackwell, 1999). An exhaustive critical analysis of shareholder theory by business ethicists can be found in Max Clarkson's collection of essays titled *The Corporation and Its Stakeholders: Classic and Contemporary Readings* (Toronto: University of Toronto Press, 1998).

37. Friedman, "A Friedman Doctrine," 123.

38. It is important to note here that the critique just outlined is normally directed against the thesis that corporations have social responsibilities beyond meeting their obligations to shareholders. It is equally germane to the thesis that corporations have human rights responsibilities inasmuch as human rights are an example of the kinds of social responsibilities that are the focus of this debate.

39. This is the basic objection of prominent critics of the view, for example, Friedman and Hayek, that corporations have social responsibilities (and by implication human rights responsibilities) beyond simply serving the interests of their shareholders. For a more recent, systematic defense of this view, see Samuel Gregg, *The Commercial Society: Foundations and Challenges in a Global Age* (Lanham, Md.: Lexington, 2007).

40. It is perhaps worth noting here how effectively this assignment of responsibilities dovetails with the preamble to the UN Declaration of Human Rights.

41. For an authoritative account of these developments, see Ruggie's report titled "Business and Human Rights."

42. Wesley Cragg, "Ethics, Globalization and the Phenomenon of Self- Regulation," in *Ethics Codes, Corporations and the Challenge of Globalization*, ed. Wesley Cragg (Cheltenham, U.K.: Edward Elgar, 2005), 1–23; John Ruggie, "Promotion and Protection of Human Rights," UN Commission on Human Rights, (E/CN.4/2006/97, February 22, 2006); Tom Campbell, "Moral Dimensions of Human Rights," in *Human Rights and the Moral Responsibilities of Corporate and Public Sector Organizations*, eds. Tom Campbell and Seumas Miller (Dordrecht: Kluwer, 2004), 11–31; Rory Sullivan ed., *Business and Human Rights* (Sheffield, U.K.: Greenleaf, 2003); Michael K. Addo, "Human Rights and Transnational Corporations," in *Human Rights Standards and the Responsibility of Transnational Corporations*, ed. Michael K. Addo, (The Hague: Kluwer Law International, 1999), 3–37; Koen De Feyter, *Human Rights: Social Justice in the Age of the Market* (London: Zed, 2005).

43. This point is developed at greater length in chapter 1 of Cragg, *Ethics Codes, Corporations and the Challenge of Globalization*. See also Hannah Arendt's description of the significance of the power that science has generated to "act into nature" and the significance of that power for our relation as human beings to nature and our capacity to

impact and alter nature and the natural environment: "The Concept of History, Ancient and Modern," in *The Portable Hannah Arendt*, ed. Peter Baehr (New York: Penguin, 2000).

44. See, for example, Roger Lowenstein, *When Genius Failed: The Rise and Fall of Long-term Capital Management* (London: Fourth Estate, 2002).

45. Ruggie notes in his report "Promotion and Protection of Human Rights," footnote 4, that "intra-firm trade amounts to some 40 per cent of United States total trade, and that does not fully reflect the related party transactions of branded marketers or retailers who do not actually manufacture anything themselves."

46. Ibid., 5.

47. For a more detailed discussion of this development, see Peter Muchlinski's discussion of the evolving understandings of the ethical responsibilities of business in "Human Rights and Multinationals: Is There a Problem?" 31–47.

48. For a detailed defense of this point, see Harry Arthurs' discussion of "Private Ordering and Workers' Rights in the Global Economy: Corporate Codes of Conduct as a Regime of Labour Market Regulation" in Cragg, *Ethics Codes*, 194–212.

49. See Ruggie, "Promotion and Protection of Human Rights," and Craig Scott, "Multinational Enterprises and Emergent Jurisprudence on Violations of Economic, Social and Cultural Rights" in *Economic, Social and Cultural Rights*, 2nd ed., ed. Asbjom Eide et al. (Dordrecht: M. Nijhoff, 2001), 563–595.

50. Bribery is not a phenomenon that globalization has introduced. As a way of influencing the behavior of public officials it is probably as old as government itself. What globalization has done is to open the door to the use of bribery as a tool for accomplishing corporate objectives on the part of wealthy and powerful corporations. It is the willingness of multinational corporations to use bribery to accomplish their objectives in international markets that has resulted in its exponential growth particularly in developing and under developed countries. For an in-depth analysis of this phenomenon, see Wesley Cragg, "The U.S. Foreign Corrupt Practices Act: The Role of Ethics, Law and Self-Regulation in Global Markets," in Cragg, *Ethics Codes*, 112–154.

51. See, for example, Mary Robinson's discussion of the impact of corruption on human rights in Transparency International's *Global Corruption Report* 2004, 7.

52. Examples include David Korten, *When Corporations Rule the World* (West Hartford, Conn.: Kumarian Press, 1995); Noreena Hertz in *The Silent Takeover: Global Capitalism and the Death of Democracy* (London: Arrow Books, 2001); Naomi Klein, *No Logo* (Toronto: Random House, 2000), and more recently, *The Shock Doctrine: The Rise of Disaster Capitalism* (Toronto: Knopf, 2008); and Robin Broad, *Global Backlash: Citizen Initiatives for a Just World Economy* (Lanham, Md.: Rowman and Littlefield, 2002).

53. For a comprehensive compendium of international codes, see note 1 above.

54. What follows is a summary critique. For a detailed analysis and critique, see Harry Arthurs, "Corporate Codes of Conduct: Profit, Power and Law in the Global Economy," in Cragg, *Ethics Codes*, 51–75.

55. For a comprehensive collection of codes, see note 1 above. See also Ruggie, "Promotion and Protection of Human Rights," 9, No. 39.

56. For a detailed analysis of the shortcomings associated with this second model, see Michael Addo's discussion of "Human Rights Perspectives of Corporate Groups," *Connecticut Law Review* 37 (3) (2005): 667–689. See also Ruggie, "Business and Human Rights," 20, and Arthurs, "Corporate Codes of Conduct," 51–75.

57. The distinction between public and private interests, goals and responsibilities, or private and common goods or interests is a common feature of the position of legal model supporters like Friedman and Hayek. The importance of the distinction is analyzed by

Kenneth E. Goodpaster, "Business Ethics and Stakeholder Analysis," *Business Ethics Quarterly* 1 (1991): 53–73. For an extended discussion of the concept of a common or public good, see John Finnis, *Natural Law and Natural Rights* (Oxford: Clarendon Press, 1980).

58. Joseph Raz, *The Morality of Freedom* (Oxford: Oxford University Press, 1986), 198, provides the following definition of a public good: "A good is a public good in a certain society if and only if the distribution of the good is not subject to voluntary control by anyone other than each potential beneficiary controlling his share of the benefit." Human rights properly enforced have this characteristic and are therefore properly described as public goods.

59. The resolution of the General Assembly setting out what has come to be called the indivisibility principle reads: "the enjoyment of civic and political freedoms and or economic, social and cultural rights are interconnected and interdependent" (Resolution 421 (V), sec. E.).

60. It would seem that this resolution was designed to emphasize that it would be contrary to endorsement of the UN Declaration of Human Rights to endorse one of the two covenants and not the other. For a more comprehensive description of the origins of the principle and its evolution and application to international human rights discourse, see Manfred Novak's discussion of the "Indivisibility of Human Rights" in *Human Rights*, ed. Rhona Smith and Christien van den Anker (London: Hodder Headline Group, 2005), 178.

61. This particular issue is a central concern of business ethics. For a discussion of the dangers attending the elision of public- and private-sector roles, see Goodpaster, "Business Ethics and Stakeholder Analysis."

62. In their article, Matten and Moon provide a detailed account of why this is the case. Dirk Matten and Jeremy Moon, " 'Implicit' and 'Explicit' CSR: A Conceptual Framework for a Comparative Understanding of Corporate Social Responsibility," *Academy of Management Review* 33 (2) (2008): 404–424.

63. The obligation to participate openly and transparently in developing and coming to conclusions about human rights obligations is discussed in more detail below.

64. Campbell, "Democratising Human Rights," in Leiser and Campbell, *Human Rights in Philosophy and Practice*, 181.

65. Ibid.

66. A useful example of a human rights impact assessment involving those impacted is the Harker Report undertaken at the request of the Canadian Government, *Human Security in the Sudan: The Report of a Canadian Assessment Mission* (Ottawa: Minister of Foreign Affairs, 2000).

67. The case of Myanmar (Burma) is an interesting one for this discussion for two reasons. First, Myanmar is an example of a country which has had and continues (at the time of writing) to have a very oppressive government and a long history of human rights abuses. Second, Myanmar has occasioned wide debate and analysis on the part of scholars specifically concerned to understand the moral responsibilities of firms active or contemplating investing in that country. See for example Ian Holliday, "Doing Business with Rights Violating Regimes: Corporate Social Responsibility and Myanmar's Military Junta," *Journal of Business Ethics* 61 (4) (2005): 329–342; Inez Louwagie, Luc Weyn, and Mathias Bienstman, *Where Do You Draw the Line?* (Brussels: Netwerk Vlaanderen, 2005); John R. Schermerhom Jr., "Terms of Global Business Engagement in Ethically Challenging Environments: Applications to Burma," *Business Ethics Quarterly* 9 (3) (1999): 485–505; Judith White, "Globalization, Divestment and Human Rights in Burma," *Journal of Corporate Citizenship* 14 (2004): 47–65.

68. For an interesting discussion of human rights impact assessment methodology, see "Rights and Democracy," *Human Rights Impact Assessments for Foreign Investment Project:*

Learning from Community Experiences in the Philippines, Tibet, the Democratic Republic of Congo, Argentina, and Peru (International Center for Human Rights and Democratic Development, Montreal, Canada (2007), http://www.dd-rd.ca/site/publications/index.php. For a similar study focused on the Sudan, see *Human Security in the Sudan: The Report of a Canadian Assessment Mission* (Ottawa: Minister of Foreign Affairs, 2000).

69. What this suggests is that John Ruggie is correct in his view that the way forward to a more effective understanding of the human rights obligations of corporations must include human rights impact assessment. Ruggie, "Business and Human Rights," 21, No. 77.

70. Samuel Huntington, *Political Order in Changing Societies* (New Haven, Conn.: Yale University Press, 1969), 12.

71. James G. March and Johan P. Olsen, *Rediscovering Institutions: The Organizational Basis of Politics* (New York: Free Press, 1989), 160.

72. B. Guy Peters, *Institutional Theory in Political Science* (London: Pinter, 1999).

73. AccountAbility is currently engaged in a broadly based consultation on Assurance Standards, http://www.accountability21.net. Social Accountability International, whose focus is more specifically labor standards, is also involved in developing assurance standards and methodologies. Its governing body draws its membership from business, academic and voluntary sector organizations. The Caux Roundtable is an international business oriented organization with connections to a variety of faith traditions.

74. For a discussion of the role of export credit agencies see "Linking Investment and Human Rights: The Case of Export Credit Agencies," Report of an NGO Strategy Session (Halifax Initiative 2002).

75. For these documents, see note 1 above.

76. John Ruggie comments at some length on these and related initiatives in section 4 of his 2007 report to the UN Secretary-General. Ruggie, "Business and Human Rights."

77. Samuel Gregg, in *The Commercial Society*, proposes that any imposition of corporate social responsibility-type values on the operation of the free market by governments or other organizations, will inevitably undermine the values on which free markets are grounded. If this argument is sound, it will apply with equal force to any model or system that assigns human rights obligations to corporations. That being the case, it is not grounds for rejecting the hybrid model as a way of determining the ethical responsibilities of corporations in a global economy in favor of the standard model.

78. This distinction between the universality of human rights and the variability of human rights obligations is a fundamental feature of human rights, as I point out in section 1 above. (See note 14, which identifies the relevant passage in section 1.) The human rights obligations of states are uniform because the powers of the state to protect and promote human rights are uniform. This is not true of individuals or corporations. It is for this reason that their obligations are variable.

SUGGESTED READING

Addo, Michael K., ed. *Human Rights Standards and the Responsibility of Transnational Corporations*. The Hague: Kluwer Law International, 1999.

Boatright, John. *Ethics in Finance*. Oxford: Blackwell, 1999.

Campbell, Tom. *Rights: A Critical Introduction*. London: Routledge, 2006.

Campbell, Tom, and Seumas Miller, eds. *Human Rights and the Moral Responsibilities of Corporate and Public Sector Organizations.* Dordrecht: Kluwer, 2004.

Cragg, Wesley, ed. *Ethics Codes, Corporations and the Challenge of Globalization.* Cheltenham, U.K.: Edward Elgar, 2005.

De Feyter, Koen. *Human Rights: Social Justice in the Age of the Market.* London: Zed, 2005.

Draft Norms, 55th Session of the Commission on Human Rights Sub-Commission on the Promotion and Protection of Human Rights (E/CN.4/Sub.2/2003/12/Rev.2).

Eide, Asbjørn, et al., eds. *Economic, Social and Cultural Rights,* 2nd ed. Dordrecht: M. Nijhoff, 2001.

Gewirth, Alan. *Reasons and Morality.* Chicago: University of Chicago Press, 1978.

———. *The Community of Rights.* Chicago: University of Chicago Press, 1996.

Goodpaster, Kenneth E. "Business Ethics and Stakeholder Analysis." *Business Ethics Quarterly* 1 (1) (1991): 55–73.

Holliday, Ian. "Doing Business with Rights Violating Regimes: Corporate Social Responsibility and Myanmar's Military Junta." *Journal of Business Ethics* 61 (4) (2005): 329–342.

Leiser, Burton M., and Tom D. Campbell, eds. *Human Rights in Philosophy and Practice.* Aldershot, U.K.: Ashgate, 2001.

Matten, Dirk, and Jeremy Moon. " 'Implicit' and 'Explicit' CSR: A Conceptual Framework for a Comparative Understanding of Corporate Social Responsibility." *Academy of Management Review* 33 (2) (2008).

Muchlinski, Peter. "Human Rights and Multinationals: Is There a Problem?" *International Affairs* 77 (1) (2001): 31–47.

Ruggie, John. "Business and Human Rights: Mapping International Standards of Responsibility and Accountability for Corporate Acts." A/HRC/4/035, February 9, 2007.

———. "Promotion and Protection of Human Rights." UN Commission on Human Rights. E/CN.4/2006/97, February 22, 2006.

Schermerhom, John R., Jr. "Terms of Global Business Engagement in Ethically Challenging Environments: Applications to Burma." *Business Ethics Quarterly* 9 (3) (1999): 485–505.

Sen, Amartya. *Development as Freedom.* New York: Anchor, 1999.

Smith, Rhona, and Christien van den Anker, eds. *Human Rights.* London: Hodder Headline Group, 2005.

Sullivan, Rory, ed. *Business and Human Rights.* Sheffield, U.K.: Greenleaf, 2003.

White, Judith. "Globalization, Divestment and Human Rights in Burma." *Journal of Corporate Citizenship* 14 (2004): 47–65.

WEB SITES

AccountAbility, http://www.accountability21.net.

Rights and Democracy, http://www.dd-rd.ca.

Transparency International, http://www.transparency.org.

Voluntary Codes: Principles, Standards and Resources, http://www.businessethicscanada.ca/capacity/tools/index.html, or http://www.yorku.ca/csr.

CHAPTER 10

MORAL ISSUES IN GLOBALIZATION

CAROL C. GOULD

GLOBALIZATION is often thought to be the defining social, political, and economic development of our times. The recent period has been marked by an intensified interconnection of economies, societies, and cultures, facilitated by the new technologies of information and communication, and the emergence of regional political systems (especially the European Union), along with some strengthening of international law and human rights regimes. The global economic reach of transnational corporations, along with global trade and the multilateral institutions—especially the World Trade Organization (WTO), the International Monetary Fund (IMF), and the World Bank that facilitate globalization and are intended to promote economic growth in the Global South—pose important new ethical questions for analysis. Political controversy also abounds, in part spearheaded by social movements for global justice, which came to prominence with the "Battle of Seattle" of 1999, and have subsequently carried out protests worldwide. Constructively, this movement has supported the rise of the World Social Forum and other bodies designed as alternatives to corporate economic globalization. Transnational civil society and nongovernmental organizations have also proliferated in this period, but the focus in this chapter will be on those aspects of globalization that are of special concern to business enterprises and the people associated with them and affected by them.

This chapter will lay out some of the key normative issues raised by globalization and will sketch some implications for business ethics and public policy, especially in regard to corporate social responsibility, the protection of the human rights of workers and other stakeholders, and the possibilities for overcoming global inequalities.

I begin with a characterization of globalization and explore some of the key problems of concern to ethicists—in business ethics and public policy—especially issues of global poverty, labor standards, outsourcing, and trade. In order to address these issues, I will consider various philosophical approaches to global justice, including that of Peter Singer, emerging conceptions of global responsibilities, including environmental ones, and the import of universal human rights fulfillment as discussed by Henry Shue and Thomas Pogge, among others. Various calls for fundamental structural changes in global trade and the global economy will also be taken up. I will also briefly touch on the challenges to global or "cosmopolitan" thinking that are posed by the diversity of cultures and the need to avoid imposing Western perspectives on societies that may not fully subscribe to them.

I then analyze three additional values posed by globalization: the need for improved transparency and accountability of multilateral institutions, as discussed by Joseph Stiglitz, the emphasis on labor standards, and the idea of sustainability and environmental justice. I conclude with a consideration of the implications of these values and norms for corporate social responsibility and stakeholder theory, and I will take note of the UN's "Global Compact," along with some new directions for strengthening the protection of human rights in the transnational contexts in which business operates.

GLOBALIZATION AND ITS DISCONTENTS

According to Thomas Friedman in *The Lexus and the Olive Tree*, globalization can be characterized as

> the inevitable integration of markets, nation-states and technologies to a degree never witnessed before—in a way that is enabling individuals, corporations and nation-states to reach around the world farther, faster, deeper and cheaper than ever before and in a way that is enabling the world to reach into individuals, corporations and nation-states farther, faster, and deeper, cheaper than ever before.[1]

Defining Globalization

Friedman points to the role of information technologies in moving both ideas and money instantaneously around the world in financial markets from New York to Hong Kong. He argues that global capitalism will in turn overwhelm old-style power politics and lead to democratization. This is summed up in the "Golden Arches Theory of Conflict Prevention," which states: "No two countries that both had McDonald's had fought a war against each other since each got its McDonald's," to which counterexamples (Israel and Lebanon, the United States and Iraq) and defenses have been mounted. Friedman's thesis is not only that global markets have new effects on nation-states but also that individuals worldwide are newly empowered to influence the decisions of these states.

Along somewhat similar lines, social and political theorists have tended to conceive globalization as a multifaceted phenomenon, marked, in David Held's terms, by "the growing interconnection of states and societies."[2] Held suggests that

> globalization can be understood in relation to a set of processes which shift the spatial form of human organization and activity to transcontinental or interregional patterns of activity, interaction and the exercise of power (see Held et al. 1999). It involves a stretching and deepening of social relations and institutions across space and time such that, on the one hand, day-to-day activities are increasingly influenced by events happening on the other side of the globe and, on the other, the practices and decisions of local groups or communities can have significant global reverberations (see Giddens 1990).[3]

Likewise, for Ulrich Beck, globalization "denotes the *processes* through which sovereign national states are criss-crossed and undermined by transnational actors with varying prospects of power, orientations, identities and networks."[4] Such a globalization process creates "transnational social links and spaces" and also "revalues local cultures," particularly in Internet communications.[5]

From the accounts of Friedman, Held, Beck, and others, we can identify several key features of this contemporary phenomenon: (1) Global economic processes, especially the free movement of capital and trade, and the development of a global marketplace; these processes may in turn result in constraints on democratic governments by unelected economic powers—including transnational corporations—that are not bound by requirements to represent the interests either of citizens or people in host countries; (2) The worldwide spread of information and communications technology and the global reach of the media, as well as attendant cultural changes, including the domination of the English language; (3) Global environmental challenges, particularly climate change and global warming; (4) The strengthening of international law and the growth of regional human rights regimes in Europe, Africa, and Latin America, through which individuals and other nonstate actors can initiate proceedings against their own governments; (5) An increasing emphasis on transnational security organizations, such as NATO, and collective defense policies; (6) Increases in transnational migration; (7) A certain globalization of care, both in problematic economic terms through the worldwide movement of care workers (e.g., to become nannies in distant households), and, in a very different sense, through the growing extent of people's care and concern with the problems of others who reside at a distance, for example, in regard to global poverty and natural disasters.

Economic globalization as involving the increased interconnection of people and countries within a world market, comprising dense networks of investment and trade, is often praised by supporters for bringing opportunities for growth, competition, and innovation to more people, whether as producers or consumers. It is held to produce new and better jobs where there is foreign investment. The claim is sometimes made that these processes have led to a diminution in world poverty and even to a decrease in income inequality. Globalization is also praised, as in the work of Friedman, for the possibilities it introduces of increasing cultural understanding through exposing people to transnational communications and to multiple sources of information, thereby potentially enabling greater democratic influence on governments. Further, it is sometimes thought to lead to a convergence on universal values, for example, of freedom, democracy, and human rights.[6] In opening up a new role for corporations, government organizations, international institutions, and NGOs, globalization is thought to introduce a useful diffusion of power and a new role for nonterritoriality, along with bringing about increases in economic efficiency.

Yet globalization in the form of what has been called "neoliberal globalization" has also been subjected to serious ethical critiques. Accordingly, social theorists including Held, Beck, Claude Ake, and others differ from Friedman in regarding globalization as a deeply contested notion, since globalization, they argue, has engendered conflict and exacerbated inequalities across societies. Accordingly, Beck distinguishes *globalization* as the interconnectedness that emerges from increased transnational communications from *globalism* as the ideology of free market world capitalism, which he criticizes.[7] For Immanuel Wallerstein, although this ideology "has been on a roll since the early 1980s," it was not a new idea. He writes:

> The ideology of neoliberal globalization...was rather the very old idea that the governments of the world should get out of the way of large, efficient enterprises in their efforts to prevail in the world market. The first policy implication was that governments, all governments, should permit these corporations freely to cross every frontier with their goods and their capital. The second policy implication was that the governments, all governments, should renounce any role as owners themselves of these productive enterprises, privatizing whatever they own. And the third policy implication was that governments, all governments, should minimize, if not eliminate, any and all kinds of social welfare transfer payments to their populations.[8]

Yet, according to Wallerstein, this ideology has met with difficulties both in former Communist regimes, where the political changes were not followed by economic success but by growing income inequality, and in the United States, with the development of a credit bubble and its uncertain future. Thus he holds that neoliberal policies are increasingly falling out of favor, with a question remaining as to what will replace them.[9]

Finally, there is also a debate as to whether globalization *itself* is a new phenomenon, in contrast to the views of Friedman and a host of others. It has been argued that in various ways the international economy was just as globalized in the late nineteenth century, in the heyday of unregulated capitalism, as it is in the present.[10] Furthermore, it is proposed that although sovereignty may have become somewhat "disaggregated" with the recent rise of global governance institutions,[11] this does not necessarily entail a diminution in the powers of nation-states to enact social democratic or welfarist agendas.[12] Nonetheless, the scale and intensity of interlinking networks of production, finance, and trade across borders and the institutions they have spawned, the intensification of intercultural communications, and the development of new regional and international governmental and nongovernmental organizations seem to create a new context with new problems that call for new norms and for innovative social and political responses.

Problems of Globalization

One of the biggest problems posed by globalization for business ethics and corporate social responsibility is that certain forms of globalization can lead to a "race to the bottom" in regard to both labor and the environment. Since transnational corporations can move and invest elsewhere if their demands are not met in a particular country, especially in what has been called the Global South, corporations are relatively free to determine workplace conditions and to disregard labor and environmental standards if they wish. Because of the competition between various countries for capital investment, governments themselves may not insist on adequate environmental controls or other regulations for these enterprises. Further, although workers in the host countries may see their new jobs as preferable to their previous situation, they are relatively powerless to deal with any exploitation they may encounter in factories and other workplaces, enabling sweatshop or other degrading conditions to proliferate. Even workers in developed countries often feel themselves to be suffering at the hands of globalization. For them, it may mean the outsourcing or "offshoring" of good jobs and a correlative loss of bargaining power at home. From this perspective, trade agreements like NAFTA and CAFTA are blamed for facilitating the movement not only of capital but of jobs outside of the United States and other developed countries in the Global North.

Herman Daly lists the problematic consequences of economic globalization with its diminution in the role of national boundaries in this way:

> (1) standards-lowering competition to externalize social and environmental costs to achieve a competitive advantage—the race to the bottom in terms of both efficiency in cost accounting and equity in income distribution; (2) increased tolerance of mergers and monopoly power in domestic markets in order to be big enough to compete internationally; (3) more intense national specialization according to the dictates of competitive advantage with the consequence of reducing the range of choices of ways to earn a livelihood, and increasing dependence on other countries. Free trade negates the freedom not to trade; (4) world-wide enforcement of a muddled and self-serving doctrine of "trade-related intellectual property rights" in direct contradiction to Thomas Jefferson's dictum that "knowledge is the common property of mankind."[13]

In explicating the first point, which is central to his critique, Daly holds that "economic integration under free market conditions promotes standards-lowering competition (a race to the bottom)"[14] and that global production tends to move to countries that do the worst job of integrating environmental and social costs into prices. He also maintains that this is accompanied by increasingly unequal income distribution in high-wage countries, such as the United States, with an abrogation of the social contract between labor and capital there. With capital mobility, Daly notes that though there may be gains in trade to the world as a whole, there is no guarantee that each nation-state will share in those gains.[15]

A second major problem, beyond these economic consequences, is that the global market disrupts and displaces local communities and traditions. Critics propose that globalization has a homogenizing effect on culture, by the creation of a "McWorld" that imposes Western—and especially United States—preferences elsewhere.[16] In this process, the global market turns people into what might be termed "abstract individuals," that is, as defined mainly in their roles as consumers of goods. This leads to the dominance worldwide of what C. B. Macpherson called possessive individualism, in which talents and the richness of personality and culture are subordinated to market ends.[17]

Third, the political consequences of economic globalization are also substantial. From the standpoint of political philosophy, a significant problem concerns the potential threat to democratic decision making itself. In place of the claim that the worldwide spread of capitalism conduces to the spread of democracy, critics have argued that economic globalization undermines the possibilities for democratic processes, at least within nation-states. This can be seen from the fact that with globalization, transnational corporations and multilateral institutions like the WTO make decisions that affect multitudes of people at a distance, as do nation-states themselves. To the degree that democracy is supposed to involve participation in decision making, globalization seems to render this more difficult, since people affected by decisions or subject to them often reside at a distance but have no input into the relevant decisions or policies. Moreover, the growing power and wealth of transnational corporations can sometimes overwhelm nation-states.[18] Some political and social theorists have addressed these difficulties by proposing to reinvigorate nation-states and their powers in various ways, while others have called for greater accountability of the institutions of global governance to those affected by their policies. Others have developed new models of transnational or global democracy that would allow forms of cross-border decision making to deal with the wide impacts of globalization processes.

Although the wealth and power of multinational corporations can overwhelm that of smaller nation-states, some have recently suggested that the relation of such corporations to the large and developed nation-states of the present is quite different. A new sort of "empire" is posited, in which currently dominant states in international affairs (particularly the United States as a global hegemon) facilitate the power of these corporations while making use of this expanding corporate scope to enlarge their own national political power and reinforce their hegemony. Yet, according to Michael Walzer, the word hegemony "denotes a looser form of rule, less authoritarian than empire is or was, more dependent on the agreement of others."[19] This perspective is illustrated by the way that the United States has used its power to advance reductions in tariffs through the General Agreement on Tariffs and Trade and subsequently the WTO. The IMF, under United States influence and the "Washington Consensus" also imposed conditionalities for its loans that diminished the self-determination of debtor countries. The United States government

repeatedly used the key role of the dollar as a global currency to facilitate its foreign policy.[20] Although in several ways unlike earlier forms of imperialism, theorists additionally point to the close interconnections between the interests of the
state and those of corporations, particularly in regard to the energy and mineral
sectors and to arms industries, along with militarization and the privatization of
security tasks.[21]

GLOBALIZATION AND JUSTICE

On the crucial question of the contribution of economic globalization to global poverty and social and economic inequalities among people worldwide, there appear
to be two countervailing trends in place: It is likely that the number of people living
in extreme poverty has decreased over the last two decades; yet the gap between the
richest and poorest (whether states or people) is larger than ever.[22]

Globalization's Impact on Poverty and Inequality

Even the impact on poverty has been questioned, particularly in terms of the World
Bank's statistical data.[23] It remains the case that roughly 44 percent of the world's
population survives below the World Bank's poverty line of $2 per day.[24] On the
positive side, it has been observed that the human development index, measuring life expectancy, literacy, and standard of living, has increased in recent years.[25]
However, based on the UN Development Programme's (UNDP) human development report and on WHO figures, Thomas Pogge writes that "the annual death toll
from poverty-related causes is around 18 million or one-third of all human deaths,
which adds up to approximately 270 million since the end of the Cold War."[26] Indeed,
Pogge further claims that "this fifteen-year death toll of 270 million is considerably
larger than the 200-million death toll from all the wars, civil wars, genocides, and
other government repressions of the entire 20th century combined."[27]

Even if extreme global poverty is diminishing, the trend of rising inequality
is well established. The richest 20 percent of the world's population (arranged by
income) receive nearly 83 percent of the total wealth, while the poorest 20 percent
receive less than 1.5 percent.[28] Moreover, the income inequalities worldwide have
often been matched by growing inequalities within countries. The states of the
Global North have tended to dominate world trade, although trade has had a differential effect among various states in the Global South. Joseph Stiglitz and others
have pointed out the ways in which the trade system and the global governance
institutions are biased against the developing countries.[29]

Global inequalities fall disproportionately upon women (approximately
70 percent of the very poor who live on a dollar or less a day are women[30]). They
shoulder the major burdens of caring for the victims of social crises like HIV-AIDS

and natural disasters like the Indonesian tsunami of 2004.[31] Moreover, the curtailment of social services in the wake of structural adjustment programs has tended to affect women differentially. Beyond this, Arlie Hochschild and others have analyzed the global care chains that result when women need to leave their own children in the care of others to move far away, taking up jobs caring for the children of affluent families in the Global North.[32] The resultant deficiency in care points to one distinctive impact of economic globalization.

The Requirements of Global Justice and Human Rights

A lively debate has taken place among philosophers with regard to the question of what to do about global poverty and global inequalities, including what the normative grounds are for addressing these difficult contemporary problems. A brief review of this literature will help in addressing the responsibilities of corporations in this context, to be discussed in the final section of this chapter.

The debate began in philosophy with Peter Singer's article "Famine, Affluence and Morality." It used a broadly consequentialist argument, subsequently developed in his book *Practical Ethics*, to the effect that we have an obligation to assist in the alleviation of global poverty.[33] Singer argued that we should give a significant portion of our income to the poor on the grounds that "if we can prevent something bad without sacrificing anything of comparable significance, we ought to do it."[34] For example, if we see a small child drowning in a pool of water, we ought to rescue it since we easily can with little cost to ourselves, which is insignificant in comparison with the avoidable death of the child.[35] He argues analogously that we should donate money to save suffering people far away, either directly or through foreign aid: "It seems safe to advocate that those earning average or above average incomes in affluent societies, unless they have an unusually large number of dependents or other special needs, ought to give a tenth of their income to reducing absolute poverty."[36]

Placing weight on institutional change instead of individual acts of charity, Charles Beitz argued for the need to implement global redistributions that deal with the injustices that are due to differential allocations of natural resources across nation-states, which takes into account the increasing interdependence of the world economy. In "Justice and International Relations" and subsequent works, Beitz argued for extending Rawls's contractarian approach and his principles of justice, initially proposed for a political society, into the domain of global distributive justice.[37]

Other philosophers, including Onora O'Neill, Henry Shue, and James Nickel presented arguments based on rights for moving toward global justice, in a way that sharply contrasted with the adoption of a lifeboat ethics of "sink or swim," as presented by Garrett Hardin in an early essay.[38] These theorists, unlike Hardin, argued for meeting the fundamental need of all people for access to means of subsistence.[39] For example, in his early work *Basic Rights*, Henry Shue argued for the interconnection of the basic rights to physical security, means of subsistence, and democratic participation.[40] He went on to reject the distinction among these as negative vs. positive, that is, that security requires only negatively refraining from interference, while subsistence or welfare rights require positive provision of means. Shue points out that protecting security also necessitates a positive provision of resources and institutions, including "police forces; criminal courts; penitentiaries; schools for training police, lawyers, and guards; and taxes to support an enormous system for the prevention, detection, and punishment of violations of personal security."[41] For Shue, the various basic rights concern our duties to alleviate helplessness. For him such human rights represent a "morality of the depths,"[42] concerned only with eliminating profound harms that people may experience. Yet, human rights and the duties they pose are increasingly being held to apply not only to traditional nation-states but also to nonstate actors, including nongovernmental organizations, corporations, and even individuals. Some of the implications of this extension will be discussed in the final section of this chapter on corporate social responsibility.

The Human Right to Means of Subsistence

Here we can take note of the increasing recognition that there is a human right to means of subsistence. The Universal Declaration of Human Rights, article 25, explicitly recognizes a right "to a standard of living adequate for the health and well-being of oneself and one's family, including food, clothing, shelter and medical care." It would seem, from this perspective, that a human rights approach requires that we work to alleviate global poverty. Thomas Pogge adopts precisely this approach in arguing that there is a negative duty to avoid harming the poor, which we do by imposing on them global institutional arrangements that prevent them from fulfilling human rights to an adequate standard of living. He claims that affluent Western governments, along with powerful actors within them such as corporations, and indeed most of their citizenry, are in fact to blame for imposing arrangements that harm poor people by exploiting them and by reproducing their massive poverty.[43]

Pogge argues against the idea that only undemocratic or corrupt national governments are responsible for the poverty of their citizens. He points to the role of global factors, including structural features of the economy and trade, through which, he claims, Western nations are complicit. Pogge highlights our recognition of the *resource privilege* that allows governments no matter how corrupt or democratic to legitimately sell their nation's resources in the world market; and the *borrowing privilege*, by which such governments can take on huge debts for which the people remain responsible into the future. These privileges serve to secure Western countries' own imports from poor countries while enabling their rulers to continue to oppress their people, denying them benefits from their own resources, and leaving them with enormous levels of indebtedness, all of which in turn serve to perpetuate poverty and misery.[44] Pogge's main concrete proposal is to institute a "global resources dividend" on the use or sale of any resources by states or governments, whereby a very small percent of the value of those resources would be put to use to alleviate severe poverty.[45] There have, in addition, been widespread calls for debt relief for developing countries.[46]

Pogge points to trade asymmetries that he argues contribute to global poverty. He criticizes the insistence by Western nations that poor countries eliminate their trade barriers, while maintaining their own protectionist policies, and that they remove subsidies on producers while wealthy countries preserve their own. Recently, Pogge has also stressed how the imposition of intellectual property regimes, particularly pharmaceuticals, deny the poor the ability to use generic drugs to counter disease, disability, and death.[47] Pogge also stresses how the global poor suffer differentially from the externalities of pollution and resource depletion imposed through economic globalization processes.[48]

Demands for a More Egalitarian Distribution

The task of eliminating severe poverty worldwide, while a central aspect of global justice and a very difficult challenge in itself, does not address the even more demanding requirement of establishing a more egalitarian distribution of wealth and income in global contexts. Even if institutional arrangements were established that enabled people to meet their human right to an adequate standard of living, some of the deep disparities in power and wealth that characterize current globalization processes would undoubtedly remain. Egalitarian philosophers have argued for overcoming these disparities if principles of justice are to be fulfilled. Accordingly, they propose, on cosmopolitan grounds—in which everyone is an equal or merits equal consideration of their interests—that it is insufficient to limit redistribution to the bounds of nation-states. These are often somewhat arbitrary in their origins, resulting from war, violence, or the results of colonialism, and states can be either lucky or not in the availability of natural and other resources. Some "luck egalitarians" argue for the need to correct for these accidental features in order to allow everyone worldwide a genuinely equal opportunity.[49]

Egalitarian principles can proceed from recognition of everyone's equal right to be free or to develop their capacities and realize long-term projects, whether individual or collective. Human rights specify the conditions that everyone needs for such self-development or self-transformative activity.[50] Among these human rights are basic ones that represent conditions for any human activity whatever (including security, liberty, and subsistence), and nonbasic ones that are conditions for the fuller development of this activity.[51] Although egalitarian principles can helpfully serve to guide our practice in various ways, for the near term it is probably sufficient to focus on the goal of putting in place social, political, and economic institutions that would enable people worldwide to fulfill their human rights, especially their basic human rights. Some implications of this approach for corporate social responsibility, and specifically the contributions that corporations can reasonably be expected to make toward the realization of human rights, will be discussed in the final section of this chapter.

Are Human Rights a Western Bias?

An objection that may be posed to human rights approaches of this sort, and also to consequentialist or contractarian theories, is that they remain tied to Western

philosophical perspectives and are thus culturally biased. The claim is sometimes advanced that in their emphasis on the universality of human beings such
approaches are oblivious to the diversity of human communities. In the priority
they give to the centrality of individuals they reflect narrowly Western frameworks
of thought and exclude more communitarian and local perspectives. This objection
raises the question of cultural relativism, which is standardly counterposed to uni-
versalist or humanistic approaches, an issue that cannot be adequately dealt with in
this chapter (but it is treated in the chapter by Beauchamp). However, as Amartya
Sen has pointed out, an emphasis on human freedom and the role of the individual
is not exclusively Western but can be found in the Indian tradition,[52] and, we might
add, in others as well. And human rights can themselves be interpreted in ways
that emphasize persons in relationships,[53] in this way bringing them closer to communitarian modes of thought. Moreover, there is currently important work going
on concerning Islamic, Confucian, and Buddhist approaches to human rights.[54]
The UN Universal Declaration on Human Rights and Covenants have been widely
endorsed by a broad swath of nation-states and peoples across cultures and play
a growing role in international law. Indeed, the rights recognized in the Universal
Declaration are not exclusively "Western." They include not only the traditional liberal individualist civil and political rights but also so-called second-generation economic and social rights and third-generation rights to culture and development. In
this way, it can be argued that they have arisen at least in part through intercultural
dialogue rather than through a simple imposition of Western perspectives. Their
future interpretation can also be seen as open to this sort of dialogue from different
perspectives, and to local and regional differences.[55]

In addition to the various approaches to global justice from consequentialist,
contractarian, and human rights perspectives, feminist theorists have proposed that
we address poverty, global inequalities, and oppression from a care ethics approach.
Theorists such as Fiona Robinson and Virginia Held have argued for an emphasis
on support for caring relationships by public agencies and institutions, and on the
establishment of networks of care and solidarity that can help to alleviate poverty
and eliminate oppression worldwide.[56] These approaches argue for the importance
of cultivating empathy and other helpful and affiliative emotions as important sup-
plements to respect for people's human rights. They also call for alleviating women's
double burden of work and care, which they argue often contributes in the Global
South to disproportional suffering and poverty of women and their children.

Another more political and grassroots approach to global justice is represented
in the World Social Forum and in related social movements, particularly in Latin
America. These movements emphasize dealing with the powerful forces of globalization by developing associations at local levels (including within cross-border
communities), as well as networks of these associations. Such networks would use
direct and consensual democratic methods to implement more egalitarian access to
public goods and welfare, and might employ solidarity economies and participatory budgeting to bring economic relations more under the control of the people
affected by them.[57]

VALUES OF DEMOCRACY, WORK, AND SUSTAINABILITY

Besides issues of global justice, economic globalization poses questions about how to devise forms of accountability for institutions of global governance such as the World Bank and the World Trade Organization, and also for the large business corporations that play such an important role in globalization processes.

Democratic Accountability

There have been calls for greater transparency within these institutions, which would allow for press and public scrutiny of their decisions and activities. With regard to global governance institutions, Joseph Stiglitz argues that transparency is more essential than it is even for governments, because the leadership of these institutions is not subject to direct election. He points out that at the WTO, negotiations tend to be carried out behind closed doors, allowing for the influence of corporate interests, while at the IMF, the financial community carries out its usual secretive methods, despite the fact that collective, public goods are involved. Transparency within these institutions, he argues, would permit criticism and more responsiveness to public needs for openness to the interests of all, as well as attention to crucial values such as environmental sustainability.[58]

A somewhat similar argument can be made for accountability and transparency in global corporations, as would be suggested also by a stakeholder approach, advocating responsibility not only to shareholders but to the variety of groups worldwide who have an important stake in the corporation's activities. For S. Prakash Sethi, such accountability extends also to a requirement for a corporation to correct for its disproportionate bargaining power and access to information by distributing some of the gains derived from such power to workers and customers. Sethi points out that the condition of imperfect competition that marks contemporary economies allows corporations to derive above-normal profits. The consequence in his view is that "corporations should be held accountable for a more equitable distribution of these above-normal profits with other groups, e.g., customers, employees, etc. who were deprived of their market-based gains because of market imperfections and corporate power."[59] Sethi proposes adding such an account of corporate social accountability to the usual notion of corporate social responsibility.

Beyond transparency and accountability in the sense of responsiveness, Stiglitz argues for introducing a measure of *democratic* accountability into the institutions of global governance. He points to the diversity of economic markets and of regional interests worldwide, along with existing differential conditions such as severe poverty. He argues that these institutions need to develop appropriate policies that suit this diversity. He proposes representation of the interests of diverse countries and regions within the deliberations of these powerful multilateral institutions.

According to Stiglitz, "Much of the rest of the world feels as if it is being deprived of making its own choices, and even forced to make choices that countries like the United States have rejected."[60]

To counter the disproportionate role of commercial and financial interests in international economic institutions, Stiglitz argues for giving voting rights to representatives of people in the developing world in the IMF and the World Bank, since they are deeply affected by its policies. At the WTO, where developing countries have seats at the table, Stiglitz proposes that more than trade ministers need to be involved.[61] Proposals have also been made to allow representatives of INGOs (international nongovernmental organizations)—for example, those concerned with human rights and development—to participate in the WTO, perhaps credentialing organizations already recognized at the United Nation for similar purposes.[62] To the objection that these NGOs are not themselves democratic and may be run by a self-appointed leadership or by Western elites, one could respond by requiring that they institute new mechanisms to ensure systematic input by their entire membership, along with forms of accountability to their members or to the people on behalf of whom these organizations speak.

Labor Rights and International Labor Standards

Among the key issues to be addressed by the newly powerful institutions of global governance is the adoption of global labor standards. Exploitation of labor—whether as child labor, forced or compulsory labor, sweatshop conditions of work, or even excessively long hours of work—is ethically unacceptable and needs to be subject to international regulation. Such cases are violations of human rights, and several international covenants adopted since the Universal Declaration of Human Rights of 1948 render them in violation of international law. Article 23 of the Universal Declaration requires "just and favorable conditions of work," along with freedom from discrimination, just and favorable remuneration, and the right to form and to join trade unions. Article 24 specifies a right to rest and leisure, including a reasonable limitation of working hours. These rights have been elaborated in the human rights covenants, particularly in the International Covenant on Economic, Social and Cultural Rights (1966), which also specifies that children should be protected from economic and social exploitation (article 10).[63]

Contemporary labor movements look to international frameworks for the adoption and implementation of a range of minimal labor standards that would mitigate some of the worst harms of globalization. These standards would contribute to equalizing the playing field among laborers in various countries by preventing the race to the bottom in terms of wages and working conditions that unregulated globalization seems to engender. A difficulty is that such labor standards, as with human rights law, must be implemented by governments within their own countries. The need to implement these standards by way of regulation can conflict with a government's concern to attract foreign investment. And there is currently only a nascent development of regional or global courts of appeal against human rights violations, though the European Union tends to be in the forefront of such developments. Even before the EU, the Council of Europe introduced the Court of Human Rights which, along with the newer European Court, has enabled appeals for the protection of human rights within the region as a whole, and even against the decisions of nation-states within it. Yet, such human rights courts (which exist also in the Inter-American context) have thus far limited their jurisprudence to the protection of civil and political rights rather than of social and economic rights including labor rights.

The International Labor Organization (ILO) has recently proposed new directions for integrating the concerns with fair globalization and decent work into the functionings of the institutions of global governance, calling for greater integration and coordination among these institutions. The ILO interprets this norm of decent work in ways that take it beyond the minimal avoidance of severe exploitation or sweatshop conditions. Among the goals that the ILO posits for making globalization fair or just are the achievement of gender equality in work, the enhancement of local communities and development, employment and enterprise creation, the establishment of a socioeconomic floor globally, and enhancing global dialogue.[64] The right to form unions and collective bargaining is also supposed to be protected.

A further norm, though one not usually counted among the conditions for decent work, is the achievement of some significant measure of worker participation in the management of work, or what might be called democratic management. The value of worker input as a condition for meaningful work—and often for the achievement of a more successful enterprise—has been articulated in the management literature over several decades.[65] The main argument for it is not only that worker participation can be effective, for example, by further motivating workers or giving them a deeper stake in the corporation, or else by taking into account their input into matters that they are knowledgeable about. Instead, the rationale is that all those engaged in cooperative forms of activity defined by shared goals, whether economic or political, should be able to codetermine this activity rather than being directed by others within these spheres of their lives. In this perspective, democratic participation is broader than a purely political notion, but it applies in all institutional settings in which people are engaged with others in joint or common projects.

Needless to say, this view is not dominant within management theory, where such democratic management may either not be recognized or may be regarded as something desirable that can nonetheless be traded for other goods such as higher wages. It is worth noting, however, that worker management has been effectively implemented in various enterprises around the world, most strikingly perhaps in the Mondragón Corporación Cooperativa, the sixth largest corporation in Spain.[66] The Mondragón group is attempting to globalize its democratic management model by working with other companies, especially in Europe, who wish to emulate its cooperative methods and its business success, but in ways suitable to their local circumstances.

Environmental Justice and Sustainability

A value that is increasingly recognized as crucial for international action is protection of the global ecosystem and the achievement of sustainable development. Without going into the extensive scientific research concerning climate change or the various public policies contemplated, "global warming" represents a crisis of enormous proportions urgently in need of concerted global action. Although there are calls for changes in consumer behavior to achieve conservation, the scale of the problem requires international agreement and regulation. These issues raise problems of sustainability and environmental justice that cannot be adequately treated in this chapter. However, the tie to economic globalization should be acknowledged. Such globalization has often been carried out in ways that have harmed the environment: through expanding resource use, especially of fossil fuels; increasing commodity consumption, generating substantial carbon emissions and polluting waste, along with its dispersal in the air, sea, and land; constructing ecologically destructive infrastructures, such as dams and ports; poisoning agricultural soil and water; and by facilitating the spread of invasive species, among other tendencies.[67]

It has been observed that "to sustain the world's population at the current consumption levels of the affluent would actually require the resources of three additional planet Earths. Even the current aggregate consumption level, which includes that of some billion people who exist in absolute poverty, is not sustainable."[68] Given that life depends on the planetary support systems and its biodiversity, it is necessary to meet people's needs in a way that preserves the ability of future generations to meet their needs, and that retains natural diversity. Accordingly, it has been proposed that a principle of sustainability requires that societies assure that

> (a) rates of resource exploitation do not exceed rates of regeneration;(b) rates of resource consumption do not exceed the rates at which renewable replacements can be phased into use; and (c) rates of pollution emissions and waste disposal do not exceed the rates of their harmless absorption. Compromising any of these three conditions puts the well-being of future generations and planetary life at grave risk.[69]

Some have addressed this challenge by appeal to an obligation that people have of environmental stewardship, which might extend not only to nature but also more broadly to the common heritage of humankind.[70] Others have proposed constitutionalizing environmental protection as a human right. Thus, Tim Hayward argues for the recognition of a "right to an environment adequate for (human) health and well-being."[71] Environmental rights have been included in numerous declarations and conventions, for example, the Stockholm Declaration of 1972, the 1989 UN Convention on the Rights of the Child, and the Aarhus Convention of 1998, in state constitutions, including several in Latin America and Africa, and in regional agreements such as the 1981 African Charter, and the 1989 Additional Protocol to the 1969 American Convention on Human Rights in the Area of Economic, Social and Cultural Rights. A further institutionalization of environmental rights appears likely over time, including substantive ones, such as freedom from pollution and environmental degradation, preservation of air, soil, water, and biological diversity, a safe and healthy work environment, and the like, as well as procedural rights such as access to information about the environment and meaningful participation in planning that affects it, and effective remedies for redressing environmental harms.[72]

A related normative approach emphasizes global environmental justice.[73] Hayward sees this justice as extending to what he calls "climate justice," which "implies a fundamental right of each individual to an equitable share of the planet's aggregate natural resources and environmental services that are available on a sustainable basis for human use. This aggregate I shall refer to as 'ecological space'... The atmosphere's capacity to absorb carbon emissions is one component of ecological space."[74] The use of more than a person's fair share would incur "ecological debt,"[75] which refers primarily to affluent people. The implications for dealing with carbon emissions is widely contested, but we can suggest that recognizing the role of broader principles of justice will be helpful in dealing with this problem by setting out the normative desiderata that need to be met through changes in existing forms of practice and the design of new ones.

Finally, I take note of the Millennium Development Goals (MDGs), which formulate eight goals that can also be seen to follow from the ethical principles for globalization discussed in this and the previous sections of this chapter. The goals to be achieved by 2015 speak to the world's main development challenges and are included in the Millennium Declaration of 2000, which was adopted by 189 nations. They are recommended as goals not only for nations and international cooperation but also for the conduct of businesses and other nonstate actors that operate within our globalizing world. The goals are as follows:

- Goal 1: Eradicate extreme poverty and hunger
- Goal 2: Achieve universal primary education
- Goal 3: Promote gender equality and empower women
- Goal 4: Reduce child mortality
- Goal 5: Improve maternal health
- Goal 6: Combat HIV/AIDS, malaria and other diseases
- Goal 7: Ensure environmental sustainability
- Goal 8: Develop a Global Partnership for Development

Some of these goals represent only aspirations at this point, whereas others—like reducing child mortality—are stated in terms that are more immediately realizable. All of them point to aspects of people's well-being worldwide that ought to be matters of wide shared concern, whether for wholly altruistic reasons or more narrowly self-interested ones. These goals also suggest the need to develop new institutional mechanisms for achieving progress about the major global problems they address. The implications of these goals, along with the requirements posed by global justice and the other crucial norms discussed earlier, for the social responsibility of business in our interconnected world, forms the topic of the final section of this chapter.

Implications for Corporate
Social Responsibility in an Increasingly
Global World

We can now consider the import of the previous analysis of globalization and global justice issues for altering notions of corporate social responsibility. In addition, the implications for enlarging the existing account of stakeholder theory will be addressed in view of the broader scope of those having a stake in corporate activity in a more globalized world. And in conclusion, two practical directions—a proposal for the wide use of human rights assessments and the UN's Global Compact initiative will be discussed.

CSR and Global Justice Norms

From the argument presented in this chapter that gives moral priority to norms of global justice, it follows that if human rights include rights against being harmed and also economic and social rights then multinational enterprises and their members have obligations to respect these rights at least by not violating them. As noted, human rights have increasingly been held to apply not only to the activities of state actors in the public sphere but also to nonstate actors as well. In addition, to the degree that human rights require individuals and other agents to participate in creating institutions that would fulfill them, there is an obligation to contribute to the degree possible to helping to fulfill people's human rights. It is difficult, of course, to determine the scope of such obligations. Controversies abound concerning how to balance obligations to those close to us as opposed to general duties on grounds of humanity to those more distant from us. Further, while some think that the latter call only for charitable acts, a stronger notion of our interdependence in meeting each other's human rights and basic human needs would support moral requirements of positively cooperating to fulfill them, especially by way of supporting institutions that would do so.

An important argument concerning the demands that human rights place on multinational corporations was presented by Thomas Donaldson, in his book *The Ethics of International Business*.[76] Although Donaldson preferred to call these fundamental rights rather than human rights, he nonetheless argued that corporations have duties to avoid violating them and to observe them in host countries. He also held that a subset of these rights imposes duties on corporations "to help protect from deprivation."[77] An example is the requirement to provide workers with protective goggles where needed to avoid injury as a condition for respecting worker's fundamental rights to physical security. Nonetheless, in keeping with what he called the "fairness-affordability" criterion,[78] Donaldson held that corporations did not have further requirements to aid the deprived, that is, to help them achieve these fundamental rights. He adopted the view that corporations are "economic animals" with primary duties to shareholders, and that they therefore have thinner duties with regard to fulfilling fundamental rights than do either individuals or governments (although, as noted, not violating human rights retains its importance for corporations as well).

Although Donaldson's guidelines impose significant duties on corporations and correspond with many people's intuitions on the subject, his account is arguably not demanding enough. Human rights are increasingly recognized as applying not only to governments but also to nonstate actors and thus would apply to corporations, which are especially important actors in view of their global power.[79] It remains to be worked out, however, which of the human rights fall within the scope of corporate power for their protection and promotion. Some human rights more clearly pertain to states, for example, the prohibition against torture, while others noted in this chapter, for example, labor rights, are more directly relevant to corporate activities.

Another argument for corporate obligations to protect and help fulfill human rights derives from Pogge's account. He argues that Western nations and multilateral institutions acting on behalf of powerful interests—including corporate ones—have in fact imposed systems on people in developing countries that are harmful, at least partly unjust, and even exploitative. In view of this, he holds that these various agents in turn have positive obligations to aid these people in fulfilling their human rights, where these obligations derive from the basic negative duty to avoid harm. It remains a difficult question to determine more precisely how these obligations devolve on the various actors—states, multilateral institutions, corporations, and individuals in Western countries—who are to different degrees complicit in imposing such harm.

Yet, even if it were claimed that corporations do not directly cause harm in this way, it can be further argued that they have legal claim to their profits only on the basis of the recognition and granting of property rights and rights of incorporation that have been allocated to them by society, and in this sense they bear a public trust that their activities will contribute to the public good. This, along with the standing of corporations as agents from a legal point of view, in turn imposes responsibilities to act in ethical ways, including respect for human rights. Such ethical obligations would be even more incumbent on the members of the corporation insofar as they are also, as individuals, obliged to act in ways that respect the equal rights of others. It can be proposed too that the primary function of corporations is to provide goods and services that are useful to people rather than simply to generate profits. To fulfill this function well corporations need to attend to the well-being of their workers and their potential customers around the world as relevant stakeholders. This observation suggests also how stakeholder theory, which has significantly enlarged the moral horizons of the corporation beyond its shareholders, proposes new responsibilities to people at a distance, in view of the increasingly global impacts of corporate decisions.

Beginning with R. Edward Freeman's path-breaking 1984 book *Strategic Management: A Stakeholder Approach*, and through its development in various other works including Donaldson and Preston's article on its import for management,[80] stakeholder theory has called attention to the range of groups that participate in a firm's activities and whose interests should be taken into account in its management. The early theory identified employees, suppliers, customers, the local community, shareholders, and management as the main stakeholders, but in the context of globalization the set of stakeholders ranges farther afield. If we take seriously Freeman's proposed definition of a stakeholder as "any group or individual which can affect or is affected by an organization,"[81] people at a distance are often affected, obligating management to consider the impacts of its decisions on distant stakeholders.

This norm may seem so broad as to be impracticable, because the unintended consequences of actions and the potential global reverberation of even local decisions would make everyone a stakeholder and hence render the model inapplicable. To address this potential difficulty, I propose a delimitation of the criterion for being importantly affected (where it concerns distant people): namely, people are to be considered as importantly affected when corporate decisions affect their possibilities of fulfilling *basic* human rights.[82] Accordingly, when a corporation contemplates actions that are likely to affect people's capacities for rights fulfillment, they need to take the fundamental interests and basic needs of these people into account. Moreover, in order to do that accurately, managers would have to go beyond imagining these impacts and would likely have to get input from these affected people or from their representatives.

Some recent directions in stakeholder theory attempt to limit the relevant groups with stakes in the firm to those who participate within it voluntarily in mutually beneficial social schemes of cooperation.[83] Although one can raise doubts about this narrower definition, this interpretation of stakeholders would nonetheless not serve to absolve corporations of responsibilities for protecting human rights because of the earlier arguments that establish the primacy of these norms and their bearing on corporate and other nonstate actors. Moreover, as has been argued by Iris Marion Young in her latest works,[84] when corporate actors are bound with others within a given social scheme, that is, when they are "socially connected" with others through economic or other forms of cooperation, their participation in such schemes itself grounds a range of global responsibilities.

An important practical application follows from the various considerations advanced thus far about human rights as fundamental moral and legal principles. Corporations, multilateral institutions of global governance, and other large actors ought to draw up *human rights assessments* as a guide for their decisions and policies, in addition to forms of assessment currently in place, such as those concerning environmental impacts or technologies.[85] Members of the corporation also need to seriously consider rights impacts in all their actions and act in ways that support rights fulfillment on the part of their workers and the members of the communities affected by their activities. What specifically is involved would necessarily vary from case to case. Even as a standard, the conception of human rights would need further elaboration in business ethics through intercultural dialogue. Nonetheless, human rights can provide important guidelines for practice and for establishing agreement on norms in transnational contexts. I suggest that such a human rights approach represents an important direction for articulating corporate social responsibility in a global world.

The UN Global Compact

We can conclude this discussion of the import of the above analysis for corporate social responsibility by taking note of an important practical direction that has been introduced in recent years. Specifically, the UN Global Compact represents "a voluntary initiative designed to help fashion a more humane world by enlisting business to follow ten principles concerning human rights, labor, the environment, and corruption."[86] The principles of the Global Compact are as follows:

Human Rights
- Principle 1: Businesses should support and respect the protection of internationally proclaimed human rights; and
- Principle 2: Make sure that they are not complicit in human rights abuses.

Labor Standards
- Principle 3: Businesses should uphold the freedom of association and the effective recognition of the right to collective bargaining
- Principle 4: Elimination of all forms of forced and compulsory labour
- Principle 5: Effective abolition of child labour.
- Principle 6: Elimination of discrimination in respect of employment and occupation;

Environment
- Principle 7: Businesses should support a precautionary approach to environmental challenges
- Principle 8: Undertake initiatives to promote greater environmental responsibility
- Principle 9: Encourage the development and diffusion of environmentally friendly technologies.

Anti-Corruption
- Principle 10: Businesses should work against corruption in all its forms, including extortion and bribery.

These principles are derived from various international declarations and agreements, such as the Universal Declaration of Human Rights, the ILO's Fundamental Principles on Rights at Work, and the Rio Principles on Environment and Development. The Compact itself is a network or partnership convened and facilitated by the United Nations, involving companies (currently over 3,700 around the world) and labor and civil society organizations, such as those concerned with human rights and sustainability. It is designed to promote core ethical principles within the corporate domain through a "good practices" approach, employing policy dialogues (concerning ways to translate the principles into corporate practices), learning forums (regarding social responsibility, including in cross-cultural and transnational contexts), the cultivation of local and sectoral networks, and partnership projects in developing countries. The organization emphasizes that the Compact does not involve codes or regulations but rather a framework for encouraging businesses to use multistakeholder dialogues and collaboration to implement the ten principles. Given the participation of large civil society and labor organizations, and governments, it is thought that the Compact will facilitate relevant monitoring and benchmarking as well as input from these other organizations into the workings of corporations and other enterprises. Although the current voluntary initiatives are very limited in scope, some theorists point to the potential they hold for a future strengthening of global governance and for bringing corporations more fully within the framework of international human rights law.[87]

Criticisms of the Global Compact

The Global Compact has been subjected to considerable criticism, particularly from the World Social Forum and from some research and advocacy groups, such as the Third World Network and the Institute for Policy Studies. These civil society organizations argue that collaboration between corporations and the United Nations is designed primarily to improve the image of big business rather than to raise social and environmental standards. They point to the fact that participating companies can pick and choose among the principles, that a focus on good practices covers up bad ones and ignores structural issues that conduce to irresponsibility, and, most centrally, that the Compact lacks mechanisms for ensuring that companies comply with the principles.[88]

Proposals for a redesigned Compact include screening of potential participants, requiring companies to report on all ten principles, enlisting more feedback from the public and noncorporate stakeholders, and introducing new forms of independent compliance monitoring.[89] Other critics propose that the United Nations focus instead on developing new forms of oversight for transnational corporations, including setting and enforcing minimum environmental and social standards, and new methods for achieving corporate accountability through effective reporting mechanisms. They also argue that the ILO ought to strengthen its own procedures for following up on and helping resolve disputes, and that it is appropriate for all the relevant UN agencies to intensify their critical research and policy analyses as these bear on transnational corporations.[90]

Conclusion

There is much more to be said about moral issues in globalization and especially concerning the cross-cultural issues implied in the choice and justification of ethical principles, beyond the brief sketch in this chapter concerning the development of human rights norms and their interpretation. For example, the importance of recognition of diversity and of making room for intercultural dialogue comes to the fore in that context. Similarly, it would be useful to consider some of the practical ethical issues that can arise for people pursuing business concerns across a variety of cultures. Nonetheless, what emerges clearly from the richness of the entire list of topics and issues reviewed here is that the field of what can be called *global business ethics* is in its infancy and now seem certain to become a prominent area of investigation in the future.[91]

NOTES

1. Thomas L. Friedman, *The Lexus and the Olive Tree* (New York: Farrar, Straus, and Giroux, 1999), 7–8.

2. David Held, "The Changing Contours of Political Community: Rethinking Democracy in the Context of Globalization," in *Global Democracy*, ed. Barry Holden (London: Routledge, 2000), 17.

3. Ibid., 19, citing David Held, Anthony McGrew et al., *Global Transformations: Politics, Economics and Culture* (Cambridge: Polity Press, 1999), and Anthony Giddens, *The Consequences of Modernity* (Cambridge: Polity Press, 1990).

4. Ulrich Beck, *What Is Globalization?*, trans. Patrick Camiller (Cambridge: Polity, 2000), 11.

5. Ibid.

6. Mathias Loenig-Archibugi, "Introduction: Globalization and the Challenge to Governance," in *Taming Globalization*, ed. David Held and Marthias Koenig-Archibugi (Cambridge: Polity, 2003), 2.

7. Ibid.

8. Immanuel Wallerstein, "2008: The Demise of Neoliberal Globalization," *Yale Global, Fernand Braudel Center*, Yale University, February 4, 2008, http://yaleglobal.yale.edu/display.article?id=10299.

9. Ibid.

10. John Quiggin, "Globalization and Economic Sovereignty," *Journal of Political Philosophy* 9 (1) (2001): 57–58, citing D. Baker, G. Epstein and R. Pollin, eds., *Globalization and Progressive Economic Policy* (Cambridge: Cambridge University Press, 1998), and J. G. Williamson, "Globalization, Labour Markets and Policy Backlash in the Past," *Journal of Economic Perspectives* 12 (4) (1998): 51–72.

11. Anne-Marie Slaughter, "Disaggregated Sovereignty: Towards the Public Accountability of Global Government Networks," *Government and Opposition* (2004): 159–190.

12. Quiggin, "Globalization and Economic Sovereignty."

13. Herman E. Daly, "Globalization and its Discontents," *Philosophy and Public Policy Quarterly* 21 (Spring/Summer 2001): 19.

14. Ibid.

15. Ibid.

16. Benjamin Barber, *Jihad vs. McWorld: How Globalism and Tribalism are Reshaping the World* (New York: Ballantine, 1995).

17. Macpherson, *The Political Theory of Possessive Individualism: Hobbes to Locke* (Oxford: Clarendon Press, 1962), and *Democratic Theory: Essays in Retrieval* (Oxford: Clarendon Press, 1973). See also Frank Cunningham, "Democracy and Globalization," in *Civilizing Globalization*, ed. Richard Sandbrook (Albany, N.Y.: SUNY Press, 2003), 139–155.

18. A report by Sarah Anderson and John Cavanaugh poses the problem starkly, observing that "1. Of the 100 largest economies in the world, 51 are now global corporations; only 49 are countries. 2. The combined sales of the world's Top 200 corporations are far greater than a quarter of the world's economic activity. 3. The Top 200 corporations' combined sales are bigger than the combined economies of all countries minus the biggest 9; that is they surpass the combined economies of 182 countries. 4. The Top 200 have almost twice the economic clout of the poorest four-fifths of humanity" (Sarah Anderson and John Cavanaugh, "Top 200: The Rise of Global Corporate Power," *Corporate Watch*, 2000), http://www.globalpolicy.org/socecon/tncs/top200.htm.

19. Michael Walzer, "Is There an American Empire?" *Dissent*, Fall 2003, http://www.dissentmagazine.org/article/?article=455.

20. See Patrick Karl O'Brien and Armand Clesse, eds., *Two Hegemonies: Britain 1846–1914 and the United States 1941–2001* (Aldershot, U.K. Asghate, 2002), and the discussion in Niall Ferguson, "Hegemony or Empire?" *Foreign Affairs* 82 (Sept/Oct 2003): 154–161.

21. Jan Nederveen Pieterse, *Globalization or Empire?* (New York: Routledge, 2004), especially 31–60.

22. David Held, *Global Covenant* (Cambridge: Polity, 2004), 35.

23. Robert Hunter Wade, "The Disturbing Rise in Poverty and Inequality: Is It All a 'Big Lie'?" in *Taming Globalization*, ed. David Held and Mathias Koenig-Archibugi (Cambridge: Polity, 2003), 18–46. For an opposing view, see Jagdish Bhagwati, *In Defense of Globalization* (New York: Oxford University Press, 2004). See also Sanjay G. Reddy and Camelia Minoiu, "Has World Poverty Really Fallen?" *Review of Income and Wealth* 53 (3) (2007): 484–502.

24. Thomas Pogge, "Symposium: World Poverty and Human Rights," *Ethics & International Affairs* 19 (1) (2005): 1, citing Shaohua Chen and Martin Ravallion, "How Have the World's Poorest Fared since the Early 1980s?" *World Bank Research Observer*, 19 (Fall 2004): 141–169.

25. Held, *Global Covenant*, 35, citing David Held and Anthony McGrew, *The Global Transformations Reader*, 2nd ed. (Cambridge: Polity, 2003), pt. 5.

26. Pogge, "Symposium: World Poverty and Human Rights," 1.

27. Thomas Pogge, "Real World Justice," *Journal of Ethics* 9 (2005): 31.

28. David Held, *Global Covenant*, 35, citing Wade (see note 21 above).

29. Joseph E. Stiglitz, "Globalization and Development," in Held and Koenig-Archibugi, *Taming Globalization*, 47–67.

30. Held, *Global Covenant*, 37. See also "Gender Equality: Striving for Justice in an Unequal World," Policy Report of the United Nations Research Institute for Social Development, http://www.unrisd.org/unrisd/website/document.nsf/0/1FF4AC64C1894EAA C1256FA3005E7201?OpenDocument.

31. Fiona Robinson, "Care, Gender and Global Social Justice: Rethinking 'Ethical Globalization,'" *Journal of Global Ethics* 2 (June 2006): 16–18, citing reports from the World Health Organization ("Ethical Choices in Long-Term Care: What Does Justice Require?" 2002, Geneva, and "Gender and Women's Health: Gender and Disaster," Regional Office for SouthEast Asia, 2005), and UNIFEM (Biennial Report, Progress of the World's Women 2000, United Nations Development Fund for Women, New York).

32. A useful summary is in Arlie Hochschild, "Global Care Chains and Emotional Surplus Value," in *Global Capitalism*, ed. Will Hutton and Anthony Giddens (New York: New Press, 2001), 130–146.

33. Peter Singer, "Famine, Affluence and Morality," *Philosophy and Public Affairs* 1 (3) (1972): 229–243; and *Practical Ethics* (Cambridge: Cambridge University Press, 1993).

34. Singer, *Practical Ethics*, 230.

35. As discussed by Singer in *Practical Ethics*, 229.

36. Ibid., 246.

37. Charles R. Beitz, "Justice and International Relations," *Philosophy and Public Affairs* 4 (Summer 1975): 360–389.

38. Garrett Hardin, "Lifeboat Ethics: the Case Against Helping the Poor," *Psychology Today*, September 1974.

39. Onora O'Neill, "Lifeboat Earth," *Philosophy and Public Affairs* 4 (1975): 273–292; Henry Shue, *Basic Rights: Subsistence, Affluence, and U.S. Foreign Policy* (Princeton, N.J.: Princeton University Press, 1980); and James W. Nickel, *Making Sense of Human Rights* (Berkeley: University of California Press, 1987).

40. Shue, *Basic Rights*.

41. Ibid., 37–38.

42. Ibid., 18.

43. Thomas Pogge, *World Poverty and Human Rights* (Cambridge: Polity Press, 2002).

44. Ibid. See also the summary and defense of the argument in Pogge, "Symposium: World Poverty and Human Rights," *Ethics & International Affairs*, 1–7.

45. Pogge, *World Poverty and Human Rights*, chap. 6; and Thomas Pogge "Eradicating Systematic Poverty: Brief for a Global Resources Dividend" *Journal of Human Development* 2 (2001): 59–77. See also the more comprehensive proposal for global taxation in Gillian Brock, "Taxation and Global Justice: Closing the Gap between Theory and Practice," *Journal of Social Philosophy* 39 (Summer 2008): 161–184.

46. Joseph Stiglitz *Globalization and its Discontents* (New York: W. W. Norton, 2002), 243–44.

47. Thomas Pogge "Human Rights and Global Health: A Research Program," *Metaphilosophy* 36 (January 2005): 182–209.

48. Pogge, "Symposium: World Poverty and Human Rights," 6–7.

49. Cf. Kok-Chor Tan *Justice Without Borders* (Cambridge: Cambridge University Press, 2004).

50. Carol C. Gould *Rethinking Democracy: Freedom and Social Cooperation in Politics, Economy, and Society* (Cambridge: Cambridge University Press, 1988), especially chap. 1 and 7; and *Globalizing Democracy and Human Rights* (Cambridge: Cambridge University Press, 2004), especially chap. 1, 8, and 9. See also the "capabilities" and "functionings" account presented by Amartya Sen and Martha Nussbaum, for example, in Martha Nussbaum "Human Capabilities, Female Human Beings," in *Women, Culture, and Development*, eds. Martha Nussbaum and Jonathan Glover (New York: Oxford University Press, 1995), 61–104; and Sen's arguments for taking these capacities as a central focus and measure for development, in his *Development and Freedom* (New York: Alfred A. Knopf, 2000).

51. Gould, *Rethinking Democracy*, chap. 7, and *Globalizing Democracy and Human Rights*, chap. 1, 8, 9.

52. Amartya Sen, "Human Rights and Asian Values," *The New Republic*, July 14–21, 1997.

53. Gould, *Rethinking Democracy*, chap. 1; and *Globalizing Democracy and Human Rights*, chap. 1, 2.

54. See, for example, Abdullahi Ahmed An-Na'im ed. *Human Rights in Cross-Cultural Perspectives: A Quest for Consensus* (Philadelphia: University of Pennsylvania Press, 1995).

55. Gould, *Globalizing Democracy and Human Rights*, especially chap. 2.

56. Fiona Robinson "Care, Gender and Global Social Justice: Rethinking 'Ethical Globalization,'" *Journal of Global Ethics* 2 (June 2006): 5–25; Virginia Held *Ethics of Care: Personal, Political, and Global* (New York: Oxford University Press, 2005), especially chap. 10. See also Carol C. Gould "Transnational Solidarities," *Journal of Social Philosophy* 38 (Spring 2007): 146–162.

57. John Cavanagh and Jerry Mander eds., *Alternatives to Economic Globalization: A Better World is Possible* (San Francisco: Berrett-Koehler, 2002).

58. Stiglitz *Globalization and its Discontents* (New York: W. W. Norton, 2002), 227–29.

59. S. Prakash Sethi "Globalization and the Good Corporation: A Need for Proactive Coexistence," *Journal of Business Ethics* 43 (2003): 21.

60. Ibid., 221.

61. Ibid., 224–26.

62. Peter Willetts "Remedying the World Trade Organisation's Deviance from Global Norms," in *Free and Fair: Making the Progressive Case for Removing Trade Barriers*, eds. P. Griffith and J. Thurston (London: Foreign Policy Centre, Nov. 2004), 131–140.

63. A minimum age for employment is also addressed in article 32 of the Convention of the Rights of the Child (1989).

64. "A Fair Globalization: The Role of the ILO," Report of the Director General on the Social Dimension of Globalization, 2004, http://www.ilo.org/wcmsp5/groups/public/—-dgreports/—-dcomm/documents/publication/kd00070.pdf.

65. See, for example, Denis Collins "The Ethical Superiority and Inevitability of Participatory Management as an Organizational System," *Organization Science* 8 (Sep.–Oct. 1997): 489–507. See also David Ellerman *The Democratic Worker-Owned Firm* (London: Unwin Hyman, 1990).

66. See Francisco Avier Forcadell "Democracy, Cooperation, and Business Success: The Case of the Mondragrón Corporación Cooperativa," *Journal of Business Ethics* 56 (2005): 255–274.

67. Cf. "Ten Principles for Sustainable Societies," in Cavanagh and Mander, *Alternatives to Economic Globalization*, 61–62.

68. Tim Hayward "Human Rights Versus Emissions Rights: Climate Justice and the Equitable Distribution of Ecological Space," *Ethics & International Affairs* 21 (4) (2007): 431–450.

69. "Ten Principles for Sustainable Societies," 62–63.

70. Ibid., 63–64.

71. Tim Hayward *Constitutional Environmental Rights* (Oxford: Oxford University Press, 2005), 29.

72. Ibid., 29–31.

73. Hayward "Human Rights Versus Emissions Rights," and "On the Nature of Our Debt to the Global Poor," *Journal of Social Philosophy* 39 (Spring, 2008): 1–19; and Simon Caney "Cosmopolitan Justice, Responsibility, and Global Climate Change," *Leiden Journal of International Law* 18 (2005): 747–775.

74. Hayward, "Human Rights Versus Emissions Rights," 445.

75. Ibid.

76. Thomas Donaldson *The Ethics of International Business* (Oxford: Oxford University Press, 1989). A useful summary of the implications for human rights is provided in the extract from that work entitled "Moral Minimums for Multinationals," in *Ethics &*

International Affairs, 2nd ed., ed. Joel H. Rosenthal (Washington, D.C.: Georgetown University Press, 1999), 455–480. In later work, Donaldson discusses global hypernorms in the context of a contractarian approach, or Integrative Social Contracts Theory. See Thomas Donaldson and Thomas W. Dunfee *Ties That Bind: A Social Contracts Approach to Business Ethics* (Boston: Harvard Business School Press, 1999).

77. Thomas Donaldson *The Ethics of International Business* (Oxford: Oxford University Press, 1989), 81–86.

78. According to Donaldson (drawing on an earlier discussion by James Nickel), this criterion requires that "rights must impose obligations or other burdens that are affordable in relation to available resources, and they must be compatible with other genuine obligations" (ibid., 74). See also James W. Nickel *Making Sense of Human Rights* (Berkeley: University of California Press, 1987), 108–119.

79. See the discussion in Steven R. Ratner "Corporations and Human Rights: A Theory of Legal Responsibility," *The Yale Law Journal* 111 (December 2001): 461–475.

80. R. Edward Freeman. *Strategic Management: A Stakeholder Approach* (Boston: Pitman, 1984); and Thomas Donaldson and Lee E. Preston "The Stakeholder Theory of the Corporation: Concepts, Evidence, and Implications," *The Academy of Management Review*, 20 (January 1995): 65–91.

81. R. Edward Freeman "Stakeholder Theory," in *Encyclopedic Dictionary of Business Ethics*, ed. Patricia H. Werhane and R. Edward Freeman (Malden, Mass.: Blackwell, 1997), 602.

82. Gould, *Globalizing Democracy and Human Rights*, 210–12.

83. See Ronald K. Mitchell Bradley R. Agle and Donna J. Wood "Toward a Theory of Stakeholder Identification and Salience: Defining the Principle of Who and What Really Counts," *Academy of Management Review* 22 (1997): 853–886; Robert A. Phillips "Stakeholder Legitimacy," *Business Ethics Quarterly* 13 (1) (2003): 25–41; and the discussion of these views in Bert van de Ven "Human Rights as a Normative Basis for Stakeholder Legitimacy," *Corporate Governance* 5 (2) (2005): 48–59.

84. Iris Marion Young "Responsibility and Global Justice: A Social Connections Model," *Social Philosophy and Policy* 23 (January 2006): 102–130; and "Responsibility and Global Labor Justice," *Journal of Political Philosophy* 12 (4) (2004): 365–388.

85. See Gould, *Globalizing Democracy and Human Rights*, 234, and Carol C. Gould "Structuring Global Democracy: Political Communities, Universal Human Rights, and Transnational Representation," *Democracy in a Globalized World*, ed. Joakim Nergelius (Oxford: Hart, 2008), based on "Transnational Representation: Extending Participation in Cross- border Decision Making," Midwest Political Science Association Meeting, Chicago, Ill., April 8, 2005. A similar proposal is in Tarek MaasaraniMargo Drakos and Joanna Pajkowska "Extracting Corporate Responsibility: Towards a Human Rights Impact Assessment," *Cornell International Law Journal* 40 (2007): 135–169.

86. Oliver Williams "The UN Global Compact: The Challenge and the Promise," *Business Ethics Quarterly* 14 (4) (2004): 755–774.

87. For a discussion of the Compact and its context, see John Gerard Ruggie, "Taking Embedded Liberalism Global: the Corporate Connection," in *Taming Globalization*, 93–129. See also Andrew Kuper "Harnessing Corporate Power: Lessons from the UN Global Compact," *Development* 47 (3) (2004): 9–19.

88. Peter Utting "The Global Compact and Civil Society: Averting a Collision Course," *Development in Practice* 12 (November 2002): 644.

89. Ibid., 645.

90. Ibid., 645–646.

91. The author gratefully acknowledges the research assistance of Francis Raven in the preparation of this chapter.

SUGGESTED READING

Beck, Ulrich. *What Is Globalization?* Translated by Patrick Camiller. Cambridge: Polity, 2000.

Bhagwati, Jagdish. *In Defense of Globalization.* New York: Oxford University Press, 2004.

Cavanagh, John, and Jerry Mander, eds. *Alternatives to Economic Globalization: A Better World is Possible.* San Francisco: Berrett-Koehler, 2002.

Cragg, Wesley. *Ethics Codes, Corporations, and the Challenge of Globalization* Cheltenham, U.K.: Edward Elgar, 2005.

Donaldson, Thomas, and Thomas W. Dunfee. *Ties That Bind.* Boston: Harvard Business School Press, 1999.

Friedman, Thomas L. *The Lexus and the Olive Tree.* New York: Farrar, Straus, and Giroux, 1999.

Gould, Carol C. *Globalizing Democracy and Human Rights.* Cambridge: Cambridge University Press, 2004.

Hayward, Tim. *Constitutional Environmental Rights.* Oxford: Oxford University Press, 2005.

Held, David. *Global Covenant.* Cambridge: Polity Press, 2004.

Held, David, and Mathias Koenig-Archibugi. *Taming Globalization: Frontiers of Governance.* Cambridge: Polity Press, 2003.

Kuper, Andrew, ed. *Global Responsibilities: Who Must Deliver on Human Rights?* London: Routledge, 2005.

Pogge, Thomas W. *World Poverty and Human Rights.* Cambridge: Polity Press, 2002.

Sen, Amartya. *Development as Freedom.* New York: Alfred A. Knopf, 2000.

Shue, Henry. *Basic Rights: Subsistence, Affluence, and U.S. Foreign Policy.* Princeton, N.J.: Princeton University Press, 1980; 2nd ed., 1996.

Singer, Peter. *One World: The Ethics of Globalization.* New Haven, Conn.: Yale University Press, 2002.

Stiglitz, Joseph E. *Globalization and its Discontents.* New York: W. W. Norton, 2002.

WEB SITES

Global Policy Forum, http://www.globalpolicy.org/.

United Nations Global Compact, http://www.unglobalcompact.org/.

UN Millennium Goals, http://www.un.org/millenniumgoals/.

World Social Forum, http://www.forumsocialmundial.org.br/index.php?cd_language=2&id_menu=.

PART V

THE USE AND PROTECTION OF INFORMATION

CHAPTER 11

DECEPTION AND INFORMATION DISCLOSURE IN BUSINESS AND PROFESSIONAL ETHICS

THOMAS L. CARSON

Business people and members of other professions frequently face moral questions about deception and about their obligations to disclose information. Few, if any, moral questions have greater bearing on the conduct of everyday business and professional practice.

This chapter (which consists of seven sections) addresses these issues. Section 1 defends a definition of deception and the related concepts of lying and withholding information. Section 2 defends a version of the Golden Rule. In section 3, I argue that my version of the Golden Rule provides a strong moral presumption against deception. I rely on this version of the Golden Rule (and the presumption against deception that it establishes) in my arguments about the moral questions addressed in sections 4–7. I attempt to make my arguments independent of appeals to disputed moral intuitions and controversial assumptions in ethical theory, for example, assumptions about the truth or falsity of utilitarianism. Section 4 defends a theory about the duties of salespeople and analyzes several cases of deception and withholding information in sales. Sections 5 and 6 discuss deception in advertising and bluffing and deception in negotiations. I argue that deceptive advertising is wrong. I also argue that lying and deception in negotiations can sometimes be justified on the grounds of "self-defense." Section 7 discusses the fiduciary obligations of professionals to act for the benefit of their clients. Professionals and business people have the duty not to lie to or deceive their clients. Those who have fiduciary duties to clients also have positive duties to answer clients' questions and to offer them relevant information that their clients need to pursue their interests. Even those who do not have fiduciary obligations have substantial obligations to provide information to customers or clients—it is not enough for them to refrain from lying and deception.

DECEPTION AND RELATED CONCEPTS

As a first approximation, we might say that to deceive someone is to cause her to have false beliefs. *The New Shorter Oxford English Dictionary* defines the verb "deceive" as "cause to believe what is false."[1]

Deception

This definition is too broad because not all cases of causing another person to have false beliefs constitute deception. If a perfectly clear and truthful statement is misinterpreted by others and causes them to have false beliefs, it is not necessarily a case of deception. An automobile salesperson does not necessarily deceive her customers if her clear and accurate description of a car, which includes the claim that the car has side and front air bags, causes a buyer to believe falsely that the car is safe in case of high-speed collisions with large vehicles. Deception requires an intention to cause others to have false beliefs.

To deceive someone, then, is to intentionally cause her to have false beliefs. However, this statement is ambiguous. It is not deception if I intentionally cause you to believe that X where X is false but I myself believe that X is true. We might say that in order for there to be deception it is necessary that the deceiver believes that what she causes the other person(s) to believe is false. Consider this definition of deception:

> D1. A person S deceives another person S1 if, and only if, S intentionally causes S1 to believe X, where X is false and S believes that X is false.

This definition is closer to the mark than the previous definition, but several questions remain. What if I intentionally cause you to believe X where X is false, and I neither believe that X is true nor believe that X is false? For example, suppose that I want you to believe X where X is false, and I have not given any thought to the question of whether X is true or false. Such statements are characteristic of bullshit.[2] To make this more concrete, suppose that a representative of a construction firm makes false claims about the features of his firm's buildings but has no idea whether what he claims is true or false. The client trusts him and believes this claim on the basis of what the representative says. If we want to count this as a case of deception, we should reject D1 in favor of something like the following:

> D2. A person S deceives another person S1 if, and only if, S intentionally causes S1 to believe X, where X is false and S does not believe that X is true.

Clearly, D1 gives sufficient conditions for deception. A person who intentionally causes another person to believe X, where X is false, and she knows or believes that X is false has clearly deceived the other person. A modified version of D2 gives necessary conditions for deception; a necessary condition of my deceiving you is that I intentionally cause you to believe something false that I do not believe to be true. Ordinary language does not give us a clear basis for choosing between D1 and D2. The kinds of cases in which D1 and D2 give conflicting results are borderline for the concept of deception. Rather than claim that one of the definitions is the correct account of deception (or is closer to being correct than the other), we should simply say that there are broader and narrower concepts of deception.

Deception vs. Withholding Information and Keeping Someone in the Dark

There is a clear distinction between the concept of withholding information and the concept of deception (or attempted deception). To withhold information is to fail to offer information that would help someone acquire true beliefs or correct false beliefs. Not all cases of withholding information constitute deception. A businessperson who withholds from his clients information about how much a product he is selling costs him does not thereby deceive (or attempt to deceive) them about his costs. However, withholding information can constitute deception if there is a clear expectation, promise, and/or professional obligation that such information will be provided. If a tax adviser is aware of a legitimate tax exemption her client can claim that would allow the client to achieve a considerable tax savings, then her failure to inform the client about it constitutes deception. She thereby intentionally causes her client to believe falsely that there is no way for him to save more money on his taxes.

Cases in which we try to prevent people from discovering the truth raise interesting questions about the concept of deception. Consider cases in which someone tries to prevent another person from learning something she does not want him to know by distracting his attention. Suppose that we are trying to close a business deal, and you are reading the contract that describes the terms of a loan I am offering you. I do not want you to read it carefully since I fear that you will be distressed by provisions that call for you to surrender collateral in case of default. You begin to read the contract, but I distract you from doing this by discussing the fortunes of our favorite baseball team or engaging you in a political argument. Since you have only a limited amount of time to look at the contract, you do not read it carefully.

You know that there are penalties in case of default, but your true beliefs about this are vague and incomplete. In this case, I have prevented you from gaining certain information. However, I have not caused you to acquire any false beliefs and, therefore, I have not deceived you about anything. Preventing someone from learning the truth about X is not the same as causing her to have false beliefs about X (deceiving her about X).

We need a term other than "deception" to describe many cases of preventing others from learning the truth. The English expression that most closely describes this is "keeping someone in the dark." Intentionally and actively preventing someone from learning something counts as keeping him or her in the dark. Sometimes withholding information or failing to correct someone's false beliefs counts as keeping someone in the dark. A lawyer keeps her client in the dark if she fails to inform him that a certain course of action she is advising him to take is likely to result in his being the subject of a lawsuit. However, not every case of failing to correct another person's false beliefs or remove his ignorance about something one knows about counts as "keeping someone in the dark." I am not, for example, keeping my neighbor in the dark if I fail to inform her about my past membership in the Cub Scouts.

Lying

Lying differs from deception in two important respects. First, unlike deception, lying requires that one use language to make statements. One can deceive another person without making a statement. For example, if my painting over the rust on a used car causes you to believe that the car body is free of rust, then I have deceived you about the condition of the car without saying anything. Second, unlike "lying," the word "deception" connotes success. An act must actually cause someone to have false beliefs if it is to count as a case of deception. Many lies are not believed and do not succeed in deceiving anyone.

There is disagreement about whether a lie must be a false statement. My linguistic intuitions suggest to me that a lie must be a false statement, but since many philosophers (and at least some dictionary definitions of lying) challenge this view,[3] I will not insist on it. A noncontroversial starting point for defining lying is this: if a statement is to count as a lie, the speaker cannot believe that it is true. Suppose that I say something false that causes you to have false beliefs. This statement cannot be a lie if I believe that what I am saying is true. Showing that one believes that what one says is true is sufficient to rebut the claim that one has told a lie. In order for a statement to constitute a lie, there must be an inconsistency between what one says and what one believes. It is not clear exactly how we should formulate this condition. We might say that in order to tell a lie one must make a statement that one believes to be false. Alternatively, we could say that one must make a statement that one does not believe to be true. The difference between these two ways of stating the condition mirrors the difference between D1 and D2. This condition is necessary for lying, but it is not sufficient. Making a statement or false statement that one believes to be false (or does not believe to be true) for the sake of humor or irony is not necessarily a case of lying. For example, suppose that I badly botch an attempt to decorate a cake and my wife says, "That looks beautiful," when we both know that the cake looks awful. Clearly some additional condition(s) is (are) required for lying. The standard view of lying holds that this additional condition is that the statement must be made with the intention of deceiving others. The reason that intentionally false humorous statements are not lies is that it they are not intended to deceive others. This leaves us with the choice between the following two definitions of lying:

> L1. To lie is to make a false statement that one does not believe to be true (or, alternatively, that one believes to be false) with the intention of causing others to have false beliefs.
>
> L2. To lie is to make a statement that one does not believe to be true (or, alternatively, that one believes to be false) with the intention of causing others to have false beliefs.

Similar definitions can be found in dictionaries and have been defended by a number of philosophers.[4]

L1 and L2 seem fairly close to the mark.[5]

The cases and issues discussed in sections 4–7 involve cases of deception, lying, and withholding information. The preceding discussion will enable us to classify these actions accurately before trying to assess them morally.

A PROOF OF THE GOLDEN RULE

For the purposes of addressing the moral questions and cases discussed in sections 4–7, I will also appeal to a version of the Golden Rule that can be proven on the basis of relatively uncontroversial assumptions.

The Proof

1. Consistency requires that I judge acts done to me in the same way I judge acts done to others, unless the acts differ in some morally relevant respect.
2. Consistency requires that our attitudes must be consistent with our moral judgments. Among other things, this means that if I think that it is morally permissible for someone to do something to me, then I must not object to her doing it to me.
   Therefore:
3. GR. Consistency requires that if I think it would be morally permissible for someone to do a certain act to another person, then I must not object to someone doing the same act to me in relevantly similar circumstances. (I am inconsistent if I think that it would be morally permissible for someone to do X, but still object to someone doing X to me in (what I recognize are)

relevantly similar circumstances.)[6] This argument is valid, and both premises are true.

Defense of Premise 1

Premise 1 is a narrower version of the universalizability principle and follows from the universalizability principle. The universalizability principle can be stated as follows:

> If one makes a moral judgment about a particular case, then one must make the same moral judgment about any similar case, unless there is a morally relevant difference between the cases.[7]

Universalizability *is* a feature of our conventional moral concepts. When using conventional moral concepts, any moral judgment we make commits us to making the same judgment about relevantly similar cases. Statements of the following sort are self-contradictory:

> Act *A* is morally permissible. Act *B* is exactly like *A* in all morally relevant respects; however, *B* is not morally permissible.

Defense of Premise 2

Premise 2 says that if I say that it is morally permissible for you to do something, I cannot object to your doing it. My thinking that it is morally permissible for you to beat me at chess does not commit me to desiring that you beat me, nor does it commit me to playing so as to allow you to beat me. If I think it is permissible for you to beat me at chess, then I cannot object to your beating me or resent you for beating me.[8] Of course, it is consistent to object to actions that one takes to be morally permissible on the grounds that they are rude, imprudent, uncool, unfashionable, or produce something ugly. However, one cannot consistently claim that one was *wronged* by an action that one takes to be morally permissible, nor can one consistently resent others or hold that they should feel guilty for doing something that one takes to be morally permissible.

CONSISTENCY ARGUMENTS AND THE MORAL PRESUMPTION AGAINST LYING AND DECEPTION

The Golden Rule implies that if I claim that it is permissible for someone to do something to another person, then, on pain of inconsistency, I cannot object if someone else does the same thing to me in relevantly similar circumstances.

The Force of Golden Rule Arguments

The force of this version of the Golden Rule derives from the fact that since we *do object* to other people doing certain things to us we cannot consistently say that it would be morally permissible for us to do these same things to them in relevantly similar circumstances.

Suppose that I judge that it would be morally right for me to do X but object when someone else does X to me or to someone I care about in relevantly similar circumstances. My judgment about my doing X is inconsistent with my attitudes about relevantly similar cases. To be consistent, I must either (1) change my moral judgments, or (2) change my attitudes about the actions in question.

Consider this example: I am a plumber and often lie to my customers. I claim that they need expensive repairs when they do not. I claim that it is morally right for me to do this. Yet, I object very strongly when I discover that my auto mechanic lies to me and claims that I need a $2,000 engine overhaul when all that I need is a tune-up that normally costs $200. On the face of it, there is no morally relevant difference between what I do and what my mechanic does. To be consistent, I must either (1) change my moral judgment about my own lying and say that it is wrong for me to lie to my customers, or (2) change my *judgment and attitudes* about what the mechanic does to me, and hold that his lying to me about my engine is morally permissible and no longer resent it or object to it. The first alternative (1) imposes other consistency demands on me. If I judge that it is wrong for me to lie to my customers, then I am inconsistent if I continue to lie to them; my lying to my customers is inconsistent with the belief that it is wrong for me to lie to them.

Here, many, perhaps most, of us will want to say that (1), *not* (2), is the appropriate response. An appeal to consistency *alone* cannot show this. The real force and power of Golden Rule arguments consist in the fact that often responses of type (2) are not a serious option. There are some things we cannot honestly consent to being done to us because of our concern for our own welfare. The present example is such a case. Since most of us do not consent and *cannot* consent to being lied to and harmed in this way because of our concern for our own interests, we cannot consistently hold that it is morally right for anyone to tell such lies. Our concern for the welfare of others also lends force to consistency arguments. I object to your defrauding my mother, and, therefore, I cannot claim that it is permissible for anyone to perform relevantly similar actions.

The Presumption against Lying and Deception

We object when others deceive us or lie to us because we object to *being harmed* in the way that those who are lied to or deceived are typically harmed (however, we also may object for reasons other than being harmed). In addition, we object when our loved ones and those we care about are harmed by lying and deception. We are often harmed when we are deceived because we cannot effectively pursue our ends and interests if we act on the basis of false beliefs. Of course, someone could be deceived about matters that are not relevant to any of her concerns or decisions. I am not harmed if someone deceives me about matters relating to the price of goats in Ethiopia during the sixteenth century. One might even benefit as a result of being deceived. For example, suppose that you lie to me by claiming that a particular stock was highly rated in the latest issue of an investment magazine. I believe you and, on the strength of what you tell me, purchase some of the stock, and its value increases many times over within a few weeks. Ordinarily, when we lie or attempt to deceive others, we do so in order to influence their attitudes or behavior. So, when we deceive others we generally deceive them about matters of interest and concern to *them*, and we try to influence them to do things or have attitudes that they would not do or have if they were not deceived; and thus ordinarily we *harm* them. This point is illustrated in many of the examples presented below in sections 4–7.

All people can be harmed by lying and deception. Lying and deception also have indirect bad consequences, such as diminishing the agent's own honesty and undermining trust between people. My Golden Rule arguments against lying and deception appeal to the fact that we object to being harmed (and object to those we care about being harmed) by the lying or deception of others. Many of us also object to people causing indirect harm by lying and deception. These arguments establish a strong presumption for thinking that lying and deception are morally wrong.

My version of the Golden Rule clearly allows for exceptions to rules against lying and deception. It is difficult to see how someone could be consistent in *always* objecting to lying or deception by others when it is necessary in order to save her life or the lives of her loved ones. Thus, my version of the Golden Rule also gives us an argument against the absolute prohibition against lying and deception.

My Golden Rule arguments about lying and deception show that, with some exceptions, it is wrong to lie or deceive others in ways that harm them. My arguments leave open whether lying and deception are wrong when they do not harm others or produce bad consequences.[9] My view has the virtue of not presupposing either the truth or the falsity of utilitarianism.

DECEPTION AND WITHHOLDING INFORMATION IN SALES

I state my view about the moral duties of salespeople in the first part of this section and defend it by appeal to my version of the Golden Rule in the second part. In the third and fourth parts, I analyze cases of deception and withholding information in sales.

The Obligations of Salespeople

Salespeople have the following moral duties regarding the disclosure of information when dealing with *rational adult consumers*:[10]

1. Salespeople should provide buyers with safety warnings and precautions about the goods and services they sell. Sometimes it is enough for salespeople to call attention to written warnings and precautions that come with goods and services. These warnings are unnecessary if it is clear the buyers already understand the dangers or precautions in question.[11]

2. Salespeople should refrain from lying and deceiving in their dealings with customers.

3. As much as their knowledge and time constraints permit, salespeople should fully answer customers' questions about the products and services they sell.[12] They should answer questions forthrightly and not evade questions or withhold information that has been asked for (even if this makes it less likely that they will make a successful sale). Salespeople are obligated to answer questions about the goods and services they themselves sell. However, they are not obligated to answer questions about competing goods and services or give information about other sellers, for example, the price that something sells for at other stores. In such cases, the salesperson should refuse to answer the question, not evade it or pretend to answer it. Similarly, salespeople should be candid about their own areas of ignorance. They should not answer or pretend to answer questions that require knowledge that they lack. If, for whatever reasons, a salesperson cannot or will not give a complete answer to a question, she should make this clear and not pretend that she has fully answered the question.

4. Salespeople should not try to "steer" customers toward purchases that they have reason to think will cause harm to customers without a compensating benefit or have reason to believe that customers will come to regret deeply. (Any means by which one tries to cause another person to purchase a particular good or service counts as "steering" him toward purchasing it.)

Duties 1–4 are prima facie duties that can conflict with other duties and are sometimes overridden by other duties. In calling these prima facie duties I am not claiming that they are ultimate, indefeasible moral obligations of the sort that Ross posits in his moral theory (see note 9). I am merely claiming that, *in ordinary circumstances*, salespeople have a moral obligation to fulfill them in the absence of weighty conflicting moral obligations.

Duties 1–4 constitute a minimal list of the duties of salespeople concerning the disclosure of information. I am inclined to think that the following are also prima facie duties of salespeople, but I am less confident that these principles can be justified:

5. Salespeople should not sell customers goods or services they have reason to think will be harmful to customers (financial harm counts) or that the customers will come to regret later, without giving the customers their reasons for thinking that this is the case.

6. Salespeople should not sell items they know to be defective or of poor quality without alerting customers to this.

Justification of Duties 1–4

Any rational and consistent moral judge who makes judgments about the moral obligations of salespeople must accept 1–4 as prima facie duties.

Duty 1. All of us have reason to fear the hazards in the world about us; we depend on others to warn us of hazards. Few people would survive to adulthood were it not for the warnings of others about such things as oncoming cars, live electric wires, approaching tornadoes, and electrified rails. No one who values her own life and health can say that she does not object to others failing to warn her of the dangers of products they sell her. Consider this: Your child or loved one is about to cross a busy street and is unaware of the dangers involved. A stranger standing by understands the dangerousness of the situation but makes no attempt to warn your loved one, who crosses the street and is seriously injured.

Duty 2. Like everyone else, a salesperson needs correct information in order to act effectively to achieve her goals and advance her interests. She objects to others deceiving her or lying to her about matters relevant to her decisions in the marketplace in order to enrich themselves.

Duty 3. All salespeople represent themselves as sources of information and as people to whom questions should be addressed. (People who do not represent themselves as available to answer questions about what is being sold are not salespeople.) It is dishonest for salespeople to misrepresent their role to customers. Salespeople have questions about the goods and services they themselves buy. They object to others who represent themselves as being available to answer questions evading or refusing to answer *their* questions. Duty 3 permits salespeople to refuse to answer questions that would force them to provide information about their competitors. Why not say instead that salespeople are obligated to answer *all questions* that customers ask? The answer is that we cannot consistently say this if we consider the full context of sales, especially the position of the salesperson's employer. A salesperson's actions affect both her customers and her employer. In applying the Golden Rule to this issue she cannot simply consider the position of the customers. Duty 3 takes into account the interests of customers, the salesperson, and her employer. We can and must recognize the legitimacy of employers' demands for loyalty. The role of being an advocate or agent for someone who is selling things is legitimate within certain limits. Duty 3 can probably be improved upon, but it is a decent first approximation. Explicit promises or disclaimers could expand or narrow the scope of Duty 3.

Duty 4. All of us are capable of being manipulated by others into doing things that harm us, especially in cases in which others are more knowledgeable than we are. We object to others manipulating us into doing things that significantly harm us whenever doing so is to their own advantage.

Salespeople who claim that it is permissible to make it a policy to deceive customers—fail to warn them about dangers, evade their questions, or manipulate them into doing things that are harmful to them whenever doing so is advantageous for them—are inconsistent because they (the salespeople) object to others doing the same to them (or their loved ones). They must allow that 1–4 are prima facie moral duties.

The Golden Rule and the theory of moral reasoning defended in section 2 above can account for cases in which duties 1–4 are overridden by other more important duties. For example, we would be willing to have other people violate 1–4 if doing so were necessary in order to save the life of an innocent person. In practice, violating 1, 2, 3, or 4 is permissible only in very rare cases. The financial interests of salespeople seldom justify violations of 1, 2, 3, or 4. The fact that a salesperson can make more money by violating 1, 2, 3, or 4 would not justify her in violating 1, 2, 3 or 4 unless she has very pressing financial obligations that she cannot meet otherwise.

Often salespeople need to meet certain minimum sales quotas to avoid being fired.[13] Suppose that a salesperson needs to make it a policy to violate 1–4 in order to meet her sales quotas and keep her job. Would this justify her in violating 1–4? *Possibly.* But, in order for this to be the case, the following conditions would have to be met: (1) she has important moral obligations such as feeding and housing her family that require her to be employed (needing money to keep one's family in an expensive house or take them to Disneyworld does not justify violating 1–4), (2) the harm that she causes her customers is not so great as to outweigh the benefits that she and her family derive from her violations of 1–4, and (3) she cannot find another job that would enable her to meet her obligations without violating 1–4 (or other equally important duties). Those salespeople who cannot keep their jobs or make an adequate income without violating 1–4 should seek other lines of employment.

Any proposed justification for violating 1–4 in order to fulfill another more important conflicting obligation must be subjected to Golden Rule consistency tests. One must ask if one objects to this being done to oneself in hypothetical cases in which the positions are reversed. We also need to imagine ourselves in the positions of the parties to whom the other conflicting obligations are owed. If done honestly, such tests will limit illegitimate justifications for violations of 1–4. But it seems likely that reasonable people will sometimes disagree about the importance of conflicting duties, and in such cases it is unclear that there is any ultimate moral truth about the matter that we can know or discover—at least my version of the Golden Rule does not enable us to find it.

This is not as troubling as it seems, since salespeople's duties to make sales for their employers do not conflict with 1–4 (see below). Duties 1–4 are duties that salespeople have to customers. Salespeople also have duties to their employers. Salespeople who work for employers arguably have a prima facie duty to serve the interests of their employers. However, this duty is not a prima facie duty to do anything whatever that promotes the interests of the employer. Rather, it is a prima facie duty to promote the interests of the employer within certain limits, while respecting other moral and legal duties (including 1–4). By the same token, one cannot create a prima facie duty to do something that is morally wrong by promising to do it. Promising to murder someone does not give one a prima facie duty to kill the person. This has important implications for our understanding of the duties of salespeople. Consider a case in which a salesperson can make a sale (and thereby promote the interests of her employer) only if she deceives her customers. We should *not* count this as a case in which a salesperson has a conflict between her duty not to deceive customers and her duty to benefit her employer. She has a duty to act for the benefit of her employer *only within* the constraints of other moral and legal duties such as the duty not to deceive customers.

The Justification of Duties 5–6

I would like to claim that duties 5–6 are also prima facie duties of salespeople, but I am not sure that 5–6 can be justified by appeal to the version of the Golden Rule defended in section 2. I object to salespeople violating 5–6. However, it would seem to be *possible* for a rational person to be consistent in holding that it is permissible for salespeople not to follow 5–6. Suppose that someone endorses a kind of "rugged individualism." She believes that competent adults should be self-reliant and, as much as possible, make their own decisions without asking for the help and advice of others. It is questionable whether those who hold this sort of view adequately consider and represent to themselves the position of people who are vulnerable, ill-informed, or unintelligent. However, without further argument that I will not provide here, this does not show that the views of those who reject 5 and 6 are inconsistent or unreasonable.

Cases of Deception in Sales

Consider the following three cases of deception in sales.

Case 1. (Actual Case.) The sales tactics of the Holland Furnace Company. I quote from Christopher Stone's description of this case:

> Holland, with gross annual sales of approximately $30 million, was the only home heating equipment manufacturer that sold through its own salesmen direct from the factory. A Holland salesman would make his way into a house by claiming himself to be an inspector from the gas company or the city, or claim he was making a "survey" of furnaces. Once inside, he would use his ostensible authority to dismantle the furnace, then flatly refuse to reassemble it on the grounds that to do so would involve grave dangers of an explosion. If the furnace was that of a Holland competitor, the salesman would inform the homeowner that it had passed its useful life, was not worth the expense involved in repairing it, or that the manufacturer had "gone out of business" and necessary replacement parts were unattainable. At this moment, though, the solution presented itself miraculously at the door: A Holland furnace man (the "inspector's" buddy who had been waiting around the corner) rang the bell and made the sale.[14]

Case 2. A used car salesperson is trying to sell a car on which the odometer has been turned back. A prospective customer asks whether the odometer reading on the car is correct. The salesperson replies by saying that it is illegal to alter odometer readings.[15]

Case 3. The director of admissions for a private university that desperately wants to increase its enrollments speaks to a group of prospective undergraduate students and their parents. She extols the virtues of her university. A parent who is concerned about the extent to which courses are taught by part-time faculty and graduate students raises this issue. The admissions director replies that 90 percent of the courses taught at the university are taught by full-time faculty. In fact, she knows that the following is the case: only 70 percent of all the class sections in the university are taught by full-time faculty members, and the course sections counted in this 70 percent figure include graduate courses and courses in the law school and medical school. Only 50 percent of the undergraduate course sections are taught by full-time faculty and, excluding small upper-division courses, the figure is 25 percent. In freshman-level courses, only 15 percent of students are taught by full-time faculty members.

Cases 1 and 3 involve lying; case 2 involves deception (or attempted deception) without lying. There is a strong moral presumption against deception in sales because of the harm it is likely to cause potential buyers. Such deception is likely to harm buyers by causing them to have false beliefs about the nature of the products in question and thereby cause some consumers to make different purchasing decisions than they would have otherwise made. In case 1, those who are deceived by this fraud are likely to be greatly harmed. Those who allow their furnace to be disassembled will need to either purchase a new furnace that they do not need, or else pay someone to reassemble the furnace. In addition, they are likely to be harmed by the inconvenience of not having a working furnace for a period of time. Suppose that in case 2 the salesperson's deceptive statements cause someone to believe that the car's mileage is 50,000 when, in fact, it is 97,000. Acting on this belief, she purchases the car for a certain price. It is likely that she would have been unwilling to purchase the car for the same price if she had known the true mileage. She might not have been willing to purchase the car at all in that case. The deception in case 3 is potentially very harmful to the student and his family. The decisions in question are very important and involve very large amounts of money (tens of thousands of dollars). This is a very serious case of fraud. It is difficult to imagine even remotely likely circumstances in which the admissions director's actions would be morally permissible.

It is *not* above and beyond the call of duty for salespeople to refrain from lying and deception, even when that means forgoing opportunities to make more money. The legitimate pursuit of one's own self-interest and the interests of one's employer are constrained by rules against lying and deception. Many of our attitudes about actual and hypothetical cases are inconsistent with the view that it is permissible for salespeople to lie or deceive others in order to promote their own interests or those of their employers. We strongly object to this being done to us or our loved ones.

What about cases in which a person benefits by being deceived? It is possible that some of the people who purchased Holland furnaces actually owned very dangerous furnaces. They likely benefited as a result of being deceived by the Holland salespeople: this deception may have even saved their lives. It is also easy to imagine how the customers in cases like 2 and 3 might have benefited as a result of being deceived. Should we say that there is nothing morally wrong with deception in such cases?

Here, it must be noted that the Holland salespeople had no reason to think that they were helping the people in question—they had reason to think that they were harming them. It is much more likely that they were causing serious safety problems by disassembling people's furnaces. We could say that this action was wrong because its expected or likely consequences were very bad. Alternatively, we could say that deceiving the person who benefits is a morally right, yet blameworthy, action.[16] In any case, from the point of view of an agent deciding what to do, such considerations are irrelevant and give no justification whatever for deceptive practices in sales. From the prospective point of view, the fact that there is a remote possibility that a certain action that is very likely to harm others might actually help them instead is no justification for doing it. Similarly, the fact that it is remotely possible that driving while intoxicated might benefit others (one's erratic driving might frighten a motorist who is nodding off to sleep and cause her to pull of the road) is no justification whatever for choosing to drive while intoxicated.

What about cases in which deceptive sales practices are likely to benefit others? Consider the following case.

Case 4. A tire salesperson exaggerates the risks of driving on inexpensive tires and thereby deceives a customer and manipulates her into purchasing a higher grade of tires than she intended to buy. He claims that his actions are justified because the customer is better off with the more expensive tires. Very conveniently, this deception also benefits him by earning him a higher commission on the sale. To claim to know better than a well-informed customer what is in the customer's best interests is presumptuous. Whether or not a purchase will benefit someone depends on facts about his personal situation, including his finances, that salespeople are seldom privy to. If the more expensive tires are really better for the customer, then the salesperson ought to be able to persuade her of this without resorting to deception. No doubt, there are cases in which this kind of paternalistic or allegedly paternalistic deception helps others; however, there are still reasons to think that paternalistic deception by salespeople is a harmful *practice.* It is harmful, in part, because it tempts one to deceive oneself about what is really in the best interests of customers in order to promote one's own self-interest. In cases in which paternalistic deception actually benefits people, my consistency arguments cannot show that this deception is wrong. Inasmuch as it seems possible to be consistent in condoning or condemning such actions, my view leaves this issue open. Ostensibly rational, consistent, and informed political philosophers disagree strongly about questions of paternalism— my version of the Golden Rule does not help to resolve this issue.

Cases of Withholding Information in Sales

Case 1. Health Insurance. (True story) I once received a one-year fellowship from the National Endowment for the Humanities. The fellowship paid for my salary but not my fringe benefits. I had the option of continuing my health insurance through the university if I paid for the premiums out of my own pocket, but the premiums seemed very high. I went to the office of Prudential Insurance agent Mr. A. O. "Ed" Mokarem. I told him that I was looking for a one-year medical insurance policy to cover me during the period of the fellowship, and that I planned to resume my university policy when I returned to teaching. He showed me a comparable Prudential policy that cost about half as much as the university's policy and explained it to me. He then told me that there was a potential problem I should consider. He said roughly the following:

> You will want to return to your free university policy next year when you return to teaching. The Prudential policy is a one-year terminal policy. If you develop any serious medical problems during the next year, Prudential will probably consider you "uninsurable" and will not be willing to sell you health insurance in the future. If you buy the Prudential policy, you may encounter the same problems with your university policy. Since you will be dropping this policy *voluntarily*, they will have the right to underwrite your application for re-enrollment. If you develop a serious health problem during the next year, their underwriting decision could be "Total Rejection," imposing some waivers and/or exclusions, or (at best) subjecting your coverage to the "pre-existing conditions clause," which would not cover any pre-existing conditions until you have been covered under the new policy for at least a year.

If I left my current health insurance for a year, I risked developing a costly medical condition for which no one would be willing to insure me. That would have been a foolish risk to take. So, I thanked him and renewed my health insurance coverage through the university.

I have discussed this case with numerous classes through the years. Most of my students regard Mr. Mokarem's actions as supererogatory or above and beyond the call of duty. Many of them endorse the following argument:

> The potential buyer should have asked about (or known about) the possibility of being turned down for medical insurance on account of pre-existing health problems. The buyer was foolish and imprudent.

Therefore,

> In this case the insurance agent had no duty to inform the buyer of the potential harm the buyer might suffer, even though it is likely that the buyer would have been seriously harmed by his purchase. The fault or blame for this harm would lie with the *buyer*, not the insurance agent.

This argument presupposes something like the following principle:

> If a person is about to harm himself through his own foolishness and rashness, others are not obligated to warn him about the harm he is likely to suffer.[17]

On examination, this principle is untenable. We are sometimes obligated to warn other people about potential harms they might suffer as the result of their own folly. For example, suppose that a drunken man wanders out onto a subway track.

He is careful to avoid oncoming trains, but he is unaware of the fact that the third rail will electrocute him if he touches it. Onlookers would be obligated to warn him about the dangers posed by the third rail. When we reflect that we and those we love and care for often do rash and foolish things, the principle in question seems even harder to consistently endorse. Some of my students also endorse the following view: "If the buyer is so stupid as to believe what he is told then he deserves what happens to him." On this view, it is morally permissible to take advantage of people who are imprudent, foolish, unintelligent, or naive. On reflection, almost no one can consistently endorse this view, since people one loves and cares for (including one's future and past self, one's descendants, and one's elderly friends and relatives) are, or might be, among those who are rash, imprudent, unintelligent, and/or naive.

If 1–4 are a salesperson's only duties concerning the disclosure of information, then Mr. Mokarem was not obligated to inform me as he did. In this case, the information in question was information about a *competing product*—the university's health insurance policy. If 5 is a prima facie duty of salespeople, then (assuming that he had no conflicting moral duties of greater or equal importance) it was his duty, all things considered, to inform me as he did. This case illustrates part of what is at stake in the question of whether 5 is a prima facie duty of salespeople.

Case 2. Steering Customers. Suppose that I am a salesperson in a large hardware store. A customer wants to purchase a propane-driven electrical generator to keep his furnace operating during power outages. We sell a rather inexpensive 1,000-watt generator that is very reliable and runs for a long time without refueling. It will only drive the furnace—not any other electrical appliances—but this is what the customer is seeking, and this model is ideal for his purposes. We also sell a more expensive 6,000-watt generator that is less reliable and does not run for as long a time, but it will run other electrical items in the house. The cheaper model would be much better for his purposes than the more expensive model. Consider the following two versions of this case.

Scenario 1. The customer tells me what he is looking for, and I show him the 6000-watt generator, stressing how many other items in the house this generator will power. He purchases the 6000-watt generator. I do not mention the 1000-watt generator or show it to him, even though it is out on the floor.

Scenario 2. The customer tells me about what he needs. He sees both models on the floor and asks me for a recommendation. I tell him that the 6000-watt model is more reliable and better for his purposes than the cheaper model.

In the first scenario, I violate duties 4 and 5. In the second scenario, I violate duties 2, 4, and 5. In the absence of conflicting obligations that are at least as important as 4 (or 2 and 4), my actions in these two scenarios are wrong.

Golden rule arguments enable us to defend rules 1–4, which give us reasonable guidance for many cases, but they leave open some difficult cases like the case of the insurance salesman. My view leaves open whether 5 and 6 are duties and also leaves open how to weigh 1–4 against conflicting duties. I am not sure that there are determinate knowable answers to these questions, since it seems possible for informed, consistent, and rational people to disagree about these matters.

Deception in Advertising

Deceptive advertising harms people in ways similar to deception in sales and tends to be wrong for similar reasons. Deceptive ads harm consumers by causing them to have false beliefs about the nature of the products being advertised and thereby causing them to make different purchasing decisions than they would have made otherwise. For example, deceptive claims about the features of a truck might cause someone to purchase a truck that is unsuitable for her needs—the ad might claim that the truck is suitable for carrying heavy loads when it is not.

The Harmfulness of Deceptive Advertising: Case Studies

Consumers are harmed if deceptive advertising causes them to spend more money for a brand-name product than a generic brand that performs just as a well. If the products in question are inexpensive, the harm to any given consumer is small, but the aggregate harm to the society as a whole can still be considerable.[18] Ivan Preston claims that ads for Bayer aspirin caused a small harm to a large number of people. Bayer ads claim that "Bayer is the world's best aspirin." According to Preston, these ads deceive many people by causing them to believe falsely that Bayer is better than other brands, when, in fact, there are no significant differences between different brands of aspirin (all aspirin has the same chemical formula). Consumers who are misled by this ad waste their money by spending more for a brand-name product that is chemically indistinguishable from cheaper generic brands. Here, one might object that this claim is mere puffery and is not deceptive. The FTC holds that such statements (bare unsupported claims to the effect that some product is the "best") are meaningless and hence not deceptive. However, empirical studies show that such ads cause roughly 20 percent of people to have false beliefs.[19] Phillip Nelson raises the following objection to these criticisms of the Bayer ads:

> Aspirins do vary in their physical characteristics. Soft aspirins dissolve in the stomach both more rapidly and more certainly than hard aspirins. In consequence, the soft aspirins are better. They are also more expensive to produce.[20]

Nelson grants that there are "non-advertised soft aspirin that sell for less than Bayer."[21] Thus, given the studies to which Preston appeals, it still seems that the Bayer ads are deceptive, because Bayer is not better than other soft aspirin. But, even though Bayer is no better than some cheaper soft aspirin, it is open to debate whether these ads *harm consumers*. As Nelson notes, "the issue is not whether the best unadvertised aspirin is as good as the most heavily advertised aspirin [Bayer]. The issue is whether purchasing one of the more heavily advertised aspirins at random gives one a better product, on average, than getting an unadvertised aspirin at random."[22] Even if we grant Nelson this point, it seems likely that Bayer's ads did harm competing manufacturers of soft aspirin.

Many consumers were harmed by ads for a Sears Kenmore dishwasher that falsely claimed that it could completely clean dishes, pots, and pans "without prior rinsing or scraping" and that its "extra hot final rinse" destroyed all harmful microorganisms.[23] The Sears ads were successful since the Kenmore dishwasher gained an increased market share.[24] Thus the ad harmed Sears competitors.[25] The FTC found that this deception caused a "substantial number" of people to purchase Sears dishwashers.[26] Since they acted on the basis of false claims, many who purchased the Kenmore dishwasher presumably would have preferred not to purchase it had they not been deceived. The harm was considerable, since the dishwashers cost hundreds of dollars. Sears clearly knew that the claims made by these ads were false. Tests that Sears ran indicated that the dishwasher would not clean the dishes unless they were first rinsed and scraped. The owner's manual instructed people to rinse and scrape the dishes prior to putting them in the dishwasher![27] Further, Sears continued to run these ads after its own consumer satisfaction surveys revealed that most purchasers of the dishwasher did not think that the dishwasher performed as advertised.[28] The false claims about killing all microorganisms might have been very harmful to anyone who relied on the dishwasher to sterilize baby bottles or jars for home canning. Sears ran one ad that claimed the final rinse would make baby bottles "hygienically clean."[29]

Finally, Vioxx, an arthritis pain medication, was aggressively marketed by Merck. Gastrointestinal problems are a common side-effect of such drugs. In 2000, Merck completed a large-scale study (VIGOR) involving 8,000 people. Merck hoped to demonstrate that Vioxx was less likely to cause gastrointestinal problems than its competitor Aleve. The VIGOR study supported this claim. However, the study also revealed that Vioxx users thought to be at high risk for heart problems were five times more likely to suffer serious heart damage due to coronary blockages than users of Aleve. Low-dose aspirin is a recommended treatment for such patients, but the aspirin was withheld from the patients for the purposes of the study. The result disturbed scientists at Merck, but they attributed the results not to the harmful effects of Vioxx but to the heart-protective effects of Aleve (they claimed that Aleve had heart-protective effects similar to aspirin). Merck offered this explanation of the VIGOR findings in a 2000 press release. Merck's marketing department attempted to quell concerns among physicians raised by the VIGOR study. It created brochures for salespeople to show physicians. These brochures made very strong claims on the basis of short-term studies of limited scientific value. The brochures claimed that Vioxx patients were eight times less likely to die of strokes and heart attacks, half as likely to die as of heart attacks as people using a placebo, and no more likely to die of heart attacks than users of other anti-inflammatory drugs. At this time, Merck was struggling with the U.S. FDA, which demanded that Merck give stronger warnings of cardiovascular risks for Vioxx. In 2002, Merck sponsored a long-term clinical trial involving 2,600 subjects to test the risks of Vioxx. The study ended abruptly eighteen months later in 2004 when a safety monitoring board found that Vioxx users had a significantly "increased relative risk for confirmed cardiovascular events, such as heart attack and stroke . . . compared to those taking a placebo."[30] Merck withdrew Vioxx from the market and has not reintroduced it.

It is not obvious the people at Merck were guilty of deliberate deception in this case. Those involved may have believed Merck's explanation of the VIGOR results. Some who have examined the case incline toward this view.[31] However, at a minimum, it seems clear that the people at Merck made false and misleading claims about the safety of Vioxx in its brochures for physicians on the basis of flimsy evidence and wishful thinking. Long after there was strong reason to question the safety of Vioxx, these claims, together with Merck's direct marketing to consumers, caused many Vioxx users to be exposed to increased risk of heart attacks and strokes. Many at Merck were aware of the reasons for questioning these claims. In September 2001, Thomas Abrams, head of the FDA's division of Drug Marketing, Advertising, and Communications wrote to Merck saying,

> Although the exact reason for the increased rate of MI's [irreversible heart damage resulting from coronary blockages] observed in the Vioxx treatment group is unknown, your promotional campaign selectively presents the following hypothetical explanation for observed increase in MI's. You assert that Vioxx does not increase the risk of MI's and that the VIGOR finding is consistent with naproxen's [Aleve's] ability to block platelet aggregation like aspirin. That is a possible explanation, but you fail to disclose that your explanation is hypothetical, has not been demonstrated by substantial evidence, and that there is another explanation, namely that Vioxx may have pro-thrombotic properties.[32]

Those at Merck who asserted that the use of Vioxx did not increase people's risk of heart attacks and strokes may have believed what they said. If so, their saying *this* did not constitute lying or attempted deception. However, the Merck marketing campaign to physicians was deceptive in that it invited reliance on the claims that those involved knew were open to serious question and in need of much further support. Inviting confident reliance on claims about such serious matters without revealing the weakness of its evidence and revealing that Merck's account of the VIGOR study was merely an untested hypothesis constitutes deception or attempted deception. It is a case of knowingly and intentionally providing a strong assurance of truth for claims that one knows are open to serious question.

In giving this assurance, the people at Merck intended to cause people to believe falsely that there was little basis for doubting the truth of the claims in question.

A person's true interests are determined by (or most closely approximated by) the decisions she would make were she fully rational and informed. To the extent that an ad causes me to have false beliefs about what I am buying, it has the potential to harm me. When deceptive advertising succeeds and causes people to make purchases that they would not have made if they had not been deceived, it usually harms competing businesses by reducing their sales.

The Wrongness of Deceptive Advertising

Are there any plausible justifications for deceptive advertising that might override the general presumption against harmful deception established in sections 3 and 4?

What about the benefits to the advertiser? Can a company justify deceptive advertising on the grounds that the company and its various stakeholders benefit from it? This is *possible*, but such cases are very rare. In any given case, it is unlikely that the benefits derived by the seller outweigh the harms to other people. Consider a case in which deception provides great benefits to a corporation and its employees and shareholders. A company that is on the verge of bankruptcy might be able to stay in business only by deceiving the public about its products. "Economic necessity" is very rarely, if ever, an adequate moral justification for deceptive practices. A firm that needs to deceive the public about the nature of its goods or services in order to stay in business is of doubtful value to society—the resources it utilizes could be put to better use in some other way. In the normal course of things, the benefit to the advertiser is likely to be counterbalanced by the harm to (honest) competitors and their employees and shareholders, to say nothing about harm to consumers and the social fabric. We should remember that, ordinarily, in such cases the alternative (or an alternative) is a mutually beneficial transaction between the buyer and some other seller who does not deceive the buyer.

Advertisers who practice deception violate the Golden Rule. They themselves are consumers who object to others deceiving them in the marketplace and causing them to base their own economic decisions on false beliefs. They object to being harmed by deception in the marketplace. They also object to their loved ones being harmed by deception. Advertisers want consumers to trust advertising and give credence to the claims of advertising. They cannot be willing to have all advertisers practice deception: if deception in advertising were a universal practice, few people would trust advertising and it would be very difficult to gain an advantage by means of deceptive advertising. Advertisers who practice deception cannot will that all other advertisers follow the same principles that they follow. They want to make a special exception for themselves.

Bluffing and Deception in Negotiations

Business people, professionals, and property owners frequently negotiate over the price and terms of goods and services. It is common, often a matter of course, for people to misstate their bargaining positions during negotiations. I will focus on the following kind of case. I am selling a house and tell a prospective buyer that $350,000 is absolutely the lowest price that I will accept, when I know that I would be willing to accept as little as $320,000 for the house. In this case, I make a deliberate false statement about my intentions and bargaining position.[33] Despite the strong presumption against lying and deception in commercial transactions established by the arguments of sections 3–5, lying and deception in negotiations can sometimes be justified on the ground of "self-defense" if others are engaging in lying or deception and thereby gaining an advantage over one.

The Economics of Bluffing

In business negotiations there is typically a range of possible agreements that each party would be willing to accept rather than reach no agreement at all. For instance, I might be willing to sell my home for as little as $320,000. (I would prefer to sell the house for $320,000 *today*, rather than continue to try to sell the house.)[34] My range of acceptable agreements extends upward without limit; I would be willing to accept any price in excess of $320,000 rather than fail to make the sale today. Suppose that a prospective buyer is willing to spend as much as $335,000 for the house. (She prefers to buy the house for $335,000 today rather than not buy it at all today.) The buyer's range of acceptable agreements presumably extends downward without limit. She would be willing to purchase the house for any price below $335,000. In this case the two bargaining positions overlap and an agreement is possible (today). Unless there is some overlap between the minimum bargaining positions of the two parties, no agreement is possible.

It can sometimes be to one's advantage to deceive others about one's own minimum bargaining position. In the present case, it would be to the seller's advantage to cause the buyer to think that $335,000 is the lowest price that he (the seller) will accept. In this case, the buyer would offer $335,000 for the house, the best possible agreement from the seller's point of view. It would also be to the buyer's advantage to deceive the seller into thinking that he is unable or unwilling to pay more than $320,000 for the house.

Attempting to mislead the other person about one's bargaining position can backfire and prevent a negotiation from reaching a mutually acceptable settlement that both parties would have preferred to no agreement at all. For example, suppose that the seller tells the buyer that he will not accept anything less than $375,000 for the house. If the buyer believes him (or believes that his statement is close to the truth) she will break off the negotiations, since, by hypothesis, she is not willing to pay $375,000 for the house. Unless he knows the other person's bargaining position, a person who misrepresents his own position risks losing the opportunity to reach an acceptable agreement.

Is it Morally Permissible to Misstate One's Negotiating Position?

Ordinarily, it is permissible to withhold information about one's bargaining position. Revealing this information is contrary to one's self-interest and, barring special circumstances, one is not obligated to act contrary to one's self-interest in this way. Even if the other party states her reservation price, one has no duty to do this oneself. Since one has reason to be skeptical of claims made by the other party, it is likely to be disadvantageous for one to report her reservation price candidly in response to the claims that other people make about their reservation price. One is not obligated to reveal one's settlement preferences or answer questions concerning them.

Is it permissible for one to attempt to gain an advantage in a negotiation by making deliberate false statements about one's intentions and reservation price? It is often permissible to misstate one's reservation price when one has good reason to think that one's negotiating partner is doing the same, and, with rare exceptions, it is impermissible to misstate one's reservation price if one does not have good reason to think that the other party is misstating her reservation price.

Whether or not the statements in question are lies (see note 33), they are intended to deceive others and thereby give one an advantage over them in the negotiations. Such statements aim at making others worse off (that is, putting others in a worse negotiating position) and are likely to do so. This is attempted deception that is likely to harm others—there is a presumption that this is morally wrong. However, when others attempt to deceive us and thereby gain an advantage over us, we are often justified in deceiving them in "self-defense." It is prima facie very wrong to use violence or deadly force against another person, but when doing so is necessary to protect ourselves from the violence or deadly force of others, then it is morally permissible. We are consistent in willing that others act to defend themselves against the violence and deception of others. Generalizing the conditions for the justifiable use of violence in self-defense to lying and deception in negotiations yields the following principle of self-defense:

> SD. It is permissible to lie or attempt to deceive others about one's negotiating position provided that (1) one's negotiating partner is doing the same and is likely to harm one thereby, (2) one cannot prevent or substantially mitigate this harm short of lying or attempting to deceive oneself, and (3) the harm one causes the other party does not greatly exceed the harm that one will suffer if one does not lie or attempt to deceive.

We can consistently hold that we and others should follow this and similar moral principles; we do not object to people making it a policy to defend themselves and not allow themselves to be prey for others.

Now let us apply this principle to the example of making deliberate false statements about one's intentions in a negotiation. First, consider a case in which it is clear that the other person is not lying. You and I are negotiating the sale of a house. You do not make any claims about your intentions or negotiating position. You just offer to pay a certain amount for the house. In this case, there is a strong moral presumption against my trying to deceive you by misstating my intentions. Barring unusual circumstances, it would be wrong for me to do this. A mere offer, however low and unrealistic, cannot be a false statement and thus cannot be a lie. Such offers typically are not deceptive either. This shows that one can bluff and engage in the process of aggressively making offers and counteroffers without making false and deceptive claims about one's intentions.

Consider now a case in which it is *clear* that the other person is misstating his intentions. You and I are negotiating the sale of a house. As the negotiations begin, you falsely claim that, because of limitations set by possible lenders, the most you can possibly pay for the house is $300,000. You do this in the hope of pressuring me to accept a low bid. Several minutes later, you offer me considerably more than $300,000 for the house. In this case, it is clear that your initial claim was false and intended to be deceptive, since the change in your offer cannot be attributed to a change in your own preferences during the heat of the negotiations. If this tends to give you an advantage in the negotiations, then (barring strong countervailing considerations) it is permissible for me to misstate my intentions.

Often in negotiations one suspects that the other party is lying or attempting to deceive one but cannot be sure that this is the case. Suppose that you make claims that I strongly suspect are false. I lean toward thinking that it would be wrong for me to lie to or attempt to deceive you. The default position should be not to lie or deceive others. Others disagree; I will not attempt to settle this issue here, and I doubt that my methodology or any other defensible methodology yields a clear answer.

An Objection

One might object that even if something like my self-defense principle (SD) is true and acceptable to rational consistent moral judges, it has very little application to the issue of bluffing in negotiations because its conditions for being justified in making false claims about one's reservation price are seldom satisfied.

Other people's lies and/or misrepresentations in negotiations can hurt one only if one chooses to remain in the negotiations. They cannot hurt one if one refuses to deal with the other person. Therefore, there cannot be cases in which misstating one's own negotiating position or intentions is necessary to avoid being harmed by the other person's misrepresentations of her position—breaking off the negotiations and dealing with someone else is always an option. If successful, the foregoing argument shows that the appeal to "self-defense" will rarely, if ever, justify a person in misrepresenting her own bargaining position.

Replies

1. Sometimes people have no acceptable alternative to negotiating with a particular party. This is often the case in labor negotiations. An employer or labor union that has entered into collective bargaining agreements is required by law to negotiate with a particular union or employer and cannot decide that it will only talk with parties who scrupulously avoid deceptive practices in the negotiations. For either party to refuse to negotiate would be viewed as an "unfair labor practice" by the law; it would constitute a failure to "negotiate in good faith."[35]

2. There are cases in which one can refuse to negotiate with a given party, but only at considerable cost to oneself. Suppose that I am trying to buy a house in a tight real-estate market. You own the only house that I can afford within a reasonable commuting distance to my job. In such cases, it is implausible to maintain that I am obligated to bear the high costs of

refusing to deal with the other person simply in order to avoid deceiving him (or lying to him) in response to *his* deception (or lies). It would be even less plausible to demand that an employee who has very limited options seek other employment rather than negotiate with an employer whose deceptive negotiating tactics are likely to put one at a disadvantage.

3. There are no doubt many cases in which it would be relatively easy for an individual involved in a negotiation to find someone else to deal with. But, given the pervasiveness of the practice of misstating one's settlement preferences, it might still be difficult for that person to find another negotiating partner who he *knows* would not also misstate her own preferences.

A Related Objection

According to my self-defense principle, a person can justify lying or deception only if (1) she has reason to think that the other party is engaging in lying or deception (or attempted deception) and (2) she has reason to think the other party is thereby harming her. However, the two conditions can never both be satisfied. I cannot be harmed by your attempted deception unless I am actually deceived by it, but, in that case, I cannot know that I am being deceived. (I cannot be harmed unless I am deceived, and if I am deceived I cannot know or believe that I am being deceived.) This objection assumes that the only way in which lies or attempted deception can harm me in a negotiation is if they cause me to have false beliefs. However, this is not the case. Attempted deception can pressure one in ways that cause one to reveal one's preferences (e.g., by expressions of emotion in response to pressures created by deception, which can give useful information to the other party). Attempted deception can also create uncertainty or fears that weaken one's resolve and bargaining position, even if one takes those fears to be irrational. Nonetheless, I concede that this objection supports the view that my self-defense principle *seldom* justifies lying or deception in negotiations.

Honesty, Professionals, and the Vulnerability of the Public

Often, professionals and others who have specialized knowledge are in a position to advance their financial interests by means of lying and deception, for example, lying to a client to manipulate her into purchasing unneeded services. This creates very serious ethical problems because often clients cannot verify the truth of what professionals tell them without great difficulty.

The Nature of the Problem

We are often at the mercy of professionals and need to rely on their honesty. Professionals ask their clients to trust their judgment and defer to their expertise. Sometimes they pressure their clients to defer to their judgment. Deception in such cases is particularly objectionable. It is treacherous to ask others to trust that one is acting for their benefit when one is planning to deceive them for one's own personal benefit. Because professionals typically have much more knowledge about the matters concerning which they advise their clients, their clients are very vulnerable to being exploited and defrauded. Here are just a few examples that illustrate this widespread phenomenon.

1. I have a water leak near my bathtub. A self-employed plumber comes to my house to repair the leak. The plumber discovers that the problem is very simple—the faucet needs a new washer. This sort of repair should cost about $100 (including the cost of the service call). However, the plumber is experiencing financial problems. He has no other house calls to make that day. He lies and tells me that the pipes behind the wall in my bathroom are leaking and need to be replaced. He will charge me about $800 for this. In addition, this will require that he destroy part of the wall by the bathtub. It will cost me about $2,000 to repair the wall and replace the tile in the bathroom. Of course, the customer could seek a "second opinion" from another plumber, but getting this opinion will take time and cost money. It will be especially difficult for the customer to do this (and thereby call the plumber's honesty and/or competence into question) if the plumber is an acquaintance or the only plumber in the area.
2. I am a self-employed attorney and am very dissatisfied with my income. A client comes to me seeking my advice as to whether she should file a lawsuit against another person. I know that if the client sues, the case is likely to be very emotionally and financially taxing. The legal precedent is clear and does not favor the plaintiff—the suit is almost certain to fail. However, I lie to my client and say that she has a 95 percent chance of winning the case. She retains my services and after two months the suit is unsuccessful. I present her with a bill for $15,000.

In such cases, professionals have clients at their mercy. This is a very serious problem. Because of the asymmetry of knowledge in such cases, there is often little chance of the professional being caught in a lie. It is difficult for anyone outside of the profession to detect lying by professionals, and many professionals are very reluctant to criticize members of their own profession. Professional organizations are often ineffective in disciplining their members and deterring them from unethical conduct. (For evidence of this in the law and medicine, see Michael Bayles's *Professional Ethics*[36] and Marc Rodwin's *Physician's Conflicts of Interest*.[37])

A *Reader's Digest* study of dishonesty in the auto repair business illustrates this problem. In 1941, two researchers took a 20,000-mile road trip through forty-eight

states. They visited 347 repair shops. They kept the car in perfect condition throughout the trip, but before visiting each shop they simply disconnected the wire from
one of the car's two coils. Then they brought the car in for diagnosis and repair.
Although the problem was minor and obvious, only 37 percent of the mechanics in
these garages reattached the wire for nothing or a nominal charge. The majority—63
percent—"overcharged, lied, invented unnecessary work, or charged for work not
done, for parts not needed, for parts not installed."[38]
      In 1987, *Reader's Digest* repeated this study.

> An automotive writer who drove a perfectly maintained three-year-old car on a
> 10,000 mile [trip]....He...visited 225 garages....Before entering each garage, he
> disconnected one spark plug wire from the engine, a problem that is as simple
> and obvious in a repair shop as an unplugged appliance is at home.[39]

In 56 percent of the cases, "mechanics performed unnecessary work, sold unnecessary parts or charged for repairs not done."[40] One recent estimate of the annual cost
of fraudulent auto repairs in the United States is $40 billion.[41]

Information Disclosure and Professional Obligations

Typically, when professionals work for clients who hire and pay them, they are obligated to act as fiduciaries for the benefit of the clients. Law and medicine are clear
examples of this. These professions have codes of ethics that require their members
to act for the benefit of their clients. Often formal business contracts state fiduciary
obligations in detail. Many other professions, including architecture, financial planning, and social work (to name just a few) also have codes of ethics that explicitly
require professionals to act for the benefit of their clients.[42] The codes for these
three professions also include explicit requirements that professionals be candid
and disclose information that is helpful to clients.[43] Since these codes of ethics are
publicly stated and used to encourage the public to trust and rely on the judgment
and services of members of the profession,[44] professionals have a duty to follow
them. Because professionals claim to have expertise and ask clients to rely on their
advice, the statements that they make in their official capacities are strongly warranted to be true. Because professionals who ask clients to rely on their advice give
a strong assurance of the truth and reliability of what they say, lying and deception
by professionals in these situations is a serious betrayal of trust. We strongly object
to being harmed by the deceptive promises of others who claim to be acting for our
benefit when they are not.
      In professional life there are often difficult cases in which professionals make
claims that they *believe* are true, but they still have serious doubts and reservations
about those claims. Professionals are obligated to be clear in communicating their
doubts and reservations about what they say. It is not enough to say what one
thinks is true and has reason to think is true. Because of the strong default warranty or assurance of truth in such cases, saying something that one believes to be
true but has serious doubts or reservations about, in a context in which what one

says is strongly warranted to be true, aims at deceiving others and often borders on lying.

The role of being an attorney, architect, or financial planner requires not only that one refrain from lying and deception; it requires that one be candid and provide one's clients with relevant information that benefits them. They are obligated to provide clients with such information even if they judge that doing so is likely to persuade the clients not to use their services or use less of their services. This obligation holds for all the many professions that have public codes of ethics requiring members to act for the benefit of clients.

Sometimes individual professionals attempt to secure the trust and reliance of others by implicitly or explicitly promising or assuring others that they are acting on their behalf or for their benefit. Such promises or assurances create the same kinds of fiduciary obligations as formal codes of ethics. Anyone who gives such assurances must deliver on them. It is very wrong to make a pretense of trying to serve the interests of the client or customer if one is not attempting to do so.

Even when no fiduciary duties are involved, it is not enough that professionals refrain from lying and deception. The arguments of section 4 about the duties of salespeople (who typically do not have fiduciary duties to customers) also apply here. At a minimum, members of professions also have the following prima facie duties with regard to disclosing information: the duty to warn others of potential health and safety hazards and the duty to refrain from steering clients or customers toward decisions they have reason to think will be harmful to them. I am not so sure about the duty to answer questions. It would seem to be possible to remove such obligations by explicitly stating that one will not provide information or answer questions. To cut costs, some services might be provided in such a way that the professional who performs the services is in a distant country and unable to communicate with the client. (There seems to be nothing wrong with this in principle.)

CONCLUSION

I have argued that there is a strong moral presumption against deception in business and professional life and have argued for the wrongness of a wide range of deceptive business and professional practices. I have argued that it is wrong for professionals and others to fail to adequately inform those to whom they have fiduciary obligations. Salespeople and other business and professional people who do not have fiduciary obligations to others still have substantial duties to offer information and give warnings. I have defended this by appealing to Golden Rule tests for the permissibility of actions. These results have far-reaching implications for business and professional ethics, because the issues in question arise frequently in most areas of business and professional life.

NOTES

1. *The New Shorter Oxford English Dictionary* (New York: Oxford University Press, 1993). Tom Beauchamp and George Brenkert offered me extensive and helpful criticisms of an earlier (and rather rough) version of this paper. Thanks also to Mark Chakoian, Christina Drogalis, and Nora Carson for helpful comments on earlier versions of this paper. The topics discussed in this paper are discussed at greater length in my book *Lying and Deception: Theory and Practice*, (forthcoming, Oxford University Press). Parts of this chapter are drawn from previously published papers. The first part of the section on sales is a substantially modified and condensed version of material published in my "Deception and Withholding Information in Sales." Two of the sales cases in this section are revised and condensed versions of cases presented in "Deception and Withholding Information in Sales," *Business Ethics Quarterly* 11 (2001): 275–306. The section on negotiations streamlines and revises material that first appeared in my paper "Second Thoughts on Bluffing," *Business Ethics Quarterly* 3 (1993): 317–341.

2. Harry Frankfurt famously claims that the essence of bullshit is unconcern with the truth (how things are) and that the bullshitter is a greater enemy of the truth than the liar (who is concerned with knowing how things are). *On Bullshit* (Princeton, N.J.: Princeton University Press, 2005), 33–34, 47–48, 56–57.

3. For some of the details on this, see my paper "The Definition of Lying," *Nous* 40 (2006): 284–306, in particular, see 284–85 and 305–6.

4. See my paper "The Definition of Lying," 286–87, 303.

5. In "The Definition of Lying," I have argued that there are clear cases of lying that do not involve any intention to deceive others. (I appeal to cases in which one is compelled or enticed to make false statements, cases of lying in which one can benefit by making false statements, even if they do not deceive others, and cases of bald-faced lies in which the liar knows that others know she is lying and therefore has no hope or intention of deceiving them.) My preferred definition of lying is the following:

> L3. A person S tells a lie if (1) S makes a false statement X, (2) S believes that x is false or probably false (or, alternatively, S does not believe that x is true), and (3) S states X in a context in which S thereby warrants the truth of X (i.e., gives an assurance or guarantee of the truth of X).
>
> However, for my purposes in this chapter, nothing turns on whether my definition is preferable to L1 and L2—all three definitions are close enough to the mark for my purposes here.

6. This argument follows Harry Gensler's defense of the Golden Rule in his paper "A Kantian Argument Against Abortion," *Philosophical Studies* 49 (1986): 89–90, but my arguments for the two premises are substantially different from Gensler's.

7. Cf. Harry Gensler, *Formal Ethics* (London: Routlege, 1996), 70. Also see Sidgwick, *The Methods of Ethics* (New York: Dover, 1966), pp. 209, 380.

8. Cf. Gensler, *Formal Ethics*, 63–64.

9. The classic statement of this view is found in W. D. Ross's *The Right and the Good* (Oxford: Oxford University Press, 1930). According to Ross, there is a prima facie duty not to lie. By this he means that not lying is one's actual duty, other things equal; it is permissible to violate this duty only if one has a conflicting obligation of equal or greater importance. Ross claims that there is a prima facie duty not to lie, but he does not claim that there is a prima facie duty not to deceive others.

10. Cases involving children or adults who are not fully rational raise special problems that I will not try to deal with here. There are also questions about whether salespeople can always identify irrational adult consumers.

11. This obligation is limited by the salesperson's knowledge. One has no obligation to warn people of dangers unless one is aware of them oneself. This raises questions about the salesperson's duties to be aware of problems and dangers that I cannot address here.

12. More needs to be said about this than I can say here. Exactly how much time and trouble salespeople should take to answer customers' questions cannot be answered in the abstract; each case must be judged on its own merits. But it is clear that a salesperson's knowledge and time constraints place limits on her obligation to fully answer questions.

13. See Guy Oakes, *The Soul of the Salesman* (Atlantic Highlands, N.J.: Humanities, 1990), 86.

14. Christopher Stone, *Where the Law Ends* (New York: Harper & Row, 1975), 175–176.

15. This case comes from David Holley, "Information Disclosure in Sales," *Journal of Business Ethics* 17 (1998): 631–641.

16. G. E. Moore and some utilitarians seem to say this; see Moore, *Ethics* (Oxford: Oxford University Press, 1965), 77–83.

17. Alternatively, one might appeal to the following principle: "If the buyer is at fault in a case that caused him/her harm, then the seller is not at fault and can't be blamed or faulted for the harm that the buyer suffers." This principle is untenable since it is at least *possible* that both the buyer and seller are at fault.

18. See Ivan Preston, *The Tangled Web They Weave: Truth, Falsity, and Advertisers* (Madison: University of Wisconsin Press, 1994), 177.

19. See Preston, *Tangled Web*, 80–81.

20. Phillip Nelson, "Advertising and Ethics," in *Ethics, Free Enterprise, and Public Policy: Original Essays on Moral Issues in Business*, ed. R. T. De George and J. A. Pitchler (Oxford: Oxford University Press, 1978), 191.

21. Ibid.

22. Ibid., 191–92.

23. *FTC Decisions* 95, "Sears, Roebuck, and Co., et al.," 1980, 406–527, http.://www.ftc.gov/bcp/guides/guides.htm.

24. Ibid., 489.

25. Ibid., 494. The FTC found this to be the case.

26. Ibid.

27. Preston, *Tangled Web*, 16–18.

28. *FTC* 95, 451.

29. Ibid., 489.

30. Ronald M. Green, "Direct-to-Consumer Advertising and Pharmaceutical Ethics: The Case of Vioxx," *Hofstra Law Review* 35 (2006): 756. My account of this case is taken from Green.

31. Ibid., 757.

32. Ibid., 758.

33. Such statements are intentional, false statements intended to deceive others. They count as lies according L1, L2, and standard dictionary definitions of lying. However, given my definition of lying, L3 (see note 5), such cases are not lies unless the negotiator warrants the truth of what he says. Imagine a negotiation between two "hardened" cynical negotiators who routinely misstate their intentions and do not object when others do this to them. Each of them recognizes that the other party is a cynical negotiator and each is aware of

the fact that the other party knows this. In this case, statements about one's minimum or maximum price are not warranted to be true and do not count as lies according to L3.

34. I make this qualification because a person's bargaining position often changes over time.

35. See "Bluffing in Labor Negotiations: Legal and Ethical Issues," Thomas Carson with Richard Wokutch and Kent Murrmann, *Journal of Business Ethics* 1 (1982): 13–22.

36. Michael Bayles, *Professional Ethics*, 2nd ed. (Belmont, Calif.: Wadsworth, 1989).

37. See Marc Rodwin, *Medicine and Morals: Physicians' Conflicts of Interest* (New York: Oxford University Press, 1993).

38. Paul Blumberg, *The Predatory Society* (Oxford: Oxford University Press, 1989), 65.

39. Ibid.

40. Ibid., 65–66.

41. David Callahan, *The Cheating Culture: Why More Americans Are Doing Wrong to Get Ahead* (New York: Harcourt World and Brace, 2004), 30.

42. See Rena Gorlin, ed., *Codes of Professional Responsibility*, 2nd ed. (Washington, D.C.: Bureau of National Affairs, 1990), 33, 79, 271.

43. Ibid., 35, 77, and 271.

44. Cf. Kenneth Arrow, "Business Codes and Economic Efficiency," in *Ethical Theory and Business*, 5th ed., ed. Tom L. Beauchamp and Norman Bowie (Upper Saddle River, N.J.: Prentice Hall, 1997), 124–126. Arrow notes that codes of ethics are intended to cause the public to trust professionals enough to use their services.

SUGGESTED READING

Barnes, J. A. *A Pack of Lies*. Cambridge: Cambridge University Press, 1993.

Bayles, Michael. *Professional Ethics*, 2nd edition. Belmont, California: Wadsworth, 1989.

Beauchamp, Tom L., and James Childress. *Principles of Biomedical Ethics*, 6th edition. New York: Oxford University Press, 2009.

Bok, Sissela. *Lying: Moral Choice in Public and Private Life*. New York: Vintage, 1979.

Carson, Thomas. "Deception and Withholding Information in Sales." *Business Ethics Quarterly* 11 (2001): 275–306.

———. *Lying and Deception: Theory and Practice*. Oxford: Oxford University Press, 2010.

Chisholm, Roderick, and Thomas Feehan. "The Intent to Deceive." *Journal of Philosophy* 74 (1977): 143–59.

Ebejer, James, and Michael Morden. "Paternalism in the Marketplace: Should a Salesman Be His Buyer's Keeper?" *Journal of Business Ethics* 7 (1988): 337–339.

Frankfurt, Harry. *On Bullshit*. Princeton: Princeton University Press, 2004.

FTC Policy Statement on Deception. http://www.ftc.gov/bcp/guides/guides.htm.

Goldman, Alan. *The Moral Foundations of Professional Ethics*. Savage, Md.: Rowman & Littlefield, 1980.

Gorlin, Rena, ed. *Codes of Professional Responsibility*, 2nd edition. Bureau of National Affairs, 1990.

Green, Ronald. "Direct-to-Consumer Advertising and Pharmaceutical Ethics: The Case of Vioxx." *Hofstra Law Review* 35 (2006): 749–759.

Holley, David. "Information Disclosure in Sales," *Journal of Business Ethics* 17 (1998): 631–641.

Leiser, Burton. "Truth in the Marketplace: Advertisers, Salesmen, and Swindlers." In *Liberty, Justice and Morals*, 2nd edition. Edited by Burton Leiser, 262–297. New York: Macmillan, 1979.

Nelson, Phillip. "Advertising and Ethics." In *Ethics, Free Enterprise, and Public Policy: Original Essays on Moral Issues in Business*. Edited by R. T. De George and J. A. Pichler, 187–198. Oxford: Oxford University Press, 1978.

Preston, Ivan. "Puffery and Other 'Loophole' Claims: How the Law's 'Don't Ask Don't Tell' Policy Condones Fraudulent Falsity in Advertising." *Journal of Law and Commerce* 18 (1998): 49–114.

———— *The Great American Blow-Up: Puffery in Advertising and Selling*. Madison: University of Wisconsin Press, 1975.

————. *The Tangled Web They Weave: Truth, Falsity, and Advertisers*. Madison: University of Wisconsin Press, 1994.

Rodwin, Marc. *Medicine and Morals: Physicians' Conflicts of Interest*. New York: Oxford University Press, 1993.

CHAPTER 12

··

INFORMATIONAL
PRIVACY

··

RICHARD A. SPINELLO

IN the years prior to the computer, it was cumbersome and expensive to gather and store information. Cybertechnology has changed this situation. The term "cybertechnology" refers to the whole range of stand-alone and distributed computer systems that manage digital data along with private networks and the Internet itself.[1] Thanks to the power of this technology, large amounts of information can be collected from diverse sources at minimal cost. Information has also become more permanent and more pliable. It can be retained longer in digital files and can be easily manipulated. As a result, businesses have greater access to information about prospective customers, employees, and other key stakeholders. They also have new ways of selling and marketing their products. Many organizations have taken advantage of the cost efficiencies and other benefits associated with networked information systems.

However, the same cybertechnology that creates these opportunities has engendered threats to personal privacy. The potential loss of privacy and security continues to cast a shadow over our social and commercial interactions in cyberspace. Cookies, for example, furtively collect digital information, while spyware—small computer programs automatically installed when users download certain software—can be programmed to track users' Web surfing habits and search engine results. Both of these technologies subject consumers to widespread surveillance in cyberspace. In the aggregate, cybertechnology is diminishing privacy and lowering our expectations for the level of privacy to which we are entitled.

Experts differ on the gravity and cumulative effects of this threat. Some argue that the erosion of privacy is not very harmful and can be constrained if users are inclined to take the necessary measures to protect themselves. Others contend that the loss of privacy is calamitous and probably irreversible. In any case, this issue will be a major ethical concern for many years. Privacy has become an issue of the same significance for the information economy as consumer protection and environmental concerns were for the industrial economy of the twentieth century.[2]

The concept of privacy is so vague and multifaceted that it is difficult to get a firm grasp on the ethical issues. We need to distinguish the definition and theoretical analysis of privacy from the normative justification of privacy rights and their preservation through public policy. Too often, these issues are not disentangled in literature on these topics, which adds to the mounting confusion.

This chapter concentrates on informational privacy, which is sometimes referred to as "data privacy." The focus on informational privacy began in the late 1960s and ushered in a new era of privacy concerns in the United States.[3] Up to this point, people were chiefly preoccupied with "physical privacy," that is, protection from an unwarranted intrusion into their homes and similarly private spaces. With the appearance of the computer and its capacity to gather massive amounts of information, personal information has become increasingly at risk.

The vagueness of the concept of informational privacy makes it imperative that we provide as precise a definition as possible. Failure to understand the nature of privacy detracts from any ethical or policy analysis and blocks our understanding of what is at stake. We will formulate a clear conception of informational privacy through the examination of several theories of privacy. We propose that a reasonable definition of informational privacy must include a condition of restricted access. Once we have delineated the nature of informational privacy, we will consider both the value of privacy and the justification of rights of privacy. Several questions arise: Is privacy an intrinsic, fundamental human good or an extrinsic, instrumental one? Is there a *right* to restrict access to one's personal information, or is it better to view informational privacy in terms of an *interest* that competes with other interests? Finally, how should we manage privacy? Assuming that a rights-based approach has validity, how can privacy rights be enforced? Should countries emulate the European model, which relies on comprehensive data protection laws to secure personal privacy rights? Or can privacy rights be adequately secured by the same type of digital technology that threatens it, that is, by privacy protection software? Some answers to these questions are purely technological, but ethical issues appear at every turn.

THE MAGNITUDE OF THREATS TO PRIVACY

We first need to have a grasp on the magnitude of the threats posed to data privacy in the information age. How big is this problem?

Cybertechnology is the main technological force behind the erosion of privacy. Information can be more easily captured, stored perpetually in a database, and recombined with other data. It can be transmitted rapidly, and unauthorized parties often gain access to data. The ease of collecting and sharing data also creates commercial incentives in favor of secondary uses in which data collected for one purpose are sold for another use. As more organizations use computerized record keeping, threats to privacy increase. For example, each time someone makes a credit card purchase the information about this transaction is digitally recorded and stored in a computer database. This type of transactional data can be kept for years and easily transmitted to credit agencies or other data collection organizations, where it is organized, combined with other data, and analyzed. This assembly of data into comprehensive databases enables the creation of "digital dossiers," a series of records that can track nearly every aspect of a person's life.[4]

How can these practices be harmful? Consider the health care industry, which has adopted electronic record keeping on a large scale. Hospitals, HMOs, and other organizations scan medical data into their computers in order to make patient records more thorough and accurate. These records are used for diagnosis, medical treatment, and claims processing. Access to this data is often shared with third parties, such as insurers. A complete medical record can sometimes include psychiatric records or other sensitive data. United States medical privacy laws neither preclude the inclusion of such data nor require that patients be informed of the precise contents of their records. Thus, a person might consent to share her medical file with an insurer or even a prospective employer, unaware of its exact contents. People who have applied for disability benefits or additional insurance coverage have been turned down based on the insurer's review of a psychotherapist's notes included in the patient's electronic medical record.[5]

A major threat comes from the process of data aggregation whereby information is collected from several sources and recombined into a single comprehensive dossier. For example, information collected by a financial institution that sells bank products can be combined with information about spending habits, online purchases, or charitable contributions. Aggregation from disparate data sources by data brokers such as ChoicePoint and Axiom poses an acute problem for the consumer.

ChoicePoint, a spin-off of the credit bureau Equifax, has collected data from multiple sources to establish dossiers on almost every adult in the United States. The company provides a range of services such as background checks on employees and risk assessment for insurance companies. It is important to recognize that ChoicePoint's consolidation of data provides key economic benefits for both vendors and customers. Banks use this service to verify information on credit and loan applications in order to reduce fraud. Also, due to the comprehensive information provided to lenders and mortgage companies, the time it takes to refinance a mortgage has been substantially reduced. Nonetheless, critics point to cases where individuals have been denied employment or fired because of faulty or questionable data in their ChoicePoint reports. Privacy experts also lament that this industry is largely unregulated and subject to minimal government oversight.[6]

The problem is exacerbated for the consumer because of the difficulty of appraising the value of information when nothing is known about future utilization or how it will be linked to other pieces of personal information. It might be that a discrete unit of information, such as a list of books and music purchased on Amazon.com, is innocuous in itself but incriminating when combined with other data and taken out of context. The fact that Joe buys Gangsta rap music on Amazon.com takes on a new light when that information is linked with the fact that he collects guns as a hobby and likes to watch violent movies. It is a mistake to assume that an aggregate of information does not violate privacy even if the different data elements, considered separately, pose no threat to someone's privacy.[7]

As a result of aggregation techniques, companies can engage in an unparalleled level of *data profiling*. This process is defined as "the gathering, assembling, and collating of data about individuals in databases that can be used to identify, segregate, categorize, and generally make decisions about individuals known to the decision maker only through their computerized profile."[8] These profiles can be profitably mined and the relevant data extracted for the purpose of targeted marketing campaigns or similar ventures.

Profiles of online activities have also proliferated. When consumers shop or browse online, many vendors monitor clickstream data—the information that is generated as a user surfs the Web and communicates with different Web sites. One way in which Web site vendors can track the browsing activities of their customers is through the use of cookies, small data files that are written and stored on the user's hard disk drive by a Web site when the user visits that site with a browser. They contain information such as passwords, lists of pages within the Web site that have been visited, and the dates when those pages were last examined. These cookies enable the monitoring of a user's movements when they visit a particular Web site. If a customer visits an online bookstore, a cookie can reveal whether she browses through sports books or is more apt to look at books on wine and gourmet foods.

Online monitoring has occasionally triggered public controversy, as it did in the so-called DoubleClick case. This company, affiliated with over 12,000 major commercial Web sites, specializes in delivering targeted advertising to those sites, which rent out available space to online advertisers. DoubleClick builds profiles of those users who traffic at its affiliates' Web sites in order to send them targeted ads. In 1999, DoubleClick agreed to purchase a direct marketing company called Abacus Direct. It quickly announced plans to merge the online information in its customer profiles with the offline data in the Abacus database in order to assemble more detailed dossiers. DoubleClick asserted that "personally identifiable information," including a user's name, address, retail, catalog and purchase history, and demographic data, would now be linked with "non-personally identifiable information" collected by DoubleClick from Web sites on the DoubleClick network. Privacy experts expressed concern that this obscure firm would be tracking the moves of consumers online and sharing information with companies eager to inundate consumers with direct-mail, telemarketing calls, and targeted Web ads. The controversy caused DoubleClick to abandon its plans to purchase Abacus.[9]

Another disturbing trend is the growing propensity towards information collection through the use of surveillance technologies embedded into music playing software or Digital Rights Management (DRM) code.[10] DRM systems are utilized to enforce access and usage rights with regard to digital content such as DVDs or e-books. Some DRM systems are designed to report to the content providers the reading or listening activities of their users. While the DRM approach may seem an ideal solution to the problem of copyright protection on the Internet, it poses some threat of invasion of privacy. These systems will allow content providers to keep precise tabs on who is accessing and using their material, which raises the demand for this information from lawyers, government officials, or other curious third parties. Also, the tracking of a person's reading habits or music tastes may shape an individual's practices of "intellectual consumption." The threat of future disclosure of this information may impede various intellectual or cultural pursuits. The loss of privacy and inability to control how this information will be used in the future might thereby impair a user's autonomous choices. Individuals with more eccentric tastes may think twice about the music they listen to if they know that their choices are being recorded and potentially transmitted to interested parties.[11]

Why do companies engage in all of this data collection, aggregation, and profiling? Aside from the protection of intellectual property and the cost efficiencies associated with digitization, a chief objective is targeted marketing and advertising. The more information a company acquires the more ability it has to tailor its marketing efforts. It is more effective to send a potential customer a targeted banner ad as opposed to a generic one. Targeted campaigns reduce risk and increase the probability of a positive response. This preoccupation with the predictive power of information is a permanent feature of modern commercial transactions.[12] Companies value detailed information because they are convinced that it will enhance their capability to market their products more effectively. The pervasive use of cookies, spyware, microchips, and self-enforcing licenses is a direct result of the market-driven push for more extensive and precise information.[13]

Is there risk for the consumer in this quest for more detailed information? Everyone realizes the negative ramifications of losing control over one's most sensitive information such as medical or financial records. But why should consumers also be concerned about the loss of control over the information they provide online or over the phone to catalog vendors if the result is merely more targeted advertising? One problem is the potential for being misconstrued or judged out of context.[14] It is easy to confuse *information* about a data subject with *knowledge* of a person. Perhaps a consumer profile is constructed of a foreign student who has purchased books about terrorism on Amazon.com, travels frequently to Canada, and has a hobby of flying a small plane. This person may have unusual interests, but these interests do not make him a terrorist. However, it would be easy to envision how someone might reach that conclusion based on a profile constructed by a data broker. Monitoring technologies, profiling, and far-reaching searches often threaten the presumption of innocence. In these situations, the burden is often placed on the consumer to establish innocence and to assure those who have collected these ambiguous facts that there is no criminal or terrorist intent.

Second, according to the perspective of "panoptic theory," which regards the indiscriminate gathering and use of personal information as a form of intrusive surveillance, there is an increased likelihood of discrimination. Oscar Gandy characterizes these activities as the "panoptic sort," which he defines as "the collection, processing, and sharing of information about individuals...used to coordinate and control their access to the goods and services that define life in the modern capitalist economy."[15] This information is transformed into "intelligence" about the person through predictive models, and it becomes a guide for marketing offers and other inducements. This "panoptic sort" is a complex discriminatory technology that constantly sorts people into different categories to qualify them for certain products, programs, or services.[16] A danger is that technology will be utilized not only to *include* individuals in a marketing program but also to *exclude* them from opportunities such as employment, insurance, bank mortgages, loans, or the use of credit.

Third, errors can lurk within data files, and they can be hard to correct once they are recorded, especially when propagated throughout multiple information systems. For example, information on "deadbeat dad" Warren J. Pierce is mistakenly entered into a database as Warren J. Pearce. This information is wrongly attributed to Mr. Pearce, who finds it exceedingly difficult to correct this inaccuracy. The credit bureau industry, which maintains credit records on over 90 million households, has been plagued with the problem of inaccurate data. These inaccuracies have led to unwarranted denials of credit.[17]

Finally, this data is vulnerable to security breaches. These information systems have become prey for criminals and hackers who want to use this data for malicious purposes such as credit card fraud and identity theft. Despite elaborate security measures, there was a serious data breach at ChoicePoint in 2002 when the company inadvertently sold personally identifiable information on over 7,000 consumers to an identity theft ring. In subsequent years there have been data breaches at companies such as Lexis-Nexis, Time-Warner, Bank of America, and a Citigroup subsidiary.[18]

Our discussion thus far has centered on the heightened threat to privacy through the rapid growth of cybertechnology. Broader access to sensitive data, including the information now contained in medical records, can have harmful effects, such as loss of insurance coverage. Because of profiling, consumers are subject to greater quantities of targeted ads, and they can become victims of various forms of discrimination, exclusion, and fraud. Now that we have reviewed the magnitude of the threat to privacy we turn to an examination of key concepts and theories of privacy.

CONCEPTS AND THEORIES OF PRIVACY

Most individuals have a strong sense that their privacy has been invaded when personal information such as a history of their credit card transactions is shared with a third party without their permission. They may be hard pressed to define "privacy" or describe what it is with any precision. Philosophers, social theorists, lawyers, and government agencies have struggled to define "privacy." Although privacy is a fundamental value in many societies, it has not been as carefully analyzed in theory or in practice.[19] It is an ambiguous concept, and even our conception of the private realm tends to be amorphous. Also, some privacy advocates add to the confusion by overemphasizing the value or worth of privacy, but its value or worth is not part of its meaning. The term "privacy" has in fact acquired and carries several different and even conflicting meanings.[20]

A *theory* of privacy should first clarify the *concept* of privacy before it considers normative issues such as whether there is a right to such privacy, whether privacy is a fundamental interest, and whether privacy protections can be justified. Our primary focus in this section is on the concept of privacy and on the question, "Under what conditions does an individual have informational privacy?"

Legal scholarship nicely illustrates both the struggle to define "privacy" and the tendency to confuse the descriptive with the normative. Legal scholars have sought to formulate a theory of privacy to guide jurisprudence. In a famous article, regarded as foundational in privacy law in the United States, Samuel Warren and Louis Brandeis described privacy in terms of "being let alone."[21] The suggestion is that privacy is invaded not necessarily by acquiring knowledge about a person but in an invasion of a person's space. This conception of privacy has given rise to "nonintrusion" theories, which analyze the notion of privacy as freedom from intrusion. The Supreme Court was apparently guided by this theory when it ruled in *Katz v. United States* that tapping a person's phone was an unacceptable intrusion into that person's personal space.[22]

These theories sometimes confuse the *condition* of privacy—or, perhaps, the *concept* of privacy—with the *right* to privacy, and they also do not carefully distinguish between privacy and liberty. In one of his judicial opinions, Brandeis defines "privacy" as "the right to be let alone—the right most valued by civilized men."[23] However, the definition of privacy as "being let alone" is too broad. For example, if a government or a corporation leaves trapped miners alone after a mine collapse, it seems bizarre to say that the miners are in a condition of privacy or that their right to privacy is being observed. The notion of privacy as "nonintrusion" (a condition of freedom from intrusion by others) has had deservedly strong resonance in the legal community. This notion correctly suggests that privacy has something to do with *limited accessibility*. As our analysis will eventually demonstrate, a strong case can be made that a person has privacy when he is able to prevent unwarranted access by others.

Another and related theory is the so-called "seclusion theory." Ruth Gavison adopts a version of this conception. She claims that a person enjoys complete or "perfect" privacy when he "is completely inaccessible to others."[24] This theory has an advantage over nonintrusion theories because it does not confuse privacy and liberty. Both theories are focused on physical privacy. Privacy exists as a condition of the restriction of access that could occur through observation or some other means. Or privacy exists under conditions of nonintrusion into someone's personal space such as one's home or back yard.[25]

Due to the emergence of cybertechnology, there is now a more pressing need to prevent the unwarranted disclosure of personal information. Hence recent privacy theories have shifted attention to informational privacy. One such theory is the control theory, which has been invoked in various judicial opinions as a justification of privacy statutes. The U.S. Supreme Court has described informational privacy as a condition of "control over information concerning his or her person."[26] Several theorists have embraced this theory. Charles Fried says that "privacy is not simply an absence of information in the minds of others, rather it is the control we have over information about ourselves."[27] In this attractive account, one has informational privacy if one has control over one's personal information.

However, the notion of control is here usually understood too broadly. The control paradigm suggests the ability to completely isolate information about oneself. How much control does one need over information to ensure privacy? It is virtually impossible to have absolute control, and therefore the degree of control, which is usually left unspecified, is important. Finally, loss of control does not entail a loss of privacy. I may not control all the ways in which my bank uses a history of my transactions, but if the information is not subsequently shared outside the bank and if it is not being improperly used within the bank, I have not lost any privacy.

Following Jim Moor and Herman Tavani, informational privacy can be understood in terms of "restricted access/limited control."[28] Our information must sometimes be shared with others so that the proper use of information must fall somewhere between total privacy and complete disclosure. The "restricted access" paradigm suggests the ability to shield personal data from some parties while sharing it with others. From this perspective, an individual has privacy "in a situation with regard to others if and only if in that situation the individual is normatively protected from intrusion, interference, and information access by others."[29] According to this definition, a "situation" can be a relationship, an activity of some sort, or any "state of affairs" in which restricted access is reasonably expected. Moor is also making a distinction between situations that are naturally private (e.g., living on a secluded island or hiking in the mountains) by contrast to normatively controlled private situations such as the lawyer-client relationship. In a situation where one is naturally protected from access by others, one has natural privacy. In a normatively private situation, norms such as laws or policies are developed to create a protective zone of privacy because the situation requires such protection.[30] Natural privacy can be lost but not violated due to the absence of norms providing a privilege to or a right to a zone of privacy. Thus, if I am sitting in a secluded place in a state forest and someone discovers me, I have lost my privacy, but I could not reasonably claim that my privacy *rights* had been violated.

As an example of this theory, consider a normatively private situation such as the doctor-patient relationship. A person expects that her medical records will only be made accessible to certain health care providers and insurers and not to the general public. The patient has privacy only if she is in a condition of *restricted access* such that those records are accessible only to doctors, medical and hospital personnel, and others who have a legitimate need. We must protect ourselves to ensure that only the right people have access to our relevant information on an as-needed basis.[31] There will be privacy if a normative zone is created through laws or ethical standards that restrict the "wrong" people from accessing this sensitive information.

Finally, what about "limited control," a vital aspect of this theory? Individuals seek as much control as is realistically possible over their personal data to ensure restricted access as they see fit. Their control will be exercised by mechanisms such as informed consent to the limited reuse and exchange of the personal information they have provided to someone for a particular purpose. People also seek to be able to correct inaccuracies. Typically, limited control is implemented by policies that help users to restrict access to their personal data and to ensure the integrity of that data.

The restricted access/limited control theory is a viable one and will be used as the basis for understanding the nature of information privacy in this chapter. It captures the important notion that one cannot have privacy without some control and without restrictions on information flows about oneself when such restrictions are warranted by one's situation. Privacy, therefore, can be defined as a *condition of limited accessibility. Invasions* of privacy, to add to this conceptual account, make an individual's information more accessible than it should be.

Privacy as an Instrumental Good

Having secured a definition of informational privacy, we can consider why privacy is valuable and ethically important. In addressing such questions we will also be positioned to demonstrate why unrestricted access to information is ethically problematic.

A condition of privacy is a "value" or a "good." The term "good" is here understood as an object of interest or desire conceived as contributing to our well-being. Privacy is certainly an end or objective that humans desire and pursue for the sake of their basic welfare and overall well-being. But what kind of "good" is privacy? It is useful to distinguish between intrinsicalist accounts of privacy—which regard privacy as an intrinsic good—and instrumental or functionalist accounts, which see privacy as a support for more important values such as security or autonomy.[32] Debate over these two accounts is beyond the scope of this essay, but it should be noted that it has proved difficult to defend privacy as an intrinsic value. Few philosophers and privacy theorists have adopted this point of view.[33]

More plausible is the thesis that privacy is an instrumental good. Westin, for example, regards privacy as instrumental "for achieving goals of self-realization."[34] To follow this line of reasoning in some depth we need to see how the good of privacy should be categorized. Almost every moral philosophy endorses some notion of the good. Even deontologists such as John Rawls, who give priority to the concept of right over the concept of good, concede the need for a "thin" theory of the good. More robust theories of the good are offered in teleological ethical frameworks, such as utilitarianism and recent natural law theory. John Finnis, for example, proposes a broader list of basic human goods that are basic not for survival but for human flourishing. Thus, thinkers as diverse as Rawls and Finnis argue that there are basic primary goods. Recently, Martha Nussbaum and others who endorse "capabilities theory" start with the notion of basic primary goods.

What are these basic human goods? A list should include the following:

1. Health
2. Safety and personal security
3. Knowledge, capacities of reasoning, and skillful performance in work and play
4. Friendship and the respect of others in personal relations
5. Community and forms of human attachment
6. Self-determination and harmony between judgments and behavior as well as between judgments and inner feelings.[35]

These are all distinct and independent aspects of basic well-being that compose a reasonable list of basic goods. A moral theory based on these goods would propose to secure a sufficient level of each dimension for each person. Although we cannot here explore theories of justice, it is arguable that the justice of societies and of the global order can be judged by how well they effect these dimensions in their political structures and social practices.

If a good is not basic for human fulfillment, it cannot qualify as a basic, intrinsic human good. Instead, it must be an instrumental good. The intelligibility of an instrumental good depends upon the intrinsic goods whose realization it facilitates. For example, external or material goods are important, but they are not basic for fulfillment. Similarly, privacy is not a basic good, since it does not directly contribute to human flourishing. Privacy is desired as a means to another end, that is, as instrumental to some further good. A monk desires solitude in order to pray more fervently, or a person on vacation enjoys solitude for the inner peace and security it affords him.

We also require privacy to ensure that our close relationships preserve their intimacy. There is a close correlation between our capacity to control who has access to us and to our information and our ability to establish and sustain intimate social relationships.[36] The intrinsic goods at stake are friendship and special relationships such as marriage. Privacy allows us to participate in these goods without inhibition. Intimacy depends on our ability to share our beliefs, aspirations, and convictions with a select few while blocking this information from everyone else.[37] Intimate information, therefore, is information that people want revealed only to a few other special people. People must be able to share such information at their discretion in order to determine the closeness of their interactions with others according to the nature of their relationship. A husband and wife will have a different relationship than an employer and his or her employee because of the different degrees of knowledge appropriate to each relationship.[38] Without the restriction of intimate information it is virtually impossible to control the conditions necessary to establish and maintain close personal relationships based on trust, love, and mutual respect.

People also desire privacy for the sake of their personal security and safety. Without privacy we cannot have adequate security. If one's financial records fall into the wrong hands one could be robbed of one's life savings. We might be victimized by identity theft or we might be judged out of context and presumed guilty even though our activities are purely innocent. In extreme cases, a person's life could be at stake if an invasion of privacy occurred.[39]

We need privacy for the sake of autonomy—that is, self-determination. It is often difficult to exercise one's autonomy without some measure of privacy. If someone openly monitors my actions or tracks my information, then he or she can alter the context of my activities. For example, if a person knows that I am watching him or monitoring his conversations, he is apt to be more self-conscious and concerned about whether his statements or actions meet my approval. It is not uncommon to find anticipatory conformity among those who are observed or whose information is tracked.[40] As Wasserstrom puts it, without privacy life is often "less spontaneous and more measured."[41] As we noted earlier, if the music I listen to is being tracked by a third party, I may be induced to alter my music listening habits, especially if they may be considered eccentric.

In summary, we have reasons for seeking out privacy that are closely connected to basic forms of human well-being. Various goods such as health, safety, and friendship could be put at risk if the flow of personal information is not restricted. The value of privacy assumes particular salience in a digital world of monitoring and data collection technologies, because it is vital for security. While privacy is not as fundamental to human flourishing and well-being as intrinsic goods such as self-determination, friendship, and knowledge, it is neither an ethical nicety nor an expendable commodity. When data privacy is impeded or destroyed without justification, the goods to which it is instrumental are also undermined. Thus, the instrumental good of privacy has an integral role to play in promoting human well-being. As we will now see, rights of privacy can be justified in terms of this instrumental account.

THE RIGHT TO PRIVACY

Is privacy not only a *good* but also a *right* to which people are entitled? If privacy is a right, do people have a legal right to privacy, a moral right, or both? Our concern here is with the moral right to informational privacy, in particular a right to the limited accessibility of one's personal information and a right to control use of that information in various ways. Analysis of legal privacy rights is beyond the scope of this discussion, though we briefly consider the efficacy of privacy law in the final section of this essay. In this section it is shown that a moral right to privacy can be expressed and justified in terms of its support for the intrinsic goods previously identified as constituting human flourishing.

Some privacy scholars believe that it is more accurate to speak of privacy in terms of an "interest" that people have, rather than a "right." Robert Clarke has high regard for the good of privacy, but he sees it as "the interest individuals have in sustaining personal space, free from interference by other people and organizations."[42] Similarly, Thomas Scanlon argues that we have a moral interest in privacy that expands or contracts based on prevailing social conventions.[43] According to his view, people may prefer the good of privacy because of the benefits it provides, but there is not necessarily a moral *entitlement* (that is, a valid claim, or right) to control the use of personal information.

Those who propose that privacy is an interest, rather than a basic human right, argue that this is a more practical and intuitive approach. Most people recognize that they have an interest in protecting their privacy, but if that interest is elevated to a right, it will be necessary to provide a philosophical justification of the right. The development and defense of such a justification often yields intractable controversy and disagreement that is counterproductive. More generally, some moral theories do not recognize rights of any sort.

Continuing to treat privacy as an individual right, however, highlights its proper worth and suggests the gravity of what is at stake when someone's privacy is breached. Our previous analysis suggests that individuals have a justified claim to privacy, given its necessity for the pursuit of basic goods. If privacy is a necessary condition for a person's realization of goods such as marriage and friendship, is not that person then entitled to privacy? The previous analysis also supports the conclusion that the right to privacy is not a fundamental moral right. Rather, it can be derived from its status as a good that is instrumental for participation in certain intrinsic goods. As H. J. McCloskey says, a right to privacy must be derived from other rights and other goods.[44]

Judith Thomson makes the same point as she argues that the "right to privacy is 'derivative' in this sense: it is possible to explain in the case of each right in the [privacy] cluster how come we have it without ever once mentioning the right to privacy."[45] We have maintained that privacy's value and importance as an instrumental good is derived from the more basic human goods that it supports such as health and friendship. As it can be plausibly demonstrated that people also have rights to those goods, such as a right to life, property, and liberty, then it also follows that privacy is not a fundamental right but a right derived from other rights. For example, security is a basic good, but people also have a right to security as part of their rights to life and property. The right to restrict access to and control over the distribution of information is not fundamental because without taking into account the damage to basic human goods that occur when one's personal information is misappropriated, such a right cannot be credibly justified.

Accordingly, privacy is not merely an interest but a moral right derived from other rights. But what exactly is a right, and how can privacy be more precisely construed as having this status? W. H. Hohfeld, in a classic work on rights theory, distinguishes between a "claim right," or a right in the "strict sense," and a liberty right. The right to privacy falls in the former category. According to Hohfeld, *A* has a claim right that *B* should do Ø if and only if *B* has a duty to *A* to do Ø.[46] When claim rights are at stake, the action in question is an action on the part of others and not on the person who has the right. A claim right is either a right to be given something, to be "assisted in some way," or a right not to be interfered with or dealt with in a certain way.[47] Otherwise, in Hofheld's terms, we would be talking about a liberty or a "privilege" instead of a claim right.

Thus, rights are *justified claims* that individuals and groups can make on other individuals or upon society. These claims entail *correlative duties* on the part of others. If one possesses a right, one is in a position to determine what others should or should not do. *Moral* rights, as opposed to legal ones, exist independently of the law and one demonstrates their existence by appealing to moral arguments about rights and duties. In Hohfeld's framework, privacy would be considered a claim-right such that one individual, the right holder, has a claim on another, the duty bearer, to assist in the process of restricting access to the right holder's personal information or not to interfere with the right holder's efforts to restrict access.

On what basis can individuals make a justified moral claim to informational privacy? Why do people have the right to restrict access and exercise limited control over their personal information? Briefly stated, there is a moral right to privacy because people *need* privacy. In most cultural contexts, privacy is a necessary condition for the pursuit of intrinsic goods that are aspects of human flourishing. As H. L. A. Hart has observed, "The core of the notion of rights is neither individual choice nor individual benefit, but basic or fundamental individual needs."[48] Because privacy is an important means to human well-being, we need privacy and the respect of others for it, and others are obligated to respect us in these ways. Correlative to this obligation is the right to privacy.

Following the Hofheld framework, we can also justifiably postulate a right where there is a positive or negative obligation or requirement imposed upon *X* not to interfere with *Y*'s activity or *Y*'s enjoyment of some form of the good.[49] If some level of privacy is essential for *Y* to participate in certain intrinsic goods such as friendship or marriage, it follows that privacy is a necessary condition for *Y*'s flourishing and well-being. It also follows that *Y* is justly owed such privacy by others because *Y* would be wronged if denied it. *Y*, therefore, has a right to privacy and *X* has a correlative duty not to impede or destroy *Y*'s privacy, lest he interfere with *Y*'s well-being and *Y*'s participation in certain basic human goods.

Thus, a claim-right provides a way of explaining what is just or moral in a given situation by focusing on the viewpoint of the other to whom something is owed or due and who would be harmed if denied that something.[50] What is just or fair in normatively private situations is restricted access to the right holder's personal information. Consider once again the situation of a doctor-patient relationship.

A patient has more than an "interest" in making sure that her medical records are not made accessible to anyone who asks for them. Given the harm that may befall her—loss of a job opportunity, denial of additional insurance coverage, or social stigma—she has a justified claim to the restriction of her medical data to her doctor and other health care providers who need that access, and she would be wronged if denied such restricted access. In the same way, a person has a right to ensure that sensitive personal information provided to a bank in order to secure a mortgage is not shared with a data broker such as ChoicePoint without that person's knowledge and consent. If, as we have proposed, privacy is a moral right, companies have a moral duty to protect personal privacy even when not required to do so by law.

This right to data privacy, however, is neither absolute nor necessarily inalienable. The exercise of one's privacy rights is limited by other rights and moral considerations because some conditions override the right to privacy. Employees should have some privacy rights in the workplace, but a suspension of those rights would be warranted if there were legitimate suspicion of criminal wrongdoing. Also, data privacy rights could be overridden to protect intrinsic goods such as security and health. It may be necessary under some urgent circumstances to breach privacy in order to preserve public health or to prevent a terrorist attack. For example, HIV-notification programs may conflict with someone's privacy rights, but they are essential because the intrinsic good of bodily health is in jeopardy.

Law, Public Policy, and Computer Code

If privacy is an instrumental good and a moral right, our policies and laws must be constructed to reflect these values. Privacy policies must ensure that individuals have the opportunity to exercise as much control over their data as realistically feasible. What does this mean, and what will it entail? At a minimum, users must be given the opportunity to consent to the release and reuse of their data. In addition, information collection and processing practices must be as transparent as possible, and users must be given reasonable opportunity to correct inaccuracies in their digital dossiers. Adherence to these principles forms the core of fair information practices that will help safeguard privacy rights.

Public policies and laws are not the only means of protecting privacy. Computer code should also have a role to play in how we manage privacy. But is it feasible to protect the right to privacy through means such as software code and self-regulation? Is law still the optimal means of securing our privacy rights?

Larry Lessig's conception of the regulatory forces at work in cyberspace is helpful for addressing these issues. He describes four distinct modalities of regulation: law, social norms, the market, and architecture (i.e., software code). Lessig's insight is that the logical constraints of code, software such as filters or digital rights systems, may be more effective than social or legal constraints. Code often controls or regulates more perfectly and completely than law, without loopholes and without ambiguities. According to Lessig, in cyberspace "the code is the law."[51] There are countless examples of how code controls our interactions on the Internet. For example, in the absence of censorship legislation, filtering software programs have proliferated throughout cyberspace. These filtering programs can be installed on individual personal computers or networked servers to block out, for example, pornographic material.

Despite the promise of this approach, a sufficient regulatory solution will usually be needed to achieve many goals. The challenge is to find ways to create the right mixture of code, law, norms, and reliance on self-correcting market mechanisms. For our discussion, the key question is which of Lessig's regulatory constraints effectively provides restricted access and the "limited control" necessary to manage privacy?

Three models for the protection of privacy rights merit attention.[52] The first model gives priority to law as the primary means for ensuring data protection and limited accessibility. The second is a market-based approach in which industry codes of conduct and other self-regulatory mechanisms are deployed. In this model, when markets fail and public welfare is jeopardized, the political state justifiably intervenes. The third approach places a heavier reliance on code. Legal protections are minimized and privacy zones are established through technical features embedded in information technology architectures. The first approach has been adopted by the European Union (EU), which has been proactive in codifying privacy requirements in law. In Europe, privacy has long been regarded as a fundamental moral right that deserves a high level of legal protection. The Europeans have preferred the suggestive term "data protection" (in preference to privacy), which is defined as "the right to control one's own data."[53] Data protection laws in Sweden date back to 1973. Most other European countries have followed suit. National statutes were eventually harmonized when the EU adopted the European Directive in 1995. This Directive, which requires member states to implement legislation incorporating its privacy standards, is unambiguous in its recognition of informational privacy as a firm legal right. Its aim is "to protect the fundamental rights and freedoms of natural persons, and in particular their right to privacy with respect to the processing of personal data."[54] The EU model firmly anchors privacy protection in a rights-based approach.

According to the Directive, every individual has the right to know about the processing of his or her data beyond the purpose of the original data collection. Users have the right to opt out of data transfers to third parties for marketing purposes, along with the right to access their data and to correct mistakes. A quality provision requires that personal data must be accurate and, where necessary, maintained up to date. Finally, there are tighter restrictions on "sensitive information," such as a person's health or genetic data. The operative principle is that personal data may not be processed without the user's consent unless "processing is necessary for the performance of a contract to which the data subject is party."[55]

The problem with European-style regulations of consumer data is the potential for high transaction and enforcement costs, which can yield a suboptimal result even when taking into account costs that are incurred when individuals' data are taken without their consent. Given the magnitude of enforcement costs along with the potential for allocative inefficiencies that often accompany government regulations, it is not obvious that comprehensive data protection laws will maximize social welfare. In addition, these laws tend to slow down the flow of information and arguably have at least some negative economic effects. Accordingly, there are warranted reservations from the perspective of social utility.

In contrast to Europe, the United States has a market policy that accords only limited legal rights of informational privacy.[56] Policy makers in the United States have preferred the invisible hand of the market to the visible hand of government regulation. The attempt to protect personal privacy has thus been highly reactive, sporadic, and unsystematic. Policy makers have maintained that responsibility for privacy protection belongs primarily with the private sector and not with the government. However, some privacy statutes such as Children's Online Privacy Protection Act (COPPA) and the Health Insurance Portability and Accountability Act (HIPAA) have been enacted in the face of egregious market failures.

The United States relies on self-regulation and the prudential privacy guidelines adopted by the private sector. Many companies such as Amazon.com and eBay have adopted privacy policies in response to market pressures or out of moral concern for the welfare of their customers. There are also privacy seals such as TRUSTe provided by independent organizations, which certify that companies are following the policies they have articulated on their Web sites. For example, the TRUSTe standard requires Web sites to disclose their use of cookies, to indicate what sort of data is collected by these cookies, and to inform users if that data will be merged with data collected from other sources.

The third model seeks more reliance on technology to help solve the very problem it has created. Technological architectures such as operating systems and application software can encompass privacy protections that reinforce privacy rights, or they can facilitate the erosion of privacy. Code, supplemented by some laws and the demands of market forces, will be the principal guardian of consumers' informational privacy. Software code will embed the limited controls necessary to manage privacy by allowing users to more easily give their informed consent for the reuse of their data. This model assumes that the needed protections of privacy involve computer software. Other problems, such as person-to-person disclosure of private information, are not considered.

This type of software is known as a Privacy Enhancing Technology (PET). A prime example of a PET is the Platform for Privacy Preferences or P3P, which standardizes the comparison between Web site privacy polices and the user's privacy preferences. This privacy protocol includes rules that guide Web browsers as they read and interpret privacy policies (in a machine-readable format) on commercial Web sites. The user's preferences will be embedded into the browser, and the PET will only allow users to provide their personal data at sites that are consistent with those preferences. The user will be warned before entering a Web site that collects more information than he or she is willing to provide or that has other data policies with which the user is uncomfortable. Presumably, the participating Web site's policy will include information such as whether it provides e-mail addresses to third parties or makes use of cookies. The goal of PET architectures is to empower users to make informed choices about whether to accept or reject a Web site's privacy practices.

These privacy statements are verbose and opaque, and users often lack the patience to read them carefully. The advantage of a code-based approach is that the code will do the tedious work of reading and assessing the policies. In this way, users can delegate the negotiating process to their computer, which will function as an electronic smart agent and represent their privacy concerns.[57] However, this model is not without defects. Code will almost certainly not be an optimal solution for helping many users to manage sensitive information.

Can we confidently rely on software code, in general, to protect medical or financial privacy? It seems unlikely, at present. Also, P3P and related PET architectures do not require commercial vendors to provide the level of information necessary to make truly informed choices. However, it also would be presumptuous to offer a *definitive* solution to the data privacy conundrum. Perhaps the best we can do is to pursue two promising avenues for protecting privacy rights. Any privacy regime will involve a combination of all four constraints delineated by Lessig: law, social norms, the market, and architecture (code). One plausible resolution relies primarily on a careful blend of code and law. This model recognizes that people vary in their sensitivity to others seeing their personal data, and it accommodates different modes of protection for certain types of information. At the highest level of protection, there will be unambiguous legal safeguards for very sensitive personal data, such as one's medical and financial background. However, consumer data may not call for the highest level of protection. We tend to find a spectrum of opinions when it comes to this sort of information. Some people are not concerned that Amazon.com knows what books they read and might sell that information to a third party; others strongly prefer that Amazon.com not include their data in any such transfers. P3P or similar software could play a major role in such a solution because it empowers users to express their preferences as rules and to restrict access if they prefer.

According to this model, there will be statutory restrictions on the use of certain categories of personal data, such as medical and financial information. Such restrictions are necessary, given the stakes of disclosure of such sensitive data and the potential for significant harm. Also, the privacy of certain classes of Internet users, such as children, will need legal protection. The law will be used to safeguard moral privacy rights and guarantee users an adequate level of control over their most sensitive data.

A code-based solution for more mundane information, such as consumer data collected by cookies (including information about shopping habits, clickstream data, and so forth), may be an adequate means for restricting access. Once a baseline level of essential privacy protection (e.g., medical privacy) has been established, a scheme of code and self-regulation can be relied upon for other types of information. In contrast to the European model, code rather than law will give people control over some of their data by allowing them to choose when to provide their information to a Web site and by facilitating the process of informed consent regarding the release and reuse of that data.

The leading problem with this model is that P3P and similar programs neither require vendors to provide adequate information about how their information will be used nor mandate transparency. Many laws also fail to require transparency along with the proper conditions for informed consent. As noted earlier, U.S. medical privacy law (HIPAA) does not oblige that patients be informed of the exact contents of their medical records. Without this knowledge, users cannot make informed decisions about whether or not this data should be shared with third parties.

Viable mechanisms of informed consent to protect consumers will need to be developed in the near future. Informed consent can only work if users are given specific and practical information about how their data is to be reused or what will happen when it is transferred to another vendor. Consent by an opt-out or opt-in mechanism will be ineffective unless people are provided with details about how their personal information will be utilized and aggregated with other data, and the mechanism must be reasonably easy to use. Hence, this model has promise so long as commercial vendors take seriously the demanding conditions of an informed consent and practical system.

A second model closely follows the example of the European Directive. It protects privacy primarily through statutory regulations. One of the proposed "model regimes" would require any U.S. company engaged in the collection and transfer of personally identifiable information to register with the Federal Trade Commission. These companies would also be required to obtain an individual's explicit consent before using any collected information for an unrelated secondary use. Since thousands of companies fall into this category, opting out has become a burden. Thus, the FTC would be mandated to develop a convenient mechanism—"a centralized do-not share registry"—so that users could exercise their opt-out privilege with one simple step.[58] Consumers would thereby be relieved of the burden of contacting multiple companies to restrict secondary usage of their personal data.

According to this model, there will be stringent limitations on sensitive data (such as medical and financial information) along with tight restrictions on the use of social security numbers for identification purposes in order to prevent identity theft. Access to personal information in public records will also be subject to statutory restrictions. Finally, individuals will be provided with a way to ensure that the personal information collected and stored by data brokers is maintained accurately. Like the European approach, the law will guarantee individuals the right to inspect and correct their information as maintained by data processors.[59]

The downside of such an extensive statutory regime is the potential cost to the economy. There should be a careful reckoning of the estimated costs of implementing these data protection polices, which will likely include significant infrastructural investment. However, giving priority to top-down regulation for privacy protection may be necessary to stop the continuing downward spiral in the erosion of privacy rights.

Both of these models are flexible enough to ensure privacy rights and autonomous choice, though the second makes it more convenient for users to exercise control over their information and thereby safeguard their privacy rights. The right to data privacy is not inalienable, and there is no problem with "tradable" privacy rights within certain boundaries, so long as users are properly informed and particularly sensitive information is adequately protected. Code may have a role to play in protecting some forms of information, but the European model, despite its costs, is the safest way to ensure privacy protection so long as the law sensibly embodies the fair information principles articulated at the beginning of this section.

CONCLUSION

Theories of privacy abound, but we have argued that the restricted access/limited control theory best captures the concept of informational privacy. Persistent threats to privacy need to be taken seriously, because privacy is more than an instrumental good that rational individuals seek out. Privacy is also a moral right. In protecting these rights, policy makers should be guided by principles of transparency and informed consent so that users can properly control access to their data. Law is the most obvious solution, but scholars such as Lessig have rightly suggested that software code may have a legitimate role to play in the management of privacy by enabling users to exercise control over data. We have, on this basis, proposed two models of privacy protection that should guide us in adequately protecting an individual's moral privacy rights.

NOTES

1. See Herman Tavani, *Ethics and Technology* (New York: Wiley, 2004), 2–4.

2. See James Gleick, "Big Brother is Us," *New York Times Magazine*, September 29, 1996, 32–35.

3. Robert Ellis Smith, *Ben Franklin's Web Site: Privacy and Curiosity from Plymouth Rock to the Internet* (Providence, R.I.: Sheridan, 2000), 312.

4. Daniel Solove, *The Digital Person: Privacy and Technology in the Information Age* (New York: New York University Press, 2004), 2.

5. Theo Francis, "Spread of Records Stirs Patient Fears of Privacy Erosion," *Wall Street Journal*, December 26, 2006, A1, A8.

6. Robert Harrow, "ID Data Conned from Firm: ChoicePoint Case Points to Huge Fraud," *Washington Post*, February 17, 2005, E1. See also Lynn Sharp Paine, "ChoicePoint A, B" (Boston: Harvard Business School, 2006).

7. Helen Nissenbaum, "Privacy as Contextual Integrity," *Washington Law Review* 79 (2004): 101.

8. Karl Belgium, "Who Leads at Half Time? Three Conflicting Versions of Internet Privacy Policy," *Richmond Journal of Law and Technology* 6 (1999): 8.

9. *In re* DoubleClick, Inc. Privacy Litigation No. 00 CIV. 0641 NRB 2001 (S.D.N.Y. 2001).

10. In 1999, RealNetworks installed software code into its JukeBox software used for playing music CDs on computers. This program monitored and recorded users' listening habits and reported this information back to RealNetworks along with the user's identity. See http://www.nytimes.com/library/tec99/11/biztech/articles/01real.html.

11. Julie Cohen, "DRM and Privacy," *Berkeley Technology Law Journal* 18 (2003): 67.

12. Albert Borgmann, *Crossing the Postmodern Divide* (Chicago: University of Chicago Press, 1992), 2.

13. Julie Cohen, "Privacy, Ideology and Technology," *Georgetown Law Journal* 89 (2001): 2040–2045.

14. Jeffrey Rosen, *The Unwanted Gaze: The Destruction of Privacy in America* (New York: Random House, 2000), 8.

15. Oscar Gandy, *The Panoptic Sort: A Political Economy of Personal Information* (Boulder, Colo.: Westview Press, 1993), 15.

16. Gandy, *The Panoptic Sort*, 53.

17. One independent study found errors in 43 percent of the credit reports maintained by the largest three bureaus: Equifax, TRW, and Trans Union. In some cases credit was denied based on these errors. See Richard A. Spinello, *Case Studies in Information and Computer Ethics* (Upper Saddle River, N.J.: Prentice-Hall, 1997), 105–111.

18. Lynn Sharp Paine, "ChoicePoint B."

19. Alan F. Westin, *Privacy and Freedom* (New York: Atheneum, 1967), 7.

20. Robert Hixson, *Privacy in a Public Society: Human Rights in Conflict* (New York: Oxford University Press, 1987), 13.

21. Samuel Warren and Louis Brandeis, "The Right to Privacy," *Harvard Law Review* 4 (1890): 193. For the significance of this article see Daniel Solove, "Conceptualizing Privacy," *California Law Review* 90 (2002): 1099.

22. *Katz v. United States*, 389 U.S. 347 (1967).

23. See his dissent in *Olmstead v. U.S.*, 277 U.S. 438 (1928).

24. Ruth Gavison, "Privacy and the Limits of the Law," *Yale Law Journal* 89 (2003): 421.

25. For more background about these two theories see Herman Tavani, "Philosophical Theories of Privacy: Implications for an Adequate Online Privacy Policy," *Metaphilosophy* 38 (2007): 1–22. As Tavani points out, Gavison is not a pure seclusion theorist, but key passages in her writings indicate that she does tend to regard privacy in this way. For another version of the seclusion theory see Michael Weinstein, "The Uses of Privacy in the Good Life," in *Nomos XIII: Privacy*, ed. J. Roland Pollock and John Chapman (New York: Atherton Press, 1971), 88–104.

26. *United States v. Reporters Comm.*, 489 U.S. 749 (1989).

27. Charles Fried, "Privacy: A Rational Context," in *Computers, Ethics, and Society*, ed. M. David Ermann, Mary Williams, and Claudio Gutierrez (New York: Oxford University Press, 1990), 54.

28. Herman Tavani and Jim Moor, "Privacy Protection, Control of Information, and Privacy-Enhancing Technologies," *Computers and Society* 31 (2003): 6–11.

29. Jim Moor, "Towards a Theory of Privacy for the Information Age," in *Readings in CyberEthics*, 2nd ed., ed. Richard Spinello and Herman Tavani (Sudbury, Mass.: Jones & Bartlett, 2004), 407–417.

30. For a lucid and extended account of the Moor and Tavani model see Herman Tavani, "Philosophical Theories of Privacy."

31. Jim Moor, "Theory of Privacy," 414.

32. See Joeren van den Hoven, "Privacy," in *Encyclopedia of Science, Technology and Ethics*, vol. 3, ed. Carl Mitcham (New York: Macmillan, 2005), vol. 1490–1492.

33. Deborah Johnson argues that privacy is an intrinsic value because "autonomy is inconceivable without privacy." See *Computer Ethics*, 2nd ed. (Upper Saddle River, N.J.: Prentice-Hall, 1994), 89.

34. Alan Westin, *Privacy and Freedom*, 39.

35. John Finnis, *Fundamentals of Ethics* (Washington, D.C.: Georgetown University Press, 1983), 124. See also John Finnis, "Liberalism and Natural Law Theory," *Mercer Law Review* 45 (1994): 687.

36. James Rachels, "Why Privacy is Important," in *Philosophical Dimensions of Privacy: An Anthology*, ed. Ferdinand Schoeman (New York: Cambridge University Press, 1984), 272.

37. Charles Fried, *An Anatomy of Values: Problems of Personal and Social Choice* (New York: Oxford University Press, 1970), 142.

38. Rachels, "Why Privacy is Important," 294.

39. *Remsburg v. Docusearch*, 149 N.H. 152 (2003). In this case, a data broker was sued because it was hired by a stalker so that he could locate and murder Amy Boyer.

40. Shoshana Zuboff, *In the Age of the Smart Machine: The Future of Work and Power* (New York: Basic Books, 1988), 344.

41. Richard Wasserstrom, "Privacy: Some Arguments and Assumptions" in *Philosophical Dimensions of Privacy*, 328.

42. Robert Clarke, "Internet Privacy Concerns Confirm the Case for Intervention," *Communications of the ACM* 42 (2) (1999): 60–67.

43. Thomas Scanlon, "Thomson on Privacy," *Philosophy and Public Affairs* 4 (1975): 315–322.

44. H. J. McCloskey, "Privacy and the Right to Privacy," *Philosophy* 55 (2) (1980): 37.

45. Judith Jarvis Thomson, *Rights, Restitution, and Risk* (Cambridge, Mass.: Harvard University Press, 1986), 77.

46. W. N. Hohfeld, *Fundamental Legal Conceptions* (New Haven, Conn.: Yale University Press, 1919), 140–44.

47. John Finnis, *Natural Law and Natural Rights* (Oxford: Oxford University Press, 1980), 200.

48. H. L. A. Hart, "Bentham on Legal Rights," *Oxford Essays in Jurisprudence: Second Series*, ed. A. W. Simpson (Oxford: Oxford University Press, 1971), 171–185.

49. See Finnis, *Natural Law and Natural Rights*, 202–210.

50. Ibid., 205.

51. Larry Lessig, *Code and Other Laws of Cyberspace* (New York: Basic Books, 1999), 5.

52. For a similar approach see Joel Reidenberg, "Privacy Protection and the Interdependence of Law, Technology and Self-Regulation," in *Cahiers du Centre de Recherches en Informatiques et Droit : Variations sur le Droit de la Société de l'Information* (Paris: Bruylant, 2001), 111–123.

53. Victor Mayer-Schonberger, "Generational Development of Data Protection in Europe," in *Technology and Privacy: The New Landscape*, ed. Phil Agre and Marc Rotenberg (Cambridge, Mass.: MIT Press, 1997), 219–242.

54. Directive 95/46/EC of the European Parliament on the Protection of Individuals with regard to Processing of Personal Data (1995), art. 1, http://europa.eu.int/eur-lex/en/lif/dat/1995.

55. Ibid., art. 8.

56. Joel Reidenberg, "Resolving Conflicting International Data Privacy Rules in Cyberspace," *Stanford Law Review* 52 (2000): 1315–1320.

57. Lessig, *Code and Other Laws of Cyberspace*, 160.

58. Daniel Solove and Chris Hoofnagle, "A Model Regime of Privacy Protection," *University of Illinois Law Review* 38 (2006): 357.

59. Solove and Hoofnagle, "A Model Regime of Privacy Protection," 372.

SUGGESTED READING

Cohen, Julie. "Privacy, Ideology and Technology." *Georgetown Law Journal* 89 (2001): 2029–2045.

DeCew, Judith. *In Pursuit of Privacy*. Ithaca, N.Y.: Cornell University Press, 1997.

Fried, Charles. "Privacy." *Yale Law Journal* 77 (1968): 475–506.

Gandy, Oscar. *The Panoptic Sort: A Political Economy of Personal Information*. Boulder, Colo.: Westview Press, 1993.

Hixson, Robert. *Privacy in a Public Society: Human Rights in Conflict*. New York: Oxford University Press, 1987.

Lessig, Larry. *Code and Other Laws of Cyberspace*. New York: Basic Books, 1999.

Mayer-Schonberger, Victor. "Generational Development of Data Protection in Europe." In *Technology and Privacy: The New Landscape*. Edited by Phil Agre and Marc Rotenberg, 219–242. Cambridge, Mass.: MIT Press, 1997.

McCloskey, H. J. "Privacy and the Right to Privacy." *Philosophy* 55 (2) (1980): 37–52.

Moor, Jim. "Towards a Theory of Privacy for the Information Age." In *Readings in CyberEthics*, 2nd ed. Edited by Richard Spinello and Herman Tavani, 407–417. Sudbury, Mass.: Jones & Bartlett, 2004.

Rachels, James. "Why Privacy Is Important." In *Philosophical Dimensions of Privacy*. Edited by Ferdinand Schoeman, 272–309. New York: Cambridge University Press, 1984.

Reidenberg, J. R. "Resolving Conflicting International Data Privacy Rules in Cyberspace." *Stanford Law Review* 52 (2000): 1315–1371.

Rosen, James. *The Unwanted Gaze: The Destruction of Privacy in America*. New York: Random House, 2000.

Schoeman, Ferdinand ed., *Philosophical Dimensions of Privacy: An Anthology*. New York: Cambridge University Press, 1984.

Smith, Robert Ellis. *Ben Franklin's Web Site: Privacy and Curiosity from Plymouth Rock to the Internet*. Providence, R.I.: Sheridan Books, 2000.

Solove, Daniel. *The Digital Person: Privacy and Technology in the Information Age*. New York: New York University Press, 2004.

Tavani, Herman. "Philosophical Theories of Privacy: Implications for an Adequate Online Privacy Policy." *Metaphilosophy* 38 (1) (2007): 1–22.

Tavani, Herman, and Jim Moor. "Privacy Protection, Control of Information, and Privacy-Enhancing Technologies." *Computers and Society* 31 (2001): 6–11.

Thomson, Judith Jarvis. "The Right to Privacy." *Philosophy and Public Affairs* 4 (Summer 1975): 295–314.

Warren, Samuel, and Louis Brandeis. "The Right to Privacy." *Harvard Law Review* 4 (1890): 193–220.

Westin, Alan. *Privacy and Freedom*. New York: Atheneum, 1967.

CHAPTER 13

THE MORAL PROBLEM IN INSIDER TRADING

ALAN STRUDLER

INSIDER trading can have sensational results.[1, 2] Its perpetrators risk finding themselves behind bars for many years and vilified in popular opinion, while their firms and the people heavily invested in them risk financial ruin. Even so, doubt may be raised about our understanding of insider trading, a doubt that should prompt concern about the justice of insider trading prosecution and about the harsh moral judgments people often make of insider traders. The doubt comes from trying to identify the moral wrong in insider trading. Candidates for this wrong abound. One might, for example, identify the wrong in consequentialist terms, that is, in terms of the unfavorable balance of harms and benefits insider trading causes. But scholars disagree deeply about whether insider trading in fact causes social harm, and even those who think it does concede that their evidence is weak.[3] One might, alternatively, say that insider trading is wrong on deontological grounds, arguing that the act of insider trading is itself wrong in ways that cannot be understood in terms of the harms and benefits it produces. As we will see, the deontological alternative has its own problems.

I will argue that the judicial treatment of insider trading aligns with a deontological interpretation: courts have consistently identified insider trading as securities fraud; the heart of securities fraud is fraud, a kind of wrongful deception; and deception is a paradigmatic deontological wrong. Establishing these claims is difficult. The deceptive element in insider trading can be elusive. To make matters worse, several moral principles, other than that proscribing deception, are commonly invoked in arguments against insider trading, including principles that proscribe theft, breach of trust, and unfair dealing. It is not obvious how insider trading might violate any of these principles, or how one should understand the relationship among them as they bear on insider trading. In this chapter I try to resolve these issues. I contend that insider trading is in fact wrong because of the deception it involves, and that establishing that contention requires establishing corollaries about other moral wrongs.

Before investigating what might make insider trading morally wrong, I mention a preliminary problem. Insider trading resists simple characterization. The standard legal analysis of insider trading says that it occurs when a corporate insider engages in a securities transaction on the basis of material, nonpublic information.[4] This analysis is schematic, relying on ideas that often seem treacherous in application: a corporate insider, material information, nonpublic information. Moreover, it excludes a perplexing and practically important class of insider trading cases, namely, those committed by so-called outsider traders—tippees (people who wrongly receive stock tips from corporate insiders) and others who wrongly trade on inside information even though they are not themselves corporate insiders. Fleshing out the standard analysis by explicating and extending the ideas in the traditional analysis would be distracting and require more space than I am allotted. I undertake much of this task elsewhere.[5] For simplicity, I will therefore restrict this discussion to cases in which the standard legal analysis of insider trading proves unproblematic. Perhaps the most famous such case is *SEC v. Texas Gulf Sulphur*, in which officers of Texas Gulf Sulphur learned of their company's rich ore strike in Canada and traded on this information before the news became public.[6] These officers, who engaged in securities transactions on the basis of material, nonpublic information, are paradigm insider traders, at least under the standard analysis. It is clear that they committed a legal wrong. We will find more challenging the matter of identifying the moral wrong in their conduct.

In the remainder of this chapter, I critically examine the leading arguments for treating insider trading as morally wrong, including arguments that insider trading is wrong because it is harmful, deceptive, unfair, constitutes theft, or breaches fiduciary duties. I conclude that these arguments, as ordinarily formulated, are unpersuasive—they either rely on dubious empirical premises or assume normative premises that are equivalent to their conclusions. But then I suggest a way to salvage at least some of the arguments. I consider a society in which insider trading was not legally prohibited, and ask about the moral viability of contracts among firms, employees, and stockholders that would license insider trading. I argue that such contracts would be unconscionable, and that facts about this unconscionability show why insider trading should always be regarded as involving morally wrongful deceit.

HARM

The argument from harm, popular among the law-and-economics scholars who dominate securities scholarship in law schools, is not a deontological argument.

Instead, it maintains that insider trading is wrong because of the social harm it causes, given that we understand "causing harm" expansively, as causing a failure to attain optimal social welfare or social good.

In a securities market there are winners and losers, people who get good prices and people who get bad prices. Other things being equal, the person with the best information about what is being bought or sold stands in the best position to find bargains and get the best price. Competing against corporate insiders, who possess superior information, thus increases the risk that one loses. Ordinary traders will balk at the risk of trading against insiders, and insider trading, then, will undermine confidence in securities markets and deter investment, increasing the price a firm must pay to raise capital and hindering both a firm's development and a society's economic growth more generally, according to the argument from harm.[7] As a society, we have good moral reason to protect ourselves against this kind of economic harm, and laws prohibiting insider trading afford the relevant protection. On this view, insider trading is wrong because it fails a cost/benefit test, depriving us of a peculiar kind of benefit, a social good whose continued existence requires the cooperation of many people in maintaining a credible securities market. The harm in insider trading may be seen as resembling the harm that occurs when people damage other social goods, for example, by gratuitously burning a forest or spoiling a lake. Healthy forests, clean lakes, and thriving securities markets all serve the social good only because we as a society protect them. It is wrong to damage the social good. The wrong in insider trading is in its compromise of this good.[8]

An empirical claim forms the core of the argument from harm: that insider trading will significantly deter investment. Influential research lends some supports to this claim. A leading article on insider trading compares the cost of capital (the price that firms must pay to raise money in a securities market) in (mostly developing) countries both before and after they begin enforcing insider trading laws, and it concludes that because this cost generally decreases after insider trading laws are enforced, social welfare improves when insider trading diminishes.[9] Does the article show that insider trading is socially harmful? Its authors acknowledge that they locate no causal link between insider trading and changes in social welfare, but merely noncausal correlation. For all we know, the securities law enforcement practices upon which these scholars focus may be mere epiphenomena reflecting more significant social forces, including economic development or the broad adoption of a securities regulation framework. Even the best social science research, then, expresses no confidence about whether insider trading deters investment in ways that prove socially harmful. Moreover, there is good reason to wonder whether insider trading will deter investment. Securities traders are accustomed to the idea that other traders may possess advantages in information, even if it is not inside information, and hardly seem deterred by this idea. Most investors do not believe that the quality of their information is as good as Warren Buffet's—or that of the stock market wizards at Goldman Sachs. If the investment public is willing to trade against Warren Buffet and the wizards at Goldman Sachs, perhaps it will not be deterred by the prospect of trading against corporate insiders, either.

In addition to doubt about the harm insider trading causes, there are other reasons for skepticism about the argument from harm: credible economic arguments purport to show that insider trading, if it causes some harm, also creates benefits—perhaps these benefits are more significant than any harms that insider trading causes.[10] Some scholars find these benefits in the idea that insider trading facilitates getting insider information to market quickly. Arguably, when market information improves, so does market performance. One may also argue that insider trading benefits the firm and hence society more generally by providing a cheap compensation device: if a firm gives its employee the valuable perquisite of a right to trade insider information, it costs the firm nothing, but it should feel warranted in asking the employee to give back some of his otherwise high salary. When the firm saves money in salary, it can pass on the benefit to others, one might think. An entirely different but equally plausible argument that insider trading is socially beneficial focuses on the costs of law enforcement. The argument is simple. If we as a society need not pay the costs of enforcing laws against insider trading, we save money. Government avoids the costs of policing and prosecuting insider trading, and firms avoid the costs of requiring their compliance programs to limit insider trading. These savings create economic benefits from which, presumably, everybody gains.

There are, then, arguments both that insider trading harms us and arguments that it benefits us. Which, if any, of these arguments should prevail in our decision making about insider trading? Scholars who examine the issue say that the economic considerations for and against insider trading seem both closely balanced and rest on speculative assumptions.[11] We should worry about accepting either the idea that insider trading is generally beneficial or that it is harmful. But that is not the largest problem for the argument from harm. Suppose that we know that allowing insider trading would create both harms (because of deterring investment) and benefits (because of facilitating information transfer, providing cheap compensation, and saving law enforcement costs). If we are to take these considerations seriously as a foundation for criminal policy and moral attitudes, we face a problem. There exists no measure for the magnitudes of these harms and benefits, and nobody knows that a reliable measure will ever emerge. So we do not know how to balance the good consequences of insider trading (if they exist) against the bad (if they exist).

So far I have been developing skepticism that our knowledge about the harm in insider trading warrants us in seeing a significant moral wrong in insider trading. There are limits to this skepticism. It does not impugn the intellectual value of the scientific project of finding causal connections between insider trading and changes to social welfare. The skepticism is limited to the idea that however interesting and important the scientific research project of understanding causal connections between insider trading and harm, the project seems not far enough along to serve as a foundation for either social policy or moral attitudes about insider trading.

If we cannot adequately explain the wrong of insider trading in terms of harm, then we must look elsewhere for a rational basis for criminalizing insider trading and for our harsh moral attitudes against insider traders. I will explore the possibility that deontological arguments, which eschew empirical speculation about the social consequences of insider trading, and instead aim to explain the wrong in terms of the inherent character of certain acts by providing a more plausible basis for understanding the morality of insider trading than do analyses in terms of costs and benefits.

DECEPTION

Courts have always seen insider trading as a kind of fraud, namely, securities fraud.[12] Historically, wrongful deception forms the heart of fraud. Hence we might look to the wrong in wrongful deception as the explanation of the wrong in insider trading. Recall *Texas Gulf Sulphur*. On the deception account, insiders deceived shareholders by buying stock from them while concealing material, nonpublic information relevant to the valuation of the securities.

The deception account allows a deontological interpretation that avoids the speculative pitfalls of the harm account. Deception can be understood as inherently wrong, apart from any harm it causes. Indeed, a standard philosophical analysis of the wrong in deception identifies it as a vicious kind of manipulation.[13] One person may wrongly deceive another when he intentionally causes that person to have a false belief in a way that compromises the autonomy of his decision making, even if doing so benefits that other person. Suppose, for example, that I intercept a phone call to you about a job offer, and hide from you the information about the call. I know that the job would be bad for you, but I also know that I cannot convince you that I am right. So I lie, telling you that no call was made. Arguably, I wrongly deceive you even if I make you better off by doing so. I manipulate you by the way in which I cause you to have a false belief. If insider trading is deceptive, then we might establish that it is similarly wrong, at least from a moral point of view, even if we cannot establish that it is socially harmful.

The deception account of insider trading has its problems. Most salient is the elusiveness of any deception that occurs in insider trading. Recall, again, the Texas Gulf Sulphur officers. As a matter of fact, these officers were responsible for a number of misstatements that appeared in the press and misled the trading public about their discoveries of ore, and these statements were used at trial against the officers. Yet insider trading law requires no false or misleading statement for a finding of liability. The law is clear that if corporate insiders trade on material, nonpublic information while silently failing to disclose the basis of their trade, their silence may ground a conviction. Thus imagine a variant on *Texas Gulf Sulphur, Texas Gulf Sulphur**. Texas Gulf Sulphur* differs from Texas Gulf Sulphur only in that Texas Gulf Sulphur* officers make no false or misleading statements about their ore find. Texas Gulf Sulphur* officers might nonetheless be convicted of insider trading. If deception is at the core of insider trading, whom do Texas Gulf Sulphur* officers deceive and how do they do it? They do not commit the most obvious kind of deception. They do not lie. Lying involves making a relevant false statement and they made none. This raises a difficulty for the idea that insider trading is wrong because it is deceptive: how can silence, saying nothing, be deceptive? In trying to resolve that difficulty, one may appeal to the fact that silence, in the right circumstances, may serve as a signal that causes false belief. Take a crude example: suppose that I tell you that if I learn that Tom is now angry, I will come to your party at 3 P.M. and then stay silent five minutes; I show up and stay appropriately silent, even though I know Tom is not angry. You believe he is angry on the basis of my silence, and you are deceived. Perhaps there are less crude examples of silence deceiving by causing a false belief. But even their possibility seems to raise a difficulty in the charge that Texas Gulf Sulphur* officers deceive. The difficulty is causal. Typically when one person deceives another, causation matters: whether by lying or not, the deceptive act causes a false belief in the deceived. Texas Gulf Sulfur* shareholders arguably do have a false belief when they buy. They falsely believe that Texas Gulf Sulphur* has no new rich ore strike that will lead to skyrocketing stock prices. But since Texas Gulf Sulphur* officers, we are supposing, say nothing relevant about this strike, it seems doubtful that they cause the relevant false belief or influence relevant shareholder beliefs in any way. Shareholders will have had their false belief even before the officers decided to buy, and the sellers will have not been influenced at all by the action of the officers. Perhaps no deception occurs.

One might understand Texas Gulf Sulphur* officers' silence as deceptive, however, even if it does not in fact influence beliefs. Suppose that these officers have a moral obligation to inform shareholders of significant firm developments before they trade on firm stock. Then, before making a trade, they have an obligation to say, if true, that there has been an important strike. By their silence they license the inference that no new strike occurred. Had the officers discharged their obligations, shareholders would have had very different beliefs—fewer relevantly false beliefs—about Texas Gulf Sulphur*. Perhaps that suffices to show that they deceive shareholders. The underlying principle, though counterfactual in form, seems appealingly realistic: If one has an obligation to be truthful to a person, and breaches that obligation in a way that leaves the person with more relevantly false belief than he would have had if one had been truthful, then one deceives that person, even if one fails to make a false or misleading statement. The queerness of this underlying principle is in its suggestion that one may do something (that is, wrongly deceive) by inaction (that is, by staying silent). Assessing this queerness would require a foray into the metaphysics of inaction and its relation to moral obligation, too much to attempt here. Luckily there seems to be a way around the metaphysical issues. We may distinguish between deception as it ordinarily occurs, which involves a discrete deceptive act, and a failure of candor, which need involve no discreet deceptive act. We may then criticize Texas Gulf Sulphur officers for their failure of candor. We may say that sometimes minimal decency requires not merely that one not conceal the truth, but instead that one reveals the truth. If your car has a massively defective engine, or if your house has a cracked foundation, it seems wrong not to disclose the fact to a prospective buyer. Indeed, the law will treat such nondisclosure as fraud, and it is no moral or legal defense that you did not lie or mislead the buyer. You should have volunteered the truth. Sometimes morality requires candor. Perhaps that is so in cases of insider trading, such as Texas Gulf Sulphur*. Having distinguished deception as it is ordinarily understood from a mere failure of candor, we may then stipulate an interpretation of "deception" to be used in discussions of fraud, including securities fraud. According to this interpretation, deception in fraud includes not only deception as it is traditionally understood but also some failures of candor. This stipulation will, I think, simplify our discussion of insider trading and track well with judicial treatment of insider trading. But it hardly solves our deeper problem of finding the moral wrong in insider trading.

No doubt Texas Gulf Sulphur* officers were not as candid as many might like. But it would be too quick to infer, without further explanation, that they should have been more candid, or that they showed a wrongful lack of candor. In a competitive business environment, one need not always be entirely candid. Suppose that you work for The Walt Disney Company, which assigns you the task of purchasing land for a new theme park. You need acquire one more plot of land to complete your assignment. On that plot sits the home of a savvy used car salesman. Should you disclose to the homeowner what Disney intends to do with his land, or even that you work for Disney? If you disclose, you risk that the homeowner, knowing how valuable the land is to Disney, will insist on an unfairly high price, and you will have no choice except to pay it.[14] I suggest that although it would plainly be wrong for you to lie to the homeowner about what you will do with the land, morality does not require you to be forthcoming. Reflection on the Disney case shows that honesty does not always require full disclosure in a competitive business environment, even when a failure to disclose denies benefits to others. How, then, do we know that Texas Gulf Sulphur* officers should disclose?

The judgment that the officers' stock sale is deceptive, even in our expansive interpretation of that term, makes little sense unless one also finds that they fail in some duty to disclose the truth. So we are left with the question: what is the moral basis for this duty to disclose? Nothing in the argument from deception begins to answer this question. In the next section, I investigate fiduciary duties, which are often invoked as the basis of a duty to disclose in securities transactions.

Fiduciary Duties

A fiduciary duty is, roughly, a duty of utmost loyalty and trustworthiness that an agent may be said to owe to his principal. These duties are a staple of legal analysis, have rich moral content, and consistently play a role in judicial thinking about insider trading. As I mentioned, a common argument in insider trading jurisprudence says that fiduciary duties form the basis of the duty to disclose that is breached when insider trading occurs.

Fiduciary duties play a central role in the "traditional theory" of insider trading, which understands insider trading as a kind of wrongful deception.[15] The traditional theory employs the notion of fiduciary duties in this way:

1. Corporate insiders stand in a fiduciary relation to shareholders.
2. Because of (1) an insider must disclose all relevant information to his principal before engaging in a securities transaction with that principal.
3. An insider's failure to disclose in a securities transaction (insider trading) constitutes wrongful deception.
4. Insider trading is wrong.

I will eventually argue that a version of this argument can be salvaged, but the argument as presented is flawed, because it relies on an idea expressed in (2), the idea that a fiduciary must always be forthcoming with his principal.

An example shows why (2) may seem attractive. Consider a paradigmatic fiduciary relationship, that between a lawyer and his client. When Fred buys property from his real estate lawyer, Ed, the lawyer must be completely forthcoming, or make himself vulnerable to an action for fraud. He cannot conceal any information that Fred might reasonably find relevant to the deal. The obligation to be candid to one's principal, legal and moral tradition argue, forms an essential part of the fiduciary's task. Suppose that the real estate would be a great purchase for Fred, but Ed does not want to tell Fred that he owns it, because he suspects that doing so would make Fred worry unreasonably about the deal, and lose money. As a matter of law, Fred must nonetheless disclose because of his fiduciary relationship with Ed.

Law and morality demand that Fred be perfectly forthcoming. There are strong reasons to doubt that fiduciaries should always be so forthcoming. Consider a standard economic argument. The fiduciary obligation that officers owe to shareholders is, we are told, to devote their utmost allegiance to advancing shareholder interests. Hence, whether a practice of insider trading should be regarded as a breach of fiduciary duty depends on whether it is socially harmful or beneficial. This argument cannot be dismissed. Why think that a fiduciary should always disclose all relevant information? In the real estate lawyers case discussed above, the answer is easy: the lawyer is hired as a counselor, a person whose task is to aid his principal in making a reasonable and informed choice; providing relevant information is essential to his task of advancing his principal's interest in making an informed judgment of his principal. But the role of corporate officers as fiduciaries seems fundamentally different, one might argue: it is not to counsel shareholders, but to make money for them, within reason. If a practice of insider trading tends to benefit shareholders, then perhaps it violates no fiduciary duty after all. At a minimum, we need some argument to regard respect for fiduciary duties as requiring not trading on insider information. A mere appeal to fiduciary duties, in the absence of argument for a specific interpretation of those duties, goes nowhere. It begs the question.

UNFAIRNESS

The argument from unfairness contends that insider traders get an unfair advantage over people with whom they engage in securities transactions and that their trades are therefore wrong on grounds of justice.[16] The supposed unfair advantage is in their use of insider information, which stock market competitors lack. The unfairness argument differs crucially from the harm argument because it does not rely on speculative empirical premises about the consequences of insider trading. It instead looks at the comparative position of buyer and seller of stock and declares these positions unacceptable on grounds of justice.

The idea that market actions can be unfair, and hence wrongful no matter what their social consequences, has ancient lineage. The Bible bans charging unfairly high prices, declaring that "when you sell something to your fellow, or buy from the hand of your fellow, don't oppress each other."[17] Aquinas asserts that it is wrong to sell something for more than it is worth.[18] Even today, courts will declare a contract to be unconscionable and hence unacceptable if its substance is acutely unfair to one party. Proponents of the unfairness objection to insider trading echo this nonconsequentialist tradition, maintaining that the wrong in insider trading can be identified apart from reflection on the social consequences of insider trading.

The unfairness argument against insider trading identifies the relevant unfairness in terms of an acute inequality of information separating buyer and seller in a securities transaction. There are certainly cases, outside the securities realm, in which an asymmetry casts doubt on the legitimacy of a sales transaction. Typically these cases involve the kind of dishonest action discussed earlier in the deception section of this essay. Hence, again, if you have a car that has a massively defective engine, or if your house has a cracked foundation, it seems wrong not to disclose the fact to a prospective buyer. One might think that the asymmetry of information that separate insider traders and parties on the other end of a securities transaction is similarly problematic.

But not all asymmetries of information are unacceptable. Suppose that Edna, an engineering genius, studies internal combustion engines for years and finds a deep design flaw in Toyota's favorite engine. She alone knows that soon most Toyotas in the world will cease functioning abruptly, as their engines melt, creating billions of dollars of liability for Toyota, and ruining its name and stock value. So Edna sells short the stock. Even though there is an acute asymmetry of information between Edna and those at the other end of her securities transactions, she does nothing wrong. Not all acute asymmetries of information in securities transactions present unfairness. Why, then, should one think that an acute asymmetry arising from inside corporate information in a securities transaction is a problem?

One might try to bolster the unfairness argument by conceding that an acute asymmetry of information does not suffice to establish the relevant unfairness, but by saying that some instances of asymmetry are problematic; in particular, one might say that the relevant unfairness occurs in instances of asymmetry that result from an unequal access to information. In general, of course, corporate insiders have greater access to corporate secrets than do outsiders. So the appeal to unequal access may appear to mark progress for the proponent of the unfairness argument. But this appearance is illusory, I believe. Sometimes the existence of unequal access does not seem to render problematic an asymmetry of information. Suppose that I am the brother of Engineer Edna, and she refuses to tell anyone but me about the defective Toyota engine. Then I have unique access to the information about the bleak future of Toyota stock. Other traders do not have access that equals mine. Yet I do nothing wrong by trading on the information Edna gives me. So the unfairness argument so far seems unconvincing.

A final modification of the unfairness argument may seem more promising. This argument identifies the unfairness in insider trading not in terms of a simple asymmetry of information between the buyer and seller of a security, or in terms of an asymmetry stemming from unequal access, but instead in terms of an asymmetry stemming from wrongly unequal access. Put more simply, the argument is that insider trading is unfair because one party trades on information stolen from the firm. The argument relies on the idea that inside information is owned by the firm. When Texas Gulf Sulphur officers use their inside information about an ore strike to get a bargain in Texas Gulf Sulphur stock, they use valuable information that belongs not to them, but to their firm. They steal something valuable, information that belongs to the firm, and hence to its shareholders. They have no right to use the information. When they do so, they act unfairly and hence wrongly.

A difficulty for the theft argument lies in explaining why one should regard the firm as possessing the relevant property rights in information. One might reason on Lockean grounds that since it is the firm's labor and investment that produces the information, the information is owned exclusively by the firm. A troubling feature of this argument is its contingent nature and hence its limited scope. The soundness of the argument depends on contingencies regarding certain contracts. Suppose that a firm's board of directors, operating in a different legal regime than the United States, legally tells managers that as a reward for their excellent performance, it grants them the right to trade on insider information. Indeed, the firm might even warn prospective shareholders of its policy to grant employees this right. It would seem that these managers do not steal anything when they trade on inside information: the owners agree to their use of the property. Thus this version of the unfairness argument has limited scope. It cannot show that it is always wrong, either legally or morally, for insiders to trade on material, nonpublic information. It would at most show that it is wrong for insiders to trade on such information unless the firm has agreed to the trades. On this argument, firms would have the authority, in the absence of legal regulation, to render legitimate insider trading. The legal acceptability of insider trading would be a matter of contract; the moral acceptability would be a matter of the validity of promises that underlie the contract. To say, however, that insider trading is wrong unless permitted by contract or promise is to find nothing inherently wrong with insider trading.

The unfairness argument thus fails to show that insider trading is wrong in any significant sense. But the construction of the argument that appeals to contract suggests a promising twist: that we look at the contracts that might license insider trading as a way to assess the morality of insider trading. In the next section I will argue that any contract sanctioning insider trading will be morally defective, and that reflecting on the defects suggests a path to salvaging some of the traditional arguments against insider trading.

UNCONSCIONABLE CONTRACTS

The argument I make in the remainder of this chapter is simple at its core, though its execution requires patience. The core idea is that insider trading acceptably occurs only if people could legitimately make contracts transferring property rights in inside information from the firm to corporate insiders. But these contracts could never be legitimately made, I will argue. Any such contract would be unconscionable and hence both legally and morally wrong. So insider trading cannot acceptably occur. Indeed, I will maintain that because insider traders can have no right to use the information on which they trade, their trades involve deception, as the traditional theory of insider trading provides. In the remainder of this section, I argue simply that contracts for insider trading would be unconscionable. In the next section, I examine the relevance of the unconscionability argument to more general arguments that insider trading is wrong.

To begin the unconscionability argument against insider trading, set aside the law of insider trading. Imagine that all jurisdictions simultaneously strike from the books all bans on insider trading. Some firms might then insist on contracts that prohibit the practice of insider trading, either because they believe that doing so will somehow create a competitive advantage over other firms, or because they find the practice objectionable; other firms might allow the practice, perhaps because of its value as a cheap compensation device. In such a strange world, whether any particular corporate officer might *permissibly* engage in insider trading would appear to be a matter of contract. But this appearance is not veridical, I will argue. A contract permitting insider trading will unavoidably have an objectionable feature: it will be unconscionable; it will therefore also be in relevant part unenforceable.

What is unconscionability? Theorists discuss two varieties—substantive and procedural. Only the substantive variety will prove relevant here. Procedural unconscionability involves cognitive or volitional defects in a contracting party, something arguably not present in common insider trading cases, because involved parties are quite sophisticated.[19] Then what is substantive unconscionability? A contract is substantively unconscionable when its terms are exploitative or grossly unfair, that is, when it requires one party to pay an unreasonably high price for the benefit the contract confers on him. This can be simplified, and it will be useful to do so, because the idea of unconscionability plays so important a role in future discussion. So let us say, "A contract is substantively unconscionable when it requires one party to pay an unreasonably high price for the benefit that the contract confers on him." Obviously, this characterization of substantive unconscionability will not by itself suffice for picking out instances of substantive unconscionability; it relies on a notion of unreasonability that I leave unanalyzed and that different people will interpret differently. Even so, the concept of unconscionability, as I characterize it, is common enough in legal reasoning and everyday moral reasoning. Consider *Hume v. U.S.*, a legal case concerning a contract for corn; the contract requires that the buyer pay the seller what amounts to forty times the market value of the corn.[20] Because of the disparity in value the contract assigned to the parties, the court upheld a lower court's decision that the contract was unconscionable and hence unenforceable with respect to the price provision. The most plausible reading of cases such as *Hume* is that courts, when reaching their legal judgments about unconscionability, rely on a moral judgment of unconscionability. I will soon contend that insider trading contracts would involve similar, though more complex, judgments of unconscionability.

Suppose that I am correct in arguing that insider trading contracts would be unconscionable. So what? Why should the law not enforce these contracts? Paternalism provides a common answer. Courts may refuse to enforce an unconscionable contract, at least with respect to its unconscionable term, on the paternalistic account, to protect a person from the consequences of his own mistaken decision to enter the contract.[21] In *Hume*, for example, the court may be understood as protecting the buyer from the consequences of his bad decision on how much to pay for corn. However plausible this paternalistic account may seem generally (and the jury is out on that question), paternalism does not seem useful in providing an explanation for why one should regard insider trading contracts as unconscionable. A paternalistic intervention seems relevant only when a person is not competent to protect his own interests, either because of his ignorance or because of problems in voluntariness.[22] The paternalistic paradigm hardly seems well suited for participants in securities markets, who tend to be comparatively sophisticated and to have a wealth of choices available to them. In the scenario I have painted, market participants are informed when a firm permits insider trading—presumably they have other investment opportunities. Their choices thus seem neither relevantly uninformed nor coerced.

Even if one resists endorsing paternalistic intervention in securities markets, there is reason to balk at unconscionable contracts. Seana Shiffrin argues that enforcing unconscionable contracts is wrong because it involves facilitating wrongdoing.[23] Her argument is not paternalistic; it does not turn simply on what courts might do to advance the welfare interests of victims in unconscionable contracts. It instead turns on government's role in the process: the government should not facilitate wrongful contracts. Shiffrin's position relies on the idea that we can distinguish between refusing to do what a person asks out of concern for his interests and refusing to do what a person asks out of respect for one's own integrity. I believe that the cogency of this distinction is needed to provide a sound nonpaternalistic explanation of our reticence to enforce unconscionable contracts, and that it illuminates social values in other realms of choice. Consider another example Shiffrin gives. One may interfere with a person smoking a cigarette out of concern for his health— doing so is paternalistic. But even a person put off by paternalism may refuse to provide cigarettes to a smoker because he does not want to assist the smoker in his objectionable activity. Similarly, our society, through the courts, may refuse to assist people in creating their unconscionable contracts.

Assume that Shiffrin is correct in asserting that courts should not enforce unconscionable contracts because it would be wrong for them to facilitate wrong doing. There are implications for contracts that would allow insider trading, because, I will contend, these contracts should be regarded as unconscionable. Insider trading contracts would be unconscionable because of the kind of disparity of benefits they confer on shareholders and corporate insiders. The involved disparity is complex, however, and not analyzable in purely financial terms. I hope that an analogy will help make clear the nature of this complex disparity.

Consider *Hooters of America, Inc. v. Phillips*, a legal case involving an arbitration agreement in an employment contract that made it extremely difficult for Hooters employees to pursue sexual harassment grievances.[24] Appealing to the unreasonable obstacles that the contract created for an employee seeking redress for sexual harassment, the court decided that the contract was unconscionable. A narrow interpretation of *Hooters* would see it as about the unconscionability of denying a person a remedy when a contract goes awry. I concede that the *Hooters* court focuses on the remedial issue: doing otherwise might seem poor judicial craftsmanship, since the remedial issue fits so neatly within legal precedent. But there is a less technical and more revealing way to think about the case, from a moral point of view. What makes Hooters contracts terrible goes beyond remedies. Hooters contracts make employees unreasonably vulnerable to sexual harassment, because they leave the employer unworried about how employees would react to harassment, in effect protecting employers. The creation of that vulnerability provides independent reason for deeming the contract unconscionable; it transforms the value of the contract for an employee in ways that cannot be translated into monetary terms or compensated by increases in salary. So there is an insurmountable disparity in the value that the contract confers on Hooters employees and the Hooters firm; while Hooters gets the benefit of diminished litigation costs and liability, the employees on the other end of the employment contract receive something much worse, even if they receive some benefits in increased pay: these employees get a package deal that includes a substantially increased vulnerability to sexual harassment. Because Hooters contracts cause one party to pay an unreasonably high price for the benefit the contract confers, they are unconscionable.

In analyzing how unconscionability makes Hooters contracts wrong, I mentioned the costs that these contracts impose on Hooters employees. Despite my reliance on the idea of costs, the analysis of unconscionability in *Hooters* cannot be understood in cost-benefit terms. If a cost-benefit analysis were correct, then it would have been appropriate for the *Hooters* court to assess the contract by asking whether the benefits that the contract created for the firm and society more generally somehow compensated for the burden imposed on Hooters employees. Yet clearly a focus on these social benefits would have been repugnant in *Hooters*. Making a person vulnerable to sexual harassment is wrong even if the Hooters firm or society more generally somehow benefits from it, and the court should play no role in facilitating this wrong. Hooters contracts were wrong as a matter of moral principle because it is wrong to make Hooters employees so vulnerable to abuses of power and control by their employers, no matter what the prospects are that the employers will actually act abusively.

The lesson I draw from *Hooters* is that when agreement to a contract causes one party to suffer vulnerability to a substantial wrong committed by the other party, there is an insurmountable disparity in benefits that the contract confers on the parties, a disparity amounting to unconscionability. This lesson has great relevance for insider trading. Insider trading contracts, like Hooters contracts, would create an environment that makes a contracting party vulnerable to wrongdoing. Of course, in the insider trading case, the relevant wrong would not be sexual harassment. It would instead be wrongs of the sort canvassed in our earlier discussion of insider trading as a breach of fiduciary duty, for example, the mismanagement that consists of creating damaging rumors in order to manipulate stock prices. Judicial enforcement of insider trading contracts would, then, facilitate wrongdoing just as enforcement of Hooters contract would facilitate wrongdoing. No court should be willing to enforce a contract that so needlessly exposes shareholders to wrong. So insider trading contracts are unconscionable.

A natural objection can be made against the unconscionability argument. One might say that the argument cannot be correct because it would implausibly undercut not only insider trading contracts but also a broad range of unquestionably legitimate contracts. The objection stems from the fact that the unconscionability in insider trading contracts, as I have argued, occurs because these contracts leave a party vulnerable to abuse. In an important sense, one may contend, most contracts leave a party similarly vulnerable to abuse: if one party performs his part of the contract and the second party thereby benefits, but then the second party opportunistically does not do his part, abuse occurs. Consider a contract that a storekeeper makes to have a new roof installed on his store. Typically a roofer requires a substantial payment before he begins work. If the roofer takes the payment, choosing to flee with the money rather than install the roof, abuse occurs. Yet from that fact, it would be rash to infer that all roofing contracts are unconscionable, even though all such contracts create the possibility that a roofer will abscond with a storekeeper's money or do a poor job. A contract may therefore make a party vulnerable to abuse, even though contracts of its kind are not generally unconscionable. So why should one think that insider trading contracts, as I have been conceiving them, are unconscionable?

Two elements seem particularly important in the analysis of vulnerability arising from contracts: a person is vulnerable to the extent that he lacks the power or information to respond to a threat. So characterized, vulnerability seems a matter of degree; some contracts make a person more vulnerable than others. The vulnerability in insider trading contracts is acute, exceeding that in the roofing contract example. Stockholders in an insider trading regime cannot protect themselves against the wrongful harm that insiders traders cause, at least in part, because it is too hard for them to get timely knowledge that it occurs. Suppose, for example, that an insider trader wishes to sell short his company's stock, and so creates unfavorable information about this firm, either by spreading false rumors, or by secretly compromising the quality of his firm's product in ways that will soon hurt the firm's reputation. In the case of spreading rumors, it is hard to trace the origins of rumors and often too late to mitigate damage when one does so; in the case of intentionally degrading product quality, it is hard to know whether the action occurs because of poor judgment or bad intent. Because it is so hard to know whether the insider trader engages in misconduct aimed at affecting stock prices, it is hard to take action to limit his misconduct or mitigate its consequences. The situation is entirely different when one is trying to protect oneself against a roofer who does not do his job. As a general matter, a person protects himself against the roofer not doing the job at all by either paying him through an escrow account or by paying him in increments as he makes progress on the job. And a person protects himself against the roofing job being done poorly through the use of warranty; indeed, courts are loathe to allow parties to make a contract that contains no warranty. The vulnerable party in a roofing contract typically has information and resources to protect himself against abuse. The stockholder in an insider trading contract we have been envisaging does not have these resources. As a practical matter, then, the vulnerability that renders an insider trading unconscionable does not affect ordinary contracts like roofing contracts. We may safely conclude that insider trading contracts would be unconscionable without embracing absurd conclusions about contracts being generally unconscionable.

The Wrong in Insider Trading

So far I have argued that contracts permitting insider trading would be wrong because they would be unconscionable. But that argument is purely counterfactual—it is about contracts that do not in fact exist. It does not say anything about actual insider trading, which does not rely on insider trading contracts. It does not show why insider trading, as it now exists, is wrong. In this section I aim to establish a connection between the unconscionability of counterfactual insider trading contracts and the moral wrong in actual insider trading. I will argue that facts about counterfactual unconscionability help show that insider trading involves both theft and wrongful deception.

Earlier I contended that there is a problem explaining how insider trading might be theft. Insider information—whether trade secrets, such as information about proprietary technologies, or confidential information, such as information about ongoing negotiations—exists for the benefit of shareholders, and hence presumptively is the property of the firm. So when an insider trades on the information, he uses information to which he has no right, presumptively committing theft. The problem with the theft argument thus stated is its limited scope. It explains why insider trading is wrong when a firm insists on keeping inside information private, but not why the firm cannot give the information to the corporate insider, thus dissolving his status as a thief. The unconscionability argument fixes the scope problem. It provides that the firm cannot rightly give the relevant information to the insider, at least for the purpose of trading on it: an attempt to do so would rely on an unconscionable contract; the property rights are therefore relevantly inalienable. So insider trading is always theft, a wrong.

Theft is not the wrong U.S. courts typically invoke in their condemnation of insider trading. Instead they accuse insider traders of engaging in fraud. The heart of fraud is deception, as we have seen. There is a problem in finding these defects in the action of the insider trader, because typically he neither lies nor makes a misleading statement. Instead he fails to state or disclose a truth. But such a failure is deceptive or otherwise dishonest only if the insider has some duty to disclose, and earlier we found no basis for that duty. The unconscionability argument suggests a basis.

Recall, again, Texas Gulf Sulphur* officers. We have now established that they stole the information that they used in their stock trade. It belongs to the firm, and derivatively, the stockholders. The fact that they use information against stockholders that they stole from them helps show that they breach a duty to disclose. Consider an analogy. Fred is shopping in an antique store when a small earthquake occurs. Price tags fall off items for sale; Fred sees an inept clerk try to replace the tags but put the wrong tags on the items. A cup tagged as $1,000 before the earthquake now has a $25 tag on it. Fred grabs the cup, takes it to the cashier, and purchases it for $25. It seems clear, and law agrees, that Fred did something wrong. He should have told the clerk about the mistake in price; he breached his obligation to disclose. Fred's failure to disclose was dishonest. The unacceptability of Fred's contact suggests the following principle of disclosure: "(D) If you have information that rightly belongs to the other party in a sales transaction, and you know that he has somehow lost it, then you must disclose it rather than using it to your advantage." Why believe (D)? Elsewhere I defend it at length,[25] but here I can only sketch the defense. Not to require disclosure is to allow Fred to deprive the antique dealer of something rightly his—not merely the information about the price of his antique cup but also the economic value of that information. That deprivation would be wrong. Now one might retort that it was not Fred but the earthquake or the incompetent clerk doing the deprivation. But that would be too generous to Fred. Absent his connivance, the value in the antique dealer's cup would lurk in his store, awaiting his next survey of merchandise. It is only when the cup leaves the store at the bargain price that the dealer loses the relevant value. The truth of (D) is, then, an implication of the antique dealer's right to retain the value attaching to information about the cup.

The antique dealer example shows that before engaging in a sales transaction with a person, one must disclose to him valuable information that one possesses but that rightfully belongs to the other party. In a typical insider trading case, one covertly trades on information that rightfully belongs to the corporation, and derivatively to the shareholders. One has no right to keep that information from them. One owes a moral obligation to disclose the information. Insider trading breaches a duty to disclose and hence constitutes wrongful deception.

In the insider cases that we have been so far discussing, the corporate insider buys stock from his own shareholder. When insiders buy stock without disclosing, they violate principle (D), because in some morally significant sense shareholders have property rights in their firm and the information owned by the firm. But principle (D) is limited in scope. It helps us understand how the corporate buyer who trades on inside information, without disclosing, may treat his shareholder unfairly and, ultimately, how the insider deceives the shareholder. Principle (D) does not explain the wrong in many other insider trading cases, however. Consider the very common cases in which an insider does not buy stock, but instead sells it to a party who does not already own stock in the insider's firm. In such cases, it makes little sense to say that the insider steals information from the buyer of stock, even derivatively, because the buyer does not yet stand in an ownership relation to the firm. Principle (D) does not directly explain the wrong that occurs when a corporate insider steals information from his firm and then relies on this information in selling stock to someone outside the firm, a stranger to the firm. How, then, should we understand this wrong? This is a complex matter that I take up at length elsewhere.[26] The argument is roughly as follows. Principle (D) helps us understand that it is unfair to get a trading advantage by using information that one has no right to use. The unfairness remains whether one wrongly acquires the information from one's trading partner (as in *Texas Gulf Sulfur*) or from another source. When a corporate insider steals information from his firm and then uses it to trade with another party (even a stranger to the firm), he treats that party unfairly. To avoid the unfairness while still making a trade, one must avoid taking advantage of the wrongfully acquired information. So one must disclose. If one fails to disclose when one should, and one's disclosure would have cured relevant false beliefs, then one engages in morally wrongful deception. Insider trading is always morally wrong because of the deception it involves.

CONCLUSION

Inside information exists for the benefit of the firm and its shareholders. It is therefore presumptive theft for a corporate insider to trade on this information without the agreement of its owners. No firm could make a morally acceptable agreement with relevant parties—its management and shareholders—that would give corporate insiders a right to trade on material, nonpublic information. Any contract purporting to assign such a right would be unconscionable; it would leave share-holders with an unreasonably bad deal in which they were overly vulnerable to man-agerial abuse. It follows that when a corporate insider trades on material, nonpublic information, he trades on information he can have no right to use, and thus steals the information from its owners—the firm and its shareholders. One may not, then, as a moral matter, trade on insider information. If one wants to make the trade, one must first assure that the information becomes public, that it is no longer insider infor-mation. If an insider nonetheless insists on trading on such information, he trades on information he has no right to keep secret from the person on the other side. He engages in wrongful deception. Such deception is wrong no matter what the social consequences. It is wrong as a matter of principle; it is a deontological wrong.

NOTES

1. For valuable discussion, I thank Tom Dunfee, Waheed Hussain, Eric Orts, Richard Shell, David Silver, and audiences at the Philosophy Department, University of Delaware, and Department of Legal Studies and Business Ethics, the Wharton School of the University of Pennsylvania. I also thank Katherina Glac for her research assistance; she would have been a coauthor had institutional barriers not complicated matters. For its generous financial support, I thank the Zicklin Center for Business Ethics Research.

2. Insider trading is illegal in the United States and in approximately one hundred other countries. In the United States and many other countries, it is treated as a felony, a serious crime. See Utpal Bhattacharya and Hazem Daouk. "The World Price of Insider Trading," *Journal of Finance* 57 (2002): 75–108. In some countries, however, insider trading is on the books as a crime, but the law is not enforced. The broad range of treatment of insider trading in different jurisdictions makes generalization difficult. For purposes of this discussion, I will limit myself to U.S. law. My discussion of insider trading as a crime will concern its status as a violation of criminal law. I will also and more fundamentally be concerned with insider trading as a moral wrong. Hence I will be concerned with whether there are good moral reasons to treat insider trading as a crime.

3. See Battacharya and Daouk, "The World Price of Insider Trading," and Andrew Metrick, "Insider Trading," in *The New Palgrave Dictionary of Economics*, 2nd ed., eds. Larry Blume and Steven Durlauf, (New York: Palgrave Macmillan, 2008).

4. For a simple overview of the legal issues, see Stephen Bainbridge, *Securities Law: Insider Trading* (New York: Foundation, 1999). The analysis of insider trading I give in the text is a partial specification of the concept, adequate for specifying paradigmatic instances of insider trading, but nothing as complete as a set of necessary and sufficient conditions for insider trading.

5. See Alan Strudler and Eric W. Orts, "Moral Principle in the Law of Insider Trading," *Texas Law Review* (1999): 375–437.

6. *SEC v. Texas Gulf Sulphur Co.*, 401 F.2d 833 (2d Cir. 1968).

7. For an unsurpassed survey of the economic issues, see Metrick, "Insider Trading."

8. Because the existence of this social good may depend on social cooperation, nonconsequentialist reasons, including reasons rooted in fairness or reciprocity, may also be triggered. But those reasons are not my concern here. Instead, I am concerned with the

purely consequentialist argument that we should promote and protect social goods to the extent that doing so satisfies the duty to bring about the best possible outcome.

9. Battacharya and Daouk, "The World Price of Insider Trading."

10. Henry Manne, *Insider Trading and the Stock Market* (New York: Free Press, 1966). For an argument against Manne, see Roy A. Schotland, "Unsafe at Any Price: A Reply to Manne, Insider Trading and the Stock Market," *University of Virginia Law Review* 53 (1967): 1425–1478.

11. For a survey of scholars reaching this conclusion see Strudler and Orts, "Moral Principle in the Law of Insider Trading," 383n24.

12. Strudler and Orts, "Moral Principle in the Law of Insider Trading."

13. See Christine M. Korsgaard, "The Right to Lie: Kant on Dealing with Evil," *Philosophy & Public Affairs* 15 (1986): 325–349; Alan Strudler, "Deception Unraveled," *Journal of Philosophy* 102 (2005): 458–473.

14. One might wonder how we know that Disney risks paying an unfairly high price, or how we know that any price is unfairly high. This is an enormously difficult issue that I cannot resolve here. In my view the seller in the Disney case, if fully informed, has so much leverage that he approaches the point of being able to engage in extortion and hence of being able to credibly demand much more than the property is worth at the time of sale. The seller is taking economic value that Disney creates and claiming it for his own. But I rely on my own subjective judgment, which I think would be widely shared. If a particular reader does not share this judgment, I ask him or her to accept for the sake of argument the idea that the well-informed buyer is in a position to ask an unfairly high price for the Disney property, and consider the argument that flows from the idea.

15. For elaboration of the traditional theory, see Strudler and Orts, "Moral Principle in the Law of Insider Trading," 389–393. For skepticism that I echo here about the traditional theory, see Frank H. Easterbrook and Daniel R. Fischel, *The Economic Structure of Corporate Law* (Cambridge: Harvard University Press, 1991), 269–270.

16. The unfairness argument is defended, in different forms, in Victor Brudney, "Insiders, Outsiders, and Informational Advantage Under the Federal Securities Laws," *Harvard Law Review* 93 (1979) 322–378; Kim Lane Scheppele, "It's Just Not Right: The Ethics of Insider Trading," *Law and Contemporary Problems* 56 (1993): 123–173; Patricia H. Werhane, "The Indefensibility of Insider Trading," *Journal of Business Ethics* 10 (1991): 729–731.

17. Leviticus 25:17.

18. Thomas Aquinas, *Summa Theologica*, II-II, q. 77, a. 4.

19. Caveat: courts strain hard to find both procedural and substantive elements of unconscionability in a contract before declaring the contract itself unconscionable. If both elements are in fact necessary for unconscionability in U.S. law, then I advocate a departure from U.S. law. U.S. law however, seems uncertain on this point. In my view, courts tend to make a purely perfunctory finding on the procedural element.

20. *Hume v. United States*, 132 U.S. 406 (1889).

21. For a discussion of in contract law, see Duncan Kennedy, "Distributive and Paternalist Motives in Contract and Tort Law, with Special Reference to Compulsory Terms and Unequal Bargaining Power," *Maryland Law Review* 41 (1982) 563–658.

22. In the text I use the term "paternalism" to signify what philosophers call *soft paternalism*, which would justify interfering with a person's self-regarding choice when it is compromised by defects in information or defects in the reasoning and decision process. Another version of paternalism, *hard* paternalism, would justify interfering with a person's self-regarding choice even in the absence of such defects, so long as a person makes a bad

choice about what is in his interests. I cannot do justice to hard paternalism in this chapter. Like many people, I find hard paternalism implausible because I find it offensive to interfere with the liberty of competent and well-informed adults to make choices about their own good.

23. Seana Shiffrin, "Paternalism, Unconscionability Doctrine, and Accommodation," *Philosophy & Public Affairs* 29 (2000): 205–250.

24. *Hooters of America, Inc. v. Phillips*, 173 F.3d 933 (4th Cir. 1999).

25. Alan Strudler, "Moral Complexity in the Law of Nondisclosure," *UCLA Law Review* 45 (1997): 337–384.

26. Strudler and Orts, "Moral Principle in the Law of Insider Trading."

SUGGESTED READING

Bainbridge, Stephen. *Securities Law: Insider Trading*. New York: Foundation, 1999.

Bhattacharya, Uptal and Hazem Daouk. "The World Price of Insider Trading." *Journal of Finance* 57 (2002): 75–108.

Brudney, Victor. "Insiders, Outsiders and Informational Advantages under the Federal Securities Laws." *Harvard Law Review* 93 (1979): 322–376.

Easterbrook, Frank and Daniel Fischel *The Economic Structure of Corporate Law*. Cambridge, Mass.: Harvard University Press, 1991.

Engelen, Peter-Jan and Luc Van Liederkerke. "The Ethics of Insider Trading Revisited." *Journal of Business Ethics* (2007) 74: 497–507.

Green, Stuart. *Lying, Cheating, and Stealing: A Moral Theory of White Collar Crime*. Oxford: Oxford University Press, 2006.

Lawson, Gary. "The Ethics of Insider Trading." *Harvard Journal of Law and Public Policy* 11 (1988): 727–783.

Leland, Hayne. "Insider Trading: Should It Be Prohibited?" *Journal of Political Economy* 100 (1992): 859–887.

Levmore, Saul. "Securities and Secrets: Insider Trading and the Law of Contracts." *Virginia Law Review* 68 (1982): 117–160.

Manne, Henry. *Insider Trading and the Stock Market*. New York: Free Press, 1966.

Metrick, Andrew. "Insider Trading." In *The New Palgrave Dictionary of Economics*, 2nd ed. Edited by Larry Blume and Steven Durlauf. New York: Palgrave MacMillan, 2008.

Moore, Jennifer. "What Is Really Unethical About Insider Trading?" *Journal of Business Ethics* 9 (1990): 171–182.

Scheppele, Kim. "It's Just Not Right: The Ethics of Insider Trading." *Law and Contemporary Problems* 56 (1993): 123–173.

Schotland, Roy. "Unsafe at Any Price: A Reply to Manne." *Virginia Law Review* 53 (1967): 1425–1478.

Shiffrin, Seana. "Paternalism, Unconscionability Doctrine, and Accommodation." *Philosophy & Public Affairs* 29 (2000): 205–250.

Strudler, Alan. "Moral Complexity in the Law of Nondisclosure." *UCLA Law Review* 45 (1997): 337–384.

Strudler, Alan and Eric Orts. "Moral Principle in the Law of Insider Trading." *Texas Law Review* 78 (1999): 375–437.

Werhane, Patricia. "The Ethics of Insider Trading." *Journal of Business Ethics* 8 (1989): 841–45.

CHAPTER 14

INTELLECTUAL PROPERTY RIGHTS

RICHARD T. DE GEORGE

INTELLECTUAL property is a contentious notion. There are disputes about what it means, about whether it can be morally justified, and, if it can be morally justified, about whether particular instances of legislation regarding it are morally justified. These disputes take place within a larger context concerned with what property is and how it is justified.

Property, in general, is anything that is owned. Ownership in turn implies either possession of or control over whatever is owned. The possession and control may be simply factual, in which case we can speak of *de facto* ownership; or it may be justified according to some criteria, in which case it is normative or *de jure*. In either case ownership involves a set of claims, and the set varies with the kind of property one has. Property, as a normative concept, consists of the rights (or justified claims) that one has in ownership. Although the basic justification for property is moral, effective or enforceable property rights of a legitimate property holder with respect to others[1] are expressed as legal rights.

There are a variety of ways of conceptualizing different kinds of property. Legally, the different kinds of property are defined as differing bundles of rights. One useful such categorization according to the nature of the property held divides property into tangible property (physical objects), real property (land and the structures built on them), intangible property (money, stocks, bonds, and other financial instruments), and intellectual property. Of these, intellectual property is the least well defined.

Although all societies have some concept of property, views differ about what can be owned and the rights that attach to the various kinds. Nomadic people frequently do not have the concept of ownership of land. Private ownership of the means of production is not allowed in communist countries, where all industry and productive resources are owned by the state, the society, or the people. Property rights (e.g., the right to exclusive use, the right to rent, the right to destroy, etc.) vary both according to the kind of property and the laws defining those rights in any given society. As a consequence, talk about the rights one has with respect to each of the different kinds of property makes most sense when those rights are specified within a social context, such as the laws of a given society. That does not mean that property, specific kinds of property, and particular laws about specific kinds of property, including intellectual property, cannot be morally evaluated. They can be and are, as we shall see. The legislative differences between nations, where there are interactions, require negotiation of the differences and frequently harmonization of the differing laws. Considerations of justice play a role, and ethical arguments can lead to pressure on governments to pass appropriate legislation.

The current period is often characterized as the Information Age. Because information (in the broad sense of products of the mind) is infinitely sharable, the Information Age has the ability to make all information available to everyone in the world. The potential for unleashing human capacities by such sharing is the hope of the postindustrial period. At the same time, the Information Age is characterized by information being the source of potential riches for those who exploit it. Thus there is a tendency to attempt to restrict its free dissemination and to claim proprietary rights over it to a much greater extent than previously. This tension between the possibility of free dissemination to all and the desire of some to control dissemination for profit forms the basis for many of the ethical debates, struggles, and problems that one finds with respect to information in the world of business, commerce, and enterprise. Consequently, it has become a major issue in the ethics of business and contemporary business ethics.

INTELLECTUAL PROPERTY

What then *is* intellectual property? The answer is by no means simple.

A first and commonsensical reply to the question would be that intellectual property must have something to do with ideas. There is an obvious sense in which each of us has ideas (or concepts or contents of cognition), and we might claim them as ours, just as we each claim our own body. I can think them even if prohibited from talking or writing about them. There is little point, however, in claiming that our ideas are our property, unless there is some threat that someone will take them from us or deprive us of them. This has nothing to do with the use I may make of my ideas but simply with their possession.

Three aspects of ideas make them problematic candidates for ownership in the ordinary sense of ownership of objects. The first is that individuals may independently arrive at similar ideas. Claiming exclusive right to an idea, in the sense that others may not think it, makes no sense. The second is that ideas (in the sense of contents of cognition) are infinitely shareable. I can give them away and still have them. In fact, this is what makes possible human history, civilization, and development. If one person has a useful idea, he or she can share that with as many others as there are, and they can all use the idea. One generation passes on to the next the knowledge it has developed. Less developed nations can learn from more developed nations. The process can go on indefinitely.

The third aspect is related to the second. Although we claim our bodies as ours as well as our possessions, land, and money, our claim to our ideas as ours is more tenuous, because we received most of our ideas as we grew up. We have received them from a large number of others and from the store of socially accumulated knowledge. They were given to us with our acquisition of language, which of course we did not invent but received from others. Our modifications to the ideas we have received from the storehouse of knowledge are usually small in the broad perspective of the accumulated knowledge acquired by humankind. Even giants such as Newton and Einstein build on what they have received from their predecessors and contemporaries. Newton and Leibniz quarreled over who was the first to develop the calculus. The fact that they both did at more or less the same time suggests that mathematics at the time had developed to the point where the calculus was within reach of those bright enough to take the needed intellectual leap.

Given these considerations, what can we claim as intellectual property, and what can any claim of intellectual property consist of? There is no natural kind called "intellectual property." The term "intellectual property" according to most sources appears for the first time in October 1845 in a Massachusetts Circuit Court ruling on a patent case.[2] Before that there were laws, which differed in the bundle of rights they granted inventors (through patents) and authors (through copyright). The term "intellectual property" developed so as to include a variety of differing bundles of rights that were recognized in law (especially trademark, trade secrecy, copyright, and patent law) for protecting what can be called various products of the mind. The rights were so recognized because someone at some point claimed that it made a difference whether they were recognized, and the difference hinged on commercial value. If what is claimed as intellectual property has no commercial value, then other than the right of attribution as the creator (which might bring with it acclaim, recognition, or some other nonmonetary reward) there seems no purpose in asserting the claim to exclusive use, much less to any notion of income from and other monetary benefits. That some people wrote books or diaries or other material that they did not want to make public does not require that they have intellectual property rights in them.[3] In fact, as the law has developed, one has property rights through copyright and patent only if the protected material is made public, and under trade secrecy laws, only if it has commercial value.

Intellectual property has come to mean the kinds of expressions of the mind that are protected by the various forms of intellectual property law. The rights that form each kind of bundle of rights has varied from time to time and place to place, as have the specific sorts of expressions covered. A full understanding of the meaning of the term, therefore, requires a fuller understanding of its history.

The Historical Background

The claim to a right to prevent others from using or profiting from or developing one's ideas does not arise to any considerable extent with respect to written material until the development of the printing press. Prior to that time the right of attribution (that is, the right to be acknowledged as the author of a work or the creator of an invention) was recognized, but expressions of ideas—be they in song or plays, in literature or science—were shared. Those who wrote the songs, minstrels for instance, earned their living by performing. Others could learn the tunes or words through their performance, but the minstrels were paid for their performance, not for the exclusive use of what they performed. The same is true of storytellers, playwrights, musicians, artists, and so on. The products of their labor, just as the products of the labor of a farmer, could become property, if embodied in some tangible form, such as a painting. The physical painting was property, not any claim to the technique used or the composition, or other forms of the idea behind the actual work. Manuscripts were copied by hand and were valuable for the work that went into producing them. One's fame as a teacher came from one's teaching not from the sale of one's books, since manuscripts were so tedious to produce that they were reproduced in very limited quantities and not available to the masses, who in any event could not read.

The printing press changed all this. The initial protection, however, was given to printers, not to authors.[4] But the step from claiming one is the original author to claiming some right to benefit from the product of one's labor, even if it is in large part intellectual labor, was a small one. Also at play in the West was the rising notion of the individual and individualism. In societies with a more collective, noncompetitive view of life, there would be less impetus to claim one's writings, songs, or poems as individual property, rather than as material to be shared, even though authorship might be noted and remembered.

Guilds did not consider their knowledge or practices as property, but they did see them as valuable, and often tried to control their dissemination exclusively to members of the guild. The practice resembles trade secrecy. In the fifteenth century, silk makers claimed ownership in their patterns and designs, and as the guild system started to break down, innovations were claimed by individuals rather than considered as guild knowledge.[5] Historically, patents or prototypical patent protection afforded by a state arose in the middle of the fifteenth century in order to protect and promote commercial interests. Similar protection did not develop in China, for instance.[6] What might be termed the first patent law was the 1624 British Statute of Monopolies, which granted monopoly protection for inventions for a period of fourteen years. The first modern copyright law was the 1709 British Act of Anne.[7]

What came to be considered intellectual property was not ideas, but their expression in some tangible form, either in books and other media or in inventions or productive processes, as protected by law.

The Legal Context

Before we look at the moral justifications for intellectual property, we should look more closely at their formulation in law, since it is primarily the protection afforded by law that is challenged and that requires justification. We should note, however, that those things that cannot be legally owned in a society cannot be legally stolen. If air cannot be owned, it cannot be stolen; if land cannot be owned, it cannot be stolen, even if it can be misappropriated or abused. Similarly, in a society that does not recognize intellectual property at all (in either a moral or a legal sense), products of the mind cannot be stolen; and in a society that does not legally recognize what others call intellectual property, a law against stealing intellectual property would make no sense. This does not mean that the society cannot hold that plagiarism, for instance, is unethical or even illegal, but in such a society its wrongfulness would come from the fact that plagiarism is a form of lying and misrepresentation about authorship, rather than any violation of property rights.

In the United States, the legal basis for the protection of what is called intellectual property comes from article 1, section 8 of the U.S. Constitution, which includes under the powers of Congress the power "to promote the Progress of Science and useful Arts, by securing for limited Times to Authors and Inventors the exclusive Right to their respective Writings and Discoveries." This implies a consequentialist pragmatic basis for the protection of intellectual property, with the emphasis on the benefit to the common good rather than the protection of individual ownership rights. It can be considered a utilitarian justification but of a restricted type in which the development of science and the useful arts is the pragmatic end to be served.

With this constitutional basis, the U.S. Congress then passed copyright and patent legislation. The first U.S. copyright law was passed in 1790.[8] The U.S. Copyright Office became a separate department of the Library of Congress in 1897. To qualify for copyright protection a work must be in a tangible form of expression, show a modicum of creativity, and be original, in the sense that it is not itself copied from some other source. Copyright originally granted to the copyright holder the exclusive right to reproduce, distribute, license, and produce derivative works from the covered written work, book, map, or chart for a period of fourteen years, renewable for another fourteen years. Over time prints, music, dramatic compositions, photographs, motion pictures, sound recordings, and in 1978, computer programs[9] were added to what could be copyrighted. In 1831, the period of protection was extended to twenty-eight years, renewable for an additional fourteen years.[10] The term of protection was extended in 1978 to the life of the author plus fifty years, and for works for hire, seventy-five years.[11] In 1989, the United States agreed to adhere to the Berne Convention for the Protection of Literary and Artistic Works,[12] and in 1998 the Sonny Bono Copyright Extension Act increased protection to the life of the author plus seventy years, or ninety-five years for a work for hire.[13]

The U.S. patent system was borrowed from the British. The first U.S. patent law was passed in the same year as the copyright law, but the period of protection was fourteen years with no provision for extension.[14] Foreign patents were not recognized, so U.S. industry could legally copy European inventions and use them for their own benefit. The United States argued that the public good was better served by importing literary works and inventions without restrictions of copyrights and patents, and that U.S. patents and copyrights were appropriate for U.S. citizens in order to stimulate creativity. The society of the United States would benefit most from that policy. Most European countries had initially also adopted a similar position, although by the middle of the nineteenth century they began to negotiate bilateral agreements.[15] From an ethical point of view one must balance the deserts of the author and inventor, the good for the society of the author or inventor in promoting new works and inventions, and the social good that results from having works and inventions available to all for the increase of culture and of economic development. One issue of dispute is whether authors and inventors have moral rights in their work independent of law or only those rights granted by law, and, if they have the former, what exactly they are. Whatever they might be, they still have to be balanced against social considerations.

In 1793, the U.S. patent system was defined to cover any "new and useful art, machine, manufacture or composition and any new and useful improvement on any art, machine, manufacture or composition of matter."[16] To be patentable an invention must pass two tests. First it must be subject matter eligible for patent. Not patentable are ideas, laws of nature, or mathematical truths. Second the invention must be new, useful, and nonobvious to "a person having ordinary skill in the area of technology relating to the invention."

In 1836, the Patent Office was established under the State Department, and the 1836 patent law was amended in 1861 to make the period of protection seventeen years.[17] The United States joined the Paris Convention for the Protection of Industrial Property in 1887,[18] and in 1995 it signed the World Trade Organization Trade Related Aspects of Intellectual Property (TRIPS) Agreement, increasing the period of protection to twenty years beginning from the patent application's filing.[19]

Copyright provides longer but weaker protection than does a patent. If two people have similar ideas and are developing their expression simultaneously but independently, both may copyright their work, as may anyone else who independently develops and expresses the same idea. Patent protection, on the other hand, is granted to the first one to file for such protection (except in the United States, where it is granted to the first to invent).[20] Those who come later, even if they develop their invention or process independently, are not allowed to exploit it commercially until the original patent expires. The difference in the kind and length of protection can be explained historically. That they should both be the same is not obvious, unless one includes both under the heading of intellectual property and maintains that all intellectual property protection should be the same. Both patent and copyright, as well as trade secrecy and trademarks, provide civil protection (unlike other kinds of property, which are protected by criminal law). If there is a violation, it is up to the owner of the protected intellectual property to sue the infringer. Violation is not a criminal offense, unless (in the United States since 1982) the copyright violation is for commercial purposes of private financial gain.[21]

Trade secrecy covers information held and protected by a business which it considers valuable and which it believes gives it a competitive advantage. Unlike what is covered by patent or copyright, a trade secret covers information or processes, formulas, devices, techniques that, as the term indicates, are not made public and that can be kept secret indefinitely. In the United States, trade secrets have been covered by state statute, although in 1980 the Uniform Trade Secrets Act was adopted by many states.[22]

A trademark is a distinctive symbol, picture, or words that identify a product, manufacturer, or seller. Trademarks have been used since ancient times to identify either the producer or the owner of goods. As early as 1282, medieval guilds gained legal protection against the misuse of their marks on goods they did not produce.[23] Trademarks both established liability on the part of the maker and were used as a guarantee of quality, identifying the product as coming from certain guilds. In the United States, trademarks can be registered with the U.S. Office of Trademarks and Patents. Initially they were covered by state common law, but since the Lanham Act (1946) federal protection has been available.[24] Like trade secrets they can be kept by a company indefinitely.

The point of this foray into the history of intellectual property is that the notion of intellectual property is neither conceptually clear nor intuitively accessible. The notion of owning (in a sense other than attribution of authorship) ideas or their expression did not spontaneously spring up as society developed. Because property rights in intellectual property are granted only for a limited period (except for trademarks and trade secrets), such property becomes available to all at some time specified by the state. The author or inventor does not relinquish ownership of what he or she owned, as with other kinds of property. Rather, after the period of protection the right simply ceases to be legally either protected or acknowledged. As a result, although one can assume, for instance, that any automobile that one sees is owned by someone, most of the expressions of ideas that one encounters are not owned but are part of the public domain, and those that are owned will cease to be owned at the time when their author's or inventor's legal ownership rights end. This is not the intuitive notion of ownership or of property. To claim that one's moral rights to ownership that were formerly protected by copyright or patent continue in the expression of one's ideas even after the legal protection and recognition has ceased is a possible position to hold. However, no society acknowledges such a right.

The upshot is that almost all writers and commentators on intellectual property mean by it whatever is protected by a diverse set of laws, especially copyright, patent, trademark, and trade secrecy. The objects that are included for the most part are those that have commercial value, and the reason the laws developed as they did was in order to protect the commercial interests of either the state or of particular groups within the state. This does not mean that one cannot ask whether the laws are morally justifiable, or whether some item that is not covered by the law should be and whether some item that is covered should not be, and so on. But it does mean that all these moral questions are most fruitfully raised in the context provided by law. These laws served reasonably well during the period of the industrial revolution and industrial development. With the move from the Industrial Age to the Information Age they are being stretched in ways they were never intended.

The General Moral Justification of Intellectual Property

The contemporary justifications given for property are basically of three types: a natural rights and justice argument based on a Lockean approach to property, a utilitarian (pragmatic) argument, and an argument based on property as an extension of one's personality.[25] In each case what is at issue is *individual* property rights—initially to the land, water, minerals, and the fruits thereof, and secondarily to the individual accumulation of wealth. Although both Aristotle and Aquinas defended some version of private property against Plato's preference for collective ownership,[26] contemporary justifications start with the modern era, with the rise of capitalism, and, in the case of Locke, with the rise of individualism and democracy. The general defenses of private ownership do not justify any particular system of property, such as capitalism, and are compatible with legal and political systems that limit individual property rights in various ways. The extent to which these general justifications apply to intellectual property, and justify it, is disputed.

The Natural Rights/Justice Argument

The Lockean justification of property begins with the assertion that "though the Earth, and all inferior Creatures be common to all Men, yet every Man has a *Property* in his own *Person*."[27] Each person has a natural right to own himself and a right to preserve his life. No person is by right a slave. Each person also owns the labor of his body and the work of his hands. What he takes out of nature and mixes with his labor, he thereby makes his property: "For this *Labor* being the unquestionable Property of the Laborer, no Man but he can have a right to what that is once joyned to, at least where there is enough, and as good left in common for others."[28] This is the "original Law of Nature for the *beginning of Property*"[29] upon which are based the positive laws that determine property. On this basis Locke justifies, as property, not only those acorns or fruits of the field that one takes from nature or the animals that one kills (although one is allowed to take only what he can use) but also the ownership of land that he cultivates or otherwise uses. One is not allowed to waste and can claim no ownership rights in more than he can use, if it would otherwise perish or spoil. But of durable things, such as gold or diamonds, which do not spoil, "he might heap up as much of these durable things as he pleased."[30] The same is true of money. According to Locke, all this was ratified by the consent of members of society and enacted into laws.[31]

This justification is a hypothetical presentation of how property arose and what societies implicitly agreed to. Although initial appropriation was justified only to the extent that one used what one possessed and that as much and as good was left for others, this latter proviso clearly had to be violated as more and more accumulation occurred, making it impossible to leave as much and as good. Thereafter, one has to assume some just method of transferring property, and of dealing with the claims of those who arrive on the scene after all the goods of the earth have been appropriated by others.

The argument from natural rights and justice is not without its critics.[32] The argument says that once someone has put his labor into an object and made it his own, it would be unjust for another simply to appropriate it. The argument has a certain intuitive appeal as giving people their due and recompensing their efforts, but its critics point out that society might arrange property rights differently, so that whatever labor one expends on land or natural resources belongs to the society as a whole rather than to the individual.[33] Moreover, the argument does not extend to the means of transfer of wealth, or to the acceptability of any given distribution of wealth that might result from individual accumulation based on effort in a society.[34]

Commentators differ on whether Locke's justification, to the extent that it justifies property at all, applies to intellectual property.[35] One reason is that ideas, which are arguably the most important products of the mind, cannot, under any of the existing systems of intellectual property, become property. One has to read Locke analogously for his theory to apply to intellectual property. In the state of nature in which everything is held in common, one draws from the commons and makes whatever one so takes one's property through one's labor. What is the commons from which one draws and to which one adds one's labor in order to justify calling it one's intellectual property? Is it the common store of language, the accumulated knowledge to which all have access, or something else? To speak of a commons here is clearly to use an analogy, but arguably the analogy does not hold. The commons of land, for instance, existed independently of human beings. But language and the storehouse of knowledge that we find when we are born into the world are all the products of human development. In addition, as opposed to taking the fruits of the field to maintain one's life, which is the justification for taking as much land as one needs, the taking from the commons of knowledge (whatever sense one may give to that) and making it one's exclusive property cannot be justified as necessary to maintain life. Everyone needs food, shelter, and clothing in order to survive. One therefore has the right to produce or procure and to use them. Which expressions of ideas that are claimed as one's individual property and that one may exclude others from using are necessary for survival? There seem to be none comparable to food, shelter, and clothing. So that part of the argument fails. By mixing one's intellectual labor with knowledge, science, information, or whatever term one chooses, one comes up with something new. But why does that belong to the one who does this? One could argue that the person has left as much and as good for others, which is true. Yet, the question raised against Locke with respect to physical objects and land applies equally to claims of ownership of expressions of ideas. Why should the new discovery or expression not become part of the general store of knowledge? In science, mathematics, and many areas of knowledge this is the rule.

Nonetheless, there is a certain appeal to the Lockean claim that if one puts a great deal of time and money into the development of the expression of an idea—whether it be writing a novel or developing an invention—a system of property that recognized private ownership would be unfair or unjust if it allowed someone else to appropriate what one developed and to benefit from it commercially before the original author or inventor had the chance to do so. That appeal, however, presupposes an existing system of property and only expresses a legitimate expectation within that system. If a society did not recognize intellectual property, then one would not have the expectation of profiting commercially from one's intellectual labor. The claim that a society that does not recognize intellectual property is morally deficient presupposes some claim to property rights in the expression of one's ideas that sees them as natural and not conventional. That claim has yet to be articulated, and Locke's approach does not provide it.

For centuries, scholars have toiled to extend knowledge, which they freely shared through their publications. The most that a Lockean justification shows is that some forms of intellectual property in some legal and social contexts can be justified if they provide for fair remuneration for one's labor. It does not show that such a system is necessary or that it is preferable to a system that does not recognize intellectual property.

The Utilitarian-Pragmatic Argument

That task is assumed for property in general, and for intellectual property in particular, by a second general defense of private property, namely, a utilitarian one. This claims that more benefit is derived for all from the existence of private property than from any alternative system. The best current evidence in support of this argument is the standard of living in the developed countries of the West as compared to what was achieved in the Soviet Union or the countries of Eastern Europe under communist governments, with socialist property systems. This utilitarian argument is often taken as a pragmatic argument as well, namely, that a society with private property works better than one without it, where "works better" is interpreted as allowing people to achieve more of what they want to achieve, whatever that is.

Similarly, the argument claims that a system that gives legal protection to authors and inventors for a limited period of time produces more benefit for the society than a system that does not give such protection. Historically, the U.S. system of patents in the nineteenth century led to such a large number of new and useful inventions that other nations changed their laws to harmonize with the U.S. law.[36] If on the whole countries with intellectual property protection have produced more benefit (in the sense of economic development and improvement in the lives of their citizens) for society through the efforts of their people per capita than societies without such protection, then, the argument asserts, this is the justification for having a system of intellectual property law, or at least for that part which consists of patent protection. The fact that other countries changed their patent laws to follow the U.S. model underlines the fact that among the various ways of protecting intellectual property some systems are better than others in advancing the promotion of socially beneficial new inventions. It should be noted, however, that the justification is not the benefit of the individual author or inventor but the benefit to society that counts. The reason is that any system of intellectual property, while providing an incentive to individuals to produce useful inventions, does so at a certain cost to those other members of society who are restrained from making improvements or otherwise freely benefiting from the creations for the period of protection. The overall good is what carries the day.

This defense is persuasive, when limited to patents. That a similar defense can be made for copyright is possible, but the data in this case are not as clear. If there were no copyright protection (there would still be the right of author attribution), would there be more or fewer works of the type presently covered by copyright? Would there be more or fewer quality works of that type, however one defines "quality"? The presumption of Western society, as expressed in its laws, is that there would be fewer. The justifying data is difficult to obtain, and the justification seems to hinge on an assumption that financial return is the prime motivator in the production of such material. Since the argument depends on the actual results of adopting a given system of intellectual property, it is possible to fault it from an ethical point of view if it fails to produce as much good as other easily adopted alternatives, if it violates human rights, or if it produces more harm than good in certain areas.

The "Personality" Argument

A third justification of property comes from Hegel, and is more influential in Europe than in the United States. This consists in the claim that property is the "outward symbol of my personality."[37] Hegel denies Locke's notion of natural rights, and his account of labor. For Hegel it is not labor that counts but rather the transference of one's will to an external object that makes it one's own. Things have no purpose of their own: "Every man has the right to turn his will upon a thing or make the thing an object of his will, that is to say, to set aside the mere thing and recreate it as his own."[38] That is what ownership means. But, "In order to fix property as the outward symbol of my personality, it is not enough that I represent it as mine and internally will it to be mine; I must also take it over into my possession."[39] By placing one's will in an object one gains control over it, which must be socially recognized for it to be secure. Hence, there is a need for appropriate legislation. With property secure, one can then carry on the activities through which one further develops oneself. The property relationship exists only as long as one continues to manifest one's will in the object.[40]

This defense of property has been criticized by many who find the notion of transferring one's will into an object a very obscure concept, and who fail to find any transfer of personality in most property, for example, money or the utilitarian objects we all use.[41] Nonetheless, the view gained prominence with respect to intellectual property in Europe, although not in the United States. The Hegelian argument, that one's property is an extension of oneself and of one's personality, became the basis for intellectual property law in the European continental tradition. In Hegel's view of intellectual property, one owns one's attainments and talents as something internal to one, but one expresses and embodies them in something external. Just as an individual cannot give up his freedom, so the author retains the right to the expression of his personality in an expression of his idea, such as a book. He may grant to others the right to produce the material books that contain his expression. Others buy the physical objects and may assimilate his ideas by reading them. But they remain his. The argument for the extension of one's personality seems clearer with respect to items that are copyrighted—books, painting, music— in which one often can identify works as being by specific individuals by their style or other characteristics than with respect to inventions. What the Hegelian approach best defends is not patents or copyrights as such but what is called "droit moral"[42] ("moral right"), which is restricted to works that are usually covered by copyright.[43] In the European tradition, the "moral right" of authorship includes the right to have one's name listed as author when the work is published, the right to prevent anyone else's name from appearing as author, the right to protection from defamation or maltreatment of the work such that it adversely affects one's reputation or honor, even after he dies, and in some jurisdictions, the right to prevent changes to a work even after the period of copyright protection has expired.[44] Some jurisdictions extend this to the author's right to restrict displays of his or her art in certain ways, or to productions of one's plays that discredit the author. This makes interpretations of an author's work by others, in producing a play, for instance, subject to the author's approval. That is stronger protection than seems reasonable to many. These extensions are not recognized as a right in U.S. law, although defamation is both unethical and illegal.

Whatever one thinks of the justice of "droit moral," the right is independent of copyright as such, does not apply to patents, and so is not a necessary part of general justifications of intellectual property.

TRADEMARK AND TRADE SECRECY LAWS

The preceding attempts at providing moral justification for intellectual property turn out to be arguments in defense either of patents (in general) or copyright (in general) or both. Those arguments do not apply to trademarks or trade secrecy, both of which are also generally considered to come under intellectual property law. Separate moral arguments must be given for these forms of intellectual property.

The least controversial kind of intellectual property law to morally justify is that which protects and enforces trademarks. Trademarks, we saw, were originally stamps that stone masons or guilds or other artisans place on their good. The modern trademark is similarly some sign or symbol that represents or stands for some commercial agent and that is used to identify a product as being made by a specific company or to advertise products made by that company. Companies wish to have trademark protection so that anyone will know that the product comes from a particular company. In addition, they have an interest in preserving their reputations and good names, and have a right to do so. Consumers also have an interest in knowing that the items they purchase come from the source indicated. The use of trademarks on goods also serves the user by identifying the company as the liable party in case of harm produced by the product. These various aims of manufacturers and users are best achieved if all parties can be reasonably secure in their reliance on trademarks, and that can be best achieved by prohibiting by law others from copying and using a company's trademark without the permission of the trademark holder.

A moral defense of trade secrecy laws is based on the intuition that one is not obliged to reveal one's thoughts. This might come under the right to freedom of conscience, or the right to freedom of speech, or the right to privacy. Human beings have no obligation to make public everything they do, think, or project; nor are they under any obligation to show their possessions to others. They have the morally defensible right to keep some things about themselves and their activities private or secret (unless they are illegal or lack of such knowledge would endanger someone else). If individuals are allowed to do this, keeping such information secret is not unethical in itself. If individuals may keep such thoughts or information secret, then groups of individuals may do so, and commercial enterprises may do so. This is widely acknowledged in a free society. Trade secrecy laws simply specify the conditions under which individuals or companies enjoy the protection of law in keeping secret their product development, techniques of doing business, or other internal activities that have commercial value and represent economic investment.

We can draw four conclusions from our discussion.

The first is that it is misleading to talk about justifications for intellectual property in the abstract as if that constituted a clear class, and as if arguments could be or are given that apply to all the members similarly.

The second is that, of all the arguments, the argument from justice and the argument from consequences (whether utilitarian or pragmatic) are the only ones that stand up to critical scrutiny. But what they justify is not intellectual property in general, but the general institutions of patents and copyrights in a society that has private property.

Third, both the argument from justice (that one has a right to the products of one's intellectual labor and legitimate property rights in them) and the argument from consequences (that more inventions and creative products that benefit society are produced if the society recognizes, grants, and protects certain claims to the products of intellectual labor) apply only in a society that has as one of its background institutions justifiable individual private property. The arguments do not show that private intellectual property rights, such as provided by patent or copyright, are morally mandatory for a society to be just.

Fourth, the justifications are very general. They do not justify any particular intellectual property laws, which is the next topic to examine.

INTELLECTUAL PROPERTY LAW AND MORALITY

Once intellectual property in general is held morally defensible, we have to consider the moral defensibility of its particular instantiations. Because we have defined intellectual property in terms of law, before turning to specific aspects of intellectual property law we should clarify several of the pertinent relations between ethics and law.

Legal Protections and Ethical Obligations

First, a law that requires people to do what is immoral cannot be morally justified, nor can a law that defends or establishes an unethical practice. If intellectual property laws did either, they could not be justified.

Second, some actions are morally wrong, whether or not they are illegal. Murder, stealing, rape, and so on are all unethical or immoral acts, whether or not they are made illegal. Making them illegal adds legal sanctions applied by state power to the preexisting moral sanctions. Stealing intellectual property, therefore, is unethical even when it is not illegal. But in the absence of appropriate law that clearly defines intellectual property rights in a given jurisdiction, disputes arise as to whether particular instances of copying or appropriation constitute stealing.

Third, many laws do not legislate morality (as criminal laws tend to do) but are passed to facilitate social interaction or promote socially desirable ends. Most intellectual property laws are of this type. From a moral point of view there is a great deal of leeway in how law may structure a society, and societies with very different civil laws may be equally just or moral societies. A law requiring motor vehicles to drive on the right in a given society is as just a law as one in another society requiring vehicles to drive on the left. The same is true with respect to differing intellectual property laws in different societies.

Fourth, citizens have a moral obligation to obey a just law passed in the proper way by a properly authorized body in a well-ordered society.[45] The four relations taken together mean that although people have no moral obligation to obey unjust laws, that is, laws that command them to do what is immoral or that forbid them from doing what they are morally required to do, a law may make legally mandatory an act that is not morally mandatory but simply morally permitted, and it may legally forbid actions that are morally permitted, but not morally required. In both cases, one has a moral as well as a legal obligation to follow the law, the moral obligation coming not from the moral nature of the act but from the fact that the law requires or forbids the action. The argument for this last statement, in a nutshell, is that the order necessary for a society to function for the general good can only be achieved if all its members obey the just laws of the society. If all members of society were to claim the moral right to disobey any law of their choosing, although risking the penalties for breaking the law if caught, civil order would be greatly disrupted. A democratic system that allows for majority rule, with protection for the rights of all, requires that its members bind themselves to obeying legally adopted laws, unless they are unjust. An unjust law may be resisted and protested by civil disobedience. If one adopts the position that it is unethical to break a law that has been passed by a legitimate body and is not in itself unethical, then to that extent some moral or ethical requirements depend on the specifications supplied by the laws in a particular jurisdiction.

The Variability of Legal Protections and Ethical Obligations

If we apply these notions to the legal protection of intellectual property, then, unless the laws that define and protect intellectual property rights are shown to be unethical (in that they require one to do what is morally prohibited or refrain from doing what is morally obligatory), members of the society have an ethical obligation to obey them. What is not permitted in this case is a function of laws, which may vary from time to time and jurisdiction to jurisdiction. This can be illustrated by the various time frames for protection that have been provided by copyright and patent law in the United States.

The period of protection afforded by copyright is currently much longer than for patents. The justification for that is that since copyright does not prevent others who develop the same idea but express it in a different way from publishing or commercializing their product, no injustice is done to independent originators of similar products. My writing a certain type of murder mystery does not prevent your simultaneously and independently writing the same type of murder mystery and publishing it a month after I do. How long should the period of protection against copying be and how much protection is required to stimulate authors or creators? As with the case of patents, the period of protection should be long enough to recoup one's investment in time and expenses, both for the creator and for the publisher or distributor. Why should protection not be indefinite, covering the life of the author and of his or her heirs as far into the future as they wish until they relinquish any ownership claims (probably because the items fail to produce any more income)? The answer, similar to the answer with patents, is that by allowing creative material to fall into the public domain, others can build on it in a way they cannot if it is protected by copyright. The right of author attribution, we have seen, is not affected by cessation of copyright protection. We have no empirical data on the correlation between length of copyright protection and the degree of creative material produced. As with patents, the copyright laws are not category specific. All items covered by copyright get the same kind and length of protection. Whether one size fits all can be questioned. Whether any given length of time is more appropriate than another length of time, for all items covered, or for different types of items, can again be questioned from a moral point of view. Yet, because the justification depends on empirical facts, in the absence of those facts, we start with the status quo, which arguably is better than no protection. The assumption is that once we have the general justification, the existing laws are morally justifiable unless shown not to be.

If we take the most recent copyright extension, which is retroactive, it protects covered works for the period of the life of the author plus seventy years, twenty years more than it did before the passage of the law. Thus, if someone published his first article at age twenty-five and his last just before he died at age eighty-five, the first would get 130 years of protection and the second seventy years. A work for hire, such as the cartoon character Mickey Mouse, which under the previous law would have fallen into the public domain in 2003, is now protected until 2019. It would have been both legal and moral to use Mickey Mouse freely after 2003 if the copyright period had not been extended. Because it has been extended, it is illegal in the Unites States to use Mickey Mouse without permission from the copyright holder, and so it is unethical to do so. The ethical character of the act of copying Mickey Mouse without permission depends on what the copyright law says. If Mickey Mouse were in the public domain because no longer covered by copyright, then it would be both legally and morally permissible to copy it. In Russia, where the copyright extension was not adopted, Mickey Mouse is in the public domain. Unless one presents an argument that U.S. law morally determines copyrighted material in the whole world, or that the only morally justifiable length of copyright protection is the current U.S. period, or that it is unethical to copy Mickey Mouse even if he is in the public domain, then in Russia Mickey Mouse may be legally, and therefore, morally freely used.

Was the latest U.S. extension morally justified? To argue that it was not is to claim that some particular period of time is the morally correct period. It is not clear how that could be argued. The extension certainly was not necessary to provide any added incentive to produce more copyrightable material, and it arguably prevents access to the many for the benefit of the very few. The last two extensions make it more difficult for the general public to know what is copyrighted, since one has to know when each author died.[46] An argument was made that by making the extension retroactive, the public was denied for an additional twenty years what it had legitimately expected to have access to.[47] The argument is not without merit, but it failed as a legal challenge to the amendment. All the negative considerations notwithstanding, the claim that no specific period of protection is uniquely morally mandatory seems valid. As a result, when the period was fourteen years that was morally justified, and now that it has been extended to the life of the author plus seventy years that too seems morally justified. At least the present period is not clearly unethical. The U.S. Congress and the various international copyright bodies do not determine the period of protection by moral considerations, and the period from a moral point of view is flexible and somewhat arbitrary. The same is true, as we shall see, with respect to what is covered. This means that the law in a specific jurisdiction determines what may be legally and hence (indirectly) morally copied.

Fair Use

Important to many issues concerning copyright is the doctrine of fair use. This is a legal doctrine that allows copying without permission for certain purposes and under certain conditions. It attempts to balance the commercial interests of authors and publishers against the claimed right of consumers to use what they purchase and the social benefits from certain specific uses. Fair use allows reproduction of portions of a work for reviews, criticism, research, or scholarship. The use must be noncommercial, the portion of the work copied proportionately small with respect to the whole work, and the effect on the potential market slight. Copying of extracts or of short pieces (such as articles from a journal) for personal or for educational use is permitted. The laws of different countries vary as to what is and what is not allowed under fair use, and even in a given country, such as the United States,[48] it is not always clear.

In a significant case, the U.S. Supreme Court ruled that VCRs used by home viewers to time shift their viewing of broadcast material was fair use.[49] One might ask whether the decision is morally defensible. I know of no argument that has been presented that claims the decision is immoral, and that despite the ruling, although it is legal to use VCRs to time shift, it is unethical to do so. A defense can be made that no injustice is done to the owners of the material being copied by the VCR because the material copied from TV is being shown to the general public, and the owners are being paid by the channels showing the material, who in turn get their revenue from the ads they show. Copying the TV programs in no way lessens the revenue either the owners of the material or the stations receive. If this is correct, then it appears that no one's property rights are being violated.[50] Now suppose the Court had ruled that the use of VCRs was illegal. Someone might argue that the Court's decision was ethically wrong. Suppose that that person makes a valid argument. The law would legally prevent people from doing something that is not immoral in itself. Yet it does not command people to do what is immoral nor does it demand that they refrain from doing what is morally obligatory. Hence it is not unethical in those senses, it is not a candidate for civil disobedience, and the proper action for those who wished would be to get legislation passed making the use of VCRs legal. Until that were done, one would have a moral obligation to obey the law, and one would have a moral obligation not to use a VCR to record programs. Given the actual way the Court decided, one does not have that moral obligation. In this sense, the morality of the action depends on the decision of the Court.

The legal doctrine of fair use is not morally mandatory. A system of private intellectual property that did not include it would not thereby be immoral. Because the fair use doctrine does not command one to do what is unethical or to refrain from what is morally required, if it was passed in a proper legally required manner in a society with a generally morally acceptable legal system, any moral challenge to the law should be made through proper legal procedures, and until the law is changed, one has the legal obligation to obey the law, and the moral obligation to do what the law requires. In particular instances, therefore, whether practices covered by fair use are legal (and therefore indirectly ethical) depends on the law.

At the present time the major disputes are not about the general justification of either property or intellectual property, but about their application to specific kinds of intellectual property.

I shall illustrate some of the ethical and legal conflicts that have arisen by looking at two different topics that have arisen in the Information Age. The first is copyright with respect to computer software and to digital information, especially music and films. The second is patents for software and for business practices, especially with respect to the Internet.

Copyright, Software, and Digital Information

Is software appropriate subject matter to be considered intellectual property, and if so, should it be covered by copyright or by patent? We have seen that simply because something is a product of the mind does not make it automatically susceptible to individual property claims, since the laws of science and the facts of mathematics are products of the mind but are not appropriate subject matter for intellectual property according to existing copyright and patent laws. The decision about whether to allow certain items copyright or patent protection is a matter of social decision, expressed in law.

When software appeared on the scene, most software was designed for particular machines and sold with it. In the early days of computing, members of the computing community for the most part freely shared their work with one another. The early programming languages were not protected by copyright or patent, nor were the early computing programs. Programs from the start have tended to build on prior programs and ideas. Subroutines developed for one program, for instance, were freely borrowed and placed into other programs. It seemed a waste of effort to rewrite a program to perform some function when that program had already been written by others and was readily available.

Computer programs are strings of commands written in a special computer language resulting in the computer's bringing about certain results. Since their purpose is to run machines, computer programs might be considered processes and so fall under patent protection. If they are embedded in chips that are parts of an engine or some other machine, they are not read or accessible to be read. If they are considered comparable to instructions in a book, then they might be considered suitable for coverage by copyright. How they should be treated in the United States was settled by the U.S. Copyright Act of 1976 (which was effective as of January 1, 1978),[51] which specifically included computer databases, computer programs, and material in digital form.

Critics, nonetheless, pointed out a number of crucial differences between software and other copyrightable material that made the extension of copyright to software at least open to criticism.

The most trenchant moral argument is raised by those who go back to the origins of computer software and claim that all software, or at least all source code, should be free. Richard Stallman in a 1988 article[52] gave the classic defense of that position. Programs from the start have tended to build on prior programs and ideas. He argues that the basic question should be the ethical one: what ought programmers do for the freedom and benefit of mankind? Hence we should not go to law for a solution but should have law conform to ethics. In particular he challenges the claim that unless software is proprietary there will be no software. Making software proprietary, he claims, makes it less available to all and results in fewer people using it; since the source code is not available, making software proprietary prevents those who want to improve the program from doing so, and it prevents people from learning from programs and basing new programs on them. Therefore, legal protection serves to impede rather than promote social benefit. Moreover, the claim that a financial incentive is necessary for people to develop programs, he asserts, is false. Programmers developed programs before they could get legal protection for them, scientists continue to contribute to the development of science even if their work is freely shared with others, and some software, such as shareware, is developed and available without proprietary impediments. The Free Software movement encourages the sharing of software and turns to other ways of supporting programmers than the market. Whether as much and as good software would be produced if source code were freely available is an empirical question that society has not tested.

The growing interest in "open source" software, in which the source code is made available under a copyright that licenses others to freely change and improve it, providing that they make their improvements available under a similar open source license, may help give society some hard data. Linux is an example of an open source operating system that is being adopted by an increasing number of firms in preference to Microsoft's operating system. Thus there is an experiment already in progress that may determine which produces more and better software. It will take decades to see which wins out. But in the interim, absent the required empirical data to show that proprietary software is unethical, the presumption is that both are morally permissible. The fact that software is protected by copyright implies the legal obligation to observe its restrictions. And, once again, the moral requirement to obey the law imposes the moral requirement to observe the existing laws on copyrighted software.

Nonetheless, copyright on programs is violated on a large scale by many ordinary people. This deserves at least some discussion.

Unauthorized Copying of Software

There are different levels and types of copying software, and it is useful to make some distinctions. The most blatant violation is the copying and commercial reselling of copyrighted programs for profit in a country in which the material is copyrighted. One can copy programs easily and cheaply. To sell them under the name of the company would be not only stealing their product but selling it under false pretenses, which would be unethical whether or not there were copyright laws. Although purchasers of stolen or pirated copies do not get any technical support, that does not justify either the copying or the sale. The same is true with respect to a third party's making copyrighted software available free on the Internet. The third party does not own the software and has no right to distribute it free. The software clearly belongs to the copyright holder and the unauthorized distribution clearly adversely affects its sales.

Copying programs for personal use arguably gets into the area of authorized fair use. The intuition of many consumers is that lending a friend a program is like lending them a book.[53] Users, upon learning that in buying a disk they are not buying something comparable to a book, find this contrary to their expectations. After all, they argue, according to the legal doctrine of first sale,[54] authors and publishers do not make any money from the second-hand market in books. If a textbook is adopted, the author and publisher make their profit on the initial sale of the book. As the secondary market of used books becomes larger and larger the sale of new books declines. The remedy of publishers and authors is to come out with a new edition. Teachers order the new edition and the cycle begins again. This is, of course, what happened with software. If the product is good, it will be copied and used by others, but after a few years, a new version will be produced. Those who purchased the original will buy the new version or be authorized to update their current version for a reduced price. Those who copied their software will have the incentive to purchase the new improved version.

The argument that the individual copying of software is unethical, whether or not it is illegal suffers from two difficulties. The first is that it implies that the doctrine of fair use is irrelevant, and all that matters is the fact that the producers of the programs are the rightful owners and as such deserve payment for their products. The difficulty with this argument is that it assumes that if there were no copyright laws, the companies would have a moral claim to their products. We have looked at that assumption already and have seen it to be a false assumption. Without laws specifying what can and cannot be considered intellectual property and what kind of protection can be justified with respect to what counts as intellectual property, we cannot intelligently discuss claims about intellectual property. Second, to say that one has intellectual property rights protected by copyright laws, but that the doctrine of fair use is not part of them, is to make one's own laws. So disputes about what constitutes fair use, which are often decided by courts, is pertinent to our understanding of what rights the producer has.

A second argument says that, if the doctrine of fair use is construed to allow individual copying, such an interpretation would be unethical because the copying causes the producing companies financial harm. That argument also suffers from two difficulties. First, it assumes companies have a right to make as much as possible and anything that cuts into its profits violates that right. The claimed right, however, is dubious and requires a defense that has not been given. Second, if financial harm is the reason, then we need facts to show the financial harm. The available facts, however, are in dispute. Those who defend the copying as morally justified claim that the copying that does take place has not prevented software companies from reaping handsome profits for useful, well-designed products. That they could make even more is an empirical claim. Some of those who do copy would not buy the product because they could not afford it. So those are not lost sales. Many of those who copy a product and become accustomed to using it—such as students—go on to buy the product once they enter the workplace. They point further to the fact that companies like Microsoft enforce their copyrights against companies that buy one license and use it on many computers but not against individual users. They simply do not support with updates or any services those who use copied version of their products. Hence, if the companies suffer no financial harm, that cannot be a valid reason for holding fair use that includes individual copying unjust. And if companies do not enforce their rights against individual infringers, that is at least some evidence that the companies do not suffer enough financial harm to make up for the cost of enforcing their rights. This does not justify copying, although it does show that one argument against a more liberal interpretation of fair us is inconclusive. However, neither does it provide a compelling argument for broadening fair use to include individual copying of programs. At present, copying of software by individuals is illegal. The best argument for its being unethical is that we have a moral obligation to obey the law.

Digital Information

This leads us to the second kind of intellectual property that has raised a good deal of discussion, namely, the copyright protection given to digital information, especially music and films. These have become central issues since the development of peer-to-peer techniques of transmitting digitalized information. The technology in itself is not unethical and is a significant advance in information technology, making possible the exchange of large amounts of digitalized information by individual users without the need to go through a central distributor. From the point of view of information distribution this technology opens up vast possibilities that have just begun to be tapped. A problem is that its use and development may be legally curtailed because of its potential to be used in ways that violate copyright law.

The issue came to a head when the rock bank Metallica sued Napster, a firm that acted as an intermediary between those requesting certain songs via the Internet and those willing to supply them without charge. A U.S. district court ordered Napster to shut down its services, and in October 2000, a U.S. appellate court ruled that Napster could only provide access to songs that were not covered by copyright.[55] Other programs immediately appeared that did not require an intermediary and allowed direct access among individual users. The music industry protested that such downloading did not constitute fair use, that it violated copyright law, and that it was costing the industry millions of dollars. Users often acknowledged that it violated copyright law, but continued to download nonetheless.[56] Some saw it as a protest against the music industry's marketing strategy of including one popular song on a CD with other songs the purchasers did not want but were forced to purchase if they wanted the popular one. Others felt that if they could loan books, they should be able to loan music. Still others claimed that since the music was available on MTV or radio and could be taped from there, sharing on the Internet was the same sort of practice. Although the various positions taken help explain why so many people downloaded music, none of them shows that the downloading was either legal or moral.

Since violation of copyright by individuals for noncommercial use is a civil offense, it is enforced through civil suit. This meant that the music industry was forced to sue its own customers. It did this to some small extent on a selective basis, going after those who downloaded or made available a very large number of songs.

Countries vary in their copyright laws with respect to downloaded music. In the United States, it is illegal to either upload or download copyrighted music. In Canada, it is illegal to upload but not illegal to download copyrighted music.[57] In Taiwan, it is legal both to upload and to download such music.[58] Is the policy of one of these countries the only morally justifiable one? Does morality dictate what the content of any nation's copyright laws and in particular its doctrine on fair use must be? We have argued so far that morality prohibits compliance with laws that mandate that one act immorally or that prohibit one from acting as morally required, but that copyright laws do neither. Does one have some moral right independent of copyright that demands, perhaps on justice grounds, that the law be one way rather than another? One might argue that a system of intellectual property law that allowed copying and sale of protected intellectual property violates the fairness condition that copyright is adopted to protect. That the fairness condition is violated by one interpretation or another of fair use, however, is far from clear. Suppose that as a result of a broader interpretation of fair use fewer people buy CDs and the profits of various compares in the music industry decline. The decline may be protested by the companies, but if they still have the opportunity to sell their product secure from commercial copying, and have the opportunity to make a profit, the fairness condition as I argued for it in discussing the justifiability of copyright is satisfied. Copyright does not have as a purpose protecting the maximum amount of profit a company may be able to make, nor does it guarantee profit at all.

The U.S., the Canadian, and the Taiwanese copyright laws, despite differences in their doctrines of fair use, all allow companies the opportunity to recoup their investment and make a profit secure from competitors using their product during the period that it is protected. What about the pragmatic aim of fostering more productivity, in this case the production of more music? So far there is no evidence that less music is being produced in any of the three countries because of the way the fair use doctrine is applied. If there were strong evidence showing a decline, then the country in question would have to decide whether to change its laws to achieve its end.

If this analysis is sound, then there is no one morally mandatory way that copyright laws have to be written, and no one morally mandatory way that fair use provisions have to be written. There are surely ways that morality prohibits. But the analysis argues that none of the three is of this type. Would it be better if the rules of the game were similar in all countries? It would promote global efficiency, and that is the point of attempts at the international harmonization of intellectual (and other) property laws. That the proper way to harmonize can be dictated by morality, rather than have morality act as a break on what is unjust or not morally justifiable, has not been shown to be the case. Most international agreements are the result of some compromise, not on principle but on what all or some of the parties feel they would prefer or is in their best interests, but which they are willing to give up to achieve more of something else they desire even more. The morality of uploading and downloading in the final analysis depends on the laws of the jurisdiction in which one resides. Clearly, the present U.S. copyright law is not very effective in deterring the practice. It is expected that as it becomes easier and quicker to download movies using peer-to-peer technology, the same problem will face the movie industry as faces the music industry. The movie industry adapted to the introduction of the VCR by introducing the movie rental business. The movie industry and the music industry are currently being challenged to adapt to peer-to-peer technology. The wide-scale illegal downloading of music led to new commercial practices and new revenue streams for music producers, such as iPod's making available individual songs for 99 cents.[59] It appears some accommodation will be achieved that will eventually be reflected in intellectual property law.

Patents for Software and Methods of Doing Business

Patents and Software

Software has typically been protected primarily by copyright. But since 1981 patent protection has been awarded to some software and to computer algorithms under certain conditions. This has been done not by legislation but initially by the Patent Office accepting such applications and subsequently by the courts ruling on cases.

In the United States, application is made to the Patent and Trademark Office. A number of examining groups have jurisdiction over various fields of technology and they decide whether to accept something for patent. If they deny a patent because the item is not new, they must document this decision. Once granted, patents can be challenged in court.

Mathematical algorithms, we noted, cannot be copyrighted. As of 1981, however, when the U.S. Supreme Court decided the case of *Diamond v. Diehr*,[60] the Patent Office has allowed the patenting of computer algorithms. The *Diamond v. Diehr* case involved a process for molding uncured synthetic rubber into rubber products through the use of a computer program that controlled the temperature and time of the rubber in the mold. In general, thereafter, algorithms that control the operation of hardware and that are part of the overall invention have been granted patent protection. Companies soon became proficient at writing patent applications for computer algorithms that presented them as part of a process. Since 1981 the number of software patents has increased dramatically and in 2004, 11,200 software patents were issued.[61]

The basic techniques of programming were developed from 1940 to 1981 and were not covered by patent because they were not considered appropriate subject matter. Much of that development lacked documentation, which is needed for many of the challenges to computer-related patents. A continuing complaint by many in the programming industry is that patents are granted for processes that are obvious to any competent programmer in the field, and that often, although used in the past, they were not documented because they were obvious. The result of the many patents granted is that it makes the cost of developing software very expensive, since one has to do a patent search on all the techniques that one may develop on one's own. Large companies such as IBM, Microsoft, Apple, Sony, Motorola, and others protect themselves by getting patents they can cross-license to other large companies, if they are accused of violating one of their patents. Microsoft, which in 2002 had applied for 1,411 software patents, had by 2004 submitted 3,780.[62] IBM alone owns more than 40,000 such patents.[63]

With the thousands of software patents that already exist, small software developers run the risk of violating some company's patents, no matter what they produce. That is as chilling an effect as one can imagine. It seems counterintuitive that although the first developer of a spreadsheet (VisiCalc) did not patent it, small improvements in the form of new algorithms or techniques for spreadsheets are now patentable.[64] Tim Berners-Lee is widely credited with being the inventor of the World Wide Web, that part of the Internet based on HTTP (Hypertext Transfer Protocol). He purposely did not seek either a patent or a copyright on his invention.[65] One can only imagine how either sort of protection would have hampered the development of the Web.

Despite the fact that these patents do not meet the original intent of establishing patents laws (which is to "promote the progress of Science and the useful Arts"), meeting that intent is not a requirement for obtaining a patent. In 2005, the European Union voted decisively against granting patents on software.[66] There seem to be good pragmatic reasons to follow the European example and no longer grant patent protection for software, since the present system of granting patents for software is already hampering and slowing growth and innovation.[67] This provides the basis for a moral argument to change the law, even though it does not show that the laws are unethical in the sense that they violate anyone's rights or require that one do what is unethical or refrain from doing what is ethically required. The moral argument is that they should be changed because they do not in fact serve the public good or promote public welfare as they should and as they could if changed.

Patents and Methods of Doing Business

The problems we find in software patents are found in a slightly different way with respect to business on the Internet. The Internet is clearly a medium in which one can transact business. Yet, the "methods of doing business" on the Internet had to be invented or developed. The U.S. Patent Office since 1998 has granted patents on "methods of doing business."[68] Most other countries do not grant such patents.[69] Since business on the Internet is new, almost any method—even if a variant on established methods in a bricks and mortar situation—is new. In 1999, the Patent Office granted Amazon.com a patent for a "method and system for placing a purchase order via a communications network" known as "one-click."[70] It lets repeat customers place a new order without repeating their information, and using one-click of the mouse instead of two clicks. Many computer programmers claim the one-click technology is obvious, even though Amazon.com was the first to put it into practice.[71] The problem with such patents is that they make any innovation on the Internet potentially costly since one has to do a patent search and the patents do not serve to motivate new developments but to hinder them.

In 2007, the U.S. Supreme Court started reigning in business methods patents by reversing the U.S. Court of Appeals for the Federal Circuit, which oversees patent law.[72] It reversed the trend of granting patents for incremental engineering advances that the court considered nonobvious because there was no prior teaching or record of the improvement.

That was a step in the direction of stimulating rather than impeding innovation. Had the Court upheld the decisions of the Court of Appeals, that would have been U.S. law, even if it seemed to many to go against the justification for intellectual property protection set forth in the U.S. Constitution. But once again, that would be compatible with arguing on moral grounds (based on the betterment of the social good), as well as on legal grounds (based on the better achievement of the aims of patents as set forth in the Constitution), either for changes in the ease with which business-practice patents are granted or for refusing to grant them at all.

CONCLUSION

The conclusion to which we are led is that although there is general moral justification for the legal protection of intellectual property rights, ethics alone does not decide the issue in many disputes about intellectual property. Ethics can say whether some legislation goes so far as to be unethical, for instance, because it violates the moral rights of some party. But most legislation concerning copyright and patent falls into the range of the morally acceptable. Legislation tends to lag too far behind new technology which changes almost daily. So, often it has been left to the courts to handle the intricacies of the changes wrought by advancing technology. Clearly, the present trend in the United States is towards increasing protection for commercial uses of intellectual property, possibly because of successful lobbying by large corporations with vested interests and ineffective lobbying by those interested and informed enough to argue for less protection. Wise legislatures and courts, however, would take note of laws that are widely flouted, since this tends to indicate a lack of match between the perceptions of the public and those of the legislatures and courts. They would also be sensitive to the needed balancing of protection on the one hand and promoting and stimulating innovation on the other hand. In most instances, given that the laws have been passed and exist in a system that is not unethical, one has the moral obligation to obey the law. Although one can raise moral concerns, the burden of argument is on those who advocate changes in the law to show why they should be changed, and more radically on those who would violate a law on moral grounds to justify their violation. While calls for drastic change in copyright or patent protection seem unlikely to succeed, changes such as the United States rescinding patent protection for computer programs or for ways of doing business, to bring it in line with most other countries, are clearly possible.

The Information Age offers unlimited possibilities for the dissemination and implementation of knowledge on a previously unimagined scale. Balancing the free access that this implies with the incentives that copyrights and patents have thus far successfully provided will be an ongoing, difficult, and delicate legal task. In this task, ethics will continue to have a role to play in morally evaluating technology as it changes, in helping champion human rights and human welfare in the evolution of business and law, and in morally evaluating specific details of the protection of intellectual property rights.

NOTES

1. On the Hohfeldian paradigm of rights, the possession of a right by one person entails an enforceable duty on the part of another or of others. In U.S. law, this is the dominant paradigm taught in law schools in discussing property. See Daniel H. Cole and Peter Z. Grossman, "The Meaning of Property 'Rights': Law vs. Economics," *Land Economics* 78 (August 2002): 317–330.

2. The case is *Davoll et al. v. Brown* (1 Woodb. & M. 53, 3 West.L.J. 151, 7 F.Cas. 197, No. 3662, 2 Robb.Pat.Cas. 303, Merw.Pat.Inv. 414), http://rychlicki.net/inne/3_West.L.J.151.pdf (accessed December 6, 2007). Christopher May and Susan K. Sell, *Intellectual Property Rights: A Critical History* (Boulder, Colo.: Lynne Rienner, 2006), 18, note that the term "appears only once in US federal court reports prior to 1900, however, and is absent in reports between 1900 and 1930." The term gains currency only later in the twentieth century.

3. For a fuller discussion of this point see the section below on the justification of intellectual property.

4. May and Sell, *Intellectual Property Rights*, 90–93; David Saunders, *Authorship and Copyright* (London: Routldge, 1992), 47–51.

5. May and Sell, *Intellectual Property Rights*, 51–52.

6. Ibid., 71–72. See also John Alan Lehman, "Intellectual Property Rights and Chinese Tradition Section: Philosophical Foundations," *Journal of Business Ethics* 69 (2006): 1–9.

7. May and Sell, *Intellectual Property Rights*, 90–93.

8. United States Copyright Office, "A Brief Introduction and History," Circular 1a, "Notable Dates in United States Copyright," May 31, 1790, http://www.copyright.gov/circs/circ1a.html (accessed November 30, 2007).

9. 17 U.S.C. § 101 (2007).

10. United States Copyright Office, "Notable Dates in United States Copyright," February 3, 1831.

11. United States Copyright Office, "Notable Dates in United States Copyright," January 1, 1978. A "work for hire" refers to work done for a firm by an author or authors (often employees) for which they are paid by the firm and to which they relinquish all rights in the product to the entity paying them.

12. United States Copyright Office, "Notable Dates in United States Copyright," March 1, 1989.

13. United States Copyright Office, "Notable Dates in United States Copyright," October 27, 1998.

14. Patent Act 1793, Section 1, cited in "History and Introduction to the U.S. Patent System," http://biojudiciary.org/subpage1.asp?tid=100 (accessed June 4, 2007).

15. May and Sell, *Intellectual Property Rights*, 111–15.

16. Patent Act 1793, Section 1, cited in "History and Introduction to the U.S. Patent System."

17. Ladas & Parry LLP, "A Brief History of the Patent Law of the United States," http://www.ladas.com/Patents/USPatentHistory.html (accessed December 3, 2007).

18. Patent Act 1793, Section 1, cited in "History and Introduction to the U.S. Patent System."

19. Ibid.

20. On the difference between the first to file and the first to invent two, see *Ius mentis*, "Differences between US and European Patents," http://www.iusmentis.com/patents/uspto-epodiff/ (accessed November 30, 2007). For details of the U.S. patent law, see "Reduction to Practice," http://www.uspto.gov/web/offices/pac/mpep/documents/2100_2138_05.htm (accessed November 30, 2007).

21. United States Copyright Office, "Notable Dates in United States Copyright," May 24, 1982.

22. David V. Radak, "The Uniform Trade Secrets Act," *TMS*, http://www.tms.org/pubs/journals/JOM/matters/matters-0601.html (accessed December 3, 2007); The Uniform Trade Secrets Act, which is a model law drafted by the National Conference of Commissioners on Uniform State Laws, http://nsi.org/Library/Espionage/usta.htm.

23. May and Sell, *Intellectual Property Rights*, 80.

24. The text of the act, with 1985 amendments, http://my.execpc.com/~mhallign/utsa85.html (accessed on November 30, 2007).

25. The arguments are referred to by various names. For a good overview of the variety of arguments, see Lawrence C. Becker, *Property Rights: Philosophic Foundations* (Boston: Routledge & Kegan Paul, 1977).

26. For a brief overview of the history of property, see Jeremy Waldron, "Property," *Stanford Encyclopedia of Philosophy*, http://plato.stanford.edu/entries/property/ (accessed on August 24, 2007). See also Anthony Parel and Thomas Flanagan, eds., *Theories of Property: Aristotle to the Present* (Waterloo, Ontario: Wilfrid Laurier University Press, 1979), which contains sixteen essays on the history of property, with articles on the theories of property of Aristotle and of Aquinas, as well as of Locke, Mill, Rousseau, and Nozick,

among others; and Robert Mayhew, "Aristotle on Property," *Review of Metaphysics* 46 (1993): 4, 803–831.

27. John Locke, *Two Treatises of Government*, ed. Peter Laslett (Cambridge: Cambridge University Press, 1988), chap. 5, sec. 27, 287.

28. Ibid., 288.

29. Ibid., sec. 30, 289.

30. Ibid., sec. 46, 300.

31. Ibid., sec. 45, 299.

32. See Becker, *Property Rights: Philosophic Foundations*, chap. 4, for a survey and assessment of a number of them.

33. See, for instance, Robert Nozick, *Anarchy, State, and Utopia* (New York: Basic Books, Inc., 1974), 174–182.

34. The issue is one of distributive justice. There is a vast literature on this topic. Central to the contemporary discussion in liberal societies is John Rawls, *A Theory of Justice* (Cambridge, Mass.: Harvard University Press, 1971). For a libertarian defense of private property see Nozick, *Anarchy, State, and Utopia*.

35. Justin Hughes, "The Philosophy of Intellectual Property," *Georgetown Law Journal* 77 (1988): 287, defends a Lockean justification as "powerful, but incomplete." Herman T. Tavani, "Locke, Intellectual Property Rights and the Information Commons," *Ethics and Information Technology* 7 (2005): 87–97, reviews the literature relating to Locke and intellectual property, and concludes Locke is helpful but "does not provide us with definitive answers to many questions underlying controversial disputes about IPRs in general" (96). E. C. Hettinger, "Justifying Intellectual Property Rights," *Philosophy & Public Affairs* 18 (1) (1989): 31–52, argues that "justifying intellectual property is a formidable task," and the application of Locke's theory to intellectual property has significant shortcomings.

36. B. Zorina Khan and Kenneth L. Sokoloff, "History Lessons: The Early Development of Intellectual Property Institutions in the United States," *Journal of Economic Perspectives* 15 (2001): 3, 234.

37. G. W. F. Hegel, *Philosophy of Right*, trans. S. W. Dyde (Amherst, Mass.: Prometheus, 1996), 56–57.

38. Ibid., 51.

39. Ibid., 57.

40. Ibid.

41. Against such criticism Richard Teichgraeber, "Hegel on Property and Poverty," *Journal of the History of Ideas* 38 (1) (1977): 47–64, argues that Hegel's view of property must be taken "within the rational development of his philosophy as a whole" (47).

42. "Moral rights" is not used in English to refer to the special intellectual rights that European law recognizes. It is used to refer to specific morally justifiable rights with respect to copyrightable material.

43. This view is embodied in the Berne Convention for the Protection of Literary and Artistic Works (Paris Text 1971), Art. 6bis, http://www.law.cornell.edu/treaties/berne/6bis.html (accessed on June 4, 2007). For a discussion of these rights, embodied in French law, see Tom G. Palmer, "Are Patents and Copyrights Morally Justified? The Philosophy of Property Rights and Ideal Objects," *Harvard Journal of Law and Public Policy* 13 (3) (1990): 817–865.

44. Article 6/bis of the Berne Convention for the Protection of Literary and Artistic Works (Paris, 1971), http://www.law.cornell.edu/treaties/berne/6bis.html (accessed August 31, 2007) deals with moral rights. The United States does not recognize these and the TRIPS Agreement does not require states to do so. See, May and Sell, *Intellectual Property Rights*, 165–66; and G. Gregory Letterman, *Basics of Internal Intellectual Property Law* (Ardsley, N.Y.: Transnational, 2001), 266.

45. An early form of the argument can be found in Thomas Aquinas, *Summa Theologica*, I-II, q. 96, a. 4. In its modern form the argument is basically utilitarian.

46. The situation is actually more complex than that, since one also has to know when the copyright first became effective and the length of protection provided at that time by the law. For a short guide to figuring out what material is probably covered, see Dennis S. Karjala, "How to Determine Whether a Work Is in the Public Domain," http://homepages.law.asu.edu/~dkarjala/OpposingCopyrightExtension/publicdomain/SearchC-R.html (accessed December 8, 2007).

47. The argument was made in *Eldred v. Ashcroft*, 537 U.S. 186 (2003), and was rejected 7–2 by the Supreme Court. See also Christina N. Gifford, "The Sonny Bono Copyright Term Extension Act," *University of Memphis Law Review* 30 (2) (1999–2000): 363–407.

48. U.S. Copyright Office, "Fair Use," http://www.copyright.gov/fls/fl102.html (accessed November 30, 2007) notes that "the distinction between 'fair use' and infringement may be unclear and not easily defined."

49. *Sony Corp. v. Universal City Studios*, 464 U.S. 417 (1984).

50. Nonetheless, VCRs may be used to copy other material, and in some instances may be used in violation of copyright laws.

51. The Copyright Act of 1976, which provides the basic framework for the current copyright law, was enacted on October 19, 1976, as Pub. L. No. 94–553, 90 Stat. 2541. The act plus amendments through 2002 are contained in Title 17 of the United States Code, http://www.copyright.gov/title17/circ92.pdf (accessed on Sept. 4, 2007). The act defines "computer program," and section 117 is titled "Limitations on exclusive right: Computer programs."

52. Richard Stallman, "Why Software Should Be Free," Free Software Foundation, Inc., http://www.gnu.org/philosophy/shouldbefree.html (accessed June 4, 2007).

53. Helen Nissenbaum, "Should I Copy My Neighbor's Software?" in *Computers, Ethics & Social Values*, ed. Deborah G. Johnson and Helen Nissenbaum (Englewood Cliffs, N.J.: Prentice Hall, 1995), 201–213, argues against the no-copy position in favor of the moral justification of copying software under certain circumstances.

54. The first-sale doctrine was codified in the Copyright Act of 1976, 17 U.S.C. § 109.

55. United States Court of Appeals for the Ninth Circuit, *A&M Records, Inc. et al. v. Napster, Inc.*, No. 0016401—(D.C. No. CV-99-05183-MHP), http://www.ca9.uscourts.gov/ca9/newopinions.nsf/69A4AA15F8D6CBD6882569F1005E7D93/$file/0016401.pdf?openelement (accessed December 7, 2007).

56. A. Harmon and J. Schwartz, "Despite Suits, Music File-Sharers Shrug Off Guilt and Keep Sharing, *New York Times*, September 19, 2003, A1, C2, cited by Richard A. Spinello, "Digital Music and Peer-to-Peer File Sharing," in *Readings in CyberEthics*, 2nd ed., ed. Richard A. Spinello and Herman A. Tavani (Sudbury, Mass.: Jones and Bartlett, 2004), 272, claims that only 36 percent of the people in the United States feel downloading MP3s is stealing.

57. John Borland, "Canada Deems P2P Downloading Legal," C/Net News.com, December 12, 2003, http://news.com.com/2100-1025_3-5121479.html (accessed August 30, 2005); Andrew Orlowski, "Canada OKs P2P Downloads," *The Register*, December 13, 2003, http://www.theregister.co.uk/2003/12/13/canada_oks_p2p_music_downloads/ (accessed August 30, 2005). Canada places a tax on MP3 music players.

58. Dan Nystedt, "Taiwan Court Rules in Favor of P-to-P Company," IDG News Service, April 4, 2005, LinuxWorld.com.au, http://www.linuxworld.com.au/index.php/

id;98332472;fp;2;fpid;1 (accessed August 30, 2005). The ruling was by a Taiwanese District Court.

59. In 2007, Apple's iTunes Store was offering 6 million songs for download at 99 cents each, http://www.apple.com/itunes/store/ (accessed on December 2, 2007).

60. *Diamond v. Diehr*, 450 U.S. 175 (1981). For a summary of the decision see, "*Oyez: Diamond v. Diehr*," http://www.oyez.org/cases/1980-1989/1980/1980_79_1112/ (accessed December 2, 2007).

61. William R. Haulbrook, "Getting a Handle on the Software Patent Explosion," Goodwin Procter, *IP Advisor*, http://www.goodwinprocter.com/~/media/3CFC3F710F8E4A 02A92F1C7AB5FC75F1.as hx (accessed December 8, 2007).

62. Roger Parloff, "Microsoft Takes on the Free World," *Fortune*, May 28, 2007, 82.

63. John Markoff, "U.S. Tackles Conflicts over Rights to Software Patents," *International Herald Tribune*, Jan 10, 2006, http://www.iht.com/articles/2006/01/10/business/patents.php. http://www.iht.com/articles/2006/01/10/business/patents.php (accessed December 8, 2007).

64. Simson L. Garfinkel, Richard M. Stallman, and Mitchell Kapor, "Why Patents are Bad for Software," *Issues in Science and Technology* (Fall 1991), http://lpf.ai.mit.edu/Links/prep.ai.mit/issues.article (accessed May 2, 2007), cite patent number 4,398,249, "which spells out the order in which to recalculate the values in a complicated model when one parameter in the model changes."

65. See Tim Berner-Lee (with Mark Fischetti), *Weaving the Web: The Original Design and Ultimate Destiny of the World Wide Web by Its Inventor* (San Francisco: Harper, 1999). See also Lawrence Lessig, *The Future of Ideas: The Fate of the Commons in a Connected World* (New York: Vintage Books, 2001), 41–44.

66. BBC News, "Software Patent Bill Thrown Out," July 2005, http://news.bbc.co.uk/1/hi/technology/4655955.stm (accessed December 8, 2007). Some countries, however, have issued patents for programs that solve certain technical problems and are considered technology patents.

67. For a fuller discussion of the case against software patents, see League for Programming Freedom, "Against Software Patents," February 28, 1991, http://lpf.ai.mit.edu/Patents/against-software-patents.html (accessed May 2, 2007). The situation since 1991 has only grown worse.

68. The U.S. Patent Office started accepting methods of doing business patents after a Federal court decision, *State Street Bank & Trust Co. v. Signal Financial Group, Inc.*, 149 F.3d 1368 (Fed. Cir. 1998) *cert. denied* 119 S. Ct. 851 (1999).

69. See, art. 52 (2) of the European Patent Convention, http://www.epo.org/about-us/press/releases/archive/2000/18082000.html (accessed December 2, 2007).

70. September 28, 1999, U.S. Pat No. 5,960,411.

71. Even one of Amazon.com's original programmers agrees, and Jeff Bezos, Amazon.com's founder, suggests shortening the length of software protection to three to five years. See, "Amazon One-Click Shopping," http://cse.stanford.edu/class/cs201/projects-99-00/software-patents/amazon.html (accessed December 8, 2007).

72. U.S. Supreme Court, *KSR International Co. v. Teleflex, Inc.*, No. 04–1350, decided Monday, April 30, 2007, http://www.usscplus.com/current/cases/PDF/9970025.pdf (accessed December 8, 2007); Anne Broache, "Supreme Court Loosens Patent 'Obviousness' Test," CNET News.com, April 30, 2007, http://www.news.com/2100-1014_3-6180220.html (accessed December 8, 2007).

SUGGESTED READING

Garfinkel, Simson L., Richard M. Stallman, Mitchell Kapor. "Why Patents Are Bad for Software." *Issues in Science and Technology,* Fall 1991. http://lpf.ai.mit.edu/Links/prep.ai.mit/issues.article (accessed May 2, 2007).

Hughes, Justin. "The Philosophy of Intellectual Property." *Georgetown Law Journal* 77 (1988): 287–366. Khan, B. Zorina, and Kenneth L. Sokoloff. "History Lessons: The Early Development of Intellecctual Property Institutions in the United States." *Journal of Economic Perspectives* 15 (2001): 233–246.

Kleve, Peter, and Leo Van der Wees. "Multimedia and Copyright." *European Journal of Law, Philosophy, and Computer Science* 1 (1) (1998): 165–174.

Lea, David. "From the Wright Brothers to Microsoft: Issues in the Moral Grounding of Intellectual Property Rights." *Business Ethics Quarterly* 16 (2006): 579–598.

League for Programming Freedom, Against Software Patents, February 28, 1991. http://lpf.ai.mit.edu/Patents/against-software-patents.html.

Lee, Timothy B. "Circumventing Competition: The Perverse Consequences of the Digital Millennium Copyright Act." Cato Institute. *Policy Analysis* no. 564 (March 21, 2006).

Lehman, Bruce A., and Ronald H. Brown. "Intellectual Property and the National Information Infrastructure: The Report of the Working Group on Intellectual Property Rights." September 1995. http://ladas.comNII.

Lehman, John Alan. "Intellectual Property Rights and Chinese Tradition Section: Philosophical Foundations." *Journal of Business Ethics* 69 (2006): 1–9

Lessig, Lawrence. *The Future of Ideas: The Fate of the Commons in a Connected World.* New York: Vintage Books, 2001.

Lewin, Peter. "Creativity or Coercion: Alternative Perspectives on Rights to Intellectual Property." *Journal of Business Ethics* 71 (2007): 441–455 Linek, Ernie. "A Brief History of Trade Secrecy Law, Part I." *BioProcess International* (October 2004): 1–4.

Palmer, Tom G. "Are Patents and Copyrights Morally Justified? The Philosophy of Property Rights and Ideal Objects." *Harvard Journal of Law and Public Policy,* 13 (3) (1990): 817–865.

Parloff, Roger. "Microsoft Takes on The Free World." *Fortune,* May 28, 2007, 77–88.

Resnik, D. B. "A Pluralist Account of Intellectual Property." *Journal of Business Ethics* 46 (2003): 319–335.

Schroeder, Jeanne L. "Unnatural Rights: Hegel and Intellectual Property." *Cardozza Law, Legal Studies Research Paper No. 80* (March 1, 2004). http://ssrn.com/abstract=518182.

Singer, Alan E. "Intellectual Property and Moral Imagination." *Journal of Economic and Social Policy* 7 (2002): 1–22.

Singer, Alan E., Jerry Calton, Ming Singer. "Profit without Copyright." *Small Business Economics* 16 (2001): 149–156.

Tavani, Herman T. "Locke, Intellectual Property Rights and the Information Commons." *Ethics and Information Technology* 7 (2005): 87–97.

PART VI

INCENTIVES AND INFLUENCE

CHAPTER 15

CONFLICTS OF INTEREST

WAYNE NORMAN
CHRIS MACDONALD

PROFESSIONAL ethics can no longer be adequately studied or effectively practiced by attending only to individuals or to associations of individuals, even professional associations. The principles of professional ethics must take seriously the special circumstances of institutional life. That does not mean that institutional ethics rests on different moral foundations, or that the problems it poses are of a completely different kind from ordinary ethics. But if we take the institutional context seriously, we ask some questions that we might not otherwise ask and consider some answers that we might otherwise neglect. The agenda of the study of professional ethics will then turn in a more fruitful direction and address problems that are more relevant for the practice of professionals today.[1]

Conflicts of interests have become a pervasive ethical concern in our professional, organizational, and political life. Rules and principles concerning conflicts of interests hold a central place in all professional, and most corporate, codes of ethics, as well as in legislation regulating the conduct of public officials and civil servants. They are a core element of the Sarbanes-Oxley Act (2002), and of other state and federal corporate-governance statutes. And they figure prominently in the basic legislation guiding national regulatory agencies such as the Securities and Exchange

Commission (SEC) and the Food and Drug Administration (FDA) in the United States. For this reason, many will be surprised to learn that the concept, as we know it, is barely half-a-century old. Aristotle, Kant, and J. S. Mill, three prominent sources of our contemporary thinking in business ethics, seem not to have pondered anything like our contemporary concerns about conflicts of interest. This curious combination of facts—that we cannot now think through the ethical stakes in commercial and professional life *without* the concept of conflict of interest, even though our greatest ethical thinkers thought they could—is in need of explanation. Exploring this puzzle leads quickly to the conclusion that the concept of conflict of interest is in many ways quite unlike other ethical concepts, and also that it has appeared in response to features in our world and in our political cultures that are much more prominent than they were before the middle of the twentieth century.

People are often confident that they can recognize a conflict of interest, as they can a good work of art, when they see one. This is true even though in most cases they will find it exceedingly difficult to give a concise and comprehensive definition of the concept. We will examine some definitions in a moment, but first consider the following list of potential conflicts of interest that might arise within a single (hypothetical but not atypical) corporation—the ABC Corporation, a large aeronautics firm and defense contractor:

- A board member owns shares in a major producer of aluminum that routinely bids for contracts from ABC.
- The CEO's husband is an executive in an airline that already owns a fleet of ABC's jetliners.
- The senior vice president of Business Development and Strategy is a retired air force general who is often perceived to favor military over civil-aviation projects.
- The accounting department makes a vague job offer to a junior member of the audit team from the accounting firm that does ABC's audits.
- A junior executive in the purchasing department has a spouse who works for a large copying-services firm with which his department regularly deals (in fact, the executive in question may have managed to get a better price for ABC for some services).
- A senior member of ABC's legal department leaves to take a job at a competing firm.
- A senior engineer leaves to take a job at the Defense Department.
- A junior engineer in the IT department has a part-time consulting business that sells IT security services.
- A respected aeronautical engineering professor from a leading university, who also advises several government agencies on purchasing decisions, is paid a handsome fee to speak at an annual training event for ABC's sales force.
- A retired general is paid by ABC to talk on the combat uses of unmanned drones (of which ABC is one manufacturer) at a major defense conference.

- ABC receives a contract from the navy to assess the combat status of its current fleet of carrier-born fighter jets, many of which were made by ABC's rival and could potentially be replaced by an ABC model already in the testing phase.
- A manager has to choose among several well-qualified subordinates—one of whom happens to be her lover—for a promotion.
- A senior executive (whose remuneration is based in part on the value of the company's stock) "leaks" misleading information about the company's product pipeline to the media, in hopes of pushing stock prices higher.

The idea here is not that these are all touchstone examples of conflicts of interest, but that they all now raise red flags. In some cases we would need more information to be sure. Situations of these sorts typically *do* qualify as conflicts of interest according to the most widely respected theories in the business ethics literature. This kind of list could be rapidly expanded with examples of conflicts of interest that might arise in or around a corporation like ABC. The list would only proliferate when we consider the vast range of conflicts of interest endemic to firms in specialized sectors such as financial services, management consulting, the pharmaceutical industry, and health care.

In this chapter we will not defend any particular formula for identifying precisely which situations do and do not qualify as conflicts of interest, though we will try to give a sense of the range of debates over such a formula. Our aim is to take stock of the substantial progress toward settling many conceptual disputes over the last couple of decades and to sketch out an agenda of both empirical and substantive normative questions that deserve more attention. This agenda is in the spirit of the "institutional turn" in professional ethics advocated by Dennis Thompson in the quote at the head of this chapter. Thompson is concerned about how both theoretical and applied ethics have tended to focus on questions at *micro-* and *macro-*levels, but neglected "ethics at the *mid-level*—the vast range of institutions that operate between the world of families, friends, and neighbors, on the one side, and the realm of governments, on the other—institutions such as hospitals, schools, corporations, and the mass media."[2] The concept of conflict of interest is so morally peculiar and so relatively novel in part because it thrives in this neglected realm. In one way or another all theorists who study conflicts of interest recognize this fact. Their analyses are illustrated by complex dilemmas in professional and quasi-professional settings. Much of the literature nevertheless seems to rely on a more traditional "microlevel" methodology, one that begins and sometimes ends with sorting out the moral obligations and interests of the lonely individual at the center of a typical conflict of interest situation. This "micro" perspective is essential for a normative theory of conflict of interest, and much progress has been made by clarifying it. We will argue that the next stage, already well underway, is to try to merge the best of these "micro" analyses with a more properly "mid-level" theory of institutional design for corporations and a "macro" theory for the design and regulation of markets in a democratic society.

THE CONCEPT OF CONFLICT OF INTEREST

In his influential study "Conflict of Interest as a Moral Category," Neil Luebke found "no use of the term 'conflict of interest' prior to the 1930s, nor any occurrence in a court decision prior to 1949."[3] Luebke noted that it was absent from the 1971 *Oxford English Dictionary* and did not appear in the *Random House Dictionary of the English Language* until 1971, albeit with a definition "that emphasizes the governmental use of the term to the virtual exclusion of the private sector." Similarly, among "standard law dictionaries it does not appear in the exhaustive *American and English Encyclopedia of Law* of 1887, in John Bouvier's *Law Dictionary and Concise Encyclopedia* of 1914, or in any edition of *Black's Law Dictionary* until 1979." Its appearance and analysis in the philosophical literature is more recent still.

Of course, we can find the words "conflict," "of," and "interest" conjoined in political philosophy texts prior to this, but in any examples we have found, this expression refers simply to the existences of what we might call "clashing interests," for example, where you and I both want something but cannot both have it.[4] Conversely, there is no question that some of the core elements of the contemporary concept of conflict of interest—including special duties for trustees, fiduciaries, judges, and professionals, as well as worries about the temptations of corruption—have been around for centuries, even if we did not use those three words to pick them out. One can surely not understand why a sultan would have insisted on having his harem attendants castrated without imagining him being keenly aware of the mostly unsupervised attendants' potential conflict of interest.

Still, there are genuinely novel features of our contemporary concept and of the ways we use it in our evaluations of individuals and the institutions within which they work. In order to begin to examine these features, let us turn now to recent scholarly attempts to define or clarify the concept. Our aim here will be both to explain the nature of conflicts of interest by way of the best of these analyses and to highlight points of consensus and of continuing dispute. Our interim conclusion will be that this project of conceptually analyzing "conflict of interest" has reached a stage of sufficient sophistication, clarity, and consensus that the community of business ethics scholars can now devote most of its energy to more substantive normative and empirical questions, which we ourselves will turn to later in this chapter.

Contemporary philosophical debates over the definition of "conflict of interest" in business ethics can be traced to a 1982 article by Michael Davis, titled simply "Conflict of Interest."[5] Davis worked to reconcile legal analysis of conflict of interest extant at the time with the one theoretically significant article he is able to cite from outside of the legal literature, namely Joseph Margolis's "Conflict of Interest and Conflicting Interests."[6] Building on the foundations of the American Bar Association's understanding of the concept and employing the methods and style of conceptual analysis current among "Anglo-American" philosophers at the time, Davis produced both a "rough formulation" and a full-blown conceptual definition with five necessary and jointly sufficient conditions for when a given person has a conflict of interest within a given role. Since this initial article, Davis has continued to work mainly with the same "rough formulation":

> On the standard view, person X has a conflict of interest if, and only if (1) X is in a relationship with another requiring X to exercise judgment in the other's, Y's, behalf and (2) X has a (special) interest tending to interfere with the proper exercise of judgment in that relationship.[7]

As Davis points out, the crucial terms here are *relationship, judgment, interest,* and *proper exercise.* His concise clarification of each of these crucial terms provides a model overview, in just three pages, of the basic issues at stake in most conceptual discussions about conflict of interest.[8] We can trace most variations in the way different scholars or institutions understand the concept of conflict of interest to different ways they interpret notions like "interest" or "relationship," or to the emphasis they place on "exercising judgment" or "fulfilling a duty."

Davis did not end all debates about the proper definition of conflict of interest in 1982. Many subsequent analyses of the concept were framed explicitly in reaction to Davis's proposed definition. For example, John Boatright argues that conflict of interest should be defined not in terms of *judgment,* but in terms of *acting in another's interest:*

> A conflict of interest occurs when a personal or institutional interest interferes with the ability of an individual or institution *to act in the interest of* another party, when the individual or institution has an ethical or legal obligation to act in that other party's interest.[9]

Another philosopher, Thomas Carson, deemphasizes the role of "interfering with the exercise of judgment" (which Davis finds so important)—and, like Boatright, stresses the centrality of fulfilling a duty. He presents what he takes to be the necessary conditions for a conflict of interest to obtain:

> In order for there to be a conflict of interest, the following conditions must be met: (1) there must be an individual X who has duties to another party Y in virtue of holding an office or a position; (2) X must be impeded or compromised in fulfilling her duties to Y; (3) the reason for X's being impeded or compromised in fulfilling her duties to Y must be that X has interests that are incompatible (or seem to her to be incompatible) with fulfilling her duties to Y.[10]

In a similar vein that is not in explicit opposition to Davis, Andrew Stark maintains that a conflict of interest "arises when a professional...possesses an interest that could impair her in executing her professional, fiduciary obligations to the principal."[11] Stark clarifies this definition by adding that he is not using the term "fiduciary" in its narrow legalistic sense, but rather to refer to the kind of heightened responsibility that typically accompanies professional roles.

It is not our intention to heap one more paper on a pile of attempts to definitively clarify the concept of conflict of interest. Instead, we will give a rough indication of the progress these conceptual discussions have made, and of how much more conceptual work is necessary for the sake of the substantive ethical and policy issues arising from conflicts of interest. In highlighting the "core idea" here, we also hope to make clearer just how novel, or at least peculiar, "conflict of interest" is as a normative concept.

The Core Idea?

So what *is* that core idea of a "conflict of interest"? The academic literature began with concerns arising within professions—although it must be emphasized that you do not have to be a member of a profession to have a conflict of interest. The archetypical example concerns a professional, like a lawyer or a physician, who has an obligation to serve her client's interests, but who is confronted with an option that would serve one of her own interests to the detriment of the client's. For example, the client trusts her to serve his interests, has good reason to trust her, and pays her based on the mutually reinforced assumption that she will indeed be dedicated to serve his interests. However, the professional herself is presented with an opportunity to serve some other interest she cares about in addition to, or instead of, serving the client's interest.

There is a lot more to be said before we can derive something like a definition, let alone a normative theory, from this kind of example. For one thing, there is a tremendous amount of normative and institutional baggage carried by the idea of a *profession* and a professional obligation. We will unpack some of this baggage later in the chapter. For now we note that there is generally assumed to be a difference between a true "conflict of interest situation" and a generic "principal-agent" problem. It may be that most conflicts of interest can be conceived of as involving at least one agent (e.g., the professional or expert in the example above) and at least one principal (e.g., the client).[12] But nobody who takes the concept of "conflict of interest" seriously will want to conflate the conflicts of interest and generic principal-agent problems.[13] In other words, there are plenty of principal-agent problems that we would *not* want to analyze in terms of conflict of interest: e.g., the standard situation of a manual laborer (the agent) who has been hired to do a relatively unsupervised job by an employer (the principal) and who has an interest in being lazy and doing as little work as he can get away with ("shirking"). It is perfectly true that there is a conflict between the employer's interest in getting as much productivity out of the worker as possible and the employee's interest in not working too hard, but this is not the kind of conflict that we are trying to get at with the specialized term of art "conflict of interest." People have always recognized the existence of this kind of "conflict." Something more conceptually and normatively interesting occurs in the kinds of situations in which professionals, executives, experts, and public servants (among others) find themselves.

Most careful definitions place a primacy on picking out a particular *kind of situation*.[14] A person has a conflict of interest because of the kind of situation she finds herself in, not simply because of the actual state of her own desires, interests, motives, and so on. This is what distinguishes the conflicted professional from the generic shirking or corrupt employee. Even cases in which the professional is morally and psychologically committed to serving her client's interests to the best of her abilities, and even when she could not conceive of being tempted or influenced by some personal interest that is in conflict with her client's, we still may say that she is in *a conflict of interest situation* and that *because* she is in such a situation she *has* a conflict of interest (not merely a potential conflict of interest). Most theorists would agree with Davis that "[O]ne can have a conflict of interest without being in the wrong. To have a conflict of interest is merely to have a moral problem. What will be morally right or wrong...is how one responds to the problem."[15] When we say that Aristotle or Kant did not think in terms of conflicts of interest in the contemporary sense, this is primarily what we are referring to. They understood the idea of trusted physicians, or politicians, or magistrates, or civil servants being tempted to enrich themselves rather than fulfilling their duties to their "principals" or to the public. But roughly speaking, for earlier thinkers, the moral analysis of such a situation would focus on the "professional" in question having (or failing to have) the courage to do the right and honorable thing and to resist the temptations of corruption. As long as this person has remained virtuous and fulfilled his primary duties, nothing morally wrong has happened. Indeed, a contemporary virtue theorist inspired by Aristotle might take the same position,[16] as would purveyors of the "everything you need to know about business ethics you learned at your mother's knee" approach.[17] There are two problems with this virtue-centric approach. First, it places too much confidence in the ability of conflicted individuals to know if their judgment is being corrupted. Second, it does not take into account the fact that the organization they work for can be harmed merely by the suspicion that the employees are being presented with "unsupervised" opportunities for corruption. We will discuss both of these issues at length later in the chapter.

We can contrast the "noble morality" of old with the "professional morality" of today, which recognizes the ethical salience of the concept of conflict of interest. Consider the case of a conflicted contemporary professional or pubic servant who decides not, for example, to disclose the conflict, but instead to follow the classical advice and simply not allow the conflicting interest to influence her decisions. Even if she made a perfectly reasonable judgment she might well be disciplined, fired, or suspended from her professional association. As the legal scholar Bayless Manning put it, as long ago as 1964, "subjective intent is not important [in conflict of interest law]...If the wrong kind of outside interest is held, *no amount of leaning over backward or purity of soul* will satisfy [a confirmation] Committee or the statutes."[18] We now find a similar primacy of the "objective" situation in conflict of interest rules in professions and firms. A person is judged to have a conflict of interest on the basis of being in a conflicted situation, whether or not that person thinks he or she is capable of resisting the temptation or corrupting influence of the interest that could interfere with her judgment. This does not mean that we are cynical about the motives or abilities of professionals or experts in this kind of situation. It is simply that we now think that finding oneself in such a situation requires that the person do more than simply resist temptation. At the end of the day, an employee or professional may be expected to exercise moral restraint to prevent her own interest from clouding her judgment, but before then she will generally be expected to take concrete steps to *escape* the conflict, *disclose* it, *have it managed*, or as a last resort *manage* it.[19] We will discuss strategies of each of these types a little later.

Different Kinds of Conflicts of Interest

There is a proliferation of *types* of conflicts of interest in our contemporary world. The "real world" of professional life typically now diverges from the context of what we might call the "small-town lawyer" or "country doctor" envisaged by the archetypical case of the lone professional facing a single client and having an interest that might interfere with the professional's duty to look after the client's interest. A typical lawyer or doctor now is more likely to work for a large law firm or hospital, or perhaps for a large corporation in, say, investment banking or the pharmaceutical industry. In these settings they may have competing principals and duties, many of which are in perpetual tension if not outright conflict. For example, a doctor may have to manage conflicting duties to two principals, patients and HMOs, several times a day.[20] Another factor in the proliferation of potential conflicts of interest is the steady emergence of new categories of professionals or quasi-professionals, also typically working in corporate settings—from practitioners of emerging services in health care, "wellness" therapies, and counseling, to experts specializing in any one of dozens of new financial services, or to consultants for just about anything. There is also an increasing professionalization of management in ways that are relevant to a concern about conflicts of interest. It is not so much that business schools have consciously taken on the trappings of professional schools, training their MBA graduates to be autonomous responsible "professionals." It is rather that modern corporations routinely place individual managers in situations where they are expected to *exercise judgment* in matters that require considerable *expertise*, including expertise that both their superiors and clients may find *difficult to evaluate*. Such managers will typically not be members of a bona fide profession (like law or accounting) with its own code of ethics, but their employers will be just as concerned as a professional association would be about ways the private interests of these managers might compromise their expert judgment or expose the firm to accusations of corruption, favoritism, or "unprofessionalism."

It is worth making clear that although we typically discuss the concept of conflict of interest with examples involving professionals, one does not have to be a bona fide professional to have a conflict of interest. The ideas of professionalism and conflict of interest are linked primarily because (for reasons we will explore later) all professions explicitly make the management of conflict of interest a central feature of their professional codes of ethics. But many organizations and groups need to minimize the chance that their members or employees will be involved in conflicts of interest and will thereby invite scandal, among other things. It is likely that public servants in many countries have lived with conflict-of-interest strictures for as long or longer than have members of many professions.

And again, such strictures have become a standard feature of most corporate codes of ethics or "conduct." Many senior managers or "officers" are treated in the law very much like professionals, with very explicit fiduciary obligations to serve others' interests ahead of their own.[21] The fiduciary obligations of senior managers were reinforced in the United States by the Sarbanes-Oxley Act of 2002 (especially Titles 3 and 4), which was prompted by the perceived lack of accountability of top management during the "Enron Era." Sarbanes-Oxley also includes provisions for another category of conflicts of interest we have barely touched upon so far, namely, conflicts that arise between different practices or services offered by the same firm. In other words, firms themselves—and not simply the individuals working for them—can be in a conflict-of-interest situation. One part of the firm, for example, may have fiduciary obligations to serve the interests of a particular principal (e.g., a client, but also perhaps the public, as in the case of auditors or engineers), but another part of the firm has an interest in selling services to that client that may not be in its (or the public's) best interests. Consequently, section 201 of Title 2 of Sarbanes-Oxley restricts firms in charge of audits from offering other consulting services to the same clients. The legitimate fear is that the judgment of the audit team may be "influenced" by the interest of their firm in maintaining good relations with the senior managers who are in a position to offer the consulting contracts—bearing in mind that the fiduciary obligations of the auditors are not to the senior managers but to the shareholders and the investing public. Title 5 of Sarbanes-Oxley, "Analyst Conflicts of Interest," focuses on the inherent conflict of interest of analysts who are supposed to give an objective assessment of the prospects of a company that may also be securing financing or IPO services from the firm (say, an investment bank) the analyst works for. The evident conflict is that the analyst may implicitly or explicitly feel pressure to paint a more optimistic picture of the company and to not jeopardize potentially lucrative contracts with his or her own firm.[22]

Does this proliferation of sites for conflicts of interest diminish our prospects for understanding both the concept and its normative stakes? Not necessarily. In his capstone article for an excellent collection on conflicts of interest in both established and emerging professions, Stark gives us some grounds for optimism. To begin with, we can usefully distinguish "out-of-role" and "in-role" conflicts of interest. By and large, "conflicts of interest arising from out-of-role sources are all alike," in that they involve conflicts between an individual's professional duties and his or her own outside private interests. The ethical problems with these kinds of conflicts are typically plain to see, and as such they tend to be less ethically and conceptually controversial (i.e., less open to debate) than what Stark calls "in-role" conflicts, which involve a tension between two or more different professional duties an individual or firm may have. Stark argues convincingly that across a broad range of professional and quasi-professional roles, we find a consistent pattern of two basic types of in-role conflicts of interest: "one that arises when a *professional occupies more than one role with respect to any given principal*; and the other, when the *professional occupies the same role with respect to many principals.*"[23] The classic example of the second, "many principals, one role," type is a lawyer with concurrent adversarial clients. However, it could also include a broker who manages accounts for multiple clients but must choose between them when allocating a security in short supply;[24] or a corporate director dealing with competing minority and majority shareholders.[25] In-role conflicts falling within Stark's first category—"many roles, one principal"— conflicts tend to emerge either (1) because "the professional simultaneously occupies a *judging* and an *advocating* role—an impartial and a partial role—in the work he does for the principal," as when professors grade graduate students, and then agree to write letters of recommendation for them with a hope of landing them jobs; or (2) because of a "tension between the professional's *diagnostic* and *service-provision* roles, his roles as both a buyer of services for, and a seller of services to, the principal," as when a dentist examines your teeth and then offers to fix the problems she "discovered."[26]

In short, there are many alternative ways one could choose to analyze and categorize different kinds or categories of conflicts of interest. Some schemes will prove more useful than others, depending on one's purposes. We believe that the scholarly community is now reaching the end of a phase that concentrated largely on the analysis of the concept of conflict of interest and is moving on increasingly to address substantive normative and institutional issues. We will, accordingly, shift (in the next section) from this conceptual discussion to some reflections on the state of conceptual debates today and the nature of the substantive questions these debates are supposed to help us address.

From Conceptual Analysis to Normative Evaluation and Institutional Design

Debates between rival explications of the concept of conflict of interest in the business ethics community (broadly construed) have reached the stage where reasonable people can agree to disagree. There seems to be substantial agreement over the "core idea" of a conflict of interest, as articulated above, as well as over what kinds of situations count as conflicts of interest and why. There is a broad consensus, for example, on the primacy of identifying conditions under which someone is in a conflict of interest *situation*. There is also a good deal of agreement over the way the concept is bound up with the need for an agent to exercise judgment involving expertise that is difficult for the principal to evaluate. There is agreement over the significance of the special or fiduciary duties of an agent to one or more principals, and of the existence of other interests that might interfere, consciously or unconsciously, with the ability or willingness of the agent to make the appropriate judgment or to carry out her fiduciary duties. This broad consensus about the concept of conflict of interest can be regarded as a basic "gestalt" created from our earlier survey of rival definitions.

A closer look at those conceptual analyses shows lively disagreements as well. Some of the leading theorists—including Davis, Boatright, Carson, and Luebke—have gone through multiple iterations of debate, in print and at scholarly conferences, without coming much closer to resolution. Any definition of conflict of interest will involve concepts that are open to different interpretations and conditions, concepts such as "judgment," "fiduciary," "interest," "relationship," and so on. Various theorists will have different intuitions about which elements of a definition are more "essential" or "core" and which ones merely follow from the core but are not part of it. So, for example, all theorists will see conflicts of interest as situations where both the agent's *judgment* and *ability to act in the interest of the principal* are potentially compromised. Still, what is the more "essential" element being interfered with—*the judgment* or *the ability to act in the other's interest* or *the ability to carry out one's duty*? This question invites related queries about which method is appropriate for settling these sorts of conceptual disputes. Many will find the answer to this question disappointing. There is no "truth" to be had in conceptual definition of this sort. There is no independently existing reality of conflicts of interest against which we can test our theories about what does and does not qualify as a conflict of interest. We cannot ask about the deep meaning of the term in ordinary language, because "conflict of interest" is a relatively recent term of art whose meaning in technical and everyday discourses is significantly vague and in flux. But as we noted at the outset, people *do* seem to be able to spot a conflict of interest. (There is a Farsi aphorism to the effect that one does not have to be a cook to smell when something is rotten in the kitchen.) So we can identify a fairly uncontroversial set of situations that we would expect a good definition of "conflict of interest" to pick out. We can also make some reasonable decisions about other kinds of situations that are adequately covered by other normative concepts (such as the general idea of a principal-agent problem, or of selfishness) and which therefore do not need to be gathered under this particular rubric. The touchstone cases and illustrations we have used so far (i.e., both clear examples of conflicts of interest and also examples that are best called something other than "conflicts of interest") would be identified correctly by any of the best of the current philosophical definitions of "conflict of interest." In the end, the question of how exactly to tweak the definition of a concept like this is pragmatic. Which aspects of the world (e.g., which kinds of situations) are worth highlighting as conflicts of interest, given our various purposes? As several scholars have noted, the concept of conflict of interest as it is used in careful legal and philosophical discourse highlights a feature of the world that had been only dimly recognized through the ages. But does our recognition of these types of situations actually help us to better understand, to evaluate, to act fairly, and the like?

As we have hinted throughout, one can pose questions of this sort at each of the three levels of ethical analysis highlighted by Thompson (and others). We need, then, an analysis of "conflict of interest" to clarify our answers to the following sorts of concrete questions:

Microlevel: Which duties does a professional or expert owe to various parties, clients, employers, or the public? What rights does she have to pursue her own interests in the context of selling a service to a client? What should she do when she recognizes she is in, or could be perceived to be in, a conflict of interest situation?

Mid-level: How should a firm or some other kind of organization employing professionals and experts be structured so that the firm itself avoids or manages its conflicts of interest, as well as the conflicts its employees may find themselves in? What rules should it have about conflicts of interest among its employees? How should it teach, monitor, and enforce these rules? Also, what rules, training, and sanctions should professions themselves have concerning the conflicts of interest of their members?

Macrolevel: Why should there be professions and when should putative professional bodies be granted a monopoly on rights to license (and to punish or expel) practitioners? Contrariwise, when should domains of experts simply be left to ply their trade in the marketplace? When are government regulations concerning conflicts of interest appropriate for the private sector? What conflict-of-interest rules and laws are appropriate for public servants, elected officials, judges, and so on?

These sample questions, albeit rather central ones, do not constitute a comprehensive list. Lying behind these relatively concrete issues are more abstract questions, such as "and what kinds of theories or principles are appropriate for justifying answers to this kind of issue?" Note that by "theories or principles" we do not want to imply that these are only ethical or even normative. Some may be prudential reasons of one sort or another. Both firms and professional bodies, for example, may decide to pay significant attention to conflicts of interest (and perceptions thereof) because doing so is the best way to secure trust from their customers and their government overseers. And trust pays.

When laid out in this way, it should be plain that the answers to the questions at different levels are linked. There is a tendency for microlevel questions to depend on answers at the mid-level, and for mid-level answers to depend on macro decisions. For example, in many cases an individual's duties in the face of a conflict of interest will depend crucially on whether or not she is a member of a bona fide profession or an employee of a firm with rules about these things. In other words, how she should answer her individualized microlevel questions depends on how the profession or firm has answered the mid-level questions. These questions may depend in part on the status of government regulations. And these kinds of regulations will be based on more abstract principles of justice and perhaps also on economic theories (e.g., about market failures, or cost-benefit analysis) and psychological theories (e.g., about the pernicious ways personal interests can unwittingly corrupt good judgments).

Over the rest of this chapter, we will illustrate how the study of conflict of interest could be advanced by thinking about the kinds of inputs that would be required to answer the relevant questions at the mid- and macrolevels. We examine next how research from the world of psychology might enrich mid-level attempts by institutions to find effective approaches to the conflicts faced by their members. We will finish with some reflections on how political philosophy might shed light on various macrolevel questions of relevance to managing conflicts of interest.

Cognitive Bias and Mid-Level Theory for Institutional Design

In the previous section, we sketched questions that might reasonably be asked about conflict of interest at each of the micro-, mid-, and macrolevels of ethical analysis. Key questions at the mid-level were about how institutions (including professions) should be structured so that those institutions and their members successfully avoid or manage conflicts of interest. But answering such questions of institutional design requires a sophisticated understanding of the capacities of the individuals who populate institutions to recognize and resist bias in oneself and others. Knowledge of these capacities of individuals is also important, in principle at least, for microlevel analysis of conflict of interest. An understanding of one's own foibles should prove useful in guarding against improper bias. But as we shall explore below, there is reason to believe that individuals often cannot make good use of information about their own cognitive capacities and biases, even when such information can be made available. Institutions, however, have at their disposal a range of artifices—policies, procedures, incentives, and oversight mechanisms—that can effectively modify human behavior. Institutions are built precisely because of their power to take human intentions and tendencies as their raw material and turn them to constructive purposes. Accurate information about human psychology seems essential here. Folk understandings of what motivates and biases decision makers are often inaccurate and are surely a poor basis on which to structure important institutions. And the tools of analytic philosophy—which have given us such a good understanding of the core concept of conflict of interest—do little to illuminate empirical questions about the actual human capacities that play a significant role in institutional solutions. Michael Davis highlights this problem in a useful thought experiment about refereeing his son's soccer game:

> *I do not know* whether I would be harder on him [his son] than an impartial referee would be, easier, or just the same. What I do know is that…I could not be as reliable as an (equally competent)…[referee] would be…The same would be true even if I refereed a game in which my son did not play but I had a strong dislike for several players on one team. Would I call more fouls against that team, fewer (because I was "bending over backwards to be fair"), or the same as a similarly qualified referee who did not share my dislike? Again, *I do not know.*[27]

Presumably, these are just the sorts of questions that need to be answered by institutions seeking to institute any but the most alarmist of prophylactic measures. Reasonable estimates of the cognitive and motivational tendencies typically experienced by human beings are precisely the kind of data that must inform reasonably nuanced institutional policies. In order to put in place effective incentives and deterrents, for example, institutions need a reasonably accurate understanding of just what factors actually incentivize and deter people. So it is not surprising that successful entrepreneurs with "gut instincts" about these things will also, when the firm grows larger, come to rely on the expertise of human resource managers trained in behavioral sciences to design systems of incentives, promotion, compliance, and deterrence.

Fortunately, a recent trend in conflict-of-interest research has seen empirical research by psychologists and experimental economists applied to the issue in ways that are instructive. In particular, this research has brought experimental and statistical methods to bear on questions such as the range and force of psychological factors at play in conflicts of interest, and the likely effectiveness of various remedial strategies. This empirical research complements nicely the analytic work done by philosophers and political theorists like Davis, Boatright, and Stark. While philosophers were analyzing the concept of conflict of interest, debating its key features, and fleshing out arguments concerning why and when conflict of interests are morally problematic, psychologists and experimental economists have been exploring the workings of the minds of the human individuals who actually find themselves in such conflicts. They have tried to understand how an interest can *interfere with* a judgment or a motivation to serve one's client's interests (even in a person of good will and virtuous character). This is incredibly important for good institutional design because it points to a need not just to educate personnel about what the definition of conflict of interest is but also to structure institutions themselves so that judgment is effectively insulated from interests that might otherwise interfere.

This empirical work on conflict of interest is rooted in a voluminous literature elucidating the large number of cognitive and motivational biases to which humans are subject—psychological mechanisms influencing decision making in ways that are often invisible to the decision maker, and that are often surprising. The touchstone for this topic is the work of Daniel Kahneman, Paul Slovic, and Amos Tversky investigating the cognitive biases (patterned deviations of human cognition from the predictions of rational choice theory) and motivational biases (biases rooted in the tendency for judgment to be affected by the individual's own interests) to which humans are subject.[28] These biases have been demonstrated to affect perception and choice in an incredible range of ways, in everything from the way individuals evaluate the seriousness of various risks and the desirability of particular outcomes, to the way they perceive connections between cause and effect, as well as their ability to summon memories and even their own understandings of what motivates them to do the things they do.

A classic example of cognitive bias is the "framing effect," which consists in the tendency for decision makers to be influenced by irrelevant factors such as the way in which a particular decision or risk is described, or framed. The exact same facts described in two different ways (e.g., listed in a different order) can result in different decisions. A highway safety initiative, for example, may be received differently by the public if it is framed in terms of "lives saved" rather than in terms of "deaths avoided," even though both descriptions are mathematically identical. Examples of well-documented biases more closely related to the study of conflict of interest include the *consistency bias* (the tendency to remember one's current behavior or decisions as being consistent with past behavior or decisions)[29] and *in-group bias* (the preference given to people whom the decision maker sees—even for seemingly spurious reasons—as being part of his or her "group").[30]

The collective wisdom of this body of literature is that *human judgment is consistently and persistently biased in ways that are often counterproductive, nearly invisible, and hard for individuals to compensate for.* Recently, researchers in the field of cognitive and motivational bias have also found fertile ground for the application of their work in the study of conflict of interest. Fundamental to the notion of conflict of interest is that someone's *judgment* is being affected or stands to be affected. Unfortunately, some theories and definitions of conflict of interest are vague, and others are narrow, regarding just which biasing conditions and causal mechanisms may be at play. The literature on cognitive and motivational biases has stepped into this breach with a body of empirical and theoretical knowledge concerning which factors bias human judgment, to what extent, and under what circumstances. Mid-level (e.g., organizational) attempts at recognizing and resolving conflicts of interest seem bound to be facilitated by a more well-substantiated understanding of the psychological causal factors at play. What sorts of things actually do bias people's judgments? What sorts of incentives (if any) can institutions put in place that are likely to be effective at getting people to exercise judgment objectively? There is reason to think that the institutional level is the right level at which to use answers to such questions. If consistent and persistent biases are found at the level of the individual, it seems unlikely that effective solutions are going to be found through the self-reflective practices of those consistently and persistently biased individuals.

Scholars have recently begun to draw on the literature on cognitive and motivational bias to shed light upon conflicts of interest that obtain in various professional and quasi-professional fields. Key examples include studies of the conflicts faced by physicians, financial analysts, and auditors. We will now examine evidence from each of these briefly before moving to suggest a path towards an empirically grounded normative theory of conflict of interest.

Dana and Loewenstein studied the conflict of interest faced by physicians who accept gifts from the pharmaceutical industry.[31] They considered in particular the impact of the *size* of such gifts. Many institutions (corporations, hospitals, professions) permit the acceptance of small, "token" gifts, based on the commonsense assumption that such gifts could not plausibly be thought to influence a professional's judgment. However, these authors note that, according to the literature on bias, "small gifts may be surprisingly influential." This casts doubt on the way in which the line between gifts that are permitted and those that are forbidden is so often drawn. Further, these authors point out that it is unhelpful, and likely inaccurate, to equate the claim that physicians accepting gifts are involved in a conflict of interest with the claim that such physicians are either corrupt or otherwise engaging in intentional impropriety: the literature on cognitive and motivational biases suggests that such biases typically affect judgment without the individuals involved being aware of it.

The psychological evidence concerning cognitive and motivational biases has also been applied to the investigation of conflict of interest in the field of financial analysis. Michaely and Womack, for example, point to the existence of cognitive biases as plausibly implying that analysts are often not just *unwilling*, but psychologically *unable*, "to accept the statistical reality that many of their IPOs will turn out to be average or below average."[32] This suggests the possibility of a trenchant bias in financial analysis, the response to which is much more likely to be found in institutional design (including features imposed by government regulations of the sort we examined earlier from the Sarbanes-Oxley Act) than in individual commitment. Scholars have paid even more attention to what is likely the most well-publicized category of conflict of interest in recent years, namely, the conflict faced by accountants engaged to audit the books of publicly traded firms. Moore, Loewenstein, Tanlu, and Bazerman present experimental data suggesting that auditors may be unable to overcome biases in favor of their clients *even* when motivated financially to make their audits accurate, rather than favorable.[33] Nelson reviews an enormous amount of empirical literature on auditor conflict of interest, concluding that the "experimental literature generally provides evidence of consistent (and persistent) effects of auditors' incentives on their reporting decisions."[34] This sort of evidence provides a key input to be used by those engaged in designing institutions in ways that will help avoid and mitigate conflicts of interest.

Toward an Empirically Informed Normative Theory

The study of cognitive and motivational biases is useful and important for several reasons relevant to mid-level ethical analysis of conflict of interest.[35] It reveals, as we have seen, a range of factors that can, and commonly do, affect judgment, and against which institutions must guard in their efforts to design systems to assist in the avoidance and mitigation of conflict of interest. This range of factors stretches beyond the kind of material (primarily financial) interest to which conflict of interest policies typically attend. As Miller notes, the idea that one can remove all possibility of bias simply by divesting oneself of a financial interest is "psychologically naive." After all, "divesting yourself financially from a concern does not ensure that you will have divested yourself emotionally from that concern."[36] These results are consistent with the trend, which Stark has observed within U.S. public institutions, to adopt increasingly "subjective" interpretations of "conflictable" interests. The law increasingly considers not just "objective" pecuniary interests but an increasing array of "subjective" interests derived from "influences, loyalties, concerns, emotions, predispositions, prejudices, animuses, biases, affiliations, experiences, relationships, attachments, moral constraints, [and] ideological agendas." All of these, Stark argues, "at one time or another, have been viewed as every bit as encumbering of official judgment as pecuniary interest itself."[37]

This empirical literature sheds light on questions of how conflicts of interest should be handled and which policy options are likely to prove fruitful. Most of what it implies about the prospects for effectively countering conflict of interest does not warrant optimism. According to Tenbrunsel, "The investigation of psychological processes and their relationship to conflicts of interest and unethical behavior is important but depressing for it reveals innate barriers that seem impermeable."[38] To see the significance of this psychological literature for mid-level analysis, one need only glance at the range of responses typically offered in the face of conflict of interest. Boatright discusses a list of methods for managing conflict of interest, including:

- Avoidance (Avoiding acquiring any interest that would jeopardize one's judgment.)
- Alignment (The arrangement of incentives such that the decision-maker's interests are aligned with those of the persons being served.)
- Objectivity (A psychological commitment to the objective exercise of one's duties. This is, in effect, the "classical" virtue-based prescription.)
- Disclosure (Disclosing conflict of interest to those who would be affected.)
- Independent Judgment (Seeking to obtain the judgment of an objective third party.)
- Competition (Imposing competitive pressure on firms to incentivize them to eliminate conflict of interest where conflicts threaten efficiency.)
- Rules and Policies (Including especially institutional remedies that prevent *potential* conflicts of interest from evolving into *actual* conflicts of interest.)
- Structural Changes (Ways of arranging operations so as to make conflicts of interest less likely, such as separating the auditing and consulting functions of accounting firms).[39]

This wide-ranging list is useful, and many of the items on it are precisely the kind of mid-level solution we have mentioned. They are strategies to be implemented or at least imposed by institutions. One reason this makes sense is because the empirical evidence suggests that individuals will typically be insufficiently self-aware to implement even apparently simple strategies such as "Objectivity" and "Disclosure." Many of these management strategies require certain psychological capacities on the part of individual institutional members. Institutional rules requiring *avoidance*, for example, will only work if the individuals involved are psychologically capable of reliably recognizing conflict-of-interest situations. Efforts to use incentives to *align* decision makers' interests with the interests of those whom they advise will only be effective if the individuals involved are susceptible to such incentives and not tempted to "game" them.[40] Whether *disclosure* will be effective depends on whether those to whom conflict is disclosed are willing to act upon such disclosure. The existence and strength of such capacities has heretofore been relegated to the realm of commonsense and folk psychology. Fortunately, as the literature on cognitive biases demonstrates, whether people in general, and professionals in particular, actually possess these capacities is something that can be investigated empirically.

A good example of the extent to which empirical research can illuminate institutional solutions relates to one of the standard remedial steps urged by almost all conflict of interest policies and theorists, namely disclosure. Interestingly, Cain et al. found evidence casting doubt on the usefulness of disclosure as a remedy. According to them, there is a substantial body of research suggesting (1) that clients are unlikely to be able to effectively use professional disclosures of conflict of interest to correctly discount advice they are given, and (2) that professionals making such disclosures may, in fact, give more biased advice than professionals who fail to make such disclosures.[41] In short: disclosure may be useless or even counterproductive. This is instructive regarding the sort of mid-level analysis we are advocating, for it implies a serious worry about the efficacy of one standard microlevel remedial strategy. The empirical literature also provides insights regarding the usefulness of focusing on avoiding or disclosing specifically *financial* conflicts of interest. Despite the common assumption that financial interests are the ones that need to be watched most carefully, Moore et al. found that "the social ties between auditors and their clients may be more of a problem than their financial incentives *per se*."[42]

This empirical evidence, however useful it may be for mid-level analysis and remediation of conflict of interest, has limitations and failings. One potential failing is its tendency to focus only on outcomes. This tendency is understandable. Empirical methods concentrate on measurable findings. But this focus on outcomes—consequences—may result in a neglect of other ethically important perspectives on conflict of interest. Research that finds that a particular kind of incentive is ineffective at changing behavior may too quickly lead to the conclusion that such incentives are useless, without considering other moral reasons favoring those incentives. For example, the useful finding by Cain et al. that disclosure is not likely to be *effective* at producing better decision making leaves unanswered the question of whether the clients or patients of conflicted professionals are nonetheless *owed* that information.[43] From a moral point of view, institutions of various kinds ought to be concerned with policies that result in those institutions and their members *doing the right thing*, not just with producing optimal measurable outcomes.

A second limitation of the empirical literature lies in its occasional tendency to focus on what is measurable, and in so doing to lose sight of the analytic and definitional rigor achieved by philosophers such as Davis and Boatright and political theorists like Stark. In some cases, this leads to an unhelpful blurring of the concept of conflict of interest. One example is a paper by Tom Tyler, featured prominently in an edited volume on empirical approaches to conflict of interest. Although the term "conflict of interest" occurs in Tyler's title, the paper is really about how people deal with "conflicts between self-interest and social values."[44] But conflict of interest is not about those generic interpersonal conflicts. Neither self-interest nor social values is a necessary ingredient of conflict of interest. An institution implementing a conflict-of-interest policy aiming to remedy the much wider range of conflicts implied by Tyler's analysis might well end up with a policy that lacks focus, and that might indeed give bad advice. "Avoidance," for example, might sometimes be a plausible management strategy for certain kinds of conflict of interest, but it is a very poor strategy for dealing with the much more pervasive conflicts between self-interest and social values. Empirical research must stay clearly focused if it is to achieve its promised utility.

Despite these limitations, the empirical research discussed in this section will prove useful to those seeking to structure organizations in ways that stand a reasonable chance of dealing effectively with conflict of interest. We cannot stress enough the fact that these are still very early days for this cognitive-bias research, and especially for its application to problems of conflict of interest and institutional design. All we hope to have provided here is a hint and a sketch of how potentially useful this kind of research could be for our understanding of conflicts of interest and their management.

Toward a Macrolevel Political Theory of Conflict of Interest

One aim in this chapter has been to take stock of the progress that has been made on understanding conflicts of interest in organizations and to look ahead to issues in greater need of exploration. Business ethics scholars have mostly moved on from the conceptual disputes that characterized the first three decades of work on conflicts of interest. The focus now must be on questions of the "management" and "regulation" of conflicts of interest, broadly construed. The minor revolution that took place in the latter half of the twentieth century was the recognition that responsibility for managing what we now call conflicts of interest cannot merely be left to the honor and courage of the professional or public official. It is not that professionals suddenly became dishonorable, cowardly, or corrupt. The cognitive bias literature confirms intuitive suspicions that "interests" really do interfere with the judgment of even honorable and courageous professionals. As we highlighted in the last section, the first place to look for oversight and management of conflict of interest situations is in the organizations, firms, or professional bodies within which the conflicted professionals and experts typically work. There is still a tremendous amount of work to do to grapple with the design challenges of conflict of interest policies and their normative justification.[45] Among the most comprehensive and philosophically adept works to try to make sense of the ethics, law, and politics of these mid-level institutional solutions is Stark's *Conflict of Interest in American Public Life*. However, as the title makes clear, it is set within the institutions of government. Other important texts with a similar scope have been written for the management of conflicts of interest within specific professions, especially law and medicine.[46] But the agenda for a mid-level ethics and institutional design for conflicts of interest in business is, as yet, vaguely formulated. This should not be surprising, given the often unique conflict-of-interest challenges that arise within so many different industry sectors. However, inasmuch as this chapter attempts to say something about the state of the art concerning the study of conflict of interest in business ethics, we cannot avoid the interim conclusion that the art is still in a rather primitive state.

If a *mid-level* ethical focus on conflict of interest at the intersection of business and the professions is only just starting to be explored in detail, a *macro* ethical analysis of the issue is still very much on the horizon. Why should society or the state care about conflicts of interest that arise in the private sector and what should it do about them? Is there a special political or social dimension to conflicts of interest that is not already taken care of through choices in the marketplace (e.g., the choice to avoid untrustworthy "experts") and normal avenues of recourse for shoddy or fraudulent service? In macrolevel questions about conflict of interest, the heart of the issue concerns the social, political, and legal status of professions and quasi-professions (or expert-centered services). If mid-level ethical questions ask (among other things) how professions should try to regulate and manage the conflicts of interest of their members, macrolevel questions ask why the state should "privatize" this form of regulation to a putative professional body (or to the codes of ethics of individual organizations). As Allen Buchanan argues, "Professions are *social constructs*, not facts of nature. As such, they are appropriate subjects of critical appraisal. It makes sense to evaluate them and, indeed, to ask whether it is a good thing that they exist."[47] Many of the long-established professions like medicine, law, and accounting, are characterized by

> special status for members of the group (public acknowledgment of worth, marks of prestige, etc.) and special privileges, including financial advantages (such as public subsidies for training and education and insulation from economic competition) and a significant sphere of autonomy, that is, substantial freedom from external regulation of the characteristic activity.[48]

Professions, then, are "*socially constructed inequalities*... and it is appropriate to ask: What is the justification for this unequal treatment? Why should some occupational groups (such as physicians) and not others (such as automobile mechanics or butchers) receive special status, reap exceptional financial rewards, and be accorded an exceptional degree of freedom from external regulation of their activities"— including, crucially, the way they choose to manage their conflicts of interest?[49] As Buchanan notes, neither "the identification of situations involving conflicts of interest, nor the development of policies to minimize these conflicts need involve the special expertise of [the members of the profession] to such an extent that external regulation is not feasible."[50]

Buchanan is not claiming that this status cannot be justified, and he is correct in implying that we do not often enough ask ourselves, either as citizens or political philosophers, what this status ought to be and why. In the early post-Enron era, leading politicians, opinion makers, and even spokespeople at the SEC began to wonder aloud whether the long "experiment" with professional self-regulation in the accounting industry had failed. As we saw earlier, the Sarbanes-Oxley Act of 2002 was an attempt to bring regulation of conflicts of interest for auditing firms back within the ambit of the federal government (and also to reign in various non-professionals such as financial analysts). As this volume goes to press there are signs that a similar federal response—this time with respect to the regulation of less well-established professions and quasi-professions in financial services, bond-rating, and mortgage brokering—is likely to follow the so-called subprime mortgage collapse in 2008.

However, such examples of rolling back the autonomy of professions seem like exceptions that prove the rule. The more typical trend in recent decades is in the opposite direction: A trade association develops more of the trappings of a professional body and eventually succeeds in lobbying the state for some degree of licensing authority (which accords market power in the provision of some service) and self-regulation.[51] Again, we do not want to imply that the granting of autonomy to professions—especially with respect to the regulation of their own conflicts of interest—is a bad thing; we want simply to note that it is a strategic political choice in need of (macrolevel ethical) justification. Typically, the granting of this autonomy is seen (or rationalized) as a social contract where the profession and its members are granted significant privileges in return for taking on significant social obligations. One reason for the state to "privatize" the regulation of conflicts of interest in this way is that it might be cost-efficient with respect to many costs, including straightforward financial ones. As the experience of companies trying to comply with Sarbanes-Oxley seems to have made clear to many observers, as if for the first time, regulating conflicts of interest can be expensive—costly enough that some would argue that it is better to risk allowing some conflicts of interest than to try to manage them all.[52] The point is that these macrolevel questions deserve much more discussion in the business ethics literature on conflict of interest, not to mention in debates about justice and political economy among political theorists.

Another way to think about the importance of the "macro" political dimensions of a theory of conflict of interest is to pose the question we introduced at the outset: Why did we not seem to need the concept of conflict of interest before the latter half of the twentieth century? How could it be that this moral category—which is now absolutely central to ethics in the professions, public service, and most corporate codes of conduct—was only vaguely and imperfectly understood before World War II? We have already given part of an answer: more traditional ethical schools of thought were inclined to think that the only morally relevant prescriptive advice in what we are now calling "conflict-of-interest situations" would be to instruct the "conflicted" individual to resist temptation, maintain objectivity, and carry out his or her duty. What we now recognize is that this response is naïve: conflicted individuals can have their judgment interfered with even when they try their best to "correct" for the influence of the conflicting interest (think of Davis's soccer referee). In many cases, they may not even be aware of the influence some source of bias may have over them, as in the case of physicians influenced by the trinkets left by pharmaceutical representatives. But we believe that this response does not adequately explain the "discovery" of the concept of a conflict of interest or its dominance in our ethical thinking over the past half century. Such an explanation is still too focused on the microethical perspective to do the job.

Boatright and Davis both offer further, and complementary, explanations that begin to adopt a more mid-level ethical perspective. Davis concedes that we still have "no authoritative answer" to the question of why "both the term and the concept [of conflict of interest] are as new as they seem to be."[53] "The best explanation now available," he continues,

> seems to be the replacement of the enduring personal relationships of master and servant by the briefer encounters characteristic of the free market, big city, and big business. We are now much more dependent on the judgment of others, much less able to evaluate their judgment decision by decision, and indeed generally know much less about those individuals than we would have even fifty years ago.

But surely this cannot be the whole story. For one thing, it does not explain why the concept "appeared" and became so prominent only in the postwar years. The trends Davis is highlighting have been in play since the dawn of the industrial revolution. They have accelerated since the 1950s, but they are not novel. It also not clear who the "we" are who are less and less able to evaluate the judgments and decisions of professionals. The relatively uneducated agrarian and industrial workers in the nineteenth century were never in a particularly good position to evaluate the judgments of professionals, bureaucrats or, say, church leaders.

Boatright also thinks that the recent appearance and prominence of the concept of conflict of interest "invite speculation," and his response to this speculation can be seen as fleshing out the one offered by Davis:

> Society became much more dependent on fiduciaries and agents, especially those in the professions, while, at the same time, market forces have come to play a larger role in their activities. When the professions—most notably, medicine, law, accounting—began to be practiced more and more in a market economy based on financial incentives, both the benefits and the harms of this development were recognized. In order to enjoy the benefits, it was necessary to develop a concept that identified the source of the potential harms and to devise means for reducing the harmful consequences.[54]

This seems more plausible, not least because of the way it begins to shift the focus away from the moral relations between an individual client and a professional service provider and to emphasize a larger-scale issue of institutional design and regulation. In Boatright's explanation, the concept is not a way of better understanding the moral obligations of professionals to their clients, as Davis's explanation seems to have it, but rather as a way of legitimizing and regulating more effective, efficient, and fair ways of supplying goods and services in an advanced market economy.

But Boatright's speculative explanation is also incomplete. It implicitly overemphasizes the individual rights of the buyers of expert services. Consider his answer to the question, "what is wrong with conflict of interest?" which immediately follows the passage just quoted. The moral wrong, he says, "is simple: a person in a conflict of interest—a fiduciary, agent, or professional—has failed to fulfill an obligation, one for which he or she has accepted an engagement and, usually, compensation." This is often true—though it need not be, since it is certainly possible to be in a conflict-of-interest situation and still faithfully fulfill one's duty to the principal in question. But it is not the whole story, and it is not the whole reason we now place such great emphasis on conflict of interest. The other half of the story is about why the professional body that agent is a member of, or the firm or government agency that agent works for, cares about conflicts of interest. They care not only because they fear individuals being harmed by their members but also because they rely crucially on a stock of trust from clients or the public at large. This stock of trust is what Alan Greenspan once usefully called "capitalized reputation"; it is literally part of the capital of a profession or an organization. In short, professions and organizations care about conflicts of interest in part because they care about, say, their clients, but also because they care about themselves and their ability to continue to operate effectively and efficiently. The very legitimacy of professions, governments, nongovernmental organizations, and many kinds of firms depends on trust. Without trust their status may be taken away from them, or their ability to effectively carry out their missions may be compromised. And conflicts of interest—even wrongly perceived or apparent conflicts of interest—corrode trust.

By focusing on how major social and political institutions come to see it in *their* interest to reduce and manage conflicts of interest, we get a fuller sense of why the concept arose when it did. Davis's and Boatright's basic explanations are silent about the simultaneous appearance and prominence of concerns for conflicts of interest in *public* institutions in the postwar world. This rise coincided with a massive expansion of the role and size of government and the number of facets of people's lives affected by large state institutions. It also coincided with the ever-growing prominence of the mass media (aided now by the Internet) and its ability to uncover and publicize even a whiff of corruption or abuse of privilege. Along with both of these trends came a more democratic, and less deferential, expectation of citizens for propriety in large institutions in both the public and private sector. It is also the precise period when virtually every sector of the economy became heavily regulated, often for the first time. So businesses, NGOs, civil servants, and professions have all become keenly aware that if the public sees them abusing positions of trust or privilege, there is always a credible threat of renewed and tighter state regulation.

However much conflicts of interest may harm individual clients of businesses or professional services, we cannot fully appreciate either the recent appearance or the sudden prominence of this normative category without seeing the threat conflicts of interest pose to large-scale social, political, and economic institutions. This is why a full understanding of the rationale and justification of regimes for regulating conflicts of interest much be part and parcel of the macrolevel political theories that guide our design and justification of these institutions. To date, our normative theories of conflict of interest have worked "upwards," so to speak, from the classic situation of the small-town lawyer and his client to ever more complicated relations between corporate lawyers and their bosses, clients, and other principals. It is time for significantly more investigation into the way we might elucidate the ethics of conflict of interest by working "downward" from our theories of justice and democratic legitimacy for the major social, political, and economic institutions that constitute what John Rawls called the basic structure of society.[55]

CONCLUSION

By now we hope to have given some insight into the puzzle with which we began: why our contemporary concept of conflict of interest was only dimly appreciated before the second half of the twentieth century even though we cannot now think our way through the challenges of organizational and professional ethics without it. Of course, conquering the most overt manifestations of conflict-of-interest— from bribery and corruption to nepotism and the use of public office for private gain—has always been recognized as one of the great challenges for civilized societies. We now realize much more clearly, however, that conflict-of-interest *situations* pose a problem even when they are not exploited in these corrupt ways. This is in part because conflicting personal and even professional interests can impair the judgment of even the most dedicated and conscientious expert. We have had solid empirical evidence of this only in the past decade or two. We also worry about even "unexploited" conflicts of interest more now because of a heightened concern for the legitimacy of institutions as diverse as governments, state bureaucracies, businesses, NGOs, religious institutions, and professions. Many of these organizations rely for their survival, or at least their efficient operation, on a stock of trust from members, clients, or society at large. And this trust is imperiled if people *even suspect* that experts or officeholders, who are inherently difficult to monitor, might be in a position to improperly profit from their privileged status. For both of these reasons, the task of ethical theory cannot rest at what we have been calling the "microlevel" with exhortations for conflicted professionals to resist temptation. It must move decisively to mid-level issues of institutional design and justification. How can institutions and associations best protect the interests of those they serve while also preserving the trust and support of these and other constituencies? Indeed, it is now only by answering these questions that we are in a position to appropriately dispense microlevel ethical advice to the individual expert or officeholder, and this advice will be much more complicated than exhortation to resist temptation (though that will certainly remain part of it). Finally, we have argued that a thorough understanding of the ethics of conflict of interest requires going beyond understanding why private-sector and civil-society institutions may wish to enhance and protect their own perceived legitimacy. We must also ask whether or why they are *actually* legitimate in a democratic society. For example, why do they have a right to self-regulate rather than to be regulated by the state? And what responsibilities do they have to members, customers, or to society at large given the privileges they are granted? Answers to these "macrolevel" ethical questions will surely have a bearing on both the appropriate design and the justification of conflict of interest provisions adopted by institutions, and ultimately therefore on the moral expectations we have for the members working within these institutions.

NOTES

1. Dennis Thompson *Restoring Responsibility* (New York: Cambridge University Press, 2005), 275.

2. Ibid., 268. Clearly, at some level this claim of Thompson's is false or at least overstated. There are now substantial concentrations of experts in, for example, business ethics and medical ethics who *live* at this "mid-level" of ethical analysis. That said, Thompson's exhortation to pay more attention to ethics for the mid-level might seem rather radical indeed to anyone who took the tables of contents of leading journals like *Ethics* or *Philosophy and Public Affairs* as their guide to the field of academic ethics.

3. Neil Luebke "Conflict of Interest as a Moral Category," *Business and Professional Ethics Journal* 6 (1987): 67.

4. Consider the following passage from John Rawls *A Theory of Justice* (Cambridge, Mass.: Harvard University Press, 1971), 4: "although a society is a cooperative venture for mutual advantage, it is typically marked by a conflict as well as by an identity of interests. There is an identity of interests since social cooperation makes possible a better life for all than any would have if each were to live solely by his own efforts. There is a *conflict of interests* since persons are not indifferent as to how the greater benefits produced by their collaboration are distributed, for in order to pursue their ends they each prefer a larger to a lesser share" (our italics). For reasons that should become clear as we discuss definitions of "conflict of interest," below, John Rawls is not talking about our notion, he is merely using the same words to mark a different idea. According to the concept we are discussing here, the conflict is not between two different people's interests but, if you will, within one single person. It is, in a sense, a conflict between that person's interest in being a good provider of expert advice or service, on the one hand, and some other interest she happens to have, on the other hand. Hence we now talk about how an individual herself might be "conflicted."

5. Michael Davis "Conflict of Interest," *Business and Professional Ethics Journal* 1 (Summer 1982): 17–27.

6. Joseph Margolis "Conflict of Interest and Conflicting Interests," in *Ethical Theory and Business*, ed. Tom L. Beauchamp and Norman B. Bowie (Englewood Cliffs, N.J.: Prentice Hall, 1979).

7. Michael Davis "Introduction," in *Conflict of Interest in the Professions*, ed. Michael Davis and Andrew Stark (New York: Oxford University Press, 2001), 8. Many of the proffered definitions of "conflict of interest" by different theorists use different letter placeholders for the person with the conflict, the other person that first person owes a duty to, and so on. We will lightly edit each author's definition to make these placeholders consistent: so X will be used for the person with the possible conflict, and Y and Z for the parties X might owe duties to.

8. Davis, "Introduction," 8–11.

9. John Boatright, "Financial Services," in Davis and Stark, *Conflict of Interest in the Professions*, 219, emphasis added.

10. Thomas L Carson "Conflict of Interest and Self-Dealing in the Professions: A Review Essay," *Business Ethics Quarterly* 14 (2004): 165.

11. Andrew Stark "Why Are (Some) Conflicts of Interest in Medicine So Uniquely Vexing?" in *Conflicts of Interest: Challenges and Solutions in Business, Law, Medicine, and Public Policy*, ed. Don A. Moore, Daylian M. Cain, George Loewenstein, and Max H. Bazerman (New York: Cambridge University Press, 2005), 152–53.

12. Note that X may be entrusted to exercise judgment on behalf of Y, or to promote Y's interests, without X being Y's agent and Y being X's principal. X may, for example, be a trustee.

13. See, for example, Thomas Carson "Conflicts of Interest," *Journal of Business Ethics* 13 (1994): 391, and Carson, "Conflict of Interest and Self-Dealing in the Professions." It must be said that many authors who work casually with the concept of conflict of interest, but who are not specifically offering an analysis of it, do sometimes seem to include all potential selfish motives of a professional as sources of conflicts of interest.

14. The definition we gave from Davis early in the previous section was preceded, for example, by the sentence: "A conflict of interest is *a situation* in which some person X (whether an individual or a corporate body) stands in a certain relation to one or more decisions" (Davis, "Introduction," 8, our italics). His quoted definition then lays out what he takes to be the salient features of such a situation. This aspect of the definition immediately sets this concept apart from most other moral concepts like virtues and vices which focus more directly on character and behavior.

15. Davis, "Introduction," 13. This quote from Davis raises an interesting question: whether "conflict of interest" is actually a *moral* concept. This used to be a very hot topic in the era when conceptual analysis, rather than normative justification, was the primary concern of moral philosophers; and when Julius Kovesi's little book *Moral Notions* (London: Routledge and Kegan Paul, 1967) highlighted the significance of a range of concepts that were, in effect, hybrids of fact and value, normative and descriptive. All of the definitions of "conflict of interest" that we have examined here actually contain clear references to ethical duties or obligations (namely, of X having a duty to look after Y's interests); and thus have a clear normative dimension. But the concept also refers to elements of a situation that are descriptive: for example, that X has interests, that these interests can interfere psychologically with X's judgment or abilities to act; perhaps also that Y has expectations that X will act impartially, and so on. In sum: "conflict of interest" would seem to be a normative-descriptive hybrid. That said, one could hardly do better in explaining succinctly the nature of its normative content than Davis does in this quote.

16. A textbook by the British philosopher Jennifer Jackson *An Introduction to Business Ethics* (Oxford: Blackwell, 1996), is a good example. It explicitly rejects utilitarian and deontological ethical traditions in favor of a virtue-based approach that "relies on the judgment of those who have virtues, for resolving particular dilemmas and problems" (109). And despite attempting to offer very practical decision-making advice on the problems facing business people, it does not seem ever to discuss conflicts of interest or why such situations might require more than just virtuous judgment by the professional with the dilemma.

17. See, for example, John C. Maxwell *There's No Such Thing as "Business Ethics": There's Only One Rule for Making Decisions* (New York: Warner Business, 2003). This bestseller, which purports to tell you everything you need to know about being ethical in business, does not seem to mention conflicts of interest—even though it begins with a

discussion of Enron, a case that can normally not be explained without reference to insidious and crippling conflicts of interest. Its advice throughout is simply to follow the golden rule and resist temptations to wrong others for your own gain.

18. Bayless Manning, "The Purity Potlatch: An Essay on Conflict of Interest, American Government, and Moral Escalation," *Federal Bar Journal* 24 (1964): 252–53, quoted in Andrew Stark, *Conflicts of Interest in American Public Life* (Cambridge, Mass.: Harvard University Press, 2000), 5 (our italics).

19. See, for example, Davis, "Introduction," 13–15.

20. Or consider the focus of this recent book: Janine Griffiths-Baker, *Serving Two Masters: Conflicts of Interest in the Modern Law Firm* (Oxford: Hart, 2002).

21. It is true that courts, in the United States at least, are historically reluctant to second-guess managers who are accused of making decisions that serve other interests than those of owners. They generally adopt the "business judgment rule," acknowledging their own inability to evaluate the senior manager's decision. See, for example, Frank H. Easterbrook and Daniel R. Fischel, *The Economic Structure of Corporate Law* (Chicago: University of Chicago Press, 1991), 93–100. Note that the basic justification the courts use for backing off is itself a primary reason for thinking of senior managers as quasi-professionals with potential conflicts of interest: namely, that they are being called upon to make expert judgments that are difficult for any outsiders, including Delaware judges, to evaluate.

22. For a comprehensive survey of conflicts of interest in the financial services industry see John Boatright, *Ethics in Finance* (Oxford: Blackwell, 1999), and John Boatright, "Financial Services," 217–236. Note that we do not want to give the impression that conflicts of interest for firms themselves (as opposed to, or in addition to, conflicts of interest for the individuals working within firms) occur only in financial services. For a fascinating illustration of multiple and overlapping conflicts in the "hospital group purchasing" industry, see the case of *Premier, Inc.* as described in the case of the same name by Anne T. Lawrence and published by Babson College Case Publishing. This case is centered around an investigation by Walt Bogdanich, Barry Meier, and Mary Williams Walsh, "Medicine's Middlemen: Questions Raised of Conflicts at Two Hospital Buying Groups," *New York Times*, March 2, 2002, A1, A18.

23. Stark, "Comparing Conflict," 336, emphasis added.

24. See Boatright, *Ethics in Finance*, chap. 3.

25. Stark "Comparing Conflict," 341, and Eric Orts, "Conflict of Interest on Corporate Boards," in Davis and Stark, *Conflict of Interest in the Professions*, 129–55.

26. Stark, "Comparing Conflict," 337.

27. Davis, "Introduction," 16, emphasis added.

28. See especially Daniel Kahneman, Paul Slovic, and Amos Tversky, eds. *Judgment Under Uncertainty: Heuristics and Biases* (Cambridge: Cambridge University Press, 1982).

29. See, for example, Benjamin R. Karney and Robert H. Coombs, "Memory Bias in Long-term Close Relationships: Consistency or Improvement?" *Personality and Social Psychology Bulletin* 26 (2000): 959–70.

30. Deborah J. Terry and Anne T. O'Brien, "Status, Legitimacy, and In-group Bias in the Context of an Organizational Merger," *Group Processes & Intergroup Relations* 4 (2001): 271–89.

31. J. Dana and G. Loewenstein, "A Social Science Perspective on Gifts to Physicians from Industry," *JAMA* 290 (2) (2003): 252–55.

32. Michaely, R. and K. L. Womack, "Conflict of Interest and the Credibility of Underwriter Analyst Recommendations," *Review of Finance* 12 (1999): 653–86.

33. Moore, D. A., G. Loewenstein, L. Tanlu, M. H. Bazerman, "Auditor Independence, Conflict of Interest, and the Unconscious Intrusion of Bias." Harvard Business School Working Paper #03–116 (2003).

34. Nelson, Mark W. "A Review of Experimental and Archival Conflicts-of-Interest Research in Auditing," in Moore et al., *Conflict of Interest*.

35. Note: we are not by any means claiming that it is the *only*, or even the most central, component of a mid-level theory for this problem. Our aim here is to illustrate how this kind empirical information can and should inform a sophisticated normative theory in institutional contexts.

36. Dale T. Miller, "Commentary: Psychologically Naïve Assumptions about the Perils of Conflict of Interest," in Moore et al., *Conflict of Interest*, 129.

37. Stark, *Conflicts of Interest in American Public Life*, 119.

38. Anne E. Tenbrunsel, "Commentary: Bounded Ethicality and Conflict of Interest," in Moore et al., *Conflict of Interest*, 100.

39. The brief parenthetical comments are ours. See John Boatright, "Conflict of Interest," in *Encyclopedia of Business Ethics and Society*, ed. Robert W. Kolb (Thousand Oaks, Calif.: Sage, 2007) for much fuller explanations.

40. Perhaps the most troubling example of gaming such strategies can be found in (1) the attempt by boards of directors to align the CEO's interests with that of the shareholders by tying much of his or her compensation to increases in the share value; and (2) having the CEO find increasingly "creative" ways of artificially and temporarily inflating the share price, to the medium- and long-term detriment of the firm.

41. Daylain M. Cain, George Loewenstein, and Don A Moore, "Coming Clean but Playing Dirtier: The Shortcomings of Disclosure as a Solution to Conflicts of Interest," in Moore et al., *Conflict of Interest*.

42. Moore et al., "Auditor Independence."

43. Cain, Loewenstein, and Moore, "Coming Clean but Playing Dirtier: The Shortcomings of Disclosure as a Solution to Conflicts of Interest."

44. Tom Tyler, "Managing Conflicts of Interest Within Organizations: Does Activating Social Values Change the Impact of Self-Interest on Behavior?" in Moore et al., *Conflict of Interest*.

45. It must be said that there is an absolutely voluminous literature that falls under article or book titles of roughly the form, "*Conflicts of Interest in X*," where "X" is the name of a profession, a trade, a managerial task (like supply-chain management, human-resource management, or purchasing), a business sector (e.g., consulting, biotech, health-care, banking), or a realm of public administration. These analyses are generally useful for enumerating the typical kinds of conflict-of-interest situations in each of these domains, as well as some of the standard ways of managing them. Our very informal survey of this literature confirms both the general typology we have borrowed from Stark of the *basic types* of conflicts of interest, and Boatright's list of options for dealing with conflicts of interest. Not surprisingly, one does not tend to find anything like a comprehensive normative theory lying behind these piecemeal attempts to get a handle on the challenges of recognizing and managing conflicts of interest in quite specific realms.

46. See, for example, Marc Rodwin *Medicine, Money, and Morals: Physicians' Conflicts of Interest* (New York: Oxford University Press, 1993); Susan P. Shapiro *Tangled Loyalties: Conflict of Interest in Legal Practice* (Ann Arbor: University of Michigan Press, 2002).

47. Allen Buchanan "Is There a Medical Profession in the House?" in *Conflicts of Interest in Clinical Practice and Research*, eds. R. Spece, D. Shimm, and A. Buchanan (Oxford: Oxford University Press, 1996), 109.

48. Ibid.

49. Ibid.

50. Ibid., 112.

51. See, for example, Keith MacDonald *The Sociology of the Professions* (Thousand Oaks, Calif.: Sage, 1995); M. T. Law and S. Kim "Specialization and Regulation: The Rise of Professionals and the Emergence of Occupational Licensing Regulation," *The Journal of Economic History* 65 (3) (2005): 723–56.

52. See, for example, John Boatright, "Reluctant Guardians: The Moral Responsibility of Gatekeepers," *Business Ethics Quarterly* 17 (4): 613–32, and John Boatright "Individual Responsibility in the American Corporate System: Does Sarbanes-Oxley Strike the Right Balance?" *Business & Professional Ethics Journal* 23 (1&2) (2004): 9–41.

53. Davis, "Introduction," 17. The quotes immediately following from Davis are from the same page.

54. Boatright, "Conflict of Interest."

55. For Rawls the "basic structure of society" is the primary subject of justice. See his *A Theory of Justice*, 7–11; and *Political Liberalism* (New York: Columbia University Press, 1993), especially lecture 7.

SUGGESTED READING

Boatright, John. "Conflict of Interest." In *Encyclopedia of Business Ethics and Society*. Edited by Robert W. Kolb. Thousand Oaks, Calif.: Sage, 2007.

Carson, Thomas L. "Conflict of Interest and Self-Dealing in the Professions: A Review Essay." *Business Ethics Quarterly* 14 (1) (2004): 161–82.

———. "Conflicts of Interest." *Journal of Business Ethics* 13 (1994): 387–404.

Dana, J., and G. Loewenstein. "A Social Science Perspective on Gifts to Physicians from Industry." *JAMA* 290 (2) (2003): 252–55.

Davis, Michael. "Conflict of Interest." *Business and Professional Ethics Journal* 1 (Summer 1982): 17–27.

Davis, Michael, and Andrew Stark, eds. *Conflict of Interest in the Professions*. New York: Oxford University Press, 2001.

Griffiths-Baker, Janine. *Serving Two Masters: Conflicts of Interest in the Modern Law Firm*. Oxford: Hart, 2002.

Luebke, Neil. "Conflict of Interest as a Moral Category." *Business and Professional Ethics Journal* 6/1 (1987): 66–81.

MacDonald, Chris, Wayne Norman, and Michael McDonald. "Charitable Conflicts of Interest." *Journal of Business Ethics* 39 (1–2) (2002): 67–74.

Michaely, R., and Womack, K. L. "Conflict of Interest and the Credibility of Underwriter Analyst Recommendations." *Review of Finance* 12 (1999): 653–86.

Moore, Don A., Daylian M. Cain, George Loewenstein, Max H. Bazerman, eds., *Conflicts of Interest: Challenges and Solutions in Business, Law, Medicine, and Public Policy*. New York: Cambridge University Press, 2005.

Rodwin, Marc. *Medicine, Money, and Morals: Physicians' Conflicts of Interest*. New York: Oxford University Press, 1993.

Shapiro, Susan P. *Tangled Loyalties: Conflict of Interest in Legal Practice*. Ann Arbor: University of Michigan Press, 2002.

Spece, R., D. Shimm, and A. Buchanan, eds. *Conflicts of Interest in Clinical Practice and Research*. Oxford: Oxford University Press, 1996.

Stark, Andrew. *Conflicts of Interest in American Public Life*. Cambridge, Mass.: Harvard University Press, 2000.

Williams-Jones, Bryn, and Chris MacDonald. "Conflict of Interest Policies at Canadian Universities: Clarity and Content." *Journal of Academic Ethics* 6 (2008): 79–90.

CHAPTER 16

CORRUPTION AND BRIBERY

MANUEL VELASQUEZ

ACCORDING to the World Bank, bribes paid out by businesses and other parties cost them over one trillion dollars a year, more than 3 percent of the total estimated world economy.[1] Businesses are not the only ones that engage in bribery, of course, but businesses have been singled out as one of the main suppliers of the bribes that are paid today to corrupt government officials.[2] Moreover, because arranging, paying, and monitoring bribes is a time-intensive activity, bribery also imposes heavy nonmonetary costs on businesses. Bribery forces managers to take time away from productively running their enterprises and instead devote their energies to queuing, negotiating, covering up, and ensuring that bribed parties will not renege on the deal or demand additional payments. While companies sometimes calculate that the benefits of paying a particular bribe (for example, to secure a lucrative government contract) will outweigh the costs of the bribe, these calculations often fail to take into account the costs that bribery imposes on other parties. For corruption also imposes significant costs on societies.[3] The bribes that firms pay to conduct business in a given country act much like a tax that drives foreign companies away, thereby lowering the country's overall foreign investment, a consequence of corruption that is particularly damaging to developing nations. Corruption also distorts a country's public expenditures as public monies are diverted away from education, health care, redistribution, and poverty reduction and are invested instead into projects where it is easier to extract bribes from businesses, such as purchasing military hardware and putting together large construction projects. And bribery lowers the quality of public projects since less qualified businesses can use bribes to secure contracts for public projects; they subsequently try to cover the costs of the bribe by using cheaper materials and then bribe inspectors to overlook cheap quality and shoddy construction.

In view of the social and private costs associated with corruption in general and bribery in particular, it is not surprising that these are now viewed as major problems that both businesses and governments need to address. Their importance is recognized by the recent explosion of activity aimed at understanding corruption and bribery and at controlling the extent to which international businesses engage in these. Numerous articles and book-length studies of the causes and consequences of corruption have been published during the last twenty-five years that have greatly enhanced our understanding of the social and economic effects of business bribery and of the conditions that engender it. Nongovernmental organizations (NGOs) like Transparency International have been founded to fight corruption and to provide measurements of its extent and costs. While every nation has long had laws prohibiting its businesses from bribing its own government officials, a large number of the world's nations have recently adopted laws that prohibit their businesses from bribing the officials of other nations. The United States, of course, criminalized the bribery of foreign officials by U.S. companies in 1977 when it passed the Foreign Corrupt Practices Act (FCPA) after investigations by the Securities and Exchange Commission discovered that more than 400 U.S. businesses were engaged in bribing foreign officials. In December 1997, the member countries of the Organization of Economic Cooperation and Development (OECD) adopted the "Convention on Combating Bribery of Foreign Public Officials in International Business Transactions," which required OECD countries to adopt legislation modeled on the FCPA that would criminalize the bribery of foreign officials by multinational businesses. Other regional groups of countries have adopted similar conventions including the Inter-American Convention Against Corruption, the African Union's Convention on Preventing and Combating Corruption, and the Anti-Corruption Initiative for Asia and the Pacific. Moreover, the World Bank, the International Monetary Fund, and several other financial institutions have adopted rules that prohibit businesses that pay bribes from participating in any projects they fund. In June 2004, the United Nations adopted Principle 10 of its Global Compact, which calls on businesses to "work against corruption in all its forms."[4]

In spite of the tremendous attention now being paid to corruption and bribery, our growing understanding of their costs, and the numerous legislative attempts governments have made to criminalize corrupt activities, relatively little attention has been paid to the ethical issues raised when businesses engage in corruption and bribery. Both the extensive new literature on corruption and the recent legislative initiatives criminalizing bribery and corruption assume that it is wrong for businesses to engage in the bribery and corruption of government officials. Yet very few attempts have been made to examine this assumption. I propose to take a close look at this key assumption. I will begin by discussing the difficult issue of articulating suitable definitions of corruption and bribery. I discuss first the definition of corruption, which is the broader and more generic term and which raises some difficult issues, and then discuss the definition of bribery, which is a specific kind of corruption and whose definition is somewhat less troublesome. Next, I turn to the ethics of corruption with the aim of critically examining the main arguments put forth to show that corruption is wrong. I will show that although these arguments provide some reason for thinking that corruption is generally wrong, each of the arguments has significant limitations. I will end by looking at what these conclusions imply about how businesses should deal with the issues of corruption and bribery.

My focus throughout is on bribery and corruption as they relate to business and primarily to the issues that arise when businesses offer bribes to government officials or otherwise engage in the corruption of government. Businesses can, of course, offer bribes to parties other than government officials. A business can, for example, bribe another company's purchasing agent in order to induce the agent to buy the products of the business. I will have only a little to say about such business-to-business forms of bribery and corruption. I set these forms of bribery and corruption aside because, as I explain in the next section, the form of bribery and corruption that is currently of most concern is the bribery of government officials by businesses.[5] Although much of what I say below will be applicable to the payment of bribes to members of other kinds of (nongovernmental) organizations, such forms of bribery lie outside the focus of this essay.

WHAT ARE CORRUPTION AND BRIBERY?

The earliest discussions of corruption, comprising what I will call the "classic" view of corruption, saw corruption primarily as a property of whole institutions, particularly of political institutions.[6] The term "corruption" itself, of course, denotes deterioration or falling away from some ideal or pristine or healthy state, a form of decline, decay, or degeneration. Plato and Aristotle used the term to describe what they characterized as the deterioration of what they believed were ideal political arrangements. Aristotle, for example, wrote that "there are three kinds of government and an equal number of deviations, or, as it were, corruptions of these three kinds." The three kinds of "right" government are those in which "the one, or the few, or the many govern with an eye to the common good," while the corrupt forms are those "administered with an eye to the private interest of either the one or the few or the many rulers."[7]

An important feature of the classic conception of corruption is the idea that what constitutes corruption of an institution is defined relative to the ideal state of that institution. In terms of the teleological views that Aristotle and other classical thinkers favored, the ideal state of an entity is defined by its proper end, and since in his view the proper end of government is the achievement of the common good of all, government becomes corrupt when it is turned to achieving the limited interests of a ruler or a ruling group. A second important feature of the classic conception of corruption is the idea that corruption involves the pursuit of personal interests instead of the pursuit of an institution's proper end. As we will see, this feature is one that remains present in those current conceptions of corruption that are extensions of the classic concept.

The idea that political institutions become corrupt when they deviate from achieving a certain ideal end can be extended to many different kinds of institutions. While the classical tradition tended to apply the term "corruption" to political institutions, we today often extend the term to apply also to commercial institutions. A business organization can be said to be corrupt when the organization has deviated from the pursuit of its proper end and is instead improperly put at the service of other private ends. This can happen, for example, when a company's purchasing agents regularly buy only from suppliers who provide kickbacks instead of purchasing the goods that will best meet the company's needs, or when management issues misleading financial statements to owners or shareholders, or when dishonesty, fraud, nepotism, or embezzlement are endemic in the company. The phenomenon of corrupt business institutions is an interesting one, and many of the arguments and claims I will make below can, with appropriate adjustments, be applied to business institutions. But I mention the concept of corrupt business institutions here only to set it aside since it is not where the most important issues lie. The enormous attention that is today being paid to corruption around the globe is concerned not with the corruption of business institutions but with the extent to which businesses, particularly multinational businesses, are corrupting the political institutions of our world.[8] I will here, therefore, focus my discussion on the ethical issues that surround the large and growing number of businesses that seem to be engaged in the corruption of our political institutions.

The Contemporary View of Corruption

Contemporary discussions of corruption differ from the classic view insofar as today we tend to see corruption not primarily as a feature of whole institutions but of individual actions performed by individual persons, including not only those who hold institutional roles but also those who exert influence on those who hold institutional roles through bribes or other means.[9] This modern broader conception of corruption can still be tied to the classic idea that sees corruption as involving the deviation of an institution from the pursuit of its proper ends. The corrupt action can then be characterized either as one in which individuals who hold institutional roles—such as government officials—divert an institution from the pursuit of its own proper end and instead have it serve other personal ends, or as one in which individuals—such as business people—seek to influence those (e.g., government officials) who hold institutional roles so as to cause them to so divert their institution from the pursuit of its proper ends. In this classically based but modernized conception the emphasis is on the act that brings about the corruption of the institution. Still, the classic idea is preserved that a corrupted institution is one that is made to deviate from the pursuit of its proper ends.

The classic view that corruption is a matter of an institution's being made to deviate from serving its own proper end or the act (or act of influence) that brings about such a deviation carries with it two significant problems. First, the view assumes that there is some more or less clearly definable end at which our institutions should aim. But there is, and always has been, disagreement about what the nature and purpose of our most basic institutions should be, not only of our political institutions but also of the institutions of business. Some claim that our political institutions should aim at the "common good"; others see political institutions in terms of a legitimate competition of factions or parties for power and resources; still others, as we will see, look at government as the personal property of an absolute monarch whose ends it appropriately serves. Thus, many British observers condemn as "corruption" the willingness of U.S. legislators to support the interests of campaign donors while most Americans see this as the normal accompaniment of competitive politics;[10] and we today would label as "corruption" the sale of government offices and their use as sources of personal income, pursuits that were common and honorable during the sixteenth, seventeenth, and eighteenth centuries in the absolute monarchies of France, Spain, England, Austria, Prussia and, China.[11] The classically based conception of corruption, then, is subject to significant ambiguity insofar as it appeals to a concept (the end or purpose of government) whose meaning is not fixed.

Second, the classical view tends to break down when it is used to try to identify corruption in an international context, which is where much of the attention now being paid to corruption is focused. Different cultures tend to have very different views about the nature of their basic social institutions and the behaviors that are appropriate for various institutional actors. Writing about Nepali society during the twentieth century, T. Louise Brown notes that

> the traditional Nepali Hindu institution of *chakari* [the bestowal of flattery and gifts upon a patron who is expected to favor the client] was important because it was the basic mechanism through which clientelism and patronage networks operated. And it was through patronage networks that Nepal was governed...What foreigners considered to be corruption was, in the Nepali context, deemed a practical way of making the system work.[12]

Because of such differences, what counts as a corrupt deviation in one culture might be viewed as normal and benign in another.

Three Contemporary Definitions of Corruption

These problems have led contemporary social scientists to set aside the classic conception of corruption and to try to construct a definition of corruption that is not afflicted by these ambiguities and difficulties. One such contemporary approach to defining corruption focuses on the idea that corruption is the violation of the formal duties of one's office for the sake of personal gain. The economist Joseph Nye, for example, characterized corruption in political contexts as "behavior which deviates from the formal duties of a public role because of private-regarding,... pecuniary, or status gains; or violates rules against the exercise of certain types of private-regarding influence. This includes such behavior as bribery;... nepotism;... and misappropriation."[13] By "formal duties," Nye refers to the duties spelled out in the law, in the explicit contract one makes with one's employer organization, or in the unwritten public norms that are believed to govern a public role.

Nye's definition, although widely cited, does not seem to be a significant improvement on the classic conception of corruption. The definition employs several ambiguous concepts including "deviates," "formal duties," "private-regarding," and "rules." What, for example, are the formal rules to which Nye's definition appeals? If these are simply codified laws or written contracts, then the definition cannot easily be applied in international contexts since laws and contracts differ significantly from country to country. If these are, instead, unwritten public norms then the definition faces the problem that public views are not monolithic within a given nation, much less between nations of different cultures, and so it will be difficult, at best, to apply this view to international contexts. Nye's definition does not seem, then, to surmount the problems and ambiguities that are attributed to the classic definition.

A second modern approach, and the one that is today prevalent among economists and other social scientists, focuses on the idea that corruption in political contexts is the misuse of something that belongs to the public for private gain. This is, for example, the kind of definition proposed by the United Nations Development Programme, which states that corruption is "the misuse of public power, office, or authority for private benefit—through bribery, extortion, influence peddling, nepotism, fraud, speed money, or embezzlement."[14] A similar definition is proposed by the economist Susan Rose-Ackerman who writes, simply, that "corruption is the misuse of public power for private gain."[15]

This second definition also seems to provide but little improvement on the classic definition. The second definition relies on a distinction between the public and private realms. But this distinction is a relatively recent Western invention.[16] Because the distinction between the public and the private is of relatively recent vintage, it is difficult to apply the concept to those earlier periods of history when the distinction did not exist, such as the absolute monarchies of the sixteenth, seventeenth, and eighteenth centuries I mentioned earlier. It is also difficult to apply the concept to those cultures where the distinction is even today not fully recognized, such as many of the nations of sub-Saharan Africa.[17] Moreover, this second definition is also subject to other ambiguities. The definition assumes that some uses of public power are "misuses." But how is one to distinguish legitimate ways of using public power to help a private party (for example, when a police officer protects the victim of a crime), from "misusing" public power for such a purpose? For reasons we have already seen, whether one relies on codified laws or on unwritten norms to determine what constitutes a "misuse," the definition will be problematic when it is applied in international contexts.

A third approach characterizes corruption in terms of damage to a group, organization, or government. Carl Friedrich, for example, writes, corruption may therefore be said to exist whenever a power holder who is charged with doing certain things, that is a responsible functionary or office holder, is by monetary or other rewards..., induced to take actions which favor whoever provides the reward and thereby damage the group or organization to which the functionary belongs, more specifically the government.[18]

Like the earlier two approaches, this third approach does not seem to provide a significant advance over the ambiguities that are said to afflict the classic definition. Friedrich's definition appeals to the concept of "damage" to the group or organization. But he leaves unexplained what constitutes damage to an organization and, more importantly, it is not clear that such damage is inflicted by all acts of corruption. Suppose a businessman secretly bribes a customs official into allowing him to move through customs at a normal rate rather than the delayed rate that the officials impose to solicit bribes. Or suppose a Jew bribes a Nazi official in order to escape death or imprisonment. Both acts, one can argue, are beneficial, not harmful. Corruption, as indicated earlier, can inflict significant costs on society, but not every individual act of corruption does so and, consequently, such harm cannot be taken as a defining characteristic of corruption.

I conclude that the definitions that recently have been proposed to replace the classic concept of corruption do not succeed in overcoming its ambiguities and problems. Indeed, to this day no definition of corruption is universally accepted as unproblematic.[19] It would seem, then, that the classic definition of corruption, in spite of its evident ambiguities and the difficulties it raises when it is applied to cross-cultural contexts, is as good as any we are going to get. This result points to an important conclusion: the concept of corruption is an inherently ambiguous one whose meaning depends on background cultural assumptions about the nature and purposes of our social institutions. Because these background assumptions vary from one period of time to another and from one culture to another, what is counted as corruption in one time and place will not count as corruption in different times and places. This aspect of corruption, as we will see in the final section of this essay, has important moral implications.

The modern definitions I have examined, however, should not be rejected as useless, for each yields valuable insights and can serve to complement the classic view of corruption, even if they do not eliminate its ambiguities. Nye's idea that corruption involves the violation of the rules that govern institutional roles reminds us that institutional roles and the rules that structure them are designed to achieve institutional ends or purposes, so that violating such rules forces the institution to deviate from its proper ends. The definition of corruption as the misuse of public power for private gain can be viewed as a modern version of the classic claim that the purpose of political institutions is to serve the interests of all, so that corruption ensues when they are made to serve the private interests of "one or the few." And Friedrich's attempt to define corruption in terms of the damage it causes is a useful reminder that although corruption is not definable by such harm, nevertheless corruption generally imposes significant costs on society.

I will return to these modern definitions when, below, I turn to discussing the ethical aspects of corruption and bribery. As we will see, these definitions are also valuable insofar as each suggests a distinct kind of argument in support of the view that corruption and bribery are unethical. Now, however, I must turn to examining how bribery can best be defined.

Bribery

Bribery is a species of corruption. Besides bribery, corruption includes a wide range of deviant institutional behaviors such as nepotism, favoritism, fraud, embezzlement, extortion, and buying votes. Bribery, however, is the paradigm case of corruption.[20] It is also the form of corruption on which virtually all the recent anticorruption legislative initiatives I discussed above have focused, and so it is the species of corruption that is today considered the most important. But what exactly is bribery?

Some recent attempts to define "bribery" are clearly mistaken. Consider, for example, the definition proposed by James: "A bribe is a payment, made by a third party to an agent of a principal, in which the agent explicitly or implicitly agrees to take an action that is contrary to his duty as an agent of the principal and is thus not in the interest of the principal."[21] This definition is too narrow. Consider, first, that there are some bribes that are not paid to "an agent of a principal." For example, an athlete, as I noted earlier, can be bribed to lose a contest when the athlete is not an "agent of a principal." Instead, the athlete is bribed into doing something that he is required not to do as a participant in the sport. Second, the person who is bribed might not be bribed to "take an action that is contrary to his duty as an agent of the principal." For example, a customs official who refuses to clear some goods through customs that he should clear might be bribed into clearing those goods as he should. In such a case the official is not being bribed to "agree to take an action that is contrary to his duty as an agent of the principal." On the contrary, the purpose of the bribe is to get the official to comply with his duty. Similar problems of narrowness afflict the proposal of Danley, who states that bribery is "offering or giving something of value with a corrupt intent to induce or influence an action of someone in a public or official capacity."[22] Danley assumes that only public officials can be bribed, and so, like James, Danley cannot accommodate the case of an athlete who is bribed to lose a contest nor of a seller who bribes the purchasing agent of a firm.

A more careful and more adequate definition of bribery is proposed by Philips, who offers the following: "P accepts a bribe from R if and only if P agrees for payment to act in a manner dictated by R rather than doing what is required of him as a participant in his practice."[23] Philip's definition of a bribe adequately captures the fact that when an athlete is paid to lose a contest, we characterize the payment as a "bribe": the athlete is paid to refrain from doing what he is required to do (strive to win) as a participant in his sport. The definition also covers the case of the customs official who is given a bribe in order to induce him to comply with his duty. For although the official is paid to do what he should do, nevertheless he is charging to do what he—as a customs official—is required to do gratuitously.

Philip's definition of bribery seems to provide a characterization of the concept that is adequate enough for our purposes. For the reasons delineated above it seems to escape the problems that afflict other definitions, and it seems to adequately capture the kinds of exchanges we would want to count as bribes. I should note, however, that, like the classic definition of corruption that I described above, this definition of bribery is also subject to ambiguity. What, for example, is to count as a "practice" and who is to count as a "participant"? Moreover, how are we to determine the requirements of a practice, particularly when the requirements are unwritten norms? While Philip's definition of bribery is good enough for our purposes, it is clear that what counts as a bribe by his definition will depend on the background beliefs we have about the nature and requirements of the various practices that surround us, beliefs that can differ from one time and place to another. In the discussion that follows, however, I will assume that Philip's definition is a sufficiently adequate characterization of bribery and turn to the question of why bribery in particular and corruption in general are viewed as morally wrong.

THE ETHICS OF BRIBERY AND CORRUPTION

The legislative initiatives that I mentioned earlier—such as the Foreign Corrupt Practices Act—take aim at businesses that pay bribes to government officials (as distinct from the officials who receive those bribes). They assume, that is, that it is wrong for a business to *give* a bribe to a government official, and they attempt to render this act illegal. What rationale underlies this assumption that it is wrong to *offer* bribes to government officials (or, for that matter, to bribe the agent of any organization)? Consider that it is at least a bit more immediately obvious why it is morally wrong for an official to *accept* a bribe. In accepting a bribe the official agrees to act in a way that subverts the role he has agreed to play as a government official. Rules governing the official's role may, of course, be formally spelled out in the explicit organizational rules, or legal rules, that define his role but they need not be. It is enough that he has agreed to serve in a way that rules out accepting bribes to perform the act the briber asks him to perform. The official who accepts a bribe, therefore, violates the role that he has agreed to play as a government official. Still, the question remains why is it wrong for the bearer of the payment—the party that supplies the bribe—to give the payment to a government official? Why should the act of this other party, the one who provides the benefit, be rendered illegal as the various legislative initiatives propose to do?

The standard answer—and, I believe, the fundamentally correct answer—is that it is morally wrong for a business person to bribe a government official—even in the absence of any legal rule prohibiting it—because by doing so he or she is causing, helping, or participating in the morally wrongful act of that official. The giving of a bribe to an official is wrong because by giving the bribe the briber leads the official to violate the standards that govern his role: The briber does wrong because he causes (or helps) an official to do wrong, and if it is wrong for a person to do something, then it is wrong to intentionally cause or help that person to do it. The moral wrongfulness of the act of giving a bribe, then, depends on—is parasitic on—the moral wrongfulness of the act of accepting a bribe. If this is correct, then bribing a government official is wrong because it is wrong for a government official to accept a bribe. This conclusion is supported by another consideration. Suppose that there were nothing morally wrong with having an official accept a bribe. Would there then be anything morally wrong with offering the official the bribe? The answer, I think, is that there would not be. Suppose, to take an earlier example, that a German Jew gives a Nazi official something of value so that the official will not kill or imprison him as he has been officially ordered to do. Then the Jew has bribed the official according to the definition of bribery I accepted above. But in letting the Jew escape the official has not done something that is morally wrong, and neither has the Jew behaved immorally by giving the bribe. Thus the giving of a bribe is not in itself an immoral act. Bribery becomes immoral when, as in the usual case, it causes or helps to cause an immoral act.

Why, then, is it wrong for a government official to accept a bribe; or, more broadly, why is it wrong for a government official to engage in corruption? I believe that the best way to answer this question is by returning to the three kinds of definitions of corruption that I discussed earlier. The three approaches to defining corruption that I outlined above each suggest a distinct response to the question of why it is wrong for an official to accept a bribe. Each suggests an analysis of the ethics of corruption that is more or less distinct from the analysis to which one is led by the other definitions. Accordingly, I will now turn to considering the arguments suggested by each of the definitions in order to see whether they provide an adequate justification of the view that it is wrong for a government official to accept a bribe and, therefore, wrong for a business to offer a bribe.

The "Formal Duties" Argument

Consider the thought behind the definition of "corruption" by Joseph Nye: corruption is "behavior which deviates from the formal duties of a public role because of private-regarding...gains."[24] The idea here is that there are certain rules or fiduciary obligations (embodied in written laws or unwritten public norms) that attach to the role of the government official, and corrupt acts are those by which the official violates the obligations attaching to his or her role. Corruption in government is wrong, then, because the corrupt public official does what the rules of his office require him not to do. A variant of this argument is a teleological argument claiming that political institutions have certain specific purposes (e.g., to secure the common good of all and not the private interests of those who provide bribes) and that it is wrong for officials to violate these purposes. Corrupt acts are acts in which an agent violates or undermines the rules and purposes that define the role he has accepted.

Why is it wrong for the official to transgress these rules or to violate these purposes? It is wrong, the argument continues, because in accepting her office the official implicitly or explicitly agrees to abide by these rules and to work to achieve those purposes.[25] Corruption, according to this argument, is a failure to live up to one's agreements—a failure to do what one has, in effect, promised to do. Corruption is wrong, therefore, because it is wrong to break one's promises. For a business to bribe an official, is wrong because by doing so the business is wrongly inducing the official to transgress the very rules and purposes of office to which the official has promised to adhere.

There are several problems with this argument. First, it is not clear exactly what normative rules or obligations are supposed to attach to any particular office. The legal rules that govern public service, of course, may be more or less clear, and, arguably, one has an ethical obligation to obey the law. But from a normative point of view, these legal rules cannot be taken as definitive: law is not the same as morality. What are the moral norms that govern public service? It is these that are not everywhere obvious. It is not clear, as we saw above, that all societies are in agreement about the norms that should govern public service.[26] In particular, there are some societies—such as parts of rural India and of Africa—in which it is acceptable for public officials to openly accept bribes, particularly if the salaries of those officials are so inadequate to live on that everyone expects and accepts that they must augment their income with bribes.[27]

Second, it is not clear that individuals always actually make any kind of explicit or implicit promise to abide by a set of rules that excludes corruption when they accept a job in government. As just noted, in societies in which it is widely accepted that poorly paid government officials will provide their services only if they are paid (i.e., bribed) to do so, individuals who enter government service may have no intention to refrain from corruption by, say, taking bribes. When an individual in such a society accepts public office, far from making an implicit agreement to refrain from taking bribes, the individual may instead accept the position with the understanding that it will be perfectly legitimate for him to take bribes in order to supplement his salary.[28] And even in industrialized societies where bribes are widely rejected, individuals do not always understand themselves to be making a special kind of agreement when they accept a government job, particularly if they have received no training about the nature of public service and have no understanding of the norms to which they are expected to adhere.[29]

The argument is only partially successful. The argument provides some support for the claim that corruption is wrong within societies where bribery is clearly not accepted and where people who accept a job in government do so with the explicit understanding that they are not to engage in corrupt activities to supplement their income. This would be the case, for example, in societies where government officials are given training that makes this understanding clear, or are provided with codes of conduct that make the prohibitions on bribery explicit, or where public media—such as daily newspapers or news programs—regularly highlight the idea that public officials are prohibited from accepting bribes. Such societies may well include most of the developed nations. But, not all officials in all societies accept their positions in government with this understanding and so the argument fails for them.

The Public-Private Argument

Consider, next, the idea that underlies the second definition of corruption I looked at above and that is favored by many economists: "corruption is the misuse of public power for private gain." The idea here is that government resources and services belong to the public and any monies accruing to those resources or services likewise belong to the public. When the government official extracts a fee for providing his services and then pockets the fee, he has taken for his private use what belongs to the public: the corrupt official appropriates as his property what is public property. Corruption is, therefore, a kind of theft of property and since theft is immoral, corruption is immoral. On this view, therefore, for a business to bribe an official is wrong because by doing so the business is getting the official to steal what belongs to the public and to put it at the private service of the briber's business.

This argument on the wrongfulness of corruption depends on a distinction between the public nature of government and the private realm. But this distinction is not present in all political systems, and so the argument cannot be unqualifiedly accepted.[30] The modern distinction between the public and the private is, as I noted above, a relatively recent one that emerged in the mid- and late nineteenth century with the development of modern governments characterized by what Weber calls "bureaucracy."[31] A bureaucracy is a system of offices, each with defined duties such that

> office holding is not considered ownership of a course of income, to be exploited
> for rents or emoluments in exchange for the rendering of certain
> services...Rather, entrance into an office...is considered an acceptance of a
> specific duty of fealty to the purpose of the office in return for the grant of a
> secure existence. It is decisive for the modern loyalty to an office that, in the pure
> type, it does not establish a relationship to a person, like the vassal's or disciple's
> faith under feudal or patrimonial authority, but rather is devoted to impersonal
> and functional purposes.[32]

Weber contrasts this modern ideal of government with what he calls "patrimonial authority," a form of governance based on the kind of personal authority exercised by the master of a household whose household members exhibit a "strictly personal loyalty" to the master in the exercise of their household duties. Patrimonial governments arise when one master establishes domination over other masters, creating the need for a system of offices to administer the increased complexity and extent of the ruler's domain. However, notes Weber, "the patrimonial office lacks above all the bureaucratic separation of the private [from] . . . the official sphere. For the political administration [of patrimonial governance], too, is treated as a purely personal affair of the ruler, and political power is considered part of his personal property which can be exploited by means of contributions and fees."[33] Because the state and its administration are the personal property of the ruler (and not of the public), the ruler can give or sell an office and its rents[34] to a subject (what in medieval Europe was called a "fee benefice").[35] Both the office and its rents then become the private property of the person occupying the office.

Weber's description of the patrimonial state is significant because it describes a regime in which the concept of corruption as "the abuse of public office for private interests" makes little sense; offices in the patrimonial state are seen not as the property of the public but as the private property of the ruler or the persons to whom the ruler has given or sold the offices. Prior to the seventeenth century, as I noted above, most states were organized as patrimonial states including the Mogul empires of the seventeenth and eighteenth centuries in India, the dynastic kingdoms of China from the Chin dynasty to the fall of the Empire in the twentieth century, the great Egyptian kingdoms of antiquity, and the absolute monarchies of France (until the French Revolution), Spain (until the Thirty Years War), and England (until the civil wars in the middle of the seventeenth century).[36] Throughout these periods in these regimes "corruption" was not thought of as "the misuse of public office for private benefit" because offices were not considered public but private. Moral condemnations of "corruption" were common in Europe and England during this period, but in every case the condemnations were aimed at churchmen or judges and their "corruption" did not involve "the abuse of public office for private interests." In the case of churchmen, corruption referred to the sale of spiritual goods (i.e., simony) which, because such goods ultimately belonged to God, should have been freely given; in the case of judges, corruption meant they showed favoritism or accepted bribes and so failed to resolve disputes between the ruler's subjects in the impartial manner desired by the ruler who had put them in charge of his courts.[37] Neither churchmen nor judges were thought of as misusing a "public" office.

Moving to a more recent period, several observers of less developed nations have argued that many today are patrimonial or "neopatrimonial" states. Zolberg has argued that the single-party regimes of West Africa are patrimonial states;[38] Roth has claimed the same of the regimes of Morocco, the sheikhdoms of the Gulf, and Thailand.[39] Medard has argued that the nations of sub-Saharan Africa are "neopatrimonial."[40] These central African nations were colonized by Europeans when these nations were full fledged patrimonial regimes. Although they adopted the external forms of European bureaucracies, they retained a tribal conception of political office as the private property of the officeholder. The result is a "mixed" system where the values of patrimonialism now exist side by side with the external structures of bureaucracy, but where the distinction between the public and private domains "is made, but rarely internalized, and even when it is, it is not respected."[41] In these patrimonial and neopatrimonial systems government is conceived as the property of the leader and offices as the property of those who have bought or been given these offices. Corruption, defined as the abuse of public office for private interests, is a concept that is alien to these patrimonial and neopatrimonial states, and it is particularly alien to the consciousness of the great masses of people who have not been schooled in Western ways and who daily participate in exchanges that we would label as "corrupt."[42]

The argument, then, that corruption and bribery are wrong because they involve the private taking of what belongs to the public does not hold for these patrimonial and neopatrimonial states.[43] It does not follow, however, that the argument is completely defective. For the argument sheds valuable light on the wrongness of corruption in modern bureaucratic states where the public-private distinction is tightly built into the structure of government and the worldviews of citizens. In relation to such fully bureaucratized states the argument seems correct: it is wrong for the government official to demand or accept a bribe because in doing so the official is appropriating for his private use what is recognized as belonging to the public. But the applicability of this argument is limited to modern bureaucratic states where the private-public distinction is prevalent and, in particular, does not apply to patrimonial or neopatrimonial states.

The "Harm" Argument

A third kind of argument in support of the claim that corruption and bribery are wrong is based on the idea that an act of corruption is, as I quoted Friedrich above as stating, one in which an "office holder is…induced to take actions which favor whoever provides the reward and thereby damages the group." The idea here is that corruption has harmful consequences to the larger group of society—it damages the "public interest"—and so, on utilitarian grounds, is unethical. The business that bribes the government official, then, is getting the official to harm society and so is engaged in wrongdoing.

Such an argument, of course, will not show that every single act of corruption is wrong since, as we have seen, it is at least conceivable that in some cases, under some circumstances, a particular act of corruption might have such good consequences that they outweigh that particular act's harmful consequences. Rather, the argument appeals to a form of rule-utilitarianism, that is, it is an argument that purports to show that the practice of corruption generally leads to bad consequences and therefore, such acts should be prohibited by a moral rule.

Such consequentialist arguments have been particularly prevalent in economists' discussions of corruption. One recent stream of empirical research on corruption demonstrates that corruption has a negative impact on the ratio of (domestic and foreign) investment to a country's gross domestic product (GDP). That is, the more corruption that exists in a given country, the lower its investment rate and, consequently, the lower its economic growth rate.[44] Other recent empirical studies have shown that corruption drives away foreign direct investment.[45] This effect of corruption is similar to that produced by a tax on foreign investment except that the negative effects of corruption are worse since they are more arbitrary and unpredictable.

Empirical studies have also shown that bonds issued by countries with high levels of corruption carry a higher risk premium than those issued by countries with lower levels of corruption and that corruption therefore increases a country's cost of capital.[46] Corruption has been shown to be inversely correlated with per capita Gross Domestic Product so that the higher a country's level of corruption, the lower that country's per capita GDP.[47] Higher levels of corruption are also associated with lower levels of growth of GDP.[48]

Other studies have shown that corruption is associated with misallocation of public funds. High levels of corruption, for example, are correlated with lower government investments in the provision of public health services and of education, both of which offer few opportunities for rent-seeking.[49] But, high levels of corruption are associated with overinvestment in large infrastructure projects[50] and arms procurement,[51] both of which offer greater opportunities for rent-seeking. Corruption is also associated with higher levels of environmental pollution due, presumably, to lowered investments in government oversight.[52]

Despite the plethora of recent studies showing that corruption has bad consequences, it is not clear that these studies provide adequate support for the claim that corruption is therefore wrong from a rule-utilitarian or consequentialist point of view. First, these empirical studies are not completely unproblematic. Because corruption is always covert, there is no direct way of measuring how much corruption is prevalent in a given country. Accordingly, all of the empirical studies noted above rely on surveys that ask business people and others how much corruption they believe is present in a given country. Such subjective judgments form a problematic basis for empirical studies of corruption particularly in light of the fact that, as we saw when I discussed the various definitions of corruption, what one observer in one culture will count as corruption may not be seen as corruption by observers of other cultures. Indeed if there is any consistency in the responses provided by the respondents to such surveys, that consistency can be credited to the fact that many or most of the respondents being surveyed are members of Western or industrialized societies who share similar bureaucratic conceptions of government and public service.

Secondly, there are studies of some countries that suggest that corruption can have good consequences. It has been argued, for example, that corruption can reduce risk for investors, can motivate officials to relax costly regulations, and can encourage efficiency since the most efficient firms, presumably, can pay the highest bribes.[53] Others have argued that corruption can reduce red tape and excessive bureaucratic rules, thereby also encouraging greater efficiency.[54] And it has been argued that in nations where corruption is deeply entwined into a nation's political and cultural institutions, corruption has a stabilizing effect and so the elimination of corruption could lead to instability and anarchy.[55]

Thirdly, and most importantly, entirely apart from whether corruption has good or bad consequences, an answer to the question whether the practice of corruption should be prohibited from a consequentialist point of view would have to weigh the costs of the alternative to corruption, that is, the costs of doing away with corruption. In some nations so-called "corrupt" practices are embedded in cultural practices (such as gift exchanges) that are valued by participants. The anthropologist Alex Kondos, for example, has argued on the basis of his ethnographic studies that in Nepal interactions with government officials are considered interpersonal exchanges to be mediated by flattery, praise, and the bestowal of gifts upon government officials, who in turn are expected to show favoritism and partiality toward the devout gift giver.[56] Despite the fact that Westerners see such gifts and the resulting lack of impartiality as instances of corruption, the Nepalese, he claims, prefer these kinds of interactions, embedded as they are in Hindu traditions that associate the gifts given to government representatives with the offerings to deities, gurus, and other Hindu rituals that give meaning and a cultural context to life. Others have made analogous claims about Bengal[57] and China.[58] If these cultural anthropologists are correct, then, arguably, to try to do away with such "corrupt" practices could be a costly matter that would inflict some level of cultural harm on the populations of these countries. The economic costs of corruption may well outweigh such noneconomic costs of doing away with corruption, but that has never been demonstrated.

The "harm" argument against corruption, then, while somewhat persuasive, still leaves room for doubt as a basis on which to prohibit corruption. While there is considerable empirical evidence that the practice of corruption has significantly harmful or costly consequences, this empirical evidence suffers from methodological problems. More importantly, little is known about the other side of the issue, that is, about the beneficial noneconomic consequences of corruption (if any) or about the costs associated with doing away with corruption. Therefore, little is known about what utilitarian theories most value: the on-balance benefits and costs of practices. The various arguments do demonstrate that the practice of corruption has costly consequences, but some corrupt activities certainly have acceptable consequences even if most do not.

What can we conclude from this examination of the three main arguments for the claim that corruption is unethical? Each of the arguments seems to provide some support for the claim that corruption is wrong, although each has its problems and these problems limit the applicability of the arguments. On balance it appears to this author that the arguments above show that corruption is generally unethical within modern Western cultural contexts where the norms governing institutional roles are clear and where key concepts like the public-private distinction are well entrenched. However, the arguments do not show that corruption is unethical where the norms governing institutional roles are not widely known or accepted and where government is not understood as having the kind of public purpose that it is assumed to serve by members of Western societies. Below I will discuss the implications of these conclusions.

I argued earlier that it is wrong for businesses to engage in bribery to the extent that it is wrong for officials to accept bribes. This led us to examine the arguments that purport to show that it is wrong for officials to accept bribes. I have now concluded that while the arguments show that it is generally wrong for officials to accept bribes within modern Western cultural contexts, the arguments do not show that it is in itself wrong for officials to accept bribes in societies that view their institutions as having a nature and a purpose that differs from our own view of their nature and purpose. This would imply that it is not necessarily wrong for businesses to provide bribes in such societies.

This is a troubling conclusion. How should businesses deal with this unsettling moral ambiguity? If bribery and corruption are sometimes but not always morally wrong, then what are businesses to do when confronted with the outstretched hands of foreign officials? I will conclude with a discussion of this important question.

DEALING WITH THE MORAL AMBIGUITIES
OF BRIBERY AND CORRUPTION

Let us begin by discussing first how businesses should deal with bribery and corruption in countries where the norms and expectations that govern official roles are relatively clear and well known, and where the public-private distinction is recognized, accepted, and well entrenched in the bureaucratic institutions of the society. The developed nations and many of the developing ones fall into this category.

The arguments above imply that in such societies it is morally wrong for officials to accept bribes because in doing so, first, they violate the explicit norms of the roles they have knowingly agreed to accept; second, they appropriate for their private purposes the power and property that belongs to the public and that is to be used to further public ends; and third, they engage in practices that have costly and harmful consequences. It is wrong, therefore, for business people to offer bribes to officials in such societies since by doing so they cause or help to cause the wrongful acts of those officials and so are direct accessories to the immoral corrupt act of the official. To ensure that employees recognize the wrongness of offering bribes in such cases and that they abide by this recognition, it is important, of course, that businesses develop and implement clear policies and procedures regarding bribes, and there are now several guides available that can assist companies in the development and implementation of such policies and procedures such as Transparency International's "Six Step Implementation Process," a "practical guide for companies implementing anti-bribery policies and procedures."[59]

Still, even in the developed societies described in the paragraph above, it may not be wrong for a business to give an official a bribe. Discussions of the ethics of bribery often distinguish wrongfully offering a bribe, on the one hand, from yielding to "extortion" on the other. The distinction turns on whether the act of bribery is initiated by the person giving the bribe or by the person receiving the bribe. In the former case the briber offers the bribe to an official as an inducement to be treated favorably by the recipient in violation of the official's duties; in the latter case, the official demands the bribe from the giver of the bribe and makes the threat that if the bribe is not paid, the official will withhold something that the giver needs and without which the giver will suffer some harm. Suppose, for example, that a government purchasing agent has agreed to buy the highly perishable goods of a business and the business ships the goods to the agent. While the goods are en route the government agent tells the business that he will renege on the sale unless the business pays him a "fee" equal to 10 percent of the value of the sale. The official is here engaged in extortion.

A substantial number of ethicists have agreed that even where it is normally wrong to offer bribes to officials, it is not necessarily wrong to comply with the demands of an extortionist.[60] Thomas Carson argues, for example, that in many cases meeting the demand of the extortionist will not have economically injurious consequences.[61] Moreover, if the victim of the extortionist risks suffering significant harm if he does not meet the extortionist's demand, then the victim is not under an obligation to prevent the extortionist's immoral behavior. For no one is obligated to sacrifice one's own substantial interests in order to prevent someone else's moral failure, particularly if one's sacrifice will do nothing to help curb such failures in the future.

The arguments of Carson and others appear to be sound: in itself, acceding to the demands of an extortionist is not morally wrong provided that paying the bribe will not create significant social costs, and provided that the business will suffer significant harm if the demands of the extortionist are not met. It should be noted, however, that although acceding to extortion is not morally wrong in itself, it may be, and generally is, *legally* wrong to do so. The Foreign Corrupt Practices Act, for example, has no provision that allows the payment of extorted bribes, nor does the OECD Convention on Combating Bribery of Foreign Public Officials in International Business Transactions.

There is a second set of circumstances in which it may be morally permissible to pay a bribe even though it would ordinarily be wrong to bribe government officials. Such circumstances are those that involve what are called "facilitating payments." A facilitating payment, sometimes referred to as a "grease payment," is a relatively small payment made to a low-level government official to get the official to perform in a timely manner a routine duty that the official is required to perform and to which the payer has a right. Facilitating payments are thus distinct from bribes given to induce an official to do something that violates the official's role duties and so to which the payer has no right.

The FCPA explicitly does not prohibit citizens from paying officials to expedite a "routine governmental action," although under the laws of most countries it is illegal for government officials to receive such payments and illegal to make them. Specific examples of the kind of "routine governmental actions" specifically allowed by the FCPA include obtaining permits, licenses, or other official documents; processing governmental papers such as visas and work orders; providing police protection, mail pick-up, and delivery; providing phone service, power and water supply; loading and unloading cargo or protecting perishable products; and scheduling inspections associated with contract performance or transit of goods across country. Most of the laws of other countries that prohibit the bribery of foreign officials also allow facilitating payments.

Although the FCPA and the anticorruption laws of other nations explicitly allow facilitating payments, ethicists have disagreed about whether making such payments is ethical.[62] Those who condemn facilitating payments as unethical point out that the official who receives the bribe is violating his role obligation to provide his services without payment. Thus, the person who provides the payment is encouraging a moral (and legal) failure. This point, however, can be countered. Those (such as this author) who defend facilitating payments as ethical in some circumstances, respond that unlike other forms of bribery, the person making a facilitating payment has a right to the service and the person receiving the bribe has an institutional obligation to render that service. Thus, the person paying the bribe is paying for something to which he is morally entitled, and he is providing the official with an incentive to fulfill his moral obligations. How could this be considered unethical? Moreover, when facilitating payments are demanded it is often the case that the person making the payment will suffer significant harm or inconvenience if the official demanding the payment follows through on his threat to withhold his services. A business that is in the process of constructing a building, for example, can suffer costly delays if it does not pay the petty officials who control building permits and who will delay processing the permits if they are not given a facilitating payment. Under such conditions, the payment is given involuntarily and so the giver of the payment cannot be morally blameworthy for making the payment, particularly if the payment has relatively insignificant social consequences, while his own losses would be large. Facilitating payments appear to be ethical, provided that (1) the person being bribed has an institutional obligation to provide the service for which he or she is being paid, (2) the person paying the official is entitled to the service and so is not asking the official to, say, lie or steal for him, (3) the person making the payment will suffer a relatively significant harm or major inconvenience if the service is not rendered, and (4) making this particular payment will have relatively insignificant costly consequences for society.

Doing Business in Societies with Different Normative Understandings

But more vexing questions arise when the business person finds himself or herself operating in a society where the conditions outlined above do not obtain, that is, societies where the normative understandings that govern official roles are significantly different from our own view that office holders should not accept bribes, societies where these understandings are simply not part of the consciousness of the average citizen, or societies where the public-private distinction is neither widely recognized nor widely accepted. Such societies may be rife with bribery, nepotism, favoritism, and other activities that we would label as corrupt. I have argued that in such societies the payment of bribes by businesses is not necessarily morally wrong. Yet, as I also noted, the practice of bribery in such countries has significant social and private costs, which would imply that, at the least, bribery in such societies must be subjected to moral scrutiny. To be sure, the payment of bribes may be legally prohibited by the antibribery laws of the business's home country, such as the U.S. Federal Corrupt Practices Act, as well as by the unenforced laws of the host country. But from a moral point of view, and setting aside such laws, under what circumstances is the payment of bribes by businesses, in such societies, morally permissible in spite of the possibility of both social and private costs?

We can begin to answer this question by observing that much of the bribe paying that goes on in such societies takes the form of facilitating payments. Such payments, as I argued, are in themselves morally permissible provided that the payment is made to an official who has a duty to perform the service, the payer is entitled to the service (and so the service is not an illicit one) and would suffer significant harm if it is not rendered, and the payment has only negligible harmful side effects. Furthermore, in such societies much of the bribe paying that goes on is also the result of extortion: officials threaten citizens with significant harm unless they pay what they demand. I have argued that paying extorted bribes is not morally wrong provided that doing so will not lead to significant social costs and the harm threatened by the extortionist is substantial. To be sure, it is not easy to make the judgments that are called for when evaluating whether it is morally permissible to pay an extortionist or make a facilitating payment. Particularly in societies where corruption is widespread it is easy, but wrong, to think that since so many others are paying bribes, one is justified in doing so oneself, and that since everyone is going to engage in corruption anyway, one's own example will have little harmful effect on others. In addition, self interest can influence one's judgment and lead one to wrongly decide that a relatively minor inconvenience constitutes a substantial injury.

But what about situations where the bribe in question is neither a facilitating payment nor one that involves extortion and where the issue of bribery arises in a society where citizens lack the kind of understanding of bureaucratic offices that is common in the developed world? What about cases of bribes where the government is not understood as a public entity serving the interests of the public but where, instead, the boundary between the public and the private interests of the individual is blurred? As I noted above, following several anthropologists, there are numerous examples of such countries among the Arab sheikhdoms including the sultanate of Oman, Qatar, and the United Arab Emirates, as well as several non-Arab developing nations such as Nepal, Thailand, and those postcolonial regimes of sub-Saharan Africa in which tribal conceptions of rulership still operate such as the Democratic Republic of Congo, Equatorial Guinea, Uganda, Zimbabwe, Cameroon, and Nigeria. In all of these countries, according to Transparency International, corruption and bribery are widespread. How are businesses to deal with bribery and corruption in such societies?

The Case of Nigeria

To make our discussion more concrete, let us take the example of Nigeria, a sub-Saharan African nation of 132 million people with substantial oil reserves.[63] In spite of the vast wealth that flows from its oil, about 60 percent of the population lives under crushing poverty on less than US$1 per day. The World Bank has estimated that about 80 percent of Nigeria's oil revenues flow into the hands of 1 percent of its people. According to the U.S. Department of State's *2005 Human Rights Report*, Nigerian government officials are responsible for or allow serious human rights abuses including politically motivated killings, hostage seizing, the beating and torture of suspects, extortion of citizens, violence, discrimination, child labor, and human trafficking. Corruption is endemic in Nigeria, which in 2007 was ranked 147 out of 179 countries by Transparency International, which ranks countries according to their level of perceived corruption.

Nigeria is a patrimonial state, of the sort that I discussed earlier.[64] Within the patrimonial state, as I noted, the distinction between what belongs to the "public" and what belongs to the private individual does not exist. Government is assumed to be the personal property of the ruler, who doles out offices to his followers and relatives who then are expected to use these offices as their own personal property. In such a context, as Patrick Chabal and Jena-Pascal Daloz point out, corruption and bribery are not perceived as wrong:

> Provided the beneficiaries of graft do not hoard too much of what they accumulate by means of the resources made available to them through their position, and provided they redistribute along lines that are judged to be socially desirable, their behavior is deemed acceptable. Corruption is not, therefore, a matter of a few "rotten apples" or of a venal "class," even less as an "evil" to be eradicated by means of vigorous "ethical" campaigns. On the contrary, it is a habitual part of everyday life, an expected element of every social transaction. This ought not to surprise us. As we have already emphasized, there is in Africa a marked reluctance to abide by the abstract and universalist norms of the legal-bureaucratic order that are the foundations of Western polities.... Expectations of probity, therefore, appear to be limited to one's kith and kin, the members of one's community, but they obviously cease to apply beyond. The usual response by Nigerians to the charge that their country is deemed by some to be the most corrupt on earth is: "This is how we do things in Nigeria!"[65]

Chabal and Daloz concede that "corruption is rarely condoned and, even, that it is frequently condemned in countries, like Nigeria, where it has reached gargantuan proportions."[66] However, they argue, "with few exceptions, such anti-corruption discourse is primarily rhetorical and... the recurrent purges which follow are, more often than not, convenient devices for eliminating political rivals rather than a real attempt to reform the political 'order.'"[67] How should companies deal with corruption in a country like Nigeria?

First, and obviously, companies are not forced to do business with, or in, high corruption societies like that of Nigeria. If, before entering a country, a business perceives that operating there is very likely to require it to engage in activities that will violate or compromise its own standards of conduct and impose significant costs on the company and possibly on the host country, it is better for the company to take its business elsewhere before it makes large investments from which it cannot easily extricate itself. Moreover, the regimes of many high-corruption nations like Nigeria are repressive and systematically violate the human rights of their citizens. This has been the case throughout the series of military and civilian regimes that have dominated Nigeria until now.[68] Contributing to such repressive regimes by providing bribes or kickbacks to ruling elites helps the regime continue its human rights violations and is best avoided regardless of whether or not bribery is wrong in itself.

Secondly, when a company provides jobs, services, or goods that the government of a high-corruption nation strongly desires, it is possible for the company to simply refuse to give officials any bribes and, even, to engage the government in instituting reforms. Shell Oil, for example, is a British company that has operated in Nigeria for several decades. During the early 1990s, Shell cooperated with a series of corrupt and abusive Nigerian regimes and did not seem to have cared whether it engaged in bribery or cooperated with these Nigerian governments who were regularly violating the human rights of their citizens. The company's stance was severely criticized by Amnesty International and other NGOs who argued that the company was complicit in the government's persecution of the Ogoni—including extrajudicial executions, torture, and the destruction of Ogoni homes—an ethnic minority on whose tribal lands Shell and other oil companies were drilling and whose lands Shell had helped to turn into an environmentally polluted disaster. In 1995, Shell was further accused of being complicit in the government's execution on trumped up charges of Ogoni activist Ken Saro-Wiwo and eight other Ogoni tribespeople who had led a nonviolent movement protesting the environmental damage being inflicted on their homeland. The deaths of Saro-Wiwo and his Ogoni companions were met with enormous international outrage, much of it focused on Shell. Stung by the ferocity of criticism, Shell responded with a remarkable turnaround. The company not only adopted one of the world's most progressive environmental programs but also began to annually issue a "Sustainability Report" that openly describes how well or poorly it is doing with respect to a number of social indicators, including its use of armed security, employee deaths, its monitoring of child labor, its environmental pollution, and the number of bribes it has offered. Shell proclaims in its reports that "we are a 'no bribes' fair competition business" and its audited "Sustainability Reports" seem to bear this out.[69] Thus, Shell's example shows that it is possible for a company, even when operating in a nation as corrupt as Nigeria, to successfully avoid bribery. Moreover, the company notes in its reports that its policy of "engagement" with the government has helped reform local security forces and supported initiatives that have led to greater investment in education, health care, and other social programs. Thus, when a company has committed itself to doing business in a country like Nigeria, it should not assume that it has no choice but to bribe, but instead should examine (1) whether it is in a position to avoid bribery completely and (2) whether it has sufficient standing to engage the government in making reforms that may reduce the country's corruption levels or, at least, its human rights violations.

Thirdly, I have argued that in patrimonial societies like Nigeria, the giving of bribes is not in itself necessarily unethical. But that does not end the matter. While the giving of a bribe may not in itself be unethical in nations like Nigeria, any particular act of bribery may still have consequences that make that particular bribe unethical. As indicated above, before 1995 Shell was probably engaged in paying bribes to various political regimes in Nigeria that in turn were violating the human rights of citizens. These regimes, moreover, were actively pursuing policies that unjustly increased inequality and fostered discrimination against minorities such as the Ogoni. The bribes also imposed heavy social costs on Nigeria insofar as the ruling elites siphoned off enormous amounts of oil monies that could have been invested in health care, education, housing, and other investments that could improve the welfare of its desperately poor citizens; these monies were, instead, spent on "consumption of imported consumer items, acquisition of a Mercedes, taking a new wife, or throwing a big party."[70] No doubt, the bribes also imposed costs on Shell managers who would have had to spend substantial amounts of time negotiating with government officials. And, finally, the bribes in some cases may have required officials to engage in deception, theft, or other illicit activity, for example by undervaluing a customs declaration, or canceling legitimate taxes, or paying for goods that will not be delivered.[71] All of these consequences are important moral considerations that imply that any bribes Shell was paying were morally unjustified because of these consequences even if in themselves the acts were morally neutral. Thus, even when bribery occurs in a cultural context in which bribery is in itself a morally neutral act, the agent must ask whether this otherwise morally neutral act (1) will contribute to substantial violations of the human rights of others, (2) will have distributive effects that are significantly unjust or unfair, (3) will generate large social and personal costs, or (4) will require serious deception, theft, or other similar illicit activity. If any of these questions is answered in the affirmative, then it is probable that the act is unethical. If all are answered in the affirmative, then it is virtually certain. It is only when all of the questions can clearly and honestly be answered in the negative that bribery can be presumed to be morally acceptable in patrimonial societies like Nigeria.

Other Patrimonial Societies

Not all societies, of course, are like Nigeria. I have purposely taken Nigeria as an example because it raises in sharp relief the kinds of oppressive conditions that are found in many high-corruption countries and that must be taken into account when evaluating the ethics of particular acts of bribery. But in patrimonial societies that are more benign than Nigeria, bribery can itself be a more benign act. Examples of such relatively benign societies include Arab nations like the sheikdoms of the United Arab Emirates and the sultanate of Oman; in both nations citizens enjoy a relatively high standard of living due to their oil resources and their governments enjoy wide support and stability.[72] While what Transparency International would characterize as "corruption" in the Emirates and Oman is not at the high levels found in Nigeria, Transparency International, nevertheless, holds that there is a substantial amount of "corruption" in both countries. But in both countries the private-public distinction is not recognized and the apparatus of the state is seen as belonging to the reigning monarch. As a Sudanese observer notes:

> In the Arab [world], where there are absolute autocratic regimes, the concept of corruption loses all meaning, as the law is the ruler's will; he decides what is permitted and what is forbidden, and his bonuses and gifts are a legitimate livelihood. If the ruler so decides, he will give his sons a monopoly on import or export; will permit them to purchase abroad at a tenth of [the merchandise's] value and be reimbursed for the full price by the state treasury; will allow his friends and cronies to use public property or state revenues, or will give them land. In these cases, we are talking of the embodiment of legitimate gain.[73]

The sultanate of Oman and the sheikdoms of the United Emirates are the kind of "absolute autocratic regimes" where "the concept of corruption loses all meaning." Moreover, in such regimes the four questions about particular bribes that I noted in the last paragraph—what impact does the act have on human rights, on distributive justice, on social and personal costs, and on illicit behavior?—will sometimes be answered in the negative. In such cases, and from a moral point of view, a particular act of bribery will be morally benign.

CONCLUSION

I have tried to show, then, that while corruption and bribery in most developed and developing nations are unethical, there are specific and identifiable cultural contexts within which they may be morally indifferent acts. I have argued, moreover, that even where corruption and bribery are unethical, there are circumstances that can render them morally acceptable, while even where corruption and bribery are morally indifferent acts, there are circumstances that can render particular instances of such acts morally wrong. In both instances, I have tried to identify the kind of difficult questions that a business person should consider when trying to decide how to approach ethical decision making on this difficult subject. This chapter can be seen as a prolonged plea for bringing a thoughtful and careful analysis to the cultural context, and the particular circumstances, within which moral decisions regarding corruption and bribery must be made. It is as much a mistake to think that a blanket condemnation of corruption and bribery can settle all questions in this culturally and morally ambiguous area, as it is a mistake to think that an approval of corruption and bribery in certain societies can relieve one of having to think about the ethics of what one is doing.

NOTES

1. World Bank, "The Costs of Corruption," press release, Washington, D.C., April 8, 2004.

2. Transparency International, "Transparency International Publishes 1997 Corruption Perceptions Index," press release, (Berlin), July 31, 1997, which quotes Dr. Peter Eigen, chairman of Transparency International, as saying: "I urge the public to recognize that a large share of the corruption is the explicit product of multinational corporations, headquartered in leading industrialized countries, using massive bribery and kickbacks to buy contracts in the developing world and the countries in transition."

3. Susan Rose-Ackerman, *Corruption and Government: Causes, Consequences, and Reform* (New York: Cambridge University Press, 1999).

4. United Nations, "United Nations Global Compact," http://www.unglobalcompact. org/aboutthegc/thetenprinciples/index.html (accessed April 1, 2008).

5. In fact, all of the legislative initiatives described in the preceding paragraphs are aimed at controlling the payment of bribes to government officials, and such bribes have been the focus of virtually all of the studies of the costs of corruption. I know of no studies that have looked at the costs of any other kind of bribery.

6. Michael Johnson, "The Search for Definitions: the Vitality of Politics and the Issue of Corruption," *International Social Science Journal* 48 (1996): 321–335.

7. Aristotle, *Politics*, 1279a.

8. Transparency International, for example, "the global civil society organization leading the fight against corruption," devotes virtually no attention whatsoever to business-to- business corruption (see http://www.transparency.org), nor does the anticorruption unit of the World Bank (http://go.worldbank.org/QYRWVXVH40). Moreover, none of the legislative initiatives criminalizing bribery and corruption that numerous countries have adopted in response to the 1997 OECD convention on bribery concern themselves with the issue of business-to-business corruption.

9. Johnson, "Search for Definitions," 322–325.

10. See D. Nissenbaum, "Davis at Center of International Trade Dispute," *San Jose Mercury News*, June 29, 2002, which notes that the kind of favoritism California governor Grey Davis showed to the industry of a key campaign donor was criticized as an abuse of power by British observers.

11. Koenraad W. Swart, *Sale of Offices in the Seventeenth Century* (The Hague: Martinus Nijhoff, 1949).

12. T. Louise Brown, *The Challenge to Democracy in Nepal* (New York: Routledge, 1996), 72.

13. Joseph S. Nye, "Corruption and Political Development: A Cost-Benefit Analysis," *American Political Science Review* 61 (1967): 419.

14. United Nations Development Program, *Fighting Corruption to Improve Governance* (New York: United Nations Development Programme, 1999), 7.

15. Rose-Ackerman, *Corruption and Government*, 91; see also A. W. Goudie and D. Stasavage, *Corruption: The Issues* (Paris: OECD, 1997), and Robert Klitgaard, "National and International Strategies for Reducing Corruption," *OECD Symposium on Corruption and Good Governance* (Paris: OECD, 1996), 37–54.

16. Koenraad Walter Swart, *Sale of Offices in the Seventeenth Century* (The Hague: Martinus Nijhoff, 1949); Robert Williams, "New Concepts for Old?" *Third World Quarterly* 20 (1999): 503–513.

17. Jean-Francois Medard, "Patrimonialism, Neo-patrimonialism, and the Study of the Post-colonial State in Sub-Saharan Africa," in *Improved Natural Resource Management: The Role of Formal Organizations and Informal Networks and Institutions*, ed. H. S. Marcussen (Roskilde, Denmark: Roskilde University, Institute of International Development Studies, 1996), 76–97.

18. Carl J. Friedrich, "Corruption Concepts in Historical Perspective," in *Political Corruption: A Handbook*, ed. Arnold J. Heidenheimer, Michael Johnston, and Victor T. LeVine. (New Brunswick, N.J.: Transaction, 2007), 15.

19. A. W. Goudie, and D. Stasavage, *Corruption: The Issues* (Paris: OECD, 1997)

20. John T. Noonan, *Bribes* (New York: Macmillan, 1984).

21. H. S. James Jr., "When Is a Bribe a Bribe? Teaching a Workable Definition of Bribery," *Teaching Business Ethics* 6 (2002): 199–217.

22. John Danley, "Toward a Theory of Bribery," *Business and Professional Ethics Journal* 2 (1984): 19–39.

23. Michael Philips, "Bribery," *Ethics* 94 (1984): 623.

24. Nye, "Corruption and Political Development," 419.

25. Thomas L. Carson, "Bribery, Extortion, and 'The Foreign Corrupt Practices Act,'" *Philosophy and Public Affairs* 14 (1985): 66–90.

26. Colin Leys, "What Is the Problem of Corruption?" *Journal of Modern African Studies* 3 (1965): 215–230.

27. Akhil Gupta, "Blurred Boundaries: the Discourse of Corruption, the Culture of Politics, and the Imagined State," *American Ethnologist* 22 (1995): 375–402; see also G. Blundo and J.-P. Olivier de Sardan, *Everyday Corruption and the State* (New York: Zed, 2006), who quote a public official as implying that the bribes he collects are "just remuneration" when he says, "I believe that the corruption at the town hall can be tolerated up to a certain level. Because it is [perpetrated by] officials who are badly paid and are the victims of many social problems" (112).

28. Alex Kondos, "The Question of 'Corruption' in Nepal," *Mankind* 17 (1987): 15–29.

29. Several years ago I used to provide ethics training to people who aspired to careers in local California politics. Part of the training included a discussion of conflict of interests. Invariably, at least a third of the participants would indicate that they previously had not known that office holders are obligated to refrain from using their public office to serve a private interest.

30. Manuel Velasquez, "Is Corruption Always Corrupt?" in *Corporate Integrity and Accountability*, ed. George G. Brenkert (Thousand Oaks, Calif.: Sage, 2004), 148–165.

31. Max Weber, *Economy and Society: An Outline of Interpretive Sociology*, ed. G. Roth and C. Wittich (Berkeley: University of California Press, 1956).

32. Ibid., 959.

33. Ibid., 1028–1029.

34. Weber uses the term "rent" to refer to the monies that an office holder is able to extract from his clients in exchange for the services provided by his office.

35. Weber, *Economy and Society*, 1031ff.

36. R. Theobald, *Corruption, Development and Underdevelopment* (London: The Macmillan Press, Ltd., 1990), 19–20; Weber, *Economy and Society*, 956.

37. Noonan, *Bribes*.

38. A. Zolberg, *Creating Political Order: The Party-States of West Africa* (Chicago: Chicago University Press, 1966).

39. Gunther Roth, "Personal Rulership, Patrimonialism, and Empire-building in the New States," *World Politics* 20 (1968): 194–206.

40. Medard, "Patrimonialism, Neo-patrimonialism, and the Study of the Post-colonial State in Sub-Saharan Africa."

41. Ibid., 85.

42. T. K. O. de Sardan, "A Moral Economy of Corruption," *Journal of Modern African Studies* 37 (1999): 25–52.

43. Velasquez, "Is Corruption Always Corrupt?"

44. A. Brunetti, G. Kisunko and B. Wedger, "Credibility of Rules and Economic Growth: Evidence from a World Wide Private Sector Survey," *The World Bank Economic Review* 12 (1998): 353–384; P. Keefer, and S. Knack, "Institutions and Economic Performance: Cross-Country Tests Using Alternative Institutional Measures," *Economics and Politics* 7 (1995): 207–227; P. Mauro, "Corruption and Growth," *Quarterly Journal of Economics* 110 (1995): 681–712.

45. S.-J. Wei, "How Taxing is Corruption on International Investors?" *Review of Economics and Statistics* 82 (2000): 1–11; J. Graf Lambsdorff and P. Cornelius, "Corruption, Foreign Investment and Growth," *The Africa Competitiveness Report 2000/2001*, ed. K. Schwab et al. (Oxford: Oxford University Press, 2000), 70–78; J. Doh, and H. Teegan, "Private Telecommunications Investment in Emerging Economies—Comparing the Latin American and Asian Experience," *Management Research* 1 (2003): 9–26.

46. F. Ciocchini, E. Durbin, and D. T. C. Ng, "Does Corruption Increase Emerging Market Bond Spreads?" *Journal of Economics and Business* 55 (2003): 503–528.

47. David Kaufmann, A. Kraay, and P. Zoido-Lobaton, "Aggregating Governance Indicators," *World Bank Policy Research Working Paper* no. 2195 (Washington D.C,: World Bank, 1999).

48. P. Mauro, "The Effects of Corruption on Growth, Investment, and Government Expenditure: A Cross-Country Analysis," *Corruption and the Global Economy*, (Washington, D.C: Institute for International Economics, 1997), 83–107.

49. S. Gupta, H. Davoodi, and E. R. Tiongson, "Corruption and the Provision of Health Care and Education Services," *The Political Economy of Corruption*, ed. A. K. Jain (London: Routledge, 2001), 111–141. Note that the term "rent-seeking" is here being used in the economist's sense of seeking to make money by manipulating the legal or economic environment rather than through some productive activity. The term "rent" here, therefore, does not refer to income derived from the ownership of land.

50. D. Esty and M. Porter, "National Environmental Performance Measurement and Determinants," in *Environmental Performance Measurement: The Global Report 2001–2002*, ed. D. Esty and P. Cornelius (New York: Oxford University Press, 2002).

51. Sanjeev Gupta, L. De Mello, and R. Sharan, "Corruption and Military Spending," *European Journal of Political Economy* 17 (2001): 749–777.

52. H. Welsch, "Corruption, Growth, and the Environment: A Cross-Country Analysis," *Environment and Development Economics* 9 (2004): 663–693.

53. Nathaniel H. Leff, "Economic Development through Bureaucratic Corruption," *American Behavioural Scientist* 8 (1964): 8–14.

54. D. H. Bayley, "The Effects of Corruption in a Developing Nation," *Western Political Quarterly* 19 (1966): 719–732; F. Lui, "An Equilibrium Queuing Model of Bribery," *Journal of Political Economy* 933 (1985): 760–781; Nye, "Corruption and Political Development: A Cost-Benefit Analysis."

55. J. Charap and C. Harm, "Institutionalized Corruption and the Kleptocratic State," in *Governance, Corruption, and Economic Performance*, ed. George T. Abed and Sanjeev Gupta (Washington, D.C.: International Monetary Fund, 2002).

56. Alex Kondos, "The Question of Corruption in Nepal," *Mankind* 17 (1987): 15–29.

57. A. E. Ruud, *Corruption as Everyday Practice: Rules and Rule-bending in Local Indian Society* (Working Paper 1998.4), Center for Development and the Environment, University of Oslo (1998).

58. Mayfair Mei-Hut Yang, "The Gift Economy and State Power in China," *Comparative Studies in Society and History* 31 (1989): 25–54.

59. Available on the Transparency International Web site, www.transparency.org/global_priorities/private_sector/business_principles/six_step_implementation_process.

60. Mark Pastin and Michael Hooker, "Ethics and the Foreign Corrupt Practices Act," in *Profit and Responsibility: Issues in Business and Professional Ethics*, ed. Patricia Werhane (New York: Mellen, 1985), 169–177; Antonio Argandona, "Corruption and Companies: The Use of Facilitating Payments," *Journal of Business Ethics* 60 (2005): 251–264.

61. Carson, "Bribery, Extortion, and 'The Foreign Corrupt Practices Act.'"

62. Transparency International, for example, takes the position that facilitating payments are wrong, see Transparency International, "Business Principles for Countering Bribery: Guidance Document", Issue III, November 2004, 23–24, http://www.transparency.org/global_priorities/private_sector/business_principles/guidance_document.

63. The information in this paragraph is drawn from Library of Congress—Federal Research Division, *Country Profile: Nigeria*, June 2006, http://lcweb2.loc.gov/frd/cs/profiles/Nigeria.pdf (accessed November 20, 2007).

64. Patrick Chabal and Jean-Pascal Daloz, *Africa Works: Disorder as Political Instrument* (Indianapolis: Indiana University Press, 1999).

65. Chabal and Daloz, *Africa Works*, 99–100.

66. Ibid., 104.

67. Ibid.

68. Amnesty International, *Amnesty International Report 2007*, http://www.amnesty.org/en/region/africa/west-africa/nigeria (accessed November 22, 2007).

69. "The Short Arm of the Law," *The Economist*, March 2, 2002, 63–65.

70. T. J. Biersteker, *Multinationals, the State, and Control of the Nigerian Economy* (Princeton, N.J.: Princeton University Press, 1987), 148.

71. Giorgio Blundo and Jean-Pierre Olivier de Sardan, *Everyday Corruption and the State: Citizens and Public Officials in Africa* (New York: Zed, 2006), 73.

72. The information in this paragraph is drawn from Helen Chapin Metz, ed., *Persian Gulf States: Country Studies* (Washington D.C.: Federal Research Division, Library of Congress, 1993), http://lcweb2.loc.gov/frd/cs/profiles (accessed November 20, 2007).

73. Abd Al-Whhab Al-Effendi, "Fighting Corruption [in the Arab World] is Like Fighting Catholicism in the Vatican." *Dar Al-Hayat* [London-based Arabic daily], August 6, 2002, http://memri.org/bin/articles.cgi?Page=archives&Area=sd&ID=SP41102#_edn1 (accessed December 10, 2007).

SUGGESTED READING

Andvig, Jens Chr. Odd-Helge Fjeldstad Inge Amundsen Tone Sissener and Tina Soreide. *Research on Corruption: A Policy Oriented Survey, Final Report.* Commissioned by NORAD. Bergen, Norway: Chr Michelsen Institute, 2000. http://www.icgg.org/downloads/contribution07_andvig.pdf.

Argandona, Antonio. "Corruption and Companies: The Use of Facilitating Payments." *Journal of Business Ethics* 60 (2005): 251–264.

Carson, Thomas L. "Bribery, Extortion, and 'The Foreign Corrupt Practices Act.'" *Philosophy and Public Affairs* 14 (1985): 66–90.

Danley, John. "Toward a Theory of Bribery." *Business and Professional Ethics Journal* 2 (1984): 19–39.

Heidenheimer, Arnold J., and Michael Johnston, eds., *Political Corruption: Concepts and Contexts*, 3rd ed. New Brunswick, N.J.: Transaction, 2007.

Johnston, Michael. "The Search for Definitions: The Vitality of Politics and the Issue of Corruption." *International Social Science Journal* 48 (1996): 321–335.

Lambsdorff, Johann Graf. *Consequences and Causes of Corruption—What Do We Know from a Cross-Section of Countries?* (Passau: Passau University, 2006). Http://www.icgg.org/downloads/Causes%20and%20Consequences%20of%20Corruption%20-%20Cross-Section.pdf/.

Mauro, P. "The Effects of Corruption on Growth, Investment, and Government Expenditure: A Cross-Country Analysis." In *Corruption and the Global Economy.* Edited by Kimberly Ann Elliott, 83–107. Washington, D.C.: Institute for International Economics, 1997.

Miller, Seumas, Peter Roberts, and Edward Spence, *Corruption and Anti-Corruption: An Applied Philosophical Approach.* New Jersey, N.J.: Prentice Hall, 2005.

Myint, U. "Corruption: Causes, Consequences and Cures." Asia-*Pacific Development Journal* 7 (2000): 33–58.

Nye, Joseph S. "Corruption and Political Development: A Cost-Benefit Analysis." *American Political Science Review* 61 (1967): 417–427.

Philips, Michael. "Bribery." *Ethics* 94 (1984): 621–636.

Rose-Ackerman, Susan. *Corruption and Government: Causes, Consequences, and Reform.* New York: Cambridge University Press, 1999.

———. *International Handbook on the Economics of Corruption.* Williston, Vt.: Edward Elgar, 2006.

Sissener, Tone Kristin. "Anthropological Perspectives on Corruption." Working paper. Bergen, Norway: Chr. Michelsen Institute, Development Studies and Human Rights, 2001. http://www.cmi.no/publications/2001/wp/wp2001-5.pdf.

Theobald, R. *Corruption, Development and Underdevelopment.* London: The Macmillan Press, Ltd., 1990.

Velasquez, Manuel. "Is Corruption Always Corrupt?" In *Corporate Integrity and Accountability*. Edited by George G. Brenkert, 148–165. Thousand Oaks, Calif: Sage, 2004.

Wei, S.-J. "How Taxing is Corruption on International Investors?" *Review of Economics and Statistics* 82 (2000): 1–11.

Williams, Robert. "New Concepts for Old?" *Third World Quarterly* 20 (1999): 503–513.

Web Sites

http://www.transparency.org
http://www.eitransparency.org
http://www.publishwhatyoupay.org
http://www.worldbank.org/anticorruption

CHAPTER 17

BUSINESS IN POLITICS: LOBBYING AND CORPORATE CAMPAIGN CONTRIBUTIONS

ANDREW STARK

CORPORATE political activity confronts managers with a potential conflict between two principles. The first speaks to a government in which public officials are free from corruption. The second provides for the robust engagement of individuals—and groups of individuals such as corporations—in the full and free expression of their views on matters of public policy. The ethics of corporate political activity—of corporate lobbying and corporate involvement in campaign finance—requires of businesses that they pursue the second principle while not threatening the first.[1]

Both are in fact among the core principles of a democratic political system. Corruption, in its broadest sense, refers to any situation in which an official makes a decision for reasons other than her best judgment as to where the public interest lies: for example, because she has a personal pecuniary interest at stake in the matter, or because someone has offered her something of pecuniary value in return for a favorable decision. The reason why corruption is inconsonant with democratic norms is obvious. Democratic officials are entrusted with power by the citizenry on the condition that they make decisions based on no other consideration than the interest of the public: that they represent exclusively the interests of those whom they ultimately serve.

Freedom of expression, as a democratic principle, secures a right to citizens and a good to society. The right to freedom of expression requires that each adult person be allowed to speak for herself, and assert her own views, in public debate. The good that freedom of expression promotes arises because the more such viewpoints that enter into debate, challenging one another, the more likely it is that wise public decisions will be made.

Although I have described freedom of expression as a principle for individuals, it also extends, through the closely related principle of "freedom of association," to groups, such as corporations. True, issues of *internal* democracy arise for business corporations in a way that they might not for other kinds of groups, such as the Sierra Club. If the purpose of a given business is to produce wealth for shareholders, while that of the Sierra Club is to take positions on environmental issues, then objections can arise to certain kinds of corporate political activity on the grounds that, by engaging in them, the corporation is not reflecting the (inevitably disparate) political views of the shareholders. This is an important issue. But I will set it aside here, because even if it is resolved, the ethical question for any manager would still remain: under what circumstances will a contemplated type of corporate political activity threaten the functioning of the democracy *external* to the corporation, the one in which we all live? In any event, the issue of "internal democracy"—of shareholders' rights—is alleviated to some extent, in the United States, by the requirement that corporations contribute to or spend on candidate campaigns not via their treasury funds, but through associated political action committees (PACs), which raise their monies from the "voluntary" contributions of shareholders and employees. When it comes to "external democracy," however—and in particular the risk of corrupting public officials—there is no reason why corporate PAC funds should not pose exactly the same threats that corporate treasury funds do. Finally, because I focus on the politically active corporation's effect on "external" democracy, where matters of the corporate form—and in particular, dealings with shareholders—are less relevant,[2] I will use the terms "business" and "corporation" interchangeably.

For purposes of simplicity, but also because this is where both the moral discourse and the cases are richest, the "democracy" I analyze will be the United States at the federal level. That moral discourse will include the reasoning of judges and advocates in court cases concerning corporate political activity. My point in drawing on this material, however, will be to advance ethical principles that should guide corporations in lobbying and campaign finance. Those principles do—as we shall see—forbid much conduct that is not prohibited by law. And though both politicians and civil servants are recipients of lobbying, only politicians are recipients of campaign finance. Hence, in what follows, the discussion and examples will focus on business's interactions with politicians—and in particular, legislators.

I will examine the interplay between the two democratic principles—against corruption and supportive of political expression—drawing out of them the ethical guidelines that should govern eight of the most common types of corporate political activity. Four of these have to do with lobbying, and the other four with corporate involvement in campaign finance. "Lobbyists," in what follows, will refer equally to government relations personnel in the direct employment of corporations, third-party lobbying firms that a corporation might hire, and any other employees, including the CEO, who lobbies on behalf of the corporation. Lobbyists pursue the democratic right and good of free expression in the following four principal ways: (i) presenting briefs, testimony, and arguments to legislators and their staffs, (ii) buttonholing them at receptions or charity events, (iii) developing relationships with them over time in one-on-one dinners or other acts of hospitality, and (iv) furnishing legislators with drafts bills and regulations reflective of their corporations' views. The potential for corruption arises whenever, at the same time, the lobbyist is doing pecuniary favors for legislators: raising money for their campaigns, hosting a reception for legislators, buying a ticket to their favorite charity, taking legislators out for dinner, or—by providing them with research and drafting that assist their lawmaking—relieving them of official expenses.

When it comes to corporate activity in electoral campaigns, the four categories I examine include (i) corporate PACs contributing to candidate campaigns or (ii) spending independently on advertising in support of candidates, and (iii) corporations contributing to party voter-mobilization efforts or (iv) spending independently on advertising to advance a particular position on a specific policy issue. Here, there is a closer link between corruption and expression. Each of these activities is itself, at one and the same time, both a potentially corruptive favor and an expressive act.

In the first section, I explore the meaning of corruption, fleshing out norms that will be useful in evaluating the eight kinds of corporate political activity. In the second section, I apply those norms, concluding that all eight involve a risk of corruption, although in four cases the kind of corruption risked is less significant than in the other four. My point in making this observation is not to argue that the risk of a less significant form of corruption is itself permissible while that of a more significant form is not. Rather, the distinction will be useful because, as I show in the final section of this chapter, the kinds of democratic expression in which corporations engage can also be classed in an analogous way. In four of the eight kinds of corporate political activity, that expression is more democratically valuable than in the remaining four. In cases where the corruption risked is the less substantial sort, but the expression involved is the more valuable kind, corporations may engage in the practice, possibly with some safeguards. In all other cases—where the expression is less valuable or the corruption risked more serious or both—corporations, I will argue, should not engage in the practice. Both the analysis of the kind of corruption and an understanding of the kinds of expression involved are necessary to make moral judgments on the eight classes of corporate political activity.

Violating Democratic Norms:
The Risk of Corruption

The U.S. Supreme Court has offered a good point of departure for any attempt to specify the democratic norm against corruption. Corruption, the Court declared in *Buckley v. Valeo*, involves a quid pro quo: an officeholder doing something in office in return for money or some other favor provided by another individual or entity (for our purposes, a corporation). The problem, however, is that in principle there can be a quid—the money or favor offered by the business to the official—and a quo—the action taken by the official that benefits the business—without any clear evidence of a pro, that is, that the two are connected. The absence of evidence could result from the fact that such deals are generally made in secret. But, more likely, they are never made explicitly in the first place. The "pro," the connection between quid and quo, might take place only inside the minds of the official and business-person concerned. But of course officials will claim that their decisions were made on the merits, that they were the right thing to do, and that the favor done by the businessperson—whether taking them for lunch to lobby them or contributing to their campaigns—had no influence on them.

Dealing with corruption, accordingly, poses two initial problems. First, in a democratic-pluralistic society in which people have different points of view, the merits of any official decision are likely to be contestable. What this means is that we cannot use the quo itself as indirect evidence for the pro. We cannot simply say: this was a bad decision and therefore the official must have made it under the influence of the favor. There is no independent, objective notion of a bad decision to which we can appeal. Second, because any connection forged between quid and quo will generally exist only in the mind of the official and possibly the businessperson, we cannot directly controvert either when they deny the "pro." Only they have access to the content of their minds.

This is not to deny that political scientists have attempted to determine whether quids and quos are linked by pros. Their findings, however, are conflicting, and concededly limited by their inability to really know for sure.[3] More important, they are ultimately of little normative bearing because citizens are entitled to be spared even the slightest grounds to suspect the existence of a pro. For there are only two alternatives: either we permit businesses to provide quids and officials to provide quos, relying on their unprovable denials of a pro, or we require them to avoid any pattern of quid and quo for which a pro could be inferred. Only a norm of the latter sort can preserve democratic confidence in government.

Here is one candidate for such a norm. On it, an unacceptable risk of corruption—an unacceptable risk that a quid pro quo has occurred—arises whenever an officeholder (1) does something in office—a quo—that favorably affects the interests of a private party, for example, a corporation, from whom the officeholder (2) has received something of value—a quid—for which the officeholder has provided no offsetting private-market consideration in return. Note that it is entirely possible for an officeholder and a private party to be in such a situation without there being any "pro," any connection between quid and quo. But because we can never know that for sure, and because corruption is so corrosive of democratic values, businesspeople and officials should never put themselves in this situation.

Of course, even a norm like this—as does any norm—has its own gray areas. I want to call attention to one kind of gray area in particular, because it will prove to be a key feature distinguishing some of the eight types of corporate political activity from the others. It concerns the quo, the kind of benefit that the corporation receives from the official and its relationship to democratic norms.

First, consider the most serious kind of quo, the one that commentators usually have in mind when they discuss corruption. It arises when a legislator does something in office—in the cases here, something to benefit a corporation—that the legislator would not otherwise have done (the quo) in the wake of, or in advance of, having received a campaign donation from the corporation, say, or a personal gift from its lobbyist (quid(s)). The quo, in other words, involves the legislator changing her positions on a subject of sufficient importance that the legislator had, in fact, developed a prior view concerning it. We might assume that the legislator came to that prior view on the basis of a diligent consideration of the merits, filtered through a genuinely arrived at set of political principles or ideology, but because we cannot peer into the legislator's mind, we cannot know that for sure. All we know is that this view numbers among the positions the legislator arrived at without any extraneous influences, any quids, at play.[4] These positions are the ones the legislator is committed to pursuing in office. They make up the agenda the legislator ran on and for whose execution the legislator has received a democratic mandate from her electorate. Furthermore, the legislator's agenda roughly orders her various issue-positions, such that some are more important to the legislator than others; in office, the legislator will devote a proportionately greater share of her time to those higher up on her agenda.

Against that backdrop, if the quo undertaken in wake of the quid provided by the corporation involves the legislator reversing or even modifying a position she had taken on an agenda issue, then the most serious kind of corruption has occurred—serious, because the quo involves the legislator altering a position that she has been entrusted to execute, a direct violation of democratic norms. It is this kind of quo that many commentators on business corruption of the political process seem to have in mind. Ken Kollman, for example, is most troubled by situations in which, in wake of a quid from a lobbyist, there is a "change [in] policy-makers' decisions."[5] "One common view of business lobbyists," Beth Leech and Frank Baumgartner write, "depicts them as arm-twisters who force government officials to go against their better judgment to do the group's bidding."[6] Likewise with corporate involvement in campaign finance: "Just as bribes cause public officials to do things they otherwise would not do," John Samples writes, "contributions induce legislators to vote in ways that are unexpected given their political ideology, their party identification, the concern of their constituents, or other political variables. That difference indicates the improper influence of money in politics."[7] Mark A. Smith is thinking along similar lines when he writes that "business power is...the ability of business to cause lawmaking to deviate from the path established by public opinion and elections."[8]

If the quo for a quid-dispensing business involves the officeholder actually changing an agenda position, then it risks the greatest threat to democratic norms. Four of the eight kinds of corporate political activity, as we shall see, tend to raise the danger of exactly such full-blown quos. The other four, however, tend more to center on two other kinds of quo. Each of these embodies one half but not the other half of the full-blown type of quo just mentioned and so, by comparison, I will call them "half-quos."

In the wake of a favor done by a lobbyist or a corporate campaign contribution or expenditure (quid), the legislator might, by way of a quo, adopt a new position on a particular issue, but one that lies outside of her agenda. Unexpected issues will constantly emerge on which the legislator has taken no position or on which she holds no strong view. A lobbyist, say, might—after raising contributions for a legislator's campaign—ask her to earmark a $2,000,000 subsidy for a corporate client's new venture. But in complying, the legislator will not have altered her agenda in any way. The legislator will remain committed to pursuing the exact same views on which she campaigned, and to doing so in exactly the order of priorities her agenda had set out.

Usually, the new issue on which the legislator adopts a position will be a "one-off" affair, meaning that her stance on it will carry no implications for—and hence pose no conflict with—the rest of her agenda, requiring no rearrangement in its priorities. At first glance, this kind of quo would seem to involve no violation of democratic norms, in the sense that it necessitates no betrayal of the commitments the legislator made to her constituents. If it is wrong, we will need a further argument as to why, and I will offer one shortly. I note here that corporations are more likely than individuals to seek this kind of half-quo, because corporations are more likely than individuals to care about matters that, while not forming part of a legislator's electoral agenda, will nevertheless come before the legislator for official action. For example, corporations will routinely have interests in new contracts, procurements, grants, tax breaks, and earmarks that deal with off-agenda matters, while individuals are, as a comparative statement, less likely to be in that position. As Issacharoff and Karlan say, there "are a variety of issues on which most voters have no...opinion," such as "all sorts of special-interest pork."[9]

One type of half-quo, then, involves the legislator taking a new position, but on a nonagenda issue. The second type involves an agenda issue, but not a new position on it; instead, it entails a reinforcement, a reemphasis, of the legislator's existing position. Much lobbying, corporate or otherwise, is (as political scientists have observed) so-called "friendly" lobbying.[10] The lobbyist lobbies a legislator who already shares the lobbyist's client's view on a particular issue—here, then, the issue is one on which the legislator does hold an agenda position—but the point of the lobbying is not to change but to reinforce, entrench, and endow the legislator with new arguments and enthusiasm for that already-existing issue position. Corporate involvement in campaign finance often seeks the same result.

In such cases, it cannot be said that the legislator's position on any issue changes as a consequence of the corporation's lobbying or campaign intervention. What could change, though, is the legislator's agenda ordering. For example, a lobbyist, by reinforcing the legislator's position on a particular issue, might cause the legislator to move it higher up on her agenda and devote more time and energy to it at the expense of other matters. The legislator will thus have changed her priorities without changing her position on any issue.

Corporations are more likely than individuals to seek this kind of half-quo because, while corporations might have interests in a greater number of nonagenda items such as contracts and earmarks than individuals do, they also have interests in a smaller number of agenda items. Corporations will—and, indeed, legally are bound to—care about only those (principally economic) issues that affect the corporation, while individuals are more likely to care about the full range of social and moral as well as the economic policy issues on which the legislator takes a stance and which compose her agenda. Caring about only a subsection, perhaps a small subsection, of the issue-positions a legislator takes, a corporation will have an interest in reinforcing them so that they advance up the hierarchy on the legislator's agenda.

So corruption can involve a full quo in which the legislator adopts a new position on an agenda item, or one or the other of two half-quos: the legislator might adopt a new position without altering her agenda, or alter her agenda without adopting a new position. And though half-quos do violate democratic norms, they do not do so to the extent that a full quo does. The point of making such a distinction is that any kind of corporate political activity that habitually risks only half-quos, but involves the most democratically valuable form of political expression (discussed below), will, on balance, be permissible on democratic norms.

What Is Wrong with Half-Quos?

What, if anything, is wrong with the half-quos? Here is one way to begin thinking about them. Whether or not half-quos are less violative of democratic norms against corruption than full quos, they are certainly more violative than official conduct that involves no quid pro quo at all. If it is the case, however, that certain kinds of relationships between legislators and business entities—while entailing absolutely no risk of any kind of quid pro quo—can nevertheless still violate democratic norms, then surely there is something wrong with a half-quo situation, let alone a full quo. And, in fact, this is the case.

Consider, for example, the situation of "private gain from public office": an EPA official, say, is hired by an executive training firm to teach a weekend seminar on a policy issue related to the official's government work. Or a navy procurement officer contracts with a publisher to write a manual on how to do business with the officer's bureau. In these examples, neither element of quid pro quo need be present. First, the private payer—the training firm in the case of the EPA official, for example, or the publisher in the case of the navy procurement official—is not one whose interests the official can in any way affect through her particular government office;

hence there is no possibility of a quo. Second, since the official provides compensating private-market consideration (a lecture, a manual) for whatever pecuniary gain she derives from the paying training or publishing company, she is not formally beholden to it: she has wiped out any quid in a legitimate way through nonofficial services rendered, eliminating any indebtedness.[11]

It is thus "possible to imagine an official who acts impartially, does not play favorites, and is a model of public decorum"—in other words, there is neither quid nor quo—but who nevertheless falls afoul of norms against "the use of public office for private gain."[12] The private gain, of course, is the money the EPA or naval officials are able to earn only because of the knowledge and expertise they have gleaned in public office. What is wrong with this conduct is that the official violates the outward reaches of her fiduciary responsibility. In an abundance of caution, the fiduciary concept does not merely prohibit the fiduciary (i.e., the official) from risking harm to the principal's (i.e., the public's) interests. The fiduciary principle bars the official or fiduciary from profiting from the relationship even if her doing so does not come in any way at the public or principal's expense: even if no injury or impairment is done to the public or principal's interests.[13]

With this understanding of private gain from public office in mind, we can see that while half-quos involve a smaller corruptive risk than full quos, they also pose a greater risk than private gain from public office: they occupy a middle terrain. On the one hand, half-quos in no way involve the legislator in changing a position on an item in her agenda; hence they do not entail a repudiation of any part of her mandate. In that central sense, the performance of a half-quo is less violative of her fiduciary duty—her duty to honor the commitments she has undertaken—than a full quo. On the other hand, half-quos still involve the legislator doing something in office to benefit a corporation from whom she has received a quid, and so in that sense they involve a more serious violation of her fiduciary duty than does private gain from public office. And so half-quos occupy a moral terrain between full quid pro quo and private gain from public office, involving not as substantial a breach of democratic norms as the former, but a greater breach than the latter.

What follows from this? Simply the possibility that a powerful countervailing democratic norm—the value of free expression—might in some cases be sufficient to override our democratically grounded concern with half-quos but fail to do so with full quos. But first, I turn to the eight major kinds of corporate political activity and indicate which of them carry the hazard of full quos, and which half-quos.

FULL QUOS, HALF-QUOS, AND THE EIGHT KINDS OF CORPORATE POLITICAL ACTIVITY

In discussing the eight kinds of corporate political activity, I will employ a device that is common to practical ethics and is particularly suited to moral reasoning about corporate political activity. I have indicated that citizens cannot be expected to determine whether or not a pro, a connection between quid and quo, exists in the mind of a given officeholder. But citizens labor under another obstacle as well: the quo itself, whether full or half, will not always be apparent. We are rightly concerned when a business does a favor—gives a quid in the form of a gift or aids the campaign—for an officeholder who is merely in a position to affect the business's interests, even when no quo, full or half, has evidently been executed. Many congressional ethics rules reflect just this concern.[14]

Why is this? Consider, for example, the type of half-quo in which a legislator reinforces or reemphasizes an existing position she holds on an agenda issue, thereby lending it higher priority. Such a half-quo is unlikely to be apparent. After all, who can tell whether a legislator has subtly adjusted the time or energy with which she advances a particular issue-position favored by a corporate giver?[15] Or consider the half-quo in which the legislator adopts a position on a new issue, one outside of her agenda, such as promoting a corporation's interest in a government contract. Often such a half-quo will itself be executed behind closed doors.

Even full quos—in which a legislator changes or modifies her position on an agenda issue—often will not be immediately clear. Although "health care providers disagree with many of the Democrats' specific proposals," the New York Times reported recently, they are contributing heavily to the presidential campaigns of the leading contenders.[16] The fact that health care providers are giving financial assistance to political candidates with whom they disagree but who can affect their interests is, itself, a source of normative concern—precisely because it risks a full quo. And knowing this is about as much as we may ever know about the situation. That is because agenda positions are frequently broadly stated, not detailed. So even if a Democratic president, say, introduced universal health insurance, it would be impossible to know whether any given detail is less universal in breadth or depth than it otherwise would have been in the absence of the insurance industry's contributions to the president's campaign. In other words, even a full quo, let alone a half-quo or a pro, can remain invisible.

Consequently, I will be classifying some of the eight types of corporate political activity as situations that risk full quos, and others as situations that risk half-quos, not on the basis of any empirical evidence—no adequate data exists—but because of the organizational and structural logic of the eight kinds of activity. Just as every case where one violates the speed limit is not dangerous driving, and every case where one abides by the speed limit is not safe driving, not every case of what I will call "small-money" lobbying will risk only half-quos, nor will every case of "big information" corporate campaign finance risk full quos. Nevertheless, that is what the structure of these kinds of corporate political activity suggests. To do practical moral reasoning, one must reason about, and from, the structure of the situation, determining what norms best apply to it. One must reason, as Dennis Thompson has argued, on the basis of "institutional tendencies"—the tendencies suggested by the organizational structure of the different kinds of corporate political activity.[17] This is how I proceed here.

Corporate Lobbying I: Big Money, Small Information

The first kind of corporate political activity is what I will call "big-money" lobbying: "big" because the lobbyist raises a large number of campaign contributions for a legislator from the lobbyist's corporate clients or colleagues. Given that any one individual may contribute only $2,300 annually to a candidate's campaign, lobbyists who can "bundle" large numbers of such contributions for a particular legislator provide a valuable quid. The telecommunications corporation SBC, whose lobbyists raised $1.8 million in bundled contributions for federal legislators during the 2004 election cycle, did so, as spokesman Dave Pacholczyk says, because "our future as a regulated company—as one of the most heavily regulated companies in the country—depends on the decision of policy-makers. We need to make sure policy-makers are educated and informed on the issues." Or, as one newspaper report put it, SBC "wants to convince lawmakers and regulators that it has sufficiently opened its local markets to competition and that it should therefore face fewer rules governing how it sells access to its network to rivals."[18]

The question here is: what kind of quo—full or half—is there an "institutional tendency" for the legislator to perform in light of the bundling quid? The barely veiled statements about "educat[ing]," "inform[ing]," and "convincing" legislators are suggestive. There is nothing about the structure of the big-money lobbying situation— unlike some other kinds of lobbying we will examine—to inhibit or bar a full quo, that is, the danger that a recipient legislator will change or modify a position she holds. Moreover, the lobbyist's campaign fundraising, unlike (say) a gift of hospitality or a donation to the legislator's favorite charity, provides not a personal but a political resource. The legislator may well calculate that the votes she can win by using the bundled money cancels out any she might lose by changing her position on an agenda issue.

The situational structure differs with a second kind of lobbying, what I will call "small-information" lobbying. Instead of presenting educative or informative briefs or testimony to legislators in their offices or other official settings, at issue here are lobbyists stealing moments to make a pitch for a corporate client or employer in nonofficial social situations such as cocktail receptions or the legislator's favorite charity golfing event. The information is "small" in the sense that the constraints of time—usually only a few minutes are involved, and space, usually the forum is widely attended—circumscribe the amount of information that the lobbyist can impart to the legislator.

Consider, as an example, a reception that United Technologies president George David held for members of Congress, many of them overseeing Pentagon contracts that the corporation was seeking, at the National Gallery of Art. It was "a night to drink in Vermeer's magic, sift through the capital's juiciest gossip, and," as the *Hartford Courant* put it, "talk a little—just a little—about business."[19] With small-information lobbying, there will either be many legislators with ears to bend at once, as with the United Technologies reception, or one legislator with many lobbyists bending the legislator's ear, as when lobbyists buy a ticket to a legislator's favorite charity golf tournament, and in return get to play a few holes with the legislator.

Now: Is it justifiable to treat such "small information" lobbying as posing a less significant corruptive risk than "big money" lobbying? I believe it is, but not for the reason typically advanced. On that typical argument, the quid—the corporate lobbyist's hosting a reception for many legislators, or, along with many lobbyists, donating to a charity favored by a particular legislator—is too small to cause any given legislator to feel indebted. If the correspondingly "small" information (the "little talk about business") imparted happens to sway the legislator, it could therefore be only because the legislator finds it persuasive on the merits.[20] The normative problem, on this argument, is that other groups—nonbusiness groups who do not have the capacity to contribute to charity events or host receptions—do not have similar access. And so, although the legislator may genuinely accept the lobbyist's perspective on the merits, she will not have been exposed to an opposing view. Although the legislator's perspective might not be corrupted, it can become skewed. In the language of quid pro quo, the concern is that a legislator might well change her mind on an agenda issue—a full blown quo—but do it because her views, her best judgment, have really (in the absence of her hearing any opposing arguments from nonbusiness groups) changed, not because she is returning a favor: hence, there is no pro.

The concern here may be legitimate. But it is really a critique of democratic norms themselves, not an objection to a practice that violates those norms. The fact is that for any number of reasons, some every bit as capricious and fortuitous as one's having the means to access a charity event or host a reception, legislators are always going to get snatches of information from some sources but not others. Their staffers will always have more access to them than their supporters; some supporters will have more access than some constituents; their friends and family might trump all of them, and so on. We also expect and hope that new information can change a legislator's genuine views. Neither the haphazard lopsidedness of the information legislators receive, nor their changing their minds genuinely on the basis of receiving it, violate democratic norms—or at least the norms of any democracy that currently exists. One can certainly critique those norms— one can certainly advance a vision of democracy on which access to a legislator is perfectly equally allotted to all sides of any given issue—but that is not an extant norm. It may or may not be worth reforming democratic systems so that they come closer to that ideal. But that would not be a principle of business ethics, a principle as to how business should conduct itself in dealing with democratic government as it is.

If the concern with small-information lobbying is merely unequal access, then there is no obligation on business lobbyists not to engage in it. But there is another way of looking at what is ethically troubling about "small-information" lobbying. On the one hand, it is too hasty to say that the lobbyist's donation to a charity event, or the lobbyist's hosting of a reception, represent quids so insignificant that the legislator will not feel any indebtedness or gratitude, any obligation to do something in return. For embedded in our norm against corruption is the fact that we can never look into a legislator's mind and exclude the possibility of a "pro." On the other hand, we can look at the external structure of the small-information situation—at the fact that it takes place at receptions and charity events—and if that structure itself acts to restrict the magnitude of the quo, then we can draw reasonable conclusions about the ethics of the conduct concerned. If we do so, we will see that the institutional tendency of the small-information situation is for it to risk the two kinds of half-quos.

Small information, taking place as it does in hurried and crowded encounters, is, as a statement about "institutional tendencies," too brief—too small—to be able to overcome a contrary existing view that the legislator holds;[21] too small to routinely risk full quos.

It is more likely, as with the first type of half-quo, that in the time allotted, the lobbyist can merely reinforce a legislator's already existing view of a particular issue, and in so doing, raise the issue to a higher level of salience: shifting the issue's place in the legislator's agenda, but not her position on it. It is also possible—as with the second type of half-quo—to bring to the legislator, at a reception or charity event, small information that supports a position favorable to the lobbyist's corporate client or employer, but on an issue of sufficient unimportance to the legislator that it lies outside her agenda, an issue the legislator had previously not known or at least not particularly cared about. Here, the small-information lobbyist induces the legislator to take a position on a new issue without shifting her agenda. A "lot of issues... are low in importance for the representative," lobbyist John Plebani says, such that the representative has no position on them.[22] Concerning such issues, "legislators often [find] it difficult to assess the issue's relevance to their constituents, so other variables (such as lobbying) could tip the balance."[23]

So small-information corporate lobbying does not, as a statement about institutional tendencies—about the structural constraints that allow for just "a little talk about business"—lead legislators to change their considered positions on an issue. If small-information lobbying is going to cause a legislator to take a new position, it will be on an issue outside the legislator's agenda, about which the legislator had not previously thought or cared. If it is going to deal with an issue within the legislator's agenda, it will typically reinforce a position that the legislator already holds, possibly causing the legislator to lend it a higher priority. Small-information lobbying tends to risk half-quos.

Corporate Lobbying II: Small Money, Big Information

We can now turn to the two other kinds of corporate lobbying, what I will call "small-money" and "big-information" lobbying. "Small-money" lobbying involves not six- or seven-figure bundles of campaign contributions, but the twenty-five dollar meals on the lobbyist's tab that some representatives or senators fight so hard to preserve, and other "gifts and favors considered desirable yet negligible in value, such as catered food, flowers, candy,... rides to work, [and] tickets to athletic events."[24] It is true that such gifts can, if they come fast and furiously, add up to sizeable money. But congressional ethics regulations limit them, and the question is whether, even within limits, there is anything wrong with small-money lobbying. As

Frank Coleman, senior lobbyist at the Distilled Spirits Council puts it, it is "critically important for lobbyists to be able to engage at length with [legislators and their staff] on their issues…Obviously, meals…make sure you've got [that] chance."[25]

The typical critique mounted against small-money lobbying, however, fails to grasp the ethical issue involved. That typical concern is that small gifts are able to make the legislator, unconsciously and by degrees, genuinely warmer, better disposed, and more inclined to take the lobbyist's view; such gifts are thought to subtly alter what the legislator truly does believe, on the merits. A recent article analyzes this phenomenon in the case of doctors receiving pens or notepads from drug companies and who—as a result—naturally and imperceptibly come to believe in the companies' products.[26] A big monetary gift would offend them, but precisely because a small gift cannot "buy" them, they let their guard down. There seems to be no reason why the same should not be true for politicians. While a big monetary gift can make a legislator feel uncomfortable toward a lobbyist, it will also make the legislator feel beholden. The problem with small gifts, on this argument, is that while they may not make a legislator feel beholden, they can make the legislator come to genuinely feel comfortable with the lobbyist—and with the views the lobbyist represents.

Let me push this a little further because, again, it cannot be wrong, *per se*, for politicians to genuinely change their views on particular issue positions because they have developed a personal trust in or warmth for those arguing for the changes. Worded this way, the concern would be that while there may be a full quo—a legislator might change her position on an agenda issue, just as a doctor might change his prescribing habits—there's no pro. Small money, on this argument, causes the legislator to change an issue-position because she has been persuaded on the merits by someone whose views and judgment she has come to trust and feel comfortable with, not because—though she actually believes it is the wrong thing to do—she is paying back someone who has bought her lunch over the years. But understood this way, small-money lobbying ultimately involves no violation of democratic norms. Legislators cannot function without giving relatively greater credence to the views of individuals whom they have grown to trust. Democratic functioning is compatible with this inevitable kind of inequality, and so there can be no obligation on a corporate lobbyist to avoid it.

This, however, does not mean that small-money lobbying accords with democratic norms. It is just that the democratic-normative issue is a different one. In small-money situations, we cannot, in fact, exclude the possibility of a pro, the possibility that the legislator's views shift because of a feeling of gratitude for lunches over the years, and not simply by a consideration of the merits as presented by someone trusted. We cannot exclude that possibility because, as noted above, we cannot look into the legislator's mind. We can, however, look to the external, visible structure of the small-money situation and draw from it general conclusions about the kinds of quo involved. Doing so, we will see that the institutional tendency is for small-money quos to be half-quos.

It is true that with small money, the lobbyist, slowly and over lengthy periods, and in iterative steps assisted by meals and other small tokens, aims to build a relationship with the legislator, so that gradually the legislator will develop an affinity for the lobbyist, coming to trust him. But for precisely this reason, small-money lobbying can be considered unlikely to cause legislators to change their positions on agenda items—unlikely, that is, to seek a full quo. After all, the entire point of the slow and steady encounters facilitated by small money is to enable the lobbyist to develop a relationship of trust with the legislator. Its purpose is to make the legislator view the lobbyist as simpatico across the broad range of issues about which the legislator cares—her agenda.

That is why lobbyists with Republican sympathies tend to lobby Republicans, and likewise with Democrats. Via meals and other such small relationship-building acts, a "lobbyist and legislator get to know one another," and as they do, "mutual confidence, trust, and understanding grow."[27] As Nolan McCarty and Lawrence S. Rothenberg put it, "politicians, usually legislators, need time to develop trust in the information that they receive from organizations" such as corporations and interest groups.[28] Such time is afforded by small acts of hospitality over long periods, and the point, as McCarty and Rothenberg make clear, is not to force the legislator into taking a position in which she does not believe, but to develop a relationship of trust, based on a demonstrated political like-mindedness, with the legislator across her agenda of issue positions.

Understood in this way, the institutional tendencies of small-money lobbying channel it toward seeking one or the other kind of half-quo. First, small-money lobbying can allow the lobbyist, at the right time, to get the legislator to adopt a position on a new issue, one lying outside of her agenda. The lobbyist says to the legislator, in effect, "here's how to extrapolate your agenda, that philosophy that you and I share, to reach a stand on this new question. What I am proposing fits in with your already existing agenda; it is compatible." Second, small money can enable the lobbyist to use his relationship with the legislator to change the priority the legislator gives to an agenda issue, but not the view she holds on it. If the lobbyist tried to change the legislator's view, he would be eroding the trust he would have built with the legislator by emphasizing their mutual simpatico. To do so would be to eat into the social capital the lobbyist has built; instead, the lobbyist wants to earn returns from it. To do so, though, the lobbyist must either extend their shared agenda to a new issue or reinforce a shared existing position on an agenda issue, but not attempt to get the legislator to adopt a new position on an agenda issue. As a matter of institutional tendencies, small-money lobbying thus tends to risk half-quos.

Now I want to turn to the last kind of lobbying, "big-information" lobbying. Here, the lobbyist is not merely building a relationship over time in social settings, but is actually entering the legislator's office or participating in closed committee sessions and drafting legislation for the legislator. Such drafts are what I call "big information," since, in an obvious sense, they represent the most extensive conceivable reach of lobbyist information provision, injected as it is into the very core of the legislative process. In 1995, Republican senator Slade Gorton of Washington wanted to move some amendments to the Endangered Species Act. The amendments' principal effect would have been to weaken the act by requiring the secretary of the interior to give an affirmative answer to the question, "Is this species so important that a single person should lose their job over it?," before acting to protect it. Lobbyists from lumber or utility groups drafted the amendments for Gorton, and when queried about it, he acknowledged, "I don't think [this is] how good public policy should be made, but I'm perfectly willing to get the free services of good lawyers in drafting my views."[29]

In a turnabout of the troubling tendency for legislators to persuade lobbyists to hire their former staff, legislators—with big-information lobbying—are getting their staff-work done by lobbyists. As Richard L. Hall and Alan V. Deardorff write, legislators would face a substantial "budgetary problem" if they had to construct such legislation, policy, and amendments on their own. Hence, Hall and Deardorff say, its provision by a lobbyist represents a "grant or income supplement" to the legislator.[30] It represents a quid, or, as Senator Gorton puts it, "free services."

As for the quo, there is nothing in the external structure of such situations to exclude the possibility of a full quo. It is true that when it comes to the immediate issue, the Endangered Species Act, the senator's existing views get reinforced. But this is not a situation in which the senator expends greater staff and resources on an existing issue position in response to a quid from a lobbyist; that would be a half-quo. Instead, the quid itself is the provision of staff and resources by the lobbyist, which leaves open the question as to what the quo might be. That is why it is Senator Gorton who feels he got a gift, not the industry.

There is nothing, then, in the institutional tendencies of big-information lobbying to constrain the lobbyist from later approaching the legislator for a full quo on a matter entirely different from the one for which the lobbyist has provided the big information, asking the legislator to change an already existing issue position in her agenda. The lobbyist's gift of bill drafting, as Hall and Deardorff say, constitutes "income"—cash—because it is fungible: it saves staff and resources that the legislator can devote to other items. Of course, this cash—this money freed up in the legislator's official budget—can be used only for political purposes, the purposes of advancing the legislator's political agenda, and not for personal purposes such as food, drink, and recreation. Still, it may well be that those saved resources, suitably redeployed, will allow the legislator to reap more votes than she will lose from changing an agenda position, as a full quo for the lobbyist, on some issue other than the one for which the lobbyist has provided the staff and resources.

A kind of divide, then, emerges from the four major areas of corporate lobbying. Big money (lobbyists bundling campaign contributions for the legislator) and big information (lobbyists providing staff and resources to furnish legislative content) contain no structural impediments to a legislator's delivery of a full quo. With small information (lobbyists buttonholing legislators at receptions and charity events) and small money (lobbyists extending personal hospitality to the legislator), by contrast, the structure of the situation—its institutional tendencies—work against full quos and more toward half-quos. Whether corporations should engage in any of them remains to be seen below when the expressive values of the different forms of lobbying will be weighed against their corruptive potential. I note that lobbyists often combine tactics. So, for example, a lobbyist might impart small information to a legislator at a reception against the background of the lobbyist's having recently raised some big money for the legislator. But in principle, small information and big money take place as business lobbying practices in and of themselves, and so they each should bear scrutiny to determine the kinds of corruption they bring on their own.

Corporate Campaign Finance I: Small Money, Big Money

Corporate involvement in political campaigns also breaks into categories that can usefully be labeled "small money," "big money," "small information" and "big information." Although, as we shall see, these terms each carry a different meaning than their counterparts in lobbying, they still offer a useful way of carving up different types of corporate involvement in campaign finance. Let me turn to the corruptive potential of each in turn, beginning with money, small and big.

"Small money" consists of financial contributions made directly to candidates for the purposes of aiding their campaigns. For a century, corporations have been barred from making such contributions out of corporate treasuries. A corporation can do so only via its political action committee (PAC), a separate entity managed by the corporation but whose funds come from the "voluntary" (and limited) donations of corporate employees, officers, or shareholders. The contributions that corporate PACs, in turn, can make to candidate campaigns are capped in amount by law at $5,000 annually.[31] Hence, for purposes here—because corporations can make no such contributions directly and only in a limited way via PACs—I will refer to corporate contributions to candidate campaigns as "small money" (though the generally used term for them is "hard money"). A particularly revealing example occurred in 1993 when NAFTA was before Congress: corporate PACs supporting the agreement gave amounts totaling in the millions of dollars in direct small-money contributions to legislators' campaign funds. Referring to these contributions, the White House NAFTA coordinator William Daley said, "Money is an important ingredient [in winning support for NAFTA]. It's getting too important."[32]

Until recently, however, any given corporation could make unlimited contributions, directly from its own treasury funds, to a political party for so-called party-building purposes, in particular, voter-registration and get-out-the-vote initiatives targeted at the party's supporters. Such contributions are meant to benefit the party as a whole and its entire slate of candidates. Consequently, it is illegal to channel them toward any individual candidate's campaign.[33] Due to the so-called Levin amendment to the Bipartisan Campaign Reform Act (BCRA), these voter-mobilizing contributions are now limited to $10,000 a year. But by exploiting loopholes in BCRA, it is still possible for corporations to contribute unlimited amounts to organizations that are formally independent of the parties. These organizations can then use this money for, among other things, the mobilization of voters supportive of a particular party.[34]

The allowable amounts here are considerably greater than those just discussed regarding "small-money" corporate contributions to individual candidate campaigns. Consequently, I will call such contributions for partisan voter mobilization "big money" (though here the generally used term is "soft money"). A typical example of such big- money contributions occurred in 2002, when Westar Energy of Kansas ponied up $25,000 to the Republican Party in hopes of getting a favorable provision inserted in an energy bill. As the firm's vice president for public affairs, Doug Lawrence, wrote in a company e-mail explaining the contribution, "[Tom] DeLay is the House majority leader. His agreement is necessary before the House conferees can push the language we have in place in the House bill."[35]

Is there any good normative reason, as the different limitations imposed by the law suggest there might be, why corporate contributions to individual candidates for their campaigns should be thought to pose a greater corruptive risk than corporate contributions to parties for voter mobilization? And if so, what would that imply about whether—and how—the ethical corporation should engage in each? One possible response is that because legislators themselves, not parties, are the ones who deliver quos, we have less reason to fear corruption when contributions go to parties, not legislators' own campaigns. As Nathaniel Persily puts it, a "candidate allegedly will not feel beholden to a contributor whose money principally benefits the party and only indirectly benefits the candidate."[36] Along similar lines, a recent legal brief declared that "a candidate will feel less indebted...to a donor for contributing [big money], which will affect his own election only indirectly and partially (if at all) than to another donor who contributes [small money], which can be used directly and entirely to support his election."[37]

Such arguments, however, involve a speculation about the pro, the feeling of "indebtedness" or "beholdenness" that might (or might not) exist in the legislator's mind as a result of party-voter-mobilization donations compared with contributions for the legislator's own campaign. Such observations do not get around the democratic norm that, since we can never know whether a pro does or does not exist, assurances or guesses that a pro does not exist cannot defeat the public's right to feel certain that it does not. Even though Westar contributed big money to the Republican Party, not to DeLay's own campaign, Doug Lawrence evidently believed that DeLay would feel indebted as a result. Instead, I will argue, the difference between big money contributions for party-voter-mobilization and small-money contributions to candidate campaigns is this: Big-money party contributions invite a kind of quo that the external structure of the situation tends to constrain, making it into a half-quo. No similar constraint operates with small-money candidate contributions, where the risk is of a full quo.

Big money mobilizes voters who have already decided to support the party, and hence its candidates, because they agree with its (and their) overall ideology, with its positions across a range of issues. What the big-money party-voter-mobilization contributor is doing, then, is paying for overt support of a recognized partisan agenda, and that support will have value to any given candidate only if she sticks to that agenda on the range of issues it contains. If the candidate veers from it, as a favor for the contributor, she risks alienating some of that support. The value to the candidate of a big-money contribution to the party, which is restricted to delivering party voters, will thus necessarily diminish if she changes her position on a party agenda issue.

This structural element restricts the possibility of full quos in the case of big-money party-voter-mobilization contributions. The most that a candidate can deliver by way of a quo, without eroding the value of a big-money quid, would be for her to adopt a view on an issue on which she, and potential party supporters, have held no prior view: a half-quo. Such "issues … are [not] ideological, partisan … and salient," but "narrower, less visible issues" that lack the usually dominant influences of party, district, leadership, and mass opinion."[38] In other words, they tend to be nonagenda items, such as the technical changes Westar wanted to see inserted into the energy bill.

By contrast, small-money contributions made directly to a candidate's campaign are not restricted, in their usage, to bringing out voters who will be of value to the candidate only as long as she sticks close to their views across a range of issues. Small-money contributions to specific candidate campaigns are not "in kind" in this way; they take the form of cash that can be used by the candidate for any campaign purpose, including the effort not only to get out voters who agree with her but to advertise to win voters who are not currently supporters. Small-money contributions can retain their full utility for the candidate, then, even if she alters her position on an agenda issue as a full quo to the contributor. Having altered her position, the candidate can use the money to win over new voters on that issue or on any others. Many of the ultimately pro-NAFTA legislators who received small-money contributions to their campaigns were initially dubious about the agreement.

There is thus a difference—a difference in the structure of the situation—between corporate contributions to parties for voter mobilization and to candidates for their campaigns. It is not a difference in the extent of the pro, the extent of the indebtedness felt by the legislator, in either case, for that is something we cannot measure, and we cannot exclude the possibility of its existing in either case. The only difference we can identify, the observable structural difference, is that the quos involved in party-voter-mobilization contributions encounter a kind of constraint—an inhibition on changing positions on agenda issues—that does not exist in the case of contributions to candidate campaigns. The institutional tendencies are for big-money contributions for party voter mobilization to risk half-quos, and small-money contributions for individual candidacies to risk full quos.

Corporate Campaign Finance II: Big Information, Small Information

Finally, the domain of campaign finance also displays its own versions of what might be called "small information" and "big information." Both involve expenditures made by a corporation, or its PAC, on its own campaign-related advertising, that is, the conveyance of political information directly to the electorate, as opposed to monetary contributions to candidates or parties. The difference between "small" and "big" information is this: "Small information" consists of advertising that advances the corporation's position on a particular policy issue, but excludes mention of any candidate, and so any effect it might have on a candidate election is indirect. "Big information" ads support a candidate; "big information" is an apt term for such candidate-oriented ads because they in effect communicate support for an entire agenda of issue positions—that of the candidate—while "small information" communicates support for just one particular issue position. Corporations are legally permitted to fund small-information (i.e., issue-focused) ads from their treasuries, and to do so in unlimited amounts, but they can fund big–information (i.e., candidate-oriented) ads only out of their PACs.

Is there any normative reason why corporate small-information (issue-focused) advertising should—as the law seems to imply—be deemed less troubling than big-information (candidate-oriented) ads? Again, there is a common—but, I believe, unsatisfactory—answer to this question. Even if an issue ad takes the same view of a particular policy matter that a candidate does, this argument goes, the candidate—not being referenced in this kind of small-information ad—will benefit only indirectly, namely, to the extent that viewers know the candidate's stance and are prepared to vote for her on that issue. The candidate in question would therefore have a minimal reason to feel grateful. Think, for example, of the insurance industry's famous $10 million "Harry and Louise" ad campaign in 1993, in which a worried couple pored over the Clinton health plan. Though the ads argued a Republican position, it was only one position in an extensive Republican agenda. They did not mention any candidate by name, and—so the argument goes—any sense of indebtedness on the part of any particular Republican candidate would have been insignificant.

By contrast, the candidate herself would be the explicit focus of an electioneering (big information) ad, and would hence derive from it a greater advantage, thus feeling more indebted. Green Mountain Energy investor Sam Wyly spent $2.5 million during the 2000 Republican primaries supporting George W. Bush and attacking his opponent, John McCain. The ad campaign was given some measurable credit for Bush's victory. And commentators have speculated as to what kind of debt the Bush administration might have felt it owed Wyly and his company.[39]

On the typical argument, then, corporate small-information (issue-focused) ads are less violative of democratic norms than corporate big-information (candidate-oriented) ads because, in the former case, any given candidate will feel less indebted, less beholden to do something in return. This argument, however, in fact does not conform to democratic norms. According to those norms, voters should not have to even entertain speculations as to the existence or magnitude of a pro in the mind of the politician. We simply cannot rule out the possibility that Newt Gingrich appreciated and felt grateful to the insurance industry for the boost Harry and Louise gave to the Republican cause, however indirect.[40]

There is, though, a way of viewing the external structure of the two kinds of corporate information-dissemination that would allow us to classify—as a matter of "institutional tendencies"—the quo typically risked in issue advertising as less disturbing of democratic functioning than the quo generally risked in candidate advertising. As a statement about the structural tendencies of the situation, small-information advertising in support of a particular position on a given issue tends to risk a half-quo: it will induce any candidate holding the same issue position in her agenda to lend it more emphasis or a heightened priority.

Issue advertising, though it cannot (thanks to BCRA) mention a candidate's name, will obviously be of value to the candidate only to the extent that it supports a position the candidate already holds. In that sense, it is a form of in-kind support for her, and it exerts an influence on her behavior, as all in-kind assistance does. In this case, the assistance—the ad's support for a particular issue position—becomes more valuable to the candidate precisely to the extent that she elevates that issue-position in her agenda and emphasizes her commitment to it. Those Republican candidates who underscored their opposition to the Clinton health care proposal were most likely to benefit from the Harry and Louise ads. And, by increasing popular support for that position via the ad, the insurance industry provided additional political reason for candidates to act with greater alacrity on it in office. Issue advertising carries a ready-made structure channeling any quo the candidate makes into the half-quo sort, leading her not to change but reemphasize an agenda issue-position: the one that the ad supports.

Corporate sponsorship of big–information advertising, by contrast, does not similarly constrain the quo a candidate might deliver. Such advertising is focused on the candidate herself, and either explicitly or implicitly on her general agenda, instead of any particular issue. It is entirely possible that such advertising would do a candidate more good than any particular change in an already-existing issue position in her agenda—as a quo for the corporate backer—will do her harm.[41] She would have to calculate whether the votes she might lose via that change would be compensated by the support she would pick up with the ad. Certainly Sam Wyly sought to divert the Bush administration toward a more proactive clean-energy stance—something that would benefit his company, Green Mountain—and he acknowledged that such a stance was not part of the president's agenda. In criticizing Wyly, Daniel Becker of the Sierra Club—who is also sympathetic to a proactive clean-energy stance—nevertheless said, "even if he [Wyly] were giving our position [on] the government's energy plan," the money he spent aiding Bush "smells to high heaven."[42] Becker's criticism here—a legitimate one—is that Wyly's support of Bush could easily have induced Bush to shift his environmental position, which in turn would suggest that whatever support Bush might have lost among opponents of green energy by changing his position (quo) would be worth the broader support (quid) the ad would have attracted.

It is for this reason, rooted in the differing institutional tendencies of the two situations, that issue advertising runs a lower risk of violating democratic norms than candidate advertising. It is not that the pro, the candidate's feeling of indebtedness, is less significant with issue advertising; we cannot know that. Rather, with issue advertising, the structure of the situation furnishes a constraint that makes the legislator's act more likely to be a half-quo, one that involves no change in any issue position in her agenda.

WEIGHING THE EXPRESSIVE RIGHTS AND GOODS INVOLVED IN CORPORATE POLITICAL ACTIVITY AGAINST THE CORRUPTIVE RISKS

Having assessed the differing degrees of harm these various kinds of corporate political activity risk for democratic functioning (table 17.1), I now turn to weigh the countervailing value they provide. Such values ultimately have to do with the nature of the political expression involved in each of the eight cases.

Freedom of expression is both a democratic right and a democratic good. It is a right because each individual is best qualified to speak for herself and to assert her own views in public debate, and this right applies not just to any given individual but to any association of individuals, such as corporations. Freedom of expression is a good insofar as the more viewpoints that are expressed, the more likely we are to reach good policy decisions.

The *Buckley* Court usefully fleshed out these twin notions of right and good. The democratic right of free expression, the Court observed, requires that speech should enjoy greater protection to the extent that it reflects the speaker's own views, views she herself has come to on the basis of her own reasoned consideration, as opposed to her merely voicing the views of another. The democratic good of free expression—the good of coming to the best policy decision—suggests, as the *Buckley* Court also observed, that speech should enjoy greater protection to the extent that it offers reasoned argumentation, as opposed to expression that is merely symbolic or that simply signals one's preferences without providing a rationale.

The *Buckley* Court confined its usage of these criteria to an examination of campaign contributions. But in fact they offer a useful moral guide for assessing all

Table 17.1. Corruptive Risks

Full Quo: New Position on Agenda Issue	Half Quo: New Position on Non-Agenda Issue	Half Quo: No New Position but New Agenda Ordering
Big Money Lobbying	Small Info Lobbying	Small Info Lobbying
Big Info Lobbying	Small Money Lobbying	Small Money Lobbying
Small Money Corporate Campaign Finance	Big Money Corporate Campaign Finance	Small Info Corporate Campaign Finance
Big Info Corporate Campaign Finance		

eight kinds of corporate political activity—for determining which involve the most democratically valuable speech and which fall short. Just because an act of speech falls short, I emphasize, does not mean that there is anything wrong with corporations engaging in it in itself. The point is that, if it is exercised either via or along with the kinds of quids we have been discussing, it might do more harm on democratic corruptive norms—depending on the kinds of quos it risks—than benefit on democratic expression norms.

A given act of political expression, then, fulfills the speaker's democratic rights most fully when it reflects the speaker's own reasoned, thought-out views. But unfortunately, we can never know in a direct way whether this has happened, since that would require our looking into the speaker's mind. Similarly, a given act of political expression most fully conduces to the democratic good of reaching the best decision when it is well reasoned and argued. But, unfortunately, we can never know directly whether this is the case, since that would require our pluralistic society to agree on the strengths of various argumentative claims. Instead, we have to look to the external structure of each particular speech situation involved in the eight kinds of corporate political activity to determine whether—as a matter of structural tendencies—the expression involved likely reflects the speaker's own reasoned views and/or is expressed in a reasoning manner. Sometimes it will do neither, sometimes one but not the other, and sometimes it will do both. Only in the latter kinds of cases can we say that the speech is the most democratically valuable sort. And then, for each of the eight kinds of corporate political activity, we must balance its expressive value against the corruption risked—full quo or half-quo—to determine whether democratic norms are ultimately better served by allowing or prohibiting it.

More specifically, the expressive rights and goods involved in a given corporate political activity must be more significant than the corruptive risks for it be an ethical one. In such cases, the centrality to democracy of expression that represents an exercise of rights and conduces to the good, and the fact that we are talking not about corruption *per se* but the risk of corruption, argues for permissibility. But if the corruptive risks are as significant as or even more significant than the expressive rights and goods involved, then the activity in question is unethical.

Lobbying: Reasoned Beliefs, Reasoning Speech

Recall that in cases of "big-money" lobbying, the lobbyist, having raised substantial sums for a legislator's campaign, then communicates with the legislator on behalf of a corporate client or employer. The twin criteria for assessing the democratically valuable nature of such communications are these: Are the views being expressed the lobbyist's own—that is, a reflection of the speaker's own reasoned thoughts—or are they the views of others? And are they being expressed in a reasoning way, that is, with arguments and justifications, or less articulately in the form more of a gesture of support?

The views that the corporate lobbyist expresses are not his own as a citizen, but those of others who have hired him. Given that the lobbyist would not be uttering those views but for the fact that he has been retained either by a corporate client or a corporate employer, it is reasonable to say that such views were not fully generated by his unencumbered, reasoned consideration of the merits. Instead, his adopting them would have been motivated right from the beginning by extraneous pecuniary considerations. In discussing a particular policy debate, lobbyist Wayne Thevenot told the journalist Jeffrey Birnbaum: "Who's got the better argument is anybody's guess. That's one I don't feel strongly about one way or the other…I don't have a dog in that fight, and don't have a position…I will have a position as soon as I get a dog."[43] Such sentiments do not reflect the most robust exercise of the democratic right of expression.

True, corporations can express their views only through agents, such as lobbyists. But only lobbyists as individuals—not as corporate agents—are entitled to dispense the quid: in this case, raise bundled contributions for legislators' campaigns. Such activity is prohibited to corporations as entities, and hence to agents acting on their behalf. The question of whose expressive rights are to be evaluated, for purposes of balancing the rights and goods of democratic expression against the risk of corruption, is governed by the consideration of who is threatening the corruption. The answer here is that it is the lobbyist as a person, not as a corporate agent. And as a matter of situational tendencies, the lobbyist is not, as Thevenot's statement suggests, expressing his own reasoned views.

Now, is there any reason—any tendency in the structure of the big-money lobbying situation—to believe that political expression by lobbyists to legislators will take the form of mere unreasoned gestures of support for a particular issue position, thereby failing to advance the democratic good that public decisions be fully informed? No. In fact, more the opposite is the tendency. Big-money lobbyists operate under no structural constraint against providing the legislator with as much argumentative ammunition as they can. As Dave Pacholczyk says, SBC's lobbyists, who engaged in big-money fundraising, sought to "educate" and "inform" legislators.

As a statement about the structural tendencies of his situation, then, the corporate lobbyist-fundraiser falls short on one of the two criteria of democratically valuable political expression. That expression may take reasoning form, but it does not represent the speaker's, that is, the lobbyist's, own reasoned beliefs. In addition, big-money lobbying—as shown above—harbors no structural tendencies precluding the most serious form of corruption, a full quo. Given that the expression involved is not the most valuable, while the quo risked is the most serious, it violates on balance democratic norms for corporate lobbyists to bundle campaign contributions for candidates. Attempts are repeatedly made to prohibit the practice through regulation; so far they have failed. But whatever the state of the law, *corporate big-money lobbying—that is, campaign fundraising by corporate lobbyists—is not justifiable on democratic norms.*

Now what of small-information lobbying? What of the lobbyist buttonholing a senator at a reception, or on a golf course, with a pitch for a client or employer? Again, the question arises as to whose expressive rights are to be evaluated—the corporation's, given that the lobbyist is its agent, or the lobbyist himself as an individual. The institutional tendencies suggest that it is the lobbyist himself. Businesses cannot deduct lobbying expenses. So even though a corporation itself might pay for a reception it holds for legislators, if it lists the expense as a business deduction—as it would have a normal tendency and an incentive to do—then any small-information lobbying done at the event would have to be constructively undertaken by its employees as individuals.[44] As for charity events, certainly "third-party" or "hired-gun" lobbyists or lobbying firms, not their corporate clients, pay for the tickets, and while there is nothing preventing a corporation from paying for its employee to attend a charity event, the greater constraints that govern corporate as opposed to individual charitable contributions create an institutional tendency for the lobbyist as an individual to be the dispenser of the quid.

Under these circumstances, it is the lobbyist himself, not the corporation, whose exercise of expressive rights has to be weighed. And again, the structure of the situation—namely, that the lobbyist is being paid to express the views of a corporate client or employer—tends to diminish the likelihood that the lobbyist is expressing his own considered views, views he came to on a reasoned, unencumbered consideration of the merits. It falls short of being the fullest kind of exercise of the right of democratic expression.

But does the small-information lobbyist at least express his client's or his employer's views with a full set of reasons and arguments, thus contributing to the democratic good of informed decision making? The structure of small-information lobbying—born of access at a cocktail party, or a golf event, or any such rushed or packed venue—suggests a negative response. All that is possible, as a general statement, are brief snatches of argument that communicate (to borrow from *Buckley*) more a "general expression of support for the . . . view"—and possibly "a rough index of the intensity of the [lobbyist's] support"—"but . . . not . . . the underlying basis for it." All that is possible, as with George David's reception for United Technologies, is a "little" talk about business.

Neither expressive of his own reasoned, considered views, nor communicated by him in a fully reasoned, informative way, the lobbyist's small-information expression, as a matter of institutional tendencies, falls short on both criteria of democratically valuable expression.[45] Small-information lobbying's structural tendency is also to fall short of threatening the most democratically destructive form of corruption. It poses only half-quo risks, risks that the legislator will either adopt a new position on a nonagenda item or else shift her agenda without adopting any new positions within it. Even so, since the speech involved is far from the most democratically valuable, and since half-quos are violative of democratic norms even if not in the most serious way, *small-information lobbying— lobbying at receptions, charitable events or in other widely attended social venues—is not a democratically justifiable practice.*

What of big information—the kind of information that involves lobbyists writing legislation or policy for the legislator? Since the corporation itself pays for the quid—the resources that provide the legislator with draft legislation and policy—it is the corporation itself whose expressive rights are to be weighed. And there is no reason—nothing in the structure of the situation—to suggest that the views expressed in such legislation are anything other than the corporation's own considered views, as indeed they are of the legislator. But big-information lobbying generally falls short of supplying reasons for those views, and so fails to conduce most effectively to the democratic good of reasoned decision making. Big-information lobbying typically provides the end products of democratic debate—legislation, policy, or amendments—but not the reasons for them. This kind of lobbying in effect bypasses the argumentative process and certainly does not contribute to it. Instead, the lobbyist enshrines the corporation's or industry's views whole cloth, and with inadequate challenge, into the content of legislation.

So while big-information lobbying bespeaks the corporation's own reasoned views, it does not do so in a reasoning fashion. Moreover, as shown above, big–information lobbying harbors no institutional tendencies precluding the most serious form of corruption, a full quo. Risking as it does the most serious form of corruption, while redeeming itself only partially with a less than fully valuable form of expression, *big information lobbying—the drafting by lobbyists of legislation and policy for legislators—is not justified on democratic norms.*

Finally, what of small-money lobbying—the careful building of a relationship over time between lobbyist and legislator through meals, small gifts, and other forms of minor hospitality all paid for by the lobbyist? In these encounters, the lobbyist establishes broad philosophical sympathies with the legislator's agenda, so that the legislator, coming to trust the lobbyist, will rely—more heavily than she might otherwise have—on the lobbyist's views. The structure of these kinds of encounters—meetings over time, often during which no specific client or employer issues are discussed[46]—suggests that what the lobbyist is communicating are his own views of the world, ones he came to for reasons apart from the exigencies of a particular client or employer relationship. Republican lobbyists, by expressing their views over time in such settings, cultivate like-minded legislators; the same with Democrats. Accordingly, such communications represent the highest—most valuable—exercise of the lobbyist's democratic expressive right. If a specific issue then does come up, the lobbyist advances a position consistent with his own philosophy and the politician's agenda.

Again, it is the lobbyist's expressive rights, not the corporation's, whose exercise we must evaluate in these situations. The lobbyist is expressing his own personal views in these encounters, doing so on the entire range of agenda issues that go well beyond those of interest to the corporation and developing a relationship with the legislator that only individuals can have with one another. Often, this relationship will have begun prior to the lobbyist's employment or contract with the corporation, when he was a supporter or perhaps staffer for the legislator, and the bulk of these small-money expenditures—the investment in social capital—would thus not have been underwritten by the corporation. Indeed, legislators are not permitted to receive gifts of home hospitality from lobbyists unless those lobbyists qualify as personal friends, in which case, their expenditures must be made personally, not underwritten by a corporate employer or client.[47]

So the small-money lobbyist is the speaker whose expressive rights are in question, and here, the lobbyist does express his own reasoned views. But does the small-money lobbyist express those views in a reasoning way, a way that contributes to the democratic good of fully reasoned decision making? The structure of the situation supplies no visible constraint on his doing so. Small-money lobbying involves venues for conversation such as restaurant meals or home hospitality, and hence for the reasoned, elaborated expression of one's views. As Coleman of the Distilled Spirits Council says, they allow for "lobbyists...to engage at length" with legislators.

If we are evaluating the quality of the expression involved in small-money lobbying, as a general statement about its structure, we would thus have to give it the highest of marks on democratic norms: as both a fully exercised democratic right and as conducing most highly to the democratic good. If we then turn to the kinds of corruptive risks posed by small-money lobbying, discussed in the second section, we recall that the institutional tendencies are for small-money lobbying to involve half-quos—quos in which the legislator might take a new position on a nonagenda issue, or reemphasize an existing position on an agenda issue, but not reverse a position on an agenda issue. When the structural tendency is for an act of expression to be of the highest value as both a right and a good, while the corruption risked does not pose the most serious form of violation, then, on the balance of democratic norms, it is permissible. That is not to say that small-money lobbying—gifts of hospitality and other small relationship–building expenses—should not be regulated, capped in amount or with disclosure required (as indeed they are). It means only that, as the applicable democratic norms of free expression and anticorruption weigh out against each other, *small-money lobbying—the provision of modest meals, hospitality, and other such venues—is an ethical practice for business lobbyists to engage in.*

Corporate Campaign Finance: Reasoned Beliefs, Reasoning Speech

Now, what about the democratically expressive credentials of corporate contributions to and expenditures on political campaigns? Small money—contributions to candidate campaigns, the kind that corporations cannot make at all from their treasuries and only in limited amounts via their PACs—is the kind of speech activity that least conforms to democratic norms. With contributions, if anybody's own reasoned views are being expressed, it is more the candidate's than the contributor's, and hence is not the fullest kind of exercise of the latter's expressive rights. As the *Buckley* Court put it, "while contributions may result in political expression if spent by a candidate...to present views to the voters," they are the views of "someone other than the contributor."[48]

Nor does the expressive act the contributor makes by contributing take a reasoning form; hence it fails to conduce most fully to the democratic good of fully reasoned decision making. As the *Buckley* Court noted, a contribution serves only "as a general expression of support for the candidate and his views, but does not communicate the underlying basis for the support...The expression rests solely on the undifferentiated, symbolic act of contributing." It "do[es] not communicate the reasons for that support."[49]

Small-money corporate campaign finance—contributions to candidate campaigns—thus falls short on both criteria of democratic expression. Moreover, its structural tendency is to risk the most serious form of democratic corruption, a full quo. On balance, then, the democratic norms that generate the ethics regime for corporate political activity suggest that *corporate PACs should not engage in small-money campaign finance; that is, they should not contribute money to candidate campaigns.*

True, there is a collective action problem here. It may be difficult for businesses to unilaterally cease contributing if their competitors continue to do so. Nevertheless, major businesses—and business organizations—have complained about the "shakedown" that corporate PAC contributions involve. They are right to do so, and to attempt to orchestrate a collective termination of the practice.[50]

Now, what of big money—the contributions that corporations can channel, directly from their treasuries as well as from PACs, to political parties (and allied entities) for voter mobilization? The most significant act of expression that big money enables—when it does what it is intended to do—is to make possible a substantial amount of voting that would not have occurred otherwise. In other words, it allows voters to express their own true convictions, their reasoned beliefs, at the ballot box: the highest and most protected form of democratic expression rights.

But is voting a reasoning form of expression? Is it the kind of expression that contributes most fully to the good of reasoned democratic decision making? Or is it more like the mere "expression of support for [a] candidate," bereft of any accompanying argumentation or reasoning, that *Buckley* associates with campaign contributions? The latter seems a more apt description of voting, which is why democratic theorists generally take the view that the simple act of voting is a necessary but far from maximally optimal form of individual civic participation.[51] The kind of expression that soft money most centrally enables—which happens to be the political expression of the voter, not the contributor—is, then, based on the speaker's (voter's) own reasoned views, but is structurally constrained not to be reasoning in form.

Bringing in an earlier discussion, we are reminded that the structural tendency of big-money party-voter mobilization is to risk half-quos, not full quos. Yet even a half-quo violates democratic norms. And since the speech enabled by big-money contributions also falls short on one of the two criteria of democratically valuable expression, on balance *big-money contributions—contributions by corporations to parties' voter mobilization efforts—violate democratic norms.*

What of big-information corporate campaign finance, corporate expenditures on electioneering advertisements that promote or oppose specific candidates? Consider D. Bruce La Pierre's observation that corporate "expenditures for advertisements and brochures urging voters to elect particular candidates...deny these candidates an opportunity to frame the messages being attributed to them and may force candidates to defend statements and positions that they would not have pursued."[52] The claim here is that if we view a corporation's ad campaign advancing a candidate's cause as, in fact, the speech not of the corporation but the candidate—on the grounds that in some basic way it will be attributed to or reflect on her—then such ads may indeed fail to represent the speaker's (i.e., the candidate's) own reasoned views. Such ads may well use words of reason and argument—they are not simply a mute gesture of support—and so conduce to the democratic good of reasoned decision making. But they put those words in the candidate's mouth. They do not bespeak the candidate's own reasoned beliefs, yet they will be attributed to her, and so violate her democratic expressive rights.[53] George W. Bush made just such a complaint about Wyly's ad campaign supporting his candidacy.[54]

If the views being attributed to an individual are not her own reasoned beliefs, even though they may well be expressed in a reasoning way, they do not constitute the most valuable form of democratic expression. Moreover, corporate PACs, though they are legally entitled to advertise on behalf of candidates, risk the most serious form of corruption—a full quo—without clearly achieving the most valued form of expression. Thus, *big-information corporate campaign finance—candidate-centered advertising by corporations—on balance violates democratic norms.*

Finally, what of small-information (issue) advertising by corporations? Of all forms of corporate political contributions/spending, small information comes closest to satisfying democratic expressive norms. There is no reason to believe that such issue advertising represents anything other than the considered thoughts, the reasoned views, of the corporate spenders, on a particular issue of interest to them, hence constituting the fullest exercise of their democratic expressive rights. And the small-information advertising format allows the corporate spender sufficient capacity to not only express its views but offer reasons, hence conducing to the democratic good, the social capacity to make the most fully reasoned decisions.

Small-information—that is, issue-focused—advertising thus involves corporations in the most democratically valuable form of political expression. Moreover, the structural tendency is for small-information issue-advertising to risk half-quos. Because it involves the risk of a less serious form of democratic corruption while entailing the most fully valuable form of democratic expression, *small-information corporate campaigns, for example, issue advertising, is not unethical for corporations to engage in.*

Table 17.2. Weighing Expressive Values against Corruptive Risk

Neither the speaker's own reasoned views nor reasoned speech	*The speaker's own reasoned views but not reasoned speech*	*Not the speaker's own reasoned views but reasoned speech*	*The speaker's own reasoned views and reasoned speech*
small info lobbying	**big info lobbying**	**big money lobbying**	small money lobbying
small money corporate campaign finance	big money corporate campaign finance	**big information corporate campaign finance**	small info corporate campaign finance

Full quo situations in bold face; half-quos in regular

CONCLUSION

Of the eight kinds of corporate political activity discussed in this essay, only two—small-money lobbying involving minor acts of hospitality, and small-information advertising in which the corporation advances its views on particular issues of interest—are ethically permissible on democratic norms. As a general statement about their structures, they involve (see the right-hand column of table 17.2) the most valuable form of democratic expression, while risking only half-quos. All other forms of lobbying activity—such as corporate lobbyists bundling campaign contributions (big money), buttonholing legislators at charity events or cocktail parties (small information), or drafting legislation for legislators (big information), violate democratic norms against risking corruption, whether full quos or half-quos, without offering a countervailing democratic value of sufficient weight in terms of the expression involved. The same is true of corporate PACs contributing to candidate campaigns (small money), PAC advertising on behalf of candidates (big information), and corporations contributing to parties for voter mobilization (big money). One day the law might prohibit some or all of these corporate political activities; indeed, initiatives to do so are always in play. But regardless of the state of the law, for reasons argued—reasons rooted in governing democratic norms— they are not ethical business practices.

NOTES

1. An earlier version of this chapter was presented at the Conference on Corruption and Democracy, Centre for the Study of Democratic Institutions, University of British Columbia, June 7–9, 2007. I am grateful to participants, as well as to the editors of this volume, for their helpful suggestions.

2. Robert H. Sitkoff, "Politics and the Business Corporation," *Regulation* (Winter 2003): 36.

3. Douglas D. Roscoe and Shannon Jenkins, "A Meta-Analysis of Campaign Contributions' Impact on Roll Call Voting," *Social Science Quarterly* 86 (2005): 52.

4. Daniel Hays Lowenstein, "On Campaign Finance Reform: The Root of All Evil Is Deeply Rooted," *Hofstra Law Review* 18 (1989), 318.

5. Ken Kollman, *Outside Lobbying: Public Opinion and Interest Group Strategies* (Princeton, N.J.: Princeton University Press, 1998), 72.

6. Beth L. Leech and Frank R. Baumgartner "Lobbying Friends and Foes in Washington," in *Interest Group Politics*, 5th ed., ed. Allan J. Cigler and Burdett A. Loomis (Washington, D.C.: Congressional Quarterly Press, 1998), 218.

7. John C. Samples, *The Fallacy of Campaign Finance Reform* (Chicago: University of Chicago Press, 2006), 88.

8. Mark A. Smith, *American Business and Political Power: Public Opinion, Elections, and Democracy* (Chicago: University of Chicago Press, 2000), 122.

9. Samuel Issacharoff and Pamela S. Karlan, "The Hydraulics of Campaign Finance Reform," *Texas Law Review* 77 (1999): 1721.

10. Richard L. Hall and Frank W. Wayman, "Buying Time: Moneyed Interests and the Mobilization of Bias on Congressional Committees," *American Political Science Review* 84 (1990): 799, 802–3; see also Samples, *Fallacy*, 257.

11. Andrew Stark, *Conflict of Interest in American Public Life* (Cambridge, Mass.: Harvard University Press, 2000), chap. 7.

12. Association of the Bar of the City of New York, *Conflict of Interest and Federal Service* (Cambridge, Mass.: Harvard University Press, 1960), 7.

13. For a fuller discussion of private gain from public office and the fiduciary principle than I can give here, see Andrew Stark, "Beyond Quid Pro Quo: What's Wrong with Private Gain from Public Office?" *American Political Science Review* 91 (1997), 108–120.

14. Stark, *Conflict of Interest*, pt. 1.

15. Richard L. Hall and Alan V. Deardorff "Lobbying as Legislative Subsidy," *American Political Science Review* 100 (2006): 84.

16. Raymond Hernandez and Robert Pear, "Health Sector Puts Its Money on Democrats," *New York Times*, October 29, 2007.

17. Dennis F. Thompson, "Two Concepts of Corruption," paper presented at the Conference on Corruption and Democracy, University of British Columbia, June 8–9, 2007, 7.

18. Sanford Nowlin, "Money & Politics: Law Doesn't Keep Companies' Cash from Reaching Its Intended Targets," *San Antonio Express-News*, October 3, 2004, 1L.

19. Michael Remez, "Wining, Dining, Lobbying," *Hartford Courant*, December 24, 1995, A1.

20. See some of the discussion in Justice Kennedy's opinion in *McConnell v FEC*, slip op., 11.

21. Richard A. Smith, "Advocacy, Interpretation and Influence in the U.S. Congress," *American Political Science Review* 78 (1984): 59.

22. Quoted in Steven E. Schier, *By Invitation Only: The Rise of Exclusive Politics in the United States* (Pittsburgh, Pa.: University of Pittsburgh Press, 2000), 172; see also Anthony J. Nownes, *Total Lobbying: What Lobbyists Want (and How They Get It)* (Cambridge: Cambridge University Press, 2006), 66.

23. Steven John, *The Persuaders: When Lobbyists Matter* (New York: Palgrave, 2002), 53, discussing M. Margaret Conway, "PACs in the Political Process," in *Interest Group Politics*, 3rd ed., eds. Allan Cigler and Burdette Loomis (Washington, D.C.: Congressional Quarterly Press, 1991), 211, 212.

24. Nownes, *Total Lobbying*, 19.

25. Juliet Eilperin, "Gift Rules Regularly Flouted on Hill, Insiders Say; House Ethics Chairman Acknowledges Enforcement Breakdown," *Washington Post*, October 14, 2002, A27.

26. Dana Katz Arthur L. Caplan and Jon F. Merz "All Gifts Large and Small," *American Journal of Bioethics* 3 (2003): 39–46.

27. Kay Lehman Schlozman and John T. Tierney *Organized Interests and American Democracy* (New York: Harper & Row, 1986), 292.

28. Nolan McCarty and Lawrence S. Rothenberg, "Commitment and the Campaign Contribution Contract," *American Journal of Political Science* 40 (1996): 874.

29. Timothy Egan, "Industries Affected by Endangered Species Help a Senator to Rewrite Its Provisions," *New York Times*, April 13, 1995, A20.

30. Hall and Deardorff, "Lobbying as Legislative Subsidy," 74.

31. 2 U.S.C. § 441a.

32. Jill Abramson and Bob Davis, "Expensive Battle over Nafta Has Each Side Claiming Its Being Outgunned and Outspent," *Wall Street Journal*, November 15, 1993, A14.

33. Burt Neuborne, "Is Money Different?" *Texas Law Review* 77 (1999): 1610.

34. Thomas B. Edsall, "New Routes To Channel 'Soft Money' On Horizon; FEC Puts Exemption In Finance Rules," *Washington Post*, June 23, 2002, A7.

35. Edsall, "New Routes," A7.

36. Nathaniel Persily, "Contested Concepts in Campaign Finance," *University of Pennsylvania Journal of Constitutional Law* 6 (2003): 125; see also Richard Briffault, "What Did They Do and What Does it Mean? The Three-Judge Court Decision in *McConnell v. FEC* and the Implications for the Supreme Court," *University of Pennsylvania Journal of Constitutional Law* 6 (2003): 68.

37. *Brief for Appellants/Cross-Appellees Senator Mitch McConnell et al.*, July 8, 2003, 24; see also *McConnell v. FEC*, slip op., 18.

38. Smith, *American Business*, 125; see also Jonathan S. Krasno and Frank J. Sorauf, "Report: Evaluating the Bipartisan Campaign Reform Act," *NYU Review of Law and Social Change* 28 (2003): 124.

39. Andrew Wheat, "Green Mountain's Other Faces: The Dirty Side of Clean Energy," *Multinational Monitor* (27) (Sept./Oct. 2006): 41.

40. Thomas Brazaitis, "Battle Over Health Care to Get Ugly: Legislators Must Also Face Voter Reaction," *The Plain Dealer*, July 17, 1994, 1A.

41. Adam Winkler, "Beyond *Bellotti*," *Loyola Law Review* 32 (1998): 133.

42. Craig Gordon, "The Fight for Computer Associates," *Newsday*, July 2, 2001, A3.

43. Jeffrey H. Birnbaum *The Lobbyists: How Influence Peddlers Get Their Way in Washington* (New York: Times Books, 1992), 32.

44. Treas. Reg. § 1.162.

45. *Buckley v. Valeo*, 424 U.S. 1 (1976), 21.

46. Edward O. Laumann et al., "Lawyers and Others: The Structure of Representation in Washington," *Stanford Law Review* 37 (1985), 37.

47. House Rule 25 5 (a) (3) (P); Senate Rule 1(c) (7).

48. *Buckley v. Valeo*, 21.

49. *Colorado Republican Federal Campaign Committee v. FEC*, 518 U.S. 604 (1996) 635.

50. Sitkoff, "Politics and the Business Corporation," 36.

51. Carole Pateman, *Participation and Democratic Theory* (Cambridge: Cambridge University Press, 1970).

52. D. Bruce La Pierre, "The Bipartisan Campaign Reform Act, Political Parties, and the First Amendment: Lessons from Missouri," *Washington University Law Quarterly* 80 (2003), 1149.

53. Cong. Rec. H372 (February 13, 2002) (statement of Rep. Matheson).

54. Walter Shapiro "Anti-McCain Tactics Dangerous to Voters' Decision," *USA Today*, March 6, 2002, 10A.

SUGGESTED READING

Hall, Richard L. and Alan V. Deardorff. "Lobbying as Legislative Subsidy." *American Political Science Review* 100 (2006): 69–84.

Hall, Richard L. and Frank W. Wayman. "Buying Time: Moneyed Interests and the Mobilization of Bias on Congressional Committees." *American Political Science Review* 84 (1990): 797–820.

Heinz, John P. et al. *The Hollow Core: Private Interests in National Policy Making.* Cambridge, Mass.: Harvard University Press, 1993.

Issacharoff, Samuel and Pamela S. Karlan. "The Hydraulics of Campaign Finance Reform." *Texas Law Review* 77 (1999): 1705–1738.

John, Steven. *The Persuaders: When Lobbyists Matter.* New York: Palgrave, 2002.

Leech, Beth L., and Frank R. Baumgartner. "Lobbying Friends and Foes in Washington." In *Interest Group Politics,* 5th ed. Edited by Allan J. Cigler and Burdett A. Loomis, 217–233. Washington, D.C.: Congressional Quarterly Press, 1998.

Lowenstein, Daniel Hays. "On Campaign Finance Reform: The Root of All Evil Is Deeply Rooted." *Hofstra Law Review* 18 (1989): 301–335.

McCarty, Nolan and Lawrence S. Rothenberg. "Commitment and the Campaign Contribution Contract." *American Journal of Political Science* 40 (1996): 872–904.

McChesney, Fred. *Money for Nothing: Politicians, Rent Extraction and Political Extortion.* Cambridge, Mass.: Harvard University Press, 1997.

Nownes, Anthony J. *Total Lobbying: What Lobbyists Want (and How They Get It)* Cambridge: Cambridge University Press, 2006.

Pateman, Carole. *Participation and Democratic Theory.* Cambridge: Cambridge University Press, 1970.

Samples, John C. *The Fallacy of Campaign Finance Reform.* Chicago: University of Chicago Press, 2006.

Schier, Steven E. *By Invitation Only: The Rise of Exclusive Politics in the United States.* Pittsburgh, Pa.: University of Pittsburgh Press, 2000.

Sitkoff, Robert H. 2002. "Management and Control of the Modern Business Corporation: Corporate Speech and Citizenship: Corporate Political Speech, Political Extortion, and the Competition for Corporate Charters." *University of Chicago Law Review* 69 (2002): 1067–1102.

Smith, Mark A. *American Business and Political Power: Public Opinion, Elections, and Democracy.* Chicago: University of Chicago Press, 2000.

Smith, Richard A. "Advocacy, Interpretation and Influence in the U.S. Congress." *American Political Science Review* 78 (1984): 44–63.

Stark, Andrew. *Conflict of Interest in American Public Life.* Cambridge, Mass.: Harvard University Press, 2000.

Stark, Andrew. "Corporate Electoral Activity, Constitutional Discourse, and Conceptions of the Individual." *American Political Science Review* 86 (1992): 626–637.

Thompson, Dennis F. *Ethics in Congress.* Washington, D.C.: Brookings Institution, 1995.

Wright, J. Skelly. "Money and the Pollution of Politics: Is the First Amendment an Obstacle to Political Equality." *Columbia Law Review* 82 (1982): 609–644.

PART VII

EMPLOYEE RIGHTS AND CORPORATE RESPONSIBILITIES

DISCRIMINATION, AFFIRMATIVE ACTION, AND DIVERSITY IN BUSINESS

BERNARD BOXILL

SINCE the mid-1960s, several U.S. policies and laws have encouraged or required corporations and other institutions to advertise jobs fairly and to promote the hiring and promotion of members of groups formerly and currently discriminated against, most notably women and minority ethnic groups. Implementation of both the letter and the spirit of these federal requirements have often involved employment goals and targeted employment outcomes intended to eliminate the vestiges of discrimination and apparently intractable prejudice and systemic favoritism. These goals and policies are the core of affirmative action. The problem of affirmative action is whether such policies can be justified and, if so, under which conditions.

"DISCRIMINATION" AND THE LANGUAGE OF "AFFIRMATIVE ACTION"

The original meaning of "affirmative action" was minimalist. It referred to plans to safeguard equal opportunity, advertise positions openly, ensure fair recruitment, and create scholarship programs for specific groups. Few, if any, now oppose these means to the end of equal treatment. However, "affirmative action" has come to have broader meanings—some advanced by proponents, others by opponents. Most importantly, the term has become closely associated—especially through its opponents—with quotas and preferential policies that target specific groups, primarily women and minorities, for preferential treatment. Stern critics of affirmative action therefore maintain that "affirmative action" today means little more than naked preference by race. Possibly they assume that all racial discrimination must be unfair. Some dictionaries report that the word "discrimination" often connotes bias and partiality. The enemies of affirmative action appeal to these connotations and often use "reverse discrimination" as a synonym for "affirmative action," insinuating that affirmative action that involves racial, sexual, and ethnic discrimination must be as unfair as the old common racial, sexual, and ethnic-minority discrimination, even if it puts the old discrimination in reverse.

This equating of affirmative action and invidious discrimination or reverse discrimination should be rejected. Strictly, the term "discrimination," understood as the mere act of drawing distinctions, does not imply unfairness. Indeed, understood in this strict sense, it is something that all living creatures must do to stay alive, and the complicated lives of humans require them to make more and finer discriminations—for example, between right and wrong, good and bad, and beautiful and ugly. Drawing such distinctions, discriminating, in other words, is ubiquitous and necessary. The question is whether it is justified.

Moral issues have arisen over the principles used to determine if discrimination is justified. Although racism and sexism—the primary sources of discrimination in the history of affirmative action—are commonly envisioned as *intentional* forms of favoritism and exclusion, the intent to discriminate unfairly is not a necessary condition for there to be discrimination that is unjustified in the relevant sense. Employees are frequently hired through networks that exclude women or minority groups from the pool of individuals who are considered for employment, even if such networks are not designed or intended to have that result. For example, hiring may occur through personal connections or by word of mouth, or by the "old boy" network, and layoffs may be controlled by a seniority system. Where these practices exist, women or minority groups may be in effect unfairly discriminated against even if those engaged in the practices do not intend to discriminate unfairly against them or are not fully aware of the unfair consequences of their practices. Consequently, the intent to discriminate should not be taken as a necessary condition of discrimination in the relevant sense. The point is important to make since it is easy to camouflage even intentional discrimination with plausible protestations that no one is intending to discriminate or is even aware that any discrimination is taking place.

Accordingly, we need to scrutinize practices for evidence of unfair discrimination even when those engaged in them are not aware of any such discrimination, and we need to discuss the limits that the law may justifiably place on the hiring practices of businesses, including whether "affirmative action" may be such a limit.

I will consider two major and widely respected moral theories as possible bases for affirmative action—utilitarianism and natural rights theory. I will argue that utilitarianism supports many forward-looking arguments for affirmative action, primarily those that support affirmative action on the basis of its good consequences. I will also argue that natural rights theory can be used to support both forward-looking and backward-looking arguments for affirmative action, the latter being arguments that support affirmative action on the ground that it is compensation for the harmful effects of past injustices.[1] This result is significant since natural rights theory has particular salience for U.S. society, as we will see, and supports arguments for affirmative action that rely less on contestable factual assumptions than utilitarian arguments. Finally, I will consider and defend a particular version of the most popular contemporary ground for affirmative action, namely, that it supports diversity in the workplace.

Utilitarian Theory as a Defense of Affirmative Action

One mainstream type of utilitarian theory (the one focused on here) takes happiness to be the only fundamental good. A corollary is that unhappiness is the only fundamentally bad thing. A second corollary is that happiness is good and unhappiness is bad wherever they occur. Having stated what is fundamentally good and bad, utilitarianism proceeds to define what actions or policies are to be considered right or obligatory. According to utilitarian theory, our basic moral obligation is to act so as to maximize the balance of happiness over unhappiness in the world.[2] Since utilitarianism maintains that happiness is not better and unhappiness is not worse because of whose happiness or unhappiness it is, utilitarianism implies that each person should act so as to maximize overall happiness, counting his or her own happiness or misery as no more important than the happiness or unhappiness of others. A common mistake is to suppose that utilitarianism implies that an action is right if it produces more happiness than unhappiness. Utilitarianism supposes that one's obligation is to *maximize* happiness, not only increase it. It follows that in order to do the right thing, individuals and firms must ordinarily make estimates of what the good and bad consequences of their actions are likely to be, though because even the most careful estimates may be mistaken, firms and individuals with the best intentions may still choose to act in ways that fail to maximize overall happiness, and therefore fail to act rightly, according to this utilitarian theory.

Generations of philosophers have attempted to demonstrate that utilitarianism is mistaken. One objection is that happiness is not sufficiently well defined or understood. Sometimes it is said to be pleasure, but pleasure seems to vary in intensity and also, as some have suggested, in quality, and it remains unclear how differences in the qualities of the pleasures or happiness affect the rightness of actions. Another problem is that it is often hard to form reliable estimates of how happy people are. Appearances can give us clues: a man gleefully waving a winning lottery ticket is almost certainly happier than a man looking dejectedly at an eviction notice. A related difficulty is that the distribution of the goods and conditions that are normally believed to lead to or to cause happiness does not always give reliable information about how happy different people are. Joan and John need not be equally happy just because they are equally paid. Joan may need more money than John to make her happy because she is pregnant; John may need more money than Joan to make him happy because he is sick. The theory that as a general rule giving equal increases of income to the rich and the poor generally adds more to the happiness of the poor than to the happiness of the rich, and consequently that as a general rule the utilitarian should recommend equalizing salaries, backfires if the firm must use high salaries to entice qualified people to do the more difficult work that is necessary for it to maintain the high quality of its products, and if lowering the quality of its products will reduce overall happiness.

The most insistent objection raised against utilitarianism is that circumstances can be imagined in which slavery maximizes happiness, even if we weigh fully the misery it inflicts on the slaves, and that utilitarianism must therefore endorse slavery in such circumstances as the right policy. I wonder whether the critics who raise this objection so confidently seriously consider the miseries that slavery is likely to cause. Slavery does not only make slaves miserable, it also makes many nonslaves miserable. I am not referring mainly to the moral uneasiness of slave masters or their worries that their throats will be cut while they sleep, although these worries and uneasiness must be counted against slavery. I am referring to the anxieties of people who live with the fear that they will be enslaved. Americans reduced these costs of slavery by stipulating that only blacks could be enslaved, thus allowing whites some composure. But this stipulation did not allow a similar composure to the free blacks living in the United States who lived in continual fear of being kidnapped and sent to the South to be enslaved, especially after the fugitive slave act of 1850. To their fears we must add the fears of Africans on the coast of West Africa, who too must have lived in constant apprehension of being hunted down, packed into the slave ships, and taken to where they did not know. New World slaves were also probably miserable in ways ancient slaves never dreamed of. Perhaps because anyone could be enslaved in ancient Greece, the idea that slaves were natural slaves never caught on there, although it was an ancient Greek, Aristotle, who invented it. However, it caught on for various reasons in the United States where blacks were held to be the perfect archetype of Aristotle's idea. Consequently, while the Greek slave could think of his enslavement as simply very bad luck, the U.S. slave had to live with the mortifying disquietude that he might be an inherently and morally inferior being, cursed by God or nature, and deservedly enslaved. These unexpected costs of slavery suggest that the favorite example of the blunders of utilitarianism may be ill founded.

But its critics have more objections, for example, that since people do not worry about evils they do not suspect exist, utilitarianism will recommend implementing evil practices like slavery if these practices will maximize happiness, and the public can be kept from knowing about them. Unfortunately, however, the critics never seem to appreciate fully the grave dangers to happiness of deception on the scale they propose. Utilitarianism's most effective response to the objections now being considered against it is that those urging these objections do not stop to consider where the intuitions they rely on come from. According to the utilitarian, education, culture, the example of our elders, and societal pressures and influences generally train our intuitions to help us to reliably behave rightly in the common circumstances of life. Consequently, it is to be expected that these same intuitions may fail us when we are confronted by the fantastic, perhaps empirically impossible, "counterexamples" that the critics of utilitarianism urge as decisive proof against it. Given its account of how our intuitions are formed, utilitarianism must allow that we should consider not following our intuitions where following them would clearly fail to produce the greatest balance of happiness over unhappiness and so frustrate the very point of morality. Utilitarianism also warns of the dangers to the overall happiness of not following our intuitions, especially the danger of weakening those intuitions, and therefore perhaps failing to act rightly in the vast number of common circumstances that we have to deal with. Finally, it is worth pointing out that even the most relentless critics of utilitarianism concede that there are circumstances—the Supreme Emergency Exemption—when they would recommend breaking the rules to avoid disaster.[3] Their standard example for illustrating their position is the British bombing of German cities in the early days of the World War II, which they argue was justified as a last resort aimed at preventing the looming Nazi victory and the ensuing collapse of civilization. They insist that they are not therefore utilitarians because they recommend breaking the rule against bombing civilians only in order to avoid certain disaster, never in order to gain marginal increases in happiness. But they never consider that the utilitarian almost always has good utilitarian reasons not to break the rules for what might appear to be marginal gains in happiness, and that their efforts to rule out these reasons fall back again on the use of fantastic examples.

For these and other reasons I intend to take utilitarianism seriously as giving reasonably good guidance in most matters of social policy. It will be useful to begin with three general empirical claims that I think most people will concede to be true. The first of these claims is that being poor usually makes people very unhappy or at least makes them less happy than they would be if they were better off. The second is that the employed are usually better off than the unemployed. The third is that black unemployment rates are usually higher than white unemployment rates and consequently that a disproportionately large number of the poorest people in the society are black. Given these three uncontroversial factual claims, laws requiring firms to give preference to poor black applicants seem likely to increase the total happiness of society, and consequently to be justifiable on utilitarian grounds. This argument is open to many fairly obvious objections, but it is presented as only the beginning of what will turn out to be a far more complicated and qualified argument.

To arrive at that argument let us begin with the objection that the argument seems to merely shift misery from one part of the society to another with no overall gain in happiness, and that it supports preferential treatment for the poor generally, not specifically the black poor. These objections have considerable force. The result of giving preference to black applicants for positions will be that better qualified nonblack applicants will fail to be hired. Indeed, it may seem that they will be unhappier than the black unemployed, for they are also likely to burn with painful feelings of resentment for being denied positions for which they believe they were the most qualified. These forceful objections can be softened by various considerations, but it must be admitted that at best the practice the argument recommends is likely to net only a small increase in overall happiness. A better way, it seems, would be to take from the rich and well-to-do and give it to the poor, both white and black. Making sure that a hundred black poor have work will subtract more unhappiness from the society and consequently more effectively raise the overall happiness of the society than making sure that a rich man can buy a bigger yacht.

It may be objected that the argument above is not an argument for affirmative action, but an argument for shifting resources from the rich to the poor, and moreover that it cannot be turned into an argument for affirmative action—for example, by giving the poor preference in the competition for jobs that the rich and middle class vie for. Since the poor are unlikely to have the skills for such jobs, this kind of affirmative action would give them jobs they cannot do well. The standard answer to this objection is that preferential treatment does not recommend hiring incompetents, but that answer still seems incompatible with utilitarianism, which requires that we maximize good outcomes, not merely get jobs done competently. Supposing that jobs done as well as possible add more to the overall happiness than jobs only done merely competently, utilitarianism it seems must insist that jobs be filled with people who can do them as well as possible.

This argument is probably not decisive when preference is given to some people in the competition for jobs requiring few skills. The difference between the work of skilled and unskilled mailmen or porters probably makes little difference to the overall happiness. However, the argument becomes more important when preference is given to some in the competition for jobs or positions requiring skills of a high order. Everyone would feel safer and therefore probably happier if commercial airlines hired not merely competent pilots but the best pilots.

This conclusion strongly suggests that taking jobs from the rich and the middle class and giving them to the poor is unlikely to increase overall happiness. But if the utilitarian will therefore not endorse affirmative action of this kind, she may endorse affirmative action that gives the poor preferences for admission into institutions that provide training for good jobs. Affirmative action of this sort would begin early, at the most elementary levels, since introducing it later would probably leave its beneficiaries academically unprepared to take advantage of the opportunities it offers them. If it is successful, the poor will acquire the skills to become serious competitors for the jobs that the rich and middle class monopolize.

So far the argument has focused on affirmative action for the poor, given that poor people who cannot feed, clothe, and shelter themselves adequately are generally unhappy, and that relieving their poverty, for example, by affirmative action is more likely to help maximize overall happiness than helping the rich to get richer. Of course the poor are not always unhappy, but the importance of this possibility has often been exaggerated—by Adam Smith, for example. Although he had great respect for wealth, declaring famously that the rich are "led by an invisible hand to make nearly the same distribution of the necessities of life, which would have been made, had the earth been divided into equal portions among all its inhabitants, and thus without intending it, without knowing it, advance the interest of society, and afford the means to the multiplication of the species," he also depreciated the contribution wealth makes to happiness, and the contribution a little of it would make to the happiness of the poor. After observing how much money the rich waste on "trinkets of frivolous utility" he concluded that "in ease of body and peace of mind, all the different ranks of life are nearly on a level, and the beggar, who suns himself on the side of the highway, possesses that security which kings are fighting for."[4]

I will pass over Smith's observation about the happiness of the rich because it is irrelevant to the argument for affirmative action under consideration, namely, that it can increase overall happiness by making the poor better off. To that argument Smith's observation about the happiness of the beggar is relevant. First, Smith asks us to imagine a beggar sunning himself by the side of the highway, apparently forgetting that the side of the highway is sometimes icy rather than sunny, and that physical discomforts normally add to unhappiness. But this is the least of his fallacies. He also seems to completely overlook the possibility that the beggar sunning himself on the side of the highway may also be mourning the deaths of his children, whom a little money might have saved. The rich suffer from somewhat similar tragedies, for no one avoids them altogether, but they befall the poor far oftener than they befall the rich. Smith also seems to forget that the poor suffer from knowing how badly others think of them, though he would probably reply that the rich suffer in the same way from the slights they receive both real and imagined. But if the rich suffer from imagined slights, it is their fault, and a utilitarian would do better to let them help themselves and focus on helping those who need help.

Perhaps Smith did not overlook that poor have painful sentiments, but simply denied that they had them. As Rousseau suggested, Smith may have misunderstood the stolidity of the poor, inferring from it that the poor did not feel the sting of insults, when he should have understood that they simply saw no point in explaining and expressing their feelings. If so, Rousseau certainly had the better of Smith for people without feelings do not explode into vengeful and bloody riots. But if Smith drew mistaken inferences from the stolidity of the poor, he should have recoiled from them. If the poor feel less sorrow for the death of their children than the rich feel when their children die, it can only be because the poor love their children less; or if the poor are less hurt when they are treated contemptuously than the rich feel when they are slighted, this can only be because they have less of a sense of their own human dignity than the rich. Cognitivists in the theory of emotions may argue that the loves and self-esteems of the poor must be as a rule cruder than those of the well-to-do because the poor simply lack the ideas necessary to make the evaluative judgments that constitute the most poignant emotions. But even if the rich and the poor have different ideas, and therefore different emotions, it does not follow that the painful emotions of the one are more piteous and profound than the painful emotions of the other. Some slave women killed their own children rather than see them grow up as slaves. Could their refined mistresses have feelings that are more harrowing than the feelings of these women?

But perhaps Smith was not making any claim about the poor in general, but only a claim about beggars sunning themselves on the sides of highways. Such individuals often affect a humility unmixed with any trace of wounded pride and seem to have adopted the Stoic philosophy, which allegedly enables its followers to be happy in whatever circumstances they happen to be in. However, I doubt that a utilitarian would countenance spreading Stoicism among today's poor as a more effective way to increase happiness rather than affirmative action that takes from the rich and gives to the poor.

The utilitarian case for affirmative action thus far is that affirmative action for the poor at the expense of the rich helps to maximize overall happiness. This may seem to suggest that utilitarianism can support only affirmative action for the poor. The concession that affirmative action in the competition for jobs is least problematic when applied to jobs requiring skills of a relatively low order seems to confirm that implication. If positions requiring skills of a high order must always be filled by the most qualified applicants with no preference given to anyone because of race or sex or ethnic origin, it also seems to follow that affirmative action should play no part in the competition for positions that middle class women and middle class black men are likely vie for. But this conclusion is unwarranted. The argument for it starts out safely enough with the assumption that as a general rule jobs done excellently produce more happiness than jobs done only competently when the jobs in question involve skills of a very high order. But the conclusion that it is impossible to build a utilitarian defense of affirmative action for positions demanding the exercise of skills of a high order is unwarranted. For high skills to maximally produce happiness in a society, a lot depends on what the skills are used to do and on how they are exercised.

Suppose that one society has many highly skilled doctors but most of them treat a small class of rich people who spend a great deal of money on nontherapeutic cosmetic surgery. Suppose that another society has only a few of such highly skilled doctors but many more reasonably competent doctors who are employed in keeping the great majority of the people healthy. Even if we concede that those rich enough to afford nontherapeutic cosmetic surgery in the first society will be ecstatic with their new and better looks, I doubt that their happiness will be enough to make up for the unhappiness of its sickly and surgically unimproved majority and make their society happier overall than the second society with their healthier majority, even its doctors are less skilled. A similar point holds for business skills. When firms argue that they want to fill positions with the most highly skilled people available, their objective is to increase profits. But when businesses maximize their profits, overall happiness is not necessarily maximized. Increasing profits may only make the rich a whole lot richer, and the poor a whole lot poorer, and the result may be a decrease in overall happiness.

Suppose, however, that allowing firms to hire the most qualified applicants will increase the total wealth of the society and that government can tax and redistribute the increased wealth among the general population. If an increase in the overall wealth of a society suitably distributed can increase its overall happiness, it may seem that utilitarianism should oppose affirmative action. The most serious difficulty for this argument is that it is not always clear what qualifications are and how to go about identifying those who have the best. At the entry level, the most qualified are typically identified by their credentials—including their grades at the educational institutions they attended, the ranking of these institutions, the letters of recommendation from their teachers and advisers, and the professional standing and credibility of these teachers and professors. At more senior levels, a person's experience in business and letters of recommendation from previous employers become increasingly important. These "qualifications" entitle persons to positions because they are predictors of *future* good work; they do not entitle persons to positions in the way that past good work makes persons deserving of rewards. We should thus be wary of the idea that good grades in college or professional school are the best or only qualifications for jobs requiring high skills. They are evidence that the applicant with them has done good work. They are not always good evidence that he will do good work.

It will be objected that if good grades are rewards for outstanding work in the past in the university classroom or laboratory, they are also the best predictors of outstanding work in the future, in making money for the firm. I concede that good grades are good predictors of future good work. Firms are well aware of this truth and generally hire people with the best grades after investigating which universities, departments, and professors educate its students well and assigns them grades that do not only report that they have done good work but also predict that they will do good work. But even exceptional grades are not always the best predictors of a person's likelihood to do exceptional work in the future. Would a firm looking for an accountant to keep its books straight conclude that the most qualified candidate was a man with brilliant grades and a keen interest in research in theoretical statistics, but with little taste for keeping books? Would a small village looking for a doctor to keep its people healthy think that a brilliant medical researcher with no interest in caring for the sick was most qualified for its job? Or consider a firm that has two applicants for a position requiring energy, resilience, resourcefulness, and know-how. One of the applicants has top grades from an Ivy League college and rich doting parents who spared no money in giving their son the best education possible. The other applicant was orphaned when she was very young, grew up in rough foster homes, and started a small business that thrived but eventually failed.

Though undaunted, she started a second business, and she has good but not outstanding grades from a state college that she attended part time paying her own way. Is it so clear that the firm should hire the applicant from the Ivy League college if it wants to make money? I think it might prefer to hire the second candidate, the determined upwardly mobile woman, not because doing so is required by affirmative action, but for purely self-interested monetary reasons.

Presented in this way, it seems a commonplace that grades are not the only or best indication of the productivity of an applicant for a position. I labor it here because when it is applied to affirmative action, the critics of affirmative action think that they can rebut the case for affirmative action by simply parading the fact that the beneficiaries of affirmative action often have lower grades than some of the applicants who failed to gain positions.

The argument just completed could be successful, but it relies on a long series of steps from increasing profits to, taxing these profits, to redistributing the proceeds, to increasing overall happiness, which may collapse at every step. For example, the step of taxing the increased profits is endangered by the fact that trying to help the weak by enabling the strong to get even stronger usually fails. In this particular case, enabling the rich to become even richer puts them in an excellent position to resist being taxed. Consequently, utilitarians should search for a less circuitous way to help the poor and maximize happiness. One possibility is to preferentially admit to lower schools or professional schools those who are eventually most likely to improve the services available to the poor.

This change in strategy changes the standard characteristics of those most qualified. To see this, begin with the obvious fact that the qualities that most qualify a person for a job depend on what the job is. The example of preferential admissions for blacks to medical schools effectively illustrates this point. Let us make three plausible assumptions. First, the job is to provide good medical service for the black poor. Second, black doctors are more likely than white doctors to practice medicine in black ghettos. Third, a policy of admitting applicants to medical schools using a highest-scores measure would result in only a very few black applicants being admitted. If these three suppositions are sound, a policy of giving some preference to black applicants for medical schools would reduce human misery to a greater extent than a policy of admitting applicants with the highest scores. That policy might end up with more and more highly skilled white male doctors lavishing medical attention for every ailment major and minor, real or imagined, that the rich white complain of while the black poor get no medical attention even for serious illnesses. This is not the way to maximize happiness.

Similar arguments may justify preferential admission of women in medical schools, given the plausible assumption that female doctors are more likely to win the trust of their female patients and as a result may provide them with better medical attention than male doctors—even if we make the highly dubious assumption that female doctors are somewhat less highly technically skilled than male doctors. In the case of business, a firm may serve communities it would otherwise not serve by having an appropriate mix of races and sexes among its top officers.

One serious problem with the present argument in favor of affirmative action is its heavy dependence on contestable empirical claims. The most prominent is that black doctors are more likely to practice in black ghettos than white doctors. If this claim is false because affirmatively admitted black doctors will choose to simply swell the number of doctors already pampering the rich, then the argument just presented for preferentially admitting black applicants to medical school falls to the ground. Still the claim that black doctors are more likely to practice in black ghettoes is plausible. White prejudice or at least doubts about the competence of blacks remain, especially if the competence that is required is of a high order and where its absence may prove disastrous. This suggests that white patients are likely to prefer being treated by white doctors than by black doctors, especially if it is widely suspected that the black doctors were affirmatively admitted to medical school. Further, even setting aside the doubts of some whites about the *competence* of black doctors, many whites may be put off by the idea of being examined by black doctors, especially black male doctors. But these conjectures could easily turn out to be false. I am not aware of any empirical studies that support their truth. The narcissism of rich and well-to-do whites that supports their craving to be cosseted for every minor and imagined aliment may overcome their prejudice and draw black doctors into their orbit.

Another difficulty for the argument in question is that people in the ghettos may have the same doubts about the competence of black doctors as white people, again especially if they hear that these doctors were affirmatively admitted to medical school, and they might complain that affirmative action is designed to provide them with inferior medical services. This difficulty cannot be met by arguing that everything considered affirmatively admitted applicants are likely to acquire the same strictly medical skills as regular applicants. We have already considered that argument and agreed that it supports affirmative action insofar as it is sound. The argument now under consideration is that there is a utilitarian case for preferentially admitting black applicants to medical schools even if these applicants are, everything considered, less qualified than white applicants, and consequently likely to become less skillful doctors. We can meet the difficulty it raises if we remember that even if happiness would be maximized if everyone got equal medical attention, sometimes trying to equalize medical attention may backfire and reduce overall happiness. For example, if we tried to equalize medical attention by compelling white, more highly skilled doctors to work in black ghettos, we could end up with a lot of sick people, since compelled work is usually not of the highest quality. A better alternative might be to use monetary inducements to attract such doctors to the black ghettos, but this also has possible drawbacks. Money may induce people to do work they dislike, but it probably does not make them do their work well. In the end, preferentially admitting blacks to medical schools may be the alternative most likely to get poor black people good medical attention, even if that attention is not quite as good as the attention rich white people get. Although it may offend the strictest egalitarians, they cannot protest that it is another example of utilitarianism's penchant for sacrificing some people in order to increase overall happiness.

LOCKEAN NATURAL RIGHTS AS A DEFENSE
OF AFFIRMATIVE ACTION

In the United States, the Lockean natural rights view of justice is more widely accepted than utilitarianism. According to authorities of U.S. political culture, Americans tend to be intuitive Lockeans.[5] Locke's hold on the American mind has a long history, apparently predating Thomas Jefferson's Lockean defense of the colonies' separation from Britain in the Declaration of Independence. When a critic contended that Jefferson "copied" Locke when penning the famous opening lines of the second paragraph of the Declaration of Independence, Jefferson responded that he had written it with no intention of inventing new ideas but simply as an "expression of the American mind."[6] This would explain the perennial popularity of the Declaration of Independence in the United States and confirm Locke as a major influence on U.S. political thought. The point is not that Americans are able to identify John Locke as the source of their main views about justice. It is rather that Locke's ideas of natural right have now become part of U.S. culture and tradition and consequently many Americans take these ideas to be intuitively, and perhaps unquestionably, true.

Consider, for example, that according to Jefferson in the Declaration of Independence, Americans "hold" the "truths" about the rights he listed to be "self-evident."[7] Since the truths in question, even if true, are certainly not self-evidently true, at least in any common epistemological sense of the expression, it can only mean that Americans *take* the truths to be unquestionably true. It is therefore important to consider carefully the Lockean and Jeffersonian view of natural rights when debating the question of affirmative action in the United States. We can be sure that affirmative action will be rejected out of hand or at least viewed with considerable suspicion if it seems to violate the truths that according to the Declaration of Independence Americans hold to be self-evident. However, as we will now see, these truths strongly support many affirmative action policies.

Lockean natural rights are intended to protect a person's most basic and important interests. Among these interests he listed life, liberty, and the pursuit of happiness so that when Jefferson drew up his famous trilogy of natural rights in the Declaration of Independence, the rights to life, liberty, and the pursuit of happiness, he was following Locke.[8] Locke also believed that we have a basic and important interest in property and consequently a natural right to property.[9] Jefferson did not list that right in the Declaration, but he also believed that human beings have very important natural rights to property.

In claiming that the right to property was a natural right, Locke implied that it is a right that human beings have independently of government or society or contracts they may make with one another. Indeed, according to Locke, human beings create political society in order to protect the property that they have a natural right to accumulate. In that case, it might seem that governments may not justifiably interfere with a person's enjoyment of his property and to tell him whom to hire or not hire in his business. Locke's theory of natural property rights also seems to put affirmative action off limits for publicly owned businesses. Such businesses make contracts with investors to do their best to make money for them and governments are supposed to enforce contracts, not to tell businesses to adopt affirmative action programs in order to maximize the overall happiness. This seems like interfering with contracts rather than enforcing them.

But Locke never held that governments must ensure that persons are not prevented from doing whatever they want with their property. Such a view would have committed him to the absurd view that government must not prevent me from burying my ax in your brain just because it is *my* ax. In general, the fact of owning something does not necessarily entitle the owner to do whatever he pleases with it. Other people have rights too and these rights must be protected as carefully as the rights to property.

Does Locke's theory of natural rights oppose affirmative action? To return to the ax example, the fact that I may and should be prevented from using my ax to kill you does not imply that I may and should be compelled to use it to help you, or that I cannot use it to prevent you from advancing your interests. For example, if you are having a hard time clearing a patch of forest in order to plant a food garden, Locke's theory does not imply that I may and should be compelled to use my ax to help you clear the patch or even that I ought to lend it to you. Indeed, the theory is fully consistent with my using my ax to clear and take possession of a patch of forest that you had an eye on for yourself. These claims must be qualified. For example, Locke's claim that we all have a general obligation to "preserve Mankind" obliges me to help you if you are likely to die of exhaustion or starvation without my assistance; his theory also obliges me to help you if I had promised to help you, or if I had violated some of your rights and injured you, and you claimed correctly that helping you to clear the patch of forest would be just reparation for the harm I unjustly caused you. Aside from a few qualifications, however, Locke's theory imposes no obligation on me to help you. Similarly, it may be argued that if a business has made no special contracts to hire specific others, or owes them no reparation, or does not have to hire them to save their lives, it has no obligation not to hire whomever it pleases. After all, its owners and investors made their own way, and as long as they do not stand in the way of others and violate their rights in doing so, it has no obligation to help them other than those following from the general obligation to preserve mankind.

This can, however, be challenged on the basis of other considerations that may also be derived from Locke's theory, and they are even more readily derivable from Jefferson's version of Locke's theory. This should make it of some interest for at least two reasons. First, Jefferson's version of Locke's theory is in this respect better than Locke's theory. Second, Jefferson's version of Locke's theory is very close to the common heritage of Americans.

According to Locke, God gave each person ownership of his body and his talents—and gave the rest of the world to human beings *in common*. This presented a problem because human beings had to own parts of the world in order to be able to use God's bounty for their preservation and happiness, and they had to do so without violating others' rights. Locke solved this problem by arguing that since every person owned his own labor, he could come to own a portion of the world by mixing his labor with it, provided that no one else had done so already. Before money was invented and in wide circulation, a person acted wrongly if he appropriated large portions of the world that he could not use himself because this would lead to waste, which was against God's will; moreover, he acted stupidly because such appropriation meant that he had labored to no purpose. After money was invented and widely used, however, appropriating large portions of the world became both consistent with God's will, if it did not violate others' rights, and smart too, for the appropriations themselves or their produce could be exchanged for money, which does not spoil, and the money can be used to buy necessities and luxuries.[10]

In such circumstances with individuals having rights to appropriate as property unlimited portions of the world, it follows that the time would eventually come when there was not enough left for latecomers to appropriate.[11] Locke did not write them off, for they were human beings with the same rights to life, liberty, and property as the property owners. He argued that the latecomers would be hired by the large properties, businesses for example, and with the money they thus earned they could buy food, clothing, and shelter. Even their rights to property would be secured because their earnings were property that could be saved and used to buy more property. Indeed, since Locke believed that large appropriations led to dramatically improved productivity, he concluded that the rights of the latecomers were better secured than they would have been had money never been widely used.

Locke also provided for the latecomers who found no one to employ them. On his account, the rich with a surplus would be obliged to help them. He wrote that "as *Justice* gives every Man a Title to the products of his honest Industry," so also "*Charity* gives every Man a Title to so much out of another's Plenty, as will keep him from extream want, where he has no means to subsist otherwise."[12] Locke is saying that even if a person has acquired his property honestly, if he has a surplus, the destitute have "title" to use that surplus to save their lives or to enable them to have decent lives, and the owner is obligated to allow them to use it for this purpose. To appreciate the strength of his position here we should draw attention to the fact that his use of the word "charity" is misleading and obscures some of the surprising implications of his argument. Typically, obligations and rights are correlated—if one person has an obligation, usually another has a right to what he is obliged to do, and vice versa. But some writers say that charity is obligatory, yet not an obligation that is correlated to any rights others' have. That is, although we may have a duty to be charitable, no one can claim our charity as his right. As a result, charity is in an important sense up to the agent. She must be charitable, but she is also free to choose when to give her charity and whom to give it to. No one can confront her and demand her charity as his right.

Locke seems to have understood charity somewhat differently. As he understood it, the charity the rich owe the poor is correlated with a "title" in them to the plenty of the rich, and by this title to the plenty of the rich, he evidently meant a right to the plenty of the rich. This right he went on to say is similar to the right a person has to the products of his own industry, which in Locke's theory made it similar to a property right, and consequently a very important right indeed. In securing from another what you have a right to, you incur no debts to him, and consequently he is not permitted to attach any strings to what you get from him. The common idea of charity suggests that the beneficiaries of charity should be deeply thankful to their benefactors and can even be expected to display a certain subservience and obsequiousness in their presence—at least it is assumed that they should shower their benefactors with thanks and praises. Evidently Locke was rejecting this common idea. "A man," he wrote, "can no more justly make use of another's necessity to force him to become his Vassal, by with-holding that Relief, God requires him to afford to the wants of his Brother, than he that has more strength can seize upon a weaker, master him to his Obedience, and with a Dagger at his Throat offer him Death or Slavery."[13] Since a vassal is a dependent, Locke was saying that the rich must allow the poor to use their surplus without insisting that they become their dependents, or in other words, their lackeys. They must give up their surplus to the poor as the right of the poor and consequently with no strings attached.

Locke's foundation for the right to property was the right to life and consistently with this foundation he denied that the right to property could be allowed to trump the right to live. Consequently, although he justified a right to unlimited appropriation and anticipated that the exercise of such a right could lead to a class of people without property and threaten their rights to life, he took care to find a way to protect them against that threat. To this end he proposed obligating the rich to be charitable to the poor. But since he was troubled by large appropriations only when they led to destitution and threatened the lives of the destitute, he saw no reason to limit rights to large appropriations if the charity of the rich could save the lives of the destitute. Knowing that charity threatens the *independence* of its beneficiaries, he tried to secure their independence with his innovative idea that the poor had a right to charity of the rich, neglecting, however, to explain why the rich would comply with their obligation to the poor without making them into their vassals. Conceivably, the government would compel them to, but if the rich remain rich they would be likely to control the government. This suggests that Locke's concern for the independence of the poor was an afterthought. Had he been concerned for it from the first or prized it from the first, and had he seen from the first that the right to unlimited appropriations would threaten it, he might not have allowed it to be so dangerously threatened, and he would not have tried to save it with the desperate idea of a right to charity. Jefferson must have understood that this idea was desperate and unlikely to succeed, and being more concerned with independence than Locke, he decided not to rely on makeshift strategies to save it after it had been threatened. Consequently, he proposed to prevent very large inequalities from arising, and where they did already exist, he proposed policies to gradually divide up to make individual holdings eventually become more equal.

He came to this position when he noticed how unlimited holdings could threaten life. During his stay in France, he was shocked by the consequences of the vast inequalities in property between the rich and the poor. The rich kept immense tracts of their estates uncultivated so that they would have enough open space uncluttered by food gardens and orchards to chase down and kill wild animals, while large numbers of desperately poor people could not find work. Outraged, Jefferson wrote to James Madison that "whenever there is in any country, uncultivated lands and unemployed poor, it is clear that the laws of property have been so far extended as to violate natural right" and consequently that "legislators cannot invent too many devices for subdividing property."[14] Among such devices he suggested abolishing primogeniture and exempting the poor from taxation while taxing the rich in geometric progression.

His solution to the problem of unlimited accumulation went considerably beyond Locke's charity solution; he did not try to solve that problem with charity, because he was trying to save not only the lives of the poor but also their independence. Charity might save their lives, but it would not save their independence. Jefferson believed that a redistribution of property that would prevent destitution from arising in the first place would avoid threatening the independence of the poor. He was not making light of natural property rights, but giving them a new foundation. His foundation for such rights was expressed in terms of our interests in life and our interest in independence. He believed that a person without property was not only in danger of losing his life but also dependent, and of the dire consequences of dependence he had no doubt. "Dependence," he declared, "begets subservience and venality, suffocates the germ of virtue, and prepares fit tools for the designs of ambition."[15] Probably, he acquired that interest from republican writers who were widely studied in the period of the Founding, for Locke was not the only philosopher that Americans read. According to Jefferson, property rights that allow accumulation beyond that required for life and independence are not natural rights, but the positive rights of a state, and they are wrong and should be repealed when they threaten the lives and independence of citizens. The French nobility's rights to large estates were positive rights, and they were wrong because they violated the rights to life and independence of the French poor.

These considerations suggest that businesses do not always have a perfect freedom to hire whomever they please for whatever reason they please. Suppose that large and prospering businesses exist, as they often do, alongside large numbers of poor people who cannot find employment and whose lives and independence are therefore endangered. Locke's theory is that these poor people have rights to life and independence that entitles them to the surpluses of the owners of such businesses. Further, since their use of these surpluses must not endanger their independence, turning them into the vassals of the rich, they should have a chance to earn it, working at respectable jobs, with some assurances of continued employment. If affirmative action is necessary to establish such opportunities for the poor, it can be viewed as a conservative way of dealing with the poor. A more radical way of dealing with the poor, also American by tradition in that it stems directly from Jefferson, would be to redistribute vast and unequal holdings that threaten the lives and independence of the poor.[16] In such redistribution benefits should obviously be directed affirmatively to the poorest. All of the above considerations are forward-looking arguments for affirmative action.

The Lockean natural rights theory also supports backward-looking arguments for affirmative action. Reparation for injuries sustained by the victims of wrongful action is a central aspect of that theory, and many different ethnic minorities have sustained grave injuries as a result of wrongful discrimination directed against them. Among these injuries we should include not only those resulting from current and recent unjust racial discrimination but those resulting from the enslavement of the ancestors of those alive today. There are subtle difficulties involved in making the case that many of the disadvantages that groups such as blacks endure today are a result of the enslavement of their ancestors, and even greater difficulties in showing that present-day businesses are responsible for making compensation for those disadvantages. But Locke's theory provides the tools for overcoming these difficulties, especially the importance it accords the right of reparation, "which he who has suffered the damage has a Right to demand in his own name, and he alone can remit," and the right of inheritance.[17] I have shown elsewhere how these tools can enable us to overcome the difficulties in question.[18]

DIVERSITY

I come, finally, to the idea that affirmative action may be justified as a means to diversity. Here we encounter a difficulty that we did not encounter when we considered the utilitarian and natural rights arguments for affirmative action. Utilitarianism asks us to maximize happiness, and all of us, utilitarians as well as nonutilitarians, agree that happiness is a great good even if we do not all agree on what it is exactly or that it is the only good or the greatest good. Similarly for natural rights theory. It asks us to respect and secure natural rights, but though some deny that there are such rights, I doubt that any deny that the interests they are meant to protect are very important. However, is diversity a comparable value?

First, we must get clearer on what it is. In the relevant context, when people speak of diversity they refer to a diversity, variety, or plurality of groups of individuals. However, this still leaves the value of diversity very unclear. Why is a diversity of groups of individuals valuable? Is it more valuable than homogeneity? Perhaps it is more aesthetically pleasing. Rainbows are beautiful perhaps because of the variety of colors in them. Perhaps similar considerations make a society with a variety of groups of people more pleasing than a homogenous society. But this suggestion gives diversity only an aesthetic value, and, although such values must not be depreciated, they are not generally the object of ethics and politics. We must narrow down our inquiry and ask what the *political* value of diversity is. Would a homogenous society improve itself politically by enticing outsiders to join it? The majority of human societies have not thought so. Human beings tend to be xenophobes who fear and distrust outsiders, and this attitude may be defensible. Homogeneity in a society strengthens the mutual sympathy of its members, and such sympathy is a glue that helps to hold the society together.

The important issues this claim raises may not be pertinent here because the relevant calls for diversity are made in societies that are *already* diverse. These calls are therefore not calls for homogenous societies to make themselves diverse; they are calls for diverse societies to have the various groups composing them appropriately represented in their most noticeable, influential, and prestigious positions. The justification for calls for such representation depends on the nature of the groups that make societies diverse. Such groups are collections of individuals who strongly identify and sympathize with each other. They are not therefore necessarily internally homogenous. Jews are a group in the relevant sense, but they are not homogenous. They can be white, brown, or black; rich or poor; and conservative or liberal. The same is true of Hispanics and blacks in the United States, who are also groups in the relevant sense. Something marks the individuals composing the group as members of the group, but although that mark is sometimes hard to miss—for example, it may be black skin—this is certainly not always the case. Sometimes it may be barely discernible, if it is discernible at all, even to the members of the group. For example, some blacks are so white looking that no one, not even other blacks, can spot them as black. Consequently, although the mark by which members of the group are identified helps to account for the reason why the members of the group identify and sympathize with each other, it is never in fact the reason why they do so. The reason why is typically a consciousness of a common history, sometimes mainly glorious, but always with suffering, for the members of the group identify with each other through identifying with their common ancestors. And as Rousseau suggested, we more readily put ourselves in the place of the pitiable than in the place of the happy. In some groups this consciousness is mainly of the group—for example, its history of defeating and prevailing against its enemies, and of a preponderance of heroic and victorious struggles against adversity.

In others, the consciousness is mainly of suffering endured with honor, and of the patience and stamina of ancestors, but always there are heroes, sly tricksters who outsmarted powerful oppressors, or men and women of great courage who sacrificed themselves for the group enabling it to remain undaunted even in defeat. In the bleakest cases where the consciousness is of a recent past of great suffering, there is often a fear, sometimes vivid, sometimes only a vague uneasiness, that despite all appearances to the contrary, powerful and numerous outsiders may be incited or are even preparing to try to make the group relive the suffering of its ancestors. Finally, the consciousness includes a feeling, veridical or illusory, of being eyed with disdain or contempt, or at least with the unsettling attention normally given to a scientific or historical curiosity.

This complex combination and mixture of shared thoughts, feeling, fears, prides, and hopes binds the members of the group more firmly to each other than to most of the other members of the society, who always remain to some degree outsiders. They often have reason to dislike and even hate each other of course, but they tend to care about anonymous insiders; to wish them well; to feel elated and proud at their successes, and deflated and shamed at their failures; and to feel some obligation to help them, although they do not usually act on these feelings. At crucial points, it is even as if they can read each other's minds. They have similar and often intense relations to outsiders, but these are usually well-known outsiders. As a result, the members of the groups in question tend to identify and sympathize with the anonymous members of their group more strongly than they identify and sympathize with the other anonymous individuals in the society. Or to put it another way, members of a group tend to identify and sympathize with each other unless they have a special reason not to; and they identify and sympathize with the rest of the society only if they have a special reason to do so.

These considerations help explain why societies that are diverse in the relevant sense so often demand diversity at the top. The sympathy that the members of groups feel for each other disposes them to be elated, proud, and happy when they are represented at the top, even when they believe that they do not have a chance of getting there themselves; and some of them not at the top come to believe and hope that they can get there, just because others of their group did. Finally, having representatives at the top makes the members of the groups feel a little safer, first because it makes them feel that they are among people who appreciate their talents and genius and treat them fairly; but also because their long experience of sympathizing with each other moves them to believe and hope that their representatives will continue to sympathize with them not at the top, will not forsake them, but will be moved to use their prestige, power, and influence to intercede on their behalf, protect them from mistreatment, and clear the way for their advancement.

These considerations, if sound, provide grounds for a plausible case for affirmative action, providing that it is used to assure that the groups that make a society diverse are appropriately represented in its more visible, influential, and powerful positions. Surely helping the members of the society to feel safer, happier, more hopeful, and more trusting of each other is a worthy goal, and if affirmative action is a means to that goal this is certainly something in its favor. Also in its favor is the fact I have described of how the members of the groups that are not represented at the top tend to feel. The groups are likely to have lots of resentful, fearful, anxious, and unhappy people. For that reason, they may also to be unstable and in danger even of dissolution.

As we have seen, utilitarianism and natural rights theory readily support affirmative action for the poor, without regard to their color, race, sex, or ethnicity, and though they may also support affirmative action for middle class blacks, women, Hispanics, and other disadvantaged groups, they do so only if some contestable empirical claims are granted. However, the case for affirmative action to achieve diversity at the top seems to straightforwardly support affirmative action for members of the middle and upper classes of the groups that make the society diverse, supposing that these individuals will be more likely that the poorer members of their groups to have the skill and education to represent their groups with credit and distinction in the high positions of their society. Such a case must be analyzed to determine whether it too depends on contestable empirical claims.

Strong doubts about it are liable to linger even if the considerations I have given in its favor are sound. For example one may ask reasonably whether it is fair, whether it is likely to arouse resentments and dissension rather than amity, and whether there are other more effective and more righteous means to secure the laudable ends that the affirmative action it supports is supposed to secure.

Let us begin by reminding ourselves that what diversity of the sort under consideration puts at stake are the stability and perhaps the very survival of the society. Diverse societies are disposed to instability and dissolution, unless effective measures are taken to counter those dispositions. Political philosophers have long conceded this fact, at least tacitly, in their frequent disquisitions on the dangerous consequences of factions, for as I will now show, the groups I described as the source of diversity in society are factions. A faction, according to James Madison's famous description, is "a number of citizens, whether amounting to a majority or minority of the whole, who are united and actuated by some common impulse of passion, or of interest, adverse to the rights of other citizens, or to the permanent and aggregate interests of the community."[19] Clearly, on this definition the groups that make societies diverse qualify as factions; the fears, anxieties, suspicions, distrusts, and apprehensions of their members, their tendency to a righteous partiality for themselves and their groups, sometimes even to vengefulness and paranoia, are certainly passions adverse to the safety and stability of the society they are in. Of course, they differ in some important aspects from other factions, but this cannot count against the claim that they are factions because there are a great many kinds of factions that also differ in important respects from each other. For example, while Madison noted that "the most common and durable source of factions, has been the various and unequal distribution of property," he also acknowledged that factions can have a great variety of sources.

These ideas, even if sound, are not enough to justify affirmative action to achieve diversity at the top. As I noted, political philosophers have long studied factions and devised schemes to control the mischief they are likely to cause. One or the other of these schemes may be more acceptable and effective than affirmative action in controlling the consequences of the kind of faction now under consideration. Madison's famous scheme in *Federalist* 10 may seem especially pertinent here because he devised it to control majority factions, and the faction that needs to be controlled to secure diversity at the top is the white majority. However, Madison's scheme depends on empirical claims that may have been plausible in his day but that are very contestable and almost certainly false today. Before presenting his own scheme, Madison saw fit to consider other schemes, dismissing Rousseau's scheme to deal with the problem of factions by preventing them from arising on the ground that the latent causes of faction are "sown in the nature of man."[20]

His first argument is that human beings differ in their abilities and desires to accumulate property and these differences result in citizens having rights to different amounts and kinds of property, and therefore government's "first object" is to protect such differences, and such differences, if protected, always lead to factions. His second argument is that human reason is such that, if it is allowed freedom, always leads to passionately held differences of opinion, which always lead to factions. Rawls's famous contemporary argument that, in free societies, human reason leads to groups of individuals holding different comprehensive doctrines is similar though not identical to Madison's second argument.[21]

But these objections against Rousseau's scheme must be set aside as irrelevant to our concern here, which is to consider whether the kinds of factions under consideration can ever be prevented from arising. Such groups do not arise due to differences of property or opinion. Blacks did not become the group that they are because being free to reason as they pleased they came to hold opinions different from the views that others held. Neither did blacks become the faction that they are because, being free to reason, they came to hold different comprehensive doctrines; there are black Catholics and black Protestants of every variety; there are black Jews, black liberals, black conservatives, and black utilitarians. Taking the other cause of faction that Madison discussed, blacks did not become the faction that they are because they were free to accumulate different amounts and kinds of property. Similarly, although Jews do generally hold a comprehensive doctrine that most others do not hold, they did not become the group that the are in the relevant sense because they held that doctrine; if it were otherwise, atheist Jews would not be Jews in the relevant sense, but of course they are. In sum, Madison's arguments against Rousseau's proposal only show that it cannot prevent *all* kinds of factions from arising without violating freedom. They do not show that it cannot prevent *some* kinds of factions from arising without violating freedom.

I will now demonstrate that Rousseau's proposal can work to prevent at least some among the kind of faction now under consideration. The source of that kind of faction is neither the freedom to reason nor the freedom to use our abilities to accumulate property—it is a history of persecution. Blacks and Jews, for example, became the groups that they are because they were persecuted. The consciousness of a history of common suffering, the fears, the anxieties, the partiality, the touchiness and sensitivity, the desperate search for heroes, and the suspiciousness of outsiders all stem from a long history of being persecuted by the ancestors of these same outsiders or by people who identify with their descendants. It may be objected that blacks became the faction that they are because of racism, and racism arose because people were free to reason; in other words, being free to reason, and reason being fallible, people came to passionately hold racist opinions. This is a desperate conclusion. Suppose I grant, but only for the sake of argument, that the freedom to reason led to racism. It does not follow that the freedom to reason led to blacks becoming a faction. Even if that freedom led to racism, and racism led to people disliking blacks, hating them, and even holding them in contempt, these attitudes even held passionately by certain people are not enough to make those they are directed at into a faction. Perhaps most people would prefer that no one dislike them, hate them, or hold them in contempt, but they are not likely to *suffer* because others feel this way about them, at least if there are enough other people who affirm their worth. Of course, even in that case they will suffer if those who dislike, hate, and contemn them are able to enslave them, lynch them, and violate their rights, but if people have the freedom to reason they certainly do not have the freedom to treat others in this way. Similar considerations are enough to dispose of the idea that the unequal ability to accumulate property is the cause of blacks being a faction. Suppose I grant, again only for the sake of argument, that blacks have fewer of the abilities that are necessary to accumulate property. The resulting unequal amounts of property held by blacks and whites that would result would not make blacks into a faction, especially if we keep in mind the limits on such inequalities imposed by Jefferson's just extension of Locke's theory discussed earlier.

This discussion suggests that Rousseau's scheme for preventing factions from arising could work for at least for some of the kind of factions under consideration. In fact, I think it has eliminated some of these factions. Consider, for example, that the Germans and the Irish in colonies and the United States in the eighteenth and nineteenth centuries were among the factions under consideration. Like these other factions, the Germans and the Irish did not become factions in the relevant sense just because they had different abilities to accumulate property, although this might have been the case; or just because they had peculiar opinions that they held passionately, even though they might have held such opinions passionately, or just because they held comprehensive doctrines that differed from the comprehensive doctrines that others held, passionately, even though again they might have held comprehensive doctrines that no one else held. They became such factions because others persecuted them. Had others not persecuted them, or had others only disliked and hated them, they would not have become such factions. In fact, however, others picked out something about them, their appearance, names, accents, or language, to identify them by, and for some reason or other, denied them their rights, exploited them, and in general, made them suffer. But these things happened some time ago. Today no one would think of treating the Germans and the Irish in these ways, for they are now members of the white majority, which of course is also a faction, though of a different kind from the kind that the Germans and Irish used to be.

This conclusion raises a difficulty for the case for affirmative action to achieve diversity at the top. I speculated earlier that a survey of the schemes political philosophers have proposed to handle the problem of factions could conceivably uncover a scheme that could be used to handle the problems raised by the groups that make a society diverse. In particular, if diversity of the sort under consideration can be eliminated, as it was in the case of the Germans and the Irish, we do not need diversity at the top, and we therefore do not need affirmative action to achieve such diversity. Since the Germans and the Irish stopped being factions of the particular sort under consideration because others stopped persecuting them, the proposal is therefore that similar factions, both those that existed alongside the Germans and Irish factions in the eighteenth and nineteenth centuries, and any that might have formed more recently, can possibly be eliminated in the same way.

But the success of the Germans and Irish in ceasing to be factions was due at least in part to the same mechanism that those who endorse affirmative action for diversity at the top hope will help eliminate present-day factions. In other words, we must not overlook the help that the earlier and well-placed members of the groups extended to the newcomers, whom they could not help regarding as their kith and kin. As Martin Delany, one of the most astute observers of these matters in the nineteenth century, expressed the same point, "Nor was it until their influence became too great, by the political position occupied by their brethren in the new republic, that the German and Irish peasantry ceased to be sold as slaves for a term of years fixed by law, for the repayment for their passage money."[22] Further, people have many different reasons for persecuting others, and these differences make a difference to how readily they can be stopped or persuaded from continuing to do so. The reasons they had for persecuting the Germans and the Irish in the eighteenth and nineteenth centuries stemmed from earlier animosities in Europe, reinforced by the xenophobia normally aroused by the presence of strange-looking people who are not well understood and therefore not trusted. Time and increasing familiarity gradually removed these obstacles to acceptance into the mainstream.

The reasons for the persecution of blacks were, and still are today, very different. The German and Irish peasantry may have been sold as slaves for a term of years but they received something valuable in exchange, passage to the New World and its opportunities. Blacks were the only group who were enslaved for life, and they got nothing but grief and an evil reputation in exchange for it. To excuse their toleration or participation in this crime, most, though not all, white Americans came to accept ideas no one had taken seriously before. For example, the Aristotelian idea of the natural slave was revived after centuries of well-deserved neglect and applied to blacks, finally finding people sufficiently gullible or self-deceived to be persuaded of it. The resulting implication that blacks were stupid, servile, and incapable of being left to fend for themselves was then "proved" by the example of selected blacks whom slavery had already ruined. This pseudoscience was supported by aesthetic and other reactions to blacks that easily became revulsion, repugnance, and disgust. It is easy to detect these emotions in Thomas Jefferson, even when he was observing with an affected scientific detachment that blacks have "a very strong and disagreeable odour," and that the "immovable veil of black" that covers all their emotions accounts for their lack of beauty compared to whites, which they declare by their preference for whites, "as uniformly as is the preference of the Oranootan for the black woman over his own species."[23]

The supporters of slavery sought hard to find ways to plant such attitudes, beliefs, and desires deeply and firmly in the European mind in the United States in order to persuade it to tolerate the practice of enslaving blacks; although slavery had once been common throughout Europe, it had been abolished and condemned there for centuries before Europeans revived the institution in America, though taking care to reserve it for nonwhites. The supporters of slavery must have found what they sought and succeeded only too well in applying it because the attitudes, beliefs, and desires in question persist a century and a half after the abolition of slavery and almost a half century after being subjected regularly to stern and cogent criticism. The most important consequence of these considerations is that the membership of factions formed and sustained as the black faction are the most permanent of all factions. The membership of economic factions is always liable to change as dynasties rise and fall, as farmers become businessmen, and businessmen become farmers, and as the rich become poor, and the poor rich. The membership of factions based on opinion also changes as people change their opinions, or as ideologies evolve and people find that they can no longer accept them. But the factions like the black faction never change membership except by death and birth. Blacks may change from rich to poor and vice versa, and from liberal to conservative, but as they sometimes say, "the only things I have to do is to stay black and die." In this respect the faction most similar to the black faction are Jews, who go through similar changes but always remain Jews, and the same goes for women, at least if we set aside sex changes. As a result, the members of these factions can find no respite, and no refuge in other groups or in the mainstream. Their consciousness of themselves as endangered stays with them wherever they go, whomever they surround themselves with, and however they disguise themselves. Consequently they have remained potential sources of instability.

The implication of the above discussion is that if Madison was right that freedom leads to factions, given human nature, it is also true that the violation of freedom can also lead to factions, given human nature, and further that some of these factions may persist even when the violation of freedom that caused them to arise is corrected. In this sort of case, it is not reason's tendency to become passionately attached to certain opinions (even demonstrably false ones) that is the source of the trouble. Blacks do not remain a faction because whites are free to reason and to passionately hold racist beliefs; nor are they a faction because they are free to reason and to passionately hold certain beliefs about whites. They are a faction because of a still vivid memory of persecution, and because of a fear that such persecution may be repeated. No one can justifiably dismiss that fear as an unfounded fear after the unexpected appearance of the Nazis in Europe seventy years ago.

To successfully calm the reasonable apprehensions of groups that are factions because of such apprehensions, it is not enough to resort to a strategy of persuading people to give up their racist beliefs. Madison was right that when human beings are given the freedom to reason, no one can be confident that their self-love, and the fallibility of their reason, will not lead them to hold passionately opinions that could be dreadfully cruel and false. Nor would it be enough to make sincere verbal promises of protection from persecution. The unreliability of such promises is well established. What is needed is to act positively to enable the faction to defend itself, and if Delany was right about the causes of the rise of the Germans and Irish, one of the ways to do this is to use affirmative action to help enable an appropriate number of them to hold influential, respected, and powerful positions in the society. They will not forsake and abandon the less fortunate members of their group. Their sympathy for these others will not permit them to, because it was forged and is sustained by the ineradicable memory of their common history of suffering.

Here we must not be too quick to object that if the Germans' sympathy for each other helped the whole rise, and the sympathy of the Irish for each other had a correspondingly good result, both groups arose without benefit of affirmative action. In helping their own kith and kin rise, powerful Germans and Irish certainly did not object to and, on the contrary, probably helped support segregation and antiblack laws. Such laws gave preference to whites of whatever ethnicity over blacks, and since the Germans and Irish were always white, these laws were in effect affirmative action for Germans and Irish. I think it would also be unfair to object that the argument for affirmative action would not work because well-placed blacks care nothing for less fortunate blacks. Well-placed blacks feel insecure, and this feeling, perfectly justified, sometimes makes them fearful of expressing their sympathy for less fortunate blacks, or perhaps prevents that sympathy from even arising. As they become more secure they will also become more sympathetic and more helpful.

The case I have just made for affirmative action to achieve diversity at the top bears some resemblance to Lani Guinier's argument for proportional representation to try to ensure that generally disadvantaged groups get appropriate political representation.[24] There is no reason why they cannot work together. Appropriate political representation for such groups would then be seconded by the sympathy of their well-placed members. But her argument is more broadly applicable than mine, for my argument does not recommend affirmative action to achieve diversity at the top for every disadvantaged group. Disadvantaged groups will benefit from affirmative action to achieve diversity at the top only if they are factions of the sort I described, that is, groups of individuals with a recent or sufficiently powerful memory of persecution that creates and sustains a strong mutual sympathy for each other as well as well founded anxieties about the likelihood of continuous fair treatment from outsiders.

This argument is not utilitarian because its object is not to maximize utility, but it is a forward-looking argument because its object lies in the future, namely, the stability of the society. It is also backward looking because its roots are in the past. New generations do not open their eyes on pristine landscapes. They come of age in circumstances that are always deeply marked by the past, and if they are willing to accept the benefits of the past they must also be prepared to fix the evils that the past has left them to deal with. Here the responsibility of businesses is immensely important. Businesses are often built on inheritances, and consequently they must fix some of the problems that the accumulation of these inheritances have left us with. Prominent among these problems is that of factions of the sort I have emphasized. If affirmative action to achieve diversity is a way to help eliminate these factions, businesses must make it a moral priority to affirmatively hire members of these factions in the most influential and powerful positions.

CONCLUSION

I have used an approach to the problem of affirmative action that differs from those that I and many others have used in the past. Instead of defending affirmative action with whatever arguments come to mind, I have presented two well-known and widely accepted conceptions of justice and tried to show that they support both forward-and backward-looking arguments for affirmative action. In the case of utilitarianism, my aim was not to show that it supports iron-clad arguments for affirmative action. Utilitarianism cannot do this because the policies it recommends depend on factual premises that can always be challenged, however implausibly. My objective was to show that if plausible or even if contestable factual assumptions are granted, utilitarianism can support arguments for affirmative action. I have been more concerned, however, to show that Locke's natural rights theory can readily support affirmative action. As noted, authorities tell us that this theory has so suffused the culture that Americans take it to be intuitively correct. To show that it supports affirmative action should therefore be a matter of some practical importance even if it is not theoretically decisive. Finally, I presented an argument for affirmative action that would help secure the stability of the society by bringing representatives of a certain faction to the top. This argument was not meant to support affirmative action to achieve a diversity of cultures at the top. I am not convinced that there is any general and compelling reason to go out of our way to achieve such a diversity.

NOTES

1. Bernard Boxill, "The Morality of Reparations," *Social Theory and Practice* 2 (1972): 113–124. I first made the distinction between forward- and backward-looking arguments for affirmative action in this essay.

2. The standard modern treatment of utilitarianism is Richard Brandt, *A Theory of the Good and the Right* (Oxford: Clarendon Press, 1979).

3. John Rawls, *The Law of Peoples* (Cambridge, Mass.: Harvard University Press, 1999), 98.

4. Adam Smith, *The Theory of Moral Sentiments* (Indianapolis, Ind.: Liberty, 1979), 184–185.

5. Louis Hartz, *The Liberal Tradition in America* (New York: Harcourt Brace, 1955).

6. Thomas Jefferson, "To James Madison," 1823 and "To Henry Lee," 1825, in *Jefferson: Political Writings*, ed. Joyce Appleby and Terence Ball (Cambridge: Cambridge University Press, 1999), 146, 148.

7. Jefferson, "The Declaration of Independence," in Appleby and Ball, *Jefferson: Political Writings*, 102.

8. John Locke, *An Essay Concerning Human Understanding*, ed. Peter Nidditch (Oxford: Clarendon Press, 1979), 266.

9. John Locke, "The Second Treatise of Government," "Of Property," chap. 5, in *Locke: Two Treatises of Government*, ed. Peter Laslett (Cambridge: Cambridge University Press, 1988), 285–302.

10. Ibid.

11. At one point Locke does write that a man has a right to what he has mixed his labor with "at least where there is enough, and as good left in common for others." See

Locke, "Second Treatise," 288. It makes most sense to suppose that he meant that leaving enough and as good for others was a sufficient and not a necessary condition for appropriation. See the argument in Jeremy Waldron, "Enough and as Good Left for Others," *Philosophical Quarterly* 29 (1979).

 12. Locke, "First Treatise," "Of Adam's Title to Sovereignty by Donation," chap. 4, sec. 42, in *Locke: Two Treatises of Government*, 170.

 13. Ibid.

 14. Thomas Jefferson, "Letter to James Madison," 1785, in *Jefferson: Political Writings*, 107.

 15. Thomas Jefferson, "Notes on the State of Virginia: Query XIX," in *Jefferson*, ed. Merrill D. Peterson (New York: Library of America, 1984), 290–291.

 16. I am not speaking of what the racial views of Locke and of Jefferson, as they saw it, commit them to. Jefferson, for example, wanted to expel black people from America. See Jefferson, "Query XIV," in *Jefferson*, 264–265.

 17. Locke, *Second Treatise of Government* (Cambridge: Cambridge University Press), 274, 394.

 18. Bernard Boxill, "A Lockean Argument for Black Reparations," *The Journal of Ethics* 7 (2003): 63–91.

 19. James Madison, "The Federalist No. 10," in *The Federalist*, ed. Jacob E. Cooke (Middleton, Conn.: Wesleyan University Press, 1961), 56–65. Rousseau's discussion of faction is in Jean-Jacques Rousseau, *On the Social Contract* (New York: St. Martin's Press, 1978), 61–62.

 20. Ibid., 58.

 21. John Rawls, *Political Liberalism* (New York: Columbia University Press, 2005), 54.

 22. Martin R. Delany, *The Condition, Elevation, Emigration, and Destiny of the Colored People of the United States* (New York: Humanity, 2004), 50.

 23. Thomas Jefferson, *Political Writings*, 475.

 24. Lani Guinier, *The Tyranny of the Majority* (New York: Free Press, 1994).

SUGGESTED READING

Anderson, Terry H. *The Pursuit of Fairness: A History of Affirmative Action*. Oxford: Oxford University Press, 2004.

Bowen, W. G., and D. Bok. *Shape of the River*. Princeton, N.J.: Princeton University Press, 1998.

Boxill, B., and J. Boxill. "Affirmative Action." In *A Companion to Applied Ethics*. Edited by R. G. Frey and Christopher H. Wellman. Oxford: Blackwell, 2003.

Cahn, S., ed. *The Affirmative Action Debate*. New York: Rutledge, 1995.

Cohen, Carl, and James P. Sterba. *Affirmative Action and Racial Preference: A Debate*. Oxford: Oxford University Press, 2003.

Cohen, M., et al. *Equality and Preferential Treatment*. Princeton, N.J.: Princeton University Press, 1977.

Dworkin, R. "Reverse Discrimination." In *Taking Rights Seriously*. Cambridge: Harvard University Press, 1977.

———. "Affirmative Action: Does it Work?" and "Affirmative Action: Is it Fair?" In *Sovereign Virtue*. Cambridge: Harvard University Press, 2000.

Ezorsky, G. *Racism and Justice: The Case for Affirmative Action.* Ithaca, N.Y.: Cornell
     University Press, 1991.
Guinier, Lani, and Susan Strum. *Who's Qualified?* Boston: Beacon, 2001.
Gurin, Patricia, Jeffrey S. Lehman, and E. Lewis. *Defending Diversity: Affirmative Action at
     the University of Michigan.* Ann Arbor: University of Michigan Press, 2007.
Kershnar, Stephen. *Justice for the Past.* Albany: State University of New York Press, 2004.
Roberts, Rodney, C. *Injustice and Rectification.* New York: Peter Lang, 2002.
Thompson, Janna. *Taking Responsibility for the Past.* Oxford: Polity, 2002.

CHAPTER 19

WHISTLE-BLOWING, MORAL INTEGRITY, AND ORGANIZATIONAL ETHICS

GEORGE G. BRENKERT

WHISTLE-BLOWING has attracted considerable interest, both popular and academic, during the past one hundred years. Although one can find examples of whistle-blowing prior to the twentieth century, whistle-blowing is largely a contemporary phenomenon that has increased in frequency and extent. Changes in job structures, attitudes toward authority, and the size and complexity of organizations are among the reasons cited for this increase.

Whistle-blowers evoke widely different responses. On the one hand, some are perceived as brave and even heroic. Jeffrey Wigand, who exposed the actions of Brown & Williamson, a tobacco company that allegedly manipulated the effects of nicotine in cigarettes, has generally been portrayed in the media as a courageous person. Three whistle-blowers, Sherron Watkins, Cynthia Rowland, and Coleen Rowley, were celebrated as "Persons of the Year" in 2002 by *Time* magazine. On the other hand, whistle-blowers are also viewed as snitches, traitors, and spies. The former president of General Motors, James Roche, is frequently quoted as calling whistle-blowers the "enemies of business" and accusing them of "spreading disunity and creating conflict."[1]

Business ethicists have examined this important phenomenon by considering, in general, two major issues.

First, how may we best analyze the concept of whistle-blowing? Since the term is recent, answers to this question are not simply reports of how the term is standardly defined, but are attempts to identify the phenomenon to be analyzed. How may we best capture the characteristics to which people refer when they speak of whistle-blowing? Second, ethical discussions of whistle-blowing have tended to focus on the question of how, if at all, whistle-blowing may be justified in individual cases. This is an ethical problem of enormous significance for those directly involved. It deserves the ethical consideration it has received.

Nevertheless, there are other important issues to which answers regarding the justification of this or that act of whistle-blowing may only be a partial, and frequently ineffective, response. Accordingly, a third issue business ethicists need to consider concerns whistle-blowing in its organizational and social context. What problem does whistle-blowing answer and how effectively does it do so? If the difficulties that give rise to whistle-blowing can be reduced or eliminated, we may be able to avoid the moral dilemmas and predicaments that whistle-blowing raises. This broader set of questions looks to the nature of the ethical organization and its implications for whistle-blowing, rather than simply at the harms or injuries to which particular acts of whistle-blowing may seek to respond.

WHAT IS WHISTLE-BLOWING?

Many definitions of whistle-blowing have been offered over the past half century.[2] Some are relatively informal and careless in their formulation, others more meticulous. Many include the following conditions: (1) An individual has some privileged status with regard to an organization (usually he or she is a member or former member) that permits knowledge of inside, confidential, or private information regarding activities undertaken by individuals within the organization; (2) This individual reports some activity that he or she considers to be illegal, immoral, or opposed to the basic values or purposes of the organization; (3) The reporting may be done internally or externally to person(s), not in the direct line of reporting, who is (are) believed to be capable and willing to stop or prevent such wrongdoing either directly or indirectly; (4) The wrongdoing is of a substantive or serious nature; (5) This wrongdoing affects the public interest, though not necessarily immediately or directly. Hence, cases of sexual harassment or racial discrimination that applied only to members of an organization might prompt whistle-blowing, because they are matters of significant public interest.

Accordingly, John Boatright suggests that

> whistle-blowing is the voluntary release of nonpublic information, as a moral
> protest, by a member or former member of an organization outside the normal
> channels of communication to an appropriate audience about illegal and/or
> immoral conduct in the organization or conduct in the organization that is
> opposed in some significant way to the public interest.[3]

Norman Bowie holds that

> a whistle blower is an employee or officer of any institution, profit or nonprofit, private or public, who believes either that he/she has been ordered to perform some act or he/she has obtained knowledge that the institution is engaged in activities which (a) are believed to cause unnecessary harm to third parties, (b) are in violation of human rights or (c) run counter to the defined purpose of the institution and who inform the public of this fact.[4]

Much more simply, Sissela Bok says that "whistle-blowers sound an alarm from within the very organization in which they work, aiming to spotlight neglect or abuses that threaten the public interest."[5] Finally, Janet Near and Marcia Miceli contend that whistle-blowing is "the disclosure by organization members (former or current) of illegal, immoral, or illegitimate practices under the control of their employers, to persons or organizations that may be able to effect action."[6] This last definition has been widely used in social scientific discussions of whistle-blowing.

These definitions differ in various ways among themselves and from the characteristics I noted above. The following paragraphs offer a resolution of these differences in the pursuit of a coherent account concept of whistle-blowing.

First, whistle-blowers do not have to be current members of the organization. They can be former members, applicants, suppliers, or auditors.[7] The Sarbanes-Oxley Act of 2002, a federal law enacted in response to corporate and accounting scandals, recognizes both present and former employees, as well as applicants, as whistle blowers.[8] More generally, it seems that the whistle-blower is a person "with privileged access to an organization's data or information"[9] that he has gained due to his official relationship with the organization. Because of one's relationship with the organization, one is assumed to have obligations of confidentiality and loyalty to the organization. Thus a potential whistle-blower must be bound by norms of confidentiality, privacy, and loyalty that govern the operations of that organization.

Second, whistle-blowing may occur inside or outside an organization. Some reject this view and argue that whistle-blowing within an organization involves processes and procedures that are part of the organization. Thus, one who reports internally is not whistle-blowing but only following standard procedures. This view is mistaken. There are many examples in which people have blown the whistle within their organizations—Cynthia Cooper blew the whistle internally on accounting practices at WorldCom.[10] The mistake made by those who oppose the notion of internal whistle-blowing is the failure to see that one can report "bad" information internally in ways that do not follow the normal chain of command and which are not, therefore, simply standard procedures. When I inform my supervisor that something wrong or harmful is going on, that is fulfilling my role responsibility. When I have to circumvent my supervisor because he will not do something to correct a harm or wrong, but tries to block the information from getting to appropriate individuals, then a situation of internal whistle-blowing arises. Accordingly, Sarbanes-Oxley speaks of whistle-blowing in an internal context.[11] Near and Miceli capture the underlying point when they note that whistle-blowing is "a challenge to the organization's authority and therefore threatens its basic mode of operation."[12] And, "It is this characteristic that, in part, makes the specter of whistle-blowing anathema to organizations."[13]

Third, whistle-blowing is a deliberate act. One does not blow the whistle by accident. Instead, one must decide and initiate a course of action to release confidential information in order to correct a wrong the whistle-blower believes someone in the organization is committing. If an employee accidentally left a document detailing wrongdoing within an organization on the desk of a journalist or a top executive in the organization who might redress that wrongdoing, it would not be a case of whistle-blowing.

Even though whistle-blowing must be a deliberate act, any particular whistle-blower might not want his or her name associated with the act of whistle-blowing. He or she may seek to blow the whistle anonymously. Sarbanes-Oxley explicitly mandates the possibility of anonymous whistle-blowing.[14] The implications of anonymity for the justification of any particular case of whistle-blowing are strongly disputed. Particularly in Europe, anonymous whistle-blowing has been viewed as unjustified.[15] Whichever route one takes to blow the whistle may have practical consequences for the whistle-blower and the charges brought against him or her, but it does not alter the fact that he or she has engaged in an act of whistle-blowing.

Fourth, the wrongdoing that is the object of whistle-blowing must be substantial.[16] Very minor transgressions in a firm or organization might be the occasion for someone to report their occurrence to someone outside the chain of command or even to people outside the organization. For example, suppose someone goes to a person higher in the hierarchy or to the press with a report that someone has taken a few pencils home from work, charging that this act is theft and ought to be stopped. The person revealing this action does what a whistle-blower would do, but the object of the action lacks the significance whistle-blowing requires. To begin with, the wrong is a common one, and though organizations oppose employees taking company property home for their personal use, this is not the appropriate occasion for complaining to higher officials or the press. It is too minor. Further, whistle-blowing occurs within a context in which the act and/or information regarding the act is not public or open. Indeed it is viewed as confidential or secret to the organization. The potential whistle-blower is viewed as having an obligation not to make the information known to the public. In trivial matters such confidentiality and obligations are themselves trivial or nonexistent. The situation does not rise to the level of whistle-blowing. However, this does not mean that there are any sharp lines here. There are not. Those who say that "an opportunity for whistle-blowing occurs with every questionable activity...[and that] therefore, the potential for whistle-blowing is widespread"[17] are exaggerating. Instead, as Bowie and Duska correctly note, "whistle-blowing is reserved conceptually only for...serious moral faults."[18] And although other faults might be involved, for example, legal ones, they are correct on the required serious or substantial nature of the situation that may occasion whistle-blowing.[19]

Fifth, in blowing the whistle, an individual must direct his or her report at some person or organization (e.g., a newspaper) that the whistle-blower believes can do something to correct the purported wrongdoing. Since what one divulges may relate to past, present, or future wrongdoings, the whistle-blower's report seeks to stop, prevent, or rectify some wrongdoing. In any case, the report must be to someone the whistle-blower believes can set in process changes that will accomplish these aims. Hence, whistle-blowing need not be to someone in authority, though frequently it will be.[20] It would not be whistle-blowing if one simply told one's spouse or a friend.

An ironical result of this analysis is that whistle-blowing, so understood, is a complex phenomenon that has evolved away from its simpler origins in sporting activities, where the referee or umpire "blows the whistle" to stop some infraction. In sports, it is the role of the officials to blow the whistle; they are (in general) respected parts of the game; they are not members of a team, but outsiders, hired by the league; what they "reveal" is not something hidden or confidential, but something that has occurred in public that they have witnessed and any careful spectator might also have seen. Though whistle-blowers do still try to stop infractions, the preceding characteristics of officials in sports are not replicated in whistle-blowing as we know it today.[21]

Justifying Whistle-Blowing

Most ethical literature regarding whistle-blowing concerns the manner in which particular acts of whistle-blowing are justified. Whistle-blowing is seen as something that confronts an individual who must morally decide what to do. This perspective on whistle-blowing naturally emerges from the previous conceptual account of whistle-blowing that focuses on the conditions under which an individual may be said to be a whistle-blower.

Three major accounts have appeared in the literature that discusses this difficult moral issue: the Harm Theory, the Complicity Theory, and the Good Reasons Theory. Each of them captures important aspects of the situation facing an individual whistle- blower. However, each falls short of adequately addressing the ethical issues whistle-blowing raises.

The Harm Theory

The most prominent theory of whistle-blowing appeals to harm that has occurred or is occurring in or through the actions of certain people or systems within a business. Among the business ethicists who have most prominently defended such an account are De George, Boatright, Bowie, Duska, and James. Inasmuch as De George's analysis is one of the most frequently cited, I will focus on his views in the following discussion.

De George's account focuses on instances in which serious bodily harm is being inflicted on others through the actions of those in profit-making firms.[22] Assuming that one's motivation is moral, De George asks about the conditions under which one might justifiably engage in whistle-blowing.[23] His answer distinguishes between whistle-blowing as being morally permissible or morally obligatory. Whistle-blowing is morally permissible if and only if:

> 1. The firm...will do serious and considerable harm to employees or to the public; 2. Once employees identify a serious threat to the user of a product or to the general public, they should report it to their immediate superior and make their moral concern known; 3. If one's immediate supervisor does nothing effective about the concern or complaint, the employee should exhaust the internal procedures and possibilities within the firm.[24]

When these three conditions have been fulfilled, a person is morally permitted to blow the whistle externally.

If two additional conditions are fulfilled, De George argues that it would be morally obligatory for that person to blow the whistle externally:

> 4. The whistle-blower must have, or have accessible, documented evidence that would convince a reasonable, impartial observer that one's view of the situation is correct; and 5. The employee must have good reasons to believe that by going public the necessary changes will be brought about. The chance of being successful must be worth the risk one takes and the danger to which one is exposed.[25]

The harm account identifies several important considerations in the justification of whistle-blowing. Crucial to this account is that mere knowledge of harmful acts does not permit or require whistle-blowing. Further, potential whistle-blowers are not urged immediately to go outside of the firm, but to recognize their responsibilities to report such harms to those in the organizational chain of command. In addition, whistle-blowers are not required to report such harm regardless of the effects of reporting on them or their family: "Employees do not have an obligation to put themselves at serious risk without some compensating advantage to be gained."[26]

There are a number of reasons why we should not be fully satisfied with this account. First, De George builds his model on the basis of "serious bodily harm, possibly death, that threatens either the users of a product or innocent bystanders."[27] The paradigm case of whistle-blowing involves the threat of physical harm or death.[28] The problem with this approach is that a large number of illegal or unethical actions that are the object of whistle-blowing do not include serious bodily harm, for example, fraud (in its plethora of forms), corruption, graft, mistreatment of others, or discrimination. Accordingly, the physical paradigm seems unwarranted. De George does indicate that his account can be extended to financial harm, tax evasion, and the like.[29] However, some worry that De George's paradigm leaves us with little or no guidance when we are confronted with more usual situations that do not involve any physical harm.[30] For example, consider the case of Roger Boisjoly, who blew the whistle in the Challenger disaster. In this instance, Michael Davis notes,

Boisjoly was seeking to prevent falsification of the record regarding this disaster.[31] He was not attempting to prevent serious physical harm. Davis concludes that that "if whistleblowers must have...'good reason to believe that revealing the threat will (probably) prevent the harm,' then the history of whistle-blowing virtually rules out the moral justification of whistle-blowing."[32] Accordingly, any account of whistle-blowing must take into account not only a wider view of wrongs or injuries that are caused by or through an organization but also the possibility that a whistle-blower may be responding to past harms rather than future harms.

Second, Davis criticizes De George's account for neglecting to take into account the high rate of failure of whistle-blowers and the significant costs blowing the whistle imposes on them. As Davis notes, the chances for success for whistle-blowers are not good. Kermit Vandivier blew the whistle on a faulty jet brake design at B. F. Goodrich, for which he was fired, while those who advocated the faulty design were promoted.[33] His experience is not atypical.

Similarly, the costs of whistle-blowing are frequently quite high and all but unknowable in advance. Jeffrey Wigand blew the whistle on Brown & Williamson's handling of its tobacco products and lost his job, his home, his wife, and his career. De George himself notes that "whistle-blowers usually fare poorly at the hands of their company....Most are fired."[34] Thus, Gene James argues that De George's fifth condition is too weak.[35] James argues that the view that "'one does not have an obligation to put oneself at serious risk without some compensating advantage to be gained' is...false. Sometimes doing one's duty requires one to undertake certain risks."[36]

Third, on the above account external whistle-blowing is permissible only once one has done everything possible within the organization. De George takes this to be the manner in which one discharges one's obligation of loyalty to one's organization.[37] Loyalty requires going up the chain of command. However, by itself, this would not obviously discharge one's loyalty to the company (supposing one has such). Loyalty is a broader and deeper concept than simply exhausting internal procedures. Loyalty is not a serious part of De George's account.

Similarly, the fact that some substantial harm has occurred and one has taken one's concern up the chain of command does not obviously invalidate or override obligations of confidentiality owed to an organization. There must be some other, overriding moral principle or value that is functioning here. De George identifies this basic principle underlying his harm theory as the view that "we are morally obliged to prevent harm to others at relatively little expense to ourselves, and that we are morally obliged to prevent great harm to a great many others, even at considerable expense to ourselves."[38] But if this is so, then, whistle-blowing should not be simply morally permissible, given the first three conditions De George mentions, but rather obligatory. The two-level account of justified whistle-blowing the Harm Theory offers would then collapse into this single condition.

Finally, De George's harm account is one of external whistle-blowing. He makes clear that an account of internal whistle-blowing will look different. In short, his is not a unified account of the justification of whistle-blowing, but a dual account. With regard to internal whistle-blowing, De George maintains that "if serious harm is threatened to employees, then the first three conditions come into play and the analysis yields an obligation to internally blow the whistle."[39] So the threat (or reality) of serious and considerable harm plus the failure of one's direct report to correct that situation does generate an obligation to blow the whistle, at least when employees are threatened. In this case, one need not (apparently) have the degree of evidence De George has previously imposed on potential whistle-blowers, nor need one (apparently) consider the chances of success or the risk to oneself. This is a much stronger and less plausible account. It is tempered by De George's more general views that internal reporting may be permitted, but is not in many circumstances morally required. For example, with other wrongdoings, such as taking kickbacks from a supplier or padding an expense account, De George does not believe the employee has an obligation to blow the whistle—"unless reporting it is stated as an obligation, such as in corporate guidelines."[40] Of course, in that case it would be a legal or compliance matter, not necessarily a moral matter. Furthermore, in such cases one does not have an obligation to report wrongdoing to a superior who is the person engaged in the wrongdoing.[41] Instead, "whether it is morally required depends on the severity of the harm, one's position within the firm and vis-à-vis the perpetrator, the firm's general operating procedures, and other pertinent factors."[42]

The harm account instructs us that whistle-blowing is neither always required nor a matter of moral indifference. Sometimes it may be permitted. Though it hardly elaborates on the point, it reminds us of the importance of loyalty considerations in blowing the whistle. It correctly emphasizes the importance for whistle-blowing of being able to provide evidence for one's views. Nevertheless, we need not follow its view that whistle-blowing is, paradigmatically, linked with serious and considerable harm of the kind that is involved in physical injury or harm (including death). Finally, the current forms of the Harm Theory tend to avoid close consideration of the nature of organizations, let alone business organizations, and the roles or relationship that people have to such organizations.[43]

The Complicity Theory

A rather different justification of whistle-blowing has been offered by Davis, whose theory of the justification for blowing the whistle rests upon one's complicity in wrongdoing. In his theory, whistle-blowing is tightly connected with one's job in an organization. In addition, he does not distinguish between permissibility and obligation in whistle-blowing. Instead, he argues that employees who are involved in wrongdoing at work "are morally required to reveal what [they]...know to the public (or to a suitable agent or representative of it)."[44] The particular conditions he identifies requiring whistle-blowing are the following:

> (C1) What you will reveal derives from your work for an organization;
> (C2) You are a voluntary member of that organization;
> (C3) You believe that the organization, though legitimate, is engaged in serious moral wrongdoing;

(C4) You believe that your work for that organization will contribute (more or less directly) to the wrong if (but not only if) you do not publicly reveal what you know;
(C5) You are justified in beliefs C3 and C4; and
(C6) Beliefs C3 and C4 are true.[45]

This theory of whistle-blowing has some advantages over the Harm Theory as Davis is quick to point out. For example, it "requires moral wrong, not harm, for justification." This addresses the problem noted above with the Harm Theory that there may be instances of whistle-blowing in which harm, in any ordinary sense, does not appear to be at issue. In addition, "the wrong need not be a new event." It may concern something that has already happened. Still, the wrong must be a serious one. Finally, "the complicity theory does not require that the whistle-blower have enough evidence to convince others of the wrong in question.... [But it does require] that the whistle-blower be (epistemically) justified in believing both that his organization is engaged in wrongdoing and that he will contribute to that wrong unless he blows the whistle."[46]

Nevertheless, the Complicity Theory has serious weaknesses. Primary among them is that it is tied to an overly narrow view of whistle-blowing requiring that "what the whistle-blower reveals must derive from his work for the organization."[47] It must concern "information with which one is *entrusted.*"[48] The significance of this requirement is that if an employee of a firm simply learns about illegal or immoral acts committed within a firm, but has not been entrusted with that information, then whistle-blowing is not at stake. Davis maintains that this allows us to distinguish the whistle-blower from a spy. He argues that if an employee reports on the wrongdoing by someone else in his or her organization, he or she is not a whistle-blower but a spy. Such a view is out of line with almost all accounts of the nature of whistle-blowing. Whistle-blowing does not necessarily concern wrongdoing that an employee is involved in or that derives from his or her work. When Cynthia Cooper blew the whistle on the accounting fraud at WorldCom, the accounting wrongs she identified did not derive from her work. When Dan Gellert, a pilot at Eastern Air Lines, reported the software defects in the autopilot system of the Lockheed 1011, neither the defects nor the subsequent management cover-up was due to his work. Finally, Joe Darby blew the whistle on prisoner abuse at Abu Gharib, but he was not involved in causing any of this abuse. Many others examples have the same implication, namely, one can blow the whistle on information with which one was not entrusted at one's place of work.

This narrow view of whistle-blowing is captured in the moral basis for the Complicity Theory that rests upon our obligation "to avoid doing moral wrongs." According to Davis, "when, despite our best efforts, we nonetheless find ourselves engaged in some wrong, we have an obligation to do what we reasonably can to set things right."[49] However, this principle would not offer a moral basis for much of what is widely recognized as whistle-blowing because that does not involve wrongdoing on the part of the whistle-blowers. We require some other ethical basis for whistle-blowing.

Given this moral basis, it is puzzling that Davis holds that the whistle-blower must be "a *voluntary* participant in the organization in question." Even if a person is being coerced to do something, we might still think that the person is responsible, depending upon the nature and extent of the coercion, for wrongs he or she did. For example, a person might be conscripted (i.e., a form of coercion) into the army, do something wrong, and feel morally obligated to set things right. This individual would not be a voluntary participant, and yet still would meet all Davis's other conditions for being a whistle-blower. Contrariwise, a person might be conscripted into the military and yet come upon knowledge of war crimes in which he played no role, but feel obligated to report to this information to his superiors or the media. According to all other accounts of whistle-blowing, but contrary to the Complicity Theory, this would also be a case of whistle-blowing.

On Davis's views, whistle-blowers need not believe that their blowing the whistle will do anything to prevent or undo the wrong. All they must believe is that their work has contributed to the wrong in question and that revealing this wrong will prevent their complicity in this wrong.[50] In short, Davis advocates confession even though no correction is possible. However, whistle-blowing is not simply an effort to wash one's hands of some wrong (e.g., through confession), all the while the wrong continues or goes uncorrected. Instead, it is an attempt either to prevent or correct that wrong, or to modify current or future practices so that that wrong does not occur again.

What Davis incorrectly captures, but importantly introduces, is the notion of an individual's integrity and the manner in which it is bound up with whistle-blowing. Rothschild and Miethe better formulate this situation when they claim that "the experience of whistle-blowers teaches that while resistance in the workplace challenges the practices, the ideology and the authority of those in power, it is also about the struggle for dignity and integrity in work organizations."[51] Still, one need not be directly involved in wrongdoing taking place in an organization to believe that one's integrity is diminished by wrongdoing brought about by the organization of which one is a member. This notion of integrity and whistle-blowing will be discussed below in the next major section of this chapter.

Finally, Davis claims that the Complicity Theory does not say anything about going through channels. The Complicity Theory does not reject going through channels, but for Davis's view this is simply "a way of finding out what the organization will do, not an independent requirement of justification."[52] The problem with this view is that Davis's theory gives no regard to matters of loyalty that a member of an organization owes to others in the organization. On behalf of one's own non-complicity, Davis implies, the employee is justified in speaking to whoever may be able to help him or her wash his or her hands. This is absolution with little regard for one's other organizational responsibilities.

We should not accept the Complicity Theory.

The Good Reasons Theory

A third approach to the justification of whistle-blowing, "Good Reasons Theory," is held by a number of other ethicists, of whom Sissela Bok is an important representative. On this view, we are not to focus on the complicity of the whistle-blower. Furthermore, she does not offer an account that focuses on harm in the manner that the Harm Theory does.

Instead, she offers a threefold account that is linked to her analysis of the nature of whistle-blowing. "Whistle-blowers," Bok tells us, "sound an alarm from within the very organization in which they work, aiming to spotlight neglect or abuses that threaten the public interest."[53] Such acts, she contends, involve three elements: dissent, breach of loyalty, and accusation.[54] The justification of any particular act of whistle-blowing flows from several "requirements" that are bound up within these elements of whistle-blowing. Bok does not distinguish between instances in which whistle-blowing is permissible as opposed to being required or obligatory. Finally, Bok focuses on external whistle-blowing, as do Davis and De George.

First, Bok argues that a whistle-blower must decide "whether, other things being equal, speaking out is in fact in the public interest."[55] This is the dissent side of whistle-blowing. A potential whistle-blower has "an obligation to consider the nature of this benefit and to consider also the possible harm that many come from speaking out."[56] In making this determination, whistle-blowers must consider how imminent and serious the threat in question is.[57] Accordingly, the underlying normative basis for Bok's view appears to be an obligation that each person has to "serve the public interest" or to "benefit the public."[58] Bok does not elaborate on this obligation. She does, however, mention additional obligations, responsibilities, risks, and their supporting arguments that one must appraise so as to arrive at a "considered choice."

Second, whistle-blowers must determine what responsibilities they owe to their colleagues and to the institution for which they work. These responsibilities must be weighed against one's responsibility to the public interest. A requirement in making this judgment is that one must ask whether existing avenues for change within the organization have been explored. If there is not time to go through the organization or the organization is corrupt, then one might go outside immediately.[59] However, one's loyalty to the organization must be taken seriously. Any breach of loyalty should be minimized. Whistle-blowing is, or should be, a last resort for alerting the public to an impending disaster.[60]

Third, the accusation one brings must meet requirements of accuracy and fairness. Does the whistle-blower have his facts straight? And, can the accusation one is considering be something one can fairly make? Or will it intrude on personal privacy and undermine trust? It is unjustified when it makes public matters related to political or sexual life that are legitimately private. In short, is the message one to which the public is entitled?[61] Here Bok raises questions of fairness to those individuals who are supposedly linked with the abuses and neglect. It is within this condition that Bok requires that one's motives be ethically appropriate and one's responsibilities to oneself adequately considered. With regard to one's motives, "one should be scrupulously aware of any motive that might skew their message."[62] Whistle-blowing is "starkly inappropriate when in malice."[63] To avoid bias, she suggests that whistle-blowers seek objective advice from others.[64] Both she and De George require that the motivation be morally appropriate.

Bok places great emphasis on the correctness of one's complaint, and on the accuracy and objectivity of the whistle-blower's complaint. She does not, as De George does, suggest different standards of evidence for whistle-blowing being permissible or obligatory. But she does urge a potential whistle-blower to seek "as much and as objective advice regarding his choice [to blow the whistle] as he can *before* going public."[65] It seems likely that she would not think whistle-blowing morally justified unless it fulfilled some robust standard of evidence. She does not invoke, as Davis does not, De George's distinction between permitted and obligatory whistle-blowing.

Bok's view does not invoke the complicity features on which Davis bases his account. Her account does not focus on wrongs to which one's work will contribute. Nor are physical harms, for her, the paradigm occasion for whistle-blowing as it is for De George. Instead, she refers more broadly to neglects, abuses, and risks to the public interest.[66] At other times, she speaks simply of the "injustice" the problem represents.[67] Further, these must be something that seriously and imminently affects the public interest. On her view, something that has happened in the past could not be the occasion of whistle-blowing unless it could be shown to have serious and imminent effects in the present. However, Bok does not say how to determine what that public interest is, and how directly it must be affected.

Bok does not spend much time considering internal whistle-blowing. Given the first condition above, internal whistle-blowing would only be justified if its cause seriously and imminently affected the public interest. In this case, however, she would be presenting a unified account—as opposed to that of De George—of whistle-blowing. Still, Bok gives much greater importance than De George or Davis to considerations of loyalty. However, like De George and unlike Davis, she urges whistle-blowers to exhaust internal resources for change, unless one's organization is thoroughly corrupt.

Bok is also concerned, as is De George but not Davis, with the effectiveness of whistle-blowing. Her focus is on the receptiveness of the audience to such a complaint: "When the audience is not free to receive or to act on the information—when censorship or fear of retribution stifles response—then the message rebounds to injure the whistle-blower."[68] Accordingly, the effectiveness of whistle-blowing does not depend simply on the whistle-blower, but on the situation of the audience that receives the whistle-blower's message. However, Bok does urge whistle-blowers to act openly, rather than anonymously, because doing so is "more likely to be taken seriously."[69]

Finally, Bok does not suggest, as De George does, that there may be limits to how much morality can demand or that one's obligation to blow the whistle must be measured against a reasonable cost to oneself. Though Bok mentions threats to whistle-blowers of retaliation and the damage it may do to them, their careers, and their families, she does not suggest any guidance by way of these considerations. The normative principle that appears to lie at the heart of her views remains unexamined. In short, though her theory of justified whistle-blowing identifies many relevant considerations, we need a theory that is more detailed in its discussion of these crucial items. Indeed, all three preceding theories identify important justificatory elements of whistle-blowing. We can draw upon their valuable points to form a more adequate account.

An Integrity Theory
of Whistle-Blowing

In formulating an integrity theory, I will begin by focusing on the notion of wrong-doing and the responsibilities one has to report wrongdoing associated with the organization of which one is a member. Through one's association or membership with an organization, one takes on certain responsibilities one would not otherwise have. In considering this role or position, I concentrate on wrongdoing rather than harm that occurs through one's organization, since some harm might be justifiably imposed on others. For an example, a supervisor might desire to learn certain intimate details about an employee's private life, but though this desire is harmed when it is blocked, still it is justified to block that desire. The supervisor has not been wronged. Such incidents are not an occasion for whistle-blowing. Instead, it is unjustified harms, or wrongs that raise the issue of whistle-blowing. The action or policy that is the object of whistle-blowing must violate some important rule, law, or value according to which the business, or those within the business, should operate.

In such a context, I will argue that in accordance with a Principle of Positional Responsibility (PPR) a person has a responsibility to blow the whistle. The scope and stringency of this responsibility is dependent, in part, upon one's other responsibilities to the organization, the possibility of effectively reporting the wrongdoing, and the risks to oneself, one's other responsibilities and projects. However, only some whistle-blowing is obligatory. Other acts of whistle-blowing are supererogatory. Whether one is justified in blowing the whistle, all things considered, depends on how one's responsibility under the Principle of Positional Responsibility coheres with other responsibilities and ideal forms of behavior to which the person is also committed. Which are most important? Which should take precedence? In acting in accord with the Principle of Positional Responsibility or other responsibilities and values one holds, how may one best maintain one's integrity? In each situation potentially involving whistle-blowing, one must not simply consider whether there are good moral reasons to blow the whistle but also whether one should, all things considered, blow the whistle given the balance of responsibilities and ideal forms of behavior to which he or she is committed. This is a question of one's integrity. Thus, this account is a two-part, mixed account of justified whistle-blowing: a Principle of Positional Responsibility and the integrity considerations of one's commitment to PPR and other normative demands and values that define one.

Duties of Employees

To develop an account of the Principle of Positional Responsibility it will be helpful to begin by considering what responsibility a person, qua employee, has to report a serious wrongdoing occurring within or through one's organization. By exploring these employee responsibilities we can seek to determine whether an employee has a responsibility not only to report serious wrongdoings to his or her superiors but also to do so under circumstances that would constitute whistle-blowing.

The employer/employee relationship has both legal and moral aspects. Since both the law and applications of moral standards differ from society to society, these differences will have an impact on the justification of whistle-blowing in different societies. For this chapter, I have assumed an Anglo-American setting. In this context, one crucial aspect is that people have agreed to work for the business and have (thereby) acquired various responsibilities. This is a historically developed relation that involves various norms and expectations. Among the responsibilities most relevant to the present discussion are the following: confidentiality, loyalty, obedience, and reporting to proper superiors or authorities.

Each employee has a duty of confidentiality with regard to legitimately private matters within the organization for which one works. There are certain matters that are private or confidential in any such relationship. Sometimes this is interpreted in the sense that "what happens here, stays here." However, regardless of how strongly some insist on this duty, the duty of confidentiality is prima face, not unconditioned or absolute. In some instances, it can and should be overridden, for example, when doing so may prevent serious wrongdoing.

Members of an organization also have a duty of obedience. Phillip Blumberg pointed out that in the Restatement of Agency an employee has "a duty to obey all reasonable directions' of the principal."[70] So too there is a prima facie responsibility that one has to one's supervisors to follow their directions. However, as Blumberg also notes, this duty does not imply "that an agent has a duty to perform acts which … are *illegal or unethical.*"[71]

As an employee, one also has duties of loyalty to the business for which one works. With regard to one's employer, the Restatement of Agency says that "one has a duty to his principal to act solely for the benefit of the principal in all matters connected with his agency."[72] Again, this is best taken as a prima facie duty. However, one also has duties of loyalty to one's fellow employees. One learns things about them one could not otherwise know, for example, certain vulnerabilities they have. One becomes part of a team or a group whose performance depends upon what one does. Any action that might jeopardize their jobs or the company may be viewed as disloyal and undercutting what they hold important. A person of integrity would seriously regard each of these duties.[73]

In addition, the Third Restatement of Agency also specifies a "duty to provide information." This says that

> an agent has a duty to use reasonable effort to provide the principal with facts that the agent knows, has reason to know, or should know when (1) the agent

knows or has reason to know that the principal would wish to have the facts; or, subject to any manifestation by the principal, the facts are material to the agent's duties to the principal; and (2) the facts can be provided to the principal without violating a duty owed by the agent to another person.[74]

If we assume that the principal would want to know about wrongdoing so that he or she could correct it, then an employee would be justified, on the basis of this job responsibility, to report the wrongdoing to his principal. If an employee saw someone breaking into the business, setting fire to the business's property, or taking goods out the front door, that person has a responsibility to say something to her supervisor or to someone who might correct this situation. Similarly, if an employee knows that someone from outside the business is stealing the organization's property or resources, they would have a responsibility to make this known to some appropriate person who can address this situation.

But what if the principal did not want to know certain facts? Does the agent then not have a responsibility to provide that information? What if the supervisor tells one to forget what one saw or learned and to mind one's own business? In such a case, when this duty to report is interpreted to refer to what a supervisor wants to hear, there is no responsibility to report anything other than what the principal would wish to have.

In fact, it is this situation that raises the question of whistle-blowing. If one simply reports to one's supervisor some wrongdoing, one is not, as such, whistle-blowing. One is doing one's job, though perhaps exceeding even that. Still, it need not be whistle-blowing. Instead, whistle-blowing occurs when the person one reports to has rejected one's notice regarding some wrongdoing. Perhaps the potential whistle-blower is urged to be a team player; she is instructed that there "really" is not a problem; or she is told to just to stick to her job. In this situation, the whistle-blower potentially faces a double failure. There is the wrongdoing itself and the refusal by one's supervisor to deal with it. This means that if one were to report the wrongdoing in question to anyone else, one would be challenging the power and authority of the supervisor, if not the organization. One would be engaging in both an act of disclosure as well as one of disobedience. Such disobedience is generally taken to be a sign of disloyalty. Thus, whistle-blowing only occurs when one does not follow the usual hierarchical order of reporting. If one breaks ranks, as it were, to inform someone not in one's usual line of reporting—someone in upper-level management, say—one then becomes a whistle-blower. One must consider whether such further action is warranted and what that justification might be.

The Duty of Loyalty

At this point, some appeal to the duty of loyalty. Though we are told that this requires an agent "to act solely for the benefit of the principal in all matters connected with his agency," we might follow the suggestion of Larmer and distinguish between the principal's avowed interests and his best interests.[75] Loyalty might then involve challenging the avowed interests of those to whom one is loyal in order to protect their best interests. Thus, Larmer has argued that a person must consider not simply the expressed interests of a supervisor or others but what their own "best interests" are. If one accepts Larmer's view that a person's best interests may never be ranged against morality, then it would be in the best interests of one's supervisors and colleagues to report the wrongdoing to them (and perhaps beyond them to others in the hierarchy). For example, if a supervisor is engaging in sexual harassment of a subordinate, this is not something that, qua immoral, can be in his best interests. Confronting him with his mistaken behavior is to act in his best interests. And, if this did not work, one would be justified, again in his best interests, in reporting his behavior to other organizational authorities. In this way, Larmer seeks to gain some traction in the argument that someone is justified not only in reporting serious wrongdoing but also in blowing the whistle, internally, and, if necessary, externally. To do so would be to serve the best interests of those involved and, at the same time, an act of loyalty.[76]

I do not, however, think this argument can gain a lot of traction. To begin with, although it may purport to give a justification for whistle-blowing within the bounds of loyalty to one's supervisors and colleagues, this does not mean that they will agree with the assessment of their "best interests." Unless one can convince them that they are misinterpreting their interests, they may well remain adamantly opposed to one's report and any attempt to correct the situation. It is hard to imagine, for example, Andy Fastow or Jeff Skilling at Enron being convinced by a subordinate (or even a colleague) that their business dealings were not in their "best interests." It is true that a loyal friend might do things for another person that that person does not, at the time, want or approve, and do this on the basis of what the person's "best" interests are. However, if one's assent to a view of one's interests is not required, then others may well impose on one a host of measures that one might vehemently reject. Isaiah Berlin has nicely written about the dangers of people interpreting the "real self" of others and imposing it on them. It may well be, in the present case, that one's supervisor(s) and colleagues do not come to agree. Thus this account of loyalty and whistle-blowing is highly questionable.

The importance of Larmer's view is to affirm that one must have good evidence regarding any purported wrongdoing as well as its objective (nonbiased) implications for all those involved. In effect, Larmer urges employees to be loyal to moral principles and to identify those moral principles with the best interests of their employers. One is then said to be loyal to their employers. It is more straightforward simply to drop talk of loyalty to one's employer in such a case, and speak of the primary importance of acting morally. Though loyalty to an employer must allow for some criticism of the employer—otherwise it is a "blind loyalty"—it does not follow that such loyalty is simply the same as acting morally towards the employer. Accordingly, one cannot appeal to the loyalty responsibility of employees to provide a general grounding for reporting wrongdoing and whistle-blowing.

A different, though related, approach has been suggested by Vandekerckhove and Commers, who remind us that an organization is more than simply the individuals who occupy it. It is based on certain legal statutes and finds its legitimacy in various principles and values that it supports, or at least does not contravene.[77] Employees have a responsibility to be loyal to these norms and standards. If these values, principles, or laws are broken, the legitimacy of the organization may be at stake. The more serious the wrongdoing that contravenes these principles or laws the more the organization's legitimacy is undercut. Individuals who violate the values, norms, or ends that justify an organization's existence undermine the legitimacy of the organization.

Accordingly, if an employee "finds herself in a situation where organizational behavior diverts from its explicit mission, goals and values, then rational loyalty— loyalty to the explicit mission, goals and values—would demand of her to blow the whistle."[78] Such a stance appears to be captured in the statement of Barron Stone, who blew the whistle on accounting irregularities at Duke Power in the late 1990s, when he said that "I felt I had an obligation to the 2 million customers and to Duke's own business ethics policy, which talks about honesty, loyalty and integrity."[79] Thus, employee loyalty may require one to report wrongdoings and even to blow the whistle when the underlying values and norms of an organization are being violated.

The difficulty with this proposal lies in connecting most employees with an ethical responsibility to defend the underlying values and norms that define a business. In some cases, businesses have not laid out what their basic values and norms are. They do not have a mission statement or code of conduct. In other cases, a business might identify some religious character, for example, Christianity, as part of its mission. Unless they make explicit that each employee is also supposed to further that part of the mission statement, and not simply the top executives, there seems little reason to accept that a person becomes committed to such values by taking a job in accounting or plant maintenance at such a business. The only limit that Vandekerckhove and Commers appear to place on the mission, norms, and values of an organization is that they be "acceptable to the wider society."[80] But, in some cases, the society a business operates in might be racist, sexist, or indifferent to the environment. Accordingly, this position faces a dilemma. Either it must qualify the values and norms an organization identifies to be those that are morally justified, or it must simply accept whatever values and norms the business identifies (if it does so). In the former case, we are back in the situation discussed above with regard to Larmer's views. In the latter case, whistle-blowing might be called for by the present view in situations that lead to protecting moral views and norms of questionable justifiability. Consequently, we must look elsewhere to determine the nature and extent of one's responsibility to provide information to one's supervisors and hence to report good, as well as bad, news to them.

The upshot of the preceding argument is that the extent of one's responsibility to report wrongdoing, as derived from simply the employment relation itself, is a limited one. There are, however, other factors that affect the robustness of this responsibility. These lie beyond one's mere employment or privileged relation with the organization.

For example, when the wrongdoing involves a felony, one has a legal responsibility to report it to an appropriate government official. Otherwise one could be charged with misprision of a felony. In addition, one's responsibility to report wrongdoing will also depend on one's position in the organization. If one occupies certain higher positions, then one will have a responsibility to report that is more robust. Beaver writes that a person has a legal responsibility to report when one is a director or member of the governing board; an officer; in an expert or professional relationship with the organization; or an ERISA fiduciary.[81] It is not surprising then that those blowing the whistle are frequently higher-level employees or managers who do have greater responsibilities for the organization than those lower down. For example, all three of the whistle-blowers who were named *Time*'s "Persons of the Year" in 2002 held middle- to high-level positions in their organizations.

In addition, the robustness of one's responsibility to report will depend upon whether one is a professional in one's position, such as an accountant, an engineer, a nurse, a physician, or a lawyer.[82] Joseph Rose, a lawyer, felt it his responsibility to the members of Associated Milk Producers Inc. (AMPI) to reveal and stop its illegal political contributions.[83] Dan Gellert was a pilot. Sherron Watkins and Cynthia Cooper were accountants at Enron and WorldCom respectively.

Finally, one's responsibility to report will also depend on structures and procedures put into place in the organization to encourage, require, and protect the reporting of "bad news." For example, many business, educational, and governmental organizations are quite explicit that an employee has a responsibility to report ethical misconduct. Bok notes that the U.S. Code of Ethics for Government Service asks civil servants "to expose corruption wherever uncovered."[84] She also notes that the professional ethics code of the "largest professional engineering association requires members to speak out against abuses threatening the safety, health, and welfare of the public."[85] In agreeing to work for one of these organizations, an employee undertakes to fulfill this responsibility.

The preceding legal, occupational, professional, and organizational responsibilities are in addition to those governed simply by the employment relationship. They may apply rather variously in different situations. Still, these extensions of one's responsibility to report do not identify a moral basis to do so that would apply to any one in a whistle-blower situation.

Accordingly, we should ask more generally what would be the responsibilities to report of a person who was a member of an organization but whose values and responsibilities were not solely defined by the organization but were rooted in the fact that he or she was a moral agent? Some broader or more general moral consideration is required.

A General Duty of Beneficence

De George proposes the following general moral principle as an answer to how we, as moral agents, ought always to act: "we are morally obliged to prevent harm to others at relatively little expense to ourselves, and that we are morally obliged to prevent great harm to a great many others, even at considerable expense to ourselves."[86] In short, De George adopts a principle of beneficence as the normative basis of his Harm Theory. On the basis of this principle, a potential whistle-blower who is aware of serious harm being caused by an organization should report it, if doing so would help to prevent it. And if the harm is great, a person would be morally obligated to report this fact even at considerable expense to himself and his family.

This broad principle speaks to the need of a general ethical basis for whistle-blowing. It applies to all moral agents, including employees. It is, however, implausibly strong since it seems to apply to any harm that a person might do something to reduce. It commits us to responses that seem excessive and unreasonable. There need be no connection with the harm, apparently, other than the fact of one's knowledge of it. Given that harm, one is obliged to (try to) prevent it, whether at little or great expense to ourselves, depending on the greatness of the harm. This would have us ever involved in the affairs of others, preventing little harms and, occasionally, great harms. And since there are great harms suffered by a very many—genocide in Sudan, ethnic cleansing in other countries, wars in Afghanistan and Iraq, and so on—this principle appears to imply that each one of us should give up a great deal in order to try to stop them.

Though De George says little regarding "how much" we must give up, he might draw upon Peter Singer, who has, of course, offered a suggestion with regard to our responsibility to prevent bad things from happening. At one point, Singer suggested that the criterion was our ability to do so "without having to sacrifice anything of comparable moral importance."[87] This extremely demanding criterion was later modified to the more modest one of donating "a round percentage of one's income" of 10 percent to address such harms as absolute poverty.[88] In any case, the demands of this principle remain a matter of considerable contention.

In addition, this principle provides us with no means to distinguish between the various harms that we should undertake to prevent. As I have argued before, there are thousands of harms that fit the De George principle. Why focus on the ones at work? Almost without exception, there are many other, more serious harms being done elsewhere in the world. If this were the case and we were to pick the most serious harms to correct, then De George's principle would lead most people away from blowing the whistle at their place of work. This would be an ironic result to the principle offered to underlie whistle-blowing.

Finally, De George's principle is stated in terms of harms, rather than of wrongs. With whistle-blowing we face a situation in which wrongful harms are being generated. Whistle-blowing does not concern the question of harms that have, perhaps, naturally occurred through disasters, that is, situations for which people have not acted wrongfully. No one blows the whistle to say that his or her firm is not doing enough to feed the poor of the world. Nor should whistle-blowing be simply a dispute over different policies that may impose harms on some stakeholders. Something wrongful needs to be at stake.

Accordingly, we need a normative basis for whistle-blowing that would not commit us to a range of actions that would morally undo us, as well as one that speaks to the wrongs whistle-blowers seek to correct. The whistle-blower needs something that speaks more directly to his or her situation.

The Integrity Theory

The first part of my twofold integrity account of justified whistle-blowing can now be stated. The preceding discussion has prepared the ground for this principle by arguing that previously offered, competing normative views are inadequate. It has also made clear the importance of a practical normative basis for whistle-blowing.

The Principle of Positional Responsibility

Underlying our responsibility to report wrongdoing is a Principle of Positional Responsibility. This principle morally obliges people to report wrongdoings to those who might prevent or rectify them, when the wrongdoings are of a significant nature (either individually or collectively), when one has special knowledge due to one's circumstances that others lack, when one has a privileged relationship with the organization through which the wrongdoing is occurring (or has occurred), and when others are not attempting to correct the wrongdoing.[89]

This is not a general principle of doing good or even preventing harm. It is a limited principle of reporting wrongdoing, under specific circumstances and conditions, with the intention of preventing or stopping it. We do not have a general duty to correct the wrongs of the world. If we did, we would be constantly involved in the affairs of others in order to fulfill our moral obligations. And, since we have limited time, abilities, and means, we would also need some means to distinguish among the various wrongs that deserved our attention. However, the Principle of Positional Responsibility tells us that due to a special organizational or situational position we occupy involving knowledge of wrongdoing, as well as our ability to have an effect on correcting a wrong of some importance through making it known, a person acquires a responsibility to speak out. That is, through these special circumstances we have a specific duty or responsibility to take steps that will lead to the correction of wrongs.

This principle concerns wrongdoings that are of a serious nature. Though this notion lacks specificity and precision, so too does much of life in business.[90] Still, we can differentiate between those wrongs that might regard small or inconsequential matters and those involving matters of great importance and/or harm to large numbers of people. The elevator inspector who shut down poorly operating elevators that were improperly licensed was addressing a serious wrongdoing.[91] An employee who reports on improper city road contracts is also concerned about serious matters, as was the FAA flight controller who worried about colliding planes.[92] Sometimes the wrongdoing is much more abstract as when it involves accounting procedures. For example, at WorldCom various expenditures were treated as capital expenditures rather than ordinary expenses. This different accounting approach allowed WorldCom to record significant profits when, according to ordinary accounting rules, it was losing money. Part of the reason that the wrongdoing must be serious is that if a person sought to report a trivial matter, for example, a few missing pencils, to someone in upper management or to the media, he would be viewed as an annoyance, rather than a whistle-blower. If the wrongdoing were very minor, it would not rise to the level of whistle-blowing, whether or not it was justified in the particular case.[93]

The Principle of Positional Responsibility requires, it should be noted, that one is connected with the organization (or situation) through which one or more people are engaged in wrongdoing. It does not tell us, absent this connection, that one has any particular responsibilities. In short, it is this connection that gives a person the position or "standing" to reveal and attempt to correct the wrongs of others. This "standing" arises because as a member of the organization (or one who has privileged access) one supports the organization through one's actions (or even sometimes one's inactions), one is more likely to have verifiable knowledge unavailable to others through such an association, and by having access to officials in the organization there may be an initial presumption one may more easily and effectively bring about change. It is true that through the media and the Internet one might become aware of a host of wrongdoings around the world. But that knowledge is not part of the special circumstances in which one is a member of an organization through which wrongdoing is taking place.

Finally, this principle requires that we can have some effect to stop the wrongdoing or to correct it, though we need not be able to do this directly or individually. It is sufficient that the whistle-blower provide the impetus or the occasion that may lead, through others, to the correction of this wrongdoing.[94] The whistle-blower need not be able to change the situation all by herself. However, by shining the light of day upon the wrongdoing, her reporting may play a crucial role in the correction process.

It is worth noting that the Principle of Positional Responsibility is compatible with widely held views regarding an individual's responsibility to report and, if possible, prevent wrongdoings associated with one's position, knowledge, and abilities. Some of this is captured in the law. For example, as earlier noted, one might be accused of a "misprision of a felony" if one fails to report felonious behavior of which one is aware.

Nonlegal, moral examples would include our responsibility to alert our neighbors and the police if we know that someone is breaking into our neighbor's house. Under these circumstances we have a responsibility to report crimes in our neighborhoods in the city. Crime Awareness campaigns and Neighborhood Crime Reports build on this notion of responsibility to report wrongs of which one becomes aware. These are responsibilities we have both as moral agents and as members of society.

This principle is also clearly related to what has been called the "Kew Gardens principle" that was formulated to capture the responsibilities of eyewitnesses to the brutal murder of Kitty Genovese in the Kew Gardens section of New York.[95] In this case, some thirty-eight people witnessed some portion of her murder but did nothing. The Kew Gardens principle argued that in cases when there is a person with a critical need, and someone is proximate to this situation, has the capability to do something to meet that need, and others are not rendering aid, that person has a responsibility to respond. One difference is that the Kew Gardens principle is formulated on the basis of critical need, the principle of positional responsibility is formulated with regard to wrongdoing. In addition, this is not a case of whistle-blowing, so much as civic duty and bystander apathy. Still, in the situation of Kitty Genovese there was clearly wrongdoing that needed to be stopped. Someone should have notified the police.

In contrast to a general principle of beneficence, a Principle of Positional Responsibility would prioritize the wrongs to be addressed based upon the above contextual conditions of organizational membership, knowledge, and ability to have an effect on correcting the alleged wrongs. As a moral agent employed by a business, one occupies a special position that others do not have. Employees are subject to the Principle of Positional Responsibility and have an obligation to report wrongdoing. Recognizing this principle helps to explain the moral outrage people express when they learn that someone knew of some important wrong he might have helped stop by calling attention to it, but did nothing. It is for this reason that we are morally troubled when we learn that executives at the Johns-Manville Corporation knew about the asbestos dangers to its employees in the 1930s, 1940s, and 1950s but not only did not tell them but also hid the dangers from them. We wonder why someone did not "blow the whistle" during these years. Hence, a special responsibility falls on one due to the circumstances defined by Principle of Positional Responsibility.

Implications of the Principle of Positional Responsibility

Still, we need to ask more specifically about the responsibilities that flow from this principle with regard to the employee reporting of wrongdoings. What are its implications for the employee whose supervisor has proven to be an obstacle? Does one have a responsibility to report further up the organization outside of standard hierarchical routes? Must one exhaust all internal sources to which one might report? When should one report externally?

By itself, the Principle of Positional Responsibility does not answer such questions. Instead, we must interpret this principle within two related contexts that relate to the scope or extent of the principle, on the one hand, and its weight or stringency, on the other.

First, in order to define the *scope* or extent of this principle, we must look to other relevant principles and values. PPR is a second-order principle. Rather than telling us not to lie or not to harm other people, it tells us that we should report the wrongdoings of others under certain circumstances as part of an effort to prevent or to correct those wrongs. But how far we should take this and in what manner, it does not say. For this we require, in part, other principles and values, for example. the value of loyalty to an organization; principles of responsibility to friends and family; the public interest.

Second, PPR lays out a responsibility we have within its own narrow framework, but does not define the weight or *stringency* we should attribute to it. This framework must be further determined by one's abilities and what might reasonably be expected of a person in a whistle-blowing situation. How should we weigh significant threats to potential whistle-blowers that may ruin their careers, destroy their family, alienate them from their peers, conflict with other important responsibilities, and/or bankrupt them? Ethicists commonly distinguish between obligations we have and admirable actions that go beyond our duties.[96] Ideal and even heroic acts are termed *supererogatory*. Might not some whistle-blowing acts fall into this category rather than being strictly obligatory? These are issues of the stringency of the Principle of Positional Responsibility that we must also consider.

The Scope of the Principle of Positional Responsibility

Previously, I have identified an employee-based responsibility to inform or report to one's supervisor, as well as duties of loyalty, obedience, and confidentiality. How do these norms relate to the Principle of Positional Responsibility when one's supervisor has told one that one's concerns regarding some putative wrongdoing are not serious or relevant and that one should get back to work? What does this principle direct one to do? How far should one proceed in reporting? This is one way to approach questions of the scope or extent of this principle.

We may begin by assuming that some serious wrong is being done to someone or some group and that all the conditions for PPR are relevantly fulfilled. Prima facie, one ought to report the wrongdoing. Similarly, one's other duties of loyalty, obedience, as well as respect for those one works for are also prima facie. They can be overridden in serious cases. Consequently, PPR might, given appropriate circumstances, override them.

One's obligation to report should be directed internally (at least initially and subject to overriding conditions) because the source of the wrongdoing comes through the organization. One's loyalty is not simply to one's supervisor but also to the organization.[97] The wrongdoing may also have significant implications for the organization (loss of reputation, legal fees, fines). Under these circumstances, to permit those closest to the wrongdoing (and responsible to correct it) the opportunity to do so is to respect their authority and self-determination. To report externally, as long as there were other reasonable internal venues, would be to undercut their responsibilities and not give them a chance to do what they should do. In addition, the internal route might also be the most efficient way to address the situation. The organization could then deal with the fact that a serious legal or moral wrong has been done. In the case of a serious legal wrongdoing, the corporation would have to self-report the problem to legal authorities. This inside approach would give the leadership of the organization a chance to know about the problem before the media or court system does, to announce the problem to the responsible legal officials, and to begin to address the organizational dimensions of the problem even before a full legal accounting took place. In general, this would be desirable both practically and ethically for an organization. However, should the internal route pose significant danger to the potential whistle-blower or the strong likelihood of a pointless result, then one's obligation to report would be to external agents.

An employee does not have a responsibility to challenge insurmountable barriers. He or she does not have a responsibility to reform the organization so that reports of wrongdoing make it to the top levels. If each person the whistle-blower goes to in the hierarchy does not act on the information but resists and punishes the whistle-blower, then there is something wrong with the organization, its processes, and procedures. Though many organizations have rules and policies requiring employees to report wrongdoing, still, the de facto corporate culture may oppose such reporting as a form of snitching or betrayal. The more a business undercuts the conditions required for the fulfillment of one's responsibility to report internally, the weaker is this responsibility to the organization. It is not surprising that one of the reasons empirical accounts report why people do not blow the whistle is that they believe nothing will be done. This is a direct reflection on the failure of the organization's internal mechanisms and culture.

If under these circumstances, an employee continues to try to report up the corporate chain of command, then they go above and beyond the call of duty. Doing so may even be foolish. It may also be that one's actions are of a supererogatory nature, presenting us with an ideal, if not heroic, form of loyalty. However, morality does not require that one take such steps or that one uselessly sacrifice oneself in this manner, even if the aim is noble. Instead, one's reporting responsibility is to make genuine efforts to report the wrongdoing to responsible officials. When it becomes clear that the organizational response is not going to change, it would be unreasonable to require one to go through each level of the organization. Instead, the Principle of Positional Responsibility and loyalty require that one give the organization a fair and meaningful chance to address the charges and to correct the problem.

If internal reporting has failed or is certain to fail, when would one's responsibility to report require that one report externally? The answer is not that one needs additionally strong evidence. Even to report internally one should have reasonable evidence that wrongdoing has taken place. Whether one reports internally or externally one should not be reporting rumors or hunches. Instead, one must consider the significance of the wrongdoing and the possibility that this wrong can be corrected. The more serious the wrongdoing and the greater the chance that reporting will correct the situation, the stronger is one's obligation to report it.

Should one also consider potential risks to the organization from reporting? For example, the revelation of the wrongs committed by some employees of Arthur Andersen and its subsequent indictment and conviction in the Enron auditing case, led to the demise of Arthur Andersen. The actions of a handful of people resulted in tens of thousands of others being thrown out of their jobs. This appears to many to be a case in which justice was done, though the heavens fell. However, for a whistle-blower to make such judgments he would have to know whether the wrongdoing he knows about is a single instance, or part of a pattern. He would have to know about the future actions of the media, the courts, and top executives. This is not something any whistle-blower is in a situation to know. This means that though the whistle-blower must act on the basis of a known wrongdoing, he can do so with only a very limited comprehension of the full situation. It is this that, in part, makes whistle-blowing a risky and dangerous undertaking for others as well as the whistle-blower himself. It does not mean that he does not have a responsibility to report serious wrongdoings externally. However, it does emphasize the importance of being accurate in the charges one brings.

The Stringency of the Principle of Positional Responsibility

The question of the weight or stringency that one should attribute to the principle of positional responsibility arises also with regard to risks to oneself. There are different studies on this topic, but there is certainly the possibility that one will suffer—perhaps even dramatically—if one reports wrongdoing, but particularly if one does so externally. Some businesses have responded with a viciousness that is appalling. The treatment of Dan Gellert by Eastern Airlines is a good example. As a pilot at Eastern Airlines, Gellert became aware of a defect in the autopilot control system on Lockheed 1011 aircraft. At times it would disengage in a manner that could lead to a crash. In fact, one plane did crash. Others had near crashes. For his efforts to bring this situation to the attention of management and get it corrected, he was given flight schedules that tested his physical well-being, mental exams that challenged his psychological fitness, told to appear in courtrooms in other cities in a time frame that was impossible, and so on. All this was part of an effort to discredit him. In short, what a whistle-blower should know is that her life will change—and may change significantly—as a result of her report.

This risk to oneself directly affects one's moral responsibility to blow the whistle since it may negatively affect many of one's other responsibilities, important interests, and projects. One has multiple responsibilities and interests that have defined one's life prior to this unexpected event. One has built up relationships at work and outside of work that depend upon one fulfilling the responsibilities that constitute these other relationships. Will one act consistently on these principles, or will one compromise some of them? Which principles and values are most important? How courageous is one prepared to be? How courageous is one capable of being? How would other moral agents who are courageous act, and what risks would they undertake, in this situation? What about one's duty of confidentiality and obedience that are part of one's job? What about one's responsibilities to one's peers and one's family? The Principle of Positional Responsibility, by itself, cannot answer these questions.[98]

The extent of one's responsibilities under this principle will be difficult to determine in any particular case and certainly cannot be ascertained precisely in many cases. A soldier's responsibilities may include placing himself in harm's way such that he might possibly be killed. A physician has a responsibility to his patients that may involve contracting life-threatening sicknesses. However, employees do not, ordinarily, have a responsibility—unless they so choose—to sacrifice their health, lives, or futures for a business by helping to prevent the damage that the wrongdoing of others may do to them. Rather, their whistle-blowing responsibilities are tied, most closely, to those who are wronged (or may be wronged) by the employees of the business for which they work.

Assuming that some serious wrongdoing has taken (or will take) place, that the person has reasonable evidence of this wrongdoing, that the agents normally responsible are not fulfilling their duties, and that one has a reasonable prospect of effectively changing the situation, one has a responsibility to proceed with bringing the wrongdoing to the attention of others who can do something about it. And, particularly, if whistle-blowing would have very minimal, short-term effects on one's life, but correct a serious wrong, then an employee has a responsibility to try to make the information public.

However, if the chance of success is limited and the implications for the whistle-blower are themselves so significant that his or her life will be dramatically injured as a result, it is much less obvious that the person is responsible to blow the whistle. After all, the wrongdoing is not itself a failure of the potential whistle-blower, but of others in the organization. Further, it is plausible that a person does not have an obligation to report the wrongdoings of others when doing so will destroy himself or turn him simply into a means whereby the organization's wrongs are corrected. Schmidtz comments, on a related situation, that "when we help out in a one-shot emergency, we are inconvenienced, may be even at risk, but we are not abandoning life as a member of a kingdom of ends and replacing it with a new life as a mere means."[99]

Accordingly, a person doing his duty by blowing the whistle may at the same time justifiably seek to avoid grave risks to himself. Some whistle-blowers have anonymously blown the whistle. However, this option is not always available—in some cases if one says anything, it will be quite clear to others who spoke up. Further, it is often said that anonymous reporting is viewed as less authoritative and less persuasive than when a person places her name on the report. It is easier then to judge its authenticity and the motivations of the person doing the reporting.

How should we respond when the harsh consequences for the whistle-blower can not be avoided? In general, the greater the seriousness of the wrongdoing, the more certain the evidence of such wrongdoing, and the greater the likelihood that publicly reporting it will correct the wrongdoing, the greater will be one's responsibility to make it known. However, there will be a point, due to the negative effects on the whistle-blower—and this may differ for individuals—when we may say that blowing the whistle is beyond the call of ordinary duty. It is not a moral requirement that one is obliged to fulfill. One is not blameworthy if one does not do it. In such cases, whistle-blowing may be supererogatory. It constitutes an ideal or heroic action that is admirable, but beyond what is morally demanded. It makes sense to encourage such actions in a society. It is important to protect those who engage in them. We should even, on many occasions, seek to emulate such actions and encourage others to do so as well. Nevertheless, they are not morally obligatory in the sense that if a person does not do them he or she is morally blameworthy and should be condemned or morally punished. Those who do blow the whistle in such circumstances have displayed great moral courage. But in destroying their family, losing their house, incurring large debts to support their efforts, they have clearly gone beyond any call of ordinary moral duty.[100]

Integrity Considerations

In making these decisions regarding whistle-blowing, one must place the Principle of Positional Responsibility within the context of other values and norms one justifiably stands for.[101] We are concerned in whistle-blowing situations with one's faithfulness or commitment not only to this principle but also to other important values, norms, and ideals that define one. Is one prepared to act and live by them even when confronted with situations that impose threats and costs—sometimes even of a considerable nature—on one? These are considerations of integrity, inasmuch as a person of integrity will defend her values and norms even when doing so is inconvenient or difficult. As Lynn Sharp Paine says, "persons of integrity have a set of anchoring beliefs or principles that define who they are and what they believe in. They stand for something and remain steadfast when confronted with adversity or temptation."[102]

Beyond this, assuming that our values, responsibilities, and ideals may conflict at times, a person of integrity will integrate these normative facets of her life into some reasonably coherent whole. Those responsibilities and values of greatest importance will receive the greatest priority. Integrity, we are told, "involves recognition that some desires are more important and more desirable than others; that some commitments make a greater claim upon us than others; that some values are deeper than others; and that some principles take priority over others."[103] Which of these principles, ideals, and values are the most important ones to support and at what cost to oneself as well as others? To which values and norms is one prepared to remain faithful? Is one prepared to sacrifice other important values (e.g., family, career) to correct the wrongdoing one has discovered?

When an instance of whistle-blowing arises, the justified course of action will be filtered through these different normative dimensions of one's justified values and norms. Does this area central to who a person is shrink, at such times, to a small island focused simply on protecting oneself? Does it encompass others and the full range of one's values, norms, and ideals? The decision one makes on implementing the Principle of Positional Responsibility will be a decision regarding one's integrity as one decides what one justifiably stands for. One might say that this situation is the flip side of complicity. It is not because one is involved in wrongdoing that one must decide whether or not one will blow the whistle, but because one must choose between the different principles of obligation and duty that pertain to one, the ideals by which one lives, and the kind of person one wishes to be. Even with internal whistle-blowing, one must decide to step outside the security, protections, and relative anonymity of the normal hierarchy to make a moral stand for what ought to be done. It is inherently a situation that requires courage and commitment to one's values and principles.

Consider then an employee, Debra, who knows of wrongdoing in the business for which she works; others who work there are afraid to say anything. Her supervisor and peers say that she ought to forget it about it: "That's just the way things are done around here." Debra is certain that wrongdoing is going on and has evidence to back up her view. This wrongdoing bothers her greatly; she understands the implications of PPR. Thus, Debra takes her information to top management or goes to an outside source to change things, even knowing that there are considerable risks. However, in doing so she does not blow the whistle simply because this is the implication of PPR, but because it fits with her ongoing concerns for honesty, for not wronging others, and for accountability. These values and norms have defined Debra's life and her relations with others. Not to blow the whistle would be to retreat and compromise these, as well as PPR. It is a question of integrity—of knowing what was going on, of having certain values and views, and of living them. Contrariwise, if she had these values, norms, and character traits and did not act on them, she would be a hypocrite and her integrity tarnished.

Contrast this with Jim, who comes to know of serious wrongdoing that is going on regarding accounting measures at his firm. No one is being physically harmed, but the company is misreporting its financial status and various activities. When this fraud becomes known, this will affect investors and possibly employees and suppliers. Jim reports his knowledge of the wrongdoing to his supervisor, who says that he will take care of it and that Jim should stick to his own job. There are suggestions that if he does not do this he will be in trouble. Jim is convinced that the supervisor will do nothing, and if he (Jim) does not do anything else, this wrongdoing will continue (at least for the present). Though there are other people (with authority) in the organization who know the wrong doing is going on, there is a conspiracy of silence amongst a small group of people. Jim is aware of the implications of PPR, but Jim has other important responsibilities as well that have shaped his life. He is the sole provider for his family. He is also the chairperson of a regional group that focuses on providing disadvantaged children with educational support. His role has been critical in moving this group from one that is largely ineffective to one that makes an important impact on children in the area. Since this area is conservative, Jim believes that if he became involved in revealing the corporate wrongdoing his position in this regional organization would be jeopardized and the aid they are providing disrupted. He is also not certain that if he blew the whistle anyone would listen. He knows about the retaliation against other whistle-blowers, and he has his family to think about. He decides that there are other, more important things he should be doing than correcting this particular wrong in his company by whistleblowing. He also has other, more direct responsibilities that would be crippled if he blew the whistle. Ideally, of course, he would do both. But this is not an ideal world. He can maintain his integrity by resigning, even if it means taking a lowerpaying job, while fulfilling the other important responsibilities he has undertaken and which are crucial to him and those to whom he is responsible.

In each of these cases, the integrity of those involved has played a role in how the Principle of Positional Responsibility is applied. If one's responsibility to blow the whistle does not significantly disrupt one's other responsibilities and projects, one has a responsibility to blow the whistle. One would be wrong not to do so, whether internally or, if necessary, externally. However, all too frequently, in deciding to blow the whistle, one may be making a life-altering decision that will affect oneself as well as others. It is not like calling the police to report a neighborhood crime, which may take a few minutes or few hours, after which it will be over. Due to the responses of fellow workers, the recrimination to which one may render oneself vulnerable, the amount of time and money one must expend to defend one's claims, the pressures it will place on one's personal life and family relationships, whistle-blowing may simply change the course of one's life. It is too easy to say, abstractly considered, one has a moral obligation to blow the whistle without placing this obligation within the broader context of the other responsibilities, values, and practical implications for the whistle-blower. One cannot appropriately respond to PPR by simply considering this principle itself, separated from the rest of one's life. Instead, one's response must arise out of how this principle, in a particular set of circumstances, coheres with the rest of who we are, namely, our other values, principles, and ideals as we have integrated them into our lives. The question is not simply and abstractly, "Would it be justified for some person or other to blow the whistle in this situation?" But rather the question is, "Would it be justified for this person in this situation to blow to whistle?" Here the risks a person must take play a legitimate role in her decision as well as how this action coheres with other values and norms she supports. In answering these questions, one defines what kind of person one is and reaffirms (or undercuts) one's integrity.

Hence, the present account of justified whistle-blowing is a mixed one. The Principle of Positional Responsibility and integrity play joint roles. But because PPR plays its role within the broader context of our integrity, I have called it the Integrity Theory.

Whistle-Blowing and the Design of Organizations

The preceding accounts of whistle-blowing ask what justifies an individual engaging in whistle-blowing. The Integrity Theory, I believe, is the best response to that question.

However, focusing on this question distracts us from the underlying problem of the misconduct occurring in (or through) organizations that organizations themselves fail to identify and correct. Whistle-blowers have played a vital role in bringing to light many of these wrongdoings. They have provided an admirable service to the public. For this they deserve protection. However, depending on the measures adopted, this way of correcting wrongdoing may not be very successful. In any case, such an approach treats the symptoms and not the underlying problems. It is a Band-Aid approach.

Accordingly, we should also be asking about the situation that gives rise to the need for individual whistle-blowing. What, in short, is the problem to which whistle-blowing is the supposed answer? What is the design problem (as McDonough would say) to which blowing the whistle is the answer?[104] The unsurprising, but important, answer is whistle-blowing is necessary when there has been a failure within the organization. It is one way by which we discover and seek to correct important wrongs or abuses by organizations when some of their members do not wish to recognize or correct them. In short, the wrong doing whistle-blowers target is both an individual and an organizational failure.

There are two striking features of this answer. First, this answer tends to imperil, and sometimes destroy, the people who report the wrongdoing. There are numerous reports of the terrible retaliation whistle-blowers have experienced.[105] And though the empirical evidence does not demonstrate that all whistle-blowers suffer significant retaliation, far too many do.[106] Second, whistle-blowing is, often, not terribly effective. The evidence regarding how often claims of whistle-blowing successfully result in the wrongs or harms reported being corrected is extremely difficult to come by, given the nature of these actions.[107] One measure is to consider those who have filed under the Whistle-blower Protection Act. On this score, whistle-blowers have had "a minuscule success rate. Only 1 percent of such cases since 2001 was referred to agency heads for investigation. Of the last 95 such cases that reached the federal circuit court of appeals, only one whistle-blower won."[108] Accordingly, whistle-blowing as a response to wrongdoing by organizations and the people in them has considerable weaknesses. The whistle-blowing answer to our design problem is not an obviously good answer—even if an individual is justified in blowing the whistle. Those who blow the whistle are themselves often wronged or abused. And the result of their efforts is quite frequently that needed changes do not take place. Yet these changes were the point of the whistle-blowing. As such, the current focus on individual whistle-blowing is often the justification of sacrificial victims on behalf of ineffective efforts.

This suggests that we need more discussion of organizational conditions that would forestall the necessity of whistle-blowing. If organizations were designed to obviate the necessity of whistle-blowing, then the gut-wrenching stories of the fate of whistle-blowers might be considerably reduced and the occasions of individual whistle-blowing become much more infrequent. In short, the discussion of organizational designs that would reduce or eliminate the need for whistle-blowing should be primary, and any justification of individual whistle-blowing should be secondary.[109]

The real ethical problem whistle-blowing raises is how do we create self-correcting organizations that catch violations by themselves and do not rely on individuals (who experience retaliation) to identify and demand their correction? How can we avoid the results of bureaucracies and organizations that devote "inordinate amounts of energy to the construction of barriers to review and account"?[110] For such self-correcting organizations, individual whistle-blowing would be, at best, a second—or third choice—as a way to address these problems.

Needless to say, the solution to this problem is something that I can only briefly touch upon here. However, for present purposes I do not need to provide a complete account. Instead, what I must do is to indicate the general features of self-correcting organizations that would work to obviate the necessity of whistle-blowing.

The relevant design question regarding organizations is not simply a matter of trying to protect whistle-blowers but of creating organizations in which external whistle-blowing is not necessary (or at the least minimized), and in which internal whistle-blowing (should it be necessary) is received with a positive response. Such organizations must be able to detect and acknowledge mistakes or wrongful acts, receive bad news, and take steps to correct those problems. Unless organizations are serious about this, we cannot be serious about whistle-blowing. If they were serious, they would be self-regulating and self-enforcing organizations. Such organizations would, thereby, be faithful to their own values, purposes, and legitimating bases. They would be organizations of integrity.

Self-Correcting Organizations

What features would characterize a self-correcting organization?

First, they would seek information regarding problems and violations from all those who are members of (or who have a privileged relation with) the organization. They cannot rely simply on monitors, auditors, or the like. If an organization's self-correcting method is dependent simply on monitors or auditors to detect its problems, then it will always be inadequate since such an approach can never have a monitor in each office and for every action.

Second, the members of organizations must also have an acknowledged responsibility to come forward when they see misconduct. Organizations can seek to capture this responsibility in codes of ethics, through ethics and compliance programs, and those in charge of overseeing ethical and legal complaints. Nevertheless, these methods will not be adequate unless this responsibility is acknowledged through a corporate culture that values, rather than denigrates, the reporting of bad news and misconduct. The most direct way for this to occur is for those involved to self-report problems, errors, wrongful acts, and so on. As in experimental sciences, these failures may be the occasion of important learning and redirection of the individuals, departments, and businesses involved.

Third, there must be means to receive the reports and to initiate examination of them and, as appropriate, institute needed changes. The point, after all, of bringing such charges forward is, when warranted, to make changes. At the same time, there are stories about employees being told they have a responsibility to report misconduct and then not being protected when they do.[111] Both these situations suggest the importance of structural and cultural changes. These do not, however, take place spontaneously. They require the good will of management and executives, the "buy-in" of employees, but also the need of the law, social pressures, and stakeholder pressures on behalf of such behavior. The law must play an important role here, giving not only some measure of protection to whistle-blowers but also incentives to organizations to be self-correcting.[112]

Fourth, self-correcting organizations would have to institute measures to foster an attitude among employees willing to push back against directions to engage in illegal or unethical behaviors. They would have to encourage them to fulfill their responsibilities to identify substantive wrongdoings and to resist efforts to remain quiet. This would require important cultural changes for many organizations and individuals. In particular, cultural changes are necessary to address the situation that has often been reported of insiders who see wrong things being done but tend not to report them.[113]

The other side of this equation would require that organizations be structured, and their members trained, to accept bad news, to confront wrongdoing, and seek ways to change it. To encourage these attitudes it is necessary to address negative attitudes employees and supervisors may have regarding resistance to their views and the reporting of misconduct.[114] This involves, but is not limited to, integrating ethics into performance evaluations and feedback surveys, linking the value of loyalty to the legitimating bases of the organization, and protecting and commending those who identify problems and misconduct.[115] This involves programs and initiatives far beyond whistle-blowing situations. These initiatives speak to a general condition for how those who have power and authority over others should treat those subordinate to them when the latter inform their leaders of illegal, immoral, or illegitimate activities going on in the organization. The organizational dimension of this question is the fundamental ethical issue that whistle-blowing raises.

Finally, since an organization is not a wholly self-contained system but exists only within the political, economic, social, and legal context of its time, there is a role for the broader social and political system in the preceding, for example, for the government to provide penalties for harming or harassing whistle-blowers and incentives for whistle-blowers to come forward with valuable information.[116] Since we are dealing with "the crooked timber" of humanity, there must always be means, internally and externally, for people in an organization to circumvent wrongdoers when these are the people to whom one would ordinarily report the wrongdoing. More generally, however, we should work to create organizations and a social and political system that renders whistle-blowing and such sacrifices unnecessary. We need to transform organizations that shape and form our lives so that the wrong, the harms, and the abuses that occur through them can be identified and corrected. We may not be able to ensure that this is always the case, but we can do a better job than we have.

The preceding points are not designed simply to protect whistle-blowers. Rather, they are about how organizations ought to be designed so that the need for whistle-blowing is minimized and not the only answer to the correction of wrongdoing within or through organizations. Since there are different kinds of organizations, the answers here will vary. They may seek to accomplish their ends in a variety of ways. But the general points made above remains the same.

This is the project on which those truly concerned about whistle-blowing should be focused. It is this project of revising corporate activities that will address the real problem that lies behind whistle-blowing.

CONCLUSION

Though there remains some disagreement over the nature of whistle-blowing, there is general agreement on the main features of whistle-blowing. What constitutes whistle-blowing is not, however, where the majority of philosophical discussions have focused.

Most philosophical studies of whistle-blowing have focused on the justification of particular acts of whistle-blowing. Three prominent views—the Harm Theory, the Complicity Theory, and the Good Reasons Theory—have played a prominent role in this discussion. Each one makes important contributions but is also subject to important limitations and deficiencies.

In their stead, I have offered an Integrity Theory that draws on these different views, and yet is itself a distinct approach. It builds on responsibilities one has as an employee and as a moral agent to report wrongdoings that fall within a special set of circumstances related to one's relation to some particular organization. Even these circumstances can only obligate a person in some cases to blow the whistle. Dependent upon the risks to oneself and others, the actions of others, and the seriousness of the wrongdoing, there will be other occasions on which blowing the whistle falls outside of any strict responsibility and is part of an ideal or even heroic course of action. In either case, however, whether one engages in whistle-blowing will depend upon how it fits within a larger set of considerations regarding who and what one is. It is this larger set of considerations that raise questions of one's integrity.

Though a justificatory schema can be given for those facing possible whistle-blowing, no algorithms or simply check-off boxes can be given to make this decision. Most worrisome, however, are the retaliation and reprisals to which far too many whistle-blowers have been subjected. As I argued at the end of this chapter, we should look not simply to what laws may protect whistle-blowers but at what we can do to create and foster self-correcting organizations that would reduce the necessity of whistle-blowing, which too often takes the form of a sacrifice that society call upon some of its members to make to correct the errors of the major organizations of that society. It is here that business ethicists need to focus more of their energies in the future.[117]

NOTES

1. James M. Roche, "The Competitive System to Work, to Preserve, and to Protect," *Vital Speeches of the Day* (May 1971): 455.

2. The term "whistle-blowing" was first coined in the twentieth century. Obviously, this does not mean that whistle-blowing did not previously occur. Nevertheless, I will focus on whistle-blowing as it appears in business today.

3. John R. Boatright *Ethics and the Conduct of Business*, 3rd ed. rev. (Upper Saddle River, N.J.: Prentice-Hall, 2000), 109.

4. Norman Bowie *Business Ethics* (Englewood Cliffs, N.J.: Prentice-Hall, Inc., 1982), 142.

5. Sissela Bok "Whistleblowing and Professional Responsibility," *New York University Education Quarterly* 11 (1980): 2.

6. Janet Near and Marcia Miceli "Organizational Dissidence: The Case of Whistle-Blowing," *Journal of Business Ethics* 4 (1985): 4.

7. See Peter B. Jubb "Whistleblowing: A Restrictive Definition and Interpretation," *Journal of Business Ethics* 21 (1999): 83.

8. Terry Morehead Dworkin "SOX and Whistleblowing," *Michigan Law Review* 105 (2007): 1762.

9. Jubb, "Whistleblowing," 83.

10. WorldCom was a communications services company that eventually had to declare bankruptcy when its various devious accounting practices came to light. Among such practices were the overvaluation of acquisitions and the treatment of operating costs as capital expenditures.

11. Dworkin, "SOX and Whistleblowing," 1759ff.

12. Near and Miceli, "Organizational Dissidence," 4.

13. Ibid.

14. Dworkin, "SOX and Whistleblowing,"1760.

15. Paul Betts, "Europe's Gag on Corporate Whistle Blowing," *Financial Times*, http://proquest.umi.com/pqdweb?did=924242721&sid=13&FMT=3&clientID=5604&RQT=309&VName=PQD (accessed July 17, 2007).

16. Accordingly, the accounts of whistle-blowing that Alan Westin relates all involve "issues of major social importance"; see Alan F. Westin *Whistle-Blowing: Loyalty and Dissent in the Corporation* (New York: McGraw-Hill, 1981), 2.

17. Marcia P. Miceli and Janet P. Near *Blowing the Whistle* (New York: Lexington, 1992): 3, 19–20.

18. Norma E. Bowie and Ronald F. Duska *Business Ethics*, 2nd ed. rev. (Englewood Cliffs, N.J.: Prentice-Hall, 1990), 74.

19. The position defended here requires that some meaning be given to "serious" or "substantial." This is often done by organizations in terms of the risk the action poses to the health or safety to those involved, the unlawfulness of the action, or the negligence involved. They might also look to the nature and extensiveness of the consequences, or to the corrupting influence of the action on the organization, institutions, and people involved.

20. Miceli and Near, *Blowing the Whistle*, 16.

21. For a similar point see Westin, *Whistle-Blowing: Loyalty and Dissent in the Corporation*, 1–2.

22. Richard De George *Business Ethics*, 6th ed. rev. (Upper Saddle River, N.J.: Pearson Prentice-Hall, 2006), 301–302.

23. De George, *Business Ethics*, 302. Accordingly, on De George's model the whistle-blower does not ask herself about the morality of her motivations. This difficult topic is assumed to have been solved. Questions of moral integrity are left in the background.

24. Ibid., 308–314.

25. Ibid., 313.

26. Ibid., 312.

27. Ibid., 302.

28. Ibid., 319.

29. Ibid., 302, 309, 314.

30. Gene G. James "Whistle Blowing: Its Moral Justification," in *Business Ethics*, eds. W. Michael Hoffman and Jennifer Mills Moore (New York: McGraw-Hill, 1990), 336.

31. Michael Davis "Some Paradoxes of Whistleblowing," *Business & Professional Ethics Journal* 15 (1996): 9.

32. Davis, "Some Paradoxes of Whistleblowing," 10.

33. See Kermit Vandivier "Why Should My Conscience Bother Me?" in *In The Name of Profit*, ed. Robert L. Heilbroner (New York: Doubleday, 1972), 3–31.

34. De George, *Business Ethics*, 304.

35. James makes the argument in light of the Pinto case that DeGeorge himself uses; see James, "Whistle Blowing," 337.

36. James, "Whistle Blowing," 340.

37. De George, *Business Ethics*, 310.

38. Ibid., 314; also see 308.

39. Ibid., 315.

40. Ibid.; also see 300.

41. Ibid., 316.

42. Ibid.

43. The importance of this point will come out in the last major section of this chapter.

44. Davis, "Some Paradoxes of Whistleblowing," 11.

45. Ibid.

46. Ibid., 13.

47. Ibid., 11.

48. Ibid., 5–6.

49. Ibid., 10.

50. Ibid., 12.

51. Joyce Rothschild and Terance D. Miethe "Whistleblowing as Resistance in Modern Work Organizations," in *Resistance and Power in Organizations*, ed. J. M. Jermier, D. Knights, and W. R. Nord (London: Routledge, 1994): 267. See also Tina Uys "The Politicisation of Whistleblowers: A Case Study," *Business Ethics: A European Review* 9 (2000): 259–267.

52. Davis, "Some Paradoxes of Whistleblowing," 14.

53. Bok, "Whistleblowing and Professional Responsibility," 2.

54. Ibid., 3.

55. Ibid., 2.

56. Ibid., 5.

57. Ibid.

58. Ibid., 2, 5.

59. Ibid., 5.

60. Ibid. Bok gives this much more weight than De George or Davis.

61. Ibid.

62. Ibid.

63. Ibid., 4.

64. Ibid., 6.

65. Ibid.

66. Ibid., 2–3.

67. Ibid., 5.

68. Ibid., 4.

69. Ibid., 5.

70. Phillip I. Blumberg "Corporate Responsibility and the Employee's Duty of Loyalty and Obedience," in *Ethical Theory and Business*, ed. Tom L. Beauchamp and Norman E. Bowie (Englewood Cliffs, N.J.: Prentice-Hall, 1979), 307.

71. Ibid.

72. Ibid.

73. Bowie's comment is appropriate: "In assuming a job (a role), one assumes special relations with one's employer and colleagues and as a result assumes obligations to his or her employer or colleagues that one does not have to all workers or to all employees" (Bowie, *Business Ethics*, 11).

74. Restatement (Third) of Agency § 8.11 (2006), http://www.wmitchell.edu/academics/curriculum/courses/assignments/Restatement%20T hird%20of%20Agency.pdf (accessed July 14, 2008).

75. Robert A. Larmer "Whistleblowing and Employee Loyalty," *Journal of Business Ethics* 11 (1992): 127–128.

76. Corvino takes a similar approach to loyalty and business. He too argues that one's loyalty to a business may require its public criticism and even whistle-blowing. See John Corvino "Loyalty in Business?" *Journal of Business Ethics* 41 (2002): 183–185.

77. Wim Vandekerckhove and M. S. Ronald Commers "Whistle Blowing and Rational Loyalty," *Journal of Business Ethics* 53 (2004): 225–233.

78. Vanderkerckhove and Commers, "Whistle Blowing and Rational Loyalty," 230.

79. Stella Hopkins and Ted Reed, "Duke Power Audit—Page One," 2, http://www.dukeemployees.com/audit/shtml (accessed December 28, 2007).

80. Vanderkerckhove and Commers, "Whistle Blowing and Rational Loyalty," 230.

81. John P. Beavers, "When to Blow the Whistle (With Respect to a Private Organization)," http://www.bricker.com/publications/articles1022.asp (accessed June 30, 2008). "ERISA" stands for the "Employee Retirement Income Security Act."

82. See Bowie, *Business Ethics*, 6.

83. See Westin, *Whistle-Blowing: Loyalty and Dissent in the Corporation*, 31–38.

84. Bok, "Whistleblowing and Professional Responsibility," 2.

85. Ibid.

86. De George, *Business Ethics*, 314; also see 308. Somewhat similarly, though much more narrowly, Vandekerckhove and Commers contend that we "have an obligation to prevent harm to my community"; see "Whistle Blowing and Rational Loyalty," 227.

87. Peter Singer "Famine, Affluence, and Morality," *Philosophy and Public Affairs* 1 (3) (1972): 231.

88. Peter Singer *Practical Ethics* (Cambridge: Cambridge University Press, 1979), 181.

89. These conditions draw upon the Kew Gardens principle that Simon, Power, and Gunneman have set out. See John G. Simon Charles W. Powers and Jon P. Gunneman *The Ethical Investor: Universities and Corporate Responsibility* (New Haven, Conn.: Yale University Press, 1972), 22–25.

90. Both De George and Bowie link whistle-blowing with serious harms or wrongdoings. See De George, *Business Ethics*, 308–9; Bowie, *Business Ethics*, 142, 144.

91. Yolanda Woodlee, "Former D.C. Workers Say Law Doesn't Prevent Retaliation," *The Washington Post*, April 28, 2008, B1.

92. Del Quentin Wilber, "More Step Up to Complain about FAA," *The Washington Post*, May 31, 2008, D1.

93. If the referee in a sporting match, be it soccer, basketball, and so on blew the whistle for each minor infraction, the game would be considerably slowed. We accept that there will be some minor infractions; the referee is there to catch the serious ones. If he

called the game very strictly according to the rules, the game might be stifled. There is an analogy here, as well, with union slow downs when they do everything according to the book in order to protest some grievance.

94. De George's principle makes it seem that the whistle-blower himself must accomplish the end of preventing the harm. This is unlikely in most cases.

95. See Simon, Powers, and Gunneman, *The Ethical Investor: Universities and Corporate Responsibility*, 22–25.

96. This is the title of the *Time* article on Bunnatine Greenhouse, who blew the whistle on Pentagon a no-bid contract to a subsidiary of Halliburton to restore Iraq's oil facilities. Adam Zagorin and Timothy J. Burger, "Beyond the Call of Duty," http://www.time.com/time/magazine/article/0,9171,733760,00.html (accessed April 5, 2008).

97. See Vandekerckhove and Commer, "Whistle Blowing and Rational Loyalty." Also Restatement of Agency.

98. In taking this position, I am assuming that a person has many different obligations and responsibilities, and that they do not all fit together into a neat, harmonious package. So one must decide: Which obligations and responsibilities should take precedence? When an employee allows those at work to predominate, this suggests the extent to which we are today defined by our jobs.

99. Schmidtz, "Islands in a Sea of Obligation," 700–701.

100. *Time* magazine's reporting of Bunnatine Greenhouse's whistle-blowing had the title "Beyond the Call of Duty."

101. One might develop an account of integrity that accepts whatever values one stands for. However, since I am interested in a justified account of whistle-blowing, I limit these values in this case to those that are themselves justifiable. Hence, a person whose values included arbitrarily manipulating people and sexual domination of others might be faithful to these values and do so in a manner that is coherent with other values he holds. I suppose we could speak of the integrity of such a person. But it would be in a neutral or descriptive sense of "integrity" and not in a normative sense that would lend itself to an account of whistle-blowing.

102. Lynn Sharp Paine "Integrity," in *The Blackwell Encyclopedic Dictionary of Business Ethics*, ed. Patricia H. Werhane and R. Edward Freeman (Malden, Mass.: Blackwell, 1997), 335.

103. Damian Cox Marguerite La Caze and Michael P. Levine *Integrity and the Fragile Self* (Aldershot, U.K.: Ashgate, 2003), 8.

104. See William A. McDonough, "A Boat for Thoreau," in *Business Ethics Quarterly: Ruffin Series*, vol. 2, "Environmental Challenges to Business" (2000), 115–133.

105. Marlene Winfield "Whistleblowers as Corporate Safety Net," in *Whistleblowing: Subversion or Corporate Citizenship?* ed. Gerald Vinten (New York: St. Martin's, 1994), 22.

106. Near and Miceli report that "fewer than half of the responding whistle-blowers [in a study they made] reported that they experienced any retaliation." See Janet P. Near and Marcia P. Miceli "Whistle-blowers in Organizations: Dissidents or Reformers?" in *Research in Organizational Behavior*, ed. B. M. Staw and L. L. Cummings (Greenwich, Conn.: JAI Press, 1987), 356. The data for this finding were gathered from the public sector where there are (were) greater protections for whistle-blowers.

107. See Marica P. Miceli and Janet P. Near "Understanding Whistle-Blowing Effectiveness: How Can One Person Make a Difference?" in *The Accountable Corporation: Business-Government Relations*, vol. 4, ed. Marc J. Epstein and Kirk O. Hanson (Westport, Conn.: Praeger, 2006).

108. Mark Clayton, "Hard Job of Blowing the Whistle Gets Harder," *The Christian Science Monitor* (January 20, 2005), http://www.csmonitor.com/2005/0120/p13s02-sten.html (accessed June 20, 2008). We should also consider the many employees who simply do not speak out but remain silent witnesses to wrongdoing; see Marcia P. Miceli and Janet P. Near *Blowing the Whistle* (New York: Lexington, 1992).

109. Alhough many accounts of whistle-blowing by business ethicists, such as those discussed above in "Justifying Whistle-blowing," do turn to legal and organizational methods of protecting whistle-blowers, for example, Boatright and De George, these are secondary to their accounts of the justification of whistle-blowing.

110. Martin Landau, "On the Concept of a Self-Correcting Organization," *Public Administration Review* (Nov.–Dec. 1973): 534.

111. See Marlene Winfield, "Whistleblowers as Corporate Safety Net," 27.

112. This is one of the aims of the U.S. Federal Sentencing Guidelines. See http://www4.globalcompliance.com/knowledge-center/articles-and-editorial/authored-by-global-compliance/does-your-ethics-and-compliance-program-meet-the-federal-sentencing-guidelines-sentencing-guidelines.html (accessed August 13, 2008).

113. Miceli and Near, "Understanding Whistle-Blowing Effectiveness: How Can One Person Make a Difference?" 201.

114. Carl R. Oliver and Francis J. Daly, "Encouraging Internal Whistleblowing (and More!)," http://www.scu.edu/ethics/practicing/focusareas/business/whistleblowing-update.html (accessed May 10, 2008).

115. The points are made in Oliver and Daly, "Encouraging Internal Whistleblowing (and More!)."

116. Geoffrey Christopher Rapp, "Beyond Protection: Invigorating Incentives for Sarbanes Oxley Corporate and Securities Fraud Whistleblowers," 2007, http://www.soxfirst.com/50226711/rapp.pdf (accessed May 8, 2008). "Qui tam" suits are another means by which whistle-blowers may assist in the prosecution of wrongdoing and receive at least part of the financial penalty imposed by the courts; see http://www.lectlaw.com/def2/q069.htm (accessed July 11, 2006).

117. This paper has benefited from the comments and observations of Tom Beauchamp and John Hasnas. I appreciate their help in developing this paper.

SUGGESTED READING

Alford, C. Fred. *Whistleblowers: Broken Lives and Organizational Power*. Ithaca, N.Y.: Cornell University Press, 2001.

Boatright, John. *Ethics and the Conduct of Business*, 3rd ed. Chapter 5: "Whistle-Blowing." Upper Saddle River, N.J.: Prentice-Hall, 1999.

Bok, Sissela. "Whistleblowing and Professional Responsibilities." *New York University Education Quarterly* 11 (1980): 2–7.

Davis, Michael. "Some Paradoxes of Whistleblowing." *Business & Professional Ethics Journal* 15 (1) (1996): 3–19.

De George, Richard. "Ethical Responsibilities in Large Organizations: The Pinto Case." *Business & Professional Ethics Journal* 1 (1) (1981): 1–14.

———. *Business Ethics*. Chapter 12: "Whistle Blowing." Upper Saddle River, N.J.: Pearson Prentice-Hall, 2006.

Duska, Ronald. "Whistleblowing and Employee Loyalty." In *Contemporary Issues in Business Ethics*. Edited by J. R. Desjardins and J. J. McCall, 295–300. Belmont, Calif.: Wadsworth, 1985.

Dworkin, Terry Morehead. "SOX and Whistleblowing." *Michigan Law Review* 105 (2007): 157–178.

Ellison, Frederick A. "Civil Disobedience and Whistleblowing." *Journal of Business Ethics* 1 (1982): 23–28.

James, Gene. "Whistle Blowing: Its Nature and Justification." *Philosophy in Context* 10 (1980): 99–117.

Jubb, Peter B. "Whistleblowing: A Restrictive Definition and Interpretation." *Journal of Business Ethics* 21 (1999): 77–94.

Larmer, Robert. "Whistleblowing and Employee Loyalty." *Journal of Business Ethics* 11 (1992): 125–128.

Miceli, Marcia P., and Janet P. Near. *Blowing the Whistle*. New York: Lexington Books, 1992.

———. "Understanding Whistle-Blowing Effectiveness: How Can One Person Make a Difference?" In *The Accountable Corporation*: Business-Government Relations, vol. 4. Edited by Marc J. Epstein and Kirk O. Hanson. Westport, Conn.: Praeger, 2006.

Near, Janet P., and Marcia P. Miceli. "Organizational Dissidence: The Case of Whistle-Blowing." *Journal of Business Ethics* 4 (1985): 1–16.

———. "Effective Whistle-Blowing." *Academy of Management Review* 20 (1995): 679–708.

Rothschild, J., and T. D. Miethe. "Whistleblowing as Resistance in Modern Work Organizations." In *Resistance and Power in Organizations*. Edited by J. M. Jermier, D. Knights, and W. R. Nord, 252–273. London: Routledge, 1994.

Vandekerckhove, Wim, and M. S. Ronald Commers. "Whistle Blowing and Rational Loyalty." *Journal of Business Ethics* 53 (2004): 225–233.

Westin, Alan F. *Whistle-Blowing: Loyalty and Dissent in the Corporation*. New York: McGraw-Hill, 1981.

WEB SITES

Government Accountability Project (GAP), http://www.whistleblower.org/template/index.cfm

National Whistleblower Center, http://www.whistleblowers.org/

Worldwide Whistleblowers, http://www.worldwidewhistleblowers.com/home/index.php

CHAPTER 20

EMPLOYMENT AT WILL AND EMPLOYEE RIGHTS

JOHN J. MCCALL
PATRICIA H. WERHANE

THE United States and Western Europe have developed dramatically different understandings of employment over the past century. In the United States, the understanding of employment derives from a long-standing common law doctrine known as Employment at Will (EAW) and from social norms that give primacy to individualism, liberty, and private property. The result is that most employees in the United States must rely upon bargaining under conditions of competitive market exchange in order to secure many of their employment related rights. By contrast, most Western European countries understand employees to be a critical "social partner" in sustaining economic performance. As a result, they have developed an extensive network of both legally and socially recognized protections for employees.

In this chapter we discuss whether there are good moral reasons for preferring one of these two approaches to employment and employee rights over the other. We use the term "job-security rights" to refer to the bundle of rights that are commonly afforded to employees in most of Western Europe. These include rights to protection from abusive treatment and arbitrary termination, to due process and grievance procedures, and to political free expression in the workplace. We do not argue that employees have unconditional rights to be employed and never be fired or dismissed.

Our first section focuses on the different understandings of employment by examining how legal job-security rights have developed over time in the United States and in Europe and other developed nations. The second section presents an account of moral rights that we use in the third section to evaluate the relative moral strength of the respective legal approaches to job-security rights. The objective is to provide a model of moral analysis that can be applied to evaluate whether other rights ought to be granted to employees. Our basic conclusion is that there are good moral reasons for holding that employees are entitled to employment-related rights that extend beyond those currently recognized in U.S. law. In the final section we discuss the outlook for such employee rights given the current trends in a globalized labor market.

Job-Security Rights in the United States and Europe

In this section, we describe ways in which the United States and Western European countries provide different levels of legal job security to their workers. Job-security questions arise in the context of rules governing both the termination of an individual and collective dismissals or layoffs. The two different cultural environments exhibit substantial disparities with respect to both contexts of separation from employment.

The United States: Modified Employment at Will

Employment law in the United States has its source in early Anglo-Saxon practices that contributed to English common law. The U.S. legal system adopted much from this English tradition, including the doctrine of Employment at Will. EAW states that in the absence of any countervailing laws or contracts, employment relationships are "at will," meaning that an employer may hire, fire, or demote an employee at any time for good reasons, for no reasons, and even for morally bad reasons without thereby being guilty of a legal wrong.[1] Similarly, in the absence of specific law or contract provisions to the contrary, employees accept job offers at their will and may quit their positions at any time without having to give reason or notice. The doctrine of EAW thus gives employers wide, almost absolute discretionary power to terminate employees and gives employees equally wide discretion in leaving their jobs. While the U.S. legal system retains EAW as its background legal assumption in matters of employment, there have been legal changes over the years that have incrementally limited the scope of the doctrine. How those limits have developed and how substantial they are can best be seen by looking separately at the U.S. rules for individual termination and for layoffs.

Individual Termination in the United States

Individual employment contracts may supersede EAW if they contain terms contrary to the at-will assumption. Most unionized employees' contracts have explicit grievance procedures governing the dismissal of individuals. Union employees are, in this regard, not subject to EAW because they have rights under superseding contractual agreements. Similarly, public-sector workers are protected under constitutional guarantees because their employer, the government, is bound by constitutional limitations on government actions. Nonetheless, EAW still serves as the background condition for approximately 70 percent of employees in the United States.[2] The scope of EAW in individual dismissal has been incrementally limited over time by statute and by precedent-setting court decisions. Legislative limits on the authority of employers to fire individuals began in earnest in the 1930s with the passage of the National Labor Relations Act (NLRA). The NLRA bars employers from dismissing workers for certain union organizing activities. Later limitations are found in sections of the Civil Rights Act of 1964 that bar dismissal on grounds of race, sex, color, religion, national origin, and ethnicity. In addition, the Americans with Disabilities Act of 1990 requires employers to make reasonable accommodations, for example, in eliminating physical obstacles to access to employment sites, in order to avoid discriminating in hiring or discharge against those with disabilities.

Employees have been granted some rights through judicial action as well, often in precedents set at the level of individual state jurisdiction. Past decisions, for example, reinstated a worker's yearly bonus that had been denied him because he was discharged without cause just prior to the date of bonus issuance (an "implied covenant of good faith" exception to EAW)[3] or held unacceptable a dismissal for alerting authorities to misleading product labeling (a "public policy" exception).[4] Courts have also tried to limit the scope of EAW by finding an implied contract in the language used in employee handbooks, for instance, in clauses suggesting that dismissal will only be for legitimate cause.[5]

While these legal actions have, over time, seemed to reduce the scope of an employer's discretionary authority to discharge, there are reasons why many feel that legal job-security rights remain inadequate and that the core doctrine of EAW is alive and well in the U.S. workplace. First, employers have been successful in blocking the effectiveness of judicial precedents. They have, for instance, responded to the Implied Contract exception by requiring workers to sign waivers indicating that they understand that they are employed at will. These waivers have become ubiquitous in corporate America, and they have been accepted by courts as superseding any language in employee handbooks that suggests that dismissal be for just cause only.

Second, the approach to legal limits on EAW has been to enumerate the reasons for dismissal that are especially objectionable, such as dismissal on grounds of racial animosity. However, this approach leaves acceptable innumerable reasons for dismissal. Employers are free to use any other reason, or no reason, to legally justify a termination. As Bruce Barry has detailed, employees have in recent years been fired for expressing, outside of work, political opinions that their employers found disagreeable or even for refusing to participate in acts of political expression organized by their employers.[6] While citizens in the United States have constitutional guarantees of free speech, these guarantees do not extend into the sphere of the private-sector workplace.

Finally, the U.S. system places the initial burden of proof on aggrieved discharged employees to establish that they have been fired for one of the listed unacceptable reasons. Given the expense of litigation and the permissibility of employers firing an employee for no reason, the job-security protections established over the years by the legislative and judicial limits on EAW are not particularly robust. This is not to imply that employees have no protections. The threat of a civil rights discrimination lawsuit can cause employers to be reluctant to discharge. Further, many corporations voluntarily adopt internal grievance systems that provide some due process for employees. These systems, however, are not required by law and, given the impact of the waivers discussed above, the protection these procedures provide may not be substantial.[7]

While there have been legislative attempts in many states to move away from this modified EAW system towards a system that limits employers' broad discretion in dismissal cases, they have generally been successfully resisted by corporate lobbying efforts. In only one state, Montana, has the EAW approach been replaced by rules requiring notice and limiting the reasons available for termination. So, while the doctrine of EAW has been subject to incremental changes that attempt to limit employers' discretion to discharge, the practical significance of these changes for employees' job security is relatively minor.

Layoffs in the United States

The discretion of employers to layoff groups of workers is even more unfettered in the United States than their ability to discharge a single individual. The sole legal limit on layoffs was created by the Worker Adjustment and Retraining Notification Act of 1988 (WARN). That act requires that plants with more than 100 workers provide sixty days notice of impending layoffs if the layoff will affect more than one third of the workforce. For larger plants, the notification threshold is 500 workers affected, even in circumstances where that would be less than one-third of the plant's total workforce. Employees in the United States thus have, under certain circumstances, a legal right to advance notice if they are to be subject to a layoff.

There are many questions about the effectiveness of these notice provisions. The 100-employee plant-level threshold effectively exempts over 90 percent of U.S. employees from coverage by the WARN Act. Further, there are questions about the degree of employer compliance and the success of the WARN Act's enforcement mechanism, which relies on workers filing suits under the provisions of the act. The Government Accounting Office found that 75 percent of employers who would have been covered failed to provide required notice and only 1 percent of violations were enforced through employee suits.[8] These numbers are explained, in part, by conscious attempts by employers to evade the law's requirements.[9]

Workers in the United States are not, in general, entitled to severance payments in cases of layoffs. Such payments are either voluntary gestures by the employer or are agreed upon as items in a contract negotiation. Estimates are that approximately 20 percent of U.S. private-sector workers are eligible for employer-provided severance benefits.[10] For that one-fifth of eligible workers, the severance formula is commonly one week of pay for every year of continuous service to the employer, usually with a cap of twenty-six weeks.[11]

Some laid-off employees in the United States are legally entitled to government supplied unemployment insurance, even if they are not entitled to company provided severance benefits. However, the United States is relatively less generous than many industrialized nations. The benefit replacement rate (the average rate at which prior salary is replaced) is 47 percent. The maximum benefit period is generally six months. Only about 40 percent of those who are unemployed actually collect benefits, in part because of state eligibility requirements, and nearly 20 percent of the unemployed have been unemployed for more than the usual twenty-six-week benefit provision.[12] As we will see, the rights of workers in Western Europe have been historically stronger in regard to individual termination, layoffs, and income insurance during periods of unemployment.

Western Europe: Just Cause and "Social Partnership"

Western Europe exhibits a different pattern in recognizing job-security rights from that displayed by the United States. While there are differences among the European countries themselves, they have historically shared norms that tended to push policies in a common direction. More recently, the creation of the European Union has led to greater harmonization between national employment practices. In Europe, individual dismissals are governed by a just-cause legal principle that provides greater job protection than does the modified EAW of the United States. Western European approaches to layoffs also generally provide employees with greater rights to advance notice and income insurance than does the United States.[13]

Just-Cause Dismissal Rules

In Europe, and in almost the entire developed world, individual employee terminations are governed by a just-cause system. Under typical just-cause legal rules, employees are guaranteed both substantive and procedural rights in dismissal proceedings. The goal of such rules is to reduce the probability of an abusive or arbitrary exercise of managerial power that could jeopardize a worker's income and employment. After a probationary period, usually of a matter of months, workers under just-cause rules have procedural rights to be given both notice of intent to dismiss as well as the reasons for the intended termination. Typically, they have the ability to challenge the dismissal in an internal pretermination hearing, though a dismissal may be provisionally effected more immediately in cases where there are serious reasons.

More substantively, European employers wishing to terminate an individual are limited to a set of permissible reasons that are enumerated by law and by prior decisions of labor courts and arbitrators. This approach contrasts to the U.S. model, which enumerates merely a set of impermissible reasons and then allows employers to use any reason not specified, or to offer no reason at all. The set of permissible reasons includes poor performance, excessive absenteeism, theft, and the like. As a result, employers are not permitted to discharge on the basis of political opinion, religion, race, and personal bias of managers. Employers bear the initial burden of proof requiring that they provide evidence to support the alleged reason for dismissal. If, say, an employer wishes to terminate an employee for poor work performance, the employer must establish that there were clear, previously announced performance standards and must provide evidence that the particular employee has failed to meet those standards.

Finally, if a dismissal is carried out, employees are entitled to challenge the action in an arbitration hearing or in a labor court. If the arbitrator or court finds that the termination was without acceptable cause, the employee is entitled to either monetary compensation amounting to some small multiple of yearly wages or to reinstatement, though the latter is rare. This is in contrast to the remedies in the United States for dismissals found to be for legally identified unacceptable reasons. For instance, in the United States, a dismissal found to have been a violation of the Civil Rights Act prohibition on racial discrimination may result in sizable monetary judgments against the corporation. However, this possibility of large damage awards only holds for classes of workers who are given specially protected status under the law.

The European just-cause approach places greater limits on the discretion of employers to dismiss than does the modified EAW of the United States. As such, it provides European workers with legislated job-security rights and some protections against abusive or arbitrary managerial action, that their U.S. peers lack. The European laws also serve as a device for communicating and reinforcing social norms with the result that employers are less likely to engage in arbitrary action.

Layoffs, European Style

European workers are legally entitled to notice of impending layoffs and entitled to more generous severance pay and unemployment compensation than are U.S. workers. The historical European approach to downsizing and collective dismissals is the product of an understanding among the state, the employer, unions, and employees. In European parlance, these "social partners" have coordinated policies that discourage the use of layoffs as well as soften the impact on workers when layoffs become necessary.

Notice requirements for an impending layoff are a matter of law and are applicable to a broader range of employers than is required by the U.S. WARN Act. For instance, in Germany, notice is required for layoffs of five or more workers in firms with fewer than fifty employees. In Belgium, the threshold is ten or more workers for firms with fewer than 100 employees. Requirements are similar in most Western European nations.[14] Most often, the law also requires the employer to negotiate or consult with representatives of workers, either through formal unions or through company works-councils. The required consultation can include discussions about alternatives to the layoff, the process, and criteria used in selecting those laid off, and the severance compensation to be paid in the event of a layoff. Individual collective bargaining agreements between firms and unions may add further constraints on when and how a collective dismissal occurs. The impact of collective bargaining agreements is often broader than one might suspect by looking only at the density of union membership in a given country because such agreements are often sectoral, that is, extended to all workers in a given sector regardless of union membership.[15]

Because of the legal consultation requirements, common practice results in greater job-security rights. In many cases where the decreased demand for labor is expected to be temporary, companies reach agreements to reduce not the number of workers but the number of hours each worker works. Workers on "short hours" are sometimes subsidized by government funding.[16] When reductions in workforce numbers are enacted, severance pay is more broadly available and more generous than in the United States.[17] One report, quoting a survey of European severance payments, notes that the average redundancy pay in the EU was £11,000 for a worker with ten years of service and a salary of £20,000 per year. The range of severance paid varied by country from £5,000 to £25,000.[18] These payments provide greater income support than would be the case under the common U.S. practice, cited above, of one week's severance pay for each year of employment. A worker in the United States with ten years of service would receive less than 20 percent of annual salary as compared with the more than 50 percent received by the average European severance recipient.

State-provided unemployment compensation is also more generous in Europe than the United States, although the degree of that generosity varies across countries. Notwithstanding intercountry differences, most major continental European nations exhibit more generosity in both amount and duration when replacing income with unemployment compensation benefits. For instance, replacement rates for lost wages in continental Europe typically are in the 60–70 percent range, and benefit duration typically extends for a year or more.[19]

This collection of legislative mandates and common practices means that European workers also possess greater entitlements when it comes to layoffs. The longer notice and wider and more generous severance arrangements serve as a disincentive for companies to engage in collective dismissals. The severance and unemployment benefits provide income entitlements that cushion job loss when it eventually occurs. Up until the most recent decade, these arrangements were generally accepted as part of the social partnership for ensuring the welfare of citizens generally. In fact, anecdotally, interviews of about a dozen executives conducted in the early 1990s by McCall showed almost universal acceptance on the part of management for both the legal rules and social norms governing individual and collective dismissals.[20]

In the mid-1990s, however, spurred by opinions offered in Organization for Economic Cooperation and Development (OECD) documents on employment, a growing sentiment developed on the continent that European labor markets needed greater "flexibility." This sentiment was, in large measure, due to a concern over the high rates of unemployment that the major European economies were experiencing at a time when the unemployment experience of the U.S. economy was registering improvement. The most recent series of OECD "Employment Outlooks" have trumpeted a call for relaxing legislated employment protections, and the European Commission has begun to echo that call in its recent communications to the European Parliament. The Commission's stance is that Europe needs to develop a system of "flexicurity" that will provide companies with increased labor market flexibility while assuring workers socially provided income and job training. Accordingly, while the United States and Europe have had divergent approaches to legal job-security rights for workers, recent developments on the continent raise a question about whether there will be convergence on an approach that is closer to the U.S. experience than to the European tradition.[21]

We have seen, then, that different nations have taken different legal approaches to employee rights, in particular in the degree to which they extend job-security rights. The United States, relying on its traditional EAW rules, offers fewer legal employee rights while the nations of Western Europe offer more. In the remainder of this chapter, we discuss whether there are arguments for claiming that one approach to employee rights is morally superior to the other. To pursue that discussion fruitfully, we will need to consider the role and justification of moral rights.

THE ROLE OF RIGHTS IN MORALITY

Moral rights can be distinguished into broad categories according to the reasons offered in their justification. Some rights are justified because they are essential for showing proper respect to individual persons. These rights give expression to basic beliefs about the moral standing of persons. Other rights are justified because of their contribution to the realization of other social goals. The function of these rights is thus instrumental. We can distinguish, then, between basic and instrumental rights by identifying the reasons offered for the rights. Attending to these different kinds of reasons that might be offered in support of a right will help us later in evaluating the competing approaches to employee rights.

Basic Rights

Basic rights show a commitment to the inherent value of persons. Often, in both secular and religious traditions, this belief in inherent value is linked to a capacity seen as unique to persons. For example, in the Judeo-Christian tradition, it is the capacity for deliberative choice that distinguished Adam and Eve from the rest of creation. In the secular philosophic tradition, dating to the Greeks, rationality defined persons and grounded the distinctive moral status conferred on persons. In contemporary language, it is autonomy, the ability to act freely based on reason, that provides persons with their claim to dignity and that allows us to ascribe to them responsibility for their choices. We will see, however, that respecting the dignity of persons requires that we identify certain of their interests for protection from threats posed by the actions of other persons.

Immanuel Kant expressed this idea when he argued that we must treat persons as ends in themselves and not merely as means. If we were always ready to use the frustration of another's interest as a tool for our own satisfaction, or for the satisfaction of our collective purposes, how could we be said to regard her as having inherent value? The commitment to the inherent value of persons requires that there are some things we will not do to persons out of respect for their dignity and autonomy.[22] This idea is often lost in contemporary discussions of issues such as torture. These discussions center on the effectiveness of torture in eliciting crucial information. They commonly fail to discuss whether certain acts are fundamentally incompatible with treating another person with dignity and respect. If we are willing to perform even the most gruesome acts on another, it is hard to imagine that we treat her as anything other than a means for our own ends.

Thus, one function that the language of rights performs in morality is to express a core moral commitment to persons as having a distinctive moral status, a moral status that demands they be treated with dignity and respect. Basic rights express this idea by marking off some interests of persons for protection from the actions of others. The critical questions are, "Which particular personal interests ought to be protected and how much protection is required if we are to capture effectively the fundamental moral intuition about the value of individuals?"

A right to life is a usual candidate for status as a basic right. It would be questionable to say that we respect the dignity of another if we were to regard her very life merely as a tool for our purposes. Sometimes rights to the material means necessary for sustaining a decent human existence are also held to be basic rights. Others have held a right to be free from avoidable threats to physical integrity to be essential to respecting the dignity of autonomous persons. Still others have held that some right to free speech and expression is basic because the exchange and consideration of ideas is integral to the capacity for reasoned deliberation, to the exercise of autonomy.

Whichever rights are identified as basic, it is important to circumscribe the content of the rights carefully, identifying which protections should be accorded to the interests selected as candidates for basic rights. Even the right to life will have limits on what it requires. Your right to life does not necessarily mean that I must do everything to keep you alive, nor even that there are no circumstances when I may legitimately kill you. The right to be free, too, is circumscribed by the equal rights of others, and free expression in particular does not entail rights to lie or otherwise libel others. Our point here is not to exhaustively enumerate those rights that are basic but to identify the critical feature of basic rights, which is that they are equal rights and that they are integrally connected to treating autonomous beings with dignity and respect.

It is also important to note that a basic right, one essential for capturing the idea that persons have inherent value, might also be a right with instrumental value. The right to free speech is often seen in this way. Not only is a right to free speech necessary for respecting a person's capacity to engage in reasoned deliberation, it can also be an instrument for protecting other rights by allowing citizens to express grievances against the government.

The rights that we categorize as basic are frequently identified as human rights or natural rights. The use of the terms "natural" and "human" is an attempt to signify a belief that some rights are possessed merely by virtue of being a human person. As such, natural or human rights are held to be entitlements whose justification does not depend on particular forms of social organization. The right to life, for example, differs from a right to a secondary education. The latter right might be justified as an instrument for effective participation in the complex social life of advanced democracies. But it could only exist in a society with a particular state of development and with particular educational institutions. The right to life, however, can be seen as an entitlement that applies to all persons in every society. For this reason, rights designated as "natural rights" and "human rights" are also often called "universal rights" in order to indicate that they are seen as valid claims in every society and valid even where they may not be, in fact, respected.

Important philosophical questions surround these claims about natural, human, or universal rights. For instance, there are some who question whether all and only members of the human species possess these rights. Others question whether it makes sense to speak of moral entitlements that are logically prior to all forms of social organization. Similarly, some question whether the content of basic rights can be truly universal, and whether instead their content might permissibly vary between social or cultural contexts. While these are important questions, their answers are not generally required for the analysis of employee rights that we propose because few employee rights could be argued to be basic. The rights to be paid for work done, a right to be free from slavery or forced labor, or to be free from physical abuse at work might be examples. But most employee rights, and particularly most of the job-security rights we have discussed, more likely will fall into a second category of rights, which we will call instrumental rights.

Instrumental Rights

Instrumental rights gain their legitimacy not because they are integral for expressing commitment to the inherent value of persons but because they are instruments for achieving goals that society finds desirable. These goals may vary considerably, from protecting basic rights to promoting the common good. For instance, the First Amendment right to a free press in the U.S. Constitution can be given a moral justification as a device for providing an external check that can limit abuses of government power. Similarly, the Second Amendment right to bear arms, if it can be justified as an individual right to possess weapons, would be justified as an instrument for helping persons protect their lives. Other instrumental rights are justified not because they provide a means for protecting basic rights but merely because they are instruments for achieving the common good, an argument used, as we will see, for a right to private property. These examples show that purely instrumental rights are not essential for respecting the dignity of persons but are tools for the fulfillment of other purposes. A free press, the ability to own weapons, or even the private ownership of goods would be hard to defend as necessary in order to treat persons with respect. There have, after all, been historical social arrangements in which persons were treated with respect and yet property was possessed in common rather than privately, there was no independent press, and the individual possession of weapons was not sanctioned.

Instrumental rights perform a different function in morality than do basic rights, but classification of a right as instrumental does not mean that it is of little importance. The rationale for any particular instrumental right must typically rest on factual evidence that recognizing such a right would have a significant probability of achieving the espoused social objective. In our case example, the right to notice before dismissal or the right to contest a pending dismissal may be very important in the life of a worker; these rights might have substantial consequences for employers and society at large as well. Instrumental status for a right is not equivalent to low status.

Since instrumental rights are a means to an end, it is unlikely that they are universal. It is reasonable to expect that instrumental rights may permissibly vary across societies and cultures. Social circumstances vary significantly, and any given end might be achieved through a variety of means. Different sets of instrumental rights with different members might equally well achieve a particular moral objective. This is not to say, however, that we need to accept as a brute difference any variation between societies with regard to the instrumental rights that they recognize. A society's recognition (or lack thereof) for an instrumental right might still be subject to reasonable critical analysis by asking whether the right, as currently recognized and embedded within social structures, effectively achieves a legitimate moral objective. It may be that an instrumental right that is de facto recognized in a particular society either fails to achieve its avowed social objective or achieves an objective that is morally suspect in itself. For instance, a legal right that gave persons the discretion to determine how much tax to pay based on their assessment of the relative importance of particular government functions would not likely achieve the society's objective of having sufficient resources for government to function effectively. Or, a right that granted some individuals the power to buy and sell others would be a right that furthered a morally objectionable social goal. Thus, the possibility of legitimate variation between societies over the recognition of rights does not entail a vitiating form of moral relativism.

In the next section, we apply this analysis of rights to assess the respective effectiveness of the U.S. and European approaches to employee job security rights.

Assessing Different Approaches to Employee Rights

We have seen that the United States differs from most Western European countries, and in fact from most other industrialized countries, in the degree to which it grants job-security rights to employees by law. In particular, there are differences over the provision of advance notice before termination, the need to provide the reasons for the proposed termination to the employee in advance, the employee's right to contest a firing before it occurs, the degree to which employers are limited in the reasons they may use, the initial burden of proof, the provision of severance benefits in layoffs, and the employer's need to consult with employee representatives before instituting a layoff. Many of the rights possessed by workers in the different environments will fall into the category of instrumental rights, though some of these instrumental rights will function to protect basic rights.

A conditional workplace right not to be fired for engaging in political expression outside of work, for example, would fall into this latter category since it serves to facilitate the exercise of a more basic right to free expression. Whether a society provides employees an explicit legal protection for free expression may be a function of whether it believes that political expression is likely to be chilled by employers' actions and whether it believes that there are other effective mechanisms for deterring such chilling behaviors. In the United States, some have argued that market forces and the potential for reputational losses are sufficient devices to deter employers from such behavior and from arbitrary discharge in general.[23] These arguments try to convince us that legal rules prohibiting discharge for political expression are unnecessary because there are other instruments that do as good a job in allowing citizens to engage in political debates. So, even in the attempt to protect a basic right such as the right to free expression, different societies might adopt different instrumental approaches. Some might preclude employers from dismissing workers for outside political expression; others might try to use the market to minimize the potential for such dismissals. As we noted above, however, a particular society's choice about which instruments it adopts for a given social end is a choice that can be subject to critical assessment. It might be a choice that is an ineffective one.

How might different societies understand and morally justify their respective approaches to job security rights? To address this question, we begin with the rationales usually presented for the U.S. resistance to an expanded set of legislated job security rights. We then provide an explanation of the broader European job-security rights and evaluate the relative adequacy of the differing sets of rights for achieving the respective social objectives. The analysis we present is meant also as a model for addressing other claimed employee rights.

Sources of U.S. Resistance: Utility, Property, and Liberty

The U.S. perspective derives from a belief that employment is primarily a matter of private contracting. Historically, this U.S. exceptionalism has been supported by appeals to utility, property, and liberty.

Economists often look back to Adam Smith to justify as little intervention in private transactions as possible. The argument is that the imposition of restrictions on individual economic exchange causes costly deviations from the most efficient economic outcomes. Better, it is argued, to leave the economy to the invisible hand of the market than to impose legislated mandates on exchange. One should be reminded, however, that Smith concluded that the market works most efficiently and effectively under a rule of law that protects basic rights and fair exchanges.[24]

In the context of employment protection legislation, the favored analysis in much of the United States is that mandating notice, requiring severance payments, limiting grounds for termination, and providing generous unemployment insurance all produce undesirable results that harm the society. For instance, the OECD has for years held that the strictness of European job-security legislation causes firms both to forgo hiring (because shedding labor is both more costly and more time consuming) and to delay adjustment to changing market conditions. The purported result is lower overall levels of employment and higher rates of unemployment as well as longer spells of unemployment for those who are looking for work.[25] These purported consequences of job-security rights are claimed to cause a drag on the overall efficiency of the economy and place many citizens in situations in which their lives are less satisfying than they otherwise would be. Many U.S. commentators echo this view that restrictions on employer discretion to fire have significantly negative aggregate welfare consequences.[26] Overall utility thus is alleged to be lower because of job security rights.

The U.S. approach to job-security rules is also defended as most adequately respecting the private property rights of owners. Consider, some suggest, that legislated job-security rights interfere with corporate owners' rights to control who has access to their property. We would claim a right for ourselves to determine who has access to our home or our car, and we would claim a right to do so without having to justify our decision to those who were denied access. Why should we not similarly accept a corporate owner's right to deny continued access to a business' facilities? Under this account, requiring advance notice, restricting the reasons available for limiting access, and requiring due process and severance payments are seen as unjustifiable interferences with property rights.[27]

Finally, the U.S. approach is often justified by appeal to liberty rights, in particular, rights to freely determine the terms of contracts.[28] Legislated mandates on employment arrangements are alleged to interfere with both employers and employees by placing outside the law contracts that both might prefer. Workers, for instance, might prefer, and employers might offer, less job security in exchange for higher wages. To preclude them, in advance, from reaching that agreement is held to be an interference with their legitimate liberty rights.

In the United States, with its emphasis on individualism and economic freedom, these moral arguments have great attraction for many. We will need, however, to analyze each of these three arguments in greater detail. We will need to assess the accuracy of the economic predictions made by the utilitarian argument against job-security regulations. We will also need to assess the reasons behind both property and free contract rights. We leave the utilitarian argument for later discussion. Now, we should address the reasons available in support of the private property and freedom of contract arguments.

There is a long tradition of moral justifications for property rights. That tradition identifies three main grounds for private property. First, private control over goods has been argued to contribute to aggregate welfare. This justification claims that providing the ability for persons to acquire goods privately both spurs greater industriousness and assures that goods are put to their most efficient use. The failures of the Soviet planned economy are often used to underscore both points: without the possibility of differential acquisition, workers had little incentive to produce; and the "dead hand" of the controlling central Soviet bureaucracy prevented the invisible hand of the market from directing resources to their most efficient uses. The result was too little bread and too little vodka on the store shelves.

Second, private property has been recommended for its instrumental contribution to individual autonomy. As far back as John Locke's *Second Treatise on Government* in 1688,[29] the secure private possession of property was seen as enhancing a person's ability to choose and to control his life. Locke described the increased independence from the crown that would be provided by a secure title to land. Today, we sometimes refer to the very rich as "independently wealthy," signifying that their wealth allows them a greater range of choice and greater control over the course of their lives.

Third, private property has been justified as contributing to fair treatment. Again, Locke is a classic source in his development of a labor theory of value. Locke argued that if a person were to clear, plant, and tend a plot of land, thereby improving it and making it into something of value, that person should have control rights over the land and its produce.[30] In contemporary discussions, owners of corporate property are described as bearing the risk of investing money and thus entitled by fairness to the residual gains (profits) produced.

Rights to freedom of contract have similar historical rationales. To give individuals the right to contract for themselves places decisions in the hands of those who best know their own interests. It can also be argued that individuals pursuing their own ends will be led "as if by an invisible hand" to contribute to the general welfare.[31] In addition to this utilitarian justification, freedom of contract can be argued to contribute to autonomy since it allows a person to have greater influence over important aspects of her life rather than to have the content of economic agreements dictated to her by outside parties.

The U.S. legal treatment of employment as a matter of private contracting, which is exceptional among developed, industrial nations, therefore has moral arguments behind it. What we need to assess is whether these arguments provide compelling reasons for resisting the more expansive legislated job-security rights that exist in the European nations. To assess that, we need to ask whether the U.S. set of entitlements promotes goals of utility, autonomy, and fairness more effectively than does the alternative. We will turn to that task after consideration of the rationales for the alternative, European picture of job-security rights.

Europe: Differing Rights, Similar Foundations

As we have seen, the European approach to job security differs dramatically from that of the United States in the set of instrumental rights that it accords to employees. Perhaps surprisingly, rationales for the European approach are remarkably similar to those used for the U.S. allocation of legal rights to employees.

Consider the job-security rights related to individual dismissal: advance notice before dismissal, limits on reasons that employers may use in justifying a termination, the ability to contest a firing in advance at an internal grievance hearing, the burden of proof falling first on an employer to establish the legitimacy of a dismissal. Each of these rights, and the set collectively, may be defended as contributing to fairness, autonomy, and utility, the same values used in justification of the U.S. approach. The goal of job-security rules is to reduce the exposure of employees to arbitrary and abusive exercise of employer authority. The introduction of these procedural rights treats the workplace as an arena in which institutional power exists and needs to be moderated in order to assure fairness, just as it needs to be in the use of governmental authority.[32]

These same procedural rights of notice and limits on employer discretion to discharge can facilitate the exercise of individual autonomy in that they help to assure security of income. While in Locke's time, secure possession of land gave some measure of economic independence, today, most persons rely upon the security of their wages and property for whatever economic security they possess. Abrupt loss of wage carries with it a substantial decrease in one's control over life choices, an impact made more significant by the probability that one's future employment will be at reduced wages. Studies of the wage experience of U.S. workers displaced by layoffs indicate that those finding new, full-time jobs after being laid off earn up to 17 percent less on average in their new positions. Wage losses are even greater among those with longer tenure at previous jobs and among those with higher levels of education.[33] Further, job-security rights that preclude discharge for the exercise of political speech can facilitate autonomy by allowing employees to participate, without risk to their livelihood, in collectively determining policy choices that have important consequences for their lives.

Finally, one can argue that job-security rights produce a utility gain. The individual with those job-security rights who is subject to impending dismissal may gain some measure of utility if the rights allow him to avoid job loss or at least find new employment sooner by providing him an opportunity to begin his job search process earlier. Others in the workplace may gain a greater sense of security from the knowledge that their jobs are less subject to abrupt and arbitrary termination. It is even possible to argue that employers gain from the introduction of just-cause systems by the inducement of greater loyalty and a sense of commitment to the firm from workers who believe that they will be treated fairly, believe that they have some future with the firm, and believe that their welfare is bound up with the long-term welfare of the firm. In fact, empirical research on the impact of human resource strategies on firm performance provides evidence that firm productivity can be increased by policies that extend conditional job security rights to employees.[34]

Consider next the severance and consultation rights connected with layoffs. These, too, may be defended on fairness, autonomy, and utility grounds. Severance pay can be argued to be fair compensation for past contributions to a firm as well as a cushion against economic conditions that are not the fault of workers. It can enhance control in the same way as do procedural rights, and it can increase welfare both by spreading the costs of difficult economic conditions across a larger pool of people and by helping to sustain consumer spending. Consultation rights have been defended as assuring a collective voice that increases the chance that workers are treated fairly and as providing the institutional structure that increases cooperation and in turn increases productivity.[35]

Assessing Relative Effectiveness

We have seen that competing institutional designs grant differing sets of legal rights to different constituencies, each design purporting to enhance utility, autonomy, and fair treatment. There are three possibilities in evaluating the competing claims with respect to each goal: it may be that each system does an equally effective job of achieving the respective objective; it may be that the market-based U.S. system does a better job in its emphasis on private property and freedom of contract; or it may be that the European social market approach with employment protection is more successful. Note that it would be a mistake to describe this as a contest between legal mandates and their absence. Both cultures have made choices about which legal entitlements they will enforce and which they will not. Europe has chosen to enforce by law broad job-security protections; the United States has chosen to enforce by law stronger notions of property and free contract. How, then, do the respective legal systems succeed as instruments for securing the common social and moral objectives?

Given the space available, we cannot presume to suggest that our analysis is anything near exhaustive or conclusive. The arguments to be considered are too numerous and too complex to discuss fully. What we offer is more suggestive than an ideally adequate analysis. We do not suggest, however, that we believe there is no preponderance of argument on these issues. We have both argued for the need for a broadened scope of employee rights in the United States.[36]

Assessment of the aggregate welfare or utility provided under the different job-security rules will largely turn on evidence about the economic consequences of those rules. OECD reports have fingered employment protections as the cause of the malaise in Western European labor markets, some of which have experienced high unemployment and lower overall levels of employment during the period after the recessions of the early 1990s. During this same period, the less regulated U.S. labor market saw declining unemployment and greater job growth. The OECD economic account is that the more highly regulated and inflexible European labor markets produce sclerotic employment results. That account has been repeated by many and has recently been echoed by the European Commission.[37]

The OECD story, though frequently repeated, has some evidentiary problems. Even the OECD has now acknowledged that empirical evidence linking employment protections to high and persistent unemployment is unavailable.[38] As the OECD admits, and a number of commentators clearly show, there is no consistent pattern of correlation between countries with high unemployment and countries with strong job-protection rights. Some European economies, such as Germany's, have high unemployment but other, comparably regulated labor markets, such as Austria, Denmark, the Netherlands, and Norway, have low unemployment, often lower than that of the United States. In the ten years since 1997, for example, those four countries have each regularly had lower unemployment than the United States. On just three occasions did Austria and Denmark have higher unemployment than the United States; the Netherlands and Norway were always below the U.S. rates.[39] Legislated job-security rights, therefore, cannot by themselves be the cause of the employment problems suffered by some European economies. Other variables that could have a significant impact on unemployment, often neglected in the push for relaxing job-security protections, include rigidities in European product markets (such as tariffs, foreign ownership barriers, price controls, and costly administrative burdens on the creation of corporations) and weak aggregate demand, perhaps worsened by high interest rates.[40] As for overall employment effects, even the OECD's own analysis now suggests that job protections have negligible effect on overall employment. While they may depress labor "take-up" by decreasing the propensity to hire new workers, that effect is likely washed out by decreased labor "shedding" since employers are also less likely to dismiss workers.[41]

Although the evidence for employment-security rights as a sufficient causal factor in unemployment is lacking, some argue that job security increases social exclusion by making unemployment spells longer and making youth unemployment worse.[42] However, others note that social exclusion as measured by income inequality, poverty, youth unemployment, and low levels of economic mobility is often worse in the

United States than in more protected labor markets.[43] Analysis of youth unemployment in France, at supposedly high levels, and the United States, with supposedly lower levels, shows that the apparent difference is largely due to the small number of French youth who are employed, a fact influenced by the relatively larger number of French youth who are full-time students. When youth unemployment is measured relative to the overall youth population instead of those desiring employment (the sum of the employed and those seeking work but not employed), youth unemployment rates in the two nations are nearly the same.[44] Again, the empirical evidence does not establish that exclusion of particular groups from economic life is robustly related to the degree of job-security protections workers receive.

The utility argument that faults job security as the cause of unemployment and social exclusion is therefore unconvincing. There is thus no apparent reason sufficient to suppose that net welfare is damaged by job-security rules, and, since there are other reasons for suspecting that job security increases productivity by inducing loyalty and commitment,[45] there may be some reason to believe that it is enhanced.

To assess the relative impacts of the alternatives on personal autonomy, we have to ask which of the following paired choices would enhance autonomy more: (1) pursuing a private contracting approach to employment with strong property and free contract rights while rejecting job-security entitlements, or (2) enacting protection for job security and free political expression in the workplace and rejecting the idea that employment protections are primarily a matter for private market bargaining. Property rights can increase independence, as Locke instructs. Secure ownership rights give an individual greater ability to make choices and to control her life. However, given the separation of ownership from control in the modern corporation, the autonomy-enhancing effect of corporate property ownership derives primarily from the realizable monetary value of the shares owned. That is, other things being equal, the greater the monetary value of one's economic holdings, the greater one's ability to plan and to have control over life choices. As noted above, those with substantial capital are called "independently wealthy" for a reason. So, if job-security protections are to damage the autonomy provided by share ownership, they must somehow cause a reduction in share values. Some suggest that providing advance notice in cases of either individual dismissal or group layoff exposes a company to economic risks due to sabotage by disgruntled employees. This claim appears to be a red herring, however, since employees targeted for individual dismissal may be given a suspension with pay pending a hearing. And in circumstances of both individual and collective dismissals, abruptly separating workers can have devastating effects on the morale of surviving employees, which in turn can damage firm productivity. As noted above, and as Bowie, Ichniowski, and Pfeffer show, properly designed job security can enhance firm value and productivity.[46]

Job loss typically has dramatic impact on personal and family finances, leading to decreased levels of choice and control. We could, of course, soften that effect without job-security protections such as advance notice and limits on reasons for dismissal if we provided social subsidies to the unemployed. In the United States, however, unemployment insurance is not generous and is relatively limited in dura-tion and, as we saw above, new employment acquired subsequent to a job loss most often offers significantly lower wages. There are also social and personal costs asso-ciated with job loss that go beyond lost income. Social connections, for example, are often centered on one's workplace. It would appear that legally requiring advance notice, limiting the reasons available for dismissal, and shifting the initial burden of proof onto the employer would enhance autonomy more than would the adoption of an U.S. system of private contracting for job-security rights.

The assertion that autonomy is adequately assured by allowing workers to freely contract the terms of their employment has a number of serious difficulties. First, it assumes that the background conditions under which bargaining occurs are con-ditions of relatively equal leverage. If one party has substantially more leverage in negotiations, it would be hard to say that agreements provide adequately for the autonomous choice of both parties. Most employees need their jobs more than the employer needs them—their continued income is usually critical to the quality of their lives. Bargaining under these conditions does not provide employees with much real choice or control over the terms of their employment. An "autonomy" which meant only that a person had the ability to select from among whatever options the market placed before her would not be a capacity worthy of much moral significance. Rather, if "autonomy" is to refer to a capacity that grounds the dignity of persons, respecting and promoting that autonomy must involve attempts to assure that person's delibera-tive choices are ones that can be made, as much as humanly possible, without sacrific-ing goods critical to the quality of life. Mere freedom of contract under conditions of unequal bargaining, then, would not be sufficient to respect autonomy in any mor-ally important sense. Second, the free contract argument presumes that workers who choose to forgo job-security protections will receive a wage premium, but it appears that absence of security generally does not come with higher wages. Workers with job security in the United States are typically higher paid professionals or unionized workers.[47] That fact further underscores the likelihood that bargaining over contract terms for most workers is done from an unequal market position.

Finally, evaluating the respective fairness of the competing approaches requires that we have some operationalized meaning for the term "fair." One way to under-stand the term is as a synonym for "reasonable" and as in opposition to "arbitrary." Job-security protections such as advance notice and limits on the reasons for dis-missal are, in fact, attempts to assure that workers are not removed from their jobs without good reason. Absent such protections, workers are subject to abusive and arbitrary exercise of employer authority. In the U.S. system, operating under modified EAW, managers are not required to give reasons for their decisions to terminate. By law, they are even permitted to use "morally wrong" reasons. This approach provides ample opportunity for arbitrary discharge. Under the meaning of "fairness" as "non-arbitrary," it is hard to see how employee job-security rights are in conflict with norms of fairness. We do not believe, for instance, that markets offer sufficient deterrence against suppression of employees' political speech or against arbitrary discharge. Nor do we believe that an employer's fear of reputational loss that damages the ability to recruit future employees or customers is enough to prevent managers from acting arbitrarily against employees. Were it the case that the market so deterred employers, we would not see that plaintiffs prevailed in jury verdicts in 64 percent of cases or that an estimated 200,000 employees are unjustly dismissed each year.[48] It appears that the U.S. approach often falls short as a device for assuring fair treatment.

Another way to understand "fairness" in the context of a cooperative activity, such as production with the joint contributions of labor and capital, would be to say that the benefits and burdens were distributed in proportion to contributions made or risks assumed by the respective parties. Certainly, shareholders bear risk when they invest their assets in an enterprise. As risk bearers, they deserve their share of the benefits. But workers can also claim that they too contribute and bear risk. While shareholders bear financial risk, they most often can diversify that risk by investing in a number of firms. Employees, however, cannot similarly diversify the financial risks of unemployment. They thus bear the risk of loss of income (often due to poor management) were they to lose their job. In addition, employees also bear other, nonfinancial risks at work, such as risks to health and safety.

It might be argued that employees have been fully compensated for these risks by the wages already paid. However, whether past wages are full and fair compensation is open to question on a number of grounds. First, employers often communicate, whether explicitly or implicitly, messages about expectations of continued employment. Such representations are a useful device for inducing loyalty and commitment. Some suggest that corporate wage structures include an element of deferred wages. Wages tend to rise over time in a way that pays workers less than their worth to the firm initially and more than their worth later.[49] Similarly, in sports, young players are often paid well below their value to a team, while to many fans veteran players appear to be overpaid. If this correctly describes wages within a firm over time, it could be said that firms defer wages as a device for binding workers to the firm. A worker who leaves early is giving up part of the value he contributed but would only recoup at a later date. A worker's awareness of deferred wages will also save the firm money by reducing its turnover costs. However, if a firm were able to terminate a worker before the deferred wages are paid, it would not be true to assert that wages already received were full and fair compensation for past contributions. A specific example of this would be the termination of an employee just before a promised bonus for yearly performance or just before a pension benefit vested. Firms in those cases opportunistically seize something that was owed to a worker.

Thus there are reasons for denying that, at every point during a worker's career, past contribution and risk have been fairly compensated by wages paid. Further, we argue that permitting termination for no reason, as the U.S. system does, is the epitome of arbitrary, that is, without good reason, treatment. Fairness, of course, requires that we avoid harming a person's interests arbitrarily. We argue similarly against terminations for reasons unconnected to worker performance or firm profitability, such as termination for outside political speech.[50] So, job-security protections such as advance notice, limits on reasons employers may use, and even severance can be effective devices for assuring against unfair treatment of workers. In weighing the impact on fairness, we would argue that legal job-security rights provide for a greater balance of fairness. It is hard to see how the absence of such rights, as in the U.S. modified EAW approach, could enhance overall fairness in a more effectively.

In short, the same moral values are offered in support of both the U.S. approach, which legally protects private property and freedom of contract, and the European approach, which legally extends specific job-security rights to employees. We have sketched arguments to the effect that the European approach is more effective at promoting the moral goals purportedly pursued by the two cultures' differing sets of rights. While property and freedom of contract are reasonable rights for a society to recognize, limiting their scope by extending to workers the rights to advance notice of termination, stronger limits on reasons for termination, and severance payments is more effective if we are pursuing the goals of increased utility, autonomy, and fairness. This appears to be a case in which one set of instrumental rights functions as a better tool for achieving the espoused shared objectives of the two social and economic systems.

BEYOND JOB SECURITY AND THE FUTURE

This chapter has focused on employee rights in the area of job security. We argued against the modified EAW of the United States and in favor of worker rights to free political expression, advance notice, due process, severance payments, limited reasons for dismissal, and the like. The analysis we provided may be extended beyond the narrow issue of job-security rights to a wider menu of employee rights. The above method of assessing right claims, particularly instrumental right claims, can offer recommendations on the rights of workers in the global economy. While we cannot provide the analysis in the space provided here, employee rights to living wages, to safe working conditions, and to reasonable weekly hours are all amenable to the strategies we have used. Consider, for example, how it might apply to arguments about the aggregate welfare, autonomy, or fairness of requiring employees in sweatshops to work sometimes more than sixty hours a week, seven days a week without a day for rest and for income that is sufficient for little more than subsistence. Do such practices increase utility or enhance autonomy? This is not to suggest that all work in the factories of developing economies is morally suspect, but there are many circumstances in which workers deserve more.[51]

In essence, we have provided an argument against the claim that the content of employee entitlements ought to be left to bargaining in a private market unconstrained by moral and legal rights. A purely market-based view of employment is deficient in that it fails to accommodate the very moral values on which it purportedly relies for its justification. Private property and freedom of contract are not unconditioned and self-evident rights. They are instrumental rights that aim to achieve important moral objectives. However, expansive understandings of property and freedom of contract are likely not to be effective in achieving those objectives. The moral goals are better realized when property and freedom of contract are balanced by the recognition of moral and legal rights for employees. Those countervailing rights are not items whose provision should be left to the vagaries of the market to provide. They are conditions without which the market system loses its moral justification. Careful attention to employee rights is a requirement, under our analysis, for markets to have a moral justification.

We see, however, a looming problem for the moral evaluation of the global marketplace. We argued for an expanded view of employee rights, at least expanded beyond what has traditionally been the case in the United States. Europe's social market with a partnership between capital, labor, and government provided an alternative as well an aspirational moral goal for labor markets. However, recent years have seen a concerted effort in Europe to reduce employee rights. The European Commission's recent call for a new "flexicurity" model recommends reducing job-protection rights, giving firms greater labor flexibility, and providing workers security instead through government subsidized training as well as unemployment compensation. This is, however, being advocated in circumstances where public coffers are increasingly strained by a dominant understanding that taxes are inefficient interferences with private market transactions.[52]

We believe that this European Commission recommendation moves in the wrong direction and that the economic rationale it depends on is theoretically and empirically flawed, for example, in its insistence on the claim that job-security rights are the primary cause of European labor market woes. Europe, once the exemplar of a morally preferable alternative, appears to be increasingly moving toward the U.S. market model. If it continues in this direction, the prospects for worker rights in a global marketplace of fluid capital and easily transferable work are not good. What is needed, apparently, is a model of work and of economies that can compete with a dominant model that reduces everything to a market exchange and sees everything in light of a narrow understanding of efficiency. An alternative model will have to understand the central role of moral rights in economic life and to evaluate economic conditions by their impact on the flourishing and dignity of the human persons who live within them.

NOTES

1. Lawrence Blades, "Employment at Will vs. Individual Freedom: On Limiting the Abusive Exercise of Employee Power," *Columbia Law Review* 67 (1967): 1404–1477.

2. Frank and Breslow, PC, "Employment at Will," http://laborlaws.com/block4/item414/.

3. *Fortune v. National Cash Register Company*, 364 N.E.2d 1251 (1977).

4. *Sheets v. Teddy's Frosted Foods, Inc.*, 427 A.2d 385 (1980).

5. *Toussaint v. Blue Cross and Blue Shield of Michigan*, 292 N.W.2d 880 (1980).

6. Bruce Barry, *Speechless: The Erosion of Free Expression in the American Workplace* (San Francisco: Berrett-Koehler, 2007).

7. See Patricia Werhane, *Persons, Rights and Corporations* (Englewood Cliffs, N.J.: Prentice Hall, 1985); Patricia Werhane, Tara Radin and Norman Bowie, *Employment and Employee* Rights (Boston: Basil Blackwell, 2004); John McCall, "A Defense of Just Cause Dismissal Rules," *Business Ethics Quarterly* 13 (2003): 151–175.

8. Government Accounting Office, *Dislocated Workers: Worker Adjustment and Retraining Notification Act Not Meeting Its Goals* GAO-HRD-93–18 (Washington, D.C., 1993); Government Accounting Office, *Worker Adjustment and Retraining Notification Act: Revising the Act and Educational Materials Could Clarify Employer Responsibilities and Employee Rights* GAO-03–1003 (Washington, D.C.: 2003).

9. Government Accounting Office, *Worker Adjustment and Retraining Notification Act* (2003).

10. Bureau of Labor Statistics, *Documenting Benefits Coverage for All Workers*, May 26, 2004, http://www.bls.gov/opub/cwc/tables/cm20040518ar01t3.htm.

11. Donald O. Parsons, "Benefit Generosity in Voluntary Severance Plans: The U.S. Experience," http://ssrn.com/abstract=877903.

12. United States Department of Labor, Employment and Training Administration 2004, http://worforcesecurity.doleta.gov/unemploy/content/chartbook/descript.asp.

13. Organization for Economic Cooperation and Development, *OECD Employment Outlook 2004* (Paris, 2004); Parsons, "Benefit Generosity," (2005).

14. Organization for Economic Cooperation and Development, *Employment Outlook 2004*.

15. Ibid.

16. Susan N. Houseman, "The Equity and Efficiency of Job Security: Contrasting Perspectives on Collective Dismissal Laws in Western Europe," in *New Developments in the Labor Market: Toward a New Institutional Paradigm*, ed. Katherine G. Abraham and Robert B. McKersie (Cambridge, Mass.: MIT Press, 1990).

17. Parsons, "Benefit Generosity"; Jonas Pontusson, *Inequality and Prosperity: Social Europe vs. Liberal America* (Ithaca, N.Y.: Cornell University Press, 2005).

18. Larry Schlesinger, "UK Offers Worst Redundancy Pay in Europe," *Accountancy Age*, June 2, 2003, http://www.accountancyage.com/accountancyage/news/2032964/uk-offers-worst-redundancy-pay-europe.

19. Organization for Economic Cooperation and Development, *OECD Employment Outlook 2006*.

20. McCall conducted a series of interviews with a variety of executives across the European Union in 1992. Executives were from Germany, France, Italy, Belgium, the Netherlands, and the United Kingdom, and their firms ranged from large manufacturing to small family-run manufacturing to large retail to banking. With one exception, all executives voiced support for just-cause termination, notice before collective dismissals, severance, and consultation with employees before a layoff.

21. Organization for Economic Cooperation and Development, *The 1994 OECD Jobs Study*; OECD, *Employment Outlook 1999, 2004, 2006*; The European Commission, *Employment in Europe: Flexibility and Security in the EU Labour Markets* (Brussels, 2006).

22. Immanuel Kant, *The Foundations of the Metaphysics of Morals*, trans. Lewis White Beck (Indianapolis: Bobbs Merrill, 1959).

23. Richard Epstein, "In Defense of Contract at Will," *University of Chicago Law Review* 51 (1984): 947.

24. Patricia H. Werhane, *Adam Smith and His Legacy for Capitalism* (New York: Oxford University Press, 1991).

25. OECD, *1994 Jobs Study; Employment Outlooks 1999, 2004, and 2006.*

26. Michael DeBow and Dwight Lee "Shareholders, Nonshareholders and Corporate Law: Communitarianism and Resource Allocation," *Delaware Journal of Corporate Law* 18 (1993): 393; Epstein, "In Defense"; Ian Maitland, "Rights in the Workplace," *Journal of Business Ethics* 8 (1989): 951, and "Distributive Justice in Firms: Do the Rules of Corporate Governance Matter?" *Business Ethics Quarterly* 11 (2001): 129; Jonathan Macey, "An Economic Analysis of the Various Rationales for Making Shareholders the Exclusive Beneficiaries of Corporate Fiduciary Duties," *Stetson Law Review* 21 (1991): 23; Richard A. Posner, *Economic Analysis of Law* (Boston: Little, Brown, 1992).

27. Epstein, "Contract at Will"; Maitland, "Rights," and "Distributive Justice": Jan Narveson, "Democracy and Economic Rights," in *Economic Rights*, ed. Ellen Paul, Jeffrey Paul, and Fred D. Miller (New York: Cambridge University Press, 1992).

28. Maitland, "Rights," and "Distributive Justice;" Jan Narveson, "Democracy and Economic Rights," Paul, et al., *Economic Rights*; Robert Nozick *Anarchy, State and Utopia* (New York: Basic Books, 1974).

29. John Locke *The Second Treatise of Government* (New York: Macmillan, 1956).

30. We should note, however, that this represents an interpretation of Locke. Locke himself believed that one acquired a natural right to land and its products by mixing one's labor with the land, improving it, and producing fruits from it. Since one had a natural right to one's labor, one thereby acquired a right to the improved land and its product. We find this account unsatisfactory. Why, for instance, would we not just forfeit our labor? To us, the only way to make sense of this labor-mixing account is to couch it in terms of a fairness claim. This is, admittedly, a variation from Locke's own account, but we think it is the only reasonable way to make his account defensible. This also explains why we disagree with Locke's assertion that property is a natural right.

31. Adam Smith *The Wealth of Nations*, ed. R. H. Campbell and A. S. Skinner (Oxford: Oxford University Press, 1976), IV.ii.9. One should be reminded that in the same book, Smith also wrote that "every man, as so long as he does not violate the laws of justice, is left perfectly free to pursue his own interest in his own way" (IV.ix.51).

32. See Thomas Scanlon "Due Process," in *Due Process*, ed. J. Roland Pennock and John Chapman (New York: New York University Press, 1977).

33. See Jeffrey R. Kling, "Wage-Loss Insurance and Temporary Earnings Replacement Accounts," Brookings Institution, http://brookings.edu/papers/2006/09unemployment_kling.aspx. See also Henry S. Farber, "What Do We Know about Job Loss in the United States?" Federal Reserve Bank of Chicago, http://www.chicagofed.org/publications/economicperspectives/ep_2qtr2005_part2_farber.pdf.

34. See Norman Bowie *Business Ethics: A Kantian Perspective* (Malden, Mass.: Blackwell, 1999); Casy Ichniowski, "Human Resource Management and Productive Labor-Management Relations," *Research Frontiers in Industrial Relations and Human Resources*, ed. David Lewin, Olivia Mitchell, and Peter Sherer (Madison, Wisc.: Industrial Relations Research Association, 1992); Jeffrey Pfeffer, *The Human Equation* (Boston: Harvard Business School Press, 1998); Werhane, Radin, and Bowie, *Employment and Employee Rights.*

35. Joel Rogers "The United States: Lessons from Home and Abroad," in *Works Councils*, ed. Joel Rogers and Wolfgang Streeck (Chicago: University of Chicago Press, 1995); Joel Rogers and Wolfgang Streeck "Workplace Representation Overseas: The Works Council Story," in *Working under Different Rules*, ed. Richard B. Freeman (New York: Russell Sage Foundation, 1994).

36. Patricia H. Werhane "Individual Rights in Business," in *Just Business: New Introductory Essays in Business Ethics*, ed. Tom Regan (New York: Random House, 1983); Werhane, Radin, and Bowie, *Employment and Employee Rights*; John J. McCall, "Employee Voice in Corporate Governance: A Defense of Strong Participation Rights," *Business Ethics Quarterly* 11 (2001): 195; McCall, "Just Cause."

37. See the references in note 21 and note 26 above.

38. OECD, *Employment Outlooks 2004 and 2006.*

39. OECD Standardised Unemployment Rates, http://stats.oecd.org/WBOS/ViewHTML.aspx.

40. David Howell, "Fighting Unemployment: Why Labor Market 'Reforms' Are Not the Answer," Center for Economic Policy Analysis, http://www.newschool.edu/cepa/research/workingpapers/employmentprotection_Howell_ FightingUnemployment_051103.pdf.

41. OECD, *Employment Outlook 2004*; Pontusson, *Inequality and Prosperity.*

42. OECD, *Employment Outlooks 1999 and 2004*; European Commission, *Towards Common Principles of Flexicurity: More and Better Jobs Through Flexibility and Security* (Brussels, 2007).

43. John Schmitt and Ben Zipperer, "Is the U.S. a Good Model for Reducing Social Exclusion in Europe?" Center for Economic and Policy Research, http://www.cepr.net/documents/social_exclusion_2006_08.pdf.

44. David Howell and John Schmitt, "Employment Regulation and French Unemployment: Were the French Students Right after All?" Center for Economic and Policy Research, http://www.cepr.net/documents/04_06_Howell_French_Students_20pdf.

45. Bowie, *Business Ethics*; Ichniowski, "Human Resource Management"; David Levine and Laura D'Andrea Tyson "Participation, Productivity and the Firm's Environment," *Paying for Productivity*, ed. Alan Blinder (Washington, D.C.: Brookings Institution, 1990); Pfeffer, *The Human Equation*; Werhane, Radin, and Bowie, *Employment and Employee Rights.*

46. Bowie, *Business Ethics*; Pfeffer, *Human Equation*; Ichniowski, "Human Resource Management."

47. McCall, "Just Cause."

48. Stephen F. Befort "Labor and Employment Law at the Millenium: An Historical Overview and Critical Assessment," *Boston College Law Review* 43 (2002): 351–460. See also ACLU Briefing Paper #12, http://www.lectlaw.com/files/emp08.htm.

49. Edward Lazear, "Compensation, Productivity and the New Economics of Personnel," Lewin et al., *Research Frontiers*, 1992.

50. Clearly, there can be some political activity that threatens the efficiency and effectiveness of the firm. In light of this, we do not claim an absolute right to be free from dismissal for such political activity. We do, however, claim that employees must have some limited but substantial right to protection from discharge due to political expression. We suggest that such a right's content ought to be fleshed out in arbitration or labor courts as are other prohibitions on the employer's ability to discharge under just cause rules.

51. For differing perspectives on the situation of labor in the developing world, see Denis Arnold and Norman Bowie "Sweatshops and Respect for Persons," *Business Ethics Quarterly* 13 (2003): 221; Denis Arnold and Laura Hartman "Worker Rights and Low Wage Industrialization: How to Avoid Sweatshops," *Human Rights Quarterly* 28 (2006): 678; Pietra Rivoli, *Travels of a T-Shirt in the Global Economy: An Economist Examines the Markets, Power and Politics of World Trade* (Hoboken, N.J.: John Wiley and Sons, 2005). See also the Workers Rights Consortium for case studies of working conditions, http://www.workersrights.org.

52. The European Commission, *Towards Common Principles.*

SUGGESTED READING

Abraham, Katherine, and Susan Houseman. *Job Security in America*. Washington, D.C.: Brookings Institution, 1993.

Barry, Bruce. *Speechless: The Erosion of Free Expression in the American Workplace*. San Francisco: Berrett-Koehler, 2007.

Blades, Lawrence. "Employment at Will vs. Individual Freedom: On Limiting the Abusive Exercise of Employer Power." *Columbia Law Review* 67 (1967): 1404–1435.

Blank, Rebecca, ed. *Social Protection versus Economic Flexibility*. Chicago: University of Chicago Press, 1994.

Bowie, Norman. *Business Ethics: A Kantian Perspective*. Malden, Mass.: Blackwell, 1999.

Epstein, Richard. "In Defense of Contract at Will." *University of Chicago Law Review* 51 (1984): 947–982.

European Commission. *Employment in Europe: Flexibility and Security in European Labor Markets*. Brussels, 2006.

Lewin, David, Olivia Mitchell, and Peter Scherer, eds. *Research Frontiers in Industrial Relations and Human Resources*. Madison, Wisc.: Industrial Relations Research Association, 1992.

Locke, John. *The Second Treatise of Government*. New York: Macmillan, 1956.

Maitland, Ian. "Rights in the Workplace." *Journal of Business Ethics* 8 (1989): 951–954.

McCall, John. "A Defense of Just Cause Dismissal Rules." *Business Ethics Quarterly* 13 (2003): 151–175.

Organization for Economic Cooperation and Development. *The 1994 OECD Jobs Study*. Paris, 1994.

———. *OECD Employment Outlook*. Paris, 1999, 2004, 2006.

Smith, Adam. *The Wealth of Nations*. Edited by R. H. Campbell and A. S. Skinner. Oxford: Oxford University Press, 1976.

Werhane, Patricia. *Persons, Rights and Corporations*. Englewood Cliffs, N.J.: Prentice Hall, 1985.

———. *Adam Smith and His Legacy for Capitalism*. New York: Oxford University Press, 1991.

Werhane, Patricia, Tara Radin, and Norman Bowie. *Employment and Employee Rights*. Boston: Basil Blackwell, 2004.

INTERNET SOURCES

Howell, David. "Fighting Unemployment: Why Labor Market 'Reforms' Are Not the Answer." Center for Economic Policy Analysis Working Paper, 2005. http://www.newschool.edu/cepa/research/workingpapers/employmentprotection_Howell_FightingUnemployment_051103.pdf.

Schmitt, John, and Ben Zipperer. "Is the U.S. a Good Model for Reducing Social Exclusion in Europe?" Center for Economic and Policy Research, 2006. http://www.cepr.net/documents/social_exclusion_2006_08.pdf.

CHAPTER 21

WORKING CONDITIONS: SAFETY AND SWEATSHOPS

DENIS G. ARNOLD

BROADLY construed, worker safety includes both injuries that occur as a result of violent workplace events, such as a massive explosion at the BP, Texas City oil refinery that killed 15 and injured 170, and diseases and injuries that are the result of exposure to toxic substances or repetitive motion, such as pneumoconiosis (black lung disease) and carpal tunnel syndrome. Workers in the United States and other industrialized nations enjoy many robust workplace regulations regarding workplace safety. Despite this, thousands of workers in industrial nations are killed or injured on the job each year. On average, over 5,000 persons are killed on the job in private industry each year in the United States, and over 4 million workers experience nonfatal injuries and illnesses.[1] In developing nations, workers typically enjoy fewer regulations and lax enforcement of the existent regulations. Worldwide, between 300,000 and 400,000 workers die each year as a result of workplace injuries, and it is estimated that a total of 2.2 million die each year as a result of injuries or work-related diseases.[2]

That employers have obligations to protect workers from workplace hazards is uncontentious. The contentious issues concern the extent of those obligations and the degree to which they ought to be mitigated or modified by competing obligations or interests. Employers, union leaders, and regulators must balance a variety of competing interests in seeking to protect the safety of workers. Among these interests are the property rights of the owners of capital, the health and safety of workers, employment opportunities, and the freedom of all parties to enter into contracts.

In the early part of the twenty-first century, one of the most contentious issues regarding employee safety concerns working conditions in the third-world sweatshops that are at the base of many supply chains in the apparel, footwear, electronics, toy, and other industries. Evidence shows that many of these factories are noncompliant with local labor laws, and that workers are subjected to unsafe working conditions, forced to work overtime, and paid wages that allow them to do little more than simply survive. Critics allege that the large multinational corporations that utilize these factories are complicit in human rights violations and demand either that they take steps to improve working conditions and wages, or that governments restrict the importation of goods made in these factories. Many economists and some social theorists defend these sweatshops as inevitable features of economic development that employ desperately poor workers and attract foreign capital to nations with few resources other than large labor pools. Business ethicists have tended to side with sweatshop critics, at least in so far as they have called for compliance with local labor laws and the voluntary improvement of working conditions. However, as we shall see, not all theorists agree that such actions are in the best interest of workers.

SAFETY

The duty of employers to provide safe working conditions is often grounded in the moral or human rights of workers. Typically, such arguments are made in reference to a right to life (or to a derivative right not to be injured) or to a right to well-being.[3] The content of a right not to be injured is self-evident, but a right to well-being requires some explanation. In the sense most relevant for present purposes, the right to well-being entails a right to physical well-being, which includes both a right not to be injured or killed and a right to basic health care.[4] If one assumes that such rights can be defended, then intentionally or negligently subjecting workers to unsafe working conditions that may result in injury or serious harm constitutes a prima facie violation of the duty not to injure or kill other persons. To justify the employment of workers in unsafe working conditions, one would need to defend at least two claims. The first is that rights are alienable in the sense that individuals should be permitted to waive or give up such rights in market transactions.[5] Second, that there are compelling interests that trump the right not to be killed or injured. Alternatively, one could argue that the right not to be killed or injured is inalienable and that employers must therefore ensure that certain minimal working conditions are met. When the cost of providing such working conditions is prohibitive, compensation to employers can be provided in various ways, such as lower employee wages, higher costs for consumers, or tax subsidies.

An employer's duty to protect workers from workplace hazards can also be grounded in the Kantian idea of respect for persons. The central idea here is that because persons are capable of acting in a manner consistent with moral principles, they have unique dignity, or intrinsic value, that must be respected.[6] This dignity serves to differentiate persons from things that have mere instrumental value. As self-governing beings, workers have a dignity that machines and capital do not possess. When employers fail to protect workers adequately from workplace hazards, they treat workers more like objects with mere instrumental value, such as tools or raw materials, rather than as beings with intrinsic value. While the idea of respect for persons is most commonly associated with Kantian ethics, theorists of a wide range of perspectives and commitments can embrace the notion of respect discussed here. This is because the idea of respect for persons is grounded in the widely shared view that persons are rational, self-governing beings.[7]

It has been argued that respecting the dignity of workers entails at least two general duties concerning safety. First, when workplace hazards exist, an employer has an obligation to inform workers in advance regarding workplace hazards so that individual workers can make informed decisions about the work and the conditions they find acceptable.[8] Second, employers have an obligation to ensure that minimum health and safety conditions exist, especially when the cost of doing so measured as a percentage of revenue is small in comparison to profits as a percentage of revenue.[9] Failure to do so violates the moral requirement that employers be concerned with the physical welfare of their employees.[10]

The Libertarian View

Libertarians emphasize the right of workers to bargain freely and contract with employers for their labor.[11] Beginning with the assumption that all individuals enjoy a right to freedom, libertarians argue that workers ought to be free to sell their labor for the price they deem appropriate. In so doing, workers will take into account such factors as wages and working conditions. Since most workers value their health and safety, safer work will normally be more attractive to workers than unsafe or dangerous work. This will be especially true of workers with dependents such as children or elderly parents. Workers who encounter poor safety conditions will seek work elsewhere. To attract and retain workers in a competitive labor market, employers will need to improve working conditions. To attract workers to inherently dangerous professions, such as fishing, logging, and iron work, employers must pay a premium over prevailing wages in the local economy. Individual workers who value the higher wages over increased risk to their personal health and safety will be free to choose more dangerous occupations. When workers and employers negotiate the terms of employment in a competitive market the freedom of both workers and employers is maximized.

Libertarians argue that when governments intervene in the contracting process by imposing safety regulations on employers, both the freedom of employers to exercise their property rights and the freedom of workers to enter into employment contracts of their choosing is unjustifiably curtailed. Such paternalism is thought by libertarians to be unjustified for two reasons. First, it falsely assumes that employers lack the right to enter into mutual agreements regarding the use of their property on their own terms.[12] Second, it treats workers as if they are "helpless, inefficacious, inept persons."[13] Most libertarians acknowledge that employers have some moral obligations to protect employee welfare. In particular, the main obligation of employers is to disclose safety risks to employees during the contracting process. Here the libertarian view is essentially identical to the Kantian view. Employers have an obligation to provide information about workplace hazards sufficient for workers to make informed judgments about where they work. However, libertarians deny that the state is justified in enforcing moral obligations via public policies such as the Occupational Safety and Health Act of 1970 (OSHA). Instead they believe that workers, acting on their own behalf, are sufficiently powerful to hold employers accountable for failures to meet minimum moral duties. Tibor Machan illustrates this point with the example of an employer who owns a coal mine, but who lacks the financial means to make the mine very safe: "When the prospective employees appear and are made aware of the type of job being offered, and its hazards, they are at liberty to (a) accept or reject, (b) organize into a group and insist on various terms not in the offing, (c) bargain alone or together with others and set terms that include improvements, or (d) pool workers' resources, borrow, and purchase the firm."[14] According to libertarians, since workers have these options the employer has no duty to improve mine safety.

This libertarian view that business owners with legitimate property rights do not owe workers salubrious working conditions, so long as they disclose workplace hazards, requires closer examination. Libertarians appear to be arguing that the property rights of the business owner trump other ethical considerations that may be applicable. This is not obviously the case in all circumstances. A distinction is needed here between two levels at which business owners might improve working conditions for workers. First, measures can be taken to significantly improve occupational safety that will cost the business owners little or nothing. These include providing clear warning signs regarding workplace hazards for literate workers and color-coded symbols for illiterate workers. They might also include routine maintenance on equipment, the prompt cleaning of spills on the factory floor, and basic fire safety and suppression equipment such as fire alarms and handheld fire extinguishers. Second, safety measures that involve significant fixed and recurring costs can be taken to improve occupational safety. These measures include industrial venting systems, integrated fire suppression systems, worker training, machinery upgrades, and appropriate safety equipment.

If we grant that respecting the rights of workers, or treating them with dignity, requires that employers be concerned with the physical welfare of their employees, business owners have, at a minimum, a prima facie obligation to take steps to improve worker safety when doing so will have significant positive impact on the welfare of employees. To do otherwise would be to treat workers with callous disregard.

The question of whether employers have a duty to make substantial fixed and recurring improvements to worker safety involves two main possibilities. First, the cost as a percentage of revenues of substantially improving working conditions (for example, the cost of raising standards in non-U.S. factories to meet U.S. standards) by an employer such as a multinational corporation may be minor in comparison to profits as a percentage of revenues. It might be objected that the fiduciary obligations to shareholders trumps the obligation to improve working conditions for workers.[15] However, if we keep in mind that these standards help prevent death and serious injuries, such as the loss of limbs and neurological damage from exposure to toxic chemicals, the primary obligation of the corporation becomes clear. Any increase in individual shareholder return as a result of poor safety conditions in factories is likely to be marginal. Given this scenario, it is difficult to understand what argument could be deployed to defend the claim that these marginal returns should trump the prima facie obligation to protect workers. This point is made more acute when it is recognized that in many developing nations in which multinational corporations operate, the unemployed labor pool is so vast that those who are offered jobs often face dire consequences if they decline the work.

Second, the cost as a percentage of revenue of improving working conditions may be substantial in comparison to profits as a percentage of revenues. This is likely to be the case with smaller businesses and in capital-intensive industries such as oil refining, mineral refining and smelting, and nuclear energy. It might be objected that in such cases the voluntary implementation of substantially improved working conditions by any one company may result in financial noncompetitiveness and eventual closure of the business. One response to this objection is that in such cases the cost of improving working conditions may result in increased worker productivity. As Laura Hartman and I have argued elsewhere, workers who are not forced to work overtime, who are not exposed to toxic chemicals and airborne pollutants, who are provided clean water and hygienic lavatories, and who are provided basic health care when sick or injured at work, will be healthier and more loyal than employees who are not provided with these benefits. Better worker health and enhanced loyalty often results in greater productivity. In at least some cases, this increase in worker productivity may be sufficient to offset the costs of improved safety conditions.[16]

In industries such as mining, steel production, and nuclear energy where productivity gains cannot offset substantial fixed and recurring costs for appropriate safety standards, and where competitors may be unwilling or unable to improve working conditions on a voluntary basis, a strong regulatory model is to be preferred. OSHA-type regulations are justified on the ground that they increase the freedom of workers by enhancing or improving their bargaining position while at the same time helping to preserve their life and welfare.[17] Furthermore, because all businesses are required to adhere to such regulations, the costs of implementing appropriate safety measures in capital intensive industries is be spread fairly across businesses within those industries. Well-crafted OSHA-type regulations also have advantages for noncapital intensive industries because they provide uniform standards and regulations that better allow for the rapid adaptation of effective health and safety practices.

The Importance of Disclosing Workplace Hazards

The claim that business owners have a moral obligation to disclose workplace hazards may be based on the view that a failure to disclose workplace hazards is fraudulent.[18] Machan maintains this view and argues that the proper recourse for workers in such circumstances is to take the business owners to court.[19] From the point of view of many libertarians and economists, workers who do not sue their employers, and who do not quit their hazardous jobs, may be assumed to have weighed the relevant costs and benefits and decided that keeping the hazardous job was in their best interest despite the fraudulent actions of their employers. This position is doubtful on several grounds. First, typical workers lack the economic resources to sue their employers. While some lawyers may take a case on a contingency fee basis, it cannot reasonably be assumed that most typical workers will have access to such lawyers. Second, typical workers are "at-will" employees who risk losing their job and accrued benefits if they take legal action against their employers. Such workers normally lack mobility and cannot simply exit their employment relationship and take a job elsewhere. Elizabeth Anderson makes the point in this way:

> Many workers in hazardous jobs do not regard themselves as fully mobile in the way that cost-benefit analysis assumes. They learn about most hazards involved in their work on the job, not before beginning employment. Many of these hazards, such as a loss of fertility and increased risk of cancer, are discovered only after years on the job, not before beginning employment. By then the costs of exit are high. When workers quit after several years invested in a job, they lose seniority, their pension, extra benefits, pay, and vacation time. Their skills are often not easily transferable to less risky jobs. Many people in such circumstances do not see themselves as having acceptable alternatives... If people make choices under circumstances they view as putting them in duress or as having no decent alternative, one cannot infer that they find the costs encountered on the job they choose to be acceptable.[20]

Legal action for fraud is one mechanism workers may use to punish employers for failing to disclose workplace hazards, but it will be a difficult means for typical employees to utilize; and legal action will likely not result in the employees' health being restored to the preexposure or preinjury state of the worker when she initially contracted with the employer.

The Reasonable Person Standard

Given the weak and vulnerable position of typical workers in relation to employers, the claim that a threat of legal action is a uniformly adequate remedy to circumstances in which workers find themselves fraudulently subject to unsafe working conditions is unpersuasive. However, it remains to be determined which specific obligations employers owe workers with respect to the disclosure of workplace hazards. How much information ought to be shared with employees? The U.S. Department of Labor answers this question with a reasonable person standard:

This standard is what a fair and informed member of the relevant community believes is needed. Under this standard, no employer, union, or other party should be held responsible for disclosing information beyond that needed to make an informed choice about the adequacy of safety precautions, industrial hygiene, long-term hazards, and the like, as determined by what the reasonable person in the community would judge to be the worker's need for information.[21]

Such a standard has the obvious benefit of being suitable to a wide range of employees in a wide range of industries.

Ruth Faden and Tom Beauchamp defend a modified reasonable person standard. They argue that the reasonable person standard fails to adequately deal with exposure to serious hazards where different workers may have different subjective needs. They argue that a reasonable person standard should be supplemented by a subjective standard whereby employees are invited to request any information pertinent to their individual circumstances. According to Faden and Beauchamp, employers have an obligation to provide employees with additional information based on the employees' unique individual circumstances and relevant needs.[22] These standards impose increasingly robust obligations on the employer.

The use of a reasonable person standard for assessing the amount of information that should be communicated to workers is not without difficulty, even when modified to include the subjective standard recommended by Faden and Beauchamp. Questions arise when one attempts to establish what such a standard might amount to in different contexts. For example, a reasonable person standard in the United States is likely to be very different than a reasonable person standard in a newly industrialized country such as China or India. Developing and newly industrialized nations often have large numbers of unemployed workers that will do almost any work in any conditions to better their circumstances. Consider the case of the ship-breakers of Alang in India. In the United States, "ship-breaking"—the process of disassembling and recycling old ships—is a capital intensive and expensive process. In India, the process has been labor intensive and much less expensive as a result of lower labor costs. Rather than making use of heavy machinery, thousands of Indian men with blowtorches and little or no protective gear disassemble ocean-going vessels. They risk injury from blowtorch mishaps; heavy and unwieldly ship components; falls from or into the ship itself; exposure to toxic substances such as asbestos, polychlorinated biphenyls (PCBs), lead paint, and oil fumes; explosions, and the like.[23] And, according to one account, "They suffer broken ankles, severed fingers, smashed skulls, malarial fevers, cholera, dysentery and tuberculosis. Some are burned and some are drowned."[24]

In this context, with tens of thousands of workers willing to take these jobs rather than risk death by starvation, one would need to determine what "a fair and informed" member of the 35,000-man Alang ship-breaking community would determine to be reasonable information regarding the health and safety risks of their employment. It is likely that illiterate workers with relatively short life expectancy who have lived and worked their entire lives in such circumstances would not regard the failure to be provided information about carcinogens and other harmful substances that would affect their health later in life as unreasonable. The difficulty with this outcome for the proponent of a context-specific reasonable person standard is that this standard of disclosure appears to be incompatible with basic human dignity and the rights to life and survival discussed at the beginning of this section. The proponent of a reasonable person standard has two choices. Accept this outcome and allow that the degree of respect for such rights is context specific, or defend a revised version of the reasonable person standard, one that can justifiably be utilized in a global context.

What sort of reasonable person standard could be applied in the global context? One possibility is a Kantian standard grounded in the categorical imperative. On this approach one would determine which reasonable person standard is universalizable. The appropriate standard by which to measure universalizability in this instance is the pragmatic contradiction test.[25] A pragmatic contradiction occurs when one acts on principles that promote an action that is inconsistent with one's purpose when acted upon by all agents in similar circumstances. In other words, an employer or manager needs to ask himself what information about occupational health and safety conditions he would want to be provided prior to deciding whether or not to accept a job. Call that baseline standard of information B. If the employer or manager would not be willing to accept a world in which the amount of information disclosed to him on at least some occasions was $<B$, then B is the appropriate minimum standard of disclosure. This account assumes that B would be relatively constant across cultures. This assumption is not unwarranted because employers or on-site managers commonly understand better than others the actual working conditions and known hazards of a workplace. Because of this asymmetry of information, average employers, unlike average workers, are well situated to make a reasonable determination regarding appropriate workplace standards. This *universal disclosure standard*, then, constitutes an important ethical tool for corporations conducting global business.[26]

Numerous additional ethical issues can be raised regarding occupational safety in a globalized economic environment. For example, which occupational health and safety standards are multinational corporations justified in using in their global operations? When multinational corporations outsource production to contractors, what level of moral responsibility do they have for ensuring that ethically justified occupational health and safety standards are met? These and related issues will be taken up in the next section.

SWEATSHOPS

The term "sweatshop" has a pejorative and imprecise meaning. The term is frequently used to describe illegal garment factories in the United States, Canada, and Europe where illegal aliens toil under difficult conditions for illegal, subminimum wages. These workers are often held captive by their employers, or coerced into compliance via the threat of being turned over to immigration authorities. Because there is little or no controversy over the ethical illegitimacy of such labor practices they will not be discussed in this essay.

The term "sweatshop" is also commonly used to describe factories in developing nations where workers produce export goods for multinational corporations (MNCs).[27] Working conditions in these factories are often hazardous. Workers are exposed to malfunctioning equipment and toxic chemicals, fire doors are locked, workspaces are poorly ventilated, and access to water is limited. In addition, the hours are long, the pay is low, and supervisors are often verbally, and sometimes physically, abusive.[28] Because there is considerable controversy regarding the ethical legitimacy of these practices, they will be the focus of the remainder of this essay.

The modern sweatshop debate emerged at approximately the same time that economic globalization began to rapidly increase. During the 1980s and 1990s there was a significant increase in foreign direct investment (FDI) on the part of MNCs. Between 1985 and 1998 global investment outflows increased from $60 billion annually to around $645 billion annually.[29] One result of the outflow of capital from industrialized nations to developing nations was an increase in the number of textile mills and factories employing low-skilled workers to manufacture apparel, footwear, toys, electronics, and a variety of other consumer goods. These factories are sometimes owned by MNCs, but often they are owned by entrepreneurs from newly industrialized nations, such as Taiwan and South Korea, or by indigenous entrepreneurs. In the 1980s and 1990s, reports of abusive labor conditions in these factories emerged. One of the most famous was the subject of a leaked January 1997 Ernst & Young internal audit of the Tae Kwang Vina Industrial Ltd. shoe factory outside Ho Chi Min City in Vietnam. This factory was completed in 1995, built for the purpose of manufacturing Nike shoes under contract.[30] The leaked documents were unique in that, rather than being the product of labor or human rights activists, the report was produced by a consulting firm at the request of a corporate client. The factory employed 10,000 workers, most of them women, mainly between the ages of eighteen and twenty-four. The report documented the following problems in the factory: Employment of underage workers, overtime work above the legal cap, underpayment of legal earnings, inadequate ventilation, insufficient or absent safety equipment leading to exposure to airborne pollutants and toxic chemicals up to 177 times the legal standard, heat and noise above legally mandated standards, and a lack of water for the use of workers.[31] Reports such as these and others issued by nongovernmental organizations have led many to criticize multinational corporations and their contractors for the unethical treatment of workers in global supply chains.[32] Critics allege that the basic dignity or basic rights of workers are violated by such practices.[33]

More Sweatshops Needed?

Partly in response to these criticisms many economists and some social theorists argue for a contrary conclusion.[34] They argue that the best way to enhance the overall welfare of the world's poorest populations is to increase the number of sweatshops in the developing world. The argument may be summarized as follows. All developing nations have a common, underexploited resource—large pools of unemployed or underemployed workers. FDI bring much needed capital to developing nations. Some of the capital is used to build manufacturing infrastructure in these nations. Once constructed, these factories employ tens of thousands of workers and more foreign capital is invested in the nation in the form of wages. The working conditions and wages in these factories are those demanded by the market, and no more, because employers are interested in profit maximization. Most workers in factories producing goods for export were previously unemployed or making less money in the informal sector of local economies. Increased income for these workers results in increased spending that improves the local economy. As the local economy improves, the competition for workers increases. To secure the best workers, factories producing goods for export must improve working conditions. Poor and hazardous working conditions and low wages are, in this view, a necessary stage in the economic development of all nations. But it is also a temporary stage that will eventually be supplanted by improved working conditions and wages.

Defenders of sweatshops tend to make two distinct, but unwarranted, assumptions. First, they assume that multinational corporations always act with instrumental practical reason aimed at self-interested profit maximization.[35] Such a view is empirically inaccurate.[36] Many multinational corporations explicitly recognize ethical constraints on their policies and practices and in so doing reject the idea that profit maximization is or should be the organization's only goal.[37] Further, proponents of sweatshops ignore the possibility, defended earlier in this essay, that employers have *duties* grounded in basic moral norms, such as dignity or rights, which require that they meet certain minimum standards regarding the treatment of workers above market-driven standards. The core normative function of business ethics is to plausibly defend the ethical obligations of business organizations. Economists and social theorists who assume that no such obligations are operative seem to fall into one of two camps. Either they maintain a naive view of corporations or they fail to analyze the sweatshop problem as an *ethical* problem.

A second faulty assumption of defenders of sweatshops is that operating factories on a profit-maximizing basis always results in the enhanced welfare of workers. Such an assumption is unwarranted given the actual harm that can result to workers and surrounding communities. For example, workers at the Tae Kwang Vina factory are susceptible to a long-term respiratory disease as a result of airborne fabric particles that were not properly vented, and to permanent neurological damage resulting from direct exposure to excessive levels of Toluene and other toxic chemicals. Workers at other factories routinely lose limbs by traumatic amputation, contract carpal tunnel syndrome from repetitive motion work, and experience hearing loss due to repeated exposure to noise pollution. The substantial and increasingly well-documented environmental harm caused to communities around some of these factories harms workers directly by polluting their ground water and indirectly by harming the environment in which their families live.[38] Defenders of sweatshops have yet to conduct analyses of the aggregate impact of sweatshops on workers in specific labor markets, one that takes into account both the benefits and harms such employment brings to workers. Until such analyses are undertaken, the claims of sweatshop defenders should be regarded with skepticism. Furthermore, even if such studies were conducted and the predictions proved correct, this by itself would not demonstrate that the ethical obligations of employers have been met. For it is possible to enhance the welfare of impoverished persons without having discharged all of one's moral duties as an employer. For example, an employer may marginally improve the income of workers while simultaneously failing to disclose workplace hazards to the workers or physically punishing them for failing to meet production quotas.

Two Further Problems with Sweatshop Defenses

In addition to the two preceding unwarranted assumptions, there are two perplexing features of the arguments of most proponents of sweatshops. First, these authors either deny or tacitly approve the widespread violation of local labor laws that take place in global sweatshops, such as at the Tae Kwan Vina factory.[39] The widespread violations of local labor laws regarding wages and benefits, working hours, collective bargaining, and worker safety has been well documented.[40] When Gap began to assess and report on vendor compliance with local labor laws, it found that between 25 and 50 percent of its contract factories lacked full compliance with local labor laws in North Asia, Southeast Asia, the Indian subcontinent, sub-Saharan Africa, Mexico, Central America, and the Caribbean, and South America. In China, more than 50 percent of its contract factories lacked full compliance with local labor laws.[41] These violations were taking place in a context in which Gap was attempting to ensure full compliance with local labor laws. If a company expends considerable resources to ensure that local labor laws are followed and fails to garner greater compliance than Gap has thus far achieved, it is reasonable to surmise that violations are more widespread in factories working for multinationals that are not seeking to ensure compliance with local labor laws.

The tacit approval of labor law violations is a perplexing feature of pro-sweatshop arguments because it is difficult to justify widespread violations of the law. For example, Milton Friedman, the iconic defender of a libertarian view of business ethics in which the primary obligation of corporations is to maximize profits in the interest of shareholders, denies that it is legitimate for corporations to violate the law.[42] Friedman's position is grounded in the idea that citizens and responsive democracies determine the laws that should govern corporate behavior. Corporations, in his view, have no basis for undermining or contravening the will of the people by violating democratically determined laws. Their existence is predicated on the consent of the people. It is only because a framework of democratically determined laws exists that corporate executives are free to focus on profit maximization.

On these premises, it is difficult to understand why defenders of sweatshops would countenance the violation of labor laws in democracies such as India,

Mexico, and El Salvador. In addition, if a company elects to set up factories in non-democratic nations such as China, Vietnam, and Bangladesh, there is a presumption that they do so with an understanding of the legal framework in place and the expectation that their own legal rights will be enforced and protected. As a matter of consistency, companies have a prima facie obligation to respect the legal framework they themselves call upon for protection.[43] There are, of course, unjust laws where people of good conscience can agree that the most ethical course of action is to ignore or challenge the law. However, this is not the case with respect to laws governing the compensation and safety of workers in developing nations. These laws are intended to provide workers with minimum working conditions and wages to ensure, in the words of the International Labour Organization, "decent and productive work, in conditions of freedom, equity, security and human dignity."[44] The systematic violation of local labor laws requires an ethical justification, something that defenders of sweatshop practices have yet to acknowledge, let alone provide.

The second perplexing feature of the arguments of most proponents of sweatshops is that they ignore the failure of employers to disclose hazards to workers. Workers at factories across the globe are routinely exposed to neurotoxins, carcinogens, dangerous or malfunctioning equipment, or other hazards, without full disclosure of the risks of such work. If one grants the force of the arguments presented above regarding the fraudulent nature of such employment and the right of workers to be informed about workplace hazards prior to being employed, then such employment practices must be regarded as impermissible. However, defenders of sweatshops do not qualify their calls for more sweatshops with the stipulation that employers disclose workplace hazards to workers, nor do they provide reasons for thinking that the employers of sweatshop laborers should be exempted from this moral requirement.[45]

Improving Working Conditions

My analysis thus far yields two minimum obligations on the part of business owners. First, there is an obligation to adhere to local labor laws. Second, there is an obligation to disclose workplace hazards to employees in a manner consistent with the universal disclosure standard defended earlier in this essay. These standards are ones that constitute the reasonable minimum among business ethicists of diverse theoretical perspectives, including libertarians and Kantians. Theorists who accept the force of Kantian or rights-based arguments defend additional obligations on the part of business owners regarding the treatment of workers. From these perspectives, business owners have an obligation to improve workplace safety beyond the minimal standards legally mandated by many developing nations under two circumstances: first, when doing so can be done at little or no cost and, second, when the cost as a percentage of revenues of doing so is marginal in comparison to profits as a percentage of revenues.

Many companies that have either outsourced or moved the production of labor-intensive goods, such as apparel, footwear, and furniture, from the United

States and Europe to Asia and Latin America have considerable expertise in occupational safety. This expertise can be utilized to improve working conditions in factories operating in nations with little occupational safety expertise. Companies such as Nike, adidas, Pentland, and Gap have publicly committed to utilizing their expertise in overseas factories. These companies have implemented low-cost safety improvements, and some claim to have raised the standards in overseas factories to meet or exceed U.S. OSHA standards. For example, in 1998, Nike, partly in response to criticism that resulted from its leaked Tae Kwan Vina factory audit, promised to adapt the personal exposure limits of OSHA as the standard for indoor air quality at all footwear factories.[46] Nike has clearly improved the working conditions in many of its factories.[47] However, nongovernmental, organization-based critics allege that Nike has failed to fully implement all of its promised reforms.[48] None of these companies has identified cost as a barrier to enhancing workplace safety. The main implementation barrier that is identified by companies is directly related to the lax safety standards that were previously tolerated. For example, in 2004 when Gap began to release public reports about its efforts to ensure compliance in all of its factories with its "Code of Vendor Conduct," it found that it was difficult to garner vendor compliance with its own code and with local labor laws.[49] Contract factories that had long operated without strict enforcement of occupational safety rules and procedures found it difficult to embrace a culture of enhanced safety.

The efforts undertaken by Nike, Gap, and other companies to improve working conditions in factories that they did not own but instead contracted with to manufacture their products raise important questions about moral responsibility. In particular, is it reasonable to hold such companies accountable for their contractors' treatment of workers? It has been argued that given that the corporation has done something positive for the workers by providing them with jobs, it is unreasonable to expect anything more from the corporation in the way of fair treatment of contract factory workers in developing nations.[50] According to proponents of this view:

> It is unreasonable to expect any bargain struck between two parties to redress every issue of fairness or desert that may apply to one party. [Corporations] are in some sense "taking advantage" of background conditions in the Third World when they outsource their production, but this alone does not make them responsible for the poverty that makes their sourcing decisions profitable.[51]

In other words, if the unsafe working conditions are a standard feature of work in these nations, the corporations that outsource to these factories, and take advantage of these lower standards, ought not be burdened with additional obligations that are the responsibility of governments. This argument implies that if the terms of the contract preclude the possibility that the contract factory can provide the legally mandated wages, working hours, and working conditions, the illegal labor practices would not be the responsibility of the corporation.

One argument in defense of the claim that it is reasonable to hold corporations responsible for the treatment of contractors is grounded in the power that corporations wield over the owners and managers of such factories. Corporations normally dictate the quantity, quality, design, and delivery date of goods manufactured in overseas factories. This imbalance in power is partly due to an oversupply of export factories. The oversupply of factories is a result of a rapid increase in the number and size of export processing zones and free trade zones established by developing nations competing for jobs and foreign investment. Corporations can shop around for suppliers who charge the lowest prices for the specified quality goods delivered in the shortest amount of time after orders are placed. Factory owners are often locked in fierce competition for orders and frequently must accept the terms offered to them by large corporations or shut down. While factory owners can provide low-cost safety features such as hazard signs and routine equipment maintenance, they may have difficulty providing costlier safety improvements (or adhering to local labor laws) if the financial terms dictated by the corporations are onerous. The coercive power that corporations exert has a causal relationship to the actual working conditions in contract factories. Given this causal relationship, it is reasonable to regard corporations as causally responsible for the safety standards of their contractors. If corporations are causally responsible for working conditions, and have the power to alter these conditions, it is difficult to understand why they ought not be regarded as morally responsible for working conditions. It is up to sweatshop defenders to provide reasons for thinking that causal responsibility ought not entail moral responsibility in these cases. Without such arguments we may conclude that, given the economic and coercive power corporations wield, they have a duty grounded in a recognition of the rights or dignity of workers to ensure that the terms of their contracts aid rather than impede the ability of factory managers to protect workers.[52]

In fact, the last fifteen years have seen a major transformation in the management of the health and safety labor practices of many multinational corporations. Companies such as Nike, adidas, Gap, and Mattel have publicly committed to respecting local labor laws, improving working conditions, monitoring factories, and reporting on their efforts in annual social reports.[53] They join companies such as Levi Strauss and Motorola, which have always sought to ensure the health and safety of workers in their supply chains. During this same period, Alcoa aggressively pursued a goal of zero injuries for both its 130,000-person global workforce and the hundreds of thousands of contractors that worked for the company.[54]

One of the most comprehensive and successful reorganizations of health and safety systems by any corporation in recent years has taken place at Mattel. In 1997, Mattel announced the creation of Global Manufacturing Principles for its production facilities and contract manufacturers. It then spent millions of dollars to upgrade its manufacturing facilities to improve worker health, safety, and comfort. It also facilitated the creation of a comprehensive independent external monitoring program to help ensure that it would meet its self-imposed standards.[55] Mattel has empowered the safety auditors of its factories and suppliers to publish all of their findings without regard to content. In this way Mattel has made its efforts to improve working conditions transparent. The examples of such companies are, perhaps, the best responses to those social theorists who cling to the idea that economic growth in developing nations must inevitably come at the cost of the safety and welfare of workers.

In summary, the main arguments that defenders of sweatshops deploy are unpersuasive. Further, defenders of sweatshops tend to make unwarranted assumptions that, once understood and analyzed, further undermine their claims. The exercise of corporate power in developing nations plays a large role in determining the working conditions in overseas factories. Corporations that fail to exercise that power in such a way as to help ensure that factory conditions are compatible with the basic rights or dignity of workers are properly regarded as blameworthy for their actions. Further, the claims of sweatshop defenders are undermined by the many corporations, in a variety of industries, that routinely expend substantial corporate resources to help ensure safe and healthy working conditions for workers. Evidence demonstrates that corporations can help protect the welfare of workers in their global supply chain while remaining economically competitive. But what about wages? Do corporations have obligations to ensure that these workers are paid an ethically appropriate wage? If so, can they afford to pay such wages while remaining economically competitive? These questions will be taken up in the last major section.

Exploitative Wages

One of the most contentious issues concerning global sweatshops is the question of whether workers are paid *exploitative* wages. Historically, the concept of exploitation has often been connected to the work of Karl Marx. His account of exploitation holds that capitalists exploit workers by expropriating the bulk of worker productivity, or what Marx referred to as their surplus labor. In this view, regular technological innovation results in labor-saving manufacturing techniques that ensure large pools of unemployed workers. The unemployed are forced to choose between accepting subsistence wages or remaining unemployed. Capitalists benefit from the surplus labor of workers, and workers have little choice but to accept meager wages. There is controversy among Marx's interpreters as to whether or not Marx thought exploitation was unjust, though it seems clear that he believed that exploitation undermines human flourishing.[56] Critics of Marxian accounts of exploitation argue that such accounts ignore the risks involved in capital investment and fail to acknowledge the importance of managerial expertise for profitable business enterprises.

In recent years the debate over the nature and moral significance of exploitation has shifted away from Marxian accounts. The most influential non-Marxian account of exploitation is provided by Alan Wertheimer.[57] Wertheimer restricts his account to mutually advantageous exchanges typical of market transactions. In such transactions, both parties gain something from the transaction, even if one party gains considerably more than the other party. Wertheimer argues that exploitation takes place when one person takes *unfair* advantage of another person relative to a specific baseline or standard. Because fairness is a moral consideration, Wertheimer's theory of exploitation is moralized.[58] The moral baseline that Wertheimer defends is that of a hypothetical market price that would be generated by an imperfect competitive market, one in which buyers and sellers lack perfect information.[59] This hypothetical market price is intended to reflect the cost of providing a service, as well as the price informed consumers are willing to pay in reasonably competitive circumstances. Such a price is to be differentiated from the price generated in a perfectly competitive market, a market in which the many buyers and sellers have perfect information.[60] This baseline is not intended to reflect a principle of desert or justice. Instead this baseline "is a price at which neither party takes special unfair advantage of particular defects in the other party's decision-making capacity or special vulnerabilities in the other party's situation."[61] Exploitation, on this account, always involves taking special unfair advantage of at least one party in a mutually advantageous market transaction. An example will help to illustrate this view. Imagine a tow-truck driver who comes across a stranded motorist in a snowstorm. The stranded motorist has no means to call for help. The tow-truck driver offers to tow the motorist to safety for ten times the prevailing towing fee in that area. The driver, facing dire circumstances, accepts the offer. On Wertheimer's account this transaction is exploitative because the driver took special unfair advantage of the stranded motorist, charging that individual a rate well in excess of the hypothetical market price. And since exploitation is always morally objectionable on a moralized view, the driver is morally blameworthy.

Are sweatshop workers paid exploitative wages on Wertheimer's account? To focus our discussion, consider the well-known cases of alleged exploitation of sweatshop workers by Nike in Indonesia. In the 1990s, critics alleged that a Nike contractor paid employees the equivalent of $2.60 per day in Jakarta, Indonesia, while the amount necessary to cover basic food, clothing, and shelter needs was approximately $4.00 per day.[62] Assume, for the sake of argument, that these facts are correct. On Wertheimer's account, Nike contract workers in Jakarta are not exploited because they benefit from their employment and the wages they earn are generated by a competitive labor market.[63] The workers freely choose to work for Nike's contractors in Indonesia because the wages they earn are better than those they could make elsewhere. One implication of understanding exploitation in this way is that it is not possible to pay a worker exploitative wages if workers voluntarily show up for work in a minimally competitive labor market. In other words, Wertheimer's position is just the opposite of Marx's: Capitalists never exploit workers, at least with respect to wages in minimally competitive labor markets.

One might object to this conclusion by pointing out that during the period in question, Indonesia had an authoritarian government that suppressed dissent with the aid of the military. Human rights violations were widespread and government policies created significant barriers to union organizing.[64] Given these unjust background conditions and a lack of negotiating power, one might argue that the workers were forced to accept the Nike contractor's terms. A critic also might argue that Nike exploited the workers by taking advantage of their desperate circumstances. Wertheimer's response is that unjust or unfair background conditions do not necessarily result in exploitative agreements. On his account, unless Nike and its contractors take special unfair advantage of the Indonesian workers, their agreement should be regarded as fair.[65] Some readers may find an account of exploitation that reaches these conclusions regarding Nike's Indonesian workers implausible and unworthy of consideration. Nonetheless, Wertheimer's account of exploitation has been utilized to argue that few, if any, sweatshop workers are exploited.[66] Furthermore, Wertheimer's position tends to support the presumption of libertarians who believe that so long as workers are not physically forced to enter the factory each day their wages cannot be regarded as exploitative.[67]

On Wertheimer's theory of exploitation, if one party exploits another the exploiter is morally blameworthy in all cases. However, the idea of justified exploitation is consistent with ordinary language use of the term. For example, we do not normally criticize a chess player who exploits a defect in the strategy of an opponent (within the rules of the game) of acting unfairly. This feature of our understanding of the concept of exploitation is part of the reason that many theorists defend a nonmoralized view. In contrast to moralized theories, empirical theories do not settle the question of the moral status of the act. Empirical theories of social concepts maintain that the criteria for determining whether a particular phenomenon has occurred rest in an evaluation of the facts involved and do not depend upon moral baseline or standards.

Perhaps the most compelling empirical account of exploitation has been defended by Allen Wood. According to Wood, exploitation occurs when one person takes advantage of the weakness or vulnerability of another to derive some benefit from the target of exploitation.[68] In this case, the question of whether exploitation takes place depends upon factual matters, such as the individual's level of vulnerability measured in categories such as economic or social power. Wood's empirical theory of exploitation suggests a different conclusion regarding the case of Nike's workers in Indonesia. On his account, Nike exploited the workers in their Indonesian factories because it took advantage of the workers' impoverished circumstances to benefit from their cheap labor. According to Wood, "Marx was right: Capital virtually always exploits wage labor. At least this is self-evident if it is granted that those who own the means of production enjoy a decisive bargaining advantage over those who own little besides their capacity to labor, and that this fundamental vulnerability on the part of labor decisively influences the terms of wage contracts."[69]

According to Wood, exploitation is morally objectionable when it is disrespectful of others.[70] Popular criticism of the wages paid to sweatshop workers is frequently grounded in a belief that these workers are treated disrespectfully, like disposable tools of production. As we saw above, Kant and his interpreters have provided a philosophical defense of the idea that the basic dignity of persons should be respected. Anyone concerned with the dignity of workers needs to determine what compensation would be consistent with respectful treatment. How many hours should employees be required to work each week? What minimum wage should they be paid for a work week? Elsewhere I have argued that to respect workers, employers must provide wages that enable them to meet basic needs and satisfy certain capabilities necessary for their well-being.[71] Specifically, Norman Bowie and I have argued that, at a minimum, respecting employees requires that they be paid wages for a forty-eight-hour workweek that allows two working adults to keep an average-sized (for a given area) family out of overall poverty. Thus, two parents would earn sufficient income to ensure that their average-sized family can afford basic food needs, shelter, clothing, energy, transportation, and basic health care with an additional 10 percent for discretionary spending.[72] Having these needs met helps to ensure the physical well-being and independence of employees, contributes to the development of their rational capacities, and provides them with the necessary conditions for the cultivation of self-esteem. So while it may be true that multinational corporations exploit the labor pools of developing nations in order to gain competitive advantages, and consumers reward such companies by purchasing lower-priced goods, companies that pay wages compatible with human dignity, while ensuring decent working conditions, do nothing wrong.

Economic Considerations

Defenders of sweatshops commonly assume that higher wages will result in increased unemployment. Given these assumptions, it is important to consider relevant economic considerations. While it is not possible to canvas the range of economic issues relevant to this debate, it will be helpful to briefly address some pertinent issues.

The labor cost of production for a sweatshirt that retails for $35.00 has been put at 45 cents, or 1.29 percent of the retail value.[73] Because the increase in labor costs necessary to ensure that workers are paid a living wage is comparatively small as a percentage of retail value, workers' rights advocates argue that the cost of providing a living wage is sufficiently small as to be absorbed as an operating expense.[74] Productivity gains can offset such a modest increase in costs: "Put simply, workers whose minimum daily dietary requirements are met and who have basic non-food needs met, will have more energy and better attitudes at work; will be less likely to come to work ill; and will be absent with less frequency."[75] Defenders of sweatshops respond by arguing that no matter how small the costs, voluntary increases in wages must result in lower employment by firms as they seek to offset increased costs.[76]

Such views tend to presuppose that corporations always operate with instrumental practical reason but, as was argued earlier in this essay, such a view is not plausible. Many corporations explicitly recognize ethical constraints regarding their treatment of employees and did so prior to being publicly criticized for disrespectful labor practices. It is also the case that defenders of sweatshops tend to ground their arguments in textbook economics, rather than in actual studies of labor markets. Few studies have been conducted of labor markets in which corporations have voluntarily increased wages. However, one recent study found that when wages were voluntarily increased in Indonesian contract factories as a result of antisweatshop campaigns, employment levels actually increased as a result.[77] In cases in which such increased costs cannot be easily absorbed as operating expenses and in which increased productivity does not offset the increase in labor costs, evidence demonstrates that the costs may be passed on to consumers via higher retail prices.[78]

Few companies that utilize large work forces in developing nations have done more to improve wages than pledge to pay all legally mandated wages and benefits. However, in 2003, adidas undertook an initiative to ensure that all workers in its global supply chains were paid a "fair wage." The company set as its goal the establishment of a wage-setting mechanism that "is transparent and has the direct input" of workers, "benchmarks basic pay at a level that is higher than the minimum wage," and "takes into account data on general cost of living and workers needs."[79] Although adidas ran a workshop and produced a report on the issue relating to its Indonesian work force, it is not clear that it has made progress toward its stated goals.[80]

Critics allege that multinational corporations wrongfully exploit workers by paying them wages incompatible with basic human dignity. Our analysis shows that much depends on the account of exploitation that one defends. On an ordinary language account of exploitation, corporations nearly always exploit workers. However, when corporations pay workers a wage that respects their humanity, they do not *wrongfully* exploit workers.

CONCLUSION

If we grant that workers enjoy basic rights such as freedom, noninjury, and well-being, and that they have dignity worthy of respect, then employers have a duty to ensure that minimum health and safety conditions are maintained in the workplace. Given that many workers are forced to take hazardous work, and given that some companies in capital- intensive industries may not be able to stay in business if they voluntarily improve health and safety conditions, OSHA-type standards are typically justified in industrialized nations. In many developing nations, OSHA-type standards cannot reasonably be enforced by local governments. In such contexts corporate employers have a duty to help ensure that respectful health and safety conditions are in place in their global supply chains. Further, all employees are entitled to be informed in the hiring process of the workplace hazards they will encounter in a manner consistent with the universal disclosure standard. Finally, the respectful treatment of workers requires that they be paid a weekly wage consistent with basic human dignity. Such a wage may or may not exceed the minimum wage in developing nations, but when it does exceed the minimum wage there are good reasons for believing that corporations have a duty to ensure that the appropriate above-minimum wage is paid to these workers. Companies that fulfill these minimal duties will play a constructive role in reducing the millions of workplace injuries and deaths that occur across the globe each year, as well as the exploitation to which countless others are subjected.

NOTES

1. Marisol Concha-Barrientos et al., "The Global Burden Due to Occupational Safety," *American Journal of Industrial Medicine* 48 (2005): 470–481; and John Zarocostas, "International Labour Organisation Tackles Work Related Injuries," *British Medical Journal* 331 (2005): 656.

2. U.S. Department of Labor, Bureau of Labor Statistics, *Census of Fatal Occupational Injuries* (2006), Table A-1: "Fatal occupational injuries by industry and event or exposure," http://www.bls.gov/iif/oshcfoi1.htm#2006.

3. Patricia H. Werhane, *Persons, Rights, and Corporations* (Englewood Cliffs, N.J.: Prentice Hall, 1985), 132; Alan Gewirth, "Human Rights and the Prevention of Cancer," in his *Human Rights: Essays on Justification and Applications* (Chicago: University of Chicago Press, 1982); Denis G. Arnold, "Moral Reasoning, Human Rights, and Global Labor Practices," in Rising *Above Sweatshops: Innovative Management Approaches to Global Labor Practices*, eds. Laura P. Hartman, Denis G. Arnold, and Richard Wokutch, (Wesport, Conn.: Praeger, 2003); and Denis G. Arnold, *The Ethics of Global Business* (Malden, Mass.: Blackwell, 2010).

4. For discussion see Amartya Sen, "Well-being, Agency and Freedom: The Dewey Lectures 1984," *Journal of Philosophy* 197 (1985): 82; and Arnold, *The Ethics of Global Business*, chap. 3.

5. Mark MacCarthy, "A Review of Some Normative and Conceptual Issues in Occupational Safety and Health," *Boston College Environmental Affairs Law Review* 9 (4) (1981): 782–787; Arnold, *The Ethics of Global Business*, chapter 3.

6. Immanuel Kant, *Foundations of the Metaphysics of Morals*, trans. Lewis White Beck (New York: Macmillan, 1990); Norman E. Bowie, *Business Ethics: A Kantian Perspective* (Malden, Mass.: Blackwell, 1999), 41–81; and Denis G. Arnold andNorman E. Bowie, "Sweatshops and Respect for Persons," *Business Ethics Quarterly* 13 (2) (2003): 221–242. For more detailed discussion of the concept of dignity as it is used here, see Thomas E. Hill Jr., *Dignity and Practical Reason* (Ithaca, N.Y.: Cornell University Press, 1992), especially 202–203.

7. For discussion see Joseph Raz, *Value, Respect, and Attachment* (Cambridge: Cambridge University Press, 2001), chap. 4. For an account of respect that owes much to Kant, but is intended to be pluralistic in the sense that it is compatible with a wide range of ethical theories, see Ruth Sample, *Exploitation: What It is and Why It's Wrong* (Lanham, Md.: Rowman & Littlefied, 2003).

8. Tibor Machan, "Rights and Myths in the Workplace," in *Moral Rights in the Workplace*, ed. Gertrude Ezorsky (Albany: State University of New York Press, 1987). Libertarian business ethicists, such as Machan, typically appeal to the work of Nozick in defending negative rights. Nozick famously defends the view that all persons have negative rights, but that positive rights come into existence only when people voluntarily agree to undertake the obligations that correspond to such rights (e.g., through valid contracts).

What is much less well understood is that, to the extent that he grounds such rights, Nozick does so by utilizing Kant's doctrine of respect for persons: "Side constraints upon action reflect the underlying Kantian principle that individuals are ends and not merely means; they may not be sacrificed or used for the achieving of others ends without their consent. Individuals are inviolable." See Robert Nozick, *Anarchy, State, and Utopia* (New York: Basic Books, 1974), 30–31. See also G. A. Cohen, "Are Disadvantaged Workers Who Take Hazardous Jobs Forced to Take Hazardous Jobs?" in Ezorsky, *Moral Rights in the Workplace.*

9. This does not imply that in cases where companies have no profits they have no obligations to employees regarding safety. It needs to be kept in mind that many basic safety measures can be implemented with little or no cost. Such practices should be implemented by all companies for the reasons discussed above. For discussion of cases in which the costs of improving conditions is higher and the solutions more complex, see below.

10. Arnold and Bowie, "Sweatshops," 232–233.

11. Machan, "Rights and Myths."

12. Ibid., 47–50.

13. Ibid., 49.

14. Ibid.

15. Such an objection might be grounded in a straightforward application of the position defended by Milton Friedman in "The Social Responsibility of Business is to Increase Its Profits," in *Ethical Theory and Business*, 8th ed., eds. Tom L. Beauchamp, Norman E. Bowie, and Denis G. Arnold (Englewood Cliffs, N.J.: Pearson Prentice-Hall, 2009), 51–55. Originally published in *New York Times Magazine*, September 13, 1970.

16. See Denis G. Arnold and Laura P. Hartman, "Worker Rights and Low Wage Industrialization: How to Avoid Sweatshops," *Human Rights Quarterly* 28 (3) (August 2006): 676–700, especially 694–696.

17. Norman Daniels advances the view that OSHA-type regulations can be justified in this way. See Norman Daniels, *Just Health Care* (Cambridge: Cambridge University Press, 1985), chap. 7.

18. See Cohen, "Are Disadvantaged Workers Who Take Hazardous Jobs Forced to Take Hazardous Jobs?"

19. Machan, "Rights and Myths," 48.

20. Elizabeth Anderson, *Values in Ethics and Economics* (Cambridge, Mass.: Harvard University Press, 1995), 197. Anderson is reporting on the work of Dorothy Nelkin and Michael Brown in their *Workers at Risk: Voices from the Workplace* (Chicago: University of Chicago Press, 1984).

21. Faden, Ruth and Tom L. Beauchamp, "The Right to Risk Information and the Right to Refuse Workplace Hazards," in Beauchamp et al., *Ethical Theory and Business*, 129–136.

22. Ibid., 132.

23. Paul R. Krugman and Maurice Obstfeld, *International Economics: Theory and Policy*, 6th ed. (New York: Addison Wesley, 2003), 289–290.

24. Gary Cohen and Will Englund, "A Third World Dump for America's Ships?" *The Baltimore Sun*, December 9, 1997.

25. For discussion see Barbara Herman, *The Practice of Moral Judgment* (Cambridge, Mass.: Harvard University Press, 1993), 47ff.

26. My initial defense of the universal disclosure standard appears in Arnold, *The Ethics of Global Business*, chap. 5.

27. For a sociological overview of modern sweatshops, see Ellen Israel Rosen, *Making Sweatshops: The Globalization of the U.S. Apparel Industry* (Berkeley: University of California Press, 2002).

28. Furthermore, children are often employed as workers in these factories. For discussions of child labor see Debra Satz, "Child Labor: A Normative Perspective," *The World Bank Economic Review* 17 (2) (2003): 297–309; and J. Lawrence French and Richard E. Wokutch, "Child Workers, Globalization and International Business Ethics: A Case Study in Brazil's Export-Oriented Shoe Industry," *Business Ethics Quarterly* 15 (4) (October 2005): 615–640.

29. World Trade Organization, "FDI Flows and Global Integration," *Some Facts and Figures: Stats for Seattle*, 1999, http://www.wto.org/english/theWTO_e/minist_e/min99_e/english/about_e/22fact_e.htm. See also Theodore H. Moran, *Beyond Sweatshops: Foreign Direct Investment and Globalization in Developing Nations* (Washington, D.C.: Brookings Institution, 2002), chap. 2.

30. Nike helped pioneer the concept of a consumer goods company that emphasizes design and marketing, but does not itself manufacture any of the products that it sells.

31. Ernst & Young, "Environmental and Labor Practices Audit of the Tae Kwang Vina Industrial Ltd. Co., Vietnam," January 13, 1997, http://www.corpwatch.org/article.php?id=2488.

32. See, for example, National Labor Committee, "The U.S. in Haiti: How to Get Rich on 11 Cents an Hour," 1995, http://www.nlcnet.org/Haiti/0196/index.htm; Human Rights Watch, "A Job or Your Rights: Continued Sex Discrimination in Mexico's Maquiladora Sector" Volume 10, No. 1(B) December 1998, http://www.hrw.org/reports98/women2/; and Timothy Conner, "We Are Not Machines: Indonesian Nike and adidas Workers," published by the Clean Clothes Campaign, Global Exchange, Maquila Solidarity Network, Oxfam Canada, and Oxfam Community Abroad, March 2002, 1–36.

33. See, for example, Michael A. Santoro, *Profits and Principles: Global Capitalism and Human Rights in China* (Ithaca, N.Y.: Cornell University Press, 2000); Arnold "Moral Reasoning, Human Rights, and Global Labor Practices," in Hartman et al., *Rising Above Sweatshops*; Arnold and Bowie, "Sweatshops and Respect for Persons;" Denis G. Arnold and Laura P. Hartman, "Moral Imagination and the Future of Sweatshops," *Business and Society Review* 108 (4) (Winter 2003): 425–461; S. Prakash Sethi, *Setting Global Standards: Guidelines for Creating Codes of Conduct in Multinational Corporations* (Hoboken, N.J.: John Wiley & Sons, 2003); Denis G. Arnold and Laura P. Hartman, "Beyond Sweatshops: Positive Deviancy and Global Labor Practices," *Business Ethics: A European Review* 14 (3) (July 2005): 206–222; Arnold and Hartman, "Worker Rights and Low Wage Industrialization: How to Avoid Sweatshops," *Human Rights Quarterly* and Arnold and Bowie, "Respect for Workers in Global Supply Chains."

34. See, for example, Ian Maitland, "The Great Non-Debate Over International Sweatshops," reprinted in *Ethical Theory and Business*, 9th ed., eds. Tom L. Beauchamp, Norman E. Bowie, and Denis G. Arnold (Upper Saddle River, N.J.: Pearson Prentice-Hall, 2009), 597–607 [first published in *British Academy of Management Conference Proceedings* (1997): 240–265]; Paul Krugman, "In Praise of Cheap Labor: Bad Jobs at Bad Wages are Better Than No Wages At All," in his *The Accidental Theorist and other Dispatches from the Dismal Science* (New York: W. W. Norton, 1999); Nicholas D. Kristof, "Brutal Drive," in *Thunder From the East: Portrait of a Rising Asia*, eds. Nicholas D. Kristof and Sheryl WuDunn (New York: Knopf, 2000); Academic Consortium on International Trade, *Letter to University Presidents* (July 29, 2000), http://www.fordschool.umich.edu/rsie/acit/

Documents/Anti-SweatshopLetterPage.html; David Henderson, *Misguided Virtue: False Notions of Corporate Social Responsibility* (London: Institute of Economic Affairs, 2001); Johan Norberg, *In Defense of Global Capitalism* (Washington, D.C.: Cato Institute, 2003); and Jagdish Bhagwati, *In Defense of Globalization* (New York: Oxford University Press, 2004).

35. See, for example, Krugman, "In Praise of Cheap Labor"; Kristof, "Brutal Drive"; and Henderson, *Misguided Virtue*. See also David Held, "Globalization, Corporate Practice and Cosmopolitan Social Standards," *Contemporary Political Theory* 1 (2002): 71.

36. Onora O'Neill makes a similar point in her "Agents of Justice" in *Global Justice*, ed. Thomas Pogge (Malden, Mass.: Blackwell, 2001).

37. For evidence see Oliver F. Williams, ed., *Global Codes of Conduct: An Idea Whose Time Has Come* (South Bend, Ind.: University of Notre Dame Press, 2000); and S. Prakash Sethi and Oliver F. Williams, *Economic Imperatives and Ethical Values in Global Business* (South Bend, Ind.: University of Notre Dame Press, 2001).

38. There are negative externalities for others members of local populations as well. For examples see Jane Spencer, "Ravaged Rivers: China Pays Steep Price as Textile Exports Boom," *Wall Street Journal*, August 22, 2007.

39. Bhagwati explicitly denies that such violations take place in his *In Defense of Globalization*, 173. Nearly all other defenders of sweatshops cited in this essay ignore the issue.

40. For discussion see Arnold and Hartman, "Worker Rights and Low Wage Industrialization," 686–690.

41. In 2003, between 25 and 50 percent of its contract factories lacked full compliance with local labor laws in North Asia Southeast Asia, the Indian subcontinent, sub-Saharan Africa, Mexico, Central America, and the Caribbean, and South America. In China, more than 50 percent of its contract factories lacked full compliance with local labor laws. Gap Inc., *Social Responsibility Report* 14 (2003), http://ccbn.mobular.net/ccbn/7/645/696/index.html.

42. Friedman, "The Social Responsibility of Business is to Increase Its Profits."

43. For a defense of this view see Arnold and Bowie, "Sweatshops and Respect for Persons," 227–228.

44. International Labour Organization, International Labour Office, Report of the Director General, "Decent Work" (Geneva, 1999), http://www.ilo.org/public/english/standards/relm/ilc/ilc87/rep-i.htm#1.%20The%20primary%20goal.

45. See, for example, Maitland, "*The Great Non-Debate Over International Sweatshops*"; Krugman, "In Praise of Cheap Labor"; Kristof, "Brutal Drive"; Henderson, *Misguided Virtue*; Norberg, *In Defense of Global Capitalism*; and Bhagwati, *In Defense of Globalization*.

46. Philip Knight, "New Labor Initiatives," speech delivered to the National Press Club, Washington D.C., May 12, 1998.

47. See Laura P. Hartman and Richard E. Wokutch, "Nike, Inc.: Corporate Social Responsibility and Workplace Standard Initiatives in Vietnam," In Hartman et al., *Rising Above Sweatshops*, 145–190.

48. See Tim Connor, "Still Waiting for Nike to Do It," (San Francisco: Global Exchange, May 2001).

49. Gap Inc., *Social Responsibility Report* 14 (2003), http://ccbn.mobular.net/ccbn/7/645/696/index.html.

50. Gordon Sollars and Fred Englander, "Sweatshops: Kant and Consequences," *Business Ethics Quarterly* 17 (1) (January 2007): 113–115.

51. Ibid.

52. For a different defense of the same conclusion, see Santoro, *Profits and Principles*, 161.

53. For case studies highlighting positive, proactive labor practices at companies such as Nike, Levi Strauss, adidas, Dow Chemical, and Chiquita, see Hartman et al., *Rising above Sweatshops*.

54. Sandy Smith, "America's Safest Companies," *Occupational Hazards*, October 21, 2002.

55. S. Prakash Sethi, "Codes of Conduct for Multinational Corporations: An Idea Whose Time Has Come," *Business and Society Review* 104 (3) (1999): 225–241; and Sethi, *Setting Global Standards*, chap. 13.

56. See, for example, Richard J. Arneson, "What's Wrong with Exploitation?" *Ethics* 91 (1981): 202–227; John Roemer, *A General Theory of Exploitation and Class*, (Cambridge, Mass.: Harvard University Press, 1982); Justin Schwartz, "In Defence of Exploitation," *Economics and Philosophy* 11 (1995): 275–307; the essays collected in Kai Nelson and Robert Ware, *Exploitation* (Atlantic Highlands, N.J.: Humanities, 1997); and Allen W. Wood, *Karl Marx*, 2nd ed. (New York: Routledge, 2004), chap. 16.

57. Alan Wertheimer, *Exploitation* (Princeton, N.J.: Princeton University Press, 1996). For an alternative moralized account of exploitation see Sample, *Exploitation*. Sample characterizes exploitation as disrespectful interaction. Her account is an improvement over Wertheimer's insofar as it is able to account for exploitative relationships and not merely exploitative transactions. However, her view has the same defect as all moralized account of exploitation insofar as it cannot account for morally neutral cases of exploitation. Furthermore, if exploitation always involves disrespect, little seems to be added to the concept of disrespect by calling it exploitative. My exposition and critique of Wertheimer's views track a similar discussion in my "Exploitation and the Sweatshop Quandary," *Business Ethics Quarterly* 13 (2) (April 2003): 243–256.

58. Wertheimer defends a moralized theory of coercion in *Coercion*. For an outline of an empirical theory of coercion see Denis G. Arnold, "Coercion and Moral Responsibility," *American Philosophical Quarterly* 38 (1) (January 2001): 53–67.

59. Wertheimer, *Exploitation*, 230.

60. Ibid., 217. A hypothetical market price "abstracts from some features of an actual market, such as defects in information and noncompetitiveness, [but] it does not abstract from other background characteristics of the buyers and sellers, such as risk" (231).

61. Ibid., 230.

62. Pamela Varley, ed., *The Sweatshop Quandary: Corporate Responsibility on the Global Frontier* (Washington, D.C.: Investor Responsibility Research Center, 1998), 258–259.

63. Defenders of sweatshops such as Matt Zwolinski and Benjamin Powell, assume that such labor markets are competitive, but it is not clear that such an assumption is warranted. In many nations employers have monopsony power over workers. For discussion of the concept of monopsony power in labor markets see William M. Boal and Michael R. Ransom, "Monopsony in the Labor Market." *Journal of Economic Literature* 35 (March 1997): 86–112. See also Matt Zwolinski, "Sweatshops, Choice, and Exploitation," *Business Ethics Quarterly* 17 (4) (October 2007): 689–727; and Benjamin Powell, "Sweatshop Sophistries," *Human Rights Quarterly* 28 (2006): 1031–1042.

64. Varley, *The Sweatshop Quandary*, 215–221.

65. Wertheimer, *Exploitation*, 298–299.

66. Zwolinski, "Sweatshops, Choice, and Exploitation."

67. Ibid. See also Maitland, "The Great Non-Debate over International Sweatshops."

68. Wood, "Exploitation," 141–147.

69. Ibid., 155.

70. Ibid., 151.

71. Arnold and Bowie, "Sweatshops and Respect for Persons," 233–239. See also Arnold and Hartman, "Worker Rights and Low Wage Industrialization."

72. This does not entail that both parents would be working in a factory. For example, one person might remain at home caring for young children while working a field or tending to a cottage industry. It is likely that any living-wage standard would need to be attentive to the options available to the spouses and factory workers in different areas and regions in order to meet the goals of the wage. The general topic of an area or context specific living wages is one that deserves considerably more attention from scholars that it has received.

73. Amy Rolph, "Students Protest Foreign Sweatshops," *Seattle Post-Intelligencer*, June 18, 2007.

74. Ibid.

75. Arnold and Bowie, "Sweatshops and Respect for Persons," 237. For more detailed discussion and additional sources see this article.

76. Powell, "Sweatshop Sophistries"; and Sollars and Englander, "Sweatshops."

77. Ann Harrison and Jason Scorse, "Improving the Conditions of Workers: Minimum Wage Legislation and Anti-Sweatshop Activism," *California Management Review* 48 (2) (2006): 144–160, especially 158.

78. A recent study of this issue found that consumers are willing to pay increased prices for products made under good working conditions. See Robert Pollin et al., "Global Apparel Production and Sweatshop Labour: Can Raising Retails Prices Finance Living Wages?" *Cambridge Journal of Economics* 28 (2) (2004): 153–171.

79. Adidas Group, "Fair Wages," http://www.adidas-group.com/en/sustainability/suppliers_and_workers/exploring_labour_standards/fair_wag es.asp.

80. Thee Kian Wie and Chris Manning, "Report on the Fair Wage Workshop: Jakarta 20–21 May, 2003," August 2003, http://www.adidas-group.com/en/sustainability/suppliers_and_workers/exploring_labour_standards/fair_wag es.asp.

SUGGESTED READING

Arnold, Denis G., and Norman E. Bowie. "Sweatshops and Respect for Persons." *Business Ethics Quarterly* 13 (2) (April 2003): 221–242.

Arnold, Denis G., and Laura P. Hartman. "Worker Rights and Low Wage Industrialization: How to Avoid Sweatshops." *Human Rights Quarterly* 28 (3) (August 2006): 676–700.

———. "Beyond Sweatshops: Positive Deviancy and Global Labor Practices." *Business Ethics: A European Review* 14 (3) (July 2005): 206–222.

Bhagwati, Jagdish. *In Defense of Globalization.* New York: Oxford University Press, 2004.

Cohen, G. A. "Are Disadvantaged Workers Who Take Hazardous Jobs Forced to Take Hazardous Jobs?" In *Moral Rights in the Workplace.* Edited by Gertrude Ezorsky. Albany: State University of New York Press, 1987.

Faden, Ruth, and Tom L. Beauchamp. "The Right to Risk Information and the Right to Refuse Workplace Hazards." In *Ethical Theory and Business*, 8th ed. Edited by Tom

L. Beauchamp, Norman E. Bowie, and Denis G. Arnold, 129–136. Englewood Cliffs, N.J.: Pearson Prentice-Hall, 2009.

French, J. Lawrence, and Richard E. Wokutch. "Child Workers, Globalization and International Business Ethics: A Case Study in Brazil's Export-Oriented Shoe Industry," *Business Ethics Quarterly* 15 (4) (October 2005): 615–640.

Harrison, Ann, and Jason Scorse. "Improving the Conditions of Workers: Minimum Wage Legislation and Anti-Sweatshop Activism." *California Management Review* 48 (2) (2006): 144–160.

Hartman, Laura P., Denis G. Arnold, and Richard Wokutch, eds. *Rising above Sweatshops: Innovative Management Approaches to Global Labor Challenges.* Westport, Conn.: Praeger, 2003.

Hartman, Laura P., Bill Shaw, and Rodney Stevenson. "Exploring the Ethics and Economics of Global Labor Standards: A Challenge to Integrated Social Contract Theory." *Business Ethics Quarterly* 13 (2) (2003): 193–220.

Kaplan, Jonathan "Import Bans and Tying One's Hands: Weakness of Will as a Justification for Trade Restrictions." *Public Affairs Quarterly* 15 (4) (2001): 355–372.

Machan, Tibor. "Rights and Myths in the Workplace." In *Moral Rights in the Workplace.* Edited by Gertrude Ezorsky. Albany: State University of New York Press, 1987.

Maitland, Ian. "The Great Non-Debate over International Sweatshops." In *Ethical Theory and Business*, 9th ed. Edited by Tom L. Beauchamp, Norman E. Bowie, and Denis G. Arnold, 597–607. Upper Saddle River, N.J.: Pearson Prentice-Hall, 2009.

Moran, Theodore H. *Beyond Sweatshops: Foreign Direct Investment and Globalization in Developing Nations.* Washington, D.C.: Brookings Institution, 2002.

Powell, Benjamin. "Sweatshop Sophistries." *Human Rights Quarterly* 28 (2006): 1031–1042.

Santoro, Michael A. *Profits and Principles: Global Capitalism and Human Rights in China.* Ithaca, N.Y.: Cornell University Press, 2000.

Satz, Debra. "Child Labor: A Normative Perspective." *The World Bank Economic Review* 17 (2) (2003): 297–309.

Sethi, S. Prakash. *Setting Global Standards: Guidelines for Creating Codes of Conduct in Multinational Corporations.* Hoboken, N.J.: John Wiley & Sons, 2003.

Wertheimer, Alan. *Exploitation.* Princeton, N.J.: Princeton University Press, 1996.

Zwolinski, Matt. "Sweatshops, Choice, and Exploitation," *Business Ethics Quarterly* 17 (4) (October 2007): 689–727.

PART VIII

SAFETY, RISK, AND HARM

CHAPTER 22

ENVIRONMENTAL ETHICS AND BUSINESS

LISA H. NEWTON

THIS chapter is an analysis of the patterns of interaction between the for-profit corporation and the natural environment and its protectors. First, we trace the rapid growth of environmental awareness from the 1960s, of public knowledge and interest in the natural environment, and of the groups dedicated to protecting it. In the wake of the environmental regulation that emerged from the first Earth Day in 1970, the corporation found itself subject to a new, unfamiliar, and troubling imperative—to protect the natural environment at home and abroad. Second, we track the evolving stages of corporate response to this new imperative—to environmental regulation from the public sector, to the emerging environmental initiatives from the Non-Governmental Organizations (NGOs) of the third sector, and eventually to the natural environment itself. Finally, we address the dimensions of that imperative—in the new duties that must be acknowledged, the new ethical frameworks in which the natural environment must be included, and the emerging environmental agenda to be addressed in the twenty-first century.

AWARENESS AND REGULATION

The origin of the current controversies between industry and the defenders of the natural environment, at least in Europe and in North America, can be traced to the early 1960s, when the first wave of reaction against the postwar industrial culture rose. In the United States, the first truly influential work was Rachel Carson's

Silent Spring.[1] Carson, a biologist by profession and a naturalist by persuasion, had many excellent portrayals of the beauty of nature in and near the sea to her credit. But the theme of the book was not that we ought to preserve nature for its beauty, but that our imposition of industrial methods and profit motives on nature, in the form of the widespread use of the pesticide DDT, was death-dealing in its effects on nontarget species. Humans, for instance, at the time she wrote, carried large burdens of DDT in their bodies. Pesticides in the body mimic chemicals in the endocrine system and may have serious negative effects on reproduction. As she wrote, the reproductive failures of the magnificent raptors, our prized eagles and falcons, which fed on the birds and fish contaminated by the insecticide, had already been documented.[2] That our industrial agricultural chemicals might be dangerous to higher species had been suggested for decades, but Carson had proof and a powerful style to deliver it.

With *Silent Spring* the long process of environmental regulation began, and it characterized the "green" movement for the next decades. As businesses expanded, they would take over new areas, build facilities to store waste products, and pursue activities that could pollute the environment; when that happened, an NGO or other "citizens' group" would protest and petition; strident debates among the parties would follow, and amid the congressional hearings, lobbying, and motions on the floors of the legislatures, the matter would be resolved by legislation or the courts. Through this movement of the campaign to save the natural environment, the posture of opposition, protestor vs. industry, became so well known as to become defining of the campaign to save the natural environment. Environmentalism was only recognizable as an attack on some industry or other, and any such NGO attack on any corporation, no matter what the subject, ironically became part of the green movement.[3]

The attacks on Rachel Carson launched in the period immediately following the publication of *Silent Spring* often came from the chemicals industry and foreshadowed the unfortunate future of these confrontations. They included personal denigration, with loudly voiced doubts about the ability of women to do science, scorn for women's scientific credentials and methods, and ultimately, a total disregard for the facts. Ezra Taft Benson, secretary of agriculture under Eisenhower, is credited with wondering "why a spinster with no children was so concerned with genetics?" He was not alone in deciding that she was "probably a Communist."[4] The pesticide industry trade group, the National Agricultural Chemicals Association, spent well over a quarter of a million dollars (about $1.4 million in today's dollars) in campaigns against Carson's conclusions and *ad hominem* attacks on her as an emotional female alarmist. They saw, more accurately than most others, that if her work were to be generally accepted, they would not only lose pesticide sales but also public trust, and could potentially face massive regulation. In this fear, they turned out to be right.[5]

Within a remarkably short period of time, environmental consciousness on many matters was raised all over the country. Citizens noticed that you had to turn on your headlights at noon in Pittsburgh, that there were days in Los Angeles when you could not comfortably breathe the air, and that the Cuyahoga River in Cleveland, Ohio, was on fire. The new concern came to an unprecedented culmination in the celebration of the first Earth Day in 1970, which had been proposed by Wisconsin senator Gaylord Nelson. The Baby Boomers, the healthiest and best-educated generation in history, came on the scene twenty million strong, determined and in force, in massive pro-environment demonstrations.

Galvanized into action, Congress passed landmark legislation to protect the environment—the Clean Air Act, the Clean Water legislation (the Water Quality Improvement Act, and significant amendments to the Water Pollution and Control Act), acts requiring recycling (the Resource Recovery Act and the Resource Conservation and Recovery Act), the Toxic Substances Control Act, the Endangered Species Act, the Marine Mammal Protection Act, among others—and created the Environmental Protection Agency (EPA) and the offices designed to make it function properly.[6] The natural environment in the United States came under highly effective protection, perhaps the best in the world, and in the process a pattern was established, at least for the time being: It was assumed that industry has little responsibility of its own to work to preserve the environment, but if harm to higher forms of life are suspected, industry may expect nasty confrontations with environmentally aware citizens, and the situation will elicit government action.

From the middle of the nineteenth century, legislation to preserve the natural environment had turned on the strong desire of the leading citizens to preserve its beauty for future generations. Now a new imperative took its place beside beauty: *To act for our own health and safety*. It is the state, acting through its police power, carrying out its duty to protect the safety and health of the people, which bears the responsibility of regulating industry's activities that adversely affect our health. Despite the always-popular rhetoric in defense of the Free Market vs. the Bureaucrats, the public had much faith in the government to protect our natural world. On the whole, it was justified. So when environmental disasters struck, by extension, the public turned to government. For instance, when Love Canal, an abandoned (and capped) waste dump of a Hooker Chemical (later Occidental Petroleum) plant in Niagara Falls, New York, was cut into by construction and overflowed in 1978, sickening the residents of a suburban community and threatening its school, it seemed natural to demand that Congress and New York State act immediately to remedy the situation. In the wake of the confrontation tactics of the mid-1970s, it also seemed natural to hold visiting congressmen hostage until they promised to do something about it. Government responded: hundreds of families were relocated, the EPA sued Hooker Chemical (and Occidental) for $117.6 million in damages to clean up the site. Legislation was prepared to make sure that it did not happen again.[7] (In the deed that Hooker had conveyed to the city of Niagara Falls when the land passed out of its ownership was a clause identifying the location of the dump and prohibiting any building on or near it; such matters tend to be forgotten as city offices change hands.)

That post–Love Canal legislation that emerged from Congress, the Comprehensive Environmental Response, Compensation, and Liability Act (CERCLA), commonly known as "Superfund," was enacted by Congress on December 11, 1980. The act taxed chemical and petroleum industries to create a fund for cleaning up toxic dumps. In the first five years of its existence, $1.6 billion was collected. It provided broad federal authority to respond directly to releases or threatened releases of hazardous substances that might endanger the public health or the environment. CERCLA established prohibitions and requirements concerning closed and abandoned hazardous waste sites, created liability for persons responsible for releases of hazardous waste at these sites, and established that fund to provide for cleanup when no responsible party could be identified.

CERCLA also enabled the revision of the National Contingency Plan (NCP), which provided the guidelines and procedures needed to respond to releases and threatened releases of hazardous substances, pollutants, or contaminants. The NCP also established a National Priorities List, designating those sites eligible for more long-term remediation. CERCLA was amended by the Superfund Amendments and Reauthorization Act (SARA) on October 17, 1986, which essentially refined and focused the work of the Superfund, encouraging more state and citizen participation in determining sites for remediation and in carrying out the work.[8]

REGULATION AND THE ETHICAL CRITIQUE OF BUSINESS

During this period of reform-minded criticism of U.S. industry, serious abuses were discovered abroad. Corruption of foreign governments and foreign trading partners, especially in East Asia and elsewhere in the developing world, seemed to have become routine. Lockheed Corporation, one of premier manufacturers of airplanes in the United States, paid about $3 million in bribes (routed through a Mafia operative) to Prime Minister Kakuei Tanaka's office during a 1976 campaign to entice Japan to buy their L-1011 planes for their national airline instead of Douglas DC-10s.[9] Litigation went on for ten years. Americans were asked to consider as a matter of business ethics, whether we ought to tolerate, or even support, bribery abroad, since bribery was (allegedly) the custom in these places and all our competitors were freely employing it to do business. The congressional response was a decided negative, in the form of the American Foreign Corrupt Practices Act (1977, later updated), which made it illegal for U.S. persons and businesses to bribe foreign government officials.

The case, and others of its sort, had nothing to do with the natural environment. But its shadow covered environmental matters as well as financial; the indignation felt against U.S. corporations throwing their weight around abroad, added to the memories of Love Canal, introduced a new ethical imperative for multinational corporations: just as it is unacceptable to pay bribes abroad even where bribery is accepted practice, so it is unacceptable to adhere to lower environmental standards abroad simply because the governments of the states where the plants are located permit it.[10]

Unnoticed at that point was the environmental damage caused by the involvement of the Bretton Woods institutions, the International Monetary Fund (IMF), and the World Bank in the economies of the developing world. The initial charge to these institutions—determined at an international conference of the wartime Allies in 1944 at Bretton Woods, New Hampshire—was to obtain stability of currency and trade. The ideas for these institutions evolved from the experience of the 1930s, when the priority of nationalistic goals, self-interested actions to obtain them, and simple ignorance of the economic consequences of these actions resulted in shortsighted policies such as high tariffs and competitive devaluations, which contributed to economic breakdown, domestic political instability, and international war. The lesson learned was that without a high degree of collaboration, the economic warfare would inevitably lead to the military kind. To ensure economic stability and political peace, then, states agreed to cooperate in regulating the international economic system. The pillar of the system was free trade, eliminating tariffs and quotas, which would bring about a market-based justice good for capitalism, good for markets, and ultimately good for countries that at that time did not have access to global markets.[11] Doubts have been raised about these glowing predictions for the poorer countries involved in the agreements, where traditionally the income for the government from tariffs has been high, and may not be easily replaceable—especially when the Bretton Woods policies urge developing nations to keep internal taxes down to attract foreign direct investment (FDI).

One major emergent role for the Bretton Woods institutions was providing loans for developing nations that could build up their economies to join the global market system. Such loans to developing nations tend to finance the infrastructure—dams, roads, electrical grids, sewers and sewage treatment plants, and power plants of many types—all intended to allow the economy to function as it did in Europe and the United States. Virtually every plan they proposed took a toll on the environment: the asphalt roads that were to truck goods to market, the dams that were to provide electricity for large regions, and the coal-burning power plants that were to permit machines to do the work that had been done by hand. Environmental consequences were rarely taken into account. But the major environmental and social problems arose when the loans had to be paid back. The developing world could produce nothing competitively except agricultural products—there were few high-value, small-volume niche products that they could produce at a profit. If they were not willing to default on the loans, they were left with no alternatives but to dedicate large amounts of land to monocultures of crops for export—pineapples, sugar, soya, coffee, and tea. The farmers' subsistence agriculture was displaced, their families could not afford to buy the export crops (which in general were not nutritious anyway), and over large parts of the developing world, the agricultural villages suffered severe food shortages.[12]

Meanwhile, the land was exhausted and the water tables dropped, although in the first years of these new economic arrangements little attention was paid to these problems. The deteriorating conditions did not seem to be the responsibility of any of the eligible targets, that is, of any offending multinational corporation. Only recently have the NGOs been moving to influence the policies of the Bretton Woods institutions to take account of environmental damage as well as economic growth when they extend loans to developing nations. The events are all connected: the attention paid to U.S. and European companies operating abroad and spurring the passage in 1977 of the Foreign Corrupt Practices Act laid the foundations for later attention to all environmental effects of corporate action, and in consequence, to the effects of the World Bank loans (and the IMF austerity measures to ensure that the loans were repaid).[13]

Even as other dimensions of the interaction between environment and business come into new focus, this original confrontation between environmental protection and business interests continues. Governments must protect the safety and health of their people, and business will continue to seek shareholder wealth and sometimes these efforts conflict. Industry does not always win. Rachel Carson ultimately (posthumously) won the pesticide battle, and set the precedent that assaults, intentional or otherwise, on the health and safety of people and animals are unacceptable. The environment also loses on occasion. In July 2007, for instance, the EPA agreed not to enforce a broader range of wetland protection directives "after intense lobbying from property owners, mine owners and developers."[14] In December of that year, after equally intense lobbying from automobile manufacturers, the agency ruled that states cannot set carbon emissions standards higher than federal standards.[15] Over a period of years, since the industry-friendly administrations of the late twentieth century, proposed Wilderness Areas (which would have to bear no permanent marks of human use) have been given over to mining interests and off-road vehicles, rendering them ineligible for Wilderness protection.[16] It might be preferable to protect our lands with good will and common sense, but government action at several levels is still the only way we can deal with problems that extend over large areas and the long run. This limitation is a serious disadvantage for the environmental protection movement, for the degree of vigilance that can be expected of government environmental agencies can be predicted from the political persuasions of the current administration, and it is easier to undo the protections of the last administration than it is to repair the damage that was done.

THE INTEGRATION OF BUSINESS ETHICS AND ENVIRONMENTAL PROTECTION

We have traced a brief history of opposition: of business interests, and the business imperative to increase the shareholders' wealth, in opposition to efforts to protect and preserve the natural environment. A critical participant in the events is government. The police power of the state has repeatedly been called upon to protect the life and health of humans and other living things from unintentional harm from certain profit-oriented activities of industry. To the extent that businesses here and abroad have begun to develop environmentally protective policies and practices, the motivation for such concern was the regulation of the late 1960s and the 1970s, not any access of moral concern for the green earth. Businesses cannot be expected to undertake initiatives for the public good without being able to make an adequate business case. The managers of corporations have undertaken, by their acceptance of their positions, to be good stewards of the assets of the investors whom they serve. They may be public-spirited citizens in their private lives, and in the use of corporate assets dedicated to public use, but by the role they have accepted in the economic organization that hires them, they are obligated to do nothing that will harm the economic interests of the corporation.[17]

The development of the business case for environmental protection illustrates an evolving understanding about the ways that business and the environment can work together in combined action toward separate ends. The first step, taken by any company in consultation with the legal department, is to ensure that the company is in compliance with all applicable law. This step corresponds with the first "shade of green": *light, or legal*, green, as described in R. Edward Freeman's *Environmentalism and the New Logic of Business*.[18] The importance of compliance is no longer seriously debated. Whatever the odds may be of getting caught in lawbreaking, the stakes are too high to risk, not only because of the fines but also because the public disgrace that follows an unfavorable verdict can seriously reduce the company's profits. In addition, the odds of prosecution may be greater than they appear to be when an antiregulatory administration is in office. Recall that antiregulatory administrations are usually followed by pro-regulatory administrations with long memories. Further, citizen organizations have shown themselves to be capable of hiring their own biologists to measure environmental damage, and of bringing action against a firm through the civil courts—or the media.

Restrictive regulation, even when passed with hostile intent toward industry, will not necessarily have consequences harmful to the industry targeted. It can spur innovation—and even an industry-wide change in attitude.[19] Several manufacturing industries, notably the petrochemical and energy industries, became pro-active in their approach to environmental protection, at least where the public's health and safety was concerned. This model for drawing business into environmental protection continues to be effective.[20]

Other models joined it. By the end of the 1970s iconic "win-win" cases had emerged, where measures taken to improve environmental performance within a company turn out to save money. Among the famous accounts of cost-lowering environmental measures is 3M's success with its Preventing Pollution Pays (3P) program.[21] Begun in 1975 as an attempt to eliminate sources of pollution, 3P saved millions of dollars in the first year, and nearly a billion by 2005. They restructured their entire manufacturing process, reformulated products, and redesigned equipment so that all the material that entered the plant was used in the product and not disposed of as waste. 3M was really just engaging in good process stewardship and proved that environmental progress can be financially beneficial.[22] It served as an example for the country: if we can do something that we have to do cheaper and more efficiently, then the business case is easy to make. The advantages to the environment can be viewed as an additional, secondary, argument for the improvement.

Toward the end of the 1970s the phenomenon of "green marketing" increased substantially, riding on a popular wave of enthusiasm for all things environmental. As Freeman points out, the logic of this (slightly darker) shade of green is the old-fashioned rule, give the customer what he wants![23] A not insignificant cohort of consumers are willing to "buy green," to pay a premium for products that can be seen as beneficial, or not harmful, to the environment. Corporations that locked into this trend were able to charge premium prices for products whose competitors were spread across the market and competed only in price. Leaving commodity competition for a "niche" market had long been understood as an excellent way of increasing profits, and so the environment became a niche. Among the best-known examples from this period is crusading entrepreneur Anita Roddick's Body Works chain, which specialized in "natural" products from the rainforest in her cosmetics and health compounds, which are developed and produced without the use of animal testing. (Cosmetics prior to Roddick had commonly been tested for safety by the "Draize Test," entailing spraying or rubbing the product into the exposed eyes of rabbits, causing pain and sometimes destroying the animal's eyes.) Roddick, a passionate environmentalist, was stung by criticism that while her products were not developed with animal tests, some of the components she used in her products were not so "natural." To preserve the brand, she was forced to look upstream, to take responsibility for the practices in her supply chain. She and her critics set a precedent that still governs business practice today: each manufacturer shall be responsible not only for his own products but also for any ethical or environmental problems that attend the origins of his products' components.[24]

Another example of the new environmental trend in business was Ben and Jerry's Ice Cream, where their environmental and ethical practices were featured in their marketing. Their Rainforest Crunch included Brazil Nuts bought from rainforest cooperatives, and they would only buy cream for their ice cream from cows that had not been treated with rBST—recombinant (artificial) bovine somatotrophin hormones—used in some commercial dairies to increase the milk production.[25] As part of the new vigilance on the environmental implications of the upstream course to manufacturing of products, new scrutiny was given the downstream consequences: it is no help to the environment if large quantities of your product, especially a product (like computers) with toxic materials in it, ends up in the landfill. The whole operation, including upstream sources and downstream consequences, must be environmentally harmless. Not all of this new scrutiny was accepted immediately. But current efforts by IBM and other corporations to recycle all their materials demonstrate that the cradle-to-grave imperative had gotten some traction. The suggestion that these materials might be reused in different products eventually gave rise to the "cradle-to-cradle" movement spearheaded by architect William McDonough.

In the course of attempts to protect the natural environment from the natural consequences of careless capitalist endeavors, especially in the developing world, the green movement worked with the human rights NGOs to urge that the workers in the multinational corporations' export platforms be paid a living wage. Payment to workers, and to agricultural cooperatives, has come to occupy a significant territory in this marketing niche. It is now possible to buy "Fair Trade" goods, notably coffee, grown in the shade to preserve mountainsides, and paying a fair wage to the people who harvest it. An increasing presence in our supermarkets is the product of the entire organic food industry, which is the most rapidly growing sector of the agricultural market. It is possible to be cautiously optimistic about the development of the Green Consumer, who responds to programs that reduce packaging, or make it recyclable, and to programs that invite the consumer to return products (especially computers) for up-to-date replacements.

Businesses need not honor the environment only in its responses to government action, or merely in search of niche markets. There is at least one example of a company that has made its whole mission the preservation of the environment. Business editors tend not to include Patagonia, a producer of outdoor clothing and gear, in their environmental lists because it is small, it is private, and often it is quirky. *Fortune* featured it as a very special case, the product of a vision of a single person, enthralled by the idea of creating perfect gear for the sports he loves, and saving the environment in the process. Yvon Chouinard loves the outdoors, created Patagonia to serve the outdoors, and luckily found a profitable niche market, while creating a new model for green business. It remains to be seen whether this model can be transplanted to a diverse array of markets.

A New Model for Business: Revolution in Design

We have seen that there is a basic "business case" for the protection of the environment, an area of common ground even under standard business assumptions. But a new generation of commentators on the ethical obligations of business for the natural environment has called for nothing less than a new industrial revolution.

Natural Capitalism by Paul Hawken, Amory Lovins and Hunter Lovins,[26] the prophetic work in this movement, points out that radically transformed ways of working, producing, and living would sharply increase resource efficiency and environmental friendliness. By the late 1990s, when the book appeared, there was a felt need for a new paradigm of environmental progress. Environmentalism seemed to have run out of steam. Industries still lobbied for an end to all regulation, and Detroit's automobile makers insisted that the mileage requirements for their automotive fleet could not possibly be increased, or they would surely be bankrupt (and all their workers unemployed). No government agency was pushing for more stringent regulation. President Ronald Reagan and his administration, over the course of the 1980s, seemed successful in their efforts to break the spirit of regulation.[27]

A new administration made little more progress. Even with a committed environmentalist as vice president of the United States, starting in 1993, little new legislation was passed. Business, still willing to operate within the law, had little inclination to go beyond the law for ethical reasons, for the sake of the common good, or for the care for future generations. Only arguments from profitability would receive a favorable audience.

It was in this context that Hawken et al. argued for environmental protection based on the idea that measures undertaken to save the environment can themselves be profitable—even highly profitable. The major difference between their conclusions and the conclusions reached by the followers of the 3M model is that the projected changes would be far more radical, modifying whole industries. *Natural Capitalism* called on business to take profitable advantage of environmental efficiencies that were already known. The automobile, mainstay of much of the U.S. twentieth-century economy, provides a good example. The purpose of the car is to transport the driver from one place to another. Of all the energy the car consumes, 80 percent is lost to operating the engine itself or dissipated in heat, leaving 20 percent to move the automobile and the driver; given the weight of the car, 95 percent of that 20 percent moves the car, and 5 percent of 20 percent moves the driver, who was the object of the enterprise.[28] It would seem we could do better.

The trends in consumption in the early part of the twenty-first century were no cause for comfort. There was evidence that new high-end housing tended to allow for three cars per family, and for a while the most popular vehicle on the road was the heavy Sport-Utility Vehicles (SUV), built on the model of trucks.[29] Should the trend continue, the atmosphere will have to cope with additional greenhouse gases: while the average U.S. car puts an alarmingly high 10,168 pounds of carbon dioxide into the air yearly, the SUV puts out 11,972 pounds.[30] More significantly, U.S. trends aside, American habits of consumption are spreading over the rest of the world, especially to China and the developing world, ensuring that any gains in prosperity among those nations will not improve the condition of the natural environment.[31]

This trend is not inevitable. The automotive industry can change. Technology is now available to make the U.S. car safer while putting much less demand on environmental resources. Most automobiles are made of steel, which is strong, attractive, and heavy. Using lighter but more expensive materials like aluminum and magnesium, molded composite materials, embedding carbon, Kevlar, glass, and other fibers in molded plastics, concept cars have been developed that can reduce the weight by two-thirds. A smaller sedan might weigh as little as 1,000 pounds. The lighter car translates into greater efficiency in several ways: since much less power is needed to accelerate the car, the engine can be smaller and lighter; since much less power is needed to stop the car, the brakes can be lighter; and since there is less weight on the tires, they lose less energy in heat.[32] (As the car becomes lighter, some features, like power steering and power brakes, might become completely unnecessary.)

None of this is new. Prototypes of extra light "hypercars," which can attain 90 miles per gallon, have existed for decades. Along the same lines, Boeing Corporation has a prototype of a lighter airplane, the 787 (launched on July 8, 2007), made largely of composites, that will save massive amounts of fuel (conserving fossil fuels and lowering emissions). Its launch was the most successful in aircraft history, selling hundreds of airplanes on the opening day, reminding us that the audience for environmentally friendly technology is very strong. If it is correct to say that a moral imperative to conserve the natural environment bears on the private sector, we may conclude that business is morally obligated to make those changes that will reduce the environmental impact of private transport; yet the authors of *Natural Capitalism* argue only that there are interesting profits in such a change.

In transportation and most other industries, the most serious environmental impact comes from the release of carbon into the atmosphere. Carbon in the air is causing the "greenhouse effect" or global warming, serious enough by now to threaten severe long-term climate change that will radically alter the conditions of life on earth. The highways are not the only source of climate-altering carbon. The suburban home idealized in the middle of the twentieth century, and by the construction industry that created and duplicates it, requires its own revolution. The suburbs are themselves dependent upon the car, and therefore are damaging to the natural environment. From this perspective, the freestanding house, surrounded by a large lawn on a large lot in the suburbs, is an independent and major assault on the environment. In comparison to the city apartment, it requires much more fuel to light, to heat, and to supply electricity for the entertainment centers, computers, fax machines, and kitchen appliances. Out of doors, the tally of taxation on electricity must include the amount of gasoline burned in mowing the lawn with power mowers or blowing leaves into a pile with power-driven leaf blowers so that they can be vacuumed into a gasoline-driven truck and driven to the dump.

Yet buildings have been designed, and in some places built, that use much less energy through superinsulation, efficient heating plants, and double windows; and where photovoltaic panels already available are attached, they can, like a tree, create more energy than they use. Much more can be accomplished from the careful design of industrial and office buildings. We could take the entire industrial system of the developed world, wring out the waste, redesign the basics, dramatically lower the environmental impact, and make a profit in the process. It is less the technology and more the mind of the technologist that needs changing. The consumer is the key to the change that is needed—there will be no New Industrial Revolution unless there is a demand for it.

For such a revolution to occur, we may have to tap more deeply into the extraordinary technological sophistication of the natural world. For instance, all of our clean water is the product of a water filtration governed entirely by natural processes. Our medicines are derived, often in one step, from the incredible variety of plants in the natural biodiversity of the threatened rainforests.[33] Nature's riches and nature's services do not often make the news until we suddenly find them slipping away. Recently we have heard repeated alarms over "colony collapse disorder," which is destroying our honeybees, the pollinators on which many of our fruit, seed, and nut crops depend.[34] If the bees are lost, science has no means of replacing them. Currently, we cannot even place a price on "nature's services": we have no standard economic procedures to estimate what might be lost if the bees disappear (the loss of income to the beekeeper is the tiniest fraction of that cost). We may find that we have another reason for preserving (wild) nature: *Because nature contains resources and models processes that we need to use and to know in order to carry on vital economic activities.*

Recently, the business environmental imperative has been given stronger impetus. As early as 1970, Barry Commoner had pointed out that there was no such place as "away," and that therefore we really could not throw anything there; what we thought we threw there actually stayed with us, rotting and polluting.[35] What can we do with waste that cannot be thrown away? William McDonough, the revolutionary green architect, proclaimed a new paradigm for industry, "waste is food": The standard model of industrial "throughput," resources entering at one end of a factory, product exiting at the other end, waste departing to someplace "away" through a pipe or in a truck, had to be abandoned. Adopting the perspective of biomimicry—the attempt to model economic processes on biological processes— he pointed out that in the natural world, nothing is lost;[36] every bit of waste from one natural process becomes the raw material for the next life. Our 1970s intolerance for wastes that persist in our environment and eventually endanger our health has led to the requirement that we shepherd our products to some safe end, "cradle to grave." McDonough's new prescription insisted that we follow them "cradle to cradle"—from the creation of one product to the resources necessary for the next.[37] One of the more prominent adherents of this new wave is Ray Anderson, founder and CEO of Interface, Inc., which has developed furnishings that are completely sustainable—using only dyes that are biodegradable and nontoxic, materials that can be recycled, and minimizing the use of fossil fuels.[38]

A Synthesis and a Serious Agenda

It might be that business's adaptation to a greener age is upon us, more than we are aware, from food to cars to architecture to joint ventures by NGOs and for-profit firms.[39] Environmental concern and preservation are now incorporated to same extent into the day-to-day operations of the business system—to preserve the beauty of the environment, to preserve human and animal health and safety, and to protect those resources and services provided by nature that we cannot replace. Business persons know well that the time of conceiving of environmentalism as a matter of "personal virtue" is long past. The protection of the environment is not a series of options but a firm set of imperatives. The most recent reflection on the implications of environmental concerns for business is an excellent treatise by Daniel Esty and Andrew Winston, *Green to Gold*.[40] It is a treatise on how competitive businesses will profit from environmental requirements, while companies that have not been alert to them will suffer. Interestingly, they envision the consumer lawsuit, replacing government regulatory agencies, as the centerpiece of reform in the twenty-first century for those businesses that continue to pollute the environment.

Business will have to include all environmental agendas in all their dealings from now on. The most important reasons for this track the motivations we have discovered in this chapter.

First, there is the health and safety argument. We will no longer tolerate operations in violation of health and safety of human beings, or, for that matter, of non-human animals. Governmental action in the name of health is always possible, and the effects on economic planning can be devastating. The first example cited by Esty and Winston is of a video game launcher from which a reasonable profit was expected, locked in a European warehouse for months because traces of a forbidden carcinogenic substance were employed in its Chinese manufacture. Europe will not allow products to be sold that contain substances banned for reasons of health or safety; and the United States is not far behind. Regulation is still present, it can become more stringent, and exceptions will prove harder to buy.

Second, the efficiency argument, with 3M still as its icon, prevails now by presumption. Every bit of waste placed in the environment is wasted product and poor process. Here Freeman and Esty/Winston join with McDonough, Anderson, and Amory Lovins. The future will reward those who rethink industrial processes for efficiency, not just in any company or process but across the entire spectrum of economic activity. One of Amory Lovins's favorite examples is the inefficient design of buildings, which results from the fact that the designer is responsible only for the costs of designing, the general contractor only for the cost of building, and neither has any incentive to think about the costs of operating what has been built. So the builders do everything for the lowest cost compatible with the building codes, skimping on insulation and routing the plumbing in any way that does not increase the cost of the building. When the building is in use, of course, the energy costs are painfully high, and for some reason very expensive pumps are needed to pump the water to the top floor. Most of the costs of any building are determined by the design; if the costs of building and operating were thought through as one unit, greater efficiencies could be realized.[41]

Third, the environment deserves preservation for its beauty. This is where we started, with the movement to establish National Parks, National Forests, and National Wilderness Areas. We are not sure of the immediate implications of the beauty of the natural environment for business, but the implications for human life are significant. At this point it becomes clear that we need to rethink not just business but human life, and that when we do, the implications for profitable business will be enormous.

The recent history of the growth of environmental concern has left U.S. businesses with a heavy agenda. The key to addressing this agenda will be collaboration among regulators, the state, federal, and international environmental agencies, and increasingly, collaboration with the environmental NGOs. The political difficulties that attend that last type of cooperation are well known—both parties to the negotiation tend to lose credibility with the hardliners on their own side, and the agreements are fragile. But the attempts continue,[42] and many may be successful.

What ongoing and deeply rooted problems stand out as requiring immediate attention? They are not new. A summary follows.

Enforcing the law and eliminating the historical lose-lose practices. Undoubtedly the worst danger to the planet is posed by deforestation, which contributes to global warming and deprives the earth of the means to recover from it. Much of the lumber industry in the world is being carried on illegally (as determined by the laws of the country in which the logs are taken). Some of this logging is in the American Pacific Northwest, but most of it is abroad, in the global South. Should international and NGO assistance be made available to these nations? Businesses can help by establishing and supporting international efforts to designate as "certified" lumber that has been taken legally and in an environmentally sound manner. But the logging industry is not the only culprit. There are industry practices that are not good either for business or the environment, which have become entrenched through regional configurations of interests. Mining, still essentially subsidized under the 1872 Mining Law, is a good example. These must simply be stopped—it is the responsibility of the business community to lend support to efforts to stop them.

Supporting new legislation and regulation, where necessary, to halt environmentally destructive practices. If oil prices rise, the free market will take the SUVs off our roads and create a preference for small houses and green offices, but the market will not act quickly enough to prevent the worst effects of carbon pollution. The housing and office siting patterns, and the entire transportation arrangement, for the nation will have to be radically changed by a creative combination of private and public enterprise.

Monitoring and remediating the environmental effects of economic initiatives across the world, especially in developing nations. In the present economic system, developing nations need foreign direct investment, namely, firms based in the North willing to take on the risks and inconveniences of carrying on operations in the South. It could be argued that whatever the environmental depredations, generally responsible EU and U.S. companies will do less damage and more good for the local economies than the unregulated enterprises locally grown—or imported from elsewhere. Those who prosper in the developed world will have to take responsibility for the problems that have been created for the developing world by the free market that we defend. Possibly we will have to follow the advice of Jeffrey Sachs and forgive the developing world's loans.[43]

Reforming agricultural practices in the United States and monitoring agricultural practices carried on by U.S. companies abroad. Many of our environmental problems started with the introduction of various forms of agriculture.[44] For unknown reasons, business ethics as a field has not, save marginally, dealt with farming as a business.[45] But what agribusiness is doing to our land is of paramount concern. The systematic consideration of the conduct of agribusiness, from an ethical standpoint, should now be one of the major agenda items on the list for business and environmental ethics.

Restoring the woods and fields. Ultimately, we must restore the woods and the fields, and with them, the biodiversity rapidly disappearing in the world. Biodiversity, rich soils, and extensive forests are the insurance policy to protect life from destructive shocks caused by us or by others. Programs of reforestation, at home but especially in the drought-ravaged areas of the global South, are possibly the most important step.

For this weighty load of problems, simple solutions are not available, which should not surprise us. There are obvious measures that are easily within our powers and that will make a start on our agenda quickly and effectively. Within the bounds of reason, they should not make an undue demand on resources. But a major player in any such an environmental agenda is government. Three major government initiatives merit attention here because they call for the cooperation of business in their implementation.

First, as per the first item on the agenda above, the law must be enforced, and enforced across international boundaries. Trade in items illegally obtained— such as illegally logged lumber, rare animal pelts, and smuggled antiquities, for instance— must be stopped; the collaboration of public and private sectors in this effort is critical. It seems strange to insist on this, but business and all citizens should be sure that the heads of enforcement agencies take the laws seriously and are willing to make sure that they are obeyed.

Second, the business community should support a heavy carbon tax, doubling or tripling the cost of all fossil fuels for all purposes. The Intergovernmental Panel on Climate Change, the UN body set up to report on global warming, suggests a price on CO_2 emissions of \$20–\$50 per ton of CO_2 emitted, which should stabilize CO_2 at a safe level by the end of the century.[46] Revenues could be set at a level adequate to supply fuel and other vital items to the poor, or others disproportionately injured by the tax. Such a tax would create an incentive to develop efficient alternative fuels, "green" cars (rendering mileage standards unnecessary), and environmentally friendly housing. Meanwhile, if the tax incentives work as they are supposed to work, goods that are now trucked will have to travel by train, forcing the upgrading of the rail system to take over most of the present work of the highways and airways. Travel by air will become much more expensive, travel by train or boat, which puts many fewer strains on the environment, will eventually be much less expensive in comparison. Automobile travel will be limited to local trips.

Third, the business community should collaborate in the termination of all major industry subsidies. Agricultural subsidies are the worst offenders and have done more to harm the land, and the income of farmers here and abroad, than anything else; but they are not alone. Business ethics should take a close look at the sources and consequences of all direct transfers of funds from government to business; in the process, it should take a much harder look at the campaign contributions that persuade legislators to authorize such transfers. Ending such subsidies will not cost us any money at all, and will bring our economy more in line with our moral claims about business. We claim to believe in the free market system—and accept the demise of the noncompetitive—let's take our money away from where our mouth isn't. We may enjoy the revival of the free market. With an end to agricultural subsidies, for instance, especially in combination with the carbon tax, local food from local farms will become profitable, because it will not be competing with the subsidized mass food of agribusiness transported by fossil-fueled trucks. Not only is it environmentally sound, but it tastes better. Meanwhile, the relatively minor subsidies extended to research on solar and wind technology can easily be paid for by the savings.[47]

In the end, there should be no permanent opposition between the interests of business and the protection of the environment. Should only such reforms as are listed above be brought into existence, we may hope to restore the land to the place it has always occupied in human industry—clearly a matter of prime concern. As David Brower has pointed out, there is no business to be done on a dead planet.[48]

NOTES

1. Rachel Carson, *Silent Spring* (Boston: Houghton-Mifflin, 1962).

2. Ibid., 118–122.

3. For instance, in the middle of a discussion of population problems and the natural environment, G. Tyler Miller Jr. includes a sidebar ("spotlight") on the 1970s story of infants in the developing world suffering from malnutrition, allegedly because of inappropriate use of infant feeding products, contaminated with the local water, or because they were too expensive for the family to purchase in sufficient quantity. Nestlé S.A. was accused of inappropriate promotion of the products. The infant formula case never at any point had anything to do with the natural environment; the INFACT protest had only to do with Nestlé's marketing practices and the health of babies in the developing world. Nothing substantially connected the two discussions, save that an NGO was opposing an industrial giant. G. Tyler Miller Jr. *Living in the Environment*, 11th ed. (Pacific Grove, Calif.: Brooks/Cole, 2000), 272.

4. Linda Lear, *Rachel Carson: Witness for Nature* (New York: Henry Holt, 1997), 429.

5. Ibid. In general, for the industry reaction to *Silent Spring* see Lear, "Rumblings of an Avalanche," in *Rachel Carson*, chap. 18.

6. The legislative history is too long to be discussed in this chapter; a brief list was excerpted from Gaylord Nelson, "Earth Day '70: What It Meant," *EPA Journal*, 1980, accessed June 16, 2007, http://www.epa.gov/history.

7. For an account of the Love Canal toxic waste incident, see Lisa Newton and Catherine Dillingham, *Watersheds: Cases in Environmental Ethics* (Belmont, Calif.: Wadsworth, 1991), chap. 1, and the references cited in that chapter.

8. http://www.epa.gov/superfund/action/law/sara.htm (accessed February 11, 2008).

9. The information is from the Lockheed "answers" Web site, http://www.answers.com/topic/lockheed-corporation (accessed June 14, 2007).

10. The situation gave special prominence to an industrial accident in Bhopal, India. Union Carbide India Limited, an affiliate of Union Carbide Company, owned a plant in Bhopal that made the insecticide SEVIN to support India's agricultural sector. It was never profitable, and its bad luck culminated on December 3, 1984, when a disgruntled employee opened a garden hose into a tank of methyl isocyanate (MIC), blowing up the tank, killing possibly 3,800 people and injuring thousands others in the plume of the resulting toxic gas. The fact that the chemicals industry was now involved in more injury to the hapless neighbors of its toxic plants was not lost on the U.S. public, and was the trigger for the passage of SARA, the update of the Superfund authorization.

11. Sources for this description include Wikipedia, http://www.en.wikipedia.org/wiki/Bretton_Woods_System (accessed September 12, 2007).

12. Vandana Shiva, *Water Wars: Privatization, Pollution and Profit* (Cambridge, Mass.: South End, 2002).

13. Joseph Stiglitz, *Globalization and Its Discontents* (New York: Norton, 2002).

14. John M. Broder, "After Lobbying, Wetland Rules Are Narrowed," *New York Times*, July 6, 2007.

15. John M. Broder and Felicity Barringer, "E.P.A. Says 17 States Can't Set Greenhouse Gas Rules for Cars," *New York Times*, December 20, 2007, A1.

16. Felicity Barringer and William Yardley, "A Surge in Off-Roading Stirs Dust and Debate in the West," *New York Times*, December 30, 2007, A1, 19.

17. See the argument to this effect in John R. Boatright, "Does Business Ethics Rest on a Mistake?" *Business Ethics Quarterly* 9 (4) (1999): 583–591.

18. R. Edward Freeman, Jessica Pierce, and Richard H. Dodd, *Environmentalism and the New Logic of Business: How Firms Can Be Profitable and Leave Our Children a Living Planet* (New York: Oxford University Press, 2000), 39.

19. An excellent illustration of this shift is found in the efforts of the Chemical Manufacturers Association (now the American Chemistry Council) to recover from Superfund. In July 1982, Attorney General Abrams said that two studies showed that the levels of dioxin in homes next to Love Canal (see above) were among the highest that had been found near where people lived. So in June 1983, contemplating further unfavorable regulation, outgoing chairman of the CMA, Bill Simeral of Du Pont, recommended that chemical companies take the initiative to ensure public safety and conform the conduct of the industry to a standard of ethical and environmental responsibility. The code that they composed, Responsible Care, was widely publicized and accepted in the industry by the time of the incident in Bhopal. Bhopal triggered the updating of Superfund to SARA, and to the CMA's delight, the drafters of SARA adopted whole sections of those provisions for SARA's Title III, almost word for word. A few years later Jon Holtzman of the CMA commented on this development: "It taught us that if we were willing to attack a problem that the public is interested in—where government wants success—government will cherry-pick our program and write it into law. Government will buy into our experience because they don't want to fail either."

20. A more complete account of the Responsible Care initiative is found in Lisa Newton and David Schmidt, *Wake-Up Calls: Classic Cases in Business Ethics* (Belmont, Calif.: Wadsworth, 1995).

21. See John Elkington's account in *Cannibals With Forks: The Triple Bottom Line of 21st Century Business* (Gabriola Island, B.C.: New Society, 1998), 53–54.

22. A good description of the 3M project can be obtained from Jim Kotsmith, 3P Program Leader, P.O. Box 33331, 3M Company, St. Paul, MN, 55133–3331.

23. Freeman et al., *Environmentalism*, 14.

24. Roddick sold Body Works to L'Oreal in 2006, netting roughly $200 million; many consider her a model environmentalist/entrepreneur combination. Jon Entine, her most persistent critic, thinks to this day that the Body Works philosophy was more hype and PR than environmentalist substance.

25. The industry is still not happy with the BST fuss; see the Op-Ed piece in the *New York Times*, June 29, 2007 (Henry I. Miller, Hoover Institution, "Don't Cry Over rBST Milk"), insisting that milk prices would go so high that poor people would no longer be able to buy milk if rBST were taken out of use.

26. Paul Hawken Amory Lovins and Hunter Lovins, *Natural Capitalism: Creating the New Industrial Revolution* (Boston: Little Brown, 1999).

27. To President Reagan is attributed the famous motto: "Government won't solve your problems; government *is* the problem."

28. Hawken et al., *Natural Capitalism*, 24.

29. What accounts for the increased demand for super-sized vehicles? Ironically, the most frequent answer given is "increased safety," as if the typical automobile accident were a head-on collision between cars, where, like dueling bison, the heavier one would inevitably crush the lighter one. These large vehicles, top-heavy and prone to rollovers, turn out to be less safe than ordinary-weight cars.

30. Brian Lavendel, "GreenHouse," *Audubon* (March-April 2001): 78.

31. Thomas L. Friedman, *Hot, Flat and Crowded* (New York: Farrar Straus Giroux, 2008), especially chapter 3.

32. Lavendel, "GreenHouse," 27–29.

33. For a start at accounting these services, see Gretchen Daily ed. *Nature's Services: Societal Dependence on Natural Ecosystems* (Washington, D.C.: Island, 1997); also Robert Costanza et al., "The Value of the World's Ecosystems and Natural Capital," *Nature* 387 (1997): 253–260.

34. To quote the entomologists of Cornell University Agricultural School, "Recent reports in the news have highlighted a dramatic loss of honey bee colonies in as many as 24 states, and the number is growing. Honey bees are a critical player in the production of many fruit, vegetable and seed crops grown throughout the country, adding between $8 and $12 billion worth of value to U.S. agriculture each year. Substantial losses, such as are currently being experienced, pose a serious threat to crops that rely on bees for pollination and portend diminished profits for growers and higher prices for consumers at the supermarket," http://www.entomology.cornell.edu/ithacacampus/articles/beecolonycolla pse (accessed September 12, 2007).

35. Barry Commoner, *The Closing Circle: Nature, Man and Technology* (New York: Knopf, 1971).

36. Janine M. Benyus, *Biomimicry: Innovation Inspired by Nature* (New York: Harper Perennial, 2002).

37. William McDonough and Michael Braungart, *Cradle to Cradle: Remaking the Way We Make Things* (New York: Farrar, Straus, and Giroux, 2002).

38. Ray C. Anderson, *Mid-Course Correction: Toward a Sustainable Enterprise: the Interface Model*, self-published, distributed by Chelsea Green (White River Junction, Vt., 1998).

39. For example, the April 2007 issue of *The Ecologist* is devoted to the new consumer-driven business environmentalism, as the "Buyer's Guide to the Future." Colleen O'Connor, "Going Green: Green Revolution May Be Just Around the Corner," *Connecticut Post*, April 9, 2007, B11 (comment "A green lifestyle seems to be growing faster than kudzu"). As global warming increases, and the cost of scarce resources goes up with it, pressure is felt by producers to innovate new ways to make products (Matthew L. Wald and Alexei Barrionuevo, "Chasing a Dream Made of Waste: As Corn Prices Soar, Pressure Builds to Make a Cheap Cellulosic Ethanol," *New York Times*, April 17, 2007, C1, C5), and also on retailers to green up and fly right. Michael Barbaro, "Home Depot to Display an Environmental Label," *New York Times*, April 17, 2007, C1, C4. See also Vivian Marino, "A Starring Role for 'Green' Construction," *New York Times*, April 29, 2007, 28; and Jerry Adler, "Moment of Truth," the lead essay on a special report on "Leadership and the Environment," *Newsweek*, April 16, 2007, 45ff. The thesis of the report, to which the whole issue is dedicated, is that the looming crises are real, but strong responses are coming from surprising quarters, including key political sources. The April 2007 issue of *Connecticut Cottages and Gardens*, "The Green Scene," contains articles about ecofriendly architecture, allergen-free homes, an impassioned campaign against lawns, and new recyclable rugs. The food sections emphasize organic. A new magazine premiered in spring 2007 called *VERDANT, Smarter Choices for Better Living*. Its central thesis, "The Greening of America," was discussed in such articles as "Hydrogen Cars: How Soon?" "No More E-Waste!" "Investing in Clean Tech," and "Healthy Organic Booze?"; Stephanie Strom, "Make Money, Save the World: Businesses and Nonprofits Are Spawning Corporate Hybrids," *New York Times*, May 6, 2007, Sunday Business, sec. 3, 1, 8.

40. Daniel C. Esty and Andrew S. Winston, *Green to Gold: How Smart Companies Use Environmental Strategy to Innovate, Create Value, and Build Competitive Advantage* (New Haven, Conn.: Yale University Press, 2006).

41. See William McDonough, "A Boat for Thoreau," *Environmental Challenges to Business*, Ruffin Series #2, a publication of the Society for Business Ethics, 2000, 115–134.

42. See Stephanie Strom, "Make Money, Save the World" op.cit.

43. In addition to Jeffrey Sachs, *The End of Poverty: Economic Possibilities for Our Time* (New York: Penguin, 2005), see Noreena Hertz, *The Debt Threat: How Debt Is Destroying The Developing World…and Threatening Us All* (New York: HarperCollins, 2004).

44. See Clive Ponting, *A Green History of the World: The Environment and the Collapse of Great Civilizations* (New York: Penguin, 1991).

45. There are some anthologies edited by biologists and chemists, centering on the notion of agricultural sustainability—Saroja Raman, ed. *Agricultural Sustainability: Principles, Processes and Prospects* (New York: Food Products, 2006); Raymond Poincelot, *Sustainable Horticulture* (Upper Saddle River, N.J.: Prentice Hall, 2004); Charles A. Francis Raymond P. Poincelot, George W. Bird eds. *Developing and Extending Sustainable Agriculture: A New Social Contract* (New York: Food Products Press, 2006)—but nothing by business scholars or ethicists. There is, to my knowledge, only one volume on environmental ethics that is centered on agriculture: Paul B. Thompson, *The Spirit of the Soil: Agriculture and Environmental Ethics* (London: Routledge, 1995). For work on agribusiness (and related topics), look for short articles in Robert Kolb ed. *Encyclopedia of Business Ethics and Society* (Thousand Oaks, Calif.: Sage, 2007), authored by Lisa Newton, Keith Warner, and Dustin Mulvaney.

46. Cited from "Cleaning Up," lead editorial in *The Economist*, June 2–8, 2007, 13.

47. A variety of popular books have addressed the problems caused by agricultural subsidies and documented the rise of the organic/fresh and local food movement. See at

least Michael Pollan, *The Omnivore's Dilemma: A Natural History of Four Meals* (New York: Penguin, 2006), and *In Defense of Food: An Eater's Manifesto* (New York: Penguin, 2008); also Barbara Kingsolver's *Animal, Vegetable, Miracle* (New York: HarperCollins, 2008).

48. I am not aware of the place of this quotation in Brower's works, but it is Patagonia's motto.

SUGGESTED READING

Anderson, Ray C. *Mid-Course Correction: Toward a Sustainable Enterprise.* Self-published, distributed by Chelsea Green. White River Junction, Vt., 1998.

Benyus, Janine M. *Biomimicry: Innovation Inspired by Nature.* New York: Harper Perennial, 2002.

Commoner, Barry. *The Closing Circle: Nature, Man and Technology.* New York: Knopf, 1971.

DesJardins, Joseph R. *Business, Ethics and the Environment: Imagining a Sustainable Future.* Upper Saddle River, N.J.: Pearson Prentice Hall, 2007.

Elkington, John. *Cannibals with Forks: The Triple Bottom Line of 21st Century Business.* Gabriola Island, B.C.: New Society, 1998.

Esty, Daniel C., and Andrew S. Winston. *Green to Gold: How Smart Companies Use Environmental Strategy to Innovate, Create Value, and Build Competitive Advantage.* New Haven, Conn.: Yale University Press, 2006.

Freeman, R. Edward, Jessica Pierce, and Richard H. Dodd. *Environmentalism and the New Logic of Business: How Firms Can Be Profitable and Leave Our Children a Living Planet.* New York: Oxford University Press, 2000.

Harvard Business Review on Business and the Environment. Boston: Harvard Business School Press, 2000.

Hawken, Paul, Amory Lovins, and L. Hunter Lovins. *Natural Capitalism: Creating the Next Industrial Revolution.* Boston: Little Brown, 1999.

McDonough, William, and Michael Braungart. *Cradle to Cradle: Remaking the Way We Make Things.* New York: Farrar, Straus, and Giroux, 2002.

Nattrass, Brian and Mary Altomare. *The Natural Step For Business: Wealth, Ecology and the Evolutionary Corporation.* Gabriola Island, B.C.: New Society, 1999.

Newton, Lisa H. *Business Ethics and the Natural Environment.* Malden, Mass.: Blackwell, 2005.

———. *Ethics and Sustainability: Sustainable Development and the Moral Life.* Upper Saddle River, N.J.: Pearson Prentice Hall, 2003.

Pollan, Michael. *In Defense of Food: An Eater's Manifesto.* New York: Penguin, 2008.

———. *The Omnivore's Dilemma: A Natural History of Four Meals.* New York: Penguin, 2007.

Ponting, Clive. *A Green History of the World: the Environment and the Collapse of Great Civilization.* New York: Penguin, 1991.

Roodman, David Malin. *The Natural Wealth of Nations: Harnessing the Market for the Environment.* New York: Norton, 1998.

Sagoff, Mark. *Price, Principle, and the Environment.* New York: Cambridge University Press, 2004.

———. *The Economy of the Earth: Philosophy, Law, and the Environment.* New York: Cambridge University Press, 1988.

Stiglitz, Joseph E. *Globalization and Its Discontents.* New York: Norton, 2002.

CHAPTER 23

THE MIRAGE OF PRODUCT SAFETY

JOHN HASNAS

A mirage is an image of something that appears to exist from a distance, but becomes less distinct as one approaches it, until it dissipates completely. As such, it is a good analog for the concept of product safety. Do businesses have an ethical obligation to produce safe products? At first glance, the question seems to answer itself. How could it be otherwise? However, closer inspection causes one's confidence in the answer to fade; indeed, one begins to doubt whether the question is even meaningful.

This chapter begins by examining the treatment—generally a scarce treatment—that product safety has received in the business ethics literature. I then argue that because safety is a relational concept whose definition is inherently a matter of subjective evaluation, the concept of an obligation to produce safe products is not well formed, and hence that businesses do not have an ethical obligation to produce safe products. I conclude by arguing that businesses do have an ethical obligation not to produce deceptively dangerous products, but that this obligation derives from the general duty of honest dealing, not a distinct duty of product safety.

THE STATE OF THE LITERATURE

The concept of product safety has received surprisingly little direct treatment by business ethicists. This may be because the subject is naturally assimilated into discussions of the obligations that arise from the law of tort. Whatever the reason, consideration of the ethical obligation to provide safe products has been sparse.

Manuel Velaquez provides what may be considered the standard treatment of the subject in his discussion of manufacturers' ethical obligations to consumers.[1] Velaquez describes three distinct accounts of a manufacturer's duty to protect the safety of the consuming public that he labels "the contract view, the 'due care' view, and the social costs view."[2] The contract view holds that a manufacturer's duty to provide safe products is determined by the contract between the manufacturer and the purchaser, and consists of the "duty to provide a product whose use involves *no greater risks* than those the seller *expressly* communicates to the buyer or those the seller *implicitly* communicates by the implicit claims made when marketing the product for a use whose normal risk level is well known."[3] The due care view holds that in addition to honoring all express and implied claims of product safety, a manufacturer "has a duty to exercise due care to prevent others from being injured by the product, *even if the manufacturer explicitly disclaims such responsibility and the buyer agrees to the disclaimer*," where due care is understood as "the care that a reasonable person could have foreseen would be necessary to prevent others from being harmed by use of the product."[4] The social costs view holds that "a manufacturer should pay the costs of *any* injuries sustained through any defects in the product, *even when the manufacturer exercised all due care in the design and manufacture of the product and has taken all reasonable precautions to warn users of every foreseen danger*."[5] To the extent that the social cost view is an account of a manufacturer's duty to provide safe products rather than a theory of who should bear the costs of accidents, it invests manufacturers with an absolute duty to provide products free from injury-producing defects.

Velasquez's alternative accounts of manufacturers' duty to protect consumers is frequently cited in business ethics literature.[6] Yet, surprisingly little has been written in the effort to determine which of the three views is correct. An exception to this is supplied by George Brenkert, who has argued in favor of the social costs theory.[7] Brenkert argues that a duty to compensate consumers injured by defective products regardless of fault on the part of manufacturers can be derived from the commitment to equality of opportunity inherent in the capitalist system and the need to maintain a market in which all parties benefit from voluntary exchange. With a little expansion, this can be shaped into a claim that manufacturers have a duty to provide products free from injury-producing defects. However, other than Brenkert, few business ethicists seem to have addressed this point directly.

In what follows, I provide an argument for an approach that resembles Velasquez's contract theory. However, my argument consists of neither a direct defense of the contract theory nor an attack on the due care or social costs theories. I contend that unless one is willing to tolerate excessive and undue interference with individual autonomy, any theory of product safety will collapse into something like the contract view.

THE CONCEPT OF PRODUCT SAFETY

It is not novel to assert that product safety is a relative concept—that is, that safety is not a property of products *per se*, but has different meanings in different circumstances. However, given that product safety is actually shorthand for a complex set of relationships among risks, harms, costs, benefits, and persons, the assertion may be an understatement.

Safety is a concept that varies along at least these five dimensions, each of which could use some specification. In the context of product safety, risk refers to a possible future harm, where harm is defined as a setback to interests, particularly in life, health, and welfare. Expressions such as minimal risk, reasonable risk, and high risk are often used to refer to the chance of a harm's occurrence—its probability—but may also refer to the severity of the harm if it occurs—its magnitude. With regard to product safety, harm usually refers to a physical injury, but may include psychological injury or purely economic damage as well. Costs refer to the resources that must be expended to attain a benefit and the negative consequences of pursuing and realizing that benefit. In the context of product safety, costs consist of the sacrifices made in the attempt to prevent injury to the users of commercial products. In contrast to risks, costs are usually expressed in monetary terms, as is typical of cost-benefit analyses. Benefits refer to the value that can be derived from the use of the relevant commercial product—the improvement to one's life that the product provides. Like costs, benefits are often measured in monetary terms, although they need not be. Finally, the value provided by commercial products and the potential for injury varies from person to person.

Risk is an irredeemably relative concept. Products can pose anything from an infinitesimal risk of harm, such as a bottle of pure water, to a near certain risk of death, as in the case of a bottle of agitated nitroglycerine. Many of the products commonly used in developed countries pose only small risks of serious harm. How much risk renders a product unsafe? A risk of 1 in 10,000? 1 in 1,000? 1 in 100? Cigarettes, the archetypical unsafe product, pose a 321 in 10,000 risk that a fifty-year-old man who has smoked a pack of cigarettes a day for thirty years will develop lung cancer in the succeeding ten years as compared with a 16 in 10,000 risk for a nonsmoker.[8] So a 305 in 10,000 increase in the risk of serious harm must be sufficient to render a product unsafe, right?[9]

Talk of risk in the abstract is pointless, however. Whether a risk is acceptable or not depends on a host of exogenous factors, such as the benefits provided by the product, the cost of avoiding the harm, the magnitude of the potential harm, who may be harmed, and the circumstances in which the product is used. Consider benefits first. A steak knife presents a much greater risk of harm than a child's butter knife, but it provides a significant benefit to those interested in eating steak. Anticancer drugs can be extremely toxic and pose a high risk of harm or death, but if they work, the benefit they confer is life itself. Those who consider cigarettes to be inherently unsafe do so because they evaluate the benefits cigarettes provide, for example, physical pleasure, the psychological feeling of being "cool," and so on, as insignificant in comparison to the elevated risk of death from disease later in life. Soldiers or others facing a high likelihood of an early death from nonnatural causes may weigh those benefits differently.

The acceptability of a risk also inherently depends upon the cost of avoiding the potential harm. Many serious injuries from automobile accidents have been avoided at relatively low cost by installing seat belts in cars. Many more such injuries could be avoided by building cars like tanks, but this is a relatively expensive proposition. As the costs incurred to avoid injuries increase, the benefits of the safer products become affordable to a decreasing number of people. At some point, the improvements in product safety completely consume the benefits of using the product. How do we determine the point at which it costs too much to make a product safer?

Further, although many products pose some risk of death or serious bodily harm, most pose significantly greater risks of less serious, minor injury. What magnitude of harm renders a product unsafe? To be safe, does a product merely have to reduce its risk of serious harm? Is a product that poses the risk of serious bruising unsafe? How do we compare the safety of rollerblades, which pose relatively high risks of cuts, scrapes, and broken bones, with that of small, two-passenger airplanes, which pose a smaller risk of death? Do paper manufacturers have an obligation to strive to eliminate the possibility of paper cuts?

Finally, there is the question of who may be harmed. It is one thing to design a product with the safety of the purchaser, who receives the product new and with instructions, in mind. It is another to design it with the safety of any potential user in mind. It is yet another to design it with the safety of the members of society at large in mind. Automobiles have been made much safer for drivers and passengers over the past several decades. This has had the unanticipated consequence of making the world less safe for pedestrians as more secure drivers exercise less care in driving.[10] As economist Gordon Tullock has pointed out, if the purpose of automotive design is to maximize the number of lives saved, the most effective safety device is a sharp dagger mounted on the steering column and pointed directly at the driver's chest.[11]

AN ECONOMIC CONCEPTION OF SAFETY

For there to be an obligation to produce safe products, there must be a criterion of what constitutes a safe product. Given the relativistic nature of the concept of safety, is it possible to provide such a criterion?

An economist might have no trouble answering this question. He or she might respond, "Just place the burden of taking precautions against injury on the least cost avoider."[12] Either the manufacturer or the consumer of a product or both may take steps to prevent injuries. Manufacturers can design their products to make injuries less likely to occur. For example, the manufacturer of power saws can install hand-guards and kill switches to reduce the likelihood that users will be cut. By the same token, consumers may take precautions to protect themselves from harm. For example, the purchaser of a power saw can wear goggles whenever using it.

Whether precautions are taken by the manufacturer or the consumer, they are costly. Hand-guards and kill switches constitute expenses for power saw manufacturers; goggles constitute an expense for power saw users. But such precautions are usually not equally costly for manufacturers and consumers. It is relatively expensive for drivers to install seat belts in their automobiles, whereas economies of scale make it considerably less so for automakers to incorporate seat belts into the design of their cars. It would be exceedingly difficult and expensive for parents to have to monitor their children's behavior sufficiently to prevent them from playing on an unfenced railroad turntable, but exceedingly inexpensive for the railroad to install a simple lock that prevents the turntable from moving and injuring children whose limbs may get caught in the joints.[13] Automakers can probably do little to prevent injuries to jaywalking pedestrians no matter how much they spend, but pedestrians can protect themselves virtually cost-free by refraining from jaywalking.

An economist would point out that the most efficient way of preventing injuries is to place the burden of avoiding them on the party that can do so at the lowest cost.[14] When manufacturers can protect consumers from injury more cheaply than the consumers can protect themselves, they should do so. Thus, because building hand-guards and kill switches into power saws protects users against cuts more cheaply than any measures power saw users can take to protect themselves, manufacturers should install them. However, when it is cheaper for consumers to take care to protect themselves, they should do so. Thus, because purchasing and wearing goggles is a less expensive way to prevent eye injuries when using a power saw than adding cumbersome shields to the saws themselves, manufacturers should not add such shields. To an economist, therefore, a safe product is one that incorporates all cost-justified precautions, that is, one designed to avoid all injuries for which the manufacturer is the least cost avoider.

Is there any reason to believe that the economic conception of product safety corresponds to the ethical one? Is there an ethical obligation to produce products designed to avoid all and only those injuries for which the manufacturer is the least cost avoider? If the maximization of social wealth is the summum bonum, the answer may be yes. Injuries are a drain on society's material resources. Preventing as many of them as possible in the most cost-effective way tends to maximize these resources. If one believes that there is a fundamental and overriding moral duty to maximize social wealth, one can argue that manufacturers are ethically obligated to sell only those products that conform to the economic definition of safety. Thus, for thoroughgoing utilitarians who define the good in terms of material welfare, there is no need to read further. The question has been answered.

However, there are well-known objections to this form of utilitarianism. As Steven Kelman has pointed out, it leaves no room for the commitment to moral principles or the recognition of individual moral entitlements or rights.[15] If social wealth would be maximized by killing an unproductive member of society and distributing his or her organs to five more productive people who need transplants to survive, the utilitarian must concede that there is an ethical obligation to do so. In addition, it assumes that the only thing of value is material wealth, implying that health, peace of mind, and even life itself have no intrinsic value. Under this form of utilitarianism, there is nothing that cannot be sacrificed for a material improvement to society—nothing that possesses a dignity and therefore is "not for sale."[16]

For those who do not accept these implications and thus have reason to doubt the correctness of a purely materialistic utilitarianism, one's ethical obligations with regard to product safety remain an open question. Further, in rejecting this form of utilitarianism, one is not rejecting the importance of cost considerations. There is no need to deny that maximizing social wealth can, all things considered, be a good thing, in order to deny that it is the *only* good thing.

Are there any other grounds on which to base the claim that the ethical conception of product safety is identical to the economic conception? Perhaps, but they are not readily apparent. It is difficult to see how deontological, perfectionist, or pluralistic ethical theories can lead to the conclusion that the ethical value of an individual's safety is identical to its monetary value. For example, Kant's injunction to treat all persons as ends in themselves and never merely as a means seems unlikely to lead to a conclusion that the value of an individual's safety should be determined purely by its effect on collective material well-being. Even preference utilitarians might struggle to demonstrate that a conception of safety that maximizes material wealth is equivalent to one that maximizes the satisfaction of human desires. It is possible that in the case of product safety, all other ethically relevant considerations cancel each other out, and cost avoidance is left as the ethically determinative factor.[17] But until we have reason to believe that this is the case, we should view the claim that the ethical and the economic conceptions of product safety are identical with some skepticism.

A LEGAL CONCEPTION OF SAFETY

A lawyer may give a different answer to the question of what constitutes product safety. He or she may assert that manufacturers have an obligation to manufacture their products with the degree of care necessary to protect the users of their products against unreasonable risk of injury—meaning, in legal language, to exercise reasonable care. The problem with this response is that it merely pushes the enquiry back one step. To know what constitutes a safe product, one must now know what constitutes reasonable care.

Lawyers have two distinct conceptions of reasonable care, specifying it either in terms of "optimal deterrence" or "corrective justice." Unfortunately, neither specification advances our understanding of manufacturers' ethical obligations. Under the optimal deterrence approach, reasonable care consists of taking all cost-justified precautions.[18] However, this definition merely identifies reasonable care with the economic definition of safety. And we have just seen that we have, as yet, no clear reason to believe that this corresponds to the ethical definition of safety. Hence, this definition of reasonable care cannot advance our analysis. Under the corrective justice approach, reasonable care consists of exercising the degree of care necessary to avoid all injuries caused by wrongful conduct.[19] However, this definition is circular. We are seeking to determine the extent to which manufacturers are ethically obligated to prevent injury to the users of their products. It does not advance our understanding to answer that manufacturers are ethically obligated to avoid all wrongfully caused injuries. Which injuries are wrongfully caused is precisely what we are trying to determine. Under this definition, reasonable care provides a synonym for product safety, not an explication of it.

The Irrelevance of the Standard of Safety in a Market

Another resolution of the problem of the proper standard of product safety is, Who cares? This response derives from the observation that in a market the standard of safety serves as a default condition that manufacturers and consumers are free to alter at will.[20]

Assume that we find a compelling argument for the conclusion that the ethically appropriate standard of safety is *caveat venditor*—that the manufacturer must take all possible precautions to prevent injury to consumers. We now know that manufacturers must bear 100 percent of the burden of protecting the public against injury from their products, and the members of the public need take no precautions to protect themselves. To comply with this standard, manufacturers will have to incorporate features designed to prevent all preventable injuries into the design of their products, rendering them considerably more expensive. This may be an acceptable state of affairs for the most risk-averse members of the public who are happy to pay more to ensure their safety. However, it will not be acceptable to those who are less risk-averse and would prefer to incur some risk of injury in return for less expensive products. It will also not be acceptable to the less affluent members of the public who have been priced out of the market. The members of these groups will offer to waive their right to be protected by the manufacturers in return for more affordable products. The competitive forces of the market will cause manufacturers or entrepreneurs to attempt to satisfy this unmet demand by offering less safe, but less expensive, products to those willing to waive their entitlement to complete protection against injury. Before long, products offering widely varying amounts of protection against injury at a variety of price points would be available. A *caveat venditor* standard may initially require all cars to be as safe as the top of the line Volvo, but there can be little doubt that a significant portion of the car-buying public would waive some of this protection to avoid paying the price of such a vehicle. Some might even waive enough of it to permit purchase of a Volkswagen Beetle.

Now assume that we find a compelling argument for the conclusion that the ethically appropriate standard of safety is *caveat emptor*—that consumers must take all necessary precautions to protect themselves against injury from dangerous products. The members of the public now bear 100 percent of the burden of protecting themselves, and manufacturers need take no precautions to ensure the safety of the public. Freed of the obligation to include expensive safety features, manufacturers will be able to offer their products to the public at considerably reduced prices. This may be an acceptable state of affairs to the most ruggedly individualistic members of the public who are happy to have the responsibility to protect themselves. However, it will not be acceptable to those who are more risk-averse and would prefer to pay more for less dangerous products. Again, the competitive forces of the market will cause manufacturers or entrepreneurs to attempt to satisfy this unmet demand by offering less dangerous, but more expensive, products to those willing to pay the premium for increased safety.[21] Before long, products offering widely varying amounts of protection against injury at a variety of price points would be available. For example, even though federal and state governments inspect and regulate the nation's food and water supplies, a significant proportion of consumers are willing to purchase an increased level of safety by buying bottled water and shopping at organic groceries, such as Whole Foods.

Finally, assume we find a compelling argument for the conclusion that the ethically appropriate standard of safety requires manufacturers to exercise reasonable care to protect consumers against injury by their product, whatever reasonable care turns out to be. Manufacturers and the members of the public must now split the burden of safety precautions. Manufacturers will have to incorporate some features designed to prevent injury into the design of their products, rendering them somewhat more expensive then they would otherwise be. This may be an acceptable state of affairs for the members of the public who have a moderate tolerance for risk and are willing to pay a small premium for increased safety. However, it will not be acceptable to either the rugged individualists, who prefer more personal responsibility and cheaper products, or the intensely risk-averse, who prefer more protection and more expensive products. The competitive forces of the market will cause manufacturers or entrepreneurs to endeavor to satisfy the unmet demand of both groups. Before long, products offering widely varying amounts of protection against injury at a variety of price points would be available.

This line of argument sees the socially accepted standard of safety, whatever it may be, as a starting point from which manufacturers and consumers are free to depart by agreement. Markets allow individuals to purchase the amount of safety each desires and can afford. The importance of the standard of safety that establishes the starting point is not that it determines how much safety the members of the public receive, but that it determines the level of transaction costs the public must bear to attain its preferred distribution of product safety. The standard matters only because the expenses involved in bargaining away from certain starting points may be greater than others. For example, the costs of obtaining waivers from the large number of people who will want cheaper products under a *caveat venditor* regime may be greater than the costs of obtaining waivers from the smaller number of people wanting cheaper products under a regime of reasonable care. But apart from transaction costs, it makes no difference which standard society chooses. As long as parties are free to depart from the standard by agreement, who cares what the standard is?

A possible response to this line of argument is that it misses the point of ethical analysis. Ethics, by its very nature, is designed to place restraints on self-interested action in markets. Skeptics may claim that market imperfections mean that the market mechanism cannot be relied upon to produce just results for all parties. In the case of product safety, they may argue that the interests of the poor, who may want greater safety, but cannot afford to pay the premium for it, are not adequately represented. No one should be denied safe products because he or she cannot afford them when the costs of safety can be shifted to manufacturers who can more readily bear them.[22] A substantive ethical standard of safety is necessary precisely to prevent the distribution of product safety that would result from unrestrained bargaining in a market. Therefore, the ethically appropriate standard of product safety cannot be a mere default condition, but must require manufacturers to supply the appropriate amount of safety regardless of any agreement to accept less by the consumer.

Whether one agrees or disagrees with the response, it requires some measure by which to determine what constitutes the "appropriate amount of safety." But there's the rub. For other than the economic conception, it is not clear that there is any useful *objective* conception of safety.[23]

THE INHERENT SUBJECTIVITY
OF PRODUCT SAFETY

We began by noting that product safety can vary along at least five dimensions: risk, benefit, cost, magnitude of harm, and person. The problem with identifying an ethically appropriate realm of product safety is not merely that safety varies along these five dimensions, but that three of them, namely, benefit, cost, and person, are inherently subjective. For this reason, it is difficult for all but a certain class of utilitarians to supply an objective definition of product safety.

Benefits are always benefits to particular individuals and must always be determined in the context of the individual's life plans and value schemes. A hang glider may provide massive benefits to one who loves the feeling of floating free and observing lovely scenery. It provides no benefit to one who has a fear of heights. Convertible sports cars apparently provide sufficient benefits to certain young singles and those undergoing mid-life crises to compensate for their relatively lower safety rating. They provide no benefit to the soccer mom with three children. Breast implants may provide intense benefits to one whose dream in life is to be a Playboy centerfold or to one who has had a mastectomy. They provide no benefit to a woman satisfied with her body's appearance.

Costs are similarly subjective. The side effects of chemotherapy are acceptable costs to a relatively young cancer patient with a good chance of survival. They may be unacceptable to an elderly patient whose life can only be briefly extended. Affluent parents may consider the costs of "child-proofing" their home to be acceptable. Less wealthy parents do not and prefer to exercise heightened personal vigilance. The cost of a ski helmet may be trivial to one who loves to ski fast, but unacceptable to the more restrained skier who finds helmets inconvenient and uncomfortable.

The same is true with regard to persons, whose varying physical characteristics and differing relationships to the product's use mean that products will inevitably affect different persons differently. Air bags make automobiles safer for most people, but more dangerous for very small and very large people.[24] Better football helmets made football safer for the wearer, but as the more protected players learned to use their heads as battering rams, the sport became more dangerous for those being blocked and tackled.[25] Vioxx was a safer anti-inflammatory medication for those susceptible to stomach bleeding, but was less safe for those without that sensitivity.[26]

The basic difficulty with providing an objective standard of product safety is that safety consists of protection against an intolerable level of risk. But since tolerability varies from person to person, there is no conception of safety that is independent of the risk preferences of individuals. What standard of protection against intolerable risk could an ethicist advocate that prevented individuals from bargaining for the level of risk that they are willing to tolerate? If safety is inherently a product of individual preferences, how can one construct a standard that guarantees safety while simultaneously frustrating these preferences?

One is always free to ignore the essential nature of safety and simply propose a regulatory standard designed to realize other ends. For example, utilitarians who subscribe to an objective definition of the good that is not dependent on individual autonomy or preferences are not interested in safety per se, but in maximizing their prescribed ends. Hence, a utilitarian who defines good in terms of material wealth has no trouble demonstrating that the proper standard for product safety is that which is attained by placing the burden of precautions on the party that can prevent the relevant harm at the lowest cost. Similarly, a utilitarian who defined the good as the preservation of human life without regard to individual assessments of its quality would identify the proper level of product safety as that which maximizes collective life-years—an approach that makes the previously mentioned Tullock safety device for automobiles look pretty good. A Benthamite who defines good in terms of pleasure would contend that the proper level of product safety is that which maximizes the pleasure experienced by members of society—a standard that places cigarettes in a whole new light.

All such proposals will rise or fall with the adequacy of the proposed utilitarian standard on which they are based. However, as previously noted, there is reason to doubt the soundness of such naturalistic forms of utilitarianism.[27] Beyond this, I have nothing to say other than that I am skeptical of any ethical theory that places no value on either the satisfaction of human desires or human autonomy. Yet any theory that allows respect for individual preferences or autonomy to play a significant role will have difficulty specifying an objective standard of product safety.

For example, consider preference utilitarianism, which defines the good as the satisfaction of human desires and posits a fundamental ethical obligation to maximize satisfied human desires. Since safety consists of protection against intolerable risk, the proper standard of product safety for a preference utilitarian would be one under which as few people as possible are exposed to risks they find intolerable, consistent with the minimum frustration of people's other desires. Preference utilitarians could argue for a standard under which most people receive the amount of safety they are comfortable with and the number of dissatisfied outliers is minimized—perhaps a somewhat amorphous reasonable care standard. But at most, this provides an argument for an initial default condition. Preference utilitarians may be able to show that the correct *starting point* is the standard under which most people's desire for safety is satisfied. However, this cannot provide an argument for a standard of product safety that restrains individual manufacturers and consumers from bargaining for more or less protection against injury. Every such bargain would result in either a greater amount of protection against intolerable risk or a smaller amount of frustrated desires for cheaper products, and hence, a morally superior outcome. Thus, for preference utilitarians the ethically appropriate standard of safety would mirror the standard determined by the market.[28] And this difficulty is likely to be even more pronounced for any nonconsequentialist ethical theory that either takes seriously the injunction to treat individuals as ends in themselves and therefore respect their autonomously arrived at decisions[29] or values individual self-actualization or self-perfection.

To argue that ethics requires us to prevent individuals in a market from bargaining for the level of product safety that they want, one must either reject the subjective conception of safety as protection against intolerable risk or show that something other than the market mechanism does a better job of delivering the desired level of protection. The former approach requires one to have a conception of the level of protection against risk that individuals should have whether they find it intolerable or not. Because this requires continual interference with individuals' value choices and life plans, I reject this approach. But what about the latter approach? Is there reason to believe that the market is not the best mechanism for providing individuals with protection against intolerable risk?

REJECTION OF A GENERAL DUTY
OF PRODUCT SAFETY

Can one argue that there should be restrictions on the ability of individuals to bargain for the level of product safety they find tolerable in order to better provide precisely that level of safety? If one can show that individuals are not the best judges of the level of safety that they desire, the answer is yes. But to do this, one would have to show either that individuals do not know what they really desire or that certain features of the market make individuals unable to form accurate assessments of what will provide their desired level of safety.

I believe the first strategy to be unavailing. The claim that people do not know what they really desire is frequently misapplied, and when it is not, it is irrelevant. It is misapplied when it is used to mean not that people do not know what they desire, but that people do not desire what they should. Critics of individual choice contend that if people were properly enlightened, they would choose differently than they do. Such critics might contend, for instance, that nineteen-year-old college students would not choose to smoke if they truly appreciated the relative value of long-term health and short-term physical pleasure. Some who make such claims assert more than merely that people do not have sufficient information to choose correctly or that they are choosing irrationally given their own values and goals; rather, they assert that people choose incorrectly because they do not value things correctly— that they do not appreciate what is truly good or truly in their best interest. To paraphrase John Stuart Mill, one who would choose the life of the satisfied fool over that of the dissatisfied Socrates does so because he or she does not appreciate the "intrinsic superiority" of the latter.[30] Since anyone who correctly perceived the value of things would choose the more valuable, one who chooses the less valuable does not really know what he or she desires.

I characterize this approach as a misapplication because it is essentially a disingenuous way of smuggling in an ostensibly objective definition of the good under the guise of respect for autonomy. Assuming that, despite their expressed preferences, people *really* desire what is truly good eliminates rather than vindicates the role of individual autonomy. Further, this move is useful only under the assumption that one possesses the correct objective conception of the good. But in the present context, this is precisely what we are *not* assuming.

The claim that people do not know what they really desire need not be misapplied, however. People frequently make decisions that do not advance their own values or life goals. People often confront complex situations in which it is difficult either to determine how the instant decision will affect their overall goals or to integrate it into their overall scheme of values. Indeed, people's values schemes may be internally inconsistent or poorly integrated, making it exceedingly difficult for them to make rational decisions that advance their own ends.

These observations, while undeniably true, are also irrelevant (unless they refer to the informational asymmetries discussed below). There is no practical alternative for improving the outcome. Individuals may be poor judges of what they desire, but they are nonetheless the best judges. How can one human being gain access to another's intimate values and life plans? How can one attain greater understanding of what another person genuinely wants? Even if one could obtain such access and understanding, what could he or she do with it? Every individual has his or her own scheme of values and life plans. Each strikes his or her unique balance between decreasing risk of harm and increasing price. There is no reason to believe that these balances are similar enough for one to devise a set of general restrictions on individual choice that will result in all or even most individuals obtaining the level of protection they really desire. Although it is theoretically possible to design a set of custom-made restrictions for each individual that would produce this result, this has no practical value in designing a general standard of product safety. How can businesses be required to research each of its customers' values, goals, and life plans sufficiently to understand the balance between protection and cost that a specific customer really desires in purchasing their products better than the individual? Yet, this is what would be necessary for businesses to paternalistically refrain from making sales that are contrary to their customers' "real will."

This leaves the second strategy of showing that certain features of the market make individuals unable to form accurate assessments of what will provide their desired level of safety. One such argument is based on the claim that significant information asymmetries exist between manufacturers and consumers that make it impossible for consumers to become knowledgeable enough to make appropriate decisions about product safety. This claim asserts that contemporary products are so sophisticated and complex that the ordinary consumer is unable to understand how they work or appreciate the dangers they pose. As long ago as 1973, it was argued that the modern product's

> functional validity and usefulness often depend on the application of electronic, chemical, or hydraulic principles far beyond the ken of the average consumer. Advances in the technologies of materials, of processes, of operational means have put it almost entirely out of the reach of the consumer to comprehend why or how the article operates, and thus even farther out of his reach to detect when there may be a defect or a danger present in its design or manufacture. In today's world, it is often only the manufacturer who can fairly be said to know and to understand when an article is suitably designed and safely made for its intended purpose.[31]

The argument proceeds by claiming that the informational asymmetry renders consumers unable to protect their own interests. Hence, they are vulnerable to overreaching by manufacturers: "Because manufacturers are in a more advantaged position, they have a duty to take special 'care' to ensure that consumers' interests are not harmed by the products that they offer them... *even if the manufacturer explicitly disclaims such responsibility and the buyer agrees to the disclaimer.*"[32] Here then is an argument for placing restrictions on individuals' ability to bargain for a desired level of product safety.

It is a rather poor argument, however. Informational asymmetry between manufacturer and consumer is not a modern phenomenon, but a function of the division of labor that dates back centuries if not longer.[33] The truth of the claim that not every individual can understand the workings of complex products does not imply that information about the quality and safety of complex products is unavailable to such individuals or that consumers have no way of judging the relative level of risk associated with a product. For decades, quality assurance and reporting organizations such as *Consumer Reports*, Underwriters' Laboratory, and *Good Housekeeping* have supplied the product information necessary for consumers to protect their interests and performed independent evaluations of the relative safety of products. Sears became one of the nation's leading retailers by testing all the products it sold and providing an assurance of quality and safety. Today, product safety information and evaluations are only a click away on the Internet, and it is even easier for consumers to overcome informational asymmetries.[34] It may be true that utilizing these resources imposes costs in time, money, and effort on consumers, but this does not imply that it is impossible for consumers to protect their interests. The most dangerous and complex product most consumers buy is the automobile, and, like me, most consumers have only a vague idea of what takes place under the hood. Yet we have no trouble distinguishing relatively safe cars from relatively unsafe ones. It is no coincidence that the more dangerous and complex the product, for example, power tools, the more frequently it tends to be reviewed by both the public and private consumer protection services.

However, even if this were false, and consumers were unable to obtain the information necessary to make safety assessments, the most that this would imply is that manufacturers have an obligation to furnish the information in a sufficiently accessible form to allow consumers to make an informed choice, not that manufacturers are obligated to paternalistically make the choice for the consumer. If the requirement of informed consent is adequate to protect patients' interests when they are making life and death medical decisions, it should certainly be adequate to protect consumers' interests when shopping.

Are there any other features of the market that justify placing restrictions on individuals' ability to bargain for the level of product safety they desire? None are readily apparent. There are certainly many critiques of the market. For example, critics point out that in markets suppliers respond only to *economic* demands. It is claimed that this is unfair to the poor who, because they cannot afford to pay the "safety premium," are unable to obtain the level of product safety that they desire. Such critics may further point out that because the poor are less likely to have the money, education, and sophistication required to utilize safety-reporting resources such as *Consumer Reports* and Underwriters Laboratories, they really do labor under an informational asymmetry that renders them unable to form accurate assessments of what will provide their desired level of safety.[35]

In the present context, however, such observations are *non sequiturs*. The market may unfairly prevent the poor from obtaining the level of product safety they desire, and justice may require that something be done to rectify the situation. Perhaps manufacturers should be required to provide the poor with safety information at no cost to alleviate the effect of informational asymmetries.[36] But whatever should be done, individuals should not be prevented from bargaining for the safety-to-price ratio they prefer, *especially if this restriction is coupled with a heightened standard of care for manufacturers*. It is difficult to see how a rule that prevents the poor from voluntarily bargaining for cheaper products while simultaneously requiring manufacturers to make more expensive products can redress any injustice to the poor. It may be unfortunate or even unjust that a carpenter is too poor to afford a power saw with hand-guards and kill switches. But if the carpenter is willing to run an increased risk of injury to purchase a cheaper saw without the safeguards, how does it correct any injustice to impede manufacturers from selling such a saw to him or her?

Product safety depends on several inherently subjective elements. What constitutes a safe product varies from individual to individual on the basis of how much benefit the individual receives, how much cost the individual incurs, and the status of the individual, for example, driver or pedestrian, arthritis sufferer with or without susceptibility to stomach bleeding. For manufacturers to have a general obligation to provide safe products that cannot be altered by the mutual consent of consumers and the manufacturers, there must be a set of objectively specifiable conditions that would protect all or most people against what they considered intolerable risk more effectively then those people could protect themselves by bargaining for their desired level of risk in the market. I am unable to identify any such set of conditions. Hence, I conclude that manufacturers have no general obligation to provide safe products.

THE DUTY NOT TO PRODUCE DECEPTIVELY DANGEROUS PRODUCTS

Does the lack of an obligation to meet an objective standard of product safety mean that manufacturers are free to disregard consumers' interest in being protected against intolerable risk? Certainly not. All manufacturers are under a duty not to produce deceptively dangerous products.

Human beings enter the marketplace vested with a wide array of moral obligations. One of the most fundamental of these is the obligation to respect the autonomy of others. And one of the most important manifestations of this obligation is the duty to refrain from using deception to override the free will of one's fellows. In markets, individuals constantly use each other as means to their desired ends. There is nothing morally objectionable about this as long as all parties obtain the knowing, voluntary consent of the others when doing so. However, employing deception and trickery to obtain fraudulent consent uses others *merely* as means to one's own ends. Subverting other human beings' ability to realize their autonomously chosen ends in this way is a quintessential violation of the obligation to respect the personhood of others. Hence, there is a basic obligation not to employ fraudulent practices in one's business activities, that is, a fundamental duty of honest dealing.

The same obligation can be derived from the nature of market activity itself. Markets do not function well in the face of widespread fraud. The costs associated with having to protect oneself against active misrepresentation and concealment of material information in every business transaction are sufficient to prevent the formation of many wealth-generating contracts. Unless contracting parties have a duty not to misrepresent material information (or conceal material nonpublic information), markets become inefficient. Hence, the obligation to refrain from fraud, which is the basic obligation of honest dealing, has been described as part of the "implicit morality of the market itself: the moral rules without which markets fail."[37]

Applying this fundamental obligation of honest dealing to the field of product safety yields a duty for manufacturers not to misrepresent the dangers associated with the use of their products. Manufacturers may not be obligated to make many representations about a product's safety, but whatever representations they make must be true. Cigarette makers may ethically sell cigarettes despite their addictive properties and the increased risk of disease associated with their use. They may advertise them as tasting good and providing a pleasant experience. They may disclaim all warranties of product safety. However, they may not claim that they are good for your health, or that they are not addictive, or that they do not increase the user's risk of cancer and heart disease.

The obligation of honest dealing thus requires manufacturers to refrain from fraudulently exposing consumers to risks associated with the use of their products. Does it yield any more extensive duty to protect consumers against intolerable risk? Generally speaking, the answer is no. Neither the duty to respect autonomy nor the nature of markets requires contractors to affirmatively protect other parties' interests. One does not fail to respect another's autonomy by not protecting that person against his or her own lack of industry or failure to exercise proper care. Further, for markets to function efficiently, it is not necessary for contracting parties to ensure that their negotiating partners have exercised due diligence. When all relevant information is publicly obtainable, each party is able to protect his or her own interests. Requiring each party to do the other's homework as well as his or her own creates a wasteful duplication of effort and thus, greater inefficiency. Hence, no duty to see that one's contracting partner is adequately informed can be derived from the nature of a well-functioning market. Ordinarily, the parties to a contract are required to bear their own research costs.

Nevertheless, a reasonable argument can be made that manufacturers do have a more extensive duty—a duty to warn the public about nonobvious risks associated with the use of their products. Although consumers are generally able to obtain the information necessary to protect their own interests, there are at least two circumstances in which this is not the case. The first is when the information is not publicly available—when manufacturers are aware of significant risks posed by their products *that are not detectible through independent testing*. The second is when the consumer is a member of a vulnerable subgroup of the population who is either too impoverished to shoulder the required research costs or too undereducated to effectively utilize the available research tools. In these cases, the informational asymmetry argument previously discussed[38] has real bite.

These cases demonstrate that the duty of honest dealing requires more than merely refraining from fraudulent representations. Intentionally concealing material, *nonpublic* safety information from consumers can subvert consumers' ability to realize their autonomously chosen ends and undermine market efficiency just as much as outright falsehoods. Thus, the duty of honest dealing requires manufacturers to disclose such information before marketing their products. Coca-Cola may ethically conceal its formula for Coke as a trade secret. But if it knows that the formula contains a chemical that may produce an allergic reaction in some users and is not easily detectable, it must reveal this fact to the public.

Furthermore, if manufacturers wish to market their products to vulnerable consumers known by the manufacturers to be unable to bear the research costs necessary to protect their interests, respect for their potential customers' autonomy requires the manufacturers to assume these costs.[39] The simplest way to do this is not to purchase subscriptions to *Consumer Reports* and tutors for vulnerable potential customers, but to inform them of any material, nonobvious risks posed by the products. Thus, manufacturers who wish to market their products to impoverished, undereducated, or otherwise vulnerable consumers may be said to have a duty to warn such consumers of nonobvious risks. But since it is easier and cheaper simply to issue a blanket warning than to attempt to warn only the vulnerable, this is equivalent to saying that manufacturers have a general duty to warn the public at large.

It appears that a duty for manufacturers not only to refrain from misrepresenting the risks associated with their products but also to warn consumers against any nonobvious risks attendant upon their use may be derived from the basic ethical obligation of honest dealing. When these duties are satisfied, consumers are in a position to decide for themselves what level of risk they wish to bear in return for less expensive products. These duties, then, which may be jointly described as the duty not to produce deceptively dangerous products, identifies manufacturers' obligations to protect the safety of their consumers. Succinctly expressed, manufacturers have no duty to paternalistically interfere with consumers' autonomous choices about how to balance the risks associated with a product's use against its expense, but, on the contrary, have a duty not to deceptively (or otherwise) undermine consumers' ability to make such choices.[40]

CONCLUSION

I have argued that manufacturers have no general duty to provide safe products. Because safety is an inherently subjective concept, there is no general standard that can guarantee each consumer his or her desired level of safety at a price he or she would be willing to pay. Only a market can do this. This explains why the duty that manufacturers have—the duty not to produce deceptively dangerous products— derives directly from the basic requirement for a well-functioning market, which is the duty of honest dealing.

This is a fairly negative conclusion and one that may be unsatisfying to some. But perhaps a slightly more positive implication can be drawn. Recall that when we considered the economic conception of safety, we noted the possibility that if all other ethically relevant considerations canceled each other out, cost avoidance could be the ethically determinative factor.[41] This is very close to the actual situation. As long as manufacturers and individual consumers are free to bargain for the safety-to-price ratio they mutually prefer, the initial standard of safety is basically irrelevant. There is, then, no moral imperative to choose one general standard of safety over another. In such a case, the utilitarian gain that can be realized may justify selecting the economic conception of safety as the initial default condition.[42] Thus, we can say that when consumers have expressed no preference for a higher or lower level of protection, manufacturers should take all and only those precautions for which they are the least cost avoiders. Although this does not provide a substantive standard of product safety, it does provide a very useful starting point. For if we begin at an economically efficient point and insist that any departure from it be made by mutual consent where manufacturers have both taken steps not to misrepresent the dangers posed by their products and warned consumers of all nonobvious risks, we can arrive at a point at which economic efficiency[43] and morally appropriate behavior coincide. Economic efficiency can serve as a "tie-breaker" that permits us to escape agnosticism with regard to the initial standard of product safety. Hence, we can derive a somewhat more positive formulation of manufacturers' obligations to protect consumers as the duty to take all and only those precautions for which they are the least cost avoiders unless consumers voluntarily agree to accept less protection or to pay for more.

Admittedly, even this positive formulation pales in comparison to the image of a definite, objective duty to provide safe products. Such an image must be as appealing to consumers as the image of an oasis in the desert is to a thirsty traveler. But it is also only a mirage. Because product safety is an inherently subjective concept, it, like beauty, is in the eye of the beholder.[44]

NOTES

1. See Manuel G. Velasquez, *Business Ethics: Concepts and Cases*, 4th ed. (Englewood Cliffs, N.J.: Prentice-Hall., 1998), 321–341.

2. Ibid., 325.

3. Ibid., 330 (emphasis in the original).

4. Ibid., 335 (emphasis in the original).

5. Ibid., 339 (emphasis in the original).

6. See, for example, John Dienhart and Jordan Curnutt, *Business Ethics: A Reference Handbook* (Santa Barbara, Calif.: ABC-CLIO, 1998); John Boatright, *Ethics and the Conduct of Business*, 3rd ed. (Upper Saddle River, N.J.: Prentice-Hall, 2000), 290–300.

7. See George Brenkert, "Strict Products Liability and Compensatory Justice," in *Ethical Theory and Business*, 7th ed., ed. Tom L. Beachamp and Norman E. Bowie (Upper Saddle River, N.J.: Prentice-Hall, 2004), 184–89.

8. These figures were derived by employing the cancer risk assessment tool provided by the government, http://smokefree.gov/smokersrisk.

9. This is a serious question. I do not actually know whether this is the correct calculation of the increase in risk, but you get the idea.

10. Clifford Winston, Vikram Maheshri, and Fred Mannering, "An Exploration of the Offset Hypothesis Using Disaggregate Data: The Case of Airbags and Antilock Brakes," *Journal of Risk and Uncertainty* 32 (2006): 84–85.

11. This is the so-called Tullock safety device. See Richard B. McKenzie and Gordon Tullock, *The New World of Economics*, 3rd ed. (Homewood, Ill.: R. D. Irwin, 1981), 40–41.

12. See R. H. Coase, "The Problem of Social Costs," *Journal of Law and Economics* 3 (1960): 1–44. The seminal article on the application of the least cost avoider principle to the problem of product safety is Richard Posner, "A Theory of Negligence," *Journal of Legal Studies* 1 (1972): 29–96.

13. See *Chicago, B. & Q. R. Co. v. Krayenbuhl*, 65 Neb. 889, 91 N.W. 880 (1902).

14. For a definition of cost, see above.

15. Steven Kelman, "Cost-Benefit Analysis: An Ethical Critique," *Regulation* 5 (1981): 33–40.

16. Kelman, "Cost-Benefit Analysis," 38.

17. See below.

18. This definition of reasonable care is associated with law and economics scholars and derived from Richard Posner's seminal article, "A Theory of Negligence."

19. This definition of reasonable care is derived from Ernest Weinreb's seminal article on corrective justice, "Toward a Moral Theory of Negligence Law," *Law and Philosophy* 2 (1983): 37–62.

20. The discussion in the present section is limited to the manufacture and sale of consumer products. It does not address questions of "ultra-hazardous" commercial activities that are typically subject to strict liability such as blasting within a city, operating a nuclear power or chemical manufacturing plant in a residential area, or operating a damn upstream of a populated area.

21. The problem of uninformed consumers who are ignorant of the risks associated with the use of certain products will be addressed in the subsequent discussion of the duty to warn.

22. Indeed, this was the argument behind the adoption of products liability in U.S. law as embodied in the second Restatement of Torts in 1965. See Restatement (Second) of Torts § 402A (1965); William Prosser, *Handbook of the Law of Torts* (St. Paul, Minn.: West, 1941), 202.

23. In this chapter, I use the term "objective" to refer to something that is specifiable in terms of an interpersonal standard of value, and hence is not dependent on the personal preferences or evaluations of individuals. In contrast, I use "subjective" to refer to determinations that inherently depend on individual assessments of value that can vary from person to person.

24. See Craig Newgard and K. John McConnell, "Stature, Body Weight, and Serious Injury from Air Bags among Adult Drivers and Passengers Involved in Motor Vehicle Crashes," *Academic Emergency Medicine* 14 (2007): 108; Richard Kent, David C. Viano, and Jeff Crandall, "The Field Performance of Frontal Air Bags: A Review of the Literature," *Traffic Injury Prevention* 6 (2005): 12.

25. See Brent Hagel and Willem Meeuwisse, "Risk Compensation: A 'Side Effect' of Sport Injury Prevention?" *Clinical Journal of Sports Medicine* 14 (2004): 194.

26. See Martin J. Stillman and M. Thomas Stillman, "Choosing Nonselective NSAIDs and Selective Cox-2 Inhibitors in the Elderly: A Clinical Use Pathway," *Geriatrics* 62 (2007): 26.

27. See the discussion of utilitarianism above.

28. A sophisticated preference utilitarian would not have accepted my earlier characterization of the situation. He or she would have said that the correct starting point is the not the one with the most presently satisfied desires, but the one that required the lowest transaction costs to reach the state of affairs in which satisfied desires were maximized.

29. See the discussion of autonomy below.

30. John Stuart Mill, *Utilitarianism*, ch. 2 (1863).

31. *Codling v. Paglia*, 32 N.Y.2d 330, 340, 298 N.E.2d 622, 627, 345 N.Y.S.2d 461, 468 (1973).

32. Velasquez, *Business Ethics*, 186.

33. My uncle used to tell the story of how he and my grandparents regarded the light bulb as a mysterious and unfathomable marvel of modern technology when their section of Brooklyn converted from gas to electric lighting.

34. See Steven D. Levitt and Stephen J. Dubner, *Freakonomics* (New York: HarperCollins, 2005), 66–68.

35. In my opinion, there is little empirical evidence to support this claim. The poor tend to be very careful shoppers, often utilizing sophisticated word-of-mouth networks to obtain useful product information. As previously noted, Sears became a major retail institution precisely by providing quality and safety assurance to the poor and less educated portion of the population. However, because the poor's inability to pay for available product information is a theoretical possibility, I consider it for the sake of completeness.

36. See the discussion of the duty to warn below.

37. Dennis P. Quinn and Thomas M. Jones, "An Agent Morality View of Business Policy," *Academy of Management Review* 20 (1995): 34.

38. See pages 689–90.

39. This claim is controversial. I am not sure that the principle of respect for persons can be stretched far enough to generate this conclusion. In the alternative, there may be arguments based on considerations of social or distributive justice that can justify the conclusion. However, I do not intend to pursue the matter in this context. For purposes of this article, I will assume that a duty for manufacturers to assume the research costs of vulnerable potential consumers can be established.

40. I have spoken in terms of the manufacturer's duty to the consumer despite the fact that products pose dangers not only to those who use them but also to the public at large. Automobiles, for example, are dangerous for pedestrians as well as for drivers and passengers. The reason for this apparent neglect is that in all relevant respects the relationship between manufacturers and the public at large is the same as that between manufacturers and consumers. The members of the general public need protection against injury from products as much as consumers do. As with consumers, the question is how much of the burden of preventing such accidents should be borne by the manufacturer and how much by the members of the public themselves. And, as with consumers, the members of the general public have widely varying preferences with regard to how much safety they are willing to forgo for less expensive products. The fact that members of the public may be injured by products that they themselves did not purchase does not change the analysis. For they do purchase products, and differ with regard to the size of the premium they are willing to pay to have manufacturers protect them against injury as a third party. Hence, the inherent subjectivity of the concept of safety infects the analysis of manufacturers' obligations to the public in the same way as it does the analysis of their obligations to consumers.

41. See above.

42. I use the word "may" advisedly. For a reasonable argument can be made that the proper default condition is the one that requires the lowest transaction costs to move to market solution, and this may not be identical to the one that places the burden of avoiding injury on the party that can do so at the lowest cost.

43. Trades entered into under these conditions make both parties better off and therefore produce a Pareto superior outcome. Hence, all such moves preserve and enhance the economic efficiency of the starting point.

44. The author wishes to thank George Brenkert and Tom L. Beauchamp of Georgetown University for the opportunity to produce this article, Ann C. Tunstall of SciLucent, LLC, for her insightful comments and literary guidance, and Annette Hasnas of the Montessori School of Northern Virginia and Ava Hasnas of Falls Church, Virginia, for causing him to be intensely concerned about the matter of product safety.

SUGGESTED READING

Brenkert, George. "Strict Products Liability and Compensatory Justice." In *Ethical Theory and Business,* 7th ed. Edited by Tom L. Beauchamp and Norman E. Bowie (Upper Saddle River, N.J.: Prentice-Hall, 2004), 184–89.

Calabresi, Guido. *The Costs of Accidents.* New Haven, Conn.: Yale University Press, 1970.

Coase, R. H. "The Problem of Social Costs," *Journal of Law and Economics* 3 (1960): 1–44.

Codling v. Paglia, 32 N.Y.2d 330, 340, 298 N.E.2d 622, 627, 345 N.Y.S.2d 461, 468 (1973).

Fletcher, George P. "Fairness and Utility in Tort Theory." *Harvard Law Review* 85 (1972): 537–573.

Greenman v. Yuba Power Products, 59 Cal. 2d 57 (1963).

Henningsen v. Bloomfield Motors, 161 A.2d 69 (1960).

Holmes, Oliver Wendell. *The Common Law.* Boston: Little, Brown & Co., 1881.

Kelman, Steven. "Cost-Benefit Analysis: An Ethical Critique." *Regulation* 5 (1981): 33–40.

Mallott, Robert M. "Let's Restore the Balance to Product Liability Law." *Harvard Business Review* 61 (3) (May-June 1983): 67–74.

Posner, Richard. "A Theory of Negligence." *Journal of Legal Studies* 1 (1972): 29–96.

Restatement of the Law, Second, Torts 2d (St. Paul, Minn.: American Law Institute Publishers, 1965–1979): Section 402A.

Velasquez, Manuel G. *Business Ethics: Concepts and Cases,* 4th ed. Englewood Cliffs, N.J.: Prentice-Hall, 1998.

Weinreb, Ernest. "Toward a Moral Theory of Negligence Law." *Law and Philosophy* 2 (1983): 37–62.

PART IX

CREATING MORAL ORGANIZATIONS

CHAPTER 24

ORGANIZATIONAL INTEGRITY AND MORAL CLIMATES

NORMAN E. BOWIE

ORGANIZATIONS have personalities that many refer to as a "culture." Some organizations are perceived as having an ethical culture, while others are perceived as having an amoral or unethical culture. Organizational cultures do not change easily. In this chapter the following questions will be addressed about these cultures: What are the marks of an organization that has integrity? What factors are important? What ostensibly important factors turn out to be less so? What factors hinder organizational integrity?

In his book *Competing with Integrity*, Richard De George says, "Acting with integrity is the same as acting ethically or morally."[1] De George chooses the word "integrity" rather than "ethics" because of the negative connotations that "ethics" has in some business circles. For example, "integrity" does not have the connotations of moralizing that words like "ethics" and "morality" have for some people. I follow a similar approach here.

For the purpose of this chapter, I assume that an organization with integrity is an organization with a certain sort of moral climate. Detailing the characteristics of a moral climate for an organization is a goal of this essay. Some features we associate with individual integrity are also characteristic of organizational integrity. For example, both individuals and organizations with integrity are steadfast in their commitment and actions to moral principle. However, I will argue that an organization with integrity has several characteristics that distinguish it from individual integrity (i.e., personal moral integrity) and that some central characteristics of individual integrity are less important for organizational integrity. Individuals with integrity are individuals who accept responsibility for any negative consequences caused by their actions. But, achieving organizational integrity may require that managers de-emphasize or even, in certain situations, ignore issues of personal responsibility. Also, an organization with integrity must have certain kinds of organizational structures or organizational incentives. This language does not apply to individuals with integrity. Indeed the key notion of organizational integrity, "moral climate," cannot be meaningfully applied to individual integrity.

I begin with the central idea of organizational integrity: moral climate. I then identify the norms and values that contribute to a moral climate, including a commitment to stakeholder management, a commitment to seeing the purpose of the organization as a cooperative enterprise, and both substantive and procedural norms of fairness. Finally, I consider the role of incentives as they support or inhibit organizational integrity, identify conditions that work against moral integrity, and conclude by considering whether for-profit organizations can instill organizational integrity and remain profitable.

The Importance of a Moral Climate

Moral climate can be described as having "shared perceptions of prevailing organizational norms established for addressing issues with a moral component."[2] A moral climate involves ethical commitments that are value-based and are embodied in the character of the organizational members and the organization's routines and incentive structures. One of the characteristics of an organization with a moral climate is that the organization takes the moral point of view with respect to organizational actions.

An essential characteristic of taking the moral point of view is to consider the interests of those affected by actions. For individuals, taking the moral point of view is straightforward—it requires that one consider the impact of one's actions on others. With respect to an organization, matters are a bit more complex. For an organization to take the moral point of view, it must have leaders and a decision-making structure that allow it to consider the interests of those it affects, with special emphasis on those it wrongs or harms.

An organization with a moral climate has two different attributes. It has both shared perceptions as to what constitutes moral behavior and processes for dealing with ethical issues. Some of these shared perceptions are core values that guide the organization. In an organization with integrity, core values govern corporate activity. A full picture of what constitutes a moral climate requires a lengthy discussion of the norms and values that constitute a moral climate, the task to which we now turn.

Stakeholder Management

One feature of an organization with a good moral climate is that its behavior is consistent with its purposes, which also must be morally justified. There is a close analogy here between individual integrity and organizational integrity. An individual has integrity when he or she exhibits good character and is steadfast in the face of adversity or temptation, and an organization displays integrity when it is true to its goals or purposes, especially when there are obstacles impeding them or temptations to deviate from them.

Strict consistency with and adherence to the organization's purpose is not sufficient for a good moral climate. The purpose must also be morally appropriate or at least not inconsistent with morality. For instance, the standard view of the purpose of a for-profit public company in the United States is the creation of shareholder wealth. Stockholders are the owners, and managers are the agents of the owners. It is the manager's responsibility to provide financial returns to the owners because that is what the owners want. This view is often attributed to Milton Friedman and is the standard view taught to students in U.S. business school classes. This view is a *moral* position in that owners have moral rights and managers have moral obligations to them.

Business ethicists generally do not regard this classic position as the best account of a corporation's purpose from the moral point of view. Many business ethicists think that something like R. Edward Freeman's account of stakeholders is closer to the mark: Business ought to be a value-creating institution, and it should be managed to promote the interests of the various corporate stakeholders. The creation of wealth is a critical value, but it is not the only one. For example, employment that provides meaningful work and income for a decent standard of living are other pertinent values. I endorse Freeman's account of the purpose of the corporation, but I will not defend it here. This defense has been well articulated in the business ethics literature, but stakeholder theory remains controversial, and there are business ethicists who believe that the traditional Friedmanite view is superior. Defenders of Friedman's view acknowledge that stakeholder theory is instrumentally correct, meaning that managers who believe their moral obligation is to increase shareholder wealth must still manage from a stakeholder perspective. These managers realize they can only increase shareholder wealth if the interests of all corporate stakeholders are taken into account and promoted.

By endorsing stakeholder theory as the goal or purpose of the corporation, I am also accepting it as a correct normative position of how the firm ought to be managed. Managers may sometimes be morally required to put the interests of other stakeholder groups ahead of the interests of the stockholders. The managers of an organization with a moral climate recognize that the interests of various stakeholders have intrinsic value. Of course, we need to elaborate further on the nature of a moral climate. However, stakeholder theory provides the basic moral framework for organizational integrity.

Seven Substantive Moral Principles

I have argued elsewhere and will here assume that morality requires that a business organization be viewed as a moral community and not simply as a set of economic relationships.[3] I will now argue that how we look at and understand the purpose of an organization affects how we will behave in it. If the individuals in an organization view it purely instrumentally, these individuals are predisposed to behave in ways that harm organizational integrity. John Rawls's insight that organizations are social unions constituted by certain norms is useful here. Organizations are not mere instruments for achieving individual goals. To develop this notion of a social union, Rawls contrasts two views of how human society is held together:[4] In the private view, human beings form social institutions after calculating that it would be advantageous to do so; in the social view human beings form social institutions because they share final ends and value common institutions and activities as intrinsically good. In a social union, cooperation is a key element of success because each individual in a social union knows that he cannot achieve his interests within the group by himself. The cooperation of others is necessary as it provides stability to the organization, enables it to endure, and enables individuals both to realize their potential and to see the qualities of others that lead to organizational success.

In an organization with a moral climate, the organization should be managed in ways that benefit the interests of the stakeholders. This can be accomplished only if the stakeholders in control do not treat the organization merely instrumentally, but rather as a cooperative enterprise or social union. (See the chapter by Kenneth Goodpaster in this volume. He augments this point considerably.)

How should cooperation be achieved in an organization characterized as having a moral climate? An organization with an effective moral climate must be governed by a set of substantive moral *principles* and be characterized as having certain *processes* (or procedures) for decision making. In short, there are both substantive and procedural elements required for organizational integrity. The following outline reflects a Kantian theory of what the business firm should be. It provides a foundation on which to build and to discuss other, non-Kantian approaches:

1. The firm should consider the interests of all the affected stakeholders in any decision that it makes.
2. The firm should have those, or representatives of those, affected by the firm's rules and policies participate in the determination of those rules and policies before they are implemented.
3. The interests of one stakeholder should not take priority over the interests of all other stakeholders for all decisions.
4. When a situation arises in which it appears that the interests of one set of stakeholders must be sacrificed for the interests of another set of stakeholders, that decision cannot be made solely on the grounds that there is a greater number of stakeholders in one group than in another.
5. No principle is acceptable if it is inconsistent with the principle that we should never treat a person merely as a means to our own ends.

6. Every profit-making firm has an imperfect duty of social beneficence (benefit to society).

7. Each business firm must establish procedures to ensure that relations among stakeholders are governed by the rules of justice.[5]

These principles can be easily accepted by all who work within Rawls's or Kant's ethical theory. I recognize that many business ethicists work from a different normative ethical theory. However, I believe these principles are consistent with the conclusions reached in many other ethical theories as well. My interest here is in building on these principles by pointing to the norms that managers who view an organization as a social union might use to help create a moral climate.

Norms of Fairness

I now move from the seven moral principles for creating a moral climate to norms of fairness. Insights from both moral philosophy and organizational theory are useful here. Both ethicists and many social scientists working in organizational theory recognize the importance of fairness. Some economists such as Robert Frank have used the sense of fairness to explain why people sometimes complete transactions that are not in their short-term interest.[6] A principal concept of economics is that economic transactions are free actions in which each party perceives that he or she will benefit from it. If I am willing, for instance, to sell my house for $500,000 and someone is willing to pay $520,000 for it, each party will benefit if we make the deal. But for what price should the house actually sell? In real estate, the selling price is determined by negotiation. Our intuitions seem to suggest that a fifty-fifty split is most fair. With that in mind and without negotiation, the fair price is $510,000. With respect to the surplus of economic value generated by an economic activity, Frank argues that fairness requires that the surplus be divided equally.

Frank's principle cannot be applied directly to organizations because we need to consider not only the fairness in the distribution of an organization's outputs but also the contributions that each individual makes to the organization. Recently, Robert Phillips has argued that fairness in an organizational context requires that benefits be distributed on the basis of the relative contribution to the organization (the equitable proportionality condition).[7] Phillips's principle is that benefits derived from organizational activity should be distributed according to the level of contribution that individuals have made to the organizational activity. Thus if Jones contributes twice as much as Smith, Jones should receive twice the benefits of Smith. Both Frank's egalitarian principle and Phillips's proportionality principle have an intuitive appeal and can be reconciled as a combined principle of fairness: Where contribution can be measured, the reward should be proportional to the contribution made. Where there is a surplus as a result of cooperative endeavor in which contribution cannot be measured, those cooperating should share the surplus equally. For managers of a firm with organizational integrity, the question is, How should the rewards of a cooperative enterprise be distributed in a firm with a moral climate? The appropriate principle is that the rewards should be distributed fairly as a function of productivity. Where productivity cannot be measured, the surplus value that results from cooperative economic activity should be equally distributed.

Issues of fairness in an organization are not limited to the internal distribution of profits. One of Frank's major contributions to economic theory has been to show the power and moral importance of perceptions of fairness in many economic transactions. Issues of fairness arise in many of the relations that an organization with integrity has with its various stakeholders. Organizations that violate widely held norms of fairness in their stakeholder relations do so at great peril, including a cost to their perceived status as an organization of integrity. One instance of this is the Coca-Cola soft drink dispenser that can adjust the price of a Coke to the temperature outside.[8] When Coca-Cola's CEO at the time reported the existence of this machine his announcement was met with outrage because people perceived that changing the price of a Coke in response to changes in temperature was unfair. Thus, a Coca-Cola dispenser that adjusts the price of a Coke to temperature was never manufactured. Other companies, though, have similar campaigns, such as the use of frequent flier miles as a means for priority boarding that are accepted by consumers. This demonstrates that while human reasoning is often inconsistent, any violation of strongly held norms of fairness will lead to the perception that an organization lacks integrity.

Procedural Norms

In addition to the substantive principle of fairness, notions of procedural fairness are important in achieving a moral climate. Rawls believed that his account of justice was basically procedural. With respect to the principles of justice for the basic structure of society (i.e., society's most basic institutions and forms of organization) a fair procedure would result in principles that were just. Rawls's emphasis on the importance of fair procedures has parallels in the organizational behavior literature. From that literature we learn that perceptions about the justice of the procedure affect perceptions about the justice of the outcomes. This finding has led some in the organizational behavior field to develop the concept of "organizational justice."

One of the more important empirical findings in organizational justice is that people are more inclined to accept an adverse result that does not benefit them—if they have had a role in determining how decisions are to be made. In other words, input into the design of the process increases acceptance of adverse decisions. This finding is especially important in employee evaluations, because if employees have had input into the evaluation process, then a negative evaluation of any employee will likely be accepted by that employee. What the organizational justice literature shows is that an organization is more effective if the procedures are just. Decisions regarding reward and task support will be more often accepted if everyone affected has participated in the development of the procedures.

Of course, the fact that people will likely accept adverse results if they believe they have been involved or consulted in setting the procedures does not mean that their acceptance is justified. Here we need to relate social science accounts of how organizational justice is perceived and its effects on efficiency with normative ethical theory on just procedures. An obvious key to a just procedure is impartiality. The procedure cannot be biased in a direction that shows self-interest or that uses criteria unrelated to merit.

To achieve organizational integrity, the procedures for decision making in the organization need input from all organizational stakeholders. Moreover, the procedures must not be biased against or merely reflect the self-interest of one group of stakeholders.

One way to solidify this discussion of justice, both substantive and procedural, is to examine a particular instance of remuneration, namely, the remuneration of CEO's and other high executives in a for-profit business. Many journalists and business ethicists believe that executive compensation is too high and that executives are being rewarded unfairly at the expense of the rest of the employees and perhaps also at the expense of the stockholders. In terms of our discussion above, these executives receive an unfair share of the surplus generated by profitable businesses.

Some defend the current level of executive pay by appeal to the market. They argue that markets set executive compensation, and therefore they are procedurally just. However, critics deny that markets set executive compensation. They point out that compensation committees composed primarily of other CEOs set the compensation. This process creates an obvious bias in favor of CEOs because people have a cognitive bias toward overvaluing their personal contributions and of blaming their shortcoming on either others or impersonal forces beyond their control. CEOs are not exempt from cognitive bias and consequently will tend to overreward CEOs. Having other CEOs set CEO salaries contributes to what Garrison Keillor of the Prairie Home Companion refers to as the Lake Wobegon effect, a situation in which all the children are above average. In this case, it is the CEOs who are all above average. (Numerous additional aspects of moral problems about CEO compensation are discussed in the chapter by John R. Boatright in this volume.)

Many sorts of wrong procedures have an adverse effect on organizational integrity. To continue the point about setting executive compensation, I turn to agency theory. Agency theory has been used by researchers in a wide range of organizational fields, such as economics, sociology, marketing, accounting, political science, and organizational behavior. Much of the scholarly literature on executive pay is grounded in agency theory and is accompanied by suggestions that may solve the agency problem. The "agency problem" is the tendency of the agent to choose his or her interests when they conflict with the interests of the principal. Within management theory, the typical application of this framework is to view shareholders as principals and managers as agents. In management, the agency problem exists when the managers put their own interests, especially their financial interests, ahead of the interests of stockholders.

Agency theorists have a long history with incentive systems. A central issue for agency theorists is how to monitor or create incentives so that the agent acts not on his or her own behalf, but rather on behalf of the principals. With respect to corporate managers, including the CEO, the issue was aligning the incentives of the organization so that managers would work to the shareholders' benefit, rather than for their own benefit. Business history presents many cases in which CEOs have promoted their own interests at the shareholders' expense. This seemed especially prevalent at the beginning of the twenty-first century.

One device for aligning the objectives of top-level managers with stockholders that became increasingly popular was the use of stock options. However, in path-breaking research, Jared Harris and Philip Bromiley examined the effect that certain compensation schemes, especially the granting of stock options, had on the likeli-hood of a firm having an accounting restatement as a result of misrepresentation.[9] They also wanted to see what effect poor performance—either as compared to peers in the industry or to past benchmarks of the firm itself—had on similar accounting restatements. In other words, to what extent do these factors serve as pressures to cheat? Using a matched sample data set, they found two similar companies in which one had experienced an accounting restatement due to an accounting irregularity and one that had not. The U.S. General Accounting Office provided the data on the accounting irregularities. What might explain the difference between two simi-lar companies? Harris and Bromiley showed conclusively that granting of a large amount of stock options significantly increased the likelihood of accounting mis-representation, whereas the comparatively smaller bonuses did not have that effect. In addition, they demonstrated that poor performance relative to other firms in the industry also increased the likelihood of accounting misrepresentation.

What lessons for organizational integrity can we extract from this? There has been a tendency for agency theorists and others who work with incentive systems to ignore the dark side of human nature—the possibility that those responding to incentive systems will not always behave ethically. They assumed that because people behaved in a self-interested way, it did not mean that people would cross the line and behave unethically. This oversight seems unrealistic, and agency theo-rists should have been the first to consider this possibility. Agency theory assumes that human beings are self-serving and that each will pursue his or her interest at the expense of the principals. One might argue that self-regarding behavior at the expense of a principal on the agent's part is always unethical. Perhaps agency theorists have not been cynical enough. They recognized that employees could be self-serving, but they usually have not gone the next step to show that when the incentives are wrong, agents may be acting illegally or immorally.

Incentives to motivate behavior are a key part of the management of any orga-nization, but under what conditions do they become morally suspect? In Harris and Bromiley's research, bonuses were not correlated with accounting irregularities, but stock options were. What differentiates stock options from bonuses in influ-encing managers to commit accounting irregularities? One answer is that bonuses are usually much smaller than stock options. People are less likely to cheat when the gains are small. Executives who manage for organizational integrity need to be knowledgeable and realistic about human nature. Organizational integrity cannot be achieved by assuming that people will do the right thing.

Many have reacted to the recent wave of corporate scandals by saying that executives are overly greedy: a character flaw. But why have some executives become greedy? The explanation is in the distinction between viewing an organization as merely an instrument to satisfying one's individual needs and seeing an organization as a social union. If the organization is seen as a means to personal enrichment and not seen as a cooperative enterprise of all those in the organization, it should come as no surprise that the executives of such an organization feel entitled to the rewards. Psychological theorists have shown that people tend to take credit when things go well and blame bad luck or circumstances beyond one's control when things go badly. Thus a CEO takes all the credit when an organization performs well but blames the general economy or other factors when things go poorly. This human tendency is predictable when executives look at organizations instrumentally.

I have been arguing that the key to organizational integrity is the existence of a good moral climate. In summary, the following elements are essential for a good moral climate: (1) commitment to a moral purpose for the organization, (2) a view of the organization as a social union rather than merely a means for achieving individual goals, and (3) management in accord with a set of substantive moral principles (including those of fairness) and in accord with a set of procedures that at a minimum avoid bias and give the employees a voice in the rules governing the organization.

Considerations That May or May Not Contribute to Organizational Integrity

A common criticism of philosophical ethics is that philosophers tend to write about ethics from an ideal standpoint, meaning that they tend to think that the task of ethical thinking is to discover the right thing to do free of conflicts and practical impediments.

The Perspective of Ideal Theory

Once the right thing to do is determined, then people will have a blueprint of what should be done and will follow that blueprint. As John Rawls once wrote, "The other limitation on our discussion is that for the most part I examine the principles of justice that would regulate a well ordered society. Everyone is presumed to act justly and to do his part in upholding just institutions."[10]

Approaching organizational integrity from an ideal standpoint is not an adequate practical perspective for those managing for organizational integrity. Nobel laureate Amartya Sen—in a keynote address on the occasion of the twentieth anniversary of Harvard's Safra Foundation Center for Ethics—noted that research in professional ethics could not be based on what he called "transcendent ethics." Such an approach to ethics will be of some but not much help in pinpointing moral integrity in organizations. Since organizations are composed of people, we need to take the findings of psychology, sociology, and economics into account in order to achieve organizational integrity.[11] Ethical theory always exists in tension: On the one hand, ethics should tell us what ought to be the case; on the other hand, what we ought to do cannot be so demanding that it requires what we cannot do or cannot reasonably expect to be done. What we can or cannot do is often an empirical question best addressed by the social and biological sciences. In managing for organizational integrity, executives must balance the ideal, the practical, and the possible. They must take account of legal requirements, cost considerations, risk-benefit analyses, community standards, and the like.

In business ethics, it is vital to keep ethical requirements of a theory close to what is known about human behavior. When I developed a Kantian account of business ethics, I tried to balance being faithful to Kant with Kantian prescriptions that were consistent with what we know about human behavior. As noted earlier, people will accept adverse decisions if they have a role in deciding the rules that govern how decisions are made. With this in mind, Kant's demand that persons not be treated as a means merely but also as an end takes on a concrete reality. To respect persons in a business organization, we arguably do not have to find a way to end up with a win-win every time. In certain situations, giving stakeholders voices in the rule-making and decision-making process may be all that is required to respect them as persons.

Assessing the Characteristics of a Workforce

Another step in structuring a realistic and practical account of organizational integrity is to understand how humans respond to incentives, which helps establish appropriate and inappropriate incentives. Organizational theory has much to tell us here. Over forty years ago, Douglas McGregor published *The Human Side of Enterprise*, in which he contrasted two theories about human nature known as theory X and theory Y. Theory X assumed that people had an inherent dislike of work and would avoid it if possible and that they seek to avoid responsibility. Theory Y assumes the opposite: employees like work, but prefer it when self-directed. They want to act imaginatively, creatively, and are willing to assume responsibility. They also act morally much of the time and can be trusted. Theory Y people are less susceptible to the agency problems mentioned earlier, in which agency theorists assume that workers would rather do something instead of work, thus suggesting that workers would underperform in their jobs. The more theory Y people an organization has, the greater the likelihood that the organization will exhibit organizational integrity, since theory Y people do not view either their jobs or the organization instrumentally. Rather, theory Y people extract meaning from their work. Thus, it is easier to align individual goals and the conditions for organizational integrity when you have a large number of theory Y people. This conclusion does not mean that organizational integrity is impossible in an organization composed mostly of theory X people, but it is more difficult because theory X people view the organization instrumentally.

People are not purely theory X or theory Y, but this broad categorization is nonetheless useful. The first task of management is to assess accurately whether theory X or theory Y persons dominate one's labor force and then to manage in ways that increase the predominance of theory Y employees. Accurate knowledge of the characteristics of one's work force will help manage for organizational integrity. The second task of management is to find ways to convert theory Xs into theory Ys. If a person stubbornly remains theory X, it is probably in the best interest of organizational integrity to terminate the person.

The Importance of Incentive Structures

If incentives are structured to promote self-serving or even unethical behavior, then an increase in self-serving or unethical behavior is to be expected. Mere exhortations to be moral are of limited value. Management scholars and managers know this, and when employees accept structured incentives and then do something that is self-serving or unethical, management must take some, and perhaps most, of the responsibility. This point can be illustrated with two much-discussed Harvard Business School cases.

First, the Sears Auto Centers case concerns allegations that surfaced in June 1992. The charge was that Sears Auto Centers had been performing unnecessary repairs on customer vehicles.[12] Many believe that changes in the compensation system were part of the problem. Mechanics had always been under a production quota, but on January 1, 1992, the production quota was raised by 60 percent. In addition, compensation changed from strictly an hourly wage to an hourly wage equal to 83 percent of former earnings plus a variable on work actually performed. This increased pressure on mechanics to speed up work and to surpass minimum production quotas. The California attorney general at the time said that the structure "made it totally inevitable that the consumer would be oversold."

Second, a case from the 1970s involved the H. J. Heinz Company (the Administration of Policy case):[13] Certain Heinz divisions, including the Star Kist division, had engaged in accounting irregularities. Expenses were recorded in one year, but the good or service was not received until the following year. The result was a decrease in income in the former year and an increase in income during the latter. In addition, sales were recorded in one fiscal period that should have been recorded in an earlier one. Why do that? If you have met your numbers for the year and the next year is uncertain, there is an incentive to increase expenses this year and lower them next year. The conclusion of an investigating audit committee focused on "poor control consciousness." The committee said, "World headquarters senior management apparently did not consider the effect on individuals in the [divisions] of the pressures to which they were subjected."[14] Other factors cited included the lack of an effective code of ethics, an effective compliance procedure, a monitoring process, competent personnel at world headquarters, including those competent in finance, and an electronic data processing manager.

Incentives are a key part of the management of any organization, but when are incentives and goals permissible and when are they morally suspect? Recall Harris and Bromiley's research in which bonuses were not correlated with accounting irregularities, but stock options were. An important task of those seeking organizational moral integrity is to think creatively about incentive structures. Managers need to think about what unforeseen consequences on ethical behavior or lack thereof the incentives might produce. The devising of incentive systems requires what Patricia Werhane refers to as moral imagination.[15]

In addition, as we see in the Heinz case, one needs competent people in the right places, effective monitoring, and an effective compliance program. These conditions are essential for organizational integrity. In her discussion of the Sears case, Lynn Sharp Paine argues that the incentive structures must be made to fit into an organization that already has integrity. Incentives can be helpful, but they can also be abused. In diagnosing the problem at Sears, an ethical climate did not preexist. Quality control and audit systems were absent and there were inadequate guidelines on what was to be considered legitimate preventive maintenance. In a telling comment, Paine says, "There is no evidence in the case that Sears has encouraged professionalism, integrity, or self-restraint.... Problems arise when companies introduce such compensation programs without insuring that quality controls, audits, cultural values, and disincentives for abuse are sufficiently strong to counter this potential."[16]

Codes of Ethics

In the public arena, people concerned about organizational ethics, especially if moral problems have arisen, often ask, "Does the organization have a code of ethics?" Many people think that codes of ethics are important for the creation of a moral climate and for the maintenance of organizational ethics. However, my view of codes of ethics is more nuanced. Codes of ethics by themselves are not a good indicator of an organization's commitment to ethics. For a code of ethics to be effective, it needs to be part of a broader moral climate. If the moral climate is absent, a code of ethics is likely to be window dressing. Enron, for instance, had one of the best codes of ethics of any corporation, yet the ethical climate at Enron was seriously degraded even before its collapse. A code of ethics is useful only if the other factors that contribute to organizational integrity are present. A powerful argument for this position is provided by a branch of economics. To explore it we must first consider transaction cost economics and the distinction between high and low asset specificity.

From the transaction cost perspective, the first and perhaps most important attribute for assessing a transaction is the degree to which individuals involved in the transaction must invest dedicated assets.[17] Dedicated assets are transaction specific and have high asset specificity. To illustrate this concept, suppose a large retailer seeks a supplier to provide a product with specifications that are unique to that retailer. To provide the product, the supplier must invest in the resources that enable it to meet the unique specifications of the retailer. Those resources would be dedicated assets and have high asset specificity. But, suppose a supplier provides products for a number of retailers all of whom have the same or similar specifications. In these circumstances, the resources of the supplier can be used for any of the retailers; the resources are not specific to one retailer. In such cases, we say that the resources have low asset specificity as they are not dedicated to one retailer.

Transaction cost economists have shown how suppliers with resources that were characterized by high asset specificity could be subject to "the hold-up problem": the supplier invests in the resources to make the specific product, only to face demands by the retailer to lower the prices. Since the supplier's resources are dedicated to that retailer, he has little choice but to lower the price. It is alleged that many of Wal-Mart's suppliers were subject to the hold-up problem.

I want to use the insights of transaction cost economics and the distinction between high and low asset specificity to establish my claim that codes of ethics alone play only a minor role in determining the moral climate of an organization. Codes of ethics have low asset specificity and are easily copied. Even a company with a bad moral climate can have a good code of ethics, as the Enron example illustrates. Thus, a good code of ethics is not a reliable indicator of whether an organization has high ethical standards or low ethical standards. However, when a code of ethics is supported by a pervasive moral climate, it can be a useful device for guiding employee and even management conduct, especially if the code is quite specific in its norms. Perhaps the best-known example of a code of ethics that has made a difference in management decision making and that does legitimately contribute to organizational integrity is Johnson and Johnson's Credo (J and J Credo), which is not simply a document on which all employees must sign off. It is a living, pervasive, and enforced document. The Credo is evaluated periodically to determine if it still reflects the values and vision of the company and if it is still useful as a tool for helping resolve ethical issues or dilemmas the company might face. Thus there is a symbiotic relationship between the ethical climate at J and J and the J and J credo. This is a worthy goal for every business organization.

Determining Individual Responsibility

To achieve organizational integrity and a pervasive moral climate, one cannot assume that solving moral issues within the organization is always a matter of focusing on individual responsibility. Determining individual responsibility is part of what is required to create an appropriate moral climate, but sometimes trying to determine who is responsible for a moral failure obstructs and retards necessary organizational reform. Moral imagination is required to decide when to focus on individual responsibility or to ignore issues of individual responsibility and to focus on technological fixes or structural organizational reform.

As we saw in the California Sears Auto Centers case, the incentive system encouraged Sears auto repairmen to do unnecessary repairs. From the paradigm of individual responsibility, it seems strange to blame the incentive system. The incentive system is not an intentional actor, yet much literature in business and business ethics suggests that the incentive system is to be blamed. However, an incentive system is established by individuals, and they must assume responsibility for adverse ethical effects of the system they initiate. Contending that the incentive system is responsible for the behavior should be understood as shorthand for saying that the individuals who created the incentive system are responsible for consequent unethical behavior. At Sears it seems that it was the managers who were responsible for the overcharging by the Sears repairmen, not the repairmen.

This determination is not quite right, however, because the problem is one of shared responsibility. Being *influenced* by incentives to act unethically does not absolve one of all responsibility. It is appropriate to place some responsibility on those who created the incentive system and some on those who acted on the incentives. Both are responsible for the moral climate that results. Of course, in many cases, we must decide how to distribute greater or lesser responsibility to different individuals when all bear some degree of responsibility.

Sometimes an effective moral climate results from balancing responsibilities, but in other circumstances determining individual responsibility is not important at all. Focusing on individual responsibility can even detract from organizational integrity. One example is the problem created by medical mistakes in hospitals. In the late 1990s, it was estimated that medical errors caused 100,000 deaths per year. Organizational integrity requires that medical organizations do everything possible to eliminate such mistakes. Evidence shows that rather than blaming individuals each time something goes wrong, the best approach is having an organizational system that searches for and implements technical fixes and related ways of reducing medical error.

To make this point, I use an extended example. In 1996, a two-month-old baby boy named Jose Eric Martinez died after being given the wrong dose (ten times the recommended amount) of the drug Digoxin. An investigation established the causal sequence that resulted in the accidental overdose as follows: [18] The first step in the sequence was the determination of the appropriate amount of Digoxin to be administered. The attending physician and resident did the calculations and determined that the correct dose was .09 milligrams. However, when the resident wrote the order on Jose's chart, he made a slip of the pen and entered 0.9 milligrams—a dose that was ten times too high. When the physician checked the chart, the mistake went unnoticed.

The Digoxin order was faxed to the pharmacy. The pharmacist thought the amount too high, so he placed the order on the coffee pot—the location of the unofficial important pile and then paged the resident to discuss the order. However, the resident had left for the day and did not receive the page. A back up copy of the order that had been sent by messenger arrived and was filled by a technician. The technician filled a vial with .9 milligrams of Digoxin and left it for the pharmacist to check. By the time the pharmacist checked the dosage, he had forgotten his original concerns. Since the order and the dosage in the vial matched, the pharmacist sent the prescription out.

That was not the end of the opportunities to correct the error. The nurse who received the vial thought that the dosage was incorrect, so she approached the resident on call, who was not the same resident who made the initial error. This resident redid the math and got the correct dosage of .09; but when he looked on the vial he failed to notice that the decimal point was in the wrong place and the dosage on the vial actually read 0.9.

There is a clear causal chain here, but which individual was responsible for the death of Jose Martinez? Are all the individuals who contributed to the mistake in some measure responsible for it? If one is concerned about organizational integrity, these questions may not be the right ones to start with. This suspicion is supported when a few more facts of the case are added. The pharmacy was one person short the night the order was filled. A policy existed that the phone must be answered within four rings and that visitors should be greeted within five seconds—a policy that put pressure on an understaffed unit. The nurse who questioned the order was from a country in which women rarely confront men and in which women rarely confront doctors. Cultural practices and some well-intentioned policies played a role in the events that occurred.

Hermann Hospital (as it was known in 1996)[19] in Houston, where this tragic mistake occurred, did not try to improve organizational integrity by investigating who was responsible. No one was fired, and no new rules for individuals to follow were introduced. Rather, technological solutions were instituted. The hospital's computer would automatically flag questionable orders for the most dangerous drugs, and the hospital looked for a paging system that would alert a caller when the person being paged had his pager deactivated.

In a 1995 hospital case at Martin Memorial Hospital South in Stuart, Florida, a seven-year-old boy died when he was given the wrong medication. Instead of receiving lidocaine as prescribed, the syringe contained a highly concentrated dose of adrenaline that was suitable for external use only. The procedure, which was common in hospitals throughout the United States, was to put the lidocaine into a cup and then empty the contents of the cup into the syringe. Instead, the syringe was filled from the wrong cup. By putting a cap on the vial of lidocaine, it could be drawn directly out of the bottle into a labeled syringe. The cup—and thus the possibility of that kind of error—was eliminated.[20]

In these cases, the search for individuals responsible for the medical mistake appears to do more to inhibit organizational integrity than to advance it. What was needed was a reassessment of procedures and an honest and transparent discussion of what happened and what needed to be changed. If the focus was on identifying and punishing the individuals involved, the parties would have been trying to protect themselves rather than change procedures. In these cases, not looking for those responsible wound up helping to improve both the quality of the operations and moral climate.

Sometimes even the fear that individuals will be held responsible inhibits the introduction of technology that would improve safety. This is especially true in a litigious society like the United States. Fear of lawsuits and civil punishment created some resistance to an open discussion of the issues in the medical error cases discussed previously. To use another example, it is my understanding that a technological innovation can track all the actions of pilots on commercial aircraft. Using this device, mistakes or tendencies that might lead to disastrous consequences can be discovered and possibly corrected before a tragedy occurs. It is my understanding that the system is apparently operative on British Airways planes. However, it is also my understanding that union pilots in the United States have apparently resisted this technology on grounds that it will be used to "punish" them. A litigious society like the United States may make organizational integrity more difficult under such circumstances.

Organizational integrity is thus not simply a matter of having a mechanism for holding individuals responsible. It is the result of a myriad of complex factors that are both individual and institutional. Sometimes it is important to resolve problems of a lapse of ethics by holding individuals responsible, but often it is most important to solve a crisis of organizational integrity by changing procedures or creating a technological fix.

Elements That Inhibit
the Development of a Moral Climate

We now discuss three things that can inhibit the development of a moral climate: groupthink, teleopathy, and conflict of interest.

Groupthink

One of the biggest dangers in the path of achieving a high level of organizational integrity is the danger of groupthink. The concept of groupthink was first introduced by William H. Whyte in an article in *Fortune*. In his construal, groupthink referred to open use of group values to achieve expedient and right outcomes. Later the term took on a negative connotation, especially at the hands of its major discussant, Irving Janus. Janus thought of it as the thinking of a cohesive in-group often driven by a desire more for unanimity rather than for realistic appraisal. Janus regarded it as a faulty decision procedure resulting from group pressures that lead to a deterioration of "mental efficiency, reality testing, and moral judgment."[21] Psychologists have identified a number of factors that lead to groupthink. These factors include (1) overestimation of the group, (2) close-mindedness, (3) pressures toward uniformity and unanimity, (4) the stereotyping of outsiders, (5) self-censorship, (6) direct pressure on dissenters, (7) mindguards,[22] and (8) the illusion of invulnerability.

It has been argued that a paradigm case of groupthink occurred among those involved in deliberations and conference calls surrounding the Challenger Launch in January 1986. The Challenger exploded shortly after liftoff. The launch was initially scheduled six days earlier, but mechanical problems caused a delay. The O-rings in the booster rockets became an engineering concern. A recommendation by Martin Thiokol engineers not to launch because the safety of the O-rings could not be guaranteed in the predicted cold weather was belittled and eventually overruled, in large part because NASA was eager to get the mission underway. Some have argued that groupthink at NASA was the chief explanation for the flawed decision to proceed.

It is widely believed that it is difficult to change a corporate culture. Seventeen years later on February 1, 2003, the Columbia was lost as it exploded on reentry over Texas. Subsequent investigation showed that requests to photograph the tiles that had been damaged during takeoff were denied. The report on the Columbia disaster had a disconcerting similarity to the official report on the Challenger disaster. Again groupthink may have been a primary cause.

Groupthink can be seen as the dark side of teamwork. Given that teamwork is important for organizational success, how can groupthink be avoided? The quality and character of the team leader are key considerations.[23] The most important factor in avoiding groupthink is an environment in which different opinions and questioning is encouraged. The group's leader will have to avoid being too directive. Sometimes it may be necessary to appoint critical evaluators with the specific responsibility to raise questions or challenge consensus. The more the members of a team think alike, the more groupthink is likely to occur. Moral failure often occurs when the leader of an organization surrounds himself or herself with "yes men," who are those who tell the boss only what he or she wants to hear. Moral failure can also result when meetings are seen as inefficient and brain storming or other activities designed to encourage a multiplicity of ideas for solving a problem or achieving an organizational goal are discouraged. Commentators have pointed out how John F. Kennedy instinctively followed all these suggestions during the Cuban missile crisis. He was sometimes absent during the discussions so that he would not stifle them. He sought the advice of people with different points of view, including some with unpopular opinions. Kennedy's behavior here is in contrast with George W. Bush, who did just the opposite in deciding to go to war in Iraq. Whereas Kennedy's strategy proved successful, Bush's did not.

Of course, analysis paralysis must be avoided but so must groupthink. As with so much in organizational ethics, balance is important. However, groupthink is clearly a very serious threat to organizational integrity.

Teleopathy

Another error in decision making to be avoided has drawn the attention of Kenneth Goodpaster in his work in business ethics.[24] This error, known as teleopathy, is defined as "the unbalanced pursuit of purpose in either individuals or organizations." The principle components of teleopathy are fixation, rationalization, and detachment. Goodpaster shows how many important cases in business ethics can be explained as instances of teleopathy. Consider shareholder theory—the theory that the obligation of the manager is to increase shareholder wealth. If organizational integrity requires stakeholder management, then the single-minded focus on only one stakeholder—the shareholder—will lead the organization astray by ignoring the interests of other stakeholders. The most common criticism made by critics of public corporations is that they are slaves of Wall Street and focus entirely on making the quarterly numbers so they can maximize profits for shareholders. A number of failures to achieve organizational integrity have resulted from this single-minded focus on shareholder profit. Even if a manger is single-minded about profit, as Friedman, Jensen, and others recommend, the manager will only succeed if he or she does not always give priority to what is most profitable. To increase shareholder wealth, the manager must often give special attention to other stakeholders whose support is vital to the success of the firm. Avoiding teleopathy is both good business and necessary for organizational integrity.

If a corporation is to be single-minded, it should be so in pursuit of creating value for corporate stakeholders. However, being single-minded here does not make the manager guilty of teleopathy, since the single-minded goal requires balancing the goals and interests of all stakeholders. Being single-minded in that respect requires great flexibility with respect to the management of a public corporation.

Conflicts of Interest

Another significant danger for an organization—especially when the organization is viewed instrumentally rather than as a social union or cooperative enterprise—is the possibility that the members of the organization will permit conflicts of interest. A standard definition of a conflict of interest is the following: a person has a conflict of interest if (1) he is in a relationship of trust with another person or institution requiring him to exercise judgment in that other's service, and (2) he himself has an interest that tends to interfere with the proper discharge of responsibility to the other party.[25]

If members see their organization solely as a means to their own private interest, it should come as no surprise that when the opportunity arises for them to put their own interests ahead of the interests of others in the organization, they will be tempted to do so. This situation is represented in the classic agency problem discussed earlier. The accounting scandals at the turn of the twenty-first century sparked a renewed discussion of conflicts of interest in business. None was more notorious than the relationship that existed between Enron (a U.S. energy company) and Arthur Andersen, a "big-five" accounting firm. Andersen had huge consulting contracts with Enron, and questions arose about how objective they could be when they performed as auditors. In addition, some of Andersen's personnel functioned as internal auditors at Enron—a clear violation of generally accepted accounting principles and a clear case of a conflict of interest. Moreover, a virtual revolving door existed between Andersen and Enron in which employees who worked for one would end up working for the other.

On Wall Street, the mergers of investment brokerages and banks created another example of conflict of interest. Investment analysts such as Henry Blodget and Jack Grubman would hype the stock of firms that provided IPO (Initial Public Offerings) funds and merger and acquisition business to the banking side of the business. The projections on stock growth given to investors were not based on an objective analysis of the future value of the firms, but rather were designed to increase artificially the value of the stock to the benefit of the bank and its client.

To see more precisely why the examples above constitute a conflict of interest we must ask to whom the auditors and the investment analysts properly owed their allegiance. The client of public auditing firms is the investment public (the idea behind the notion of "certified public accountant"). The investment public is also the client of investment advisers. In both cases, the allegiance should have been to the investing public, but instead the personal interests of the investment advisers and the interests of Arthur Andersen and the banking side of such corporations as Citicorp were given priority. The auditors of public companies are in a position of trust with respect to the investing public, as are investment analysts. However, in these cases this trust was violated because personal or institutional interests prevented the objective professional analysis that was required. E-mails show that Grubman disparaged stocks in private that he publicly recommended.[26]

Even if one takes a Friedmanite view about the purpose of a public corporation—namely, that it should be managed in the interests of the stockholders—the activities described above are wrong and indicate a lack of organizational integrity. These individuals and firms violated a number of the conditions required for organizational integrity that have been enumerated and defended in this chapter. These events provide additional evidence that the agency theorists who postulate a cynical psychological egoism may not have been cynical enough. They assumed that the manager's self-interest would stop at the point of illegality or blatant immorality. The widespread existence of conflict of interests—both financial and nonfinancial conflicts—within organizations stands as a significant impediment to organizational integrity.

WHY FIRMS WITH ORGANIZATIONAL INTEGRITY SHOULD BE SUCCESSFUL

Business people will want more than an account of organizational integrity in this chapter. They will want to know if business organizations with integrity can be financially successful. Ideals of organizational integrity must be shown to be practical and affordable. The starting point of the argument that organizations with integrity can be successful is the claim made by some corporations that their reputation as organizations with integrity gives them a competitive advantage in the marketplace. Their reputation for organizational integrity is part of their brand. Marketing theorists and finance theorists know that a brand can be highly valuable, even though it is intangible. Firms such as Johnson and Johnson have organizational integrity as part of their brand and believe that their brand gives them a competitive advantage.

We need an argument to show that there is some reason to accept what Johnson and Johnson takes to be true—that their reputation as an organization of integrity gives them a competitive advantage. Transaction cost economics—the theory we used to show why codes of ethics by themselves are not good indicators of a moral climate—is the theoretical basis for the argument. Key to the argument is the fact that organizational integrity is grounded in the values and routines of the firm, an idea that is evident in the list of items I have identified as characterizing organizational integrity. Those values tend to be knowledge-based, embodied in individual employees or firm routines, and characterized by high asset specificity. Assets characterized by high asset specificity are difficult to copy because they are unique or nearly unique to the firm that possesses them. Experience confirms the theory that moral climates are difficult to copy.

What evidence backs this claim? Both scholarly literature and business experience suggest that it is difficult to change moral climate once it has become a part of the corporate culture. A good example is the contrast between Ashland Oil Company and Exxon-Mobil. When Ashland was involved in an oil spill in January 1988, the CEO and other corporate officers quickly went to Pittsburgh, admitted fault, and directed the clean-up. This action was wise from both an ethical and a business perspective. Ashland had its fines reduced and suffered less litigation as a result of its behavior. Executives also gained respect as running an ethically responsible company. In March 1989, Exxon, as it was known then, experienced the Exxon Valdez oil spill in Prince William Sound off the coast of Alaska. Exxon's CEO never visited Alaska and belatedly sent a taped message of apology. Exxon has stayed in an adversarial mode since the beginning. Exxon apparently had learned nothing from the Ashland incident and thus was subjected to much litigation and a serious blow to its reputation. The courts awarded $287 million dollars for actual damages and (on appeal) punitive damages of $2.5 billion dollars.[27] Exxon did not learn from Ashland's successful handling of the crisis and thus suffered both financially and in terms of its reputation. Why did Exxon behave as it did? To use our earlier language, the answer is that corporate culture and specifically a moral climate have high asset specificity and—unlike codes of ethics—are not easily copied.

In strategic management, a competitive ideal is to occupy a position in which the firm has an asset that is difficult to copy and gives it a competitive advantage. An organization that has integrity is in that position. Because of this competitive advantage, organizations with integrity should be successful. However, there are some disturbing recent trends in corporate America showing that the argument mentioned thus far is not sufficiently persuasive.

A Pessimistic Concern and a Topic for Future Research

Although the moral climates of organizations with integrity are difficult to copy, they can be lost. That is, an organization that has integrity can lose it. That seems to be happening. Let us look at some of the companies that business ethicists have held up as shining examples of organizational integrity over the past thirty-five years in order to see how integrity can easily be lost. The "Hewlett-Packard Way"—the credo that had guided the firm for generations—was exemplary, but after its merger with Compaq HP it ran into trouble. The HP board became dysfunctional, and corporate officials engaged in illegal activity to determine who was leaking information about board deliberations to the public. There were massive layoffs as a result of the merger, and morale plummeted. The Hewlett Packard Way became ineffective. There is general consensus in the literature that HP lost critical dimensions of its integrity—or at least that it was severely tarnished.

Merck and other companies supply similar examples. Merck had achieved acclaim for manufacturing a drug to cure river blindness, but its reputation became tarnished by the Vioxx scandal. Merck was accused of promoting Vioxx while knowing of its dangerous side effects. Likewise, British Petroleum, which established the motto "Beyond Petroleum," has been cited for major safety violations in a U.S. refinery in which workers died in a fiery explosion. British Petroleum also has been criticized as environmentally insensitive in a series of Alaskan pipeline leaks allegedly caused by inadequate maintenance. Shell had tried to instill a culture of corporate social responsibility after the Brent Spar affair and its appearance of insensitivity to human rights in the Siro-Wiwa affair in Nigeria. Yet shortly after much fanfare and success in communicating its corporate social responsibility, the company admitted to accounting irregularities with respect to its oil reserves. Finally, the HB Fuller Company, which originally provided a model of the enlightened corporation under the leadership of Elmer Andersen followed by his son Tony Andersen, became just another company focused on quarterly returns. The company that resisted Wall Street came to pay it homage.

Good research is necessary to help us understand what happened to so many of our shining examples of organizational integrity. One thing is clear. Achieving organizational integrity is difficult, and once achieved is characterized by high asset specificity. Thus, it is difficult to copy. Yet, these examples tell us that departures from organizational integrity can have an immediate impact on the reputation of the firm and that once a reputation is lost, it is difficult to regain. If these generalizations are correct, one has reason to be pessimistic about the future. Are firms with organizational integrity an endangered species?

CONCLUSION

I have argued that organizational integrity exists when an organization has a moral climate. This culture exists only if the organization adheres to certain substantive ethical norms. Other features of a moral climate include fair procedures and the existence of incentive structures that support moral conduct rather than incentive structures that are perverse with respect to moral conduct. Groupthink, teleopathy, and conflicts of interest must be avoided. Corporate codes of ethics are no substitute for a moral climate, but once embedded in an organization with integrity, such codes can be useful as general guides. In an organization with integrity, the organization is not viewed as a mere instrument for individual personal advancement, but rather is seen as a cooperative endeavor of those within the organization that provides value to its corporate stakeholders. Organizational ethics is the set of norms and actions that create a moral climate, but these must be embedded at the highest level and constantly monitored. The managers, especially top executives, should show leadership with respect to organizational ethics. Sadly, we still have a great deal of work to do in creating organizational integrity, but at least many are now seriously engaged in the endeavor.

NOTES

1. Richard De George, *Competing with Integrity* (New York: Oxford University Press, 1993), 5.
2. Bart Victor and John B. Cullen, "The Organizational Basis of Ethical Work Climates," *Administrative Science Quarterly* 33 (1988): 101–125.
3. Norman E. Bowie, "The Firm as a Moral Community," in *Morality, Rationality and Efficiency: New Perspectives on Socio-Economics*, ed. Richard M. Coughlin (Armonk, N.Y.: M. E. Sharpe, 1991), 169–183.
4. John Rawls, *A Theory of Justice*, rev. ed. (Cambridge, Mass.: Harvard University Press, 1999), 58–60.
5. Norman E. Bowie, *Business Ethics: A Kantian Perspective* (Malden, Mass.: Blackwell, 1999).
6. See Robert Frank, *Passions Within Reason* (New York: W. W. Norton, 1988).
7. Robert Phillips, *Stakeholder Theory and Organizational Justice* (San Francisco: Berrett-Koehler, 2003).
8. See Coca-Cola's New Vending Machine A. (Harvard Business School Case 9-500-068).
9. Jared Harris and Philip Bromiley, "Incentives to Cheat: The Influence of Executive Compensation and Firm Performance on Financial Misrepresentation," *Organization Science* 13 (2007), 350–367.
10. Rawls, *Theory of Justice*, 7–8.
11. Richard Brandt excelled in using the insights of the social sciences including psychology and anthropology.

12. Sears Auto Centers, Harvard Business School Case 9-394-009.

13. Harvard Business School Case 9-382-034.

14. Kenneth E. Goodpaster, Laura L. Nash, and Henri-Claude de Bettignies, *Business Ethics, Policies and Persons* (Boston: Irwin McGraw Hill, 2006), 121.

15. Patricia Werhane, *Moral Imagination and Management Decision Making* (New York: Oxford University Press, 1999).

16. Lynn Sharp Paine, *Instructor's Manual: Cases in Leadership, Ethics, and Organizational Integrity* (Burr Ridge, Ill.: Irwin, 1997), 80–81.

17. The development of transaction cost economics is primarily attributed to Oliver E. Williamson. See his *Markets and Hierarchies* (New York: Free Press, 1975), and his *The Economic Institutions of Capitalism* (New York: Free Press, 1985).

18. Lisa Belk, "How Can We Save the Next Victim?" *New York Times Magazine*, June 15, 1997.

19. After a 1997 merger the merged hospitals were referred to as Memorial Hermann.

20. The details of this case are in Belk, "How Can We Save the Next Victim?"

21. Irving Janus, *Victims of Groupthink* (New York: Houghton Mifflin, 1972), 9.

22. Mindguards occur when members protect the group and the leader by withholding information that is problematic or contradictory to the group's cohesiveness.

23. This chapter has not emphasized leadership as an ingredient in organizational integrity. This is not because the quality of the leader is unimportant. However, leadership is addressed elsewhere in this volume.

24. For example, see his *Conscience and Corporate Culture* (Malden, Mass.: Blackwell, 2007).

25. Michael Davis, "Conflict of Interest," *Business and Professional Ethics Journal* 1 (Summer 1982).

26. One of the most complete and best accounts of this era is Gasparino's *Blood on the Street*. If Arthur Andersen's decline and fall is of interest, see Barbara Ley Toffler's *Final Accounting*.

27. This decision of the 9th U.S. Circuit Court of Appeals has been appealed by Exxon to the U.S. Supreme Court. Litigation continues nearly twenty years after it occurred.

SUGGESTED READING

Bowie, Norman E. *Business Ethics: A Kantian Perspective.* Malden, Mass.: Blackwell, 1999.

Bowie, Norman E., with Patricia H. Werhane. *Management Ethics.* Malden, Mass.: Blackwell, 2005.

Brown, Marvin T. *Corporate Integrity.* New York: Cambridge University Press, 2005.

Cohen, Deborah Vidaver. "Creating Ethical Work Climates: A Socio-economic Perspective." *Journal of Socioeconomics* 24 (1995): 317–343.

———. "Organizational Moral Climate." In *Encyclopedic Dictionary of Business Ethics.* Edited by Patricia H. Werhane and R. Edward Freeman. Malden, Mass.: Blackwell, 1997.

De George, Richard T. *Competing with Integrity.* New York: Oxford University Press, 1993.

Freeman, R. Edward, Jeffrey S. Harrison, and Andrew Wicks. *Managing for Stakeholders: Survival, Reputation, and Success.* New Haven, Conn.: Yale University Press, 2007.

Goodpaster, Kenneth E. *Conscience and Corporate Culture.* Malden Mass.: Blackwell, 2007.

Greenberg, Jerald, and Jason Colquitt. *Handbook of Organizational Justice*. Mahwah, N.J.: Lawrence Erlbaum Associates, 2005.

Halfon, Mark A. *Integrity: A Philosophical Inquiry*. Philadelphia: Temple University Press, 1989.

Kaptein, Muel, and Johan Wempe. *The Balanced Company: A Theory of Corporate Integrity*. New York: Oxford University Press, 2002.

Kramer, Robert M. ed. *Organizational Trust: A Reader*. New York: Oxford University Press, 2006.

Milla, Ann. "Moral Climate" In *The Blackwell Encyclopedia of Management: Business Ethics*, 2nd ed. Edited by Patricia H. Werhane and R Edward Freeman. Malden, Mass.: Blackwell, 2005.

Paine, Lynn Sharp. *Cases in Leadership, Ethics, and Organizational Integrity: A Strategic Perspective*. Chicago: Irwin, 1997.

———. "Managing for Organizational Integrity." *Harvard Business Review* 72 (1994): 106–117.

Petrick, Joseph A. "Integrity." In *Encyclopedia of Business Ethics and Society*. Edited by Robert W Kolb. Thousand Oaks, Calif.: Sage, 2008.

Phillips, Robert. *Stakeholder Theory and Organizational Justice*. San Francisco: Berrett-Koehler, 2003.

Trevino, Linda Klebe, and Gary R. Weaver. *Managing Ethics in Business Organizations*. Stanford, Calif.: Stanford University Press, 2003.

Victor, Bart, and John B. Cullen. "The Organizational Basis of Ethical Work Climates." *Administrative Science Quarterly/* 33 (1988): 101–125.

Werhane, Patricia H. *Moral Imagination*. New York: Oxford University Press, 1999.

INDEX

Absolute moral norms, 244, 342, 379, 678
Acceptable risk, 64, 248, 679–80, 683–86. *See also* Hazards; Safety
Access to health care
  adverse selection and mandatory insurance, 204–10, 223
  and employer-provided insurance, 218–19, 222, 349
  and exclusions from coverage by insurance, 204, 221–23, 349
  and free-riding and cost-shifting, 203, 208–15, 219–21, 223, 225
  mandatory, compulsory insurance coverage, 207–9, 219
  and market segmentation techniques, 205–07, 218, 224
  Menzel on just access, 8, 202–31
  rationing care and efficiency, 224–25
  universal coverage and, 202, 206, 208
Accountability, 27, 35, 278–79, 284, 306, 316
AdvaMed Code of Ethics, 148
Advertising
  campaign-related, 518
  deception in, 11, 54, 57, 257, 351–54
  direct-to-consumer, 148
  and the ethics of creating desire, 65–66, 214–15
  issue, 520, 528
  pharmaceutical, 142
  targeted, 370
  See also Deception
Affirmative action
  Boxill on, 15, 535–62
  the concept of, 535–37
  as group preferential treatment, 62–63, 536, 540, 544
  and the idea of discrimination, 535–37, 551
  Lockean natural rights as a defense of, 546–51
  as a means to diversity, 551–59
  and reverse discrimination, 536
  shifting resources through, 540
  utilitarian theory as a defense of, 537–45
  See also Discrimination; Justice; Prejudice
Agency problems and agency theory, 175, 177, 178, 190, 707–08
Allocation of scarce resources. *See* Access to health care
Anderson, Elizabeth, 88–89, 633
Animals on factory farms, 241–42, 662

Aristotle and Aristotelian theories, 56–60, 65, 415, 442, 473, 538, 557. *See also* Virtue theory
Arrogance (cultural), 255
Arthur Andersen Accounting, 35, 150, 239, 718–19
Ashland Oil Co., 720
Authority
  bureaucratic, 116–19
  and consent of employees, 100, 102, 106–08
  and cooperation, 110–15
  distinguished from power, 102–04
  de facto, 103
  employer, 616, 620
  the integrated structure of social, 111–14
  McMahon on legitimate managerial, 8, 100–24
  morally objectionable uses of managerial, 107–13
  patrimonial, 482
  political authority as the root model, 101–03, 111, 116, 119–21
  and property, 105–06
  subordinate, 115–17
Automobile industry, 336, 662, 665–67, 680
Autonomy, 270, 272–73, 286, 291, 314, 374, 376, 384, 461, 610, 619–20, 686. *See also* Respect for autonomy

Beauchamp, Tom, 10, 634
Bebchuk, Lucien, 179–80, 182, 184, 190
Beck, Ulrich, 307
Beinhocker, Eric, 86
Beitz, Charles, 312
Ben and Jerry's ice cream, 169, 664
Beneficence, 57, 62–64, 258, 580–81. *See also* Charity
Benevolence, 62, 84, 249
Bentham, Jeremy, and Benthamism, 58, 686. *See also* Utilitarianism
Biomedical ethics, 3
Bluffing in negotiations, 11, 24, 335, 354–58
Board of directors, 132, 135, 163, 170, 176, 179, 181, 188
Boatright, John, 9, 34, 132–33, 457, 462–63, 564
Body Works (Anita Roddick's), 664
Bok, Derek, 38–39, 169
Bok, Sissela, 565, 572–575, 580
Bowie, Norman, 18, 25, 565–66, 645
Brenkert, George, 15, 34–35, 678
Bretton Woods institutions, 661–62

Bribery
  as a corporate strategy, 282
  different normative views on, 489–94
  effects of, 282, 471, 490
  ethics of, 54, 472, 479–87, 493–95
  extent of, 471–72
  and extortion, 487–88, 490
  facilitating payments in, 488–90
  the formal duties argument, 480–82
  the harm argument, 484–87
  laws against, 472
  the nature of, 473, 478–79
  in Nigeria, 491–93
  the patrimonial societies view, 491–94
  the private-public argument, 482–84
  Velasquez on, 13–14
  See also Corruption
British Act of Anne, 411
British American Tobacco, 141–42
British Statute of Monopolies, 411
Brown, Marvin, 151
Buchanan, Allen, 460
Business Ethics
  corporate responsibility and, 127
  education in, 37–39
  ethical theory and, 46–50
  empirical study and, 4, 37
  the field of, 132
  globalization and, 309
  levels of analysis, 126
  libertarian view of, 638
  public policy and, 305–06
  regrettable views of, 5–6
  two understandings of, 3–5
  whether a universal or a particular morality,
    260
  See also Codes of ethics; Conflicts of interest;
    Ethical theory; Ethics officers; Methods of
    business ethics; Professional ethics

Campbell, Tom, 271, 273, 290
Capitalism
  and business ethics, 74
  capitalist ownership, 75–81
  creative destruction and, 173
  democratic, 126, 130, 133
  democracy and, 310
  Gaus on, 7–8
  and markets, 81–89
  nature and meaning of, 7–8
  and socialism, 91–93
  See also Free markets
Carson, Rachel, 657–58, 662
Carson, Thomas, 445, 488
Categorical imperative (Kant's), 25, 57–58, 60, 62,
  635. See also Kantian ethics
Catholics, 555
Caux Round Table, 30, 145, 292

Charity, 109, 241, 259, 312, 368, 548–50
Cheating, 28, 37, 49, 51, 203, 708
Coase, R. M., 81–83, 90–91
Coca-Cola, 11, 692, 706
Codes of ethics, 238, 243–44, 360–61, 712–13
Coercion, 36, 54, 85, 239, 572
Common morality, 236, 240–47, 250, 257, 260
Common sense intuitionism, 60–61
Compassionate use, 216
Comprehensive moral thinking, 128, 146,
  148, 150
Comprehensive social awareness, 143
Conceptual analysis, 30, 54–55, 65–66, 74
Confidentiality, 236, 239, 244
Conflict of interest
  cognitive bias and, 453–56
  the concept of, 442–48, 450–52, 461
  different kinds of, 448–50
  empirical work on, 454–56, 457–58
  ethical concerns about, 441, 443
  importance of, 442–43
  institutional approaches to, 443, 451–56
  justified and unjustified, 242, 247
  macro-level theory of, 459–64
  methods for managing, 456–59
  Norman and MacDonald on, 13
  normative theory of, 456–58
  and organizational integrity, 718–19
  and Sarbanes-Oxley, 441, 449, 456, 460–61
Conflict (moral) and disagreement, 243–48
Conscience, 137–39, 145, 245
Conscientiousness, 61, 237, 240
Consent as a ground of managerial authority,
  106–8. See also Authority; Informed consent
Consequentialism. See Utilitarianism
Consumers, 204–05, 347, 351–52, 366–71, 380–83,
  664–69, 678, 680–94, 706
Contractarian theories and relations, 6, 25, 29,
  30–31, 249, 546–47
Cooperation, 29, 84–85, 110–18, 704–06, 718, 722
Copyrights
  and bundles of rights, 410
  compared to patents, 413
  copyright law, 12, 411–12, 414, 422–30
  defense of, 418–20
  fair use, 424–25, 427–29
  and personality, 419
  their protection on the Internet, 370
  software and, 430–31
Corporate boards, 34, 278
Corporate campaign contributions, 14, 55, 501ff, 672
Corporate cultures and climates, 701–09
Corporate governance, 34, 48, 104, 115, 132, 137,
  163, 189–92
Corporate responsibility
  and comprehensive moral thinking, 128, 146,
    148, 150
  and constituents, 129, 151
  the dualistic model, 128

Corporate responsibility (*continued*)
  its global implications, 305, 306, 309, 314, 321, 324
  and individual responsibility, 713–14
  Goodpaster on, 8
  and moral projection, 131
  non-fiduciary responsibilities of, 135–36
  as a subfield of business ethics, 23
  three levels of responsibility, 126
  the tripartite model, 127, 129, 140, 144, 151
Correlativity of rights and obligations, 251.
    See also Rights
Corruption
  dealing with, 487, 504
  effects of, 471–72
  ethics of, 13–14, 35, 473
  extent of, 210, 282, 660
  the formal duties argument, 480–82
  and the harm argument, 484–87
  the nature of, 473–78, 501, 503–04, 507
  and the private-public argument, 482–84
  See also Bribery
Cosmopolitan theories, 258–59
Cost-benefit analysis, 59, 679
Cost shifting and health insurance, 208–09, 220.
    See also Access to health care
Cultural imperialism, 254–57
Cybertechnology, 366ff. *See also* Privacy

Daly, Herman, 309
Danley, John, 478
Davis, Michael, 444–45, 447, 453, 461–63, 568–72
Dayton Hudson Corporation, 149–50
De George, Richard, 12, 34, 568–70, 573–74,
    580–81, 701
Deception
  in advertising, 11, 54, 57, 257, 351–54
  and bluffing in negotiations, 24, 335, 354–58
  and bribery, 493
  Carson on, 11, 335–65
  the concept of, 336–38, 522
  fraud and, 394, 403
  and honesty, 358–61
  in sales, 342–50
  insider trading and, 388–89, 392–94
  and withholding information, 337–38, 342–50
  wrongful, 388–89, 392, 395, 402, 404–05
  See also Advertising; Corruption; Lying
Democracy
  capitalism and, 310
  corporate, 114–15, 119, 122
  democratic accountability, 316–17
  democratic management, 318
  democratic norms and principles, 501–03, 511, 523
  and freedom of expression, 502, 521
  and participation, 310
  and universal values, 308
Deontological theories, 29, 375, 682. *See also*
    Kantian theories

Digital information, 428
Disclosure of and withholding information, 11,
    335–65. *See also* Informed consent;
    Information disclosure
Discretion, 23, 34, 121, 376
Discrimination, 15, 206–10, 535ff, 551, 605, 607.
    See also Affirmative action; Equal treatment;
    Equality of opportunity
Diversity, corporate
  Boxill on, 15, 535–62
  utilitarian value of, 63
  in the workforce, 537, 551–59
  See also Affirmative action; Discrimination
Donaldson, Thomas, 29–30, 240, 319
Drucker, Peter, 130, 149, 169
Due care duties, 678
Dunfee, Thomas, 29–30, 240

Efficiency in markets, 74, 78, 81–88, 90–91, 224–25,
    691–94. *See also* Capitalism; Free markets
Egalitarian principles, 224, 258, 705
Employees
  employee rights, 613–14, 622, 623
  and job-security rights, 602–03, 613–14,
    617, 622
Employment at will
  autonomy and, 619–20
  common law doctrine of, 602–03
  its core doctrines, 14–15, 603–05
  European views of, 602–03, 616–17
  and fairness, 620–22
  and the "flexicurity" model, 623
  and freedom of contract, 615–16
  and individual termination, 604–07
  and job-security rights, 602–03, 608, 613–14,
    617, 622
  and just-cause dismissal rules, 606–07
  and layoffs (in Europe), 607–09
  and layoffs (in the U.S.), 605–06
  liberty rights, 615
  limits on, 604–05
  property rights and, 615
  the relative effectiveness of, 617–22
  and the utility argument, 617–19
  and U.S. views of employment, 602–03, 614–16
  and the WARN Act, 605
Enron case, 35, 64, 239, 578, 580, 586, 712–13,
    718–19
Entrepreneurs, 7, 92–94, 162, 167, 173–75, 184, 186,
    191, 454, 664, 683–84
Environmental protection
  and environmental justice, 319
  and environmental responsibilities, 289
  governmental attempts to foster, 289, 659–62
  history of since the early 1960s, 657–60
  its integration into business ethics, 662–65
  justice and, 319–320
  models of, for business, 665–68

Environmental protection (*continued*)
   Newton on, 17, 657–76
   pollution control, 4, 16, 81–82, 721
   recommendations in need of attention, 670–72
   standards, 309, 324–25
   as a value, 120
Equal treatment, 55–56, 59, 536. *See also*
      Discrimination
Equality of opportunity, 63, 224, 238, 535, 678
Epistemology, 52–54, 66, 546
Ethical corporate culture, 6, 17–18, 208–09, 224,
   701–22
Ethical investors, 218, 220
Ethical theory
   Audi on, 7, 46–69
   uses and varieties in types of, 26–27, 39, 239,
      244, 375, 705
   its goals and place in business ethics, 6–7, 26
   the tasks of, 464
   See also Common morality; Morality
Ethics officers, 4, 17
European Union (EU), 318, 380, 431, 606
Executive compensation
   and annual bonuses, 163–64
   base salary issues, 163–64
   Boatright on, 9, 161ff
   the CEO labor market argument, 176–77
   and compensation committees, 162–63, 175
   the evolution of executive pay, 165–67
   and executives acting as bureaucrats, 162, 167, 191
   and executives as entrepreneurs, 162, 167,
      173–75, 186, 191
   and fiduciary duties, 162
   long-term incentive plans and, 163, 164
   the managerial power thesis, 179–86, 190
   moral issues in, 247, 707
   objections to high, 168–71
   a principal-agent approach to, 177–79
   principles justifying, 161–62, 171–75
   and shareholder power, 163, 167
   and stock options, 164–67, 170, 180, 186–88
   the structure of executive pay, 163–65
   tying pay to performance, 186–90
   See also Justice; Wages
Exploitation (in labor), 85, 216, 239, 254, 309, 317–19
Exploitative wages
   the concept of, 642–45
   and human dignity, 644–46
   Marx on, 642–44
   the unfairness of, 643–44, 646
   and vulnerability, 644
   Wertheimer on, 642–44
   Wood, Allen, on, 644
   See also Wages
Exxon-Mobil, 720

Faden, Ruth, 634
Fair share, 203, 208, 211–14, 219, 223, 707

Fairness, norms of, 114–15, 202–08, 222–25, 318,
   424–25, 427–29, 620–22, 705–09. *See also* Fair
   share; Justice
Families, 208, 345, 659
Federal sentencing guidelines (U.S.), 4, 17, 35
Fidelity, 50, 56, 61, 64, 240
Fiduciary relationships and duties, 11–12, 132,
   134–35, 183, 236, 246, 336, 360–61, 394–95, 508,
Finnis, John, 375
Food and Drug Administration (FDA), 210–11,
   214, 216, 225, 228, 352–53
Foreign Corrupt Practices Act, 35, 472, 479, 488–89
Fossil fuel, 667–68, 671
Fraud (corporate), 35, 84, 347, 359–60, 368, 371,
   691–92
Freedom of expression, 14, 250–51, 282
Free markets
   and capitalism, 7–8, 34, 38, 73ff
   and environmental problems, 670, 672
   executive compensation in, 8, 162, 171–73, 178
   and lower standards, 309
   vs. the bureaucrats, 659
   See also Capitalism; Efficiency in markets
Free riding (and medical costs), 203, 208–09, 211–15,
   219–21, 223–25. *See also* Access to health care
Freeman, R. Edward, 22, 25, 33, 36, 322, 663–64,
   669, 703
Fried, Jesse, 179, 180, 182, 184, 190
Friedman, Milton, 24, 133–34, 173, 278, 638, 703,
   718–19
Friedman, Thomas, 38, 306
Friedrich, Carl, 476–477
Friendship, 88, 375–78
Future generations, 5, 659

Gender equality, 30–31, 238. *See also* Equal treatment;
   Equality of opportunity
Gender and preferential treatment, 94, 247
Gender-based discrimination, 14. *See also*
   Discrimination
Genetic discrimination (in health insurance),
   206–08, 210, 218, 224. *See also* Access to
   health care; Discrimination
Genetic information, 206–07
Gewirth, Alan, 270
Global Reporting Initiative, 292–93
Globalization
   the conditions of, 279–281
   corporate social responsibility and, 321–24
   corporations and, 282, 297
   the definition of, 306–09
   and democratic accountability, 316–17
   and development, 305
   egalitarian principles and, 314
   and global social justice, 257–59
   globalism, 308
   Gould on, 10–11
   inequalities and, 311–12

Globalization (*continued*)
    justice and, 311–14, 321
    labor standards and, 317–18
    problems of, 309–12
    and the race to the bottom, 309
    sustainability and, 319–20
    See also Equality of opportunity; Rights;
        Universal norms and universal morality
Golden handshakes, 163, 168
Golden parachutes, 164, 168
Golden rule
    its role in business ethics, 11, 56, 139, 249, 335,
        340, 345–46
    and the presumption against lying and
        deception, 340–42, 354
    a proof of, 339–40
    See also Universalizability
Good and well-being, theories of, 375
Greed, 23, 49, 54, 170–71, 709
Gregor, Douglas, 710
Griffin, James, 270
Groupthink, 716–17, 722

Handy, Charles, 136–37
Harm
    corruption and, 477, 484–89
    to the environment, 664, 672
    exposures to, 244, 629, 637, 680, 685–86,
        688–89
    from lack of privacy, 379, 382
    from lying and deception, 342–44, 347–48,
        351–53, 358, 360
    from past injustices, 537
    from practices, 368, 371, 663
    to organizational integrity, 704
    to others, 76, 78, 205, 237, 341, 356–57, 447, 508,
        584, 614, 678–80
    to self, 348
    types of risk of, 16–17, 50, 64
    whistle-blowing and, 567–571, 573–75, 580–81
    See also Corruption; Environmental protection;
        Hazards; Safety; Worker safety
Hayek, F. A., 87, 89, 92–94
Hayward, Tim, 319–20
Hazards
    to health and safety, 361, 660
    workplace, 16, 245, 240, 252, 628–31, 633–35,
        639, 646
    See also Harm; Safety; Worker safety
Health care, just access to. *See* Access to health care
Health Maintenance Organization (HMO), 368
Hegel, Georg Wilhelm Friedrich, 418–19
Heinz Company, 711–12
Held, David, 307
Hermann Hospital case, 715
Hierarchical firms, 89–95, 115
HIPAA (privacy law), 227, 381, 383. *See also*
    Privacy

Hewlett-Packard, 721
Holmstron, Bengt, 181–82
Honesty and deception
    honest dealing, duty of, 17, 394, 677, 691–93
    in sales, 342–50, 358–61
    and withholding information, 337–38, 342–50
Hooters of America, Inc. v. Phillips, 400–01
Human dignity, 140, 144–47, 149, 270–71, 276, 635,
    639, 645–46
Human equality, 270–71, 273, 276. *See also* Equal
    treatment; Equality of opportunity
Human rights. *See* Rights, human
Hume v. U.S., 399
Hume, David, 53, 84
Hypernorms, 30–31, 240

Ideal theory, 709–10
Immigration (illegal), 149
Incentive structures, 58, 82, 102–05, 224–25, 702,
    711–12, 722
Individualism, 15, 32, 224, 310, 346, 411, 415, 602,
    615, 684
Individual responsibility, 126, 132, 143
Inequalities, 8, 259, 549–50, 556
Information age, 409, 433
Informed consent, 374, 381, 383–84, 690
Information disclosure
    Carson on, 11, 335–64
    Spinello on, 366–86
Insider trading
    arguments from harm, 389–92
    and breach of fiduciary duties, 394–95
    and breach of trust, 389
    corporate, 389, 390, 392, 395, 397–98, 400, 403–04
    differing assessments of, 236
    results of, 388
    Strudler on, 12
    and unconscionable contracts, 389, 396, 398–02
    unfairness questions about, 396–98, 404
    and wrongful deception, 388–89, 392–94, 403, 405
    the wrongness of, 388–89, 402–04
Insurance, health, 202–25, 348–50. *See also* Access
    to health care; Genetic discrimination (in
    health insurance)
Integrative social contracts theory (Donaldson
    and Dunfee), 29–31, 240
Integrity
    Brenkert on moral, 15, 563ff
    Organizational, 18, 33, 701–22
    Personal, 15, 108–9, 240, 245
Intellectual property
    the concept of, 12, 370, 408–09
    a contentious notion, 408
    and copyrights, 413, 419–20, 428, 433
    copyright law on, 411–12, 422–23, 427–30
    De George on, 12
    and digital information, 425, 428–30
    its historical background, 411

Intellectual property (*continued*)
   intellectual property law, 410, 417, 419, 421–31
   justifications of, 412, 415–19
   its legal contexts, 411–15
   and natural rights and justice arguments,
      414–17, 419
   the nature of, 409–10
   patents and, 411–14, 417–20, 422, 425, 430–32
   and the personality argument, 418–19
   software as, 425–28, 430–32
   and trade secrecy, 410, 413–14, 419–20
   and trademarks, 410, 413–14, 419–20, 430
   utilitarian-pragmatic arguments about,
      417–419
   See also Property
International Labor Organization (ILO), 318
International Monetary Fund (IMF), 305, 310,
   316–17, 661
Investor obligations, 217–18

James, H. S., 478
Jefferson, Thomas, 546–50, 556–57
Jensen, Michael, 166, 187
John Paul II, 143–44, 148
Johnson and Johnson, 713, 720
Jurisprudence, 372
Justice
   in access to vital goods (Menzel on), 8, 202–31
   and affirmative action, 63, 535–37, 546, 551, 560
   compensatory, 92
   in contractarian theory, 30–31
   corrective, 682
   distributive, 172–75, 312, 494
   economic, 8–9
   in egalitarian theory, 55, 224, 258, 314, 319, 705
   environmental, 319–20
   in free markets, 8–9, 17, 84, 661
   global, 9, 257–59, 306, 312, 314–16, 320–21
   and inequality, 8, 255, 257–59, 321, 549–50, 556
   and intellectual property, 415–16, 420
   procedural, 706–07, 709
   social, 129, 140, 145
   See also Affirmative action; Equality of
      opportunity; Fairness

Kant, Immanuel, 57, 270, 442, 610, 644, 710
Kantian ethical theory, 25–26, 57–58, 61
Kaplan, Steve, 181–82
Kimberly Process, 294
Kirzner, Israel, 174–75
Kyosei, 145

Larmer, Robert, 577–78
Legislation, 35, 115–16, 209, 380, 659, 666
Liability (legal)
   Hasnas on product liability, 17, 677ff

for environmental damage, 659–60
Lobbying
   and big information, 512, 514–15, 518–20,
      524–25, 527–28
   and big money, 510, 515, 517–18, 523, 527
   the Bipartisan Campaign Reform Act (BCRA),
      516, 520
   as corporate political activity, 501–03, 508–09,
      521–22, 529
   and freedom of expression, 501–02, 508, 521–22
   full quos, 506–09, 513, 518
   half quos, 506–09, 512
   the nature of, 14, 146, 503, 505
   quid pro quo, 504–06, 511
   reasoned beliefs and speech, 522–28
   and small information, 510–12, 518–20, 523–24,
      528
   and small money, 512–14, 516–18, 525–27
   Stark on, 14
   and ways to find value congruence, 146
Locke, John, 77, 79, 132, 174, 415–18, 515–16, 619
Love Canal, 659–60
Loyal agents, 178
Luebke, Neil, 444
Lying
   Carson on, 11, 335–65
   consequences of, 52
   the concept of, 11, 54–55, 338–39, 392–93, 412
   See also Deception

Madison, James, 554
Managerial authority. *See* Authority
Managerial decision making, 23–24, 29, 32–37,
   100, 116–24. *See also* Authority
Managerial power thesis, the, 179–86
Manipulative influences, 13, 58, 65–66, 344, 348,
   358, 366
Margolis, Joseph, 444
Market solutions and product safety, 680–81,
   684–85, 693–94. *See also* Capitalism; Free
   market
Martin Memorial Hospital case, 715
Marx, Karl, 75, 78, 89, 93–94, 642, 644
Medtronic, 135–36, 148
Merck, 352–53, 721
Metaethics, 27, 47, 56, 66
Methods of business ethics
   Audi on ethical theory and, 7, 46–67
   and business ethics education, 26–27, 31–32,
      37–39
   centrality of the case method, 28
   conceptual analysis as a method, 54–55
   Donaldson and Dunfee on, 29–31, 240
   empirical, 28–31
   Green and Donovan on, 6–7, 21–39
   and the mission of business ethics, 22–24
   philosophical and ethical, 24–28
   See also Business ethics

Mill, J. S., 58–59, 75, 79, 90, 442, 688
Millennium Development Goals (MDGs), 320
Minorities
    Boxill on ethnic, 15, 535ff
    cultural suppression of, 254–57, 493
    and job hiring, 63, 248
    See also Affirmative action; Discrimination
Mirandola, Pico Della, 270
Moore, G. E., 143
Moral climates and cultures, 17–18, 701–24
Moral free space, 30, 257
Moral life, the, 137–39, 144–45, 242, 245
Moral point of view, theories of the, 49–50, 65,
    248–50, 702–03
Moral psychology, 53–54, 65–66
Moral realism, 50–51
Moral status, 27, 610, 644
Morality
    contrasted with law, 421–22, 429, 481
    and moral awareness, 137
    its nature, 6, 10, 46–47, 60, 240–43, 251, 260,
        313, 394, 447, 578, 586, 704
    and the role of rights in, 609–13
    See also Ethical theory; Rights
Muchlinski, Peter, 268
Multiculturalism, 15, 253–57. See also Rights;
    Universal norms and universal morality
Multinational corporations, 9–10, 116, 251–53,
    660–62, 665
Mutual benefit in markets, 83–84

Nagel, Thomas, 137–39, 144–45
Natural law and natural rights theories, 79–80,
    375, 415–16, 418, 537, 546–51, 611
Nozick, Robert, 85, 172, 174
Nussbaum, Martha, 375
Nye, Joseph, 475–76

Okin, Susan, 256

Paine, Lynn Sharp, 712
Patagonia, 665
Patents, 411–13, 417–19, 422, 430–33
Paternalism, 348, 399–400, 630, 689–90, 693
Personhood (the model of), 80–81, 691
Pharmaceutical practices and pricing
    Canadian and U.S. customs compared, 203,
        214–15
    and "compassionate use" policies, 216
    and industry standards, 210–18
    "me-too" and non-innovative drugs, 211–15, 225
    Menzel on, 8, 202–32
    and orphan drugs, 202, 211, 215–17, 220, 223–25
    reimportation of pharmaceuticals, 211–15
Philips, Michael, 478
Plato, 52, 75, 415, 473

Pluralistic societies, 107. See also Multiculturalism
Pogge, Thomas, 258–59, 306, 311, 313–14, 322
Political philosophy, 8, 34, 36, 92, 100–02, 107, 118,
    554, 556
Poverty, 258–59, 311, 541
Prejudice (and discrimination), 535ff, 545. See
    also Affirmative action; Discrimination
Prima facie obligations, 60, 63, 67, 244, 272,
    343–46, 361, 631–32, 639
Principal-agent, 135, 177–78, 446, 451
Privacy
    concepts and theories of, 367, 371, 374
    Gavison on seclusion theory, 372–73
    and Hohfeld's rights theory, 378
    and hospital patients' records, 368, 373–74
    informational, 11, 245, 250, 366–87
    legal scholarship about, 372
    loss of, threatened by cybertechnology, 366–71
    Moor and Tavani on restricted access, 373
    protections of in law and public policy, 379–84
    rights of, 367, 372, 376–79
    Thomson's cluster theory, 377
    use of private information in marketing and
        advertising, 370–71
    Warren and Brandeis on, 372
    See also Rights
Professional ethics, 5, 11, 101, 243, 360–61, 710
Promising, 60, 100–02, 106–12, 245, 344–45, 361
Property
    concept of, 408
    defense of, 415–19
    intellectual. See Intellectual property
    ownership of, 408–10
    private, 73, 75–81, 84, 90, 105–06, 132, 174, 408,
        420, 475, 482–83, 491, 614–15, 617, 622
    property rights, 172, 322, 398, 409, 415–17, 424
    See also Capitalism; Rights
Public good(s), 101, 113–16, 119–21, 212–14, 663
Public health, 379, 660
Public policy, 76, 219, 258–60

Rationing health care, 224–25. See also Access to
    health care
Rawls, John, 25–26, 39, 81, 249–50, 258, 375, 555,
    704–06, 709
Reasonable person standard, 678
Reflective equilibrium, 26, 52–53, 65. See also Rawls
Relativism, moral (and cultural)
    Beauchamp on, 10, 235–48, 260
    Donaldson and Dunfee in opposition to,
        29–30
    encouraged by methods of education, 27
Religion and ethics, 55–56
Reparations, 60–63, 547, 551
Respect for autonomy, 376, 678, 686, 688, 691,
    693. See also Autonomy
Respect for persons, 25, 58, 696
Respectfulness, 61

Richardson, Henry, 116, 246
Right to health care. *See* Access to health care; Rights
Rights
    basic, 610–11
    and business responsibilities, 251–53, 267–68, 279–92, 313, 321–24
    complicity in human rights abuses, 290–91
    the concept and nature of, 244, 250, 269, 271–73, 314, 609
    the correlativity of rights and obligations, 251
    Cragg on human, 10
    the draft-norms model, 284–87, 288
    globalization and, 282, 305–08, 313–14, 317–19, 321–22
    the hybrid model of, 269, 293–96
    and impact analyses, 323
    their institutionalization, 272–74, 292–93
    instrumental rights, 612–13
    the International Bill of Rights, 282, 288
    legal models of, 273–79, 283, 288, 294
    McCall and Werhane on employee, 15
    moral foundations of, 269–71
    overriding, 272–73, 286–88
    property, 75–83, 88–89, 105–03
    and responsibilities of the state, 267–68, 279–83, 313
    the right to means of subsistence, 313–14
    rights-based approaches in ethical theory, 380
    the voluntary self-regulatory model, 268–69, 283–84, 288
    universal, 10, 235, 250–52, 271–73, 275–76, 283, 285, 288, 291
    Universal Declaration of Human Rights, 269, 275, 276, 313, 315, 317
    violations of, 297, 629
    Western bias in favor of (alleged), 254–55, 314–17
    See also Equality of opportunity; Universal norms and universal morality
Role models, 56
Rose-Ackerman, Susan, 476–77
Ross, W. D., 60, 62, 244
Royce, Josiah, 131–32, 134, 144
Ruggie, John, 276–77, 280–81

Sacrifices, 110, 222, 552, 679
Safety
    Arnold on workplace, 16, 628ff
    and caveat emptor and caveat venditor, 683
    the concept of product safety, 678–83
    employee, 621
    general duties of product safety, 687–93
    Hasnas on product safety, 17, 677–97
    the inherent subjectivity of product safety, 687
    the literature on product, 677–78
    types of risk and, 16
    See also Harm; Hazards; Worker safety

Sales, deception in, 342–50. *See also* Deception
Sarbanes-Oxley Act, 35, 150, 180, 441–42, 449, 460–61, 565–66
Schmidtz, David, 78
Sears Auto Centers, 711
SEC v. Texas Gulf Sulphur, 389, 392–94, 397, 403–04
Self-interest, 49, 84, 109, 222, 217, 221, 249, 347–48, 355, 544, 661, 685, 707. *See also* Agency theory; Greed
Selznick, Philip, 131, 149
Sen, Amartya, 256, 315, 710
Sethi, S. Prakash, 316
Sexism, 536. *See also* Women, rights of
Shareholders (as principals)
    CEO pay, 162–63, 170, 175, 177, 179–80, 187–88
    fiduciary obligations to, 632
    and the nomination of boards, 185
    risks to, 621
    roles in corporations of, 127–28, 132
    shareholder control, 167, 181, 186, 188
    shareholder interests, 94, 132, 135, 140, 162, 167, 179, 183, 191, 638
    shareholder wealth, 178–179, 187, 189, 502
    See also Executive compensation; Insider trading; Stakeholders; Stockholders
Shell Oil Company, 492
Shiffrin, Seana, 399–400
Shue, Henry, 306, 312–13
Singer, Peter, 258, 306, 312, 581
Smith, Adam, 249, 541, 614
Specification of norms, 245–46
Stakeholders and stakeholder theory
    and corporate moral climates, 702–06, 710, 718
    corporate stakeholders, 127
    and the draft norms model, 287
    expanded corporate moral horizons of, 322–23
    Freeman's theory, 22–23, 25, 32–33, 35–36, 118
    and pharmaceutical company obligations, 217, 220
    as a reaction to prior theories, 25
    stakeholder dialogues, 294
    stakeholder fallacy, 133
    the stakeholder paradox, 134–35
    stakeholder management, 18, 93, 133, 137, 322, 366, 702–05, 718
    stakeholder thinking, 127–32, 134, 136, 138–40, 142–44, 146, 149–51
    See also Shareholders; Stockholders
Stallman, Richard, 426
Stark, Andrew, 445, 449–50, 456, 459
Stiglitz, Joseph, 306, 316–17
Stockholders
    boards represent, 133
    and corporate moral climates, 703, 707–08, 719
    insider trading and, 402–04
    legal concerns of, 141
    moral responsibilities of, 132–34, 140–41
    obligations to, 24, 64, 132, 134–35, 278
    preoccupation with, 127, 130–31
    profits for, 129, 137, 143

Stockholders (*continued*)
  proximate beneficiaries, 133
  See also Shareholders; Stakeholders
Stone, Christopher, 346
Subjective evaluations of safety, 17, 677, 685–87,
    691–94. *See also* Harm; Hazards; Safety;
    Worker safety
Sullivan Principles, 294
Sunstein, Cass, 88
Supererogation, 349, 575, 585–86, 588
Superfund, 660
Supreme Court, U.S., 372–73
Sustainability, 10, 319, 492
Sweatshops
  conditions in, 622, 629, 638–41
  criticisms of, 637–39
  defense of, 636–39, 642, 645
  definition of, 635–36
  and human dignity, 636–37, 639, 641–42
  and improving working conditions, 14, 16,
    108–09, 252–53, 255, 639–42

Tamir, Yael, 257
Teleopathy, 717–18, 722
Texaco, 252
Texas Gulf Sulphur, 389, 392–94, 397, 403–04
3M Co., 663, 666, 669
Thompson, Dennis, 443
Trade secrets, 12, 402, 414, 692
Transaction costs, 91, 206, 684, 695, 712–13, 720
Transparency, 179, 294, 306, 316, 379, 383–84
Tripartite model, 127, 129, 144, 150–51
Trustworthiness, 240
Truthfulness, 59, 64, 236, 240, 336
Tyler, Tom, 458

U. N. Global Compact for Business, 10, 268, 284,
    321, 306, 324–25, 472
Unions, 36, 189, 238, 317–18, 357, 604, 608, 643, 716
Unionization, 109, 115, 143
Universal norms and universal morality
  Beauchamp on, 10, 240–43, 248–57
  Donaldson and Dunfee on, 30–31, 240
  globalization and, 10
  human rights and, 10
  primary issues of, 9–10
  See also Globalization; Rights
Universalizability (principle of), 57–64, 340
Utilitarianism, 26, 58–64, 258, 537–45, 551, 560,
    681–82, 686–87. *See also* Bentham; Mill; Singer

Veil of ignorance, 249–50. *See also* Rawls; Reflective
    equilibrium
Velasquez, Manuel, 678
Velsicol Chemical Corporation, 146–47
Veracity, 50, 52, 54, 59

Vices, 57, 240
Virtue ethics, 25, 32, 56–58, 65–66
Voluntary codes of conduct, 268, 283–84, 294. *See
    also* Codes of ethics

Wages
  economic considerations about, 219, 221, 645–46
  exploitative, 90, 252, 258, 642
  Marx on, 94, 642–44
  Wertheimer on, 642–44
  Wood on, 644
  See also Executive compensation
Wallerstein, Immanuel, 308
Wal-Mart, 86, 713
Walzer, Michael, 310
Weber, Max, 482–83
Whistle-Blowing
  Audi on, 7, 63–65
  the background of, 563
  Brenkert on, 15
  and complicity theory, 570–72
  the concept of, 564–67
  and duties of employees, 576–80
  and the duty of beneficence, 580–81, 584
  and the duty of confidentiality, 576
  and the duty of loyalty, 577–80
  and good reasons theory, 572–75
  and harm theory, 567–70
  and integrity theory, 575–77, 582–91, 595
  the Kew Gardens principle, 583
  the principle of positional responsibility,
    575–76, 582–588
  and organizational design, 564, 591–94
  reservations about, 63–64, 241–42
  and the restatement of agency, 576
  and self-correcting organizations, 593–94
Women, rights of, 238–39, 250, 254–56, 535–36,
    658, 715
World Bank, 283, 293–94, 305, 311, 316–17, 471–72,
    491, 661–62
WorldCom, 565, 571, 580, 582
World Social Forum, 305, 315
World Trade Organization (WTO), 258, 281, 305,
    310, 316–17
Worker participation and the Mondragón
    Corporación Cooperativa, 318
Worker safety
  dignity and, 630–31, 635, 637, 641, 644–46
  and the disclosure of hazards, 633
  and employer obligations, 628–31, 639–42
  Hasnas on product safety, 677–94
  injuries, 628, 634
  the libertarian view of, 630–32
  OSHA, 631–32, 640, 646
  the reasonable person standard, 633–35
  and the right to life, 629, 635
  and the right to well-being, 629
  See also Harm; Hazards; Safety

9 780199 916221